Authors and Titles with AP Writing Prompts

• •

AP® EDITION

PERRINE'S

LITERATURE

AP® EDITION

PERRINE'S

LITERATURE

STRUCTURE, SOUND, AND SENSE

Twelfth Edition

Greg Johnson
Kennesaw State University

Thomas R. Arp
Southern Methodist University

With AP® Contributions by
Donna Carlson Tanzer
Martin Beller
Robert Brown
Suzanne Loosen

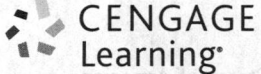

CENGAGE
Learning·

Australia • Brazil • Japan • Korea • Mexico • Singapore • Spain • United Kingdom • United States

CENGAGE
Learning·

AP® Edition of Perrine's Literature: Structure, Sound & Sense, Twelfth Edition

Greg Johnson and Thomas R. Arp

Product Director: Monica Eckman

Product Manager: Kate Derrick

Content Developer: Helen Triller-Yambert

Associate Content Developer: Erin Bosco

Content Coordinator: Danielle Warchol

Product Assistant: Katie Walsh

Media Developer: Janine Tangney

Marketing Manager: Lydia Lestar

Content Project Manager: Dan Saabye

Art Director: Marissa Falco

Manufacturing Planner: Betsy Donaghey

Rights Acquisition Specialist: Jessica Elias

Production Service: S4-Carlisle Publishing Services

Text Designer: Anne Bell Carter, a bell design company

Cover Designer: Sarah Bishins

Compositor: S4-Carlisle Publishing Services

Associate Content Developer, Advanced and Elective Products Program: Ashley Bargende

Senior Media Developer, Advanced and Elective Products Program: Philip Lanza

For product information and technology assistance, contact us at **Cengage Learning Customer & Sales Support, 1-888-915-3276.**

For permission to use material from this text or product, submit all requests online at **www.cengage.com/permissions.** Further permissions questions can be emailed to **permissionrequest@cengage.com.**

Library of Congress Control Number: 2013957164

ISBN-13: 978-1-285-46234-9
ISBN-10: 1-285-46234-3

Cengage Learning
200 First Stamford Place, 4th Floor
Stamford, CT 06902
USA

Cengage Learning is a leading provider of customized learning solutions with office locations around the globe, including Singapore, the United Kingdom, Australia, Mexico, Brazil and Japan. Locate your local office at **international.cengage.com/region.**

Cengage Learning products are represented in Canada by Nelson Education, Ltd.

To find online supplements and other instructional support, please visit **www.cengagebrain.com.**

AP® and Advanced Placement Program® are trademarks registered and/or owned by the College Board, which was not involved in the production of, and does not endorse, this product.

Printed in the United States of America
8   17

BRIEF CONTENTS

Writing about Literature 1

FICTION

The Elements of Fiction 55

Stories for Further Reading 525

POETRY

The Elements of Poetry 679

Poems for Further Reading   973

DRAMA

The Elements of Drama   1067

Plays for Further Reading   1503

CONTENTS

FICTION

The Elements of Fiction   55

CHAPTER ONE   Reading the Story   56

CHAPTER TWO   Plot and Structure   97

CHAPTER THREE   Characterization   142

POETRY

The Elements of Poetry   679

CHAPTER ONE   What Is Poetry?   680

CHAPTER TWO   Reading the Poem   699

CHAPTER THREE Denotation and Connotation 720

CHAPTER FOUR Imagery 732

CHAPTER FIVE   Figurative Language 1:
Simile, Metaphor, Personification, Apostrophe, Metonymy   747

CHAPTER SIX   Figurative Language 2:
Symbol, Allegory   765

CHAPTER SEVEN Figurative Language 3:
Paradox, Overstatement, Understatement, Irony 791

CHAPTER EIGHT Allusion 810

CHAPTER NINE   Meaning and Idea   824

CHAPTER TEN   Tone   838

CHAPTER ELEVEN   Musical Devices   856

CHAPTER TWELVE   Rhythm and Meter   874

FEATURED POETS

The following poems appear as illustrations in various chapters of the book, but these three poets are represented by a sufficient number of poems to warrant studying them as individual artists. Approaches to analysis and writing are suggested on pages 8–9 of this book.

A CONTEMPORARY COLLECTION

These five contemporary poets are represented by at least six poems each, included at various points in the book. They offer students the opportunity to sample at greater lengths the works of poets of their own time. Approaches to analysis and writing are suggested on pages 8–9 of this book.

Poems for Further Reading 973

DRAMA

The Elements of Drama   1067

CHAPTER ONE   The Nature of Drama   1068

PREFACE

In preparing this twelfth edition of *Perrine's Literature: Structure, Sound, and Sense,* I have striven to be faithful to the principles established by Laurence Perrine more than fifty years ago while acknowledging the evolving nature of literature. I have been guided not only by my own experience but also by the rich legacy of Thomas R. Arp, who joined Perrine in 1979, and by the helpful suggestions of many teachers who have contributed the results of their classroom experience. Many of them are identified in the "Professional Acknowledgments" pages. They have helped me in replacing more than twenty-five percent of the literature printed in the previous edition.

Here I must expand briefly on the contribution of Thomas R. Arp, whose work on *Literature* for more than thirty years has left an indelible and invaluable imprint. Professor Arp's depth of knowledge and experience with the book as a whole, combined with his perspicacity in choosing material to illustrate the principles of each chapter, has been a source of inspiration to me during the twelve years I have worked with him, and here I wish to salute his achievement and wish him well in his retirement. Though any faults in this new edition are mine alone, I have continued to benefit from his wisdom and insight since he has consented to serve in a consulting role for the present and the foreseeable future. Thus his name, I am happy to say, continues to grace the cover of the book, a fitting reminder of his past contributions and his continuing involvement.

In keeping with Perrine's and Arp's shared principles, the book works to balance the classic with the contemporary, to represent a wide diversity of writers, and to emphasize the importance of understanding the elements of literature as the avenue to enjoy and appreciate it. Although there are many flourishing approaches to literature and its effects, all three of us have always believed that the initial step must be understanding the major elements of fiction, poetry, and drama.

This book is written for the student who is beginning a serious study of literature. It seeks to give that student a sufficient grasp of the nature and variety of fiction, poetry, and drama; some reasonable means for reading with appreciative understanding; and a few primary ideas of how to evaluate literature. The separate chapters gradually introduce the student to the elements of literature, putting the emphasis always on *how* and *why: How* can the reader use these elements to get at the meaning of the work, to interpret it correctly, and to respond to it adequately? *Why* does the writer use these elements? What values have they for the writer and the reader?

In matters of theory, some issues are undoubtedly simplified, but I hope none seriously, and some more sophisticated theoretical approaches have had to be excluded. The purpose has always been to give the beginning student something to understand and use. The first assumption of *Literature* is that literature needs to be read carefully and considered thoughtfully, and that, when so read, it gives its readers continuing rewards in experience and understanding. I also assume that some works repay more richly than others the trouble and effort expended in reading them, and my objective is to help the student identify, understand, enjoy, and prefer such works. To this end, the book examines the major elements of literature and suggests some criteria for judgment.

The organization and structure of the book reinforce the step-by-step approach to understanding literature. Each chapter contains two parts: (1) a discussion of the topic indicated by the chapter title, with illustrative works, and (2) a relevant selection of additional works with study questions for further illustration of the topic. Also, in each chapter I include a list of review topics for the materials, and a list of Suggestions for Writing about those materials as they are illustrated elsewhere in the book.

The book opens with a section on "Writing about Literature," which embraces the important assumption that the fullest understanding and appreciation of a literary work arises from a reader's ability to express in language its meaning and emotional effects. The process of finding the right words to make these clear, and the additional clarity that results from the correct and effective presentation of these materials, is a significant part of making a work part of one's experience.

Although the book emphasizes the study of literature, not writers, I have continued the practice of representing some authors with a sufficient number of works to support the study of them as individual artists. In the fiction section, I include three stories each by one of the modernist masters of the short story form (D.H. Lawrence), by a great twentieth-century writer (Flannery O'Connor), and by a major contemporary author (Joyce Carol Oates). In this edition, there are also five poets amply represented as "Featured Poets": John Donne from the Renaissance, John Keats and Emily Dickinson from the nineteenth century, and Robert Frost and Elizabeth Bishop from the modern era. The table of contents gathers the titles of their poems in a boxed format for easy reference.

This edition also presents a "Contemporary Collection," five poets represented by six or more poems each, placed throughout the text. These too are identified in a boxed format in the table of contents. Among them for the first time is Pulitzer Prize-winning poet Natasha Trethewey.

Finally, to provide an introduction to the further works of individual poets, the book contains at least three poems each by more than two dozen writers, both classic and modern. These poems can easily be referenced in the index of the book.

In the drama section, I have maintained the practice of including a number of one-act plays so as to provide a wider range of dramatic styles and approaches, and to include contemporary playwrights of diverse backgrounds.

An Instructor's Manual has again been prepared to accompany this book. It is available to all teachers who adopt the book for their classes. The manual contains an analytical article on every selection, suggesting approaches to interpretation and providing information that places the works in their contexts. These articles are the work of the author who prepared this edition as well as the man who created the first edition, Laurence Perrine, and the man who worked on the series for several decades, Thomas R. Arp. In the interests of space, the main text does not provide extended biographical information about the writers, but instructors and students who feel the need for such material are urged to consult Wadsworth's valuable "Literature Resource Center" at http://trials.galegroup.com/thomson.

Through the twelve editions of this book, which originated in the middle of the twentieth century, *Literature: Structure, Sound, and Sense* has evolved in many ways, responding to shifts in interest, concern, and taste expressed by its users. However, certain abiding principles remain as relevant in this new century as they were in the last. Among these are the convictions that the close reading of a text is basic to understanding and appreciating it, that to understand the means by which a work achieves its ends is an essential part of experiencing it fully, and that reading imaginative literature is important to the development of the whole person.

G.J.

AP® Edition

This AP edition contains helpful features for students preparing for the AP® English Literature and Composition Examination. There are more than 80 AP practice prompts akin to the poetry essay question, prose essay question, and open essay question students will find on the AP Literature and Composition Exam. There is also an introduction to the AP course and exam that offers strategies students can use both in preparing for the exam and taking it. Finally, writers who appear in the College Board's list of representative authors are indicated in the table of contents.

AP® and Advanced Placement Program® are trademarks registered and/or owned by the College Board, which was not involved in the production of, and does not endorse, this product.

AP® Teacher Support

For this edition, there is a corresponding Teacher's Guide for the Advanced Placement Program, which includes information and lesson suggestions for teachers in the AP course. Teachers who adopt the book can request *Classroom Practice Exercises*, which includes a set of additional multiple-choice questions in AP format. In addition, the ExamView® Computerized and Online Testing available for this edition offers more than 300 questions that will help students practice for the multiple-choice section of the AP exam. Teachers also have the option to easily generate their own questions within the ExamView "Quick Test Wizard."

AP® Student Support

Fast Track to a 5: Preparing for the AP® English Literature and Composition Examination is a test-preparation manual that includes an introduction for students about the exam, chapters on each type of question, and two complete practice tests. It can be purchased either with the text or separately.

AP® Contributors

Donna Carlson Tanzer A former AP Literature teacher for the West Allis, Wisconsin, school district, Donna Tanzer teaches writing and humanities at the Milwaukee Institute of Art and Design and has taught at Marian University. She co-authored *Interpreting Poetry* with Martin Beller, with whom she has presented at several AP Annual Conferences and NCTE national conventions. Ms. Tanzer co-authored the AP Guide to accompany this textbook Claudia Klein Felske, along with several editions of an *AP Guide for Perrine's Literature*, and wrote AP content for Perrine's AP edition. She has been an AP Reader since 2004.

Martin Beller Martin Beller is a Visiting Professor in the English Department at Texas Southern University. Dr. Beller is co-author, with Donna Tanzer, of *Interpreting Poetry*, a text for AP and pre-AP classes, and has presented workshops on teaching poetry, with Ms. Tanzer, at AP Annual Conferences and at annual meetings of the NCTE. He taught both AP English courses during ten years as a high school teacher, and has served as an AP Reader since 2006.

Robert Brown Rob Brown teaches AP English and leads the English Department at Rice Memorial High School in South Burlington, Vermont, where he has taught for more than 30 years. As a College Board-endorsed consultant, Rob has presented workshops and institutes throughout the northeast as well as at the 2010 AP Annual Conference. He has served as an AP Reader since 1999.

Suzanne Loosen Suzanne Loosen has been teaching AP English Literature and Composition since she was a first year teacher at Milwaukee School of Languages. In 2011, she was honored as a "Teacher of the Year" by the Milwaukee Metropolitan Alliance of Black School Educators.

PROFESSIONAL ACKNOWLEDGMENTS

The following high school instructors have offered helpful reactions and suggestions for this 12th edition of *Perrine's Literature: Structure, Sound, and Sense.*

Tracy Amaral
Medway High School

Sara Berry
School for Creative and Performing Arts

Scott Bokash
South Lake High School

Keri Bostwick
Bartlesville High School

Fred Bracher
Castle High School

Elizabeth Brammer
Robstown High School

Susan Buice
Cherokee High School

Diane Clark
Sherman High School

Brad Edom
East Union High School

Deborah Gill
Jenks High School

Michelle Goins
Union-Endicott High School

Sheri Goldstein
Ida Crown Jewish Academy

Nicholas Jackson
Herbert Hoover High School

Mary Jindra
Mayfield High School

Melissa Kevonian
Utica High School

William Kolbe
Northern Garrett High School

Eric Larew
Pleasant Valley High

John Manear
Seton-LaSalle High School

Shanna Miller
Fruita Monument High School

Raymond Nighan
St. Johns

Kelly Stollings
Watauga High School

Michele Sullivan
Patchogue Medford High School

Roberta Teran
Lakewood High School

Michelle Waters
Deep Creek High School

Sarah Whittier
City and Country School

Wendi Wooddell
Winter Haven High School

Sharon Wright
Heritage High School

Leah Zika
Prairie High School

Deidre Zongker
Olathe North High School

FOREWORD
TO STUDENTS

You've been reading stories ever since you learned to read; your first exposure to verse came with "Pat-a-cake, pat-a-cake, baker's man"; you've been watching dramatized life since your family planted you in front of the TV. You've developed your own tastes and your own attitudes toward what these varieties of "literature" can give you. In a sense, there's no need to take an introductory course in reading literature, because you've moved beyond the "introductory" phase. Let's say, then, that it's time to become familiar and friendly with the literary arts.

But let's take stock of where you stand. What have you been getting out of the things that you enjoy reading and watching? For most people, the first answer is "vicarious experience," the impression that you are temporarily able to live in some other world than your own private one—a world that may be as familiar as your own neighborhood or as alien to your experience as space travel in some future time or the adventures of explorers of the past. What you want is for the author to take you to where you have never been, so that you can imagine yourself as a person in a world other than your own.

You probably also want to be able to "relate" to the characters in the things you read or watch, discovering in them some features of yourself or some qualities that you would like to have. Or you like to share vicariously the excitements, joys, and sorrows of people who are not very much like you, but whose lives seem rich and interesting. Or you get a lift from watching some characters making major mistakes with their lives, and turning themselves around just in time—or maybe you are thrilled to see such people brought to justice and punished for misdeeds.

Whatever the sources of your pleasure and enjoyment from reading, you may now be ready to find both broader and deeper reasons for continuing that pastime. No matter how much experience you bring to the study of these works, you're in for a few surprises. Some of them will be the surprises that come from broadening your vicarious experience, from "traveling" with us to India and Russia, to Paris and Pittsburgh and Dublin, to sixteenth-century London and seventeenth-century Massachusetts and nineteenth-century Wall Street. Some will be the surprises that come from penetrating to the secret recesses of the human mind and soul in joys and agonies, from observing people whom you have never met or imagined and with whom you have nothing in common but your humanness.

And, we hope, there will be the surprises and pleasures that come from feeling yourself growing in control or even mastery of your responses and reactions as you learn *how* literature does what it does. This, of course, is what the formal study of literature can bring you. We all know how we *feel* when we first read through a work. We probably start by thinking "I like this" or "it doesn't say much to me" or "what in the world is that supposed to mean?" If you could, you'd act on your first reaction and read the work again, or try to see what it's trying to say, or drop it and go on to do something more pleasurable.

But you're in a special situation. You're taking a course (either by your own choice or because you're required to), and one of the rules of the game is that you're supposed to move from your initial reaction to some sort of "serious" response that will satisfy your teacher. If you like something and want to reread it, your teacher will pester you with wanting to know *why* you liked it, and might even insist that you offer reasons why other people should like it too. If you are only a little bit curious about it, or think that it is a waste of time, your teacher will lead (or nudge, or bash) you into finding things in it that might change your first opinion. In any case, the terms of your special situation, as a student in a course with a grade on the horizon, make it necessary for you to have more than an initial reaction. You'll need to have a developing understanding of the work, and you'll need to show in discussion or writing both what you understand and how the work itself led to that understanding.

That's where this book will help. In addition to a systematic guide for discovering how and what a literary work means, we've provided you with Suggestions for Writing at the ends of the chapters and standards for your written work in the first section of the book.

Why is writing so important? It's the most straightforward way of sorting out your feelings and ideas, putting them into shape, nailing down your own experience. All writing about literature has a double motive—it sharpens your grasp of the work, and it helps you to lead other people to share your experience. Writing about literature is writing persuasively, and persuading others to see what you see helps you to see it more clearly.

So at the most basic level, we want to help you with reading and writing. But you have every right to ask, "Why literature?" That's a good question, because in our world there are so many ways of gaining experience and insight into our lives and the lives of others that focusing on one resource based on the spoken and written word may seem narrow and old-fashioned. We're willing to grant that, and we'll go even further: in a sense, it is also elitist, and turning to literature as a source of experience will set you apart from the majority of people. Thus, literature provides not only vicarious experience and opportunities to relate to others' lives, but it also permits you to join a special group of scholars, instructors, critics, and other students who share in the wealth of enjoyment and intellectual challenge that it has to offer.

PREPARING TO SUCCEED ON THE AP® ENGLISH LITERATURE AND COMPOSITION EXAMINATION

by Donna Carlson Tanzer

Every May, well over 350,000 students sit down to a rigorous exam in close reading and analytical writing about literature: the Advanced Placement English Literature and Composition Exam. In 2013 that number was 366,647. For most of these students, the exam is the culmination of a classroom course in AP Literature; others may have been home-schooled, may have taken an online course, or may have decided to take the exam independently. These test-takers hope to demonstrate that they are ready for the rigors of college composition and literature courses. Many hope to perform well enough to earn college credits and waive introductory college composition courses.

You are most likely among the many students studying AP Literature (or a similarly rigorous course of literature study), and you may wonder just what you can do to best prepare for this rigorous exam. You may have heard that the exam is challenging; you may wonder how you will fare or even whether or not you should take the exam. Many test prep books are available, including Cengage's *Fast Track to a 5: Preparing for the AP® English Literature and Composition Examination*, which will take you step-by-step through the exam process, and you can find abundant tips online; an entire industry has been built around Advanced Placement preparation in *all* subject areas. And it is true that there are good test-taking strategies you can learn to help you succeed. Familiarizing yourself with the test format will no doubt allow you to enter the exam room with more confidence than if you have no idea what you will face. This chapter aims to provide you an overview of the exam and some good working strategies that will help you succeed.

Yet more important than any test-taking strategy is intelligent analysis based on close reading. As AP Literature teacher Martin Beller states, to perform well on the AP Literature Exam you need to be "lit smart"–intuitive, observant, sensitive, and skilled at reading and analyzing literature. Does that mean you should just throw up your hands and figure your "lit smarts" are a matter of fate or genes, that nothing can change your AP Lit destiny? Not at all. No matter how naturally smart you are, you can develop your literary I.Q. through careful and close reading and rereading and by learning to write well about literature. The College Board states that students' reading in preparation for this exam must be "wide and deep." To read widely means to have studied literature from all genres and a range of eras. To read deeply means to read with insight and understanding: to look beyond the obvious surface meaning. The College Board suggests that you should have experience with literature from the sixteenth through the twenty-first century. This reading should ideally span over your entire high school career; the skills you will build from this in-depth reading and study develop and improve over time.

The best way to succeed on the AP Literature exam is not by trying to study *the exam itself* but by reading and understanding the kind of material the exam covers—poetry, fiction, and drama of literary excellence. By familiarizing yourself with a wide range of good literature in all these genres, you are prepared to read, comprehend, and analyze an excerpt or short work of literature you've never seen before—one of the tasks the AP exam will demand of you. You will be able to read short passages, such as those appearing in the exam's multiple-choice section, quickly and with attention to tone, diction, and other elements of literature that often form the basis of these questions. The qualities the exam tests are those that persistent, focused readers of excellent literature can develop over time: sensitivity to nuance, attention to detail, a solid working vocabulary, and the skills of critical analysis. You are far better off developing these skills than agonizing over what the current year's exam will cover or trying to second guess the test developers.

You have at your fingertips this very moment an exceptional resource to help you develop these very skills: *Perrine's Literature: Structure, Sound and Sense*. This book provides analysis and guidance that will prepare you well for the complex questions asked on the multiple-choice portion of the AP exam as well as for writing the exam's free response essay question. Read the chapter analyses closely as you study the stories, poems, and plays assigned in your class. If you are assigned to answer the questions that accompany the poems, answer them in depth or detail rather than rushing through them. These questions do not ask for a quick "right answer" but are geared to point you toward a solid understanding and interpretation of the poem. Many questions can lead to lively, intense class discussions—discussions of the meanings of word choices, poetic voice, and interpretation. Such discussions, in turn, prepare you to find and support your own ideas about a work of literature, a skill you will use during the AP exam. The text's thought-provoking, incisive questions point you toward the most significant elements of a given poem. Read each poem both silently and aloud, and return to each poem for at least one more reading as you study the text analysis or work through the questions. Muse over even those questions that are not assigned in your class, and let them lead you to comprehension and deeper insights. Writing about literature is also an excellent way to learn. As soon as you have read a piece of literature, write a response in your journal. Use the questions to guide your journal writing, or write your immediate and genuine response. Return to your journal often as you sort through your reactions to the ambiguities and layered meanings found in good literature. All these steps—reading, rereading, discussing, responding to questions, and writing—are the basics every good reader of literature knows and follows. They are the most effective way of becoming not just an expert on the AP exam, but an expert *reader* who is solidly prepared to take this exam.

The Exam: Multiple-Choice

The three-hour exam consists of two parts: a one-hour multiple-choice section and a two-hour essay section. During the first section of the exam, you will have one hour to answer 55 multiple-choice questions. The multiple-choice exam usually includes four excerpts or poems although some exams have included five. You will be asked to read each of these excerpts or poems and answer about 10 to 14 multiple-choice questions based on them. These questions often test your ability to recognize and discern tone; for example, you may be asked which of five possible tones is reflected in a passage or poem. Often these questions test your ability to work through convoluted syntax simply to determine what is being said in a lengthy sentence or a stanza of poetry. You may be tested on your ability to infer a literary character's traits or purpose based on the information provided in a passage. Some questions may test your ability to recognize literary devices such as metaphor, apostrophe, or oxymoron. However, these questions are always based on the context of the passage or poem. You would never be expected to define a literary device in the abstract; rather, you may be asked about the effect or impact of a particular device or choice of words. Thus, while familiarity with literary terminology is important and often useful in the multiple-choice section of the exam, the ability to discern how literary elements function within a work is more essential and will more likely result in a better test outcome.

The Free Response Essay Questions

The essay portion of the AP Lit exam lasts two hours and consists of three free-response essay questions or prompts. Although the suggested time allotment is 40 minutes per essay, you will have access to all three essay prompts and may write them in any order and allocate your two hours however you choose.

Question 1: Poetry

Question 1, the poetry question, may be based on a single poem or excerpt of poetry, or it may require a comparison-contrast essay about two poems. You will receive a prompt that asks you to address specific aspects of the poem. Although the prompt asks one unified question, it usually includes two or more steps. For example, one step may ask an incisive question about the meaning or significance of the poem, and another step will almost always ask you how the literary devices in the poem contribute to the meaning. It might be helpful to think of these steps as the "what" and the "how" of the question, and it is essential to read and answer the prompt thoroughly.

Question 2: Prose

Question 2 usually includes an excerpt from prose fiction and is therefore often referred to informally as the "prose question." However, the passages provided for analysis in past years have come from plays and nonfiction (though nonfiction has not appeared for over 20 years) as well as from novels or short stories. In a few cases, a complete short story, usually a very brief one, has formed the basis of this question. You may be asked to look at details of characterization, including how two or more characters relate to each other, and you may be asked how certain details in the excerpt contribute to its overall effect. Many Q2 questions from past years have asked students to analyze the effect of setting, dialogue, comic effect, and other basic literary elements. In all cases you will be expected to find a connection between the focus of this question and the literary work's overall meaning. As you study the questions and prompts in Perrine's, you will notice that many prompts are based on the entire short story, usually much longer than a passage from the AP exam. It should be apparent that the study of these short stories in their entirety and the elements that convey their meanings is excellent practice for the AP Lit Question 2.

Question 3: The "Open" Question

Question 3, the "open" question, is often a favorite of students because of the choices it offers. This question consists of a general prompt, usually thematic or character-based, that you will apply specifically to any one novel or play of literary merit. Although the question usually stipulates "novel or play," in past years the question has included "epic poem," and if you can write well about an epic poem, you may do so without fear of penalty. Following the question, the College Board provides a list of novels and plays that are applicable to the year's particular question. You need not choose your selection from this list, however, and often many of the more interesting and well-written responses are based on a literary work from outside the list. Some AP Lit teachers advise their students to cover up the list of choices as they read the question and consider what novel or play they know well that will work best. However, other students prefer to peruse the list in the hopes that they will recognize a title they know and about which they can write well. The plays in Perrine's are all of recognized literary merit; any full-length play from Perrine's that suits a given year's prompt would be a fine choice for Question 3.

Writing the Exam: Tips for Success

Answering Multiple-Choice Questions

The key to success on the multiple-choice questions is your ability to read and comprehend a wide range of literature of all genres from the sixteenth to the twenty-first century. No one knows what passages will appear on the multiple-choice exam, and, although familiarity with the question format is helpful, practicing many old multiple-choice tests is unlikely to help you as much as improving your overall ability to understand literature. It is important to read the passage carefully and to read the questions and all the options closely. You will want to read slowly enough to discern significant details but quickly enough to finish the 55 questions in the hour provided. This is where some practice can be helpful. You will want to achieve a pace that allows you to read the four passages and also answer 55 questions— about a question every 40 seconds. You also need to learn how to eliminate the distracters—the wrong answers. As you read through the choices, try to eliminate the ones that are obviously wrong at first so that you can narrow your choices. Note that there is no penalty for wrong answers; you simply don't get credit for them. So you should answer every question, even if you have to guess. Being able to take challenging multiple-choice tests involves not only good reading but good critical thinking as you work through the syntax of the questions and possible answers. After you finish the multiple-choice, you will need to use the break provided to clear your head so that you can do your very best on the free response essay questions.

You can find sample multiple-choice questions at http://www.collegeboard.com/student/testing/ap/sub_englit.html?englit (click on the download link immediately after the title). Click on "Exam Practice" found in the green heading. When you get to "Exam Practice," click on the AP Literature and Composition Course Description PDF under "Exam Resources." This entire document offers valuable practice—for AP Language and Composition as well as Literature. The exam practice for literature begins on page 54. Among the selections offered for practice is the poem "The Eolian Harp" by Samuel Taylor Coleridge. Find the poem on page 65. Read the poem carefully first and then refer back to it as you answer the questions. The first stanza of the poem reads:

The Eolian Harp

My pensive Sara! thy soft cheek reclined
Thus on mine arm, most soothing sweet it is
To sit beside our Cot, our Cot o'ergown
With white-flower'd Jasmin, and the broad-leav'd Myrtle,
(Meet emblems they of Innocence and Love!)
And watch the clouds, that late were rich with light,
Slow saddening round, and mark the star of eve
Serenely brilliant (such should Wisdom be)
Shine opposite! How exquisite the scents
Snatch'd from yon bean-field! and the world *so* hush'd!
The stilly murmur of the distant Sea
Tells us of silence.

Notice first that two words you might not understand, "Eolian Harp" and "Cot," are defined for you in the footnotes as a stringed instrument and a cottage. You should also be able to recognize that these lines are addressed to a woman called "Sara," who is described as "pensive," or thoughtful. Clearly the speaker loves Sara: in the poem's opening phrase he calls her "*My* pensive Sara," and her cheek is resting on his arm. (Poet Samuel Taylor Coleridge was engaged to marry Sara Fricker when he began writing "The Eolian Harp," but you don't need to know this background information in order to explore the poem.) You should also be able to see that the speaker and Sara are sitting outside their cottage watching the clouds, taking in nature's scents ("How exquisite the scents / Snatch'd from yon bean-field!")

and sounds ("the stilly murmur of the distant sea"). If you had trouble figuring out this basic setting, ask yourself some basic questions when you first read a poem: Who is the speaker? Where is he or she? What is happening?

The first multiple-choice question on this poem, no. 34, asks us to determine the mood of these opening lines:

34. In the first section of the poem (lines 1–12), the speaker seeks to convey a feeling of
    (a) curiosity
    (b) contentment
    (c) remoteness
    (d) resignation
    (e) foreboding

Read lines 1-12 again quickly, asking yourself how the diction choices convey a specific feeling. For this kind of question, it is often helpful to imagine someone reading the poem aloud—hear it with the "voice" inside your head. The sound of that voice can help you find the right mood and the correct answer. You can easily eliminate "a" as there are no words or phrases to suggest that the speaker is curious about anything. The intimacy suggested by Sara's cheek on the speaker's arm and the couple's seating right outside the cottage completely contradict the idea of "remoteness." Therefore, you have eliminated "c." Now look at "d": resignation. What is there to feel "resigned" about? The poem does not give us any indication that the speaker is "resigned"—that is, that he has given up or accepted something reluctantly. Nor is there any suggestion in the text of foreboding ("e"). In fact, the speaker seems quite contented sitting there with his beloved. Obviously, "b" is the correct answer—"contentment."

If you merely glance at the poem's words without considering meaning and context, there is a slight possibility that the word "saddening" in line 7 might lead you to think that the speaker is not content—that he is vexed or melancholy. But you need to consider the context of "saddening," which no. 35 asks you to do:

35. In context, "saddening" (line 7) suggests that the:
    (a) clouds have become darker
    (b) speaker is increasingly melancholy
    (c) happiness of the speaker will fade
    (d) security of the couple will be threatened
    (e) prospect of night vexes the speaker

The correct answer is "a." If you look carefully at the context of the phrase "slow saddening round," you will see that the speaker and Sarah "watch the clouds, that late were rich with light, / Slow saddening round." The clouds, once bright, are now darkening ("saddening") as night falls and the "star of eve" (evening) appears. Nothing in this description of day transitioning into evening suggests that the speaker is sad or melancholy (b); we know he is still sitting with Sara's cheek upon his arm. Nothing in these lines suggests that the speaker's happiness is short-lived (c), and we are not given any reason to think the couple's security will be threatened (d). And although the lines do describe the approaching nightfall, nothing suggests that this occurrence in any way vexes the speaker (e). Clearly, "a" is the only viable answer. Note that all these distracters attempt to lure you into assumptions that are not supported by the text.

Another multiple-choice question, from a past College Board released exam, refers to Henry Fielding's *Tom Jones*. The opening paragraph of the exam passage reads:

> Mr. Jones, of whose personal accomplishments we have hitherto said very little, was, in reality, one of the handsomest young fellows in the world. His face, besides being the picture of health, had in it the most apparent marks of sweetness and good-nature. These qualities were indeed so characteristical in his countenance, that, while the spirit and sensibility in his eyes, though they must have been perceived by an accurate observer, might have escaped the notice of the less discerning, so strongly was this good-nature painted in his look, that it was remarked by almost every one who saw him.

Notice that the first two sentences mention Mr. Jones' handsome face, especially the sweetness and good nature that are most noticeable. One of the multiple-choice questions asks you to focus on the third sentence, beginning in line 5:

> The structure of the sentence beginning in line 5 does which of the following?
> (a) It stresses the variety of Mr. Jones's personal attributes.
> (b) It implies that Mr. Jones is a less complicated personality than the speaker suggests.
> (c) It disguises the prominence of Mr. Jones's sensitive nature and emphasizes his less readily discerned traits.
> (d) It reflects the failure of some observers to recognize Mr. Jones's spirit and sensibility.
> (e) It belies the straightforward assertion made in the previous sentence.

The correct answer is d. Notice that the question asks you to look closely at the structure of the sentence. We can readily eliminate "a" because the sentence is not stressing variety; it is dealing only with the spirit and sensibility in Mr. Jones' eyes. We can also eliminate "b" because the sentence *is* suggesting a complication—that is, that the spirit and sensibility are only apparent to those who are discerning. The answer "c" is clearly wrong: the sentence does just the opposite. And "e " is clearly wrong because the sentence supports and builds on the assertions in the previous sentences; it does not "belie" them (show them to be untrue). This leaves us with "d," the correct answer. The sentence tells us that *though* some astute observers see this quality in Mr. Jones, it "might have escaped the notice of the less discerning." This is clearly the correct response.

These examples demonstrate the importance of a solid vocabulary and how important it is for you to follow the ideas through the syntax of complicated lines and sentences in both poetry and prose. Although practicing a few multiple-choice questions can help you sharpen these abilities, the most important quality is an ability to read with discernment and strong critical thinking. Only intensive close reading and analysis of poetry and of passages from prose literature can help you truly develop this ability.

Writing the Free-Response Essays

The key to writing three solid essays is often summed up in a mnemonic for "AP"—address the prompt. Read each question slowly and carefully. You are allowed to write on the green test sheets, and most students find it helpful to underline parts of the question in order to ensure that they have covered all steps. For Questions 1 and 2, which are based on poems and passages or stories provided for you, it is helpful to annotate the poem or passage, underlining pertinent phrases that you may want to cite as you write your essay. Your handwritten essay is considered a draft so don't worry about crossing off words or phrases or, if you must, starting over (keeping the time factor in mind). If you need to insert a sentence or two or even a full paragraph, try to do so clearly, boxing the inserted material and pointing to where it goes; the exam readers will make every effort to follow your thinking. Read through all three questions quickly before deciding on the order in which you will answer them. Although the order is completely up to you, many teachers as well as former AP students recommend that you begin with the essay you feel you are able to answer best. This will boost your confidence as you approach the remaining questions, but more importantly, if you do go over the suggested time allotted to each essay (40 minutes), you will at least have spent the greater proportion of your time on your strongest essay. You don't want to find yourself facing the question you know best with only 15 minutes left. You are advised to spend exactly

40 minutes on each question, but these are general guidelines, and the exact allocation of your two hours is up to you.

Despite the time pressure of the exam, most students are also better off resisting the temptation to plunge right into the writing. In addition to the close reading and annotating already recommended, you might want to jot down a rough outline or plan for your writing. Although insightful reading and interpretation of literature is the focus of this exam, it is also a test of writing skills. It is important that you write in an organized fashion with a clear thesis. The exam readers are instructed to treat your essay as a draft and normally disregard minor errors, but it is still to your best advantage to write as accurately and eloquently as you can. Avoid spending too much time on an elaborate introduction, especially one that is unrelated to the topic and that is intended as an "attention-getter." You will want to write a brief and pertinent introduction that does not merely repeat the prompt, but you will also want to stay clear of what exam readers and teachers call "dawn of time" intros ("For as long as literature has existed, authors have written about _____." As you respond to the question, try to write analytically, answering the specific question and supporting your insights with details and, for Questions 1 and 2, with direct citations. Be sure that you explain quoted passages; integrating quotations effectively into your own sentences is an excellent skill, but you don't want to become so enamored of this technique that you end up just repeating a literary passage with an essay that is heavy on quotations but light on analysis. Try to demonstrate why words or lines you cite are significant and *how* they "address the prompt." As you cite passages, you need not include line numbers, as you would in a researched essay, because the readers have the passage right in front of them and will know it well.

One point may seem obvious, but it is worth remembering. For all three essays, be sure you write something. Sometimes students lose track of time, spending all their time on two essays. Wear a watch or keep one close by in case your exam room has no clock. (You will not be allowed to have your cell phone with you.) If you should decide it is a wise decision to go over the suggested time for one or even two essays, save enough time to write at least a brief third essay. It is always surprising to exam readers to see exam books in which students evidently put forth considerable effort on two essays, only to leave the third one blank. In a worst-case scenario, even if you only have time to write a paragraph, you might still earn a score that could make a difference in your overall exam results. The complex scoring formula includes a multiplier for each of the essays so even a low score will boost your overall score more than skipping an essay. And it should go without saying that the "something" you write needs to be relevant to the question. You may find the exam frustrating, but you are only hurting yourself if you decide to rant about your teacher or about the bad day you're having. These off-topic essays receive the same score as an essay left blank, and the time you could use writing to the best of your ability, even on the hardest question, can yield a positive outcome. It is also helps you develop good habits of mind as you prepare for the exams you will take in college and the challenging situations you may find yourself in all through your life. Giving up won't do anything for you, but staying with a task that seems daunting can help you develop your mental and emotional stamina.

Writing Question 1: Poetry

As you read and prepare Question 1, the poetry question, read the poem once before you read the prompt, and read it again, slowly, with the prompt in mind. Poetry is intended to be read aloud, to be heard, and although you can't read the poem aloud during the exam, you can read it to yourself as if you were *hearing* it read aloud. Allow the voice in your head to help you mentally "hear" the poem's sounds and rhythms. For many students, a high-stakes test is more nerve-inducing than fun, but if you try to enjoy the poem as you mentally "listen" to it, you may find enjoyment and relaxation that will open the door to better understanding and a better essay. Ask yourself, "Who is the speaker in the poem?" and listen closely to that speaker's poetic voice. Consider why the poet chose this speaker and why the speaker is important in conveying the meaning of the poem. You will find that one part of the prompt addresses meaning and another addresses poetic devices or elements, and the prompt may point you in the direction of some devices that contribute to the meaning of the poem.

It is always helpful to address the meaning of the poem first—it is the "what," the essence of the poem and of the prompt. The devices are the "how"—they help us to see how the poet conveys meaning. A student who answers the "meaning" portion of the poetry question without analyzing devices will always fare better than one who addresses only devices devoid of meaning. The best essays include both, and of these, the very best integrate the discussion of meaning and technique seamlessly without belaboring devices. Avoid a "laundry list" of devices, such as "the poet uses diction, tone, and imagery to..." For example, an analysis of the poet's diction (word choices) may be an effective means of addressing the prompt, but focus on the meaning of the poem and the words as the doorway to discussing this element. Keep in mind, too, that when the prompt says "analyze how the poet uses devices (or elements) *such as*," the words "such as" offer you the choice to choose other elements not indicated in the prompt. The prompts are user-friendly; that is, they give you strong indicators of what will lead to a good essay so you may well want to discuss those devices suggested by the prompt. But if the prompt points toward "paradox" and you either don't see paradox in the poem or have temporarily forgotten what paradox means, choose another literary element you can discuss intelligently and that is clearly significant in the poem. It cannot be emphasized strongly enough that any devices you choose to discuss are secondary to meaning. Don't create a list of devices you think you understand and then try to twist and mold them to fit the prompt. Thinking about the poet's techniques as tools of the craft as opposed to "devices" may help you avoid this pitfall and write an integrated essay that answers the prompt well.

A close look at the 2012 Question 1 prompt might clarify the procedure for you. The poem, "Thou Blind Man's Mark" by Sir Philip Sydney, can be found online at AP Central (http://www.collegeboard.com/student/testing/ap/english_lit/samp.html?englit) by clicking on the link for the 2012 free-response questions. The prompt reads: "In the following poem by Sir Philip Sidney (1554-1586), the speaker addresses the subject of desire. Read the poem carefully. Then write a well-developed essay in which you analyze how poetic devices help to convey the speaker's complex attitude toward desire." It often helps to consider each prompt as "friendly"—that is, a solid direction to help you, not intimidate you—in which every word is important. The first sentence tells us that Sir Philip Sydney's sixteenth-century poem addresses the subject of *desire*. This is key to understanding the poem. Underline the word *desire*.

The second sentence reminds you that you need to write a well-developed essay, one with a solid thesis statement that does not merely echo the prompt, and which is clearly organized and supported. You are asked to "analyze," which means to examine the structure or makeup of something (in this case the poem) closely and methodically for the purpose of interpretation or explanation. This word reminds you that your answer should include the overall meaning of the poem and show how the poet creates that meaning. You may want to underline "well-developed" and "analyze," but the essence of the prompt comes in the next phrase. You are asked to analyze "how poetic devices help to convey the speaker's complex attitude toward desire." The word "complex," which appears frequently in AP prompts, is significant. It tells you that there is something in the speaker's attitude that is complicated and that may not be obvious on a first reading. The word "complex" signals layered or often contradictory emotions. As you look for this complexity, your task is to look for nuances and even contradictions regarding the speaker's attitude. You already know that *desire* is the subject he is addressing: now look closely to see how he *feels* about desire. You should read the poem first quickly to get a general sense of these feelings. This initial reading will let you know that he sees desire as negative ("Fond fancy's scum," "Band of all evils") and hurtful ("thou has my ruin sought"). A closer reading will help you to discover and analyze just how the speaker conveys this negative attitude: though literary devices. Although you want to avoid that laundry list of devices, identifying and pointing out how the devices communicate meaning is exactly what the prompt is asking you to do.

With a Renaissance poem such as "Thou Blind Man's Mark," it is essential to look at the clear direction of the speaker's ideas and not to let the sixteenth-century language intimidate you. Even in modern times, you undoubtedly know about Cupid (the blind man) and his arrow (aiming at the "mark" in the title): you have just discovered an allusion in the poem. The poem's diction is particularly intense ("scum," "snare," "ruin"), and alliteration ("cradle of causeless care," "worthless ware") works effectively to underscore the intensity with which the speaker scorns desire. If you can see the poem's pattern as a sonnet (three quatrains followed by a couplet), then you can clearly follow and discuss the speaker's argument. The first four lines directly address desire (apostrophe) and show how it evokes foolishness. Desire drives people to act like fools: desire is "thy fool's self-chosen snare" (it traps us); it makes people act without reason and haphazardly ("causeless... "dregs of scattered thought"). In the second quatrain, the speaker complains that he has wasted his time on the object of his desire: "I have too deeply bought, / With price of mangled mind, thy worthless ware." He states that desire's ware is "worthless," yet he has sacrificed his sanity ("price of mangled mind") for it. In other words, he drove himself crazy with desire.

The speaker repeats this theme in the third quatrain: He acted like a crazy fool, and "in vain" (for nothing). He did not achieve what he wanted—note the repetition of "in vain"—even though he gave up his rational mind for it. Notice the metaphor "thou kindlest all thy smoky fire"—again "in vain" but with the hot intensity we associate with desire. The closing couplet lets us know the speaker's goal. He now desires only to "kill desire"—a paradox.

By creating a free account on the College Board's exam practice page, you will have access to the 2011 poetry question, "A Story" by Li-Young Lee, which contrasts sharply with 2012's sixteenth-century sonnet. The 2011 prompt reads, "The following poem is by the contemporary poet Li-Young Lee. Read the poem carefully. Then write a well-developed essay in which you analyze how the poet conveys the complex relationship of the father and son through the use of literary devices such as point of view and structure." This is again a "friendly" prompt offering clear direction. The first sentence identifies Li-Young Lee as a contemporary poet, thus implying that the situation and theme of the poem may involve contemporary concerns. Underline or circle the word "contemporary" to remind you to keep this situation in mind as you read the poem.

The second sentence reminds you again (as with the 2012 example) to write a well-developed essay. You may want to underline "well-developed" and "analyze," but the essence of the prompt comes in the next sentences. You are asked to analyze "how the poet conveys the complex relationship of the father and the son." There's that word "complex" again, alerting you to look for something in the relationship between father and son that you might not see right away. In this poem, such a reminder is particularly important because the poem may at first seem deceptively accessible. As you write about the nuanced relationship between these two characters, include the father's mental projection of their future relationship when the son is a young man looking for car keys. You might want to underline "complex relationship" and the words "father" and "son."

The final phrase "through the use of literary devices such as point of view and structure" is also important. Although you know that the phrase "such as" allows you to examine the literary elements you are most comfortable with (perhaps tone or diction), you might want to at least take a close look at point of view and structure, which work closely together in this poem. The poem is structured with three distinct voices, or speakers: a narrator describing events in the third person, the father, whose concerns are expressed in the first person, and the son, also speaking plaintively in the first person. But it is never enough merely to identify these devices; good writers show how these disparate points of view work together to suggest the father's tongue-tied anxiety, his worries as he projects himself into the future, and the "silence" (the highly significant last word of the poem) that is present despite the father's deep love. Like the third-person narrator who introduces the characters and then steps aside, we watch the father struggle with the worries about the future that prevent him from holding fast to the present. Notice how the structure of the poem also leads us to jump through time from the present to the future fraught with conflict and distance and then back again to the present. While this is not the only approach to this poem, it is one that will work for you if you make the best use of the prompt itself.

This approach can also keep you from falling into the traps that ensnare so many student writers. If you see the three voices in the poem, you will resist the temptation to think only from the young person's point of view—understandable because you are young but disastrous for this poem—or to fall into another weak approach and give advice to the father (or to any character in literature you are examining). Likewise, the prompt does not ask you to praise Li-Young Lee for his contemporary awareness or his moving scenario. Stick to the prompt, and show *how* Lee—or any poet represented on a given year's exam—communicates his theme.

Writing Question 2: Passage Analysis (Prose)

Question 2, the prose question, also demands careful reading, planning, and annotating a literary passage before you write. You've heard this before, and it may be tempting to shrug it off, but this is *highly* important: you need to notice and keep track of significant details. Again, you will be making a connection between the "what" (the content) and the "how" (the literary elements). The passage, most often an excerpt from a novel or short story, is often the equivalent of about two Perrine's pages and may involve complicated syntax, detailed plotting, or complex characterization. If the passage is short, you may need to pay close attention to its subtext—to what is being said between the lines or "beneath the text" as opposed to explicitly. In any event, you will once again need to read the passage carefully. As with *all* of the essay questions, it is crucial that you read the prompt carefully, paying close attention to the different parts of the question. Annotating both the prompt and the passage will help you to stay focused on both the different steps within the question and those aspects of the passage that are most important in responding to the prompt.

Many previous prose questions have left most of the specific analysis choices to the writer. Several of these past questions provided a passage and then asked how the author of the passage used language to achieve his or her effect. For example, the 1995 prose question directs students to read "Eleven" by Sandra Cisneros and then to "write an essay analyzing how the author, Sandra Cisneros, uses literary techniques to characterize Rachel." In this case, your only specific direction is to focus on characterization. What is Rachel like? *How* (literary techniques) does Cisneros create Rachel and show her to us? The 2005 prose question directed students to read a very short story, "The Birthday Party," and then, in the essay, to "show how the author uses literary devices to achieve her purpose." Your only specific direction is to focus on purpose: why did the author write this piece? What does she want you to think about as you read it? And *how* does she create her effect (literary techniques)?

However, if the prompt does provide you with a clearer direction, be sure to take advantage of this by reading and annotating the prompt closely. The 2011 Question 2 prompt was based on a fairly challenging passage from George Eliot's nineteenth-century novel *Middlemarch*. (This excerpt and prompt are also found at the link for 2011 free response questions at http://www.collegeboard.com/student/testing/ap/english_lit/samp.html?englit. You do need to create a free account to log in.) Despite the difficulty level of the passage, the prompt offered considerable help to the student writers:

> The following passage is from the novel *Middlemarch* by George Eliot, the pen name of Mary Ann Evans (1819–1880). In the passage, Rosamond and Tertius Lydgate, a recently married couple, confront financial difficulties.
>
> Read the passage carefully. Then write a well-developed essay in which you analyze how Eliot portrays these two characters and their complex relationship as husband and wife. You may wish to consider such literary devices as narrative perspective and selection of detail.

The prompt offers insight into the content of the passage immediately by introducing the characters, Rosamond and Tertius Lydgate, and providing the context that they are newly married and confronting financial difficulties. You should underline these facts. Underline as well "how Eliot portrays these two characters" and "complex relationship." The fact that the two characters are newly married is enormously helpful, and you should keep in mind the difficulties of adjusting to life with new partner as you read the passage. Notice the word "complex" again, which refers in this case to complexity of meaning as opposed to technique. Rosamond and Tertius, like real and complicated human beings, do not always react to each other in predictable ways. It is the mark of a superior writer, such as Eliot and others likely to be represented on the AP Lit exam, to reveal human nature in all its ambivalence. And it is your job to uncover the ambiguities and contradictions that infuse the shifts and turns in the dialogue as you analyze the passage. It is not enough, ever, to simply repeat the word "complex" as in "Their complex relationship..." You need to *show* with examples and specific quotations from the passage where this complexity lies.

This prompt also gives you some helpful direction as you analyze how Eliot reveals this complex relationship. You are asked to refer to her literary techniques *such as* narrative perspective and selection of detail. Again, the phrase "such as" offers you the option of considering other literary techniques, such as figurative language, or tone, but you should realize that the two *suggested* elements are key to grappling with this passage. Narrative perspective, another term for point of view (though perhaps slightly broader), is particularly significant in helping us to see the complexity of the relationship. In this passage, the omniscient narration helps direct and then redirect our sympathies. By paying close attention to the nuanced shifts of consciousness throughout the passage, you are not only examining narrative perspective in detail, you are also responding to the prompt's question about the married couple's "complex relationship."

It is important to remain alert as you read the passage and as you write your essay. Too many exam writers seem to make up their minds about the direction of a passage after reading only a few sentences, thus missing the very subtleties it holds. Read with an open mind and pen in hand, underlining specific details, shifts, and ambiguities as you go. Keep in mind at all times that you are *analyzing*—not merely summarizing—the passage, as you look for key details and citations that support what the prompt is asking. To prevent falling into the trap of too much plot summary, ask yourself if your examples from the plot are examples in service of your thesis. Do they support your analysis of the characters (or whatever the given year's prompt is asking of you), or are you starting to summarize the passage merely for summary's sake? Pay close attention to the way you open and close your paragraphs—a plot summary will simply take off with another plot element; that is, it will tell what happened next. An analysis that uses plot developments only to exemplify an analytical observation will first make the point about theme or characterization and then follow it with the example.

Writing Question 3: The "Open" Question

The novels, plays, and epic poems you read and study throughout your AP Literature course will prepare you to write this question. Most Question 3 topics are thematic in nature though many in past years have also dealt with such literary elements as setting, characterization, or symbolism. The work you choose as the basis for your essay should be of strong literary merit. Young adult novels and bestselling commercial novels (see "Chapter Eight: Evaluating Fiction" in this book) are not appropriate choices for this question primarily because they do not provide you with enough depth of characterization and richness of theme to write a solid essay. Students who choose such works usually find themselves writing mere plot summary and little to no analysis.

The question of just what constitutes a work of "literary merit" is a challenging one, and educators continue to debate the relative merit of the most contemporary works. The classics you have read in school—canonical titles from the sixteenth through early twentieth century—have left a lasting literary imprint. Although these books may be challenging to read, their enduring qualities leave readers with much to discuss. With contemporary novels, a good question to ask yourself is how much you would glean from a novel if you were to reread it. Challenging works of literary merit can be read over and over again; each time the reader gains a new perspective or insight. Popular commercial fiction usually does not stand up to more than one reading, and there is usually little to discuss beyond plot. Characters may be stereotypical and one-dimensional, lacking the "complexity" that comes into play in so many of the AP Literature exam questions. If you are in doubt, look up reviews of the work and see what critical reviewers from *The New York Times* and *The New York Times Book Review* say about the work. Ask your teacher's opinion, or perhaps stick to the works you have studied in your Advanced Placement Literature class. Texts that appear most frequently on the AP Lit exam include many you may have studied in class: *Invisible Man*, *Wuthering Heights*, *Crime and Punishment*, *Great Expectations*, *Jane Eyre*, and *Moby Dick*. The authors represented in this text (with the exception of a few whose more commercial works are included for contrast) are all highly respected writers whose full-length novels and plays would be excellent choices for the open question. For example, *Perrine's* includes Jhumpa Lahiri's "The Interpreter of Maladies." You should not choose a short story for Question 3, but Larhiri's *The Namesake* is a novel of respected literary merit. Novels by Edith Wharton, Kazuo Ishigaro, Joyce Carol Oates, Nadine Gordimer, D. H. Lawrence, and Gabriel Garcia Marquez—only a fraction of the authors represented in *Perrine's*—would all unquestionably meet the test of literary merit. Of course, it is also essential that the novel or play be a suitable choice with which to answer the prompt.

It will help you to be well prepared to write about works that are varied in content, style, theme, and literary era. Several experienced AP Lit teachers suggest having in mind a focus list of possibly three to five novels or plays that you can write about effectively, including a Shakespeare play and two or more novels that contrast markedly in style and substance (perhaps at least one that is canonical and one that is a high-quality contemporary work). Prior to the exam, review the major characters and the plot and theme of the works of literary merit you have chosen for your focus list so that you don't have to spend too much precious writing time trying to remember details. However, if the three or so works you have selected do not seem to suit the prompt, do not hesitate to abandon your plan and to choose something else you know. There is little worse than twisting or distorting the question to fit what you've already decided to write about ahead of time. Readers readily spot these attempts, which do not effectively show your ability to think critically and creatively under the time pressure.

Read the question closely, thinking as you read of different full-length works of literature that can allow you, once again, to address the prompt. Before looking at the list of novel and play titles that are provided, quickly write down whichever titles from your focus list apply to the thrust of the question. Then you have two choices. If you are certain that you will use one of these titles, skip the list of suggested titles altogether and begin planning your essay. However, if you are still a bit undecided, let the list of suggested titles jog your memory of the novels and plays you know. Circle or place a check mark by titles you are considering. Be sure to think of works that you know well and can discuss thoroughly, but don't be afraid to think creatively about *how* a work might effectively answer the thematic question. Be sure that with the work you choose you can answer all parts of the question; more importantly, make certain that the "work as a whole" (an oft-repeated phrase in Question 3 prompts) relates meaningfully to the question. For example, the 2009 Form B AP Literature Exam Question 3 asks exam writers to choose a novel or play that focuses on political or social issues. If you were to choose a novel where a political issue is only peripheral, you would not be able to answer that portion of the question that asks you to apply how the social or political issue "contributes to the meaning of the work as a whole." Similarly, the 2002 AP Literature Exam Question 3 asked students to write about a novel or a play with a "morally ambiguous character" who "plays a pivotal role" in a work. If you were to choose a character who is morally ambiguous but whose role is not central to the work, you would be unable to answer the question fully.

But what if don't see anything you've studied on the list of suggested titles, or you don't even recognize any of the titles? Don't allow yourself to become frantic or depressed; keep in mind that this is only a *suggested* list. Panicking will only prevent you from thinking clearly. Instead, calmly ask yourself, "What *have* I read?" Mentally review the works you *do* know, those you have studied in school or even read on your own, and you will find you probably know more than one work that could apply to the prompt. The AP Literature Question 3 is always written sufficiently broadly to apply to a wide range of choices. Most students who have taken an AP Literature course, as well as previous courses in English, will be able to recall a novel, play, or epic poem that suits the question well. If you are undecided among works, choose the one that would elicit the best essay from you; trust yourself and your knowledge base.

The 2011 Question 3 prompt, like many others, focuses on a thematic concern: the issue of justice. The complete prompt is:

> In a novel by William Styron, a father tells his son that life "is a search for justice."
>
> Choose a character from a novel or play who responds in some significant way to justice or injustice. Then write a well-developed essay in which you analyze the character's understanding of justice, the degree to which the character's search for justice is successful, and the significance of this search for the work as a whole.
>
> You may choose a work from the list below or another work of comparable literary merit. Do not merely summarize the plot.

It is essential to choose a novel, play, or epic poem in which the search for justice or response to injustice imbues the entire work. To answer this question, think closely about what the word "justice" means, just as you would consider in some depth the meaning of any thematic word included in the open question prompt. For example, if you were to apply the justice prompt to *Jane Eyre*, you could certainly find a justice component in the novel, but this would not mean Jane's falling in love with Rochester. Rochester's treatment of his psychotic wife and his refusal to trust Jane are clear instances of injustice; Jane's departure from Thornfield Hall reflects her response to this injustice and a search for the justice she later realizes. Jay Gatsby's yearning for Daisy and his desire to recapture the past are not a "search for justice" in *The Great Gatsby*, but consider how Fitzgerald portrays the effects of wealth and social inequality: Tom and Daisy's wealth either completely destroys people like Myrtle and George Wilson, or leaves them behind to "clean up" the Buchanans' messes—a clear social injustice. Determine a focus for your novel that truly explores justice: racial inequality in *Invisible Man*, individual conscience and the consequences of criminal action in *Crime and Punishment*, the lasting injustice of slavery in *Beloved*, the enduring questions of justice in *The Merchant of Venice* and *King Lear*. *Heart of Darkness* could make a compelling choice if you were to focus on Marlow, not Kurtz: be sure to think incisively about the character and whether or not he or she is truly engaged in the pursuit of justice. All these works are clearly relevant and rich with examples that support the question.

As with Questions 1 and 2, it is a good idea to mark up the prompt before you begin to write. It is also an effective use of your time to take time to draft a good thesis statement, one that incorporates what is asked by the prompt but does not mimic the prompt directly. You may want to devote some time to a brief outline or list of ideas, keeping in mind that your ability to write clearly and well is also being tested. You don't want to ramble incoherently, and even a brief outline will help you stay on track. In this prompt, you might want to underline the words "character," "justice or injustice," "search for justice," and "meaning of the work as a whole." The phrase "the meaning of the work as a whole," which appears in almost all Question 3 prompts, reminds you to include the book's overall thematic purpose. If justice or injustice predominates in the novel, this task should be an integral part of your analysis. It is not necessary to explicitly call attention to this phrase (as in "the meaning of the work as a whole is...") if you have clearly examined the thematic thrust of the book. It is a sign of weakness to repeat the actual words of the prompt too closely or too often, and the phrase "the meaning of the work as a whole," when removed from the prompt and placed into your essay, can seem awkward and forced. It is more important to ensure that you have managed this task than to call explicit attention to it. Similarly, if your essay deals integrally with justice or injustice, you need not sprinkle the word "justice" liberally throughout the essay; an eloquent discussion of justice as demonstrated within a well-chosen novel will effectively announce itself.

Underline the reminder to avoid mere plot summary. With this particular essay prompt, avoiding plot summary is a challenge because it can be difficult to discuss the search for justice or the experience of injustice without alluding to plot. Just remember that you need to keep the issue of justice firmly in mind, again using your plot examples to support your point about the overarching theme of justice. Don't allow yourself to abandon the justice theme and write only about "what happened next" (merely plot); however, do not hesitate to use compelling examples from the plot and, especially, from the author's characterization, to support your point. It needs to be clear that these are, indeed, *examples* in *support* of your thesis about justice—or whatever the Question 3 topic is—and that the plot details are not the main thrust of your essay. Ask "how?" and "why?" and try to answer these questions as they relate to plot developments. Several of the prompts provided in the drama section of this book will help you wrestle with the challenge of using plot examples (for example, the development of a character throughout a work) for support but not allowing yourself to write *only* a plot summary. Since this challenge applies to both Question 2 and 3, you will benefit from writing essays of analysis that focus on theme, characterization, setting, or another literary element in which you call on plot details only as supporting details in your writing.

More Reminders for All Free Response Essays

A few more important reminders apply to all three free response essays. Remember to focus on what is actually present in the novel, play, passage, or poem. If you know a work well, or read a passage astutely, you will find sufficient content with which to address the prompt. You need not speculate on what would have happened in the book or the passage if something else *had not happened*. The word "happened" should alert you that you are considering only plot (though the speculation of what might have been different is limitless); more importantly, your task is to analyze the content that is present, not to go off into the realm of speculation. Speculating about how the novel or the passage might have been written differently does not serve you well and robs you of time you can devote to *what* the author does have to say and *how* he or she says it.

Your style of writing and level of diction are also an important consideration. You may study vocabulary extensively in your AP class (a study that will certainly pay off as you answer the multiple-choice questions), but the free response essays are not the place to grandstand and show off your knowledge of obscure words. Write eloquently and cogently, but most of all clearly. You should also take care to avoid slang and colloquial diction. Stating that that father in "A Story" (Question 1) needs to "chill out" or that King Lear "freaks out in the storm" does not do justice to your own knowledge of literature and ability to analyze; such colloquial diction is at best a distraction. In addition to your style of writing, consider your hand-writing. At this point, the AP Literature exam free response essays are still handwritten although you probably write most of your papers for school on a computer. You should practice writing at least some essays, especially timed writings, by hand, writing them as clearly as you can. If you have very small handwriting, practice writing larger so that your work can be read. Readers are told to "reward students for what they do well," and it is true they will make every effort to decipher and read poor or overly small handwriting. But many times the effort it takes the exam reader to put your work under a microscope and decipher such writing will call attention to minor flaws and lapses that may otherwise miss the reader's attention. At the very least, it may distract the reader from the valid ideas you are com-municating. In addition to taking advantage of your best writing voice and your clearest handwriting, allow at least a few minutes to proofread your exam. Minor errors may not affect your overall score, but an accumulation of errors, especially those you can find easily and correct, could distract from your message and result in a lower score than you deserve.

Finally, although length alone is not a criterion, high-scoring essays almost always exceed two handwritten pages. It is not the length that earns the high score; essays that ramble on without saying anything for three or four pages are not successful. It is a matter of having something worthwhile to say and saying it completely, with good reasons, details and examples supporting a solid thesis. Writing a sufficiently long and substantial essay is not something you can suddenly learn to do while taking the exam; rather, this ability will be nurtured throughout your Advanced Placement Literature class and reflects your ability to write long, sustained essays of literary analysis in addition to the timed writings you will practice based on AP prompts. The prompts included in this book include some that are suitable for timed writings and others that might be better used for longer, more fully developed essays, including those you work on at home and over time. Both kinds of writing will help you develop the ability to write essays of appropriate length and substantial content for the AP exam, just as the reading, discussion, and analysis of literature throughout all your English classes contribute to your becoming "lit smart" and being able to analyze and write quickly and astutely. Regardless of the score you ultimately earn on your AP Lit exam, these qualities will take you far in college and later, no matter what profession you choose.

Scoring the Essays: The Scoring Guide

An understanding of the essay scoring process can help you feel more comfortable about the exam and the validity of your score. More significantly, it can help you as you write your essays. An exam reader who is exclusively reading one of the three essays scores your essay on a 0-9 point scale. The exam reader and table leader will search through your booklet to find your essays regardless of the order in which you write them, and they will leaf through blank pages, too, to ensure that they read everything you provide. The scores you receive are not arbitrary or capricious on the part of the exam reader but reflect careful training. Readers do not add up or take off points. They score holistically, determining which of the descriptors on the scoring guide most closely matches what you have written. Examining scoring guides from past years' exams, as well as generic scoring guides that some teachers have developed, can help you learn where you need to improve as you write practice essays. A score of seven, for example, means something *specific* and there are clear and exact descriptors that raise it up to more than a five or a six. Past years' scoring guides are available at the College Board website: http://www.collegeboard.com/student/testing/ap/english_lit/samp.html?englit (scroll down to "scoring guidelines"). An online search will readily supply generic scoring guides that apply to any AP Literature timed writing. When your teacher scores your in-class writings with a scoring guide, read each score point descriptor carefully to learn how you can improve your essays and raise your scores. Above all, take comfort in the directive readers continually receive to "reward students for what they do well." Readers want to help you earn the best score you can and are delighted to they read fine and substantive essays that reveal students' ability to analyze unfamiliar passages and to showcase their knowledge of excellent literature.

AP Lit Culture in the Classroom

The most important element of the Advanced Placement Literature classroom, as already stated, is the exposure to excellent literature and the opportunity to learn to analyze literature with insight and sensitivity. There are also aspects of "AP Classroom Culture" that have caught on in the land of AP Lit courses and that may help you as you prepare for this challenging exam. Among these is a short story "boot camp" that AP Literature teacher Tim Averill originated; it is intended to immerse you in an intense study of literature as you read many short stories quickly during the opening weeks of class. Should your class include such a boot camp, embrace this opportunity for an intense, concentrated exposure to fine short stories, several essays written quickly over a few weeks, and the opportunity to study literary elements closely. In some classrooms, teachers have adapted Mr. Averill's boot camp to poetry boot camps, while other teachers try to immerse you in poetry all year long. As the exam approaches in the spring, you may find that AP Question 3 "Speed Dating," an activity designed by AP teacher Mary Filak, helps familiarize you with the format of Question 3 as you look very quickly, as in real-life speed dating, at different questions from past years to determine which novels and plays you've read would be suitable choices (dates). Your teacher may ask you to prepare 5" by 7" note cards with information from the books you've studied all year to help you remember them for the exam, or you and your classmates make give brief review presentations on these works. All these classroom activities contribute to your comfort level with literature and with the Advanced Placement exam.

The Last Minute

Preparing for the AP Literature exam means learning to read and love literature and learning to analyze it cogently, a process that takes many years of schooling and time both in your classes and on your own. While your class may involve some writing and reviewing from past AP exams or from AP prep books, there is really no way that you can "cram" for the AP Literature exam. When the night before the exam arrives, remind yourself that you have read good literature, developed your vocabulary, and written essays of literary analysis. At this point the best preparation is a good night's sleep. Eat a good breakfast the morning of the exam and stay hydrated. Bring sharpened pencils for the multiple-choice section and two black or blue pens for the essays. Wear layered, comfortable clothing so you can add or remove a layer depending on the room's temperature. Take a deep breath, read the test questions carefully, and do your best.

Remember, although you may think of this as a high stakes exam, and its results can help you get a head start on college, it is only a snapshot in time. The reading, writing, learning, and critical thinking you have done to prepare for this exam are far more important and will prepare you well for life, not just one day's exam. Be proud of the work you have completed in Advanced Placement Literature and try to enjoy the test as an opportunity to read and write about powerful, enduring literature.

(Thanks go to Martin Beller and Robert Brown for their contributions.)

Writing about

Literature

I. Why Write about Literature?

Written assignments in a literature class have two purposes: (1) to give you additional practice in writing clearly and persuasively, and (2) to deepen your understanding of literary works by leading you to read and think about a few works more searchingly than you might otherwise do. But these two purposes are private. To be successful, your paper must have a public purpose as well: it should be written to enlighten others besides yourself. Even if no one else ever reads your paper, you should never treat it as a private note to your instructor. You should write every paper as if it were intended for publication.

II. For Whom Do You Write?

The audience for whom you write will govern both the content and the expression of your paper. You need to know something about your readers' backgrounds—national, racial, social, religious—and be able to make intelligent guesses about their knowledge, interests, and previous reading. In writing about George Herbert's "Peace" (page 774) for a Hindu audience, you would need to include explanations of Christian belief and biblical stories that would be unnecessary for a western European or American audience. In presenting Graham Greene's "The Destructors" (page 105), your editors have felt it necessary to provide information (in footnotes) that would not be needed by a British audience; for "Los Vendidos" by Luis Valdez (page 1228), footnotes provide translations and explanations that would not be necessary for an audience familiar with the Spanish-language slang of contemporary America. But the most crucial question about an audience is: *Has it read the work you are writing about?* The book reviewer in your Sunday paper generally writes about a newly published book that the audience has not read. A reviewer's purpose is to let readers know something of what the book is about and to give them some notion of whether they will enjoy or profit from reading it. At an opposite extreme, the scholar writing in a specialized scholarly journal can generally assume an audience that *has* read the work, that has a knowledge of previous interpretations of the work, and that is familiar with other works in its period or genre. The scholar's purpose, not infrequently, is to persuade this audience that some new information or some new way of looking at the work appreciably deepens or alters its meaning or significance.

Clearly, essays written for such different audiences and with such different purposes differ considerably in content, organization, and style. Book reviewers reviewing a new novel will include a general idea of its plot while being careful not to reveal the outcome. Scholars will assume that readers already know the plot, and will have no compunction about discussing its outcome. Reviewers will try to write interestingly and engagingly about the novel and to persuade readers that they have valid grounds for their opinions of its worth, but their manner will generally be informal. Scholars are more interested in presenting a cogent argument, logically arranged and solidly based on evidence. They will be more formal, and may use critical terms and refer to related works that would be unfamiliar to non-specialized readers. In documentation the two types of essays will be quite different. Reviewers' only documentation is normally the identification of the novel's title, author, publisher, and price, at the top of the review. For other information and opinions, they hope that a reader will rely on their intelligence, knowledge, and judgment. Scholars, on the other hand, may furnish an elaborate array of citations of other sources of information, allowing the reader to verify the accuracy or basis of any important part of their argument. Scholars expect to be challenged, and they see to it that all parts of their arguments are buttressed.

For whom, then, should *you* write? Unless your instructor stipulates (or you request) a different audience, the best plan is to assume that you are writing for the other members of your class. Pretend that your class publishes a journal of which it also constitutes the readership. Your instructor is the editor and determines editorial policy. If you write on a work that has been assigned for class reading, you assume that your audience is familiar with it. (This kind of paper is generally of the greatest educational value, for it is most open to challenge and class discussion and places on you a heavier burden of proof.) If you compare an assigned work with one that has not been assigned, you must gauge what portion of your audience is familiar with the unassigned work and proceed accordingly. If the unassigned story were A. Conan Doyle's "The Adventure of the Speckled Band," you would probably not need to explain that "Sherlock Holmes is a detective" and that "Dr. Watson is his friend," for you can assume that *this* audience, through movies, TV, or reading, is familiar with these characters; but you could not assume familiarity with this particular story. You know that, as members of the same class, your readers have certain backgrounds and interests in common and are at comparable levels of education. Anything you know about your audience may be important for how you write your paper and what you put in it.

Assuming members of your class as your audience carries another advantage: you can also assume that they are familiar with the definitions and examples given in this book, and therefore you can avoid wasting space by quoting or paraphrasing the book. There will be no need to tell them that an indeterminate ending is one in which the central conflict is left unresolved, or that Emily Dickinson's poems are untitled, or that Miss Brill is an unmarried Englishwoman living in France.

III. Two Basic Approaches

In a beginning study of literature, most writing will focus on a careful reading of details of the assigned work as the basis for any further exploration. Traditionally, the approach will be structured as an *explication* or an *analysis*.

1. Explication

An *explication* (literally, an "unfolding") is a detailed elucidation of a work, sometimes line by line or word by word, which is interested not only in *what* that work means but in *how* it means what it means. It thus considers all relevant aspects of a work—speaker or point of view, connotative words and double meanings, images, figurative language, allusions, form, structure, sound, rhythm—and discusses, if not all of these, at least the most important. (There is no such thing as exhausting the meanings and the ways to those meanings in a complex piece of literature, and the explicator must settle for something less than completeness.) Explication follows from what we sometimes call "close reading"—looking at a piece of writing, as it were, through a magnifying glass.

Clearly, the kinds of literature for which an explication is appropriate are limited. First, the work must be rich enough to repay the kind of close attention demanded. One would not think of explicating "Pease Porridge Hot" (page 899) unless for purposes of parody, for it has no meanings that need elucidation and no "art" worthy of comment. Second, the work must be short enough to be encompassed in a relatively brief discussion. A thorough explication of *Othello* would be much longer than the play itself and would tire the patience of the most dogged reader. Explications work best with short poems. (Sonnets like Shakespeare's "That time of year" [page 921] and Frost's "Design" [page 829] almost beg for explication.) Explication sometimes may also be appropriate for passages in long poems, as, for example, the lines spoken by Macbeth after the death of his wife (page 812) or the "sonnet" from *Romeo and Juliet* (page 927), and occasionally for exceptionally rich or crucial passages of prose, perhaps the final paragraphs of stories like "Paul's Case" (page 243) or "Miss Brill" (page 155). But explication as a critical form should perhaps be separated from explication as a method. Whenever you elucidate even a small part of a literary work by a close examination that relates it to the whole, you are essentially explicating (unfolding). For example, if you point out the multiple meanings in the title of "Time Flies" (page 1101) as they relate to that play's themes, you are explicating the title.

For examples of explication, see the three sample essays in Part XII of this section (pages 38–54). The discussions in this book display the explicative method frequently, but except for the sample essays, there are no pure examples of explication. The discussions of "A Noiseless Patient Spider" (pages 767–768) and "Digging" (pages 770–771) come close to being explications and might have been so had they included answers to the study questions and one or two other matters. The exercises provided in "Understanding and Evaluating Poetry" on page 688 should be helpful to you in writing an explication of a poem. Not all the questions will be applicable to every poem, and you need not answer all those that are applicable, but you should start by considering all that apply and then work with those that are central and important for your explication.

2. Analysis

An *analysis* (literally a "breaking up" or separation of something into its constituent parts), instead of trying to examine all parts of a work in relation to the whole, selects for examination *one* aspect or element or part that relates to the whole. Clearly, an analysis is a better approach to longer works and to prose works than is an explication. A literary work may be usefully approached through almost any of its elements—point of view, characterization, plot, setting, symbolism, structure, and the like—so long as you relate this element to the central meaning or the whole. (An analysis of meter is meaningless unless it shows how meter serves the meaning; an analysis of the vocabulary and grammar of "Spunk" [page 564] or "The Sandbox" [page 1095] would be pointless unless related to the characterization of the speakers.) The list of exercises on pages 94–96 may suggest approaches to stories, plays, and narrative poems; the list on page 688 to anything written in verse; and that on pages 1072–1073 to dramas. As always, it is important to choose a topic appropriate to the space available. "Characterization in Lawrence's 'The Rocking-Horse Winner' " is too large a topic to be usefully treated in a few pages, but a character analysis of Paul or of his uncle and mother might fit the space neatly. For examples of analyses of three literary forms, see the sample essays in Part XII of this section (pages 38–54).

IV. Choosing a Topic

As editor of this imaginary publication, your instructor is responsible for the nature of its contents. Instructors may be very specific in their assignments, or they may be very general, inviting you to submit a paper on any subject within a broadly defined area of interest. They will also have editorial policies concerning length of papers, preparation of manuscripts, and deadlines for submission (all of which should be meticulously heeded).

Instructors may further specify whether the paper should be entirely the work of your own critical thinking, or whether it is to be an investigative assignment—that is, one involving research into what other writers have written concerning your subject and the use of their findings, where relevant, to help you support your own conclusions.

Let us consider four kinds of papers you might write: (1) papers that focus on a single literary work, (2) papers of comparison and contrast, (3) papers on a number of works by a single author, and (4) papers on a number of works having some feature other than authorship in common.

1. Papers That Focus on a Single Literary Work

If your assignment is a specific one (How is the landscape symbolic in "The Guest" [page 360]? What emotions are evoked by the imagery in "The Widow's Lament in Springtime" [page 736]?) your task is clearcut. You have only to read the selection carefully (obviously more than once), formulate your answer, and support it with corroborating evidence from within the text as cogently and convincingly as possible. In order to convince your readers that your answer is the best one, you will need to examine and account for apparently contrary evidence as well as clearly supportive evidence; otherwise, skeptical readers, reluctant to change their minds, might simply refer to "important points" that you have "overlooked."

Specific questions like these, when they are central to the work and may be a matter of dispute, make excellent topics for papers. You may discover them for yourself when you disagree with a classmate about the interpretation of a story or poem or play. The study questions following many of the selections in this anthology frequently suggest topics of this kind.

If your assignment is more general, and if you are given some choice as to what selection you wish to write on, it is usually best to choose one you enjoyed, whether or not you entirely understood it. (You are more likely to write a good paper on a selection you liked than on one you disliked, and you should arrive at a fuller understanding of it while thinking through your paper.) You must then decide what kind of paper you will write, taking into account the length and kind of selection you have chosen and the amount of space at your disposal.

2. Papers of Comparison and Contrast

The comparison and contrast of two stories, poems, or plays having one or more features in common may be an illuminating exercise because the similarities highlight the differences, or vice versa, and thus lead to a better understanding not only of both pieces but of literary processes in general. The works selected may be similar in plot but different in theme, similar in subject but different in tone, similar in theme but different in literary value, or, conversely, different in plot but similar in theme, different in subject but similar in tone, and so on. In writing such a paper, it is usually best to decide first whether the similarities or the differences are more significant, begin with a brief summary of the less significant, and then concentrate on the more significant.

A number of selections in this collection have been included to encourage just this kind of study: "The Most Dangerous Game" and "Hunters in the Snow" in chapter 1 of the Fiction section; "The Necklace" and "Roman Fever" in chapter 8; in the Poetry section, "Spring" and "The Widow's Lament in Springtime" in chapter 4; all six pairs of poems in chapter 9; "To the Snake" and "A Narrow Fellow in the Grass," "Crossing the Bar" and "The Oxen," "Dover Beach" and "Church Going" in chapter 10; all poems in chapter 15; and "Terence, this is stupid stuff" and "Ars Poetica" in Poems for Further Reading. In addition, many of the Suggestions for Writing at the ends of chapters group together comparable works.

3. Papers on a Number of Works by a Single Author

Most readers, when they discover a work they particularly like, look for other works by the same author. The paper that focuses on a single author rather than a single work is the natural corollary of such an interest. The most common concern in a paper of this type is to identify the characteristics that make this author different from other authors and therefore of particular interest to the writer. What are the author's characteristic subjects, settings, attitudes, or themes? With what kinds of life does the author characteristically deal? What are the author's preferred literary forms? Is the author's approach ironic, witty, serious, comic, tragic? Is the author's vision directed principally inward or outward? In short, what configuration of patterns makes the author's fingerprints unique? Your paper may consider one or more of these questions.

Several writers are represented in this book by a sufficient number of works to support such a paper without turning to outside sources. In the Fiction section, three stories each by D. H. Lawrence, Flannery O'Connor, and Joyce Carol Oates are grouped together for comparative study. In the Poetry section, there are numerous poems by John Keats, John Donne, Emily Dickinson, Robert Frost and Elizabeth Bishop, six or more poems each by authors listed in the table of contents as a "Contemporary Collection," and at least three poems each by eighteen poets, both classic and modern. The author listings in the index will help you locate the multiple poems by a single author.

A more ambitious type of paper on a single author examines the works for signs of development. The attitudes that any person, especially an author, takes toward the world may change with the passing from adolescence to adulthood to old age. So also may the author's means of expressing attitudes and judgments. Though some writers are remarkably consistent in outlook and expression throughout their careers, others manifest surprising changes. To write a paper on the development of an author's work, you must have accurate information about the dates when works were written, and the works must be read in chronological order. When you have mastered the differences, you may be able to illustrate them through close examination of two or three works, one for each stage.

When readers become especially interested in the works of a particular author, they may develop a curiosity about that author's life as well. This is a legitimate interest, and, if there is sufficient space and your editor/instructor permits it, you may want to incorporate biographical information into your paper. If so, however, you should heed three caveats. First, your main interest should be in the literature itself: the biographical material should be subordinated to and used in service of your examination of the work. In general, discuss only those aspects of the author's life that bear directly on the work: biography should not be used as "filler." Second, you should be extremely cautious about identifying an event in a work with an event in the life of the author. Almost never is a story, poem, or play an exact transcription of its author's personal experience. Authors fictionalize themselves when they put themselves into imaginative works. If you consider that even in autobiographies (where they intend to give accurate accounts of their lives) writers must select incidents from the vast complexity of their experiences, that the memory of past events may be defective, and that at best writers work from their own points of view—in short, when you realize that even autobiography cannot be an absolutely reliable transcription of historical fact—you should be more fully prepared not to expect such an equation in works whose object is imaginative truth. Third, you must document the sources of your information about the author's life (see pages 22–30).

4. Papers on a Number of Works with Some Feature Other than Authorship in Common

You might also write a successful paper on works by various authors that have some features in common, such as subject matter, form, setting, point of view, literary devices, and the like; discovering the ways in which different works employ a particular feature can be illuminating. Probably the most familiar paper of this type is the one that treats works having a similar thematic concern (love, war, religious belief or doubt, art, adolescence, initiation, maturity, old age, death, parents and children, racial conflict, social injustice). But a paper may also examine particular forms of literature, for example, the Italian sonnet, the dramatic monologue, the short story with an unreliable narrator. Topics of this kind may be further limited by time or place or number—four attitudes toward death; Elizabethan love lyrics; poetry on the experience of war; satires of bureaucracy.

V. Proving Your Point

In writing about literature, your object generally is to convince your readers that your understanding of a work is valid and important and to lead them to share that understanding. When writing about other subjects, it may be appropriate to persuade your readers through various rhetorical means—through eloquent diction, structural devices that create suspense, analogies, personal anecdotes, and the like. But readers of essays about literature usually look for "proof." They want you to show them *how* the work, or the element you are discussing, does what you claim it does. Like scientists who require proof of the sort that they can duplicate in their own laboratories, readers of criticism want access to the process of inference, analysis, and deduction that has led to your conclusions, so that they may respond as you have done.

To provide this proof is no easy task, for it requires the development of your own reading and writing skills. In addition, you must have developed a responsible interpretation of the work and of the way it achieves its effect; you should be able to point out precisely how it communicates its meanings; and you should be able to present your experiences of it clearly and directly. When you have spent considerable time in coming to understand and respond to a work of literature, it may become so familiar that it seems self-evident to you, and you will need to "back off" sufficiently to be able to put yourself in your readers' position—they may have vague feelings about the work ("I like it" or "It moves me deeply"), without knowing what it is that produced those feelings. It is your job to refine the feelings and define away the vagueness.

Some forms of "proof" rarely do the job. Precision does not result from explaining a metaphor metaphorically ("When Shakespeare's Juliet calls parting from Romeo a 'sweet sorrow,' the reader is reminded of taking bitter-tasting medicine"). Nor can you prove anything about a work by hypothesizing about what it might have been if it did not contain what it does ("If Desdemona had not lost her handkerchief, Othello would never have murdered her"—this is equivalent to saying, "If the play were not what it is, it would not be what it is"). Your own personal experiences will rarely help your readers ("My anxiety, excitement, and awkwardness at my first skiing lesson were like the mixed feelings Prufrock imagines for himself at the tea party"—*your* reader hasn't shared your experience of that lesson). Even your personal history of coming to understand a literary work will seldom help, though you present it in more general terms ("At a first reading, the opening paragraphs of 'The Lottery' are confusing because they do not explain why the villagers are gathering"—most literature does not yield up its richness on a first reading, so this approach has nothing to add to your reader's understanding). Just as argument by analogy is not regarded as valid in formal logic, so in critical discourse, analogies are usually unconvincing ("Desdemona's ignorance about adultery is like a child's inability to balance a bank account"). These strategies all have in common the looseness and vagueness of trying to define something by saying what it is not, or what it is like, rather than dealing with what it *is*.

"Proof" in writing about literature is primarily an exercise in strict definition. Juliet's phrase "sweet sorrow" (quoted in the preceding paragraph) derives its feeling from the paradoxical linking of sweetness and grief as a representation of the conflicting emotions of love. To provide an appropriate definition of the effect of the phrase, you would need to identify the figure of speech as paradox and to investigate the way in which love can simultaneously inflict pain and give pleasure, and you might find it useful to point to the alliteration that ties these opposites together. Obviously, comparing this kind of proof to that required by science is inexact, since what you are doing is reminding your readers, or perhaps informing them, of feelings that are associated with language, not of the properties of chemical compounds. Furthermore, a scientific proof is incomplete if it does not present every step in a process. If that requirement were placed on literary analysis, a critical essay would be interminable, since more can always be said about any interpretive point. So, rather than attempting to prove every point that you make, you should aim to demonstrate that your *method* of analysis is valid by providing persuasive proof of your major point or points. If you have shown that your handling of a major point is sound, your readers will tend to trust your judgment on lesser matters.

VI. Writing the Paper

The general procedures for writing a good paper on literature are much the same as the procedures for writing a good paper on any subject.

7. After all is in order, prepare your final copy, being sure to follow the editorial policies of your instructor for the submission of manuscripts.

8. Read over your final copy slowly and carefully, and correct any mistakes (omissions, repetitions, typographical errors) you may have made in revising your draft. This final step—too often omitted due to haste or fatigue—is extremely important and may make the difference between an A or a C paper, or between a C paper and an F. It is easy to make careless mistakes in copying, but your reader should not be counted on to recognize the difference between a copying error and one of ignorance. Moreover, the smallest error may utterly destroy the sense of what you have written: omission of a "not" may make your paper say exactly the opposite of what you meant it to say.

VII. Writing In-Class Essays or Essay Tests

You will often be asked in your literature courses to write essays in class or to write essay tests. The topic or assignment may be given to you in advance so that you can prepare for writing in the classroom, or you may be given the topic in the class when you will do the writing. If you have the topic early enough to prepare, you will want to follow the preparatory suggestions offered for writing a formal out-of-class essay. If the topic for your essay or test is not given out in advance, the following general approaches may be useful.

1. Analyze the topic. If you are asked to compare characters, or to discuss the implications of an event, or to define a concept and exemplify it, be sure that you do so. Pay attention to key words and such instructions as *compare, show how*, and especially *define*. If asked to compare, be sure you are drawing the comparison and not just giving two summaries; if asked to define, be sure your statement is in the form of a definition and does not just give examples. And be sure that you answer all parts of a question: consider whether it contains two or even three tasks within a single instruction.

2. For each question, take a little time to jot down a few key words or ideas that seem to be essential in answering the question, to keep yourself from spending all your time on one of the points but leaving out others of equal importance. If you can, decide which points are the *most* important and be sure to include them.

3. Try to begin your answer with a topic sentence that includes all the major points you intend to use in your essay. You can often get a good

topic sentence out of the question itself: if it says "Show how the frame story of Gordimer's 'Once upon a Time' is related to the main story," you might begin your essay, "The frame story involving a writer awakened by a frightening noise in the night introduces fear, the central topic of the main story, but the kinds of fear are distinctly different."

4. Don't give summaries of actions and plots unless you need to do so. You may need to give a brief summary, for example, in order to support a point; but be sure you are doing that rather than assuming that a summary will *make* a point. An essay test is not usually the place to prove that you have read the assigned material, but that you can *use* your reading.

5. Be specific and concrete. Prove your points with facts—named characters, specific actions, concrete details of plot, and even paraphrases or quotations from speeches if you can recall them (but don't quote unless you have indeed memorized them, and do not place quotation marks around paraphrases).

6. Keep an eye on the clock and budget your time. If you are asked to write two essays with equal time allotments, and you answer only one, then your maximum score can be no more than 50 percent—no matter how well you answer the one. If you have time, review and revise your writing, making corrections as neatly as you can. When moving whole paragraphs or blocks of writing, be sure your final intention is clear. And take all the time that is allotted to you—if you think you have said everything you can, then spend the time in revision.

VIII. Introducing Quotations

In writing about literature it is often desirable, sometimes imperative, to quote from the work under discussion. Quoted material is needed (1) to provide essential evidence in support of your argument, and (2) to set before your reader any passage that you are going to examine in detail. It will also keep your reader in contact with the text and allow you to use felicitous phrasing from the text to enhance your own presentation. You must, however, be careful not to overquote. If a paper consists of more than 20 percent quotation, it loses the appearance of closely knit argument and seems instead merely a collection of quotations strung together like clothes hung out on a line to dry. Avoid, especially, unnecessary use of long quotations. Readers tend to skip them. Consider carefully whether the quoted material may not be more economically presented by paraphrase, or whether the quotation, if judged necessary, may not be effectively shortened by ellipsis (see Q9 below). Readers faced with a long quotation may reasonably expect you to examine it in some detail; that is, the longer your quotation, the more you should do with it.

As a general rule in analytical writing, quotation should be included for the purpose of supporting or proving a point, not for the purpose of re-creating the experience of a work for your reader. You may assume that your reader has already read the work and does not need to have it summarized—but on the other hand, you should not send your reader back to the book to reread in order to understand what you are referring to. Analysis is the process of demonstrating how the parts work together to create the whole; it must examine these parts in detail and show how they work together. Quoting presents details, and analysis shows how the details do what you say they do. If a quotation seems entirely self-evident to you, so that you have nothing to explain about it, then it is not really worth quoting. If it is self-evident, your reader has already understood all there is to know about it.

As with every other aspect of good writing, the use of quotation is a matter of intelligence and tact. There are no hard-and-fast rules, since the amount of material you quote and the way you explain the significance of your quotations will vary, depending on the work you are writing about and the kind of paper you are writing. In general, however, you should limit direct quotation to words, phrases, or short passages that are so well written and illuminating that to paraphrase them would dilute the force of your argument. Such quotation strengthens your own writing by showing that you have mastered the material and can offer the crucial evidence directly from the text. On the other hand, if the *content* of a passage (especially a long passage) is more significant than the specific language the author uses, then a paraphrase is probably adequate. Either way, be sure that you quote or paraphrase selectively, keeping your own ideas about the work in the foreground; and also be sure that your quotation or paraphrase directly supports your argument.

1. Principles and Guidelines

There is no legislative body that establishes laws governing the formal aspects of quoting, documenting, or any other aspect of writing. The only "rules" are the editorial policies of the publisher to whom you submit your work. (In the case of papers being written as class assignments, your "publisher" is your instructor.) There is, however, a national organization—the Modern Language Association of America—that is so influential that its policies for its own publications and its recommendations for others are adopted by most journals of literary criticism and scholarship. The instructions below are in general accord with those stated in the *MLA Handbook for Writers of Research Papers*, 7th edition, by Joseph Gibaldi (New York: MLA, 2009). In your course, your instructor will inform you of any editorial policies in effect that differ from those given here or in the *MLA Handbook*. The examples we use here are all drawn from act 5, scene 2 of *Othello*.

Q1. If the quotation is short (normally not more than four typed lines of prose or not more than two or three lines of verse), put it in quotation marks and introduce it directly into the text of your essay.

---

a   Othello, before stabbing himself, reminds his listeners, "I have done the state some service and they know 't."

b   He speaks of himself as "one that loved not wisely but too well" and compares himself to "the base Indian"

c   who "threw a pearl away / Richer than all his tribe" (5.2.338–47).

Q2. If the quotation is long (normally more than four typed lines of prose or more than three lines of verse), begin it on a new line (and resume the text of your essay on a new line also); double-space it (like the rest of your paper); and indent it twice as far from the left margin (one inch) as you do for a new paragraph indentation (one-half inch). If it is verse and has lines either too long or too short to look good with a one-inch indentation, center the quotation between the margins. Whether verse or prose, *do not enclose it in quotation marks.* Since the indentation and the line arrangement both signal a quotation, the use of quotation marks would be redundant.

In the final scene, convinced that Desdemona is entirely innocent and having decided to kill himself, Othello says to his auditors:

> I pray you, in your letters,
> When you shall these unlucky deeds relate,
> Speak of me as I am, nothing extenuate,
> Nor set down aught in malice (5.2.339–42)

The two boxed examples illustrate the "run-in" quotation (Q1), where the quotation is "run in" with the writer's own text, and the "set-off" or "block" quotation (Q2), which is separated from the writer's text.

Q3. In quoting verse, it is extremely important to preserve the line arrangement of the original because the verse line is a rhythmical unit and thus affects meaning. When more than one line of verse is run in, the lines are separated by a virgule (or diagonal slash) with one letter-space on each side, and capitalization after the first line follows that of the original (see Q1.c above).

Q4. In general, sentences containing a quotation are punctuated as they would be if there were no quotation. In Q1.a above, a comma precedes the quoted statement, as it would if there were no quotation marks. In Q2, a colon precedes the quoted sentence because it is long and complex. In Q1.b and Q1.c, there is no punctuation at all before the quotation. Do not put punctuation before a quotation unless it is otherwise called for.

Q5. Your quotation must combine with its introduction to make a grammatically correct sentence. The normal processes of grammar and syntax, like the normal processes of punctuation, are unaffected by quoting. Subjects must agree with their verbs, verbs must be consistent in tense, pronouns must have their normal relation with antecedents.

WRONG	Othello says, "One that loved not wisely but too well" (5.2.343). *(Incomplete sentence)*
RIGHT	Othello speaks of himself as "one that loved not wisely but too well" (5.2.343).

WRONG	Othello asks his auditors to "speak of me as I am" (5.2.341). *(The pronouns "me" and "I" do not agree in person with their antecedent.)*
RIGHT	Othello bids his auditors, Speak of me as I am, nothing extenuate, Nor set down aught in malice. Then must you speak Of one that loved not wisely but too well. (5.2.341–43)

WRONG	Othello says that "I have done the state some service" (5.2.338). *(Incorrect mixture of direct and indirect quotation)*
RIGHT	Othello says, "I have done the state some service" (5.2.338).

WRONG	Othello says that he "have done the state some service" (5.2.338). *(Subject and verb of subordinate clause lack agreement.)*
RIGHT	Othello says that he has "done the state some service" (5.2.338).

Q6. Your introduction must supply enough context to make the quotation meaningful. Be careful that all pronouns in the quotation have clearly identifiable antecedents.

WRONG	In the final speech of the play, Lodovico says, "Look on the tragic loading of this bed: / This is thy work" (5.2.362–63). *(Whose work?)*
RIGHT	In the final speech of the play, Lodovico says to Iago, "Look on the tragic loading of this bed: / This is thy work" (5.2.362–63).

Q7. The words within your quotation marks must be quoted *exactly* from the original.

WRONG	Though Iago bids his wife to "hold her peace," Emilia declares, "I will speak as liberally as the north wind" (5.2.218–19).

Q8. It is permissible to insert or supply words in a quotation *if* you enclose them within brackets. Brackets (parentheses with square corners) indicate *your* changes or additions. If parentheses were used, the reader might interpret the enclosed material as the *author's* (as part of what you are quoting). Avoid excessive use of brackets: they make quotations more difficult to read and comprehend. Often paraphrase will serve as well as quotation, particularly if you are not explicitly analyzing the language of a passage.

CORRECT	Though Iago bids his wife to "hold [her] peace," Emilia declares, "I will speak as liberal[ly] as the north [wind]" (5.2.218–19).
BETTER	Though Iago bids his wife to hold her peace, Emilia declares that she will speak as liberally as the north wind.

Notice that a word within brackets can either replace a word in the original (as in the substitution of *her* for "your" above) or be added to explain or complete the original (as with *-ly* and *wind* above). Since a reader understands that brackets signal either substitutions or additions, it is superfluous to include the words for which substitutions have been made.

WRONG	Iago bids his wife to "hold your [her] peace" (5.2.218).

Your sentences, including bracketed words, must read as if there were no brackets:

RIGHT | After Iago's treachery has been completely exposed, Lodovico tells Othello:

> You must forsake this room, and go with us.
> Your power and your command is taken off.
> And Cassio rules in Cyprus. For this slave [Iago],
> If there can be any cunning cruelty
> That can torment him much and hold him long,
> It shall be his. (5.2.329–31)

Q9. It is permissible to omit words from quoted material, but *only if* the omission is indicated. Three *spaced* periods are used to indicate the omission (technically they are called "ellipsis points"). If there are four periods, the first is the normal period at the end of a sentence; the other three indicate the ellipsis.

The statement just concluded, if quoted, might be shortened in the following way: "It is permissible to omit words ... *if* the omission is indicated. Three *spaced* periods are used to indicate the omission.... If there are four periods, the first is the normal period at the end of a sentence."

It is usually not necessary to indicate ellipsis at the beginning or ending of a quotation (the very act of quoting implies that something precedes and follows)—unless what you quote is in some way contradicted by its context, as for example by a "not" preceding the material you quote.

Q10. Single quotation marks are used for quotations within quotations. Thus, if the material you are quoting in a run-in quotation includes a quotation, you should reduce the original double quote marks to single quote marks. (In a block quotation, the quotation marks would remain unchanged.)

In her dying speech, Emilia asks her dead mistress, "Hark, canst thou hear me? I will play the swan, / And die in music. 'Willow, willow, willow'" (5.2.246–47)

Single quotation marks are not used for any other purposes and should not be substituted for double quotes.

Q11. At the conclusion of a run-in quotation, commas and periods are conventionally placed *within* quotation marks; semicolons and colons are placed outside. (The convention is based on appearance, not on logic.) Question marks and exclamation marks are placed inside if they belong to the quoted sentence, outside if they belong to your sentence. (This *is* based on logic.) Special rules apply when the quotation is followed by parenthetical documentation (see PD3 and PD4, page 26). The following examples are all correct:

"I am not valiant neither," says Othello (5.2.242).

Othello says, "I am not valiant neither" (5.2.242).

"Who can control his fate?" cries Othello (5.2.264).

Does Shakespeare endorse Othello's implication that no one "can control his fate"? (5.2.264).

IX. Documentation

Documentation is the process of identifying the sources of materials used in your paper. The sources are of two kinds: primary and secondary. *Primary* sources are materials written *by* the author being studied, and may be confined to the single work being discussed. *Secondary* sources are materials by other writers *about* the author or work being discussed, or materials having some bearing on that work. Documentation serves two purposes: (1) it enables your readers to check any material they may think you have misinterpreted; (2) it enables you to make proper acknowledgment of information, ideas, opinions, or phraseology that are not your own.

It is difficult to overemphasize the second of these purposes. The use of someone else's ideas or insights in your own words, since it does not require quotation marks, makes an even heavier demand for acknowledgment than does quoted material. Although you need not document matters of common knowledge, your use without acknowledgment of material that is uniquely someone else's is not only dishonest but also illegal (plagiarism), and could result in penalties ranging from an F on the paper through expulsion from school to a term in jail, depending on the magnitude of the offense.

Documentation may be given in (1) the text of your essay; (2) parentheses placed within the text of your essay; or (3) a list of Works Cited placed at the end of your essay but keyed to parenthetical references within the essay. The three methods are progressively more formal.

In any case, the type of documentation required in your class will be chosen by your instructor, who may wish to have you practice several methods so that you will learn their use.

1. Textual Documentation

Every literary essay contains textual documentation. A title like "Dramatic Irony in *Oedipus Rex*" identifies the play that will furnish the main materials in the paper. A paragraph beginning "In scene 2 ..." locates more specifically the source of what follows. An informally documented essay is one that relies on textual documentation exclusively. Perhaps the majority of articles published in newspapers and periodicals with wide circulation are of this kind. Informal documentation works best for essays written on a single short work, without use of secondary sources, for readers without great scholarly expectations. A first-rate paper might be written on Herman Melville's "Bartleby the Scrivener" using only textual documentation. The author's name and the title of the story mentioned somewhere near the beginning of the essay, plus a few phrases like "In the opening paragraph" or "When Bartleby answers the lawyer's advertisement for additional scriveners" or "At the story's conclusion" might provide all the documentation needed for this audience. The action of the story is straightforward enough that the reader can easily locate any detail within it. If the essay is intended for our hypothetical journal published by your literature class (all of whose members are using the same anthology and have presumably read the story), its readers can readily locate the story and its events. But textual documentation, although less appropriate, can also be used for more complex subjects, and can even accommodate secondary sources with phrases like "As Yvor Winters points out in his essay on Melville in *In Defense of Reason*...."

Principles and Guidelines

TD1. Enclose titles of short stories, articles, one-act plays, and poems (unless they are book-length) in quotation marks; underline or italicize titles of full-length plays, magazines, newspapers, and books. Do not underline, italicize, or use quotation marks around the title of your own paper. The general principle is that titles of separate publications are underlined or italicized; titles of selections or parts of books are put within quotation marks. Full-length plays, such as *Othello* and *Oedipus Rex*, though often reprinted as part of an anthology, are elsewhere published as separate books and should be underlined or italicized. Underlining, in manuscripts, is equivalent to italics in printed matter. Most word-processing programs include italic fonts, so you should check with your instructor for the preferred style.

TD2. Capitalize the first word and all important words in titles. Do not capitalize articles, prepositions, and conjunctions except when they begin the title ("The Lottery," "Hunters in the Snow," "To the Virgins, to Make Much of Time").

TD3. When the title above a poem is identical with its first line or a major part of its first line, there is a strong presumption that the poet left the poem untitled and the editor or anthologist has used the first line or part of it to serve as a title. In such a case you may *use* the first line as a title, but should not *refer* to it as a title. For example, you might write that "Dickinson's 'There's a certain slant of Light' is a powerful poem about a depressed psychological state." But you should not write, "Dickinson repeats her title in the first line of 'There's a certain slant of Light' because she wants to emphasize her main point." In using it as a title, capitalize only those words that are capitalized in the first line.

TD4. Never use page numbers in the body of your discussion because a page is not a structural part of a story, poem, or play. You may refer in your discussions to paragraphs, sections, stanzas, lines, acts, or scenes, as appropriate, but use page numbers *only* in parenthetical documentation where a specific edition of the work has been named.

TD5. Spell out numerical references when they precede the unit they refer to; use numbers when they follow the unit (the fifth act, or act 5; the second paragraph, or paragraph 2; the fourth line, or line 4; the tenth stanza, or stanza 10). Use the first of these alternative forms sparingly, and only with small numbers. Never write "In the thirty-fourth and thirty-fifth lines ...," for to do so is to waste good space and irritate your reader; write "In lines 34–35...."

2. Parenthetical Documentation

Parenthetical documentation makes possible fuller and more precise accrediting without a forbidding apparatus of footnotes or an extensive list of Works Cited. With a full-length play like Tennessee Williams's *The Glass Menagerie*, a phrase like "midway through scene 4" is insufficient to allow the reader to locate the passage readily. This can be done by giving a page number, within parentheses, after the passage cited. But the reader needs to know also what book or edition the page number refers to, so this information must be supplied the first time such a citation is made.

Parenthetical documentation is the method most often required for a paper using only the primary source, or, at most, two or three sources—as, for example, most of the writing assigned in an introductory literature course. The information given in parenthetical documentation should enable your reader to turn easily to the exact source of a quotation or a reference. At the first mention of a work (which may well precede the first quotation from it), full publishing details should be given, but parenthetical documentation should supplement textual documentation; that is, information provided in the text of your essay should not be repeated within the parentheses. For the readers of our hypothetical class journal, the first reference in a paper on Williams's play might look like this:

> In Tennessee Williams's *The Glass Menagerie* (reprinted in Greg Johnson and Thomas R. Arp, *Perrine's Literature: Structure, Sound, and Sense*, 12th ed. [Boston: Wadsworth, 2015] 1156–1208), Tom occasionally addresses the audience directly.

Notice in this entry that brackets are used for parentheses within parentheses. In subsequent references, provided no other source intervenes, only the page number need be given:

> Amanda defines her fear that she and Laura will be deserted when she compares Tom to his father: "He was out all hours without explanation! Then *left! Good-bye!* And me with the bag to hold" (1174).

If you use more than one source, each must be identified—if referred to a second time, by an abbreviated version of the first citation. Normally this will be the author's last name or, if you cite several works by a single author, the work's title or a shortened version of it; in any case, use the shortest identification that will differentiate the source from all others.

Principles and Guidelines

PD1. For the first citation from a book, give the author's name; the title of the selection; the name of the book from which it is taken; the editor (preceded by the abbreviation *ed.* for "edited by") or the translator (preceded by the abbreviation *trans.* for "translated by"); the edition (designated by a number) if there has been more than one; the city of publication (the first one will suffice if there is more than one); the publisher (this may be given in shortened form, dropping all but the first name); the year of publication or of most recent copyright; and the page number. The following example correctly combines textual with parenthetical documentation:

> In "Home Burial," Frost has a husband complain, " 'A man must partly give up being a man / With womenfolk' " (*The Poetry of Robert Frost*, ed. Edward Connery Lathem [New York: Holt, 1969] 52).

PD2. For your principal primary source, after the first reference, only a page number is required. Since the paragraphs of the stories in this book are numbered, your instructor may prefer you to supply the paragraph number rather than the page number. For long poems, it may be useful to give line numbers or stanza numbers rather than page numbers. If a poem is short, line numbers are unnecessary and should be omitted. For plays in verse, citation by line number (preceded by act and scene number) will usually be more useful than citation by page number—for example, *Othello* (5.2.133).

PD3. Documentation for run-in quotations always follows the quotation marks. If the quotation ends with a period, move it to the end of the documentation. If it ends with an exclamation point or question mark, leave it, but put a period after the documentation as well. The following examples are from *Othello*:

> "She was false as water" (5.2.133).

> "Alas, what cry is that?" (5.2.116).

PD4. With block quotations, parenthetical documentation follows the last mark of punctuation without further punctuation after the parentheses:

> Out and alas! That was my lady's voice.
> Help! Help, ho! Help! O lady, speak again!
> Sweet Desdemona! O sweet mistress, speak!
> (5.2.118–20)

PD5. Avoid cluttering your paper with excessive documentation. When possible, use one note to cover a series of short quotations. (See example, Q1.) Remember that short poems need no parenthetical documentation at all after the first reference. Do not document well-known sayings or proverbs that you use for stylistic purposes and that form no part of the substance of your investigation (and of course be wary of including hackneyed commonplaces in your formal writing).

PD6. It is customary in a formal paper to document all quoted materials. Do not, however, assume that *only* quotations need documentation. The first purpose of documentation (see page 22) is to allow the reader to check the primary text concerning any major or possibly controversial interpretation. If you declare that the turning point in a long story occurs with an apparently minor event, it may be more important for the reader to have a page number for that event than for any quotation from the story. Judgment must be exercised. You cannot and should not provide page numbers for every detail of a story; but neither should you think that you have necessarily done your duty if you only document all quotations.

3. Documentation by Works Cited

When your assignment involves the use of secondary sources, your instructor may require you to create a list of "Works Cited," to be located at the end of your paper. Any book, article, website, or other source you use or quote from must be referenced parenthetically in the body of your paper so that the reader can easily locate the source in your Works Cited list.

Your first step should be to create the Works Cited list (no longer called a "bibliography") in the format detailed in the *MLA Handbook for Writers of Research Papers* mentioned earlier. Then you should locate each instance in your paper where you have quoted from or paraphrased a source or where your ideas have been formed by reading a source. In order to identify the source, you should normally give the author's last name and the page number to which you are indebted.

For example, let's say you are writing a research paper on Emily Dickinson and one of your sources is David Porter's book *The Art of Emily Dickinson's Early Poetry*. Typically you would cite a reference to the book in this manner: (Porter 141). There are some instances, however, where more information might be needed. David Porter wrote a second book on Dickinson called *Dickinson: The Modern Idiom*. If both of Porter's titles are in your Works Cited list, you need to identify the source parenthetically with an abbreviation of the particular book you are citing. These might read as follows: (Porter, *Early Poetry* 141) or (Porter, *Modern Idiom* 252). The key principle is that you should keep the parenthetical citations both as brief and as clear as possible, so that the reader will have no trouble finding the particular source you are citing.

Here is another example of when you must provide some information in addition to the last name and page number: you might have two authors on your Works Cited list with the last name of Smith. In this case, you need to be specific about which of the two authors you are quoting. Thus the parenthetical citations might read (Mary Smith 88) or (John Smith 138). Note that the first name is required only when there are two sources on the Works Cited list whose authors have the same last name.

Always keep the *MLA Handbook* nearby when preparing the parenthetical documentation and the Works Cited list. Different types of sources—for instance, a newspaper story or an article from an anthology with multiple editors—require different formats, and examples of all these are located in the *Handbook*.

Here is a sample Works Cited page from a paper on Emily Dickinson. Note that the list should start on a new page and be double-spaced, and note the proper method of abbreviation for publishers' names—for example, "Harvard UP" rather than "Harvard University Press." Also remember to indent after the first line of an entry. When two titles are by the same author, like the entries for David Porter here, the second and any subsequent listings of the author's name should be replaced by a straight line.

Works Cited

Buckingham, Willis J. *Emily Dickinson: An Annotated Bibliography.* Bloomington: Indiana UP, 1970. Print.

Cameron, Sharon. *Lyric Time: Dickinson and the Limits of Genre.* Baltimore: Johns Hopkins UP, 1979. Print.

Diehl, Joanne Feit. "Dickinson and Bloom: An Antithetical Reading of Romanticism." *Texas Studies in Literature and Language.* Vol. 23. 1981: 414–41. Print.

Porter, David. *The Art of Dickinson's Early Poetry.* Cambridge: Harvard UP, 1966. Print.

——————. *Dickinson: The Modern Idiom.* Cambridge: Harvard UP, 1981. Print.

Wilson, Suzanne M. "Structural Patterns in the Poetry of Emily Dickinson." *American Literature.* Vol. 35. 1963: 53–59. Print.

4. Documentation of Electronic Sources

If your instructor encourages or permits you to do research on the Internet or other electronic sources, you need to be sure that the information is reliable, since much of what is available is uncredited or incorrect.

As with all research, the quality of your paper will be directly affected by the quality of its sources.

Electronic sources are cited in your paper as parenthetical references and then included in your list of Works Cited. Examples include personal websites; online books, magazines, and newspapers; and materials obtained from a library subscription service such as Lexis-Nexis or Expanded Academic ASAP. Unlike textual sources, which usually clearly state author, title, date of publication, and publisher, electronic sources may or may not provide such information. Whatever the format, you will need to provide information that enables your reader to access the exact source of your materials.

Your parenthetical citations normally will include the name of the author and a page number. If the source is not paginated, the name of the author may suffice; if it is divided by paragraphs, sections, or screen numbers, after the author's name use the abbreviations "par.," "sec.," or the word "screen" followed by the appropriate number. Here are some examples from a paper on James Joyce's "Araby":

A scholarly project or information database:
According to many scholars, James Joyce's "Araby" is best understood if studied at both a realistic and a symbolic level (Gray 1).

A document within a scholarly project or information database:
"Araby" was first published in *Irish Homestead* in 1904 ("James Joyce").

An article in a scholarly journal:
Most scholars contend that "Araby" is an initiation story recounting a young man's first bitter taste of reality (Coulthard).

An article in an encyclopedia:
Joyce often used stream of consciousness, a technique that allows authors to capture their character's complete flow of interior thoughts and feelings ("Stream of Consciousness" par. 2).

Works from online services:
Often lacking courage and honesty, the anti-hero reflects modern man's ambivalence towards traditional social mores ("Anti-hero" sec. 2). Dublin, and its long history of legal and cultural repression, heavily influenced Joyce's writing ("Dublin" par. 2).

A CD-ROM nonperiodical publication:
According to the *Oxford English Dictionary*, the word "araby" is a romantic word for the Middle East ("Araby").

In your list of Works Cited, Internet sources should include both the date of the electronic publication (if available) and the date you accessed the source, and should also include the URL. These are the Works Cited for the previous examples:

Gray, Wallace. "James Joyce's Dubliners: An Introduction by Wallace Gray." *World Wide Dubliners by James Joyce*. Ed. Roger B. Blumberg and Wallace Gray. 1997. Brown U. Web. 5 Sep. 2004 <http://www.mendele.com/WWD/home.html>.

"James Joyce." *Contemporary Authors*. 2003. Gale Group. Web. 3 Sep. 2004 <http://www.galenet.com/servlet/LitIndex/>.

Coulthard, A.R. "Joyce's 'Araby'." *Explicator* 52 (1994): 97–100.

Academic Search Premier. EBSCOhost. U Texas Lib. Austin, TX. Web. 6 Sept. 2004 <http://www.lib.utexas.edu/indexes/s-literaturesinenglish. html>.

"Stream of Consciousness." *Britannica Online*. 2004. Encyclopedia Britannica. Web. 2 Sep. 2004 <http://www.britannica.com>.

"Anti-hero." *Encyclopedia*. 2004. Infoplease.com. Web. 1 Sep. 2004. Keyword: James Joyce.

"Dublin." *Encyclopedia*. 2004. Infoplease.com. Web. 6 Sep. 2004. Path: James Joyce; Irish Literary Renaissance; History; Republic of Ireland.

"Araby." *The Oxford English Dictionary*. 2nd ed. CD-ROM. Oxford: Oxford UP, 2001.

The Internet and other electronic sources provide a great variety of materials, and there are many complex variations on the examples we have given you. For the fullest possible range of correct references, consult the *MLA Handbook*.

X. Stance and Style

In section II, "For Whom Do You Write?" we discussed the assumed audience for your critical writing. Now we must consider the other half of the reader/writer equation. We might ask the parallel question "Who Are You?" except that that would imply that we are asking about your own personal identity. Rather, since we defined your audience hypothetically as members of your class, we need to define "you" in terms of the voice that your audience will expect and appreciate. There are certain conventional expectations that are aroused when we read critical analyses of literature, and the following suggestions may lead you to adopt the stance that your readers will expect. If these sound prescriptive (or if your instructor suggests others), remember that writing about literature is essentially persuasive writing, its purpose being to persuade your readers to agree with your interpretation; the means of persuasion are many, and the writer's stance is only one of them. What we advise here are a few "hints" that have been valuable to students in the past, and may be helpful to you.

S1. *Avoid first-person pronouns.* This injunction warns you away from unnecessarily intruding yourself into your critical statements, with a consequent loss of power and precision. Consider the relative force of these approaches:

POOR	It seems to me that Welty uses the name Phoenix to symbolize endurance and persistence.
GOOD	Welty uses the name Phoenix to symbolize endurance and persistence.
BETTER	The name Phoenix symbolizes endurance and persistence.

The first example dilutes the statement by making it sound tentative and opinionated. It allows your reader to respond, "Why should I consider that seriously, since the writer confesses that it's only a private opinion rather than a fact?" As a critic, you should adopt the stance of the sensitive person who is confident of the accuracy of her or his insights—even when in your heart you may *feel* tentative or unsure. Say it with an air of confidence.

The third example is "better" because it observes the following suggestion:

S2. *Write about the work.* When analyzing a work of literature or some aspect of it, you should be sure that the thesis or topic of a paragraph or essay (and its thesis sentence) focuses on your topic. You will usually not be writing about an *author* but about a *work*, so try to avoid using the author's name as the subject:

POOR	Welty uses the name to symbolize endurance. (*This focuses on* Welty [subject] *and* uses [verb].)
GOOD	The name symbolizes endurance. (*Subject,* name; *verb,* symbolizes.)

Try also to avoid the verb *uses*, since your focus is not on a writer using a technical device but on the result of that use; not on an author selecting a device to achieve a purpose but on the result of that selection. The easiest way to get rid of the word *use* or the idea of *using* is simply to delete them:

POOR	Welty uses the name to symbolize ...
GOOD	The name symbolizes ...

The revised version cuts the wordiness and is more direct.

S3. *Be cautious about passive constructions.* In analyzing literature, the passive voice presents three potential problems: (1) it may fail to identify its subject and thus (2) may introduce vagueness, and (3) it is often a weak and wordy way to say something that you can say directly and forcefully. It may also be a roundabout way to write about an author rather than a work:

POOR	The plot is structured on Phoenix's journey.
GOOD	Phoenix's journey gives structure to the plot.

S4. *Be cautious about praise.* Praising a work or writer with such adverbs as *cleverly, remarkably, beautifully,* and so forth, is much less effective than presenting and analyzing the details that you find praiseworthy. Your opinion is important, but your reader wants the opportunity to share it—and such labeling doesn't really afford that opportunity.

S5. *Avoid preparatory circumlocution.* Don't write a "table of contents" as an introductory paragraph, and eliminate such phrases as "in order to understand X we must examine Y." Just go ahead and examine Y, and trust your reader to recognize its relevance. Another example: "Z is a significant aspect of the poem" (or, a little worse, "It is interesting to note that Z is a significant aspect"). If Z is significant, just go ahead and say what it signifies; if it is interesting, let what is interesting about it be your topic.

Such circumlocution is sometimes called "treading water," since it is generally only a way of keeping afloat on the page until you get a good idea of the direction you really want to swim. You wouldn't walk into a room and announce, "I am now going to tell you that I'm here," or "I will tell you how interested you'll be to notice that I'm here." You'd say, "Here I am!"

It is perfectly all right to use such space-wasters in preliminary drafts—as ways of keeping your pen or keyboard in action while you are figuring out which way you are going to swim. Just be sure to edit them from your finished text.

S6. *Avoid negative hypotheses.* Negative hypothesis is introduced with an example on page 10, "Proving Your Point." Here's another: "If Phoenix Jackson's grandson had not swallowed lye, she would not have made her trip to the city." But he did, so a critical analysis can neither speculate about what might have happened under other circumstances, nor prove by comparison that what happens is better or worse—there is nothing to compare.

On the other hand, in the process of coming to understand a work (as distinct from presenting the results of that process in your writing), it can be valuable to entertain such hypotheses. For example, in discussing connotation, we suggest that imagining possible alternative words can sharpen your appreciation of the poet's actual choice (see study questions for Dickinson, "There is no Frigate like a Book" [page 721]).

XI. Grammar, Punctuation, and Usage: Common Problems

1. Grammar

G1. In discussing the action of a literary work, rely primarily on the present tense (even when the work itself uses the past), keeping the past, future, and perfect tenses available for prior or subsequent actions; for example,

> When Phoenix reaches the city she has undergone many adventures, and when she receives the soothing medicine, she will return home to give it to her grandson.

G2. Do not let pronouns refer to nouns in the possessive case. Antecedents of pronouns should always hold a strong grammatical position: a possessive is a mere modifier, like an adjective:

WRONG	In Shakespeare's play *Othello,* he writes … *(Antecedent of "he" is in possessive case.)*
RIGHT	In his play *Othello,* Shakespeare writes … *(Antecedent of "his" is the subject of the sentence.)*

2. Punctuation

P1. The insertion of a parenthetical phrase in your sentence structure (as, for example, in parenthetical documentation) does not alter the normal punctuation of the rest of the sentence. Do not, as the preceding sentence doesn't, place a comma after a parenthetical phrase unless it belonged there before the parenthesis was inserted. You wouldn't write, "Welty's story, touches upon racial issues," so don't include that comma when you insert a parenthesis.

WRONG   Welty's "A Worn Path" (rpt. in Greg Johnson and Thomas R. Arp, *Perrine's Literature: Structure, Sound and Sense,* 12th ed. [Boston: Wadsworth, 2015] 239–246), touches upon racial issues in the early twentieth century.

(Delete the comma after the parenthesis.)

And it is an inflexible rule of punctuation: never place a comma immediately before a parenthesis.

P2. Do not set off restrictive appositives with commas. A restrictive appositive is one necessary to the meaning of the sentence; a nonrestrictive appositive could be left out without changing the meaning.

WRONG   In her story, "A Worn Path," Welty …

(The title of the story is necessary to the meaning of the statement. As punctuated, the sentence falsely implies that Welty wrote only one story.)

RIGHT   In her story "A Worn Path," Welty …

RIGHT   In her story in chapter 4 of *Perrine's Literature,* "A Worn Path," Welty …

(The chapter number identifies the story. The title simply supplies additional information and could be omitted without changing the meaning.)

P3. Words used simply as words should be either underlined or italicized, or put in quotation marks.

WRONG	The word describing the seal and frame is gold. *(This statement is false; all the words in the story are black.)*
RIGHT	The word describing the seal and frame is "gold."

Since the word "gold" is quoted from the story, it has here been put in quotation marks. However, if you list a series of words from various parts of the story, you may prefer underlining or italicizing for the sake of appearance. Whichever system you choose, be consistent throughout your paper.

P4. Observe the conventions of typed manuscripts: (1) put a space after an abbreviating period (p. 7, not p.7; pp. 10–13, not pp.10–13); (2) use two hyphens to represent a dash—and do not put spaces before and after them.

P5. Observe the standard for forming possessives. For a singular noun, add an apostrophe and an *s* (a student's duty, yesterday's mail, the dress's hemline). For a plural noun, add only an apostrophe (the students' duties, seven days' mail). For proper nouns, the same rules apply (Camus's "The Guest," Chekhov's "Misery," Ives's play).

Do not confuse the contraction *it's* (it is) with the possessive *its* (belonging to it). *Its* is an exception to the general rule requiring apostrophes for possessives.

3. Usage

U1. Though accepted usage changes with time, and the distinctions between the following pairs of words are fading, many instructors will bless you if you try to preserve them.

convince, persuade   *Convince* pertains to belief (conviction); *persuade* pertains to either action or belief. The following sentences observe the distinction. In *Othello*, Iago convinces Othello that Desdemona is unfaithful. He then persuades him to strangle rather than poison her.

describe, define   *Describe* means to delineate the visual appearance of something; *define* means to state the meaning of a word or phrase, or to explain the essential quality of something. Reserve *describe* and *description* for talking about how things look.

disinterested, uninterested A disinterested judge is one who has no stake or personal interest in the outcome of a case and can therefore judge fairly; an uninterested judge goes to sleep on the bench. A good judge is interested in the case but disinterested in its outcome. An uninterested reader finds reading boring. A disinterested reader? Perhaps one who can enjoy a good book whatever its subject matter.

imply, infer A writer or speaker implies; a reader or listener infers. An implication is a meaning hinted at but not stated outright. An inference is a conclusion drawn from evidence not complete enough for proof. If you imply that I am a snob, I may infer that you do not like me.

lover, beloved In older literature, the word *lover* usually meant one of two things—a man who is sexually involved, or any person who feels affection or esteem for another person or persons. In the case of the former, *lover* generally designated the male partner and *beloved* his female partner. In the case of the latter usage, no sexual implications are involved.

quote, quotation The word *quote* was originally only a verb. Today the use of the terms "single quotes" and "double quotes" in reference to quotation marks is almost universally accepted; but, although the use of "quote" for the noun "quotation" is common in informal speech, it is still unacceptable in formal writing.

Note also that quoting is an act performed by the writer *about* literature, not by the writer *of* literature:

WRONG	Shakespeare's famous quotation "To be or not to be" ...
RIGHT	The famous quotation from Shakespeare, "To be or not to be" ...

sensuous, sensual *Sensuous* normally pertains to the finer senses, *sensual* to the appetites. Good poetry is sensuous: it appeals through the imagination to the senses. A voluptuous woman, an attractive man, or a rich dessert may have a sensual appeal that stirs a desire for possession.

U2. Some words and phrases to avoid are the following.

center around A geometrical impossibility. A story may perhaps center *on* a certain feature, but to make it center *around* that feature is to make the hub surround the wheel.

just as This phrase as a term of comparison is too precise for literary analysis because the adjective *just* means *exactly* or *identical in every possible way*, almost an impossibility when discussing literature. You should take the trouble to establish the points of similarity and dissimilarity between things that you are comparing.

lifestyle An overused neologism, especially inappropriate for use with older literature, that is too general to mean much. One dictionary defines it as "a person's typical approach to living, including his moral attitudes, preferred entertainment, fads, fashions, etc." If you wish to define someone's moral attitudes, do so; if you try to define a person's "lifestyle," you have a monumental task of all-inclusive definition. It's easier just to avoid it.

society The problem with this word is that it is too often used only vaguely as a substitute for some more precise idea. Any story, poem, or play that does deal with "society" will clearly indicate a *particular* society—the world of segregated white middle-class people in South Africa's apartheid system in "Once upon a Time," or the paternalistic society of Norway in the late nineteenth century in *A Doll House*. In those cases, once one has defined the particular society and its characteristics, the term might legitimately be used. But don't use it simply to mean "people in general at that time in that place." And it is important to avoid the glib assumption that *society* makes a person do something. A person's desire to be a member of a social group may lead to actions that appear to be imposed or forced, but what makes a person conform is the desire to be or remain a member, not the fact that there are codes of behavior.

somewhat (also *rather, more or less, as it were, in a manner*). All of these terms are specifically designed to avoid or evade precision—to create a sense of vagueness. Since clarity and precision are the goals of critical analysis, these terms should be avoided. They also sound wishy-washy, while you should strive to sound firm and convinced.

upset As an adjective to define an emotional condition, the word is just too vague. Your dictionary will tell you that its synonyms are "distressed, disturbed, agitated, perturbed, irritated," and so forth. All of those terms are more precise than *upset*, and the one that most nearly indicates your meaning should be chosen.

what the author is trying to say is The implication of this expression is that the author *failed* to say it. You don't say "I'm trying to get to Boston" if you are already there; give the author credit for having got where he or she was going.

Others suggested by your instructor:

_____   _____

_____   _____

_____   _____

_____   _____

_____   _____

XII. Writing Samples

1. Fiction Explication

The Indeterminate Ending in "Where Are You Going, Where Have You Been?"

The concluding paragraphs of Joyce Carol Oates's "Where Are You Going, Where Have You Been?" (rpt. in Greg Johnson and Thomas R. Arp, _Perrine's Literature: Structure, Sound, and Sense_, 12th ed. [Boston: Wadsworth, 2015] 487–501) have frequently been explicated by critics, in part because of their seeming indeterminacy. After her long, frightening encounter with Arnold Friend, the protagonist Connie finally submits to his wishes that she open the back screen door and join him and his sinister friend, Ellie Oscar, in Friend's bizarre golden jalopy. What happens next is unknown, however, for we are left suspended at her moment of submission, and similarly unknown is her true motive for acquiescing to Friend. Has she simply become entranced by Friend's hypnotically suggestive insistence that she submit? Is she acting out of a kind of altruism, in order to spare her family the gruesome fate at which Arnold Friend has hinted if she refuses to comply? These questions give the ending paragraphs an aura of mystery that helps make this story a perennially fascinating one for discussion and debate.

The story, it should be pointed out, has carefully prepared for this ending. Connie, only fifteen, is perhaps a "typical" teenager of her time and place, and we have seen her characterized appealingly as being naïve as well as rebellious, both of which are appropriate to her age. Arnold Friend, by contrast, is a considerably older (around thirty) and threatening, even demonic figure who tries to make himself look younger by the evident use of makeup and hair dye, and by using slang expressions popular with the teenagers with whom he mingles. In the second half of the story, after Friend arrives at Connie's house and begins his drawn-out seduction of her, wanting her to come with him and Oscar in the jalopy, Connie's mood shifts from wise-cracking dismissal and skepticism, to slow-building anxiety, and finally, by the end, to outright terror.

The final couple of pages show Connie in a state of fear so extreme that she becomes detached from her surroundings and unable to resist Friend's persistent suggestions that she open the screen door and come outside to join him. We are told of her "pounding heart" and, in a careful choice of words on the narrator's part, we are told that "She watched herself push the door slowly open" (506). Such descriptions suggest that Connie now suffers a fearfulness so extreme that she is numbed both physically and mentally, and that she no longer quite understands the possible consequences of her acquiescence to Friend.

Rather than using rough language or violent means to attain his ends, Friend continues to cajole her; his self-possession during the final scene is in marked contrast to Connie's zombie-like compliance. He calls her "My sweet little blue-eyed girl"—even though Connie has brown eyes—and speaks in a "half-sung sigh" (506). This seeming gentleness as a prelude to rape and likely murder (the story is based on the case of a serial killer who operated in Arizona and was dubbed by the media "the Pied Piper of Tucson") gives the final scene its powerfully macabre and sinister impact. The scene suggests, above all, Connie's helplessness; she knows that if Friend wanted, he could easily force his way through the screen door, and it is clear that Ellie Oscar is brandishing a gun.

The final paragraph confirms Connie's fatal detachment from her surroundings even as it provides the story's indeterminate ending. Connie fails to recognize the surrounding land she sees outside, even though she's in her own house and has viewed the landscape countless times in the past. Yet the narrator insists that this was "so much land that Connie had never seen before and did not recognize except to know that she was going to it" (506). What will happen next, however, remains outside the story's purview: Oates could have narrated a rape and murder, but the suggestiveness of the indeterminate ending is in fact more powerful, and has given rise to other interpretations of what will happen. For instance, in the film version of the story, entitled *Smooth Talk* and directed by Joyce Chopra, Arnold Friend takes Connie away in his jalopy, almost certainly for a sexual tryst, but then brings her back home, where she has the brief conversation with her sister, June, which ends the film. One can understand Chopra's predicament, for as Oates later said, the text itself provides an "unfilmable" conclusion because its effect is based on its lack of a visually presented, definite, determined fate for Connie. The director thus chose a "happy ending" rather than the tragic implications most readers take from the text itself.

By withholding a neatly determined closure in the final paragraphs, "Where Are You Going, Where Have You Been?" is in line with contemporary fiction generally, which prefers not to provide tidy narrative packages but privileges a rich suggestiveness and ambiguity that leave much to the reader's imagination. However one imagines Connie's ultimate fate, this story's ending is clearly a triumph of careful and effective storytelling that powerfully haunts the imagination and forces the reader to confront the lack of certainty and determinacy that characterizes life itself.

Comments

While this essay does not provide a line-by-line explication of the passage, its handling of key words and phrases and its limitation to one paragraph for its evidence qualify it as explicative. It summarizes the major event in the story not for purposes of narration but in order to provide necessary background material for explicating the mystery that it presents. Since there is only one documented source, the citations from the story need not use the author's name. The date of publication of the story is not documented since it is known to the hypothetical readers of the essay who have read the introductory footnote in the text.

2. Fiction Analysis

The Function of the Frame Story in "Once upon a Time"

Nadine Gordimer's "Once upon a Time" (rpt. in Greg Johnson and Thomas R. Arp, *Perrine's Literature: Structure, Sound, and Sense*, 12th ed. [Boston: Wadsworth, 2015] 247–252) is a complex, ironic presentation of the results of fear and hatred. This "children's story," so flat in its tone, characterization, and reporting of events, proceeds by gradual steps to show a family systematically barricading itself behind various security devices, the last of which has an effect opposite of what was intended in destroying the child that the parents are trying to protect.

The tale is especially harrowing because of the tone hinted at in the title. This is an easy, casual narration that repeats such standard storybook phrases as "living happily ever after" (249) and identifies its characters only by their functions and relationships, never exploring motivations or revealing the steps of their decision making. The deeper causes for fear are not defined in the tale. All these qualities, and others, establish the tone of fairy tales and other stories for children. In this story, however, no one lives "happily ever after," for in attempting to safeguard themselves, the parents destroy their lives.

But that tale doesn't begin until the ninth paragraph of Gordimer's story. What precedes it is the frame story of a writer who has been asked to write a story for a children's collection, who refuses to contribute, and then is awakened in the night by some noise that frightens her. Her fear first chillingly conjures up a burglar or murderer "moving from room to room, coming up the passage—to [her] door" (247). Then the actual cause of her waking comes to her: deep down, "three thousand feet below" her house, some rock face has fallen in the gold mine beneath (248). She is not in personal danger, then. Yet she cannot return to sleep, so she tells herself "a bedtime story" to relax her mind—and the story is of the family that grows obsessed with security and protection, the awful story of the mutilation of the little boy.

The frame story initially seems little more than an introductory explanation of how the tale came to be written, against the writer's will and purpose. Its details are unrelated to the children's tale—explicitly so, as the writer, despite her knowledge of two recent murders in her neighborhood, and the rational fears that such events arouse, has "no burglar bars, no gun under the pillow" (247), in contrast to the precautions taken in the tale. There is no fairy-tale gold mine in her life, only the knowledge of the mining of gold a half-mile beneath her. So what does this frame have to do with the tale, other than to place the reader within the literal reality of a writer's time and place, from which the imagination journeys to "once upon a time"? Is it more than an ironic contrast in subject and tone?

For answers, we need to consider the writer's time and place as parallels to those of the tale. Both are located in South Africa, both are in the present (even though the phrase "once upon a time" normally signals a long time ago, in a far-off place). The family in the tale, with their burglar bars, walls, alarms, and finally "the razor-bladed coils all round the walls of the house," are like those people in the writer's world who do keep guns under their pillows. Like the real people of the writer's neighborhood, the family focuses its fears on the black African populace who surround and outnumber them. On the one hand, in the writer's world, the fears focus on "a casual laborer ... dismissed without pay" who returns to strangle the watchdogs and knife the man who treated him unfairly (247); on the other hand, in the children's story, the fears focus on the hungry, out-of-work, and begging multitudes who fill and spoil the suburban streets of the fictitious family's neighborhood. In both worlds, unfairness, want, and deprivation mark the blacks, while the whites feel surrounded and threatened by them.

Why cannot the writer return to sleep after she has discovered the innocent cause of her awakening? Because the comforting natural explanation, which removes her from personal danger, is in fact more horrifying than a murderous prowler. She thinks of

> the Chopi and Tsonga migrant miners who might [be] down there, under [her] in the earth at that moment. The stope where the [rock] fall was could have been disused, dripping water from its ruptured veins; or men might now be interred there in the most profound of tombs. (248)

Two possibilities occur to her—one of no harm to men, the other of burial alive—both a consequence of the wage-slavery of "migrant miners" over whose heads (literally and figuratively) the white society lives in "uneasy strain ... of brick, cement, wood and glass" (248). If no miner has been harmed by *this* rock fall, others have been and will be; and moreover, being killed in that subterranean world of "ruptured veins" is not the only harm that the whites have inflicted on the original inhabitants of the country they control, nor on their own sensitivities and consciences.

The frame story of "Once upon a Time," then, foreshadows the fear, the violence, and the pain of the children's tale, and points to the ultimate cause of its terrible sacrifice of a child—the systematic mal-treatment of one race by another and the brutality and self-destruction that are its result.

Comments

This analysis has as its subject an aspect of the story that the writer can fully develop in the limited space. It is written for our hypothetical class journal, as indicated by the way in which the writer refrains from giving a detailed summary of the tale enclosed in the frame (since the audience is known to be familiar with the story), and presents details from the frame narration as they support the writer's argument. It employs some information about the author that is common knowledge to the class (her national-ity and her contemporaneity are in the introductory footnote to the story). Quotations are integrated into the writer's sentence structures, and the writer interpolates words within the extended quotation.

3. Poetry Explication

"A Study of Reading Habits"

The first noteworthy feature of Philip Larkin's "A Study of Reading Habits" (rpt. in Greg Johnson and Thomas R. Arp, *Perrine's Literature: Structure, Sound, and Sense*, 12th ed. [Boston: Wadsworth, 2015] 682) is the ironic discrepancy between the formal language of its title and the colloquial, slangy, even vulgar language of the poem itself. The title by its tone implies a formal sociological research paper, possibly one that samples a cross section of a population and draws conclusions about people's reading. The poem presents, instead, the confessions of one man whose attitudes toward reading have progressively deteriorated to the point where books seem to him "a load of crap." The poem's real subject, moreover, is not the man's reading habits but the revelation of life and character they provide.

The poem is patterned in three stanzas having an identical rhyme scheme (*abcbac*) and the same basic meter (iambic trimeter). The stanzaic division of the poem corresponds to the internal structure of meaning, for the three stanzas present the speaker at three stages of his life: as schoolboy, adolescent, and adult. Larkin signals the chronological progression in the first lines of the stanzas by the words "When," "Later," and "now." The "now" is the present out of which the adult speaks, recalling the two earlier periods.

The boy he remembers in stanza 1 was unhappy, both in his home and, even more so, at school. Perhaps small and bullied by bigger boys, probably an indifferent student, making poor grades, and scolded by teachers, he found a partial escape from his miseries through reading. The books he read—tales of action and adventure, pitting good guys against bad guys, full of physical conflict, and ending with victory for the good guy—enabled him to construct a fantasy life in which he identified with the virtuous hero and in his imagination beat up villains twice his size, thus reversing the situations of his real life.

In stanza 2 the speaker recalls his adolescence when his dreams were of sexual rather than muscular prowess. True to the prediction of "ruining [his] eyes" in stanza 1, he had to wear spectacles, which he describes hyperbolically as "inch-thick"—a further detriment to his social life. To compensate for his lack of success with girls, he envisioned himself as a Dracula figure with cloak and fangs, enjoying a series of sexual triumphs. His reading continued to feed his fantasy life, but, instead of identifying with the virtuous hero, he identified with the glamorous, sexually ruthless villain. The poet puns on the word "ripping" (the speaker "had ripping times in the dark"), implying both the British slang meaning of "splendid" and the violence of the rapist who rips the clothes off his victim.

In stanza 3 the speaker, now a young adult, confesses that he no longer reads much. His accumulated experience of personal failure and his long familiarity with his shortcomings have made it impossible for him to identify, even in fantasy, with the strong virtuous hero or the viciously potent villain. He can no longer hide from himself the truth that he resembles more closely the weak secondary characters of the escapist tales he picks up. He recognizes himself in the undependable dude who fails the heroine, or the cowardly storekeeper who knuckles under to the bad guys. He therefore has turned to a more powerful means of escape, one that protects him from dwelling on what he knows about himself: drunkenness. His final words are memorable—so "unpoetical" in a traditional sense, so poetically effective in characterizing this speaker. "Get stewed," he tells himself. "Books are a load of crap."

It would be a serious mistake to identify the speaker of the poem, or his attitudes or his language, with the poet. Poets, unless they are in a cynical or depressed mood, do not think that "books are a load of crap." Philip Larkin, moreover, an English poet and a graduate of Oxford, was for many years until his death a university librarian (Ian Hamilton, ed., *Oxford Companion to Twentieth-Century Poetry* [Oxford: Oxford UP, 1994] 288). "A Study of Reading Habits" is both dramatic and ironic. It presents a first-person speaker who has been unable to cope with the reality of his life in any of its stages and has therefore turned toward various means of escaping it. His confessions reveal a progressive deterioration of values (from good to evil to sodden indifference) and a decline in reading tastes (from adventure stories to prurient sexual novels to none) that reflect his downward slide.

Comments

The title of this paper is enclosed in quotation marks because the writer has used the title of the poem for the title of the paper. The paper uses textual and parenthetical documentation. Line numbers for quotations from the poem are not supplied because the poem is too short to require them: they would serve no useful purpose. Notice that in quoting from stanza 1, the writer has changed the phrase "ruining my eyes" to fit the essay's syntax, but has indicated the alteration by putting the changed word within brackets. The paper is written for an American audience; if it had been written for an English audience, the writer would not have needed to explain that "ripping" is British slang or to have made it a point that the poet is English. The paper is documented for an audience using this textbook. If it were directed toward a wider audience, the writer would want to refer, for his text of the poem, not to a textbook or anthology but to the volume of Larkin's poetry containing this poem (*Collected Poems*, ed. Anthony Thwaite [London: Faber, 1988] 31). Also, the writer would probably wish to include the poet's name in the title: Philip Larkin's "A Study of Reading Habits" (or) An Examination of Larkin's "A Study of Reading Habits." Since Larkin's nationality and his profession as a librarian are not common knowledge, the paper documents a biographical source where that information is found.

4. Poetry Analysis

Diction in "Spring in the Classroom"

Mary Oliver's "Spring in the Classroom" (reprinted in Greg Johnson and Thomas R. Arp, *Perrine's Literature: Structure, Sound, and Sense*, 12th ed. [Boston: Wadsworth, 2015] 700–701) surprisingly juxtaposes two contrasted concepts throughout the poem, providing much of its charm as well as its poetic unity. As the poem builds toward its surprise ending, it uses thoughtful and colorful diction to illustrate these concepts.

The poem is divided into two stanzas: in the first, the speaker sets the scene; in the second, she convincingly dramatizes the contrasted concepts through human action. The entire poem employs a first-person plural point of view, suggesting that the particular identity of the speaker is unimportant. She is simply one of a classroom full of like-minded students who while away the school hours by staring out the window and wishing they could escape outside to enjoy the beautiful spring afternoon.

In the first stanza, the two contrasted concepts become clear: one presents the "dry" (1) atmosphere of the classroom, while the other portrays the "greening woodlot" (3) typifying the natural beauty outside, which the students watch with such longing. The classroom has the teacher, "Miss Willow Bangs" (2), the boring lessons, and the barrier-like windows that keep the students inside. The woodlot, however, has "secrets and increases" (4), "hidden nests and kind" (5). Contemplating it, the children feel "warmed" (6), their "old mud blood murmuring" (7), the latter phrase emphasizing its importance through assonance and alliteration. When the students feel too bored, they carve their initials into desk with small knives, in the time-honored schoolroom tradition, and the speaker specifies that their initials are "pulsing" (11) with the "mud blood" mentioned above. The stanza concludes that the children are indignant to be confined, "without pity and beyond reason" (12) by their teacher, whose physical description suggests (deceptively, as it turns out) that she is part of the dry schoolroom atmosphere, "her eyes two stones behind glass,/Her leg thick, her heart/in love with pencils and arithmetic" (13–15).

The second stanza pulls back from such close observation to summarize the students' unhappy condition, sitting "like captives" (17) with "one gorgeous day lost after another" (16). They are so angry, the speaker asserts, that they could easily be led to "plot mutiny, even murder" (20). But then the surprising ending arrives:

> And the one day, Miss Willow Bangs, we saw you
> As we ran wild in our three o'clock escape
> Past the abandoned swings; you were leaning
> All furry and blooming against the old brick wall
> In the Art Teacher's arms. (22–26)

Here the diction once again underscores the meaning, for it turns out that Miss Willow Bangs, far from being a cruel prison warden, also must have been suffering, from the dry, unnatural confinement indoors, and longed to be "furry and blooming" in concert with the rest of the natural world outside.

Even the diction found in the poem's title implies the contrasted concepts present throughout the poem. "Spring in the Classroom," in the speaker's eyes, is almost a conflict in terms, since spring, she feels, should be a time when one is out of doors. The classroom with all its dryness and confinement represents everything against which the speaker's childlike heart rebels. Only through the careful, selective use of diction is the speaker able to dramatize this dominant theme.

Comments

The title of this paper is not set off in quotation marks—the writer uses them only to set off the title of the poem. Line numbers are given for all direct quotations, except when the quotation is being used a second time. Note that the writer does not use every possible detail in the poem to support its thesis, but simply chooses those that underscore the essay's argument most effectively. The paper includes the general meaning of the poem as an orientation for the meaningful presentation of the details, but its main focus is on the quality of language as that contributes to the general meaning.

5. Drama Explication

Iago's First Soliloquy

At the end of the first act of *Othello, the Moor of Venice* (rpt. in Greg Johnson and Thomas R. Arp, *Perrine's Literature: Structure, Sound, and Sense,* 12th ed. [Boston: Wadsworth, 2015], 1276–1371), Iago delivers the first of his several soliloquies (1.3.363–84). In this act Iago has initiated the action by leading Roderigo to announce to her father Desdemona's elopement with Othello. The result is Brabantio's violent accusation of Othello and his estrangement from his daughter. Most of Iago's time on the stage has been with Roderigo, whom he manipulates first in inducing him to cause trouble for Othello and dismay to Brabantio, and then at length in persuading him to pursue Desdemona to Cyprus (having first gathered up as much money as he can).

Iago begins the soliloquy justifying to himself spending time with such a fool as Roderigo:

> Thus do I ever make my fool my purse,
> For I mine own gained knowledge should profane
> If I would time expend with such a snipe
> But for my sport and profit.   (363–66)

That he feels the need to justify such an association is implied by the terms he uses to describe him—"fool," "snipe," and, at the end of the soliloquy, "ass." Roderigo is no fit companion for a man of such "gained knowledge"—that is, a man of Iago's accomplishments and wisdom. We may sense in this not only his contempt for Roderigo, but pride in his own superiority, a pride that is evidenced elsewhere in this soliloquy as well. For example, he alludes to Roderigo at the end when he says that Othello "will be as tenderly led by the nose / As asses are." What he gains from associating with this "snipe" is "sport and profit"—the pleasure of manipulating and controlling someone, and the monetary gain that he plans to receive. How Roderigo's money becomes Iago's, we learn much later: he persuades Roderigo to give him cash to purchase jewels to bribe Desdemona into sleeping with the young man, but of course he pockets the money rather than buying her presents (see 4.2.184–88 and 5.1.15–17).

After these four lines of self-justification, Iago turns to Othello. He has already at length told Roderigo of his duplicity in serving the general, and has given a reason for hating him: Othello has promoted Cassio ahead of Iago, thus thwarting his ambitions (1.1.8–65). In the soliloquy, ambition takes a back seat to other motives:

> I hate the Moor,
> And it is thought abroad that twixt my sheets
> He's done my office. I know not if't be true,
> But I for mere suspicion in that kind
> Will do as if for surety.   (366–70)

We must not read this too quickly, or we might miss the disconnect between the first line and what follows. He does not say "I hate the Moor" *because* I suspect him of sleeping with my wife; rather, those appear as two distinct motives, one explicit, the other general and vague. His hatred is almost abstract, a flat statement of loathing without a supporting cause. His jealousy, on the other hand, though based merely on rumors (and vigorously refuted by Emilia later in the play), is at least a humanly comprehensible motivation. And he does not repeat what he has told Roderigo, that he hates Othello because he bypassed him for promotion. Rather, that comes in as he begins to plot his revenge for having been cuckolded:

> [Othello] holds me well,
> The better shall my purpose work on him.
> Cassio's a proper man. Let me see now,
> To get his place, and to plume up my will
> In double knavery.—How, how?—Let's see.— (370–74)

He enjoys the irony that Othello's admiration for him will make the general more vulnerable to his plotting. But even more delightful to him is the proud prospect of "double knavery," taking revenge on Othello and supplanting Cassio as lieutenant, and thus "plum[ing] up [his] will" by creating a two-part plot that will bring down Cassio as well as Othello. What he has against Cassio personally (as opposed to his professional jealousy) is implied in the brief sentence referring to Cassio's handsomeness. As he explains much later, Cassio "hath a daily beauty in his life / That makes me ugly" (5.1.19–20). He is jealous of Cassio's social and physical superiority; Cassio is as far above him in grace as he himself is superior to Roderigo in craft and intelligence. And as he goes on to say, Cassio

> hath a person and a smooth dispose
> To be suspected, framed to make women false.   (377–78)

It is characteristic of Iago that he perceives the virtues in others, and in his thinking twists them into weaknesses or vices. Othello esteems him, which will make him less suspicious; Cassio is handsome, which makes him a threat to women. He goes on in this vein:

> The Moor is of a free and open nature
> That thinks men honest that but seem to be so.   (379–80)

Othello's lack of guile, his own honesty, make him the more vulnerable to a guileful, dishonest schemer like Iago. He concludes the soliloquy with an echo of an earlier remark of his:

> I have't. It is engendered. Hell and night
> Must bring this monstrous birth to the world's light.   (383–84)

In advising Roderigo to prepare for his trip to Cyprus, Iago tells him, "There are many events in the womb of time which will be delivered" (1.3.353–54). He ends the soliloquy proudly announcing that he himself has impregnated that "womb of time," and the offspring will be "monstrous."

The essence of the plot is expressed with great simplicity:

> After some time, to abuse Othello's ear
> That [Cassio] is too familiar with [Othello's] wife.   (375–76)

This monstrous lie seems to Iago a perfect revenge—and one that inadvertently suggests Iago is not in fact jealous of Othello's sleeping with Emilia, for this perfect circle of wife-for-wife will culminate not in Desdemona's infidelity but in the illusion of it. We may well wonder if Iago does in fact believe in his own wife's disloyalty, since he is plotting a lie about Desdemona's.

There is one more example of Iago's proud self-estimation in the soliloquy, his assertion of his strong will. Of Othello's supposed sexual relations with Emilia, he says,

> I know not if't be true,
> But I for mere suspicion in that kind
> Will do as if for surety.   (368–70)

His boast is that he is not the sort of man who waits and investigates (a man of "gained knowledge"), but one who will take drastic action even on "mere suspicion." It is a curious assertion, since the subsequent events seem to show the opposite—and may even be contradicted here by his plan to induce Othello's jealousy only "After some time."

What this soliloquy reveals is that Iago takes great pride in his manipulative abilities, that he has a mixture of motives, and that he is not entirely consistent. These are traits that we can follow throughout the play.

Comments

The essay restricts its references to the text of the play, so parenthetical documentation is appropriate. While it explicates the whole soliloquy, it does not simply "read" the speech from beginning to end, but rather structures its argument according to the writer's several points that characterize Iago. Its conclusion draws attention to the importance of the speech in establishing character traits that can be observed in the rest of the play.

6. Drama Analysis

Othello's Race

The subtitle of *Othello* is *The Moor of Venice,* a term that can be misleading if we rely on a standard desk dictionary for a definition of "moor." For example, the *Random House College Dictionary* defines it thus: "Moor ... a Muslim of mixed Berber and Arab people inhabiting NW Africa." *The American Heritage Dictionary* agrees with that definition and adds an alternative: "one of the Saracens who invaded Spain in the eighth century A.D." But these definitions do not match the facts in the play.

Othello is presented as a Christian, not a Muslim. Iago refers to his "baptism" (2.3.308), and in his first meeting with Desdemona on Cyprus he clearly alludes to their shared belief in Christian salvation (2.1.184–90).

But more importantly, he is throughout the play characterized as a black African. A fuller definition of the word "moor" can be found in the *Oxford English Dictionary:* "in the Middle Ages, and as late as the 17th c. . . . ., Moors were commonly supposed to be mostly black, ... and hence the word was often used for 'negro.'"

In the opening scene Roderigo refers to Othello's negroid features by calling him "the thick-lips" (1.1.66), and Iago insultingly refers to his race ("an old black ram," "a Barbary horse" [1.1.88, 110–11]). Brabantio's public denunciation of him in 1.3 is clearly calling him black. He himself in his soliloquy trying to cope with Desdemona's supposed rejection of him in favor of Cassio explicitly calls himself "black" (3.3.264), and later in that scene in referring to Desdemona's supposed sinful lust says:

> Her name, that was as fresh
> As Dian's visage, is now begrimed and black
> As mine own face.   (3.3.387–89)

The play also establishes a racist bigotry about Othello's color, chiefly in the assumptions revealed by Brabantio in his distress over Desdemona's marriage to the Moor. When he learns of it from Iago and Roderigo in 1.1, he declares to Roderigo "would you had had her" (1.1.173), though he has already reminded Roderigo that he had rejected him as a suitor for his daughter—that is, *any* white man would be preferable to a black. This attitude is supported by his assumption that a mixed marriage is "in spite of nature" and "against all rules of nature" (1.3.96, 101). That she is aware of her father's prejudices is implied in Desdemona's defense of her choice: "I saw Othello's visage in his mind" (1.3.249), not in the superficial coloring of his skin. That the racism is not limited to Brabantio is indicated by the nature of the insults mouthed to him by Iago and Roderigo, and even by the goodhearted Duke who tries to patch up the quarrel between Brabantio and Othello. He says to Brabantio, "If virtue no delighted beauty lack / Your son-in-law is far more fair than black" (1.3.286–87), by which he means that Othello's virtues outweigh his unfortunate blackness.

Surprisingly, Othello himself seems partially to subscribe to the racist argument that it is unnatural for whites and blacks to marry. Having been reminded by Iago of Brabantio's warning that Desdemona had deceived her father and therefore could deceive her husband, Othello echoes Brabantio: "nature erring from itself" (3.3.228) he says of his wife's accepting him as a husband.

The importance of correctly identifying Othello's race and recognizing the social attitude toward it is that we can more clearly see the deeply ironic reversal of expectations enacted in this tragedy. By tradition, black was the color ascribed to the devil (hence Emilia's charge that by murdering Desdemona, Othello has shown himself to be "a blacker devil" [5.2.130]). Evil itself was popularly referred to as a black deed. Again, the *OED* provides full and useful definitions of two figurative meanings of the word "black":

> Having dark or deadly purposes, malignant; pertaining to or involving death, deadly; baneful, disastrous, sinister ... Foul, iniquitous, atrocious, horribly wicked.

But in the play, the "horribly wicked" character is Iago, the white Venetian, and Othello is a great, virtuous man who makes the terrible mistake of supposing his wife to be a criminal deserving execution at the hands of "justice." The dramatic effect is overwhelming, as we see the viciousness of white Iago overcoming the virtue of black Othello.

Works Cited

"Black," "Moor." *The Compact Edition of the Oxford English Dictionary.* 1971. Print.

"Moor." *The American Heritage Dictionary of the English Language.* 1981. Print.

"Moor." *The Random House College Dictionary.* Rev. ed. 1980. Print.

Shakespeare, William. *Othello, the Moor of Venice.* Rpt. in Greg Johnson and Thomas R. Arp. *Perrine's Literature: Structure, Sound, and Sense.* 12th ed. Boston: Wadsworth, 2015. Print.

Comments

This analysis makes use of references from four sources, three dictionaries and the text of the play, so a Works Cited list is appropriate. The textual material is not presented in the order of its appearance in the play but is instead arranged according to the writer's thesis. The essay proceeds by defining Othello's race, then establishing the prevailing attitudes toward it, and finally reaching a conclusion about the effect of reversing racial expectations.

The Elements

of Fiction

CHAPTER ONE

Reading the Story

Before embarking on a study of fiction, we might ask a basic question: Why bother to read it? With so many pressing demands on our time, and with so many nonfiction books of history, memoir, politics, and cultural discussion competing for our attention, why should we spend our scarce free time on works of imagination?

The eternal answers to this question are two: enjoyment and understanding.

Since the invention of language, human beings have enjoyed hearing and reading stories, participating in the fictional experiences and adventures of imaginary people. The bedtime stories read to children, the thrillers and romances many adults take to the beach, the historical novels and inspirational fiction elderly people often enjoy—any such harmless activity that helps make life less tedious or stressful surely needs nothing else to recommend it. Simple enjoyment has always been a primary aim and justification for reading fiction.

Fiction whose sole purpose is to entertain, however, requires no serious or intensive study. Unless a story expands or refines our thinking on a significant topic or quickens our sense of life, its value is not appreciably greater than that of video games or crossword puzzles. A story written with serious artistic intentions, on the other hand, must yield not only enjoyment but also understanding.

Like all serious art, fiction of this latter kind provides an imagined experience that yields authentic insights into some significant aspect of life. "Art is a lie," Picasso said, "that leads to the truth," and since a short story is a fiction, and thus a kind of "lie," this statement perfectly sums up the kind of story that provides entertainment but also may become part of an enduring literature. Most fiction, of course, is of the other sort: it has no aspirations beyond merely entertaining the reader. In order to distinguish these types of fiction, therefore, we should begin by defining two broad classifications, employing the terms most often used today: **commercial fiction**, the kind intended solely to entertain; and **literary fiction**, which is the primary subject of this book.

Commercial fiction, such as the legal thrillers and romance novels that make up best-seller lists and the easy-to-read short stories that appear in mass-market magazines, is written and published primarily to make money, and it makes money because it helps large numbers of people escape the tedium and stress of their lives. Literary fiction, however, is written by someone with serious artistic intentions who hopes to broaden, deepen, and sharpen the reader's awareness of life. Commercial fiction takes us *away* from the real world: it helps us temporarily to forget our troubles. Literary fiction plunges us, through the author's imaginative vision and artistic ability, more deeply *into* the real world, enabling us to understand life's difficulties and to empathize with others. While commercial fiction has the reader's immediate pleasure as its object, literary fiction hopes to provide a complex, lasting aesthetic and intellectual pleasure rather than a simple, escapist diversion; its object is to offer pleasure *plus* understanding.

We should immediately make the point that these two categories of fiction are not clear-cut. Not every given story can simply be tossed into one of two bins marked "commercial" or "literary." Rather the two categories suggest opposite ends of a spectrum; some works may fall close to the middle rather than to one end, and genres normally associated with commercial purposes and categories are sometimes used successfully by authors with literary intentions. A famous work such as Harriet Beecher Stowe's *Uncle Tom's Cabin* (1852), for instance, seems to straddle the line between commercial and literary fiction; immensely popular in its own time, it was written with serious intentions but is marred by significant aesthetic flaws. Because it does have some literary quality, however, and because it is an historically important work of its century, it is still read today by general readers and scholars alike. Another example of the occasional blending of our two broad categories is Charlotte Brontë's novel *Jane Eyre* (1847), which adheres to certain conventions of the romance novel and has been commercially successful since it was first published; but it also remains one of the finest literary novels ever written. Similarly, writers such as Charles Dickens, Edith Wharton, and John Updike have published novels that were simultaneously best-sellers and highly praised by literary critics.

The terms "commercial" and "literary" should be applied to novels or stories themselves, not necessarily to their authors. Dickens, in fact, is a good example of a single author capable of writing different works that fall into one category or the other. His novel *Martin Chuzzlewit* (1844), for instance, had disappointing sales when first published but today is greatly admired and discussed by literary scholars; on the other hand, his sentimental but hugely popular *A Christmas Carol* (1843) is essentially a commercial work. More recently, Graham Greene wrote some novels he subtitled "entertainments" as a way of setting them apart from his more serious, literary novels.

It should likewise be stressed that the differences between commercial and literary fiction do not necessarily relate to the absence or presence of a "moral." A story whose incidents and characters are notably shallow may have an unimpeachable moral, while a literary story or novel may have no "moral" at all in the conventional sense; it may choose to dramatize human experience rather than to moralize about it. Similarly, the differences between commercial and literary fiction do not lie in the absence or presence of "facts." An historical romance may be packed with reliable information and yet be pure escape in its depiction of human behavior. Nor do the differences lie in the presence or absence of an element of fantasy. Commercial fiction may have the surface appearance of everyday reality— a police detective novel is a good example—but have little significance beyond the reality depicted; on the other hand, a wildly fanciful tale may impress the reader with a profound and surprising truth. The differences between the two kinds of fiction are deeper and more subtle than any of these distinctions.

Perhaps we can clarify the differences by analogy. Commercial writers are like inventors who devise a contrivance for our diversion. When we push a button, lights flash, bells ring, and cardboard figures move jerkily across a painted horizon. Such writers are full of tricks and surprises: they pull rabbits out of hats, saw beautiful women in two, and juggle brightly colored balls in the air. By contrast, literary writers are more like explorers: they take us out into the midst of life and say, "Look, here is the world in all its complexity." They also take us behind the scenes, where they show us the props and mirrors and seek to dispel the illusions. This is not to say that literary writers are merely reporters. More surely than commercial writers, they carefully shape their materials. But they shape them always with the intent that we may see, feel, and understand them better, not for the primary purpose of furnishing entertainment. In short, any fiction that illuminates some aspect of human life or behavior with genuine originality and power may be called "literary." Such a story presents an insight— whether large or small—into the nature and condition of our existence. It gives us a keener awareness of our humanity within a universe that is sometimes friendly, sometimes hostile. It helps us to understand our world, our neighbors, and ourselves.

The distinctions we have drawn between the two types of fiction are true of both the full-length novel and the short story. Since the latter form is the focus of this text, however, we should stress that the short story, by its very nature, is a more literary genre. Writers hoping to succeed as commercial authors usually work in the novel form, which has proved more popular with large masses of people than has the more refined and subtle art of the story. (A collection of short stories appearing on any best-seller list is an extremely rare event.) Although there are types of commercial short stories that appear in men's adventure magazines, mystery and horror anthologies, and women's publications, the majority of short fiction published today appears in journals that are called, in fact, "literary magazines." Because of their serious intentions and their brevity, short stories provide the ideal vehicle for studying those elements of storytelling common to all literary fiction.

As you read and reread the stories in this book, you will become aware that the term "short story" is a highly elastic one. While brevity is an obvious characteristic of the genre, short narratives have always been part of the human storytelling impulse and have shown an impressive diversity throughout history. Ancient fairy tales and fables were the precursors of the modern short story, but only in the last two centuries has the short story assumed the generally accepted characteristics, outlined in the following chapters, which constitute its uniqueness as a literary genre. Authors of short stories continually seek new ways to exploit the genre, however, using fresh techniques and storytelling approaches in order to advance and refine this sophisticated form. A seemingly conventional tale may veer in an unexpected direction; a fragmented structure may help to mirror the world of one story, while an experimental approach to language or style may distinguish another from anything you have read before. The short story's lack of commercial appeal has, in a way, helped its development as an art form, for writers of short fiction, unconstrained by the demands of the marketplace and a mass audience, are able to give free rein to their creativity and imagination. Noting the "freedom and promise of the form," author Joyce Carol Oates has observed that "radical experimentation, which might be ill-advised in the novel, is well suited for the short story." This outlook, shared by most literary writers, has helped to maintain the status of the short story as a genre capable of ongoing diversity, richness, and self-renewal.

Before beginning a serious study of fiction, you should be aware that literary fiction requires a different way of reading than commercial fiction does. When we take a novel by Stephen King or Danielle Steel to the beach, we do not want to have to think much, if at all, about what we are reading; we simply want a diverting way of passing the time. When we read a literary novel or story, however, we are seeking something different. We expect a serious work to offer some of the immediate pleasures of a well-told story—an original premise and intriguing characters, for instance; but we also know that a literary work may be more demanding of the reader in terms of its language, structure, and complexity. Ultimately we expect to come away from a literary work with an enhanced understanding of life.

In order to appreciate how it operates as a work of narrative art, we should read any piece of literary fiction *at least twice* before we can fully grasp what it has to offer. This is another reason the short story represents an ideal medium for the intensive study of fiction, since its length enables us to reread a story without making unreasonable demands on our time. As you read the stories included in this book, try following this general procedure: (1) read the story the first time simply to enjoy and familiarize yourself with it; (2) read the story a second time, more slowly and deliberately, in the attempt to understand its full artistic significance and achievement. As you proceed through the chapters, learning about plot, characterization, theme, and so forth, you will gradually develop the instincts of a serious reader: it is important to ask, for instance, why a story is constructed in a certain way, or why an author explores a specific character's inner life. With commercial fiction, such questions are irrelevant: there the focus is usually on what happens next, not on the techniques the author uses to tell the story. But with literary fiction, we are willing to invest more time and energy into reading more deliberately, and into careful rereading, because we know the personal rewards will be greater.

When we speak of different kinds of reading, of course, we aren't necessarily talking about different kinds of people. Avid readers may read both commercial and literary fiction at different times, just as an individual may sometimes want fast food, or "junk food," and at other times be willing to invest considerable time and money in savoring a gourmet meal. An English professor may buy a paperback thriller to enjoy during a vacation, while a factory worker might read *Jane Eyre* during her work breaks. So the primary distinction is between kinds of reading, not kinds of readers.

We also bring different expectations to our reading of these two different types of fiction. When we pick up a commercial novel, we come to the book with specific, fixed expectations and will feel frustrated and disappointed unless those expectations are met. Depending on the genre, some of these expectations may include (1) a sympathetic hero or heroine—someone with whom the reader can identify and whose adventures and triumphs the reader can share; (2) a defined plot in which something exciting is always happening and in which there is a strong element of suspense (thus the term "page-turner," often applied to a successful commercial novel); (3) a happy ending that sends the reader away undisturbed and optimistic about life; (4) a general theme, or "message," that affirms widely held, conventional views of the world.

By contrast, when we come to a novel or story with literary intentions, we approach the work with a different set of expectations. For one thing, we are willing to expect the unexpected: instead of adopting a conventional way of storytelling, a literary author may create a unique style or angle of vision to express his or her artistic truth; and instead of a happy or conventional ending in which everything is tied together in a neat package, a literary work may end in an unsettling or even unresolved way, forcing us to examine our own expectations about the story itself, about the way the story is told, and about our ingrained, perhaps unconscious way of viewing a certain topic or idea that may have been challenged or changed by what we have read. In short, when reading literary fiction we must keep an open mind and stay receptive to the author's imaginative vision, however different it may be from our own habits of perceiving and "reading" the world.

Reading effectively, it should be stressed, involves evaluating what we read. A typical library contains thousands of books, and any individual has time to read only a fraction of them. To choose our reading wisely, we need to know two things: (1) how to get the most out of any book we read and (2) how to choose the books that will best repay the time and attention we devote to them. The assumption of this book is that a proper selection will include both fiction and nonfiction—nonfiction as an indispensable fund of information and ideas that constitute one kind of knowledge of the world; literary fiction as an equally indispensable source of a different kind of knowledge, a knowledge of experience, felt in the emotions as well as apprehended by the mind. One aim of this book is to help you develop your understanding and judgment in evaluating what you read.

If we approach a literary story in a serious, committed way, after all, we will probably have a more memorable and satisfying reading experience than the kind we derive from commercial fiction, which we tend to forget as soon as we have consumed it. Especially if you are accustomed to reading fiction quickly and without much thought about its possible complex meanings, try to adopt a slower, more thoughtful approach as you read the stories in this and later chapters. Inevitably, as with different commercial works, you will find some of the stories in this book more appealing than others. They have been chosen carefully, however, to help you explore the elements of fiction and to illustrate the diversity of the short-story form as practiced by a broad range of writers. Ideally, a careful reading of these stories will convince you that while nonfiction may be an indispensable fund of information and ideas, and one way of knowing about the world, fiction is an equally indispensable source of knowledge, and a knowledge apprehended not only by your intellect but by your emotions and imagination as well. Through the act of reading a story and sharing an author's imaginative vision, you will gain not only a pleasurable experience but growth in your understanding of the world and of the human condition.

REVIEWING CHAPTER ONE

....

1. Differentiate between commercial fiction and literary fiction.
2. Explain the purposes of literary fiction.
3. Review the different types of short stories.
4. Describe the best way to read a short story for the purpose of serious study.
5. List the differing expectations we bring to the reading of commercial and literary fiction.

RICHARD CONNELL

The Most Dangerous Game

"Off there to the right—somewhere—is a large island," said Whitney. "It's rather a mystery—"

"What island is it?" Rainsford asked.

"The old charts call it 'Ship-Trap Island,'" Whitney replied. "A suggestive name, isn't it? Sailors have a curious dread of the place. I don't know why. Some superstition—"

"Can't see it," remarked Rainsford, trying to peer through the dank tropical night that was palpable as it pressed its thick warm blackness in upon the yacht.

5   "You've good eyes," said Whitney, with a laugh, "and I've seen you pick off a moose moving in the brown fall bush at four hundred yards, but even you can't see four miles or so through a moonless Caribbean night."

"Nor four yards," admitted Rainsford. "Ugh! It's like moist black velvet."

"It will be light in Rio," promised Whitney. "We should make it in a few days. I hope the jaguar guns have come from Purdey's. We should have some good hunting up the Amazon. Great sport, hunting."

"The best sport in the world," agreed Rainsford.

"For the hunter," amended Whitney. "Not for the jaguar."

10   "Don't talk rot, Whitney," said Rainsford. "You're a big-game hunter, not a philosopher. Who cares how a jaguar feels?"

"Perhaps the jaguar does," observed Whitney.

"Bah! They've no understanding."

THE MOST DANGEROUS GAME   First published in 1924. Richard Connell (1893–1949) was a native of New York State, graduated from Harvard, and served a year in France with the United States Army during World War I.

"Even so, I rather think they understand one thing—fear. The fear of pain and the fear of death."

"Nonsense," laughed Rainsford. "This hot weather is making you soft, Whitney. Be a realist. The world is made up of two classes—the hunters and the huntees. Luckily, you and I are the hunters. Do you think we've passed that island yet?"

"I can't tell in the dark. I hope so." 15

"Why?" asked Rainsford.

"The place has a reputation—a bad one."

"Cannibals?" suggested Rainsford.

"Hardly. Even cannibals wouldn't live in such a God-forsaken place. But it's gotten into sailor lore, somehow. Didn't you notice that the crew's nerves seemed a bit jumpy today?"

"They were a bit strange, now you mention it. Even Captain 20 Nielsen—"

"Yes, even that tough-minded old Swede, who'd go up to the devil himself and ask him for a light. Those fishy blue eyes held a look I never saw there before. All I could get out of him was: 'This place has an evil name among seafaring men, sir.' Then he said to me, very gravely: 'Don't you feel anything?'—as if the air about us was actually poisonous. Now, you mustn't laugh when I tell you this—I did feel something like a sudden chill.

"There was no breeze. The sea was as flat as a plate-glass window. We were drawing near the island then. What I felt was a—a mental chill; a sort of sudden dread."

"Pure imagination," said Rainsford. "One superstitious sailor can taint the whole ship's company with his fear."

"Maybe. But sometimes I think sailors have an extra sense that tells them when they are in danger. Sometimes I think evil is a tangible thing—with wave lengths, just as sound and light have. An evil place can, so to speak, broadcast vibrations of evil. Anyhow, I'm glad we're getting out of this zone. Well, I think I'll turn in now, Rainsford."

"I'm not sleepy," said Rainsford. "I'm going to smoke another pipe on 25 the after deck."

"Good night, then, Rainsford. See you at breakfast."

"Right. Good night, Whitney."

There was no sound in the night as Rainsford sat there, but the muffled throb of the engine that drove the yacht swiftly through the darkness, and the swish and ripple of the wash of the propeller.

Rainsford, reclining in a steamer chair, indolently puffed on his favorite brier. The sensuous drowsiness of the night was on him. "It's so dark," he thought, "that I could sleep without closing my eyes; the night would be my eyelids—"

30   An abrupt sound startled him. Off to the right he heard it, and his ears, expert in such matters, could not be mistaken. Again he heard the sound, and again. Somewhere, off in the blackness, some one had fired a gun three times.

Rainsford sprang up and moved quickly to the rail, mystified. He strained his eyes in the direction from which the reports had come, but it was like trying to see through a blanket. He leaped upon the rail and balanced himself there, to get greater elevation; his pipe, striking a rope, was knocked from his mouth. He lunged for it; a short, hoarse cry came from his lips as he realized he had reached too far and had lost his balance. The cry was pinched off short as the blood-warm waters of the Caribbean Sea closed over his head.

He struggled up to the surface and tried to cry out, but the wash from the speeding yacht slapped him in the face and the salt water in his open mouth made him gag and strangle. Desperately he struck out with strong strokes after the receding lights of the yacht, but he stopped before he had swum fifty feet. A certain cool-headedness had come to him; it was not the first time he had been in a tight place. There was a chance that his cries could be heard by some one aboard the yacht, but that chance was slender, and grew more slender as the yacht raced on. He wrestled himself out of his clothes, and shouted with all his power. The lights of the yacht became faint and ever-vanishing fireflies; then they were blotted out entirely by the night.

Rainsford remembered the shots. They had come from the right, and doggedly he swam in that direction, swimming with slow, deliberate strokes, conserving his strength. For a seemingly endless time he fought the sea. He began to count his strokes; he could do possibly a hundred more and then—

Rainsford heard a sound. It came out of the darkness, a high screaming sound, the sound of an animal in an extremity of anguish and terror.

35   He did not recognize the animal that made the sound; he did not try to; with fresh vitality he swam toward the sound. He heard it again; then it was cut short by another noise, crisp, staccato.

"Pistol shot," muttered Rainsford, swimming on.

Ten minutes of determined effort brought another sound to his ears—the most welcome he had ever heard—the muttering and growling of the sea breaking on a rocky shore. He was almost on the rocks before he saw them; on a night less calm he would have been shattered against them. With his remaining strength he dragged himself from the swirling waters. Jagged crags appeared to jut into the opaqueness; he forced himself upward, hand over hand. Gasping, his hands raw, he reached a flat place at the top. Dense jungle came down to the very edge of the cliffs. What perils that tangle of trees and underbrush might hold for him did not concern Rainsford just then. All he knew was that he was safe from his enemy, the sea, and that utter weariness was on him. He flung himself down at the jungle edge and tumbled headlong into the deepest sleep of his life.

When he opened his eyes he knew from the position of the sun that it was late in the afternoon. Sleep had given him new vigor; a sharp hunger was picking at him. He looked about him, almost cheerfully.

"Where there are pistol shots, there are men. Where there are men, there is food," he thought. But what kind of men, he wondered, in so forbidding a place? An unbroken front of snarled and ragged jungle fringed the shore.

He saw no sign of a trail through the closely knit web of weeds and 40 trees; it was easier to go along the shore, and Rainsford floundered along by the water. Not far from where he had landed, he stopped.

Some wounded thing, by the evidence a large animal, had thrashed about in the underbrush; the jungle weeds were crushed down and the moss was lacerated; one patch of weeds was stained crimson. A small, glittering object not far away caught Rainsford's eye and he picked it up. It was an empty cartridge.

"A twenty-two," he remarked. "That's odd. It must have been a fairly large animal too. The hunter had his nerve with him to tackle it with a light gun. It's clear that the brute put up a fight. I suppose the first three shots I heard was when the hunter flushed his quarry and wounded it. The last shot was when he trailed it here and finished it."

He examined the ground closely and found what he had hoped to find—the print of hunting boots. They pointed along the cliff in the direction he had been going. Eagerly he hurried along, now slipping on a rotten log or a loose stone, but making headway; night was beginning to settle down on the island.

Bleak darkness was blacking out the sea and jungle when Rainsford sighted the lights. He came upon them as he turned a crook in the coast line, and his first thought was that he had come upon a village, for there were many lights. But as he forged along he saw to his great astonishment that all the lights were in one enormous building—a lofty structure with pointed towers plunging upward into the gloom. His eyes made out the shadowy outlines of a palatial château; it was set on a high bluff, and on three sides of it cliffs dived down to where the sea licked greedy lips in the shadows.

"Mirage," thought Rainsford. But it was no mirage, he found, when 45 he opened the tall spiked iron gate. The stone steps were real enough; the massive door with a leering gargoyle for a knocker was real enough; yet about it all hung an air of unreality.

He lifted the knocker, and it creaked up stiffly, as if it had never before been used. He let it fall, and it startled him with its booming loudness. He thought he heard steps within; the door remained closed. Again Rainsford lifted the heavy knocker, and let it fall. The door opened then, opened as suddenly as if it were on a spring, and Rainsford stood blinking in the river of glaring gold light that poured out. The first thing Rainsford's eyes discerned was the largest man Rainsford had ever seen—a gigantic creature, solidly made and black-bearded to the waist. In his hand the man held a long-barreled revolver, and he was pointing it straight at Rainsford's heart.

Out of the snarl of beard two small eyes regarded Rainsford.

"Don't be alarmed," said Rainsford, with a smile which he hoped was disarming. "I'm no robber. I fell off a yacht. My name is Sanger Rainsford of New York City."

The menacing look in the eyes did not change. The revolver pointed as rigidly as if the giant were a statue. He gave no sign that he understood Rainsford's words, or that he had even heard them. He was dressed in uniform, a black uniform trimmed with gray astrakhan.

50 "I'm Sanger Rainsford of New York," Rainsford began again. "I fell off a yacht. I am hungry."

The man's only answer was to raise with his thumb the hammer of his revolver. Then Rainsford saw the man's free hand go to his forehead in a military salute, and he saw him click his heels together and stand at attention. Another man was coming down the broad marble steps, an erect, slender man in evening clothes. He advanced to Rainsford and held out his hand.

In a cultivated voice marked by a slight accent that gave it added precision and deliberateness, he said: "It is a very great pleasure and honor to welcome Mr. Sanger Rainsford, the celebrated hunter, to my home."

Automatically Rainsford shook the man's hand.

"I've read your book about hunting snow leopards in Tibet, you see," explained the man. "I am General Zaroff."

55 Rainsford's first impression was that the man was singularly handsome; his second was that there was an original, almost bizarre quality about the general's face. He was a tall man past middle age, for his hair was a vivid white; but his thick eyebrows and pointed military mustache were as black as the night from which Rainsford had come. His eyes, too, were black and very bright. He had high cheek bones, a sharp-cut nose, a spare, dark face, the face of a man used to giving orders, the face of an aristocrat. Turning to the giant in uniform, the general made a sign. The giant put away his pistol, saluted, withdrew.

"Ivan is an incredibly strong fellow," remarked the general, "but he has the misfortune to be deaf and dumb. A simple fellow, but, I'm afraid, like all his race, a bit of a savage."

"Is he Russian?"

"He is a Cossack," said the general, and his smile showed red lips and pointed teeth. "So am I."

"Come," he said, "we shouldn't be chatting here. We can talk later. Now you want clothes, food, rest. You shall have them. This is a most restful spot."

Ivan had reappeared, and the general spoke to him with lips that   60
moved but gave forth no sound.

"Follow Ivan, if you please, Mr. Rainsford," said the general. "I was about to have my dinner when you came. I'll wait for you. You'll find that my clothes will fit you, I think."

It was to a huge, beam-ceilinged bedroom with a canopied bed big enough for six men that Rainsford followed the silent giant. Ivan laid out an evening suit, and Rainsford, as he put it on, noticed that it came from a London tailor who ordinarily cut and sewed for none below the rank of duke.

The dining room to which Ivan conducted him was in many ways remarkable. There was a medieval magnificence about it; it suggested a baronial hall of feudal times with its oaken panels, its high ceiling, its vast refectory table where twoscore men could sit down to eat. About the hall were the mounted heads of many animals—lions, tigers, elephants, moose, bears; larger or more perfect specimens Rainsford had never seen. At the great table the general was sitting, alone.

"You'll have a cocktail, Mr. Rainsford," he suggested. The cocktail was surpassingly good; and, Rainsford noted, the table appointments were of the finest—the linen, the crystal, the silver, the china.

They were eating *borsch*, the rich, red soup with whipped cream so dear   65
to Russian palates. Half apologetically General Zaroff said: "We do our best to preserve the amenities of civilization here. Please forgive any lapses. We are well off the beaten track, you know. Do you think the champagne has suffered from its long ocean trip?"

"Not in the least," declared Rainsford. He was finding the general a most thoughtful and affable host, a true cosmopolite. But there was one small trait of the general's that made Rainsford uncomfortable. Whenever he looked up from his plate he found the general studying him, appraising him narrowly.

"Perhaps," said General Zaroff, "you were surprised that I recognized your name. You see, I read all books on hunting published in English, French, and Russian. I have but one passion in my life, Mr. Rainsford, and it is the hunt."

"You have some wonderful heads here," said Rainsford as he ate a particularly well-cooked filet mignon. "That Cape buffalo is the largest I ever saw."

"Oh, that fellow. Yes, he was a monster."

70 "Did he charge you?"

"Hurled me against a tree," said the general. "Fractured my skull. But I got the brute."

"I've always thought," said Rainsford, "that the Cape buffalo is the most dangerous of all big game."

For a moment the general did not reply; he was smiling his curious red-lipped smile. Then he said slowly: "No. You are wrong, sir. The Cape buffalo is not the most dangerous big game." He sipped his wine. "Here in my preserve on this island," he said in the same slow tone, "I hunt more dangerous game."

Rainsford expressed his surprise. "Is there big game on this island?"

75 The general nodded. "The biggest."

"Really?"

"Oh, it isn't here naturally, of course. I have to stock the island."

"What have you imported, general?" Rainsford asked. "Tigers?"

The general smiled. "No," he said. "Hunting tigers ceased to interest me some years ago. I exhausted their possibilities, you see. No thrill left in tigers, no real danger. I live for danger, Mr. Rainsford."

80 The general took from his pocket a gold cigaret case and offered his guest a long black cigaret with a silver tip; it was perfumed and gave off a smell like incense.

"We will have some capital hunting, you and I," said the general. "I shall be most glad to have your society."

"But what game—" began Rainsford.

"I'll tell you," said the general. "You will be amused, I know. I think I may say, in all modesty, that I have done a rare thing. I have invented a new sensation. May I pour you another glass of port, Mr. Rainsford?"

"Thank you, general."

85 The general filled both glasses, and said: "God makes some men poets. Some He makes kings, some beggars. Me He made a hunter. My hand was made for the trigger, my father said. He was a very rich man with a quarter of a million acres in the Crimea, and he was an ardent sportsman. When I was only five years old he gave me a little gun, specially made in Moscow for me, to shoot sparrows with. When I shot some of his prize turkeys with it, he did not punish me; he complimented me on my marksmanship. I killed my first bear in the Caucasus when I was ten. My whole life has been one prolonged hunt. I went into the army—it was expected of noblemen's sons—and for a time commanded a division of Cossack cavalry, but my real interest was always the hunt. I have hunted every kind of game in every land. It would be impossible for me to tell you how many animals I have killed."

The general puffed at his cigaret.

"After the debacle in Russia I left the country, for it was imprudent for an officer of the Czar to stay there. Many noble Russians lost everything. I, luckily, had invested heavily in American securities, so I shall never have to open a tea room in Monte Carlo or drive a taxi in Paris. Naturally, I continued to hunt—grizzlies in your Rockies, crocodiles in the Ganges, rhinoceroses in East Africa. It was in Africa that the Cape buffalo hit me and laid me up for six months. As soon as I recovered I started for the Amazon to hunt jaguars, for I had heard they were unusually cunning. They weren't." The Cossack sighed. "They were no match at all for a hunter with his wits about him, and a high-powered rifle. I was bitterly disappointed. I was lying in my tent with a splitting headache one night when a terrible thought pushed its way into my mind. Hunting was beginning to bore me! And hunting, remember, had been my life. I have heard that in America businessmen often go to pieces when they give up the business that has been their life."

"Yes, that's so," said Rainsford.

The general smiled. "I had no wish to go to pieces," he said. "I must do something. Now, mine is an analytical mind, Mr. Rainsford. Doubtless that is why I enjoy the problems of the chase."

"No doubt, General Zaroff." 90

"So," continued the general, "I asked myself why the hunt no longer fascinated me. You are much younger than I am, Mr. Rainsford, and have not hunted as much, but you perhaps can guess the answer."

"What was it?"

"Simply this: hunting had ceased to be what you call 'a sporting proposition.' It had become too easy. I always got my quarry. Always. There is no greater bore than perfection."

The general lit a fresh cigaret.

"No animal had a chance with me any more. That is no boast; it is 95 a mathematical certainty. The animal had nothing but his legs and his instinct. Instinct is no match for reason. When I thought of this it was a tragic moment for me, I can tell you."

Rainsford leaned across the table, absorbed in what his host was saying.

"It came to me as an inspiration what I must do," the general went on.

"And that was?"

The general smiled the quiet smile of one who has faced an obstacle and surmounted it with success. "I had to invent a new animal to hunt," he said.

"A new animal? You're joking."

"Not at all," said the general. "I never joke about hunting. I needed a 100 new animal. I found one. So I bought this island, built this house, and here

I do my hunting. The island is perfect for my purposes—there are jungles with a maze of trails in them, hills, swamps—"

"But the animal, General Zaroff?"

"Oh," said the general, "it supplies me with the most exciting hunting in the world. No other hunting compares with it for an instant. Every day I hunt, and I never grow bored now, for I have a quarry with which I can match my wits."

Rainsford's bewilderment showed in his face.

105   "I wanted the ideal animal to hunt," explained the general. "So I said: 'What are the attributes of an ideal quarry?' And the answer was, of course: 'it must have courage, cunning, and, above all, it must be able to reason.'"

"But no animal can reason," objected Rainsford.

"My dear fellow," said the general, "there is one that can."

"But you can't mean—" gasped Rainsford.

"And why not?"

110   "I can't believe you are serious, General Zaroff. This is a grisly joke."

"Why should I not be serious? I am speaking of hunting."

"Hunting? Good God, General Zaroff, what you speak of is murder."

The general laughed with entire good nature. He regarded Rainsford quizzically. "I refuse to believe that so modern and civilized a young man as you seem to be harbors romantic ideas about the value of human life. Surely your experiences in the war—"

"Did not make me condone cold-blooded murder," finished Rainsford stiffly.

115   Laughter shook the general. "How extraordinarily droll you are!" he said. "One does not expect nowadays to find a young man of the educated class, even in America, with such a naive, and, if I may say so, mid-Victorian point of view. It's like finding a snuff-box in a limousine. Ah, well, doubtless you had Puritan ancestors. So many Americans appear to have had. I'll wager you'll forget your notions when you go hunting with me. You've a genuine new thrill in store for you, Mr. Rainsford."

"Thank you, I'm a hunter, not a murderer."

"Dear me," said the general, quite unruffled, "again that unpleasant word. But I think I can show you that your scruples are quite ill founded."

"Yes?"

"Life is for the strong, to be lived by the strong, and, if need be, taken by the strong. The weak of the world were put here to give the strong pleasure. I am strong. Why should I not use my gift? If I wish to hunt, why should I not? I hunt the scum of the earth—sailors from tramp ships—lascars, blacks, Chinese, whites, mongrels—a thoroughbred horse or hound is worth more than a score of them."

120   "But they are men," said Rainsford hotly.

"Precisely," said the general. "That is why I use them. It gives me pleasure. They can reason, after a fashion. So they are dangerous."

"But where do you get them?"

The general's left eyelid fluttered down in a wink. "This island is called Ship-Trap," he answered. "Sometimes an angry god of the high seas sends them to me. Sometimes, when Providence is not so kind, I help Providence a bit. Come to the window with me."

Rainsford went to the window and looked out toward the sea.

"Watch! Out there!" exclaimed the general, pointing into the night. 125 Rainsford's eyes saw only blackness, and then, as the general pressed a button, far out to sea Rainsford saw the flash of lights.

The general chuckled. "They indicate a channel," he said, "where there's none: giant rocks with razor edges crouch like a sea monster with wide-open jaws. They can crush a ship as easily as I crush this nut." He dropped a walnut on the hardwood floor and brought his heel grinding down on it. "Oh, yes," he said, casually, as if in answer to a question, "I have electricity. We try to be civilized here."

"Civilized? And you shoot down men?"

A trace of anger was in the general's black eyes, but it was there for but a second, and he said, in his most pleasant manner: "Dear me, what a righteous young man you are! I assure you I do not do the thing you suggest. That would be barbarous. I treat these visitors with every consideration. They get plenty of good food and exercise. They get into splendid physical condition. You shall see for yourself tomorrow."

"What do you mean?"

"We'll visit my training school," smiled the general. "It's in the cel- 130 lar. I have about a dozen pupils down there now. They're from the Spanish bark *San Lucar* that had the bad luck to go on the rocks out there. A very inferior lot, I regret to say. Poor specimens and more accustomed to the deck than to the jungle."

He raised his hand, and Ivan, who served as waiter, brought thick Turkish coffee. Rainsford, with an effort, held his tongue in check.

"It's a game, you see," pursued the general blandly. "I suggest to one of them that we go hunting. I give him a supply of food and an excellent hunting knife. I give him three hours' start. I am to follow, armed only with a pistol of the smallest caliber and range. If my quarry eludes me for three whole days, he wins the game. If I find him"—the general smiled— "he loses."

"Suppose he refuses to be hunted?"

"Oh," said the general, "I give him his option, of course. He need not play that game if he doesn't wish to. If he does not wish to hunt, I turn him over to Ivan. Ivan once had the honor of serving as official knouter to the Great White Czar, and he has his own ideas of sport. Invariably, Mr. Rainsford, invariably they choose the hunt."

135   "And if they win?"

The smile on the general's face widened. "To date I have not lost," he said.

Then he added, hastily: "I don't wish you to think me a braggart, Mr. Rainsford. Many of them afford only the most elementary sort of problem. Occasionally I strike a tartar. One almost did win. I eventually had to use the dogs."

"The dogs?"

"This way, please. I'll show you."

140   The general steered Rainsford to a window. The lights from the windows sent a flickering illumination that made grotesque patterns on the courtyard below, and Rainsford could see moving about there a dozen or so huge black shapes; as they turned toward him, their eyes glittered greenly.

"A rather good lot, I think," observed the general. "They are let out at seven every night. If anyone should try to get into my house—or out of it—something extremely regrettable would occur to him." He hummed a snatch of song from the Folies Bergère.

"And now," said the general, "I want to show you my new collection of heads. Will you come with me to the library?"

"I hope," said Rainsford, "that you will excuse me tonight, General Zaroff. I'm really not feeling at all well."

"Ah, indeed?" the general inquired solicitously. "Well, I suppose that's only natural, after your long swim. You need a good, restful night's sleep. Tomorrow you'll feel like a new man, I'll wager. Then we'll hunt, eh? I've one rather promising prospect—"

145   Rainsford was hurrying from the room.

"Sorry you can't go with me tonight," called the general. "I expect rather fair sport—a big, strong black. He looks resourceful—Well, good night, Mr. Rainsford; I hope you have a good night's rest."

The bed was good, and the pajamas of the softest silk, and he was tired in every fiber of his being, but nevertheless Rainsford could not quiet his brain with the opiate of sleep. He lay, eyes wide open. Once he thought he heard stealthy steps in the corridor outside his room. He sought to throw open the door; it would not open. He went to the window and looked out. His room was high up in one of the towers. The lights of the château were out now, and it was dark and silent, but there was a fragment of sallow moon, and by its wan light he could see, dimly, the courtyard; there, weaving in and out in the pattern of shadow, were black, noiseless forms; the hounds heard him at the window and looked up, expectantly, with their green eyes. Rainsford went back to the bed and lay down. By many methods he tried to put himself to sleep. He had achieved a doze when, just as morning began to come, he heard, far off in the jungle, the faint report of a pistol.

General Zaroff did not appear until luncheon. He was dressed faultlessly in the tweeds of a country squire. He was solicitous about the state of Rainsford's health.

"As for me," sighed the general, "I do not feel so well. I am worried, Mr. Rainsford. Last night I detected traces of my old complaint."

To Rainsford's questioning glance the general said: "Ennui. Boredom." 150

Then, taking a second helping of Crêpes Suzette, the general explained: "The hunting was not good last night. The fellow lost his head. He made a straight trail that offered no problems at all. That's the trouble with these sailors; they have dull brains to begin with, and they do not know how to get about in the woods. They do excessively stupid and obvious things. It's most annoying. Will you have another glass of Chablis, Mr. Rainsford?"

"General," said Rainsford firmly, "I wish to leave this island at once."

The general raised his thickets of eyebrows; he seemed hurt. "But, my dear fellow," the general protested, "you've only just come. You've had no hunting—"

"I wish to go today," said Rainsford. He saw the dead black eyes of the general on him, studying him. General Zaroff's face suddenly brightened.

He filled Rainsford's glass with venerable Chablis from a dusty bottle. 155

"Tonight," said the general, "we will hunt—you and I."

Rainsford shook his head. "No, general," he said. "I will not hunt."

The general shrugged his shoulders and delicately ate a hothouse grape. "As you wish, my friend," he said. "The choice rests entirely with you. But may I not venture to suggest that you will find my idea of sport more diverting than Ivan's?"

He nodded toward the corner to where the giant stood, scowling, his thick arms crossed on his hogshead of chest.

"You don't mean—" cried Rainsford. 160

"My dear fellow," said the general, "have I not told you I always mean what I say about hunting? This is really an inspiration. I drink to a foeman worthy of my steel—at last."

The general raised his glass, but Rainsford sat staring at him.

"You'll find this game worth playing," the general said enthusiastically. "Your brain against mine. Your woodcraft against mine. Your strength and stamina against mine. Outdoor chess! And the stake is not without value, eh?"

"And if I win—" began Rainsford huskily.

"I'll cheerfully acknowledge myself defeated if I do not find you by 165 midnight of the third day," said General Zaroff. "My sloop will place you on the mainland near a town."

The general read what Rainsford was thinking.

"Oh, you can trust me," said the Cossack. "I will give you my word as a gentleman and a sportsman. Of course you, in turn, must agree to say nothing of your visit here."

"I'll agree to nothing of the kind," said Rainsford.

"Oh," said the general, "in that case—But why discuss that now? Three days hence we can discuss it over a bottle of Veuve Cliquot, unless—"

170 The general sipped his wine.

Then a businesslike air animated him. "Ivan," he said to Rainsford, "will supply you with hunting clothes, food, a knife. I suggest you wear moccasins; they leave a poorer trail. I suggest too that you avoid the big swamp in the southeast corner of the island. We call it Death Swamp. There's quicksand there. One foolish fellow tried it. The deplorable part of it was that Lazarus followed him. You can imagine my feelings, Mr. Rainsford. I loved Lazarus; he was the finest hound in my pack. Well, I must beg you to excuse me now. I always take a siesta after lunch. You'll hardly have time for a nap, I fear. You'll want to start, no doubt. I shall not follow till dusk. Hunting at night is so much more exciting than by day, don't you think? Au revoir, Mr. Rainsford, au revoir."

General Zaroff, with a deep, courtly bow, strolled from the room.

From another door came Ivan. Under one arm he carried khaki hunting clothes, a haversack of food, a leather sheath containing a long-bladed hunting knife; his right hand rested on a cocked revolver thrust in the crimson sash about his waist. . . .

Rainsford had fought his way through the bush for two hours. "I must keep my nerve. I must keep my nerve," he said through tight teeth.

175 He had not been entirely clear-headed when the château gates snapped shut behind him. His whole idea at first was to put distance between himself and General Zaroff, and, to this end, he had plunged along, spurred on by the sharp rowels of something very like panic. Now he had got a grip on himself, had stopped, and was taking stock of himself and the situation.

He saw that straight flight was futile; inevitably it would bring him face to face with the sea. He was in a picture with a frame of water, and his operations, clearly, must take place within that frame.

"I'll give him a trail to follow," muttered Rainsford, and he struck off from the rude paths he had been following into the trackless wilderness. He executed a series of intricate loops; he doubled on his trail again and again, recalling all the lore of the fox hunt, and all the dodges of the fox. Night found him leg-weary, with hands and face lashed by the branches, on a thickly wooded ridge. He knew it would be insane to blunder on through the dark, even if he had the strength. His need for rest was imperative and he thought: "I have played the fox, now I must play the cat of the fable." A big tree with a thick trunk and outspread branches was nearby, and, taking care to leave not the slightest mark, he climbed up into the crotch, and stretching out on one of the broad limbs, after a fashion, rested. Rest brought him new confidence and almost a feeling of security. Even so zealous a hunter as General Zaroff could not trace him there, he told himself; only the devil himself could follow that complicated trail through the jungle after dark. But, perhaps, the general was a devil—

An apprehensive night crawled slowly by like a wounded snake, and sleep did not visit Rainsford, although the silence of a dead world was on the jungle. Toward morning when a dingy gray was varnishing the sky, the cry of some startled bird focused Rainsford's attention in that direction. Something was coming through the bush, coming slowly, carefully, coming by the same winding way Rainsford had come. He flattened himself down on the limb, and through a screen of leaves almost as thick as tapestry, he watched. The thing that was approaching was a man.

It was General Zaroff. He made his way along with his eyes fixed in utmost concentration on the ground before him. He paused, almost beneath the tree, dropped to his knees and studied the ground. Rainsford's impulse was to hurl himself down like a panther, but he saw the general's right hand held something metallic—a small automatic pistol.

The hunter shook his head several times, as if he were puzzled. Then he straightened up and took from his case one of his black cigarets; its pungent incense-like smoke floated up to Rainsford's nostrils.

Rainsford held his breath. The general's eyes had left the ground and were traveling inch by inch up the tree. Rainsford froze there, every muscle tensed for a spring. But the sharp eyes of the hunter stopped before they reached the limb where Rainsford lay; a smile spread over his brown face. Very deliberately he blew a smoke ring into the air; then he turned his back on the tree and walked carelessly away, back along the trail he had come. The swish of the underbrush against his hunting boots grew fainter and fainter.

The pent-up air burst hotly from Rainsford's lungs. His first thought made him feel sick and numb. The general could follow a trail through the woods at night; he could follow an extremely difficult trail; he must have uncanny powers; only by the merest chance had the Cossack failed to see his quarry.

Rainsford's second thought was even more terrible. It sent a shudder of cold horror through his whole being. Why had the general smiled? Why had he turned back?

Rainsford did not want to believe what his reason told him was true, but the truth was as evident as the sun that had by now pushed through the morning mists. The general was playing with him! The general was saving him for another day's sport! The Cossack was the cat; he was the mouse. Then it was that Rainsford knew the full meaning of terror.

185   "I will not lose my nerve. I will not."

He slid down from the tree, and struck off again into the woods. His face was set and he forced the machinery of his mind to function. Three hundred yards from his hiding place he stopped where a huge dead tree leaned precariously on a smaller, living one. Throwing off his sack of food, Rainsford took his knife from its sheath and began to work with all his energy.

The job was finished at last, and he threw himself down behind a fallen log a hundred feet away. He did not have to wait long. The cat was coming again to play with the mouse.

Following the trail with the sureness of a bloodhound, came General Zaroff. Nothing escaped those searching black eyes, no crushed blade of grass, no bent twig, no mark, no matter how faint, in the moss. So intent was the Cossack on his stalking that he was upon the thing Rainsford had made before he saw it. His foot touched the protruding bough that was the trigger. Even as he touched it, the general sensed his danger and leaped back with the agility of an ape. But he was not quick enough; the dead tree, delicately adjusted to rest on the cut living one, crashed down and struck the general a glancing blow on the shoulder as it fell; but for his alertness, he must have been smashed beneath it. He staggered, but he did not fall; nor did he drop his revolver. He stood there, rubbing his injured shoulder, and Rainsford, with fear again gripping his heart, heard the general's mocking laugh ring through the jungle.

"Rainsford," called the general, "if you are within the sound of my voice, as I suppose you are, let me congratulate you. Not many men know how to make a Malay man-catcher. Luckily, for me, I too have hunted in Malacca. You are proving interesting, Mr. Rainsford. I am going now to have my wound dressed; it's only a slight one. But I shall be back. I shall be back."

190   When the general, nursing his bruised shoulder, had gone, Rainsford took up his flight again. It was flight now, a desperate, hopeless flight, that carried him on for some hours. Dusk came, then darkness, and still he pressed on. The ground grew softer under his moccasins; the vegetation grew ranker, denser; insects bit him savagely. Then, as he stepped forward, his foot sank in the ooze. He tried to wrench it back, but the muck sucked viciously at his foot as if it were a giant leech. With a violent effort, he tore loose. He knew where he was now. Death Swamp and its quicksand.

His hands were tight closed as if his nerve were something tangible that some one in the darkness was trying to tear from his grip. The softness of the earth had given him an idea. He stepped back from the quicksand a dozen feet or so, and, like some huge prehistoric beaver, he began to dig.

Rainsford had dug himself in in France when a second's delay meant death. That had been a placid pastime compared to his digging now.

The pit grew deeper; when it was above his shoulders, he climbed out and from some hard saplings cut stakes and sharpened them to a fine point. These stakes he planted at the bottom of the pit with the points sticking up. With flying fingers he wove a rough carpet of weeds and branches and with it he covered the mouth of the pit. Then, wet with sweat and aching with tiredness, he crouched behind the stump of a lightning-charred tree.

He knew his pursuer was coming; he heard the padding sound of feet on the soft earth, and the night breeze brought him the perfume of the general's cigaret. It seemed to Rainsford that the general was coming with unusual swiftness; he was not feeling his way along, foot by foot. Rainsford, crouching there, could not see the general, nor could he see the pit. He lived a year in a minute. Then he felt an impulse to cry aloud with joy, for he heard the sharp crackle of the breaking branches as the cover of the pit gave way; he heard the sharp scream of pain as the pointed stakes found their mark. He leaped up from his place of concealment. Then he cowered back. Three feet from the pit a man was standing, with an electric torch in his hand.

"You've done well, Rainsford," the voice of the general called. "Your Burmese tiger pit has claimed one of my best dogs. Again you score. I think, Mr. Rainsford, I'll see what you can do against my whole pack. I'm going home for a rest now. Thank you for a most amusing evening."

At daybreak Rainsford, lying near the swamp, was awakened by the 195 sound that made him know that he had new things to learn about fear. It was a distant sound, faint and wavering, but he knew it. It was the baying of a pack of hounds.

Rainsford knew he could do one of two things. He could stay where he was and wait. That was suicide. He could flee. That was postponing the inevitable. For a moment he stood there, thinking. An idea that held a wild chance came to him, and, tightening his belt, he headed away from the swamp.

The baying of the hounds drew nearer, then still nearer, nearer, ever nearer. On a ridge Rainsford climbed a tree. Down a watercourse, not a quarter of a mile away, he could see the bush moving. Straining his eyes, he saw the lean figure of General Zaroff; just ahead of him Rainsford made out another figure whose wide shoulders surged through the tall jungle weeds; it was the giant Ivan, and he seemed pulled forward by some unseen force; Rainsford knew that Ivan must be holding the pack in leash.

They would be on him any minute now. His mind worked frantically. He thought of a native trick he had learned in Uganda. He slid down the tree. He caught hold of a springy young sapling and to it he fastened his hunting knife, with the blade pointing down the trail; with a bit of wild grapevine he tied back the sapling. Then he ran for his life. The hounds raised their voices as they hit the fresh scent. Rainsford knew now how an animal at bay feels.

He had to stop to get his breath. The baying of the hounds stopped abruptly, and Rainsford's heart stopped too. They must have reached the knife.

200   He shinnied excitedly up a tree and looked back. His pursuers had stopped. But the hope that was in Rainsford's brain when he climbed died, for he saw in the shallow valley that General Zaroff was still on his feet. But Ivan was not. The knife, driven by the recoil of the springing tree, had not wholly failed.

"Nerve, nerve, nerve!" he panted, as he dashed along. A blue gap showed between the trees dead ahead. Ever nearer drew the hounds. Rainsford forced himself on toward that gap. He reached it. It was the shore of the sea. Across a cove he could see the gloomy gray stone of the château. Twenty feet below him the sea rumbled and hissed. Rainsford hesitated. He heard the hounds. Then he leaped far out into the sea. . . .

When the general and his pack reached the place by the sea, the Cossack stopped. For some minutes he stood regarding the blue-green expanse of water. He shrugged his shoulders. Then he sat down, took a drink of brandy from a silver flask, lit a perfumed cigaret, and hummed a bit from *Madame Butterfly*.

General Zaroff had an exceedingly good dinner in his great paneled dining hall that evening. With it he had a bottle of Pol Roger and half a bottle of Chambertin. Two slight annoyances kept him from perfect enjoyment. One was the thought that it would be difficult to replace Ivan; the other was that his quarry had escaped him; of course the American hadn't played the game—so thought the general as he tasted his after-dinner liqueur. In his library he read, to soothe himself, from the works of Marcus Aurelius. At ten he went up to his bedroom. He was deliciously tired, he said to himself, as he locked himself in. There was a little moonlight, so, before turning on his light, he went to the window and looked down at the courtyard. He could see the great hounds, and he called: "Better luck another time," to them. Then he switched on the light.

A man, who had been hiding in the curtains of the bed, was standing there.

205   "Rainsford!" screamed the general. "How in God's name did you get here?"

"Swam," said Rainsford. "I found it quicker than walking through the jungle."

The general sucked in his breath and smiled. "I congratulate you," he said. "You have won the game."

Rainsford did not smile. "I am still a beast at bay," he said, in a low, hoarse voice. "Get ready, General Zaroff."

The general made one of his deepest bows. "I see," he said. "Splendid! One of us is to furnish a repast for the hounds. The other will sleep in this very excellent bed. On guard, Rainsford. . . ."

He had never slept in a better bed, Rainsford decided.   210

QUESTIONS

1. Discuss the two meanings of the title.
2. How important is suspense in the story? How is it developed and sustained? What roles do chance and coincidence play in the story?
3. Discuss the characterizations of Rainsford and General Zaroff. Which one is more fully characterized? Are both characters plausible?
4. Why does Connell include the "philosophical" discussion between Whitney and Rainsford at the beginning of the story (paragraphs 7–24)? Does it reveal a personal limitation on Rainsford's part? Does Rainsford undergo any significant changes in the course of the story? Do we come to know him better as the story proceeds?
5. Compare the discussion between Whitney and Rainsford and the after-dinner conversation between Rainsford and Zaroff (paragraphs 68–145). In these discussions, is Rainsford more like Whitney or Zaroff? How does he differ from Zaroff? Does the end of the story resolve that difference?
6. As you read the story, do you develop any expectations of how it might be resolved? Are these expectations met or overturned?
7. As you go through the story a second time, do you find more significance in any of the action or description than you noticed during the first reading?
8. Would you describe this story as commercial fiction or literary fiction? Support your answer.

TOBIAS WOLFF
Hunters in the Snow

Tub had been waiting for an hour in the falling snow. He paced the sidewalk to keep warm and stuck his head out over the curb whenever he saw lights approaching. One driver stopped for him but before Tub could wave the man on he saw the rifle on Tub's back and hit the gas. The tires spun on the ice.

The fall of snow thickened. Tub stood below the overhang of a building. Across the road the clouds whitened just above the rooftops, and the street lights went out. He shifted the rifle strap to his other shoulder. The whiteness seeped up the sky.

HUNTERS IN THE SNOW   First published in 1981. Tobias Wolff (b. 1945), a winner of the PEN/Faulkner award, has also won many awards for his short fiction, including places in the annual *Prize Stories: The O. Henry Awards* and *The Best American Short Stories* volumes. Raised in the state of Washington, he dropped out of high school and worked as an apprentice seaman, then later served as a paratrooper in Vietnam. He then earned degrees at Oxford University and Stanford, where he now teaches.

A truck slid around the corner, horn blaring, rear end sashaying. Tub moved to the sidewalk and held up his hand. The truck jumped the curb and kept coming, half on the street and half on the sidewalk. It wasn't slowing down at all. Tub stood for a moment, still holding up his hand, then jumped back. His rifle slipped off his shoulder and clattered on the ice, a sandwich fell out of his pocket. He ran for the steps of the building. Another sandwich and a package of cookies tumbled onto the new snow. He made the steps and looked back.

The truck had stopped several feet beyond where Tub had been standing. He picked up his sandwiches and his cookies and slung the rifle and went up to the driver's window. The driver was bent against the steering wheel, slapping his knees and drumming his feet on the floorboards. He looked like a cartoon of a person laughing, except that his eyes watched the man on the seat beside him. "You ought to see yourself," the driver said. "He looks just like a beach ball with a hat on, doesn't he? Doesn't he, Frank?"

5   The man beside him smiled and looked off.

"You almost ran me down," Tub said. "You could've killed me."

"Come on, Tub," said the man beside the driver. "Be mellow. Kenny was just messing around." He opened the door and slid over to the middle of the seat.

Tub took the bolt out of his rifle and climbed in beside him. "I waited an hour," he said. "If you meant ten o'clock why didn't you say ten o'clock?"

"Tub, you haven't done anything but complain since we got here," said the man in the middle. "If you want to piss and moan all day you might as well go home and bitch at your kids. Take your pick." When Tub didn't say anything he turned to the driver. "Okay, Kenny, let's hit the road."

10   Some juvenile delinquents had heaved a brick through the wind shield on the driver's side, so the cold and snow tunneled right into the cab. The heater didn't work. They covered themselves with a couple of blankets Kenny had brought along and pulled down the muffs on their caps. Tub tried to keep his hands warm by rubbing them under the blanket but Frank made him stop.

They left Spokane and drove deep into the country, running along black lines of fences. The snow let up, but still there was no edge to the land where it met the sky. Nothing moved in the chalky fields. The cold bleached their faces and made the stubble stand out on their cheeks and along their upper lips. They stopped twice for coffee before they got to the woods where Kenny wanted to hunt.

Tub was for trying someplace different; two years in a row they'd been up and down this land and hadn't seen a thing. Frank didn't care one way or the other, he just wanted to get out of the goddamned truck. "Feel that," Frank said, slamming the door. He spread his feet and closed his eyes and leaned his head way back and breathed deeply. "Tune in on that energy."

"Another thing," Kenny said. "This is open land. Most of the land around here is posted."

"I'm cold," Tub said.

Frank breathed out. "Stop bitching, Tub. Get centered."   15

"I wasn't bitching."

"Centered," Kenny said. "Next thing you'll be wearing a nightgown, Frank. Selling flowers out at the airport."

"Kenny," Frank said, "you talk too much."

"Okay," Kenny said. "I won't say a word. Like I won't say anything about a certain babysitter."

"What babysitter?" Tub asked.   20

"That's between us," Frank said, looking at Kenny. "That's confidential. You keep your mouth shut."

Kenny laughed.

"You're asking for it," Frank said.

"Asking for what?"

"You'll see."   25

"Hey," Tub said, "are we hunting or what?"

They started off across the field. Tub had trouble getting through the fences. Frank and Kenny could have helped him; they could have lifted up on the top wire and stepped on the bottom wire, but they didn't. They stood and watched him. There were a lot of fences and Tub was puffing when they reached the woods.

They hunted for over two hours and saw no deer, no tracks, no sign. Finally they stopped by the creek to eat. Kenny had several slices of pizza and a couple of candy bars; Frank had a sandwich, an apple, two carrots, and a square of chocolate; Tub ate one hard-boiled egg and a stick of celery.

"You ask me how I want to die today," Kenny said, "I'll tell you burn me at the stake." He turned to Tub. "You still on that diet?" He winked at Frank.

"What do you think? You think I like hard-boiled eggs?"   30

"All I can say is, it's the first diet I ever heard of where you gained weight from it."

"Who said I gained weight?"

"Oh, pardon me. I take it back. You're just wasting away before my very eyes. Isn't he, Frank?"

Frank had his fingers fanned out, tips against the bark of the stump where he'd laid his food. His knuckles were hairy. He wore a heavy wedding band and on his right pinky another gold ring with a flat face and an "F" in what looked like diamonds. He turned the ring this way and that. "Tub," he said, "you haven't seen your own balls in ten years."

35   Kenny doubled over laughing. He took off his hat and slapped his leg with it.

"What am I supposed to do?" Tub said. "It's my glands."

They left the woods and hunted along the creek. Frank and Kenny worked one bank and Tub worked the other, moving upstream. The snow was light but the drifts were deep and hard to move through. Wherever Tub looked the surface was smooth, undisturbed, and after a time he lost interest. He stopped looking for tracks and just tried to keep up with Frank and Kenny on the other side. A moment came when he realized he hadn't seen them in a long time. The breeze was moving from him to them; when it stilled he could sometimes hear Kenny laughing but that was all. He quickened his pace, breasting hard into the drifts, fighting away the snow with his knees and elbows. He heard his heart and felt the flush on his face but he never once stopped.

Tub caught up with Frank and Kenny at a bend of the creek. They were standing on a log that stretched from their bank to his. Ice had backed up behind the log. Frozen reeds stuck out, barely nodding when the air moved.

"See anything?" Frank asked.

40   Tub shook his head.

There wasn't much daylight left and they decided to head back toward the road. Frank and Kenny crossed the log and they started downstream, using the trail Tub had broken. Before they had gone very far Kenny stopped. "Look at that," he said, and pointed to some tracks going from the creek back into the woods. Tub's footprints crossed right over them. There on the bank, plain as day, were several mounds of deer sign. "What do you think that is, Tub?" Kenny kicked at it. "Walnuts on vanilla icing?"

"I guess I didn't notice."

Kenny looked at Frank.

"I was lost."

45   "You were lost. Big deal."

They followed the tracks into the woods. The deer had gone over a fence half buried in drifting snow. A no hunting sign was nailed to the top of one of the posts. Frank laughed and said the son of a bitch could read. Kenny wanted to go after him but Frank said no way, the people out here didn't mess around. He thought maybe the farmer who owned the land would let them use it if they asked. Kenny wasn't so sure. Anyway, he figured that by the time they walked to the truck and drove up the road and doubled back it would be almost dark.

"Relax," Frank said. "You can't hurry nature. If we're meant to get that deer, we'll get it. If we're not, we won't."

They started back toward the truck. This part of the woods was mainly pine. The snow was shaded and had a glaze on it. It held up Kenny and Frank but Tub kept falling through. As he kicked forward, the edge of the crust bruised his shins. Kenny and Frank pulled ahead of him, to where he couldn't even hear their voices any more. He sat down on a stump and wiped his face. He ate both the sandwiches and half the cookies, taking his own sweet time. It was dead quiet.

When Tub crossed the last fence into the road the truck started moving. Tub had to run for it and just managed to grab hold of the tailgate and hoist himself into the bed. He lay there, panting. Kenny looked out the rear window and grinned. Tub crawled into the lee of the cab to get out of the freezing wind. He pulled his earflaps low and pushed his chin into the collar of his coat. Someone rapped on the window but Tub would not turn around.

He and Frank waited outside while Kenny went into the farmhouse 50 to ask permission. The house was old and paint was curling off the sides. The smoke streamed westward off the top of the chimney, fanning away into a thin gray plume. Above the ridge of the hills another ridge of blue clouds was rising.

"You've got a short memory," Tub said.

"What?" Frank said. He had been staring off.

"I used to stick up for you."

"Okay, so you used to stick up for me. What's eating you?"

"You shouldn't have just left me back there like that." 55

"You're a grown-up, Tub. You can take care of yourself. Anyway, if you think you're the only person with problems I can tell you that you're not."

"Is something bothering you, Frank?"

Frank kicked at a branch poking out of the snow. "Never mind," he said.

"What did Kenny mean about the babysitter?"

"Kenny talks too much," Frank said. "You just mind your own 60 business."

Kenny came out of the farmhouse and gave the thumbs-up and they began walking back toward the woods. As they passed the barn a large black hound with a grizzled snout ran out and barked at them. Every time he barked he slid backwards a bit, like a cannon recoiling. Kenny got down on all fours and snarled and barked back at him, and the dog slunk away into the barn, looking over his shoulder and peeing a little as he went.

"That's an old-timer," Frank said. "A real graybeard. Fifteen years if he's a day."

"Too old," Kenny said.

Past the barn they cut off through the fields. The land was unfenced and the crust was freezing up thick and they made good time. They kept to the edge of the field until they picked up the tracks again and followed them into the woods, farther and farther back toward the hills. The trees started to blur with the shadows and the wind rose and needled their faces with the crystals it swept off the glaze. Finally they lost the tracks.

65   Kenny swore and threw down his hat. "This is the worst day of hunting I ever had, bar none." He picked up his hat and brushed off the snow. "This will be the first season since I was fifteen I haven't got my deer."

"It isn't the deer," Frank said. "It's the hunting. There are all these forces out here and you just have to go with them."

"You go with them," Kenny said. "I came out here to get me a deer, not listen to a bunch of hippie bullshit. And if it hadn't been for dimples here I would have, too."

"That's enough," Frank said.

"And you—you're so busy thinking about that little jailbait of yours you wouldn't know a deer if you saw one."

70   "Drop dead," Frank said, and turned away.

Kenny and Tub followed him back across the fields. When they were coming up to the barn Kenny stopped and pointed. "I hate that post," he said. He raised his rifle and fired. It sounded like a dry branch cracking. The post splintered along its right side, up towards the top. "There," Kenny said. "It's dead."

"Knock it off," Frank said, walking ahead.

Kenny looked at Tub. He smiled. "I hate that tree," he said, and fired again. Tub hurried to catch up with Frank. He started to speak but just then the dog ran out of the barn and barked at them. "Easy, boy," Frank said.

"I hate that dog." Kenny was behind them.

75   "That's enough," Frank said. "You put that gun down."

Kenny fired. The bullet went in between the dog's eyes. He sank right down into the snow, his legs splayed out on each side, his yellow eyes open and staring. Except for the blood he looked like a small bearskin rug. The blood ran down the dog's muzzle into the snow.

They all looked at the dog lying there.

"What did he ever do to you?" Tub asked. "He was just barking."

Kenny turned to Tub. "I hate you."

80   Tub shot from the waist. Kenny jerked backward against the fence and buckled to his knees. He folded his hands across his stomach. "Look," he

said. His hands were covered with blood. In the dusk his blood was more blue than red. It seemed to belong to the shadows. It didn't seem out of place. Kenny eased himself onto his back. He sighed several times, deeply. "You shot me," he said.

"I had to," Tub said. He knelt beside Kenny. "Oh God," he said. "Frank. Frank."

Frank hadn't moved since Kenny killed the dog.

"Frank!" Tub shouted.

"I was just kidding around," Kenny said. "It was a joke. Oh!" he said, and arched his back suddenly. "Oh!" he said again, and dug his heels into the snow and pushed himself along on his head for several feet. Then he stopped and lay there, rocking back and forth on his heels and head like a wrestler doing warm-up exercises.

Frank roused himself. "Kenny," he said. He bent down and put his 85
gloved hand on Kenny's brow. "You shot him," he said to Tub.

"He made me," Tub said.

"No no no," Kenny said.

Tub was weeping from the eyes and nostrils. His whole face was wet. Frank closed his eyes, then looked down at Kenny again. "Where does it hurt?"

"Everywhere," Kenny said, "just everywhere."

"Oh God," Tub said. 90

"I mean where did it go in?" Frank said.

"Here." Kenny pointed at the wound in his stomach. It was welling slowly with blood.

"You're lucky," Frank said. "It's on the left side. It missed your appendix. If it had hit your appendix you'd really be in the soup." He turned and threw up onto the snow, holding his sides as if to keep warm.

"Are you all right?" Tub said.

"There's some aspirin in the truck," Kenny said. 95

"I'm all right," Frank said.

"We'd better call an ambulance," Tub said.

"Jesus," Frank said. "What are we going to say?"

"Exactly what happened," Tub said. "He was going to shoot me but I shot him first."

"No sir!" Kenny said. "I wasn't either!" 100

Frank patted Kenny on the arm. "Easy does it, partner." He stood. "Let's go."

Tub picked up Kenny's rifle as they walked down toward the farmhouse. "No sense leaving this around," he said. "Kenny might get ideas."

"I can tell you one thing," Frank said. "You've really done it this time. This definitely takes the cake."

They had to knock on the door twice before it was opened by a thin man with lank hair. The room behind him was filled with smoke. He squinted at them. "You get anything?" he asked.

105   "No," Frank said.

"I knew you wouldn't. That's what I told the other fellow."

"We've had an accident."

The man looked past Frank and Tub into the gloom. "Shoot your friend, did you?"

Frank nodded.

110   "I did," Tub said.

"I suppose you want to use the phone."

"If it's okay."

The man in the door looked behind him, then stepped back. Frank and Tub followed him into the house. There was a woman sitting by the stove in the middle of the room. The stove was smoking badly. She looked up and then down again at the child asleep in her lap. Her face was white and damp; strands of hair were pasted across her forehead. Tub warmed his hands over the stove while Frank went into the kitchen to call. The man who had let them in stood at the window, his hands in his pockets.

"My friend shot your dog," Tub said.

115   The man nodded without turning around. "I should have done it myself. I just couldn't."

"He loved that dog so much," the woman said. The child squirmed and she rocked it.

"You asked him to?" Tub said. "You asked him to shoot your dog?"

"He was old and sick. Couldn't chew his food any more. I would have done it myself but I don't have a gun."

"You couldn't have anyway," the woman said. "Never in a million years."

120   The man shrugged.

Frank came out of the kitchen. "We'll have to take him ourselves. The nearest hospital is fifty miles from here and all their ambulances are out anyway."

The woman knew a shortcut but the directions were complicated and Tub had to write them down. The man told them where they could find some boards to carry Kenny on. He didn't have a flashlight but he said he would leave the porch light on.

It was dark outside. The clouds were low and heavy-looking and the wind blew in shrill gusts. There was a screen loose on the house and it banged slowly and then quickly as the wind rose again. They could hear it all the way to the barn. Frank went for the boards while Tub looked for

Kenny, who was not where they had left him. Tub found him farther up the drive, lying on his stomach. "You okay?" Tub said.

"It hurts."

"Frank says it missed your appendix."   125

"I already had my appendix out."

"All right," Frank said, coming up to them. "We'll have you in a nice warm bed before you can say Jack Robinson." He put the two boards on Kenny's right side.

"Just as long as I don't have one of those male nurses," Kenny said.

"Ha ha," Frank said. "That's the spirit. Get ready, set, *over you go*," and he rolled Kenny onto the boards. Kenny screamed and kicked his legs in the air. When he quieted down Frank and Tub lifted the boards and carried him down the drive. Tub had the back end, and with the snow blowing into his face he had trouble with his footing. Also he was tired and the man inside had forgotten to turn the porch light on. Just past the house Tub slipped and threw out his hands to catch himself. The boards fell and Kenny tumbled out and rolled to the bottom of the drive, yelling all the way. He came to rest against the right front wheel of the truck.

"You fat moron," Frank said. "You aren't good for diddly."   130

Tub grabbed Frank by the collar and backed him hard up against the fence. Frank tried to pull his hands away but Tub shook him and snapped his head back and forth and finally Frank gave up.

"What do you know about fat," Tub said. "What do you know about glands." As he spoke he kept shaking Frank. "What do you know about me."

"All right," Frank said.

"No more," Tub said.

"All right."   135

"No more talking to me like that. No more watching. No more laughing."

"Okay, Tub. I promise."

Tub let go of Frank and leaned his forehead against the fence. His arms hung straight at his sides.

"I'm sorry, Tub." Frank touched him on the shoulder. "I'll be down at the truck."

Tub stood by the fence for a while and then got the rifles off the   140
porch. Frank had rolled Kenny back onto the boards and they lifted him into the bed of the truck. Frank spread the seat blankets over him. "Warm enough?" he asked.

Kenny nodded.

"Okay. Now how does reverse work on this thing?"

"All the way to the left and up." Kenny sat up as Frank started forward to the cab. "Frank!"

"What?"

145 "If it sticks don't force it."

The truck started right away. "One thing," Frank said, "you've got to hand it to the Japanese. A very ancient, very spiritual culture and they can still make a hell of a truck." He glanced over at Tub. "Look, I'm sorry. I didn't know you felt that way, honest to God I didn't. You should have said something."

"I did."

"When? Name one time."

"A couple of hours ago."

"I guess I wasn't paying attention."

150 "That's true, Frank," Tub said. "You don't pay attention very much."

"Tub," Frank said, "what happened back there, I should have been more sympathetic. I realize that. You were going through a lot. I just want you to know it wasn't your fault. He was asking for it."

"You think so?"

"Absolutely. It was him or you. I would have done the same thing in your shoes, no question."

155 The wind was blowing into their faces. The snow was a moving white wall in front of their lights; it swirled into the cab through the hole in the windshield and settled on them. Tub clapped his hands and shifted around to stay warm, but it didn't work.

"I'm going to have to stop," Frank said. "I can't feel my fingers."

Up ahead they saw some lights off the road. It was a tavern. Outside in the parking lot there were several jeeps and trucks. A couple of them had deer strapped across their hoods. Frank parked and they went back to Kenny. "How you doing, partner," Frank said.

"I'm cold."

"Well, don't feel like the Lone Ranger. It's worse inside, take my word for it. You should get that windshield fixed."

160 "Look," Tub said, "he threw the blankets off." They were lying in a heap against the tailgate.

"Now look, Kenny," Frank said, "it's no use whining about being cold if you're not going to try and keep warm. You've got to do your share." He spread the blankets over Kenny and tucked them in at the corners.

"They blew off."

"Hold on to them then."

"Why are we stopping, Frank?"

165 "Because if me and Tub don't get warmed up we're going to freeze solid and then where will you be?" He punched Kenny lightly in the arm. "So just hold your horses."

The bar was full of men in colored jackets, mostly orange. The waitress brought coffee. "Just what the doctor ordered," Frank said, cradling the steaming cup in his hand. His skin was bone white. "Tub, I've been thinking. What you said about me not paying attention, that's true."

"It's okay."

"No. I really had that coming. I guess I've just been a little too interested in old number one. I've had a lot on my mind. Not that that's any excuse."

"Forget it, Frank. I sort of lost my temper back there. I guess we're all a little on edge."

Frank shook his head. "It isn't just that."   170

"You want to talk about it?"

"Just between us, Tub?"

"Sure, Frank. Just between us."

"Tub, I think I'm going to be leaving Nancy."

"Oh, Frank. Oh, Frank." Tub sat back and shook his head.   175

Frank reached out and laid his hand on Tub's arm. "Tub, have you ever been really in love?"

"Well—"

"I mean *really* in love." He squeezed Tub's wrist. "With your whole being."

"I don't know. When you put it like that, I don't know."

"You haven't then. Nothing against you, but you'd know it if you 180 had." Frank let go of Tub's arm. "This isn't just some bit of fluff I'm talking about."

"Who is she, Frank?"

Frank paused. He looked into his empty cup. "Roxanne Brewer."

"Cliff Brewer's kid? The babysitter?"

"You can't just put people into categories like that, Tub. That's why the whole system is wrong. And that's why this country is going to hell in a rowboat."

"But she can't be more than—" Tub shook his head.   185

"Fifteen. She'll be sixteen in May." Frank smiled. "May fourth, three twenty-seven p.m. Hell, Tub, a hundred years ago she'd have been an old maid by that age. Juliet was only thirteen."

"Juliet? Juliet Miller? Jesus, Frank, she doesn't even have breasts. She doesn't even wear a top to her bathing suit. She's still collecting frogs."

"Not Juliet Miller. The real Juliet. Tub, don't you see how you're dividing people up into categories? He's an executive, she's a secretary, he's a truck driver, she's fifteen years old. Tub, this so-called babysitter, this so-called fifteen-year-old has more in her little finger than most of us have in our entire bodies. I can tell you this little lady is something special."

Tub nodded. "I know the kids like her."

"She's opened up whole worlds to me that I never knew were there." 190

"What does Nancy think about all of this?"

"She doesn't know."

"You haven't told her?"

"Not yet. It's not so easy. She's been damned good to me all these years. Then there's the kids to consider." The brightness in Frank's eyes trembled and he wiped quickly at them with the back of his hand. "I guess you think I'm a complete bastard."

195   "No, Frank. I don't think that."

"Well, you *ought* to."

"Frank, when you've got a friend it means you've always got someone on your side, no matter what. That's the way I feel about it, anyway."

"You mean that, Tub?"

"Sure I do."

200   Frank smiled. "You don't know how good it feels to hear you say that."

Kenny had tried to get out of the truck but he hadn't made it. He was jackknifed over the tailgate, his head hanging above the bumper. They lifted him back into the bed and covered him again. He was sweating and his teeth chattered. "It hurts, Frank."

"It wouldn't hurt so much if you just stayed put. Now we're going to the hospital. Got that? Say it—I'm going to the hospital."

"I'm going to the hospital."

"Again."

205   "I'm going to the hospital."

"Now just keep saying that to yourself and before you know it we'll be there."

After they had gone a few miles Tub turned to Frank. "I just pulled a real boner," he said.

"What's that?"

"I left the directions on the table back there."

210   "That's okay. I remember them pretty well."

The snowfall lightened and the clouds began to roll back off the fields, but it was no warmer and after a time both Frank and Tub were bitten through and shaking. Frank almost didn't make it around a curve, and they decided to stop at the next roadhouse.

There was an automatic hand-dryer in the bathroom and they took turns standing in front of it, opening their jackets and shirts and letting the jet of hot air breathe across their faces and chests.

"You know," Tub said, "what you told me back there, I appreciate it. Trusting me."

Frank opened and closed his fingers in front of the nozzle. "The way I look at it, Tub, no man is an island. You've got to trust someone."

"Frank—"   215

Frank waited.

"When I said that about my glands, that wasn't true. The truth is I just shovel it in."

"Well, Tub—"

"Day and night, Frank. In the shower. On the freeway." He turned and let the air play over his back. "I've even got stuff in the paper towel machine at work."

"There's nothing wrong with your glands at all?" Frank had taken   220 his boots and socks off. He held first his right, then his left foot up to the nozzle.

"No. There never was."

"Does Alice know?" The machine went off and Frank started lacing up his boots.

"Nobody knows. That's the worst of it, Frank. Not the being fat, I never got any big kick out of being thin, but the lying. Having to lead a double life like a spy or a hit man. This sounds strange but I feel sorry for those guys, I really do. I know what they go through. Always having to think about what you say and do. Always feeling like people are watching you, trying to catch you at something. Never able to just be yourself. Like when I make a big deal about only having an orange for breakfast and then scarf all the way to work. Oreos, Mars Bars, Twinkies. Sugar Babies. Snickers." Tub glanced at Frank and looked quickly away. "Pretty disgusting, isn't it?"

"Tub. Tub." Frank shook his head. "Come on." He took Tub's arm and led him into the restaurant half of the bar. "My friend is hungry," he told the waitress. "Bring four orders of pancakes, plenty of butter and syrup."

"Frank—"   225

"Sit down."

When the dishes came Frank carved out slabs of butter and just laid them on the pancakes. Then he emptied the bottle of syrup, moving it back and forth over the plates. He leaned forward on his elbows and rested his chin in one hand. "Go on, Tub."

Tub ate several mouthfuls, then started to wipe his lips. Frank took the napkin away from him. "No wiping," he said. Tub kept at it. The syrup covered his chin; it dripped to a point like a goatee. "Weigh in, Tub," Frank said, pushing another fork across the table. "Get down to business." Tub took the fork in his left hand and lowered his head and started really chowing down. "Clean your plate," Frank said when the pancakes were gone, and Tub lifted each of the four plates and licked it clean. He sat back, trying to catch his breath.

"Beautiful," Frank said. "Are you full?"

"I'm full," Tub said. "I've never been so full."   230

Kenny's blankets were bunched up against the tailgate again.

"They must have blown off," Tub said.

"They're not doing him any good," Frank said. "We might as well get some use out of them."

Kenny mumbled. Tub bent over him. "What? Speak up."

235 "I'm going to the hospital," Kenny said.

"Attaboy," Frank said.

The blankets helped. The wind still got their faces and Frank's hands but it was much better. The fresh snow on the road and the trees sparkled under the beam of the headlight. Squares of light from farmhouse windows fell onto the blue snow in the fields.

"Frank," Tub said after a time, "you know that farmer? He told Kenny to kill the dog."

"You're kidding!" Frank leaned forward, considering. "That Kenny. What a card." He laughed and so did Tub. Tub smiled out the back window. Kenny lay with his arms folded over his stomach, moving his lips at the stars. Right overhead was the Big Dipper, and behind, hanging between Kenny's toes in the direction of the hospital, was the North Star, Pole Star, Help to Sailors. As the truck twisted through the gentle hills the star went back and forth between Kenny's boots, staying always in his sight. "I'm going to the hospital," Kenny said. But he was wrong. They had taken a different turn a long way back.

QUESTIONS

1. Discuss the way Tub is presented in the opening scene. Does your assessment of his character change in the later scenes?

2. How does the cold, hostile environment in the story relate to its meaning?

3. Which is the most sympathetic of the three characters? The story deals, in part, with the power struggle among the characters. Which character is the most powerful? Do the balance of power and alliances between the characters shift as the story proceeds?

4. How do the physical descriptions of the characters help us to understand them? For example, how is Tub's obesity relevant to his character?

5. The second half of the story includes some surprising twists and turns. How are these more meaningful and substantial than the random plot twists one might find in a purely commercial work of fiction?

6. What other elements of the story suggest that this is a serious, literary work rather than merely an entertaining yarn about three hapless hunters?

7. What is the purpose of the scene in which Frank and Tub stop at the tavern for food and coffee, leaving the wounded Kenny in the back of the truck? During their conversation, Frank analyzes his own character and expresses remorse. Are his insights and remorse genuine? Why or why not?

8. The final plot twist comes in the last two sentences of the story. Here the narrator speaks directly to the reader, giving us information the characters don't know. How is this an appropriate conclusion to the story? What final statement is being made about the characters?

SUGGESTIONS FOR WRITING

1. After reviewing the distinguishing characteristics of literary and commercial fiction, and bearing in mind that the two types of fiction represent a spectrum of qualities rather than hard-and-fast opposites, examine one of the following stories for its mix of literary and commercial characteristics:
   a. Fitzgerald, "Babylon Revisited" (page 200).
   b. Hurston, "Spunk" (page 564).
   c. Poe, "The Cask of Amontillado" (page 657).
   d. Maupassant, "The Necklace" (page 382).
   On balance, determine whether your choice is predominantly commercial or literary.
2. Connell's "The Most Dangerous Game" and Wolff's "Hunters in the Snow" both deal with the "sport" of hunting. In a comparative essay, determine which is the literary and which is the commercial story.

UNDERSTANDING AND EVALUATING FICTION

Most of the stories in this book are accompanied by study questions that are by no means exhaustive. The following is a list of questions that you may apply to any story. You may be unable to answer many of them until you have read further in the book.

Plot and Structure

1. Who is the protagonist of the story? What are the conflicts? Are they physical, intellectual, moral, or emotional? Is the main conflict between sharply differentiated good and evil, or is it more subtle and complex?
2. Does the plot have unity? Are all the episodes relevant to the total meaning or effect of the story? Does each incident grow logically out of the preceding incident and lead naturally to the next? Is the ending happy, unhappy, or indeterminate? Is it fairly achieved?
3. What use does the story make of chance and coincidence? Are these occurrences used to initiate, to complicate, or to resolve the story? How improbable are they?
4. How is suspense created in the story? Is the interest confined to "What happens next?" or are larger concerns involved? Can you find examples of mystery? Of dilemma?
5. What use does the story make of surprise? Are the surprises achieved fairly? Do they serve a significant purpose? Do they divert the reader's attention from weaknesses in the story?
6. To what extent is this a "formula" story?

Characterization

7. What means does the author use to reveal character? Are the characters sufficiently dramatized? What use is made of character contrasts?
8. Are the characters consistent in their actions? Adequately motivated? Plausible? Does the author successfully avoid stock characters?
9. Is each character fully enough developed to justify its role in the story? Are the main characters round or flat?
10. Is any of the characters a developing character? If so, is the change a large or a small one? Is it a plausible change for such a person? Is it sufficiently motivated? Is it given sufficient time?

Theme

11. Does the story have a theme? What is it? Is it implicit or explicit?
12. Does the theme reinforce or oppose popular notions of life? Does it furnish a new insight or refresh or deepen an old one?

Point of View

13. What point of view does the story use? Is it consistent in its use of this point of view? If shifts are made, are they justified?
14. What advantages does the chosen point of view have? Does it furnish any clues as to the purpose of the story?
15. If the point of view is that of one of the characters, does this character have any limitations that affect her or his interpretation of events or persons?
16. Does the author use point of view primarily to reveal or conceal? Is important information known to the central character ever unfairly withheld?

Symbol, Allegory, and Fantasy

17. Does the story make use of symbols? If so, do the symbols carry or merely reinforce the meaning of the story?
18. Does the story make use of symbolic settings?
19. Does the story employ allegory? Is the use of allegory clear-cut or ambiguous?
20. Does the story contain any elements of fantasy? If so, what is the initial assumption? Does the story operate logically from this assumption?
21. Is the fantasy employed for its own sake or to express some human truth? If the latter, what truth?

Humor and Irony

22. If the story employs humor, is the humor present merely for its own sake or does it contribute to the meaning?
23. Does the story anywhere use irony of situation? Dramatic irony? Verbal irony? What functions do the ironies serve?

General

24. Is the primary interest of the story in plot, character, theme, or some other element?

25. What contribution to the story is made by its setting? Is the particular setting essential, or could the story have happened anywhere?
26. What are the characteristics of the author's style? Are they appropriate to the nature of the story?
27. What light is thrown on the story by its title?
28. Do all the elements of the story work together to support a central purpose? Is any part irrelevant or inappropriate?
29. What do you conceive to be the story's central purpose? How fully has it achieved that purpose?
30. Is the story commercial or literary? How significant is the story's purpose?
31. Is the story more or less impressive on a second reading?

PRACTICE AP WRITING PROMPTS

Richard Connell, "The Most Dangerous Game" (pp. 62)

40-minute prompt: Read carefully paragraphs 28 (top of p. 63) through 46 (p. 66). Write a well-organized essay in which you show how Connell uses point of view, imagery, and sound devices to establish the mood and setting of "The Most Dangerous Game."

CHAPTER TWO

Plot and Structure

Plot is the sequence of incidents or events through which an author constructs a story; skilled authors are careful to present the sequence in a significant order. When described in isolation, the plot bears about the same relationship to a story that a map does to a journey. Just as a map may be drawn on a finer or grosser scale, so may a plot be recounted with lesser or greater detail. A plot summary may include what characters say or think, as well as what they do, but it leaves out description and analysis and concentrates primarily on major events.

Plot should not be confused with the content of the work. The plot is not the action itself, but the way the author *arranges* the action toward a specific end. In commercial fiction, the plot may include many surprising twists and turns and a culminating, climactic incident; because the main goal is to keep the reader turning the pages, a commercial author is likely to use a tried-and-true, fairly conventional **structure** in arranging the plot elements. The story may follow a standard chronology, for instance, and may employ familiar structural patterns. Connell's "The Most Dangerous Game" has a chronological structure and includes the familiar structural tactic (one as old as the story of Goldilocks and the Three Bears) of using a three-part sequence in narrating Rainsford's attempts to entrap General Zaroff: first he tries the Malay man-catcher, and fails; then he tries the Burmese tiger pit, and fails; but on the third try, with the "native trick" learned in Uganda, he manages to kill Ivan and ultimately outwit Zaroff. Although Wolff's "Hunters in the Snow" also employs a chronological structure, the plot elements are arranged in a complex way in order to explore the relationships among the three principal characters. Compared with "The Most Dangerous Game," the plot structure in "Hunters in the Snow" is more experimental and unpredictable, taking unexpected excursions into the thought processes of all three characters. For a literary writer, a complex structure is often required to convey complex meanings. In Wolff's story, the *significance* of the action is more important than the action itself, and subtle exchanges of words among characters may be just as significant as the more action-oriented sequences of the hunting expeditions.

Ordinarily, however, both the surface excitement required in commercial fiction and the significant meaning found in literary fiction arise out of some sort of **conflict**—a clash of actions, ideas, desires, or wills. Characters may be pitted against some other person or group of persons (conflict of person against person); they may be in conflict with some external force—physical nature, society, or "fate" (conflict of person against environment); or they may be in conflict with some elements in their own natures (conflict of person against himself or herself). The conflict may be physical, mental, emotional, or moral. There is conflict in a chess game—during which the competitors sit quite still for hours—as surely as in a wrestling match; emotional conflict may be raging within a person sitting alone in a silent room.

The central character in a conflict, whether sympathetic or unsympathetic as a person, is called the **protagonist**; occasionally there may be more than one protagonist in a story. (The technical term "protagonist" is preferable to the popular term "hero" or "heroine" because it is less ambiguous. The protagonist is simply the central character; the term "hero" or "heroine" implies that the central character has heroic qualities, which is often not the case.) Any force arranged against the protagonist—whether persons, things, conventions of society, or the protagonist's own character traits—is the **antagonist**. In some stories the conflict is single, clear-cut, and easily identifiable. In others it is multiple, various, and subtle. A person may be in conflict with other individuals, with social norms or nature, and with herself or himself all at the same time, and sometimes may be involved in conflict without being aware of it.

"The Most Dangerous Game" illustrates most of these kinds of conflict. Rainsford, the protagonist, is pitted first against other men—against Whitney and General Zaroff in the discussions preceding the manhunt, against Zaroff and Ivan during the manhunt. Early in the story he is pitted against nature when he falls into the sea and cannot get back to the yacht. At the beginning of the manhunt, he is in conflict with himself when he tries to fight off panic by repeating to himself, "I must keep my nerve. I must keep my nerve." The various conflicts illuminated in this story are physical (Rainsford against the sea and Zaroff), mental (Rainsford's initial conflict of ideas with Whitney and his battle of wits with Zaroff during the manhunt, which Zaroff refers to as "outdoor chess"), emotional (Rainsford's efforts to control his terror), and moral (Rainsford's refusal to "condone cold-blooded murder," in contrast to Zaroff's contempt for "romantic ideas about the value of human life").

Excellent literary fiction has been written utilizing all four of these major kinds of conflict. Much commercial fiction, however, emphasizes only the confrontation between man and man, depending on the element of physical conflict to supply the primary excitement. For instance, it is hard to conceive of a western story without a fistfight or a gunfight. Even in the most formulaic kinds of fiction, however, something more will be found than mere physical action. Good people will be arrayed against bad ones, and thus the conflict will also be between moral values. In commercial fiction this conflict often is clearly defined in terms of moral absolutes: the "good guy" versus the "bad guy." In literary fiction, the contrasts are usually less distinct. Good may be opposed to good, or half-truth to half-truth. There may be difficulty in determining what *is* good or bad, causing internal conflict rather than physical confrontation. In the real world, of course, significant moral issues are seldom sharply defined—judgments are difficult, and choices are complex rather than simple. Literary writers are aware of this complexity and are more concerned with displaying its various shadings of moral values than with presenting glaring, simplistic contrasts of good and evil, right and wrong.

Suspense is the quality in a story that makes readers ask "What's going to happen next?" or "How will this turn out?" Such questions compel them to keep reading. Suspense increases when a reader's curiosity is combined with anxiety about the fate of a likable, sympathetic character. Thus, in old serial movies—often appropriately called "cliff-hangers"—a strong element of suspense was created at the end of each episode by leaving the hero hanging from the edge of a cliff or the heroine tied to railroad tracks with an express train rapidly approaching. In murder mysteries—often called "whodunits"—the main element of suspense is the reader's desire to know who committed the murder. In love stories the reader wants to know if the boy will win the girl, or if the lovers will be reunited.

In more literary forms of fiction the suspense often involves not so much the question *what* as the question *why*—not "What will happen next?" but "Why is the protagonist behaving this way? How is the protagonist's behavior to be explained in terms of human personality and character?" The forms of suspense range from crude to subtle and may involve not only actions but psychological considerations and moral issues as well. Writers use two common devices to create suspense: they introduce an element of **mystery** (an unusual set of circumstances for which the reader craves an explanation) or they place the protagonist in a **dilemma** (a position in which he or she must choose between two courses of action, both undesirable). But suspense can readily be created for most readers by placing *anybody* on a seventeenth-story window ledge or simply by bringing together two attractive, sexy young people.

In "The Most Dangerous Game," the author initiates suspense in the opening sentences with Whitney's account of the mystery of "Ship-Trap Island," of which sailors "have a curious dread"—a place that seems to emanate evil. The mystery grows when, in this out-of-the-way spot, Rainsford discovers an enormous château with a leering gargoyle knocker on its massive door and confronts a bearded giant pointing a long-barreled revolver straight at his heart. Connell introduces a second mystery when General Zaroff tells Rainsford that he hunts "more dangerous game" on this island than the Cape buffalo. He then frustrates Rainsford's (and the reader's) curiosity for some thirty-six paragraphs before revealing what the game is. Meanwhile, by placing the protagonist in physical danger, Connell introduces a second kind of suspense. Initiated by Rainsford's fall into the sea and his confrontation with Ivan, this second kind becomes the principal source of suspense in the second half of the story. Simply put, the issues of whether Rainsford will escape and how he will escape are what keep the reader absorbed in the story. The manhunt itself begins with a dilemma. Rainsford must choose among three undesirable courses of action: he can hunt men with Zaroff; he can let himself be hunted; or he can submit to a presumably torturous death at the hands of Ivan. During the hunt, he is faced with other dilemmas. For instance, on the third day, pursued by Zaroff's hounds, "Rainsford knew he could do one of two things. He could stay where he was and wait. That was suicide. He could flee. That was postponing the inevitable."

Suspense is usually the most important criterion for good commercial fiction; unless a story makes us want to keep reading it, it can have little merit. In literary fiction, however, suspense is less important than other elements the author uses to engage the reader's interest: such a story may be amusing, well written, morally penetrating, peopled by intriguing characters; or it may feature some combination of all these elements. One test of a literary story is to determine whether it creates a desire to read it again. Like a play by Shakespeare, a successful literary story should create an even richer reading experience on the second or third encounter—even though we already know what is going to happen—than on a first reading. By contrast, when an author creates suspense artificially—by the simple withholding of vital information, for instance—readers will feel that the author's purpose is simply to keep them guessing what will happen next, not to reveal some insight into human experience. Either a commercial or a literary story could be written, for example, about the man on the seventeenth-story window ledge; but the literary story would focus less upon whether the man will jump than upon the psychological factors and life experiences that brought him to the ledge in the first place. The commercial story would keep us asking, "What happens next?" The literary story will make us wonder, "*Why* do things happen as they do?" or "What is the significance of this event?"

Closely connected with the element of suspense in fiction is the element of **surprise**. If we know ahead of time exactly what is going to happen in a story and why, there can be no suspense; as long as we do not know, whatever happens comes with an element of surprise. The surprise is proportional to the unexpectedness of what happens; it becomes pronounced when the story departs radically from our expectation. In the short story, such radical departure is most often found in a **surprise ending**: one that features a sudden, unexpected turn or twist. In this book, Kate Chopin's "The Story of an Hour" (page 536) is a good example of a tale with such an ending.

As with physical action and suspense, commercial fiction tends to feature a surprise ending more frequently than literary fiction. But in either type of story, there are two ways by which the legitimacy and value of a surprise ending may be judged: (1) by the fairness with which the surprise is achieved and (2) by the purpose that it serves. If the surprise is contrived through an improbable coincidence or series of coincidences, or by the planting of false clues (details whose only purpose is to mislead the reader), or through the arbitrary withholding of information, then we may well dismiss it as a cheap trick. If, on the other hand, the ending that at first is such a surprise comes to seem, the more we think about it and look back over the story, perfectly logical and natural, we will feel the surprise was achieved fairly. Again, a surprise ending may be judged as trivial if it exists simply for its own sake—to shock or to titillate the reader. We may judge it as a fraud if it serves, as it does in more formulaic commercial fiction, to conceal earlier weaknesses in the story by giving us a shiny bauble at the end to absorb and concentrate our attention. We will consider a surprise ending justified, however, when it serves to broaden or to reinforce the meaning of the story. In literary fiction, the surprise is one that furnishes meaningful illumination, not just a reversal of expectation.

Whether or not a commercial story has a surprise ending, it almost always has a **happy ending**: the protagonist must solve her problems, defeat an adversary, win her man, "live happily ever after." A common obstacle confronting readers who are making their first attempt to enjoy literary fiction is that such fiction often (though certainly not always) ends unhappily. They are likely to label such stories as "depressing" and to complain that "real life has enough troubles of its own" or, conversely, that "real life is seldom as unhappy as all that."

Two justifications may be made for the **unhappy ending**. First, many situations in real life do have unpleasant outcomes; therefore, if fiction is to reflect and illuminate life, it must acknowledge human defeats as well as triumphs. Commercial writers of sports fiction usually write of how an individual or a team achieves victory against formidable odds. Yet if one team wins the pennant, thirteen others must lose it; if a golfer wins a tournament, fifty or a hundred others must fail to win. In situations like these, at least, success is much less frequent than failure. Varying the formula, a sports writer might tell how an individual lost the game but learned some important moral lesson—for instance, the importance of fair play. But here again, in real life, people achieve such compensations only occasionally. Defeat, in fact, sometimes embitters people and makes them less able to cope with life than before. Thus we need to understand and perhaps expect defeat as well as victory.

The second justification for an unhappy ending is its value in forcing us to ponder the complexities of life. The story with a happy ending has been "wrapped up" for us: it sends the reader away feeling pleasantly and vaguely satisfied with the world, and it requires no further thought. The unhappy ending, on the other hand, may cause readers to brood over the outcome, to relive the story in their minds, and by searching out its implications to get much more meaning and significance from it. Just as we can judge individuals better when we see how they behave in times of trouble, so we can see deeper into life when it is pried open for inspection. The unhappy ending is also more likely to raise significant issues. Shakespeare's tragedies reverberate in our minds much longer and more resonantly than his comedies. The ending of "The Most Dangerous Game" resolves all our anxieties, but the ending of "Hunters in the Snow" forces us to think about the mysteries and contradictions of human nature.

Readers of literary fiction evaluate an ending not by whether it is happy or unhappy but by whether it is logical within the story's own terms and whether it affords a full, believable revelation. An ending that meets these tests can be profoundly satisfying, whether happy or unhappy. In fact, some artistically satisfying stories have no ending at all in the sense that the central conflict is resolved in favor of protagonist or antagonist. In real life some problems are never solved and some battles never permanently won. A story, therefore, may have an **indeterminate ending**, one in which no definitive conclusion is reached. There must be some kind of conclusion, of course; a story, which must have artistic unity, cannot simply stop. But the conclusion need not be in terms of a resolved conflict. We cannot be sure whether Tub and Frank in "Hunters in the Snow" will maintain their alliance, or what the ultimate fate of their "friendship" might be. But the story is more effective without a definite resolution, for it leaves us to ponder the complex psychological dynamics that operate within human relationships.

Artistic unity is essential to a good plot. There must be nothing in the story that is irrelevant, that does not contribute to the meaning; there should be nothing there for its own sake or its own excitement. Good writers exercise rigorous selection: they include nothing that does not advance the central intention of the story. But they not only select; they also arrange. Authors place the story's incidents and scenes in the most effective order, which is not necessarily the chronological order (although, when we place them in chronological order, they must form a logical progression). In a carefully unified story, each event grows out of the preceding one and leads logically to the next. The author links scenes together in a chain of cause and effect. With such a story the reader should not feel that events might as easily have taken one turn as another; at the same time, the author's handling of plot should not be heavy-handed but should have a quality of natural inevitability, given the specific set of characters and the initial situation.

An author who includes a turn in the plot that is unjustified by the situation or the characters is indulging in **plot manipulation**. An unmotivated action is one instance of such manipulation. Similarly, the reader feels manipulated if the plot relies too heavily on chance or on coincidence to provide a resolution to a story. This kind of resolution is sometimes called a **deus ex machina** (Latin for "god from a machine") after the practice of some ancient Greek dramatists in having a god descend from heaven at the last minute (presented in the theater by means of a mechanical stage device) to rescue the protagonist from some impossible situation. But while this was an accepted convention in Greek drama, such a resolution is seldom convincing in fiction. The action should grow organically out of the plot rather than end with an arbitrary, chance resolution for which the author has laid no groundwork earlier in the story.

Chance cannot be barred from fiction, of course, any more than it can be barred from life; the same is true of **coincidence**. Chance is the occurrence of an event that has no apparent cause in previous events or in predisposition of character, while coincidence is the chance occurrence of *two* events that may have a peculiar correspondence. But if an author uses an improbable chance event to resolve a story, the story loses its sense of conviction and thus its power to move the reader. The use of coincidence in fiction is even more problematic, since coincidence is chance compounded. Coincidence may justifiably be used to initiate a story, and occasionally to complicate it, but not to resolve it. Its use is objectionable in proportion to its improbability, its importance to the story, and its nearness to the ending. If two characters in a story both start talking of the same topic at once, it may be a coincidence but not necessarily an objectionable one. But if both decide suddenly and at the same time to kill their mothers, the coincidence would be less believable. The use of even a highly improbable coincidence may be perfectly appropriate at the start of a story. Just as a chemist may wonder what will happen if he places certain chemical elements together in a test tube, an author may wonder what will happen if two former lovers accidentally meet in Majorca, where they longed as young lovers to go, many years after they have each married someone else. The improbable initial situation is justified because it offers a chance to observe human nature in conditions that may be particularly revealing, and readers of literary fiction should demand only that the author develop a story logically from that initial situation. But the writer who uses a similar coincidence to resolve a story is imposing an unlikely pattern on human experience rather than revealing any human truth. It is often said that fact is stranger than fiction: in fact, convincing fiction often cannot include some of the more bizarre occurrences (including chance and coincidence) that sometimes happen in life. In life, almost any sequence of events is possible; but in a story the sequence must be plausible in order to convince and hold the reader.

There are various approaches to the analysis of plot. We may, if we wish, draw diagrams of different kinds of plots or trace the development of **rising action, climax,** and **falling action.** Tracing such structural patterns, however, if they are concerned only with examining the plot in isolation, will not take us very far into the story. A more profitable approach is to consider the *function* of plot in trying to understand the relationship of each incident to the larger meaning of the story. In literary fiction, plot is important for what it reveals. Analyzing a story by focusing on its central conflict may be especially fruitful, for this quickly takes the reader to the primary issue in the story. In evaluating fiction for its quality, it is useful to examine the way incidents and scenes are connected as a way of testing the story's plausibility and unity. In any good story, plot is inextricable from other elements of fiction to be considered in later chapters: characterization, point of view, and so forth. It provides a kind of map, or guide, but it cannot serve as a substitute for the reader's journey into the author's fictional landscape.

REVIEWING CHAPTER TWO

1. Define the term "plot."
2. Describe the importance of conflict in fiction.
3. Differentiate between the protagonist and the antagonist in a story.
4. Explore the importance of the element of surprise in fiction.
5. Consider the differences between a happy, an unhappy, and an indeterminate ending.
6. Review the importance of artistic unity in literary fiction.

GRAHAM GREENE
The Destructors

1

It was the eve of August Bank Holiday° that the latest recruit became the leader of the Wormsley Common Gang. No one was surprised except Mike, but Mike at the age of nine was surprised by everything. "If you don't shut your mouth," somebody once said to him, "you'll get a frog down it." After that Mike had kept his teeth tightly clamped except when the surprise was too great.

The new recruit had been with the gang since the beginning of the summer holidays, and there were possibilities about his brooding silence that all recognized. He never wasted a word even to tell his name until that was required of him by the rules. When he said "Trevor" it was a statement of fact, not as it would have been with the others a statement of shame or defiance. Nor did anyone laugh except Mike, who finding himself without support and meeting the dark gaze of the newcomer opened his mouth and was quiet again. There was every reason why T., as he was afterwards referred to, should have been an object of mockery—there was his name (and they substituted the initial because otherwise they had no excuse not to laugh at it), the fact that his father, a former architect and present clerk, had "come down in the world" and that his mother considered herself better than the neighbors. What but an odd quality of danger, of the unpredictable, established him in the gang without any ignoble ceremony of initiation?

The gang met every morning in an impromptu car-park, the site of the last bomb of the first blitz. The leader, who was known as Blackie, claimed to have heard it fall, and no one was precise enough in his dates to point out that he would have been one year old and fast asleep on the down platform of Wormsley Common Underground Station. On one side of the car-park leant the first occupied house, No. 3, of the shattered Northwood Terrace—literally leant, for it had suffered from the blast of

THE DESTRUCTORS   First published in 1954. The setting is London nine years after the conclusion of World War II (1939–1945). During the first sustained bombing attacks on London ("the first blitz") from September 1940 to May 1941, many families slept in the Underground (i.e., subway) stations, which were used as bomb shelters. "Trevor" was typically an upper-class English name. Sir Christopher Wren (1632–1723), England's most famous architect, designed St. Paul's Cathedral and many other late seventeenth- and early eighteenth-century buildings. Graham Greene (1904–1991), who was born just outside London, lived in that city at various stages of his life.
Bank Holiday: three-day weekend in Britain, one of several during the year

the bomb and the side walls were supported on wooden struts. A smaller bomb and some incendiaries had fallen beyond, so that the house stuck up like a jagged tooth and carried on the further wall relics of its neighbor, a dado, the remains of a fireplace. T., whose words were almost confined to voting "Yes" or "No" to the plan of operations proposed each day by Blackie, once startled the whole gang by saying broodingly, "Wren built that house, father says."

"Who's Wren?"

5 "The man who built St. Paul's."

"Who cares?" Blackie said. "It's only Old Misery's."

Old Misery—whose real name was Thomas—had once been a builder and decorator. He lived alone in the crippled house, doing for himself: once a week you could see him coming back across the common with bread and vegetables, and once as the boys played in the car-park he put his head over the smashed wall of his garden and looked at them.

"Been to the lav," one of the boys said, for it was common knowledge that since the bombs fell something had gone wrong with the pipes of the house and Old Misery was too mean to spend money on the property. He could do the redecorating himself at cost price, but he had never learnt plumbing. The lav was a wooden shed at the bottom of the narrow garden with a star-shaped hole in the door: it had escaped the blast which had smashed the house next door and sucked out the window-frames of No. 3.

The next time the gang became aware of Mr. Thomas was more surprising. Blackie, Mike and a thin yellow boy, who for some reason was called by his surname Summers, met him on the common coming back from the market. Mr. Thomas stopped them. He said glumly, "You belong to the lot that play in the car-park?"

10 Mike was about to answer when Blackie stopped him. As the leader he had responsibilities. "Suppose we are?" he said ambiguously.

"I got some chocolates," Mr. Thomas said. "Don't like 'em myself. Here you are. Not enough to go round, I don't suppose. There never is," he added with somber conviction. He handed over three packets of Smarties.

The gang were puzzled and perturbed by this action and tried to explain it away. "Bet someone dropped them and he picked 'em up," somebody suggested.

"Pinched 'em and then got in a bleeding funk," another thought aloud.

"It's a bribe," Summers said. "He wants us to stop bouncing balls on his wall."

15 "We'll show him we don't take bribes," Blackie said, and they sacrificed the whole morning to the game of bouncing that only Mike was young enough to enjoy. There was no sign from Mr. Thomas.

Next day T. astonished them all. He was late at the rendezvous, and the voting for the day's exploit took place without him. At Blackie's suggestion the gang was to disperse in pairs, take buses at random and see how many free rides could be snatched from unwary conductors (the operation was to be carried out in pairs to avoid cheating). They were drawing lots for their companions when T. arrived.

"Where you been, T.?" Blackie asked. "You can't vote now. You know the rules."

"I've been *there*," T. said. He looked at the ground, as though he had thoughts to hide.

"Where?"

"At Old Misery's." Mike's mouth opened and then hurriedly closed 20 again with a click. He had remembered the frog.

"At Old Misery's?" Blackie said. There was nothing in the rules against it, but he had a sensation that T. was treading on dangerous ground. He asked hopefully, "Did you break in?"

"No. I rang the bell."

"And what did you say?"

"I said I wanted to see his house."

"What did he do?"   25

"He showed it to me."

"Pinch anything?"

"No."

"What did you do it for then?"

The gang had gathered round: it was as though an impromptu court 30 were about to form and to try some case of deviation. T. said, "It's a beautiful house," and still watching the ground, meeting no one's eyes, he licked his lips first one way, then the other.

"What do you mean, a beautiful house?" Blackie asked with scorn.

"It's got a staircase two hundred years old like a corkscrew. Nothing holds it up."

"What do you mean, nothing holds it up. Does it float?"

"It's to do with opposite forces, Old Misery said."

"What else?"   35

"There's paneling."

"Like in the Blue Boar?"

"Two hundred years old."

"Is Old Misery two hundred years old?"

Mike laughed suddenly and then was quiet again. The meeting was 40 in a serious mood. For the first time since T. had strolled into the car-park on the first day of the holidays his position was in danger. It only needed a single use of his real name and the gang would be at his heels.

"What did you do it for?" Blackie asked. He was just, he had no jealousy, he was anxious to retain T. in the gang if he could. It was the word "beautiful" that worried him—that belonged to a class world that you could still see parodied at the Wormsley Common Empire° by a man wearing a top hat and a monocle, with a haw-haw accent. He was tempted to say, "My dear Trevor, old chap," and unleash his hell hounds. "If you'd broken in," he said sadly—that indeed would have been an exploit worthy of the gang.

"This was better," T. said. "I found out things." He continued to stare at his feet, not meeting anybody's eye, as though he were absorbed in some dream he was unwilling—or ashamed—to share.

"What things?"

"Old Misery's going to be away all tomorrow and Bank Holiday."

45   Blackie said with relief, "You mean we could break in?"

"And pinch things?" somebody asked.

Blackie said, "Nobody's going to pinch things. Breaking in—that's good enough, isn't it? We don't want any court stuff."

"I don't want to pinch anything," T. said. "I've got a better idea."

"What is it?"

50   T. raised his eyes, as grey and disturbed as the drab August day. "We'll pull it down," he said. "We'll destroy it."

Blackie gave a single hoot of laughter and then, like Mike, fell quiet, daunted by the serious implacable gaze. "What'd the police be doing all the time?" he asked.

"They'd never know. We'd do it from inside. I've found a way in." He said with a sort of intensity, "We'd be like worms, don't you see, in an apple. When we came out again there'd be nothing there, no staircase, no panels, nothing but just walls, and then we'd make the walls fall down—somehow."

"We'd go to jug," Blackie said.

"Who's to prove? And anyway we wouldn't have pinched anything." He added without the smallest flicker of glee, "There wouldn't be anything to pinch after we'd finished."

55   "I've never heard of going to prison for breaking things," Summers said.

"There wouldn't be time," Blackie said. "I've seen housebreakers at work."

"There are twelve of us," T. said. "We'd organize."

"None of us know how . . ."

"I know," T. said. He looked across at Blackie. "Have you got a better plan?"

Wormsley Common Empire: a music hall for revues and popular entertainments

"Today," Mike said tactlessly, "we're pinching free rides . . ."   60

"Free rides," T. said. "You can stand down, Blackie, if you'd rather . . ."

"The gang's got to vote."

"Put it up then."

Blackie said uneasily, "It's proposed that tomorrow and Monday we destroy Old Misery's house."

"Here, here," said a fat boy called Joe.   65

"Who's in favor?"

T. said, "It's carried."

"How do we start?" Summers asked.

"He'll tell you," Blackie said. It was the end of his leadership. He went away to the back of the car-park and began to kick a stone, dribbling it this way and that. There was only one old Morris in the park, for few cars were left there except lorries: without an attendant there was no safety. He took a flying kick at the car and scraped a little paint off the rear mudguard. Beyond, paying no more attention to him than to a stranger, the gang had gathered round T.; Blackie was dimly aware of the fickleness of favor. He thought of going home, of never returning, of letting them all discover the hollowness of T.'s leadership, but suppose after all what T. proposed was possible—nothing like it had ever been done before. The fame of the Wormsley Common car-park gang would surely reach around London. There would be headlines in the papers. Even the grown-up gangs who ran the betting at the all-in wrestling and the barrow-boys would hear with respect of how Old Misery's house had been destroyed. Driven by the pure, simple and altruistic ambition of fame for the gang, Blackie came back to where T. stood in the shadow of Misery's wall.

T. was giving his orders with decision: it was as though this plan had 70 been with him all his life, pondered through the seasons, now in his fifteenth year crystallized with the pain of puberty. "You," he said to Mike, "bring some big nails, the biggest you can find, and a hammer. Anyone else who can better bring a hammer and a screwdriver. We'll need plenty of them. Chisels too. We can't have too many chisels. Can anybody bring a saw?"

"I can," Mike said.

"Not a child's saw," T. said. "A real saw."

Blackie realized he had raised his hand like any ordinary member of the gang.

"Right, you bring one, Blackie. But now there's a difficulty. We want a hacksaw."

"What's a hacksaw?" someone asked.   75

"You can get 'em at Woolworth's," Summers said.

The fat boy called Joe said gloomily, "I knew it would end in a collection."

"I'll get one myself," T. said. "I don't want your money. But I can't buy a sledgehammer."

Blackie said, "They are working on No. 15. I know where they'll leave their stuff for Bank Holiday."

80   "Then that's all," T. said. "We meet here at nine sharp."

"I've got to go to church," Mike said.

"Come over the wall and whistle. We'll let you in."

2

On Sunday morning all were punctual except Blackie, even Mike. Mike had had a stroke of luck. His mother felt ill, his father was tired after Saturday night, and he was told to go to church alone with many warnings of what would happen if he strayed. Blackie had had difficulty in smuggling out the saw, and then in finding the sledgehammer at the back of No. 15. He approached the house from a lane at the rear of the garden, for fear of the policeman's beat along the main road. The tired evergreens kept off a stormy sun: another wet Bank Holiday was being prepared over the Atlantic, beginning in swirls of dust under the trees. Blackie climbed the wall into Misery's garden.

There was no sign of anybody anywhere. The lav stood like a tomb in a neglected graveyard. The curtains were drawn. The house slept. Blackie lumbered nearer with the saw and the sledgehammer. Perhaps after all nobody had turned up: the plan had been a wild invention: they had woken wiser. But when he came close to the back door he could hear a confusion of sound hardly louder than a hive in swarm: a clickety-clack, a bang bang, a scraping, a creaking, a sudden painful crack. He thought: it's true, and whistled.

85   They opened the back door to him and he came in. He had at once the impression of organization, very different from the old happy-go-lucky ways under his leadership. For a while he wandered up and down stairs looking for T. Nobody addressed him: he had a sense of great urgency, and already he could begin to see the plan. The interior of the house was being carefully demolished without touching the outer walls. Summers with hammer and chisel was ripping out the skirting-boards in the ground floor dining-room: he had already smashed the panels of the door. In the same room Joe was heaving up the parquet blocks, exposing the soft wood floorboards over the cellar. Coils of wire came out of the damaged skirting and Mike sat happily on the floor clipping the wires.

On the curved stairs two of the gang were working hard with an inadequate child's saw on the banisters—when they saw Blackie's big saw they signaled for it wordlessly. When he next saw them a quarter of the banisters had been dropped into the hall. He found T. at last in the bathroom—he sat moodily in the least cared-for room in the house, listening to the sounds coming up from below.

"You've really done it," Blackie said with awe. "What's going to happen?"

"We've only just begun," T. said. He looked at the sledgehammer and gave his instructions. "You stay here and break the bath and the wash-basin. Don't bother about the pipes. They come later."

Mike appeared at the door. "I've finished the wires, T.," he said.

"Good. You've just got to go wandering round now. The kitchen's in the basement. Smash all the china and glass and bottles you can lay hold of. Don't turn on the taps—we don't want a flood—yet. Then go into all the rooms and turn out drawers. If they are locked get one of the others to break them open. Tear up any papers you find and smash all the ornaments. Better take a carving-knife with you from the kitchen. The bedroom's opposite here. Open the pillows and tear up the sheets. That's enough for the moment. And you, Blackie, when you've finished in here crack the plaster in the passage up with your sledgehammer."

"What are you going to do?" Blackie asked.

"I'm looking for something special," T. said.

It was nearly lunch-time before Blackie had finished and went in search of T. Chaos had advanced. The kitchen was a shambles of broken glass and china. The dining-room was stripped of parquet, the skirting was up, the door had been taken off its hinges, and the destroyers had moved up a floor. Streaks of light came in through the closed shutters where they worked with the seriousness of creators—and destruction after all is a form of creation. A kind of imagination had seen this house as it had now become.

Mike said, "I've got to go home for dinner."

"Who else?" T. asked, but all the others on one excuse or another had brought provisions with them.

They squatted in the ruins of the room and swapped unwanted sandwiches. Half an hour for lunch and they were at work again. By the time Mike returned, they were on the top floor, and by six the superficial damage was completed. The doors were all off, all the skirtings raised, the furniture pillaged and ripped and smashed—no one could have slept in the house except on a bed of broken plaster. T. gave his orders—eight o'clock next morning, and to escape notice they climbed singly over the garden wall, into the carpark. Only Blackie and T. were left: the light had nearly gone, and when they touched a switch, nothing worked—Mike had done his job thoroughly.

"Did you find anything special?" Blackie asked.

T. nodded. "Come over here," he said, "and look." Out of both pockets he drew bundles of pound notes. "Old Misery's savings," he said. "Mike ripped out the mattress, but he missed them."

90

95

"What are you going to do? Share them?"

100   "We aren't thieves," T. said. "Nobody's going to steal anything from this house. I kept these for you and me—a celebration." He knelt down on the floor and counted them out—there were seventy in all. "We'll burn them," he said, "one by one," and taking it in turns they held a note upwards and lit the top corner, so that the flame burnt slowly towards their fingers. The grey ash floated above them and fell on their heads like age. "I'd like to see Old Misery's face when we are through," T. said.

"You hate him a lot?" Blackie asked.

"Of course I don't hate him," T. said. "There'd be no fun if I hated him." The last burning note illuminated his brooding face. "All this hate and love," he said, "it's soft, it's hooey. There's only things, Blackie," and he looked round the room crowded with the unfamiliar shadows of half things, broken things, former things. "I'll race you home, Blackie," he said.

3

Next morning the serious destruction started. Two were missing—Mike and another boy whose parents were off to Southend and Brighton in spite of the slow warm drops that had begun to fall and the rumble of thunder in the estuary like the first guns of the old blitz. "We've got to hurry," T. said.

Summers was restive. "Haven't we done enough?" he said. "I've been given a bob for slot machines. This is like work."

105   "We've hardly started," T. said. "Why, there's all the floor left, and the stairs. We haven't taken out a single window. You voted like the others. We are going to *destroy* this house. There won't be anything left when we've finished."

They began again on the first floor picking up the top floorboards next to the outer wall, leaving the joists exposed. Then they sawed through the joists and retreated into the hall, as what was left of the floor heeled and sank. They had learnt with practice, and the second floor collapsed more easily. By the evening an odd exhilaration seized them as they looked down the great hollow of the house. They ran risks and made mistakes: when they thought of the windows it was too late to reach them. "Cor," Joe said, and dropped a penny down in the dry rubble-filled well. It cracked and span among the broken glass.

"Why did we start this?" Summers asked with astonishment; T. was already on the ground, digging at the rubble, clearing a space along the outer wall. "Turn on the taps," he said. "It's too dark for anyone to see now, and in the morning it won't matter." The water overtook them on the stairs and fell through the floorless rooms.

It was then they heard Mike's whistle at the back. "Something's wrong," Blackie said. They could hear his urgent breathing as they unlocked the door.

"The bogies?"° Summers asked.

"Old Misery," Mike said. "He's on his way." He put his head between   110
his knees and retched. "Ran all the way," he said with pride.

"But why?" T. said. "He told me . . ." He protested with the fury of
the child he had never been, "It isn't fair."

"He was down at Southend," Mike said, "and he was on the train
coming back. Said it was too cold and wet." He paused and gazed at the
water. "My, you've had a storm here. Is the roof leaking?"

"How long will he be?"

"Five minutes. I gave Ma the slip and ran."

"We better clear," Summers said. "We've done enough, anyway."   115

"Oh, no, we haven't. Anybody could do this—" "This" was the shattered hollowed house with nothing left but the walls. Yet the walls could
be preserved. Façades were valuable. They could build inside again more
beautifully than before. This could again be a home. He said angrily,
"We've got to finish. Don't move. Let me think."

"There's no time," a boy said.

"There's got to be a way," T. said. "We couldn't have got this far . . ."

"We've done a lot," Blackie said.

"No. No, we haven't. Somebody watch the front."   120

"We can't do any more."

"He may come in at the back."

"Watch the back too." T. began to plead. "Just give me a minute and
I'll fix it. I swear I'll fix it." But his authority had gone with his ambiguity.
He was only one of the gang. "Please," he said.

"Please," Summers mimicked him, and then suddenly struck home
with the fatal name. "Run along home, Trevor."

T. stood with his back to the rubble like a boxer knocked groggy against   125
the ropes. He had no words as his dreams shook and slid. Then Blackie acted
before the gang had time to laugh, pushing Summers backward. "I'll watch
the front, T.," he said, and cautiously he opened the shutters of the hall. The
grey wet common stretched ahead, and the lamps gleamed in the puddles.
"Someone's coming, T. No, it's not him. What's your plan, T.?"

"Tell Mike to go out to the lav and hide close beside it. When he hears
me whistle he's got to count ten and start to shout."

"Shout what?"

"Oh, 'Help,' anything."

"You hear, Mike," Blackie said. He was the leader again. He took a
quick look between the shutters. "He's coming, T."

"Quick, Mike. The lav. Stay here, Blackie, all of you till I yell."   130

bogies: police

"Where are you going, T.?"

"Don't worry. I'll see to this. I said I would, didn't I?"

Old Misery came limping off the common. He had mud on his shoes and he stopped to scrape them on the pavement's edge. He didn't want to soil his house, which stood jagged and dark between the bombsites, saved so narrowly, as he believed, from destruction. Even the fan-light had been left unbroken by the bomb's blast. Somewhere somebody whistled. Old Misery looked sharply round. He didn't trust whistles. A child was shouting: it seemed to come from his own garden. Then a boy ran into the road from the car-park. "Mr. Thomas," he called. "Mr. Thomas."

"What is it?"

135   "I'm terribly sorry, Mr. Thomas. One of us got taken short, and we thought you wouldn't mind, and now he can't get out."

"What do you mean, boy?"

"He's got stuck in your lav."

"He'd no business . . . Haven't I seen you before?"

"You showed me your house."

140   "So I did. So I did. That doesn't give you the right to . . ."

"Do hurry, Mr. Thomas. He'll suffocate."

"Nonsense. He can't suffocate. Wait till I put my bag in."

"I'll carry your bag."

"Oh no, you don't. I carry my own."

145   "This way, Mr. Thomas."

"I can't get in the garden that way. I've got to go through the house."

"But you *can* get in the garden this way, Mr. Thomas. We often do."

"You often do?" He followed the boy with a scandalized fascination. "When? What right? . . ."

"Do you see . . .? The wall's low."

150   "I'm not going to climb walls into my own garden. It's absurd."

"This is how we do it. One foot here, one foot there, and over." The boy's face peered down, an arm shot out, and Mr. Thomas found his bag taken and deposited on the other side of the wall.

"Give me back my bag," Mr. Thomas said. From the loo° a boy yelled and yelled. "I'll call the police."

"Your bag's all right, Mr. Thomas. Look. One foot there. On your right. Now just above. To your left." Mr. Thomas climbed over his own garden wall. "Here's your bag, Mr. Thomas."

"I'll have the wall built up," Mr. Thomas said. "I'll not have you boys coming over here, using my loo." He stumbled on the path, but the boy caught his elbow and supported him. "Thank you, thank you, my

---

loo: outdoor toilet (an older term for "lav")

boy," he murmured automatically. Somebody shouted again through the dark. "I'm coming, I'm coming," Mr. Thomas called. He said to the boy beside him, "I'm not unreasonable. Been a boy myself. As long as things are done regular. I don't mind you playing round the place Saturday mornings. Sometimes I like company. Only it's got to be regular. One of you asks leave and I say Yes. Sometimes I'll say No. Won't feel like it. And you come in at the front door and out at the back. No garden walls."

"Do get him out, Mr. Thomas."   155

"He won't come to any harm in my loo," Mr. Thomas said, stumbling slowly down the garden. "Oh, my rheumatics," he said. "Always get 'em on Bank Holiday. I've got to go careful. There's loose stones here. Give me your hand. Do you know what my horoscope said yesterday? 'Abstain from any dealings in first half of week. Danger of serious crash.' That might be on this path," Mr. Thomas said. "They speak in parables and double meanings." He paused at the door of the loo. "What's the matter in there?" he called. There was no reply.

"Perhaps he's fainted," the boy said.

"Not in my loo. Here, you come out," Mr. Thomas said, and giving a great jerk at the door he nearly fell on his back when it swung easily open. A hand first supported him and then pushed him hard. His head hit the opposite wall and he sat heavily down. His bag hit his feet. A hand whipped the key out of the lock and the door slammed. "Let me out," he called, and heard the key turn in the lock. "A serious crash," he thought, and felt dithery and confused and old.

A voice spoke to him softly through the star-shaped hole in the door. "Don't worry, Mr. Thomas," it said, "we won't hurt you, not if you stay quiet."

Mr. Thomas put his head between his hands and pondered. He had   160
noticed that there was only one lorry in the car-park, and he felt certain that the driver would not come for it before the morning. Nobody could hear him from the road in front, and the lane at the back was seldom used. Anyone who passed there would be hurrying home and would not pause for what they would certainly take to be drunken cries. And if he did call "Help," who, on a lonely Bank Holiday evening, would have the courage to investigate? Mr. Thomas sat on the loo and pondered with the wisdom of age.

After a while it seemed to him that there were sounds in the silence—they were faint and came from the direction of his house. He stood up and peered through the ventilation-hole—between the cracks in one of the shutters he saw a light, not the light of a lamp, but the wavering light that a candle might give. Then he thought he heard the sound of hammering and scraping and chipping. He thought of burglars—perhaps they had employed the boy as a scout, but why should burglars engage in what sounded more and more like a stealthy form of carpentry? Mr. Thomas let out an experimental yell, but nobody answered. The noise could not even have reached his enemies.

4

Mike had gone home to bed, but the rest stayed. The question of leadership no longer concerned the gang. With nails, chisels, screwdrivers, anything that was sharp and penetrating, they moved around the inner walls worrying at the mortar between the bricks. They started too high, and it was Blackie who hit on the damp course and realized the work could be halved if they weakened the joints immediately above. It was a long, tiring, unamusing job, but at last it was finished. The gutted house stood there balanced on a few inches of mortar between the damp course and the bricks.

There remained the most dangerous task of all, out in the open at the edge of the bomb-site. Summers was sent to watch the road for passers-by, and Mr. Thomas, sitting on the loo, heard clearly now the sound of sawing. It no longer came from his house, and that a little reassured him. He felt less concerned. Perhaps the other noises too had no significance.

A voice spoke to him through the hole. "Mr. Thomas."

165   "Let me out," Mr. Thomas said sternly.

"Here's a blanket," the voice said, and a long grey sausage was worked through the hole and fell in swathes over Mr. Thomas's head.

"There's nothing personal," the voice said. "We want you to be comfortable tonight."

"Tonight," Mr. Thomas repeated incredulously.

"Catch," the voice said. "Penny buns—we've buttered them, and sausage-rolls. We don't want you to starve, Mr. Thomas."

170   Mr. Thomas pleaded desperately. "A joke's a joke, boy. Let me out and I won't say a thing. I've got rheumatics. I got to sleep comfortable."

"You wouldn't be comfortable, not in your house, you wouldn't. Not now."

"What do you mean, boy?" but the footsteps receded. There was only the silence of night: no sound of sawing. Mr. Thomas tried one more yell, but he was daunted and rebuked by the silence—a long way off an owl hooted and made away again on its muffled flight through the soundless world.

At seven next morning the driver came to fetch his lorry. He climbed into the seat and tried to start the engine. He was vaguely aware of a voice shouting, but it didn't concern him. At last the engine responded and he backed the lorry until it touched the great wooden shore that supported Mr. Thomas's house. That way he could drive right out and down the street without reversing. The lorry moved forward, was momentarily checked as though something were pulling it from behind, and then went on to the sound of a long rumbling crash. The driver was astonished to see bricks bouncing ahead of him, while stones hit the roof of his cab. He put on his brakes. When he climbed out the whole landscape had suddenly altered. There was no house beside the car-park, only a hill of rubble. He went round and examined the back of his car for damage, and found a rope tied there that was still twisted at the other end round part of a wooden strut.

The driver again became aware of somebody shouting. It came from the wooden erection which was the nearest thing to a house in that desolation of broken brick. The driver climbed the smashed wall and unlocked the door. Mr. Thomas came out of the loo. He was wearing a grey blanket to which flakes of pastry adhered. He gave a sobbing cry. "My house," he said. "Where's my house?"

"Search me," the driver said. His eye lit on the remains of a bath and 175 what had once been a dresser and he began to laugh. There wasn't anything left anywhere.

"How dare you laugh," Mr. Thomas said. "It was my house. My house."

"I'm sorry," the driver said, making heroic efforts, but when he remembered the sudden check to his lorry, the crash of bricks falling, he became convulsed again. One moment the house had stood there with such dignity between the bomb-sites like a man in a top hat, and then, bang, crash, there wasn't anything left—not anything. He said, "I'm sorry. I can't help it, Mr. Thomas. There's nothing personal, but you got to admit it's funny."

QUESTIONS

1. Who is the protagonist in this story—Trevor, Blackie, or the gang? Who or what is the antagonist? Identify the conflicts of the story.
2. How is suspense created?
3. This story uses the most common basic formula of commercial fiction: protagonist aims at a goal, is confronted with various obstacles between himself and his goal, overcomes the obstacles, and achieves his goal. How does this story differ from commercial fiction in its use of this formula? Does the story have a happy ending?
4. Discuss the gang's motivations, taking into account (a) the age and beauty of the house, (b) Blackie's reasons for not going home after losing his position of leadership, (c) the seriousness with which the boys work at their task, and their loss of concern over their leadership, (d) the burning of the pound notes, (e) their consideration for Old Misery, (f) the lorry driver's reaction. What characteristics do the gang's two named exploits—pinching free rides and destroying the house—have in common?
5. Of what significance, if any, is the setting of this story in blitzed London? Does the story have anything to say about the consequences of war? About the causes of war?

6. Explain as fully as you can the causes of the gang's delinquency, taking into account (a) their reaction to the name Trevor, (b) their reaction to Old Misery's gift of chocolates, (c) Blackie's reaction to the word "beautiful," (d) Trevor's comments on "hate and love," (e) Summers's reaction to the word "Please," (f) the setting.
7. What good qualities do the delinquents in this story have? Do they differ as a group from other youth gangs you have read or know about? If so, account for the differences.
8. On the surface this is a story of action, suspense, and adventure. At a deeper level it is about delinquency, war, and human nature. Try to sum up what the story says about human nature in general.

ALICE MUNRO
How I Met My Husband

We heard the plane come over at noon, roaring through the radio news, and we were sure it was going to hit the house, so we all ran out into the yard. We saw it come over the treetops, all red and silver, the first close-up plane I ever saw. Mrs. Peebles screamed.

"Crash landing," their little boy said. Joey was his name.

"It's okay," said Dr. Peebles. "He knows what he's doing." Dr. Peebles was only an animal doctor, but had a calming way of talking, like any doctor.

This was my first job—working for Dr. and Mrs. Peebles, who had bought an old house out on the Fifth Line, about five miles out of town. It was just when the trend was starting of town people buying up old farms, not to work them but to live on them.

5   We watched the plane land across the road, where the fairgrounds used to be. It did make a good landing field, nice and level for the old race track, and the barns and display sheds torn down now for scrap lumber so there was nothing in the way. Even the old grandstand bays had burned.

"All right," said Mrs. Peebles, snappy as she always was when she got over her nerves. "Let's go back in the house. Let's not stand here gawking like a set of farmers."

She didn't say that to hurt my feelings. It never occurred to her.

I was just setting the dessert down when Loretta Bird arrived, out of breath, at the screen door.

HOW I MET MY HUSBAND   First published in her collection *Something I've Been Meaning to Tell You* in 1974. Alice Munro (b. 1931) grew up in rural southwestern Ontario, where much of her fiction is set. She attended the University of Western Ontario for two years and moved to British Columbia, where she lived until 1972; she now lives in Clinton, Ontario. She is the author of twelve collections of short fiction, most recently *Dear Life* (2012). She won the Nobel Prize for Literature in 2013.

"I thought it was going to crash into the house and kill youse all!"

She lived on the next place and the Peebleses thought she was a country- 10
woman, they didn't know the difference. She and her husband didn't farm,
he worked on the roads and had a bad name for drinking. They had seven
children and couldn't get credit at the HiWay Grocery. The Peebleses made
her welcome, not knowing any better, as I say, and offered her dessert.

Dessert was never anything to write home about, at their place. A dish
of Jell-O or sliced bananas or fruit out of a tin. "Have a house without a
pie, be ashamed until you die," my mother used to say, but Mrs. Peebles
operated differently.

Loretta Bird saw me getting the can of peaches.

"Oh, never mind," she said. "I haven't got the right kind of a stomach
to trust what comes out of those tins, I can only eat home canning."

I could have slapped her. I bet she never put down fruit in her life.

"I know what he's landed here for," she said. "He's got permission to 15
use the fairgrounds and take people up for rides. It costs a dollar. It's the
same fellow who was over at Palmerston last week and was up the lakeshore
before that. I wouldn't go up, if you paid me."

"I'd jump at the chance," Dr. Peebles said. "I'd like to see this
neighborhood from the air."

Mrs. Peebles said she would just as soon see it from the ground. Joey
said he wanted to go and Heather did, too. Joey was nine and Heather was
seven.

"Would you, Edie?" Heather said.

I said I didn't know. I was scared, but I never admitted that, especially
in front of children I was taking care of.

"People are going to be coming out here in their cars raising dust and 20
trampling your property, if I was you I would complain," Loretta said. She
hooked her legs around the chair rung and I knew we were in for a lengthy
visit. After Dr. Peebles went back to his office or out on his next call and
Mrs. Peebles went for her nap, she would hang around me while I was trying to do the dishes. She would pass remarks about the Peebleses in their
own house.

"She wouldn't find time to lay down in the middle of the day, if she
had seven kids like I got."

She asked me did they fight and did they keep things in the dresser
drawer not to have babies with. She said it was a sin if they did. I pretended
I didn't know what she was talking about.

I was fifteen and away from home for the first time. My parents had
made the effort and sent me to high school for a year, but I didn't like it.
I was shy of strangers and the work was hard, they didn't make it nice for
you or explain the way they do now. At the end of the year the averages

were published in the paper, and mine came out at the very bottom, 37 percent. My father said that's enough and I didn't blame him. The last thing I wanted, anyway, was to go on and end up teaching school. It happened the very day the paper came out with my disgrace in it, Dr. Peebles was staying at our place for dinner, having just helped one of our cows have twins, and he said I looked smart to him and his wife was looking for a girl to help. He said she felt tied down, with the two children, out in the country. I guess she would, my mother said, being polite, though I could tell from her face she was wondering what on earth it would be like to have only two children and no barn work, and then to be complaining.

When I went home I would describe to them the work I had to do, and it made everybody laugh. Mrs. Peebles had an automatic washer and dryer, the first I ever saw. I have had those in my own home for such a long time now it's hard to remember how much of a miracle it was to me, not having to struggle with the wringer and hang up and haul down. Let alone not having to heat water. Then there was practically no baking. Mrs. Peebles said she couldn't make pie crust, the most amazing thing I ever heard a woman admit. I could, of course, and I could make light biscuits and a white cake and dark cake, but they didn't want it, she said they watched their figures. The only thing I didn't like about working there, in fact, was feeling half hungry a lot of the time. I used to bring back a box of doughnuts made out at home, and hide them under my bed. The children found out, and I didn't mind sharing, but I thought I better bind them to secrecy.

25   The day after the plane landed Mrs. Peebles put both children in the car and drove over to Chesley, to get their hair cut. There was a good woman then at Chesley for doing hair. She got hers done at the same place, Mrs. Peebles did, and that meant they would be gone a good while. She had to pick a day Dr. Peebles wasn't going out into the country, she didn't have her own car. Cars were still in short supply then, after the war.

I loved being left in the house alone, to do my work at leisure. The kitchen was all white and bright yellow, with fluorescent lights. That was before they ever thought of making the appliances all different colors and doing the cupboards like dark old wood and hiding the lighting. I loved light. I loved the double sink. So would anybody new-come from washing dishes in a dishpan with a rag-plugged hole on an oilcloth-covered table by light of a coal-oil lamp. I kept everything shining.

The bathroom too. I had a bath in there once a week. They wouldn't have minded if I took one oftener, but to me it seemed like asking too much, or maybe risking making it less wonderful. The basin and the tub and the toilet were all pink, and there were glass doors with flamingos painted on them, to shut off the tub. The light had a rosy cast and the mat sank under your feet like snow, except that it was warm. The mirror was three-way. With the mirror all steamed up and the air like a perfume cloud, from things I was allowed to use, I stood up on the side of the tub and admired myself naked, from three directions. Sometimes I thought about the way we lived out at home and the way we lived here and how one way was so hard to imagine when you were living the other way. But I thought it was still a lot easier, living the way we lived at home, to picture something like this, the painted flamingos and the warmth and the soft mat, than it was anybody knowing only things like this to picture how it was the other way. And why was that?

I was through my jobs in no time, and had the vegetables peeled for supper and sitting in cold water besides. Then I went into Mrs. Peebles' bedroom. I had been in there plenty of times, cleaning, and I always took a good look in her closet, at the clothes she had hanging there. I wouldn't have looked in her drawers, but a closet is open to anybody. That's a lie. I would have looked in drawers, but I would have felt worse doing it and been more scared she could tell.

Some clothes in her closet she wore all the time, I was quite familiar with them. Others she never put on, they were pushed to the back. I was disappointed to see no wedding dress. But there was one long dress I could just see the skirt of, and I was hungering to see the rest. Now I took note of where it hung and lifted it out. It was satin, a lovely weight on my arm, light bluish-green in color, almost silvery. It had a fitted, pointed waist and a full skirt and an off-the-shoulder fold hiding the little sleeves.

Next thing was easy. I got out of my own things and slipped it on. I was ³⁰ slimmer at fifteen than anybody would believe who knows me now and the fit was beautiful. I didn't, of course, have a strapless bra on, which was what it needed, I just had to slide my straps down my arms under the material. Then I tried pinning up my hair, to get the effect. One thing led to another. I put on rouge and lipstick and eyebrow pencil from her dresser. The heat of the day and the weight of the satin and all the excitement made me thirsty, and I went out to the kitchen, got-up as I was, to get a glass of ginger ale with ice cubes from the refrigerator. The Peebleses drank ginger ale, or fruit drinks, all day, like water, and I was getting so I did too. Also there was no limit on ice cubes, which I was so fond of I would even put them in a glass of milk.

I turned from putting the ice tray back and saw a man watching me through the screen. It was the luckiest thing in the world I didn't spill the ginger ale down the front of me then and there.

"I never meant to scare you. I knocked but you were getting the ice out, you didn't hear me."

I couldn't see what he looked like, he was dark the way somebody is pressed up against a screen door with the bright daylight behind them. I only knew he wasn't from around here.

"I'm from the plane over there. My name is Chris Watters and what I was wondering was if I could use that pump."

35   There was a pump in the yard. That was the way the people used to get their water. Now I noticed he was carrying a pail.

"You're welcome," I said. "I can get it from the tap and save you pumping." I guess I wanted him to know we had piped water, didn't pump ourselves.

"I don't mind the exercise." He didn't move, though, and finally he said, "Were you going to a dance?"

Seeing a stranger there had made me entirely forget how I was dressed.

"Or is that the way ladies around here generally get dressed up in the afternoon?"

40   I didn't know how to joke back then. I was too embarrassed.

"You live here? Are you the lady of the house?"

"I'm the hired girl."

Some people change when they find that out, their whole way of looking at you and speaking to you changes, but his didn't.

"Well, I just wanted to tell you you look very nice. I was so surprised when I looked in the door and saw you. Just because you looked so nice and beautiful."

45   I wasn't even old enough then to realize how out of the common it is, for a man to say something like that to a woman, or somebody he is treating like a woman. For a man to say a word like *beautiful*. I wasn't old enough to realize or to say anything back, or in fact to do anything but wish he would go away. Not that I didn't like him, but just that it upset me so, having him look at me, and me trying to think of something to say.

He must have understood. He said good-bye, and thanked me, and went and started filling his pail from the pump. I stood behind the Venetian blinds in the dining room, watching him. When he had gone, I went into the bedroom and took the dress off and put it back in the same place. I dressed in my own clothes and took my hair down and washed my face, wiping it on Kleenex, which I threw in the wastebasket.

The Peebleses asked me what kind of man he was. Young, middle-aged, short, tall? I couldn't say.

"Good-looking?" Dr. Peebles teased me.

I couldn't think a thing but that he would be coming to get his water again, he would be talking to Dr. or Mrs. Peebles, making friends with them, and he would mention seeing me that first afternoon, dressed up. Why not mention it? He would think it was funny. And no idea of the trouble it would get me into.

50   After supper the Peebleses drove into town to go to a movie. She wanted to go somewhere with her hair fresh done. I sat in my bright

kitchen wondering what to do, knowing I would never sleep. Mrs. Peebles might not fire me, when she found out, but it would give her a different feeling about me altogether. This was the first place I ever worked but I really had picked up things about the way people feel when you are working for them. They like to think you aren't curious. Not just that you aren't dishonest, that isn't enough. They like to feel you don't notice things, that you don't think or wonder about anything but what they liked to eat and how they liked things ironed, and so on. I don't mean they weren't kind to me, because they were. They had me eat my meals with them (to tell the truth I expected to, I didn't know there were families who don't) and sometimes they took me along in the car. But all the same.

I went up and checked on the children being asleep and then I went out. I had to do it. I crossed the road and went in the old fairgrounds gate. The plane looked unnatural sitting there, and shining with the moon. Off at the far side of the fairgrounds, where the bush was taking over, I saw his tent.

He was sitting outside it smoking a cigarette. He saw me coming.

"Hello, were you looking for a plane ride? I don't start taking people up till tomorrow." Then he looked again and said, "Oh, it's you. I didn't know you without your long dress on."

My heart was knocking away, my tongue was dried up. I had to say something. But I couldn't. My throat was closed and I was like a deaf-and-dumb.

"Did you want to ride? Sit down. Have a cigarette."   55

I couldn't even shake my head to say no, so he gave me one.

"Put it in your mouth or I can't light it. It's a good thing I'm used to shy ladies."

I did. It wasn't the first time I had smoked a cigarette, actually. My girlfriend out home, Muriel Lowe, used to steal them from her brother.

"Look at your hand shaking. Did you just want to have a chat, or what?"

In one burst I said, "I wisht you wouldn't say anything about that dress."   60

"What dress? Oh, the long dress."

"It's Mrs. Peebles'."

"Whose? Oh, the lady you work for? Is that it? She wasn't home so you got dressed up in her dress, eh? You got dressed up and played queen. I don't blame you. You're not smoking the cigarette right. Don't just puff. Draw it in. Did anybody ever show you how to inhale? Are you scared I'll tell on you? Is that it?"

I was so ashamed at having to ask him to connive this way I couldn't nod. I just looked at him and he saw *yes*.

"Well I won't. I won't in the slightest way mention it or embarrass 65
you. I give you my word of honor."

Then he changed the subject, to help me out, seeing I couldn't even thank him.

"What do you think of this sign?"

It was a board sign lying practically at my feet.

SEE THE WORLD FROM THE SKY. ADULTS $1.00, CHILDREN 50¢. QUALIFIED PILOT.

70   "My old sign was getting pretty beat up, I thought I'd make a new one. That's what I've been doing with my time today."

The lettering wasn't all that handsome, I thought. I could have done a better one in half an hour.

"I'm not an expert at sign making."

"It's very good," I said.

"I don't need it for publicity, word of mouth is usually enough. I turned away two carloads tonight. I felt like taking it easy. I didn't tell them ladies were dropping in to visit me."

75   Now I remembered the children and I was scared again, in case one of them had waked up and called me and I wasn't there.

"Do you have to go so soon?"

I remembered some manners. "Thank you for the cigarette."

"Don't forget. You have my word of honor."

I tore off across the fairgrounds, scared I'd see the car heading home from town. My sense of time was mixed up, I didn't know how long I'd been out of the house. But it was all right, it wasn't late, the children were asleep. I got in bed myself and lay thinking what a lucky end to the day, after all, and among things to be grateful for I could be grateful Loretta Bird hadn't been the one who caught me.

80   The yard and borders didn't get trampled, it wasn't as bad as that. All the same it seemed very public, around the house. The sign was on the fairgrounds gate. People came mostly after supper but a good many in the afternoon, too. The Bird children all came without fifty cents between them and hung on the gate. We got used to the excitement of the plane coming in and taking off, it wasn't excitement anymore. I never went over, after that one time, but would see him when he came to get his water. I would be out on the steps doing sitting-down work, like preparing vegetables, if I could.

"Why don't you come over? I'll take you up in my plane."

"I'm saving my money," I said, because I couldn't think of anything else.

"For what? For getting married?"

I shook my head.

85   "I'll take you up for free if you come sometime when it's slack. I thought you would come, and have another cigarette."

I made a face to hush him, because you never could tell when the children would be sneaking around the porch, or Mrs. Peebles herself listening in the house. Sometimes she came out and had a conversation with him. He told her things he hadn't bothered to tell me. But then I hadn't thought to ask. He told her he had been in the war, that was where he learned to fly a plane, and now he couldn't settle down to ordinary life, this was what he liked. She said she couldn't imagine anybody liking such a thing. Though sometimes, she said, she was almost bored enough to try anything herself, she wasn't brought up to living in the country. It's all my husband's idea, she said. This was news to me.

"Maybe you ought to give flying lessons," she said.

"Would you take them?"

She just laughed.

Sunday was a busy flying day in spite of it being preached against from 90 two pulpits. We were all sitting out watching. Joey and Heather were over on the fence with the Bird kids. Their father had said they could go, after their mother saying all week they couldn't.

A car came down the road past the parked cars and pulled up right in the drive. It was Loretta Bird who got out, all importance, and on the driver's side another woman got out, more sedately. She was wearing sunglasses.

"This is a lady looking for the man that flies the plane," Loretta Bird said. "I heard her inquire in the hotel coffee shop where I was having a Coke and I brought her out."

"I'm sorry to bother you," the lady said. "I'm Alice Kelling, Mr. Watters' fiancée."

This Alice Kelling had on a pair of brown and white checked slacks and a yellow top. Her bust looked to me rather low and bumpy. She had a worried face. Her hair had had a permanent, but had grown out, and she wore a yellow band to keep it off her face. Nothing in the least pretty or even young-looking about her. But you could tell from how she talked she was from the city, or educated, or both.

Dr. Peebles stood up and introduced himself and his wife and me and 95 asked her to be seated.

"He's up in the air right now, but you're welcome to sit and wait. He gets his water here and he hasn't been yet. He'll probably take his break about five."

"That is him, then?" said Alice Kelling, wrinkling and straining at the sky.

"He's not in the habit of running out on you, taking a different name?" Dr. Peebles laughed. He was the one, not his wife, to offer iced tea. Then she sent me into the kitchen to fix it. She smiled. She was wearing sunglasses too.

"He never mentioned his fiancée," she said.

I loved fixing iced tea with lots of ice and slices of lemon in tall glasses. 100 I ought to have mentioned before, Dr. Peebles was an abstainer, at least around the house, or I wouldn't have been allowed to take the place. I had to fix a glass for Loretta Bird too, though it galled me, and when I went out she had settled in my lawn chair, leaving me the steps.

"I knew you was a nurse when I first heard you in that coffee shop."

"How would you know a thing like that?"

"I get my hunches about people. Was that how you met him, nursing?"

"Chris? Well yes. Yes, it was."

105   "Oh, were you overseas?" said Mrs. Peebles.

"No, it was before he went overseas. I nursed him when he was stationed at Centralia and had a ruptured appendix. We got engaged and then he went overseas. My, this is refreshing, after a long drive."

"He'll be glad to see you," Dr. Peebles said. "It's a rackety kind of life, isn't it, not staying one place long enough to really make friends."

"Youse've had a long engagement," Loretta Bird said.

Alice Kelling passed that over. "I was going to get a room at the hotel, but when I was offered directions I came on out. Do you think I could phone them?"

110   "No need," Dr. Peebles said. "You're five miles away from him if you stay at the hotel. Here, you're right across the road. Stay with us. We've got rooms on rooms, look at this big house."

Asking people to stay, just like that, is certainly a country thing, and maybe seemed natural to him now, but not to Mrs. Peebles, from the way she said, oh yes, we have plenty of room. Or to Alice Kelling, who kept protesting, but let herself be worn down. I got the feeling it was a temptation to her, to be that close. I was trying for a look at her ring. Her nails were painted red, her fingers were freckled and wrinkled. It was a tiny stone. Muriel Lowe's cousin had one twice as big.

Chris came to get his water, late in the afternoon just as Dr. Peebles had predicted. He must have recognized the car from a way off. He came smiling.

"Here I am chasing after you to see what you're up to," called Alice Kelling. She got up and went to meet him and they kissed, just touched, in front of us.

"You're going to spend a lot on gas that way," Chris said.

115   Dr. Peebles invited Chris to stay for supper, since he had already put up the sign that said: NO MORE RIDES TILL 7 P.M. Mrs. Peebles wanted it served in the yard, in spite of the bugs. One thing strange to anybody from the country is this eating outside. I had made a potato salad earlier and she had made a jellied salad, that was one thing she could do, so it was just a matter of getting those out, and some sliced meat and cucumbers and fresh leaf lettuce. Loretta Bird hung around for some time saying, "Oh, well, I guess I better get home to those yappers," and, "It's so nice just sitting here, I sure hate to get up," but nobody invited her, I was relieved to see, and finally she had to go.

That night after rides were finished Alice Kelling and Chris went off somewhere in her car. I lay awake till they got back. When I saw the car lights sweep my ceiling I got up to look down on them through the slats of my blind. I don't know what I thought I was going to see. Muriel Lowe and I used to sleep on her front veranda and watch her sister and her sister's boyfriend saying good night. Afterward we couldn't get to sleep, for longing for somebody to kiss us and rub up against us and we would talk about suppose you were out in a boat with a boy and he wouldn't bring you in to shore unless you did it, or what if somebody got you trapped in a barn, you would have to, wouldn't you, it wouldn't be your fault. Muriel said her two girl cousins used to try with a toilet paper roll that one of them was a boy. We wouldn't do anything like that; just lay and wondered.

All that happened was that Chris got out of the car on one side and she got out on the other and they walked off separately—him toward the fairgrounds and her toward the house. I got back in bed and imagined about me coming home with him, not like that.

Next morning Alice Kelling got up late and I fixed a grapefruit for her the way I had learned and Mrs. Peebles sat down with her to visit and have another cup of coffee. Mrs. Peebles seemed pleased enough now, having company. Alice Kelling said she guessed she better get used to putting in a day just watching Chris take off and come down, and Mrs. Peebles said she didn't know if she should suggest it because Alice Kelling was the one with the car, but the lake was only twenty-five miles away and what a good day for a picnic.

Alice Kelling took her up on the idea and by eleven o'clock they were in the car, with Joey and Heather and a sandwich lunch I had made. The only thing was that Chris hadn't come down, and she wanted to tell him where they were going.

"Edie'll go over and tell him," Mrs. Peebles said. "There's no problem." 120

Alice Kelling wrinkled her face and agreed.

"Be sure and tell him we'll be back by five!"

I didn't see that he would be concerned about knowing this right away, and I thought of him eating whatever he ate over there, alone, cooking on his camp stove, so I got to work and mixed up a crumb cake and baked it, in between the other work I had to do; then, when it was a bit cooled, wrapped it in a tea towel. I didn't do anything to myself but take off my apron and comb my hair. I would like to have put some makeup on, but I was too afraid it would remind him of the way he first saw me, and that would humiliate me all over again.

He had come and put another sign on the gate: NO RIDES THIS P.M. APOLOGIES. I worried that he wasn't feeling well. No sign of him outside and the tent flap was down. I knocked on the pole.

125   "Come in," he said, in a voice that would just as soon have said *Stay out*. I lifted the flap.

"Oh, it's you. I'm sorry. I didn't know it was you."

He had been just sitting on the side of the bed, smoking. Why not at least sit and smoke in the fresh air?

"I brought a cake and hope you're not sick," I said.

130   "Why would I be sick? Oh—that sign. That's all right. I'm just tired of talking to people. I don't mean you. Have a seat." He pinned back the tent flap. "Get some fresh air in here."

I sat on the edge of the bed, there was no place else. It was one of those fold-up cots, really: I remembered and gave him his fiancée's message.

He ate some of the cake. "Good."

"Put the rest away for when you're hungry later."

"I'll tell you a secret. I won't be around here much longer."

135   "Are you getting married?"

"Ha ha. What time did you say they'd be back?"

"Five o'clock."

"Well, by that time, this place will have seen the last of me. A plane can get further than a car." He unwrapped the cake and ate another piece of it, absentmindedly.

"Now you'll be thirsty."

140   "There's some water in the pail."

"It won't be very cold. I could bring some fresh. I could bring some ice from the refrigerator."

"No," he said. "I don't want you to go. I want a nice long time of saying good-bye to you."

He put the cake away carefully and sat beside me and started those little kisses, so soft, I can't ever let myself think about them, such kindness in his face and lovely kisses, all over my eyelids and neck and ears, all over, then me kissing back as well as I could (I had only kissed a boy on a dare before, and kissed my own arms for practice) and we lay back on the cot and pressed together, just gently, and he did some other things, not bad things or not in a bad way. It was lovely in the tent, that smell of grass and hot tent cloth with the sun beating down on it, and he said, "I wouldn't do you any harm for the world." Once, when he had rolled on top of me and we were sort of rocking together on the cot, he said softly, "Oh, no," and freed himself and jumped up and got the water pail. He splashed some of it on his neck and face, and the little bit left, on me lying there.

"That's to cool us off, miss."

145   When we said good-bye I wasn't at all sad, because he held my face and said, "I'm going to write you a letter. I'll tell you where I am and maybe you can come and see me. Would you like that? Okay then. You wait." I was

really glad I think to get away from him, it was like he was piling presents on me I couldn't get the pleasure of till I considered them alone.

No consternation at first about the plane being gone. They thought he had taken somebody up, and I didn't enlighten them. Dr. Peebles had phoned he had to go to the country, so there was just us having supper, and then Loretta Bird thrusting her head in the door and saying, "I see he's took off."

"What?" said Alice Kelling, and pushed back her chair.

"The kids come and told me this afternoon he was taking down his tent. Did he think he'd run through all the business there was round here? He didn't take off without letting you know, did he?"

"He'll send me word," Alice Kelling said. "He'll probably phone tonight. He's terribly restless, since the war."

"Edie, he didn't mention to you, did he?" Mrs. Peebles said. "When you took over the message?"   150

"Yes," I said. So far so true.

"Well why didn't you say?" All of them were looking at me. "Did he say where he was going?"

"He said he might try Bayfield," I said. What made me tell such a lie? I didn't intend it.

"Bayfield, how far is that?" said Alice Kelling.

Mrs. Peebles said, "Thirty, thirty-five miles."   155

"That's not far. Oh, well, that's really not far at all. It's on the lake, isn't it?"

You'd think I'd be ashamed of myself, setting her on the wrong track. I did it to give him more time, whatever time he needed. I lied for him, and also, I have to admit, for me. Women should stick together and not do things like that. I see that now, but didn't then. I never thought of myself as being in any way like her, or coming to the same troubles, ever.

She hadn't taken her eyes off me. I thought she suspected my lie.

"When did he mention this to you?"

"Earlier."   160

"When you were over at the plane?"

"Yes."

"You must've stayed and had a chat." She smiled at me, not a nice smile. "You must've stayed and had a little visit with him."

"I took a cake," I said, thinking that telling some truth would spare me telling the rest.

"We didn't have a cake," said Mrs. Peebles rather sharply.   165

"I baked one."

Alice Kelling said, "That was very friendly of you."

"Did you get permission," said Loretta Bird. "You never know what these girls'll do next," she said. "It's not they mean harm so much, as they're ignorant."

"The cake is neither here nor there," Mrs. Peebles broke in. "Edie, I wasn't aware you knew Chris that well."

170   I didn't know what to say.

"I'm not surprised," Alice Kelling said in a high voice. "I knew by the look of her as soon as I saw her. We get them at the hospital all the time." She looked hard at me with her stretched smile. "Having their babies. We have to put them in a special ward because of their diseases. Little country tramps. Fourteen and fifteen years old. You should see the babies they have, too."

"There was a bad woman here in town had a baby that pus was running out of its eyes," Loretta Bird put in.

"Wait a minute," said Mrs. Peebles. "What is this talk? Edie. What about you and Mr. Watters? Were you intimate with him?"

"Yes," I said. I was thinking of us lying on the cot and kissing, wasn't that intimate? And I would never deny it.

175   They were all one minute quiet, even Loretta Bird.

"Well," said Mrs. Peebles. "I am surprised. I think I need a cigarette. This is the first of any such tendencies I've seen in her," she said, speaking to Alice Kelling, but Alice Kelling was looking at me.

"Loose little bitch." Tears ran down her face. "Loose little bitch, aren't you? I knew as soon as I saw you. Men despise girls like you. He just made use of you and went off, you know that, don't you? Girls like you are just nothing, they're just public conveniences, just filthy little rags!"

"Oh, now," said Mrs. Peebles.

"Filthy," Alice Kelling sobbed. "Filthy little rags!"

180   "Don't get yourself upset," Loretta Bird said. She was swollen up with pleasure at being in on this scene. "Men are all the same."

"Edie, I'm very surprised," Mrs. Peebles said. "I thought your parents were so strict. You don't want to have a baby, do you?"

I'm still ashamed of what happened next. I lost control, just like a six-year-old, I started howling. "You don't get a baby from just doing that!"

"You see. Some of them are that ignorant," Loretta Bird said.

But Mrs. Peebles jumped up and caught my arms and shook me.

185   "Calm down. Don't get hysterical. Calm down. Stop crying. Listen to me. Listen. I'm wondering, if you know what being intimate means. Now tell me. What did you think it meant?"

"Kissing," I howled.

She let go. "Oh, Edie. Stop it. Don't be silly. It's all right. It's all a misunderstanding. Being intimate means a lot more than that. Oh, I wondered."

"She's trying to cover up, now," said Alice Kelling. "Yes. She's not so stupid. She sees she got herself in trouble."

"I believe her," Mrs. Peebles said. "This is an awful scene."

"Well there is one way to find out," said Alice Kelling, getting up. 190
"After all, I am a nurse."

Mrs. Peebles drew a breath and said, "No. No. Go to your room, Edie.
And stop that noise. This is too disgusting."

I heard the car start in a little while. I tried to stop crying, pulling
back each wave as it started over me. Finally I succeeded, and lay heaving
on the bed.

Mrs. Peebles came and stood in the doorway.

"She's gone," she said. "That Bird woman too. Of course, you know
you should never have gone near that man and that is the cause of all this
trouble. I have a headache. As soon as you can, go and wash your face in
cold water and get at the dishes and we will not say any more about this."

Nor we didn't. I didn't figure out till years later the extent of what I 195
had been saved from. Mrs. Peebles was not very friendly to me afterward,
but she was fair. Not very friendly is the wrong way of describing what she
was. She had never been very friendly. It was just that now she had to see
me all the time and it got on her nerves, a little.

As for me, I put it all out of my mind like a bad dream and concentrated
on waiting for my letter. The mail came every day except Sunday, between
one-thirty and two in the afternoon, a good time for me because Mrs. Peebles
was always having her nap. I would get the kitchen all cleaned and then go up
to the mailbox and sit in the grass, waiting. I was perfectly happy, waiting, I
forgot all about Alice Kelling and her misery and awful talk and Mrs. Peebles
and her chilliness and the embarrassment of whether she had told Dr. Peebles
and the face of Loretta Bird, getting her fill of other people's troubles. I was
always smiling when the mailman got there, and continued smiling even
after he gave me the mail and I saw today wasn't the day. The mailman was
a Carmichael. I knew by his face because there are a lot of Carmichaels living
out by us and so many of them have a sort of sticking-out top lip. So I asked
his name (he was a young man, shy, but good-humored, anybody could ask
him anything) and then I said, "I knew by your face!" He was pleased by that
and always glad to see me and got a little less shy. "You've got the smile I've
been waiting on all day!" he used to holler out the car window.

It never crossed my mind for a long time a letter might not come. I
believed in it coming just like I believed the sun would rise in the morning.
I just put off my hope from day to day, and there was the goldenrod out
around the mailbox and the children gone back to school, and the leaves
turning, and I was wearing a sweater when I went to wait. One day walking back with the hydro bill stuck in my hand, that was all, looking across
at the fairgrounds with the full-blown milkweed and dark teasels, so much

like fall, it just struck me: *No letter was ever going to come.* It was an impossible idea to get used to. No, not impossible. If I thought about Chris's face when he said he was going to write to me, it was impossible, but if I forgot that and thought about the actual tin mailbox, empty, it was plain and true. I kept on going to meet the mail, but my heart was heavy now like a lump of lead. I only smiled because I thought of the mailman counting on it, and he didn't have an easy life, with the winter driving ahead.

Till it came to me one day there were women doing this with their lives, all over. There were women just waiting and waiting by mailboxes for one letter or another. I imagined me making this journey day after day and year after year, and my hair starting to go gray, and I thought, I was never made to go on like that. So I stopped meeting the mail. If there were women all through life waiting, and women busy and not waiting, I knew which I had to be. Even though there might be things the second kind of women have to pass up and never know about, it still is better.

I was surprised when the mailman phoned the Peebleses' place in the evening and asked for me. He said he missed me. He asked if I would like to go to Goderich, where some well-known movie was on, I forget now what. So I said yes, and I went out with him for two years and he asked me to marry him, and we were engaged a year more while I got my things together, and then we did marry. He always tells the children the story of how I went after him by sitting by the mailbox every day, and naturally I laugh and let him, because I like for people to think what pleases them and makes them happy.

QUESTIONS

1. Describe the plot structure in the story. How is the arrangement of the plot elements effective? At which points were your expectations as a reader overturned?
2. How does the story generate suspense? Which developments of the plot help to increase the suspense?
3. How do minor characters like Loretta Bird and Mrs. Peebles help advance the plot? What else do they add to the story?
4. Is Edie a sympathetic character? How does her status as "the hired girl" affect the way you respond to her as a reader?
5. Evaluate Chris Watters as a potential husband for Edie. Does her evaluation of him differ from the reader's?
6. The title "How I Met My Husband" suggests a reminiscence told from a much later, more mature vantage point. Can you detect the voice of an older, wiser Edie who is distinct from the young girl working for Dr. and Mrs. Peebles?
7. Discuss the role of Alice Kelling in advancing the plot and in the story as a whole. Could she be described as the antagonist? Why or why not?
8. Discuss the effectiveness of the surprise ending. How does Carmichael differ from Chris Watters? Can it be argued that the surprise ending is also inevitable and appropriate?

KAZUO ISHIGURO

A Family Supper

Fugu is a fish caught off the Pacific shores of Japan. The fish has held a special significance for me ever since my mother died through eating one. The poison resides in the sexual glands of the fish, inside two fragile bags. When preparing the fish, these bags must be removed with caution, for any clumsiness will result in the poison leaking into the veins. Regrettably, it is not easy to tell whether or not this operation has been carried out successfully. The proof is, as it were, in the eating.

Fugu poisoning is hideously painful and almost always fatal. If the fish has been eaten during the evening, the victim is usually overtaken by pain during his sleep. He rolls about in agony for a few hours and is dead by morning. The fish became extremely popular in Japan after the war. Until stricter regulations were imposed, it was all the rage to perform the hazardous gutting operation in one's own kitchen, then to invite neighbors and friends round for the feast.

At the time of my mother's death, I was living in California. My relationship with my parents had become somewhat strained around that period, and consequently I did not learn of the circumstances surrounding her death until I returned to Tokyo two years later. Apparently, my mother had always refused to eat fugu, but on this particular occasion she had made an exception, having been invited by an old schoolfriend whom she was anxious not to offend. It was my father who supplied me with the details as we drove from the airport to his home in the Kamakura district. When we finally arrived, it was nearing the end of a sunny autumn day.

"Did you eat on the plane?" my father asked. We were sitting on the tatami floor of his tea-room.

"They gave me a light snack."

"You must be hungry. We'll eat as soon as Kikuko arrives." 5

My father was a formidable-looking man with a large stony jaw and furious black eyebrows. I think now in retrospect that he much resembled Chou En-lai,° although he would not have cherished such a comparison, being particularly proud of the pure samurai blood that ran in the family. His general presence was not one which encouraged relaxed conversation; neither were things helped much by his odd way of stating each remark as

A FAMILY SUPPER   First published in 1982. Kazuo Ishiguro (b. 1954) was born in Japan but has lived most of his life in England. His novels include the Booker Prize-winning *The Remains of the Day* (1989) and *The Unconsoled* (1995).

Chou En-lai: Chou En-lai (1898–1976), the first Premier of the People's Republic of China

if it were the concluding one. In fact, as I sat opposite him that afternoon, a boyhood memory came back to me of the time he had struck me several times around the head for "chattering like an old woman." Inevitably, our conversation since my arrival at the airport had been punctuated by long pauses.

"I'm sorry to hear about the firm," I said when neither of us had spoken for some time. He nodded gravely.

"In fact the story didn't end there," he said. "After the firm's collapse, Watanabe killed himself. He didn't wish to live with the disgrace."

10 "I see."

"We were partners for seventeen years. A man of principle and honor. I respected him very much."

"Will you go into business again?" I said.

"I am—in retirement. I'm too old to involve myself in new ventures now. Business these days has become so different. Dealing with foreigners. Doing things their way. I don't understand how we've come to this. Neither did Watanabe." He sighed. "A fine man. A man of principle."

The tea-room looked out over the garden. From where I sat I could make out the ancient well which as a child I had believed haunted. It was just visible now through the thick foliage. The sun had sunk low and much of the garden had fallen into shadow.

15 "I'm glad in any case that you've decided to come back," my father said. "More than a short visit, I hope."

"I'm not sure what my plans will be."

"I for one am prepared to forget the past. Your mother too was always ready to welcome you back—upset as she was by your behavior."

"I appreciate your sympathy. As I say, I'm not sure what my plans are."

"I've come to believe now that there were no evil intentions in your mind," my father continued. "You were swayed by certain—influences. Like so many others."

20 "Perhaps we should forget it, as you suggest."

"As you will. More tea?"

Just then a girl's voice came echoing through the house.

"At last." My father rose to his feet. "Kikuko has arrived."

Despite our difference in years, my sister and I had always been close. Seeing me again seemed to make her excessively excited and for a while she did nothing but giggle nervously. But she calmed down somewhat when my father started to question her about Osaka and her university. She answered him with short formal replies. She in turn asked me a few questions, but she seemed inhibited by the fear that her questions might lead to awkward topics. After a while, the conversation had become even sparser than prior to Kikuko's arrival. Then my father stood up, saying:

"I must attend to the supper. Please excuse me for being burdened down by such matters. Kikuko will look after you."

My sister relaxed quite visibly once he had left the room. Within a few 25 minutes, she was chatting freely about her friends in Osaka and about her classes at university. Then quite suddenly she decided we should walk in the garden and went striding out onto the veranda. We put on some straw sandals that had been left along the veranda rail and stepped out into the garden. The daylight had almost gone.

"I've been dying for a smoke for the last half-hour," she said, lighting a cigarette.

"Then why didn't you smoke?"

She made a furtive gesture back toward the house, then grinned mischievously.

"Oh I see," I said.

"Guess what? I've got a boyfriend now." 30

"Oh yes?"

"Except I'm wondering what to do. I haven't made up my mind yet."

"Quite understandable."

"You see, he's making plans to go to America. He wants me to go with him as soon as I finish studying."

"I see. And you want to go to America?" 35

"If we go, we're going to hitch-hike." Kikuko waved a thumb in front of my face. "People say it's dangerous, but I've done it in Osaka and it's fine."

"I see. So what is it you're unsure about?"

We were following a narrow path that wound through the shrubs and finished by the old well. As we walked, Kikuko persisted in taking unnecessarily theatrical puffs on her cigarette.

"Well. I've got lots of friends now in Osaka. I like it there. I'm not sure I want to leave them all behind just yet. And Suichi—I like him, but I'm not sure I want to spend so much time with him. Do you understand?"

"Oh perfectly." 40

She grinned again, then skipped on ahead of me until she had reached the well. "Do you remember," she said, as I came walking up to her, "how you used to say this well was haunted?"

"Yes, I remember."

We both peered over the side.

"Mother always told me it was the old woman from the vegetable store you'd seen that night," she said. "But I never believed her and never came out here alone."

"Mother used to tell me that too. She even told me once the old 45 woman had confessed to being the ghost. Apparently she'd been taking a short cut through our garden. I imagine she had some trouble clambering over these walls."

Kikuko gave a giggle. She then turned her back to the well, casting her gaze about the garden.

"Mother never really blamed you, you know," she said, in a new voice. I remained silent. "She always used to say to me how it was their fault, hers and Father's, for not bringing you up correctly. She used to tell me how much more careful they'd been with me, and that's why I was so good." She looked up and the mischievous grin had returned to her face. "Poor Mother," she said.

"Yes. Poor Mother."

"Are you going back to California?"

50   "I don't know. I'll have to see."

"What happened to—to her? To Vicki?"

"That's all finished with," I said. "There's nothing much left for me now in California."

"Do you think I ought to go there?"

"Why not? I don't know. You'll probably like it." I glanced toward the house. "Perhaps we'd better go in soon. Father might need a hand with the supper."

55   But my sister was once more peering down into the well. "I can't see any ghosts," she said. Her voice echoed a little.

"Is Father very upset about his firm collapsing?"

"Don't know. You can never tell with Father." Then suddenly she straightened up and turned to me. "Did he tell you about old Watanabe? What he did?"

"I heard he committed suicide."

"Well, that wasn't all. He took his whole family with him. His wife and his two little girls."

60   "Oh yes?"

"Those two beautiful little girls. He turned on the gas while they were all asleep. Then he cut his stomach with a meat knife."

"Yes, Father was just telling me how Watanabe was a man of principle."

"Sick." My sister turned back to the well.

"Careful. You'll fall right in."

65   "I can't see any ghost," she said. "You were lying to me all that time."

"But I never said it lived down the well."

"Where is it, then?"

We both looked around at the trees and shrubs. The light in the garden had grown very dim. Eventually I pointed to a small clearing some ten yards away.

70   "Just there I saw it. Just there."

We stared at the spot.

"What did it look like?"

"I couldn't see very well. It was dark."

"But you must have seen something."

"It was an old woman. She was just standing there, watching me."

We kept staring at the spot as if mesmerized.   75

"She was wearing a white kimono," I said. "Some of her hair had come undone. It was blowing around a little."

Kikuko pushed her elbow against my arm. "Oh be quiet. You're trying to frighten me all over again." She trod on the remains of her cigarette, then for a brief moment stood regarding it with a perplexed expression. She kicked some pine needles over it, then once more displayed her grin. "Let's see if supper's ready," she said.

We found my father in the kitchen. He gave us a quick glance, then carried on with what he was doing.

"Father's become quite a chef since he's had to manage on his own," Kikuko said with a laugh. He turned and looked at my sister coldly.

"Hardly a skill I'm proud of," he said. "Kikuko, come here and help."   80

For some moments my sister did not move. Then she stepped forward and took an apron hanging from a drawer.

"Just these vegetables need cooking now," he said to her. "The rest just needs watching." Then he looked up and regarded me strangely for some seconds. "I expect you want to look around the house," he said eventually. He put down the chopsticks he had been holding. "It's a long time since you've seen it."

As we left the kitchen I glanced back toward Kikuko, but her back was turned.

"She's a good girl," my father said quietly.

I followed my father from room to room. I had forgotten how large the   85
house was. A panel would slide open and another room would appear. But the rooms were all startlingly empty. In one of the rooms the lights did not come on, and we stared at the stark walls and tatami in the pale light that came from the windows.

"This house is too large for a man to live in alone," my father said. "I don't have much use for most of these rooms now."

But eventually my father opened the door to a room packed full of books and papers. There were flowers in vases and pictures on the walls. Then I noticed something on a low table in the corner of the room. I came nearer and saw it was a plastic model of a battleship, the kind constructed by children. It had been placed on some newspaper; scattered around it were assorted pieces of grey plastic.

My father gave a laugh. He came up to the table and picked up the model.

"Since the firm folded," he said, "I have a little more time on my hands." He laughed again, rather strangely. For a moment his face looked almost gentle. "A little more time."

90   "That seems odd," I said. "You were always so busy."

"Too busy perhaps." He looked at me with a small smile. "Perhaps I should have been a more attentive father."

I laughed. He went on contemplating his battleship. Then he looked up. "I hadn't meant to tell you this, but perhaps it's best that I do. It's my belief that your mother's death was no accident. She had many worries. And some disappointments."

We both gazed at the plastic battleship.

"Surely," I said eventually, "my mother didn't expect me to live here forever."

95   "Obviously you don't see. You don't see how it is for some parents. Not only must they lose their children, they must lose them to things they don't understand." He spun the battleship in his fingers. "These little gunboats here could have been better glued, don't you think?"

"Perhaps. I think it looks fine."

"During the war I spent some time on a ship rather like this. But my ambition was always the air force. I figured it like this. If your ship was struck by the enemy, all you could do was struggle in the water hoping for a lifeline. But in an aeroplane—well—there was always the final weapon." He put the model back onto the table. "I don't suppose you believe in war."

"Not particularly."

He cast an eye around the room. "Supper should be ready by now," he said. "You must be hungry."

100   Supper was waiting in a dimly lit room next to the kitchen. The only source of light was a big lantern that hung over the table, casting the rest of the room into shadow. We bowed to each other before starting the meal.

There was little conversation. When I made some polite comment about the food, Kikuko giggled a little. Her earlier nervousness seemed to have returned to her. My father did not speak for several minutes. Finally he said:

"It must feel strange for you, being back in Japan."

"Yes, it is a little strange."

"Already, perhaps, you regret leaving America."

105   "A little. Not so much. I didn't leave behind much. Just some empty rooms."

"I see."

I glanced across the table. My father's face looked stony and forbidding in the half-light. We ate on in silence.

Then my eye caught something at the back of the room. At first I continued eating, then my hands became still. The others noticed and looked at me. I went on gazing into the darkness past my father's shoulder.

"Who is that? In that photograph there?"

"Which photograph?" My father turned slightly, trying to follow my gaze. 110
"The lowest one. The old woman in the white kimono."

My father put down his chopsticks. He looked first at the photograph, then at me.

"Your mother." His voice had become very hard. "Can't you recognize your own mother?"

"My mother. You see, it's dark. I can't see it very well."

No one spoke for a few seconds, then Kikuko rose to her feet. She took 115
the photograph down from the wall, came back to the table and gave it to me.

"She looks a lot older," I said.

"It was taken shortly before her death," said my father.

"It was the dark. I couldn't see very well."

I looked up and noticed my father holding out a hand. I gave him the photograph. He looked at it intently, then held it toward Kikuko. Obediently, my sister rose to her feet once more and returned the picture to the wall.

There was a large pot left unopened at the center of the table. When 120
Kikuko had seated herself again, my father reached forward and lifted the lid. A cloud of steam rose up and curled toward the lantern. He pushed the pot a little toward me.

"You must be hungry," he said. One side of his face had fallen into shadow.

"Thank you." I reached forward with my chopsticks. The steam was almost scalding. "What is it?"

"Fish."

"It smells very good."

In amidst soup were strips of fish that had curled almost into balls. I 125
picked one out and brought it to my bowl.

"Help yourself. There's plenty."

"Thank you." I took a little more, then pushed the pot toward my father. I watched him take several pieces to his bowl. Then we both watched as Kikuko served herself.

My father bowed slightly. "You must be hungry," he said again. He took some fish to his mouth and started to eat. Then I too chose a piece and put it in my mouth. It felt soft, quite fleshy against my tongue.

"Very good," I said. "What is it?" 130
"Just fish."

"It's very good."

The three of us ate on in silence. Several minutes went by.

"Some more?"

"Is there enough?"

"There's plenty for all of us." My father lifted the lid and once more 135
steam rose up. We all reached forward and helped ourselves.

"Here," I said to my father, "you have this last piece."

"Thank you."

When we had finished the meal, my father stretched out his arms and yawned with an air of satisfaction. "Kikuko," he said. "Prepare a pot of tea, please."

My sister looked at him, then left the room without comment. My father stood up.

140

"Let's retire to the other room. It's rather warm in here."

I got to my feet and followed him into the tea-room. The large sliding windows had been left open, bringing in a breeze from the garden. For a while we sat in silence.

"Father," I said, finally.

"Yes?"

"Kikuko tells me Watanabe-San took his whole family with him."

145

My father lowered his eyes and nodded. For some moments he seemed deep in thought. "Watanabe was very devoted to his work," he said at last. "The collapse of the firm was a great blow to him. I fear it must have weakened his judgment."

"You think what he did—it was a mistake?"

"Why, of course. Do you see it otherwise?"

"No, no. Of course not."

"There are other things besides work."

150

"Yes."

We fell silent again. The sound of locusts came in from the garden. I looked out into the darkness. The well was no longer visible.

"What do you think you will do now?" my father asked. "Will you stay in Japan for a while?"

"To be honest, I hadn't thought that far ahead."

"If you wish to stay here, I mean here in this house, you would be very welcome. That is, if you don't mind living with an old man."

155

"Thank you. I'll have to think about it."

I gazed out once more into the darkness.

"But of course," said my father, "this house is so dreary now. You'll no doubt return to America before long."

"Perhaps. I don't know yet."

"No doubt you will."

160

For some time my father seemed to be studying the back of his hands. Then he looked up and sighed.

"Kikuko is due to complete her studies next spring," he said. "Perhaps she will want to come home then. She's a good girl."

"Perhaps she will."

"Things will improve then."

"Yes, I'm sure they will."

165

We fell silent once more, waiting for Kikuko to bring the tea.

QUESTIONS

1. The first two paragraphs describe the poisonous fish, fugu, while the characters are not introduced until paragraph 3. Why is this method employed? How does it set the plot into motion?
2. Why was the son chosen as the story's narrator? What is the significance of his having lived in California? What are the differences in values between him and his father?
3. Discuss the role of the narrator's sister, Kikuko. Are her values aligned with his or with those of her parents?
4. How does Mr. Watanabe's suicide relate to the plot? Why did he kill his entire family instead of only himself?
5. Discuss the story's abrupt ending. How is this ending appropriate to the story?

SUGGESTIONS FOR WRITING

1. In Wolff's "Hunters in the Snow," the plot helps to illuminate the struggle for power among the three principal characters. Write an essay in which you show how this struggle for power is elucidated by some of the elements of fiction presented in Chapter Two—such as suspense, mystery, surprise, and conflict.
2. Write an essay on the ending of one of the following stories, determining whether it is happy, unhappy, or indeterminate and how the type of ending helps define the story as an example of commercial or literary fiction:
   a. Wolff, "Hunters in the Snow" (page 79)
   b. Malamud, "The Magic Barrel" (page 612)
   c. Chopin, "The Story of an Hour" (page 536)
   d. Jackson, "The Lottery" (page 260)
3. Write an essay defining the type(s) of conflict in one of these stories:
   a. Malamud, "The Magic Barrel" (page 612).
   b. Hurston, "Spunk" (page 564)
   c. Hemingway, "Hills Like White Elephants" (page 276).
   d. Fitzgerald, "Babylon Revisited" (page 200).

PRACTICE AP WRITING PROMPTS ▮▮▮▮▮▮▮

Graham Greene, "The Destructors" (pp. 105–117)

40-minute prompt: Read Section Two of "The Destructors," paragraph 83 (p. 110) through paragraph 102 (p. 112). In a well-written essay, show how literary elements such as dialogue, selective detail, and irony contribute to the contrasting characterizations of the three main "destructors."

CHAPTER THREE

Characterization

The preceding chapter considered plot apart from characterization, as if the two were separable. Actually, along with the other elements of fiction discussed in later chapters, plot and characterization work together in any good story. In commercial fiction, plot is usually more important than in-depth characterization, while literary writers are usually more concerned with complex characters than with the mechanics of plot. Many literary fiction writers, in fact, consider characterization to be the most important element of their art.

Analyzing **characterization** is more difficult than describing plot, for human character is infinitely complex, variable, and ambiguous. Anyone can summarize what a person in a story has done, but a writer needs considerable skill and insight into human beings to describe convincingly *who* a person is. Even the most complicated plot in a detective story puts far less strain on our understanding than does human nature. This is why commercial fiction may feature an elaborate plot but offer characters who are simple and two-dimensional, even stereotypical. In such fiction the characters must be easily identifiable and clearly labeled as good or bad; the commercial author's aim is to create characters who can carry the plot forward, not to explore human psychology and motivation.

The main character in a commercial work must also be someone attractive or sympathetic. If the protagonist is male, he need not be perfect, but usually he must be fundamentally decent—honest, good-hearted, and preferably good-looking. He may also have larger-than-life qualities, showing himself to be daring, dashing, or gallant. He may defy laws made for "ordinary" people, but this makes him even more likable because he breaks the rules for a good reason: to catch a criminal, or to prevent a disaster. In commercial fiction, the reader enjoys identifying with such a protagonist, vicariously sharing his adventures, escapes, and triumphs. If the protagonist has vices, they must be the kind a typical reader would not mind or would enjoy having. For instance, the main character in successful commercial fiction may be sexually promiscuous—James Bond is a good example—and thus allow readers to indulge imaginatively in pleasures they might not allow themselves in real life.

Literary fiction does not necessarily renounce the attractive character. Jane Eyre, Huckleberry Finn, and Holden Caulfield are literary characters beloved by millions of readers; both the narrator in "A Family Supper" and Edie in "How I Met My Husband" are likable characters as well. But literary protagonists are less easily labeled and pigeonholed than their counterparts in commercial fiction. Sometimes they may be wholly unsympathetic, even despicable. But because human nature is not often entirely bad or perfectly good, literary fiction deals usually with characters who are composed of both good and evil impulses, three-dimensional human beings who live in our memory as "real" people long after we have stopped reading.

Such fiction offers an exciting opportunity to observe human nature in all its complexity and multiplicity. It enables us to know people, to understand them, and to develop compassion for them in a way we might not do without reading serious fiction. In some respects, we can know fictional characters even better than we know real people in our lives. For one thing, we observe fictional people in situations that are always significant and that serve to illuminate their characters in a way that our daily, routine exposure to real people seldom does. We can also view a character's inner life in a way that's impossible in ordinary life. Authors can show us, if they wish, exactly what is happening in a character's mind and emotions. In real life, of course, we can only guess at another person's thoughts and feelings from external behavior, which may be designed to conceal the person's inner life. Because of the opportunity literary fiction affords us of knowing its characters so thoroughly, it also enables us to understand the motives and behavior of people in real life.

Authors present their characters either directly or indirectly. In **direct presentation** they tell us straight out, by exposition or analysis, what the characters are like, or they have another character in the story describe them. In **indirect presentation** the author *shows* us the characters through their actions; we determine what they are like by what they say or do. Graham Greene uses direct presentation when he tells us about Blackie: "He was just, he had no jealousy." He uses indirect presentation when he shows Blackie allowing the gang to vote on Trevor's project, accepting the end of his leadership fairly calmly, taking orders from Trevor without resentment, burning banknotes with Trevor, and racing him home. In this story, of course, the word "just" has a slight ironic twist—it applies only to behavior within the gang—and Greene presents this indirectly. Alice Munro relies on indirect presentation to show that Chris Watters is a charming but irresponsible barnstormer; Edie never directly criticizes him, but we feel her disillusionment as she waits day after day for a letter that will never come.

Sometimes the method of direct presentation has the advantages of being clear and economical, but good writers use it sparingly. In order to involve the reader in a character, the author must *show* the character in action; the axiom "show, don't tell" is therefore one of the basics of fiction writing. If characters are merely described, then the story will read more like an essay. The direct method usually has little emotional impact unless it is bolstered by the indirect. It will give us only the explanation of a character, not the impression of a living, breathing human being. In almost all good fiction, therefore, the characters are **dramatized**. They are shown speaking and behaving, as in a stage play. If we are really to believe in the selfishness of a character, we must see the character acting selfishly. Instead of telling us that Frank in "Hunters in the Snow" is a selfish, self-deluding man, Wolff gives us dramatic scenes in which Frank exhibits his selfishness and self-delusions through his dialogue and actions. Most literary writers rely on indirect presentation and may even use it exclusively.

Good fiction follows three other principles of characterization. First, the characters are consistent in their behavior: they do not behave one way on one occasion and a different way on another unless there is a clear and sufficient reason for the change. Second, the characters' words and actions spring from **motivations** the reader can understand and believe; if we can't understand why they behave in a certain way immediately, that understanding comes by the end of the story. Finally, the characters must be plausible or lifelike. They cannot be perfectly virtuous or monsters of evil; nor can they have some impossible combination of contradictory traits. In short, the author must convince the reader that the character might well have existed so that, at least while we're reading, we have the illusion that the person is real and forget we are reading fiction at all.

In his book *Aspects of the Novel* (1927), the British novelist E. M. Forster introduced terms that have become standard in discussing types of characters; he wrote that a literary character is either "flat" or "round." **Flat characters** usually have only one or two predominant traits; they can be summed up in a sentence or two. Richard Connell's character Ivan, for instance, is a fearsome thug, and that is all we need to know about him. By contrast, **round characters** are complex and many-sided; they have the three-dimensional quality of real people. Huck Finn, for example, because Mark Twain imagined and dramatized him so successfully as an individual, lives vigorously in the imagination of millions of readers. This is not to say that flat characters cannot be memorable. Though essentially two-dimensional, they too may be made memorable in the hands of an expert author who creates some vivid detail of their appearance, gestures, or speech. Ebenezer Scrooge, in Dickens's *A Christmas Carol*, could be defined as a stereotype of the miserly misanthrope; but his "Bah! Humbug!" has helped make him an immortal character.

Whether round or flat, all characters in good fiction are dramatized to whatever extent needed to make them convincing and to fulfill their roles in the story. Most short stories, of course, will have room for only one or two round characters. Minor characters must necessarily remain flat. There are some literary stories, of course, where the exploration of individual character is not the main focus of interest—Shirley Jackson's "The Lottery" (page 260) is an example—and in such stories none of the characters may be developed fully. Such instances, however, are relatively rare.

A special kind of flat character is the **stock character**. These are stereotyped figures who have recurred so often in fiction that we recognize them at once: the strong, silent sheriff, the brilliant detective with eccentric habits, the mad scientist who performs fiendish experiments on living people, the glamorous international spy of mysterious background, the comic Englishman with a monocle, the cruel stepmother, and so forth. Commercial authors often rely on such stock characters precisely because they can be grasped quickly and easily by the reader. Such characters are like interchangeable parts that might be transferred from one story to another. When literary writers employ a conventional type, however, they usually add individualizing touches to help create a fresh and memorable character. Conan Doyle's Sherlock Holmes follows a stock pattern of the detective, but he remains more memorable than hundreds of other fictional detectives who have come and gone since he was created. Similarly, Wolff's character Tub in "Hunters in the Snow" embodies the stereotypes of the fat, comic buffoon; but certain details about him—his insecurity, his habit of hiding the food he eats so compulsively—help to make him distinctive.

Fictional characters may also be classified as either static or developing. The **static character** remains essentially the same person from the beginning of the story to the end. The **developing** (or **dynamic**) **character**, on the other hand, undergoes some distinct change of character, personality, or outlook. The change may be a large or a small one; it may be positive or negative; but it is something significant and basic, not some minor change of habit or opinion. The Irish writer James Joyce used a term that has become widely adopted today, noting that a character in a story often experiences an **epiphany**, which he termed a moment of spiritual insight into life or into the character's own circumstances. This epiphany or insight usually defines the moment of the developing character's change.

Edie in Munro's "How I Met My Husband" is a dynamic character, for she learns a painful lesson about romance and growing up that alters the entire course of her life. Many stories show a change in the protagonist as the result of some crucial situation in his or her life. This change is usually at the heart of the story, and defining and explaining the change will be the best way to arrive at its meaning. In commercial fiction, changes in character are likely to be relatively superficial, intended mainly to effect a happy ending. Readers of literary fiction, however, usually expect that a convincing change in a character meet three conditions: (1) it must be consistent with the individual's characterization as dramatized in the story; (2) it must be sufficiently motivated by the circumstances in which the character is placed; and (3) the story must offer sufficient time for the change to take place and still be believable. Essential changes in human character, after all, do not usually occur suddenly. For this reason, good fiction will not give us a confirmed criminal who miraculously reforms at the end of a story, or a lifelong racist who wakes up one day and decides to be tolerant and open-minded. If fiction is to be convincing, it must show us believable, dynamic, but often quiet changes or turning points in a character's life. When an author has carefully laid the groundwork earlier in the story, we believe in the character's change and experience the moment of epiphany as a possibly small but significant marker in the life of an individual human being.

Ultimately it is the quality of characterization by which a literary story stands or falls. Long after we have read even the greatest novels and short stories, we tend to remember not the incidents of plot but the unforgettable characters who made our reading such a rich, vibrant experience. Through the creation of character, an author can summon up a new personality, a new voice, and an entirely new and original way of seeing the world. Such characters come alive each time a reader takes up the story, renewing the miracle of the human imagination.

REVIEWING CHAPTER THREE

1. Describe the significance of characterization in literary fiction vs. commercial fiction.
2. Distinguish between direct and indirect presentation of character in fiction.
3. Review the terms "flat character," "round character," and "stock character."
4. Consider the difference between a static character and a dynamic character.
5. Explore the authors' use of characterization in the following stories.

ALICE WALKER

Everyday Use

for your grandmama

I will wait for her in the yard that Maggie and I made so clean and wavy yesterday afternoon. A yard like this is more comfortable than most people know. It is not just a yard. It is like an extended living room. When the hard clay is swept clean as a floor and the fine sand around the edges lined with tiny, irregular grooves, anyone can come and sit and look up into the elm tree and wait for the breezes that never come inside the house.

Maggie will be nervous until after her sister goes: she will stand hopelessly in corners, homely and ashamed of the burn scars down her arms and legs, eying her sister with a mixture of envy and awe. She thinks her sister has held life always in the palm of one hand, that "no" is a word the world never learned to say to her.

You've no doubt seen those TV shows where the child who has "made it" is confronted, as a surprise, by her own mother and father, tottering in weakly from backstage. (A pleasant surprise, of course: What would they do if parent and child came on the show only to curse out and insult each other?) On TV mother and child embrace and smile into each other's faces. Sometimes the mother and father weep, the child wraps them in her arms and leans across the table to tell how she would not have made it without their help. I have seen these programs.

Sometimes I dream a dream in which Dee and I are suddenly brought together on a TV program of this sort. Out of a dark and soft-seated limousine I am ushered into a bright room filled with many people. There I meet a smiling, gray, sporty man like Johnny Carson° who shakes my hand and tells me what a fine girl I have. Then we are on the stage and Dee is embracing me with tears in her eyes. She pins on my dress a large orchid, even though she had told me once that she thinks orchids are tacky flowers.

In real life I am a large, big-boned woman with rough, man-working 5 hands. In the winter I wear flannel nightgowns to bed and overalls during

---

EVERYDAY USE   First published in 1973. Alice Walker was born in Georgia in 1944, attended Spelman College for two years, earned her B.A. from Sarah Lawrence, and was active in the civil rights movement. She has taught and been writer-in-residence at various colleges including Jackson State, Tougaloo, Wellesley, the University of California at Berkeley, and Brandeis. The names adopted by two of the characters in the story reflect the practice among some members of the black community of rejecting names inherited from the period of slavery and selecting others more in keeping with their African heritage. The greetings used by Hakim and Wangero ("Asalamalakim" and "Wa-su-zo-Tean-o") are apparently adaptations of Arabic and African languages.

Johnny Carson: former host of *The Tonight Show* on NBC

the day. I can kill and clean a hog as mercilessly as a man. My fat keeps me hot in zero weather. I can work outside all day, breaking ice to get water for washing; I can eat pork liver cooked over the open fire minutes after it comes steaming from the hog. One winter I knocked a bull calf straight in the brain between the eyes with a sledge hammer and had the meat hung up to chill before nightfall. But of course all this does not show on television. I am the way my daughter would want me to be: a hundred pounds lighter, my skin like an uncooked barley pancake. My hair glistens in the hot bright lights. Johnny Carson has much to do to keep up with my quick and witty tongue.

But that is a mistake. I know even before I wake up. Who ever knew a Johnson with a quick tongue? Who can even imagine me looking a strange white man in the eye? It seems to me I have talked to them always with one foot raised in flight, with my head turned in whichever way is farthest from them. Dee, though. She would always look anyone in the eye. Hesitation was no part of her nature.

"How do I look, Mama?" Maggie says, showing just enough of her thin body enveloped in pink skirt and red blouse for me to know she's there, almost hidden by the door.

"Come out into the yard," I say.

Have you ever seen a lame animal, perhaps a dog run over by some careless person rich enough to own a car, sidle up to someone who is ignorant enough to be kind to him? That is the way my Maggie walks. She has been like this, chin on chest, eyes on ground, feet in shuffle, ever since the fire that burned the other house to the ground.

10   Dee is lighter than Maggie, with nicer hair and a fuller figure. She's a woman now, though sometimes I forget. How long ago was it that the other house burned? Ten, twelve years? Sometimes I can still hear the flames and feel Maggie's arms sticking to me, her hair smoking and her dress falling off her in little black papery flakes. Her eyes seemed stretched open, blazed open by the flames reflected in them. And Dee. I see her standing off under the sweet gum tree she used to dig gum out of; a look of concentration on her face as she watched the last dingy gray board of the house fall in toward the red-hot brick chimney. Why don't you do a dance around the ashes? I'd wanted to ask her. She had hated the house that much.

I used to think she hated Maggie, too. But that was before we raised the money, the church and me, to send her to Augusta to school. She used to read to us without pity; forcing words, lies, other folks' habits, whole lives upon us two, sitting trapped and ignorant underneath her voice. She washed us in a river of make-believe, burned us with a lot of knowledge we didn't necessarily need to know. Pressed us to her with the serious way she read, to shove us away at just the moment, like dimwits, we seemed about to understand.

Dee wanted nice things. A yellow organdy dress to wear to her graduation from high school; black pumps to match a green suit she'd made from an old suit somebody gave me. She was determined to stare down any disaster in her efforts. Her eyelids would not flicker for minutes at a time. Often I fought off the temptation to shake her. At sixteen she had a style of her own: and knew what style was.

I never had an education myself. After second grade the school was closed down. Don't ask me why: in 1927 colored asked fewer questions than they do now. Sometimes Maggie reads to me. She stumbles along good-naturedly but can't see well. She knows she is not bright. Like good looks and money, quickness passed her by. She will marry John Thomas (who has mossy teeth in an earnest face) and then I'll be free to sit here and I guess just sing church songs to myself. Although I never was a good singer. Never could carry a tune. I was always better at a man's job. I used to love to milk till I was hooked in the side in '49. Cows are soothing and slow and don't bother you, unless you try to milk them the wrong way.

I have deliberately turned my back on the house. It is three rooms, just like the one that burned, except the roof is tin; they don't make shingle roofs any more. There are no real windows, just some holes cut in the sides, like the portholes in a ship, but not round and not square, with rawhide holding the shutters up on the outside. This house is in a pasture, too, like the other one. No doubt when Dee sees it she will want to tear it down. She wrote me once that no matter where we "choose" to live, she will manage to come see us. But she will never bring her friends. Maggie and I thought about this and Maggie asked me, "Mama, when did Dee ever *have* any friends?"

She had a few. Furtive boys in pink shirts hanging about on washday 15 after school. Nervous girls who never laughed. Impressed with her, they worshipped the well-turned phrase, the cute shape, the scalding humor that erupted like bubbles in lye. She read to them.

When she was courting Jimmy T she didn't have much time to pay to us, but turned all her faultfinding power on him. He *flew* to marry a cheap city girl from a family of ignorant flashy people. She hardly had time to recompose herself.

When she comes I will meet—but there they are!

Maggie attempts to make a dash for the house, in her shuffling way, but I stay her with my hand. "Come back here," I say. And she stops and tries to dig a well in the sand with her toe.

It is hard to see them clearly through the strong sun. But even the first glimpse of leg out of the car tells me it is Dee. Her feet were always neat-looking, as if God himself had shaped them with a certain style. From the other side of the car comes a short, stocky man. Hair is all over his head a foot long and hanging from his chin like a kinky mule tail. I hear Maggie suck in her breath. "Uhnnnh," is what it sounds like. Like when you see the wriggling end of a snake just in front of your foot on the road. "Uhnnnh."

20 Dee next. A dress down to the ground, in this hot weather. A dress so loud it hurts my eyes. There are yellows and oranges enough to throw back the light of the sun. I feel my whole face warming from the heat waves it throws out. Earrings gold, too, and hanging down to her shoulders. Bracelets dangling and making noises when she moves her arm up to shake the folds of the dress out of her armpits. The dress is loose and flows, and as she walks closer, I like it. I hear Maggie go "Uhnnnh" again. It is her sister's hair. It stands straight up like the wool on a sheep. It is black as night and around the edges are two long pigtails that rope about like small lizards disappearing behind her ears.

"Wa-su-zo-Tean-o!" she says, coming on in that gliding way the dress makes her move. The short stocky fellow with the hair to his navel is all grinning and he follows up with "Asalamalakim, my mother and sister!" He moves to hug Maggie but she falls back, right up against the back of my chair. I feel her trembling there and when I look up I see the perspiration falling off her chin.

"Don't get up," says Dee. Since I am stout it takes something of a push. You can see me trying to move a second or two before I make it. She turns, showing white heels through her sandals, and goes back to the car. Out she peeks next with a Polaroid. She stoops down quickly and lines up picture after picture of me sitting there in front of the house with Maggie cowering behind me. She never takes a shot without making sure the house is included. When a cow comes nibbling around the edge of the yard she snaps it and me and Maggie and the house. Then she puts the Polaroid in the back seat of the car, and comes up and kisses me on the forehead.

Meanwhile Asalamalakim is going through motions with Maggie's hand. Maggie's hand is as limp as a fish, and probably as cold, despite the sweat, and she keeps trying to pull it back. It looks like Asalamalakim wants to shake hands but wants to do it fancy. Or maybe he don't know how people shake hands. Anyhow, he soon gives up on Maggie.

"Well," I say. "Dee."

25 "No, Mama," she says. "Not 'Dee,' Wangero Leewanika Kemanjo!"

"What happened to 'Dee'?" I wanted to know.

"She's dead," Wangero said. "I couldn't bear it any longer, being named after the people who oppress me."

"You know as well as me you was named after your aunt Dicie," I said. Dicie is my sister. She named Dee. We called her "Big Dee" after Dee was born.

"But who was she named after?" asked Wangero.

"I guess after Grandma Dee," I said.   30

"And who was she named after?" asked Wangero.

"Her mother," I said, and saw Wangero was getting tired. "That's about as far back as I can trace it," I said. Though, in fact, I probably could have carried it back beyond the Civil War through the branches.

"Well," said Asalamalakim, "there you are."

"Uhnnnh," I heard Maggie say.

"There I was not," I said, "before 'Dicie' cropped up in our family, so   35
why should I try to trace it that far back?"

He just stood there grinning, looking down on me like somebody inspecting a Model A car. Every once in a while he and Wangero sent eye signals over my head.

"How do you pronounce this name?" I asked.

"You don't have to call me by it if you don't want to," said Wangero.

"Why shouldn't I?" I asked. "If that's what you want us to call you, we'll call you."

"I know it might sound awkward at first," said Wangero.   40

"I'll get used to it," I said. "Ream it out again."

Well, soon we got the name out of the way. Asalamalakim had a name twice as long and three times as hard. After I tripped over it two or three times he told me to just call him Hakim-a-barber. I wanted to ask him was he a barber, but I didn't really think he was, so I didn't ask.

"You must belong to those beef-cattle peoples down the road," I said. They said "Asalamalakim" when they met you, too, but they didn't shake hands. Always too busy: feeding the cattle, fixing the fences, putting up salt-lick shelters, throwing down hay. When the white folks poisoned some of the herd the men stayed up all night with rifles in their hands. I walked a mile and a half just to see the sight.

Hakim-a-barber said, "I accept some of their doctrines, but farming and raising cattle is not my style." (They didn't tell me, and I didn't ask, whether Wangero [Dee] had really gone and married him.)

We sat down to eat and right away he said he didn't eat collards and   45
pork was unclean. Wangero, though, went on through the chitlins and corn bread, the greens and everything else. She talked a blue streak over the sweet potatoes. Everything delighted her. Even the fact that we still used the benches her daddy made for the table when we couldn't afford to buy chairs.

"Oh, Mama!" she cried. Then turned to Hakim-a-barber. "I never knew how lovely these benches are. You can feel the rump prints," she said, running her hands underneath her and along the bench. Then she gave a sigh and her hand closed over Grandma Dee's butter dish. "That's it!" she said. "I knew there was something I wanted to ask you if I could have." She jumped up from the table and went over in the corner where the churn stood, the milk in it clabber by now. She looked at the churn and looked at it.

"This churn top is what I need," she said. "Didn't Uncle Buddy whittle it out of a tree you all used to have?"

"Yes," I said.

"Uh huh," she said happily. "And I want the dasher, too."

50   "Uncle Buddy whittle that, too?" asked the barber.

Dee (Wangero) looked up at me.

"Aunt Dee's first husband whittled the dash," said Maggie so low you almost couldn't hear her. "His name was Henry, but they called him Stash."

"Maggie's brain is like an elephant's," Wangero said, laughing. "I can use the churn top as a centerpiece for the alcove table," she said, sliding a plate over the churn, "and I'll think of something artistic to do with the dasher."

When she finished wrapping the dasher the handle stuck out. I took it for a moment in my hands. You didn't even have to look close to see where hands pushing the dasher up and down to make butter had left a kind of sink in the wood. In fact, there were a lot of small sinks; you could see where thumbs and fingers had sunk into the wood. It was beautiful light yellow wood, from a tree that grew in the yard where Big Dee and Stash had lived.

55   After dinner Dee (Wangero) went to the trunk at the foot of my bed and started rifling through it. Maggie hung back in the kitchen over the dishpan. Out came Wangero with two quilts. They had been pieced by Grandma Dee and then Big Dee and me had hung them on the quilt frames on the front porch and quilted them. One was in the Lone Star pattern. The other was Walk Around the Mountain. In both of them were scraps of dresses Grandma Dee had worn fifty and more years ago. Bits and pieces of Grandpa Jarrell's Paisley shirts. And one teeny faded blue piece, about the size of a penny matchbox, that was from Great Grandpa Ezra's uniform that he wore in the Civil War.

"Mama," Wangero said sweet as a bird. "Can I have these old quilts?"

I heard something fall in the kitchen, and a minute later the kitchen door slammed.

"Why don't you take one or two of the others?" I asked. "These old things was just done by me and Big Dee from some tops your grandma pieced before she died."

"No," said Wangero. "I don't want those. They are stitched around the borders by machine."

60   "That'll make them last better," I said.

"That's not the point," said Wangero. "These are all pieces of dresses Grandma used to wear. She did all this stitching by hand. Imagine!" She held the quilts securely in her arms, stroking them.

"Some of the pieces, like those lavender ones, come from old clothes her mother handed down to her," I said, moving up to touch the quilts. Dee (Wangero) moved back just enough so that I couldn't reach the quilts. They already belonged to her.

"Imagine!" she breathed again, clutching them closely to her bosom.

"The truth is," I said, "I promised to give them quilts to Maggie, for when she marries John Thomas."

She gasped like a bee had stung her.   65

"Maggie can't appreciate these quilts!" she said. "She'd probably be backward enough to put them to everyday use."

"I reckon she would," I said. "God knows I been saving 'em for long enough with nobody using 'em. I hope she will!" I didn't want to bring up how I had offered Dee (Wangero) a quilt when she went away to college. Then she had told me they were old-fashioned, out of style.

"But they're *priceless!*" she was saying now, furiously; for she has a temper. "Maggie would put them on the bed and in five years they'd be in rags. Less than that!"

"She can always make some more," I said. "Maggie knows how to quilt."

Dee (Wangero) looked at me with hatred. "You just will not under-   70
stand. The point is these quilts, *these* quilts!"

"Well," I said, stumped. "What would *you* do with them?"

"Hang them," she said. As if that was the only thing you *could* do with quilts.

Maggie by now was standing in the door. I could almost hear the sound her feet made as they scraped over each other.

"She can have them, Mama," she said, like somebody used to never winning anything, or having anything reserved for her. "I can 'member Grandma Dee without the quilts."

I looked at her hard. She had filled her bottom lip with checkerberry   75
snuff and it gave her face a kind of dopey, hangdog look. It was Grandma Dee and Big Dee who taught her how to quilt herself. She stood there with her scarred hands hidden in the folds of her skirt. She looked at her sister with something like fear but she wasn't mad at her. This was Maggie's portion. This was the way she knew God to work.

When I looked at her like that something hit me in the top of my head and ran down to the soles of my feet. Just like when I'm in church and the spirit of God touches me and I get happy and shout. I did something I never had done before: hugged Maggie to me, then dragged her on into the room, snatched the quilts out of Miss Wangero's hands and dumped them into Maggie's lap. Maggie just sat there on my bed with her mouth open.

"Take one or two of the others," I said to Dee.

But she turned without a word and went out to Hakim-a-barber.

"You just don't understand," she said, as Maggie and I came out to the car.

80

"What don't I understand?" I wanted to know.

"Your heritage," she said. And then she turned to Maggie, kissed her, and said, "You ought to try to make something of yourself, too, Maggie. It's really a new day for us. But from the way you and Mama still live you'd never know it."

She put on some sunglasses that hid everything above the tip of her nose and her chin.

Maggie smiled; maybe at the sunglasses. But a real smile, not scared. After we watched the car dust settle I asked Maggie to bring me a dip of snuff. And then the two of us sat there just enjoying, until it was time to go in the house and go to bed.

QUESTIONS

1. Characterize the speaker and evaluate her reliability as a reporter and interpreter of events. Where does she refrain from making judgments? Where does she present less than the full truth? Do these examples of reticence undercut her reliability?

2. Describe as fully as possible the lives of the mother, Dee, and Maggie prior to the events of the story. How are the following incidents from the past also reflected in the present actions: (a) Dee's hatred of the old house; (b) Dee's ability "to stare down any disaster"; (c) Maggie's burns from the fire; (d) the mother's having been "hooked in the side" while milking a cow; (e) Dee's refusal to accept a quilt when she went away to college?

3. As evidence of current social movements and as innovations that the mother responds to, what do the following have in common: (a) Dee's new name and costume; (b) Hakim's behavior and attitudes; (c) the "beef-cattle peoples down the road"; (d) Dee's concern for her "heritage"?

4. Does the mother's refusal to let Dee have the quilts indicate a permanent or temporary change of character? Why has she never done anything like it before? Why does she do it now? What details in the story prepare for and foreshadow that refusal?

5. How does the physical setting give support to the contrasting attitudes of both the mother and Dee? Does the author indicate that one or the other of them is entirely correct in her feelings about the house and yard?

6. Is Dee wholly unsympathetic? Is the mother's victory over her altogether positive? What emotional ambivalence is there in the final scene between Maggie and her mother in the yard?

KATHERINE MANSFIELD
Miss Brill

Although it was so brilliantly fine—the blue sky powdered with gold and great spots of light like white wine splashed over the Jardins Publiques—Miss Brill was glad that she had decided on her fur. The air was motionless, but when you opened your mouth there was just a faint chill, like a chill from a glass of iced water before you sip, and now and again a leaf came drifting—from nowhere, from the sky. Miss Brill put up her hand and touched her fur. Dear little thing! It was nice to feel it again. She had taken it out of its box that afternoon, shaken out the moth powder, given it a good brush, and rubbed the life back into the dim little eyes. "What has been happening to me?" said the sad little eyes. Oh, how sweet it was to see them snap at her again from the red eiderdown! . . . But the nose, which was of some black composition, wasn't at all firm. It must have had a knock, somehow. Never mind—a little dab of black sealing-wax when the time came—when it was absolutely necessary . . . Little rogue! Yes, she really felt like that about it. Little rogue biting its tail just by her left ear. She could have taken it off and laid it on her lap and stroked it. She felt a tingling in her hands and arms, but that came from walking, she supposed. And when she breathed, something light and sad—no, not sad, exactly—something gentle seemed to move in her bosom.

There were a number of people out this afternoon, far more than last Sunday. And the band sounded louder and gayer. That was because the Season had begun. For although the band played all the year round on Sundays, out of season it was never the same. It was like someone playing with only the family to listen; it didn't care how it played if there weren't any strangers present. Wasn't the conductor wearing a new coat, too? She was sure it was new. He scraped with his foot and flapped his arms like a rooster about to crow, and the bandsmen sitting in the green rotunda blew out their cheeks and glared at the music. Now there came a little "flutey" bit—very pretty!—a little chain of bright drops. She was sure it would be repeated. It was; she lifted her head and smiled.

Only two people shared her "special" seat: a fine old man in a velvet coat, his hands clasped over a huge carved walking-stick, and a big old woman, sitting upright, with a roll of knitting on her embroidered apron. They did not speak. This was disappointing, for Miss Brill always looked forward to the conversation. She had become really quite expert, she

MISS BRILL   Written in 1921; first published in 1922. "Jardins Publiques" is French for Public Gardens. Katherine Mansfield (1888–1923) was born and grew up in New Zealand but lived her adult life in London, with various sojourns on the Continent.

thought, at listening as though she didn't listen, at sitting in other people's lives just for a minute while they talked round her.

She glanced, sideways, at the old couple. Perhaps they would go soon. Last Sunday, too, hadn't been as interesting as usual. An Englishman and his wife, he wearing a dreadful Panama hat and she button boots. And she'd gone on the whole time about how she ought to wear spectacles; she knew she needed them; but that it was no good getting any; they'd be sure to break and they'd never keep on. And he'd been so patient. He'd suggested everything—gold rims, the kind that curve round your ears, little pads inside the bridge. No, nothing would please her. "They'll always be sliding down my nose!" Miss Brill had wanted to shake her.

5 The old people sat on the bench, still as statues. Never mind, there was always the crowd to watch. To and fro, in front of the flower beds and the band rotunda, the couples and groups paraded, stopped to talk, to greet, to buy a handful of flowers from the old beggar who had his tray fixed to the railings. Little children ran among them, swooping and laughing; little boys with big white silk bows under their chins, little girls, little French dolls, dressed up in velvet and lace. And sometimes a tiny staggerer came suddenly rocking into the open from under the trees, stopped, stared, as suddenly sat down "flop," until its small high-stepping mother, like a young hen, rushed scolding to its rescue. Other people sat on the benches and green chairs, but they were nearly always the same, Sunday after Sunday, and—Miss Brill had often noticed—there was something funny about nearly all of them. They were odd, silent, nearly all old, and from the way they stared they looked as though they'd just come from dark little rooms or even—even cupboards!

Behind the rotunda the slender trees with yellow leaves down drooping, and through them just a line of sea, and beyond the blue sky with gold-veined clouds.

Tum-tum-tum tiddle-um! tiddle-um! tum tiddley-um tum ta! blew the band.

Two young girls in red came by and two young soldiers in blue met them, and they laughed and paired and went off arm-in-arm. Two peasant women with funny straw hats passed, gravely, leading beautiful smoke-colored donkeys. A cold, pale nun hurried by. A beautiful woman came along and dropped her bunch of violets, and a little boy ran after to hand them to her, and she took them and threw them away as if they'd been poisoned. Dear me! Miss Brill didn't know whether to admire that or not! And now an ermine toque and a gentleman in gray met just in front of her. He was tall, stiff, dignified, and she was wearing the ermine toque she'd bought when her hair was yellow. Now everything, her hair, her face, even her eyes, was the same color as the shabby ermine, and her hand, in its cleaned glove, lifted to dab her lips, was a tiny yellowish paw. Oh, she was so pleased to see him—delighted! She rather thought they were going to meet that afternoon. She described where she'd been—everywhere, here, there, along by the sea. The day was so charming—didn't he agree? And wouldn't he, perhaps?. . . But he shook his head, lighted a cigarette, slowly breathed a great deep puff into her face, and, even while she was still talking and laughing, flicked the match away and walked on. The ermine toque was alone; she smiled more brightly than ever. But even the band seemed to know what she was feeling and played more softly, played tenderly, and the drum beat, "The Brute! The Brute!" over and over. What would she do? What was going to happen now? But as Miss Brill wondered, the ermine toque turned, raised her hand as though she'd seen some one else, much nicer, just over there, and pattered away. And the band changed again and played more quickly, more gayly than ever, and the old couple on Miss Brill's seat got up and marched away, and such a funny old man with long whiskers hobbled along in time to the music and was nearly knocked over by four girls walking abreast.

Oh, how fascinating it was! How she enjoyed it! How she loved sitting here, watching it all! It was like a play. It was exactly like a play. Who could believe the sky at the back wasn't painted? But it wasn't till a little brown dog trotted on solemn and then slowly trotted off, like a little "theater" dog, a little dog that had been drugged, that Miss Brill discovered what it was that made it so exciting. They were all on stage. They weren't only the audience, not only looking on; they were acting. Even she had a part and came every Sunday. No doubt somebody would have noticed if she hadn't been there; she was part of the performance after all. How strange she'd never thought of it like that before! And yet it explained why she made such a point of starting from home at just the same time each week—so as not to be late for the performance—and it also explained why she had quite a queer, shy feeling at telling her English pupils how she spent her Sunday afternoons. No wonder! Miss Brill nearly laughed out loud. She was on the stage. She thought of the old invalid gentleman to whom she read the newspaper four afternoons a week while he slept in the garden. She had got quite used to the frail head on the cotton pillow, the hollowed eyes, the open mouth and the high pinched nose. If he'd been dead she mightn't have noticed for weeks; she wouldn't have minded. But suddenly he knew he was having the paper read to him by an actress! "An actress!" The old head lifted; two points of light quivered in the old eyes. "An actress—are ye?" And Miss Brill smoothed the newspaper as though it were the manuscript of her part and said gently: "Yes, I have been an actress for a long time."

The band had been having a rest. Now they started again. And what they played was warm, sunny, yet there was just a faint chill—a something, 10 what was it?—not sadness—no, not sadness—a something that made you want to sing. The tune lifted, lifted, the light shone; and it seemed to Miss Brill that in another moment all of them, all the whole company, would begin singing. The young ones, the laughing ones who were moving together, they would begin, and the men's voices, very resolute and brave, would join them. And then she too, she too, and the others on the benches—they would come in with a kind of accompaniment—something low, that scarcely rose or fell, something so beautiful—moving . . . . And Miss Brill's eyes filled with tears and she looked smiling at all the other members of the company. Yes, we understand, we understand, she thought—though what they understood she didn't know.

Just at that moment a boy and girl came and sat down where the old couple had been. They were beautifully dressed; they were in love. The hero and heroine, of course, just arrived from his father's yacht. And still soundlessly singing, still with that trembling smile, Miss Brill prepared to listen.

"No, not now," said the girl. "Not here, I can't."

"But why? Because of that stupid old thing at the end there?" asked the boy. "Why does she come here at all—who wants her? Why doesn't she keep her silly old mug at home?"

"It's her fu-fur which is so funny," giggled the girl. "It's exactly like a fried whiting."

"Ah, be off with you!" said the boy in an angry whisper. Then: "Tell me, ma petite chère—"

"No, not here," said the girl. "Not *yet*."

On her way home she usually bought a slice of honeycake at the baker's. It was her Sunday treat. Sometimes there was an almond in her slice, sometimes not. It made a great difference. If there was an almond it was like carrying home a tiny present—a surprise—something that might very well not have been there. She hurried on the almond Sundays and struck the match for the kettle in quite a dashing way.

But today she passed the baker's by, climbed the stairs, went into the little dark room—her room like a cupboard—and sat down on the red eiderdown. She sat there for a long time. The box that the fur came out of was on the bed. She unclasped the necklet quickly; quickly, without looking, laid it inside. But when she put the lid on she thought she heard something crying.

QUESTIONS

1. We view the people and events of this story almost entirely through the eyes and feelings of its protagonist. The author relies upon indirect presentation for her characterization of Miss Brill. After answering the following questions, write

as full an account as you can of the nature and temperament of the story's main character.
2. What nationality is Miss Brill? What is the story's setting? Why is it important?
3. How old is Miss Brill? What are her circumstances? Why does she listen in on conversations?
4. Why does Miss Brill enjoy her Sundays in the park? Why especially this Sunday?
5. Of what importance to the story is the woman in the ermine toque?
6. What is Miss Brill's mood at the beginning of the story? What is it at the end? Why? Is she a static or a developing character?
7. What function does Miss Brill's fur serve in the story? What is the meaning of the final sentence?
8. Does Miss Brill come to a realization about her life and habits, or does she manage to suppress the truths that have been presented to her?

JAMES BALDWIN
Sonny's Blues

I read about it in the paper, in the subway, on my way to work. I read it, and I couldn't believe it, and I read it again. Then perhaps I just stared at it, at the newsprint spelling out his name, spelling out the story. I stared at it in the swinging lights of the subway car, and in the faces and bodies of the people, and in my own face, trapped in the darkness which roared outside.

It was not to be believed and I kept telling myself that, as I walked from the subway station to the high school. And at the same time I couldn't doubt it. I was scared, scared for Sonny. He became real to me again. A great block of ice got settled in my belly and kept melting there slowly all day long, while I taught my classes algebra. It was a special kind of ice. It kept melting, sending trickles of ice water all up and down my veins, but it never got less. Sometimes it hardened and seemed to expand until I felt my guts were going to come spilling out or that I was going to choke or scream. This would always be at a moment when I was remembering some specific thing Sonny had once said or done.

When he was about as old as the boys in my classes his face had been bright and open, there was a lot of copper in it; and he'd had wonderfully direct brown eyes, and great gentleness and privacy. I wondered what he looked like now. He had been picked up, the evening before, in a raid on an apartment downtown, for peddling and using heroin.

SONNY'S BLUES First published in 1957. James Baldwin (1924–1987) was one of the most significant chroniclers of African American experience in the twentieth century. His influential novels include *Go Tell It on the Mountain* (1953) and *Another Country* (1962).

I couldn't believe it: but what I mean by that is that I couldn't find any room for it anywhere inside me. I had kept it outside me for a long time. I hadn't wanted to know. I had had suspicions, but I didn't name them, I kept putting them away. I told myself that Sonny was wild, but he wasn't crazy. And he'd always been a good boy, he hadn't ever turned hard or evil or disrespectful, the way kids can, so quick, so quick, especially in Harlem. I didn't want to believe that I'd ever see my brother going down, coming to nothing, all that light in his face gone out, in the condition I'd already seen so many others. Yet it had happened and here I was talking about algebra to a lot of boys who might, every one of them for all I knew, be popping off needles every time they went to the head. Maybe it did more for them than algebra could.

5   I was sure that the first time Sonny had ever had horse,° he couldn't have been much older than these boys were now. These boys, now, were living as we'd been living then, they were growing up with a rush and their heads bumped abruptly against the low ceiling of their actual possibilities. They were filled with rage. All they really knew were two darknesses, the darkness of their lives, which was now closing in on them, and the darkness of the movies, which had blinded them to that other darkness, and in which they now, vindictively, dreamed, at once more together than they were at any other time, and more alone.

When the last bell rang, the last class ended, I let out my breath. It seemed I'd been holding it for all that time. My clothes were wet—I may have looked as though I'd been sitting in a steam bath, all dressed up, all afternoon. I sat alone in the classroom a long time. I listened to the boys outside, downstairs, shouting and cursing and laughing. Their laughter struck me for perhaps the first time. It was not the joyous laughter which—God knows why—one associates with children. It was mocking and insular, its intent to denigrate. It was disenchanted, and in this, also, lay the authority of their curses. Perhaps I was listening to them because I was thinking about my brother and in them I heard my brother. And myself.

One boy was whistling a tune, at once very complicated and very simple, it seemed to be pouring out of him as though he were a bird, and it sounded very cool and moving through all that harsh, bright air, only just holding its own through all those other sounds.

I stood up and walked over to the window and looked down into the courtyard. It was the beginning of the spring and the sap was rising in the boys. A teacher passed through them every now and again, quickly, as though he or she couldn't wait to get out of that courtyard, to get those

---

horse: heroin

boys out of their sight and off their minds. I started collecting my stuff. I thought I'd better get home and talk to Isabel.

The courtyard was almost deserted by the time I got downstairs. I saw this boy standing in the shadow of a doorway, looking just like Sonny. I almost called his name. Then I saw that it wasn't Sonny, but somebody we used to know, a boy from around our block. He'd been Sonny's friend. He'd never been mine, having been too young for me, and, anyway, I'd never liked him. And now, even though he was a grown-up man, he still hung around that block, still spent hours on the street corners, was always high and raggy. I used to run into him from time to time and he'd often work around to asking me for a quarter or fifty cents. He always had some real good excuse, too, and I always gave it to him, I don't know why.

But now, abruptly, I hated him. I couldn't stand the way he looked   10
at me, partly like a dog, partly like a cunning child. I wanted to ask him what the hell he was doing in the school courtyard.

He sort of shuffled over to me, and he said, "I see you got the papers. So you already know about it."

"You mean about Sonny? Yes, I already know about it. How come they didn't get you?"

He grinned. It made him repulsive and it also brought to mind what he'd looked like as a kid. "I wasn't there. I stay away from them people."

"Good for you." I offered him a cigarette and I watched him through the smoke. "You come all the way down here just to tell me about Sonny?"

"That's right." He was sort of shaking his head and his eyes looked   15
strange, as though they were about to cross. The bright sun deadened his damp dark brown skin and it made his eyes look yellow and showed up the dirt in his kinked hair. He smelled funky. I moved a little away from him and I said, "Well, thanks. But I already know about it and I got to get home."

"I'll walk you a little ways," he said. We started walking. There were a couple of kids still loitering in the courtyard and one of them said good night to me and looked strangely at the boy beside me.

"What're you going to do?" he asked me. "I mean, about Sonny?"

"Look. I haven't seen Sonny for over a year, I'm not sure I'm going to do anything. Anyway, what the hell *can* I do?"

"That's right," he said quickly, "ain't nothing you can do. Can't much help old Sonny no more, I guess."

It was what I was thinking and so it seemed to me he had no right to   20
say it.

"I'm surprised at Sonny, though," he went on—he had a funny way of talking, he looked straight ahead as though he were talking to himself—"I thought Sonny was a smart boy, I thought he was too smart to get hung."

"I guess he thought so too," I said sharply, "and that's how he got hung. And how about you? You're pretty goddamn smart, I bet."

Then he looked directly at me, just for a minute. "I ain't smart," he said. "If I was smart, I'd have reached for a pistol a long time ago."

"Look. Don't tell *me* your sad story, if it was up to me, I'd give you one." Then I felt guilty—guilty, probably, for never having supposed that the poor bastard *had* a story of his own, much less a sad one, and I asked, quickly, "What's going to happen to him now?"

He didn't answer this. He was off by himself some place. "Funny thing," he said, and from his tone we might have been discussing the quickest way to get to Brooklyn, "when I saw the papers this morning, the first thing I asked myself was if I had anything to do with it. I felt sort of responsible."

I began to listen more carefully. The subway station was on the corner, just before us, and I stopped. He stopped, too. We were in front of a bar and he ducked slightly, peering in, but whoever he was looking for didn't seem to be there. The jukebox was blasting away with something black and bouncy and I half watched the barmaid as she danced her way from the jukebox to her place behind the bar. And I watched her face as she laughingly responded to something someone said to her, still keeping time to the music. When she smiled one saw the little girl, one sensed the doomed, still-struggling woman beneath the battered face of the semi-whore.

"I never *give* Sonny nothing," the boy said finally, "but a long time ago I come to school high and Sonny asked me how it felt." He paused, I couldn't bear to watch him, I watched the barmaid, and I listened to the music which seemed to be causing the pavement to shake. "I told him it felt great." The music stopped, the barmaid paused and watched the jukebox until the music began again. "It did."

All this was carrying me some place I didn't want to go. I certainly didn't want to know how it felt. It filled everything, the people, the houses, the music, the dark, quicksilver barmaid, with menace; and this menace was their reality.

"What's going to happen to him now?" I asked again.

"They'll send him away some place and they'll try to cure him." He shook his head. "Maybe he'll even think he's kicked the habit. Then they'll let him loose"—he gestured, throwing his cigarette into the gutter. "That's all."

"What do you mean, that's *all*?"

But I knew what he meant.

"I *mean*, that's *all*." He turned his head and looked at me, pulling down the corners of his mouth. "Don't you know what I mean?" he asked, softly.

"How the hell *would* I know what you mean?" I almost whispered it, I don't know why.

"That's right," he said to the air, "how would *he* know what I mean?"   35
He turned toward me again, patient and calm, and yet I somehow felt him
shaking, shaking as though he were going to fall apart. I felt that ice in my
guts again, the dread I'd felt all afternoon; and again I watched the barmaid, moving about the bar, washing glasses, and singing. "Listen. They'll
let him out and then it'll just start all over again. That's what I mean."

"You mean—they'll let him out. And then he'll just start working his way
back in again. You mean he'll never kick the habit. Is that what you mean?"

"That's right," he said, cheerfully. "*You* see what I mean."

"Tell me," I said at last, "why does he want to die? He must want to
die, he's killing himself, why does he want to die?"

He looked at me in surprise. He licked his lips. "He don't want to die.
He wants to live. Don't nobody want to die, ever."

Then I wanted to ask him—too many things. He could not have   40
answered, or if he had, I could not have borne the answers. I started walking. "Well, I guess it's none of my business."

"It's going to be rough on old Sonny," he said. We reached the subway
station. "This is your station?" he asked. I nodded. I took one step down.
"Damn!" he said, suddenly. I looked up at him. He grinned again. "Damn
it if I didn't leave all my money home. You ain't got a dollar on you, have
you? Just for a couple of days, is all."

All at once something inside gave and threatened to come pouring out
of me. I didn't hate him anymore. I felt that in another moment I'd start
crying like a child.

"Sure," I said. "Don't sweat." I looked in my wallet and didn't have a
dollar, I only had a five. "Here," I said. "That hold you?"

He didn't look at it—he didn't want to look at it. A terrible closed
look came over his face, as though he were keeping the number on the bill
a secret from him and me. "Thanks," he said, and now he was dying to see
me go. "Don't worry about Sonny. Maybe I'll write him or something."

"Sure," I said. "You do that. So long."   45

"Be seeing you," he said. I went on down the steps.

And I didn't write Sonny or send him anything for a long time. When
I finally did, it was just after my little girl died, he wrote me back a letter
which made me feel like a bastard.

Here's what he said:

Dear brother,

    You don't know how much I needed to hear from you. I wanted   50
to write you many a time but I dug how much I must have hurt
you and so I didn't write. But now I feel like a man who's been
trying to climb up out of some deep, real deep and funky hole and
just saw the sun up there, outside. I got to get outside.

I can't tell you much about how I got here. I mean I don't know how to tell you. I guess I was afraid of something or I was trying to escape from something and you know I have never been very strong in the head (smile). I'm glad Mama and Daddy are dead and can't see what's happened to their son and I swear if I'd known what I was doing I would never have hurt you so, you and a lot of other fine people who were nice to me and who believed in me.

I don't want you to think it had anything to do with me being a musician. It's more than that. Or maybe less than that. I can't get anything straight in my head down here and I try not to think about what's going to happen to me when I get outside again. Sometime I think I'm going to flip and *never* get outside and sometime I think I'll come straight back. I tell you one thing, though, I'd rather blow my brains out than go through this again. But that's what they all say, so they tell me. If I tell you when I'm coming to New York and if you could meet me, I sure would appreciate it. Give my love to Isabel and the kids and I was sure sorry to hear about little Gracie. I wish I could be like Mama and say the Lord's will be done, but I don't know it seems to me that trouble is the one thing that never does get stopped and I don't know what good it does to blame it on the Lord. But maybe it does some good if you believe it.

> Your brother,
> Sonny

Then I kept in constant touch with him and I sent him whatever I could and I went to meet him when he came back to New York. When I saw him many things I thought I had forgotten came flooding back to me. This was because I had begun, finally, to wonder about Sonny, about the life that Sonny lived inside. This life, whatever it was, had made him older and thinner and it had deepened the distant stillness in which he had always moved. He looked very unlike my baby brother. Yet, when he smiled, when we shook hands, the baby brother I'd never known looked out from the depths of his private life, like an animal waiting to be coaxed into the light.

"How you been keeping?" he asked me.

55 "All right. And you?"

"Just fine." He was smiling all over his face. "It's good to see you again."

"It's good to see you."

The seven years' difference in our ages lay between us like a chasm: I wondered if these years would ever operate between us as a bridge. I was remembering, and it made it hard to catch my breath, that I had been there when he was born; and I had heard the first words he had ever spoken. When he started to walk, he walked from our mother straight to me. I caught him just before he fell when he took the first steps he ever took in this world.

"How's Isabel?"

"Just fine. She's dying to see you." 60

"And the boys?"

"They're fine, too. They're anxious to see their uncle."

"Oh, come on. You know they don't remember me."

"Are you kidding? Of course they remember you."

He grinned again. We got into a taxi. We had a lot to say to each other, 65 far too much to know how to begin.

As the taxi began to move, I asked, "You still want to go to India?"

He laughed. "You still remember that. Hell, no. This place is Indian enough for me."

"It used to belong to them," I said.

And he laughed again. "They damn sure knew what they were doing when they got rid of it."

Years ago, when he was around fourteen, he'd been all hipped on the 70 idea of going to India. He read books about people sitting on rocks, naked, in all kinds of weather, but mostly bad, naturally, and walking barefoot through hot coals and arriving at wisdom. I used to say that it sounded to me as though they were getting away from wisdom as fast as they could. I think he sort of looked down on me for that.

"Do you mind," he asked, "if we have the driver drive alongside the park? On the west side—I haven't seen the city in so long."

"Of course not," I said. I was afraid that I might sound as though I were humoring him, but I hoped he wouldn't take it that way.

So we drove along, between the green of the park and the stony, lifeless elegance of hotels and apartment buildings, toward the vivid, killing streets of our childhood. These streets hadn't changed, though housing projects jutted up out of them now like rocks in the middle of a boiling sea. Most of the houses in which we had grown up had vanished, as had the stores from which we had stolen, the basements in which we had first tried sex, the rooftops from which we had hurled tin cans and bricks. But houses exactly like the houses of our past yet dominated the landscape, boys exactly like the boys we once had been found themselves smothering in these houses, came down into the streets for light and air and found themselves encircled by disaster. Some escaped the trap, most didn't. Those who got out always left something of themselves behind, as some animals amputate a leg and leave it in the trap. It might be said, perhaps, that I had escaped, after all, I was a school teacher; or that Sonny had, he hadn't lived in Harlem for years. Yet, as the cab moved uptown through streets which seemed, with a rush, to darken with dark people, and as I covertly studied Sonny's face, it came to me that what we both were seeking through our separate cab windows was that part of ourselves which had been left behind. It's always at the hour of trouble and confrontation that the missing member aches.

We hit 110th Street and started rolling up Lenox Avenue. And I'd known this avenue all my life, but it seemed to me again, as it had seemed on the day I'd first heard about Sonny's trouble, filled with a hidden menace which was its very breath of life.

75   "We almost there," said Sonny.

"Almost." We were both too nervous to say anything more.

We live in a housing project. It hasn't been up long. A few days after it was up it seemed uninhabitably new, now, of course, it's already rundown. It looks like a parody of the good, clean, faceless life—God knows the people who live in it do their best to make it a parody. The beat-looking grass lying around isn't enough to make their lives green, the hedges will never hold out the streets, and they know it. The big windows fool no one, they aren't big enough to make space out of no space. They don't bother with the windows, they watch the TV screen instead. The playground is most popular with the children who don't play at jacks, or skip rope, or roller skate, or swing, and they can be found in it after dark. We moved in partly because it's not too far from where I teach, and partly for the kids; but it's really just like the houses in which Sonny and I grew up. The same things happen, they'll have the same things to remember. The moment Sonny and I started into the house I had the feeling that I was simply bringing him back into the danger he had almost died trying to escape.

Sonny has never been talkative. So I don't know why I was sure he'd be dying to talk to me when supper was over the first night. Everything went fine, the oldest boy remembered him, and the youngest boy liked him, and Sonny had remembered to bring something for each of them; and Isabel, who is really much nicer than I am, more open and giving, had gone to a lot of trouble about dinner and was genuinely glad to see him. And she's always been able to tease Sonny in a way that I haven't. It was nice to see her face so vivid again and to hear her laugh and watch her make Sonny laugh. She wasn't, or, anyway, she didn't seem to be, at all uneasy or embarrassed. She chatted as though there were no subject which had to be avoided and she got Sonny past his first, faint stiffness. And thank God she was there, for I was filled with that icy dread again. Everything I did seemed awkward to me, and everything I said sounded freighted with hidden meaning. I was trying to remember everything I'd heard about dope addiction and I couldn't help watching Sonny for signs. I wasn't doing it out of malice. I was trying to find out something about my brother. I was dying to hear him tell me he was safe.

"Safe!" my father grunted, whenever Mama suggested trying to move to a neighborhood which might be safer for children. "Safe, hell! Ain't no place safe for kids, nor nobody."

He always went on like this, but he wasn't, ever, really as bad as he sounded, not even on weekends, when he got drunk. As a matter of fact, he was always on the lookout for "something a little better," but he died before he found it. He died suddenly, during a drunken weekend in the middle of the war, when Sonny was fifteen. He and Sonny hadn't ever got on too well. And this was partly because Sonny was the apple of his father's eye. It was because he loved Sonny so much and was frightened for him, that he was always fighting with him. It doesn't do any good to fight with Sonny. Sonny just moves back, inside himself, where he can't be reached. But the principal reason that they never hit it off is that they were so much alike. Daddy was big and rough and loud-talking, just the opposite of Sonny, but they both had—that same privacy.

Mama tried to tell me something about this, just after Daddy died. I was home on leave from the army.

This was the last time I ever saw my mother alive. Just the same, this picture gets all mixed up in my mind with pictures I had of her when she was younger. The way I always see her is the way she used to be on a Sunday afternoon, say, when the old folks were talking after the big Sunday dinner. I always see her wearing pale blue. She'd be sitting on the sofa. And my father would be sitting in the easy chair, not far from her. And the living room would be full of church folks and relatives. There they sit, in chairs all around the living room, and the night is creeping up outside, but nobody knows it yet. You can see the darkness growing against the windowpanes and you hear the street noises every now and again, or maybe the jangling beat of a tambourine from one of the churches close by, but it's real quiet in the room. For a moment nobody's talking, but every face looks darkening, like the sky outside. And my mother rocks a little from the waist, and my father's eyes are closed. Everyone is looking at something a child can't see. For a minute they've forgotten the children. Maybe a kid is lying on the rug, half asleep. Maybe somebody's got a kid in his lap and is absentmindedly stroking the kid's head. Maybe there's a kid, quiet and big-eyed, curled up in a big chair in the corner. The silence, the darkness coming, and the darkness in the faces frightens the child obscurely. He hopes that the hand which strokes his forehead will never stop—will never die. He hopes that there will never come a time when the old folks won't be sitting around the living room, talking about where they've come from, and what they've seen, and what's happened to them and their kinfolk.

But something deep and watchful in the child knows that this is bound to end, is already ending. In a moment someone will get up and turn on the light. Then the old folks will remember the children and they won't talk anymore that day. And when light fills the room, the child is filled with darkness. He knows that everytime this happens he's moved just a little closer to that darkness outside. The darkness outside is what the old folks have been talking about. It's what they've come from. It's what they endure. The child knows that they won't talk anymore because if he knows too much about what's happened to *them,* he'll know too much too soon, about what's going to happen to *him.*

The last time I talked to my mother, I remember I was restless. I wanted to get out and see Isabel. We weren't married then and we had a lot to straighten out between us.

85   There Mama sat, in black, by the window. She was humming an old church song, *Lord, you brought me from a long ways off.* Sonny was out somewhere. Mama kept watching the streets.

"I don't know," she said, "if I'll ever see you again, after you go off from here. But I hope you'll remember the things I tried to teach you."

"Don't talk like that," I said, and smiled. "You'll be here a long time yet."

She smiled, too, but she said nothing. She was quiet for a long time. And I said, "Mama, don't you worry about nothing. I'll be writing all the time, and you be getting the checks. . . ."

"I want to talk to you about your brother," she said, suddenly. "If anything happens to me he ain't going to have nobody to look out for him."

90   "Mama," I said, "ain't nothing going to happen to you *or* Sonny. Sonny's all right. He's a good boy and he's got good sense."

"It ain't a question of his being a good boy," Mama said, "nor of his having good sense. It ain't only the bad ones, nor yet the dumb ones that gets sucked under." She stopped, looking at me. "Your Daddy once had a brother," she said, and she smiled in a way that made me feel she was in pain. "You didn't never know that, did you?"

"No," I said, "I never knew that," and I watched her face.

"Oh, yes," she said, "your Daddy had a brother." She looked out of the window again. "I know you never saw your Daddy cry. But *I* did—many a time, through all these years."

I asked her, "What happened to his brother? How come nobody's ever talked about him?"

95   This was the first time I ever saw my mother look old.

"His brother got killed," she said, "when he was just a little younger than you are now. I knew him. He was a fine boy. He was maybe a little full of the devil, but he didn't mean nobody no harm."

Then she stopped and the room was silent, exactly as it had sometimes been on those Sunday afternoons. Mama kept looking out into the streets.

"He used to have a job in the mill," she said, "and, like all young folks, he just liked to perform on Saturday nights. Saturday nights, him and your father would drift around to different places, go to dances and things like that, or just sit around with people they knew, and your father's brother would sing, he had a fine voice, and play along with himself on his guitar. Well, this particular Saturday night, him and your father was coming home from some place, and they were both a little drunk and there was a moon that night, it was bright like day. Your father's brother was feeling kind of good, and he was whistling to himself, and he had his guitar slung over his shoulder. They was coming down a hill and beneath them was a road that turned off from the highway. Well, your father's brother, being always kind of frisky, decided to run down this hill, and he did, with that guitar banging and clanging behind him, and he ran across the road, and he was making water behind a tree. And your father was sort of amused at him and he was still coming down the hill, kind of slow. Then he heard a car motor and that same minute his brother stepped from behind the tree, into the road, in the moonlight. And he started to cross the road. And your father started to run down the hill, he says he don't know why. This car was full of white men. They was all drunk, and when they seen your father's brother they let out a great whoop and holler and they aimed the car straight at him. They was having fun, they just wanted to scare him, the way they do sometimes, you know. But they was drunk. And I guess the boy, being drunk, too, and scared, kind of lost his head. By the time he jumped it was too late. Your father says he heard his brother scream when the car rolled over him, and he heard the wood of that guitar when it give, and he heard them strings go flying, and he heard them white men shouting, and the car kept on a going and it ain't stopped till this day. And, time your father got down the hill, his brother weren't nothing but blood and pulp."

Tears were gleaming on my mother's face. There wasn't anything I could say.

"He never mentioned it," she said, "because I never let him mention it before you children. Your Daddy was like a crazy man that night and for many a night thereafter. He says he never in his life seen anything as dark as that road after the lights of that car had gone away. Weren't nothing, weren't nobody on that road, just your Daddy and his brother and that busted guitar. Oh, yes. Your Daddy never did really get right again. Till the day he died he weren't sure but that every white man he saw was the man that killed his brother."

She stopped, and took out her handkerchief and dried her eyes and looked at me.

100

"I ain't telling you all this," she said, "to make you scared or bitter or to make you hate nobody. I'm telling you this because you got a brother. And the world ain't changed."

I guess I didn't want to believe this. I guess she saw this in my face. She turned away from me, toward the window again, searching those streets.

"But I praise my Redeemer," she said at last, "that He called your Daddy home before me. I ain't saying it to throw no flowers at myself, but, I declare, it keeps me from feeling too cast down to know I helped your father get safely through this world. Your father always acted like he was the roughest, strongest man on earth. And everybody took him to be like that. But if he hadn't had *me* there—to see his tears!"

105 She was crying, again. Still, I couldn't move. I said, "Lord, Lord, Mama, I didn't know it was like that."

"Oh, honey," she said, "there's a lot that you don't know. But you are going to find it out." She stood up from the window and came over to me. "You got to hold on to your brother," she said, "and don't let him fall, no matter what it looks like is happening to him and no matter how evil you gets with him. You going to be evil with him many a time. But don't you forget what I told you, you hear?"

"I won't forget," I said. "Don't you worry, I won't forget. I won't let nothing happen to Sonny."

My mother smiled as though she were amused at something she saw in my face. Then, "You may not be able to stop nothing from happening. But you got to let him know you's *there*."

Two days later I was married, and then I was gone. And I had a lot of things on my mind and I pretty well forgot my promise to Mama until I got shipped home on a special furlough for her funeral.

110 And, after the funeral, with just Sonny and me alone in the empty kitchen, I tried to find out something about him.

"What do you want to do?" I asked him.

"I'm going to be a musician," he said.

For he had graduated, in the time I had been away, from dancing to the jukebox to finding out who was playing what, and what they were doing with it, and he had bought himself a set of drums.

"You mean, you want to be a drummer?" I somehow had the feeling that being a drummer might be all right for other people but not for my brother Sonny.

115 "I don't think," he said, looking at me very gravely, "that I'll ever be a good drummer. But I think I can play a piano."

I frowned. I'd never played the role of the older brother quite so seriously before, had scarcely ever, in fact, *asked* Sonny a damn thing. I sensed myself in the presence of something I didn't really know how to handle, didn't understand. So I made my frown a little deeper as I asked: "What kind of musician do you want to be?"

He grinned. "How many kinds do you think there are?"

"Be *serious*," I said.

He laughed, throwing his head back, and then looked at me. "I *am* serious."

"Well, then, for Christ's sake, stop kidding around and answer a seri- 120 ous question, I mean, do you want to be a concert pianist, you want to play classical music and all that, or—or what?" Long before I finished he was laughing again. "For Christ's *sake*, Sonny!"

He sobered, but with difficulty. "I'm sorry. But you sound so—*scared!*" and he was off again.

"Well, you may think it's funny now, baby, but it's not going to be so funny when you have to make your living at it, let me tell you *that*." I was furious because I knew he was laughing at me and I didn't know why.

"No," he said, very sober now, and afraid, perhaps, that he'd hurt me, "I don't want to be a classical pianist. That isn't what interests me. I mean"—he paused, looking hard at me, as though his eyes would help me to understand, and then gestured helplessly, as though perhaps his hand would help—"I mean, I'll have a lot of studying to do, and I'll have to study *everything*, but, I mean, I want to play *with*—jazz musicians." He stopped. "I want to play jazz," he said.

Well, the word had never before sounded as heavy, as real, as it sounded that afternoon in Sonny's mouth. I just looked at him and I was probably frowning a real frown by this time. I simply couldn't see why on earth he'd want to spend his time hanging around nightclubs, clowning around on bandstands, while people pushed each other around a dance floor. It seemed—beneath him, somehow. I had never thought about it before, had never been forced to, but I suppose I had always put jazz musicians in a class with what Daddy called "good-time people."

"Are you *serious*?"   125

"Hell, *yes* I'm serious."

He looked more helpless than ever, and annoyed, and deeply hurt.

I suggested, helpfully: "You mean—like Louis Armstrong?"

His face closed as though I'd struck him. "No. I'm not talking about none of that old-time, down home crap."

"Well, look, Sonny, I'm sorry, don't get mad. I just don't altogether 130 get it, that's all. Name somebody—you know, a jazz musician you admire."

"Bird."

"Who?"

"Bird! Charlie Parker!° Don't they teach you nothing in the goddamn army?"

I lit a cigarette. I was surprised and then a little amused to discover that I was trembling. "I've been out of touch," I said. "You'll have to be patient with me. Now. Who's this Parker character?"

135   "He's just one of the greatest jazz musicians alive," said Sonny, sullenly, his hands in his pockets, his back to me. "Maybe *the* greatest," he added, bitterly, "that's probably why *you* never heard of him."

"All right," I said, "I'm ignorant. I'm sorry. I'll go out and buy all the cat's records right away, all right?"

"It don't," said Sonny, with dignity, "make any difference to me. I don't care what you listen to. Don't do me no favors."

I was beginning to realize that I'd never seen him so upset before. With another part of my mind I was thinking that this would probably turn out to be one of those things kids go through and that I shouldn't make it seem important by pushing it too hard. Still, I didn't think it would do any harm to ask: "Doesn't all this take a lot of time? Can you make a living at it?"

He turned back to me and half leaned, half sat, on the kitchen table. "Everything takes time," he said, "and—well, yes sure, I can make a living at it. But what *i* don't seem to be able to make you understand is that it's the only thing I want to do."

140   "Well, Sonny," I said, gently, "you know people can't always do exactly what they *want* to do—"

"*No*, I don't know that," said Sonny, surprising me. "I think people *ought* to do what they want to do, what else are they alive for?"

"You getting to be a big boy," I said desperately, "it's time you started thinking about your future."

"I'm thinking about my future," said Sonny, grimly. "I think about it all the time."

I gave up. I decided, if he didn't change his mind, that we could always talk about it later. "In the meantime," I said, "you got to finish school." We had already decided that he'd have to move in with Isabel and her folks. I knew this wasn't the ideal arrangement because Isabel's folks are inclined to be dicty° and they hadn't especially wanted Isabel to marry me. But I didn't know what else to do. "And we have to get you fixed up at Isabel's."

Charlie Parker: Charlie "Bird" Parker (1920–1955), jazz musician, was one of the leading figures of the jazz movement in the 1940s   **dicty:** bossy

There was a long silence. He moved from the kitchen table to the 145
window. "That's a terrible idea. You know it yourself."

"Do you have a *better* idea?"

He just walked up and down the kitchen for a minute. He was as tall
as I was. He had started to shave. I suddenly had the feeling that I didn't
know him at all.

He stopped at the kitchen table and picked up my cigarettes. Looking
at me with a kind of mocking, amused defiance, he put one between his
lips. "You mind?"

"You smoking already?"

He lit the cigarette and nodded, watching me through the smoke. "I just 150
wanted to see if I'd have the courage to smoke in front of you." He grinned
and blew a great cloud of smoke to the ceiling. "It was easy." He looked at
my face. "Come on, now. I bet you was smoking at my age, tell the truth."

I didn't say anything but the truth was on my face, and he laughed.
But now there was something very strained in his laugh. "Sure. And I bet
that ain't all you was doing."

He was frightening me a little. "Cut the crap," I said. "We already
decided that you was going to go and live at Isabel's. Now what's got into
you all of a sudden?"

"*You* decided it," he pointed out. "*I* didn't decide nothing." He
stopped in front of me, leaning against the stove, arms loosely folded.
"Look, brother. I don't want to stay in Harlem no more, I really don't." He
was very earnest. He looked at me, then over toward the kitchen window.
There was something in his eyes I'd never seen before, some thoughtfulness, some worry all his own. He rubbed the muscle of one arm. "It's time
I was getting out of here."

"Where do you want to *go*, Sonny?"

"I want to join the army. Or the navy, I don't care. If I say I'm old 155
enough, they'll believe me."

Then I got mad. It was because I was so scared. "You must be crazy.
You goddamn fool, what the hell do you want to go and join the *army* for?"

"I just told you. To get out of Harlem."

"Sonny, you haven't even finished *school*. And if you really want to be a
musician, how do you expect to study if you're in the *army*?"

He looked at me, trapped, and in anguish. "There's ways. I might be
able to work out some kind of deal. Anyway, I'll have the G.I. Bill when
I come out."

"*If* you come out." We stared at each other. "Sonny, please. Be reason- 160
able. I know the setup is far from perfect. But we got to do the best we can."

"I ain't learning nothing in school," he said. "Even when I go." He
turned away from me and opened the window and threw his cigarette out

into the narrow alley. I watched his back. "At least, I ain't learning nothing you'd want me to learn." He slammed the window so hard I thought the glass would fly out, and turned back to me. "And I'm sick of the stink of these garbage cans!"

"Sonny," I said, "I know how you feel. But if you don't finish school now, you're going to be sorry later that you didn't." I grabbed him by the shoulders. "And you only got another year. It ain't so bad. And I'll come back and I swear I'll help you do *whatever* you want to do. Just try to put up with it till I come back. Will you please do that? For me?"

He didn't answer and he wouldn't look at me.

"Sonny. You hear me?"

165   He pulled away. "I hear you. But you never hear anything *I* say."

I didn't know what to say to that. He looked out of the window and then back at me. "OK," he said, and sighed. "I'll try."

Then I said, trying to cheer him up a little, "They got a piano at Isabel's. You can practice on it."

And as a matter of fact, it did cheer him up for a minute. "That's right," he said to himself. "I forgot that." His face relaxed a little. But the worry, the thoughtfulness, played on it still, the way shadows play on a face which is staring into the fire.

But I thought I'd never hear the end of that piano. At first, Isabel would write me, saying how nice it was that Sonny was so serious about his music and how, as soon as he came in from school, or wherever he had been when he was supposed to be at school, he went straight to that piano and stayed there until suppertime. And, after supper, he went back to that piano and stayed there until everybody went to bed. He was at the piano all day Saturday and all day Sunday. Then he bought a record player and started playing records. He'd play one record over and over again, all day long sometimes, and he'd improvise along with it on the piano. Or he'd play one section of the record, one chord, one change, one progression, then he'd do it on the piano. Then back to the record. Then back to the piano.

170   Well, I really don't know how they stood it. Isabel finally confessed that it wasn't like living with a person at all, it was like living with sound. And the sound didn't make any sense to her, didn't make any sense to any of them—naturally. They began, in a way, to be afflicted by this presence that was living in their home. It was as though Sonny was some sort of god, or monster. He moved in an atmosphere which wasn't like theirs at all. They fed him and he ate, he washed himself, he walked in and out of their door; he certainly wasn't nasty or unpleasant or rude, Sonny isn't any of those things; but it was as though he were all wrapped up in some cloud, some fire, some vision all his own; and there wasn't any way to reach him.

At the same time, he wasn't really a man yet, he was still a child, and they had to watch out for him in all kinds of ways. They certainly couldn't throw him out. Neither did they dare to make a great scene about that piano because even they dimly sensed, as I sensed, from so many thousands of miles away, that Sonny was at that piano playing for his life.

But he hadn't been going to school. One day a letter came from the school board and Isabel's mother got it—there had, apparently, been other letters but Sonny had torn them up. This day, when Sonny came in, Isabel's mother showed him the letter and asked where he'd been spending his time. And she finally got it out of him that he'd been down in Greenwich Village, with musicians and other characters, in a white girl's apartment. And this scared her and she started to scream at him and what came up, once she began—though she denies it to this day—was what sacrifices they were making to give Sonny a decent home and how little he appreciated it.

Sonny didn't play the piano that day. By evening, Isabel's mother had calmed down but then there was the old man to deal with, and Isabel herself. Isabel says she did her best to be calm but she broke down and started crying. She says she just watched Sonny's face. She could tell, by watching him, what was happening with him. And what was happening was that they penetrated his cloud, they had reached him. Even if their fingers had been a thousand times more gentle than human fingers ever are, he could hardly help feeling that they had stripped him naked and were spitting on that nakedness. For he also had to see that his presence, that music, which was life or death to him, had been torture for them and that they had endured it, not at all for his sake, but only for mine. And Sonny couldn't take that. He can take it a little better today than he could then but he's still not very good at it and, frankly, I don't know anybody who is.

The silence of the next few days must have been louder than the sound of all the music ever played since time began. One morning, before she went to work, Isabel was in his room for something and she suddenly realized that all of his records were gone. And she knew for certain that he was gone. And he was. He went as far as the navy would carry him. He finally sent me a postcard from some place in Greece and that was the first I knew that Sonny was still alive. I didn't see him anymore until we were both back in New York and the war had long been over.

He was a man by then, of course, but I wasn't willing to see it. He came by the house from time to time, but we fought almost every time we met. I didn't like the way he carried himself, loose and dreamlike all the time, and I didn't like his friends, and his music seemed to be merely an excuse for the life he led. It sounded just that weird and disordered.

Then we had a fight, a pretty awful fight, and I didn't see him for months. By and by I looked him up, where he was living, in a furnished

175

room in the Village, and I tried to make it up. But there were lots of people in the room and Sonny just lay on his bed, and he wouldn't come downstairs with me, and he treated these other people as though they were his family and I weren't. So I got mad and then he got mad, and then I told him that he might just as well be dead as live the way he was living. Then he stood up and he told me not to worry about him anymore in life, that he *was* dead as far as I was concerned. Then he pushed me to the door and the other people looked on as though nothing were happening, and he slammed the door behind me. I stood in the hallway, staring at the door. I heard somebody laugh in the room and then the tears came to my eyes. I started down the steps, whistling to keep from crying, I kept whistling to myself, *You going to need me, baby, one of these cold, rainy days.*

I read about Sonny's trouble in the spring. Little Grace died in the fall. She was a beautiful little girl. But she only lived a little over two years. She died of polio and she suffered. She had a slight fever for a couple of days, but it didn't seem like anything and we just kept her in bed. And we would certainly have called the doctor, but the fever dropped, she seemed to be all right. So we thought it had just been a cold. Then, one day, she was up, playing, Isabel was in the kitchen fixing lunch for the two boys when they'd come in from school, and she heard Grace fall down in the living room. When you have a lot of children you don't always start running when one of them falls, unless they start screaming or something. And, this time, Grace was quiet. Yet, Isabel says that when she heard that *thump* and then that silence, something happened in her to make her afraid. And she ran to the living room and there was little Grace on the floor, all twisted up, and the reason she hadn't screamed was that she couldn't get her breath. And when she did scream, it was the worst sound, Isabel says, that she'd ever heard in all her life, and she still hears it sometimes in her dreams. Isabel will sometimes wake me up with a low, moaning, strangled sound and I have to be quick to awaken her and hold her to me and where Isabel is weeping against me seems a mortal wound.

I think I may have written Sonny the very day that little Grace was buried. I was sitting in the living room in the dark, by myself, and I suddenly thought of Sonny. My trouble made his real.

One Saturday afternoon, when Sonny had been living with us, or, anyway, been in our house, for nearly two weeks, I found myself wandering aimlessly about the living room, drinking from a can of beer, and trying to work up the courage to search Sonny's room. He was out, he was usually out whenever I was home, and Isabel had taken the children to see their grandparents. Suddenly I was standing still in front of the living room window, watching Seventh Avenue. The idea of searching Sonny's room made me still. I scarcely dared to admit to myself what I'd be searching for. I didn't know what I'd do if I found it. Or if I didn't.

On the sidewalk across from me, near the entrance to a barbecue 180
joint, some people were holding an old-fashioned revival meeting. The
barbecue cook, wearing a dirty white apron, his conked hair reddish and
metallic in the pale sun, and a cigarette between his lips, stood in the
doorway, watching them. Kids and older people paused in their errands
and stood there, along with some older men and a couple of very tough-
looking women who watched everything that happened on the avenue,
as though they owned it, or were maybe owned by it. Well, they were
watching this, too. The revival was being carried on by three sisters in
black, and a brother. All they had were their voices and their Bibles and a
tambourine. The brother was testifying and while he testified two of the
sisters stood together, seeming to say, amen, and the third sister walked
around with the tambourine outstretched and a couple of people dropped
coins into it. Then the brother's testimony ended and the sister who
had been taking up the collection dumped the coins into her palm and
transferred them to the pocket of her long black robe. Then she raised
both hands, striking the tambourine against the air, and then against one
hand, and she started to sing. And the two other sisters and the brother
joined in.

It was strange, suddenly, to watch, though I had been seeing these
street meetings all my life. So, of course, had everybody else down there.
Yet, they paused and watched and listened and I stood still at the window.
"Tis the old ship of Zion," they sang, and the sister with the tambourine kept
a steady, jangling beat, *"it has rescued many a thousand!"* Not a soul under
the sound of their voices was hearing this song for the first time, not one
of them had been rescued. Nor had they seen much in the way of rescue
work being done around them. Neither did they especially believe in the
holiness of the three sisters and the brother, they knew too much about
them, knew where they lived, and how. The woman with the tambourine,
whose voice dominated the air, whose face was bright with joy, was divided
by very little from the woman who stood watching her, a cigarette between
her heavy, chapped lips, her hair a cuckoo's nest, her face scarred and swollen from many beatings, and her black eyes glittering like coal. Perhaps
they both knew this, which was why, when, as rarely, they addressed each
other, they addressed each other as Sister. As the singing filled the air the
watching, listening faces underwent a change, the eyes focusing on something within; the music seemed to soothe a poison out of them; and time
seemed, nearly, to fall away from the sullen, belligerent, battered faces, as
though they were fleeing back to their first condition while dreaming of
their last. The barbecue cook half shook his head and smiled, and dropped
his cigarette and disappeared into his joint. A man fumbled in his pockets for change and stood holding it in his hand impatiently, as though he
had just remembered a pressing appointment further up the avenue. He

looked furious. Then I saw Sonny, standing on the edge of the crowd. He was carrying a wide, flat notebook with a green cover, and it made him look, from where I was standing, almost like a schoolboy. The coppery sun brought out the copper in his skin, he was very faintly smiling, standing very still. Then the singing stopped, the tambourine turned into a collection plate again. The furious man dropped in his coins and vanished, so did a couple of the women, and Sonny dropped some change in the plate, looking directly at the woman with a little smile. He started across the avenue, toward the house. He has a slow, loping walk, something like the way Harlem hipsters walk, only he's imposed on this his own half-beat. I had never really noticed it before.

I stayed at the window, both relieved and apprehensive. As Sonny disappeared from my sight, they began singing again. And they were still singing when his key turned in the lock.

"Hey," he said.

"Hey, yourself. You want some beer?"

185 "No. Well, maybe." But he came up to the window and stood beside me, looking out. "What a warm voice," he said.

They were singing *If I could only hear my mother pray again!*

"Yes," I said, "and she can sure beat that tambourine."

"But what a terrible song," he said, and laughed. He dropped his notebook on the sofa and disappeared into the kitchen. "Where's Isabel and the kids?"

"I think they went to see their grandparents. You hungry?"

190 "No." He came back into the living room with his can of beer. "You want to come some place with me tonight?"

I sensed, I don't know how, that I couldn't possibly say no. "Sure. Where?"

He sat down on the sofa and picked up his notebook and started leafing through it. "I'm going to sit in with some fellows in a joint in the Village."

"You mean, you're going to play, tonight?"

"That's right." He took a swallow of his beer and moved back to the window. He gave me a sidelong look. "If you can stand it."

195 "I'll try," I said.

He smiled to himself and we both watched as the meeting across the way broke up. The three sisters and the brother, heads bowed, were singing *God be with you till we meet again.* The faces around them were very quiet. Then the song ended. The small crowd dispersed. We watched the three women and the lone man walk slowly up the avenue.

"When she was singing before," said Sonny, abruptly, "her voice reminded me for a minute of what heroin feels like sometimes—when it's in your veins. It makes you feel sort of warm and cool at the same time. And distant. And—and sure," He sipped his beer, very deliberately not looking at me. I watched his face. "It makes you feel—in control. Sometimes you've got to have that feeling."

"Do you?" I sat down slowly in the easy chair.

"Sometimes." He went to the sofa and picked up his notebook again. "Some people do."

"In order," I asked, "to play?" And my voice was very ugly, full of   200
contempt and anger.

"Well"—he looked at me with great, troubled eyes, as though, in fact, he hoped his eyes would tell me things he could never otherwise say— "they *think so*. And *if* they think so—!"

"And what do *you* think?" I asked.

He sat on the sofa and put his can of beer on the floor. "I don't know," he said, and I couldn't be sure if he were answering my question or pursuing his thoughts. His face didn't tell me. "It's not so much to *play*. It's *to stand* it, to be able to make it at all. On any level." He frowned and smiled: "In order to keep from shaking to pieces."

"But these friends of yours," I said, "they seem to shake themselves to pieces pretty goddamn fast."

"Maybe." He played with the notebook. And something told me that I   205
should curb my tongue, that Sonny was doing his best to talk, that I should listen. "But of course you only know the ones that've gone to pieces. Some don't—or at least they haven't *yet* and that's just about all *any* of us can say." He paused. "And then there are some who just live, really, in hell, and they know it and they see what's happening and they go right on. I don't know." He sighed, dropped the notebook, folded his arms. "Some guys, you can tell from the way they play, they on something *all* the time. And you can see that, well, it makes something real for them. But of course," he picked up his beer from the floor and sipped it and put the can down again, "they *want* to, too, you've got to see that. Even some of them that say they don't—*some*, not all."

"And what about you?" I asked—I couldn't help it. "What about you? Do *you,* want to?"

He stood up and walked to the window and remained silent for a long time. Then he sighed. "Me," he said. Then: "While I was downstairs before, on my way here, listening to that woman sing, it struck me all of a sudden how much suffering she must have had to go through—to sing like that. It's *repulsive* to think you have to suffer that much."

I said: "But there's no way not to suffer—is there, Sonny?"

"I believe not," he said and smiled, "but that's never stopped anyone from trying." He looked at me. "Has it?" I realized, with this mocking look, that there stood between us, forever, beyond the power of time or forgiveness, the fact that I had held silence—so long—when he had needed human speech to help him. He turned back to the window. "No, there's no way not to suffer. But you try all kinds of ways to keep from drowning in it, to keep on top of it, and to make it seem—well, like *you*. Like you did something, all right, and now you're suffering for it. You know?" I said nothing. "Well, you know," he said, impatiently, "why *do* people suffer? Maybe it's better to do something to give it a reason, *any* reason."

210   "But we just agreed," I said, "that there's no way not to suffer. Isn't it better, then, just to—take it?"

"But nobody just takes it," Sonny cried, "that's what I'm telling you! *Everybody* tries not to. You're just hung up on the *way* some people try—it's not *your* way!"

The hair on my face began to itch, my face felt wet. "That's not true," I said, "that's not true. I don't give a damn what other people do, I don't even care how they suffer. I just care how *you* suffer." And he looked at me. "Please believe me," I said, "I don't want to see you—die—trying not to suffer."

"I won't," he said, flatly, "die trying not to suffer. At least, not any faster than anybody else."

"But there's no need," I said, trying to laugh, "is there? in killing yourself."

215   I wanted to say more, but I couldn't. I wanted to talk about willpower and how life could be—well, beautiful. I wanted to say that it was all within; but was it? or, rather, wasn't that exactly the trouble? And I wanted to promise that I would never fail him again. But it would all have sounded— empty words and lies.

So I made the promise to myself and prayed that I would keep it.

"It's terrible sometimes, inside," he said, "that's what's the trouble. You walk these streets, black and funky and cold, and there's not really a living ass to talk to, and there's nothing shaking, and there's no way of getting it out—that storm inside. You can't talk it and you can't make love with it, and when you finally try to get with it and play it, you realize *nobody's* listening. So *you've* got to listen. You got to find a way to listen."

And then he walked away from the window and sat on the sofa again, as though all the wind had suddenly been knocked out of him. "Sometimes you'll do *anything* to play, even cut your mother's throat." He laughed and looked at me. "Or your brother's." Then he sobered. "Or your own." Then: "Don't worry. I'm all right now and I think I'll *be* all right. But I can't forget—where I've been. I don't mean just the physical place I've been, I mean where I've *been*. And *what* I've been."

"What have you been, Sonny?" I asked.

He smiled—but sat sideways on the sofa, his elbow resting on the   220
back, his fingers playing with his mouth and chin, not looking at me. "I've
been something I didn't recognize, didn't know I could be. Didn't know
anybody could be." He stopped, looking inward, looking helplessly young,
looking old. "I'm not talking about it now because I feel *guilty* or anything
like that—maybe it would be better if I did, I don't know. Anyway, I can't
really talk about it. Not to you, not to anybody," and now he turned and
faced me. "Sometimes, you know, and it was actually when I was most *out*
of the world, I felt that I was in it, that I was *with* it, really, and I could
play or I don't really have to *play*, it just came out of me, it was there.
And I don't know how I played, thinking about it now, but I know I did
awful things, those times, sometimes, to people. Or it wasn't that I *did*
anything to them—it was that they weren't real." He picked up the beer
can; it was empty; he rolled it between his palms: "And other times—well,
I needed a fix, I needed to find a place to lean, I needed to clear a space to
listen—and I couldn't find it, and I—went crazy, I did terrible things to *me*,
I was terrible *for* me." He began pressing the beer can between his hands,
I watched the metal begin to give. It glittered, as he played with it, like a
knife, and I was afraid he would cut himself, but I said nothing. "Oh well.
I can never tell you. I was all by myself at the bottom of something, stinking and sweating and crying and shaking, and I smelled it, you know? *my*
stink, and I thought I'd die if I couldn't get away from it and yet, all the
same, I knew that everything I was doing was just locking me in with it.
And I didn't know," he paused, still flattening the beer can, "I didn't know,
I still *don't* know, something kept telling me that maybe it was good to
smell your own stink, but I didn't think that *that* was what I'd been trying to do—and—who can stand it?" and he abruptly dropped the ruined
beer can, looking at me with a small, still smile, and then rose, walking
to the window as though it were the lodestone rock. I watched his face, he
watched the avenue. "I couldn't tell you when Mama died—but the reason
I wanted to leave Harlem so bad was to get away from drugs. And then,
when I ran away, that's what I was running from—really. When I came
back, nothing had changed, *I* hadn't changed, I was just—older." And he
stopped, drumming with his fingers on the windowpane. The sun had vanished, soon darkness would fall. I watched his face. "It can come again," he
said, almost as though speaking to himself. Then he turned to me. "It can
come again," he repeated. "I just want you to know that."

"All right," I said, at last. "So it can come again. All right."

He smiled, but the smile was sorrowful. "I had to try to tell you," he said.

"Yes," I said. "I understand that."

"You're my brother," he said, looking straight at me, and not smiling
at all.

225   "Yes," I repeated, "yes. I understand that."

He turned back to the window, looking out. "All that hatred down there," he said, "all that hatred and misery and love. It's a wonder it doesn't blow the avenue apart."

We went to the only nightclub on a short, dark street, downtown. We squeezed through the narrow, chattering, jam-packed bar to the entrance of the big room, where the bandstand was. And we stood there for a moment, for the lights were very dim in this room and we couldn't see. Then, "Hello, boy," said a voice and an enormous black man, much older than Sonny or myself, erupted out of all that atmospheric lighting and put an arm around Sonny's shoulder. "I been sitting right here," he said, "waiting for you."

He had a big voice, too, and heads in the darkness turned toward us.

Sonny grinned and pulled a little away, and said, "Creole, this is my brother. I told you about him."

230   Creole shook my hand. "I'm glad to meet you, son," he said, and it was clear that he was glad to meet me *there*, for Sonny's sake. And he smiled, "You got a real musician in *your* family," and he took his arm from Sonny's shoulder and slapped him, lightly, affectionately, with the back of his hand.

"Well. Now I've heard it all," said a voice behind us. This was another musician, and a friend of Sonny's, a coal-black, cheerful-looking man, built close to the ground. He immediately began confiding to me, at the top of his lungs, the most terrible things about Sonny, his teeth gleaming like a lighthouse and his laugh coming up out of him like the beginning of an earthquake. And it turned out that everyone at the bar knew Sonny, or almost everyone; some were musicians, working there, or nearby, or not working, some were simply hangers-on, and some were there to hear Sonny play. I was introduced to all of them and they were all very polite to me. Yet, it was clear that, for them, I was only Sonny's brother. Here, I was in Sonny's world. Or, rather: his kingdom. Here, it was not even a question that his veins bore royal blood.

They were going to play soon and Creole installed me, by myself, at a table in a dark corner. Then I watched them, Creole, and the little black man, and Sonny, and the others, while they horsed around, standing just below the bandstand. The light from the bandstand spilled just a little short of them and, watching them laughing and gesturing and moving about, I had the feeling that they, nevertheless, were being most careful not to step into that circle of light too suddenly: that if they moved into the light too suddenly, without thinking, they would perish in flame. Then, while I watched, one of them, the small, black man, moved into the light and crossed the bandstand and started fooling around with his drums. Then—being funny and being, also, extremely ceremonious—Creole took

Sonny by the arm and led him to the piano. A woman's voice called Sonny's name and a few hands started clapping. And Sonny, also being funny and being ceremonious, and so touched, I think, that he could have cried, but neither hiding it nor showing it, riding it like a man, grinned, and put both hands to his heart and bowed from the waist.

Creole then went to the bass fiddle and a lean, very bright-skinned brown man jumped up on the bandstand and picked up his horn. So there they were, and the atmosphere on the bandstand and in the room began to change and tighten. Someone stepped up to the microphone and announced them. Then, there were all kinds of murmurs. Some people at the bar shushed others. The waitress ran around, frantically getting in the last orders, guys and chicks got closer to each other, and the lights on the bandstand, on the quartet, turned to a kind of indigo. Then they all looked different there. Creole looked about him for the last time, as though he were making certain that all his chickens were in the coop, and then he— jumped and struck the fiddle. And there they were.

All I know about music is that not many people ever really hear it. And even then, on the rare occasions when something opens within, and the music enters, what we mainly hear, or hear corroborated, are personal, private, vanishing evocations. But the man who creates the music is hearing something else, is dealing with the roar rising from the void and imposing order on it as it hits the air. What is evoked in him, then, is of another order, more terrible because it has no words, and triumphant, too, for that same reason. And his triumph, when he triumphs, is ours. I just watched Sonny's face. His face was troubled, he was working hard, but he wasn't with it. And I had the feeling that, in a way, everyone on the bandstand was waiting for him, both waiting for him and pushing him along. But as I began to watch Creole, I realized that it was Creole who held them all back. He had them on a short rein. Up there, keeping the beat with his whole body, wailing on the fiddle, with his eyes half closed, he was listening to everything, but he was listening to Sonny. He was having a dialogue with Sonny. He wanted Sonny to leave the shoreline and strike out for the deep water. He was Sonny's witness that deep water and drowning were not the same thing—he had been there, and he knew. And he wanted Sonny to know. He was waiting for Sonny to do the things on the keys which would let Creole know that Sonny was in the water.

And, while Creole listened, Sonny moved, deep within, exactly like   235
someone in torment. I had never before thought of how awful the relationship must be between the musician and his instrument. He has to fill it, this instrument, with the breath of life, his own. He has to make it do what he wants it to do. And a piano is just a piano. It's made out of so much wood and wires and little hammers and big ones, and ivory. While there's

only so much you can do with it, the only way to find this out is to try; to try and make it do everything.

And Sonny hadn't been near a piano for over a year. And he wasn't on much better terms with his life, not the life that stretched before him now. He and the piano stammered, started one way, got scared, stopped; started another way, panicked, marked time, started again; then seemed to have found a direction, panicked again, got stuck. And the face I saw on Sonny I'd never seen before. Everything had been burned out of it, and, at the same time, things usually hidden were being burned in, by the fire and fury of the battle which was occurring in him up there.

Yet, watching Creole's face as they neared the end of the first set, I had the feeling that something had happened, something I hadn't heard. Then they finished, there was scattered applause, and then, without an instant's warning, Creole started into something else, it was almost sardonic, it was *Am I Blue*. And, as though he commanded, Sonny began to play. Something began to happen. And Creole let out the reins. The dry, low, black man said something awful, on the drums, Creole answered, and the drums talked back. Then the horn insisted, sweet and high, slightly detached perhaps, and Creole listened, commenting now and then, dry, and driving, beautiful and calm and old. Then they all came together again, and Sonny was part of the family again. I could tell this from his face. He seemed to have found, right there beneath his fingers, a damn brand-new piano. It seemed that he couldn't get over it. Then, for a while, just being happy with Sonny, they seemed to be agreeing with him that brand new pianos certainly were a gas.

Then Creole stepped forward to remind them that what they were playing was the blues. He hit something in all of them, he hit something in me, myself, and the music tightened and deepened, apprehension began to beat the air. Creole began to tell us what the blues were all about. They were not about anything very new. He and his boys up there were keeping it new, at the risk of ruin, destruction, madness, and death, in order to find new ways to make us listen. For, while the tale of how we suffer, and how we are delighted, and how we may triumph is never new, it always must be heard. There isn't any other tale to tell, it's the only light we've got in all this darkness.

And this tale, according to that face, that body, those strong hands on those strings, has another aspect in every country, and a new depth in every generation. Listen, Creole seemed to be saying, listen. Now these are Sonny's blues. He made the little black man on the drums know it, and the bright, brown man on the horn. Creole wasn't trying any longer to get Sonny in the water. He was wishing him Godspeed. Then he stepped back, very slowly, filling the air with the immense suggestion that Sonny speak for himself.

Then they all gathered around Sonny and Sonny played. Every now and 240
again one of them seemed to say, amen. Sonny's fingers filled the air with life,
his life. But that life contained so many others. And Sonny went all the way
back, he really began with the spare, flat statement of the opening phrase of
the song. Then he began to make it his. It was very beautiful because it wasn't
hurried and it was no longer a lament. I seemed to hear with what burning
he had made it his, with what buring we had yet to make it ours, how we
could cease lamenting. Freedom lurked around us and I understood, at last,
that he could help us to be free if we would listen, that he would never be
free until we did. Yet, there was no battle in his face now. I heard what he
had gone through, and would continue to go through until he came to rest in
earth. He had made it his: that long line, of which we knew only Mama and
Daddy. And he was giving it back, as everything must be given back, so that,
passing through death, it can live forever. I saw my mother's face again; and
felt, for the first time, how the stones of the road she had walked on must have
bruised her feet. I saw the moonlit road where my father's brother died. And it
brought something else back to me, and carried me past it. I saw my little girl
again, and felt Isabel's tears again, and I felt my own tears begin to rise. And
I was yet aware that this was only a moment, that the world waited outside,
as hungry as a tiger, and that trouble stretched above us, longer than the sky.

Then it was over. Creole and Sonny let out their breath, both soaking
wet, and grinning. There was a lot of applause and some of it was real. In
the dark, the girl came by and I asked her to take drinks to the bandstand.
There was a long pause, while they talked up there in the indigo light and
after a while I saw the girl put a Scotch and milk on top of the piano for
Sonny. He didn't seem to notice it, but just before they started playing
again, he sipped from it and looked toward me, and nodded. Then he put
it back on top of the piano. For me, then, as they began to play again, it
glowed and shook above my brother's head like the very cup of trembling.

QUESTIONS

1. Describe the plot structure of "Sonny's Blues." Is there a relationship between the content of the story and the way the story is constructed?
2. How are the narrator and Sonny characterized? How are they different? In what ways are they similar?
3. The story contains significant flashbacks. Isolate these flashbacks and describe their importance in achieving a full understanding of the story.
4. Why is the story told from the viewpoint of Sonny's brother?
5. Is Sonny a sympathetic character? Why or why not?
6. How does the final scene in the nightclub form an appropriate ending to the story? Is the ending happy, unhappy, or indeterminate?
7. Discuss the ways in which "Sonny's Blues" depicts significant aspects of African American experience.

JAMES JOYCE
Araby

North Richmond Street, being blind,° was a quiet street except at the hour when the Christian Brothers' School set the boys free. An uninhabited house of two storeys stood at the blind end, detached from its neighbours in a square ground. The other houses of the street, conscious of decent lives within them, gazed at one another with brown imperturbable faces.

The former tenant of our house, a priest, had died in the back drawing-room. Air, musty from having been long enclosed, hung in all the rooms, and the waste room behind the kitchen was littered with old useless papers. Among these I found a few paper-covered books, the pages of which were curled and damp: *The Abbot*, by Walter Scott, *The Devout Communicant* and *The Memoirs of Vidocq*.° liked the last best because its leaves were yellow. The wild garden behind the house contained a central apple-tree and a few straggling bushes under one of which I found the late-tenant's rusty bicycle-pump. He had been a very charitable priest; in his will he had left all his money to institutions and the furniture of his house to his sister.

When the short days of winter came dusk fell before we had well eaten our dinners. When we met in the street the houses had grown somber. The space of sky above us was the color of ever-changing violet and towards it the lamps of the street lifted their feeble lanterns. The cold air stung us and we played till our bodies glowed. Our shouts echoed in the silent street. The career of our play brought us through the dark muddy lanes behind the houses where we ran the gauntlet of the rough tribes from the cottages, to the back doors of the dark dripping gardens where odors arose from the ashpits, to the dark odorous stables where a coachman smoothed and combed the horse or shook music from the buckled harness. When we returned to the street, light from the kitchen windows had filled the areas. If my uncle was seen turning the corner we hid in the shadow until we had seen him safely housed. Or if Mangan's sister came out on the doorstep to call her brother in to his tea we watched her from our shadow peer up and down the street. We waited to see whether she would remain or go in and, if she remained, we left our shadow and walked up to Mangan's steps

ARABY   First published in 1914. James Joyce (1882–1941) was born and lived in Dublin, Ireland, until 1904 when he went to Paris, and for the rest of his life he lived abroad and wrote about Dublin. He attended Jesuit school and graduated from University College in Dublin. The short stories collected in his first book, *Dubliners*, are among the most celebrated and influential of the genre in the modern era.
blind: a dead-end street   **The Abbot:** an 1820 novel by Sir Walter Scott (1771–1834)   *The Devout Communicant:* a Roman Catholic tract published in 1813   *The Memoirs of Vidocq:* memoirs by a French detective, Francois Vidocq (1775–1857)

resignedly. She was waiting for us, her figure defined by the light from the half-opened door. Her brother always teased her before he obeyed and I stood by the railings looking at her. Her dress swung as she moved her body and the soft rope of her hair tossed from side to side.

Every morning I lay on the floor in the front parlor watching her door. The blind was pulled down to within an inch of the sash so that I could not be seen. When she came out on the doorstep my heart leaped. I ran to the hall, seized my books and followed her. I kept her brown figure always in my eye and, when we came near the point at which our ways diverged, I quickened my pace and passed her. This happened morning after morning. I had never spoken to her, except for a few casual words, and yet her name was like a summons to all my foolish blood.

Her image accompanied me even in places the most hostile to romance. 5 On Saturday evenings when my aunt went marketing I had to go to carry some of the parcels. We walked through the flaring streets, jostled by drunken men and bargaining women, amid the curses of laborers, the shrill litanies of shop-boys who stood on guard by the barrels of pigs' cheeks, the nasal chanting of street-singers, who sang a *come-all-you*° about O'Donovan Rossa,° or a ballad about the troubles in our native land. These noises converged in a single sensation of life for me: I imagined that I bore my chalice safely through a throng of foes. Her name sprang to my lips at moments in strange prayers and praises which I myself did not understand. My eyes were often full of tears (I could not tell why) and at times a flood from my heart seemed to pour itself out into my bosom. I thought little of the future. I did not know whether I would ever speak to her or not or, if I spoke to her, how I could tell her of my confused adoration. But my body was like a harp and her words and gestures were like fingers running upon the wires.

One evening I went into the back drawing-room in which the priest had died. It was a dark rainy evening and there was no sound in the house. Through one of the broken panes I heard the rain impinge upon the earth, the fine incessant needles of water playing in the sodden beds. Some distant lamp or lighted window gleamed below me. I was thankful that I could see so little. All my senses seemed to desire to veil themselves and, feeling that I was about to slip from them, I pressed the palms of my hands together until they trembled, murmuring: *O love! O love!* many times.

At last she spoke to me. When she addressed the first words to me I was so confused that I did not know what to answer. She asked me was I going to *Araby.* I forget whether I answered yes or no. It would be a splendid bazaar, she said; she would love to go.

---

come-all-you: an Irish patriotic song   **O'Donovan Rossa:** Jeremiah O'Donovan (1831–1915), an Irish nationalist

"And why can't you?" I asked.

While she spoke she turned a silver bracelet round and round her wrist. She could not go, she said, because there would be a retreat that week in her convent. Her brother and two other boys were fighting for their caps and I was alone at the railings. She held one of the spikes, bowing her head towards me. The light from the lamp opposite our door caught the white curve of her neck, lit up her hair that rested there and, falling, lit up the hand upon the railing. It fell over one side of her dress and caught the white border of a petticoat, just visible as she stood at ease.

10 "It's well for you," she said.

"If I go," I said, "I will bring you something."

What innumerable follies laid waste my waking and sleeping thoughts after that evening! I wished to annihilate the tedious intervening days. I chafed against the work of school. At night in my bedroom and by day in the classroom her image came between me and the page I strove to read. The syllables of the word *Araby* were called to me through the silence in which my soul luxuriated and cast an Eastern enchantment over me. I asked for leave to go to the bazaar Saturday night. My aunt was surprised and hoped it was not some Freemason° affair. I answered few questions in class. I watched my master's face pass from amiability to sternness; he hoped I was not beginning to idle. I could not call my wandering thoughts together. I had hardly any patience with the serious work of life which, now that it stood between me and my desire, seemed to me child's play, ugly monotonous child's play.

On Saturday morning I reminded my uncle that I wished to go to the bazaar in the evening. He was fussing at the hallstand, looking for the hat-brush, and answered me curtly:

"Yes, boy, I know."

15 As he was in the hall I could not go into the front parlor and lie at the window. I left the house in bad humor and walked slowly towards the school. The air was pitilessly raw and already my heart misgave me.

When I came home to dinner my uncle had not yet been home. Still it was early. I sat staring at the clock for some time and, when its ticking began to irritate me, I left the room. I mounted the staircase and gained the upper part of the house. The high cold empty gloomy rooms liberated me and I went from room to room singing. From the front window I saw my companions playing below in the street. Their cries reached me weakened and indistinct and, leaning my forehead against the cool glass, I looked over at the dark house where she lived. I may have stood there for an hour, seeing nothing but the brown-clad figure cast by my imagination, touched discreetly by the lamplight at the curved neck, at the hand upon the railings and at the border below the dress.

Freemason: member of a highly secretive fraternal organization

When I came downstairs again I found Mrs. Mercer sitting at the fire. She was an old garrulous woman, a pawnbroker's widow, who collected used stamps for some pious purpose. I had to endure the gossip of the tea-table. The meal was prolonged beyond an hour and still my uncle did not come. Mrs. Mercer stood up to go: she was sorry she couldn't wait any longer, but it was after eight o'clock and she did not like to be out late, as the night air was bad for her. When she had gone I began to walk up and down the room, clenching my fists. My aunt said:

"I'm afraid you may put off your bazaar for this night of Our Lord."

At nine o'clock I heard my uncle's latchkey in the halldoor. I heard him talking to himself and heard the hallstand rocking when it had received the weight of his overcoat. I could interpret these signs. When he was midway through his dinner I asked him to give me the money to go to the bazaar. He had forgotten.

"The people are in bed and after their first sleep now," he said.   20

I did not smile. My aunt said to him energetically:

"Can't you give him the money and let him go? You've kept him late enough as it is."

My uncle said he was very sorry he had forgotten. He said he believed in the old saying: *All work and no play makes Jack a dull boy.* He asked me where I was going and, when I had told him a second time he asked me did I know *The Arab's Farewell to His Steed.*° When I left the kitchen he was about to recite the opening lines of the piece to my aunt.

I held a florin° tightly in my hand as I strode down Buckingham Street towards the station. The sight of the streets thronged with buyers and glaring with gas recalled to me the purpose of my journey. I took my seat in a third-class carriage of a deserted train. After an intolerable delay the train moved out of the station slowly. It crept onward among ruinous houses and over the twinkling river. At Westland Row Station a crowd of people pressed to the carriage doors; but the porters moved them back, saying that it was a special train for the bazaar. I remained alone in the bare carriage. In a few minutes the train drew up beside an improvised wooden platform. I passed out on to the road and saw by the lighted dial of a clock that it was ten minutes to ten. In front of me was a large building which displayed the magical name.

I could not find any sixpenny entrance and, fearing that the bazaar   25
would be closed, I passed in quickly through a turnstile, handing a shilling to a weary-looking man. I found myself in a big hall girdled at half its height by a gallery. Nearly all the stalls were closed and the greater part

The Arab's Farewell to His Steed: a popular nineteenth-century song   **florin:** a coin worth two shillings

of the hall was in darkness. I recognized a silence like that which pervades a church after a service. I walked into the center of the bazaar timidly. A few people were gathered about the stalls which were still open. Before a curtain, over which the words *Café Chantant°* were written in colored lamps, two men were counting money on a salver. I listened to the fall of the coins.

Remembering with difficulty why I had come I went over to one of the stalls and examined porcelain vases and flowered tea-sets. At the door of the stall a young lady was talking and laughing with two young gentlemen. I remarked their English accents and listened vaguely to their conversation.

"O, I never said such a thing!"

"O, but you did!"

"O, but I didn't!"

30   "Didn't she say that?"

"Yes, I heard her."

"O, there's a . . . fib!"

Observing me the young lady came over and asked me did I wish to buy anything. The tone of her voice was not encouraging; she seemed to have spoken to me out of a sense of duty. I looked humbly at the great jars that stood like eastern guards at either side of the dark entrance to the stall and murmured:

"No, thank you."

35   The young lady changed the position of one of the vases and went back to the two young men. They began to talk of the same subject. Once or twice the young lady glanced at me over her shoulder.

I lingered before her stall, though I knew my stay was useless, to make my interest in her wares seem the more real. Then I turned away slowly and walked down the middle of the bazaar. I allowed the two pennies to fall against the sixpence in my pocket. I heard a voice call from one end of the gallery that the light was out. The upper part of the hall was now completely dark.

Gazing up into the darkness I saw myself as a creature driven and derided by vanity; and my eyes burned with anguish and anger.

QUESTIONS

1. Discuss the setting and the way it is described in the opening paragraphs. How is the setting related to die boy's state of mind?
2. How is the boy characterized? Roughly how old is he and how would you describe his temperament and personality?
3. Analyze the role of Mangan's sister. Why is she not given a name? How does her physical description relate to the boy's state of mind?

Café Chantant: a café with music

4. Describe the role of the boy's uncle. Can he be called the antagonist? When the uncle returns home, he is talking to himself and moving awkwardly. What are these "signs" the boy says he is able to interpret?
5. How is the bazaar described? How is it different from the reader's and the boy's expectations?
6. At the bazaar, there is an inconsequential conversation between the young salesgirl and two Englishmen. Why is this dialogue important? How does the boy react to it?
7. Why does the boy decide not to buy anything for Mangan's sister? Where in the text would you locate the moment of "epiphany"?
8. Analyze the boy's feelings as described in the story's last paragraph. Are his feelings justified? How will he be changed as a result of his experience at the bazaar?

SUGGESTIONS FOR WRITING

1. Write an essay on the direct or indirect presentation of character in one of the following:
   a. Connell, "The Most Dangerous Game" (page 62)
   b. Greene, "The Destructors" (page 105)
   c. Ishiguro, "A Family Supper" (page 133)
   d. Joyce, "Araby" (page 186)
2. Considering the three criteria that are necessary for developing a convincing character, write an essay in which you determine whether one of the following characters meets these criteria:
   a. Rainsford in Connell, "The Most Dangerous Game" (page 62)
   b. Blackie in Greene, "The Destructors" (page 105)
   c. The narrator in Ishiguro, "A Family Supper" (page 133)
   d. Sonny in Baldwin, "Sonny's Blues" (page 159)

PRACTICE AP WRITING PROMPTS ▬▬▬▬

Alice Walker, "Everyday Use" (pp. 147–154)

Shakespeare's Juliet wonders, perhaps naively, "What's in a name?" In many works of literature, the answer is "much." Characters' names may denote or simply suggest personal qualities. They may also reflect larger thematic considerations. Reflect on the characters in Alice Walker's story "Everyday Use." Write an essay in which you analyze the ways in which characters' names illuminate the meaning of the story as a whole.

Katherine Mansfield, "Miss Brill" (pp. 155)

40-minute prompt: Read "Miss Brill" from paragraph 8 (p. 156) to the end of the story (p. 158); then write an essay in which you analyze how Mansfield characterizes "Miss Brill" through her relationships to others. Refer to such elements as symbolism, point of view, and epiphany.

....

James Joyce, "Araby" (pp. 186)

40-minute prompt: Read "Araby" carefully from the beginning of the story through the end of paragraph 6 (p. 187). Then write a well-organized essay in which you analyze how Joyce creates narrative tone through literary elements such as characterization, selective detail, and imagery.

....

CHAPTER FOUR

Theme

> *"Daddy, the man next door kisses his wife every morning when he leaves for work. Why don't you do that?"*
> *"Are you kidding? I don't even know the woman."*

> *"Daughter, your young man stays until a very late hour. Hasn't your mother said anything to you about this habit of his?"*
> *"Yes, father. Mother says men haven't altered a bit."*

For readers who contemplate the two jokes above, a significant difference emerges between them. The first joke depends only upon a reversal of expectation. We expect the man to explain why he doesn't kiss his wife; instead he explains why he doesn't kiss his neighbor's wife. The second joke, though it contains a reversal of expectation, depends as much or more for its effectiveness on a truth about human life, namely, that *people tend to grow more conservative as they grow older* or that *parents often scold their children for doing exactly what they did themselves when young.* This truth, which might be stated in different ways, is the *theme* of the joke.

The **theme** of a piece of fiction is its controlling idea or its central insight. It is the unifying generalization about life stated or implied by the story. To derive the theme of a story, we must determine what its central *purpose* is: what view of life it supports or what insight into life it reveals.

Not all stories have a significant theme. The purpose of a horror story may be simply to scare readers, to give them gooseflesh. The purpose of an adventure story may be simply to carry readers through a series of exciting escapades. The purpose of a murder mystery may be simply to pose a problem for readers to try to solve (and to prevent them from solving it, if possible, until the last paragraph). The purpose of some stories may be simply to provide suspense or to make readers laugh or to surprise them with a sudden twist at the end. Theme exists only (1) when an author has seriously attempted to record life accurately or to reveal some truth about it or (2) when an author has deliberately introduced as a unifying element some concept or theory of life that the story illuminates. Theme exists in virtually all literary fiction but only in some commercial fiction. In literary fiction it is the primary purpose of the story; in commercial fiction, it is usually less important than such elements as plot and suspense.

In many stories the theme may be equivalent to the revelation of human character. If a story has as its central purpose to exhibit a certain kind of human being, our statement of theme may be no more than a concentrated description of the person revealed, with the addition, "Some people are like this." Frequently, however, through its portrayal of specific persons in specific situations a story will have something to say about the nature of all human beings or about their relationship to each other or to the universe. Whatever central generalization about life arises from the specifics of the story constitutes theme.

The theme of a story, like its plot, may be stated very briefly or at greater length. With a simple or very brief story, we may be satisfied to sum up the theme in a single sentence. With a more complex story, if it is successfully unified, we can still state the theme in a single sentence, but we may feel that a paragraph—or occasionally even an essay—is needed to state it adequately. A rich story will give us many and complex insights into life. In stating the theme in a sentence, we must pick the *central* insight, the one that explains the greatest number of elements in the story and relates them to each other. Theme is what gives a story its unity. In any story at all complex, however, we are likely to feel that a one-sentence statement of theme leaves out a great part of the story's meaning. Though the theme of *Othello* may be expressed as "Jealousy exacts a terrible cost," such a statement does not begin to suggest the range and depth of Shakespeare's play. Any successful story is a good deal more and means a good deal more than any one-sentence statement of theme that we may extract from it, for the story will modify and expand this statement in various and subtle ways.

We must never think, once we have stated the theme of a story, that the whole purpose of the story has been to yield up this abstract statement. If this were so, there would be no reason for the story: we could stop with the abstract statement. The function of literary writers is not to state a theme but to vivify it. They wish to deliver it not simply to our intellects but to our emotions, our senses, and our imaginations. The theme of a story may be little or nothing except as it is embodied and vitalized by the story. Unembodied, it is a dry backbone, without flesh or life.

Sometimes the theme of a story is explicitly stated somewhere in the story, either by the author or by one of the characters. More often, however, the theme is implied. Story writers, after all, are story writers, not essayists or philosophers. Their first business is to reveal life, not to comment on it. They may well feel that unless the story somehow expresses its own meaning, without their having to point it out, they have not told the story well. Or they may feel that if the story is to have its maximum emotional effect, they must refrain from interrupting it or making remarks about it. They are also wary of spoiling a story for perceptive readers by "explaining" it, just as some people ruin jokes by explaining them. For these reasons theme is more often left implicit than stated explicitly. Good writers do not ordinarily write a story for the sole purpose of "illustrating" a theme, as do the writers of parables or fables. They write stories to bring alive some segment of human existence. When they do so searchingly and coherently, theme arises naturally out of what they have written. Good readers may state the generalizations for themselves.

Some readers—especially inexperienced readers—look for a "moral" in everything they read, some rule of conduct that they regard as applicable to their lives. They consider the words "theme" and "moral" to be interchangeable. Sometimes the words are interchangeable. Occasionally the theme of a story may be expressed as a moral principle without doing violence to the story. More frequently, however, the word "moral" is too narrow to fit the kind of illumination provided by a first-rate story. It is hardly suitable, for instance, for the kind of story that simply displays human character. Such nouns as "moral," "lesson," and "message" are therefore best avoided in the discussion of fiction. The critical term "theme" is preferable for several reasons. First, it is less likely to obscure the fact that a story is not a preachment or a sermon: a story's *first* object is enjoyment. Second, it should keep us from trying to wring from every story a didactic pronouncement about life. The person who seeks a moral in every story is likely to oversimplify and conventionalize it—to reduce it to some dusty platitude like "Be kind to animals" or "Look before you leap" or "Crime does not pay." The purpose of literary story writers is to give us a greater awareness and a greater understanding of life, not to inculcate a code of moral rules for regulating daily conduct. In getting at the theme of the story it is better to ask not *What does this story teach?* but *What does this story reveal?* Readers who analyze Ishiguro's "A Family Supper" as being simply about a conflict between a father and his son have missed nine-tenths of the story. The theme could be stated more accurately this way: "Generational conflicts can lead to disaster unless tempered by honest communication (which the father lacks the ability to initiate) or by mutual understanding (which the father, the son, and the daughter all lack)." Obviously, this dry statement is a poor thing beside the living reality of the story. But it is a more faithful abstracting of the story's content than any pat, cut-and-dried "moral."

The revelation offered by a good story may be something fresh or something old. The story may bring us some insight into life that we had not had before, and thus expand our horizons, or it may make us *feel* or *feel again* some truth of which we have long been merely intellectually aware. We may know in our minds, for instance, that "War is horrible" or that "Old age is often pathetic and in need of understanding," but these are insights that need to be periodically renewed. *Emotionally* we may forget them, and if we do, we are less alive and complete as human beings. Story writers perform a service for us—interpret life for us— whether they give us new insights or refresh and extend old ones.

The themes of commercial and literary stories may be identical, but frequently they are different. Commercial stories, for the most part, confirm their readers' prejudices, endorse their opinions, ratify their feelings, and satisfy their wishes. Usually, therefore, the themes of such stories are widely accepted platitudes of experience that may or may not be supported by the life around us. They represent life as we would like it to be, not always as it is. We should certainly like to believe, for instance, that "motherhood is sacred," that "true love always wins through," that "virtue and hard work are rewarded in the end," that "cheaters never win," that "old age brings a mellow wisdom that compensates for its infirmity," and that "every human being has a soft spot in him somewhere." Literary writers, however, being thoughtful observers of life, are likely to question these beliefs and often to challenge them. Their ideas about life are not simply taken over ready-made from what they were taught in Sunday school or from the books they read as children; they are the formulations of sensitive and independent observers who have collated all that they have read and been taught by life itself. The themes of their stories therefore do not often correspond to the pretty little sentiments we find inscribed in greeting cards. They may sometimes represent rather somber truths. Much of the process of maturing as a reader lies in the discovery that there may be more nourishment and deeper enjoyment in these somber truths than in the warm and fuzzy optimism found in so-called "inspirational" fiction.

We do not, however, have to accept the theme of a literary story any more than we do that of a commercial story. Though we should never summarily dismiss it without reflection, we may find that the theme of a story represents a judgment on life with which, on examination, we cannot agree. If it is the reasoned view of a seasoned and serious artist, nevertheless, it cannot be without value to us. There is value in knowing what the world looks like to others, and we can thus use a judgment to expand our knowledge of human experience even though we cannot ourselves accept it. Genuine artists and thoughtful observers, moreover, can hardly fail to present us with partial insights along the way, although we disagree with the total view. Careful readers, therefore, will not reject a story because they reject its theme. They can enjoy any story that arises from sufficient depth of observation and reflection and is artistically composed, though they disagree with its theme; and they will prefer it to a shallower, less thoughtful, or less successfully integrated story that presents a theme they endorse.

Discovering and stating the theme of a story is often a delicate task. Sometimes we will *feel* what the story is about strongly enough and yet find it difficult to put this feeling into words. If we are skilled readers, it is perhaps unnecessary that we do so. The bare statement of the theme, so lifeless and impoverished when abstracted from the story, may seem to diminish the story to something less than it is. Often, however, the attempt to state a theme will reveal to us aspects of a story that we should otherwise not have noticed and will thereby lead to more thorough understanding. The ability to state theme, moreover, is a test of our understanding of a story. Careless readers often think they understand a story when in actuality they have misunderstood it. They understand the events but not what the events add up to. Or, in adding up the events, they arrive at an erroneous total. People sometimes miss the point of a joke. It is not surprising that they should occasionally miss the point of a good piece of fiction, which is many times more complex than a joke.

There is no prescribed method for discovering theme. Sometimes we can best get at it by asking in what way the main character has changed in the course of the story and what, if anything, the character has learned before its end. Sometimes the best approach is to explore the nature of the central conflict and its outcome. Sometimes the title will provide an important clue. At all times we should keep in mind the following principles:

1. Theme should be expressible in the form of a statement with a subject and a predicate. It is insufficient to say that the theme of a story is motherhood or loyalty to country. Motherhood and loyalty are simply subjects. Theme must be a statement *about* the subject. For instance, "Motherhood sometimes has more frustrations than rewards" or "Loyalty to country often inspires heroic self-sacrifice." If we express the theme in the form of a phrase, the phrase must be convertible to sentence form. A phrase such as "the futility of envy," for instance, may be converted to the statement "Envy is futile": it may therefore serve as a statement of theme.

2. The theme should be stated as a *generalization* about life. In stating theme we do not use the names of the characters or refer to precise places or events, for to do so is to make a specific rather than a general statement. The theme of "The Destructors" is not that "The Wormsley Common Gang of London, in the aftermath of World War II, found a creative

outlet in destroying a beautiful two-hundred-year-old house designed by Sir Christopher Wren." Rather, it is something like this: "The dislocations caused by a devastating war may produce among the young a conscious or unconscious rebellion against all the values of the reigning society—a rebellion in which the creative instincts are channeled into destructive enterprises."

3. We must be careful not to make the generalization larger than is justified by the terms of the story. Terms like *every, all, always* should be used very cautiously; terms like *some, sometimes, may* are often more accurate. The theme of "Everyday Use" is not that "Habitually compliant and tolerant mothers will eventually stand up to their bullying children," for we have only one instance of such behavior in the story. But the story does sufficiently present this event as a climactic change in a developing character. Because the story's narrator recalls precise details of her previous behavior that she brings to bear on her present decision, we can safely infer that this decision will be meaningful and lasting, and should feel that we can generalize beyond the specific situation. The theme might be expressed thus: "A person whose honesty and tolerance have long made her susceptible to the strong will of another may reach a point where she will exert her own will for the sake of justice," or more generally, "Ingrained habits can be given up if justice makes a greater demand." Notice that we have said *may* and *can*, not *will* and *must*. Only occasionally will the theme of a story be expressible as a universal generalization. The bleak, darkly humorous ending of "Hunters in the Snow" lets us know that Wolff views all three of his characters as hopelessly "lost" in both the geographical and moral senses of the word. The world contains many people who are essentially predatory, the story seems to say, entirely self-interested "hunters" in a cold universe; even when two individuals form temporary alliances, these are symbiotic relationships in which each person is simply trying to fulfill a selfish need through the other.

4. Theme is the *central* and *unifying* concept of a story. Therefore (a) it accounts for all the major details of the story. If we cannot explain the bearing of an important incident or character on the theme, either in exemplifying it or modifying it in some way, it is probable that our interpretation is partial and incomplete, that at best we have got hold only of a subtheme. Another alternative, though it must be used with caution, is that the story itself is imperfectly constructed and lacks unity. (b) The theme is not contradicted by any detail of the story. If we have to overlook or blink at or "force" the meaning of some significant detail in order to frame our statement, we may be sure that our statement is defective. (c) The theme cannot rely upon supposed facts—facts not actually stated or clearly implied by the story. The theme exists *inside*, not *outside*, the story. The statement of it

must be based on the data of the story itself, not on assumptions supplied from our own experience.

5. There is no *one* way of stating the theme of a story. The story is not a guessing game or an acrostic that is supposed to yield some magic verbal formula that won't work if a syllable is changed. It merely presents a view of life, and, as long as the previously stated conditions are fulfilled, that view may surely be stated in more than one way. Here, for instance, are three possible ways of stating the theme of "Miss Brill": (a) A person living alone may create a protective fantasy life by dramatizing insignificant activities, but such a life can be jeopardized when she is forced to see herself as others see her. (b) Isolated elderly people, unsupported by a network of family and friends, may make a satisfying adjustment through a pleas-ant fantasy life, but when their fantasy is punctured by the cold claw of reality, the effect can be devastating. (c) Loneliness is a pitiable emotional state that may be avoided by refusing to acknowledge that one feels lonely, though such an avoidance may also require one to create unrealistic fantasies about oneself.

6. We should avoid any statement that reduces the theme to some familiar saying that we have heard all our lives, such as "You can't judge a book by its cover" or "A stitch in time saves nine." Although such a statement *may* express the theme accurately, too often it is simply a lazy shortcut that impoverishes the essential meaning of the story in order to save mental effort. When readers force every new experience into an old formula, they lose the chance for a fresh perception. Beware of using clichés when attempting to summarize a story's theme. To decide that "love is blind" is the theme of "How I Met My Husband" is to indulge in a reduc-tive absurdity. When a readymade phrase comes to mind as the theme of a story, this may be a sign that the reader should think more deeply and thoroughly about the author's central purpose.

REVIEWING CHAPTER FOUR

1. Review the definition of "theme" in fiction.
2. Describe the best way(s) in which the theme of a story may be stated.
3. Distinguish between the theme of a story and the central purpose of a story.
4. Differentiate between the typical themes of commercial vs. literary stories.
5. Review the six principles relating to theme as described in this chapter.

F. SCOTT FITZGERALD

Babylon Revisited

1

"And where's Mr. Campbell?" Charlie asked.

"Gone to Switzerland. Mr. Campbell's a pretty sick man, Mr. Wales."

"I'm sorry to hear that. And George Hardt?" Charlie inquired.

"Back in America, gone to work."

5   "And where is the Snow Bird?"

"He was in here last week. Anyway, his friend, Mr. Schaeffer, is in Paris."

Two familiar names from the long list of a year and a half ago. Charlie scribbled an address in his notebook and tore out the page.

"If you see Mr. Schaeffer, give him this," he said. "It's my brother-in-law's address. I haven't settled on a hotel yet."

He was not really disappointed to find Paris was so empty. But the stillness in the Ritz bar was strange and portentous. It was not an American bar any more—he felt polite in it, and not as if he owned it. It had gone back into France. He felt the stillness from the moment he got out of the taxi and saw the doorman, usually in a frenzy of activity at this hour, gossiping with a *chasseur*° by the servants' entrance.

10   Passing through the corridor, he heard only a single, bored voice in the once-clamorous women's room. When he turned into the bar he travelled the twenty feet of green carpet with his eyes fixed straight ahead by old habit; and then, with his foot firmly on the rail, he turned and surveyed the room, encountering only a single pair of eyes that fluttered up from a newspaper in the corner. Charlie asked for the head barman, Paul, who in the latter days of the bull market had come to work in his own custom-built car—disembarking, however, with due nicety at the nearest corner. But Paul was at his country house today and Alix giving him information.

"No, no more," Charlie said, "I'm going slow these days."

Alix congratulated him: "You were going pretty strong a couple of years ago."

BABYLON REVISITED   First published in 1931. The ancient Mesopotamian city of Babylon is a symbol of decadence and corruption. F. Scott Fitzgerald (1896–1940) published dozens of short stories during the 1920s and 1930s, along with such celebrated novels as *The Great Gatsby* (1925) and *Tender Is the Night* (1934). He and his wife, Zelda, parents of a daughter named Scottie, lived an affluent lifestyle during the 1920s, spending much of the decade in Paris. Fitzgerald battled alcoholism for most of his adult life, and Zelda suffered from mental illness that led to her being institutionalized in the 1930s and 1940s.
chasseur: bellman

"I'll stick to it all right," Charlie assured him. "I've stuck to it for over a year and a half now."

"How do you find conditions in America?"

"I haven't been to America for months. I'm in business in Prague, 15 representing a couple of concerns there. They don't know about me down there."

Alix smiled.

"Remember the night of George Hardt's bachelor dinner here?" said Charlie. "By the way, what's become of Claude Fessenden?"

Alix lowered his voice confidentially: "He's in Paris, but he doesn't come here any more. Paul doesn't allow it. He ran up a bill of thirty thousand francs, charging all his drinks and his lunches, and usually his dinner, for more than a year. And when Paul finally told him he had to pay, he gave him a bad check."

Alix shook his head sadly.

"I don't understand it, such a dandy fellow. Now he's all bloated up—" 20 He made a plump apple of his hands.

Charlie watched a group of strident queens installing themselves in a corner.

"Nothing affects them," he thought. "Stocks rise and fall, people loaf or work, but they go on forever." The place oppressed him. He called for the dice and shook with Alix for the drink.

"Here for long, Mr. Wales?"

"I'm here for four or five days to see my little girl."

"Oh-h! You have a little girl?" 25

Outside, the fire-red, gas-blue, ghost-green signs shone smokily through the tranquil rain. It was late afternoon and the streets were in movement; the *bistros*° gleamed. At the corner of the Boulevard des Capucines he took a taxi. The Place de la Concorde moved by in pink majesty; they crossed the logical Seine, and Charlie felt the sudden provincial quality of the Left Bank.

Charlie directed his taxi to the Avenue de l'Opera, which was out of his way. But he wanted to see the blue hour spread over the magnificent façade, and imagine that the cab horns, playing endlessly the first few bars of *La Plus que Lent,*° were the trumpets of the Second Empire. They were closing the iron grill in front of Brentano's Book-store, and people were already at dinner behind the trim little bourgeois hedge of Duval's. He had never eaten at a really cheap restaurant in Paris. Five-course dinner, four francs fifty, eighteen cents, wine included. For some odd reason he wished that he had.

bistros: cafes   *La Plus que Lent:* "Slower than Slow," a piano piece by Claude Debussy (1862–1918)

"You have to be damn drunk," he thought.

55 Zelli's was closed, the bleak and sinister cheap hotels surrounding it were dark; up in the Rue Blanche there was more light and a local, colloquial French crowd. The Poet's Cave had disappeared, but the two great mouths of the Café of Heaven and the Café of Hell still yawned—even devoured, as he watched, the meager contents of a tourist bus—a German, a Japanese, and an American couple who glanced at him with frightened eyes.

So much for the effort and ingenuity of Montmartre. All the catering to vice and waste was on an utterly childish scale, and he suddenly realized the meaning of the word "dissipate"—to dissipate into thin air; to make nothing out of something. In the little hours of the night every move from place to place was an enormous human jump, an increase of paying for the privilege of slower and slower motion.

He remembered thousand-franc notes given to an orchestra for playing a single number, hundred-franc notes tossed to a doorman for calling a cab.

But it hadn't been given for nothing.

It had been given, even the most wildly squandered sum, as an offering to destiny that he might not remember the things most worth remembering, the things that now he would always remember—his child taken from his control, his wife escaped to a grave in Vermont.

60 In the glare of a *brasserie*° a woman spoke to him. He bought her some eggs and coffee, and then, eluding her encouraging stare, gave her a twenty-franc note and took a taxi to his hotel.

2

He woke upon a fine fall day—football weather. The depression of yesterday was gone and he liked the people on the streets. At noon he sat opposite Honoria at Le Grand Vatel, the only restaurant he could think of not reminiscent of champagne dinners and long luncheons that began at two and ended in a blurred and vague twilight.

"Now, how about vegetables? Oughtn't you to have some vegetables?"

"Well, yes."

"Here's *épinards* and *chou-fleur* and carrots and *haricots*."°

65 "I'd like *chou-fleur*."

"Wouldn't you like to have two vegetables?"

"I usually only have one at lunch."

The waiter was pretending to be inordinately fond of children. "*Qu'elle est mignonne la petite! Elle parle exactement comme une Française.*"°

---

brasserie: small bar-restaurant   *épinards, chou-fleur, haricots:* spinach, cauliflower, beans
"Qu'elle . . . Française": "What a precious little girl! She speaks exactly like a French child!"

"How about dessert? Shall we wait and see?"

The waiter disappeared. Honoria looked at her father expectantly.   70

"What are we going to do?"

"First, we're going to that toy store in the Rue Saint-Honoré and buy you anything you like. And then we're going to the vaudeville at the Empire."

She hesitated. "I like it about the vaudeville, but not the toy store."

"Why not?"

"Well, you brought me this doll." She had it with her. "And I've got   75
lots of things. And we're not rich any more, are we?"

"We never were. But today you are to have anything you want."

"All right," she agreed resignedly.

When there had been her mother and a French nurse he had been inclined to be strict; now he extended himself, reached out for a new tolerance; he must be both parents to her and not shut any of her out of communication.

"I want to get to know you," he said gravely. "First let me introduce myself. My name is Charles J. Wales, of Prague."

"Oh, daddy!" her voice cracked with laughter.   80

"And who are you, please?" he persisted, and she accepted a rôle immediately: "Honoria Wales, Rue Palatine, Paris."

"Married or single?"

"No, not married. Single."

He indicated the doll. "But I see you have a child, madame."

Unwilling to disinherit it, she took it to her heart and thought quickly: 85
"Yes, I've been married, but I'm not married now. My husband is dead."

He went on quickly, "And the child's name?"

"Simone. That's after my best friend at school."

"I'm very pleased that you're doing so well at school."

"I'm third this month," she boasted. "Elsie"—that was her cousin—"is only about eighteenth, and Richard is about at the bottom."

"You like Richard and Elsie, don't you?"   90

"Oh, yes. I like Richard quite well and I like her all right."

Cautiously and casually he asked: "And Aunt Marion and Uncle Lincoln—which do you like best?"

"Oh, Uncle Lincoln, I guess."

He was increasingly aware of her presence. As they came in, a murmur of ". . . adorable" followed them, and now the people at the next table bent all their silences upon her, staring as if she were something no more conscious than a flower.

"Why don't I live with you?" she asked suddenly. "Because mamma's   95
dead?"

"You must stay here and learn more French. It would have been hard for daddy to take care of you so well."

"I don't really need much taking care of any more. I do everything for myself."

Going out of the restaurant, a man and a woman unexpectedly hailed him.

"Well, the old Wales!"

100 "Hello there, Lorraine. . . . Dunc."

Sudden ghosts out of the past: Duncan Schaeffer, a friend from college. Lorraine Quarrles, a lovely, pale blonde of thirty; one of a crowd who had helped them make months into days in the lavish times of three years ago.

"My husband couldn't come this year," she said, in answer to his question. "We're poor as hell. So he gave me two hundred a month and told me I could do my worst on that. . . . This your little girl?"

"What about coming back and sitting down?" Duncan asked.

"Can't do it." He was glad for an excuse. As always, he felt Lorraine's passionate, provocative attraction, but his own rhythm was different now.

105 "Well, how about dinner?" she asked.

"I'm not free. Give me your address and let me call you."

"Charlie, I believe you're sober," she said judicially. "I honestly believe he's sober, Dunc. Pinch him and see if he's sober."

Charlie indicated Honoria with his head. They both laughed.

"What's your address?" said Duncan sceptically.

110 He hesitated, unwilling to give the name of his hotel.

"I'm not settled yet. I'd better call you. We're going to see the vaudeville at the Empire."

"There! That's what I want to do," Lorraine said. "I want to see some clowns and acrobats and jugglers. That's just what we'll do, Dunc."

"We've got to do an errand first," said Charlie. "Perhaps we'll see you there."

"All right, you snob. . . . Good-by, beautiful little girl."

115 "Good-by."

Honoria bobbed politely.

Somehow, an unwelcome encounter. They liked him because he was functioning, because he was serious; they wanted to see him, because he was stronger than they were now, because they wanted to draw a certain sustenance from his strength.

At the Empire, Honoria proudly refused to sit upon her father's folded coat. She was already an individual with a code of her own, and Charlie was more and more absorbed by the desire of putting a little of himself into her before she crystallized utterly. It was hopeless to try to know her in so short a time.

Between the acts they came upon Duncan and Lorraine in the lobby
where the band was playing.

"Have a drink?" 120

"All right, but not up at the bar. We'll take a table."

"The perfect father."

Listening abstractedly to Lorraine, Charlie watched Honoria's eyes
leave their table, and he followed them wistfully about the room, wondering what they saw. He met her glance and she smiled.

"I liked that lemonade," she said.

What had she said? What had he expected? Going home in a taxi 125
afterward, he pulled her over until her head rested against his chest.

"Darling, do you ever think about your mother?"

"Yes, sometimes," she answered vaguely.

"I don't want you to forget her. Have you got a picture of her?"

"Yes, I think so. Anyhow, Aunt Marion has. Why don't you want me
to forget her?"

"She loved you very much." 130

"I loved her too."

They were silent for a moment.

"Daddy, I want to come and live with you," she said suddenly.

His heart leaped; he had wanted it to come like this.

"Aren't you perfectly happy?" 135

"Yes, but I love you better than anybody. And you love me better than
anybody, don't you, now that mummy's dead?"

"Of course I do. But you won't always like me best, honey. You'll grow
up and meet somebody your own age and go marry him and forget you
ever had a daddy."

"Yes, that's true," she agreed tranquilly.

He didn't go in. He was coming back at nine o'clock and he wanted to
keep himself fresh and new for the thing he must say then.

"When you're safe inside, just show yourself in that window." 140

"All right. Good-by, dads, dads, dads, dads."

He waited in the dark street until she appeared, all warm and glowing,
in the window above and kissed her fingers out into the night.

3

They were waiting. Marion sat behind the coffee service in a dignified
black dinner dress that just faintly suggested mourning. Lincoln was walking up and down with the animation of one who had already been talking.
They were as anxious as he was to get into the question. He opened it
almost immediately:

"I suppose you know what I want to see you about—why I really came
to Paris."

145   Marion played with the black stars on her necklace and frowned.

"I'm awfully anxious to have a home," he continued. "And I'm awfully anxious to have Honoria in it. I appreciate your taking in Honoria for her mother's sake, but things have changed now"—he hesitated and then continued more forcibly—"changed radically with me, and I want to ask you to reconsider the matter. It would be silly for me to deny that about three years ago I was acting badly—"

Marion looked up at him with hard eyes.

"—but all that's over. As I told you, I haven't had more than a drink a day for over a year, and I take that drink deliberately, so that the idea of alcohol won't get too big in my imagination. You see the idea?"

"No," said Marion succinctly.

150   "It's a sort of stunt I set myself. It keeps the matter in proportion."

"I get you," said Lincoln. "You don't want to admit it's got any attraction for you."

"Something like that. Sometimes I forget and don't take it. But I try to take it. Anyhow, I couldn't afford to drink in my position. The people I represent are more than satisfied with what I've done, and I'm bringing my sister over from Burlington to keep house for me, and I want awfully to have Honoria too. You know that even when her mother and I weren't getting along well we never let anything that happened touch Honoria. I know she's fond of me and I know I'm able to take care of her and—well, there you are. How do you feel about it?"

He knew that now he would have to take a beating. It would last an hour or two hours, and it would be difficult, but if he modulated his inevitable resentment to the chastened attitude of the reformed sinner, he might win his point in the end.

Keep your temper, he told himself. You don't want to be justified. You want Honoria.

155   Lincoln spoke first: "We've been talking it over ever since we got your letter last month. We're happy to have Honoria here. She's a dear little thing, and we're glad to be able to help her, but of course that isn't the question—"

Marion interrupted suddenly. "How long are you going to stay sober, Charlie?" she asked.

"Permanently, I hope."

"How can anybody count on that?"

"You know I never did drink heavily until I gave up business and came over here with nothing to do. Then Helen and I began to run around with—"

160   "Please leave Helen out of it. I can't bear to hear you talk about her like that."

He stared at her grimly; he had never been certain how fond of each other the sisters were in life.

"My drinking only lasted about a year and a half—from the time we came over until I—collapsed."

"It was time enough."

"It was time enough," he agreed.

"My duty is entirely to Helen," she said. "I try to think what she 165 would have wanted me to do. Frankly, from the night you did that terrible thing you haven't really existed for me. I can't help that. She was my sister."

"Yes."

"When she was dying she asked me to look out for Honoria. If you hadn't been in a sanitarium then, it might have helped matters."

He had no answer.

"I'll never in my life be able to forget the morning when Helen knocked at my door, soaked to the skin and shivering, and said you'd locked her out."

Charlie gripped the sides of the chair. This was more difficult than he 170 expected; he wanted to launch out into a long expostulation and explanation, but he only said: "The night I locked her out—" and she interrupted, "I don't feel up to going over that again."

After a moment's silence Lincoln said: "We're getting off the subject. You want Marion to set aside her legal guardianship and give you Honoria. I think the main point for her is whether she has confidence in you or not."

"I don't blame Marion," Charlie said slowly, "but I think she can have entire confidence in me. I had a good record up to three years ago. Of course, it's within human possibilities I might go wrong any time. But if we wait much longer I'll lose Honoria's childhood and my chance for a home." He shook his head, "I'll simply lose her, don't you see?"

"Yes, I see," said Lincoln.

"Why didn't you think of all this before?" Marion asked.

"I suppose I did, from time to time, but Helen and I were getting along 175 badly. When I consented to the guardianship, I was flat on my back in a sanitarium and the market had cleaned me out. I knew I'd acted badly, and I thought if it would bring any peace to Helen, I'd agree to anything. But now it's different. I'm functioning, I'm behaving damn well, so far as—"

"Please don't swear at me," Marion said.

He looked at her, startled. With each remark the force of her dislike became more and more apparent. She had built up all her fear of life into one wall and faced it toward him. This trivial reproof was possibly the result of some trouble with the cook several hours before. Charlie became increasingly alarmed at leaving Honoria in this atmosphere of hostility against himself; sooner or later it would come out, in a word here, a shake of the head there, and some of that distrust would be irrevocably implanted in Honoria. But he pulled his temper down out of his face and shut it up inside him; he had won a point, for Lincoln realized the absurdity of Marion's remark and asked her lightly since when she had objected to the word "damn."

"Another thing," Charlie said: "I'm able to give her certain advantages now. I'm going to take a French governess to Prague with me. I've got a lease on a new apartment—"

He stopped, realizing that he was blundering. They couldn't be expected to accept with equanimity the fact that his income was again twice as large as their own.

180   "I suppose you can give her more luxuries than we can," said Marion. "When you were throwing away money we were living along watching every ten francs. . . . I suppose you'll start doing it again."

"Oh, no," he said. "I've learned. I worked hard for ten years, you know—until I got lucky in the market, like so many people. Terribly lucky. It didn't seem any use working any more, so I quit. It won't happen again."

There was a long silence. All of them felt their nerves straining, and for the first time in a year Charlie wanted a drink. He was sure now that Lincoln Peters wanted him to have his child.

Marion shuddered suddenly; part of her saw that Charlie's feet were planted on the earth now, and her own maternal feeling recognized the naturalness of his desire; but she had lived for a long time with a prejudice—a prejudice founded on a curious disbelief in her sister's happiness, and which, in the shock of one terrible night, had turned to hatred for him. It had all happened at a point in her life where the discouragement of ill health and adverse circumstances made it necessary for her to believe in tangible villainy and a tangible villain.

"I can't help what I think!" she cried out suddenly. "How much you were responsible for Helen's death, I don't know. It's something you'll have to square with your own conscience."

185   An electric current of agony surged through him; for a moment he was almost on his feet, an unuttered sound echoing in his throat. He hung on to himself for a moment, another moment.

"Hold on there," said Lincoln uncomfortably. "I never thought you were responsible for that."

"Helen died of heart trouble," Charlie said dully.

"Yes, heart trouble." Marion spoke as if the phrase had another meaning for her.

Then, in the flatness that followed her outburst, she saw him plainly and she knew he had somehow arrived at control over the situation. Glancing at her husband, she found no help from him, and as abruptly as if it were a matter of no importance, she threw up the sponge.

"Do what you like!" she cried, springing up from her chair. "She's your   190
child. I'm not the person to stand in your way. I think if it were my child
I'd rather see her—" She managed to check herself. "You two decide it. I
can't stand this. I'm sick. I'm going to bed."

She hurried from the room; after a moment Lincoln said:

"This has been a hard day for her. You know how strongly she feels—"
His voice was almost apologetic: "When a woman gets an idea in her head."

"Of course."

"It's going to be all right. I think she sees now that you—can provide
for the child, and so we can't very well stand in your way or Honoria's way."

"Thank you, Lincoln."   195

"I'd better go along and see how she is."

"I'm going."

He was still trembling when he reached the street, but a walk down
the Rue Bonaparte to the quais° set him up, and as he crossed the Seine,
fresh and new by the quai lamps, he felt exultant. But back in his room
he couldn't sleep. The image of Helen haunted him. Helen whom he had
loved so until they had senselessly begun to abuse each other's love, tear it
into shreds. On that terrible February night that Marion remembered so
vividly, a slow quarrel had gone on for hours. There was a scene at the Florida, and then he attempted to take her home, and then she kissed young
Webb at a table; after that there was what she had hysterically said. When
he arrived home alone he turned the key in the lock in wild anger. How
could he know she would arrive an hour later alone, that there would be a
snowstorm in which she wandered about in slippers, too confused to find
a taxi? Then the aftermath, her escaping pneumonia by a miracle, and all
the attendant horror. They were "reconciled," but that was the beginning
of the end, and Marion, who had seen with her own eyes and who imagined
it to be one of many scenes from her sister's martyrdom, never forgot.

Going over it again brought Helen nearer, and in the white, soft light
that steals upon half sleep near morning he found himself talking to her
again. She said that he was perfectly right about Honoria and that she
wanted Honoria to be with him. She said she was glad he was being good
and doing better. She said a lot of other things—very friendly things—but
she was in a swing in a white dress, and swinging faster and faster all the
time, so that at the end he could not hear clearly all that she said.

4

He woke up feeling happy. The door of the world was open again.   200
He made plans, vistas, futures for Honoria and himself, but suddenly he

quais: paved streets along the river

grew sad, remembering all the plans he and Helen had made. She had not planned to die. The present was the thing—work to do and someone to love. But not to love too much, for he knew the injury that a father can do to a daughter or a mother to a son by attaching them too closely: afterward, out in the world, the child would seek in the marriage partner the same blind tenderness and, failing probably to find it, turn against love and life.

It was another bright, crisp day. He called Lincoln Peters at the bank where he worked and asked if he could count on taking Honoria when he left for Prague. Lincoln agreed that there was no reason for delay. One thing—the legal guardianship. Marion wanted to retain that a while longer. She was upset by the whole matter, and it would oil things if she felt that the situation was still in her control for another year. Charlie agreed, wanting only the tangible, visible child.

Then the question of a governess. Charlie sat in a gloomy agency and talked to a cross Béarnaise and to a buxom Breton peasant, neither of whom he could have endured. There were others whom he would see tomorrow.

He lunched with Lincoln Peters at Griffon, trying to keep down his exultation.

"There's nothing quite like your own child," Lincoln said. "But you understand how Marion feels too."

205 "She's forgotten how hard I worked for seven years there," Charlie said. "She just remembers one night."

"There's another thing." Lincoln hesitated. "While you and Helen were tearing around Europe throwing money away, we were just getting along. I didn't touch any of the prosperity because I never got ahead enough to carry anything but my insurance. I think Marion felt there was some kind of injustice in it—you not even working toward the end, and getting richer and richer."

"It went just as quick as it came," said Charlie.

"Yes, a lot of it stayed in the hands of *chasseurs* and saxophone players and maîtres d'hôtel—well, the big party's over now. I just said that to explain Marion's feeling about those crazy years. If you drop in about six o'clock tonight before Marion's too tired, we'll settle the details on the spot."

Back at his hotel, Charlie found a *pneumatique°* that had been redirected from the Ritz bar where Charlie had left his address for the purpose of finding a certain man.

210 DEAR CHARLIE: You were so strange when we saw you the other day that I wondered if I did something to offend you. If so, I'm not conscious of it. In fact, I have thought about you too much

pneumatique: telegram

for the last year, and it's always been in the back of my mind that I might see you if I came over here. We *did* have such good times that crazy spring, like the night you and I stole the butcher's tricycle, and the time we tried to call on the president and you had the old derby rim and the wire cane. Everybody seems so old lately, but I don't feel old a bit. Couldn't we get together some time today for old time's sake? I've got a vile hang-over for the moment, but will be feeling better this afternoon and will look for you about five in the sweat-shop at the Ritz.

Always devotedly,

LORRAINE

His first feeling was one of awe that he had actually, in his mature years, stolen a tricycle and pedalled Lorraine all over the Étoile between the small hours and dawn. In retrospect it was a nightmare. Locking out Helen didn't fit in with any other act of his life, but the tricycle incident did—it was one of many. How many weeks or months of dissipation to arrive at that condition of utter irresponsibility?

He tried to picture how Lorraine had appeared to him then—very attractive; Helen was unhappy about it, though she said nothing. Yesterday, in the restaurant, Lorraine had seemed trite, blurred, worn away. He emphatically did not want to see her, and he was glad Alix had not given away his hotel address. It was a relief to think, instead, of Honoria, to think of Sundays spent with her and of saying good morning to her and of knowing she was there in his house at night, drawing her breath in the darkness.

At five he took a taxi and bought presents for all the Peters—a piquant cloth doll, a box of Roman soldiers, flowers for Marion, big linen handker-chiefs for Lincoln.

He saw, when he arrived in the apartment, that Marion had accepted the inevitable. She greeted him now as though he were a recalcitrant member of the family, rather than a menacing outsider. Honoria had been told she was going; Charlie was glad to see that her tact made her conceal her excessive happiness. Only on his lap did she whisper her delight and the question "When?" before she slipped away with the other children.

He and Marion were alone for a minute in the room, and on an impulse he spoke out boldly:

"Family quarrels are bitter things. They don't go according to any rules. They're not like aches or wounds; they're more like splits in the skin that won't heal because there's not enough material. I wish you and I could be on better terms."

215

"Some things are hard to forget," she answered. "It's a question of confidence." There was no answer to this and presently she asked, "When do you propose to take her?"

"As soon as I can get a governess. I hoped the day after tomorrow."

"That's impossible. I've got to get her things in shape. Not before Saturday."

220   He yielded. Coming back into the room, Lincoln offered him a drink. "I'll take my daily whisky," he said.

It was warm here, it was a home, people together by a fire. The children felt very safe and important; the mother and father were serious, watchful. They had things to do for the children more important than his visit here. A spoonful of medicine was, after all, more important than the strained relations between Marion and himself. They were not dull people, but they were very much in the grip of life and circumstances. He wondered if he couldn't do something to get Lincoln out of his rut at the bank.

A long peal at the door-bell; the *bonne à tout faire*° passed through and went down the corridor. The door opened upon another long ring, and then voices, and the three in the salon looked up expectantly; Lincoln moved to bring the corridor within his range of vision, and Marion rose. Then the maid came back along the corridor, closely followed by the voices, which developed under the light into Duncan Schaeffer and Lorraine Quarrles.

They were gay, they were hilarious, they were roaring with laughter. For a moment Charlie was astounded; unable to understand how they ferreted out the Peters' address.

225   "Ah-h-h!" Duncan wagged his finger roguishly at Charlie. "Ah-h-h!"

They both slid down another cascade of laughter. Anxious and at a loss, Charlie shook hands with them quickly and presented them to Lincoln and Marion. Marion nodded, scarcely speaking. She had drawn back a step toward the fire; her little girl stood beside her, and Marion put an arm about her shoulder.

With growing annoyance at the intrusion, Charlie waited for them to explain themselves. After some concentration Duncan said:

"We came to invite you out to dinner. Lorraine and I insist that all this chi-chi, cagy business 'bout your address got to stop."

Charlie came closer to them, as if to force them backward down the corridor.

230   "Sorry, but I can't. Tell me where you'll be and I'll phone you in half an hour."

This made no impression. Lorraine sat down suddenly on the side of a chair, and focussing her eyes on Richard, cried, "Oh, what a nice little boy! Come here, little boy." Richard glanced at his mother, but did not

bonne à tout faire: house-maid

move. With a perceptible shrug of her shoulders, Lorraine turned back to Charlie:

"Come and dine. Sure your cousins won' mine. See you so sel'om. Or solemn."

"I can't," said Charlie sharply. "You two have dinner and I'll phone you."

Her voice became suddenly unpleasant. "All right, we'll go. But I remember once when you hammered on my door at four A.M. I was enough of a good sport to give you a drink. Come on, Dunc."

Still in slow motion, with blurred, angry faces, with uncertain feet, 235 they retired along the corridor.

"Good night," Charlie said.

"Good night!" responded Lorraine emphatically.

When he went back into the salon Marion had not moved, only now her son was standing in the circle of her other arm. Lincoln was still swinging Honoria back and forth like a pendulum from side to side.

"What an outrage!" Charlie broke out. "What an absolute outrage!"

Neither of them answered. Charlie dropped into an armchair, picked 240 up his drink, set it down again and said:

"People I haven't seen for two years having the colossal nerve—"

He broke off. Marion had made the sound "Oh!" in one swift, furious breath, turned her body from him with a jerk and left the room.

Lincoln set down Honoria carefully.

"You children go in and start your soup," he said, and when they obeyed, he said to Charlie:

"Marion's not well and she can't stand shocks. That kind of people 245 make her really physically sick."

"I didn't tell them to come here. They wormed your name out of somebody. They deliberately—"

"Well, it's too bad. It doesn't help matters. Excuse me a minute."

Left alone, Charlie sat tense in his chair. In the next room he could hear the children eating, talking in monosyllables, already oblivious to the scene between their elders. He heard a murmur of conversation from a farther room and then the ticking bell of a telephone receiver picked up, and in a panic he moved to the other side of the room and out of earshot.

In a minute Lincoln came back. "Look here, Charlie. I think we'd better call off dinner for tonight. Marion's in bad shape."

"Is she angry with me?"
250
"Sort of," he said, almost roughly. "She's not strong and—"

"You mean she's changed her mind about Honoria?"

"She's pretty bitter right now. I don't know. You phone me at the bank tomorrow."

"I wish you'd explain to her I never dreamed these people would come here. I'm just as sore as you are."

255 "I couldn't explain anything to her now."

Charlie got up. He took his coat and hat and started down the corridor. Then he opened the door of the dining room and said in a strange voice, "Good night, children."

Honoria rose and ran around the table to hug him.

"Good night, sweetheart," he said vaguely, and then trying to make his voice more tender, trying to conciliate something, "Good night, dear children."

5

Charlie went directly to the Ritz bar with the furious idea of finding Lorraine and Duncan, but they were not there, and he realized that in any case there was nothing he could do. He had not touched his drink at the Peters', and now he ordered a whisky-and-soda. Paul came over to say hello.

260 "It's a great change," he said sadly. "We do about half the business we did. So many fellows I hear about back in the States lost everything, maybe not in the first crash, but then in the second. Your friend George Hardt lost every cent, I hear. Are you back in the States?"

"No, I'm in business in Prague."

"I heard that you lost a lot in the crash."

"I did," and he added grimly, "but I lost everything I wanted in the boom."

"Selling short."

265 "Something like that."

Again the memory of those days swept over him like a nightmare—the people they had met travelling; then people who couldn't add a row of figures or speak a coherent sentence. The little man Helen had consented to dance with at the ship's party, who had insulted her ten feet from the table; the women and girls carried screaming with drink or drugs out of public places—

—The men who locked their wives out in the snow, because the snow of twenty-nine wasn't real snow. If you didn't want it to be snow, you just paid some money.

He went to the phone and called the Peters' apartment; Lincoln answered.

"I called up because this thing is on my mind. Has Marion said anything definite?"

270 "Marion's sick," Lincoln answered shortly. "I know this thing isn't altogether your fault, but I can't have her go to pieces about it. I'm afraid we'll have to let it slide for six months; I can't take the chance of working her up to this state again."

"I see."

"I'm sorry, Charlie."

He went back to his table. His whisky glass was empty, but he shook his head when Alix looked at it questioningly. There wasn't much he could do now except send Honoria some things; he would send her a lot of things tomorrow. He thought rather angrily that this was just money—he had given so many people money. . . .

"No, no more," he said to another waiter. "What do I owe you?"

He would come back some day; they couldn't make him pay forever. But   275
he wanted his child, and nothing was much good now, beside that fact. He wasn't young any more, with a lot of nice thoughts and dreams to have by himself. He was absolutely sure Helen wouldn't have wanted him to be so alone.

QUESTIONS

1. Contrast Charlie's past life in Paris with his present circumstances. How does this contrast between his past and present relate to the theme of the story? Describe the theme as precisely as possible.
2. How has Charlie's character changed from past years when he lived in Paris with his wife, Helen? Is his reform authentic or feigned?
3. How is Charlie's daughter characterized? Is she similar to or different from her father?
4. Why is the Paris setting important? What details does Fitzgerald employ to bring the setting to life?
5. Describe the plot structure of the story. What is the central conflict? When does the action reach a dramatic climax?
6. Discuss the importance of Duncan Schaeffer and Lorraine Quarrles to the story. Why are they included?
7. Is Marion Peters a sympathetic character? Why or why not?
8. Analyze the story's conclusion. Is the ending happy, unhappy, or indeterminate?

ANTON CHEKHOV
Misery

The twilight of evening. Big flakes of wet snow are whirling lazily about the street lamps, which have just been lighted, and lying in a thin soft layer on roofs, horses' backs, shoulders, caps. Iona Potapov, the sledge-driver, is all white like a ghost. He sits on the box without stirring,

MISERY   First published in 1886. Translated from the Russian by Constance Garnett. Anton Chekhov (1860–1904) was raised in semi-poverty in the town of Taganrog, on the Black Sea, A scholarship enabled him to take a medical degree from Moscow University, but writing plays, stories, and sketches was his main source of income. Along with James Joyce, Chekhov is considered one of the founders of the modern short story.

bent as double as the living body can be bent. If a regular snowdrift fell on him it seems as though even then he would not think it necessary to shake it off. . . . His little mare is white and motionless too. Her stillness, the angularity of her lines, and the stick-like straightness of her legs make her look like a halfpenny gingerbread horse. She is probably lost in thought. Anyone who has been torn away from the plow, from the familiar gray landscapes, and cast into the slough, full of monstrous lights, of unceasing uproar and hurrying people, is bound to think.

It is a long time since Iona and his nag have budged. They came out of the yard before dinner-time and not a single fare yet. But now the shades of evening are falling on the town. The pale light of the street lamps changes to a vivid color, and the bustle of the street grows noisier.

"Sledge to Vyborgskaya!" Iona hears. "Sledge!"

Iona starts, and through his snow-plastered eyelashes sees an officer in a military overcoat with a hood over his head.

5   "To Vyborgskaya," repeats the officer. "Are you asleep? To Vyborgskaya!"

In token of assent Iona gives a tug at the reins which sends cakes of snow flying from the horse's back and shoulders. The officer gets into the sledge. The sledge-driver clicks to the horse, cranes his neck like a swan, rises in his seat, and more from habit than necessity brandishes his whip. The mare cranes her neck, too, crooks her stick-like legs, and hesitatingly sets off. . . .

"Where are you shoving, you devil?" Iona immediately hears shouts from the dark mass shifting to and fro before him. "Where the devil are you going? Keep to the r-right!"

"You don't know how to drive! Keep to the right," says the officer angrily.

A coachman driving a carriage swears at him; a pedestrian crossing the road and brushing the horse's nose with his shoulder looks at him angrily and shakes the snow off his sleeve. Iona fidgets on the box as though he were sitting on thorns, jerks his elbows, and turns his eyes about like one possessed, as though he did not know where he was or why he was there.

10   "What rascals they all are!" says the officer jocosely. "They are simply doing their best to run up against you or fall under the horse's feet. They must be doing it on purpose."

Iona looks at his fare and moves his lips. . . . Apparently he means to say something, but nothing comes but a sniff.

"What?" inquires the officer.

Iona gives a wry smile, and straining his throat, brings out huskily: "My son . . . er . . . my son died this week, sir."

"H'm! What did he die of?"

Iona turns his whole body round to his fare, and says:

"Who can tell! It must have been from fever. . . . He lay three days in the hospital and then he died. . . . God's will."

"Turn round, you devil!" comes out of the darkness. "Have you gone cracked, you old dog? Look where you are going!"

"Drive on! drive on!. . ." says the officer. "We shan't get there till tomorrow going on like this. Hurry up!"

The sledge-driver cranes his neck again, rises in his seat, and with heavy grace swings his whip. Several times he looks round at the officer, but the latter keeps his eyes shut and is apparently disinclined to listen. Putting his fare down at Vyborgskaya, Iona stops by a restaurant, and again sits huddled up on the box. . . . Again the wet snow paints him and the horse white. One hour passes, and then another. . . .

Three young men, two tall and thin, one short and hunchbacked, come up, railing at each other and loudly stamping on the pavement with their galoshes.

"Cabby, to the Police Bridge!" the hunchback cries in a cracked voice. "The three of us, . . . twenty kopecks!"

Iona tugs at the reins and clicks to his horse. Twenty kopecks is not a fair price, but he has no thoughts for that. Whether it is a ruble or whether it is five kopecks does not matter to him now so long as he has a fare. . . . The three young men, shoving each other and using bad language, go up to the sledge, and all three try to sit down at once. The question remains to be settled: Which are to sit down and which one is to stand? After a long altercation, ill-temper, and abuse, they come to the conclusion that the hunchback must stand because he is the shortest.

"Well, drive on," says the hunchback in his cracked voice, settling himself and breathing down Iona's neck. "Cut along! What a cap you've got, my friend! You wouldn't find a worse one in all Petersburg . . ."

"He-he! . . . he-he! . . ." laughs Iona. "It's nothing to boast of!"

"Well, then, nothing to boast of, drive on! Are you going to drive like this all the way? Eh? Shall I give you one in the neck?"

"My head aches," says one of the tall ones. "At the Dukmasovs' yesterday Vaska and I drank four bottles of brandy between us."

"I can't make out why you talk such stuff," says the other tall one angrily. "You lie like a brute."

"Strike me dead, it's the truth! . . ."

"It's about as true as that a louse coughs."

"He-he!" grins Iona. "Me-er-ry gentlemen!"

"Tfoo! the devil take you!" cries the hunchback indignantly. "Will you get on, you old plague, or won't you? Is that the way to drive? Give her one with the whip. Hang it all, give it her well."

15

20

25

30

Iona feels behind his back the jolting person and quivering voice of the hunchback. He hears abuse addressed to him, he sees people, and the feeling of loneliness begins little by little to be less heavy on his heart. The hunchback swears at him, till he chokes over some elaborately whimsical string of epithets and is overpowered by his cough. His tall companions begin talking of a certain Nadyezhda Petrovna. Iona looks round at them. Waiting till there is a brief pause, he looks round once more and says:

"This week . . . er . . . my . . . er . . . son died!"

"We shall all die . . ." says the hunchback with a sigh, wiping his lips after coughing. "Come, drive on! drive on! My friends, I simply cannot stand crawling like this! When will he get us there?"

35   "Well, you give him a little encouragement . . . one in the neck!"

"Do you hear, you old plague? I'll make you smart. If one stands on ceremony with fellows like you one may as well walk. Do you hear, you old dragon? Or don't you care a hang what we say?"

And Iona hears rather than feels a slap on the back of his neck.

"He-he! . . ." he laughs. "Merry gentlemen. . . . God give you health!"

"Cabman, are you married?" asks one of the tall ones.

40   "I? He-he! Me-er-ry gentlemen. The only wife for me now is the damp earth. . . . He-ho-ho!. . . . The grave that is!. . . Here my son's dead and I am alive. . . . It's a strange thing, death has come in at the wrong door. . . . Instead of coming for me it went for my son. . . ."

And Iona turns round to tell them how his son died, but at that point the hunchback gives a faint sigh and announces that, thank God! they have arrived at last. After taking his twenty kopecks, Iona gazes for a long while after the revelers, who disappear into a dark entry. Again he is alone and again there is silence for him. . . . The misery which has been for a brief space eased comes back again and tears his heart more cruelly than ever. With a look of anxiety and suffering Iona's eyes stray restlessly among the crowds moving to and fro on both sides of the street: can he not find among those thousands someone who will listen to him? But the crowds flit by heedless of him and his misery. . . . His misery is immense, beyond all bounds. If Iona's heart were to burst and his misery to flow out, it would flood the whole world, it seems, but yet it is not seen. It has found a hiding-place in such an insignificant shell that one would not have found it with a candle by daylight. . . .

Iona sees a house-porter with a parcel and makes up his mind to address him.

"What time will it be, friend?" he asks.

"Going on for ten. . . . Why have you stopped here? Drive on!"

45   Iona drives a few paces away, bends himself double, and gives himself up to his misery. He feels it is no good to appeal to people. But before five

minutes have passed he draws himself up, shakes his head as though he feels a sharp pain, and tugs at the reins. . . . He can bear it no longer.

"Back to the yard!" he thinks. "To the yard!"

And his little mare, as though she knew his thoughts, falls to trotting. An hour and a half later Iona is sitting by a big dirty stove. On the stove, on the floor, and on the benches are people snoring. The air is full of smells and stuffiness. Iona looks at the sleeping figures, scratches himself, and regrets that he has come home so early. . . .

"I have not earned enough to pay for the oats, even," he thinks. "That's why I am so miserable. A man who knows how to do his work, . . . who has had enough to eat, and whose horse has had enough to eat, is always at ease. . . ."

In one of the corners a young cabman gets up, clears his throat sleepily, and makes for the waterbucket.

"Want a drink?" Iona asks him.

"Seems so."

"May it do you good. . . . But my son is dead, mate. . . . Do you hear? This week in the hospital. . . . It's queer business. . . ."

Iona looks to see the effect produced by his words, but he sees nothing. The young man has covered his head over and is already asleep. The old man sighs and scratches himself. . . . Just as the young man had been thirsty for water, he thirsts for speech. His son will soon have been dead a week, and he has not really talked to anybody yet. . . . He wants to talk of it properly, with deliberation. . . . He wants to tell how his son was taken ill, how he suffered, what he said before he died, how he died. . . . He wants to describe the funeral, and how he went to the hospital to get his son's clothes. He still has his daughter Anisya in the country. . . . And he wants to talk about her too. . . . Yes, he has plenty to talk about now. His listener ought to sigh and exclaim and lament. . . . It would be even better to talk to women. Though they are silly creatures, they blubber at the first word.

"Let's go out and have a look at the mare," Iona thinks. "There is always time for sleep. . . . You'll have sleep enough, no fear. . . ."

He puts on his coat and goes into the stables where his mare is standing. He thinks about oats, about hay, about the weather. . . . He cannot think about his son when he is alone. . . . To talk about him with someone is possible, but to think of him and picture him is insufferable anguish. . . .

"Are you munching?" Iona asks the mare, seeing her shining eyes. "There, munch away, munch away. . . . Since we have not earned enough for oats, we will eat hay. . . . Yes, . . . I have grown too old to drive. . . . My son ought to be driving, not I. . . . He was a real cabman. . . . He ought to have lived. . . ."

50

55

Iona is silent for a while, and then he goes on: "That's how it is, old girl. . . . Kuzma Ionitch is gone. . . . He said goodby to me. . . . He went and died for no reason. . . . Now, suppose you had a little colt, and you were own mother to that little colt. . . . And all at once that same little colt went and died. . . . You'd be sorry, wouldn't you? . . ."

The little mare munches, listens, and breathes on her master's hands. Iona is carried away and tells her all about it.

QUESTIONS

1. What kind of man is Iona? What does this brief story tell us about him? Is he a sympathetic or unsympathetic character?
2. Does this story have a plot? How would you describe its structure? Is there a dramatic climax? a denouement?
3. How would you describe the central theme of the story? How does the final scene help illustrate the theme?
4. Describe the characterizations of the men who hire Iona for a ride in his sledge. Are they sympathetic or unsympathetic?
5. Though the story is brief, can it be argued that it offers a completed action and resolution? Why or why not?

EUDORA WELTY

A Worn Path

It was December—a bright frozen day in the early morning. Far out in the country there was an old Negro woman with her head tied in a red rag, coming along a path through the pinewoods. Her name was Phoenix Jackson. She was very old and small and she walked slowly in the dark pine shadows, moving a little from side to side in her steps, with the balanced heaviness and lightness of a pendulum in a grandfather clock. She carried a thin, small cane made from an umbrella, and with this she kept tapping the frozen earth in front of her. This made a grave and persistent noise in the still air, that seemed meditative like the chirping of a solitary little bird.

She wore a dark striped dress reaching down to her shoe tops, and an equally long apron of bleached sugar sacks, with a full pocket: all neat and tidy, but every time she took a step she might have fallen over her shoelaces, which dragged from her unlaced shoes. She looked straight ahead. Her eyes were blue with age. Her skin had a pattern all its own of

A WORN PATH   First published in 1941. Eudora Welty (1909–2001) was born in Jackson, Mississippi, where she was raised and to which she returned after studying at the University of Wisconsin and Columbia University. In the mid-1930s she was employed by the federal Work Projects Administration (WPA) to travel throughout Mississippi writing newspaper copy and taking photographs, a job that enabled her to observe many varieties of rural life in her native state.

numberless branching wrinkles and as though a whole little tree stood in the middle of her forehead, but a golden color ran underneath, and the two knobs of her cheeks were illumined by a yellow burning under the dark. Under the red rag her hair came down on her neck in the frailest of ringlets, still black, and with an odor like copper.

Now and then there was a quivering in the thicket. Old Phoenix said, "Out of my way, all you foxes, owls, beetles, jack rabbits, coons, and wild animals!. . . Keep out from under these feet, little bobwhites. . . . Keep the big wild hogs out of my path. Don't let none of those come running my direction. I got a long way." Under her small black-freckled hand her cane, limber as a buggy whip, would switch at the brush as if to rouse up any hiding things.

On she went. The woods were deep and still. The sun made the pine needles almost too bright to look at, up where the wind rocked. The cones dropped as light as feathers. Down in the hollow was the mourning dove— it was not too late for him.

The path ran up a hill. "Seem like there is chains about my feet, time   5
I get this far," she said, in the voice of argument old people keep to use with themselves. "Something always take a hold of me on this hill—pleads I should stay."

After she got to the top she turned and gave a full, severe look behind her where she had come. "Up through pines," she said at length. "Now down through oaks."

Her eyes opened their widest, and she started down gently. But before she got to the bottom of the hill a bush caught her dress.

Her fingers were busy and intent, but her skirts were full and long, so that before she could pull them free in one place they were caught in another. It was not possible to allow the dress to tear. "I in the thorny bush," she said. "Thorns, you doing your appointed work. Never want to let folks pass, no sir. Old eyes thought you was a pretty little *green* bush."

Finally, trembling all over, she stood free, and after a moment dared to stoop for her cane.

"Sun so high!" she cried, leaning back and looking, while the thick   10
tears went over her eyes. "The time getting all gone here."

At the foot of this hill was a place where a log was laid across the creek. "Now comes the trial," said Phoenix.

Putting her right foot out, she mounted the log and shut her eyes. Lifting her skirt, leveling her cane fiercely before her, like a festival figure in some parade, she began to march across. Then she opened her eyes and she was safe on the other side.

"I wasn't as old as I thought," she said.

15 But she sat down to rest. She spread her skirts on the bank around her and folded her hands over her knees. Up above her was a tree in a pearly cloud of mistletoe. She did not dare to close her eyes, and when a little boy brought her a plate with a slice of marble-cake on it she spoke to him. "That would be acceptable," she said. But when she went to take it there was just her own hand in the air.

So she left that tree, and had to go through a barbed-wire fence. There she had to creep and crawl, spreading her knees and stretching her fingers like a baby trying to climb the steps. But she talked loudly to herself: she could not let her dress be torn now, so late in the day, and she could not pay for having her arm or her leg sawed off if she got caught fast where she was.

At last she was safe through the fence and risen up out in the clearing. Big dead trees, like black men with one arm, were standing in the purple stalks of the withered cotton field. There sat a buzzard.

"Who you watching?"

In the furrow she made her way along.

20 "Glad this not the season for bulls," she said, looking sideways, "and the good Lord made his snakes to curl up and sleep in the winter. A pleasure I don't see no two-headed snake coming around that tree, where it come once. It took a while to get by him, back in the summer."

She passed through the old cotton and went into a field of dead corn. It whispered and shook and was taller than her head. "Through the maze now," she said, for there was no path.

Then there was something tall, black, and skinny there, moving before her.

At first she took it for a man. It could have been a man dancing in the field. But she stood still and listened, and it did not make a sound. It was as silent as a ghost.

"Ghost," she said sharply, "who be you the ghost of? For I have heard of nary death close by."

25 But there was no answer—only the ragged dancing in the wind.

She shut her eyes, reached out her hand, and touched a sleeve. She found a coat and inside that an emptiness, cold as ice.

"You scarecrow," she said. Her face lighted. "I ought to be shut up for good," she said with laughter. "My senses is gone. I too old. I the oldest people I ever know. Dance, old scarecrow," she said, "while I dancing with you."

She kicked her foot over the furrow, and with mouth drawn down, shook her head once or twice in a little strutting way. Some husks blew down and whirled in streamers about her skirts.

Then she went on, parting her way from side to side with the cane, through the whispering field. At last she came to the end, to a wagon track where the silver grass blew between the red ruts. The quail were walking around like pullets, seeming all dainty and unseen.

"Walk pretty," she said. "This the easy place. This the easy going."   30

She followed the track, swaying through the quiet bare fields, through the little strings of trees silver in their dead leaves, past cabins silver from weather, with the doors and windows boarded shut, all like old women under a spell sitting there. "I walking in their sleep," she said, nodding her head vigorously.

In a ravine she went where a spring was silently flowing through a hollow log. Old Phoenix bent and drank. "Sweet-gum makes the water sweet," she said, and drank more. "Nobody know who made this well, for it was here when I was born."

The track crossed a swampy part where the moss hung as white as lace from every limb. "Sleep on, alligators, and blow your bubbles." Then the track went into the road.

Deep, deep the road went down between the high green-colored banks. Overhead the live-oaks met, and it was as dark as a cave.

A black dog with a lolling tongue came up out of the weeds by the   35
ditch. She was meditating, and not ready, and when he came at her she only hit him a little with her cane. Over she went in the ditch, like a little puff of milkweed.

Down there, her senses drifted away. A dream visited her, and she reached her hand up, but nothing reached down and gave her a pull. So she lay there and presently went to talking. "Old woman," she said to herself, "that black dog come up out of the weeds to stall you off, and now there he sitting on his fine tail, smiling at you."

A white man finally came along and found her—a hunter, a young man, with his dog on a chain.

"Well, Granny!" he laughed. "What are you doing there?"

"Lying on my back like a June-bug waiting to be turned over, mister," she said, reaching up her hand.

He lifted her up, gave her a swing in the air, and set her down. "Any-   40
thing broken, Granny?"

"No sir, them old dead weeds is springy enough," said Phoenix, when she had got her breath. "I thank you for your trouble."

"Where do you live, Granny?" he asked, while the two dogs were growling at each other.

"Away back yonder, sir, behind the ridge. You can't even see it from here."

"On your way home?"

"No sir, going to town."   45

"Why, that's too far! That's as far as I walk when I come out myself, and I get something for my trouble." He patted the stuffed bag he carried, and there hung down a little closed claw. It was one of the bobwhites, with its beak hooked bitterly to show it was dead. "Now you go on home, Granny!"

"I bound to go to town, mister," said Phoenix. "The time come around."

He gave another laugh, filling the whole landscape. "I know you old colored people! Wouldn't miss going to town to see Santa Claus!"

But something held old Phoenix very still. The deep lines in her face went into a fierce and different radiation. Without warning, she had seen with her own eyes a flashing nickel fall out of the man's pocket onto the ground.

50 "How old are you, Granny?" he was saying.

"There is no telling, mister," she said, "no telling."

Then she gave a little cry and clapped her hands and said, "Git on away from here, dog! Look! Look at that dog!" She laughed as if in admiration. "He ain't scared of nobody. He a big black dog." She whispered, "Sic him!"

"Watch me get rid of that cur," said the man. "Sic him, Pete! Sic him!"

Phoenix heard the dogs fighting, and heard the man running and throwing sticks. She even heard a gunshot. But she was slowly bending forward by that time, further and further forward, the lids stretched down over her eyes, as if she were doing this in her sleep. Her chin was lowered almost to her knees. The yellow palm of her hand came out from the fold of her apron. Her fingers slid down and along the ground under the piece of money with the grace and care they would have in lifting an egg from under a setting hen. Then she slowly straightened up, she stood erect, and the nickel was in her apron pocket. A bird flew by. Her lips moved. "God watching me the whole time. I come to stealing."

55 The man came back, and his own dog panted about them. "Well, I scared him off that time," he said, and then he laughed and lifted his gun and pointed it at Phoenix.

She stood straight and faced him.

"Doesn't the gun scare you?" he said, still pointing it.

"No, sir, I seen plenty go off closer by, in my day, and for less than what I done," she said, holding utterly still.

He smiled, and shouldered the gun. "Well, Granny," he said, "you must be a hundred years old, and scared of nothing. I'd give you a dime if I had any money with me. But you take my advice and stay home, and nothing will happen to you."

60 "I bound to go on my way, mister," said Phoenix. She inclined her head in the red rag. Then they went in different directions, but she could hear the gun shooting again and again over the hill.

She walked on. The shadows hung from the oak trees to the road like curtains. Then she smelled wood-smoke, and smelled the river, and she saw a steeple and the cabins on their steep steps. Dozens of little black children whirled around her. There ahead was Natchez shining. Bells were ringing. She walked on.

In the paved city it was Christmas time. There were red and green electric lights strung and crisscrossed everywhere, and all turned on in the daytime. Old Phoenix would have been lost if she had not distrusted her eyesight and depended on her feet to know where to take her.

She paused quietly on the sidewalk where people were passing by. A lady came along in the crowd, carrying an armful of red-, green-, and silver-wrapped presents; she gave off perfume like the red roses in hot summer, and Phoenix stopped her.

"Please, missy, will you lace up my shoe?" She held up her foot.

"What do you want, Grandma?" 65

"See my shoe," said Phoenix. "Do all right for out in the country, but wouldn't look right to go in a big building."

"Stand still then, Grandma," said the lady. She put her packages down on the sidewalk beside her and laced and tied both shoes tightly.

"Can't lace 'em with a cane," said Phoenix. "Thank you, missy. I doesn't mind asking a nice lady to tie up my shoe, when I gets out on the street."

Moving slowly and from side to side, she went into the big building, and into a tower of steps, where she walked up and around and around until her feet knew to stop.

She entered a door, and there she saw nailed up on the wall the docu- 70
ment that had been stamped with the gold seal and framed in the gold frame, which matched the dream that was hung up in her head.

"Here I be," she said. There was a fixed and ceremonial stiffness over her body.

"A charity case, I suppose," said an attendant who sat at the desk before her.

But Phoenix only looked above her head. There was sweat on her face, the wrinkles in her skin shone like a bright net.

"Speak up, Grandma," the woman said. "What's your name? We must have your history, you know. Have you been here before? What seems to be the trouble with you?"

Old Phoenix only gave a twitch to her face as if a fly were bothering her. 75

"Are you deaf?" cried the attendant.

But then the nurse came in.

"Oh, that's just old Aunt Phoenix," she said. "She doesn't come for herself—she has a little grandson. She makes these trips just as regular as clockwork. She lives away back off the Old Natchez Trace." She bent down. "Well, Aunt Phoenix, why don't you just take a seat? We won't keep you standing after your long trip." She pointed.

The old woman sat down, bolt upright in the chair.

80   "Now, how is the boy?" asked the nurse.

Old Phoenix did not speak.

"I said, how is the boy?"

But Phoenix only waited and stared straight ahead, her face very solemn and withdrawn into rigidity.

"Is his throat any better?" asked the nurse. "Aunt Phoenix, don't you hear me? Is your grandson's throat any better since the last time you came for the medicine?"

85   With her hands on her knees, the old woman waited, silent, erect and motionless, just as if she were in armor.

"You mustn't take up our time this way, Aunt Phoenix," the nurse said. "Tell us quickly about your grandson, and get it over. He isn't dead, is he?"

At last there came a flicker and then a flame of comprehension across her face, and she spoke.

"My grandson. It was my memory had left me. There I sat and forgot why I made my long trip."

"Forgot?" The nurse frowned. "After you came so far?"

90   Then Phoenix was like an old woman begging a dignified forgiveness for waking up frightened in the night. "I never did go to school, I was too old at the Surrender," she said in a soft voice. "I'm an old woman without an education. It was my memory fail me. My little grandson, he is just the same, and I forgot it in the coming."

"Throat never heals, does it?" said the nurse, speaking in a loud, sure voice to old Phoenix. By now she had a card with something written on it, a little list. "Yes. Swallowed lye. When was it?—January—two, three years ago—?"

Phoenix spoke unasked now. "No, missy, he not dead, he just the same. Every little while his throat begin to close up again, and he not able to swallow. He not get his breath. He not able to help himself. So the time come around, and I go on another trip for the soothing medicine."

"All right. The doctor said as long as you came to get it, you could have it," said the nurse. "But it's an obstinate case."

"My little grandson, he sit up there in the house all wrapped up, waiting by himself," Phoenix went on. "We is the only two left in the world. He suffer and it don't seem to put him back at all. He got a sweet look. He going to last. He wear a little patch quilt and peep out holding his mouth open like a little bird. I remembers so plain now. I not going to forget him again, no, the whole enduring time. I could tell him from all the others in creation."

95   "All right." The nurse was trying to hush her now. She brought her a bottle of medicine. "Charity," she said, making a check mark in a book.

Old Phoenix held the bottle close to her eyes, and then carefully put it into her pocket.

"I thank you," she said.

"It's Christmas time, Grandma," said the attendant. "Could I give you a few pennies out of my purse?"

"Five pennies is a nickel," said Phoenix stiffly.

"Here's a nickel," said the attendant.   100

Phoenix rose carefully and held out her hand. She received the nickel and then fished the other nickel out of her pocket and laid it beside the new one. She stared at her palm closely, with her head on one side.

Then she gave a tap with her cane on the floor.

"This is what come to me to do," she said. "I going to the store and buy my child a little windmill they sells, made out of paper. He going to find it hard to believe there such a thing in the world. I'll march myself back where he waiting, holding it straight up in this hand."

She lifted her free hand, gave a little nod, turned around, and walked out of the doctor's office. Then her slow step began on the stairs, going down.

QUESTIONS

1. Write a precise, well-developed sentence that states as fully as possible the theme of the story. Remember to avoid clichés or oversimplification.
2. Apart from the story's major theme, can you isolate minor themes that help give the story richness and depth? List as many as you can.
3. Discuss the way the characterization of Phoenix contributes to the theme.
4. Analyze the minor characters. What do they reveal about Phoenix and about the world in which she lives?
5. Like many classic works of literature, "A Worn Path" features a journey and a quest. Discuss the elements of plot and structure that dramatize Phoenix's journey. What are the obstacles to her quest, and how does she overcome them?
6. In answer to a student who wrote to ask her, "Is the grandson really dead?" Welty responded, "My best answer would be: *Phoenix* is alive." What might have led the student to ask that question? How can the author's remark be seen as an answer?

NADINE GORDIMER

Once upon a Time

Someone has written to ask me to contribute to an anthology of stories for children. I reply that I don't write children's stories; and he writes back that at a recent congress/book fair/seminar a certain novelist said every writer ought to write at least one story for children. I think of sending a postcard saying I don't accept that I "ought" to write anything.

And then last night I woke up—or rather was awakened without knowing what had roused me.

A voice in the echo-chamber of the subconscious?

A sound.

5   A creaking of the kind made by the weight carried by one foot after another along a wooden floor. I listened. I felt the apertures of my ears distend with concentration. Again: the creaking. I was waiting for it; waiting to hear if it indicated that feet were moving from room to room, coming up the passage—to my door. I have no burglar bars, no gun under the pillow, but I have the same fears as people who do take these precautions, and my windowpanes are thin as rime, could shatter like a wineglass. A woman was murdered (how do they put it) in broad daylight in a house two blocks away, last year, and the fierce dogs who guarded an old widower and his collection of antique clocks were strangled before he was knifed by a casual laborer he had dismissed without pay.

I was staring at the door, making it out in my mind rather than seeing it, in the dark. I lay quite still—a victim already—the arrhythmia of my heart was fleeing, knocking this way and that against its body-cage. How finely tuned the senses are, just out of rest, sleep! I could never listen intently as that in the distractions of the day; I was reading every faintest sound, identifying and classifying its possible threat.

But I learned that I was to be neither threatened nor spared. There was no human weight pressing on the boards, the creaking was a buckling, an epicenter of stress. I was in it. The house that surrounds me while I sleep is built on undermined ground; far beneath my bed, the floor, the house's foundations, the stopes and passages of gold mines

ONCE UPON A TIME   First published in 1989. Nadine Gordimer was born in 1923 in a small town near Johannesburg, South Africa, and graduated from the University of Witwatersrand. She has taught at several American universities but continues to reside in her native country. A prolific writer, Gordimer has published more than twenty books of fiction (novels and short story collections). In addition to England's prestigious Booker Prize for Fiction, she received the Nobel Prize for literature in 1991.

have hollowed the rock, and when some face trembles, detaches and falls, three thousand feet below, the whole house shifts slightly, bringing uneasy strain to the balance and counterbalance of brick, cement, wood and glass that hold it as a structure around me. The misbeats of my heart tailed off like the last muffled flourishes on one of the wooden xylophones made by the Chopi and Tsonga° migrant miners who might have been down there, under me in the earth at that moment. The stope where the fall was could have been disused, dripping water from its ruptured veins; or men might now be interred there in the most profound of tombs.

I couldn't find a position in which my mind would let go of my body—release me to sleep again. So I began to tell myself a story; a bed-time story.

In a house, in a suburb, in a city, there were a man and his wife who loved each other very much and were living happily ever after. They had a little boy, and they loved him very much. They had a cat and a dog that the little boy loved very much. They had a car and a caravan trailer for holidays, and a swimming-pool which was fenced so that the little boy and his play-mates would not fall in and drown. They had a housemaid who was abso-lutely trustworthy and an itinerant gardener who was highly recommended by the neighbors. For when they began to live happily ever after they were warned, by that wise old witch, the husband's mother, not to take on anyone off the street. They were inscribed in a medical benefit society, their pet dog was licensed, they were insured against fire, flood damage and theft, and subscribed to the local Neighborhood Watch, which supplied them with a plaque for their gates lettered YOU HAVE BEEN WARNED over the silhouette of a would-be intruder. He was masked; it could not be said if he was black or white, and therefore proved the property owner was no racist.

It was not possible to insure the house, the swimming-pool or the car against riot damage. There were riots, but these were outside the city, where people of another color were quartered. These people were not allowed into the suburb except as reliable housemaids and gardeners, so there was nothing to fear, the husband told the wife. Yet she was afraid that some day such people might come up the street and tear off the plaque YOU HAVE BEEN WARNED and open the gates and stream in . . . Nonsense, my dear, said the husband, there are police and soldiers and tear-gas and guns to keep them away. But to please her—for he loved her very much and buses were being burned, cars stoned, and schoolchildren shot by the police in those quarters out of sight and hearing of the suburb—he

10

Chopi and Tsonga: two peoples from Mozambique, northeast of South Africa had electronically controlled gates fitted. Anyone who pulled off the sign YOU HAVE BEEN WARNED and tried to open the gates would have to announce his intentions by pressing a button and speaking into a receiver relayed to the house. The little boy was fascinated by the device and used it as a walkie-talkie in cops and robbers play with his small friends.

The riots were suppressed, but there were many burglaries in the suburb and somebody's trusted housemaid was tied up and shut in a cupboard by thieves while she was in charge of her employers' house. The trusted housemaid of the man and wife and little boy was so upset by this misfortune befalling a friend left, as she herself often was, with responsibility for the possessions of the man and his wife and the little boy that she implored her employers to have burglar bars attached to the doors and windows of the house, and an alarm system installed. The wife said, She is right, let us take heed of her advice. So from every window and door in the house where they were living happily ever after they now saw the trees and sky through bars, and when the little boy's pet cat tried to climb in by the fanlight to keep him company in his little bed at night, as it customarily had done, it set off the alarm keening through the house.

The alarm was often answered—it seemed—by other burglar alarms, in other houses, that had been triggered by pet cats or nibbling mice. The alarms called to one another across the gardens in shrills and bleats and wails that everyone soon became accustomed to, so that the din roused the inhabitants of the suburb no more than the croak of frogs and musical grating of cicadas' legs. Under cover of the electronic harpies' discourse intruders sawed the iron bars and broke into homes, taking away hi-fi equipment, television sets, cassette players, cameras and radios, jewelry and clothing, and sometimes were hungry enough to devour everything in the refrigerator or paused audaciously to drink the whiskey in the cabinets or patio bars. Insurance companies paid no compensation for single malt,° a loss made keener by the property owner's knowledge that the thieves wouldn't even have been able to appreciate what it was they were drinking.

Then the time came when many of the people who were not trusted housemaids and gardeners hung about the suburb because they were unemployed. Some importuned for a job: weeding or painting a roof; anything, *baas*,° madam. But the man and his wife remembered the warning about taking on anyone off the street. Some drank liquor and fouled the street with discarded bottles. Some begged, waiting for the man or his wife to drive the car out of the electronically operated gates. They sat about with their feet in the gutters, under the jacaranda trees that made a green tunnel of the street—for it was a beautiful suburb, spoilt only by their presence—and sometimes they fell asleep lying right before the gates in

single malt: an expensive Scotch whiskey   ***baas:*** boss

the midday sun. The wife could never see anyone go hungry. She sent the trusted housemaid out with bread and tea, but the trusted housemaid said these were loafers and *tsotsis*,° who would come and tie her and shut her in a cupboard. The husband said, She's right. Take heed of her advice. You only encourage them with your bread and tea. They are looking for their chance . . . And he brought the little boy's tricycle from the garden into the house every night, because if the house was surely secure, once locked and with the alarm set, someone might still be able to climb over the wall or the electronically closed gates into the garden.

You are right, said the wife, then the wall should be higher. And the wise old witch, the husband's mother, paid for the extra bricks as her Christmas present to her son and his wife—the little boy got a Space Man outfit and a book of fairy tales.

But every week there were more reports of intrusion: in broad day- 15 light and the dead of night, in the early hours of the morning, and even in the lovely summer twilight—a certain family was at dinner while the bedrooms were being ransacked upstairs. The man and his wife, talking of the latest armed robbery in the suburb, were distracted by the sight of the little boy's pet cat effortlessly arriving over the seven-foot wall, descending first with a rapid bracing of extended forepaws down on the sheer vertical surface, and then a graceful launch, landing with swishing tail within the property. The whitewashed wall was marked with the cat's comings and goings; and on the street side of the wall there were larger red-earth smudges that could have been made by the kind of broken run-ning shoes, seen on the feet of unemployed loiterers, that had no innocent destination.

When the man and wife and little boy took the pet dog for its walk round the neighborhood streets they no longer paused to admire this show of roses or that perfect lawn; these were hidden behind an array of differ-ent varieties of security fences, walls and devices. The man, wife, little boy and dog passed a remarkable choice: there was the low-cost option of pieces of broken glass embedded in cement along the top of walls, there were iron grilles ending in lance-points, there were attempts at reconcil-ing the aesthetics of prison architecture with the Spanish Villa style (spikes painted pink) and with the plaster urns of neoclassical façades (twelve-inch pikes finned like zigzags of lightning and painted pure white). Some walls had a small board affixed, giving the name and telephone number of the firm responsible for the installation of the devices. While the little boy and the pet dog raced ahead, the husband and wife found themselves compar-ing the possible effectiveness of each style against its appearance; and after several weeks when they paused before this barricade or that without need-ing to speak, both came out with the conclusion that only one was worth

tsotsis: hooligans

considering. It was the ugliest but the most honest in its suggestion of the pure concentration-camp style, no frills, all evident efficacy. Placed the length of walls, it consisted of a continuous coil of stiff and shining metal serrated into jagged blades, so that there would be no way of climbing over it and no way through its tunnel without getting entangled in its fangs. There would be no way out, only a struggle getting bloodier and bloodier, a deeper and sharper hooking and tearing of flesh. The wife shuddered to look at it. You're right, said the husband, anyone would think twice . . . And they took heed of the advice on a small board fixed to the wall: Consult DRAGON'S TEETH The People For Total Security.

Next day a gang of workmen came and stretched the razor-bladed coils all round the walls of the house where the husband and wife and little boy and pet dog and cat were living happily ever after. The sunlight flashed and slashed, off the serrations, the cornice of razor thorns encircled the home, shining. The husband said, Never mind. It will weather. The wife said, You're wrong. They guarantee it's rust-proof. And she waited until the little boy had run off to play before she said, I hope the cat will take heed . . . The husband said, Don't worry, my dear, cats always look before they leap. And it was true that from that day on the cat slept in the little boy's bed and kept to the garden, never risking a try at breaching security.

One evening, the mother read the little boy to sleep with a fairy story from the book the wise old witch had given him at Christmas. Next day he pretended to be the Prince who braves the terrible thicket of thorns to enter the palace and kiss the Sleeping Beauty back to life: he dragged a ladder to the wall, the shining coiled tunnel was just wide enough for his little body to creep in, and with the first fixing of its razor-teeth in his knees and hands and head he screamed and struggled deeper into its tangle. The trusted housemaid and the itinerant gardener, whose "day" it was, came running, the first to see and to scream with him, and the itinerant gardener tore his hands trying to get at the little boy. Then the man and his wife burst wildly into the garden and for some reason (the cat, probably) the alarm set up wailing against the screams while the bleeding mass of the little boy was hacked out of the security coil with saws, wire-cutters, choppers, and they carried it—the man, the wife, the hysterical trusted housemaid and the weeping gardener—into the house.

QUESTIONS

1. The opening section of the story is told by a writer awakened by a frightening sound in the night. What two causes for the sound does she consider? Ultimately, which is the more significant cause for fear? How do these together create an emotional background for the "children's story" she tells?

2. What stylistic devices create the atmosphere of children's stories? How is this atmosphere related to the story's theme?

3. To what extent does the story explore the motives for the behavior of the wife and husband, the husband's mother, the servants, and the people who surround the suburb and the house? What motives can you infer for these people? What ironies do they display in their actions?

4. Can you fix the blame for the calamity that befalls the child? What are the possible meanings of the repeated phrase "YOU HAVE BEEN WARNED"?

5. What details in the introductory section and in the children's story imply the nature of the social order in which both occur?

6. Analyze the story's final paragraph in detail. How does it help to elucidate the theme?

SUGGESTIONS FOR WRITING

1. Bearing in mind point 5 in the introduction to this chapter ("there is no *one* way of stating the theme of a story"), write out three alternative statements of theme for one or more of the following:
   a. Wolff, "Hunters in the Snow" (page 79).
   b. Munro, "How I Met My Husband" (page 118).
   c. Chekhov, "Misery" (page 217).

2. The theme of a story often is displayed in the development of the protagonist or in the epiphany that the protagonist experiences. But in some stories, there may be more than one focal character, and the theme must therefore be inferred by examining the different experiences of more than one person. Demonstrate the validity of this statement by examining the three main characters in one of the following:
   a. Wolff, "Hunters in the Snow" (page 79).
   b. Walker, "Everyday Use" (page 147).
   c. Hurston, "Spunk" (page 561).

PRACTICE AP WRITING PROMPTS

Anton Chekhov, "Misery" (pp. 217)

Read Anton Chekhov's "Misery" carefully. Then, in a well-written essay, analyze how the author employs elements such as point of view and characterization (including dialogue) to render a commentary on social behavior and human needs.

Eudora Welty, "A Worn Path" (pp. 222)

In a well-organized essay on "A Worn Path," show how Eudora Welty employs such literary elements as diction, symbolism, irony, and understatement to give significant meaning to Phoenix's journey.

CHAPTER FIVE

Point of View

Primitive storytellers, unbothered by considerations of form, simply spun their tales. "Once upon a time," they began, and proceeded to narrate the story to their listeners, describing the characters when necessary, telling what the characters thought and felt as well as what they did, and interjecting comments and ideas of their own. Modern fiction writers are artistically more self-conscious. They realize that there are many ways of telling a story; they decide upon a method before they begin, or discover one while in the act of writing, and may even set up rules for themselves. Instead of telling the story themselves, they may let one of the characters tell it; they may tell it by means of letters or diaries; they may confine themselves to recording the thoughts of one of the characters. With the growth of artistic consciousness, the question of **point of view**—of who tells the story, and, therefore, of how it gets told—has assumed special importance.

To determine the point of view of a story, we ask, "Who tells the story?" and "How much is this person allowed to know?" and, especially, "To what extent does the narrator look inside the characters and report their thoughts and feelings?"

Though many variations and combinations are possible, the basic points of view are four, as follows:

1. Omniscient	
2. Third-person limited	{ (a) Major character { (b) Minor character
3. First person	{ (a) Major character { (b) Minor character
4. Objective	

1. In the **omniscient point of view**, the story is told in the third person by a narrator whose knowledge and prerogatives are unlimited. Such narrators are free to go wherever they wish, to peer inside the minds and hearts of characters at will and tell us what they are thinking or feeling. These narrators can interpret behavior and can comment, if they wish, on the significance of their stories. They know all. They can tell us as much or as little as they please.

The following version of Aesop's fable "The Ant and the Grasshopper" is told from the omniscient point of view. Notice that in it we are told not only what both characters do and say, but also what they think and feel; notice also that the narrator comments at the end on the significance of the story. (The phrases in which the narrator enters into the thoughts or feelings of the ant and the grasshopper have been italicized; the comment by the author is printed in small capitals.)

Weary in every limb, the ant tugged over the snow a piece of corn he had stored up last summer. *It would taste mighty good at dinner tonight.*

A grasshopper, *cold and hungry*, looked on. *Finally he could bear it no longer.* "Please, friend ant, may I have a bite of corn?"

"What were you doing all last summer?" asked the ant. He looked the grasshopper up and down. *He knew its kind.*

"I sang from dawn till dark," replied the grasshopper, *happily unaware of what was coming next.*

"Well," said the ant, *hardly bothering to conceal his contempt*, "since you sang all summer, you can dance all winter."

HE WHO IDLES WHEN HE'S YOUNG
WILL HAVE NOTHING WHEN HE'S OLD

Stories told from the omniscient point of view may vary widely in the amount of omniscience the narrator is allowed. In "Hunters in the Snow," we are frequently allowed into the mind of Tub, but near the end of the story the omniscient narrator takes over and gives us information none of the characters could know. In "The Destructors," though we are taken into the minds of Blackie, Mike, the gang as a group, Old Misery, and the lorry driver, we are not taken into the mind of Trevor—the most important character. In "The Most Dangerous Game," we are confined to the thoughts and feelings of Rainsford, except for the brief passage between Rainsford's leap into the sea and his waking in Zaroff's bed, during which the point of view shifts to General Zaroff.

The omniscient is the most flexible point of view and permits the widest scope. It is also the most subject to abuse. It offers constant danger that the narrator may come between the readers and the story, or that the continual shifting of viewpoint from character to character may cause a breakdown in coherence or unity. Used skillfully, it enables the author to achieve simultaneous breadth and depth. Unskillfully used, it can destroy the illusion of reality that the story attempts to create.

2. In the **third-person limited point of view**, the story is told in the third person, but from the viewpoint of one character in the story. Such point-of-view characters are filters through whose eyes and minds writers look at the events. Authors employing this perspective may move both inside and outside these characters but never leave their sides. They tell us what these characters see and hear and what they think and feel; they possibly interpret the characters' thoughts and behavior. They know everything about their point-of-view characters—often more than the characters know about themselves. But they limit themselves to these characters' perceptions and show no direct knowledge of what *other* characters are thinking or feeling or doing, except for what the point-of-view character knows or can infer about them. The chosen character may be either a major or a minor character, a participant or an observer, and this choice also will be a very important one for the story. "Babylon Revisited," "Miss Brill," and "A Worn Path" are told from the third-person limited point of view, from the perspective of the main character. The use of this viewpoint with a minor character is rare in the short story, and is not illustrated in this book.

Here is "The Ant and the Grasshopper" told, in the third person, from the point of view of the ant. Notice that this time we are told nothing of what the grasshopper thinks or feels. We see and hear and know of him only what the ant sees and hears and knows.

> *Weary in every limb*, the ant tugged over the snow a piece of corn he had stored up last summer. *It would taste mighty good at dinner tonight. It was then that he noticed the grasshopper, looking cold and pinched.*
>
> "Please, friend ant, may I have a bite of your corn?" asked the grasshopper.
>
> He looked the grasshopper up and down. "What were you doing all last summer?" he asked. *He knew its kind.*
>
> "I sang from dawn till dark," replied the grasshopper.
>
> "Well," said the ant, *hardly bothering to conceal his contempt*, "since you sang all summer, you can dance all winter."

The third-person limited point of view, since it acquaints us with the world through the mind and senses of only one character, approximates more closely than the omniscient the conditions of real life; it also offers a ready-made unifying element, since all details of the story are the experience of one character. And it affords an additional device of characterization, since what a point-of-view character does or does not find noteworthy, and the inferences that such a character draws about other characters' actions and motives, may reveal biases or limitations in the observer. At the same time it offers a limited field of observation, for the readers can go nowhere except where the chosen character goes, and there may be difficulty in having the character naturally cognizant of all important events. Clumsy writers will constantly have the focal character listening at keyholes, accidentally overhearing important conversations, or coincidentally being present when important events occur.

A variant of third-person limited point of view, illustrated in this chapter by Porter's "The Jilting of Granny Weatherall," is called **stream of consciousness.** Stream of consciousness presents the apparently random thoughts going through a character's head within a certain period of time, mingling memory and present experiences, and employing transitional links that are psychological rather than strictly logical. (First-person narrators might also tell their stories through stream of consciousness, though first-person use of this technique is relatively rare.)

3. In the **first-person point of view,** the author disappears into one of the characters, who tells the story in the first person. This character, again, may be either a major or a minor character, protagonist or observer, and it will make considerable difference whether the protagonist tells the story or someone else tells it. In "How I Met My Husband," the protagonist tells the story in the first person. In "A Rose for Emily," presented in Part 4, the story is told in the unusual first-person plural, from the vantage point of the townspeople observing Emily's life through the years.

Our fable is retold below in the first person from the point of view of the grasshopper. (The whole story is italicized because it all comes out of the grasshopper's mind.)

> *Cold and hungry, I watched the ant tugging over the snow a piece of corn he had stored up last summer. My feelers twitched, and I was conscious of a tic in my left hind leg. Finally I could bear it no longer.*
>
> *"Please, friend ant," I asked, "may I have a bite of your corn?"*
>
> *He looked me up and down. "What were you doing all last summer?" he asked, rather too smugly it seemed to me.*
>
> *"I sang from dawn till dark," I said innocently, remembering the happy times.*
>
> *"Well," he said, with a priggish sneer, "since you sang all summer, you can dance all winter."*

The first-person point of view shares the virtues and limitations of the third-person limited. It offers, sometimes, a gain in immediacy and reality, since we get the story directly from a participant, the author as intermediary being eliminated. It offers no opportunity, however, for *direct* interpretation by the author, and there is constant danger that narrators may be made to transcend their own sensitivity, their knowledge, or their powers of language in telling a story. Talented authors, however, can make tremendous literary capital out of the very limitations of their narrators. The first-person point of view offers excellent opportunities for dramatic irony and for studies in limited or blunted human perceptiveness. In "How I Met My Husband," for instance, there is an increasingly clear difference between what the narrator perceives and what the reader perceives as the story proceeds. Even though Edie is clearly narrating her story from the vantage point of maturity—ultimately we know this from the ending and from the title itself—she rarely allows her mature voice to intrude or to make judgments on Edie's thoughts and feelings as a fifteen-year-old girl infatuated with a handsome pilot. The story gains in emotional power because of the poignancy of youthful romanticism that Edie's hopes and wishes represent, and because of the inevitable disillusionment she must suffer. By choosing this point of view, Munro offers an interpretation of the material *indirectly*, through her dramatization of Edie's experiences. In other stories, like "A Rose for Emily," the author intends the first-person viewpoint to suggest a conventional set of perceptions and attitudes, perhaps including those of the author and the reader. Identifications of a narrator's attitudes with the author's, however, must always be undertaken with extreme caution; they are justified only if the total material of the story supports them, or if outside evidence (for example, a statement by the author) supports such an identification. In "A Rose for Emily" the narrative detachment does reflect the author's own; nevertheless, much of the interest of the story arises from the limited viewpoint of the townspeople and the cloak of mystery surrounding Emily and her life inside the house.

4. In the **objective point of view,** the narrator disappears into a kind of roving sound camera. This camera can go anywhere but can record only what is seen and heard. It cannot comment, interpret, or enter a character's mind. With this point of view (sometimes called also the **dramatic point of view**) readers are placed in the position of spectators at a movie or play. They see what the characters do and hear what they say but must infer what they think or feel and what they are like. Authors are not there to explain. The purest example of a story told from the objective point of view would be one written entirely in dialogue, for as

soon as authors add words of their own, they begin to interpret through their very choice of words. Actually, few stories using this point of view are antiseptically pure, for the limitations it imposes on the author are severe. Shirley Jackson's "The Lottery," presented in this chapter, is essentially objective in its narration.

The following version of "The Ant and the Grasshopper" is also told from the objective point of view. (Since we are nowhere taken into the thoughts or feelings of the characters, none of this version is printed in italics.)

The ant tugged over the snow a piece of corn he had stored up last summer, perspiring in spite of the cold.

A grasshopper, his feelers twitching and with a tic in his left hind leg, looked on for some time. Finally he asked, "Please, friend ant, may I have a bite of your corn?"

The ant looked the grasshopper up and down. "What were you doing all last summer?" he snapped.

"I sang from dawn till dark," replied the grasshopper, not changing his tone.

"Well," said the ant, and a faint smile crept into his face, "since you sang all summer, you can dance all winter."

The objective point of view requires readers to draw their own inferences. But it must rely heavily on external action and dialogue, and it offers no opportunities for direct interpretation by the author.

Each of the points of view has its advantages, its limitations, and its peculiar uses. Ideally the choice of the author will depend upon the materials and the purpose of a story. Authors choose the point of view that enables them to present their particular materials most effectively in terms of their purposes. Writers of murder mysteries with suspense and thrills as the purpose will ordinarily avoid using the point of view of the murderer or the brilliant detective: otherwise they would have to reveal at the beginning the secrets they wish to conceal till the end. On the other hand, if they are interested in exploring criminal psychology, the murderer's point of view might be by far the most effective. In the Sherlock Holmes stories, A. Conan Doyle effectively uses the somewhat imperceptive Dr. Watson as his narrator, so that the reader may be kept in the dark as long as possible and then be as amazed as Watson is by Holmes's deductive powers. In Dostoevsky's *Crime and Punishment*, however, the author is interested not in mystifying and surprising but in illuminating the moral and psychological operations of the human soul in the act of taking life; he therefore tells the story from the viewpoint of a sensitive and intelligent murderer.

For readers, the examination of point of view may be important both for understanding and for evaluating the story. First, they should know whether the events of the story are being interpreted by a narrator or by one of the characters. If the latter, they must ask how this character's mind and personality affect the interpretation, whether the character is perceptive or imperceptive, and whether the interpretation can be accepted at face value or must be discounted because of ignorance, stupidity, or self-deception.

Next, readers should ask whether the writer has chosen the point of view for maximum revelation of the material or for another reason. The author may choose the point of view mainly to conceal certain information till the end of the story and thus maintain suspense and create surprise. The author may even deliberately mislead readers by presenting the events through a character who puts a false interpretation on them. Such a false interpretation may be justified if it leads eventually to more effective revelation of character and theme. If it is there merely to trick readers, it is obviously less justifiable.

Finally, readers should ask whether the author has used the selected point of view fairly and consistently. Even in commercial fiction we have a right to demand fair treatment. If the person to whose thoughts and feelings we are admitted has pertinent information that is not revealed, we legitimately feel cheated. To have a chance to solve a murder mystery, we must know what the detective learns. A writer also should be consistent in the point of view; if it shifts, it should do so for a just artistic reason. Serious literary writers choose and use point of view so as to yield ultimately the greatest possible insight, either in fullness or in intensity.

REVIEWING CHAPTER FIVE

1. Explain how to determine the point of view in a story.
2. Describe the characteristics of omniscient point of view.
3. Review the definition of third-person limited point of view.
4. Consider the virtues and limitations of first-person point of view.
5. Explore the use of objective point of view in Hemingway's "Hills Like White Elephants," presented in this chapter.

WILLA CATHER
Paul's Case

It was Paul's afternoon to appear before the faculty of the Pittsburgh High School to account for his various misdemeanors. He had been suspended a week ago, and his father had called at the Principal's office and confessed his perplexity about his son. Paul entered the faculty room suave and smiling. His clothes were a trifle outgrown, and the tan velvet on the collar of his open overcoat was frayed and worn; but for all that there was something of a dandy about him, and he wore an opal pin in his neatly knotted black four-in-hand, and a red carnation in his buttonhole. This latter adornment the faculty somehow felt was not properly significant of the contrite spirit befitting a boy under the ban of suspension.

Paul was tall for his age and very thin, with high, cramped shoulders and a narrow chest. His eyes were remarkable for a certain hysterical brilliancy, and he continually used them in a conscious, theatrical sort of way, peculiarly offensive in a boy. The pupils were abnormally large, as though he were addicted to belladonna, but there was a glassy glitter about them which that drug does not produce.

When questioned by the Principal as to why he was there, Paul stated, politely enough, that he wanted to come back to school. This was a lie, but Paul was quite accustomed to lying; found it, indeed, indispensable for overcoming friction. His teachers were asked to state their respective charges against him, which they did with such a rancor and aggrieved ness as evinced that this was not a usual case. Disorder and impertinence were among the offences named, yet each of his instructors felt that it was scarcely possible to put into words the real cause of the trouble, which lay in a sort of hysterically defiant manner of the boy's; in the contempt which they all knew he felt for them, and which he seemingly made not the least effort to conceal. Once, when he had been making a synopsis of a paragraph at the blackboard, his English teacher had stepped to his side and attempted to guide his hand. Paul had started back with a shudder and thrust his hands violently behind him. The astonished woman could scarcely have been more hurt and embarrassed had he struck at her. The insult was so involuntary and definitely personal as to be unforgettable. In one way and another, he had made all his teachers, men and women alike, conscious of the same feeling of physical aversion. In one class he habitually

PAUL'S CASE   Written in 1904, first published in 1905. Willa Cather (1873–1947) was born in Virginia and grew up and was educated in Nebraska. From 1895 to 1905 she lived and worked in Pittsburgh, first as a journalist, writing drama and music criticism, later as a teacher of English and Latin in two Pittsburgh high schools. In 1902 she traveled in Europe.

sat with his hand shading his eyes; in another he always looked out of the window during the recitation; in another he made a running commentary on the lecture, with humorous intent.

His teachers felt this afternoon that his whole attitude was symbolized by his shrug and his flippantly red carnation flower, and they fell upon him without mercy, his English teacher leading the pack. He stood through it smiling, his pale lips parted over his white teeth. (His lips were continually twitching, and he had a habit of raising his eyebrows that was contemptuous and irritating to the last degree.) Older boys than Paul had broken down and shed tears under that ordeal, but his set smile did not once desert him, and his only sign of discomfort was the nervous trembling of the fingers that toyed with the buttons of his overcoat, and an occasional jerking of the other hand which held his hat. Paul was always smiling, always glancing about him, seeming to feel that people might be watching him and trying to detect something. This conscious expression, since it was as far as possible from boyish mirthfulness, was usually attributed to insolence or "smartness."

5   As the inquisition proceeded, one of his instructors repeated an impertinent remark of the boy's, and the Principal asked him whether he thought that a courteous speech to make to a woman. Paul shrugged his shoulders slightly and his eyebrows twitched.

"I don't know," he replied. "I didn't mean to be polite or impolite, either. I guess it's a sort of way I have, of saying things regardless."

The Principal asked him whether he didn't think that a way it would be well to get rid of. Paul grinned and said he guessed so. When he was told that he could go, he bowed gracefully and went out. His bow was like a repetition of the scandalous red carnation.

His teachers were in despair, and his drawing-master voiced the feeling of them all when he declared there was something about the boy which none of them understood. He added: "I don't really believe that smile of his comes altogether from insolence; there's something sort of haunted about it. The boy is not strong for one thing. There is something wrong about the fellow."

The drawing-master had come to realize that, in looking at Paul, one saw only his white teeth and the forced animation of his eyes. One warm afternoon the boy had gone to sleep at his drawing-board, and his master had noted with amazement what a white, blue-veined face it was; drawn and wrinkled like an old man's about the eyes, the lips twitching even in his sleep.

10   His teachers left the building dissatisfied and unhappy; humiliated to have felt so vindictive toward a mere boy, to have uttered this feeling in cutting terms, and to have set each other on, as it were, in the gruesome game of intemperate reproach. One of them remembered having seen a miserable street cat set at bay by a ring of tormentors.

As for Paul, he ran down the hill whistling the Soldiers' Chorus from *Faust*, looking behind him now and then to see whether some of his teachers were not there to witness his light-heartedness. As it was now late in the afternoon and Paul was on duty that evening as usher at Carnegie Hall, he decided that he would not go home to supper.

When he reached the concert hall, the doors were not yet open. It was chilly outside, and he decided to go up into the picture gallery—always deserted at this hour—where there were some of Raffelli's gay studies of Paris streets and an airy blue Venetian scene or two that always exhilarated him. He was delighted to find no one in the gallery but the old guard, who sat in the corner, a newspaper on his knee, a black patch over one eye and the other closed. Paul possessed himself of the place and walked confidently up and down, whistling under his breath. After a while he sat down before a blue Rico and lost himself. When he bethought him to look at his watch, it was after seven o'clock and he rose with a start and ran downstairs, making a face at Augustus Caesar, peering out from the cast-room, and an evil gesture at the Venus of Milo as he passed her on the stairway.

When Paul reached the ushers' dressing-room, half a dozen boys were there already, and he began excitedly to tumble into his uniform. It was one of the few that at all approached fitting, and Paul thought it very becoming—though he knew the tight, straight coat accentuated his narrow chest, about which he was exceedingly sensitive. He was always excited while he dressed, twanging all over to the tuning of the strings and the preliminary flourishes of the horns in the music-room; but tonight he seemed quite beside himself, and he teased and plagued the boys until, telling him that he was crazy, they put him down on the floor and sat on him.

Somewhat calmed by his suppression, Paul dashed out to the front of the house to seat the early comers. He was a model usher. Gracious and smiling he ran up and down the aisles. Nothing was too much trouble for him; he carried messages and brought programs as though it were his greatest pleasure in life, and all the people in his section thought him a charming boy, feeling that he remembered and admired them. As the house filled, he grew more and more vivacious and animated, and the color came to his cheeks and lips. It was very much as though this were a great reception and Paul were the host. Just as the musicians came out to take their places, his English teacher arrived with checks for the seats which a prominent manufacturer had taken for the season. She betrayed some embarrassment when she handed Paul the tickets, and a *hauteur*° which subsequently made her feel very foolish. Paul was startled for a moment, and had the feeling of wanting to put her out; what business had she here among all these fine people and gay colors? He looked her over and decided

hauteur: condescension

that she was not appropriately dressed and must be a fool to sit downstairs in such togs. The tickets had probably been sent her out of kindness, he reflected, as he put down a seat for her, and she had about as much right to sit there as he had.

15   When the symphony began, Paul sank into one of the rear seats with a long sigh of relief, and lost himself as he had done before the Rico. It was not that symphonies, as such, meant anything in particular to Paul, but the first sight of the instruments seemed to free some hilarious spirit within him; something that struggled there like the Genius in the bottle found by the Arab fisherman. He felt a sudden zest of life; the lights danced before his eyes and the concert hall blazed into unimaginable splendor. When the soprano soloist came on, Paul forgot even the nastiness of his teacher's being there, and gave himself up to the peculiar intoxication such personages always had for him. The soloist chanced to be a German woman, by no means in her first youth, and the mother of many children; but she wore a satin gown and a tiara, and she had that indefinable air of achievement, that world-shine upon her, which always blinded Paul to any possible defects.

After a concert was over, Paul was often irritable and wretched until he got to sleep—and tonight he was even more than usually restless. He had the feeling of not being able to let down; of its being impossible to give up this delicious excitement which was the only thing that could be called living at all. During the last number he withdrew and, after hastily changing his clothes in the dressing-room, slipped out to the side door where the singer's carriage stood. Here he began pacing rapidly up and down the walk, waiting to see her come out.

Over yonder the Schenley, in its vacant stretch, loomed big and square through the fine rain, the windows of its twelve stories glowing like those of a lighted cardboard house under a Christmas tree. All the actors and singers of any importance stayed there when they were in Pittsburgh, and a number of the big manufacturers of the place lived there in the winter. Paul had often hung about the hotel, watching the people go in and out, longing to enter and leave schoolmasters and dull care behind him forever.

At last the singer came out, accompanied by the conductor, who helped her into her carriage and closed the door with a cordial *auf wiedersehen*°— which set Paul to wondering whether she were not an old sweetheart of his. Paul followed the carriage over to the hotel, walking so rapidly as not to be far from the entrance when the singer alighted and disappeared behind the swinging glass doors which were opened by a Negro in a tall hat and a long coat. In the moment that the door was ajar, it seemed to Paul that he, too, entered. He seemed to feel himself go after her up the steps, into the warm, lighted building, into an exotic, a tropical world of shiny, glistening

auf wiedersehen: goodbye or farewell

surfaces and basking ease. He reflected upon the mysterious dishes that were brought into the dining-room, the green bottles in buckets of ice, as he had seen them in the supper-party pictures of the Sunday supplement. A quick gust of wind brought the rain down with sudden vehemence, and Paul was startled to find that he was still outside in the slush of the gravel driveway; that his boots were letting in the water and his scanty overcoat was clinging wet about him; that the lights in front of the concert hall were out, and that the rain was driving in sheets between him and the orange glow of the windows above him. There it was, what he wanted—tangibly before him, like the fairy world of a Christmas pantomime; as the rain beat in his face, Paul wondered whether he were destined always to shiver in the black night outside, looking up at it.

He turned and walked reluctantly toward the car tracks. The end had to come sometime; his father in his night-clothes at the top of the stairs, explanations that did not explain, hastily improvised fictions that were forever tripping him up, his upstairs room and its horrible yellow wall-paper, the creaking bureau with the greasy plush collar-box, and over his painted wooden bed the pictures of George Washington and John Calvin, and the framed motto, "Feed my Lambs," which had been worked in red worsted by his mother, whom Paul could not remember.

Half an hour later, Paul alighted from the Negley Avenue car and 20 went slowly down one of the side streets off the main thoroughfare. It was a highly respectable street, where all the houses were exactly alike, and where business men of moderate means begot and reared large families of children, all of whom went to Sabbath School and learned the shorter catechism, and were interested in arithmetic; all of whom were as exactly alike as their homes, and of a piece with the monotony in which they lived. Paul never went up Cordelia Street without a shudder of loathing. His home was next to the house of the Cumberland minister. He approached it tonight with the nerveless sense of defeat, the hopeless feeling of sinking back forever into ugliness and commonness that he had always had when he came home. The moment he turned into Cordelia Street he felt the waters close above his head. After each of these orgies of living, he experienced all the physical depression which follows a debauch; the loathing of respect-able beds, of common food, of a house permeated by kitchen odors; a shud-dering repulsion for the flavorless, colorless mass of everyday existence; a morbid desire for cool things and soft lights and fresh flowers.

The nearer he approached the house, the more absolutely unequal Paul felt to the sight of it all: his ugly sleeping chamber; the old bathroom with the grimy zinc tub, the cracked mirror, the dripping spigots; his father, at the top of the stairs, his hairy legs sticking out from his nightshirt, his feet thrust into carpet slippers. He was so much later than usual that there would certainly be inquiries and reproaches. Paul stopped short before the door. He felt that he could not be accosted by his father tonight; that he could not toss again on that miserable bed. He would not go in. He would tell his father that he had no carfare, and it was raining so hard he had gone home with one of the boys and stayed all night.

Meanwhile, he was wet and cold. He went around to the back of the house and tried one of the basement windows, found it open, and raised it cautiously, and scrambled down the cellar wall to the floor. There he stood, holding his breath, terrified by the noise he had made; but the floor above him was silent, and there was no creak on the stairs. He found a soap-box, and carried it over to the soft ring of light that streamed from the furnace door, and sat down. He was horribly afraid of rats, so he did not try to sleep, but sat looking distrustfully at the dark, still terrified lest he might have awakened his father. In such reactions, after one of the experiences which made days and nights out of the dreary blanks of the calendar, when his senses were deadened, Paul's head was always singularly clear. Suppose his father had heard him getting in at the window and had come down and shot him for a burglar? Then, again, suppose his father had come down, pistol in hand, and he had cried out in time to save himself, and his father had been horrified to think how nearly he had killed him? Then again, suppose a day should come when his father would remember that night, and wish there had been no warning cry to stay his hand? With this last supposition Paul entertained himself until daybreak.

The following Sunday was fine; the sodden November chill was broken by the last flash of autumnal summer. In the morning Paul had to go to church and Sabbath School, as always. On seasonable Sunday afternoons the burghers of Cordelia Street usually sat out on their front "stoops," and talked to their neighbors on the next stoop, or called to those across the street in neighborly fashion. The men sat placidly on gay cushions placed upon the steps that led down to the sidewalk, while the women, in their Sunday "waists," sat in rockers on the cramped porches, pretending to be greatly at their ease. The children played in the streets; there were so many of them that the place resembled the recreation grounds of a kindergarten. The men on the steps—all in their shirt-sleeves, their vests unbuttoned, sat with their legs well apart, their stomachs comfortably protruding, and talked of the prices of things, or told anecdotes of the sagacity of their various chiefs and overlords. They occasionally looked over the multitude of squabbling children, listened affectionately to their high-pitched, nasal voices, smiling to see their own proclivities reproduced in their offspring, and interspersed their legends of the iron kings with remarks about their sons' progress at school, their grades in arithmetic, and the amounts they had saved in their toy banks.

On this last Sunday of November, Paul sat all afternoon on the lowest step of his "stoop," staring into the street, while his sisters, in their rockers, were talking to the minister's daughters next door about how many shirtwaists they had made in the last week, and how many waffles someone had eaten at the last church supper. When the weather was warm, and his father was in a particularly jovial frame of mind, the girls made lemonade, which was always brought out in a red-glass pitcher, ornamented with forget-me-nots in blue enamel. This the girls thought very fine, and the neighbors joked about the suspicious color of the pitcher.

Today Paul's father, on the top step, was talking to a young man who shifted a restless baby from knee to knee. He happened to be the young man who was daily held up to Paul as a model, and after whom it was his father's dearest hope that he would pattern. This young man was of a ruddy complexion, with a compressed, red mouth, and faded, nearsighted eyes, over which he wore thick spectacles, with gold bows that curved about his ears. He was clerk to one of the magnates of a great steel corporation, and was looked upon in Cordelia Street as a young man with a future. There was a story that, some five years ago—he was now barely twenty-six—he had been a trifle "dissipated," but in order to curb his appetites and save the loss of time and strength that a sowing of wild oats might have entailed, he had taken his chief's advice, oft reiterated to his employees, and at twenty-one had married the first woman whom he could persuade to share his fortunes. She happened to be an angular schoolmistress, much older than he, who also wore thick glasses, and who had now borne him four children, all nearsighted like herself.

The young man was relating how his chief, now cruising in the Mediterranean, kept in touch with all the details of the business, arranging his office hours on his yacht just as though he were at home, and "knocking off work enough to keep two stenographers busy." His father told, in turn, the plan his corporation was considering, of putting in an electric railway plant at Cairo. Paul snapped his teeth; he had an awful apprehension that they might spoil it all before he got there. Yet he rather liked to hear these legends of the iron kings, that were told and retold on Sundays and holidays; these stories of palaces in Venice, yachts on the Mediterranean, and high play at Monte Carlo appealed to his fancy, and he was interested in the triumphs of cash-boys who had become famous, though he had no mind for the cash-boy stage.

After supper was over, and he had helped to dry the dishes, Paul nervously asked his father whether he could go to George's to get some help in his geometry, and still more nervously asked for carfare. This latter request he had to repeat, as his father, on principle, did not like to hear requests for money, whether much or little. He asked Paul whether he could not go to some boy who lived nearer, and told him that he ought not to leave his school work until Sunday; but he gave him the dime. He was not a poor man, but he had a worthy ambition to come up in the world. His only reason for allowing Paul to usher was that he thought a boy ought to be earning a little.

Paul bounded upstairs, scrubbed the greasy odor of the dishwater from his hands with the ill-smelling soap he hated, and then shook over his fingers a few drops of violet water from the bottle he kept hidden in his drawer. He left the house with his geometry conspicuously under his arm, and the moment he got out of Cordelia Street and boarded a downtown car, he shook off the lethargy of two deadening days, and began to live again.

The leading juvenile of the permanent stock company which played at one of the downtown theaters was an acquaintance of Paul's, and the boy had been invited to drop in at the Sunday-night rehearsals whenever he could. For more than a year Paul had spent every available moment loitering about Charley Edwards's dressing-room. He had won a place among Edwards's following not only because the young actor, who could not afford to employ a dresser, often found him useful, but because he recognized in Paul something akin to what churchmen term "vocation."

30   It was at the theater and at Carnegie Hall that Paul really lived; the rest was but a sleep and a forgetting. This was Paul's fairy tale, and it had for him all the allurement of a secret love. The moment he inhaled the gassy, painty, dusty odor behind the scenes, he breathed like a prisoner set free, and felt within him the possibility of doing or saying splendid, brilliant things. The moment the cracked orchestra beat out the overture from *Martha*, or jerked at the serenade from *Rigoletto*, all stupid and ugly things slid from him, and his senses were deliciously, yet delicately fired.

Perhaps it was because, in Paul's world, the natural nearly always wore the guise of ugliness, that a certain element of artificiality seemed to him necessary in beauty. Perhaps it was because his experience of life elsewhere was so full of Sabbath-School picnics, petty economies, wholesome advice as to how to succeed in life, and the unescapable odors of cooking, that he found this existence so alluring, these smartly clad men and women so attractive, that he was so moved by these starry apple orchards that bloomed perennially under the limelight.

It would be difficult to put it strongly enough how convincingly the stage entrance of the theater was for Paul the actual portal of Romance. Certainly none of the company ever suspected it, least of all Charley Edwards. It was very like the old stories that used to float about London of fabulously rich Jews, who had subterranean halls, with palms, and fountains, and soft lamps and richly appareled women who never saw the disenchanting light of London day. So, in the midst of that smoke-palled city, enamored of figures and grimy toil, Paul had his secret temple, his wishing-carpet, his bit of blue-and-white Mediterranean shore bathed in perpetual sunshine.

Several of Paul's teachers had a theory that his imagination had been perverted by garish fiction; but the truth was, he scarcely ever read at all. The books at home were not such as would either tempt or corrupt a youthful mind, and as for reading the novels that some of his friends urged upon him—well, he got what he wanted much more quickly from music; any sort of music, from an orchestra to a barrel-organ. He needed only the spark, the indescribable thrill that made his imagination master of his senses, and he could make plots and pictures enough of his own. It was equally true that he was not stage-struck—not, at any rate, in the usual acceptation of the expression. He had no desire to become an actor, any more than he had to become a musician. He felt no necessity to do any of these things; what he wanted was to see, to be in the atmosphere, float on the wave of it, to be carried out, blue league after league, away from everything.

After a night behind the scenes, Paul found the schoolroom more than ever repulsive; the bare floors and naked walls; the prosy men who never wore frock coats, or violets in their buttonholes; the women with their dull gowns, shrill voices, and pitiful seriousness about prepositions that govern the dative. He could not bear to have the other pupils think, for a moment, that he took these people seriously; he must convey to them that he considered it all trivial, and was there only by the way of a joke, anyway. He had autographed pictures of all the members of the stock company which he showed his classmates, telling them the most incredible stories of his familiarity with these people, of his acquaintance with the soloists who came to Carnegie Hall, his suppers with them and the flowers he sent them. When these stories lost their effect, and his audience grew listless, he would bid all the boys goodbye, announcing that he was going to travel for a while; going to Naples, to California, to Egypt. Then, next Monday, he would slip back, conscious and nervously smiling; his sister was ill, and he would have to defer his voyage until spring.

Matters went steadily worse with Paul at school. In the itch to let his instructors know how heartily he despised them, and how thoroughly he was appreciated elsewhere, he mentioned once or twice that he had no time to fool with theorems; adding—with a twitch of the eyebrows and a touch of that nervous bravado which so perplexed them—that he was helping the people down at the stock company; they were old friends of his.

The upshot of the matter was that the Principal went to Paul's father, and Paul was taken out of school and put to work. The manager at Carnegie Hall was told to get another usher in his stead; the doorkeeper at the theater was warned not to admit him to the house; and Charley Edwards remorsefully promised the boy's father not to see him again.

The members of the stock company were vastly amused when some of Paul's stories reached them—especially the women. They were hardworking women, most of them supporting indolent husbands or brothers, and they laughed rather bitterly at having stirred the boy to such fervid and florid inventions. They agreed with the faculty and with his father, that Paul's was a bad case.

The east-bound train was plowing through a January snowstorm; the dull dawn was beginning to show grey when the engine whistled a mile out of Newark. Paul started up from the seat where he had lain curled in uneasy slumber, rubbed the breath-misted window-glass with his hand, and peered out. The snow was whirling in curling eddies above the white bottom lands, and the drifts lay already deep in the fields and along the fences, while here and there the tall dead grass and dried weed stalks protruded black above it. Lights shone from the scattered houses, and a gang of laborers who stood beside the track waved their lanterns.

Paul had slept very little, and he felt grimy and uncomfortable. He had made the all-night journey in a day coach because he was afraid if he took a Pullman he might be seen by some Pittsburgh business man who had noticed him in Denny and Carson's office. When the whistle woke him, he clutched quickly at his breast pocket, glancing about him with an uncertain smile. But the little, clay-bespattered Italians were still sleeping, the slatternly women across the aisle were in openmouthed oblivion, and even the crumby, crying babies were for the nonce stilled. Paul settled back to struggle with his impatience as best he could.

40   When he arrived at the Jersey City station, he hurried through his breakfast, manifestly ill at ease and keeping a sharp eye about him. After he reached the Twenty-third Street station, he consulted a cabman, and had himself driven to a men's furnishing establishment which was just opening for the day. He spent upward of two hours there, buying with endless reconsidering and great care. His new street suit he put on in the fitting-room; the frock coat and dress clothes he had bundled into the cab with his new shirts. Then he drove to a hatter's and a shoe house. His next errand was at Tiffany's, where he selected silver-mounted brushes and a scarf-pin. He would not wait to have his silver marked, he said. Lastly, he stopped at a trunk shop on Broadway, and had his purchases packed into various traveling-bags.

It was a little after one o'clock when he drove up to the Waldorf, and, after settling with the cabman, went into the office. He registered from Washington; said his mother and father had been abroad, and that he had come down to await the arrival of their steamer. He told his story plausibly and had no trouble, since he offered to pay for them in advance, in engaging his rooms; a sleeping-room, sitting-room, and bath.

Not once, but a hundred times Paul had planned this entry into New York. He had gone over every detail of it with Charley Edwards, and in his scrapbook at home there were pages of description about New York hotels, cut from the Sunday papers.

When he was shown to his sitting-room on the eighth floor, he saw at a glance that everything was as it should be; there was but one detail in his mental picture that the place did not realize, so he rang for the bell-boy and sent him down for flowers. He moved about nervously until the boy returned, putting away his new linen and fingering it delightedly as he did so. When the flowers came, he put them hastily into water, and then tumbled into a hot bath. Presently he came out of his white bathroom, resplendent in his new silk underwear, and playing with the tassels of his red robe. The snow was whirling so fiercely outside his windows that he could scarcely see across the street; but within, the air was deliciously soft and fragrant. He put the violets and jonquils on the taboret beside the couch, and threw himself down with a long sigh, covering himself with a Roman blanket. He was thoroughly tired; he had been in such haste, he had stood up to such a strain, covered so much ground in the last twenty-four hours, that he wanted to think how it had all come about. Lulled by the sound of the wind, the warm air, and the cool fragrance of the flowers, he sank into deep, drowsy retrospection.

It had been wonderfully simple; when they had shut him out of the theater and concert hall, when they had taken away his bone, the whole thing was virtually determined. The rest was a mere matter of opportunity. The only thing that at all surprised him was his own courage—for he realized well enough that he had always been tormented by fear, a sort of apprehensive dread which, of late years, as the meshes of the lies he had told closed about him, had been pulling the muscles of his body tighter and tighter. Until now, he could not remember a time when he had not been dreading something. Even when he was a little boy, it was always there—behind him, or before, or on either side. There had always been the shadowed corner, the dark place into which he dared not look, but from which something seemed always to be watching him—and Paul had done things that were not pretty to watch, he knew.

But now he had a curious sense of relief, as though he had at last 45 thrown down the gauntlet to the thing in the corner.

Yet it was but a day since he had been sulking in the traces; but yesterday afternoon that he had been sent to the bank with Denny & Carson's deposit, as usual—but this time he was instructed to leave the book to be balanced. There was above two thousand dollars in checks, and nearly a thousand in the banknotes which he had taken from the book and quietly transferred to his pocket. At the bank he had made out a new deposit slip. His nerves had been steady enough to permit of his returning to the office, where he had finished his work and asked for a full day's holiday tomorrow, Saturday, giving a perfectly reasonable pretext. The bank book, he knew, would not be returned before Monday or Tuesday, and his father would be out of town for the next week. From the time he slipped the banknotes into his pocket until he boarded the night train for New York, he had not known a moment's hesitation.

How astonishingly easy it had all been; here he was, the thing done; and this time there would be no awakening, no figure at the top of the stairs. He watched the snowflakes whirling by his window until he fell asleep.

When he awoke, it was four o'clock in the afternoon. He bounded up with a start; one of his precious days gone already! He spent nearly an hour in dressing, watching every stage of his toilet carefully in the mirror. Everything was quite perfect; he was exactly the kind of boy he had always wanted to be.

When he went downstairs, Paul took a carriage and drove up Fifth Avenue toward the Park. The snow had somewhat abated; carriages and tradesmen's wagons were hurrying soundlessly to and fro in the winter twilight; boys in woolen mufflers were shoveling off the doorsteps; the Avenue stages made fine spots of color against the white street. Here and there on the corners whole flower gardens blooming behind glass windows, against which the snowflakes stuck and melted; violets, roses, carnations, lilies-of-the-valley—somehow vastly more lovely and alluring that they blossomed thus unnaturally in the snow. The Park itself was a wonderful stage winter-piece.

50   When he returned, the pause of the twilight had ceased, and the tune of the streets had changed. The snow was falling faster, lights streamed from the hotels that reared their many stories fearlessly up into the storm, defying the raging Atlantic winds. A long, black stream of carriages poured down the Avenue, intersected here and there by other streams, tending horizontally. There were a score of cabs about the entrance of his hotel, and his driver had to wait. Boys in livery were running in and out of the awning stretched across the sidewalk, up and down the red velvet carpet laid from the door to the street. Above, about, within it all, was the rumble and roar, the hurry and toss of thousands of human beings as hot for pleasure as himself, and on every side of him towered the glaring affirmation of the omnipotence of wealth.

The boy set his teeth and drew his shoulders together in a spasm of realization; the plot of all dramas, the text of all romances, the nerve-stuff of all sensations was whirling about him like the snowflakes. He burnt like a faggot in a tempest.

When Paul came down to dinner, the music of the orchestra floated up the elevator shaft to greet him. As he stepped into the thronged corridor, he sank back into one of the chairs against the wall to get his breath. The lights, the chatter, the perfumes, the bewildering medley of color— he had, for a moment, the feeling of not being able to stand it. But only for a moment; these were his own people, he told himself. He went slowly about the corridors, through the writing-rooms, smoking-rooms, reception-rooms, as though he were exploring the chambers of an enchanted palace, built and peopled for him alone.

When he reached the dining-room he sat down at a table near a window. The flowers, the white linen, the many-colored wine-glasses, the gay toilettes of the women, the low popping of corks, the undulating repetitions of the "Blue Danube" from the orchestra, all flooded Paul's dream with bewildering radiance. When the roseate tinge of his champagne was added—that cold, precious, bubbling stuff that creamed and foamed in his glass—Paul wondered that there were honest men in the world at all. This was what all the world was fighting for, he reflected; this was what all the struggle was about. He doubted the reality of his past. Had he ever known a place called Cordelia Street, a place where fagged-looking business men boarded the early car? Mere rivets in a machine they seemed to Paul—sickening men, with combings of children's hair always hanging to their coats, and the smell of cooking in their clothes. Cordelia Street—Ah, that belonged to another time and country! Had he not always been thus, had he not sat here night after night, from as far back as he could remember, looking pensively over just such shimmering textures, and slowly twirling the stem of a glass like this one between his thumb and middle finger? He rather thought he had.

He was not in the least abashed or lonely. He had no especial desire to meet or to know any of these people; all he demanded was the right to look on and conjecture, to watch the pageant. The mere stage properties were all he contended for. Nor was he lonely later in the evening, in his loge at the Opera. He was entirely rid of his nervous misgivings, of his forced aggressiveness, of the imperative desire to show himself different from his surroundings. He felt now that his surroundings explained him. Nobody questioned the purple; he had only to wear it passively. He had only to glance down at his dress coat to reassure himself that here it would be impossible for anyone to humiliate him.

55   He found it hard to leave his beautiful sitting-room to go to bed that night, and sat long watching the raging storm from his turret window. When he went to sleep, it was with the lights turned on in his bedroom; partly because of his old timidity, and partly so that, if he should wake in the night, there would be no wretched moment of doubt, no horrible suspicion of yellow wallpaper, or of Washington and Calvin above his bed.

    On Sunday morning the city was practically snowbound. Paul breakfasted late, and in the afternoon he fell in with a wild San Francisco boy, a freshman at Yale, who said he had run down for a "little flyer" over Sunday. The young man offered to show Paul the night side of the town, and the two boys went off together after dinner, not returning to the hotel until seven o'clock the next morning. They had started out in the confiding warmth of a champagne friendship, but their parting in the elevator was singularly cool. The freshman pulled himself together to make his train, and Paul went to bed. He awoke at two o'clock in the afternoon, very thirsty and dizzy, and rang for ice-water, coffee, and the Pittsburgh papers.

    On the part of the hotel management, Paul excited no suspicion. There was this to be said for him, that he wore his spoils with dignity and in no way made himself conspicuous. His chief greediness lay in his ears and eyes, and his excesses were not offensive ones. His dearest pleasures were the grey winter twilights in his sitting-room; his quiet enjoyment of his flowers, his clothes, his wide divan, his cigarette, and his sense of power. He could not remember a time when he had felt so at peace with himself. The mere release from the necessity of petty lying, lying every day and every day, restored his self-respect. He had never lied for pleasure, even at school; but to make himself noticed and admired, to assert his difference from other Cordelia Street boys; and he felt a good deal more manly, more honest, even, now that he had no need for boastful pretensions, now that he could, as his actor friends used to say, "dress the part." It was characteristic that remorse did not occur to him. His golden days went by without a shadow, and he made each as perfect as he could.

    On the eighth day after his arrival in New York, he found the whole affair exploited in the Pittsburgh papers, exploited with a wealth of detail which indicated that local news of a sensational nature was at a low ebb. The firm of Denny & Carson announced that the boy's father had refunded the full amount of his theft, and that they had no intention of prosecuting. The Cumberland minister had been interviewed, and expressed his hope of yet reclaiming the motherless lad, and Paul's Sabbath-School teacher declared that she would spare no effort to that end. The rumor had reached Pittsburgh that the boy had been seen in a New York hotel, and his father had gone East to find him and bring him home.

Paul had just come in to dress for dinner; he sank into the chair, weak in the knees, and clasped his head in his hands. It was to be worse than jail, even; the tepid waters of Cordelia Street were to close over him finally and forever. The grey monotony stretched before him in hopeless, unrelieved years;—Sabbath School, Young People's Meeting, the yellow-papered room, the damp dish-towels; it all rushed back upon him with sickening vividness. He had the old feeling that the orchestra had suddenly stopped, the sinking sensation that the play was over. The sweat broke out on his face, and he sprang to his feet, looked about him with his white, conscious smile, and winked at himself in the mirror. With something of the childish belief in miracles with which he had so often gone to class, all his lessons unlearned, Paul dressed and dashed whistling down the corridor to the elevator.

He had no sooner entered the dining-room and caught the measure 60 of the music than his remembrance was lightened by his old elastic power of claiming the moment, mounting with it, and finding it all-sufficient. The glare and glitter about him, the mere scenic accessories had again, and for the last time, their old potency. He would show himself that he was game, he would finish the thing splendidly. He doubted, more than ever, the existence of Cordelia Street, and for the first time he drank his wine recklessly. Was he not, after all, one of these fortunate beings? Was he not still himself, and in his own place? He drummed a nervous accompaniment to the music and looked about him, telling himself over and over that it had paid.

He reflected drowsily, to the swell of the violin and the chill sweetness of his wine, that he might have done it more wisely. He might have caught an outbound steamer and been well out of their clutches before now. But the other side of the world had seemed too far away and too uncertain then; he could not have waited for it; his need had been too sharp. If he had to choose over again, he would do the same thing tomorrow. He looked affectionately about the dining-room, now gilded with a soft mist. Ah, it had paid indeed!

Paul was awakened next morning by a painful throbbing in his head and feet. He had thrown himself across the bed without undressing, and had slept with his shoes on. His limbs and hands were lead-heavy, and his tongue and throat were parched. There came upon him one of those fateful attacks of clear-headedness that never occurred except when he was physically exhausted and his nerves hung loose. He lay still and closed his eyes and let the tide of realities wash over him.

His father was in New York; "stopping at some joint or other," he told himself. The memory of successive summers on the front stoop fell upon him like a weight of black water. He had not a hundred dollars left; and he knew now, more than ever, that money was everything, the wall that stood between all he loathed and all he wanted. The thing was winding itself up; he had thought of that on his first glorious day in New York, and had even provided a way to snap the thread. It lay on his dressing-table now; he had got it out last night when he came blindly up from dinner—but the shiny metal hurt his eyes, and he disliked the look of it, anyway.

He rose and moved about with a painful effort, succumbing now and again to attacks of nausea. It was the old depression exaggerated; all the world had become Cordelia Street. Yet somehow he was not afraid of anything, was absolutely calm; perhaps because he had looked into the dark corner at last, and knew. It was bad enough, what he saw there; but somehow not so bad as his long fear of it had been. He saw everything clearly now. He had a feeling that he had made the best of it, that he had lived the sort of life he was meant to live, and for half an hour he sat staring at the revolver. But he told himself that was not the way, so he went downstairs and took a cab to the ferry.

65   When Paul arrived at Newark, he got off the train and took another cab, directing the driver to follow the Pennsylvania tracks out of town. The snow lay heavy on the roadways and had drifted deep in the open fields. Only here and there the dead grass or dried weed stalks projected, singularly black, above it.

Once well into the country, Paul dismissed the carriage and walked, floundering along the tracks, his mind a medley of irrelevant things. He seemed to hold in his brain an actual picture of everything he had seen that morning. He remembered every feature of both his drivers, the toothless old woman from whom he had bought the red flowers in his coat, the agent from whom he had got his ticket, and all of his fellow-passengers on the ferry. His mind, unable to cope with vital matters near at hand, worked feverishly and deftly at sorting and grouping these images. They made for him a part of the ugliness of the world, of the ache in his head, and the bitter burning on his tongue. He stooped and put a handful of snow into his mouth as he walked, but that, too, seemed hot. When he reached a little hillside, where the tracks ran through a cut some twenty feet below him, he stopped and sat down.

The carnations in his coat were drooping with cold, he noticed; all their red glory over. It occurred to him that all the flowers he had seen in the show windows that first night must have gone the same way, long before this. It was only one splendid breath they had, in spite of their brave mockery at the winter outside the glass. It was a losing game in the end, it seemed, this revolt against the homilies by which the world is run. Paul took one of the blossoms carefully from his coat and scooped a little hole in the snow, where he covered it up. Then he dozed awhile, from his weak condition, seeming insensible to the cold.

The sound of an approaching train woke him and he started to his feet, remembering only his resolution, and afraid lest he should be too late. He stood watching the approaching locomotive, his teeth chattering, his lips drawn away from them in a frightened smile; once or twice he glanced nervously sidewise, as though he were being watched. When the right moment came, he jumped. As he fell, the folly of his haste occurred to him with merciless clearness, the vastness of what he had left undone. There flashed through his brain, clearer than ever before, the blue of Adriatic water, the yellow of Algerian sands.

He felt something strike his chest—his body being thrown swiftly through the air, on and on, immeasurably far and fast, while his limbs gently relaxed. Then, because the picture making mechanism was crushed, the disturbing visions flashed into black, and Paul dropped back into the immense design of things.

QUESTIONS

1. Technically we should classify the author's point of view as omniscient, for she enters into the minds of characters at will. Nevertheless, early in the story the focus changes rather abruptly. Locate the point where the change occurs. Through whose eyes do we see Paul prior to this point? Through whose eyes do we see him afterward? What is the purpose of this shift? Does it offer any clue to the purpose of the story?

2. What details of Paul's appearance and behavior, as his teachers see him, indicate that he is different from most other boys?

3. Explain Paul's behavior. Why does he lie? What does he hate? What does he want? Contrast the world of Cordelia Street with the worlds that Paul finds at Carnegie Hall, at the Schenley, at the stock theater, and in New York.

4. Is Paul artistic? Describe his reactions to music, to painting, to literature, and to the theater. What value does he find in the arts?

5. Is Paul a static or a developing character? If the latter, at what points does he change? Why?

6. What do Paul's clandestine trips to the stock theater, his trip to New York, and his suicide have in common?

7. Compare Paul and the college boy he meets in New York (paragraph 56). Are they two of a kind? If not, how do they differ?

8. What are the implications of the title? What does the last sentence of the story do to the reader's focus of vision?

9. Are there any clues to the causes of Paul's unusual personality? How many? In what is the author chiefly interested?

10. In what two cities is the story set? Does this choice of setting have any symbolic value? Could the story have been set as validly in Cleveland and Detroit? In San Francisco and Los Angeles? In New Orleans and Birmingham?

SHIRLEY JACKSON

The Lottery

The morning of June 27th was clear and sunny, with the fresh warmth of a full-summer day; the flowers were blossoming profusely and the grass was richly green. The people of the village began to gather in the square, between the post office and the bank, around ten o'clock; in some towns there were so many people that the lottery took two days and had to be started on June 26th, but in this village, where there were only about three hundred people, the whole lottery took less than two hours, so it could begin at ten o'clock in the morning and still be through in time to allow the villagers to get home for noon dinner.

The children assembled first, of course. School was recently over for the summer, and the feeling of liberty sat uneasily on most of them; they tended to gather together quietly for a while before they broke into boisterous play, and their talk was still of the classroom and the teacher, of books and reprimands. Bobby Martin had already stuffed his pockets full of stones, and the other boys soon followed his example, selecting the smoothest and roundest stones; Bobby and Harry Jones and Dickie Delacroix—the villagers pronounced this name "Dellacroy"—eventually made a great pile of stones in one corner of the square and guarded it against the raids of the other boys. The girls stood aside, talking among themselves, looking over their shoulders at the boys, and the very small children rolled in the dust or clung to the hands of their older brothers or sisters.

Soon the men began to gather, surveying their own children, speaking of planting and rain, tractors and taxes. They stood together, away from the pile of stones in the corner, and their jokes were quiet and they smiled rather than laughed. The women, wearing faded house dresses and sweaters, came shortly after their menfolk. They greeted one another and exchanged bits of gossip as they went to join their husbands. Soon the women, standing by their husbands, began to call to their children, and the children came reluctantly, having to be called four or five times. Bobby Martin ducked under his mother's grasping hand and ran, laughing, back to the pile of stones. His father spoke up sharply, and Bobby came quickly and took his place between his father and his oldest brother.

The lottery was conducted—as were the square dances, the teenage club, the Halloween program—by Mr. Summers, who had time and

THE LOTTERY   First published in 1948. Shirley Jackson (1919–1965) was born in San Francisco and spent most of her early life in California. After her marriage in 1940 she lived in a quiet rural community in Vermont.

energy to devote to civic activities. He was a round-faced, jovial man and he ran the coal business, and people were sorry for him, because he had no children and his wife was a scold. When he arrived in the square, carrying the black wooden box, there was a murmur of conversation among the villagers, and he waved and called, "Little late today, folks." The postmaster, Mr. Graves, followed him, carrying a three-legged stool, and the stool was put in the center of the square and Mr. Summers set the black box down on it. The villagers kept their distance, leaving a space between themselves and the stool, and when Mr. Summers said, "Some of you fellows want to give me a hand?" there was a hesitation before two men, Mr. Martin and his oldest son, Baxter, came forward to hold the box steady on the stool while Mr. Summers stirred up the papers inside it.

The original paraphernalia for the lottery had been lost long ago, and 5 the black box now resting on the stool had been put into use even before Old Man Warner, the oldest man in town, was born. Mr. Summers spoke frequently to the villagers about making a new box, but no one liked to upset even as much tradition as was represented by the black box. There was a story that the present box had been made with some pieces of the box that had preceded it, the one that had been constructed when the first people settled down to make a village here. Every year, after the lottery, Mr. Summers began talking again about a new box, but every year the subject was allowed to fade off without anything's being done. The black box grew shabbier each year; by now it was no longer completely black but splintered badly along one side to show the original wood color, and in some places faded or stained.

Mr. Martin and his oldest son, Baxter, held the black box securely on the stool until Mr. Summers had stirred the papers thoroughly with his hand. Because so much of the ritual had been forgotten or discarded, Mr. Summers had been successful in having slips of paper substituted for the chips of wood that had been used for generations. Chips of wood, Mr. Summers had argued, had been all very well when the village was tiny, but now that the population was more than three hundred and likely to keep on growing, it was necessary to use something that would fit more easily into the black box. The night before the lottery, Mr. Summers and Mr. Graves made up the slips of paper and put them in the box, and it was then taken to the safe of Mr. Summers's coal company and locked up until Mr. Summers was ready to take it to the square next morning. The rest of the year, the box was put away, sometimes one place, sometimes another; it had spent one year in Mr. Graves's barn and another year underfoot in the post office, and sometimes it was set on a shelf in the Martin grocery and left there.

There was a great deal of fussing to be done before Mr. Summers declared the lottery open. There were the lists to make up—of heads of families, heads of households in each family, members of each household in each family. There was the proper swearing-in of Mr. Summers by the postmaster, as the official of the lottery; at one time, some people remembered, there had been a recital of some sort, performed by the official of the lottery, a perfunctory, tuneless chant that had been rattled off duly each year; some people believed that the official of the lottery used to stand just so when he said or sang it, others believed that he was supposed to walk among the people, but years and years ago this part of the ritual had been allowed to lapse. There had been, also, a ritual salute, which the official of the lottery had had to use in addressing each person who came up to draw from the box, but this also had changed with time, until now it was felt necessary only for the official to speak to each person approaching. Mr. Summers was very good at all this; in his clean white shirt and blue jeans, with one hand resting carelessly on the black box, he seemed very proper and important as he talked interminably to Mr. Graves and the Martins.

Just as Mr. Summers finally left off talking and turned to the assembled villagers, Mrs. Hutchinson came hurriedly along the path to the square, her sweater thrown over her shoulders, and slid into place in the back of the crowd. "Clean forgot what day it was," she said to Mrs. Delacroix, who stood next to her, and they both laughed softly. "Thought my old man was out back stacking wood," Mrs. Hutchinson went on, "and then I looked out the window and the kids were gone, and then I remembered it was the twenty-seventh and came a-running." She dried her hands on her apron, and Mrs. Delacroix said, "You're in time, though. They're still talking away up there."

Mrs. Hutchinson craned her neck to see through the crowd and found her husband and children standing near the front. She tapped Mrs. Delacroix on the arm as a farewell and began to make her way through the crowd. The people separated good-humoredly to let her through; two or three people said, in voices just loud enough to be heard across the crowd, "Here comes your Missus, Hutchinson," and "Bill, she made it after all." Mrs. Hutchinson reached her husband, and Mr. Summers, who had been waiting, said cheerfully, "Thought we were going to have to get on without you, Tessie." Mrs. Hutchinson said, grinning, "Wouldn't have me leave m'dishes in the sink, now, would you, Joe?" and soft laughter ran through the crowd as the people stirred back into position after Mrs. Hutchinson's arrival.

10 "Well, now," Mr. Summers said soberly, "guess we better get started, get this over with, so's we can go back to work. Anybody ain't here?"

"Dunbar," several people said. "Dunbar, Dunbar."

Mr. Summers consulted his list. "Clyde Dunbar," he said. "That's right. He's broke his leg, hasn't he? Who's drawing for him?"

"Me, I guess," a woman said, and Mr. Summers turned to look at her. "Wife draws for her husband," Mr. Summers said. "Don't you have a grown boy to do it for you, Janey?" Although Mr. Summers and everyone else in the village knew the answer perfectly well, it was the business of the official of the lottery to ask such questions formally. Mr. Summers waited with an expression of polite interest while Mrs. Dunbar answered.

"Horace's not but sixteen yet," Mrs. Dunbar said regretfully. "Guess I gotta fill in for the old man this year."

"Right," Mr. Summers said. He made a note on the list he was 15 holding. Then he asked, "Watson boy drawing this year?"

A tall boy in the crowd raised his hand. "Here," he said. "I'm drawing for m'mother and me." He blinked his eyes nervously and ducked his head as several voices in the crowd said things like "Good fellow, Jack," and "Glad to see your mother's got a man to do it."

"Well," Mr. Summers said, "guess that's everyone. Old Man Warner make it?"

"Here," a voice said, and Mr. Summers nodded.

A sudden hush fell on the crowd as Mr. Summers cleared his throat and looked at the list. "All ready?" he called. "Now, I'll read the names—heads of families first—and the men come up and take a paper out of the box. Keep the paper folded in your hand without looking at it until everyone has had a turn. Everything clear?"

The people had done it so many times that they only half listened 20 to the directions; most of them were quiet, wetting their lips, not looking around. Then Mr. Summers raised one hand high and said, "Adams." A man disengaged himself from the crowd and came forward. "Hi, Steve," Mr. Summers said, and Mr. Adams said, "Hi, Joe." They grinned at one another humorlessly and nervously. Then Mr. Adams reached into the black box and took out a folded paper. He held it firmly by one corner as he turned and went hastily back to his place in the crowd, where he stood a little apart from his family, not looking down at his hand.

"Allen," Mr. Summers said. "Anderson . . . Bentham."

"Seems like there's no time at all between lotteries any more," Mrs. Delacroix said to Mrs. Graves in the back row. "Seems like we got through with the last one only last week."

"Time sure goes fast," Mrs. Graves said.

"Clark . . . Delacroix."

"There goes my old man," Mrs. Delacroix said. She held her breath 25 while her husband went forward.

"Dunbar," Mr. Summers said, and Mrs. Dunbar went steadily to the box while one of the women said, "Go on, Janey," and another said, "There she goes."

"We're next," Mrs. Graves said. She watched while Mr. Graves came around from the side of the box, greeted Mr. Summers gravely, and selected a slip of paper from the box. By now, all through the crowd there were men holding the small folded papers in their large hands, turning them over and over nervously. Mrs. Dunbar and her two sons stood together, Mrs. Dunbar holding the slip of paper.

"Harburt . . . Hutchinson."

"Get up there, Bill," Mrs. Hutchinson said, and the people near her laughed.

30   "Jones."

"They do say," Mr. Adams said to Old Man Warner, who stood next to him, "that over in the north village they're talking of giving up the lottery."

Old Man Warner snorted. "Pack of crazy fools," he said. "Listening to the young folks, nothing's good enough for them. Next thing you know, they'll be wanting to go back to living in caves, nobody work any more, live that way for a while. Used to be a saying about 'Lottery in June, corn be heavy soon.' First thing you know, we'd all be eating stewed chickweed and acorns. There's always been a lottery," he added petulantly. "Bad enough to see young Joe Summers up there joking with everybody."

"Some places have already quit lotteries," Mrs. Adams said.

"Nothing but trouble in that," Old Man Warner said stoutly. "Pack of young fools."

35   "Martin." And Bobby Martin watched his father go forward. "Overdyke . . . Percy."

"I wish they'd hurry," Mrs. Dunbar said to her older son. "I wish they'd hurry."

"They're almost through," her son said.

"You get ready to run tell Dad," Mrs. Dunbar said.

Mr. Summers called his own name and then stepped forward precisely and selected a slip from the box. Then he called, "Warner."

40   "Seventy-seventh year I been in the lottery," Old Man Warner said as he went through the crowd. "Seventy-seventh time."

"Watson." The tall boy came awkwardly through the crowd. Someone said, "Don't be nervous, Jack," and Mr. Summers said, "Take your time, son." "Zanini."

After that, there was a long pause, a breathless pause, until Mr. Summers, holding his slip of paper in the air, said, "All right, fellows." For a minute, no one moved, and then all the slips of paper were opened. Suddenly, all the women began to speak at once, saying, "Who is it?" "Who's got it?" "Is it the Dunbars?" "Is it the Watsons?" Then the voices began to say, "It's Hutchinson. It's Bill." "Bill Hutchinson's got it."

"Go tell your father," Mrs. Dunbar said to her older son.

People began to look around to see the Hutchinsons. Bill Hutchinson   45
was standing quiet, staring down at the paper in his hand. Suddenly, Tessie Hutchinson shouted to Mr. Summers. "You didn't give him time enough to take any paper he wanted. I saw you. It wasn't fair."

"Be a good sport, Tessie," Mrs. Delacroix called, and Mrs. Graves said, "All of us took the same chance."

"Shut up, Tessie," Bill Hutchinson said.

"Well, everyone," Mr. Summers said, "that was done pretty fast, and now we've got to be hurrying a little more to get done in time." He consulted his next list. "Bill," he said, "you draw for the Hutchinson family. You got any other households in the Hutchinsons?"

"There's Don and Eva," Mrs. Hutchinson yelled. "Make them take their chance!"

"Daughters draw with their husband's families, Tessie," Mr. Summers   50
said gently. "You know that as well as anyone else."

"It wasn't fair," Tessie said.

"I guess not, Joe," Bill Hutchinson said regretfully. "My daughter draws with her husband's family, that's only fair. And I've got no other family except the kids."

"Then, as far as drawing for families is concerned, it's you," Mr. Summers said in explanation, "and as far as drawing for households is concerned, that's you, too. Right?"

"Right," Bill Hutchinson said.

"How many kids, Bill?" Mr. Summers asked formally.   55

"Three," Bill Hutchinson said. "There's Bill, Jr., and Nancy, and little Dave. And Tessie and me."

"All right, then," Mr. Summers said. "Harry, you got their tickets back?"

Mr. Graves nodded and held up the slips of paper. "Put them in the box, then," Mr. Summers directed. "Take Bill's and put it in."

"I think we ought to start over," Mrs. Hutchinson said, as quietly as she could. "I tell you it wasn't fair. You didn't give him time enough to choose. Everybody saw that."

Mr. Graves had selected the five slips and put them in the box, and he   60
dropped all the papers but those onto the ground, where the breeze caught them and lifted them off.

"Listen, everybody," Mrs. Hutchinson was saying to the people around her.

KATHERINE ANNE PORTER
The Jilting of Granny Weatherall

She flicked her wrist neatly out of Doctor Harry's pudgy careful fingers and pulled the sheet up to her chin. The brat ought to be in knee breeches. Doctoring around the country with spectacles on his nose! "Get along now, take your schoolbooks and go. There's nothing wrong with me."

Doctor Harry spread a warm paw like a cushion on her forehead where the forked green vein danced and made her eyelids twitch. "Now, now, be a good girl, and we'll have you up in no time."

"That's no way to speak to a woman nearly eighty years old just because she's down. I'd have you respect your elders, young man."

"Well, Missy, excuse me." Doctor Harry patted her cheek. "But I've got to warn you, haven't I? You're a marvel, but you must be careful or you're going to be good and sorry."

5   "Don't tell me what I'm going to be. I'm on my feet now, morally speaking. It's Cornelia. I had to go to bed to get rid of her."

Her bones felt loose, and floated around in her skin, and Doctor Harry floated like a balloon around the foot of the bed. He floated and pulled down his waistcoat and swung his glasses on a cord. "Well, stay where you are, it certainly can't hurt you."

"Get along and doctor your sick," said Granny Weatherall. "Leave a well woman alone. I'll call for you when I want you. . . . Where were you forty years ago when I pulled through milk-leg and double pneumonia? You weren't even born. Don't let Cornelia lead you on," she shouted, because Doctor Harry appeared to float up to the ceiling and out. "I pay my own bills, and I don't throw my money away on nonsense!"

She meant to wave good-by, but it was too much trouble. Her eyes closed of themselves, it was like a dark curtain drawn around the bed. The pillow rose and floated under her, pleasant as a hammock in a light wind. She listened to the leaves rustling outside the window. No, somebody was swishing newspapers: no, Cornelia and Doctor Harry were whispering together. She leaped broad awake, thinking they whispered in her ear.

"She was never like this, never like this!" "Well, what can we expect?" "Yes, eighty years old. . . ."

THE JILTING OF GRANNY WEATHERALL   First published in 1930. Katherine Anne Porter (1890–1980) was born and grew up in Texas, was educated at convent schools in New Orleans, and lived in Chicago, Fort Worth, Mexico, and New York City before writing this story.

Well, and what if she was? She still had ears. It was like Cornelia to 10
whisper around doors. She always kept things secret in such a public way.
She was always being tactful and kind. Cornelia was dutiful; that was the
trouble with her. Dutiful and good: "So good and dutiful," said Granny,
"that I'd like to spank her." She saw herself spanking Cornelia and making
a fine job of it.

"What'd you say, Mother?"

Granny felt her face tying up in hard knots.

"Can't a body think, I'd like to know?"

"I thought you might want something."

"I do. I want a lot of things. First off, go away and don't whisper." 15

She lay and drowsed, hoping in her sleep that the children would keep
out and let her rest a minute. It had been a long day. Not that she was tired.
It was always pleasant to snatch a minute now and then. There was always
so much to be done, let me see: tomorrow.

Tomorrow was far away and there was nothing to trouble about.
Things were finished somehow when the time came; thank God there was
always a little margin left over for peace: then a person could spread out
the plan of life and tuck in the edges orderly. It was good to have everything clean and folded away, with the hair brushes and tonic bottles sitting
straight on the white embroidered linen: the day started without fuss and
the pantry shelves laid out with rows of jelly glasses and brown jugs and
white stone-china jars with blue whirligigs and words painted on them:
coffee, tea, sugar, ginger, cinnamon, allspice: and the bronze clock with the
lion on top nicely dusted off. The dust that lion could collect in twenty-
four hours! The box in the attic with all those letters tied up, well, she'd
have to go through that tomorrow. All those letters—George's letters and
John's letters and her letters to them both—lying around for the children
to find afterwards made her uneasy. Yes, that would be tomorrow's business. No use to let them know how silly she had been once.

While she was rummaging around she found death in her mind and
it felt clammy and unfamiliar. She had spent so much time preparing for
death there was no need for bringing it up again. Let it take care of itself
now. When she was sixty she had felt very old, finished, and went around
making farewell trips to see her children and grandchildren, with a secret
in her mind: This is the very last of your mother, children! Then she made
her will and came down with a long fever. That was all just a notion like a
lot of other things, but it was lucky too, for she had once for all got over the
idea of dying for a long time. Now she couldn't be worried. She hoped she
had better sense now. Her father had lived to be one hundred and two years
old and had drunk a noggin of strong hot toddy on his last birthday. He
told the reporters it was his daily habit, and he owed his long life to that.

He had made quite a scandal and was very pleased about it. She believed she'd just plague Cornelia a little.

"Cornelia! Cornelia!" No footsteps, but a sudden hand on her cheek. "Bless you, where have you been?"

20   "Here, Mother."

"Well, Cornelia, I want a noggin of hot toddy."

"Are you cold, darling?"

"I'm chilly, Cornelia. Lying in bed stops the circulation. I must have told you that a thousand times."

Well, she could just hear Cornelia telling her husband that Mother was getting a little childish and they'd have to humor her. The thing that most annoyed her was that Cornelia thought she was deaf, dumb, and blind. Little hasty glances and tiny gestures tossed around her and over her head saying, "Don't cross her, let her have her way, she's eighty years old," and she sitting there as if she lived in a thin glass cage. Sometimes Granny almost made up her mind to pack up and move back to her own house where nobody could remind her every minute that she was old. Wait, wait, Cornelia, till your own children whisper behind your back!

25   In her day she had kept a better house and had got more work done. She wasn't too old yet for Lydia to be driving eighty miles for advice when one of the children jumped the track, and Jimmy still dropped in and talked things over: "Now, Mammy, you've a good business head, I want to know what you think of this? . . . ." Old. Cornelia couldn't change the furniture around without asking. Little things, little things! They had been so sweet when they were little. Granny wished the old days were back again with the children young and everything to be done over. It had been a hard pull, but not too much for her. When she thought of all the food she had cooked, and all the clothes she had cut and sewed, and all the gardens she had made—well, the children showed it. There they were, made out of her, and they couldn't get away from that. Sometimes she wanted to see John again and point to them and say, Well, I didn't do so badly, did I? But that would have to wait. That was for tomorrow. She used to think of him as a man, but now all the children were older than their father, and he would be a child beside her if she saw him now. It seemed strange and there was something wrong in the idea. Why, he couldn't possibly recognize her. She had fenced in a hundred acres once, digging the post holes herself and clamping the wires with just a negro boy to help. That changed a woman. John would be looking for a young woman with the peaked Spanish comb in her hair and the painted fan. Digging post holes changed a woman. Riding country roads in the winter when women had their babies was another thing: sitting up nights with sick horses and sick negroes and sick children and hardly ever losing one. John, I hardly ever lost one of them! John would

see that in a minute, that would be something he could understand, she wouldn't have to explain anything!

It made her feel like rolling up her sleeves and putting the whole place to rights again. No matter if Cornelia was determined to be everywhere at once, there were a great many things left undone on this place. She would start tomorrow and do them. It was good to be strong enough for everything, even if all you made melted and changed and slipped under your hands, so that by the time you finished you almost forgot what you were working for. What was it I set out to do? she asked herself intently, but she could not remember. A fog rose over the valley, she saw it marching across the creek swallowing the trees and moving up the hill like an army of ghosts. Soon it would be at the near edge of the orchard, and then it was time to go in and light the lamps. Come in, children, don't stay out in the night air.

Lighting the lamps had been beautiful. The children huddled up to her and breathed like little calves waiting at the bars in the twilight. Their eyes followed the match and watched the flame rise and settle in a blue curve, then they moved away from her. The lamp was lit, they didn't have to be scared and hang on to mother any more. Never, never, never more. God, for all my life I thank Thee. Without Thee, my God, I could never have done it. Hail, Mary, full of grace.

I want you to pick all the fruit this year and see that nothing is wasted. There's always someone who can use it. Don't let good things rot for want of using. You waste life when you waste good food. Don't let things get lost. It's bitter to lose things. Now, don't let me get to thinking, not when I am tired and taking a little nap before supper. . . .

The pillow rose about her shoulders and pressed against her heart and the memory was being squeezed out of it: oh, push down the pillow, somebody: it would smother her if she tried to hold it. Such a fresh breeze blowing and such a green day with no threats in it. But he had not come, just the same. What does a woman do when she has put on the white veil and set out the white cake for a man and he doesn't come? She tried to remember. No, I swear he never harmed me but in that. He never harmed me but in that . . . and what if he did? There was the day, the day, but a whirl of dark smoke rose and covered it, crept up and over into the bright field where everything was planted so carefully in orderly rows. That was hell, she knew hell when she saw it. For sixty years she had prayed against remembering him and against losing her soul in the deep pit of hell, and now the two things were mingled in one and the thought of him was a smoky cloud from hell that moved and crept in her head when she had just got rid of Doctor Harry and was trying to rest a minute. Wounded vanity, Ellen, said a sharp voice in the top of her mind. Don't let your wounded vanity get the upper hand of you. Plenty of girls get jilted. You were jilted, weren't you? Then stand up to it. Her eyelids wavered and let in streamers of blue-gray light like tissue paper over her eyes. She must get up and pull the shades down or she'd never sleep. She was in bed again and the shades were not down. How could that happen? Better turn over, hide from the light, sleeping in the light gave you nightmares. "Mother, how do you feel now?" and a stinging wetness on her forehead. But I don't like having my face washed in cold water!

30   Hapsy? George? Lydia? Jimmy? No, Cornelia, and her features were swollen and full of little puddles. "They're coming, darling, they'll all be here soon." Go wash your face, child, you look funny.

Instead of obeying, Cornelia knelt down and put her head on the pillow. She seemed to be talking but there was no sound. "Well, are you tongue-tied? Whose birthday is it? Are you going to give a party?"

Cornelia's mouth moved urgently in strange shapes. "Don't do that, you bother me, daughter."

"Oh, no, Mother. Oh, no. . . ."

Nonsense. It was strange about children. They disputed your every word. "No what, Cornelia?"

35   "Here's Doctor Harry."

"I won't see that boy again. He just left five minutes ago."

"That was this morning, Mother. It's night now. Here's the nurse."

"This is Doctor Harry, Mrs. Weatherall. I never saw you look so young and happy!"

"Ah, I'll never be young again—but I'd be happy if they'd let me lie in peace and get rested."

40   She thought she spoke up loudly, but no one answered. A warm weight on her forehead, a warm bracelet on her wrist, and a breeze went on whispering, trying to tell her something. A shuffle of leaves in the everlasting hand of God, He blew on them and they danced and rattled. "Mother, don't mind, we're going to give you a little hypodermic." "Look here, daughter, how do ants get in this bed? I saw sugar ants yesterday." Did you send for Hapsy too?

It was Hapsy she really wanted. She had to go a long way back through a great many rooms to find Hapsy standing with a baby on her arm. She seemed to herself to be Hapsy also, and the baby on Hapsy's arm was Hapsy and himself and herself, all at once, and there was no surprise in the meeting. Then Hapsy melted from within and turned flimsy as gray gauze and the baby was a gauzy shadow, and Hapsy came up close and said, "I thought you'd never come," and looked at her very searchingly and said, "You haven't changed a bit!" They leaned forward to kiss, when Cornelia began whispering from a long way off, "Oh, is there anything you want to tell me? Is there anything I can do for you?"

Yes, she had changed her mind after sixty years and she would like to see George. I want you to find George. Find him and be sure to tell him I forgot him. I want him to know I had my husband just the same and my children and my house like any other woman. A good house too and a good husband that I loved and fine children out of him. Better than I hoped for even. Tell him I was given back everything he took away and more. Oh, no, oh, God, no, there was something else besides the house and the man and the children. Oh, surely they were not all? What was it? Something not given back. . . . Her breath crowded down under her ribs and grew into a monstrous frightening shape with cutting edges; it bored up into her head, and the agony was unbelievable: Yes, John, get the Doctor now, no more talk, my time has come.

When this one was born it should be the last. The last. It should have been born first, for it was the one she had truly wanted. Everything came in good time. Nothing left out, left over. She was strong, in three days she would be as well as ever. Better. A woman needed milk in her to have her full health.

"Mother, do you hear me?"

"I've been telling you—"

"Mother, Father Connolly's here."

"I went to Holy Communion only last week. Tell him I'm not so sinful as all that."

"Father just wants to speak to you."

He could speak as much as he pleased. It was like him to drop in and inquire about her soul as if it were a teething baby, and then stay on for a cup of tea and a round of cards and gossip. He always had a funny story of some sort, usually about an Irishman who made his little mistakes and confessed them, and the point lay in some absurd thing he would blurt out in the confessional showing his struggles between native piety and original sin. Granny felt easy about her soul. Cornelia, where are your manners? Give Father Connolly a chair. She had her secret comfortable understanding with a few favorite saints who cleared a straight road to God for her. All as surely signed and sealed as the papers for the new Forty Acres. Forever . . . heirs and assigns forever. Since the day the wedding cake was not cut, but thrown out and wasted. The whole bottom dropped out of the world, and there she was blind and sweating with nothing under her feet and the walls falling away. His hand had caught her under the breast, she had not fallen, there was the freshly polished floor with the green rug on it, just as before. He had cursed like a sailor's parrot and said, "I'll kill him for you." Don't lay a hand on him, for my sake leave something to God. "Now, Ellen, you must believe what I tell you. . . ."

45

50   So there was nothing, nothing to worry about any more, except sometimes in the night one of the children screamed in a nightmare, and they both hustled out shaking and hunting for the matches and calling, "There, wait a minute, here we are!" John, get the doctor now, Hapsy's time has come. But there was Hapsy standing by the bed in a white cap. "Cornelia, tell Hapsy to take off her cap. I can't see her plain."

Her eyes opened very wide and the room stood out like a picture she had seen somewhere. Dark colors with the shadows rising towards the ceiling in long angles. The tall black dresser gleamed with nothing on it but John's picture, enlarged from a little one, with John's eyes very black when they should have been blue. You never saw him, so how do you know how he looked? But the man insisted the copy was perfect, it was very rich and handsome. For a picture, yes, but it's not my husband. The table by the bed had a linen cover and a candle and a crucifix. The light was blue from Cornelia's silk lampshades. No sort of light at all, just frippery. You had to live forty years with kerosene lamps to appreciate honest electricity. She felt very strong and she saw Doctor Harry with a rosy nimbus around him.

"You look like a saint, Doctor Harry, and I vow that's as near as you'll ever come to it."

"She's saying something."

"I heard you, Cornelia. What's all this carrying-on?"

55   "Father Connolly's saying—"

Cornelia's voice staggered and bumped like a cart in a bad road. It rounded corners and turned back again and arrived nowhere. Granny stepped up in the cart very lightly and reached for the reins, but a man sat beside her and she knew him by his hands, driving the cart. She did not look in his face, for she knew without seeing, but looked instead down the road where the trees leaned over and bowed to each other and a thousand birds were singing a Mass. She felt like singing too, but she put her hand in the bosom of her dress and pulled out a rosary, and Father Connolly murmured Latin in a very solemn voice and tickled her feet. My God, will you stop that nonsense? I'm a married woman. What if he did run away and leave me to face the priest by myself? I found another a whole world better. I wouldn't have exchanged my husband for anybody except St. Michael himself, and you may tell him that for me with a thank you in the bargain.

Light flashed on her closed eyelids, and a deep roaring shook her. Cornelia, is that lightning? I hear thunder. There's going to be a storm. Close all the windows. Call the children in. . . . "Mother, here we are, all of us." "Is that you, Hapsy?" "Oh, no, I'm Lydia. We drove as fast as we could." Their faces drifted above her, drifted away. The rosary fell out of her hands and Lydia put it back. Jimmy tried to help, their hands fumbled together, and Granny closed two fingers around Jimmy's thumb. Beads wouldn't do, it must be something alive. She was so amazed her thoughts ran round and round. So, my dear Lord, this is my death and I wasn't even thinking about it. My children have come to see me die. But I can't, it's not time. Oh, I always hated surprises. I wanted to give Cornelia the amethyst set—Cornelia, you're to have the amethyst set, but Hapsy's to wear it when she wants, and, Doctor Harry, do shut up. Nobody sent for you. Oh, my dear Lord, do wait a minute. I meant to do something about the Forty Acres, Jimmy doesn't need it and Lydia will later on, with that worthless husband of hers. I meant to finish the altar cloth and send six bottles of wine to Sister Borgia for her dyspepsia. I want to send six bottles of wine to Sister Borgia, Father Connolly, now don't let me forget.

Cornelia's voice made short turns and tilted over and crashed. "Oh, Mother, oh, Mother, oh, Mother. . . ."

"I'm not going, Cornelia. I'm taken by surprise. I can't go."

You'll see Hapsy again. What about her? "I thought you'd never come." Granny made a long journey outward, looking for Hapsy. What if I don't find her? What then? Her heart sank down and down, there was no bottom to death, she couldn't come to the end of it. The blue light from Cornelia's lampshade drew into a tiny point in the center of her brain, it flickered and winked like an eye, quietly it fluttered and dwindled. Granny lay curled down within herself, amazed and watchful, staring at the point of light that was herself; her body was now only a deeper mass of shadow in an endless darkness and this darkness would curl around the light and swallow it up. God, give a sign!

For the second time there was no sign. Again no bridegroom and the priest in the house. She could not remember any other sorrow because this grief wiped them all away. Oh, no, there's nothing more cruel than this— I'll never forgive it. She stretched herself with a deep breath and blew out the light.

QUESTIONS

1. Why is stream of consciousness appropriate in this story? What characteristics of Ellen Weatherall's condition does this narrative technique represent? How effectively does it reveal events of the past? How clearly does it reflect the present? What is gained by the lack of clarity?

2. The protagonist reveals herself to be in conflict with other persons, and with her physical environment, both in the past and in the present. Identify her antagonists. To what extent has she experienced conflicts within herself? To what extent is she now experiencing such conflicts?

3. What does her memory present as the major turning points in her life? Is it more than a coincidence that one of them occurs every twenty years? Considering the many major events in a woman's life that might have been climactic, how do the ones she recalls so vividly define her character?

4. What kind of life has Granny Weatherall made for herself? What have been her characteristic activities and attitudes? Can her "jilting" be seen as a partial cause for these activities and attitudes?
5. What is the significance of Hapsy? What religious symbolism is attached to the vision of her and her infant son (paragraph 41)?
6. Most critics understand the title to refer to two "jiltings," the one by her fiancé sixty years earlier, the other by God at the moment of her death. Can you justify this interpretation? Does the story have a determinate or indeterminate ending?

ERNEST HEMINGWAY

Hills Like White Elephants

The hills across the valley of the Ebro were long and white. On this side there was no shade and no trees and the station was between two lines of rails in the sun. Close against the side of the station there was the warm shadow of the building and a curtain, made of strings of bamboo beads, hung across the open door into the bar, to keep out flies. The American and the girl with him sat at a table in the shade, outside the building. It was very hot and the express from Barcelona would come in forty minutes. It stopped at this junction for two minutes and went on to Madrid.

"What should we drink?" the girl asked. She had taken off her hat and put it on the table.

"It's pretty hot," the man said.

"Let's drink beer."

5   "Dos cervezas," the man said into the curtain.

"Big ones?" a woman asked from the doorway.

"Yes. Two big ones."

The woman brought two glasses of beer and two felt pads. She put the felt pads and beer glasses on the table and looked at the man and the girl. The girl was looking off at the line of hills. They were white in the sun and the country was brown and dry.

"They look like white elephants," she said.

10   "I've never seen one," the man drank his beer.

"No, you wouldn't have."

"I might have," the man said. "Just because you say I wouldn't have doesn't prove anything."

HILLS LIKE WHITE ELEPHANTS First published in 1927. Ernest Hemingway (1899–1961) was born and grew up in Oak Park, Illinois, with summer vacations in northern Michigan. By the time he wrote this story he had been wounded in Italy during World War I; had traveled extensively in Europe as a newspaper correspondent and writer; had married, fathered a son, been divorced, and remarried.

The girl looked at the bead curtain. "They've painted something on it," she said. "What does it say?"

"Anis del Toro. It's a drink."

"Could we try it?"   15

The man called "Listen" through the curtain. The woman came out from the bar.

"Four reales."

"We want two Anis del Toro."

"With water?"

"Do you want it with water?"   20

"I don't know," the girl said. "Is it good with water?"

"It's all right."

"You want them with water?" asked the woman.

"Yes, with water."

"It tastes like licorice," the girl said and put the glass down.   25

"That's the way with everything."

"Yes," said the girl. "Everything tastes of licorice. Especially all the things you've waited so long for, like absinthe."

"Oh, cut it out."

"You started it," the girl said. "I was being amused. I was having a fine time."

"Well, let's try to have a fine time."   30

"All right. I was trying. I said the mountains looked like white elephants. Wasn't that bright?"

"That was bright."

"I wanted to try this new drink. That's all we do, isn't it—look at things and try new drinks."

"I guess so."

The girl looked across at the hills.   35

"They're lovely hills," she said. "They don't really look like white elephants. I just meant the coloring of their skin through the trees."

"Should we have another drink?"

"All right."

The warm wind blew the bead curtain against the table.

"The beer's nice and cool," the man said.   40

"It's lovely," the girl said.

"It's really an awfully simple operation, Jig," the man said. "It's not really an operation at all."

The girl looked at the ground the table legs rested on.

"I know you wouldn't mind it, Jig. It's really not anything. It's just to let the air in."

The girl did not say anything.   45

"I'll go with you and I'll stay with you all the time. They just let the air in and then it's all perfectly natural."

"Then what will we do afterward?"

"We'll be fine afterward. Just like we were before."

"What makes you think so?"

50   "That's the only thing that bothers us. It's the only thing that's made us unhappy."

The girl looked at the bead curtain, put her hand out and took hold of two strings of beads.

"And you think then we'll be all right and be happy."

"I know we will. You don't have to be afraid. I've known lots of people that have done it."

"So have I," said the girl. "And afterward they were all so happy."

55   "Well," the man said, "if you don't want to you don't have to. I wouldn't have you do it if you didn't want to. But I know it's perfectly simple."

"And you really want to?"

"I think it's the best thing to do. But I don't want you to do it if you don't really want to."

"And if I do it you'll be happy and things will be like they were and you'll love me?"

"I love you now. You know I love you."

60   "I know. But if I do it, then it will be nice again if I say things are like white elephants, and you'll like it?"

"I'll love it. I love it now but I just can't think about it. You know how I get when I worry."

"If I do it you won't ever worry?"

"I won't worry about that because it's perfectly simple."

"Then I'll do it. Because I don't care about me."

65   "What do you mean?"

"I don't care about me."

"Well, I care about you."

"Oh yes. But I don't care about me. And I'll do it and then everything will be fine."

"I don't want you to do it if you feel that way."

70   The girl stood up and walked to the end of the station. Across, on the other side, were fields of grain and trees along the banks of the Ebro. Far away, beyond the river, were mountains. The shadow of a cloud moved across the field of grain and she saw the river through the trees.

"And we could have all this," she said. "And we could have everything and every day we make it more impossible."

"What did you say?"

"I said we could have everything."

"We can have everything."

"No, we can't." 75

"We can have the whole world."

"No, we can't."

"We can go everywhere."

"No, we can't. It isn't ours any more."

"It's ours." 80

"No, it isn't. And once they take it away, you never get it back."

"But they haven't taken it away."

"We'll wait and see."

"Come on back in the shade," he said. "You mustn't feel that way."

"I don't feel any way," the girl said. "I just know things." 85

"I don't want you to do anything that you don't want to do—"

"Nor that isn't good for me," she said. "I know. Could we have another beer."

"All right. But you've got to realize—"

"I realize," the girl said. "Can't we stop talking?"

They sat down at the table and the girl looked across at the hills on the 90
dry side of the valley and the man looked at her and at the table.

"You've got to realize," he said, "that I don't want you to do it if
you don't want to. I'm perfectly willing to go through with it if it means
anything to you."

"Doesn't it mean anything to you? We could get along."

"Of course it does. But I don't want anybody but you. I don't want any
one else. And I know it's perfectly simple."

"Yes, you know it's perfectly simple."

"It's all right for you to say that, but I do know it." 95

"Would you do something for me now?"

"I'd do anything for you."

"Would you please please please please please please please stop talking?"

He did not say anything but looked at the bags against the wall of
the station. There were labels on them from all the hotels where they had
spent nights.

"But I don't want you to," he said. "I don't care anything about it." 100

"I'll scream," said the girl.

The woman came out through the curtains with two glasses of beer
and put them down on the damp felt pads. "The train comes in five
minutes," she said.

"What did she say?" asked the girl.

"That the train is coming in five minutes."

The girl smiled brightly at the woman, to thank her. 105

"I'd better take the bags over to the other side of the station," the man said. She smiled at him.

"All right. Then come back and we'll finish the beer."

He picked up the two heavy bags and carried them around the station to the other tracks. He looked up the tracks but could not see the train. Coming back, he walked through the barroom, where people waiting for the train were drinking. He drank an Anis at the bar and looked at the people. They were all waiting reasonably for the train. He went out through the bead curtain. She was sitting at the table and smiled at him.

"Do you feel better?" he asked.

110   "I feel fine," she said. "There's nothing wrong with me. I feel fine."

QUESTIONS

1. The main topic of discussion between the man and the girl is never named. What is the "awfully simple operation"? Why is it not named? What different attitudes are taken toward it by the man and the girl? Why?

2. What is indicated about the past life of the man and the girl? How? What has happened to the quality of their relationship? Why? How do we know? How accurate is the man's judgment about their future?

3. Though the story consists mostly of dialogue, and though it contains strong emotional conflict, it is entirely without adverbs indicating the tone of the remarks. How does Hemingway indicate tone? At what points are the characters insincere? Self-deceived? Ironic or sarcastic? To what extent do they give open expression to their feelings? Does either want an open conflict? Why or why not? Trace the various phases of emotion in the girl.

4. How sincere is the man in his insistence that he would not have the girl undergo the operation if she does not want to and that he is "perfectly willing to go through with it" if it means anything to the girl? What is "it"? How many times does he repeat these ideas? What significance has the man's drinking an Anis by himself before rejoining the girl at the end of the story?

5. Much of the conversation seems to be about trivial things (ordering drinks, the weather, and so on). What purposes does this conversation serve? What relevance has the girl's remark about absinthe?

6. What is the point of the girl's comparison of the hills to white elephants? Does the remark assume any significance for the reader beyond its significance for the characters? Why does the author use it for his title?

7. What purpose does the setting serve—the hills across the valley, the treeless railroad tracks and station? What is contributed by the precise information about time at the end of the first paragraph?

8. Which of the two characters is more "reasonable"? Which "wins" the conflict between them? The point of view is objective. Does this mean that we cannot tell whether the sympathy of the author lies more with one character than with the other? Explain your answer.

SUGGESTIONS FOR WRITING

1. Compare the effectiveness of first-person point of view in any two of the following stories. What contrasting effects do the authors achieve from the different ways they use the first person?
   a. Munro, "How I Met My Husband" (page 118).
   b. Faulkner, "A Rose for Emily" (page 538).
   c. Melville, "Bartleby the Scrivener" (page 627).
   d. Poe, "The Cask of Amontillado" (page 657).
2. Compare/contrast the use of third-person point of view in any two of the following stories. Does the author use objective, omniscient, or limited? Why is the particular point of view appropriate to each story? Focus on scenes in which the chosen point of view is especially effective.
   a. Wolff, "Hunters in the Snow" (page 79).
   b. Lahiri, "Interpreter of Maladies" (page 590).
   c. Mansfield, "Miss Brill" (page 155).
   d. Lawrence, "Odour of Chrysanthemums" (page 402).
   e. Hawthorne, "Young Goodman Brown" (page 293).
   f. García Márquez, "A Very Old Man with Enormous Wings" (page 318).
   g. Oates, "Where Are You Going, Where Have You Been?" (page 489).
   h. Jackson, "The Lottery" (page 260).

PRACTICE AP WRITING PROMPTS

Shirley Jackson, "The Lottery" (pp. 260)

Read "The Lottery" carefully. Then write an essay in which you trace the reader's shifting perception of the townspeople. Refer to such literary elements as dialogue, symbolism, and narrative pace.

....

Katherine Anne Porter, "The Jilting of Granny Weatherall" (pp. 268)

Write an essay in which you analyze how Porter foreshadows the story's ironic ending using shifts in time and Ellen (Granny) Weatherall's apparently disjoined stream of consciousness.

....

CHAPTER SIX

Symbol, Allegory, and Fantasy

Most successful stories are characterized by compression. The writer's aim is to say as much as possible as briefly as possible. This does not mean that most good stories are brief. It means only that nothing is wasted and that the author chooses each word and detail carefully for maximum effectiveness.

Talented authors achieve compression by exercising a careful selectivity. They choose the details and incidents essential to the story they have to tell and they eliminate any that do not contribute to the unified effect of the story. Because every element in a story must do as much as possible, some details and incidents may serve a variety of purposes at once. A detail that illustrates character at the same time that it advances plot is more useful than a detail that does only one or the other.

Three of the many resources available to writers for achieving compression are symbol, allegory, and fantasy. To varying degrees, each of these techniques is a way to depart from the strict adherence to factual language and representation of the kind a journalist uses, for instance, in writing a newspaper story. By modifying, enhancing, and at times even abandoning such a factual or realistic approach to storytelling, an author can increase the emotional force and resonance of a story, suggesting a much larger and richer meaning than might be achieved with a strictly realistic approach. But such narrative strategies also require close attention on the reader's part.

A literary **symbol** is something that means *more* than what it suggests on the surface. It may be an object, a person, a situation, an action, or some other element that has a literal meaning in the story but that suggests or represents other meanings as well. A very simple illustration is that of name symbolism. Most names are simply labels. A name, for instance, does not tell much about the person to whom it is attached, except possibly the individual's nationality or, in the case of first names, the person's gender. In a story, however, authors may choose names for their characters that not only label them but also suggest something about them. In "A Worn Path," for instance, the name "Phoenix" has several meanings that are relevant to Welty's character. In Egyptian mythology, a phoenix was a bird that consumed itself by fire after five hundred years, but then rose from its own ashes. It was also employed as a Christian symbol of death and resurrection in the art and architecture of the medieval period. Authors have often used this bird to suggest magical powers of renewal and endurance, and this meaning certainly relates to Phoenix Jackson's enduring love for her grandson. More generally, a phoenix also means a person of particular excellence, a meaning also applicable to Welty's protagonist. In "Everyday Use," Dee's rejection of her name and adoption of the alternative "Wangero" symbolizes for her a changed perspective on her heritage. The name of General Zaroff in "The Most Dangerous Game" is fitting for a former "officer of the Czar" who now behaves like a czar himself. Trevor's name in Greene's "The Destructors" suggests his upper-class origins. Equally meaningful in that story is the name of the Wormsley Common Gang. First, the word "Common," here designating a small public park or green, also suggests the "common people" or the lower middle and laboring classes as opposed to the upper class. More significant, when Trevor advocates his plan for gutting the old house—"We'd do it from inside. . . . We'd be like worms, don't you see, in an apple" (paragraph 52), we see that Greene's choice of the name Wormsley was quite deliberate and that it is appropriate also (as well as perfectly natural) that Wormsley Common should have an Underground Station. (The word "apple," in Trevor's speech, also has symbolic resonances. Though it is often a mistake to push symbolism too hard, the reader may well ask whether anything would be lost if Trevor had compared the gang's activities to those of worms in a peach or a pear.)

More important than name symbolism is the symbolic use of objects and actions. In some stories these symbols will fit so naturally into the literal context that their symbolic value will not at first be apparent except to the most perceptive reader. In other stories—usually stories with a less realistic surface—they will be so central and so obvious that they will demand symbolical interpretation if the story is to yield significant meaning. In the first kind of story the symbols *reinforce* and *add* to the meaning. In the second kind of story they *carry* the meaning.

Eudora Welty's "A Worn Path" superficially concerns a very old woman who walks from the back country into the city, encountering a variety of obstacles on her trip, in order to receive a bottle of soothing medicine from a charity clinic for her chronically ill grandson. The story has the familiar structure of a journey or quest and, in the old woman's ability to overcome or avert the dangers that she faces, a kind of mythic power that might remind us of *The Odyssey* or *Pilgrim's Progress*. It is a story of valor, purposefulness, and triumph, as the abiding love of the protagonist gives her the strength and shrewdness to achieve her goal.

But the symbolic meaning is more profound and moving. There are two predominant sets of symbols in the story, one made apparent by repetition, the other gradually developed by realistic details that build by accretion. The first is initially suggested by the symbolic name of the protagonist, "Phoenix" (not uncommon for a black woman in the south at the time of the story). In this example of name symbolism the character thus embodies such qualities as great age, pertinacity, persistence, and the magical ability to renew herself and regain strength and vigor.

Name symbolism, however, is only a beginning point in interpreting "A Worn Path." It adds grandeur to an otherwise apparently insignificant person, but it also initiates the repetitive references to birds that fill the story. At the onset of her trip, Phoenix's tapping of her cane sounds like "the chirping of a solitary little bird"; as she begins her journey, she warns "little bobwhites" to avoid being underfoot; and when she hears the "mourning dove" still crying down in the hollow, she symbolically interprets it as a parallel to herself: it too has persisted into the winter season. A buzzard among "big dead trees" she interprets as a reminder of death— and she brusquely dismisses it by asking, " 'Who you watching?' " When she encounters a scarecrow, she first mistakes it for a mysterious dancing man, then for a ghost. As a bird herself she is "scared" by it, then identifies it for what it is and dances with it while corn husks "whirl in streamers about her skirts," a festive dance of triumph over this enemy of birds. Immediately after, as she escapes from the "maze" of the dead cornfield into a familiar wagon track, the "quail . . . walking around like pullets, seeming all dainty and unseen" reinforce her victory over fear and confusion.

The next bird that Phoenix sees is one of those same quail, now called "bobwhite," in the hunter's bag, with "a little closed claw" and "its beak hooked bitterly to show it was dead," a symbol of the genuine dangers that all mortal birds may face—but not Phoenix, who is not frightened by the foolish, callous hunter pointing his gun at her.

Birds thus symbolize for Phoenix the dangers and the delights of her life, both past and present. They are a well-known population of her world, and all of them embody some meaning for her. She is an interpreter of symbols. She feels protective and pitying toward the vulnerable, and she scorns and dismisses the threatening. There is one bird, however, that truly disturbs her. When by her ruse of inciting a dog-fight so as to pick up the nickel dropped by the hunter (who later lies to her about having any money, pretending he wishes to be charitable), Phoenix looks up as she puts the coin in her pocket and sees "a bird [fly] by." Her interpretation links bird-life to faith and morality: "'God watching me the whole time. I come to stealing.'" What birds know and do is to her an intimation of God's commandments and love.

At the climax of the story, one final symbolic reference to birds reveals the central meaning of the story. After a momentary memory lapse at the charity clinic, Phoenix focuses again on the purpose of her trip, to relieve the suffering of her grandson. "'We is the only two left in the world,'" she says, meaning that the two of them are the last of their family but also implying their mutual need to sustain each other. She goes on, "'He wear a little patch quilt and peep out holding his mouth open like a little bird.'" She is confident that the two of them are "going to last," the loving spirit of Phoenix ever renewing itself, and the innocent "sweet" child always needing and receiving her self-sacrifice.

There is another symbolic frame of reference in this story, not so obvious but perhaps just as important. While the bird symbolism enlarges the meaning of Phoenix's trip to embrace enduring human values that transcend time and place, the story also symbolizes the historical and cultural issue of racial division in America at the time of its writing and in the years before and since the Civil War. Phoenix, who "'was too old at the Surrender'" (1865) to attend school, and now at over 100 is the oldest person she knows about, spans in her lifetime the period of slavery, emancipation, its aftermath during the Reconstruction, and the era of Jim Crow laws in the south and prejudice and bigotry throughout the country. A diligent reading will reveal a constant recurrence of "black" and "white" as words, as implied appearances, and even as moral abstractions. Because they are not always easily associated with right and wrong, good and evil, the references do not constitute an allegorical system but rather a repeated reminder of black-white oppositions. The first of these will suggest the subtlety of this symbolism: in the initial description of Phoenix's appearance, the narrator points out that the hair of this centenarian, falling on her neck "in the frailest of ringlets . . . [is] still black." Contrary to natural expectations, her hair has not turned *white*, and her racial identity is intact. Following this implied contrast of black and white, the careful reader will discover many explicit or implicit references to these colors.

Symbolically, the most impressive and touching example occurs during Phoenix's dream as she rests after the ordeal of crossing the creek. She sits down, spreads out her skirts, and assumes a girlish posture as she looks around: "Up above her was a tree in a pearly cloud of mistletoe. She did not dare to close her eyes, and when a little boy brought her a plate with a slice of marble-cake on it she spoke to him. 'That would be acceptable,' she said. But when she went to take it there was just her hand in the air." Here, as if from heaven itself (where the "pearly" gates are as white as the garments of the angels themselves), a "little boy" (perhaps reminiscent of her grandson) offers her a delicacy that displays a perfect mixing of light and dark, a promised harmony of sweet equality—but not yet, not in real life. Phoenix's understated acceptance of it as a gift offered rather than a right demanded is characteristic of the humble gratitude for small advances that was all too common at the time of the story. As a black woman, she has endured and she will keep enduring the vicissitudes of social change, a reminder of love as a remedy for hatred.

Another example of symbolic setting and action is presented in Hemingway's "Hills Like White Elephants," in which a man and a girl sit waiting for the train to Madrid, where the girl is to have an abortion. But the girl is not fully persuaded that she wants an abortion (at the deepest levels of her being, she does not). The man is aware of this and seeks to reassure her: "It's really an awfully simple operation. . . . It's not really an operation at all. . . . But I don't want you to do it if you don't really want to." The man *does* want her to do it even if she doesn't really want to; nevertheless, the decision is not irrevocable. They are at a railroad junction, a place where one can change directions. Symbolically it represents a juncture where they can change the direction of their lives. Their bags, with "labels on them from all the hotels where they had spent nights," indicate the kind of rootless, pleasure-seeking existence without responsibility they have hitherto lived. The man wants the girl to have the abortion so that they can go on living as they have before.

The railway station is situated in a river valley between two mountain ranges. On one side of the valley there is no shade and no trees and the country is "brown and dry." It is on this side, "the dry side," that the station sits in the heat, "between two lines of rails." It is also this side that the couple see from their table and that prompts the girl's remark that the hills look "like white elephants." On the other side of the valley, which the girl can see when she walks to the end of the station, lies the river, with "fields of grain and trees" along its banks, the "shadow of a cloud" moving across a field of grain, and another range of mountains in the distance. Looking in this direction, the girl remarks, "And we could have all this." The two landscapes, on opposite sides of the valley, have symbolic meaning in relation to the decision that the girl is being asked to reconfirm. The hot arid side of the valley represents sterility; the other side, with water in the river and the cloud, a hint of coolness in the cloud's moving shadow, and growing things along the river banks, represents fertility. The girl's remark about this other side shows a conscious recognition of its symbolism.

But what does the girl mean by her remark that the mountains on the dry side of the valley look "like white elephants"? Perhaps nothing at all. It is intended as a "bright" remark, a clever if far-fetched comparison made to amuse the man, as it would have in their earlier days together. But whether or not the girl means anything by it, almost certainly Hemingway means something. Or perhaps several things. Clearly the child begun in the girl's womb is a "white elephant" for the man, who says, "I don't want anybody but you. I don't want any one else." For the girl, on the other hand, the abortion itself, the decision to continue living as they have been living, without responsibility, may be considered a "white elephant." We already know that this life has lost its savor for her. When she remarks that the Anis del Toro "tastes like licorice," the man's response—"that's the way with everything"—is probably meant to apply only to the drink and food in this section of the country, but the girl's confirmation of his observation seems to enlarge its meaning to the whole life they have been living together, which consists, she says, only of looking at things and trying new drinks. Thus the licorice flavor, suggesting tedium and disillusion, joins the "hills like white elephants," the opposed sides of the river valley, and the railroad junction in a network of symbols that intensify the meaning and impact of the story.

The ability to recognize and identify symbols requires perception and tact. The great danger facing readers when they first become aware of symbolic values is a tendency to run wild—to find symbols everywhere and to read into the details of a story all sorts of fanciful meanings not legitimately supported by it. But we need to remember that most stories operate almost wholly at the literal level and that even in highly symbolic stories, the majority of the details are purely literal. A story is not an excuse for an exercise in ingenuity. It is better, indeed, to miss the symbolic meanings of a story than to pervert its meaning by discovering symbols that are nonexistent. Better to miss the boat than to jump wildly for it and drown.

The ability to interpret symbols is nevertheless essential for a full understanding of literature. Readers should always be alert for symbolic meanings but should observe the following cautions:

1. The story itself must furnish a clue that a detail is to be taken symbolically. In Mansfield's story, Miss Brill's fur is given prominence at the beginning of the story, when it is taken out of its box; at the climax of the story, when the girl on the bench compares it to "a fried whiting"; and at the end of the story, when Miss Brill puts it back in the box and thinks she hears it crying. The fur is clearly a symbol for Miss Brill herself. It comes out of a box like a dark little room or a cupboard, it is old and in need of repair, it is ridiculed by the boy and the girl on the park bench, and it is returned to its box at the end of the story. Symbolically, it is herself whom Miss Brill hears crying. In Welty's story, the repetition of references to

birds, including the name of the protagonist, signals the need to interpret them symbolically. The title "A Worn Path" explicitly refers to Phoenix's repeated journeys, and by implication symbolizes the journeys of her race toward love and full acceptance. Both items are emphasized and significant to the meaning of the story, but neither is essential to its plot. Even greater emphasis is given to the quilts in the story by Walker. Symbols nearly always signal their existence by *emphasis, repetition*, or *position*. In the absence of such signals, we should be reluctant to identify an item as symbolic.

2. The meaning of a literary symbol must be established and supported by the entire context of the story. The symbol has its meaning *in* the story, not *outside* it. For instance, in "A Worn Path," the meaning of the "pearly cloud of mistletoe" is supported by and dependent on its relation to other references within the story establishing the correlations between black and white and the dreams that Phoenix harbors. In another context a cloud of mistletoe might connote parasitism and the death of the host tree. Here, associated as it is with a proffered gift of delight from on high, the symbol reinforces Phoenix's faith and reliance on God's will.

3. To be called a symbol, an item must suggest a meaning different in *kind* from its literal meaning; a symbol is something more than the representative of a class or type. Miss Brill, for instance, is an old, odd, silent, friendless person, set in her ways, who does not realize (until the climax of the story) that she herself is old, odd, and set in her ways—like other elderly people she observes in the park each Sunday. But to say this is to say no more than that the story has a theme. Every literary story suggests a generalization about life, is more than an accounting of the specific fortunes of specific individuals. There is no point, therefore, in calling Miss Brill a *symbol* of odd, self-deluded elderly people; she *is* an odd, self-deluded elderly person: a member of the class of odd, self-deluded elderly persons. Her fur is a symbol, but she is not. We ought not to use the phrase *is a symbol of* when we can easily use *is*, or *is an example of* or *is an evidence of.* Phoenix Jackson, in "A Worn Path," through the symbolic associations attached to her name, is clearly meant to be something more than an *example* of any class or race of human beings, or of humanity in general; she is a symbol of something *within* the human spirit, of hidden possibilities latent in many people.

The quilts in Alice Walker's "Everyday Use" are *evidence* that the family has been enslaved and impoverished, evidence of a past that Dee is proud to have escaped. To her, they are valuable as artifacts of oppression. In the story, however, they *symbolize* a wealth beyond money in the family's linkages to an authentic heritage of craftsmanship and beauty.

4. A symbol may have more than one meaning. It may suggest a cluster of meanings. At its most effective, a symbol is like a many-faceted jewel: it flashes different colors when turned in the light. This is not to say that it can mean

anything we want it to: the area of possible meanings is always controlled by the context. Nevertheless, this possibility of complex meaning plus concreteness and emotional power gives the symbol its peculiar compressive value. The path in Welty's story symbolizes life itself, including its obstacles, its habits, its occasional moments of humor, pain, and beauty, and above all its nature as a journey human beings must undertake with as much courage and dignity as possible, motivated by love. The quilts in Walker's story have an equally wide range of meaning—inherited values, family attachments, independence and self-reliance, the beauty of useful objects, the virtue of craftsmanship—all in contrast to the shallow, monetary meaning expressed in Dee's acquisitive demand for them. When she says, "But they're *priceless!*" she means that they are worth a great deal of money, but in the truer sense their symbolic values cannot be reckoned at any price. The meaning is not confined to any one of these qualities: it is all of them, and therein lies the symbol's value.

An **allegory** is a story that has a second meaning beneath the surface, endowing a cluster of characters, objects, or events with added significance; often the pattern relates each literal item to a corresponding abstract idea or moral principle. It is different from symbolism in that it puts less emphasis on the literal meanings and more on the ulterior meanings. Also, those ulterior meanings are more fixed, and they usually constitute a pre-existing system of ideas or principles. Medieval and Renaissance religious allegories, for instance, were intended to illustrate the progress of a typical Christian individual through life, as in the medieval play *Everyman* and in John Bunyan's *Pilgrim's Progress*, a seventeenth-century work in which a character named "Christian" journeys toward salvation, encountering along the way such temptations as despair, labeled "The Slough of Despond," and witnessing human hypocrisy in a town called "Fair Speech." Probably the most widely read allegorical work today is Nathaniel Hawthorne's novel *The Scarlet Letter* (1850). Although Hawthorne's novel, like most more modern allegories, eschews the mechanical, one-to-one correspondences found in older allegorical works (which were written more for religious or political than literary purposes), he does provide a coherent system that evokes and critiques the seventeenth-century Puritan world in which the novel is set. The novel's allegorical pattern includes the scarlet "A" for adultery that Hester Prynne wears on her dress; the names of her husband, Chillingworth, and her daughter, Pearl; Hester's uneasy residence on the border between the wilderness, representing natural impulses, and the "civilized" Puritan culture that ostracizes her. In this chapter, Hawthorne's story "Young Goodman Brown" has a similar allegorical pattern. The title character, as his name suggests, is a typical young and virtuous man; his surname "Brown," like "Smith" in America today, is the most common name during his era, again suggesting his identity as a representative individual. His wife, "Faith," represents the steadfast virtue he is leaving behind during his journey into the wilderness, just as her pink ribbons suggest her innocence. During a crisis point in the story, Brown shouts "My Faith is gone!" and the allegorical meaning is clear, for he is talking simultaneously about his literal wife and the abstraction of his religious faith. Other elements in the story—the old man's staff that begins "writhing" like a serpent, the wilderness itself with its suggestions of moral chaos and depravity—likewise fulfill roles in Hawthorne's allegory.

It should be stressed, however, that an author employing allegory usually does not intend simply to create two levels of reality, one literal and one abstract, which readers merely identify as though connecting a series of dots. Serious writers often introduce an element of ambiguity into their allegorical meanings, undercutting easy and simplistic interpretation. For example, in Hawthorne's story, Brown's innocent wife Faith pleads with her husband not to undertake the journey, observing, "A lone woman is troubled with such dreams and such thoughts that she's afeared of herself sometimes"—a bit of dialogue that suggests her identity as more than an abstract representation of faith but also as a flesh-and-blood woman who may well encounter her own temptations and psychological turmoil when separated from her husband.

The creation of an allegorical pattern of meaning enables an author to achieve power through economy. Reading a story, you should therefore be aware of an author's use of description and detail, for these may be present not only to create a sensual apprehension of a story's characters and settings, but also to suggest meanings—moral, intellectual, emotional—beyond that reality. This ability to compress a great deal of meaning into the relatively small canvas of a short story is part of what gives the best examples of this genre their powerful narrative impact.

While some stories use factual details to suggest additional, sometimes abstract, meanings, there is another type of story that abandons factual representation altogether. The nonrealistic story, or **fantasy**, is one that transcends the bounds of known reality. After all, truth in fiction is not the same as fidelity to fact. All fiction is essentially a game of make-believe in which the author imaginatively conceives characters and situations and sets them down on paper. The purpose of any literary artist is to communicate truths by means of imagined facts. While most authors, using realistic means, attempt to create an illusion of reality in telling their stories, careful to stay in the realm of the plausible and relate something that *could have happened*, sometimes an author chooses to go a step further and create a story that is entirely implausible or even impossible. Such stories require from the reader what the poet Samuel Taylor Coleridge called "a willing suspension of disbelief": that is, the reader is willing to accept the author's premise of a strange and marvelous world, in which a character falls down a rabbit hole or climbs up a beanstalk or finds himself in an alien spaceship. Such a fantasy story introduces human beings into a world where the ordinary laws of nature are suspended or superseded and where the landscape and its creatures are unfamiliar; or, on the other hand, it may introduce ghosts, fairies, dragons, werewolves, talking animals, Martian invaders, or miraculous occurrences into the recognizable, everyday world of human beings. A recently popular form of this second approach to fantasy has been called "magical realism," in which fantastic and magical events are woven into mundane and ordinary situations, creating striking and memorable effects unavailable to either realism or fantasy alone. Such popular forms of storytelling as fables, ghost stories, and science fiction are all types of fantasy. Like stories using symbolism and allegory, fantasy stories are often highly compressed, enabling the author to convey a richly textured, resonant vision within a relatively short narrative.

The story writer begins, then, by saying, "What if. . . ." "What if," for instance, "a young, somewhat naïve girl working in a farmhouse should meet a handsome pilot visiting the area and become infatuated with him." From this initial assumption the author goes on to develop a story ("How I Met My Husband"), which, though presumably imaginary in the sense that it never happened, nevertheless reveals convincingly to us some truths of human behavior.

But now, what if the author goes a step further and supposes not just something that might very well have happened (though it didn't) but something highly improbable—something that could happen, say, only as the result of a very surprising coincidence? What if he begins, "Let's suppose that a misogynist and a charming woman find themselves alone on a desert island"? This initial supposition causes us to stretch our imaginations a bit further, but is not this situation just as capable of revealing human truths as the former? The psychologist puts a rat in a maze (certainly an improbable situation for a rat), observes its reactions to the maze, and discovers some truth of rat behavior. The author may put imaginary characters on an imagined desert island, imaginatively study their reactions, and reveal some truth of human nature. The improbable initial situation may yield as much truth as the probable one.

From the improbable it is but one step further to the impossible (as we know it in this life). Why should our author not begin "Let's suppose that a miser and his termagant wife find themselves in hell" or "Let's suppose that a primitive scapegoat ritual still survives in contemporary America." Could not these situations also be used to exhibit human traits?

Like stories employing realistic characters and events, fantasies may be purely commercial entertainment or they may be serious literary works. A story about a spaceship on its way to a distant planet might be filled with stock characters or with richly imagined human beings; it may be designed chiefly to exhibit mechanical marvels and to provide thrills and adventures, or it may be a way of creating a setting in which human behavior can be sharply observed and studied. Fantasy, like other forms of fiction, may be employed sheerly for its own sake or as a means of communicating significant insights into the world of human beings. The important point to remember is that truth in fiction is not to be identified with a realistic method. Stories that fly on the wings of fantasy may be vehicles for truth that are as powerful in their own way as such realistic stories as "Hunters in the Snow" or "Interpreter of Maladies." Fantasy may employ the techniques of symbolism or allegory, or it may simply provide an exotic, nonrealistic setting as a way of observing human nature. Some of the world's greatest works of literature have been partly or wholly fantasy: *The Odyssey, The Divine Comedy, The Tempest, Pilgrim's Progress, Gulliver's Travels*, and *Alice in Wonderland* all offer profound and significant insights into the human condition.

Clearly, then, we must not judge a story as good or bad according to whether or not it stays within the limits of the possible. Rather, we should begin reading any story by suspending disbelief—that is, by granting every story its initial premise or assumption. The writer may begin with an ordinary, everyday situation or with a far-fetched, improbable coincidence. Or the writer may be allowed to suspend a law of nature or to create a marvelous being or machine or place. But once we have accepted an impossible reality as a premise, we have a right to demand probability and consistency in the author's treatment of it. Fantasy is not an excuse for haphazard writing or a poorly imagined story. We need to ask, too, for what reason the story employs fantasy. Is it used simply for its own strangeness, or for thrills or surprises or laughs? Or is it used to illuminate truths of the reader's own experience? What, finally, is the purpose of the author's fantastic invention? Is it, like a roller coaster, simply a machine for producing a temporary thrill? Or does it, like an observation balloon, provide a unique vantage point that may change our view of the world forever?

REVIEWING CHAPTER SIX

1. Review the definition of a literary symbol.
2. Explore the uses of symbolic names, objects, and actions.
3. Summarize the use of symbolism in Welty's "A Worn Path."
4. Distinguish between symbolism and allegory.
5. Describe the importance of ambiguity in a literary allegory.
6. Define the term "fantasy" and describe the prominent features of a fantastic story.

NATHANIEL HAWTHORNE
Young Goodman Brown

Young Goodman Brown came forth at sunset into the street of Salem village, but put his head back, after crossing the threshold, to exchange a parting kiss with his young wife. And Faith, as the wife was aptly named, thrust her own pretty head into the street, letting the wind play with the pink ribbons of her cap while she called to Goodman Brown.

"Dearest heart," whispered she softly and rather sadly when her lips were close to his ear, "prithee, put off your journey until sunrise, and sleep in your own bed tonight. A lone woman is troubled with such dreams and such thoughts that she's afeard of herself, sometimes. Pray, tarry with me this night, dear husband, of all nights in the year!"

"My love and my Faith," replied young Goodman Brown, "of all nights in the year this one must I tarry away from thee. My journey, as thou callest it, forth and back again must needs be done 'twixt now and sunrise. What, my sweet, pretty wife, dost thou doubt me already, and we but three months married!"

"Then God bless you!" said Faith with the pink ribbons, "and may you find all well when you come back."

"Amen!" cried Goodman Brown. "Say thy prayers, dear Faith, and go to bed at dusk, and no harm will come to thee."   5

So they parted; and the young man pursued his way until, being about to turn the corner by the meeting-house, he looked back and saw the head of Faith still peeping after him with a melancholy air in spite of her pink ribbons.

"Poor little Faith!" thought he, for his heart smote him. "What a wretch am I, to leave her on such an errand! She talks of dreams, too. Methought, as she spoke, there was trouble in her face, as if a dream had warned her what work is to be done tonight. But no, no! 'twould kill her to think it. Well; she's a blessed angel on earth and after this one night I'll cling to her skirts and follow her to Heaven."

With this excellent resolve for the future, Goodman Brown felt himself justified in making more haste on his present evil purpose. He had

YOUNG GOODMAN BROWN   First published in 1835. "Goodman" was a title of respect, but at a social rank lower than "gentleman." "Goody" (or "Goodwife") was the feminine equivalent. Deacon Gookin in the story is a historical personage (1612–1687), as are also Goody Cloyse, Goody Cory, and Martha Carrier, all three executed at the Salem witchcraft trials in 1692. Nathaniel Hawthorne (1804–1864) was born and grew up in Salem, Massachusetts, where Hawthornes had lived since the seventeenth century. One ancestor had been a judge at the Salem witch trials; another had been a leader in the persecution of Quakers. "Young Goodman Brown" is one of several stories in which Hawthorne explored the Puritan past of New England.

taken a dreary road, darkened by all the gloomiest trees of the forest, which barely stood aside to let the narrow path creep through, and closed immediately behind. It was all as lonely as could be; and there is this peculiarity in such a solitude, that the traveler knows not who may be concealed by the innumerable trunks and the thick boughs overhead, so that with lonely footsteps he may be passing through an unseen multitude.

"There may be a devilish Indian behind every tree," said Goodman Brown to himself; and he glanced fearfully behind him as he added, "What if the devil himself should be at my very elbow!"

10 His head being turned back, he passed a crook of the road, and looking forward again beheld the figure of a man in grave and decent attire, seated at the foot of an old tree. He rose at Goodman Brown's approach and walked onward side by side with him.

"You are late, Goodman Brown," said he. "The clock of the Old South was striking as I came through Boston, and that is full fifteen minutes agone."°

"Faith kept me back awhile," replied the young man with a tremor in his voice caused by the sudden appearance of his companion, though not wholly unexpected.

It was now deep dusk in the forest, and deepest in that part of it where these two were journeying. As nearly as could be discerned, the second traveler was about fifty years old, apparently in the same rank of life as Goodman Brown, and bearing a considerable resemblance to him, though perhaps more in expression than features. Still, they might have been taken for father and son. And yet, though the elder person was as simply clad as the younger, and as simple in manner too, he had an indescribable air of one who knew the world and would not have felt abashed at the governor's dinner table or in King William's court,° were it possible that his affairs should call him thither. But the only thing about him that could be fixed upon as remarkable was his staff, which bore the likeness of a great black snake, so curiously wrought that it might almost be seen to twist and wriggle itself like a living serpent. This, of course, must have been an ocular deception, assisted by the uncertain light.

"Come, Goodman Brown!" cried his fellow-traveler, "this is a dull pace for the beginning of a journey. Take my staff if you are so soon weary."

15 "Friend," said the other, exchanging his slow pace for a full stop, "having kept covenant by meeting thee here, it is my purpose now to return whence I came. I have scruples touching the matter thou wot'st of."

---

full fifteen minutes agone: The distance from the center of Boston to the forest was over twenty miles. King William's court: William III, King of England, 1689–1702

"Sayest thou so?" replied he of the serpent, smiling apart. "Let us walk on nevertheless, reasoning as we go, and if I convince thee not, thou shalt turn back. We are but a little way in the forest yet."

"Too far, too far!" exclaimed the goodman, unconsciously resuming his walk. "My father never went into the woods on such an errand, nor his father before him. We have been a race of honest men and good Christians since the days of the martyrs. And shall I be the first of the name of Brown that ever took this path and kept—"

"Such company, thou wouldst say," observed the elder person interrupting his pause. "Well said, Goodman Brown! I have been as well acquainted with your family as with ever a one among the Puritans, and that's no trifle to say. I helped your grandfather the constable when he lashed the Quaker woman so smartly through the streets of Salem. And it was I that brought your father a pitch-pine knot kindled at my own hearth, to set fire to an Indian village, in King Philip's war.° They were my good friends, both; and many a pleasant walk have we had along this path and returned merrily after midnight. I would fain be friends with you, for their sake."

"If it be as thou sayest," replied Goodman Brown, "I marvel they never spoke of these matters. Or, verily, I marvel not, seeing that the least rumor of the sort would have driven them from New England. We are a people of prayer, and good works to boot, and abide no such wickedness."

"Wickedness or not," said the traveler with twisted staff, "I have a general acquaintance here in New England. The deacons of many a church have drunk the communion wine with me, the selectmen of divers towns make me their chairman, and a majority of the Great and General Court° are firm supporters of my interest. The governor and I, too—but these are state secrets." 20

"Can this be so!" cried Goodman Brown with a stare of amazement at his undisturbed companion. "Howbeit, I have nothing to do with the governor and council; they have their own ways and are no rule for a simple husbandman like me. But were I to go on with thee, how should I meet the eye of that good old man, our minister, at Salem village? Oh, his voice would make me tremble, both Sabbath-day and lecture-day!"

Thus far, the elder traveler had listened with due gravity but now burst into a fit of irrepressible mirth, shaking himself so violently that his snakelike staff actually seemed to wriggle in sympathy.

"Ha! ha! ha!" shouted he, again and again; then composing himself, "Well, go on, Goodman Brown, go on; but prithee, don't kill me with laughing!"

King Philip's war: a war between the colonists and Indians, 1675–1676 **Great and General Court:** the legislature of the Massachusetts Bay Colony

"Well, then, to end the matter at once," said Goodman Brown, considerably nettled, "there is my wife, Faith. It would break her dear little heart, and I'd rather break my own!"

25   "Nay, if that be the case," answered the other, "e'en go thy ways, Goodman Brown. I would not for twenty old women like the one hobbling before us that Faith should come to any harm."

As he spoke he pointed his staff at a female figure on the path in whom Goodman Brown recognized a very pious and exemplary dame who had taught him his catechism in youth and was still his moral and spiritual adviser, jointly with the minister and Deacon Gookin.

"A marvel, truly, that Goody Cloyse should be so far in the wilderness at nightfall!" said he. "But with your leave, friend, I shall take a cut through the woods until we have left this Christian woman behind. Being a stranger to you, she might ask whom I was consorting with and whither I was going."

"Be it so," said his fellow-traveler. "Betake you to the woods and let me keep the path."

Accordingly, the young man turned aside, but took care to watch his companion who advanced softly along the road until he had come within a staff's length of the old dame. She, meanwhile, was making the best of her way, with singular speed for so aged a woman, and mumbling some indistinct words, a prayer, doubtless, as she went. The traveler put forth his staff and touched her withered neck with what seemed the serpent's tail.

30   "The devil!" screamed the pious old lady.

"Then Goody Cloyse knows her old friend?" observed the traveler, confronting her and leaning on his writhing stick.

"Ah, forsooth, and is it your worship indeed?" cried the good dame. "Yea, truly is it, and in the very image of my old gossip, Goodman Brown, the grandfather of the silly fellow that now is. But would your worship believe it? my broomstick hath strangely disappeared, stolen as I suspect by that unhanged witch, Goody Cory, and that, too, when I was all anointed with the juice of smallage and cinque-foil and wolf's-bane—"

"Mingled with fine wheat and the fat of a new-born babe," said the shape of old Goodman Brown.

"Ah, your worship knows the recipe," cried the old lady, cackling aloud. "So, as I was saying, being all ready for the meeting, and no horse to ride on, I made up my mind to foot it; for they tell me there is a nice young man to be taken into communion tonight. But now your good worship will lend me your arm and we shall be there in a twinkling."

35   "That can hardly be," answered her friend. "I may not spare you my arm, Goody Cloyse, but here is my staff, if you will."

So saying, he threw it down at her feet where, perhaps, it assumed life, being one of the rods which its owner had formerly lent to the Egyptian Magi. Of this fact, however, Goodman Brown could not take cognizance.

He had cast up his eyes in astonishment, and looking down again beheld neither Goody Cloyse nor the serpentine staff, but his fellow-traveler alone, who waited for him as calmly as if nothing had happened.

"That old woman taught me my catechism!" said the young man, and there was a world of meaning in this simple comment.

They continued to walk onward while the elder traveler exhorted his companion to make good speed and persevere in the path, discoursing so aptly that his arguments seemed rather to spring up in the bosom of his auditor than to be suggested by himself. As they went he plucked a branch of maple to serve for a walking-stick, and began to strip it of the twigs and little boughs which were wet with evening dew. The moment his fingers touched them they became strangely withered and dried up, as with a week's sunshine. Thus the pair proceeded at a good free pace, until suddenly, in a gloomy hollow of the road, Goodman Brown sat himself down on the stump of a tree and refused to go any farther.

"Friend," said he stubbornly, "my mind is made up. Not another step will I budge on this errand. What if a wretched old woman do choose to go to the devil when I thought she was going to Heaven! Is that any reason why I should quit my dear Faith and go after her?"

"You will think better of this by and by," said his acquaintance composedly. "Sit here and rest yourself awhile, and when you feel like moving again, there is my staff to help you along."

Without more words, he threw his companion the maple stick and was as speedily out of sight as if he had vanished into the deepening gloom. The young man sat a few moments by the roadside, applauding himself greatly and thinking with how clear a conscience he should meet the minister in his morning walk, nor shrink from the eye of good old Deacon Gookin. And what calm sleep would be his that very night, which was to have been spent so wickedly, but purely and sweetly now, in the arms of Faith! Amidst these pleasant and praiseworthy meditations, Goodman Brown heard the tramp of horses along the road and deemed it advisable to conceal himself within the verge of the forest, conscious of the guilty purpose that had brought him thither, though now so happily turned from it.

On came the hoof-tramps and the voices of the riders, two grave old voices conversing soberly as they drew near. These mingled sounds appeared to pass along the road within a few yards of the young man's hiding place; but owing, doubtless, to the depth of the gloom at that particular spot, neither the travelers nor their steeds were visible. Though their figures brushed the small boughs by the wayside, it could not be seen that they intercepted even for a moment the faint gleam from the strip of bright sky athwart which they must have passed. Goodman Brown alternately crouched and stood on tiptoe, pulling aside the branches and thrusting forth his head as far as he durst, without discerning so much as a shadow. It vexed him the more because he could have sworn, were such a thing possible, that he recognized the voices of the minister and Deacon Gookin, jogging along quietly as they were wont to do when bound to some ordination or ecclesiastical council. While yet within hearing, one of the riders stopped to pluck a switch.

"Of the two, reverend Sir," said the voice like the deacon's, "I had rather miss an ordination dinner than tonight's meeting. They tell me that some of our community are to be here from Falmouth and beyond, and others from Connecticut and Rhode Island, besides several of the Indian powwows who, after their fashion, know almost as much deviltry as the best of us. Moreover, there is a goodly young woman to be taken into communion."

"Mighty well, Deacon Gookin!" replied the solemn old tones of the minister. "Spur up, or we shall be late. Nothing can be done, you know, until I get on the ground."

45   The hoofs clattered again, and the voices talking so strangely in the empty air passed on through the forest where no church had ever been gathered nor solitary Christian prayed. Whither, then, could these holy men be journeying, so deep into the heathen wilderness? Young Goodman Brown caught hold of a tree for support, being ready to sink down on the ground, faint and over-burthened with the heavy sickness of his heart. He looked up to the sky, doubting whether there really was a Heaven above him. Yet there was the blue arch, and the stars brightening in it.

"With Heaven above, and Faith below, I will yet stand firm against the devil!" cried Goodman Brown.

While he still gazed upward into the deep arch of the firmament and had lifted his hands to pray, a cloud, though no wind was stirring, hurried across the zenith and hid the brightening stars. The blue sky was still visible except directly overhead, where this black mass of cloud was sweeping swiftly northward. Aloft in the air, as if from the depths of the cloud, came a confused and doubtful sound of voices. Once the listener fancied that he could distinguish the accents of townspeople of his own, men and women, both pious and ungodly, many of whom he had met at the communion-table, and had seen others rioting at the tavern. The next moment, so indistinct were the sounds, he doubted whether he had heard aught but the murmur of the old forest whispering without a wind. Then came a stronger swell of those familiar tones heard daily in the sunshine at Salem village, but never, until now, from a cloud at night. There was one voice, of a young woman uttering lamentations yet with an uncertain sorrow, and entreating for some favor, which, perhaps, it would grieve her to obtain. And all the unseen multitude, both saints and sinners, seemed to encourage her onward.

"Faith!" shouted Goodman Brown in a voice of agony and desperation; and the echoes of the forest mocked him, crying "Faith! Faith!" as if bewildered wretches were seeking her all through the wilderness.

The cry of grief, rage, and terror was yet piercing the night when the unhappy husband held his breath for a response. There was a scream, drowned immediately in a louder murmur of voices fading into far-off laughter as the dark cloud swept away leaving the clear and silent sky above Goodman Brown. But something fluttered lightly down through the air and caught on the branch of a tree. The young man seized it and beheld a pink ribbon.

"My Faith is gone!" cried he, after one stupefied moment. "There is 50 no good on earth, and sin is but a name. Come, devil! for to thee is this world given."

And maddened with despair, so that he laughed loud and long, did Goodman Brown grasp his staff and set forth again at such a rate that he seemed to fly along the forest path rather than to walk or run. The road grew wilder and drearier and more faintly traced, and vanished at length, leaving him in the heart of the dark wilderness, still rushing onward with the instinct that guides mortal man to evil. The whole forest was peopled with frightful sounds—the creaking of the trees, the howling of wild beasts, and the yell of Indians; while sometimes the wind tolled like a distant church bell, and sometimes gave a broad roar around the traveler, as if all Nature were laughing him to scorn. But he was himself the chief horror of the scene, and shrank not from its other horrors.

"Ha! ha! ha!" roared Goodman Brown when the wind laughed at him. "Let us hear which will laugh loudest! Think not to frighten me with your deviltry! come witch, come wizard, come Indian powwow, come devil himself! and here comes Goodman Brown. You may as well fear him as he fear you!"

In truth, all through the haunted forest there could be nothing more frightful than the figure of Goodman Brown. On he flew among the black pines, brandishing his staff with frenzied gestures, now giving vent to an inspiration of horrid blasphemy, and now shouting forth such laughter as set all the echoes of the forest laughing like demons around him. The fiend in his own shape is less hideous than when he rages in the breast of man. Thus sped the demoniac on his course until, quivering among the trees, he saw a red light before him, as when the felled trunks and branches of a clearing have been set on fire and throw up their lurid blaze against the sky at the hour of midnight. He paused in a lull of the tempest that had driven him onward, and heard the swell of what seemed a hymn rolling solemnly from a distance with the weight of many voices. He knew the tune. It was a familiar one in the choir of the village meeting-house. The verse died heavily away, and was lengthened by a chorus not of human voices but of all the sounds of the benighted wilderness pealing in awful harmony together. Goodman Brown cried out, and his cry was lost to his own ear by its unison with the cry of the desert.

In the interval of silence he stole forward until the light glared full upon his eyes. At one extremity of an open space, hemmed in by the dark wall of the forest, arose a rock bearing some rude, natural resemblance either to an altar or a pulpit, and surrounded by four blazing pines, their tops aflame, their stems untouched, like candles at an evening meeting. The mass of foliage that had overgrown the summit of the rock was all on fire, blazing high into the night and fitfully illuminating the whole field. Each pendent twig and leafy festoon was in a blaze. As the red light arose and fell, a numerous congregation alternately shone forth, then disappeared in shadow, and again grew, as it were, out of the darkness, peopling the heart of the solitary woods at once.

55   "A grave and dark-clad company!" quoth Goodman Brown.

In truth they were such. Among them, quivering to and fro between gloom and splendor, appeared faces that would be seen next day at the council-board of the province, and others which Sabbath after Sabbath looked devoutly heavenward and benignantly over the crowded pews from the holiest pulpits in the land. Some affirm that the lady of the governor was there. At least, there were high dames well known to her, and wives of honored husbands, and widows a great multitude, and ancient maidens, all of excellent repute, and fair young girls who trembled lest their mothers should espy them. Either the sudden gleams of light flashing over the obscure field bedazzled Goodman Brown, or he recognized a score of the church members of Salem village famous for their especial sanctity. Good old Deacon Gookin had arrived and waited at the skirts of that venerable saint, his reverend pastor. But irreverently consorting with these grave, reputable, and pious people, these elders of the church, these chaste dames and dewy virgins, there were men of dissolute lives and women of spotted fame, wretches given over to all mean and filthy vice and suspected even of horrid crimes. It was strange to see that the good shrank not from the wicked, nor were the sinners abashed by the saints. Scattered also among their pale-faced enemies were the Indian priests or powwows who had often scared their native forest with more hideous incantations than any known to English witchcraft.

"But where is Faith?" thought Goodman Brown; and as hope came into his heart he trembled.

Another verse of the hymn arose, a slow and mournful strain such as the pious love, but joined to words which expressed all that our nature can conceive of sin, and darkly hinted at far more. Unfathomable to mere mortals is the lore of fiends. Verse after verse was sung, and still the chorus of the desert swelled between, like the deepest tone of a mighty organ. And with the final peal of that dreadful anthem, there came a sound as if the roaring wind, the rushing streams, the howling beasts, and every other voice of the unconverted wilderness were mingling and according with the voice of guilty man in homage to the prince of all. The four blazing pines threw up a loftier flame and obscurely discovered shapes and visages of horror on the smoke-wreaths above the impious assembly. At the same moment the fire on the rock shot redly forth and formed a glowing arch above its base, where now appeared a figure. With reverence be it spoken, the apparition bore no slight similitude both in garb and manner to some grave divine of the New England churches.

"Bring forth the converts!" cried a voice that echoed through the field and rolled into the forest.

At the word, Goodman Brown stepped forth from the shadow of the trees and approached the congregation, with whom he felt a loathful brotherhood by the sympathy of all that was wicked in his heart. He could have well-nigh sworn that the shape of his own dead father beckoned him to advance, looking downward from a smoke-wreath, while a woman with dim features of despair threw out her hand to warn him back. Was it his mother? But he had no power to retreat one step nor to resist, even in thought, when the minister and good old Deacon Gookin seized his arms and led him to the blazing rock. Thither came also the slender form of a veiled female led between Goody Cloyse, that pious teacher of the catechism, and Martha Carrier, who had received the devil's promise to be queen of hell. A rampant hag was she! And there stood the proselytes beneath the canopy of fire.

"Welcome, my children," said the dark figure, "to the communion of your race! Ye have found, thus young, your nature and your destiny. My children, look behind you!"

They turned, and flashing forth as it were in a sheet of flame, the fiend-worshippers were seen; the smile of welcome gleamed darkly on every visage.

"There," resumed the sable form, "are all whom ye have reverenced from youth. Ye deemed them holier than yourselves and shrank from your own sin, contrasting it with their lives of righteousness and prayerful aspirations heavenward. Yet here are they all in my worshipping assembly! This night it shall be granted you to know their secret deeds: how hoary-bearded elders of the church have whispered wanton words to the young maids of their households; how many a woman eager for widow's weeds has given her husband a drink at bedtime, and let him sleep his last sleep in her bosom; how beardless youths have made haste to inherit their father's wealth; and how fair damsels—blush not, sweet ones!—have dug little

60

graves in the garden and bidden me, the sole guest, to an infant's funeral. By the sympathy of your human hearts for sin, ye shall scent out all the places—whether in church, bedchamber, street, field, or forest—where crime has been committed, and shall exult to behold the whole earth one stain of guilt, one mighty blood-spot. Far more than this! It shall be yours to penetrate in every bosom the deep mystery of sin, the fountain of all wicked arts, and which inexhaustibly supplies more evil impulses than human power—than my power, at its utmost!—can make manifest in deeds. And now, my children, look upon each other."

They did so, and by the blaze of the hell-kindled torches the wretched man beheld his Faith, and the wife her husband trembling before that unhallowed altar.

65   "Lo! there ye stand, my children," said the figure in a deep solemn tone, almost sad with its despairing awfulness, as if his once angelic nature could yet mourn for our miserable race. "Depending upon one another's hearts, ye had still hoped that virtue were not all a dream! Now are ye undeceived—Evil is the nature of mankind. Evil must be your only happiness. Welcome, again, my children, to the communion of your race!"

"Welcome!" repeated the fiend-worshippers in one cry of despair and triumph.

And there they stood, the only pair as it seemed who were yet hesitating on the verge of wickedness in this dark world. A basin was hollowed naturally in the rock. Did it contain water, reddened by the lurid light? or was it blood? or, perchance, a liquid flame? Herein did the Shape of Evil dip his hand and prepare to lay the mark of baptism upon their foreheads, that they might be partakers of the mystery of sin, more conscious of the secret guilt of others both in deed and thought than they could now be of their own. The husband cast one look at his pale wife, and Faith at him. What polluted wretches would the next glance show them to each other, shuddering alike at what they disclosed and what they saw!

"Faith! Faith!" cried the husband. "Look up to Heaven, and resist the Wicked One!"

Whether Faith obeyed he knew not. Hardly had he spoken when he found himself amid calm night and solitude, listening to a roar of the wind which died heavily away through the forest. He staggered against the rock and felt it chill and damp, while a hanging twig that had been all on fire besprinkled his cheek with the coldest dew.

70   The next morning, young Goodman Brown came slowly into the street of Salem village staring around him like a bewildered man. The good old minister was taking a walk along the graveyard to get an appetite for breakfast and meditate his sermon, and bestowed a blessing as he passed on Goodman Brown. He shrank from the venerable saint as if to avoid

an anathema. Old Deacon Gookin was at domestic worship, and the holy words of his prayer were heard through the open window. "What God doth the wizard pray to?" quoth Goodman Brown. Goody Cloyse, that excellent old Christian, stood in the early sunshine at her own lattice catechizing a little girl who had brought her a pint of morning's milk. Goodman Brown snatched away the child as from the grasp of the fiend himself. Turning the corner by the meeting-house, he spied the head of Faith with the pink ribbons gazing anxiously forth, and bursting into such joy at sight of him that she skipped along the street and almost kissed her husband before the whole village. But Goodman Brown looked sternly and sadly into her face and passed on without a greeting.

Had Goodman Brown fallen asleep in the forest and only dreamed a wild dream of a witch-meeting?

Be it so, if you will. But, alas! it was a dream of evil omen for young Goodman Brown. A stern, a sad, a darkly meditative, a distrustful, if not a desperate man did he become from the night of that fearful dream. On the Sabbath-day when the congregation were singing a holy psalm, he could not listen because an anthem of sin rushed loudly upon his ear and drowned all the blessed strain. When the minister spoke from the pulpit with power and fervid eloquence and with his hand on the open Bible, of the sacred truths of our religion, and of saint-like lives and triumphant deaths, and of future bliss or misery unutterable, then did Goodman Brown turn pale, dreading lest the roof should thunder down upon the gray blasphemer and his hearers. Often awaking suddenly at midnight, he shrank from the bosom of Faith, and at morning or eventide when the family knelt down at prayer, he scowled and muttered to himself and gazed sternly at his wife and turned away. And when he had lived long and was borne to his grave a hoary corpse, followed by Faith, an aged woman, and children and grand-children, a goodly procession, besides neighbors not a few, they carved no hopeful verse upon his tombstone, for his dying hour was gloom.

QUESTIONS

1. What does Hawthorne gain by including the names of actual persons (Goody Cloyse, Goody Cory, Deacon Gookin, Martha Carrier) and places (Salem village, Boston, Old South Church)? What religion is practiced by the townspeople?
2. What is the point of view? Where does it change, and what is the result of the change?
3. What allegorical meanings may be given to Goodman Brown? His wife? The forest? Night (as opposed to day)? Brown's journey?
4. What is Brown's motive for going into the forest? What results does he expect from his journey? What does he expect the rest of his life to be like?
5. After he keeps his appointment with the traveler in the forest, Brown announces that he plans to return home. Why does he not do so immediately, and why at

each stage when he renews his intention to do so does he proceed deeper into the forest? Is there any reason to suppose he does not actually see and hear what he thinks he perceives?

6. What details of the "witch-meeting" parallel those of a church communion service? Why does the congregation include "grave, reputable, and pious people" as well as known sinners (paragraph 56)?

7. What prevents Goodman Brown from receiving baptism? What does the devil promise as the result of baptism? Is that what you usually suppose is the reward for selling your soul to the devil? Why is it an appropriate reward for Goodman Brown? Since he does not receive baptism, how do you account for his behavior when he returns to the village?

8. "Had Goodman Brown . . . only dreamed a wild dream of a witch-meeting?" (paragraph 71). How are we to answer this question? Point out other places where Hawthorne leaves the interpretation of the story ambiguous. How is such ambiguity related to the story's theme?

9. Characterize the behavior of Faith and the other townspeople after Brown's return to the village. Are Brown's attitude and behavior thereafter the result of conviction or doubt? Is he completely misanthropic?

10. Does the story demonstrate the devil's claim that "Evil is the nature of mankind" (paragraph 65)?

CHARLOTTE PERKINS GILMAN

The Yellow Wallpaper

It is very seldom that mere ordinary people like John and myself secure ancestral halls for the summer.

A colonial mansion, a hereditary estate, I would say a haunted house and reach the height of romantic felicity—but that would be asking too much of fate!

Still I will proudly declare that there is something queer about it.

Else, why should it be let so cheaply? And why have stood so long untenanted?

John laughs at me, of course, but one expects that.

5 John is practical in the extreme. He has no patience with faith, an intense horror of superstition, and he scoffs openly at any talk of things not to be felt and seen and put down in figures.

THE YELLOW WALLPAPER First published in 1892. Born in Hartford, Connecticut, Charlotte Perkins Gilman (1860–1935) is a major figure in the history of American feminism. During her busy career, she published such nonfiction works as *Women and Economics* (1898) and the Utopian novel, *Herland* (1915), which depicts a society composed entirely of women. Gilman suffered from a severe post-partum depression after the birth of her only child, and endured a "rest cure" that inspired "The Yellow Wallpaper," her most famous work.

John is a physician, and *perhaps*—(I would not say it to a living soul, of course, but this is dead paper and a great relief to my mind)—*perhaps* that is one reason I do not get well faster.

You see, he does not believe I am sick! And what can one do?

If a physician of high standing, and one's own husband, assures friends and relatives that there is really nothing the matter with one but temporary nervous depression—a slight hysterical tendency—what is one to do?

My brother is also a physician, and also of high standing, and he says the same thing.

So I take phosphates or phosphites—whichever it is—and tonics, and air and exercise, and journeys, and am absolutely forbidden to "work" until I am well again.

Personally, I disagree with their ideas.

Personally, I believe that congenial work, with excitement and change, would do me good.

But what is one to do?

I did write for a while in spite of them; but it *does* exhaust me a good deal—having to be so sly about it, or else meet with heavy opposition.

I sometimes fancy that in my condition, if I had less opposition and more society and stimulus—but John says the very worst thing I can do is to think about my condition, and I confess it always makes me feel bad.

So I will let it alone and talk about the house.

The most beautiful place! It is quite alone, standing well back from the road, quite three miles from the village. It makes me think of English places that you read about, for there are hedges and walls and gates that lock, and lots of separate little houses for the gardeners and people.

There is a *delicious* garden! I never saw such a garden—large and shady, full of box-bordered paths, and lined with long grape-covered arbors with seats under them.

There were greenhouses, but they are all broken now.

There was some legal trouble, I believe, something about the heirs and coheirs; anyhow, the place has been empty for years.

That spoils my ghostliness, I am afraid, but I don't care—there is something strange about the house—I can feel it.

I even said so to John one moonlight evening, but he said what I felt was a *draught*, and shut the window.

I get unreasonably angry with John sometimes. I'm sure I never used to be so sensitive. I think it is due to this nervous condition.

But John says if I feel so I shall neglect proper self-control; so I take pains to control myself—before him, at least, and that makes me very tired.

I don't like our room a bit. I wanted one downstairs that opened onto the piazza and had roses all over the window, and such pretty old-fashioned chintz hangings! But John would not hear of it.

He said there was only one window and not room for two beds, and no near room for him if he took another.

He is very careful and loving, and hardly lets me stir without special direction.

I have a schedule prescription for each hour in the day; he takes all care from me, and so I feel basely ungrateful not to value it more.

30   He said he came here solely on my account, that I was to have perfect rest and all the air I could get. "Your exercise depends on your strength, my dear," said he, "and your food somewhat on your appetite; but air you can absorb all the time." So we took the nursery at the top of the house.

It is a big, airy room, the whole floor nearly, with windows that look all ways, and air and sunshine galore. It was a nursery first, and then play-room and gymnasium, I should judge, for the windows are barred for little children, and there are rings and things in the walls.

The paint and paper look as if a boys' school had used it. It is stripped off—the paper—in great patches all around the head of my bed, about as far as I can reach, and in a great place on the other side of the room low down. I never saw a worse paper in my life. One of those sprawling, flam-boyant patterns committing every artistic sin.

It is dull enough to confuse the eye in following, pronounced enough constantly to irritate and provoke study, and when you follow the lame uncertain curves for a little distance they suddenly commit suicide—plunge off at outrageous angles, destroy themselves in unheard of contradictions.

The color is repellent, almost revolting: a smouldering unclean yellow, strangely faded by the slow-turning sunlight. It is a dull yet lurid orange in some places, a sickly sulphur tint in others.

35   No wonder the children hated it! I should hate it myself if I had to live in this room long.

There comes John, and I must put this away—he hates to have me write a word.

We have been here two weeks, and I haven't felt like writing before, since that first day.

I am sitting by the window now, up in this atrocious nursery, and there is nothing to hinder my writing as much as I please, save lack of strength.

John is away all day, and even some nights when his cases are serious.

40   I am glad my case is not serious!

But these nervous troubles are dreadfully depressing.

John does not know how much I really suffer. He knows there is no *reason* to suffer, and that satisfies him.

Of course it is only nervousness. It does weigh on me so not to do my duty in any way!

I meant to be such a help to John, such a real rest and comfort, and here I am a comparative burden already!

Nobody would believe what an effort it is to do what little I am able— 45 to dress and entertain, and order things.

It is fortunate Mary is so good with the baby. Such a dear baby!

And yet I *cannot* be with him, it makes me so nervous.

I suppose John never was nervous in his life. He laughs at me so about this wallpaper!

At first he meant to repaper the room, but afterward he said that I was letting it get the better of me, and that nothing was worse for a nervous patient than to give way to such fancies.

He said that after the wallpaper was changed it would be the heavy 50 bedstead, and then the barred windows, and then that gate at the head of the stairs, and so on.

"You know the place is doing you good," he said, "and really, dear, I don't care to renovate the house just for a three months' rental."

"Then do let us go downstairs," I said. "There are such pretty rooms there."

Then he took me in his arms and called me a blessed little goose, and said he would go down to the cellar, if I wished, and have it whitewashed into the bargain.

But he is right enough about the beds and windows and things.

It is as airy and comfortable a room as anyone need wish, and, of course, 55 I would not be so silly as to make him uncomfortable just for a whim.

I'm really getting quite fond of the big room, all but that horrid paper.

Out of one window I can see the garden—those mysterious deep-shaded arbors, the riotous old-fashioned flowers, and bushes and gnarly trees.

Out of another I get a lovely view of the bay and a little private wharf belonging to the estate. There is a beautiful shaded lane that runs down there from the house. I always fancy I see people walking in these numerous paths and arbors, but John has cautioned me not to give way to fancy in the least. He says that with my imaginative power and habit of storymaking, a nervous weakness like mine is sure to lead to all manner of excited fancies, and that I ought to use my will and good sense to check the tendency. So I try.

I think sometimes that if I were only well enough to write a little it would relieve the press of ideas and rest me.

But I find I get pretty tired when I try. 60

It is so discouraging not to have any advice and companionship about my work. When I get really well, John says we will ask Cousin Henry and Julia down for a long visit; but he says he would as soon put fireworks in my pillow-case as to let me have those stimulating people about now.

I wish I could get well faster.

But I must not think about that. This paper looks to me as if it *knew* what a vicious influence it had!

There is a recurrent spot where the pattern lolls like a broken neck and two bulbous eyes stare at you upside down.

65 I get positively angry with the impertinence of it and the ever-lastingness. Up and down and sideways they crawl, and those absurd unblinking eyes are everywhere. There is one place where two breadths didn't match, and the eyes go all up and down the line, one a little higher than the other.

I never saw so much expression in an inanimate thing before, and we all know how much expression they have! I used to lie awake as a child and get more entertainment and terror out of blank walls and plain furniture than most children could find in a toy-store.

I remember what a kindly wink the knobs of our big old bureau used to have, and there was one chair that always seemed like a strong friend.

I used to feel that if any of the other things looked too fierce I could always hop into that chair and be safe.

The furniture in this room is no worse than inharmonious, however, for we had to bring it all from downstairs. I suppose when this was used as a playroom they had to take the nursery things out, and no wonder! I never saw such ravages as the children have made here.

70 The wallpaper, as I said before, is torn off in spots, and it sticketh closer than a brother—they must have had perseverance as well as hatred.

Then the floor is scratched and gouged and splintered, the plaster itself is dug out here and there, and this great heavy bed, which is all we found in the room, looks as if it had been through the wars.

But I don't mind it a bit—only the paper.

There comes John's sister. Such a dear girl as she is, and so careful of me! I must not let her find me writing.

She is a perfect and enthusiastic housekeeper, and hopes for no better profession. I verily believe she thinks it is the writing which made me sick!

75 But I can write when she is out, and see her a long way off from these windows.

There is one that commands the road, a lovely shaded winding road, and one that just looks off over the country. A lovely country, too, full of great elms and velvet meadows.

This wallpaper has a kind of subpattern in a different shade, a particularly irritating one, for you can only see it in certain lights, and not clearly then.

But in the places where it isn't faded and where the sun is just so—I can see a strange, provoking, formless sort of figure that seems to skulk about behind that silly and conspicuous front design.

There's sister on the stairs!

Well, the Fourth of July is over! The people are all gone, and I am tired out. John thought it might do me good to see a little company, so we just had Mother and Nellie and the children down for a week.

Of course I didn't do a thing. Jennie sees to everything now.

But it tired me all the same.

John says if I don't pick up faster he shall send me to Weir Mitchell° in the fall.

But I don't want to go there at all. I had a friend who was in his hands once, and she says he is just like John and my brother, only more so!

Besides, it is such an undertaking to go so far.

I don't feel as if it was worthwhile to turn my hand over for anything, and I'm getting dreadfully fretful and querulous.

I cry at nothing, and cry most of the time.

Of course I don't when John is here, or anybody else, but when I am alone.

And I am alone a good deal just now. John is kept in town very often by serious cases, and Jennie is good and lets me alone when I want her to.

So I walk a little in the garden or down that lovely lane, sit on the porch under the roses, and lie down up here a good deal.

I'm getting really fond of the room in spite of the wallpaper. Perhaps *because* of the wallpaper.

It dwells in my mind so!

I lie here on this great immovable bed—it is nailed down, I believe— and follow that pattern about by the hour. It is as good as gymnastics, I assure you. I start, we'll say, at the bottom, down in the corner over there where it has not been touched, and I determine for the thousandth time that I *will* follow that pointless pattern to some sort of a conclusion.

I know a little of the principle of design, and I know this thing was not arranged on any laws of radiation, or alternation, or repetition, or symmetry, or anything else that I ever heard of.

It is repeated, of course, by the breadths, but not otherwise.

Looked at in one way, each breadth stands alone; the bloated curves and flourishes—a kind of "debased Romanesque" with *delirium* tremens— go waddling up and down in isolated columns of fatuity.

But, on the other hand, they connect diagonally, and the sprawling outlines run off in great slanting waves of optic horror, like a lot of wallowing sea-weeds in full chase.

The whole thing goes horizontally, too, at least it seems so, and I exhaust myself trying to distinguish the order of its going in that direction.

Weir Mitchell: S. Weir Mitchell (1829–1914), a prominent physician who invented the so-called "rest cure" for women suffering from psychological disturbances. Gilman was one of Mitchell's patients.

They have used a horizontal breadth for a frieze, and that adds wonderfully to the confusion.

100   There is one end of the room where it is almost intact, and there, when the crosslights fade and the low sun shines directly upon it, I can almost fancy radiation after all—the interminable grotesque seems to form around a common center and runs off in headlong plunges of equal distraction.

It makes me tired to follow it. I will take a nap, I guess.

I don't know why I should write this.

I don't want to.

I don't feel able.

105   And I know John would think it absurd. But I *must* say what I feel and think in some way—it is such a relief!

But the effort is getting to be greater than the relief.

Half the time now I am awfully lazy, and lie down ever so much. John says I mustn't lose my strength, and has me take cod liver oil and lots of tonics and things, to say nothing of ale and wines and rare meat.

Dear John! He loves me very dearly, and hates to have me sick. I tried to have a real earnest reasonable talk with him the other day, and tell him how I wish he would let me go and make a visit to Cousin Henry and Julia.

But he said I wasn't able to go, nor able to stand it after I got there; and I did not make out a very good case for myself, for I was crying before I had finished.

110   It is getting to be a great effort for me to think straight. Just this nervous weakness, I suppose.

And dear John gathered me up in his arms, and just carried me upstairs and laid me on the bed, and sat by me and read to me till it tired my head.

He said I was his darling and his comfort and all he had, and that I must take care of myself for his sake, and keep well.

He says no one but myself can help me out of it, that I must use my will and self-control and not let any silly fancies run away with me.

There's one comfort—the baby is well and happy, and does not have to occupy this nursery with the horrid wallpaper.

115   If we had not used it, that blessed child would have! What a fortunate escape! Why, I wouldn't have a child of mine, an impressionable little thing, live in such a room for worlds.

I never thought of it before, but it is lucky that John kept me here after all; I can stand it so much easier than a baby, you see.

Of course I never mention it to them any more—I am too wise—but I keep watch for it all the same.

There are things in the wallpaper that nobody knows about but me, or ever will.

Behind that outside pattern the dim shapes get clearer every day.

It is always the same shape, only very numerous.   120

And it is like a woman stooping down and creeping about behind that pattern. I don't like it a bit. I wonder—I begin to think—I wish John would take me away from here!

It is so hard to talk with John about my case, because he is so wise, and because he loves me so.

But I tried it last night.

It was moonlight. The moon shines in all around just as the sun does.

I hate to see it sometimes, it creeps so slowly, and always comes in by   125
one window or another.

John was asleep and I hated to waken him, so I kept still and watched the moonlight on that undulating wallpaper till I felt creepy.

The faint figure behind seemed to shake the pattern, just as if she wanted to get out.

I got up softly and went to feel and see if the paper *did* move, and when I came back John was awake.

"What is it, little girl?" he said. "Don't go walking about like that— you'll get cold."

I thought it was a good time to talk, so I told him that I really was not   130
gaining here, and that I wished he would take me away.

"Why, darling!" said he. "Our lease will be up in three weeks, and I can't see how to leave before."

"The repairs are not done at home, and I cannot possibly leave town just now. Of course, if you were in any danger, I could and would, but you really are better, dear, whether you can see it or not. I am a doctor, dear, and I know. You are gaining flesh and color, your appetite is better, I feel really much easier about you."

"I don't weigh a bit more," said I, "nor as much; and my appetite may be better in the evening when you are here but it is worse in the morning when you are away!"

"Bless her little heart!" said he with a big hug. "She shall be as sick as she pleases! But now let's improve the shining hours by going to sleep, and talk about it in the morning!"

"And you won't go away?" I asked gloomily.   135

"Why, how can I, dear? It is only three weeks more and then we will take a nice little trip for a few days while Jennie is getting the house ready. Really, dear, you are better!"

"Better in body perhaps—" I began, and stopped short, for he sat up straight and looked at me with such a stern, reproachful look that I could not say another word.

"My darling," said he, "I beg you, for my sake and for our child's sake, as well as for your own, that you will never for one instant let that idea enter your mind! There is nothing so dangerous, so fascinating, to a temperament like yours. It is a false and foolish fancy. Can you trust me as a physician when I tell you so?"

So of course I said no more on that score, and we went to sleep before long. He thought I was asleep first, but I wasn't, and lay there for hours trying to decide whether that front pattern and the back pattern really did move together or separately.

140   On a pattern like this, by daylight, there is a lack of sequence, a defiance of law, that is a constant irritant to a normal mind.

The color is hideous enough, and unreliable enough, and infuriating enough, but the pattern is torturing.

You think you have mastered it, but just as you get well under way in following, it turns a back-somersault and there you are. It slaps you in the face, knocks you down, and tramples upon you. It is like a bad dream.

The outside pattern is a florid arabesque, reminding one of a fungus. If you can imagine a toadstool in joints, an interminable string of toadstools, budding and sprouting in endless convolutions—why, that is something like it.

That is, sometimes!

145   There is one marked peculiarity about this paper, a thing nobody seems to notice but myself, and that is that it changes as the light changes.

When the sun shoots in through the east window—I always watch for that first long, straight ray—it changes so quickly that I never can quite believe it.

That is why I watch it always.

By moonlight—the moon shines in all night when there is a moon—I wouldn't know it was the same paper.

At night in any kind of light, in twilight, candlelight, lamplight, and worst of all by moonlight, it becomes bars! The outside pattern, I mean, and the woman behind it is as plain as can be.

150   I didn't realize for a long time what the thing was that showed behind, that dim subpattern, but now I am quite sure it is a woman.

By daylight she is subdued, quiet. I fancy it is the pattern that keeps her so still. It is so puzzling. It keeps me quiet by the hour.

I lie down ever so much now. John says it is good for me, and to sleep all I can.

Indeed he started the habit by making me lie down for an hour after each meal.

It is a very bad habit, I am convinced, for you see, I don't sleep.

155   And that cultivates deceit, for I don't tell them I'm awake—oh, no!

The fact is I am getting a little afraid of John.

He seems very queer sometimes, and even Jennie has an inexplicable look.

It strikes me occasionally, just as a scientific hypothesis, that perhaps it is the paper!

I have watched John when he did not know I was looking, and come into the room suddenly on the most innocent excuses, and I've caught him several times *looking at the paper!* And Jennie too. I caught Jennie with her hand on it once.

She didn't know I was in the room, and when I asked her in a quiet, a   160
very quiet voice, with the most restrained manner possible, what she was doing with the paper, she turned around as if she had been caught stealing, and looked quite angry—asked me why I should frighten her so!

Then she said that the paper stained everything it touched, that she had found yellow smooches° on all my clothes and John's and she wished we would be more careful!

Did not that sound innocent? But I know she was studying that pattern, and I am determined that nobody shall find it out but myself!

Life is very much more exciting now than it used to be. You see, I have something more to expect, to look forward to, to watch. I really do eat better, and am more quiet than I was.

John is so pleased to see me improve! He laughed a little the other day, and said I seemed to be flourishing in spite of my wallpaper.

I turned it off with a laugh. I had no intention of telling him it was   165
because of the wallpaper—he would make fun of me. He might even want to take me away.

I don't want to leave now until I have found it out. There is a week more, and I think that will be enough.

I'm feeling so much better!

I don't sleep much at night, for it is so interesting to watch developments; but I sleep a good deal during the daytime.

In the daytime it is tiresome and perplexing.

There are always new shoots on the fungus, and new shades of yellow   170
all over it. I cannot keep count of them, though I have tried conscientiously.

It is the strangest yellow, that wallpaper! It makes me think of all the yellow things I ever saw—not beautiful ones like buttercups, but old, foul, bad yellow things.

But there is something else about that paper—the smell! I noticed it the moment we came into the room, but with so much air and sun it was not bad. Now we have had a week of fog and rain, and whether the windows are open or not, the smell is here.

It creeps all over the house.

I find it hovering in the dining-room, skulking in the parlor, hiding in the hall, lying in wait for me on the stairs.

smooches: smudges

175   It gets into my hair.

Even when I go to ride, if I turn my head suddenly and surprise it—there is that smell!

Such a peculiar odor, too! I have spent hours in trying to analyze it, to find what it smelled like.

It is not bad—at first—and very gentle, but quite the subtlest, most enduring odor I ever met.

In this damp weather it is awful. I wake up in the night and find it hanging over me.

180   It used to disturb me at first. I thought seriously of burning the house—to reach the smell.

But now I am used to it. The only thing I can think of that it is like is the *color* of the paper! A yellow smell.

There is a very funny mark on this wall, low down, near the mopboard. A streak that runs round the room. It goes behind every piece of furniture, except the bed, a long, straight, even *smooch*, as if it had been rubbed over and over.

I wonder how it was done and who did it, and what they did it for. Round and round and round—round and round and round—it makes me dizzy!

I really have discovered something at last.

185   Through watching so much at night, when it changes so, I have finally found out.

The front pattern *does* move—and no wonder! The woman behind shakes it!

Sometimes I think there are a great many women behind, and sometimes only one, and she crawls around fast, and her crawling shakes it all over.

Then in the very bright spots she keeps still, and in the very shady spots she just takes hold of the bars and shakes them hard.

And she is all the time trying to climb through. But nobody could climb through that pattern—it strangles so; I think that is why it has so many heads.

190   They get through and then the pattern strangles them off and turns them upside down, and makes their eyes white!

If those heads were covered or taken off it would not be half so bad.

I think that woman gets out in the daytime!

And I'll tell you why—privately—I've seen her!

I can see her out of every one of my windows!

195   It is the same woman, I know, for she is always creeping, and most women do not creep by daylight.

I see her in that long shaded lane, creeping up and down. I see her in those dark grape arbors, creeping all round the garden.

I see her on that long road under the trees, creeping along, and when a carriage comes she hides under the blackberry vines.

I don't blame her a bit. It must be very humiliating to be caught creeping by daylight!

I always lock the door when I creep by daylight. I can't do it at night, for I know John would suspect something at once.

And John is so queer now that I don't want to irritate him. I wish he would take another room! Besides, I don't want anybody to get that woman out at night but myself. 200

I often wonder if I could see her out of all the windows at once.

But, turn as fast as I can, I can only see out of one at one time.

And though I always see her, she may be able to creep faster than I can turn! I have watched her sometimes away off in the open country, creeping as fast as a cloud shadow in a wind.

If only that top pattern could be gotten off from the under one! I mean to try it, little by little.

I have found out another funny thing, but I shan't tell it this time! It does not do to trust people too much. 205

There are only two more days to get this paper off, and I believe John is beginning to notice. I don't like the look in his eyes.

And I heard him ask Jennie a lot of professional questions about me. She had a very good report to give.

She said I slept a good deal in the daytime.

John knows I don't sleep very well at night, for all I'm so quiet!

He asked me all sorts of questions too, and pretended to be very loving and kind. 210

As if I couldn't see through him!

Still, I don't wonder he acts so, sleeping under this paper for three months.

It only interests me, but I feel sure John and Jennie are affected by it.

Hurrah! This is the last day, but it is enough. John is to stay in town over night, and won't be out until this evening.

Jennie wanted to sleep with me—the sly thing; but I told her I should undoubtedly rest better for a night all alone. 215

That was clever, for really I wasn't alone a bit! As soon as it was moonlight and that poor thing began to crawl and shake the pattern, I got up and ran to help her.

I pulled and she shook. I shook and she pulled, and before morning we had peeled off yards of that paper.

A strip about as high as my head and half around the room.

And then when the sun came and that awful pattern began to laugh at me, I declared I would finish it today!

220   We go away tomorrow, and they are moving all my furniture down again to leave things as they were before.

      Jennie looked at the wall in amazement, but I told her merrily that I did it out of pure spite at the vicious thing.

      She laughed and said she wouldn't mind doing it herself, but I must not get tired.

      How she betrayed herself that time!

      But I am here, and no person touches this paper but me—not *alive!*

225   She tried to get me out of the room—it was too patent! But I said it was so quiet and empty and clean now that I believed I would lie down again and sleep all I could, and not to wake me even for dinner—I would call when I woke.

      So now she is gone, and the servants are gone, and the things are gone, and there is nothing left but that great bedstead nailed down, with the canvas mattress we found on it.

      We shall sleep downstairs tonight, and take the boat home tomorrow.

      I quite enjoy the room, now it is bare again.

      How those children did tear about here!

230   This bedstead is fairly gnawed!

      But I must get to work.

      I have locked the door and thrown the key down into the front path.

      I don't want to go out, and I don't want to have anybody come in, till John comes.

      I want to astonish him.

235   I've got a rope up here that even Jennie did not find. If that woman does get out, and tries to get away, I can tie her!

      But I forgot I could not reach far without anything to stand on!

      This bed will *not* move!

      I tried to lift and push it until I was lame, and then I got so angry I bit off a little piece at one corner—but it hurt my teeth.

      Then I peeled off all the paper I could reach standing on the floor. It sticks horribly and the pattern just enjoys it! All those strangled heads and bulbous eyes and waddling fungus growths just shriek with derision!

240   I am getting angry enough to do something desperate. To jump out of the window would be admirable exercise, but the bars are too strong even to try.

      Besides I wouldn't do it. Of course not. I know well enough that a step like that is improper and might be misconstrued.

      I don't like to *look* out of the windows even—there are so many of those creeping women, and they creep so fast.

      I wonder if they all come out of that wallpaper as I did!

      But I am securely fastened now by my well-hidden rope—you don't get *me* out in the road there!

I suppose I shall have to get back behind the pattern when it comes   245
night, and that is hard!

It is so pleasant to be out in this great room and creep around as
I please!

I don't want to go outside. I won't, even if Jennie asks me to.

For outside you have to creep on the ground, and everything is green
instead of yellow.

But here I can creep smoothly on the floor, and my shoulder just fits in
that long smooch around the wall, so I cannot lose my way.

Why, there's John at the door!   250

It is no use, young man, you can't open it!

How he does call and pound!

Now he's crying to Jennie for an axe.

It would be a shame to break down that beautiful door!

"John, dear!" said I in the gentlest voice. "The key is down by the front   255
steps, under a plantain leaf!"

That silenced him for a few moments.

Then he said, very quietly indeed, "Open the door, my darling!"

"I can't," said I. "The key is down by the front door under a plantain
leaf!" And then I said it again, several times, very gently and slowly, and
said it so often that he had to go and see, and he got it of course, and came
in. He stopped short by the door.

"What is the matter?" he cried. "For God's sake, what are you doing!"

I kept on creeping just the same, but I looked at him over my shoulder.   260

"I've got out at last," said I, "in spite of you and Jane. And I've pulled
off most of the paper, so you can't put me back!"

Now why should that man have fainted? But he did, and right across
my path by the wall, so that I had to creep over him every time!

QUESTIONS

1. Why did the author choose first-person point of view for this story? In what
   ways is this point of view appropriate?
2. Is the narrator reliable or unreliable? Cite specific passages to support your
   answer.
3. Describe the characterization of the narrator's husband, John. Is he a sympathetic
   or unsympathetic character?
4. Most of the story is narrated in very brief paragraphs. Why is this the case and
   why is it appropriate?
5. What does the yellow wallpaper symbolize?
6. What is the significance of the characters' names? What do their names imply
   about them?
7. Discuss the setting. How is the setting appropriate?
8. What is the story's theme? What does it say about the position of women in
   nineteenth-century America?

GABRIEL GARCÍA MÁRQUEZ

A Very Old Man with Enormous Wings

On the third day of rain they had killed so many crabs inside the house that Pelayo had to cross his drenched courtyard and throw them into the sea, because the newborn child had a temperature all night and they thought it was due to the stench. The world had been sad since Tuesday. Sea and sky were a single ash-gray thing and the sands of the beach, which on March nights glimmered like powdered light, had become a stew of mud and rotten shellfish. The light was so weak at noon that when Pelayo was coming back to the house after throwing away the crabs, it was hard for him to see what it was that was moving and groaning in the rear of the courtyard. He had to go very close to see that it was an old man, a very old man, lying face down in the mud, who, in spite of his tremendous efforts, couldn't get up, impeded by his enormous wings.

Frightened by that nightmare, Pelayo ran to get Elisenda, his wife, who was putting compresses on the sick child, and he took her to the rear of the courtyard. They both looked at the fallen body with mute stupor. He was dressed like a ragpicker. There were only a few faded hairs left on his bald skull and very few teeth in his mouth, and his pitiful condition of a drenched great-grandfather had taken away any sense of grandeur he might have had. His huge buzzard wings, dirty and half-plucked, were forever entangled in the mud. They looked at him so long and so closely that Pelayo and Elisenda very soon overcame their surprise and in the end found him familiar. Then they dared speak to him, and he answered in an incomprehensible dialect with a strong sailor's voice. That was how they skipped over the inconvenience of the wings and quite intelligently concluded that he was a lonely castaway from some foreign ship wrecked by the storm. And yet, they called in a neighbor woman who knew everything about life and death to see him, and all she needed was one look to show them their mistake.

"He's an angel," she told them. "He must have been coming for the child, but the poor fellow is so old that the rain knocked him down."

On the following day everyone knew that a flesh-and-blood angel was held captive in Pelayo's house. Against the judgment of the wise neighbor woman, for whom angels in those times were the fugitive survivors of

A VERY OLD MAN WITH ENORMOUS WINGS First published in 1955. Translated by Gregory Rabassa. Born in Colombia in 1928, Gabriel García Márquez studied law and worked as a newspaper reporter before publishing his first book of stories, *Leaf Storm* (1955). His best-known novels, which exemplify the unique blend of realistic and fantastic detail known as magical realism, include *One Hundred Years of Solitude* (1969) and *Love in the Time of Cholera* (1988). He won the Nobel Prize for literature in 1982.

a celestial conspiracy, they did not have the heart to club him to death. Pelayo watched over him all afternoon from the kitchen, armed with his bailiff's club, and before going to bed he dragged him out of the mud and locked him up with the hens in the wire chicken coop. In the middle of the night, when the rain stopped, Pelayo and Elisenda were still killing crabs. A short time afterward the child woke up without a fever and with a desire to eat. Then they felt magnanimous and decided to put the angel on a raft with fresh water and provisions for three days and leave him to his fate on the high seas. But when they went out into the courtyard with the first light of dawn, they found the whole neighborhood in front of the chicken coop having fun with the angel, without the slightest reverence, tossing him things to eat through the openings in the wire as if he weren't a supernatural creature but a circus animal.

Father Gonzaga arrived before seven o'clock, alarmed at the strange news. By that time onlookers less frivolous than those at dawn had already arrived and they were making all kinds of conjectures concerning the captive's future. The simplest among them thought that he should be named mayor of the world. Others of sterner mind felt that he should be promoted to the rank of five-star general in order to win all wars. Some visionaries hoped that he could be put to stud in order to implant on earth a race of winged wise men who could take charge of the universe. But Father Gonzaga, before becoming a priest, had been a robust woodcutter. Standing by the wire, he reviewed his catechism in an instant and asked them to open the door so that he could take a close look at that pitiful man who looked more like a huge decrepit hen among the fascinated chickens. He was lying in a corner drying his open wings in the sunlight among the fruit peels and breakfast leftovers that the early risers had thrown him. Alien to the impertinences of the world, he only lifted his antiquarian eyes and murmured something in his dialect when Father Gonzaga went into the chicken coop and said good morning to him in Latin. The parish priest had his first suspicion of an impostor when he saw that he did not understand the language of God or know how to greet His ministers. Then he noticed that seen close up he was much too human: he had an unbearable smell of the outdoors, the back side of his wings was strewn with parasites and his main feathers had been mistreated by terrestrial winds, and nothing about him measured up to the proud dignity of angels. Then he came out of the chicken coop and in a brief sermon warned the curious against the risks of being ingenuous. He reminded them that the devil had the bad habit of making use of carnival tricks in order to confuse the unwary. He argued that if wings were not the essential element in determining the difference between a hawk and an airplane, they were even less so in the recognition of angels. Nevertheless, he promised to write a letter to his bishop so that the latter would write to

5

his primate so that the latter would write to the Supreme Pontiff in order to get the final verdict from the highest courts.

His prudence fell on sterile hearts. The news of the captive angel spread with such rapidity that after a few hours the courtyard had the bustle of a marketplace and they had to call in troops with fixed bayonets to disperse the mob that was about to knock the house down. Elisenda, her spine all twisted from sweeping up so much marketplace trash, then got the idea of fencing in the yard and charging five cents admission to see the angel.

The curious came from far away. A traveling carnival arrived with a flying acrobat who buzzed over the crowd several times, but no one paid any attention to him because his wings were not those of an angel but, rather, those of a sidereal bat. The most unfortunate invalids on earth came in search of health: a poor woman who since childhood had been counting her heartbeats and had run out of numbers; a Portuguese man who couldn't sleep because the noise of the stars disturbed him; a sleep-walker who got up at night to undo the things he had done while awake; and many others with less serious ailments. In the midst of that shipwreck disorder that made the earth tremble, Pelayo and Elisenda were happy with fatigue, for in less than a week they had crammed their rooms with money and the line of pilgrims waiting their turn to enter still reached beyond the horizon.

The angel was the only one who took no part in his own act. He spent his time trying to get comfortable in his borrowed nest, befuddled by the hellish heat of the oil lamps and sacramental candles that had been placed along the wire. At first they tried to make him eat some mothballs, which, according to the wisdom of the wise neighbor woman, were the food prescribed for angels. But he turned them down, just as he turned down the papal lunches that the penitents brought him, and they never found out whether it was because he was an angel or because he was an old man that in the end he ate nothing but eggplant mush. His only supernatural virtue seemed to be patience. Especially during the first days, when the hens pecked at him, searching for the stellar parasites that proliferated in his wings, and the cripples pulled out feathers to touch their defective parts with, and even the most merciful threw stones at him, trying to get him to rise so they could see him standing. The only time they succeeded in arousing him was when they burned his side with an iron for branding steers, for he had been motionless for so many hours that they thought he was dead. He awoke with a start, ranting in his hermetic language and with tears in his eyes, and he flapped his wings a couple of times, which brought on a whirlwind of chicken dung and lunar dust and a gale of panic that did not seem to be of this world. Although many thought that his reaction had been one not of rage but of pain, from then on they were careful not to annoy him, because the majority understood that his passivity was not that of a hero taking his ease but that of a cataclysm in repose.

Father Gonzaga held back the crowd's frivolity with formulas of maid-servant inspiration while awaiting the arrival of a final judgment on the nature of the captive. But the mail from Rome showed no sense of urgency. They spent their time finding out if the prisoner had a navel, if his dialect had any connection with Aramaic, how many times he could fit on the head of a pin, or whether he wasn't just a Norwegian with wings. Those meager letters might have come and gone until the end of time if a providential event had not put an end to the priest's tribulations.

It so happened that during those days, among so many other carnival attractions, there arrived in town the traveling show of the woman who had been changed into a spider for having disobeyed her parents. The admission to see her was not only less than the admission to see the angel, but people were permitted to ask her all manner of questions about her absurd state and to examine her up and down so that no one would ever doubt the truth of her horror. She was a frightful tarantula the size of a ram and with the head of a sad maiden. What was most heart-rending, however, was not her outlandish shape but the sincere affliction with which she recounted the details of her misfortune. While still practically a child she had sneaked out of her parents' house to go to a dance, and while she was coming back through the woods after having danced all night without permission, a fearful thunderclap rent the sky in two and through the crack came the lightning bolt of brimstone that changed her into a spider. Her only nourishment came from the meatballs that charitable souls chose to toss into her mouth. A spectacle like that, full of so much human truth and with such a fearful lesson, was bound to defeat without even trying that of a haughty angel who scarcely deigned to look at mortals. Besides, the few miracles attributed to the angel showed a certain mental disorder, like the blind man who didn't recover his sight but grew three new teeth, or the paralytic who didn't get to walk but almost won the lottery, and the leper whose sores sprouted sunflowers. Those consolation miracles, which were more like mocking fun, had already ruined the angel's reputation when the woman who had been changed into a spider finally crushed him completely. That was how Father Gonzaga was cured forever of his insomnia and Pelayo's courtyard went back to being as empty as during the time it had rained for three days and crabs walked through the bedrooms.

The owners of the house had no reason to lament. With the money they saved they built a two-story mansion with balconies and gardens and high netting so that crabs wouldn't get in during the winter, and with iron bars on the windows so that angels wouldn't get in. Pelayo also set up a rabbit warren close to town and gave up his job as bailiff for good, and Elisenda bought some satin pumps with high heels and many dresses of

10

iridescent silk, the kind worn on Sunday by the most desirable women in those times. The chicken coop was the only thing that didn't receive any attention. If they washed it down with creolin and burned tears of myrrh inside it every so often, it was not in homage to the angel but to drive away the dungheap stench that still hung everywhere like a ghost and was turning the new house into an old one. At first, when the child learned to walk, they were careful that he not get too close to the chicken coop. But then they began to lose their fears and got used to the smell, and before the child got his second teeth he'd gone inside the chicken coop to play, where the wires were falling apart. The angel was no less standoffish with him than with other mortals, but he tolerated the most ingenious infamies with the patience of a dog who had no illusions. They both came down with chicken pox at the same time. The doctor who took care of the child couldn't resist the temptation to listen to the angel's heart, and he found so much whistling in the heart and so many sounds in his kidneys that it seemed impossible for him to be alive. What surprised him most, however, was the logic of his wings. They seemed so natural on that completely human organism that he couldn't understand why other men didn't have them too.

When the child began school it had been some time since the sun and rain had caused the collapse of the chicken coop. The angel went dragging himself about here and there like a stray dying man. They would drive him out of the bedroom with a broom and a moment later find him in the kitchen. He seemed to be in so many places at the same time that they grew to think that he'd been duplicated, that he was reproducing himself all through the house, and the exasperated and unhinged Elisenda shouted that it was awful living in that hell full of angels. He could scarcely eat and his antiquarian eyes had also become so foggy that he went about bumping into posts. All he had left were the bare cannulae of his last feathers. Pelayo threw a blanket over him and extended him the charity of letting him sleep in the shed, and only then did they notice that he had a temperature at night, and was delirious with the tongue twisters of an old Norwegian. That was one of the few times they became alarmed, for they thought he was going to die and not even the wise neighbor woman had been able to tell them what to do with dead angels.

And yet he not only survived his worst winter, but seemed improved with the first sunny days. He remained motionless for several days in the farthest corner of the courtyard, where no one would see him, and at the beginning of December some large, stiff feathers began to grow on his wings, the feathers of a scarecrow, which looked more like another misfortune of decrepitude. But he must have known the reason for those changes, for he was quite careful that no one should notice them, that no one should hear the sea chanteys that he sometimes sang under the stars. One morning Elisenda was cutting some bunches of onions for lunch when a wind that seemed to come from the high seas blew into the kitchen. Then she went to the window and caught the angel in his first attempts at flight. They were so clumsy that his fingernails opened a furrow in the vegetable patch and he was on the point of knocking the shed down with the ungainly flapping that slipped on the light and couldn't get a grip on the air. But he did manage to gain altitude. Elisenda let out a sigh of relief, for herself and for him, when she saw him pass over the last houses, holding himself up in some way with the risky flapping of a senile vulture. She kept watching him even when she was through cutting the onions and she kept on watching until it was no longer possible for her to see him, because then he was no longer an annoyance in her life but an imaginary dot on the horizon of the sea.

QUESTIONS

1. At what point in the story did you first know that it included elements of fantasy? Discuss the effect of the second sentence: "The world had been sad since Tuesday."

2. What is the symbolic significance of the old man and his enormous wings? Since he's called an "angel," is there a religious significance to his physical appearance? Why does the narrator stress such details as his "dirty and half-plucked" wings and his grossly physical, animalistic traits? How is the oxymoron "flesh-and-blood angel" central to the meaning?

3. The author wrote that this was "a tale for children." In what ways is it a tale for children but also a story for adults?

4. Discuss the blend of realistic and fantastic details. Does this blend make the story more or less effective? Does it require a different way of reading than other stories you've read that contain no elements of fantasy?

5. The story contains almost no dialogue. Why is this appropriate? How does it relate to the point of view the author has chosen?

6. What is the major theme of the story? How do the fantastic elements help provide insights into the way human beings actually think and behave?

RAY BRADBURY
There Will Come Soft Rains

In the living room the voice-clock sang, *Tick-tock, Seven o'clock, time to get up, time to get up, seven o'clock!* as if it were afraid that nobody would. The morning house lay empty. The clock ticked on, repeating and repeating its sounds into the emptiness. *Seven-nine, breakfast time, seven-nine!*

THERE WILL COME SOFT RAINS   First published in 1950. Ray Bradbury (1920–2012) was a highly prolific author of science fiction, mystery, and horror. He published hundreds of short stories in addition to such celebrated novels as *Fahrenheit 451* (1953) and *Something Wicked This Way Comes* (1962).

In the kitchen the breakfast stove gave a hissing sigh and ejected from its warm interior eight pieces of perfectly browned toast, eight eggs sunnyside up, sixteen slices of bacon, two coffees, and two cool glasses of milk.

"Today is August 4, 2026," said a second voice from the kitchen ceiling, "in the city of Allendale, California." It repeated the date three times for memory's sake. "Today is Mr. Featherstone's birthday. Today is the anniversary of Tilita's marriage. Insurance is payable, as are the water, gas, and light bills."

Somewhere in the walls, relays clicked, memory tapes glided under electric eyes.

5   *Eight-one, tick-tock, eight-one o'clock, off to school, off to work, run, run, eight-one!* But no doors slammed, no carpets took the soft tread of rubber heels. It was raining outside. The weather box on the front door sang quietly: "Rain, rain, go away; rubbers, raincoats for today . . ." And the rain tapped on the empty house, echoing.

Outside, the garage chimed and lifted its door to reveal the waiting car. After a long wait the door swung down again.

At eight-thirty the eggs were shriveled and the toast was like stone. An aluminum wedge scraped them into the sink, where hot water whirled them down a metal throat which digested and flushed them away to the distant sea. The dirty dishes were dropped into a hot washer and emerged twinkling dry.

Nine-fifteen, sang the clock, *time to clean.*

Out of warrens in the wall, tiny robot mice darted. The rooms were acrawl with the small cleaning animals, all rubber and metal. They thudded against chairs, whirling their mustached runners, kneading the rug nap, sucking gently at hidden dust. Then, like mysterious invaders, they popped into their burrows. Their pink electric eyes faded. The house was clean.

10   *Ten o'clock.* The sun came out from behind the rain. The house stood alone in a city of rubble and ashes, This was the one house left standing. At night the ruined city gave off a radioactive glow which could be seen for miles.

Ten-fifteen. The garden sprinklers whirled up in golden founts, filling the soft morning air with scatterings of brightness. The water pelted windowpanes running down the charred west side where the house had been burned evenly free of its white paint. The entire west face of the house was black, save for five places. Here the silhouette in paint of a man mowing a lawn. Here, as in a photograph, a woman bent to pick flowers. Still farther over, their images burned on wood in one titanic instant, a small boy, hands flung into the air; higher up, the image of a thrown ball, and opposite him a girl, hands raised to catch a ball which never came down.

The five spots of paint—the man, the woman, the children, the ball—remained. The rest was a thin charcoaled layer.

The gentle sprinkler rain filled the garden with falling light.

Until this day, how well the house had kept its peace. How carefully it had inquired, "Who goes there? What's the password?" and, getting no answer from lonely foxes and whining cats, it had shut up its windows and drawn shades in an old-maidenly preoccupation with self-protection which bordered on a mechanical paranoia.

It quivered at each sound, the house did. If a sparrow brushed a 15 window, the shade snapped up. The bird, startled, flew off! No, not even a bird must touch the house!

The house was an altar with ten thousand attendants, big, small, servicing, attending, in choirs. But the gods had gone away, and the ritual of the religion continued senselessly, uselessly.

Twelve noon.

A dog whined, shivering, on the front porch.

The front door recognized the dog voice and opened. The dog, once huge and fleshy, but now gone to bone and covered with sores, moved in and through the house, tracking mud. Behind it whirred angry mice, angry at having to pick up mud, angry at inconvenience.

For not a leaf fragment blew under the door but what the wall panels 20 flipped open and the copper scrap rats flashed swiftly out. The offending dust, hair, or paper, seized in miniature steel jaws, was raced back to the burrows. There, down tubes which fed into the cellar, it was dropped into the sighing vent of an incinerator which sat like evil Baal in a dark corner.

The dog ran upstairs, hysterically yelping to each door, at last realizing, as the house realized, that only silence was here.

It sniffed the air and scratched the kitchen door. Behind the door, the stove was making pancakes which filled the house with a rich baked odor and the scent of maple syrup.

The dog frothed at the mouth, lying at the door, sniffing, its eyes turned to fire. It ran wildly in circles, biting at its tail, spun in a frenzy, and died. It lay in the parlor for an hour.

Two o'clock, sang a voice.

Delicately sensing decay at last, the regiments of mice hummed out as 25 softly as blown gray leaves in an electrical wind.

Two-fifteen.

The dog was gone.

In the cellar, the incinerator glowed suddenly and a whirl of sparks leaped up the chimney.

Two thirty-five.

Bridge tables sprouted from patio walls. Playing cards fluttered onto 30 pads in a shower of pips. Martinis manifested on an oaken bench with egg-salad sandwiches. Music played.

But the tables were silent and the cards untouched.

At four o'clock the tables folded like great butterflies back through the paneled walls.

Four-thirty.

The nursery walls glowed.

35   Animals took shape: yellow giraffes, blue lions, pink antelopes, lilac panthers cavorting in crystal substance. The walls were glass. They looked out upon color and fantasy. Hidden films clocked through well-oiled sprockets, and the walls lived. The nursery floor was woven to resemble a crisp, cereal meadow. Over this ran aluminum roaches and iron crickets, and in the hot still air butterflies of delicate red tissue wavered among the sharp aroma of animal spoors! There was the sound like a great matted yellow hive of bees within a dark bellows, the lazy bumble of a purring lion. And there was the patter of okapi feet and the murmur of a fresh jungle rain, like other hoofs, falling upon the summer-starched grass. Now the walls dissolved into distances of parched weed, mile on mile, and warm endless sky. The animals drew away into thorn brakes and water holes.

It was the children's hour.

Five o'clock. The bath filled with clear hot water.

Six, seven, eight o'clock. The dinner dishes manipulated like magic tricks, and in the study a *click.* In the metal stand opposite the hearth where a fire now blazed up warmly, a cigar popped out, half an inch of soft gray ash on it, smoking, waiting.

Nine o'clock. The beds warmed their hidden circuits, for nights were cool here.

40   *Nine-five.* A voice spoke from the study ceiling:

"Mrs. McClellan, which poem would you like this evening?"

The house was silent.

The voice said at last, "Since you express no preference, I shall select a poem at random." Quiet music rose to back the voice. "Sara Teasdale. As I recall, your favorite. . . .

*"There will come soft rains and the smell of the ground,
And swallows circling with their shimmering sound;*

*And frogs in the pools singing at night,
And wild plum-trees in tremulous white;*

Sara Teasdale: Sara Teasdale (1884–1933) was an American poet; the poem "There Will Come Soft Rains" appeared in her 1920 collection, *Flame and Shadow.*

Robins will wear their feathery fire
Whistling their whims on a low fence-wire.

And not one will know of the war, not one
Will care at last when it is done.

Not one would mind, either bird nor tree
If mankind perished utterly;

And Spring herself, when she woke at dawn,
Would scarcely know that we were gone."

The fire burned on the stone hearth and the cigar fell away into a   45
mound of quiet ash on its tray. The empty chairs faced each other between
the silent walls, and the music played.

At ten o'clock the house began to die.
The wind blew. A falling tree bough crashed through the kitchen
window. Cleaning solvent, bottled, shattered over the stove. The room was
ablaze in an instant!
"Fire!" screamed a voice. The house lights flashed, water pumps shot
water from the ceilings. But the solvent spread on the linoleum, licking,
eating under the kitchen door, while the voices took it up in chorus: "Fire,
fire, fire!"
The house tried to save itself. Doors sprang tightly shut, but the windows were broken by the heat and the wind blew and sucked upon the fire.
The house gave ground as the fire in ten billion angry sparks moved   50
with flaming ease from room to room and then up the stairs. While scur-
rying water rats squeaked from the walls, pistoled their water, and ran for
more. And the wall sprays let down showers of mechanical rain.
But too late. Somewhere, sighing, a pump shrugged to a stop. The
quenching rain ceased. The reserve water supply which had filled baths and
washed dishes for many quiet days was gone.
The fire crackled up the stairs. It fed upon Picassos and Matisses in the
upper halls, like delicacies, baking off the oily flesh, tenderly crisping the
canvases into black shavings.
Now the fire lay in beds, stood in windows, changed the colors of
drapes!
And then, reinforcements.
From attic trapdoors, blind robot faces peered down with faucet   55
mouths gushing green chemical.
The fire backed off, as even an elephant must at the sight of a dead
snake. Now there were twenty snakes whipping over the floor, killing the
fire with a clear cold venom of green froth.

But the fire was clever. It had sent flame outside the house, up through the attic to the pumps there. An explosion! The attic brain which directed the pumps was shattered into bronze shrapnel on the beams.

The fire rushed back into every closet and felt of the clothes hung there.

The house shuddered, oak bone on bone, its bared skeleton cringing from the heat, its wire, its nerves revealed as if a surgeon had torn the skin off to let the red veins and capillaries quiver in the scalded air. Help, help! Fire! Run, run! Heat snapped mirrors like the first brittle winter ice And the voices wailed Fire, fire, run, run, like a tragic nursery rhyme, a dozen voices, high, low, like children dying in a forest, alone, alone. And the voices fading as the wires popped their sheathings like hot chestnuts. One, two, three, four, five voices died.

60   In the nursery the jungle burned. Blue lions roared, purple giraffes bounded off. The panthers ran in circles, changing color, and ten million animals, running before the fire, vanished off toward a distant steaming river. . . .

Ten more voices died. In the last instant under the fire avalanche, other choruses, oblivious, could be heard announcing the time, playing music, cutting the lawn by remote-control mower, or setting an umbrella frantically out and in the slamming and opening front door, a thousand things happening, like a clock shop when each clock strikes the hour insanely before or after the other, a scene of maniac confusion, yet unity; singing, screaming, a few last cleaning mice darting bravely out to carry the horrid ashes away! And one voice, with sublime disregard for the situation, read poetry aloud in the fiery study, until all the film spools burned, until all the wires withered and the circuits cracked.

The fire burst the house and let it slam flat down, puffing out skirts of spark and smoke.

In the kitchen, an instant before the rain of fire and timber, the stove could be seen making breakfasts at a psychopathic rate, ten dozen eggs, six loaves of toast, twenty dozen bacon strips, which, eaten by fire, started the stove working again, hysterically hissing!

The crash. The attic smashing into kitchen and parlor. The parlor into cellar, cellar into sub-cellar. Deep freeze, armchair, film tapes, circuits, beds, and all like skeletons thrown in a cluttered mound deep under.

65   Smoke and silence. A great quantity of smoke.

Dawn showed faintly in the east. Among the ruins, one wall stood alone. Within the wall, a last voice said, over and over again and again, even as the sun rose to shine upon the heaped rubble and steam:

"Today is August 5, 2026, today is August 5, 2026, today is . . ."

QUESTIONS

1. This futuristic fantasy was published in 1950. Now we are much closer to the date of the story, 2026. How much of what Bradbury predicted in the story has come true? What elements of present-day culture turned out to exceed even Bradbury's imagination?
2. The family who has occupied the house is notably absent. What has happened to them?
3. Bradbury employs short, lyrical paragraphs throughout the story. Why is this an effective means of narration?
4. Discuss the Sara Teasdale poem from which the story's title is derived. What is the relationship between the poem and the story?
5. What does the story's ending say about contemporary society? Why is the use of repetition effective here?

SUGGESTIONS FOR WRITING

1. Compare the use of symbolism in any two of the following stories, clarifying how each achieves compression through the use of symbols:
   a. Mansfield, "Miss Brill" (page 155).
   b. Joyce, "Araby" (page 186).
   c. Gordimer, "Once upon a Time" (page 230).
   d. Faulkner, "A Rose for Emily" (page 538).
   e. Hurston, "Spunk" (page 564).
   f. Ishiguro, "A Family Supper" (page 133).
2. Argue that any one of the following stories does, or does not, contain elements of fantasy. Carefully support your argument.
   a. Connell, "The Most Dangerous Game" (page 62).
   b. Mansfield, "Miss Brill" (page 155).
   c. Porter, "The Jilting of Granny Weatherall" (page 268).
   d. Hawthorne, "Young Goodman Brown" (page 293).
   e. Lawrence, "The Rocking-Horse Winner" (page 432).
   f. Jackson, "The Lottery" (page 260).
   g. Poe, "The Cask of Amontillado" (page 657).

PRACTICE AP WRITING PROMPTS ▬▬▬

Nathaniel Hawthorne, "Young Goodman Brown" (pp. 293–303)

Even when narrators do not appear as characters in the stories they relate, they often exhibit personalities, opinions, and viewpoints. Carefully read paragraphs 7 through 18 from "Young Goodman Brown." In a well-written essay, analyze the ways in which the narrator employs such resources as connotation, symbol, foreshadowing, and irony to convey an attitude toward Goodman Brown and the community he lives in.

Charlotte Perkins Gilman, "The Yellow Wallpaper" (pp. 304)

Write an essay in which you analyze how Gilman explores the boundary between madness and sanity in "The Yellow Wallpaper." Pay particular attention to such literary elements as symbolism and point of view.

....

Gabriel García Márquez, "A Very Old Man with Enormous Wings" (pp. 318)

40-minute prompt: Read carefully from the beginning of "A Very Old Man with Enormous Wings" to the end of paragraph 4 (p. 318): the arrival of the angel. Analyze how Gabriel García Márquez combines realistic detail with fantasy (magical realism) to shape his attitude toward the angel.

....

CHAPTER SEVEN

Humor and Irony

In previous chapters, we have sometimes used the term "serious" to describe a story or writer whose intentions are literary and artistic rather than primarily commercial. In this context, however, it's important to understand that a serious story is not necessarily a solemn one. In fact, many of the world's great works of serious literature have employed humor in conveying major truths about the human condition. The ancient Greek and Roman dramatists wrote raucous comic plays; Shakespeare's humor is an important dimension of his work, in tragedies such as *Hamlet* and *King Lear* as well as in his famous comedies. Writers as diverse as Geoffrey Chaucer, Jonathan Swift, Jane Austen, Charles Dickens, Mark Twain, and Flannery O'Connor have used humor as a central element in their art.

Novels and short stories that employ humor often use the technique we call **irony**, a term which has a range of meanings that all involve some sort of discrepancy or incongruity. All the above-named writers are master ironists, employing incongruous situations and characters that evoke laughter in the reader even as they express a significant insight into human nature. Irony should not be equated with mere sarcasm, which is simply language one person uses to belittle or ridicule another. Irony is far more complex, a technique used to convey a truth about human experience by exposing some incongruity of a character's behavior or a society's traditions. Operating through careful, often subtle indirection, irony helps to critique the world in which we live by laughing at the many varieties of human eccentricity and folly. It may be useful here to distinguish three distinct kinds of irony found in literary fiction.

Verbal irony, usually the simplest kind, is a figure of speech in which the speaker says the opposite of what he or she intends to say. (This form of irony is, in fact, often employed to create sarcasm.) In "Hunters in the Snow," when Kenny says to Tub, "You're just wasting away before my very eyes," he is speaking ironically—and sarcastically—for of course Tub is obese, and Kenny intends to hurt him.

In **dramatic irony** the contrast is between what a character says or thinks and what the reader knows to be true. The value of this kind of irony lies in the truth it conveys about the character or the character's expectations. In "How I Met My Husband," for instance, Loretta Bird says about Mrs. Peebles, "She wouldn't find time to lay down in the middle of the day, if she had seven kids like I got." The reader grasps the irony of this remark, since Loretta herself often "finds time" to sit gossiping at the Peebles farm instead of staying home with her children. Another effective example comes when Miss Brill, sitting in the park, thinks about the other people around her:

> Other people sat on the benches and green chairs, but they were nearly always the same, Sunday after Sunday, and—Miss Brill had often noticed—there was something funny about nearly all of them . . . from the way they stared they looked as though they'd just come from dark little rooms or even—even cupboards!

It is ironic that the judgment she makes of them is exactly the same one the story makes of her—even including the word "funny," which the young girl later uses about her beloved fur. Miss Brill is unaware that her phrase "nearly always the same, Sunday after Sunday" describes her own behavior, which she unwittingly reveals when she thinks that she "had *often* noticed" them. And of course the irony of the statement about the "cupboards" they must have come from becomes overt when she returns at the end of the story to "her room like a cupboard." Perhaps the most poignant of the dramatic ironies involving Miss Brill lies in her boastful thought, "Yes, I have been an actress for a long time," for she has indeed created a fictitious role for herself—not that of a glamorous stage actress in a romantic musical play, but that of a perceptive, happy, and self-sufficient woman. First-person stories similarly use dramatic irony to suggest that the narrator is not reliable. In Porter's "The Jilting of Granny Weatherall," for example, Granny confusedly reports that ants are biting her when she is actually receiving a hypodermic injection, and that the priest is tickling her feet when really he is administering extreme unction (the last rites in Roman Catholicism). The result is an ironic portrayal of Granny's bewildered mental state.

In **irony of situation**, usually the most important kind for the fiction writer, the discrepancy is between appearance and reality, or between expectation and fulfillment, or between what is and what would seem appropriate. In "The Most Dangerous Game," it is ironic that Rainsford, "the celebrated hunter," should become the hunted, for this is a reversal of his expected and appropriate role. In "The Destructors," it is ironic that Old Misery's horoscope should read, "Abstain from any dealings in first half of week. Danger of serious crash," for the horoscope is valid in a sense that is quite different from what the words appear to indicate. In "Interpreter of Maladies" (page 590), it is ironic that Mr. Das's guidebook to India "looked as if it had been published abroad," and that the Indian tour guide Mr. Kapasi watches the American television show *Dallas* but the American-born Tina Das has never heard of the program. In "Hunters in the Snow," it is ironic that inside the diner Frank and Tub encourage one another's self-indulgent behavior—Frank's lust for a teenage babysitter, Tub's gluttony—and view themselves as forming a noble, trusting alliance, when all the while their companion Kenny is lying wounded and freezing outside in the back of their truck.

Irony, like symbol and allegory, is often a means for the author to achieve compression. By creating an ironic situation or perspective, the author can suggest complex meanings without stating them. In "Miss Brill," we do not need to be told how difficult it is for an aging, solitary woman to cope with her aloneness; we witness her plight and the incongruous means by which she attempts to deny it and therefore endure it. In "Hunters in the Snow," we do not need to be told that these three hunting buddies are not "friends" in any meaningful sense of that word; we witness their cruel, self-absorbed behavior. In these and other stories, the ironic contrast between appearances and reality generates a complex set of meanings.

One reason that irony is such an important technique is that a story, like other art forms, achieves its effects through indirection. "Tell all the truth," Emily Dickinson advised, "but tell it slant"— advice as valid for fiction writers as for poets. In art, the truth must be produced indirectly because a flat statement—as in an essay, or a dry plot summary—can have no emotional impact on the reader. We must *feel* the truth a story conveys with our whole being, not simply understand it with our intellect. If a story has no emotional impact, it has failed as a work of art.

Humor and irony are important because they help an author to achieve such an impact. A reader will not respond to a story, for instance, that contrives its emotions and attempts to "play upon" the reader's feelings directly. An ironic method can help to temper and control the emotional content of a story, evoking responses that are intellectual and emotional at once. At the end of "Interpreter of Maladies," we feel Mr. Kapasi's disillusionment even as we understand the hopelessness of his attraction to Mrs. Das. The narrator's cool, dispassionate stance, complete with its ironic observations and its undercurrent of humor, helps to keep the story's emotional content more honest, genuine, and believable.

By contrast, stories that try to elicit easy or unearned emotional responses are guilty of **sentimentality**. Sentimentality in fiction is not the same as genuine emotion; rather, it is contrived or excessive emotion.

A novel such as Harriet Beecher Stowe's *Uncle Tom's Cabin* (1852), for instance, often tries to wring tears from the reader over the plight of African American slaves; for this reason, the novel is much less powerful as a work of art than Toni Morrison's *Beloved* (1987), which uses carefully restrained, artful language and a frequently biting irony in its castigation of slavery. A narrative contains genuine emotion when it treats life faithfully and perceptively. A sentimental narrative oversimplifies and exaggerates emotion in the attempt to arouse a similarly excessive emotion in the reader.

Genuine emotion, like character, is presented indirectly—it is dramatized. It cannot be produced by words that identify emotions, like *angry, sad, pathetic, heart-breaking,* or *passionate.* A writer draws forth genuine emotion by producing a character in a situation that deserves our sympathy and showing us enough about the character and the situation to make them real and convincing.

Sentimental writers are recognizable by a number of characteristics. First, they often try to make words do what the situation faithfully presented by itself will not do. They **editorialize**—that is, comment on the story and, in a manner, instruct us how to feel. Or they overwrite and **poeticize**—use an immoderately heightened and distended language to accomplish their effects. Second, they make an excessively selective use of detail. All artists, of course, must be selective in their use of detail, but good writers use representative details while sentimentalists use details that all point one way—toward producing emotion rather than conveying truth. The little child who dies will be shown as always uncomplaining and cheerful under adversity, never as naughty, querulous, or ungrateful. It will possibly be an orphan or the only child of a mother who loves it dearly; in addition, it may be lame, hungry, ragged, and possessed of one toy, from which it cannot be parted. The villain will be *all* villain, with a cruel laugh and a sharp whip, though he may reform at the end, for sentimentalists are firm believers in the heart of gold beneath the rough exterior. In short, reality will be unduly heightened and drastically oversimplified. Third, sentimentalists rely heavily on the stock response—an emotion that has its source outside the facts established by the story. In some readers certain situations and objects—babies, mothers, grandmothers, young love, patriotism, worship—produce an almost automatic response, whether the immediate situation warrants it or not. Sentimental writers, to affect such readers, have only to draw out certain stops, as on an organ, to produce an easily anticipated effect. They depend on stock materials to produce a stock response. They thus need not go to the trouble of picturing the situation in realistic and convincing detail. Finally, sentimental writers present, nearly always, a fundamentally "sweet" picture of life. They rely not only on stock characters and situations but also on stock themes. For them every cloud has its silver lining, every bad event its good side, every storm its rainbow.

If the little child dies, it goes to heaven or makes some life better by its death. Virtue is characteristically triumphant: the villain is defeated, the ne'er-do-well redeemed. True love is rewarded in some fashion; it is love—never hate—that makes the world go round. In short, sentimental writers specialize in the sad but sweet. The tears called for are warm tears, never bitter. There is always sugar at the bottom of the cup.

The writers we value most are able to look at human experience in a clear-eyed, honest way and to employ literary techniques such as humor and irony as a way to enhance, not reduce, the emotional impact of their stories. Though not every first-rate story contains humor, there are few that do not involve some blend on the author's part of human empathy and ironic detachment. After reading "Hills Like White Elephants," "Miss Brill," and "A Rose for Emily," for example, we experience a similarly blended response to the protagonists of these stories. A complex human reality requires a complex narrative technique, and in this way the best storytellers always have attempted to portray the whole of human experience—from its most tragic misery to its most absurd folly—in a single, integrated artistic vision.

REVIEWING CHAPTER SEVEN

1. Distinguish between verbal irony and dramatic irony.
2. Define the term "irony of situation."
3. Explore the reasons why sentimentality is an undesirable trait in literary fiction.
4. List the major characteristics of sentimental writing.
5. Describe the particular types of irony found in the following stories.

LORRIE MOORE

You're Ugly, Too

You had to get out of them occasionally, those Illinois towns with the funny names: Paris, Oblong, Normal. Once, when the Dow-Jones dipped two hundred points, the Paris paper boasted a banner headline: NORMAL

YOU'RE UGLY, TOO   First published in 1990. Lorrie Moore (b. 1957) earned an M.F.A. degree in creative writing from Cornell University and has taught for many years at the University of Wisconsin. The author of three novels, Moore is best-known for her three collections of short stories, many of which have been reprinted in the *Best American Short Stories* and *Prize Stories: The O. Henry Awards* series. Her fiction has been critically praised for its innovative and humorous explorations of contemporary American life.

MAN MARRIES OBLONG WOMAN. They knew what was important. They did! But you had to get out once in a while, even if it was just across the border to Terre Haute, for a movie.

Outside of Paris, in the middle of a large field, was a scatter of brick buildings, a small liberal arts college with the improbable name of Hilldale-Versailles. Zoë Hendricks had been teaching American History there for three years. She taught "The Revolution and Beyond" to freshmen and sophomores, and every third semester she had the Senior Seminar for Majors, and although her student evaluations had been slipping in the last year and a half—*Professor Hendricks is often late for class and usually arrives with a cup of hot chocolate, which she offers the class sips of*—generally, the department of nine men was pleased to have her. They felt she added some needed feminine touch to the corridors—that faint trace of Obsession and sweat, the light, fast clicking of heels. Plus they had had a sex-discrimination suit, and the dean had said, well, it was time.

The situation was not easy for her, they knew. Once, at the start of last semester, she had skipped into her lecture hall singing "Getting to Know You"—both verses. At the request of the dean, the chairman had called her into his office, but did not ask her for an explanation, not really. He asked her how she was and then smiled in an avuncular way. She said, "Fine," and he studied the way she said it, her front teeth catching on the inside of her lower lip. She was almost pretty, but her face showed the strain and ambition of always having been close but not quite. There was too much effort with the eyeliner, and her earrings, worn no doubt for the drama her features lacked, were a little frightening, jutting out from the side of her head like antennae.

"I'm going out of my mind," said Zoë to her younger sister, Evan, in Manhattan. *Professor Hendricks seems to know the entire sound track to* The King and I. *Is this history?* Zoë phoned her every Tuesday.

5   "You always say that," said Evan, "but then you go on your trips and vacations and then you settle back into things and then you're quiet for a while and then you say you're fine, you're busy, and then after a while you say you're going crazy again, and you start all over." Evan was a part-time food designer for photo shoots. She cooked vegetables in green dye. She propped up beef stew with a bed of marbles and shopped for new kinds of silicone sprays and plastic ice cubes. She thought her life was "OK." She was living with her boyfriend of many years, who was independently wealthy and had an amusing little job in book publishing. They were five years out of college, and they lived in a luxury midtown high-rise with a balcony and access to a pool. "It's not the same as having your own pool," Evan was always sighing, as if to let Zoë know that, as with Zoë, there were still things she, Evan, had to do without.

"Illinois. It makes me sarcastic to be here," said Zoë on the phone. She used to insist it was irony, something gently layered and sophisticated, something alien to the Midwest, but her students kept calling it sarcasm, something they felt qualified to recognize, and now she had to agree. It wasn't irony. *What is your perfume?* a student once asked her. *Room freshener,* she said. She smiled, but he looked at her, unnerved.

Her students were by and large good Midwesterners, spacey with estrogen from large quantities of meat and cheese. They shared their parents' suburban values; their parents had given them things, things, things. They were complacent. They had been purchased. They were armed with a healthy vagueness about anything historical or geographic. They seemed actually to know very little about anything, but they were extremely good-natured about it. "All those states in the East are so tiny and jagged and bunched up," complained one of her undergraduates the week she was lecturing on "The Turning Point of Independence: The Battle at Saratoga." "Professor Hendricks, you're from Delaware originally, right?" the student asked her.

"Maryland," corrected Zoë.

"Aw," he said, waving his hand dismissively. "New England."

Her articles—chapters toward a book called *Hearing the One About: Uses of Humor in the American Presidency*—were generally well received, though they came slowly for her. She liked her pieces to have something from every time of day in them—she didn't trust things written in the morning only—so she reread and rewrote painstakingly. No part of a day, its moods, its light, was allowed to dominate. She hung on to a piece for over a year sometimes, revising at all hours, until the entirety of a day had registered there.

The job she'd had before the one at Hilldale-Versailles had been at a small college in New Geneva, Minnesota, Land of the Dying Shopping Mall. Everyone was so blond there that brunettes were often presumed to be from foreign countries. *Just because Professor Hendricks is from Spain doesn't give her the right to be so negative about our country.* There was a general emphasis on cheerfulness. In New Geneva you weren't supposed to be critical or complain. You weren't supposed to notice that the town had overextended and that its shopping malls were raggedy and going under. You were never to say you weren't fine thank you and yourself. You were supposed to be Heidi. You were supposed to lug goat milk up the hills and not think twice. Heidi did not complain. Heidi did not do things like stand in front of the new IBM photocopier, saying, "If this fucking Xerox machine breaks on me one more time, I'm going to slit my wrists."

But now, in her second job, in her fourth year of teaching in the Midwest, Zoë was discovering something she never suspected she had: a crusty edge,

10

brittle and pointed. Once she had pampered her students, singing them songs, letting them call her at home, even, and ask personal questions. Now she was losing sympathy. They were beginning to seem different. They were beginning to seem demanding and spoiled.

"You act," said one of her Senior Seminar students at a scheduled conference, "like your opinion is worth more than everybody else's in the class."

Zoë's eyes widened. "I *am* the teacher," she said. "I *do* get paid to act like that." She narrowed her gaze at the student, who was wearing a big leather bow in her hair, like a cowgirl in a TV ranch show. "I mean, otherwise *everybody* in the class would have little offices and office hours." *Sometimes Professor Hendricks will take up the class's time just talking about movies she's seen.* She stared at the student some more, then added, "I bet you'd like that."

15   "Maybe I sound whiny to you," said the girl, "but I simply want my history major to mean something."

"Well, there's your problem," said Zoë, and with a smile, she showed the student to the door. "I like your bow," she added.

Zoë lived for the mail, for the postman, that handsome blue jay, and when she got a real letter, with a real full-price stamp, from someplace else, she took it to bed with her and read it over and over. She also watched television until all hours and had her set in the bedroom, a bad sign. *Professor Hendricks has said critical things about Fawn Hall, the Catholic religion, and the whole state of Illinois. It is unbelievable.* At Christmastime she gave twenty-dollar tips to the mailman and to Jerry, the only cabbie in town, whom she had gotten to know from all her rides to and from the Terre Haute airport, and who, since he realized such rides were an extravagance, often gave her cut rates.

"I'm flying in to visit you this weekend," announced Zoë.

"I was hoping you would," said Evan. "Charlie and I are having a party for Halloween. It'll be fun."

20   "I have a costume already. It's a bonehead. It's this thing that looks like a giant bone going through your head."

"Great," said Evan.

"It is, it's great."

"Alls I have is my moon mask from last year and the year before. I'll probably end up getting married in it."

"Are you and Charlie getting *married?*" Foreboding filled her voice.

25   "Hmmmmmmnnno, not immediately."

"Don't get married."

"Why?"

"Just not yet. You're too young."

"You're only saying that because you're five years older than I am and *you're* not married."

"*I'm* not married? Oh, my God," said Zoë. "I forgot to get married."   30

Zoë had been out with three men since she'd come to Hilldale-Versailles. One of them was a man in the Paris municipal bureaucracy who had fixed a parking ticket she'd brought in to protest and who then asked her to coffee. At first she thought he was amazing—at last, someone who did not want Heidi! But soon she came to realize that all men, deep down, wanted Heidi. Heidi with cleavage. Heidi with outfits. The parking ticket bureaucrat soon became tired and intermittent. One cool fall day, in his snazzy, impractical convertible, when she asked him what was wrong, he said, "You would not be ill-served by new clothes, you know." She wore a lot of gray-green corduroy. She had been under the impression that it brought out her eyes, those shy stars. She flicked an ant from her sleeve.

"Did you have to brush that off in the car?" he said, driving. He glanced down at his own pectorals, giving first the left, then the right, a quick survey. He was wearing a tight shirt.

"Excuse me?"

He slowed down at a yellow light and frowned. "Couldn't you have picked it up and thrown it outside?"

"The ant? It might have bitten me. I mean, what difference does it   35 make?"

"It might have bitten you! Ha! How ridiculous! Now it's going to lay eggs in my car!"

The second guy was sweeter, lunkier, though not insensitive to certain paintings and songs, but too often, too, things he'd do or say would startle her. Once, in a restaurant, he stole the garnishes off her dinner plate and waited for her to notice. When she didn't, he finally thrust his fist across the table and said, "Look," and when he opened it, there was her parsley sprig and her orange slice, crumpled to a wad. Another time he described to her his recent trip to the Louvre. "And there I was in front of Géricault's *Raft of the Medusa,* and everyone else had wandered off, so I had my own private audience with it, all those painted, drowning bodies splayed in every direction, and there's this motion in that painting that starts at the bottom left, swirling and building, and building, and building, and going up to the right-hand corner, where there's this guy waving a flag, and on the horizon in the distance you could see this teeny tiny boat. . . ." He was breathless in the telling. She found this touching and smiled in encouragement. "A painting like that," he said, shaking his head. "It just makes you shit."

"I have to ask you something," said Evan. "I know every woman complains about not meeting men, but really, on my shoots, I meet a lot of men. And they're not all gay, either." She paused. "Not anymore."

"What are you asking?"

40   The third guy was a political science professor named Murray Peterson, who liked to go out on double dates with colleagues whose wives he was attracted to. Usually the wives would consent to flirt with him. Under the table sometimes there was footsie, and once there was even kneesie. Zoë and the husband would be left to their food, staring into their water glasses, chewing like goats. "Oh, Murray," said one wife, who had never finished her master's in physical therapy and wore great clothes. You know, I know everything about you: your birthday, your license plate number. I have everything memorized. But then that's the kind of mind I have. Once at a dinner party I amazed the host by getting up and saying goodbye to every single person there, first *and* last names."

"I knew a dog who could do that," said Zoë, with her mouth full. Murray and the wife looked at her with vexed and rebuking expressions, but the husband seemed suddenly twinkling and amused. Zoë swallowed. "It was a Talking Lab, and after about ten minutes of listening to the dinner conversation this dog knew everyone's name. You could say, 'Bring this knife to Murray Peterson,' and it would."

"Really," said the wife, frowning, and Murray Peterson never called again.

"Are you seeing anyone?" said Evan. "I'm asking for a particular reason, I'm not just being like mom."

"I'm seeing my house. I'm tending to it when it wets, when it cries, when it throws up." Zoë had bought a mint-green ranch house near campus, though now she was thinking that maybe she shouldn't have. It was hard to live in a house. She kept wandering in and out of the rooms, wondering where she had put things. She went downstairs into the basement for no reason at all except that it amused her to own a basement. It also amused her to own a tree. The day she moved in, she had tacked to her tree a small paper sign that said *Zoë's Tree.*

45   Her parents, in Maryland, had been very pleased that one of their children had at last been able to afford real estate, and when she closed on the house they sent her flowers with a Congratulations card. Her mother had even UPS'd a box of old decorating magazines saved over the years, photographs of beautiful rooms her mother used to moon over, since there never had been any money to redecorate. It was like getting her mother's pornography, that box, inheriting her drooled-upon fantasies, the endless wish and tease that had been her life. But to her mother it was a rite of passage that pleased her. "Maybe you will get some ideas from these," she had written. And when Zoë looked at the photographs, at the bold and beautiful living rooms, she was filled with longing. Ideas and ideas of longing.

Right now Zoë's house was rather empty. The previous owner had wall-papered around the furniture, leaving strange gaps and silhouettes on the walls, and Zoë hadn't done much about that yet. She had bought furniture, then taken it back, furnishing and unfurnishing, preparing and shedding, like a womb. She had bought several plain pine chests to use as love seats or boot boxes, but they came to look to her more and more like children's coffins, so she returned them. And she had recently bought an Oriental rug for the living room, with Chinese symbols on it she didn't understand. The salesgirl had kept saying she was sure they meant *Peace* and *Eternal Life,* but when Zoë got the rug home, she worried. What if they didn't mean *Peace* and *Eternal Life?* What if they meant, say, *Bruce Springsteen.* And the more she thought about it, the more she became convinced she had a rug that said *Bruce Springsteen,* and so she returned that, too.

She had also bought a little baroque mirror for the front entryway, which she had been told, by Murray Peterson, would keep away evil spirits. The mirror, however, tended to frighten *her,* startling her with an image of a woman she never recognized. Sometimes she looked puffier and plainer than she remembered. Sometimes shifty and dark. Most times she just looked vague. *You look like someone I know,* she had been told twice in the last year by strangers in restaurants in Terre Haute. In fact, sometimes she seemed not to have a look of her own, or any look whatsoever, and it began to amaze her that her students and colleagues were able to recognize her at all. How did they know? When she walked into a room, how did she look so that they knew it was her? Like this? Did she look like this? And so she returned the mirror.

"The reason I'm asking is that I know a man I think you should meet," said Evan. "He's fun. He's straight. He's single. That's all I'm going to say."

"I think I'm too old for fun," said Zoë. She had a dark bristly hair in her chin, and she could feel it now with her finger. Perhaps when you had been without the opposite sex for too long, you began to resemble them. In an act of desperate invention, you began to grow your own. "I just want to come, wear my bonehead, visit with Charlie's tropical fish, ask you about your food shoots."

She thought about all the papers on "Our Constitution: How It Affects   50
Us" she was going to have to correct. She thought about how she was going in for ultrasound tests on Friday, because, according to her doctor and her doctor's assistant, she had a large, mysterious growth in her abdomen. Gallbladder, they kept saying. Or ovaries or colon. "You guys practice medicine?" asked Zoë aloud, after they had left the room. Once, as a girl, she brought her dog to a vet, who had told her, "Well, either your dog has worms or cancer or else it was hit by a car."

She was looking forward to New York.

"Well, whatever. We'll just play it cool. I can't wait to see you, hon. Don't forget your bonehead," said Evan.

"A bonehead you don't forget," said Zoë.

"I suppose," said Evan.

55   The ultrasound Zoë was keeping a secret, even from Evan. "I feel like I'm dying," Zoë had hinted just once on the phone.

"You're not dying," said Evan. 'You're just annoyed."

"Ultrasound," Zoë now said jokingly to the technician who put the cold jelly on her bare stomach. "Does that sound like a really great stereo system, or what?" She had not had anyone make this much fuss over her bare stomach since her boyfriend in graduate school, who had hovered over her whenever she felt ill, waved his arms, pressed his hands upon her navel, and drawled evangelically, "Heal! Heal for thy Baby Jesus' sake!" Zoë would laugh and they would make love, both secretly hoping she would get pregnant. Later they would worry together, and he would sink a cheek to her belly and ask whether she was late, was she late, was she sure, she might be late, and when after two years she had not gotten pregnant, they took to quarreling and drifted apart.

"OK," said the technician absently.

The monitor was in place, and Zoë's insides came on the screen in all their gray and ribbony hollowness. They were marbled in the finest gradations of black and white, like stone in an old church or a picture of the moon. "Do you suppose," she babbled at the technician, "that the rise in infertility among so many couples in this country is due to completely different species trying to reproduce?" The technician moved the scanner around and took more pictures. On one view in particular, on Zoë's right side, the technician became suddenly alert, the machine he was operating clicking away.

60   Zoë stared at the screen. "That must be the growth you found there," suggested Zoë.

"I can't tell you anything," said the technician rigidly. "Your doctor will get the radiologist's report this afternoon and will phone you then."

"I'll be out of town," said Zoë.

"I'm sorry," said the technician.

Driving home, Zoë looked in the rearview mirror and decided she looked—well, how would one describe it? A little wan. She thought of the joke about the guy who visits his doctor and the doctor says, "Well, I'm sorry to say you've got six weeks to live."

65   "I want a second opinion," says the guy. *You act like your opinion is worth more than everyone else's in the class.*

"You want a second opinion? OK," says the doctor. "You're ugly, too." She liked that joke. She thought it was terribly, terribly funny.

She took a cab to the airport, Jerry the cabbie happy to see her.
"Have fun in New York," he said, getting her bag out of the trunk.
He liked her, or at least he always acted as if he did. She called him "Jare."
"Thanks, Jare."
"You know, I'll tell you a secret: I've never been to New York. I'll tell   70
you two secrets: I've never been on a plane." And he waved at her sadly as she
pushed her way in through the terminal door. "Or an escalator!" he shouted.
The trick to flying safe, Zoë always said, was never to buy a discount
ticket and to tell yourself you had nothing to live for anyway, so that when
the plane crashed it was no big deal. Then, when it didn't crash, when you
had succeeded in keeping it aloft with your own worthlessness, all you had
to do was stagger off, locate your luggage, and, by the time a cab arrived,
come up with a persuasive reason to go on living.

"You're here!" shrieked Evan over the doorbell, before she even opened
the door. Then she opened it wide. Zoë set her bags on the hall floor and
hugged Evan hard. When she was little, Evan had always been affectionate
and devoted. Zoe had always taken care of her, advising, reassuring, until
recently, when it seemed Evan had started advising and reassuring *her*. It
startled Zoë. She suspected it had something to do with Zoë's being alone.
It made people uncomfortable. "How, *are* you?"
"I threw up on the plane. Besides that, I'm OK."
"Can I get you something? Here, let me take your suitcase. Sick on
the plane. Eeeyew."
"It was into one of those sickness bags," said Zoë, just in case Evan   75
thought she'd lost it in the aisle. "I was very quiet."
The apartment was spacious and bright, with a view all the way downtown along the East Side. There was a balcony and sliding glass doors. "I
keep forgetting how nice this apartment is. Twentieth floor, doorman . . ."
Zoë could work her whole life and never have an apartment like this. So
could Evan. It was Charlie's apartment. He and Evan lived in it like two
kids in a dorm, beer cans and clothes strewn around. Evan put Zoë's bag
away from the mess, over by the fish tank. "I'm so glad you're here," she
said. "Now what can I get you?"
Evan made them a snack—soup from a can, and saltines.
"I don't know about Charlie," she said, after they had finished. "I feel
like we've gone all sexless and middle-aged already."
"Hmmm," said Zoë. She leaned back into Evan's sofa and stared out the
window at the dark tops of the buildings. It seemed a little unnatural to live
up in the sky like this, like birds that out of some wrongheaded derring-do
had nested too high. She nodded toward the lighted fish tank and giggled.
"I feel like a bird," she said, "with my own personal supply of fish."

80   Evan sighed. "He comes home and just sacks out on the sofa, watching fuzzy football. He's wearing the psychic cold cream and curlers, if you know what I mean."

Zoë sat up, readjusted the sofa cushions. "What's fuzzy football?"

"We haven't gotten cable yet. Everything comes in fuzzy. Charlie just watches it that way."

"Hmmm, yeah, that's a little depressing," Zoë said. She looked at her hands. "Especially the part about not having cable."

"This is how he gets into bed at night." Evan stood up to demonstrate. "He whips all his clothes off, and when he gets to his underwear, he lets it drop to one ankle. Then he kicks up his leg and flips the underwear in the air and catches it. I, of course, watch from the bed. There's nothing else. There's just that."

85   "Maybe you should just get it over with and get married."

"Really?"

"Yeah. I mean, you guys probably think living together like this is the best of both worlds, but . . ." Zoë tried to sound like an older sister; an older sister was supposed to be the parent you could never have, the hip, cool mom. ". . . I've always found that as soon as you think you've got the best of both worlds"—she thought now of herself, alone in her house; of the toad-faced cicadas that flew around like little caped men at night, landing on her screens, staring; of the size fourteen shoes she placed at the doorstep, to scare off intruders; of the ridiculous inflatable blow-up doll someone had told her to keep propped up at the breakfast table—"it can suddenly twist and become the worst of both worlds."

"Really?" Evan was beaming. "Oh, Zoë. I have something to tell you. Charlie and I *are* getting married."

"Really." Zoë felt confused.

90   "I didn't know how to tell you."

"Yes, well, I guess the part about fuzzy football misled me a little."

"I was hoping you'd be my maid of honor," said Evan, waiting. "Aren't you happy for me?"

"Yes," said Zoë, and she began to tell Evan a story about an award-winning violinist at Hilldale-Versailles, how the violinist had come home from a competition in Europe and taken up with a local man, who made her go to all his summer softball games, made her cheer for him from the stands, with the wives, until she later killed herself. But when she got halfway through, to the part about cheering at the softball games, Zoë stopped.

"What?" said Evan. "So what happened?"

95   "Actually, nothing," said Zoë lightly, "She just really got into softball. I mean, really. You should have seen her."

Zoë decided to go to a late-afternoon movie, leaving Evan to chores she needed to do before the party—*I have to do them alone,* she'd said, a little tense after the violinist story. Zoë thought about going to an art museum, but women alone in art museums had to look good. They always did. Chic and serious, moving languidly, with a great handbag. Instead, she walked over and down through Kips Bay, past an earring boutique called Stick It in Your Ear, past a beauty salon called Dorian Gray's. That was the funny thing about *beauty,* thought Zoë. Look it up in the yellow pages, and you found a hundred entries, hostile with wit, cutesy with warning. But look up *truth*—ha! There was nothing at all.

Zoë thought about Evan getting married. Would Evan turn into Peter Pumpkin Eater's wife? Mrs. Eater? At the wedding would she make Zoë wear some flouncy lavender dress, identical with the other maids'? Zoë hated unisex forms, had even, in the first grade, refused to join Elf Girls, because she didn't want to wear the same dress as everyone else. Now she might have to. But maybe she could distinguish it. Hitch it up on one side with a clothespin. Wear surgical gauze at the waist. Clip to her bodice one of those pins that said in loud letters, SHIT HAPPENS.

At the movie—*Death by Number*—she bought strands of red licorice to tug and chew. She took a seat off to one side in the theater. She felt strangely self-conscious sitting alone and hoped for the place to darken fast. When it did and the coming attractions came on, she reached inside her purse for her glasses. They were in a Baggie. Her Kleenex was also in a Baggie. So were her pen and her aspirin and her mints. Everything was in Baggies. This was what she'd become: *a woman alone at the movies with everything in a Baggie.*

* * *

At the Halloween party, there were about two dozen people. There were people with ape heads and large hairy hands. There was someone dressed as a leprechaun. There was someone dressed as a frozen dinner. Some man had brought his two small daughters: a ballerina and a ballerina's sister, also dressed as a ballerina. There was a gaggle of sexy witches—women dressed entirely in black, beautifully made up and jeweled. "I hate those sexy witches. It's not in the spirit of Halloween," said Evan. Evan had abandoned the moon mask and dolled herself up as a hausfrau, in curlers and an apron, a decision she now regretted. Charlie, because he liked fish, because he owned fish, collected fish, had decided to go as a fish. He had fins and eyes on the side of his head. "Zoë! How are you! I'm sorry I wasn't here when you first arrived!" He spent the rest of his time chatting up the sexy witches.

"Isn't there something I can help you with here?" Zoë asked her sister. "You've been running yourself ragged." She rubbed her sister's arm, gently, as if she wished they were alone. 100

"Oh, God, not at all," said Evan, arranging stuffed mushrooms on a plate. The timer went off, and she pulled another sheetful out of the oven. "Actually, you know what you can do?"

"What?" Zoë put on her bonehead.

"Meet Earl. He's the guy I had in mind for you. When he gets here, just talk to him a little. He's nice. He's fun. He's going through a divorce."

"I'll try." Zoë groaned. "OK? I'll try." She looked at her watch.

105   When Earl arrived, he was dressed as a naked woman, steel wool glued strategically to a body stocking, and large rubber breasts protruding like hams.

"Zoë, this is Earl," said Evan.

"Good to meet you," said Earl, circling Evan to shake Zoë's hand. He stared at the top of Zoë's head. "Great bone."

Zoë nodded. "Great tits," she said. She looked past him, out the window at the city thrown glitteringly up against the sky; people were saying the usual things: how it looked like jewels, like bracelets and necklaces unstrung. You could see Grand Central station, the clock of the Con Ed building, the red-and-gold-capped Empire State, the Chrysler like a rocket ship dreamed up in a depression. Far west you could glimpse the Astor Plaza, its flying white roof like a nun's habit. "There's beer out on the balcony, Earl—can I get you one?" Zoë asked.

"Sure, uh, I'll come along. Hey, Charlie, how's it going?"

110   Charlie grinned and whistled. People turned to look. "Hey, Earl," someone called, from across the room. "Va-va-va-voom."

They squeezed their way past the other guests, past the apes and the sexy witches. The suction of the sliding door gave way in a whoosh, and Zoë and Earl stepped out onto the balcony, a bonehead and a naked woman, the night air roaring and smoky cool. Another couple was out here, too, murmuring privately. They were not wearing costumes. They smiled at Zoë and Earl. "Hi," said Zoë. She found the plastic-foam cooler, dug into it, and retrieved two beers.

"Thanks," said Earl. His rubber breasts folded inward, dimpled and dented, as he twisted open the bottle.

"Well," sighed Zoë anxiously. She had to learn not to be afraid of a man, the way, in your childhood, you learned not to be afraid of an earthworm or a bug. Often, when she spoke to men at parties, she rushed things in her mind. As the man politely blathered on, she would fall in love, marry, then find herself in a bitter custody battle with him for the kids and hoping for a reconciliation so that despite all his betrayals she might no longer despise him, and in the few minutes remaining, learn, perhaps, what his last name was and what he did for a living, though probably there was already too much history between them. She would nod, blush, turn away.

"Evan tells me you're a professor. Where do you teach?"

"Just over the Indiana border into Illinois."   115

He looked a little shocked. "I guess Evan didn't tell me that part."

"She didn't?"

"No."

"Well, that's Evan for you. When we were kids we both had speech impediments."

"That can be tough," said Earl. One of his breasts was hidden behind   120
his drinking arm, but the other shone low and pink, full as a strawberry moon.

"Yes, well, it wasn't a total loss. We used to go to what we called peach pearapy. For about ten years of my life I had to map out every sentence in my mind, way ahead, before I said it. That was the only way I could get a coherent sentence out."

Earl drank from his beer. "How did you do that? I mean, how did you get through?"

"I told a lot of jokes. Jokes you know the lines to already—you can just say them. I love jokes. Jokes and songs."

Earl smiled. He had on lipstick, a deep shade of red, but it was wearing off from the beer. "What's your favorite joke?"

"Uh, my favorite joke is probably . . . OK, all right. This guy goes into   125
a doctor's office and—"

"I think I know this one," interrupted Earl, eagerly. He wanted to tell it himself. "A guy goes into a doctor's office, and the doctor tells him he's got some good news and some bad news—that one, right?"

"I'm not sure," said Zoë. "This might be a different version."

"So the guy says, 'Give me the bad news first,' and the doctor says, 'OK. You've got three weeks to live.' And the guy cries, 'Three weeks to live! Doctor, what is the good news?' And the doctor says, 'Did you see that secretary out front? I finally fucked her.'"

Zoë frowned.

"That's not the one you were thinking of?"   130

"No." There was accusation in her voice. "Mine was different."

"Oh," said Earl. He looked away and then back again. "You teach history, right? What kind of history do you teach?"

"I teach American, mostly—eighteenth and nineteenth century." In graduate school, at bars, the pickup line was always: "So what's your century?"

"Occasionally I teach a special theme course," she added, "say, 'Humor and Personality in the White House.' That's what my book's on." She thought of something someone once told her about bowerbirds, how they build elaborate structures before mating.

135   "Your book's on *humor?*"

"Yeah, and, well, when I teach a theme course like that, I do all the centuries." *So what's your century?*

"All three of them."

"Pardon?" The breeze glistened her eyes. Traffic revved beneath them. She felt high and puny, like someone lifted into heaven by mistake and then spurned.

"Three. There's only three."

140   "Well, four, really." She was thinking of Jamestown, and of the Pilgrims coming here with buckles and witch hats to say their prayers.

"I'm a photographer," said Earl. His face was starting to gleam, his rouge smearing in a sunset beneath his eyes.

"Do you like that?"

"Well, actually I'm starting to feel it's a little dangerous."

"Really?"

145   "Spending all your time in a darkroom with that red light and all those chemicals. There's links with Parkinson's, you know."

"No, I didn't."

"I suppose I should wear rubber gloves, but I don't like to. Unless I'm touching it directly, I don't think of it as real."

"Hmmm," said Zoë. Alarm buzzed through her, mildly, like a tea.

"Sometimes, when I have a cut or something, I feel the sting and think, *shit.* I wash constantly and just hope. I don't like rubber over the skin like that."

150   "Really."

"I mean, the physical contact. That's what you want, or why bother?"

"I guess," said Zoë. She wished she could think of a joke, something slow and deliberate, with the end in sight. She thought of gorillas, how when they had been kept too long alone in cages, they would smack each other in the head instead of mating.

"Are you ... in a relationship?" Earl suddenly blurted.

"Now? As we speak?"

155   "Well, I mean, I'm sure you have a relationship to your *work.*" A smile, a weird one, nestled in his mouth like an egg. She thought of zoos in parks, how when cities were under siege, during world wars, people are the animals. "But I mean, with a *man.*"

"No, I'm not in a relationship with a *man.*" She rubbed her chin with her hand and could feel the one bristly hair there. "But my last relationship was with a very sweet man," she said. She made something up. "From Switzerland. He was a botanist—a weed expert. His name was Jerry. I called him 'Jare.' He was so funny. You'd go to the movies with him and all he would notice were the plants. He would never pay attention to the plot.

Once, in a jungle movie, he started rattling off all these Latin names, out loud. It was very exciting for him." She paused, caught her breath. "Eventually he went back to Europe to, uh, study the edelweiss." She looked at Earl. "Are you involved in a relationship? With a *woman?*"

Earl shifted his weight, and the creases in his body stocking changed, splintering outward like something broken. His pubic hair slid over to one hip, like a corsage on a saloon girl. "No," he said, clearing his throat. The steel wool in his underarms was inching toward his biceps. "I've just gotten out of a marriage that was full of bad dialogue, like "You want more *space?* I'll give you more space!' *Clonk.* Your basic Three Stooges."

Zoë looked at him sympathetically. "I suppose it's hard for love to recover after that."

His eyes lit up. He wanted to talk about love. "But *I* keep thinking love should be like a tree. You look at trees and they've got bumps and scars from tumors, infestations, what have you, but they're still growing. Despite the bumps and bruises, they're . . . straight."

"Yeah, well," said Zoë, "where I'm from, they're all married or gay.   160
Did you see that movie *Death by Number?*"

Earl looked at her, a little lost. She was getting away from him. "No," he said.

One of his breasts had slipped under his arm, tucked there like a baguette. She kept thinking of trees, of gorillas and parks, of people in wartime eating the zebras. She felt a stabbing pain in her abdomen.

"Want some hors d'oeuvres?" Evan came pushing through the sliding door. She was smiling, though her curlers were coming out, hanging bedraggled at the ends of her hair like Christmas decorations, like food put out for the birds. She thrust forward a plate of stuffed mushrooms.

"Are you asking for donations or giving them away," said Earl, wittily. He liked Evan, and he put his arm around her.

"You know, I'll be right back," said Zoë.   165

"Oh," said Evan, looking concerned.

"Right back. I promise."

Zoë hurried inside, across the living room, into the bedroom, to the adjoining bath. It was empty; most of the guests were using the half bath near the kitchen. She flicked on the light and closed the door. The pain had stopped and she didn't really have to go to the bathroom, but she stayed there anyway, resting. In the mirror above the sink she looked haggard beneath her bonehead, violet grays showing under the skin like a plucked and pocky bird. She leaned closer, raising her chin a little to find the bristly hair. It was there, at the end of the jaw, sharp and dark as a wire. She opened the medicine cabinet, pawed through it until she found some tweezers. She lifted her head again and poked at her face with the metal tips, grasping and pinching and missing. Outside the door she could hear two people talking low. They had come into the bedroom and were discussing something. They were sitting on the bed. One of them giggled in a false way. She stabbed again at her chin, and it started to bleed a little. She pulled the skin tight along the jawbone, gripped the tweezers hard around what she hoped was the hair, and tugged. A tiny square of skin came away with it, but the hair remained, blood bright at the root of it. Zoë clenched her teeth. "Come on," she whispered. The couple outside in the bedroom were now telling stories, softly, and laughing. There was a bounce and squeak of mattress, and the sound of a chair being moved out of the way. Zoë aimed the tweezers carefully, pinched, then pulled gently away, and this time the hair came, too, with a slight twinge of pain and then a great flood of relief. "Yeah!" breathed Zoë. She grabbed some toilet paper and dabbed at her chin. It came away spotted with blood, and so she tore off some more and pressed hard until it stopped. Then she turned off the light and opened the door, to return to the party. "Excuse me," she said to the couple in the bedroom. They were the couple from the balcony, and they looked at her, a bit surprised. They had their arms around each other, and they were eating candy bars.

Earl was still out on the balcony, alone, and Zoë rejoined him there.

170 "Hi," she said. He turned around and smiled. He had straightened his costume out a bit, though all the secondary sex characteristics seemed slightly doomed, destined to shift and flip and zip around again any moment.

"Are you OK?" he asked. He had opened another beer and was chugging.

"Oh, yeah. I just had to go to the bathroom." She paused. "Actually I have been going to a lot of doctors recently."

"What's wrong?" asked Earl.

"Oh, probably nothing. But they're putting me through tests." She sighed. "I've had sonograms. I've had mammograms. Next week I'm going in for a candygram." He looked at her worriedly. "I've had too many gram words," she said.

175 "Here, I saved you these." He held out a napkin with two stuffed mushroom caps. They were cold and leaving oil marks on the napkin.

"Thanks," said Zoë, and pushed them both in her mouth. "Watch," she said, with her mouth full. "With my luck, it'll be a gallbladder operation."

Earl made a face. "So your sister's getting married," he said, changing the subject. "Tell me, really, what you think about love."

"*Love?*" Hadn't they done this already? "I don't know." She chewed thoughtfully and swallowed. "All right. I'll tell you what I think about love. Here is a love story. This friend of mine—"

"You've got something on your chin," said Earl, and he reached over to touch it.

"*What?*" said Zoë, stepping back. She turned her face away and 180 grabbed at her chin. A piece of toilet paper peeled off it, like tape. "It's nothing," she said. "It's just—it's nothing."

Earl stared at her.

"At any rate," she continued, "this friend of mine was this award-winning violinist. She traveled all over Europe and won competitions; she made records, she gave concerts, she got famous. But she had no social life. So one day she threw herself at the feet of this conductor she had a terrible crush on. He picked her up, scolded her gently, and sent her back to her hotel room. After that she came home from Europe. She went back to her old hometown, stopped playing the violin, and took up with a local boy. This was in Illinois. He took her to some Big Ten bar every night to drink with his buddies from the team. He used to say things like 'Katrina here likes to play the violin,' and then he'd pinch her cheek. When she once suggested that they go home, he said, 'What, you think you're too famous for a place like this? Well, let me tell you something. You may think you're famous, but you're not *famous* famous.' Two famouses. 'No one here's ever heard of you.' Then he went up and bought a round of drinks for everyone but her. She got her coat, went home, and shot a gun through her head."

Earl was silent.

"That's the end of my love story," said Zoë.

"You're not at all like your sister," said Earl. 185

"Ho, really," said Zoë. The air had gotten colder, the wind singing minor and thick as a dirge.

"No." He didn't want to talk about love anymore. "You know, you should wear a lot of blue—blue and white—around your face. It would bring out your coloring." He reached an arm out to show her how the blue bracelet he was wearing might look against her skin, but she swatted it away.

"Tell me, Earl. Does the word *fag* mean anything to you?"

He stepped back, away from her. He shook his head in disbelief. "You know, I just shouldn't try to go out with career women. You're all stricken. A guy can really tell what life has done to you. I do better with women who have part-time jobs."

"Oh, yes?" said Zoë. She had once read an article entitled "Profes- 190 sional Women and the Demographics of Grief." Or no, it was a poem: *If there were a lake, the moonlight would dance across it in conniptions.* She remembered that line. But perhaps the title was "The Empty House: Aesthetics of Barrenness." Or maybe "Space Gypsies: Girls in Academe." She had forgotten.

Earl turned and leaned on the railing of the balcony. It was getting late. Inside, the party guests were beginning to leave. The sexy witches were already gone. "Live and learn," Earl murmured.

"Live and get dumb," replied Zoë. Beneath them on Lexington there were no cars, just the gold rush of an occasional cab. He leaned hard on his elbows, brooding.

"Look at those few people down there," he said. "They look like bugs. You know how bugs are kept under control? They're sprayed with bug hormones, female bug hormones. The male bugs get so crazy in the presence of this hormone, they're screwing everything in sight: trees, rocks— everything but female bugs. Population control. That's what's happening in this country," he said drunkenly. "Hormones sprayed around, and now men are screwing rocks. Rocks!"

In the back the Magic Marker line of his buttocks spread wide, a sketchy black on pink like a funnies page. Zoë came up, slow, from behind and gave him a shove. His arms slipped forward, off the railing, out over the street. Beer spilled out of his bottle, raining twenty stories down to the street.

195   "Hey, what are you doing?!" he said, whipping around. He stood straight and readied and moved away from the railing, sidestepping Zoë. "What the *hell* are you doing?"

"Just kidding," she said. "I was just kidding." But he gazed at her, appalled and frightened, his Magic Marker buttocks turned away now toward all of downtown, a naked pseudowoman with a blue bracelet at the wrist, trapped out on a balcony with—with *what? "Really, I was just kidding!"* Zoë shouted. The wind lifted the hair up off her head, skyward in spines behind the bone. If there were a lake, the moonlight would dance across it in conniptions. She smiled at him, and wondered how she looked.

QUESTIONS

1. What is the significance of Zoë's many eccentricities—for instance, her keeping all her pocketbook items in Baggies, and her unusual way of interacting with her students? Does her eccentricity make her more or less sympathetic as a character?
2. At the Halloween party in New York, Zoë and the other characters wear ludicrous costumes. How do these costumes and the way they are described contribute to the meaning of the story? How do they help us to understand Zoë and her generation of affluent, well educated young adults?
3. This story makes extensive use of jokes. Discuss the importance of jokes to the characterization of Zoë and to the story as a whole.
4. Early in the story (paragraph 6), Zoë thinks about the distinction between irony and sarcasm. Find an instance in the story when Zoë speaks sarcastically to another character, then find another instance when she speaks ironically. How do they differ?

5. Discuss the ways in which the story achieves humor through incongruity. How do these passages help elucidate the theme?
6. Zoë's ill-fated relationships with men offer examples of dramatic irony. What do we learn about these men through their words and actions that the men themselves do not grasp? In the final scene, Zoë drops her ironic mask and exhibits outright hostility to Earl. What brings about this change? Have earlier passages helped to prepare for the change? How does this scene reveal an important truth about Zoë's life?
7. Can you find examples of situational irony? In what ways are they significant?

MARK TWAIN
Cannibalism in the Cars

I visited St. Louis lately, and on my way West, after changing cars at Terre Haute, Indiana, a mild, benevolent-looking gentleman of about forty-five, or maybe fifty, came in at one of the way stations and sat down beside me. We talked together pleasantly on various subjects for an hour, perhaps, and I found him exceedingly intelligent and entertaining. When he learned that I was from Washington, he immediately began to ask questions about various public men, and about congressional affairs; and I saw very shortly that I was conversing with a man who was perfectly familiar with the ins and outs of political life at the capital, even to the ways and manners, and customs of procedure of senators and representatives in the chambers of the national legislature. Presently two men halted near us for a single moment, and one said to the other: "Harris, if you'll do that for me, I'll never forget you, my boy."

My new comrade's eye lighted pleasantly. The words had touched upon a happy memory, I thought. Then his face settled into thoughtfulness— almost into gloom. He turned to me and said, "Let me tell you a story, let me give you a secret chapter of my life—a chapter that has never been referred to by me since its events transpired. Listen patiently, and promise that you will not interrupt me."

I said I would not, and he related the following strange adventure, speaking sometimes with animation, sometimes with melancholy, but always with feeling and earnestness.

On the nineteenth of December, 1853, I started from St. Louis on the evening train bound for Chicago. There were only twenty-four passengers,

CANNIBALISM IN THE CARS First published in 1868. "Mark Twain," the pen name of Samuel L. Clemens, was perhaps the most celebrated American writer of the nineteenth century, the author of such classics as *Innocents Abroad* (1868) and *The Adventures of Huckleberry Finn* (1884). In much of his work, including "Cannibalism in the Cars," Twain's sense of humor is clearly combined with a cynical outlook on the human race.

all told. There were no ladies and no children. We were in excellent spirits, and pleasant acquaintanceships were soon formed. The journey bade fair to be a happy one; and no individual in the party, I think, had even the vaguest presentiment of the horrors we were soon to undergo.

5   At 11:00 P.M. it began to snow hard. Shortly after leaving the small village of Welden, we entered upon that tremendous prairie solitude that stretches its leagues on leagues of houseless dreariness far away toward the Jubilee Settlements. The winds, unobstructed by trees or hills, or even vagrant rocks, whistled fiercely across the level desert, driving the falling snow before it like spray from the crested waves of a stormy sea. The snow was deepening fast; and we knew, by the diminished speed of the train, that the engine was plowing through it with steadily increasing difficulty. Indeed, it almost came to a dead halt sometimes, in the midst of great drifts that piled themselves like colossal graves across the track. Conversation began to flag. Cheerfulness gave place to grave concern. The possibility of being imprisoned in the snow, on the bleak prairie, fifty miles from any house, presented itself to every mind, and extended its depressing influence over every spirit.

At two o'clock in the morning I was aroused out of an uneasy slumber by the ceasing of all motion about me. The appalling truth flashed upon me instantly—we were captives in a snowdrift! "All hands to the rescue!" Every man sprang to obey. Out into the wild night, the pitchy darkness, the billow snow, the driving storm, every soul leaped, with the consciousness that a moment lost now might bring destruction to us all. Shovels, hands, boards—anything, everything that could displace snow, was brought into instant requisition. It was a weird picture, that small company of frantic men fighting the banking snows, half in the blackest shadow and half in the angry light of the locomotive's reflector.

One short hour sufficed to prove the utter uselessness of our efforts. The storm barricaded the track with a dozen drifts while we dug one away. And worse than this, it was discovered that the last grand charge the engine had made upon the enemy had broken the fore-and-aft shaft of the driving wheel! With a free track before us we should still have been helpless. We entered the car wearied with labor, and very sorrowful. We gathered about the stoves, and gravely canvassed our situation. We had no provisions whatever—in this lay our chief distress. We could not freeze, for there was a good supply of wood in the tender. This was our only comfort. The discussion ended at last in accepting the disheartening decision of the conductor, *viz.*, that it would be death for any man to attempt to travel fifty miles on foot through snow like that. We could not send for help, and even if we could it would not come. We must submit, and await, as patiently as we might, succor or starvation! I think the stoutest heart there felt a momentary chill when those words were uttered.

Within the hour conversation subsided to a low murmur here and there about the car, caught fitfully between the rising and falling of the blast; the lamps grew dim; and the majority of the castaways settled themselves among the flickering shadows to think—to forget the present, if they could—to sleep, if they might.

The eternal night—it surely seemed eternal to us—wore its lagging hours away at last, and the cold gray dawn broke in the east. As the light grew stronger the passengers began to stir and give signs of life, one after another, and each in turn pushed his slouched hat up from his forehead, stretched his stiffened limbs and glanced out of the windows upon the cheerless prospect. It was cheerless, indeed!—not a living thing visible anywhere, not a human habitation; nothing but a vast white desert; uplifted sheets of snow drifting hither and thither before the wind—a world of eddying flakes shutting out the firmament above.

All day we moped about the cars, saying little, thinking much. 10 Another lingering dreary night—and hunger.

Another dawning—another day of silence, sadness, wasting hunger, hopeless watching for succor that could not come. A night of restless slumber, filled with dreams of feasting—wakings distressed with the gnawings of hunger.

The fourth day came and went—and the fifth! Five days of dreadful imprisonment! A savage hunger looked out at every eye. There was in it a sign of awful import—the foreshadowing of a something that was vaguely shaping itself in every heart—a something which no tongue dared yet to frame into words.

The sixth day passed—the seventh dawned upon as gaunt and haggard and hopeless a company of men as ever stood in the shadow of death. It must out now! That thing which had been growing up in every heart was ready to leap from every lip at last! Nature had been taxed to the utmost— she must yield. Richard H. Gaston of Minnesota, tall, cadaverous, and pale, rose up. All knew what was coming. All prepared—every emotion, every semblance of excitement was smothered—only a calm, thoughtful seriousness appeared in the eyes that were lately so wild.

"Gentlemen: It cannot be delayed longer! The time is at hand! We must determine which of us shall die to furnish food for the rest!"

MR. JOHN J. WILLIAMS of Illinois rose and said: "Gentlemen—I 15 nominate the Reverend James Sawyer of Tennessee."

MR. WM. R. ADAMS of Indiana said: "I nominate Mr. Daniel Slote of New York."

MR. CHARLES J. LANGDON: "I nominate Mr. Samuel A. Bowen of St. Louis."

MR. SLOTE: "Gentlemen—I desire to decline in favor of Mr. John A. Van Nostrand, Jr., of New Jersey."

MR. GASTON: "If there be no objection, the gentleman's desire will be acceded to."

20   Mr. Van Nostrand objecting, the resignation of Mr. Slote was rejected. The resignations of Messrs. Sawyer and Bowen were also offered, and refused upon the same grounds.

MR. A. L. BASCOM of Ohio: "I move that the nominations now close, and that the House proceed to an election by ballot."

MR. SAWYER: "Gentlemen—I protest earnestly against these proceedings. They are, in every way, irregular and unbecoming. I must beg to move that they be chopped at once, and that we elect a chairman of the meeting and proper officers to assist him, and then we can go on with the business before us understandingly."

MR. BELL of Iowa: "Gentlemen—I object. This is no time to stand upon forms and ceremonious observances. For more than seven days we have been without food. Every moment we lose in idle discussion increases our distress. I am satisfied with the nominations that have been made— every gentleman present is, I believe—and I, for one, do not see why we should not proceed at once to elect one or more of them. I wish to offer a resolution—"

MR. GASTON: "It would be objected to, and have to lie over one day under the rules, thus bringing about the very delay you wish to avoid. The gentleman from New Jersey—"

25   MR. VAN NOSTRAND: "Gentlemen—I am a stranger among you; I have not sought the distinction that has been conferred upon me, and I feel a delicacy—"

MR. MORGAN of Alabama (interrupting): "I move the previous question."

The motion was carried, and further debate shut off, of course. The motion to elect officers was passed, and under it Mr. Gaston was chosen chairman, Mr. Blake, secretary, Messrs. Holcomb, Dyer and Baldwin a committee on nominations, and Mr. R. M. Howland, purveyor, to assist the committee in making selections.

A recess of half an hour was then taken, and some little caucusing followed. At the sound of the gavel the meeting reassembled, and the committee reported in favor of Messrs. George Ferguson of Kentucky, Lucien Herrman of Louisiana and W. Messick of Colorado as candidates. The report was accepted.

MR. ROGERS of Missouri: "Mr. President—The report being properly before the House now, I move to amend it by substituting for the name of Mr. Herrman that of Mr. Lucius Harris of St. Louis, who is well and honorably known to us all. I do not wish to be understood as casting the least reflection upon the high character and standing of the gentleman from Louisiana—far from it. I respect and esteem him as much as any gentleman here present possibly can; but none of us can be blind to the fact that he had lost more flesh during the week that we have lain here than any among us—none of us can be blind to the fact that the committee has been derelict in its duty, either through negligence or a graver fault, in thus offering for our suffrages a gentleman who, however pure his own motives may be, has really less nutriment in him—"

THE CHAIR: "The gentleman from Missouri will take his seat. The   30 Chair cannot allow the integrity of the committee to be questioned save by the regular course, under the rules. What action will the House take upon the gentleman's motion?"

MR. HALLIDAY of Virginia: "I move to further amend the report by substituting Mr. Harvey Davis of Oregon for Mr. Messick. It may be urged by gentlemen that the hardships and privations of a frontier life have rendered Mr. Davis tough; but, gentlemen, is this a time to cavil at toughness? Is this a time to be fastidious concerning trifles? Is this a time to dispute about matters of paltry significance? No, gentlemen, bulk is what we desired—substance, weight, bulk—these are the supreme requisites now—not talent, not genius, not education. I insist upon my motion."

MR. MORGAN (excitedly): "Mr. Chairman—I do most strenuously object to this amendment. The gentleman from Oregon is old, and furthermore is bulky only in bone—not in flesh. I ask the gentleman from Virginia if it is soup we want instead of solid sustenance? if he would delude us with shadows? if he would mock our suffering with an Oregonian specter? I ask him if he can look upon the anxious faces around him, if he can gaze into our sad eyes, if he can listen to the beating of our expectant hearts, and still thrust this famine-stricken fraud upon us? I ask him if he can think of our desolate state, of our past sorrows, of our dark future, and still unpityingly foist upon us this wreck, this ruin, this tottering swindle, this gnarled and blighted and sapless vagabond from Oregon's inhospitable shores? Never! [Applause.]"

The amendment was put to vote, after a fiery debate, and lost. Mr. Harris was substituted on the first amendment. The balloting then began. Five ballots were held without a choice. On the sixth, Mr. Harris was elected, all voting for him but himself. It was then moved that his election should be ratified by acclamation, which was lost, in consequence of his again voting against himself.

Mr. Radway moved that the House now take up the remaining candidates, and go into an election for breakfast. This was carried.

On the first ballot there was a tie, half the members favoring one   35 candidate on account of his youth, and half favoring the other on account of his superior size. The president gave the casting vote for the latter,

Mr. Messick. This decision created considerable dissatisfaction among the friends of Mr. Ferguson, the defeated candidate, and there was some talk of demanding a new ballot; but in the midst of it a motion to adjourn was carried, and the meeting broke up at once.

The preparations for supper diverted the attention of the Ferguson faction from the discussion of their grievance for a long time, and then, when they would have taken it up again, the happy announcement that Mr. Harris was ready drove all thought of it to the winds.

We improvised tables by propping up the backs of car seats, and sat down with hearts full of gratitude to the finest supper that had blessed our vision for seven torturing days. How changed we were from what we had been a few short hours before! Hopeless, sad-eyed misery, hunger, feverish anxiety, desperation, then; thankfulness, serenity, joy too deep for utterance now. That I know was the cheeriest hour of my eventful life. The winds howled, and blew the snow wildly about our prison house, but they were powerless to distress us anymore. I liked Harris. He might have been better done, perhaps, but I am free to say that no man ever agreed with me better than Harris, or afforded me so large a degree of satisfaction. Messick was very well, though rather high-flavored, but for genuine nutritiousness and delicacy of fiber, give me Harris. Messick had his good points—I will not attempt to deny it, nor do I wish to do it—but he was no more fitted for breakfast than a mummy would be, sir—not a bit. Lean?—why, bless me!—and tough? Ah, he was very tough! You could not imagine it—you could never imagine anything like it.

"Do you mean to tell me that—"

"Do not interrupt me, please. After breakfast we elected a man by the name of Walker, from Detroit, for supper. He was very good. I wrote his wife so afterward. He was worthy of all praise. I shall always remember Walker. He was a little rare, but very good. And then the next morning we had Morgan of Alabama for breakfast. He was one of the finest men I ever sat down to—handsome, educated, refined, spoke several languages fluently—a perfect gentleman—he was a perfect gentleman, and singularly juicy. For supper we had that Oregon patriarch, and he *was* a fraud, there is no question about it—old, scraggy, tough, nobody can picture the reality. I finally said, 'Gentlemen, you can do as you like, but *I* will wait for another election.' And Grimes of Illinois said, 'Gentlemen, *I* will wait also. When you elect a man that has *something* to recommend him, I shall be glad to join you again.' It soon became evident that there was general dissatisfaction with Davis of Oregon, and so, to preserve the good will that had prevailed so pleasantly since we had had Harris, an election was called, and the result of it was that Baker of Georgia was chosen. He was splendid! Well, well—after that we had Doolittle, and Hawkins, and McElroy (there was some complaint about McElroy, because he was uncommonly short and thin), and Penrod, and two Smiths, and Bailey (Bailey had a wooden leg, which was clear loss, but he was otherwise good), and an Indian boy, and an organ-grinder and a gentleman by the name of Buckminster—a poor stick of a vagabond that wasn't any good for company and no account for breakfast. We were glad we got him elected before relief came."

"And so the blessed relief *did* come at last?"   40

"Yes, it came one bright, sunny morning, just after election. John Murphy was the choice, and there never was a better, I am willing to testify; but John Murphy came home with us, in the train that came to succor us, and lived to marry the widow Harris—"

"Relict of—"

"Relict of our first choice. He married her, and is happy and respected and prosperous yet. Ah, it was like a novel, sir—it was like a romance. This is my stopping-place, sir; I must bid you goodbye. Any time that you can make it convenient to tarry a day or two with me, I shall be glad to have you. I like you, sir; I have conceived an affection for you. I could like you as well as I liked Harris himself, sir. Good day, sir, and a pleasant journey."

He was gone. I never felt so stunned, so distressed, so bewildered in my life. But in my soul I was glad he was gone. With all his gentleness of manner and his soft voice, I shuddered whenever he turned his hungry eye upon me; and when I heard that I had achieved his perilous affection, and that I stood almost with the late Harris in his esteem, my heart fairly stood still!

I was bewildered beyond description. I did not doubt his word; I could   45
not question a single item in a statement so stamped with the earnestness of truth as his; but its dreadful details overpowered me, and threw my thoughts into hopeless confusion. I saw the conductor looking at me. I said, "Who is that man?"

"He was a member of congress once, and a good one. But he got caught in a snowdrift in the cars, and like to have been starved to death. He got so frostbitten and frozen up generally, and used up for want of something to eat, that he was sick and out of his head two or three months afterward. He is all right now, only he is a monomaniac, and when he gets on that old subject he never stops till he has eat up that whole carload of people he talks about. He would have finished the crowd by this time, only he had to get out here. He has got their names as pat as *ABC*. When he gets them all eat up but himself, he always says: 'Then the hour for the unusual election for breakfast having arrived, and there being no opposition, I was duly elected, after which, there being no objections offered, I resigned. Thus I am here.'"

I felt inexpressibly relieved to know that I had only been listening to the harmless vagaries of a madman instead of the genuine experiences of a bloodthirsty cannibal.

QUESTIONS

1. This story is notable for its use of a "frame device": in this case, an outside narrator—he gives the stage, so to speak, to a character who was actually present when the train wrecked—who then reappears at the end. Why is this device effective? What would be lost if this outside narrator were removed from the story altogether?
2. How would you describe the tone of the story? Is it comic or is it serious, or is it a blend of both? What is the source of the story's humor?
3. How does this story differ from other Mark Twain works you have read? Does it take a different approach from that found in his more typical work?
4. Discuss the ending. Is the story more or less effective for being revealed as a madman's deranged fantasy? If the story were presented as factual realism, would it still be believable?

ALBERT CAMUS

The Guest

The schoolmaster was watching the two men climb toward him. One was on horseback, the other on foot. They had not yet tackled the abrupt rise leading to the schoolhouse built on the hillside. They were toiling onward, making slow progress in the snow, among the stones, on the vast expanse of the high, deserted plateau. From time to time the horse stumbled. Without hearing anything yet, he could see the breath issuing from the horse's nostrils. One of the men, at least, knew the region. They were following the trail although it had disappeared days ago under a layer of dirty white snow. The schoolmaster calculated that it would take them half an hour to get onto the hill. It was cold; he went back into the school to get a sweater.

He crossed the empty, frigid classroom. On the blackboard the four rivers of France, drawn with four different colored chalks, had been flowing toward their estuaries for the past three days. Snow had suddenly fallen in mid-October after eight months of drought without the transition of rain, and the twenty pupils, more or less, who lived in the villages scattered over the plateau had stopped coming. With fair weather they would return.

THE GUEST   First published in 1957. Translated into English by Justin O'Brien. Algeria, now a republic, was until midcentury a French territory with a population about 88 percent Muslim (either Arab or Berber). Daru and Balducci, in the story, are French civil servants. Algeria gained its independence as a result of the Algerian War, 1954–1962, a Muslim revolt against French rule. Albert Camus (1913–1960), though a Frenchman, was born in northeastern Algeria, was educated in Algiers, and did not see France until 1939. In 1940, with the fall of France to Germany, he returned to Algiers and taught for two years in a private school in Oran, on the seacoast. In 1942 he returned to Paris and engaged actively in the Resistance movement by writing for the underground press. He continued his residence in Paris after World War II.

Daru now heated only the single room that was his lodging, adjoining the classroom and giving also onto the plateau to the east. Like the class windows, his window looked to the south too. On that side the school was a few kilometers from the point where the plateau began to slope toward the south. In clear weather could be seen the purple mass of the mountain range where the gap opened onto the desert.

Somewhat warmed, Daru returned to the window from which he had first seen the two men. They were no longer visible. Hence they must have tackled the rise. The sky was not so dark, for the snow had stopped falling during the night. The morning had opened with a dirty light which had scarcely become brighter as the ceiling of clouds lifted. At two in the afternoon it seemed as if the day were merely beginning. But still this was better than those three days when the thick snow was falling amidst unbroken darkness with little gusts of wind that rattled the double door of the classroom. Then Daru had spent long hours in his room, leaving it only to go to the shed and feed the chickens or get some coal. Fortunately the delivery truck from Tadjid, the nearest village to the north, had brought his supplies two days before the blizzard. It would return in forty-eight hours.

Besides, he had enough to resist a siege, for the little room was cluttered with bags of wheat that the administration left as a stock to distribute to those of his pupils whose families had suffered from the drought. Actually they had all been victims because they were all poor. Every day Daru would distribute a ration to the children. They had missed it, he knew, during these bad days. Possibly one of the fathers or big brothers would come this afternoon and he could supply them with grain. It was just a matter of carrying them over to the next harvest. Now shiploads of wheat were arriving from France and the worst was over. But it would be hard to forget that poverty, that army of ragged ghosts wandering in the sunlight, the plateaus burned to a cinder month after month, the earth shriveled up little by little, literally scorched, every stone bursting into dust under one's foot. The sheep had died then by thousands and even a few men, here and there, sometimes without anyone's knowing.

In contrast with such poverty, he who lived almost like a monk in his 5 remote schoolhouse, nonetheless satisfied with the little he had and with the rough life, had felt like a lord with his whitewashed walls, his narrow couch, his unpainted shelves, his well, and his weekly provision of water and food. And suddenly this snow, without warning, without the foretaste of rain. This is the way the region was, cruel to live in, even without men— who didn't help matters either. But Daru had been born here. Everywhere else, he felt exiled.

He stepped out onto the terrace in front of the schoolhouse. The two men were now halfway up the slope. He recognized the horseman as

Balducci, the old gendarme he had known for a long time. Balducci was holding on the end of a rope an Arab who was walking behind him with hands bound and head lowered. The gendarme waved a greeting to which Daru did not reply, lost as he was in contemplation of the Arab dressed in a faded blue jellaba, his feet in sandals but covered with socks of heavy raw wool, his head surmounted by a narrow, short *chèche*. They were approaching. Balducci was holding back his horse in order not to hurt the Arab, and the group was advancing slowly.

Within earshot, Balducci shouted: "One hour to do the three kilometers from El Ameur!" Daru did not answer. Short and square in his thick sweater, he watched them climb. Not once had the Arab raised his head. "Hello," said Daru when they got up onto the terrace. "Come in and warm up." Balducci painfully got down from his horse without letting go the rope. From under his bristling mustache he smiled at the schoolmaster. His little dark eyes, deep-set under a tanned forehead, and his mouth surrounded with wrinkles made him look attentive and studious. Daru took the bridle, led the horse to the shed, and came back to the two men, who were now waiting for him in the school. He led them into his room. "I am going to heat up the classroom," he said. "We'll be more comfortable there." When he entered the room again, Balducci was on the couch. He had undone the rope tying him to the Arab, who had squatted near the stove. His hands still bound, the *chèche* pushed back on his head, he was looking toward the window. At first Daru noticed only his huge lips, fat, smooth, almost Negroid; yet his nose was straight, his eyes were dark and full of fever. The *chèche* revealed an obstinate forehead and, under the weathered skin now rather discolored by the cold, the whole face had a restless and rebellious look that struck Daru when the Arab, turning his face toward him, looked him straight in the eyes. "Go into the other room," said the schoolmaster, "and I'll make you some mint tea." "Thanks," Balducci said. "What a chore! How I long for retirement." And addressing his prisoner in Arabic: "Come on, you." The Arab got up and, slowly, holding his bound wrists in front of him, went into the classroom.

With the tea, Daru brought a chair. But Balducci was already enthroned on the nearest pupil's desk and the Arab had squatted against the teacher's platform facing the stove, which stood between the desk and the window. When he held out the glass of tea to the prisoner, Daru hesitated at the sight of his bound hands. "He might perhaps be untied." "Sure," said Balducci. "That was for the trip." He started to get to his feet. But Daru, setting the glass on the floor, had knelt beside the Arab. Without saying anything, the Arab watched him with his feverish eyes. Once his hands were free, he rubbed his swollen wrists against each other, took the glass of tea, and sucked up the burning liquid in swift little sips.

"Good," said Daru. "And where are you headed?"

Balducci withdrew his mustache from the tea. "Here, son." 10

"Odd pupils! And you're spending the night?"

"No. I'm going back to El Ameur. And you will deliver this fellow to Tinguit. He is expected at police headquarters."

Balducci was looking at Daru with a friendly little smile.

"What's this story?" asked the schoolmaster. "Are you pulling my leg?"

"No, son. Those are the orders." 15

"The orders? I'm not . . ." Daru hesitated, not wanting to hurt the old Corsican. "I mean, that's not my job."

"What! What's the meaning of that? In wartime people do all kinds of jobs."

"Then I'll wait for the declaration of war!"

Balducci nodded.

"O.K. But the orders exist and they concern you too. Things are brewing, 20 it appears. There is talk of a forthcoming revolt. We are mobilized, in a way."

Daru still had his obstinate look.

"Listen, son," Balducci said. "I like you and you must understand. There's only a dozen of us at El Ameur to patrol throughout the whole territory of a small department and I must get back in a hurry. I was told to hand this guy over to you and return without delay. He couldn't be kept there. His village was beginning to stir; they wanted to take him back. You must take him to Tinguit tomorrow before the day is over. Twenty kilometers shouldn't faze a husky fellow like you. After that, all will be over. You'll come back to your pupils and your comfortable life."

Behind the wall the horse could be heard snorting and pawing the earth. Daru was looking out the window. Decidedly, the weather was clearing and the light was increasing over the snowy plateau. When all the snow was melted, the sun would take over again and once more would burn the fields of stone. For days, still, the unchanging sky would shed its dry light on the solitary expanse where nothing had any connection with man.

"After all," he said, turning around toward Balducci, "what did he do?" And, before the gendarme had opened his mouth, he asked: "Does he speak French?"

"No, not a word. We had been looking for him for a month, but they 25 were hiding him. He killed his cousin."

"Is he against us?"

"I don't think so. But you can never be sure."

"Why did he kill?"

"A family squabble, I think. One owed the other grain, it seems. It's not at all clear. In short, he killed his cousin with a billhook. You know, like a sheep, *kreezk*!"

30   Balducci made the gesture of drawing a blade across his throat and the Arab, his attention attracted, watched him with a sort of anxiety. Daru felt a sudden wrath against the man, against all men with their rotten spite, their tireless hates, their blood lust.

But the kettle was singing on the stove. He served Balducci more tea, hesitated, then served the Arab again, who, a second time, drank avidly. His raised arms made the jellaba fall open and the schoolmaster saw his thin, muscular chest.

"Thanks, kid," Balducci said. "And now, I'm off."

He got up and went toward the Arab, taking a small rope from his pocket.

"What are you doing?" Daru asked dryly.

35   Balducci, disconcerted, showed him the rope.

"Don't bother."

The old gendarme hesitated. "It's up to you. Of course, you are armed?"

"I have my shotgun."

"Where?"

40   "In the trunk."

"You ought to have it near your bed."

"Why? I have nothing to fear."

"You're crazy, son. If there's an uprising, no one is safe, we're all in the same boat."

"I'll defend myself. I'll have time to see them coming."

45   Balducci began to laugh, then suddenly the mustache covered the white teeth.

"You'll have time? O.K. That's just what I was saying. You have always been a little cracked. That's why I like you, my son was like that."

At the same time he took out his revolver and put it on the desk.

"Keep it; I don't need two weapons from here to El Ameur."

The revolver shone against the black paint of the table. When the gendarme turned toward him, the schoolmaster caught the smell of leather and horseflesh.

50   "Listen, Balducci," Daru said suddenly, "every bit of this disgusts me, and first of all your fellow here. But I won't hand him over. Fight, yes, if I have to. But not that."

The old gendarme stood in front of him and looked at him severely.

"You're being a fool," he said slowly. "I don't like it either. You don't get used to putting a rope on a man even after years of it, and you're even ashamed—yes, ashamed. But you can't let them have their way."

"I won't hand him over," Daru said again.

"It's an order, son, and I repeat it."

55   "That's right. Repeat to them what I've said to you: I won't hand him over."

Balducci made a visible effort to reflect. He looked at the Arab and at Daru. At last he decided.

"No, I won't tell them anything. If you want to drop us, go ahead; I'll not denounce you. I have an order to deliver the prisoner and I'm doing so. And now you'll just sign this paper for me."

"There's no need. I'll not deny that you left him with me."

"Don't be mean with me. I know you'll tell the truth. You're from hereabouts and you are a man. But you must sign, that's the rule."

Daru opened his drawer, took out a little square bottle of purple ink, the red wooden penholder with the "sergeant-major" pen he used for making models of penmanship, and signed. The gendarme carefully folded the paper and put it into his wallet. Then he moved toward the door.

"I'll see you off," Daru said.

"No," said Balducci. "There's no use being polite. You insulted me."

He looked at the Arab, motionless in the same spot, sniffed peevishly, and turned away toward the door. "Good-by, son," he said. The door shut behind him. Balducci appeared suddenly outside the window and then disappeared. His footsteps were muffled by the snow. The horse stirred on the other side of the wall and several chickens fluttered in fright. A moment later Balducci reappeared outside the window leading the horse by the bridle. He walked toward the little rise without turning around and disappeared from sight with the horse following him. A big stone could be heard bouncing down. Daru walked back toward the prisoner, who, without stirring, never took his eyes off him. "Wait," the schoolmaster said in Arabic and went toward the bedroom. As he was going through the door, he had a second thought, went to the desk, took the revolver, and stuck it in his pocket. Then, without looking back, he went into his room.

For some time he lay on his couch watching the sky gradually close over, listening to the silence. It was this silence that had seemed painful to him during the first days here, after the war. He had requested a post in the little town at the base of the foothills separating the upper plateaus from the desert. There, rocky walls, green and black to the north, pink and lavender to the south, marked the frontier of eternal summer. He had been named to a post farther north, on the plateau itself. In the beginning, the solitude and the silence had been hard for him on these wastelands peopled only by stones. Occasionally, furrows suggested cultivation, but they had been dug to uncover a certain kind of stone good for building. The only plowing here was to harvest rocks. Elsewhere a thin layer of soil accumulated in the hollows would be scraped out to enrich paltry village gardens. This is the way it was: bare rock covered three quarters of the region. Towns sprang up, flourished, then disappeared; men came by, loved

60

one another or fought bitterly, then died. No one in this desert, neither he nor his guest, mattered. And yet, outside this desert neither of them, Daru knew, could have really lived.

65   When he got up, no noise came from the classroom. He was amazed at the unmixed joy he derived from the mere thought that the Arab might have fled and that he would be alone with no decision to make. But the prisoner was there. He had merely stretched out between the stove and the desk. With eyes open, he was staring at the ceiling. In that position, his thick lips were particularly noticeable, giving him a pouting look. "Come," said Daru. The Arab got up and followed him. In the bedroom, the school-master pointed to a chair near the table under the window. The Arab sat down without taking his eyes off Daru.

"Are you hungry?"

"Yes," the prisoner said.

Daru set the table for two. He took flour and oil, shaped a cake in a frying-pan, and lighted the little stove that functioned on bottled gas. While the cake was cooking, he went out to the shed to get cheese, eggs, dates, and condensed milk. When the cake was done he set it on the win-dow sill to cool, heated some condensed milk diluted with water, and beat up the eggs into an omelette. In one of his motions he knocked against the revolver stuck in his right pocket. He set the bowl down, went into the classroom, and put the revolver in his desk drawer. When he came back to the room, night was falling. He put on the light and served the Arab. "Eat," he said. The Arab took a piece of the cake, lifted it eagerly to his mouth, and stopped short.

70   "And you?" he asked.

"After you. I'll eat too."

The thick lips opened slightly. The Arab hesitated, then bit into the cake determinedly.

The meal over, the Arab looked at the schoolmaster. "Are you the judge?"

"No, I'm simply keeping you until tomorrow."

"Why do you eat with me?"

75   "I'm hungry."

The Arab fell silent. Daru got up and went out. He brought back a folding bed from the shed, set it up between the table and the stove, perpendicular to his own bed. From a large suitcase which, upright in a corner, served as a shelf for papers, he took two blankets and arranged them on the camp bed. Then he stopped, felt useless, and sat down on his bed. There was nothing more to do or to get ready. He had to look at this man. He looked at him, therefore, trying to imagine his face bursting with rage. He couldn't do so. He could see nothing but the dark yet shining eyes and the animal mouth.

"Why did you kill him?" he asked in a voice whose hostile tone surprised him.

The Arab looked away.

"He ran away. I ran after him."

He raised his eyes to Daru again and they were full of a sort of woeful 80
interrogation. "Now what will they do to me?"

"Are you afraid?"

He stiffened, turning his eyes away.

"Are you sorry?"

The Arab stared at him openmouthed. Obviously he did not understand. Daru's annoyance was growing. At the same time he felt awkward and self-conscious with his big body wedged between the two beds.

"Lie down there," he said impatiently. "That's your bed." 85

The Arab didn't move. He called to Daru:

"Tell me!"

The schoolmaster looked at him.

"Is the gendarme coming back tomorrow?"

"I don't know." 90

"Are you coming with us?"

"I don't know. Why?"

The prisoner got up and stretched out on top of the blankets, his feet toward the window. The light from the electric bulb shone straight into his eyes and he closed them at once.

"Why?" Daru repeated, standing beside the bed.

The Arab opened his eyes under the blinding light and looked at him, 95
trying not to blink.

"Come with us," he said.

In the middle of the night, Daru was still not asleep. He had gone to bed after undressing completely; he generally slept naked. But when he suddenly realized that he had nothing on, he hesitated. He felt vulnerable and the temptation came to him to put his clothes back on. Then he shrugged his shoulders; after all, he wasn't a child and, if need be, he could break his adversary in two. From his bed he could observe him, lying on his back, still motionless with his eyes closed under the harsh light. When Daru turned out the light, the darkness seemed to coagulate all of a sudden. Little by little, the night came back to life in the window where the starless sky was stirring gently. The schoolmaster soon made out the body lying at his feet. The Arab still did not move, but his eyes seemed open. A faint wind was prowling around the schoolhouse. Perhaps it would drive away the clouds and the sun would reappear.

During the night the wind increased. The hens fluttered a little and then were silent. The Arab turned over on his side with his back to Daru, who thought he heard him moan. Then he listened for his guest's breathing, become heavier and more regular. He listened to that breath so close to him and mused without being able to go to sleep. In this room where he had been sleeping alone for a year, this presence bothered him. But it bothered him also by imposing on him a sort of brotherhood he knew well but refused to accept in the present circumstances. Men who share the same rooms, soldiers or prisoners, develop a strange alliance as if, having cast off their armor with their clothing, they fraternized every evening, over and above their differences, in the ancient community of dream and fatigue. But Daru shook himself; he didn't like such musings, and it was essential to sleep.

A little later, however, when the Arab stirred slightly, the schoolmaster was still not asleep. When the prisoner made a second move, he stiffened, on the alert. The Arab was lifting himself slowly on his arms with almost the motion of a sleepwalker. Seated upright in bed, he waited motionless without turning his head toward Daru, as if he were listening attentively. Daru did not stir; it had just occurred to him that the revolver was still in the drawer of his desk. It was better to act at once. Yet he continued to observe the prisoner, who, with the same slithery motion, put his feet on the ground, waited again, then began to stand up slowly. Daru was about to call out to him when the Arab began to walk, in a quite natural but extraordinarily silent way. He was heading toward the door at the end of the room that opened into the shed. He lifted the latch with precaution and went out, pushing the door behind him but without shutting it. Daru had not stirred. "He is running away," he merely thought. "Good riddance!" Yet he listened attentively. The hens were not fluttering; the guest must be on the plateau. A faint sound of water reached him, and he didn't know what it was until the Arab again stood framed in the doorway, closed the door carefully, and came back to bed without a sound. Then Daru turned his back on him and fell asleep. Still later he seemed, from the depths of his sleep, to hear furtive steps around the schoolhouse. "I'm dreaming! I'm dreaming!" he repeated to himself. And he went on sleeping.

100   When he awoke, the sky was clear; the loose window let in a cold, pure air. The Arab was asleep, hunched up under the blankets now, his mouth open, utterly relaxed. But when Daru shook him, he started dreadfully, staring at Daru with wild eyes as if he had never seen him and such a frightened expression that the schoolmaster stepped back. "Don't be afraid. It's me. You must eat." The Arab nodded his head and said yes. Calm had returned to his face, but his expression was vacant and listless.

The coffee was ready. They drank it seated together on the folding bed as they munched their pieces of the cake. Then Daru led the Arab under the shed and showed him the faucet where he washed. He went back into the room, folded the blankets and the bed, made his own bed and put the

room in order. Then he went through the classroom and out onto the terrace. The sun was already rising in the blue sky; a soft, bright light was
bathing the deserted plateau. On the ridge the snow was melting in spots.
The stones were about to reappear. Crouched on the edge of the plateau,
the schoolmaster looked at the deserted expanse. He thought of Balducci.
He had hurt him, for he had sent him off in a way as if he didn't want to
be associated with him. He could still hear the gendarme's farewell and,
without knowing why, he felt strangely empty and vulnerable. At that
moment, from the other side of the schoolhouse, the prisoner coughed.
Daru listened to him almost despite himself and then, furious, threw a
pebble that whistled through the air before sinking into the snow. That
man's stupid crime revolted him, but to hand him over was contrary to
honor. Merely thinking of it made him smart with humiliation. And he
cursed at one and the same time his own people who had sent him this
Arab and the Arab too who had dared to kill and not managed to get away.
Daru got up, walked in a circle on the terrace, waited motionless, and then
went back into the schoolhouse.

The Arab, leaning over the cement floor of the shed, was washing his
teeth with two fingers. Daru looked at him and said: "Come." He went
back into the room ahead of the prisoner. He slipped a hunting-jacket on
over his sweater and put on walking-shoes. Standing, he waited until the
Arab had put on his *chèche* and sandals. They went into the classroom and
the schoolmaster pointed to the exit, saying: "Go ahead." The fellow didn't
budge. "I'm coming," said Daru. The Arab went out. Daru went back
into the room and made a package of pieces of rusk, dates, and sugar. In
the classroom, before going out, he hesitated a second in front of his desk,
then crossed the threshold and locked the door. "That's the way," he said.
He started toward the east, followed by the prisoner. But, a short distance
from the schoolhouse, he thought he heard a slight sound behind them.
He retraced his steps and examined the surroundings of the house; there
was no one there. The Arab watched him without seeming to understand.
"Come on," said Daru.

They walked for an hour and rested beside a sharp peak of limestone.
The snow was melting faster and faster and the sun was drinking up the
puddles at once, rapidly cleaning the plateau, which gradually dried and
vibrated like the air itself. When they resumed walking, the ground rang
under their feet. From time to time a bird rent the space in front of them
with a joyful cry. Daru breathed in deeply the fresh morning light. He
felt a sort of rapture before the vast familiar expanse, now almost entirely
yellow under its dome of blue sky. They walked an hour more, descending
toward the south. They reached a level height made up of crumbly rocks.
From there on, the plateau sloped down, eastward, toward a low plain

where there were a few spindly trees and, to the south, toward outcroppings of rock that gave the landscape a chaotic look.

Daru surveyed the two directions. There was nothing but the sky on the horizon. Not a man could be seen. He turned toward the Arab, who was looking at him blankly. Daru held out the package to him. "Take it," he said. "There are dates, bread, and sugar. You can hold out for two days. Here are a thousand francs too." The Arab took the package and the money but kept his full hands at chest level as if he didn't know what to do with what was being given him. "Now look," the schoolmaster said as he pointed in the direction of the east, "there's the way to Tinguit. You have a two-hour walk. At Tinguit you'll find the administration and the police. They are expecting you." The Arab looked toward the east, still holding the package and the money against his chest. Daru took his elbow and turned him rather roughly toward the south. At the foot of the height on which they stood could be seen a faint path. "That's the trail across the plateau. In a day's walk from here you'll find pasturelands and the first nomads. They'll take you in and shelter you according to their law." The Arab had now turned toward Daru and a sort of panic was visible in his expression. "Listen," he said. Daru shook his head: "No, be quiet. Now I'm leaving you." He turned his back on him, took two long steps in the direction of the school, looked hesitantly at the motionless Arab, and started off again. For a few minutes he heard nothing but his own step resounding on the cold ground and did not turn his head. A moment later, however, he turned around. The Arab was still there on the edge of the hill, his arms hanging now, and he was looking at the schoolmaster. Daru felt something rise in his throat. But he swore with impatience, waved vaguely, and started off again. He had already gone some distance when he again stopped and looked. There was no longer anyone on the hill.

105   Daru hesitated. The sun was now rather high in the sky and was beginning to beat down on his head. The schoolmaster retraced his steps, at first somewhat uncertainly, then with decision. When he reached the little hill, he was bathed in sweat. He climbed it as fast as he could and stopped, out of breath, at the top. The rock-fields to the south stood out sharply against the blue sky, but on the plain to the east a steamy heat was already rising. And in that slight haze, Daru, with heavy heart, made out the Arab walking slowly on the road to prison.

A little later, standing before the window of the classroom, the schoolmaster was watching the clear light bathing the whole surface of the plateau, but he hardly saw it. Behind him on the blackboard, among the winding French rivers, sprawled the clumsily chalked-up words he had just read: "You handed over our brother. You will pay for this." Daru looked at the sky, the plateau, and, beyond, the invisible lands stretching all the way to the sea. In this vast landscape he had loved so much, he was alone.

QUESTIONS

1. What is the central conflict of the story? Is it external or internal? Can it be defined in terms of dilemma?
2. Compare and contrast the attitudes of Daru and Balducci toward the prisoner and the situation. What is their attitude toward each other? Is either a bad or a cruel man? How does the conflict between Daru and Balducci intensify the central conflict?
3. Why does Daru give the prisoner his freedom? What reasons are there for not giving him his freedom?
4. In what respect is the title ironic? Why does "The Guest" make a better title than "The Prisoner"? And why does the French title "L'Hôte" (which can mean either "The Guest" or "The Host") make an even better title than its English translation?
5. This story contains the materials of explosive action—a revolver, a murderer, a state of undeclared war, an incipient uprising, a revenge note—but no violence occurs in the story. In what aspect of the situation is Camus principally interested?
6. This story has as its background a specific political situation—the French Algerian crisis in the years following World War II. How does Daru reflect France's plight? Is the story's meaning limited to this situation? What does the story tell us about good and evil and the nature of moral choice? How does the story differ in its treatment of these things from the typical Western story or the patriotic editorial?
7. In what respect is the ending of the story ironic? What kind of irony is this? What does it contribute to the meaning of the story?
8. Besides the ironies of the title and the ending, there are other ironies in the story. Find and explain them. Daru uses verbal irony in paragraph 11 when he exclaims, "Odd pupils!" Is verbal irony the same thing as sarcasm?
9. Comment on the following: (a) Daru's behavior toward firearms and how it helps reveal him; (b) Camus's reason for making the Arab a murderer; (c) the Arab's reason for taking the road to prison.

JOHN UPDIKE

A & P

In walks these three girls in nothing but bathing suits. I'm in the third check-out slot, with my back to the door, so I don't see them until they're over by the bread. The one that caught my eye first was the one in the plaid green two-piece. She was a chunky kid, with a good tan and a sweet broad soft-looking can with those two crescents of white just under it, where the

A & P   First published in 1960. John Updike (1932–2009) was one of America's most celebrated contemporary writers and a highly prolific, equally adept practitioner in many genres: the novel, the short story, poetry, and criticism. Born in Shillington, Pennsylvania, he attended Harvard University and shortly after his graduation began publishing short stories in *The New Yorker*, the magazine with which his work is strongly identified. In his most characteristic fiction, he portrays the anxieties of middle-class life in a style of luminous clarity and realism.

sun never seems to hit, at the top of the backs of her legs. I stood there with my hand on a box of HiHo crackers trying to remember if I rang it up or not. I ring it up again and the customer starts giving me hell. She's one of these cash register-watchers, a witch about fifty with rouge on her cheekbones and no eyebrows, and I know it made her day to trip me up. She'd been watching cash registers for fifty years and probably never seen a mistake before.

By the time I got her feathers smoothed and her goodies into a bag— she gives me a little snort in passing, if she'd been born at the right time they would have burned her over in Salem—by the time I get her on her way the girls had circled around the bread and were coming back, without a push-cart, back my way along the counters, in the aisle between the check-outs and the Special bins. They didn't even have shoes on. There was this chunky one, with the two-piece—it was bright green and the seams on the bra were still sharp and her belly was still pretty pale so I guessed she just got it (the suit)—there was this one, with one of those chubby berry-faces, the lips all bunched together under her nose, this one, and a tall one, with black hair that hadn't quite frizzed right, and one of these sunburns right across under the eyes, and a chin that was too long—you know, the kind of girl other girls think is very "striking" and "attractive" but never quite makes it, as they very well know, which is why they like her so much—and then the third one, that wasn't quite so tall. She was the queen. She kind of led them, the other two peeking around and making their shoulders round. She didn't look around, not this queen, she just walked straight on slowly, on these long white primadonna legs. She came down a little hard on her heels, as if she didn't walk in her bare feet that much, putting down her heels and then letting the weight move along to her toes as if she was test-ing the floor with every step, putting a little deliberate extra action into it. You never know for sure how girls' minds work (do you really think it's a mind in there or just a little buzz like a bee in a glass jar?) but you got the idea she had talked the other two into coming in here with her, and now she was showing them how to do it, walk slow and hold yourself straight.

She had on a kind of dirty-pink—beige maybe, I don't know—bathing suit with a little nubble all over it and, what got me, the straps were down. They were off her shoulders looped loose around the cool tops of her arms, and I guess as a result the suit had slipped a little on her, so all around the top of the cloth there was this shining rim. If it hadn't been there you wouldn't have known there could have been anything whiter than those shoulders. With the straps pushed off, there was nothing between the top of the suit and the top of her head except just *her*, this clean bare plane of the top of her chest down from the shoulder bones like a dented sheet of metal tilted in the light. I mean, it was more than pretty.

She had sort of oaky hair that the sun and salt had bleached, done up in a bun that was unraveling, and a kind of prim face. Walking into the A & P with your straps down, I suppose it's the only kind of face you *can* have. She held her head so high her neck, coming up out of those white shoulders, looked kind of stretched, but I didn't mind. The longer her neck was, the more of her there was.

She must have felt in the corner of her eye me and over my shoulder   5 Stokesie in the second slot watching, but she didn't tip. Not this queen. She kept her eyes moving across the racks, and stopped, and turned so slow it made my stomach rub the inside of my apron, and buzzed to the other two, who kind of huddled against her for relief, and they all three of them went up the cat-and-dog-food-breakfast-cereal macaroni-rice-raisins-seasonings-spreads-spaghetti-soft-drinks-crackers-and-cookies aisle. From the third slot I look straight up this aisle to the meat counter, and I watched them all the way. The fat one with the tan sort of fumbled with the cookies, but on second thought she put the packages back. The sheep pushing their carts down the aisle—the girls were walking against the usual traffic (not that we have one-way signs or anything)—were pretty hilarious. You could see them, when Queenie's white shoulders dawned on them, kind of jerk, or hop, or hiccup, but their eyes snapped back to their own baskets and on they pushed. I bet you could set off dynamite in an A&P and the people would by and large keep reaching and checking oatmeal off their lists and muttering "Let me see, there was a third thing, began with A, asparagus, no, ah, yes, applesauce!" or whatever it is they do mutter. But there was no doubt, this jiggled them. A few houseslaves in pin curlers even looked around after pushing their carts to make sure what they had seen was correct.

You know, it's one thing to have a girl in a bathing suit down on the beach, where what with the glare nobody can look at each other much any-way, and another thing in the cool of the A&P, under the fluorescent lights, against all those stacked packages, with her feet paddling along naked over our checkerboard green-and-cream rubber-tile floor.

"Oh Daddy," Stokesie said beside me. "I feel so faint."

"Darling," I said. "Hold me tight." Stokesie's married, with two babies chalked up on his fuselage already, but as far as I can tell that's the only difference. He's twenty-two, and I was nineteen this April.

"Is it done?" he asks, the responsible married man finding his voice. I forgot to say he thinks he's going to be manager some sunny day, maybe in 1990 when it's called the Great Alexandrov and Petrooshki Tea Company or something.

What he meant was, our town is five miles from a beach, with a big   10 summer colony out on the Point, but we're right in the middle of town, and the women generally put on a shirt or shorts or something before they get out of the car into the street. And anyway these are usually women with six children and varicose veins mapping their legs and nobody, including them, could care less. As I say, we're right in the middle of town, and if you stand at our front doors you can see two banks and the Congregational church and the newspaper store and three real-estate offices and about twenty-seven old freeloaders tearing up Central Street because the sewer broke again. It's not as if we're on the Cape; we're north of Boston and there's people in this town haven't seen the ocean for twenty years.

The girls had reached the meat counter and were asking McMahon something. He pointed, they pointed, and they shuffled out of sight behind a pyramid of Diet Delight peaches. All that was left for us to see was old McMahon patting his mouth and looking after them sizing up their joints. Poor kids, I began to feel sorry for them, they couldn't help it.

Now here comes the sad part of the story, at least my family says it's sad but I don't think it's sad myself. The store's pretty empty, it being Thursday afternoon, so there was nothing much to do except lean on the register and wait for the girls to show up again. The whole store was like a pinball machine and I didn't know which tunnel they'd come out of. After a while they come around out of the far aisle, around the light bulbs, records at discount of the Caribbean Six or Tony Martin Sings or some such gunk you wonder they waste the wax on, sixpacks of candy bars, and plastic toys done up in cellophane that fall apart when a kid looks at them anyway. Around they come, Queenie still leading the way, and holding a little gray jar in her hand. Slots Three through Seven are unmanned and I could see her wondering between Stokes and me, but Stokesie with his usual luck draws an old party in baggy gray pants who stumbles up with four giant cans of pineapple juice (what do these bums *do* with all that pineapple juice? I've often asked myself) so the girls come to me. Queenie puts down the jar and I take it into my fingers icy cold. Kingfish Fancy Herring Snacks in Pure Sour Cream: 49¢. Now her hands are empty, not a ring or a bracelet, bare as God made them, and I wonder where the money's coming from. Still with that prim look she lifts a folded dollar bill out of the hollow at the center of her nubbled pink top. The jar went heavy in my hand. Really, I thought that was so cute.

Then, everybody's luck begins to run out. Lengel comes in from haggling with a truck full of cabbages on the lot and is about to scuttle into that door marked MANAGER behind which he hides all day when the girls touch his eye. Lengel's pretty dreary, teaches Sunday school and the rest, but he doesn't miss that much. He comes over and says, "Girls, this isn't the beach."

Queenie blushes, though maybe it's just a brush of sunburn I was noticing for the first time, now that she was so close. "My mother asked me to pick up a jar of herring snacks." Her voice kind of startled me, the way voices do when you see the people first, coming out so flat and dumb yet kind of tony, too, the way it ticked over "pick up" and "snacks." All of a sudden I slid right down her voice into her living room. Her father and the other men were standing around in ice-cream coats and bow ties and the women were in sandals picking up herring snacks on toothpicks off a big plate and they were all holding drinks the color of water with olives and sprigs of mint in them. When my parents have somebody over they get lemonade and if it's a real racy affair Schlitz in tall glasses with "They'll Do It Every Time" cartoons stencilled on.

"That's all right," Lengel said. "But this isn't the beach." His repeating 15 this struck me as funny, as if it had just occurred to him, and he had been thinking all these years the A&P was a great big dune and he was the head lifeguard. He didn't like my smiling—as I say he doesn't miss much—but he concentrates on giving the girls that sad Sunday-school-superintendent stare.

Queenie's blush is no sunburn now, and the plump one in plaid, that I liked better from the back—a really sweet can—pipes up, "We weren't doing any shopping. We just came in for the one thing."

"That makes no difference," Lengel tells her, and I could see from the way his eyes went that he hadn't noticed she was wearing a two-piece before. "We want you decently dressed when you come in here."

"We *are* decent," Queenie says suddenly, her lower lip pushing, getting sore now that she remembers her place, a place from which the crowd that runs the A&P must look pretty crummy. Fancy Herring Snacks flashed in her very blue eyes.

"Girls, I don't want to argue with you. After this come in here with your shoulders covered. It's our policy." He turns his back. That's policy for you. Policy is what the kingpins want. What the others want is juvenile delinquency.

All this while, the customers had been showing up with their carts 20 but, you know, sheep, seeing a scene, they had all bunched up on Stokesie, who shook open a paper bag as gently as peeling a peach, not wanting to miss a word. I could feel in the silence everybody getting nervous, most of all Lengel, who asks me, "Sammy, have you rung up this purchase?"

I thought and said "No" but it wasn't about that I was thinking. I go through the punches, 4, 9, GROC, TOT—it's more complicated than you think, and after you do it often enough, it begins to make a little song, that you hear words to, in my case "Hello (*bing*) there, you (*gung*) hap-py *pee*-pul (*splat*)!"—the *splat* being the drawer flying out. I uncrease the bill, tenderly as you may imagine, it just having come from between the two smoothest scoops of vanilla I had ever known were there, and pass a half and a penny into her narrow pink palm, and nestle the herrings in a bag and twist its neck and hand it over, all the time thinking.

The girls, and who'd blame them, are in a hurry to get out, so I say "I quit" to Lengel quick enough for them to hear, hoping they'll stop and watch me, their unsuspected hero. They keep right on going, into the electric eye; the door flies open and they flicker across the lot to their car, Queenie and Plaid and Big Tall Goony-Goony (not that as raw material she was so bad), leaving me with Lengel and a kink in his eyebrow.

"Did you say something, Sammy?"

"I said I quit."

25   "I thought you did."

"You didn't have to embarrass them."

"It was they who were embarrassing us."

I started to say something that came out "Fiddle-de-doo." It's a saying of my grandmother's, and I know she would have been pleased.

"I don't think you know what you're saying," Lengel said.

30   "I know you don't," I said. "But I do." I pull the bow at the back of my apron and start shrugging it off my shoulders. A couple customers that had been heading for my slot begin to knock against each other, like scared pigs in a chute.

Lengel sighs and begins to look very patient and old and gray. He's been a friend of my parents for years. "Sammy, you don't want to do this to your Mom and Dad," he tells me. It's true, I don't. But it seems to me that once you begin a gesture it's fatal not to go through with it. I fold the apron, "Sammy" stitched in red on the pocket, and put it on the counter, and drop the bow tie on top of it. The bow tie is theirs, if you've ever wondered. "You'll feel this for the rest of your life," Lengel says, and I know that's true, too, but remembering how he made that pretty girl blush makes me so scrunchy inside I punch the No Sale tab and the machine whirs "pee-pul" and the drawer splats out. One advantage to this scene taking place in summer, I can follow this up with a clean exit, there's no fumbling around getting your coat and galoshes, I just saunter into the electric eye in my white shirt that my mother ironed the night before, and the door heaves itself open, and outside the sunshine is skating around the asphalt.

I look around for my girls, but they're gone, of course. There wasn't anybody but some young married screaming with her children about some candy they didn't get by the door of a powder-blue Falcon station wagon. Looking back in the big windows, over the bags of peat moss and aluminum lawn furniture stacked on the pavement, I could see Lengel in my place in the slot, checking the sheep through. His face was dark gray and his back stiff, as if he'd just had an injection of iron, and my stomach kind of fell as I felt how hard the world was going to be to me hereafter.

QUESTIONS

1. Is Sammy a likable, sympathetic character? Why or why not?
2. Some of John Updike's work, including this story, has been criticized for its portrayals of women. Is Sammy's attitude toward the girls "sexist"? Defend your position.

3. Analyze the importance of the setting. Why is a grocery store a significant setting for this story?
4. Who is the antagonist of this story?
5. Does Sammy have an epiphany anywhere in the story? Locate this moment and discuss its significance.

SUGGESTIONS FOR WRITING

1. Write an essay exploring the use of irony in one of the following stories, or compare the use of irony in any two of the stories:
   a. Wolff, "Hunters in the Snow" (page 79).
   b. Munro, "How I Met My Husband" (page 118).
   c. Walker, "Everyday Use" (page 147).
   d. Moore, "You're Ugly, Too" (page 335).
   e. Twain, "Cannibalism in the Cars" (page 353).
   f. O'Connor, "Everything That Rises Must Converge" (page 476).
   g. Lahiri, "Interpreter of Maladies" (page 590).
   h. Melville, "Bartleby the Scrivener" (page 627).
2. Discuss the effect of humor in any of the following stories. Apart from its entertainment value, how does the humor contribute to the theme and significance of the story?
   a. Wolff, "Hunters in the Snow" (page 79).
   b. Walker, "Everyday Use" (page 147).
   c. Moore, "You're Ugly, Too" (page 335).
   d. O'Connor, "A Good Man Is Hard to Find" (page 445).
   e. Hurston, "Spunk" (page 564).
   f. Melville, "Bartleby the Scrivener" (page 627).

PRACTICE AP WRITING PROMPTS ▬▬▬▬▬

Albert Camus, "The Guest" (pp. 360)

40-minute prompt: Carefully read "The Guest" from paragraph 65 (p. 366) through paragraph 96 (p. 367). Then write an essay in which you analyze how Camus uses such elements as diction, point of view, and selection of detail to convey Daru's complex attitude toward the Arab.

....

John Updike, "A&P" (pp. 371–376)

Read the first two paragraphs of "A&P" by John Updike. Then provide as full an account as you can of the first-person narrator's character and personality. Consider the way Updike characterizes the narrator through his tone of voice and word choices as well as through the details the narrator notices.

....

CHAPTER EIGHT

Evaluating Fiction

Our purpose in the preceding chapters has been to develop not literary critics but proficient readers—readers who choose wisely and read well. Yet good reading involves the ability to evaluate what we read, and making wise choices necessitates sound judgment. This does not mean that in order to read well we must decide whether Welty's "A Worn Path" or Lawrence's "The Rocking-Horse Winner" is the "better" story, or whether Willa Cather is a "better" writer than Katherine Anne Porter. Any such judgments would be unpredictable, since in both these pairings equally intelligent readers might choose one or the other based on personal tastes and preferences. We do need, however, to be able to discriminate between the genuine and the spurious, the consequential and the trivial, the significant and the merely entertaining. Where such distinct categories are the issue, good readers will almost always reach the same conclusions.

There are no simple rules for literary judgment. Such judgment depends ultimately on our sensitivity, intelligence, and experience; it is a product of how much and how alertly we have lived and how much and how well we have read. Yet there are at least two basic principles that may serve to help you form your own evaluations. First, *every story should be judged initially by how fully it achieves its central purpose.* In a first-rate story, every element works with every other element to accomplish the central purpose as economically and powerfully as possible. For this reason, no single element in a story should be judged in isolation.

In fact, isolating a single element for evaluation without considering the other fictional elements in a story can lead to a flawed evaluation. It would be a mistake, for instance, to criticize "The Guest" for not revealing what ultimately happens to Daru, since the theme of the story involves the unpredictability of the consequences of human choices in unfriendly conditions. We cannot say that "Miss Brill" and "Araby" are poor stories because they do not have exciting plots full of action and conflict: the effectiveness of a story's plot can be judged only in relation to the other elements in a story and to its central purpose. In "Miss Brill" and "Araby," of course, the relatively plotless quality of the narratives reflects the uneventful nature of the two characters' lives.

Every first-rate story is an organic whole. All its parts should be related and all should be essential to the central purpose. We might ask, for example, whether the plot and characterizations of "The Most Dangerous Game" help to elucidate an important theme. Near the beginning of the story, there *is* a suggestion of theme. When Whitney declares that hunting is a great sport—for the hunter, not for the jaguar—Rainsford replies, "Who cares how a jaguar feels? . . . They've no understanding." To this, Whitney counters: "I rather think they understand one thing—fear. The fear of pain and the fear of death." Evidently Rainsford has something to learn about how it feels to be hunted, and presumably during the hunt he learns it, for when General Zaroff turns back the first time—playing cat and mouse—we are told, "Then it was that Rainsford knew the full meaning of terror." Later, on the morning of the third day, Rainsford awakens to the baying of hounds—"a sound that made him know that he had new things to learn about fear." But little is made of Rainsford's terror during the hunt. The story focuses instead on Malay man-catchers, Burmese tiger pits, Ugandan knife-throwers—in short, on the colorful and entertaining action. The story ends with the physical triumph of Rainsford over Zaroff, but has Rainsford been altered by the experience? Has he learned anything significant? Has he changed his attitudes toward hunting? We cannot answer, for the author's major purpose has been not to develop these themes but to entertain the reader. There is no clear thematic connection between the final sentence—"He had never slept in a better bed, Rainsford decided"—and the question "Who cares how a jaguar feels?" Rather, the ending merely provokes a smile from the reader at Rainsford's victory and at the cleverness of the author's concluding flourish; it does not, however, encourage the reader to think further about the story as an artistic statement of any real import.

By contrast, Wolff's "Hunters in the Snow" is a far more thematically unified story. Throughout a varied group of scenes, the story develops the idea that human beings, like animals in the wild, engage constantly in a struggle for power. Tub is overweight and the most sympathetic of the three major characters, and both Frank and Kenny treat him cruelly at several key points. Once Kenny is wounded, however, and thereby becomes the "weakest" of the characters, Frank and Tub form a new alliance and Kenny becomes the odd man out. Ultimately the story makes clear that the more powerful individual in any relationship will behave in a cruel and callous way toward the weaker individual. The reader finishes this masterful story thinking not about the bleak setting or the hunting trip it depicts but about the dark complexity of human relationships.

Once you have judged a story as successful in achieving its central purpose, you may consider a second principle of judgment: *a story should also be judged by the significance of its purpose.* Once you determine that a story successfully integrates its materials into an organic unity, you should then evaluate the depth, the range, and the significance of what the story has achieved. This principle returns us to our distinction between commercial and literary fiction. If a story's chief aim is to entertain, we may judge it to have less stature and significance than a story whose aim is to reveal important truths of human experience. "The Most Dangerous Game" and "Hunters in the Snow," it could be argued, are equally successful in achieving their central purposes. But Wolff's story is far more ambitious and significant than Connell's. A critical consensus has developed that "Hunters in the Snow" is a contemporary masterpiece of short fiction, while Connell's story is less highly regarded. Using other stories from the preceding chapters, we might also argue that "Once upon a Time" has a more ambitious, significant purpose than "Cannibalism in the Cars," and that "Young Goodman Brown" has a more ambitious, significant purpose than "Miss Brill." This is not to disparage either "Cannibalism in the Cars," or "Miss Brill," both of which are excellent stories, but to suggest that certain stories stake out larger thematic terrain and plumb the depths of human experience more profoundly than others.

A related evaluative principle is simply one of length. Most fiction takes the form of novels, not short stories, and while all the aspects of fiction we have discussed are represented in both longer and shorter forms, there is no doubt that a novel has the room to explore more varieties of human experience than does the short story, and that it has the leisure to explore them in greater depth. Obviously, then, Hawthorne's *The Scarlet Letter* is a greater work than his short story "Young Goodman Brown," simply by virtue of its greater length and therefore its greater richness of characterization, plot, and language. It should be stressed, however, that length alone is not a significant criterion in evaluating a work of fiction. The very brief "Araby" is a more significant literary work, of course, than any 500-page romance or horror novel found on a best-seller list. But a serious literary author practicing the long form of the novel inevitably has greater opportunities for developing varieties of characters, exploring multiple themes, and providing richer and fuller artistic visions than the short story affords.

Again, as we stressed in discussing literary versus commercial fiction, we cannot evaluate stories by placing them into artificial categories; the evaluation of individual stories and novels is an ongoing process, and even the most informed evaluations do not remain fixed in time. For instance, the finest work of Herman Melville, author of *Moby-Dick* and "Bartleby the Scrivener," received scathing critical assessments and was virtually forgotten at the time of his death; yet today he is considered one of the most significant fiction writers of his era. Conversely, a short story called "Circumstance," published by Harriet Prescott Spofford in 1860, was one of the most famous stories of the nineteenth century, highly praised by such discriminating readers as Emily Dickinson and Henry James; but today the story is seldom read except by scholars and historians. When we evaluate a work of fiction, therefore, we must be aware that we are judging it according to the aesthetic criteria of our own time and that such criteria evolve and change. Similarly, individual readers—including professional critics—may evaluate works differently at different points in their own lives. Some readers, for instance, might respond enthusiastically to a particular novel in their twenties, but in their fifties might reread the beloved novel and wonder why they rated it so highly. While evaluating what we read is essential to developing our skill and insight, we must also be aware that any evaluation of a given work—our own, or that of the culture at large—may well change over time.

Ultimately, however, we must rely on our own judgments, based on our accumulated experience with both literature and life.

REVIEWING CHAPTER EIGHT

1. Review the two basic principles required for evaluating fiction.
2. Describe the elements that make up a first-rate story.
3. Analyze the literary quality of Connell's "The Most Dangerous Game" vs. Wolff's "Hunters in the Snow."
4. Describe the importance of length in evaluating fiction.
5. Choose any two stories in this book and evaluate them comparatively.

EXERCISE

The two stories that follow both have surprise endings, and in both cases the ending is integral to the story's full meanings. Which story, in your estimation, deserves the higher ranking? Which gives the greater insight into significant human values? Support your choice with a reasoned and thorough analysis, using the study questions for what help they may provide.

GUY DE MAUPASSANT

The Necklace

She was one of those pretty and charming girls who are sometimes, as if by a mistake of destiny, born in a family of clerks. She had no dowry, no expectations, no means of being known, understood, loved, wedded by any rich and distinguished man; and she let herself be married to a little clerk at the Ministry of Public Instructions.

She dressed plainly because she could not dress well, but she was as unhappy as though she had really fallen from her proper station, since with women there is neither caste nor rank: and beauty, grace, and charm act instead of family and birth. Natural fineness, instinct for what is elegant, suppleness of wit, are the sole hierarchy, and make from women of the people the equals of the very greatest ladies.

She suffered ceaselessly, feeling herself born for all the delicacies and all the luxuries. She suffered from the poverty of her dwelling, from the wretched look of the walls, from the worn-out chairs, from the ugliness of the curtains. All those things, of which another woman of her rank would never even have been conscious, tortured her and made her angry. The sight of the little Breton peasant, who did her humble housework aroused in her regrets which were despairing, and distracted dreams. She thought of the silent antechambers hung with Oriental tapestry, lit by tall bronze candelabra, and of the two great footmen in knee breeches who sleep in the big armchairs, made drowsy by the heavy warmth of the hot-air stove. She thought of the long *salons* fitted up with ancient silk, of the delicate furniture carrying priceless curiosities, and of the coquettish perfumed boudoirs made for talks at five o'clock with intimate friends, with men famous and sought after, whom all women envy and whose attention they all desire.

When she sat down to dinner, before the round table covered with a tablecloth three days old, opposite her husband, who uncovered the soup tureen and declared with an enchanted air, "Ah, the good *pot-au-feu!* I don't know anything better than that," she thought of dainty dinners, of shining silverware, of tapestry which peopled the walls with ancient personages and with strange birds flying in the midst of a fairy forest; and she thought of delicious dishes served on marvelous plates, and of the whispered gallantries which you listen to with a sphinxlike smile, while you are eating the pink flesh of a trout or the wings of a quail.

THE NECKLACE   First published in 1884; translated by Marjorie Laurie. Guy de Maupassant (1850–1893) was one of the most prolific short-story writers of his era, producing almost 300 stories in his short life. His work—including "The Necklace," his best-known tale—exerted an enormous influence on such subsequent writers as Kate Chopin and Joseph Conrad.

She had no dresses, no jewels, nothing. And she loved nothing but 5
that; she felt made for that. She would so have liked to please, to be envied,
to be charming, to be sought after.

She had a friend, a former schoolmate at the convent, who was rich,
and whom she did not like to go and see any more, because she suffered so
much when she came back.

But one evening, her husband returned home with a triumphant air,
and, holding a large envelope in his hand.

"There," said he. "Here is something for you."

She tore the paper sharply, and drew out a printed card which bore
these words:

"The Minister of Public Instruction and Mme. Georges Ramponneau 10
request the honor of M. and Mme. Loisel's company at the palace of the
Ministry on Monday evening, January eighteenth."

Instead of being delighted, as her husband hoped, she threw the invitation on the table with disdain, murmuring:

"What do you want me to do with that?"

"But, my dear, I thought you would be glad. You never go out, and
this is such a fine opportunity. I had awful trouble to get it. Everyone wants
to go; it is very select, and they are not giving many invitations to clerks.
The whole official world will be there."

She looked at him with an irritated glance, and said, impatiently:

"And what do you want me to put on my back?" 15

He had not thought of that; he stammered:

"Why, the dress you go to the theater in. It looks very well, to me."

He stopped, distracted, seeing his wife was crying. Two great tears
descended slowly from the corners of her eyes toward the corners of her
mouth. He stuttered:

"What's the matter? What's the matter?"

But, by violent effort, she had conquered her grief, and she replied, 20
with a calm voice, while she wiped her wet cheeks:

"Nothing. Only I have no dress and therefore I can't go to this ball.
Give your card to some colleague whose wife is better equipped than I."

He was in despair. He resumed:

"Come, let us see, Mathilde. How much would it cost, a suitable dress,
which you could use on other occasions. Something very simple?"

She reflected several seconds, making her calculations and wondering
also what sum she could ask without drawing on herself an immediate
refusal and a frightened exclamation from the economical clerk.

Finally, she replied, hesitatingly: 25

"I don't know exactly, but I think I could manage it with four hundred
francs."

He had grown a little pale, because he was laying aside just that amount to buy a gun and treat himself to a little shooting next summer on the plain of Nanterre, with several friends who went to shoot larks down there, of a Sunday.

But he said:

"All right. I will give you four hundred francs. And try to have a pretty dress."

30   The day of the ball drew near, and Mme. Loisel seemed sad, uneasy, anxious. Her dress was ready, however. Her husband said to her one evening:

"What is the matter? Come, you've been so queer these last three days."

And she answered:

"It annoys me not to have a single jewel, not a single stone, nothing to put on. I shall look like distress. I should almost rather not go at all."

He resumed:

35   "You might wear natural flowers. It's very stylish at this time of the year. For ten francs you can get two or three magnificent roses."

She was not convinced.

"No; there's nothing more humiliating than to look poor among other women who are rich."

But her husband cried:

"How stupid you are! Go look up your friend Mme. Forestier, and ask her to lend you some jewels. You're quite thick enough with her to do that."

40   She uttered a cry of joy:

"It's true. I never thought of it."

The next day she went to her friend and told of her distress.

Mme. Forestier went to a wardrobe with a glass door, took out a large jewelbox, brought it back, opened it, and said to Mme. Loisel:

"Choose, choose, my dear."

45   She saw first of all some bracelets, then a pearl necklace, then a Venetian cross, gold and precious stones of admirable workmanship. She tried on the ornaments before the glass, hesitated, could not make up her mind to part with them, to give them back. She kept asking:

"Haven't you, any more?"

"Why, yes. Look. I don't know what you like."

All of a sudden she discovered, in a black satin box, a superb necklace of diamonds, and her heart began to beat with an immoderate desire. Her hands trembled as she took it. She fastened it around her throat, outside her high necked dress, and remained lost in ecstasy at the sight of herself.

Then she asked, hesitating, filled with anguish:

50   "Can you lend me that, only that?"

"Why, yes, certainly."

She sprang upon the neck of her friend, kissed her passionately, then fled with her treasure.

The day of the ball arrived. Mme. Loisel made a great success. She was prettier than them all, elegant, gracious, smiling, and crazy with joy. All the men looked at her, asked her name, endeavored to be introduced. All the attachés of the Cabinet wanted to waltz with her. She was remarked by the minister himself.

She danced with intoxication, with passion, made drunk by pleasure, forgetting all, in the triumph of her beauty, in the glory of her success, in a sort of cloud of happiness composed of all this homage, of all this admiration, of all these awakened desires, and of that sense of complete victory which is so sweet to a woman's heart.

She went away about four o'clock in the morning. Her husband had   55 been sleeping since midnight, in a little deserted anteroom, with three other gentlemen whose wives were having a good time. He threw over her shoulders the wraps which he had brought, modest wraps of common life, whose poverty contrasted with the elegance of the ball dress. She felt this, and wanted to escape so as not to be remarked by the other women, who were enveloping themselves in costly furs.

Loisel held her back.

"Wait a bit. You will catch cold outside. I will go and call a cab."

But she did not listen to him, and rapidly descended the stairs. When they were in the street they did not find a carriage; and they began to look for one, shouting after the cabmen whom they saw passing by at a distance.

They went down toward the Seine, in despair, shivering with cold. At last they found on the quay one of those ancient noctambulant coupés which, exactly as if they were ashamed to show their misery during the day, are never seen round Paris until after nightfall.

It took them to their door in the Rue des Martyrs, and once more,   60 sadly, they climbed up homeward. All was ended, for her. And as to him, he reflected that he must be at the Ministry at ten o'clock.

She removed the wraps which covered her shoulders before the glass, so as once more to see herself in all her glory. But suddenly she uttered a cry. She no longer had the necklace around her neck!

Her husband, already half undressed, demanded:

"What is the matter with you?"

She turned madly toward him:

"I have—I have—I've lost Mme. Forestier's necklace."   65

He stood up, distracted.

"What!—how?—impossible!"

And they looked in the folds of her dress, in the folds of her cloak, in her pockets, everywhere. They did not find it.

He asked:

70   "You're sure you had it on when you left the ball?"

"Yes, I felt it in the vestibule of the palace."

"But if you had lost it in the street we should have heard it fall. It must be in the cab."

"Yes. Probably. Did you take his number?"

"No. And you, didn't you notice it?"

75   "No."

They looked, thunderstruck, at one another. At last Loisel put on his clothes.

"I shall go back on foot," said he, "over the whole route which we have taken to see if I can find it."

And he went out. She sat waiting on a chair in her ball dress, without strength to go to bed, overwhelmed, without fire, without a thought.

Her husband came back about seven o'clock. He had found nothing.

80   He went to Police Headquarters, to the newspaper offices, to offer a reward; he went to the cab companies—everywhere, in fact, whither he was urged by the least suspicion of hope.

She waited all day, in the same condition of mad fear before this terrible calamity.

Loisel returned at night with a hollow, pale face; he had discovered nothing.

"You must write to your friend," said he, "that you have broken the clasp of her necklace and that you are having it mended. That will give us time to turn round."

She wrote at his dictation.

85   At the end of a week they had lost all hope.

And Loisel, who had aged five years, declared:

"We must consider how to replace that ornament."

The next day they took the box which had contained it, and they went to the jeweler whose name was found within. He consulted his books.

"It was not I, madame, who sold that necklace; I must simply have furnished the case."

90   Then they went from jeweler to jeweler, searching for a necklace like the other, consulting their memories, sick both of them with chagrin and anguish.

They found, in a shop at the Palais Royal, a string of diamonds which seemed to them exactly like the one they looked for. It was worth forty thousand francs. They could have it for thirty-six.

So they begged the jeweler not to sell it for three days yet. And they made a bargain that he should buy it back for thirty-four thousand francs, in case they found the other one before the end of February.

Loisel possessed eighteen thousand francs which his father had left him. He would borrow the rest.

He did borrow, asking a thousand francs of one, five hundred of another, five louis here, three louis there. He gave notes, took up ruinous obligations, dealt with usurers and all the race of lenders. He compromised all the rest of his life, risked his signature without even knowing if he could meet it; and, frightened by the pains yet to come, by the black misery which was about to fall upon him, by the prospect of all the physical privation and of all the moral tortures which lie was to suffer, he went to get the new necklace, putting down upon the merchant's counter thirty-six thousand francs.

When Mme. Loisel took back the necklace, Mme. Forestier said to her, with a chilly manner: 95

"You should have returned it sooner; I might have needed it."

She did not open the case, as her friend had so much feared. If she had detected the substitution, what would she have thought, what would she have said? Would she not have taken Mme. Loisel for a thief?

Mme. Loisel now knew the horrible existence of the needy. She took her part, moreover, all of a sudden, with heroism. That dreadful debt must be paid. She would pay it. They dismissed their servant; they changed their lodgings; they rented a garret under the roof.

She came to know what heavy housework meant and the odious cares of the kitchen. She washed the dishes, using her rosy nails on the greasy pots and pans. She washed the dirty linen, the shirts, and the dishcloths, which she dried upon a line; she carried the slops down to the street every morning, and carried up the water, stopping for breath at every landing. And, dressed like a woman of the people, she went to the fruiterer, the grocer, the butcher, her basket on her arm, bargaining, insulted, defending her miserable money sou by sou.

Each month they had to meet some notes, renew others, obtain more time. 100

Her husband worked in the evening making a fair copy of some tradesman's accounts, and late at night he often copied manuscript for five sous a page.

And this life lasted for ten years.

At the end of ten years, they had paid everything, everything, with the rates of usury, and the accumulations of the compound interest.

Mme. Loisel looked old now. She had become the woman of impoverished households—strong and hard and rough. With frowsy hair, skirts askew, and red hands, she talked loud while washing the floor with great swishes of water. But sometimes, when her husband was at the office, she sat down near the window, and she thought of that gay evening of long ago, of that ball where she had been so beautiful and so fêted.

105 What would have happened if she had not lost that necklace? Who knows? Who knows? How life is strange and changeful! How little a thing is needed for us to be lost or to be saved!

But, one Sunday, having gone to take a walk in the Champs Elysées to refresh herself from the labor of the week, she suddenly perceived a woman who was leading a child. It was Mme. Forestier, still young, still beautiful, still charming.

Mme. Loisel felt moved. Was she going to speak to her? Yes, certainly. And now that she had paid, she was going to tell her all about it. Why not?

She went up.

"Good-day, Jeanne."

110 The other, astonished to be familiarly addressed by this plain goodwife, did not recognize her at all, and stammered.

"But—madam!—I do not know—you must be mistaken."

"No. I am Mathilde Loisel."

Her friend uttered a cry.

"Oh, my poor Mathilde! How you are changed!"

115 "Yes, I have had days hard enough, since I have seen you, days wretched enough—and that because of you!"

"Of me! How so?"

"Do you remember that diamond necklace which you lent me to wear at the ministerial ball?"

"Yes. Well?"

"Well, I lost it."

120 "What do you mean? You brought it back."

"I brought you back another just like it. And for this we have been ten years paying. You can understand that it was not easy for us, who had nothing. At last it is ended, and I am very glad."

Mme. Forestier had stopped.

"You say that you bought a necklace of diamonds to replace mine?"

"Yes. You never noticed it, then! They were very like."

125 And she smiled with a joy which was proud and naïve at once.

Mme. Forestier, strongly moved, took her two hands.

"Oh, my poor Mathilde! Why, my necklace was paste. It was worth at most five hundred francs!"

QUESTIONS

1. Is Mathilde a sympathetic or unsympathetic character? Does our view of her change as the story develops?

2. Describe the plot structure of "The Necklace." How does the author achieve suspense?
3. What is the relationship between Mathilde and her husband? Is theirs a normal, loving partnership? How might the story differ in this respect if written today?
4. Discuss the surprise ending. Was this ending predictable or was it a genuine surprise?
5. Does the story make a larger statement about human nature, transcending the merely surprising ending? Or was the entire story written merely to surprise and entertain the reader?

EDITH WHARTON

Roman Fever

1

From the table at which they had been lunching two American ladies of ripe but well-cared-for middle age moved across the lofty terrace of the Roman restaurant and, leaning on its parapet, looked first at each other, and then down on the outspread glories of the Palatine and the Forum, with the same expression of vague but benevolent approval.

As they leaned there a girlish voice echoed up gaily from the stairs leading to the court below. "Well, come along, then," it cried, not to them but to an invisible companion, "and let's leave the young things to their knitting"; and a voice as fresh laughed back: "Oh, look here, Babs, not actually *knitting*—" "Well, I mean figuratively," rejoined the first. "After all, we haven't left our poor parents much else to do. . . ." and at that point the turn of the stairs engulfed the dialogue.

The two ladies looked at each other again, this time with a tinge of smiling embarrassment, and the smaller and paler one shook her head and colored slightly.

"Barbara!" she murmured, sending an unheard rebuke after the mocking voice in the stairway.

The other lady, who was fuller, and higher in color, with a small deter- 5
mined nose supported by vigorous black eyebrows, gave a good-humored laugh. "That's what our daughters think of us!"

Her companion replied by a deprecating gesture. "Not of us individually. We must remember that. It's just the collective modern idea of

ROMAN FEVER   First published in 1934. Edith Wharton (1862–1937) was born into a socially prominent New York family and was privately educated by governesses and tutors. She married in 1885 and began a financially and critically successful writing career in 1890. After frequent visits to Europe beginning in her childhood, she took up permanent residence in France. Both she and her husband had a history of adulterous affairs, and she divorced him in 1913; she had no children. "Roman fever" was the name given to a type of malaria prevalent in Rome in the nineteenth century.

Mothers. And you see—" Half-guiltily she drew from her handsomely mounted black handbag a twist of crimson silk run through by two fine knitting needles. "One never knows," she murmured. "The new system has certainly given us a good deal of time to kill; and sometimes I get tired just looking,—even at this." Her gesture was now addressed to the stupendous scene at their feet.

The dark lady laughed again, and they both relapsed upon the view, contemplating it in silence, with a sort of diffused serenity which might have been borrowed from the spring effulgence of the Roman skies. The luncheon hour was long past, and the two had their end of the vast terrace to themselves. At its opposite extremity a few groups, detained by a lingering look at the outspread city, were gathering up guidebooks and fumbling for tips. The last of them scattered, and the two ladies were alone on the air-washed height.

"Well, I don't see why we shouldn't just stay here," said Mrs. Slade, the lady of the high color and energetic brows. Two derelict basket chairs stood near, and she pushed them into the angle of the parapet, and settled herself in one, her gaze upon the Palatine. "After all, it's still the most beautiful view in the world."

"It always will be, to me," assented her friend Mrs. Ansley, with so slight a stress on the "me" that Mrs. Slade, though she noticed it, wondered if it were not merely accidental, like the random underlinings of old-fashioned letter writers.

10 "Grace Ansley was always old-fashioned," she thought; and added aloud, with a retrospective smile: "It's a view we've both been familiar with for a good many years. When we first met here we were younger than our girls are now. You remember?"

"Oh, yes, I remember," murmured Mrs. Ansley, with the same undefinable stress. "There's that headwaiter wondering," she interpolated. She was evidently far less sure than her companion of herself and of her rights in the world.

"I'll cure him of wondering," said Mrs. Slade, stretching her hand toward a bag as discreetly opulent-looking as Mrs. Ansley's. Signing to the headwaiter, she explained that she and her friend were old lovers of Rome, and would like to spend the end of the afternoon looking down on the view—that is, if it did not disturb the service? The headwaiter, bowing over her gratuity, assured her that the ladies were most welcome, and would be still more so if they would condescend to remain for dinner. A full-moon night, they would remember. . . .

Mrs. Slade's black brows drew together, as though references to the moon were out of place and even unwelcome. But she smiled away her frown as the headwaiter retreated. "Well, why not? We might do worse.

There's no knowing, I suppose, when the girls will be back. Do you even know back from *where?* I don't!"

Mrs. Ansley again colored slightly. "I think those young Italian aviators we met at the Embassy invited them to fly to Tarquinia for tea. I suppose they'll want to wait and fly back by moonlight."

"Moonlight—moonlight! What a part it still plays. Do you suppose 15 they're as sentimental as we were?"

"I've come to the conclusion that I don't in the least know what they are," said Mrs. Ansley. "And perhaps we didn't know much more about each other."

"No; perhaps we didn't."

Her friend gave her a shy glance. "I never should have supposed you were sentimental, Alida."

"Well, perhaps I wasn't." Mrs. Slade drew her lids together in retrospect; and for a few moments the two ladies, who had been intimate since childhood, reflected how little they knew each other. Each one, of course, had a label ready to attach to the other's name; Mrs. Delphin Slade, for instance, would have told herself, or anyone who asked her, that Mrs. Horace Ansley, twenty-five years ago, had been exquisitely lovely—no, you wouldn't believe it, would you? . . . though, of course, still charming, distinguished. . . . Well, as a girl she had been exquisite; far more beautiful than her daughter Barbara, though certainly Babs, according to the new standards at any rate, was more effective—had more *edge*, as they say. Funny where she got it, with those two nullities as parents. Yes; Horace Ansley was—well, just the duplicate of his wife. Museum specimens of old New York. Good-looking, irreproachable, exemplary. Mrs. Slade and Mrs. Ansley had lived opposite each other—actually as well as figuratively—for years. When the drawing-room curtains in No. 20 East 73rd Street were renewed, No. 23, across the way, was always aware of it. And of all the movings, buyings, travels, anniversaries, illnesses—the tame chronicle of an estimable pair. Little of it escaped Mrs. Slade. But she had grown bored with it by the time her husband made his big *coup* in Wall Street, and when they bought in upper Park Avenue had already begun to think: "I'd rather live opposite a speakeasy for a change; at least one might see it raided." The idea of seeing Grace raided was so amusing that (before the move) she launched it at a woman's lunch. It made a hit, and went the rounds—she sometimes wondered if it had crossed the street, and reached Mrs. Ansley. She hoped not, but didn't much mind. Those were the days when respectability was at a discount, and it did the irreproachable no harm to laugh at them a little.

A few years later, and not many months apart, both ladies lost their 20 husbands. There was an appropriate exchange of wreaths and condolences, and a brief renewal of intimacy in the half-shadow of their mourning; and now, after another interval, they had run across each other in Rome, at the same hotel, each of them the modest appendage of a salient daughter. The similarity of their lot had again drawn them together, lending itself to mild jokes, and the mutual confession that, if in old days it must have been tiring to "keep up" with daughters, it was now, at times, a little dull not to.

No doubt, Mrs. Slade reflected, she felt her unemployment more than poor Grace ever would. It was a big drop from being the wife of Delphin Slade to being his widow. She had always regarded herself (with a certain conjugal pride) as his equal in social gifts, as contributing her full share to the making of the exceptional couple they were: but the difference after his death was irremediable. As the wife of the famous corporation lawyer, always with an international case or two on hand, every day brought its exciting and unexpected obligation: the impromptu entertaining of eminent colleagues from abroad, the hurried dashes on legal business to London, Paris or Rome, where the entertaining was so handsomely reciprocated; the amusement of hearing in her wake: "What, that handsome woman with the good clothes and the eyes is Mrs. Slade—*the* Slade's wife? Really? Generally the wives of celebrities are such frumps."

Yes; being *the* Slade's widow was a dullish business after that. In living up to such a husband all her faculties had been engaged; now she had only her daughter to live up to, for the son who seemed to have inherited his father's gifts had died suddenly in boyhood. She had fought through that agony because her husband was there, to be helped and to help; now, after the father's death, the thought of the boy had become unbearable. There was nothing left but to mother her daughter; and dear Jenny was such a perfect daughter that she needed no excessive mothering. "Now with Babs Ansley I don't know that I *should* be so quiet," Mrs. Slade sometimes half-enviously reflected; but Jenny, who was younger than her brilliant friend, was that rare accident, an extremely pretty girl who somehow made youth and prettiness seem as safe as their absence. It was all perplexing—and to Mrs. Slade a little boring. She wished that Jenny would fall in love—with the wrong man, even; that she might have to be watched, out-maneuvered, rescued. And instead, it was Jenny who watched her mother, kept her out of drafts, made sure that she had taken her tonic. . . .

Mrs. Ansley was much less articulate than her friend, and her mental portrait of Mrs. Slade was slighter, and drawn with fainter touches. "Alida Slade's awfully brilliant; but not as brilliant as she thinks," would have summed it up; though she would have added, for the enlightenment of strangers, that Mrs. Slade had been an extremely dashing girl; much more so than her daughter, who was pretty, of course, and clever in a way, but had none of her mother's—well, "vividness," someone had once called it. Mrs. Ansley would take up current words like this, and cite them in quotation marks, as unheard-of audacities. No; Jenny was not like her mother. Sometimes Mrs. Ansley thought Alida Slade was disappointed; on the whole she had had a sad life. Full of failures and mistakes; Mrs. Ansley had always been rather sorry for her. . . .

So these two ladies visualized each other, each through the wrong end of her little telescope.

2

For a long time they continued to sit side by side without speak-   25
ing. It seemed as though, to both, there was a relief in laying down their somewhat futile activities in the presence of the vast Memento Mori° which faced them. Mrs. Slade sat quite still, her eyes fixed on the golden slope of the Palace of the Caesars, and after a while Mrs. Ansley ceased to fidget with her bag, and she too sank into meditation. Like many intimate friends, the two ladies had never before had occasion to be silent together, and Mrs. Ansley was slightly embarrassed by what seemed, after so many years, a new stage in their intimacy, and one with which she did not yet know how to deal.

Suddenly the air was full of that deep clangor of bells which periodically covers Rome with a roof of silver. Mrs. Slade glanced at her wristwatch. "Five o'clock already," she said, as though surprised.

Mrs. Ansley suggested interrogatively: "There's bridge at the Embassy at five." For a long time Mrs. Slade did not answer. She appeared to be lost in contemplation, and Mrs. Ansley thought the remark had escaped her. But after a while she said, as if speaking out of a dream: "Bridge, did you say? Not unless you want to. . . . But I don't think I will, you know."

"Oh, no," Mrs. Ansley hastened to assure her. "I don't care to at all. It's so lovely here; and so full of old memories, as you say." She settled herself in her chair, and almost furtively drew forth her knitting. Mrs. Slade took sideway note of this activity, but her own beautifully cared-for hands remained motionless on her knee.

"I was just thinking," she said slowly, "what different things Rome stands for to each generation of travelers. To our grandmother's, Roman fever; to our mothers, sentimental dangers—how we used to be guarded!— to our daughters, no more dangers than the middle of Main Street. They don't know it—but how much they're missing!"

The long golden light was beginning to pale, and Mrs. Ansley lifted   30
her knitting a little closer to her eyes. "Yes; how we were guarded!"

"I always used to think," Mrs. Slade continued, "that our mothers had a much more difficult job than our grandmothers. When Roman fever

---

Memento Mori: reminder of mortality (Latin: literally, "remember that you must die")

90   "I suppose," said Mrs. Ansley slowly, "it's because you've always gone on hating me."

"Perhaps. Or because I wanted to get the whole thing off my mind." She paused. "I'm glad you destroyed the letter. Of course I never thought you'd die."

Mrs. Ansley relapsed into silence, and Mrs. Slade, leaning above her, was conscious of a strange sense of isolation, of being cut off from the warm current of human communion. "You think me a monster!"

"I don't know. . . . It was the only letter I had, and you say he didn't write it?"

"Ah, how you care for him still!"

95   "I cared for that memory," said Mrs. Ansley.

Mrs. Slade continued to look down on her. She seemed physically reduced by the blow—as if, when she got up, the wind might scatter her like a puff of dust. Mrs. Slade's jealousy suddenly leapt up again at the sight. All these years the woman had been living on that letter. How she must have loved him, to treasure the mere memory of its ashes! The letter of the man her friend was engaged to. Wasn't it she who was the monster?

"You tried your best to get him away from me, didn't you? But you failed; and I kept him. That's all."

"Yes. That's all."

"I wish now I hadn't told you. I'd no idea you'd feel about it as you do; I thought you'd be amused. It all happened so long ago, as you say; and you must do me the justice to remember that I had no reason to think you'd ever taken it seriously. How could I, when you were married to Horace Ansley two months afterward? As soon as you could get out of bed your mother rushed you off to Florence and married you. People were rather surprised— they wondered at its being done so quickly; but I thought I knew. I had an idea you did it out of *pique*—to be able to say you'd got ahead of Delphin and me. Girls have such silly reasons for doing the most serious things. And your marrying so soon convinced me that you'd never really cared."

100   "Yes. I suppose it would," Mrs. Ansley assented.

The clear heaven overhead was emptied of all its gold. Dusk spread over it, abruptly darkening the Seven Hills. Here and there lights began to twinkle through the foliage at their feet. Steps were coming and going on the deserted terrace—waiters looking out of the doorway at the head of the stairs, then reappearing with trays and napkins and flasks of wine. Tables were moved, chairs straightened. A feeble string of electric lights flickered out. Some vases of faded flowers were carried away, and brought back replenished. A stout lady in a dust coat suddenly appeared, asking in broken Italian if anyone had seen the elastic band which held together her tattered Baedeker.° She poked with her stick under the table at which she had lunched, the waiters assisting.

Baedeker: tourist guidebook (one of a series issued by the German publisher Karl Baedeker)

The corner where Mrs. Slade and Mrs. Ansley sat was still shadowy and deserted. For a long time neither of them spoke. At length Mrs. Slade began again: "I suppose I did it as a sort of joke—"

"A joke?"

"Well, girls are ferocious sometimes, you know. Girls in love especially. And I remember laughing to myself all that evening at the idea that you were waiting around there in the dark, dodging out of sight, listening for every sound, trying to get in—Of course I was upset when I heard you were so ill afterward."

Mrs. Ansley had not moved for a long time. But now she turned slowly 105 toward her companion. "But I didn't wait. He'd arranged everything. He was there. We were let in at once," she said.

Mrs. Slade sprang up from her leaning position. "Delphin there? They let you in?— Ah, now you're lying!" she burst out with violence.

Mrs. Ansley's voice grew clearer, and full of surprise. "But of course he was there. Naturally he came—"

"Came? How did he know he'd find you there? You must be raving!"

Mrs. Ansley hesitated, as though reflecting. "But I answered the letter. I told him I'd be there. So he came."

Mrs. Slade flung her hands up to her face. "Oh, God—you answered! 110 I never thought of your answering. . . ."

"It's odd you never thought of it, if you wrote the letter."

"Yes. I was blind with rage."

Mrs. Ansley rose, and drew her fur scarf about her. "It is cold here. We'd better go . . . I'm sorry for you," she said, as she clasped the fur about her throat.

The unexpected words sent a pang through Mrs. Slade. "Yes; we'd better go." She gathered up her bag and cloak. "I don't know why you should be sorry for me," she muttered.

Mrs. Ansley stood looking away from her toward the dusky 115 secret mass of the Colosseum. "Well—because I didn't have to wait that night."

Mrs. Slade gave an unquiet laugh. "Yes; I was beaten there. But I oughtn't to begrudge it to you, I suppose. At the end of all these years. After all, I had everything; I had him for twenty-five years. And you had nothing but that one letter that he didn't write."

Mrs. Ansley was again silent. At length she turned toward the door of the terrace. She took a step, and turned back, facing her companion.

"I had Barbara," she said, and began to move ahead of Mrs. Slade toward the stairway.

QUESTIONS

1. Characterize Grace Ansley and Alida Slade as fully as you can. By what characterizing devices does the story imply the superiority of Mrs. Slade (what gestures, what statements, what unspoken thoughts)? At what point does Mrs. Ansley begin to seem the superior person?
2. What is the meaning of the comment about "the wrong end of [the] little telescope" (paragraph 24)? How is that comment a suitable conclusion for the first part of the story?
3. Trace the revelation of the animosity that Mrs. Slade feels for Mrs. Ansley. Is Mrs. Ansley doing anything on this evening to provoke her envy? Why has Mrs. Slade always harbored negative feelings about her friend?
4. What purpose is served by the discussion of the different meanings of Rome to mothers and daughters of different generations (paragraphs 29–31)? What standards of behavior have changed from one generation to the next? What standards have remained the same? How does this discussion expand the meaning of the title of the story?
5. Discuss the surprise ending. How does Wharton prepare for this ending earlier in the story?
6. Which of the two women does the story judge more harshly? Which is more likable and sympathetic?

SUGGESTIONS FOR WRITING

1. Write an essay evaluating the relative quality of any of the following pairs of stories. Decide which is the better story, and support your argument fully:
   a. Connell, "The Most Dangerous Game" (page 62) and Glaspell, "A Jury of Her Peers" (page 546)
   b. Walker, "Everyday Use" (page 147) and Hurston, "Spunk" (page 564).
   c. Maupassant, "The Necklace" (page 382) and Wharton, "Roman Fever" (page 389)
   d. O'Connor, "Everything That Rises Must Converge" (page 476) and Poe, "The Cask of Amontillado" (page 657)
   e. Porter, "The Jilting of Granny Weatherall" (page 268) and Oates, "A Brutal Murder in a Public Place" (page 517)
2. Write an essay in which you argue for the literary quality of any one of the following stories, detailing its successful use of the elements of fiction:
   a. Lahiri, "Interpreter of Maladies" (page 590)
   b. Joyce, "Araby" (page 186)
   c. Gordimer, "Once upon a Time" (page 230)
   d. Hawthorne, "Young Goodman Brown" (page 293)
   e. Melville, "Bartleby the Scrivener" (page 627)
   f. O'Connor, "Good Country People" (page 459)
   g. Wharton, "Roman Fever" (page 389)

Three Featured

Writers

D. H. Lawrence

Flannery O'Connor

Joyce Carol Oates

D. H. LAWRENCE
Odour of Chrysanthemums

1

THE small locomotive engine, Number 4, came clanking, stumbling down from Selston with seven full wagons. It appeared round the corner with loud threats of speed, but the colt that it startled from among the gorse, which still flickered indistinctly in the raw afternoon, out-distanced it at a canter. A woman, walking up the railway line to Underwood, drew back into the hedge, held her basket aside, and watched the footplate of the engine advancing. The trucks thumped heavily past, one by one, with slow inevitable movement, as she stood insignificantly trapped between the jolting black wagons and the hedge; then they curved away towards the coppice where the withered oak leaves dropped noiselessly, while the birds, pulling at the scarlet hips beside the track, made off into the dusk that had already crept into the spinney. In the open, the smoke from the engine sank and cleaved to the rough grass. The fields were dreary and forsaken, and in the marshy strip that led to the whimsey, a reedy pit-pond, the fowls had already abandoned their run among the alders, to roost in the tarred fowl-house. The pit-bank loomed up beyond the pond, flames like red sores licking its ashy sides, in the afternoon's stagnant light. Just beyond rose the tapering chimneys and the clumsy black headstocks of Brinsley Colliery. The two wheels were spinning fast up against the sky, and the winding engine rapped out its little spasms. The miners were being turned up.

The engine whistled as it came into the wide bay of railway lines beside the colliery, where rows of trucks stood in harbour.

Miners, single, trailing and in groups, passed like shadows diverging home. At the edge of the ribbed level of sidings squat a low cottage, three steps down from the cinder track. A large bony vine clutched at the house, as if to claw down the tiled roof. Round the bricked yard grew a few wintry primroses. Beyond, the long garden sloped down to a bush-covered brook course. There were some twiggy apple trees, winter-crack trees, and ragged cabbages. Beside the path hung dishevelled pink chrysanthemums, like pink cloths hung on bushes. A woman came stooping out of the felt-covered fowl-house, half-way down the garden. She closed and padlocked the door, then drew herself erect, having brushed some bits from her white apron.

She was a tall woman of imperious mien, handsome, with definite black eyebrows. Her smooth black hair was parted exactly. For a few

ODOUR OF CHRYSANTHEMUMS First published in 1914. D. H. Lawrence (1885–1930), son of a coal miner and a school teacher, was born and grew up in Nottinghamshire, England, was rejected for military service in World War I because of lung trouble, and lived most of his adult life abroad, including parts of three years in New Mexico.

moments she stood steadily watching the miners as they passed along the railway: then she turned towards the brook course. Her face was calm and set, her mouth was closed with disillusionment. After a moment she called:

"John!" There was no answer. She waited, and then said distinctly: 5 "Where are you?"

"Here!" replied a child's sulky voice from among the bushes. The woman looked piercingly through the dusk.

"Are you at that brook?" she asked sternly.

For answer the child showed himself before the raspberry-canes that rose like whips. He was a small, sturdy boy of five. He stood quite still, defiantly.

"Oh!" said the mother, conciliated. "I thought you were down at that   10 wet brook—and you remember what I told you—"

The boy did not move or answer.

"Come, come on in," she said more gently, "it's getting dark. There's your grandfather's engine coming down the line!"

The lad advanced slowly, with resentful, taciturn movement. He was dressed in trousers and waistcoat of cloth that was too thick and hard for the size of the garments. They were evidently cut down from a man's clothes.

As they went slowly towards the house he tore at the ragged wisps of chrysanthemums and dropped the petals in handfuls among the path.

"Don't do that—it does look nasty," said his mother. He refrained, and   15 she, suddenly pitiful, broke off a twig with three or four wan flowers and held them against her face. When mother and son reached the yard her hand hesitated, and instead of laying the flower aside, she pushed it in her apron-band. The mother and son stood at the foot of the three steps looking across the bay of lines at the passing home of the miners. The trundle of the small train was imminent. Suddenly the engine loomed past the house and came to a stop opposite the gate.

The engine-driver, a short man with round grey beard, leaned out of the cab high above the woman.

"Have you got a cup of tea?" he said in a cheery, hearty fashion.

It was her father. She went in, saying she would mash. Directly, she returned.

"I didn't come to see you on Sunday," began the little grey-bearded man.

"I didn't expect you," said his daughter.   20

The engine-driver winced; then, reassuming his cheery, airy manner, he said:

"Oh, have you heard then? Well, and what do you think—?"

"I think it is soon enough," she replied.

At her brief censure the little man made an impatient gesture, and said coaxingly, yet with dangerous coldness:

25   "Well, what's a man to do? It's no sort of life for a man of my years, to sit at my own hearth like a stranger. And if I'm going to marry again it may as well be soon as late—what does it matter to anybody?"

The woman did not reply, but turned and went into the house. The man in the engine-cab stood assertive, till she returned with a cup of tea and a piece of bread and butter on a plate. She went up the steps and stood near the footplate of the hissing engine.

"You needn't 'a' brought me bread an' butter," said her father. "But a cup of tea"—he sipped appreciatively—"it's very nice." He sipped for a moment or two, then: "I hear as Walter's got another bout on," he said.

"When hasn't he?" said the woman bitterly.

"I heerd tell of him in the 'Lord Nelson,'° braggin' as he was going to spend that b— afore he went: half a sovereign that was."

30   "When?" asked the woman.

"A' Sat'day night—I know that's true."

"Very likely," she laughed bitterly. "He gives me twenty-three shillings."

"Aye, it's a nice thing, when a man can do nothing with his money but make a beast of himself!" said the grey-whiskered man. The woman turned her head away. Her father swallowed the last of his tea and handed her the cup.

"Aye," he sighed, wiping his mouth. "It's a settler, it is—"

35   He put his hand on the lever. The little engine strained and groaned, and the train rumbled towards the crossing. The woman again looked across the metals. Darkness was settling over the spaces of the railway and trucks: the miners, in grey sombre groups, were still passing home. The winding engine pulsed hurriedly, with brief pauses. Elizabeth Bates looked at the dreary flow of men, then she went indoors. Her husband did not come.

The kitchen was small and full of firelight; red coals piled glowing up the chimney mouth. All the life of the room seemed in the white, warm hearth and the steel fender reflecting the red fire. The cloth was laid for tea; cups glinted in the shadows. At the back, where the lowest stairs protruded into the room, the boy sat struggling with a knife and a piece of white wood. He was almost hidden in the shadow. It was half-past four. They had but to await the father's coming to begin tea. As the mother watched her son's sullen little struggle with the wood, she saw herself in his silence and pertinacity; she saw the father in her child's indifference to all but himself. She seemed to be occupied by her husband. He had probably gone past his home, slunk past his own door, to drink before he came in, while his

---

The "Lord Nelson": the name of a pub (a public-house), or drinking house; other pubs named later in the story are "The Prince of Wales" and "The Yew Tree."

dinner spoiled and wasted in waiting. She glanced at the clock, then took the potatoes to strain them in the yard. The garden and fields beyond the brook were closed in uncertain darkness. When she rose with the saucepan, leaving the drain steaming into the night behind her, she saw the yellow lamps were lit along the high road that went up the hill away beyond the space of the railway lines and the field.

Then again she watched the men trooping home, fewer now and fewer.

Indoors the fire was sinking and the room was dark red. The woman put her saucepan on the hob, and set a batter-pudding near the mouth of the oven. Then she stood unmoving. Directly, gratefully, came quick young steps to the door. Someone hung on the latch a moment, then a little girl entered and began pulling off her outdoor things, dragging a mass of curls, just ripening from gold to brown, over her eyes with her hat.

Her mother chid her for coming late from school, and said she would have to keep her at home the dark winter days.

"Why, mother, it's hardly a bit dark yet. The lamp's not lighted, and my father's not home." 40

"No, he isn't. But it's a quarter to five! Did you see anything of him?"

The child became serious. She looked at her mother with large, wistful blue eyes.

"No, mother, I've never seen him. Why? Has he come up an' gone past, to Old Brinsley? He hasn't, mother, 'cos I never saw him."

"He'd watch that," said the mother bitterly, "he'd take care as you didn't see him. But you may depend upon it, he's seated in the 'Prince o' Wales.' He wouldn't be this late."

The girl looked at her mother piteously. 45

"Let's have our teas, mother, should we?" said she.

The mother called John to table. She opened the door once more and looked out across the darkness of the lines. All was deserted: she could not hear the winding-engines.

"Perhaps," she said to herself, "he's stopped to get some ripping done."

They sat down to tea. John, at the end of the table near the door, was almost lost in the darkness. Their faces were hidden from each other. The girl crouched against the fender slowly moving a thick piece of bread before the fire. The lad, his face a dusky mark on the shadow, sat watching her who was transfigured in the red glow.

"I do think it's beautiful to look in the fire," said the child. 50

"Do you?" said her mother. "Why?"

"It's so red, and full of little caves—and it feels so nice, and you can fair smell it."

"It'll want mending directly," replied her mother, "and then if your father comes he'll carry on and say there never is a fire when a man comes home sweating from the pit. A public-house is always warm enough."

There was silence till the boy said complainingly: "Make haste, our Annie."

55   "Well, I am doing! I can't make the fire do it no faster, can I?"

"She keeps wafflin' it about so's to make 'er slow," grumbled the boy.

"Don't have such an evil imagination, child," replied the mother.

Soon the room was busy in the darkness with the crisp sound of crunching. The mother ate very little. She drank her tea determinedly, and sat thinking. When she rose her anger was evident in the stern unbending of her head. She looked at the pudding in the fender, and broke out:

"It is a scandalous thing as a man can't even come home to his dinner! If it's crozzled up to a cinder I don't see why I should care. Past his very door he goes to get to a public-house, and here I sit with his dinner waiting for him—"

60   She went out. As she dropped piece after piece of coal on the red fire, the shadows fell on the walls, till the room was almost in total darkness.

"I canna see," grumbled the invisible John. In spite of herself, the mother laughed.

"You know the way to your mouth," she said. She set the dust-pan outside the door. When she came again like a shadow on the hearth, the lad repeated, complaining sulkily:

"I canna see."

"Good gracious!" cried the mother irritably, "you're as bad as your father if it's a bit dusk!"

65   Nevertheless, she took a paper spill from a sheaf on the mantelpiece and proceeded to light the lamp that hung from the ceiling in the middle of the room. As she reached up, her figure displayed itself just rounding with maternity.

"Oh, mother—!" exclaimed the girl.

"What?" said the woman, suspended in the act of putting the lamp-glass over the flame. The copper reflector shone handsomely on her, as she stood with uplifted arm, turning to face her daughter.

"You've got a flower in your apron!" said the child, in a little rapture at this unusual event.

"Goodness me!" exclaimed the woman, relieved. "One would think the house was afire." She replaced the glass and waited a moment before turning up the wick. A pale shadow was seen floating vaguely on the floor.

70   "Let me smell!" said the child, still rapturously, coming forward and putting her face to her mother's waist.

"Go along, silly!" said the mother, turning up the lamp. The light revealed their suspense so that the woman felt it almost unbearable. Annie was still bending at her waist. Irritably, the mother took the flowers out from her apron-band.

"Oh, mother—don't take them out!" Annie cried, catching her hand and trying to replace the sprig.

"Such nonsense!" said the mother, turning away. The child put the pale chrysanthemums to her lips, murmuring:

"Don't they smell beautiful!"

Her mother gave a short laugh. 75

"No," she said, "not to me. It was chrysanthemums when I married him, and chrysanthemums when you were born, and the first time they ever brought him home drunk, he'd got brown chrysanthemums in his button-hole."

She looked at the children. Their eyes and their parted lips were wondering. The mother sat rocking in silence for some time. Then she looked at the clock.

"Twenty minutes to six!" In a tone of fine bitter carelessness she continued: "Eh, he'll not come now till they bring him. There he'll stick! But he needn't come rolling in here in his pit-dirt, for *I* won't wash him. He can lie on the floor— Eh, what a fool I've been, what a fool! And this is what I came here for, to this dirty hole, rats, and all, for him to slink past his very door. Twice last week—he's begun now—"

She silenced herself, and rose to clear the table.

While for an hour or more the children played, subduedly intent, 80 fertile of imagination, united in fear of the mother's wrath, and in dread of their father's home-coming, Mrs. Bates sat in her rocking-chair making a 'singlet' of thick cream-coloured flannel, which gave a dull wounded sound as she tore off the grey edge. She worked at her sewing with energy, listening to the children, and her anger wearied itself, lay down to rest, opening its eyes from time to time and steadily watching, its ears raised to listen. Sometimes even her anger quailed and shrank, and the mother suspended her sewing, tracing the footsteps that thudded along the sleepers outside; she would lift her head sharply to bid the children 'hush', but she recovered herself in time, and the footsteps went past the gate, and the children were not flung out of their play-world.

But at last Annie sighed, and gave in. She glanced at her wagon of slippers, and loathed the game. She turned plaintively to her mother.

"Mother!"—but she was inarticulate.

John crept out like a frog from under the sofa. His mother glanced up.

"Yes," she said, "just look at those shirt-sleeves!"

The boy held them out to survey them, saying nothing. Then some- 85 body called in a hoarse voice away down the line, and suspense bristled in the room, till two people had gone by outside, talking.

"It is time for bed," said the mother.

"My father hasn't come," wailed Annie plaintively. But her mother was primed with courage.

"Never mind. They'll bring him when he does come—like a log." She meant there would be no scene. "And he may sleep on the floor till he wakes himself. I know he'll not go to work to-morrow after this!"

The children had their hands and faces wiped with a flannel. They were very quiet. When they had put on their nightdresses, they said their prayers, the boy mumbling. The mother looked down at them, at the brown silken bush of intertwining curls in the nape of the girl's neck, at the little black head of the lad, and her heart burst with anger at their father, who caused all three such distress. The children hid their faces in her skirts for comfort.

90   When Mrs. Bates came down, the room was strangely empty, with a tension of expectancy. She took up her sewing and stitched for some time without raising her head. Meantime her anger was tinged with fear.

2

The clock struck eight and she rose suddenly, dropping her sewing on her chair. She went to the stair-foot door, opened it, listening. Then she went out, locking the door behind her.

Something scuffled in the yard, and she started, though she knew it was only the rats with which the place was over-run. The night was very dark. In the great bay of railway lines, bulked with trucks, there was no trace of light, only away back she could see a few yellow lamps at the pit-top, and the red smear of the burning pit-bank on the night. She hurried along the edge of the track, then, crossing the converging lines, came to the stile by the white gates, whence she emerged on the road. Then the fear which had led her shrank. People were walking up to New Brinsley; she saw the lights in the houses; twenty yards farther on were the broad windows of the 'Prince of Wales', very warm and bright, and the loud voices of men could be heard distinctly. What a fool she had been to imagine that anything had happened to him! He was merely drinking over there at the 'Prince of Wales'. She faltered. She had never yet been to fetch him, and she never would go. So she continued her walk towards the long straggling line of houses, standing back on the highway. She entered a passage between the dwellings.

"Mr. Rigley?—Yes! Did you want him? No, he's not in at this minute."

The raw-boned woman leaned forward from her dark scullery and peered at the other, upon whom fell a dim light through the blind of the kitchen window.

95   "Is it Mrs. Bates?" she asked in a tone tinged with respect.

"Yes. I wondered if your Master was at home. Mine hasn't come yet."

"'Asn't 'e! Oh, Jack's been 'ome an' 'ad 'is dinner an' gone out. 'E's just gone for 'alf an hour afore bed-time. Did you call at the 'Prince of Wales'?"

"No—"

"No, you didn't like——! It's not very nice." The other woman was indulgent. There was an awkward pause. "Jack never said nothink about—about your Master," she said.

"No!—I expect he's stuck in there!"   100

Elizabeth Bates said this bitterly, and with recklessness. She knew that the woman across the yard was standing at her door listening, but she did not care. As she turned:

"Stop a minute! I'll just go an' ask Jack if 'e knows anythink," said Mrs. Rigley.

"Oh no—I wouldn't like to put——!"

"Yes, I will, if you'll just step inside an' see as th' childer doesn't come downstairs and set theirselves afire."

Elizabeth Bates, murmuring a remonstrance, stepped inside. The other   105 woman apologised for the state of the room.

The kitchen needed apology. There were little frocks and trousers and childish undergarments on the squab and on the floor, and a litter of playthings everywhere. On the black American cloth of the table were pieces of bread and cake, crusts, slops, and a teapot with cold tea.

"Eh, ours is just as bad," said Elizabeth Bates, looking at the woman, not at the house. Mrs. Rigley put a shawl over her head and hurried out, saying:

"I shanna be a minute."

The other sat, noting with faint disapproval the general untidiness of the room. Then she fell to counting the shoes of various sizes scattered over the floor. There were twelve. She sighed and said to herself: "No wonder!"—glancing at the litter. There came the scratching of two pairs of feet on the yard, and the Rigleys entered. Elizabeth Bates rose. Rigley was a big man, with very large bones. His head looked particularly bony. Across his temple was a blue scar, caused by a wound got in the pit, a wound in which the coal-dust remained blue like tattooing.

"'Asna 'e come whoam yit?" asked the man, without any form of greet-   110 ing, but with deference and sympathy. "I couldna say wheer he is—'e's non ower theer!"—he jerked his head to signify the 'Prince of Wales'.

"'E's 'appen gone up to th' 'Yew'," said Mrs. Rigley.

There was another pause. Rigley had evidently something to get off his mind:

"Ah left 'im finishin' a stint," he began. "Loose-all 'ad bin gone about ten minutes when we com'n away, an' I shouted: 'Are ter comin', Walt?' an' 'e said: 'Go on, Ah shanna be but a'ef a minnit,' so we com'n ter th' bottom, me an' Bowers, thinkin' as 'e wor just behint, an' 'ud come up i' th' new bantle—"

He stood perplexed, as if answering a charge of deserting his mate. Elizabeth Bates, now again certain of disaster, hastened to reassure him:

115   "I expect 'e's gone up to th' 'Yew Tree', as you say. It's not the first
time. I've fretted myself into a fever before now. He'll come home when
they carry him."

"Ay, isn't it too bad!" deplored the other woman.

"I'll just step up to Dick's an' see if 'e *is* theer," offered the man, afraid
of appearing alarmed, afraid of taking liberties.

"Oh, I wouldn't think of bothering you that far," said Elizabeth Bates,
with emphasis, but he knew she was glad of his offer.

As they stumbled up the entry, Elizabeth Bates heard Rigley's wife
run across the yard and open her neighbour's door. At this, suddenly all the
blood in her body seemed to switch away from her heart.

120   "Mind!" warned Rigley. "Ah've said many a time as Ah'd fill up them
ruts in this entry, sumb'dy 'll be breakin' their legs yit."

She recovered herself and walked quickly along with the miner.

"I don't like leaving the children in bed, and nobody in the house,"
she said.

"No, you dunna!" he replied courteously. They were soon at the gate
of the cottage.

"Well, I shanna be many minnits. Dunna you be frettin' now, 'e'll be
all right," said the butty.°

125   "Thank you very much, Mr. Rigley," she replied.

"You're welcome!" he stammered, moving away. "I shanna be many
minnits."

The house was quiet. Elizabeth Bates took off her hat and shawl, and
rolled back the rug. When she had finished, she sat down. It was a few minutes past nine. She was startled by the rapid chuff of the winding-engine
at the pit, and the sharp whirr of the brakes on the rope as it descended.
Again she felt the painful sweep of her blood, and she put her hand to
her side, saying aloud: "Good gracious!—it's only the nine o'clock deputy
going down," rebuking herself.

She sat still, listening. Half an hour of this, and she was wearied out.

"What am I working myself up like this for?" she said pitiably to
herself, "I s'll only be doing myself some damage."

130   She took out her sewing again.

At a quarter to ten there were footsteps. One person! She watched for
the door to open. It was an elderly woman, in a black bonnet and a black
woollen shawl—his mother. She was about sixty years old, pale, with blue
eyes, and her face all wrinkled and lamentable. She shut the door and
turned to her daughter-in-law peevishly.

"Eh, Lizzie, whatever shall we do, whatever shall we do!" she cried.

Elizabeth drew back a little, sharply.

butty: a mine worker

"What is it, mother?" she said.

The elder woman seated herself on the sofa. 135

"I don't know, child, I can't tell you!"—she shook her head slowly. Elizabeth sat watching her, anxious and vexed.

"I don't know," replied the grandmother, sighing very deeply. "There's no end to my troubles, there isn't. The things I've gone through, I'm sure it's enough——!" She wept without wiping her eyes, the tears running.

"But, mother," interrupted Elizabeth, "what do you mean? What is it?"

The grandmother slowly wiped her eyes. The fountains of her tears were stopped by Elizabeth's directness. She wiped her eyes slowly.

"Poor child! Eh, you poor thing!" she moaned. "I don't know what 140 we're going to do, I don't—and you as you are— it's a thing, it is indeed!"

Elizabeth waited.

"Is he dead?" she asked, and at the words her heart swung violently, though she felt a slight flush of shame at the ultimate extravagance of the question. Her words sufficiently frightened the old lady, almost brought her to herself.

"Don't say so, Elizabeth! We'll hope it's not as bad as that; no, may the Lord spare us that, Elizabeth. Jack Rigley came just as I was sittin' down to a glass afore going to bed, an' 'e said: ''Appen you'll go down th' line, Mrs. Bates. Walt's had an accident. 'Appen you'll go an' sit wi' 'er till we can get him home.' I hadn't time to ask him a word afore he was gone. An' I put my bonnet on an' come straight down, Lizzie. I thought to myself: 'Eh, that poor blessed child, if anybody should come an' tell her of a sudden, there's no knowin' what'll 'appen to 'er.' You mustn't let it upset you, Lizzie—or you know what to expect. How long is it, six months—or is it five, Lizzie? Ay!"—the old woman shook her head—"time slips on, it slips on! Ay!"

Elizabeth's thoughts were busy elsewhere. If he was killed—would she be able to manage on the little pension and what she could earn?—she counted up rapidly. If he was hurt—they wouldn't take him to the hospital—how tiresome he would be to nurse!—but perhaps she'd be able to get him away from the drink and his hateful ways. She would—while he was ill. The tears offered to come to her eyes at the picture. But what sentimental luxury was this she was beginning? She turned to consider the children. At any rate she was absolutely necessary for them. They were her business.

"Ay!" repeated the old woman, "it seems but a week or two since he 145 brought me his first wages. Ay—he was a good lad, Elizabeth he was, in his way. I don't know why he got to be such a trouble, I don't. He was a happy lad at home, only full of spirits. But there's no mistake he's been a handful of trouble, he has! I hope the Lord'll spare him to mend his ways. I hope so, I hope so. You've had a sight o' trouble with him, Elizabeth, you have indeed. But he was a jolly enough lad wi' me, he was, I can assure you. I don't know how it is. . . . ."

The old woman continued to muse aloud, a monotonous irritating sound, while Elizabeth thought concentratedly, startled once, when she heard the winding-engine chuff quickly, and the brakes skirr with a shriek. Then she heard the engine more slowly, and the brakes made no sound. The old woman did not notice. Elizabeth waited in suspense. The mother-in-law talked, with lapses into silence.

"But he wasn't your son, Lizzie, an' it makes a difference. Whatever he was, I remember him when he was little, an' I learned to understand him and to make allowances. You've got to make allowances for them—"

It was half-past ten, and the old woman was saying: "But it's trouble from beginning to end; you're never too old for trouble, never too old for that—" when the gate banged back, and there were heavy feet on the steps.

"I'll go, Lizzie, let me go," cried the old woman, rising. But Elizabeth was at the door. It was a man in pit-clothes.

150 "They're bringin' 'im, Missis," he said. Elizabeth's heart halted a moment. Then it surged on again, almost suffocating her.

"Is he—is it bad?" she asked.

The man turned away, looking at the darkness:

"The doctor says 'e'd been dead hours. 'E saw 'im i' th' lamp-cabin."

The old woman, who stood just behind Elizabeth, dropped into a chair, and folded her hands, crying: "Oh, my boy, my boy!"

155 "Hush!" said Elizabeth, with a sharp twitch of a frown. "Be still, mother, don't waken th' children: I wouldn't have them down for anything!"

The old woman moaned softly, rocking herself. The man was drawing away. Elizabeth took a step forward.

"How was it?" she asked.

"Well, I couldn't say for sure," the man replied, very ill at ease. "'E wor finishin' a stint an' th' butties 'ad gone, an' a lot o' stuff come down atop 'n 'im."

"And crushed him?" cried the widow, with a shudder.

160 "No," said the man, "it fell at th' back of 'im. 'E wor under th' face, an' it niver touched 'im. It shut 'im in. It seems 'e wor smothered."

Elizabeth shrank back. She heard the old woman behind her cry:

"What?—what did 'e say it was?"

The man replied, more loudly: "'E wor smothered!"

Then the old woman wailed aloud, and this relieved Elizabeth.

165 "Oh, mother," she said, putting her hand on the old woman, "don't waken th' children, don't waken th' children."

She wept a little, unknowing, while the old mother rocked herself and moaned. Elizabeth remembered that they were bringing him home, and she must be ready. "They'll lay him in the parlour," she said to herself, standing a moment pale and perplexed.

Then she lighted a candle and went into the tiny room. The air was cold and damp, but she could not make a fire, there was no fireplace. She set down the candle and looked round. The candlelight glittered on the lustre-glasses, on the two vases that held some of the pink chrysanthemums, and on the dark mahogany. There was a cold, deathly smell of chrysanthemums in the room. Elizabeth stood looking at the flowers. She turned away, and calculated whether there would be room to lay him on the floor, between the couch and the chiffonier. She pushed the chairs aside. There would be room to lay him down and to step round him. Then she fetched the old red tablecloth, and another old cloth, spreading them down to save her bit of carpet. She shivered on leaving the parlour; so, from the dresser drawer she took a clean shirt and put it at the fire to air. All the time her mother-in-law was rocking herself in the chair and moaning.

"You'll have to move from there, mother," said Elizabeth. "They'll be bringing him in. Come in the rocker."

The old mother rose mechanically, and seated herself by the fire, continuing to lament. Elizabeth went into the pantry for another candle, and there, in the little pent-house under the naked tiles, she heard them coming. She stood still in the pantry doorway, listening. She heard them pass the end of the house, and come awkwardly down the three steps, a jumble of shuffling footsteps and muttering voices. The old woman was silent. The men were in the yard.

Then Elizabeth heard Matthews, the manager of the pit, say: "You go in first, Jim. Mind!" 170

The door came open, and the two women saw a collier backing into the room, holding one end of a stretcher, on which they could see the nailed pit-boots of the dead man. The two carriers halted, the man at the head stooping to the lintel of the door.

"Wheer will you have him?" asked the manager, a short, white-bearded man.

Elizabeth roused herself and came from the pantry carrying the unlighted candle.

"In the parlour," she said.

"In there, Jim!" pointed the manager, and the carriers backed round 175 into the tiny room. The coat with which they had covered the body fell off as they awkwardly turned through the two doorways, and the women saw their man, naked to the waist, lying stripped for work. The old woman began to moan in a low voice of horror.

"Lay th' stretcher at th' side," snapped the manager, "an' put 'im on th' cloths. Mind now, mind! Look you now—!"

One of the men had knocked off a vase of chrysanthemums. He stared awkwardly, then they set down the stretcher. Elizabeth did not look at her husband. As soon as she could get in the room, she went and picked up the broken vase and the flowers.

"Wait a minute!" she said.

The three men waited in silence while she mopped up the water with a duster.

180   "Eh, what a job, what a job, to be sure!" the manager was saying, rubbing his brow with trouble and perplexity. "Never knew such a thing in my life, never! He'd no business to ha' been left. I never knew such a thing in my life! Fell over him clean as a whistle, an' shut him in. Not four foot of space, there wasn't—yet it scarce bruised him."

He looked down at the dead man, lying prone, half naked, all grimed with coal-dust.

"'Sphyxiated', the doctor said. It *is* the most terrible job I've ever known. Seems as if it was done o' purpose. Clean over him, an' shut 'im in, like a mouse-trap"—he made a sharp, descending gesture with his hand.

The colliers standing by jerked aside their heads in hopeless comment.

The horror of the thing bristled upon them all.

185   Then they heard the girl's voice upstairs calling shrilly: "Mother, mother—who is it? Mother, who is it?"

Elizabeth hurried to the foot of the stairs and opened the door:

"Go to sleep!" she commanded sharply. "What are you shouting about? Go to sleep at once—there's nothing—"

Then she began to mount the stairs. They could hear her on the boards, and on the plaster floor of the little bedroom. They could hear her distinctly:

"What's the matter now ?—what's the matter with you, silly thing?"— her voice was much agitated, with an unreal gentleness.

190   "I thought it was some men come," said the plaintive voice of the child. "Has he come?"

"Yes, they've brought him. There's nothing to make a fuss about. Go to sleep now, like a good child."

They could hear her voice in the bedroom, they waited whilst she covered the children under the bedclothes.

"Is he drunk?" asked the girl, timidly, faintly.

"No! No—he's not! He—he's asleep."

195   "Is he asleep downstairs?"

"Yes—and don't make a noise."

There was silence for a moment, then the men heard the frightened child again:

"What's that noise?"

"It's nothing, I tell you, what are you bothering for?"

200   The noise was the grandmother moaning. She was oblivious of everything, sitting on her chair rocking and moaning. The manager put his hand on her arm and bade her "Sh—sh!!"

The old woman opened her eyes and looked at him. She was shocked by this interruption, and seemed to wonder.

"What time is it?" the plaintive thin voice of the child, sinking back unhappily into sleep, asked this last question.

"Ten o'clock," answered the mother more softly. Then she must have bent down and kissed the children.

Matthews beckoned to the men to come away. They put on their caps and took up the stretcher. Stepping over the body, they tiptoed out of the house. None of them spoke till they were far from the wakeful children.

When Elizabeth came down she found her mother alone on the parlour floor, leaning over the dead man, the tears dropping on him. 205

"We must lay him out," the wife said. She put on the kettle, then returning knelt at the feet, and began to unfasten the knotted leather laces. The room was clammy and dim with only one candle, so that she had to bend her face almost to the floor. At last she got off the heavy boots and put them away.

"You must help me now," she whispered to the old woman. Together they stripped the man.

When they arose, saw him lying in the naïve dignity of death, the women stood arrested in fear and respect. For a few moments they remained still, looking down, the old mother whimpering. Elizabeth felt countermanded. She saw him, how utterly inviolable he lay in himself. She had nothing to do with him. She could not accept it. Stooping, she laid her hand on him, in claim. He was still warm, for the mine was hot where he had died. His mother had his face between her hands, and was murmuring incoherently. The old tears fell in succession as drops from wet leaves; the mother was not weeping, merely her tears flowed. Elizabeth embraced the body of her husband, with cheek and lips. She seemed to be listening, inquiring, trying to get some connection. But she could not. She was driven away. He was impregnable.

She rose, went into the kitchen, where she poured warm water into a bowl, brought soap and flannel and a soft towel.

"I must wash him," she said. 210

Then the old mother rose stiffly, and watched Elizabeth as she carefully washed his face, carefully brushing the big blond moustache from his mouth with the flannel. She was afraid with a bottomless fear, so she ministered to him. The old woman, jealous, said:

"Let me wipe him!"—and she knelt on the other side drying slowly as Elizabeth washed, her big black bonnet sometimes brushing the dark head of her daughter-in-law. They worked thus in silence for a long time. They never forgot it was death, and the touch of the man's dead body gave them strange emotions, different in each of the women; a great dread possessed them both, the mother felt the lie was given to her womb, she was denied; the wife felt the utter isolation of the human soul, the child within her was a weight apart from her.

At last it was finished. He was a man of handsome body, and his face showed no traces of drink. He was blond, full-fleshed, with fine limbs. But he was dead.

"Bless him," whispered his mother, looking always at his face, and speaking out of sheer terror. "Dear lad—bless him!" She spoke in a faint, sibilant ecstasy of fear and mother love.

215 Elizabeth sank down again to the floor, and put her face against his neck, and trembled and shuddered. But she had to draw away again. He was dead, and her living flesh had no place against his. A great dread and weariness held her: she was so unavailing. Her life was gone like this.

"White as milk he is, clear as a twelve-month baby, bless him, the darling!" the old mother murmured to herself. "Not a mark on him, clear and clean and white, beautiful as ever a child was made," she murmured with pride. Elizabeth kept her face hidden.

"He went peaceful, Lizzie—peaceful as sleep. Isn't he beautiful, the lamb? Ay—he must ha' made his peace, Lizzie. 'Appen he made it all right, Lizzie, shut in there. He'd have time. He wouldn't look like this if he hadn't made his peace. The lamb, the dear lamb. Eh, but he had a hearty laugh. I loved to hear it. He had the heartiest laugh, Lizzie, as a lad—"

Elizabeth looked up. The man's mouth was fallen back, slightly open under the cover of the moustache. The eyes, half shut, did not show glazed in the obscurity. Life with its smoky burning gone from him, had left him apart and utterly alien to her. And she knew what a stranger he was to her. In her womb was ice of fear, because of this separate stranger with whom she had been living as one flesh. Was this what it all meant—utter, intact separateness, obscured by heat of living? In dread she turned her face away. The fact was too deadly. There had been nothing between them, and yet they had come together, exchanging their nakedness repeatedly. Each time he had taken her, they had been two isolated beings, far apart as now. He was no more responsible than she. The child was like ice in her womb. For as she looked at the dead man, her mind, cold and detached, said clearly: "Who am I? What have I been doing? I have been fighting a husband who did not exist. *He* existed all the time. What wrong have I done ? What was that I have been living with? There lies the reality, this man." And her soul died in her for fear: she knew she had never seen him, he had never seen her, they had met in the dark and had fought in the dark, not knowing whom they met nor whom they fought. And now she saw, and turned silent in seeing. For she had been wrong. She had said he was something he was not; she had felt familiar with him. Whereas he was apart all the while, living as she never lived, feeling as she never felt.

In fear and shame she looked at his naked body, that she had known falsely. And he was the father of her children. Her soul was torn from her body and stood apart. She looked at his naked body and was ashamed, as if she had denied it. After all, it was itself. It seemed awful to her. She looked at his face, and she turned her own face to the wall. For his look was other than hers, his way was not her way. She had denied him what he was—she saw it now. She had refused him as himself. And this had been her life, and his life. She was grateful to death, which restored the truth. And she knew she was not dead.

And all the while her heart was bursting with grief and pity for him. What had he suffered? What stretch of horror for this helpless man! She was rigid with agony. She had not been able to help him. He had been cruelly injured, this naked man, this other being, and she could make no reparation. There were the children—but the children belonged to life. This dead man had nothing to do with them. He and she were only channels through which life had flowed to issue in the children. She was a mother—but how awful she knew it now to have been a wife. And he, dead now, how awful he must have felt it to be a husband. She felt that in the next world he would be a stranger to her. If they met there, in the beyond, they would only be ashamed of what had been before. The children had come, for some mysterious reason, out of both of them. But the children did not unite them. Now he was dead, she knew how eternally he was apart from her, how eternally he had nothing more to do with her. She saw this episode of her life closed. They had denied each other in life. Now he had withdrawn. An anguish came over her. It was finished then: it had become hopeless between them long before he died. Yet he had been her husband. But how little!

"Have you got his shirt, 'Lizabeth?"

Elizabeth turned without answering, though she strove to weep and behave as her mother-in-law expected. But she could not, she was silenced. She went into the kitchen and returned with the garment.

"It is aired," she said, grasping the cotton shirt here and there to try. She was almost ashamed to handle him; what right had she or anyone to lay hands on him; but her touch was humble on his body. It was hard work to clothe him. He was so heavy and inert. A terrible dread gripped her all the while: that he could be so heavy and utterly inert, unresponsive, apart. The horror of the distance between them was almost too much for her—it was so infinite a gap she must look across.

At last it was finished. They covered him with a sheet and left him lying, with his face bound. And she fastened the door of the little parlour, lest the children should see what was lying there. Then, with peace sunk heavy on her heart, she went about making tidy the kitchen. She knew she submitted to life, which was her immediate master. But from death, her ultimate master, she winced with fear and shame.

220

QUESTIONS

1. Discuss the title. What is the symbolic significance of the chrysanthemums? Does their meaning change as the story proceeds?
2. How is Elizabeth Bates characterized? Does her physical description help to characterize her? Is she a likable character?
3. What kind of marriage did Elizabeth and her husband have before his death?
4. Contrast the grief felt by Walter's mother and that felt by Elizabeth. Whose grief is the more deeply felt?
5. What is the significance of Elizabeth's being pregnant with another child? How does this fact relate to Walter's death?
6. Focus on the closing paragraphs of the story. What theme is Lawrence stressing here? What is the overarching theme of the entire story?

D. H. LAWRENCE
The Horse-Dealer's Daughter

"Well, Mabel, and what are you going to do with yourself?" asked Joe, with foolish flippancy. He felt quite safe himself. Without listening for an answer, he turned aside, worked a grain of tobacco to the tip of his tongue, and spat it out. He did not care about anything, since he felt safe himself.

The three brothers and the sister sat round the desolate breakfast-table, attempting some sort of desultory consultation. The morning's post had given the final tap to the family fortunes, and all was over. The dreary dining-room itself, with its heavy mahogany furniture, looked as if it were waiting to be done away with.

But the consultation amounted to nothing. There was a strange air of ineffectuality about the three men, as they sprawled at table, smoking and reflecting vaguely on their own condition. The girl was alone, a rather short, sullen-looking young woman of twenty-seven. She did not share the same life as her brothers. She would have been good-looking, save for the impressive fixity of her face, "bull-dog," as her brothers called it.

There was a confused tramping of horses' feet outside. The three men all sprawled round in their chairs to watch. Beyond the dark holly bushes that separated the strip of lawn from the high-road, they could see a cavalcade of shire horses swinging out of their own yard, being taken for exercise. This was the last time. These were the last horses that would go through their hands. The young men watched with critical, callous look. They were all frightened at the collapse of their lives, and the sense of disaster in which they were involved left them no inner freedom.

5   Yet they were three fine, well-set fellows enough. Joe, the eldest, was a man of thirty-three, broad and handsome in a hot, flushed way. His face

THE HORSE-DEALER'S DAUGHTER   First published in 1922. See the footnote on page 402 for more information on Lawrence and his career.

was red, he twisted his black moustache over a thick finger, his eyes were shallow and restless. He had a sensual way of uncovering his teeth when he laughed, and his bearing was stupid. Now he watched the horses with a glazed look of helplessness in his eyes, a certain stupor of downfall.

The great draught-horses swung past. They were tied head to tail, four of them, and they heaved along to where a lane branched off from the high-road, planting their great hoofs floutingly in the fine black mud, swinging their great rounded haunches sumptuously, and trotting a few sudden steps as they were led into the lane, round the corner. Every movement showed a massive, slumbrous strength, and a stupidity which held them in subjection. The groom at the head looked back, jerking the leading rope. And the cavalcade moved out of sight up the lane, the tail of the last horse, bobbed up tight and stiff, held out taut from the swinging great haunches as they rocked behind the hedges in a motion-like sleep.

Joe watched with glazed hopeless eyes. The horses were almost like his own body to him. He felt he was done for now. Luckily he was engaged to a woman as old as himself, and therefore her father, who was steward of a neighboring estate, would provide him with a job. He would marry and go into harness. His life was over, he would be a subject animal now.

He turned uneasily aside, the retreating steps of the horses echoing in his ears. Then, with foolish restlessness, he reached for the scraps of bacon-rind from the plates, and making a faint whistling sound, flung them to the terrier that lay against the fender. He watched the dog swallow them, and waited till the creature looked into his eyes. Then a faint grin came on his face, and in a high, foolish voice he said:

"You won't get much more bacon, shall you, you little b——?"

The dog faintly and dismally wagged its tail, then lowered its 10 haunches, circled round, and lay down again.

There was another helpless silence at the table. Joe sprawled uneasily in his seat, not willing to go till the family conclave was dissolved. Fred Henry, the second brother, was erect, clean-limbed, alert. He had watched the passing of the horses with more *sang-froid*. If he was an animal, like Joe, he was an animal which controls, not one which is controlled. He was master of any horse, and he carried himself with a well-tempered air of mastery. But he was not master of the situations of life. He pushed his coarse brown moustache upwards, off his lip, and glanced irritably at his sister, who sat impassive and inscrutable.

"You'll go and stop with Lucy for a bit, shan't you?" he asked. The girl did not answer.

"I don't see what else you can do," persisted Fred Henry.

"Go as a skivvy,"° Joe interpolated laconically.

The girl did not move a muscle. 15

skivvy: household maid

"If I was her, I should go in for training for a nurse," said Malcolm, the youngest of them all. He was the baby of the family, a young man of twenty-two, with a fresh, jaunty *museau.*°

But Mabel did not take any notice of him. They had talked at her and round her for so many years, that she hardly heard them at all.

The marble clock on the mantelpiece softly chimed the half-hour, the dog rose uneasily from the hearth-rug and looked at the party at the breakfast-table. But still they sat in an ineffectual conclave.

"Oh, all right," said Joe suddenly, apropos of nothing. "I'll get a move on."

20   He pushed back his chair, straddled his knees with a downward jerk, to get them free, in horsey fashion, and went to the fire. Still he did not go out of the room; he was curious to know what the others would do or say. He began to charge his pipe, looking down at the dog and saying in a high, affected voice:

"Going wi' me? Going wi' me are ter? Tha'rt goin' further than tha counts on just now, dost hear?"

The dog faintly wagged his tail, the man stuck out his jaw and covered his pipe with his hands, and puffed intently, losing himself in the tobacco, looking down all the while at the dog with an absent brown eye. The dog looked up at him in mournful distrust. Joe stood with his knees stuck out, in real horsey fashion.

"Have you had a letter from Lucy?" Fred Henry asked of his sister.

"Last week," came the neutral reply.

25   "And what does she say?"

There was no answer.

"Does she *ask* you to go and stop there?" persisted Fred Henry.

"She says I can if I like."

"Well, then, you'd better. Tell her you'll come on Monday."

30   This was received in silence.

"That's what you'll do then, is it?" said Fred Henry, in some exasperation.

But she made no answer. There was a silence of futility and irritation in the room. Malcolm grinned fatuously.

"You'll have to make up your mind between now and next Wednesday," said Joe loudly, "or else find your lodgings on the kerbstone."

The face of the young woman darkened, but she sat on immutable.

35   "Here's Jack Ferguson!" exclaimed Malcolm, who was looking aimlessly out of the window.

"Where?" exclaimed Joe loudly.

"Just gone past."

"Coming in?"

museau: face (French)

Malcolm craned his neck to see the gate.

"Yes," he said.   40

There was a silence. Mabel sat on like one condemned, at the head of the table. Then a whistle was heard from the kitchen. The dog got up and barked sharply. Joe opened the door and shouted:

"Come on."

After a moment a young man entered. He was muffled up in overcoat and a purple woollen scarf, and his tweed cap, which he did not remove, was pulled down on his head. He was of medium height, his face was rather long and pale, his eyes looked tired.

"Hello, Jack! Well, Jack!" exclaimed Malcolm and Joe. Fred Henry merely said: "Jack."

"What's doing?" asked the newcomer, evidently addressing Fred Henry.   45

"Same. We've got to be out by Wednesday. Got a cold?"

"I have—got it bad, too."

"Why don't you stop in?"

"*Me* stop in? When I can't stand on my legs, perhaps I shall have a chance." The young man spoke huskily. He had a slight Scotch accent.

"It's a knock-out, isn't it," said Joe, boisterously, "if a doctor goes   50
round croaking with a cold. Looks bad for the patients, doesn't it?"

The young doctor looked at him slowly.

"Anything the matter with *you*, then?" he asked sarcastically.

"Not as I know of. Damn your eyes, I hope not. Why?"

"I thought you were very concerned about the patients, wondered if you might be one yourself."

"Damn it, no, I've never been patient to no flaming doctor, and hope   55
I never shall be," returned Joe.

At this point Mabel rose from the table, and they all seemed to become aware of her existence. She began putting the dishes together. The young doctor looked at her, but did not address her. He had not greeted her. She went out of the room with the tray, her face impassive and unchanged.

"When are you off then, all of you?" asked the doctor.

"I'm catching the eleven-forty," replied Malcolm. "Are you goin' down wi' th' trap, Joe?"

"Yes, I've told you I'm going down wi' th' trap, haven't I?"

"We'd better be getting her in then. So long Jack, if I don't see you   60
before I go," said Malcolm, shaking hands.

He went out, followed by Joe, who seemed to have his tail between his legs.

"Well, this is the devil's own," exclaimed the doctor, when he was left alone with Fred Henry. "Going before Wednesday, are you?"

"That's the orders," replied the other.

"Where, to Northampton?"

65   "That's it."

"The devil!" exclaimed Ferguson, with quiet chagrin.

And there was silence between the two.

"All settled up, are you?" asked Ferguson.

"About."

70   There was another pause.

"Well, I shall miss yer, Freddy, boy," said the young doctor.

"And I shall miss thee, Jack," returned the other.

"Miss you like hell," mused the doctor.

Fred Henry turned aside. There was nothing to say. Mabel came in again, to finish clearing the table.

75   "What are *you* going to do, then, Miss Pervin?" asked Ferguson. "Going to your sister's, are you?"

Mabel looked at him with her steady, dangerous eyes, that always made him uncomfortable, unsettling his superficial ease.

"No," she said.

"Well, what in the name of fortune *are* you going to do? Say what you mean to do," cried Fred Henry, with futile intensity.

But she only averted her head, and continued her work. She folded the white table-cloth, and put on the chenille cloth.

80   "The sulkiest bitch that ever trod!" muttered her brother.

But she finished her task with perfectly impassive face, the young doctor watching her interestedly all the while. Then she went out.

Fred Henry stared after her, clenching his lips, his blue eyes fixing in sharp antagonism, as he made a grimace of sour exasperation.

"You could bray her into bits, and that's all you'd get out of her," he said, in a small, narrowed tone.

The doctor smiled faintly.

85   "What's she *going* to do, then?" he asked.

"Strike me if *I* know!" returned the other.

There was a pause. Then the doctor stirred.

"I'll be seeing you tonight, shall I?" he said to his friend.

"Ay—where's it to be? Are we going over to Jessdale?"

90   "I don't know. I've got such a cold on me. I'll come round to the 'Moon and Stars,' anyway."

"Let Lizzie and May miss their night for once, eh?"

"That's it—if I feel as I do now."

"All's one—"

The two young men went through the passage and down to the back door together. The house was large, but it was servantless now, and desolate. At the back was a small brick house-yard and beyond that a big square, graveled fine and red, and having stables on two sides. Sloping, dank, winter-dark fields stretched away on the open sides.

But the stables were empty. Joseph Pervin, the father of the family, had 95 been a man of no education, who had become a fairly large horse dealer. The stables had been full of horses, there was a great turmoil and come-and-go of horses and of dealers and grooms. Then the kitchen was full of servants. But of late things had declined. The old man had married a second time, to retrieve his fortunes. Now he was dead and everything was gone to the dogs, there was nothing but debt and threatening.

For months, Mabel had been servantless in the big house, keeping the home together in penury for her ineffectual brothers. She had kept house for ten years. But previously it was with unstinted means. Then, however brutal and coarse everything was, the sense of money had kept her proud, confident. The men might be foul-mouthed, the women in the kitchen might have bad reputations, her brothers might have illegitimate children. But so long as there was money, the girl felt herself established, and brutally proud, reserved.

No company came to the house, save dealers and coarse men. Mabel had no associates of her own sex, after her sister went away. But she did not mind. She went regularly to church, she attended to her father. And she lived in the memory of her mother, who had died when she was fourteen, and whom she had loved. She had loved her father, too, in a different way, depending upon him, and feeling secure in him, until at the age of fifty-four he married again. And then she had set hard against him. Now he had died and left them all hopelessly in debt.

She had suffered badly during the period of poverty. Nothing, however, could shake the curious, sullen, animal pride that dominated each member of the family. Now, for Mabel, the end had come. Still she would not cast about her. She would follow her own way just the same. She would always hold the keys of her own situation. Mindless and persistent, she endured from day to day. Why should she think? Why should she answer anybody? It was enough that this was the end, and there was no way out. She need not pass any more darkly along the main street of the small town, avoiding every eye. She need not demean herself any more, going into the shops and buying the cheapest food. This was at an end. She thought of nobody, not even of herself. Mindless and persistent, she seemed in a sort of ecstasy to be coming nearer to her fulfilment, her own glorification, approaching her dead mother, who was glorified.

In the afternoon, she took a little bag, with shears and sponge and a small scrubbing-brush, and went out. It was a gray, wintry day, with saddened, dark green fields and an atmosphere blackened by the smoke of foundries not far off. She went quickly, darkly along the causeway, heeding nobody, through the town to the churchyard.

100   There she always felt secure, as if no one could see her, although as a matter of fact she was exposed to the stare of everyone who passed along under the churchyard wall. Nevertheless, once under the shadow of the great looming church, among the graves, she felt immune from the world, reserved within the thick churchyard wall as in another country.

Carefully she clipped the grass from the grave, and arranged the pinky white, small chrysanthemums in the tin cross. When this was done, she took an empty jar from a neighboring grave, brought water, and carefully, most scrupulously sponged the marble headstone and the coping-stone.

It gave her sincere satisfaction to do this. She felt in immediate contact with the world of her mother. She took minute pains, went through the park in a state bordering on pure happiness, as if in performing this task she came into a subtle, intimate connection with her mother. For the life she followed here in the world was far less real than the world of death she inherited from her mother.

The doctor's house was just by the church. Ferguson, being a mere hired assistant, was slave to the country-side. As he hurried now to attend to the out-patients in the surgery, glancing across the graveyard with his quick eye, he saw the girl at her task at the grave. She seemed so intent and remote, it was like looking into another world. Some mystical element was touched in him. He slowed down as he walked, watching her as if spellbound.

She lifted her eyes, feeling him looking. Their eyes met. And each looked away again at once, each feeling, in some way, found out by the other. He lifted his cap and passed on down the road. There remained distinct in his consciousness, like a vision, the memory of her face, lifted from the tombstone in the churchyard, and looking at him with slow, large, portentous eyes. It *was* portentous, her face. It seemed to mesmerize him. There was a heavy power in her eyes which laid hold of his whole being, as if he had drunk some powerful drug. He had been feeling weak and done before. Now the life came back into him, he felt delivered from his own fretted, daily self.

105   He finished his duties at the surgery as quickly as might be, hastily filling up the bottles of the waiting people with cheap drugs. Then, in perpetual haste, he set off again to visit several cases in another part of his round, before tea-time. At all times he preferred to walk if he could, but particularly when he was not well. He fancied the motion restored him.

The afternoon was falling. It was gray, deadened, and wintry, with a slow, moist, heavy coldness sinking in and deadening all the faculties. But why should he think or notice? He hastily climbed the hill and turned across the dark green fields, following the black cinder-track. In the distance, across a shallow dip in the country, the small town was clustered like smouldering ash, a tower, a spire, a heap of low, raw, extinct houses. And on the nearest fringe of the town, sloping into the dip, was Oldmeadow, the Pervins' house. He could see the stables and the outbuildings distinctly, as they lay toward him on the slope. Well, he would not go there many more times! Another resource would be lost to him, another place gone: the only company he cared for in the alien, ugly little town he was losing. Nothing but work, drudgery, constant hastening from dwelling to dwelling among the colliers and the iron-workers. It wore him out, but at the same time he had a craving for it. It was a stimulant to him to be in the homes of the working people, moving, as it were, through the innermost body of their life. His nerves were excited and gratified. He could come so near, into the very lives of the rough, inarticulate, powerfully emotional men and women. He grumbled, he said he hated the hellish hole. But as a matter of fact it excited him, the contact with the rough, strongly-feeling people was a stimulant applied direct to his nerves.

Below Oldmeadow, in the green, shallow, soddened hollow of fields, lay a square, deep pond. Roving across the landscape, the doctor's quick eye detected a figure in black passing through the gate of the field, down toward the pond. He looked again. It would be Mabel Pervin. His mind suddenly became alive and attentive.

Why was she going down there? He pulled up on the path on the slope above, and stood staring. He could just make sure of the small black figure moving in the hollow of the failing day. He seemed to see her in the midst of such obscurity, that he was like a clairvoyant, seeing rather with the mind's eye than with ordinary sight. Yet he could see her positively enough, whilst he kept his eye attentive. He felt, if he looked away from her, in the thick, ugly falling dusk, he would lose her altogether.

He followed her minutely as she moved, direct and intent, like something transmitted rather than stirring in voluntary activity, straight down the field toward the pond. There she stood on the bank for a moment. She never raised her head. Then she waded slowly into the water.

He stood motionless as the small black figure walked slowly and deliberately toward the center of the pond, very slowly, gradually moving deeper into the motionless water, and still moving forward as the water got up to her breast. Then he could see her no more in the dusk of the dead afternoon.

"There!" he exclaimed. "Would you believe it?"

And he hastened straight down, running over the wet, soddened fields, pushing through the hedges, down into the depression of callous wintry obscurity. It took him several minutes to come to the pond. He stood on the bank, breathing heavily. He could see nothing. His eyes seemed to penetrate the dead water. Yes, perhaps that was the dark shadow of her black clothing beneath the surface of the water.

He slowly ventured into the pond. The bottom was deep, soft clay, he sank in, and the water clasped dead cold round his legs. As he stirred he could smell the cold, rotten clay that fouled up into the water. It was objectionable in his lungs. Still, repelled and yet not heeding, he moved deeper into the pond. The cold water rose over his thighs, over his loins, upon his abdomen. The lower part of his body was all sunk in the hideous cold element. And the bottom was so deeply soft and uncertain, he was afraid of pitching with his mouth underneath. He could not swim, and was afraid.

He crouched a little, spreading his hands under the water and moving them round, trying to feel for her. The dead cold pond swayed upon his chest. He moved again, a little deeper, and again, with his hands underneath, he felt all around under the water. And he touched her clothing. But it evaded his fingers. He made a desperate effort to grasp it.

115   And so doing he lost his balance and went under, horribly, suffocating in the foul earthy water, struggling madly for a few moments. At last, after what seemed an eternity, he got his footing, rose again into the air and looked around. He gasped, and knew he was in the world. Then he looked at the water. She had risen near him. He grasped her clothing, and drawing her nearer, turned to take his way to land again.

He went very slowly, carefully, absorbed in the slow progress. He rose higher, climbing out of the pond. The water was now only about his legs; he was thankful, full of relief to be out of the clutches of the pond. He lifted her and staggered onto the bank, out of the horror of wet, gray clay.

He laid her down on the bank. She was quite unconscious and running with water. He made the water come from her mouth, he worked to restore her. He did not have to work very long before he could feel the breathing begin again in her; she was breathing naturally. He worked a little longer. He could feel her live beneath his hands; she was coming back. He wiped her face, wrapped her in his overcoat, looked round into the dim, dark gray world, then lifted her and staggered down the bank and across the fields.

It seemed an unthinkably long way, and his burden so heavy he felt he would never get to the house. But at last he was in the stable-yard, and then in the house-yard. He opened the door and went into the house. In the kitchen he laid her down on the hearth-rug and called. The house was empty. But the fire was burning in the grate.

Then again he kneeled to attend to her. She was breathing regularly, her eyes were wide open and as if conscious, but there seemed something missing in her look. She was conscious in herself, but unconscious of her surroundings.

120   He ran upstairs, took blankets from a bed, and put them before the fire to warm. Then he removed her saturated, earthy-smelling clothing, rubbed her dry with a towel, and wrapped her naked in the blankets. Then

he went into the dining-room, to look for spirits. There was a little whisky. He drank a gulp himself, and put some into her mouth.

The effect was instantaneous. She looked full into his face, as if she had been seeing him for some time, and yet had only just become conscious of him.

"Dr. Ferguson?" she said.

"What?" he answered.

He was divesting himself of his coat, intending to find some dry clothing upstairs. He could not bear the smell of the dead, clayey water, and he was mortally afraid for his own health.

"What did I do?" she asked.   125

"Walked into the pond," he replied. He had begun to shudder like one sick, and could hardly attend to her. Her eyes remained full on him, he seemed to be going dark in his mind, looking back at her helplessly. The shuddering became quieter in him, his life came back to him, dark and unknowing, but strong again.

"Was I out of my mind?" she asked, while her eyes were fixed on him all the time.

"Maybe, for the moment," he replied. He felt quiet, because his strength had come back. The strange fretful strain had left him.

"Am I out of my mind now?" she asked.

"Are you?" he reflected a moment. "No," he answered truthfully. "I   130 don't see that you are." He turned his face aside. He was afraid now, because he felt dazed, and felt dimly that her power was stronger than his, in this issue. And she continued to look at him fixedly all the time. "Can you tell me where I shall find some dry things to put on?" he asked.

"Did you dive into the pond for me?" she asked.

"No," he answered. "I walked in. But I went in over head as well."

There was silence for a moment. He hesitated. He very much wanted to go upstairs to get into dry clothing. But there was another desire in him. And she seemed to hold him. His will seemed to have gone to sleep, and left him, standing there slack before her. But he felt warm inside himself. He did not shudder at all, though his clothes were sodden on him.

"Why did you?" she asked.

"Because I didn't want you to do such a foolish thing," he said.   135

"It wasn't foolish," she said, still gazing at him as she lay on the floor, with a sofa cushion under her head. "It was the right thing to do. *I* knew best, then."

"I'll go and shift these wet things," he said. But still he had not the power to move out of her presence, until she sent him. It was as if she had the life of his body in her hands, and he could not extricate himself. Or perhaps he did not want to.

Suddenly she sat up. Then she became aware of her own immediate condition. She felt the blankets about her, she knew her own limbs. For a moment it seemed as if her reason were going. She looked round, with wild eye, as if seeking something. He stood still with fear. She saw her clothing lying scattered.

"Who undressed me?" she asked, her eyes resting full and inevitable on his face.

140   "I did," he replied, "to bring you round."

For some moments she sat and gazed at him awfully, her lips parted. "Do you love me, then?" she asked.

He only stood and stared at her, fascinated. His soul seemed to melt.

She shuffled forward on her knees, and put her arms round him, round his legs, as he stood there, pressing her breasts against his knees and thighs, clutching him with strange, convulsive certainty, pressing his thighs against her, drawing him to her face, her throat, as she looked up at him with flaring, humble eyes of transfiguration, triumphant in first possession.

145   "You love me," she murmured, in strange transport, yearning and triumphant and confident. "You love me. I know you love me, I know."

And she was passionately kissing his knees, through the wet clothing, passionately and indiscriminately kissing his knees, his legs, as if unaware of everything.

He looked down at the tangled wet hair, the wild, bare, animal shoulders. He was amazed, bewildered, and afraid. He had never thought of loving her. He had never wanted to love her. When he rescued her and restored her, he was a doctor, and she was a patient. He had had no single personal thought of her. Nay, this introduction of the personal element was very distasteful to him, a violation of his professional honor. It was horrible to have her there embracing his knees. It was horrible. He revolted from it, violently. And yet—and yet—he had not the power to break away.

She looked at him again, with the same supplication of powerful love, and that same transcendent, frightening light of triumph. In view of the delicate flame which seemed to come from her face like a light, he was powerless. And yet he had never intended to love her. He had never intended. And something stubborn in him could not give way.

"You love me," she repeated, in a murmur of deep, rhapsodic assurance. "You love me."

150   Her hands were drawing him, drawing him down to her. He was afraid, even a little horrified. For he had, really, no intention of loving her. Yet her hands were drawing him toward her. He put out his hand quickly to steady himself, and grasped her bare shoulder. A flame seemed to burn the hand that grasped her soft shoulder. He had no intention of loving her: his whole will was against his yielding. It was horrible. And yet wonderful

was the touch of her shoulders, beautiful the shining of her face. Was she perhaps mad? He had a horror of yielding to her. Yet something in him ached also.

He had been staring away at the door, away from her. But his hand remained on her shoulder. She had gone suddenly very still. He looked down at her. Her eyes were now wide with fear, with doubt, the light was dying from her face, a shadow of terrible grayness was returning. He could not bear the touch of her eyes' question upon him, and the look of death behind the question.

With an inward groan he gave way, and let his heart yield toward her. A sudden gentle smile came on his face. And her eyes, which never left his face, slowly, slowly filled with tears. He watched the strange water rise in her eyes, like some slow fountain coming up. And his heart seemed to burn and melt away in his breast.

He could not bear to look at her any more. He dropped on his knees and caught her head with his arms and pressed her face against his throat. She was very still. His heart, which seemed to have broken, was burning with a kind of agony in his breast. And he felt her slow, hot tears wetting his throat. But he could not move.

He felt the hot tears wet his neck and the hollows of his neck, and he remained motionless, suspended through one of man's eternities. Only now it had become indispensable to him to have her face pressed close to him; he could never let her go again. He could never let her head go away from the close clutch of his arm. He wanted to remain like that forever, with his heart hurting him in a pain that was also life to him. Without knowing, he was looking down on her damp, soft brown hair.

Then, as it were suddenly, he smelt the horrid stagnant smell of that water. And at the same moment she drew away from him and looked at him. Her eyes were wistful and unfathomable. He was afraid of them, he fell to kissing her, not knowing what he was doing. He wanted her eyes not to have that terrible, wistful, unfathomable look. 155

When she turned her face to him again, a faint delicate flush was glowing, and there was again dawning that terrible shining of joy in her eyes, which really terrified him, and yet which he now wanted to see, because he feared the look of doubt still more.

"You love me?" she said, rather faltering.

"Yes." The word cost him a painful effort. Not because it wasn't true. But because it was too newly true, the *saying* seemed to tear open again his newly-torn heart. And he hardly wanted it to be true, even now.

She lifted her face to him, and he bent forward and kissed her on the mouth, gently, with the one kiss that is an eternal pledge. And as he kissed her his heart strained again in his breast. He never intended to love her.

But now it was over. He had crossed over the gulf to her, and all that he had left behind had shrivelled and become void.

160   After the kiss, her eyes again slowly filled with tears. She sat still, away from him, with her face drooped aside, and her hands folded in her lap. The tears fell very slowly. There was complete silence. He too sat there motionless and silent on the hearth-rug. The strange pain of his heart that was broken seemed to consume him. That he should love her? That this was love! That he should be ripped open in this way! Him, a doctor! How they would all jeer if they knew! It was agony to him to think they might know.

In the curious naked pain of the thought he looked again to her. She was sitting there drooped into a muse. He saw a tear fall, and his heart flared hot. He saw for the first time that one of her shoulders was quite uncovered, one arm bare, he could see one of her small breasts; dimly, because it had become almost dark in the room.

"Why are you crying?" he asked, in an altered voice.

She looked up at him, and behind her tears the consciousness of her situation for the first time brought a dark look of shame to her eyes.

"I'm not crying, really," she said, watching him, half frightened.

165   He reached his hand, and softly closed it on her bare arm.

"I love you! I love you!" he said in a soft, low vibrating voice, unlike himself.

She shrank, and dropped her head. The soft, penetrating grip of his hand on her arm distressed her. She looked up at him.

"I want to go," she said. "I want to go and get you some dry things."

"Why?" he said. "I'm all right."

170   "But I want to go," she said. "And I want you to change your things."

He released her arm, and she wrapped herself in the blanket, looking at him rather frightened. And still she did not rise.

"Kiss me," she said wistfully.

He kissed her, but briefly, half in anger.

Then, after a second, she rose nervously, all mixed up in the blanket. He watched her in her confusion as she tried to extricate herself and wrap herself up so that she could walk. He watched her relentlessly, as she knew. And as she went, the blanket trailing, and as he saw a glimpse of her feet and her white leg, he tried to remember her as she was when he had wrapped her in the blanket. But then he didn't want to remember, because she had been nothing to him then, and his nature revolted from remembering her as she was when she was nothing to him.

175   A tumbling, muffled noise from within the dark house startled him. Then he heard her voice: "There are clothes." He rose and went to the foot of the stairs, and gathered up the garments she had thrown down. Then he came back to the fire, to rub himself down and dress. He grinned at his own appearance when he had finished.

The fire was sinking, so he put on coal. The house was now quite dark, save for the light of a street-lamp that shone in faintly from beyond the holly trees. He lit the gas with matches he found on the mantel-piece. Then he emptied the pockets of his own clothes, and threw all his wet things in a heap into the scullery. After which he gathered up her sodden clothes, gently, and put them in a separate heap on the copper-top in the scullery.

It was six o'clock on the clock. His own watch had stopped. He ought to go back to the surgery. He waited, and still she did not come down. So he went to the foot of the stairs and called:

"I shall have to go."

Almost immediately he heard her coming down. She had on her best dress of black voile, and her hair was tidy, but still damp. She looked at him—and in spite of herself, smiled.

"I don't like you in those clothes," she said. 180

"Do I look a sight?" he answered.

They were shy of one another.

"I'll make you some tea," she said.

"No. I must go."

"Must you?" And she looked at him again with the wide, strained, 185 doubtful eyes. And again, from the pain of his breast, he knew how he loved her. He went and bent to kiss her, gently, passionately, with his heart's painful kiss.

"And my hair smells so horrible," she murmured in distraction. "And I'm so awful, I'm so awful! Oh no, I'm too awful." And she broke into bitter, heart-broken sobbing. "You can't want to love me, I'm horrible."

"Don't be silly, don't be silly," he said, trying to comfort her, kissing her, holding her in his arms. "I want you, I want to marry you, we're going to be married, quickly, quickly—to-morrow if I can."

But she only sobbed terribly, and cried:

"I feel awful. I feel awful. I feel I'm horrible to you."

"No, I want you, I want you," was all he answered, blindly, with that 190 terrible intonation which frightened her almost more than her horror lest he should *not* want her.

QUESTIONS

1. Discuss the opening scene. What is its purpose? How do the three brothers contrast with their sister, Mabel, and how does the scene help prepare the reader for Mabel's encounter with Dr. Ferguson?

2. The title suggests that Mabel is a kind of non-entity, merely someone else's daughter. By the end of the tale, could she be considered "the doctor's wife"? Or has she become her own person?

3. Lawrence has sometimes been criticized for failing to construct strong plots for his stories. Does this story have a plot? How would you describe its structure?

4. Analyze the characterization of Dr. Ferguson. Is he a sympathetic character?
5. What is the purpose of the scene at the pond? What happens to Mabel and Dr. Ferguson there? How are they changed?

D. H. LAWRENCE
The Rocking-Horse Winner

There was a woman who was beautiful, who started with all the advantages, yet she had no luck. She married for love, and the love turned to dust. She had bonny children, yet she felt they had been thrust upon her, and she could not love them. They looked at her coldly, as if they were finding fault with her. And hurriedly she felt she must cover up some fault in herself. Yet what it was that she must cover up she never knew. Nevertheless, when her children were present, she always felt the center of her heart go hard. This troubled her, and in her manner she was all the more gentle and anxious for her children, as if she loved them very much. Only she herself knew that at the center of her heart was a hard little place that could not feel love, no, not for anybody. Everybody else said of her: "She is such a good mother. She adores her children." Only she herself, and her children themselves, knew it was not so. They read it in each other's eyes.

There were a boy and two little girls. They lived in a pleasant house, with a garden, and they had discreet servants, and felt themselves superior to anyone in the neighborhood.

Although they lived in style, they felt always an anxiety in the house. There was never enough money. The mother had a small income, and the father had a small income, but not nearly enough for the social position which they had to keep up. The father went into town to some office. But though he had good prospects, these prospects never materialized. There was always the grinding sense of the shortage of money, though the style was always kept up.

At last the mother said: "I will see if I can't make something." But she did not know where to begin. She racked her brains, and tried this thing and the other, but could not find anything successful. The failure made deep lines come into her face. Her children were growing up, they would have to go to school. There must be more money, there must be more money. The father, who was always very handsome and expensive in his tastes, seemed as if he never would be able to do anything worth doing. And the mother, who had a great belief in herself, did not succeed any better, and her tastes were just as expensive.

THE ROCKING-HORSE WINNER   First published in 1933. See the footnote on page 402 for more information on Lawrence and his career.

And so the house came to be haunted by the unspoken phrase: There 5
must be more money! There must be more money! The children could hear
it all the time, though nobody said it aloud. They heard it at Christmas,
when the expensive and splendid toys filled the nursery. Behind the shining
modern rocking horse, behind the smart doll's-house, a voice would start
whispering: "There must be more money! There must be more money!"
And the children would stop playing, to listen for a moment. They would
look into each other's eyes, to see if they had all heard. And each one saw
in the eyes of the other two that they too had heard. "There must be more
money! There must be more money!"

It came whispering from the springs of the still-swaying rocking
horse, and even the horse, bending his wooden, champing head, heard
it. The big doll, sitting so pink and smirking in her new pram, could
hear it quite plainly, and seemed to be smirking all the more self-
consciously because of it. The foolish puppy, too, that took the place of
the Teddy bear, he was looking so extraordinarily foolish for no other
reason but that he heard the secret whisper all over the house: "There
must be more money!"

Yet nobody ever said it aloud. The whisper was everywhere, and therefore no one spoke it. Just as no one ever says: "We are breathing!" in spite
of the fact that breath is coming and going all the time.

"Mother," said the boy Paul one day, "why don't we keep a car of our
own? Why do we always use uncle's, or else a taxi?"

"Because we're the poor members of the family," said the mother.

"But why are we, mother?"   10

"Well—I suppose," she said slowly and bitterly, "it's because your
father has no luck."

The boy was silent for some time.

"Is luck money, mother?" he asked, rather timidly.

"No, Paul. Not quite. It's what causes you to have money."

"Oh!" said Paul vaguely. "I thought when Uncle Oscar said filthy 15
lucker, it meant money."

"Filthy lucre° does mean money," said the mother. "But it's lucre, not
luck."

"Oh!" said the boy. "Then what is luck, mother?"

"It's what causes you to have money. If you're lucky you have money.
That's why it's better to be born lucky than rich. If you're rich, you may
lose your money. But if you're lucky, you will always get more money."

"Oh! Will you? And is father not lucky?"

"Very unlucky, I should say," she said bitterly.   20

---

filthy lucre: See New Testament, I Timothy 3:3.

The boy watched her with unsure eyes.

"Why?" he asked.

"I don't know. Nobody ever knows why one person is lucky and another unlucky."

"Don't they? Nobody at all? Does nobody know?"

25 "Perhaps God. But He never tells."

"He ought to, then. And aren't you lucky either, mother?"

"I can't be, if I married an unlucky husband."

"But by yourself, aren't you?"

"I used to think I was, before I married. Now I think I am very unlucky indeed."

30 "Why?"

"Well—never mind! Perhaps I'm not really," she said.

The child looked at her, to see if she meant it. But he saw, by the lines of her mouth, that she was only trying to hide something from him.

"Well, anyhow," he said stoutly, "I'm a lucky person."

"Why?" said his mother, with a sudden laugh.

35 He stared at her. He didn't even know why he had said it.

"God told me," he asserted, brazening it out.

"I hope He did, dear!" she said, again with a laugh, but rather bitter.

"He did, mother!"

"Excellent!" said the mother, using one of her husband's exclamations.

40 The boy saw she did not believe him; or, rather, that she paid no attention to his assertion. This angered him somewhat, and made him want to compel her attention.

He went off by himself, vaguely, in a childish way, seeking for the clue to "luck." Absorbed, talking no heed of other people, he went about with a sort of stealth, seeking inwardly for luck. He wanted luck, he wanted it, he wanted it. When the two girls were playing dolls in the nursery, he would sit on his big rocking horse, charging madly into space, with a frenzy that made the little girls peer at him uneasily. Wildly the horse careered, the waving dark hair of the boy tossed, his eyes had a strange glare in them. The little girls dared not speak to him.

When he had ridden to the end of his mad little journey, he climbed down and stood in front of his rocking horse, staring fixedly into its lowered face. Its red mouth was slightly open, its big eye was wide and glassy-bright.

"Now!" he would silently command the snorting steed. "Now, take me to where there is luck! Now take me!"

And he would slash the horse on the neck with the little whip he had asked Uncle Oscar for. He knew the horse could take him to where there was luck, if only he forced it. So he would mount again, and start on his furious ride, hoping at last to get there. He knew he could get there.

"You'll break your horse, Paul!" said the nurse.   45

"He's always riding like that! I wish he'd leave off!" said his elder sister Joan.

But he only glared down on them in silence. Nurse gave him up. She could make nothing of him. Anyhow he was growing beyond her.

One day his mother and his Uncle Oscar came in when he was on one of his furious rides. He did not speak to them.

"Hallo, you young jockey! Riding a winner?" said his uncle.

"Aren't you growing too big for a rocking horse? You're not a very   50 little boy any longer, you know," said his mother.

But Paul only gave a blue glare from his big, rather close-set eyes. He would speak to nobody when he was in full tilt. His mother watched him with an anxious expression on her face.

At last he suddenly stopped forcing his horse into the mechanical gallop, and slid down.

"Well, I got there!" he announced fiercely, his blue eyes still flaring, and his sturdy long legs straddling apart.

"Where did you get to?" asked his mother.

"Where I wanted to go," he flared back at her.   55

"That's right, son!" said Uncle Oscar. "Don't you stop till you get there. What's the horse's name?"

"He doesn't have a name," said the boy.

"Gets on without all right?" asked the uncle.

"Well, he has different names. He was called Sansovino last week."

"Sansovino, eh? Won the Ascot. How did you know his name?"   60

"He always talks about horse races with Bassett," said Joan.

The uncle was delighted to find that his small nephew was posted with all the racing news. Bassett, the young gardener, who had been wounded in the left foot in the war and got his present job through Oscar Cresswell, whose batman he had been, was a perfect blade of the "turf." He lived in the racing events, and the small boy lived with him.

Oscar Cresswell got it all from Bassett.

"Master Paul comes and asks me, so I can't do more than tell him, sir," said Bassett, his face terribly serious, as if he were speaking of religious matters.

"And does he ever put anything on a horse he fancies?"   65

"Well—I don't want to give him away—he's a young sport, a fine sport, sir. Would you mind asking him yourself? He sort of takes a pleasure in it, and perhaps he'd feel I was giving him away, sir, if you don't mind."

Bassett was serious as a church.

The uncle went back to his nephew, and took him off for a ride in the car.

"Say, Paul, old man, do you ever put anything on a horse?" the uncle asked.

70 The boy watched the handsome man closely.

"Why, do you think I oughtn't to?" he parried.

"Not a bit of it! I thought perhaps you might give me a tip for the Lincoln."

The car sped on into the country, going down to Uncle Oscar's place in Hampshire.

"Honor bright?" said the nephew.

75 "Honor bright, son!" said the uncle.

"Well, then, Daffodil."

"Daffodil! I doubt it, sonny. What about Mirza?"

"I only know the winner," said the boy. "That's Daffodil."

"Daffodil, eh?"

80 There was a pause. Daffodil was an obscure horse comparatively.

"Uncle!"

"Yes, son?"

"You won't let it go any further, will you? I promised Bassett."

"Bassett be damned, old man! What's he got to do with it?"

85 "We're partners. We've been partners from the first. Uncle, he lent me my first five shillings, which I lost. I promised him, honor bright, it was only between me and him; only you gave me that ten-shilling note I started winning with, so I thought you were lucky. You won't let it go any further, will you?"

The boy gazed at his uncle from those big, hot, blue eyes, set rather close together. The uncle stirred and laughed uneasily.

"Right you are, son! I'll keep your tip private. Daffodil, eh? How much are you putting on him?"

"All except twenty pounds," said the boy. "I keep that in reserve."

The uncle thought it a good joke.

90 "You keep twenty pounds in reserve, do you, you young romancer? What are you betting, then?"

"I'm betting three hundred," said the boy gravely. "But it's between you and me, Uncle Oscar! Honor bright?"

The uncle burst into a roar of laughter.

"It's between you and me all right, you young Nat Gould,"° he said, laughing. "But where's your three hundred?"

"Bassett keeps it for me. We're partners."

Nat Gould: a journalist and novelist (1857–1919) who wrote about horse racing

"You are, are you! And what is Bassett putting on Daffodil?"   95
"He won't go quite as high as I do, I expect. Perhaps he'll go a hundred and fifty."

"What, pennies?" laughed the uncle.

"Pounds," said the child, with a surprised look at his uncle. "Bassett keeps a bigger reserve than I do."

Between wonder and amusement Uncle Oscar was silent. He pursued the matter no further, but he determined to take his nephew with him to the Lincoln races.

"Now, son," he said, "I'm putting twenty on Mirza, and I'll put five   100
for you on any horse you fancy. What's your pick?"

"Daffodil, uncle."

"No, not the fiver on Daffodil!"

"I should if it was my own fiver," said the child.

"Good! Good! Right you are! A fiver for me and a fiver for you on Daffodil."

The child had never been to a race meeting before, and his eyes were   105
blue fire. He pursed his mouth tight, and watched. A Frenchman just in front had put his money on Lancelot. Wild with excitement, he flayed his arms up and down, yelling "Lancelot! Lancelot!" in his French accent.

Daffodil came in first, Lancelot second, Mirza third. The child, flushed and with eyes blazing, was curiously serene. His uncle brought him four five-pound notes, four to one.

"What am I to do with these?" he cried, waving them before the boy's eyes.

"I suppose we'll talk to Bassett," said the boy. "I expect I have fifteen hundred now; and twenty in reserve; and this twenty."

His uncle studied him for some moments.

"Look here, son!" he said. "You're not serious about Bassett and that   110
fifteen hundred, are you?"

"Yes, I am. But it's between you and me, uncle. Honor bright!"

"Honor bright all right, son! But I must talk to Bassett."

"If you'd like to be a partner, uncle, with Bassett and me, we could all be partners. Only, you'd have to promise, honor bright, uncle, not to let it go beyond us three. Bassett and I are lucky, and you must be lucky, because it was your ten shillings I started winning with . . . ."

Uncle Oscar took both Bassett and Paul into Richmond Park for an afternoon, and there they talked.

"It's like this, you see, sir," Bassett said. "Master Paul would get me   115
talking about racing events, spinning yarns, you know, sir. And he was always keen on knowing if I'd made or if I'd lost. It's about a year since, now, that I put five shillings on Blush of Dawn for him—and we lost.

Then the luck turned, with that ten shillings he had from you, that we put on Singhalese. And since that time, it's been pretty steady, all things considering. What do you say, Master Paul?"

"We're all right when we're sure," said Paul. "It's when we're not quite sure that we go down."

"Oh, but we're careful then," said Bassett.

"But when are you sure?" smiled Uncle Oscar.

"It's Master Paul, sir," said Bassett, in a secret, religious voice. "It's as if he had it from heaven. Like Daffodil, now, for the Lincoln. That was as sure as eggs."

120   "Did you put anything on Daffodil?" asked Oscar Cresswell.

"Yes, sir, I made my bit."

"And my nephew?"

Bassett was obstinately silent, looking at Paul.

"I made twelve hundred, didn't I, Bassett? I told uncle I was putting three hundred on Daffodil."

125   "That's right," said Bassett, nodding.

"But where's the money?" asked the uncle.

"I keep it safe locked up, sir. Master Paul he can have it any minute he likes to ask for it."

"What, fifteen hundred pounds?"

"And twenty! and forty, that is, with the twenty he made on the course."

130   "It's amazing!" said the uncle.

"If Master Paul offers you to be partners, sir, I would, if I were you; if you'll excuse me," said Bassett.

Oscar Cresswell thought about it.

"I'll see the money," he said.

They drove home again, and sure enough, Bassett came round to the garden-house with fifteen hundred pounds in notes. The twenty pounds reserve was left with Joe Glee, in the Turf Commission deposit.

135   "You see, it's all right, uncle, when I'm sure! Then we go strong, for all we're worth. Don't we Bassett?"

"We do that, Master Paul."

"And when are you sure?" said the uncle, laughing.

"Oh, well, sometimes I'm absolutely sure, like about Daffodil," said the boy; "and sometimes I have an idea; and sometimes I haven't even an idea, have I, Bassett? Then we're careful, because we mostly go down."

"You do, do you! And when you're sure, like about Daffodil, what makes you sure, sonny?"

140   "Oh, well, I don't know," said the boy uneasily. "I'm sure, you know, uncle; that's all."

"It's as if he had it from heaven, sir," Bassett reiterated.

"I should say so!" said the uncle.

But he became a partner. And when the Leger was coming on, Paul was "sure" about Lively Spark, which was a quite inconsiderable horse. The boy insisted on putting a thousand on the horse, Bassett went for five hundred, and Oscar Cresswell two hundred. Lively Spark came in first, and the betting had been ten to one against him. Paul had made ten thousand.

"You see," he said, "I was absolutely sure of him."

Even Oscar Cresswell had cleared two thousand.   145

"Look here son," he said, "this sort of thing makes me nervous."

"It needn't, uncle! Perhaps I shan't be sure again for a long time."

"But what are you going to do with your money?" asked the uncle.

"Of course," said the boy, "I started it for mother. She said she had no luck, because father is unlucky, so I thought if I was lucky, it might stop whispering."

"What might stop whispering?"   150

"Our house. I hate our house for whispering."

"What does it whisper?"

"Why—why"—the boy fidgeted—"why, I don't know. But it's always short of money, you know, uncle."

"I know it, son, I know it."

"You know people send mother writs, don't you, uncle?"   155

"I'm afraid I do," said the uncle.

"And then the house whispers, like people laughing at you behind your back. It's awful, that is! I thought if I was lucky . . ."

"You might stop it," added the uncle.

The boy watched him with big blue eyes that had an uncanny cold fire in them, and he said never a word.

"Well, then!" said the uncle. "What are we doing?"   160

"I shouldn't like mother to know I was lucky," said the boy.

"Why not, son?"

"She'd stop me."

"I don't think she would."

"Oh!"—and the boy writhed in an odd way—"I don't want her to   165
know, uncle."

"All right, son! We'll manage it without her knowing."

They managed it very easily. Paul, at the other's suggestion, handed over five thousand pounds to his uncle, who deposited it with the family lawyer, who was then to inform Paul's mother that a relative had put five thousand pounds into his hands, which sum was to be paid out a thousand pounds at a time, on the mother's birthday, for the next five years.

"So she'll have a birthday present of a thousand pounds for five successive years," said Uncle Oscar. "I hope it won't make it all the harder for her later."

Paul's mother had her birthday in November. The house had been "whispering" worse than ever lately, and, even in spite of his luck, Paul could not bear up against it. He was very anxious to see the effect of the birthday letter telling his mother about the thousand pounds.

170 When there were no visitors, Paul now took his meals with his parents, as he was beyond the nursery control. His mother went into town nearly every day. She had discovered that she had an odd knack of sketching furs and dress materials, so she worked secretly in the studio of a friend who was the chief "artist" for the leading drapers. She drew the figures of ladies in furs and ladies in silk and sequins for the newspaper advertisements. This young woman artist earned several thousand pounds a year, but Paul's mother only made several hundreds, and she was again dissatisfied. She so wanted to be first in something, and she did not succeed, even in making sketches for drapery advertisements.

She was down to breakfast on the morning of her birthday. Paul watched her face as she read her letters. He knew the lawyer's letter. As his mother read it, her face hardened and became more expressionless. Then a cold, determined look came on her mouth. She hid the letter under the pile of others, and said not a word about it.

"Didn't you have anything nice in the post for your birthday, mother?" said Paul.

"Quite moderately nice," she said, her voice cold and absent.

She went away to town without saying more.

175 But in the afternoon Uncle Oscar appeared. He said Paul's mother had had a long interview with the lawyer, asking if the whole five thousand could be advanced at once, as she was in debt.

"What do you think, uncle?" said the boy.

"I leave it to you, son."

"Oh, let her have it, then! We can get some more with the other," said the boy.

"A bird in the hand is worth two in the bush, laddie!" said Uncle Oscar.

180 "But I'm sure to know for the Grand National; or the Lincolnshire; or else the Derby. I'm sure to know for one of them," said Paul.

So Uncle Oscar signed the agreement, and Paul's mother touched the whole five thousand. Then something very curious happened. The voices in the house suddenly went mad, like a chorus of frogs on a spring evening. There were certain new furnishings, and Paul had a tutor. He was really going to Eton,° his father's school, in the following autumn. There were flowers in the winter, and a blossoming of the luxury Paul's mother had

Eton: England's most prestigious privately supported school

been used to. And yet the voices in the house, behind the sprays of mimosa and almond blossom, and from under the piles of iridescent cushions, simply trilled and screamed in a sort of ecstasy: "There must be more money! Oh-h-h, there must be more money. Oh, now, now-w! Now-w-w— there must be more money—more than ever! More than ever!"

It frightened Paul terribly. He studied away at his Latin and Greek with his tutor. But his intense hours were spent with Bassett. The Grand National had gone by: he had not "known," and had lost a hundred pounds. Summer was at hand. He was in agony for the Lincoln. But even for the Lincoln he didn't "know" and he lost fifty pounds. He became wild-eyed and strange, as if something were going to explode in him.

"Let it alone, son! Don't you bother about it!" urged Uncle Oscar. But it was as if the boy couldn't really hear what his uncle was saying.

"I've got to know for the Derby! I've got to know for the Derby!" the child reiterated, his big blue eyes blazing with a sort of madness.

His mother noticed how overwrought he was.   185

"You'd better go to the seaside. Wouldn't you like to go now to the seaside, instead of waiting? I think you'd better," she said, looking down at him anxiously, her heart curiously heavy because of him.

But the child lifted his uncanny blue eyes.

"I couldn't possibly go before the Derby, mother!" he said. "I couldn't possibly!"

"Why not?" she said, her voice becoming heavy when she was opposed. "Why not? You can still go from the seaside to see the Derby with your Uncle Oscar, if that's what you wish. No need for you to wait here. Besides, I think you care too much about these races. It's a bad sign. My family has been a gambling family, and you won't know till you grow up how much damage it has done. But it has done damage. I shall have to send Bassett away, and ask Uncle Oscar not to talk racing to you, unless you promise to be reasonable about it; go away to the seaside and forget it. You're all nerves!"

"I'll do what you like, mother, so long as you don't send me away till 190 after the Derby," the boy said.

"Send you away from where? Just from this house?"

"Yes," he said, gazing at her.

"Why, you curious child, what makes you care about this house so much, suddenly? I never knew you loved it."

He gazed at her without speaking. He had a secret within a secret, something he had not divulged, even to Bassett or to his Uncle Oscar.

But his mother, after standing undecided and a little bit sullen for 195 some moments, said:

"Very well, then! Don't go to the seaside till after the Derby, if you don't wish it. But promise me you won't let your nerves go to pieces.

Promise you won't think so much about horse racing and events, as you call them!"

"Oh, no," said the boy casually. "I won't think much about them, mother. You needn't worry. I wouldn't worry, mother, if I were you."

"If you were me and I were you," said his mother, "I wonder what we should do!"

"But you know you needn't worry, mother, don't you?" the boy repeated.

200 "I should be awfully glad to know it," she said wearily.

"Oh, well, you can, you know. I mean, you ought to know you needn't worry," he insisted.

"Ought I? Then I'll see about it," she said.

Paul's secret of secrets was his wooden horse, that which had no name. Since he was emancipated from a nurse and a nursery-governess, he had had his rocking horse removed to his own bedroom at the top of the house.

"Surely, you're too big for a rocking horse!" his mother had remonstrated.

205 "Well, you see mother, till I can have a real horse, I like to have some sort of animal about," had been his quaint answer.

"Do you feel he keeps you company?" she laughed.

"Oh, yes! He's very good, he always keeps me company, when I'm there," said Paul.

So the horse, rather shabby, stood in an arrested prance in the boy's bedroom.

The Derby was drawing near, and the boy grew more and more tense. He hardly heard what was spoken to him, he was very frail, and his eyes were really uncanny. His mother had sudden seizures of uneasiness about him. Sometimes, for half-an-hour, she would feel a sudden anxiety about him that was almost anguish. She wanted to rush to him at once, and know he was safe.

210 Two nights before the Derby, she was at a big party in town, when one of her rushes of anxiety about her boy, her first-born, gripped her heart till she could hardly speak. She fought with the feeling, might and main, for she believed in common sense. But it was too strong. The children's nursery-governess was terribly surprised and startled at being rung up in the night.

"Are the children all right, Miss Wilmot?"

"Oh, yes, they are quite all right."

"Master Paul? Is he all right?"

"He went to bed as right as a trivet. Shall I run up and look at him?"

215 "No," said Paul's mother reluctantly. "No! Don't trouble. It's all right. Don't sit up. We shall be home fairly soon." She did not want her son's privacy intruded upon.

"Very good," said the governess.

It was about one o'clock when Paul's mother and father drove up to their house. All was still. Paul's mother went to her room and slipped off her white fur coat. She had told her maid not to wait up for her. She heard her husband downstairs, mixing a whiskey-and-soda.

And then, because of the strange anxiety at her heart, she stole upstairs to her son's room. Noiselessly she went along the upper corridor. Was there a faint noise? What was it?

She stood, with arrested muscles, outside his door listening. There was a strange, heavy, and yet not loud noise. Her heart stood still. It was a soundless noise, yet rushing and powerful. Something huge, in violent, hushed motion. What was it? What in God's name was it? She ought to know. She felt that she knew the noise. She knew what it was.

Yet she could not place it. She couldn't say what it was. And on and 220 on it went, like madness.

Softly, frozen with anxiety and fear, she turned the door handle.

The room was dark. Yet in the space near the window, she heard and saw something plunging to and fro. She gazed in fear and amazement.

Then suddenly she switched on the light, and saw her son, in his green pajamas, madly surging on the rocking horse. The blaze of light suddenly lit him up, as he urged the wooden horse, and lit her up, as she stood, blonde, in her dress of pale green and crystal, in the doorway.

"Paul!" she cried. "Whatever are you doing?"

"It's Malabar!" he screamed, in a powerful, strange voice. "It's Malabar." 225

His eyes blazed at her for one strange and senseless second, as he ceased urging his wooden horse. Then he fell with a crash to the ground, and she, all her tormented motherhood flooding upon her, rushed to gather him up.

But he was unconscious, and unconscious he remained, with some brain-fever. He talked and tossed, and his mother sat stonily by his side.

"Malabar! It's Malabar! Bassett, Bassett, I know it! It's Malabar!"

So the child cried, trying to get up and urge the rocking horse that gave him his inspiration.

"What does he mean by Malabar?" asked the heart-frozen mother. 230

"I don't know," said his father stonily.

"What does he mean by Malabar?" she asked her brother Oscar.

"It's one of the horses running for the Derby," was the answer.

And, in spite of himself, Oscar Cresswell spoke to Bassett, and himself put a thousand on Malabar: at fourteen to one.

The third day of the illness was critical: they were waiting for a 235 change. The boy, with his rather long, curly hair, was tossing ceaselessly on the pillow. He neither slept nor regained consciousness, and his eyes were like blue stones. His mother sat, feeling her heart had gone, turned actually into a stone.

In the evening, Oscar Cresswell did not come, but Bassett sent a message, saying could he come up for one moment, just one moment? Paul's mother was very angry at the intrusion, but on second thought she agreed. The boy was the same. Perhaps Bassett might bring him to consciousness.

The gardener, a shortish fellow with a brown mustache, and sharp little brown eyes, tiptoed into the room, touched his imaginary cap to Paul's mother, and stole to the bedside, staring with glittering, smallish eyes, at the tossing, dying child.

"Master Paul!" he whispered. "Master Paul! Malabar came in first all right, a clean win. I did as you told me. You've made over seventy thousand pounds, you have; you've got over eighty thousand. Malabar came in all right, Master Paul."

"Malabar! Malabar! Did I say Malabar, mother? Did I say Malabar? Do you think I'm lucky, mother? I knew Malabar, didn't I? Over eighty thousand pounds! I call that lucky, don't you, mother? Over eighty thousand pounds! I knew, didn't I know I knew? Malabar came in all right. If I ride my horse till I'm sure, then I tell you, Bassett, you can go as high as you like. Did you go for all you were worth, Bassett?"

240

"I went a thousand on it, Master Paul."

"I never told you, mother, that if I can ride my horse, and get there, then I'm absolutely sure—oh, absolutely! Mother, did I ever tell you? I'm lucky."

"No, you never did," said the mother.

But the boy died in the night.

And even as he lay dead, his mother heard her brother's voice saying to her: "My God, Hester, you're eighty-odd thousand to the good and a poor devil of a son to the bad. But, poor devil, poor devil, he's best gone out of a life where he rides his rocking horse to find a winner."

QUESTIONS

1. In the phraseology of its beginning ("There was a woman . . ."), its simple style, its direct characterization, and its use of the wish motif—especially that of the wish that is granted only on conditions that nullify its desirability (compare the story of King Midas)—this story has the qualities of a fairy tale. Its differences, however—in characterization, setting, and ending—are especially significant. What do they tell us about the purpose of the story?

2. Characterize the mother fully. How does she differ from the stepmothers in fairy tales like "Cinderella" and "Hansel and Gretel"? How does the boy's mistake about *filthy lucker* (paragraph 15) clarify her thinking and her motivations? Why had her love for her husband turned to dust? Why is she "unlucky"?

3. What kind of a child is Paul? What are his motivations?

4. The initial assumptions of the story are that (a) a boy might get divinatory powers by riding a rocking horse, and (b) a house can whisper. Could the second of these be accepted as little more than a metaphor? Once we have granted these initial assumptions, does the story develop plausibly?

5. It is ironic that the boy's attempt to stop the whispers should only increase them. Is this a plausible irony? Why? What does it tell us about the theme of the story? Why is it ironic that the whispers should be especially audible at Christmas time? What irony is contained in the boy's last speech?

6. In what way is the boy's furious riding on the rocking horse an appropriate symbol for materialistic pursuits?

7. How might a commercial writer have ended the story?

8. How many persons in the story are affected (or infected) by materialism?

9. What is the theme of the story?

FLANNERY O'CONNOR

A Good Man Is Hard to Find

The grandmother didn't want to go to Florida. She wanted to visit some of her connections in east Tennessee and she was seizing at every chance to change Bailey's mind. Bailey was the son she lived with, her only boy. He was sitting on the edge of his chair at the table, bent over the orange sports section of the *Journal*. "Now look here, Bailey," she said, "see here, read this," and she stood with one hand on her thin hip and the other rattling the newspaper at his bald head. "Here this fellow that calls himself The Misfit is aloose from the Federal Pen and headed toward Florida and you read here what it says he did to these people. Just you read it. I wouldn't take my children in any direction with a criminal like that aloose in it. I couldn't answer to my conscience if I did."

Bailey didn't look up from his reading so she wheeled around then and faced the children's mother, a young woman in slacks, whose face was as broad and innocent as a cabbage and was tied around with a green head-kerchief that had two points on the top like a rabbit's ears. She was sitting on the sofa, feeding the baby his apricots out of a jar. "The children have been to Florida before," the old lady said. "You all ought to take them somewhere else for a change so they would see different parts of the world and be broad. They never have been to east Tennessee."

The children's mother didn't seem to hear her but the eight-year-old boy, John Wesley, a stocky child with glasses, said, "If you don't want to go to Florida, why dontcha stay at home?" He and the little girl, June Star, were reading the funny papers on the floor.

A GOOD MAN IS HARD TO FIND   First published in 1953. Flannery O'Connor (1925–1964) spent most of her writing life in Milledgeville, Georgia. Though a devout Roman Catholic, she wrote about the denizens of the rural South, most of whom were fundamentalist Protestants. O'Connor's people are often prideful, hardheaded southerners whose confrontation with violence and death forces them to test their capacity for grace. O'Connor insisted that her Christian vision of human life and destiny informed all her writing.

"She wouldn't stay at home to be queen for a day," June Star said without raising her yellow head.

5   "Yes and what would you do if this fellow, The Misfit, caught you?" the grandmother asked.

"I'd smack his face," John Wesley said.

"She wouldn't stay at home for a million bucks," June Star said. "Afraid she'd miss something. She has to go everywhere we go."

"All right, Miss," the grandmother said. "Just remember that the next time you want me to curl your hair."

June Star said her hair was naturally curly.

10   The next morning the grandmother was the first one in the car, ready to go. She had her big black valise that looked like the head of a hippopotamus in one corner, and underneath it she was hiding a basket with Pitty Sing, the cat, in it. She didn't intend for the cat to be left alone in the house for three days because he would miss her too much and she was afraid he might brush against one of the gas burners and accidentally asphyxiate himself. Her son, Bailey, didn't like to arrive at a motel with a cat.

She sat in the middle of the back seat with John Wesley and June Star on either side of her. Bailey and the children's mother and the baby sat in front and they left Atlanta at eight forty-five with the mileage on the car at 55890. The grandmother wrote this down because she thought it would be interesting to say how many miles they had been when they got back. It took them twenty minutes to reach the outskirts of the city.

The old lady settled herself comfortably, removing her white cotton gloves and putting them up with her purse on the shelf in front of the back window. The children's mother still had on slacks and still had her head tied up in a green kerchief, but the grandmother had on a navy blue straw sailor hat with a bunch of white violets on the brim and a navy blue dress with a small white dot in the print. Her collars and cuffs were white organdy trimmed with lace and at her neckline she had pinned a purple spray of cloth violets containing a sachet. In case of an accident, anyone seeing her dead on the highway would know at once that she was a lady.

She said she thought it was going to be a good day for driving, neither too hot nor too cold, and she cautioned Bailey that the speed limit was fifty-five miles an hour and that the patrolmen hid themselves behind billboards and small clumps of trees and sped out after you before you had a chance to slow down. She pointed out interesting details of the scenery: Stone Mountain; the blue granite that in some places came up to both sides of the highway; the brilliant red clay banks slightly streaked with purple; and the various crops that made rows of green lace-work on the ground. The trees were full of silver-white sunlight and the meanest of them sparkled. The children were reading comic magazines and their mother had gone back to sleep.

"Let's go through Georgia fast so we won't have to look at it much," John Wesley said.

"If I were a little boy," said the grandmother, "I wouldn't talk about 15 my native state that way. Tennessee has the mountains and Georgia has the hills."

"Tennessee is just a hillbilly dumping ground," John Wesley said, "and Georgia is a lousy state too."

"You said it," June Star said.

"In my time," said the grandmother, folding her thin veined fingers, "children were more respectful of their native states and their parents and everything else. People did right then. Oh look at the cute little pickaninny!" she said and pointed to a Negro child standing in the door of a shack. "Wouldn't that make a picture, now?" she asked and they all turned and looked at the little Negro out of the back window. He waved.

"He didn't have any britches on," June Star said.

"He probably didn't have any," the grandmother explained. "Little 20 niggers in the country don't have things like we do. If I could paint, I'd paint that picture," she said.

The children exchanged comic books.

The grandmother offered to hold the baby and the children's mother passed him over the front seat to her. She set him on her knee and bounced him and told him about the things they were passing. She rolled her eyes and screwed up her mouth and stuck her leathery thin face into his smooth bland one. Occasionally he gave her a faraway smile. They passed a large cotton field with five or six graves fenced in the middle of it, like a small island. "Look at the graveyard!" the grandmother said, pointing it out. "That was the old family burying ground. That belonged to the plantation."

"Where's the plantation?" John Wesley asked.

"Gone With the Wind," said the grandmother. "Ha. Ha."

When the children finished all the comic books they had brought, 25 they opened the lunch and ate it. The grandmother ate a peanut butter sandwich and an olive and would not let the children throw the box and the paper napkins out the window. When there was nothing else to do they played a game by choosing a cloud and making the other two guess what shape it suggested. John Wesley took one the shape of a cow and June Star guessed a cow and John Wesley said, no, an automobile, and June Star said he didn't play fair, and they began to slap each other over the grandmother.

The grandmother said she would tell them a story if they would keep quiet. When she told a story, she rolled her eyes and waved her head and was very dramatic. She said once when she was a maiden lady she had been courted by a Mr. Edgar Atkins Teagarden from Jasper, Georgia. She said he was a very good-looking man and a gentleman and that he brought her a watermelon every Saturday afternoon with his initials cut in it, E. A. T. Well, one Saturday, she said, Mr. Teagarden brought the watermelon and there was nobody at home and he left it on the front porch and returned in his buggy to Jasper, but she never got the watermelon, she said, because a nigger boy ate it when he saw the initials, E. A. T.! This story tickled John Wesley's funny bone and he giggled and giggled but June Star didn't think it was any good. She said she wouldn't marry a man that just brought her a watermelon on Saturday. The grandmother said she would have done well to marry Mr. Teagarden because he was a gentleman and had bought Coca-Cola stock when it first came out and that he had died only a few years ago, a very wealthy man.

They stopped at The Tower for barbecued sandwiches. The Tower was a part stucco and part wood filling station and dance hall set in a clearing outside of Timothy. A fat man named Red Sammy Butts ran it and there were signs stuck here and there on the building and for miles up and down the highway saying, TRY RED SAMMY'S FAMOUS BARBECUE. NONE LIKE FAMOUS RED SAMMY'S! RED SAM! THE FAT BOY WITH THE HAPPY LAUGH! A VETERAN! RED SAMMY'S YOUR MAN!

Red Sammy was lying on the bare ground outside The Tower with his head under a truck while a gray monkey about a foot high, chained to a small chinaberry tree, chattered nearby. The monkey sprang back into the tree and got on the highest limb as soon as he saw the children jump out of the car and run toward him.

Inside, The Tower was a long dark room with a counter at one end and tables at the other and dancing space in the middle. They all sat down at a board table next to the nickelodeon and Red Sam's wife, a tall burnt-brown woman with hair and eyes lighter than her skin, came and took their order. The children's mother put a dime in the machine and played "The Tennessee Waltz," and the grandmother said that tune always made her want to dance. She asked Bailey if he would like to dance but he only glared at her. He didn't have a naturally sunny disposition like she did and trips made him nervous. The grandmother's brown eyes were very bright. She swayed her head from side to side and pretended she was dancing in her chair. June Star said play something she could tap to so the children's mother put in another dime and played a fast number and June Star stepped out onto the dance floor and did her tap routine.

30   "Ain't she cute?" Red Sam's wife said, leaning over the counter. "Would you like to come be my little girl?"

"No I certainly wouldn't," June Star said. "I wouldn't live in a broken-down place like this for a million bucks!" and she ran back to the table.

"Ain't she cute?" the woman repeated, stretching her mouth politely.

"Aren't you ashamed?" hissed the grandmother.

Red Sam came in and told his wife to quit lounging on the counter and hurry up with these people's order. His khaki trousers reached just to his hip bones and his stomach hung over them like a sack of meal swaying under his shirt. He came over and sat down at a table nearby and let out a combination sigh and yodel. "You can't win," he said. "You can't win," and he wiped his sweating red face off with a gray handkerchief. "These days you don't know who to trust," he said. "Ain't that the truth?"

"People are certainly not nice like they used to be," said the grandmother. 35

"Two fellers come in here last week," Red Sammy said, "driving a Chrysler. It was a old beat-up car but it was a good one and these boys looked all right to me. Said they worked at the mill and you know I let them fellers charge the gas they bought? Now why did I do that?"

"Because you're a good man!" the grandmother said at once.

"Yes'm, I suppose so," Red Sam said as if he were struck with this answer.

His wife brought the orders, carrying the five plates all at once without a tray, two in each hand and one balanced on her arm. "It isn't a soul in this green world of God's that you can trust," she said. "And I don't count nobody out of that, not nobody," she repeated, looking at Red Sammy.

"Did you read about that criminal, The Misfit, that's escaped?" asked 40 the grandmother.

"I wouldn't be a bit surprised if he didn't attact this place right here," said the woman. "If he hears about it being here, I wouldn't be none surprised to see him. If he hears it's two cent in the cash register, I wouldn't be a tall surprised if he . . ."

"That'll do," Red Sam said. "Go bring these people their Co'-Colas," and the woman went off to get the rest of the order.

"A good man is hard to find," Red Sammy said. "Everything is getting terrible. I remember the day you could go off and leave your screen door unlatched. Not no more."

He and the grandmother discussed better times. The old lady said that in her opinion Europe was entirely to blame for the way things were now. She said the way Europe acted you would think we were made of money and Red Sam said it was no use talking about it, she was exactly right. The children ran outside into the white sunlight and looked at the monkey in the lacy chinaberry tree. He was busy catching fleas on himself and biting each one carefully between his teeth as if it were a delicacy.

45   They drove off again into the hot afternoon. The grandmother took cat naps and woke up every few minutes with her own snoring. Outside of Toombsboro she woke up and recalled an old plantation that she had visited in this neighborhood once when she was a young lady. She said the house had six white columns across the front and that there was an avenue of oaks leading up to it and two little wooden trellis arbors on either side in front where you sat down with your suitor after a stroll in the garden. She recalled exactly which road to turn off to get to it. She knew that Bailey would not be willing to lose any time looking at an old house, but the more she talked about it, the more she wanted to see it once again and find out if the little twin arbors were still standing. "There was a secret panel in this house," she said craftily, not telling the truth but wishing that she were, "and the story went that all the family silver was hidden in it when Sherman came through but it was never found . . ."

"Hey!" John Wesley said. "Let's go see it! We'll find it! We'll poke all the woodwork and find it! Who lives there? Where do you turn off at? Hey Pop, can't we turn off there?"

"We never have seen a house with a secret panel!" June Star shrieked. "Let's go to the house with the secret panel! Hey Pop, can't we go see the house with the secret panel!"

"It's not far from here, I know," the grandmother said. "It wouldn't take over twenty minutes."

Bailey was looking straight ahead. His jaw was as rigid as a horseshoe. "No," he said.

50   The children began to yell and scream that they wanted to see the house with the secret panel. John Wesley kicked the back of the front seat and June Star hung over her mother's shoulder and whined desperately into her ear that they never had any fun even on their vacation, that they could never do what THEY wanted to do. The baby began to scream and John Wesley kicked the back of the seat so hard that his father could feel the blows in his kidney.

"All right!" he shouted and drew the car to a stop at the side of the road. "Will you all shut up? Will you all just shut up for one second? If you don't shut up, we won't go anywhere."

"It would be very educational for them," the grandmother murmured.

"All right," Bailey said, "but get this: this is the only time we're going to stop for anything like this. This is the one and only time."

"The dirt road that you have to turn down is about a mile back," the grandmother directed. "I marked it when we passed."

55   "A dirt road," Bailey groaned.

After they had turned around and were headed toward the dirt road, the grandmother recalled other points about the house, the beautiful glass over the front doorway and the candle-lamp in the hall. John Wesley said that the secret panel was probably in the fireplace.

"You can't go inside this house," Bailey said. "You don't know who lives there."

"While you all talk to the people in front, I'll run around behind and get in a window," John Wesley suggested.

"We'll all stay in the car," his mother said.

They turned onto the dirt road and the car raced roughly along in a   60 swirl of pink dust. The grandmother recalled the times when there were no paved roads and thirty miles was a day's journey. The dirt road was hilly and there were sudden washes in it and sharp curves on dangerous embankments. All at once they would be on a hill, looking down over the blue tops of trees for miles around, then the next minute, they would be in a red depression with the dust-coated trees looking down on them.

"This place had better turn up in a minute," Bailey said, "or I'm going to turn around."

The road looked as if no one had traveled on it in months.

"It's not much farther," the grandmother said and just as she said it, a horrible thought came to her. The thought was so embarrassing that she turned red in the face and her eyes dilated and her feet jumped up, upsetting her valise in the corner. The instant the valise moved, the newspaper top she had over the basket under it rose with a snarl and Pitty Sing, the cat, sprang onto Bailey's shoulder.

The children were thrown to the floor and their mother, clutching the baby, was thrown out the door onto the ground; the old lady was thrown into the front seat. The car turned over once and landed right-side-up in a gulch off the side of the road. Bailey remained in the driver's seat with the cat—gray-striped with a broad white face and an orange nose—clinging to his neck like a caterpillar.

As soon as the children saw they could move their arms and legs, they   65 scrambled out of the car, shouting, "We've had an ACCIDENT!" The grandmother was curled up under the dashboard, hoping she was injured so that Bailey's wrath would not come down on her all at once. The horrible thought she had had before the accident was that the house she had remembered so vividly was not in Georgia but in Tennessee.

Bailey removed the cat from his neck with both hands and flung it out the window against the side of a pine tree. Then he got out of the car and started looking for the children's mother. She was sitting against the side of the red gutted ditch, holding the screaming baby, but she only had a cut down her face and a broken shoulder. "We've had an ACCIDENT!" the children screamed in a frenzy of delight.

"But nobody's killed," June Star said with disappointment as the grandmother limped out of the car, her hat still pinned to her head but the broken front brim standing up at a jaunty angle and the violet spray hanging off the side. They all sat down in the ditch, except the children, to recover from the shock. They were all shaking.

"Maybe a car will come along," said the children's mother hoarsely.

"I believe I have injured an organ," said the grandmother, pressing her side, but no one answered her. Bailey's teeth were clattering. He had on a yellow sport shirt with bright blue parrots designed in it and his face was as yellow as the shirt. The grandmother decided that she would not mention that the house was in Tennessee.

70   The road was about ten feet above and they could see only the tops of the trees on the other side of it. Behind the ditch they were sitting in there were more woods, tall and dark and deep. In a few minutes they saw a car some distance away on top of a hill, coming slowly as if the occupants were watching them. The grandmother stood up and waved both arms dramatically to attract their attention. The car continued to come on slowly, disappeared around a bend and appeared again, moving even slower, on top of the hill they had gone over. It was a big black battered hearse-like automobile. There were three men in it.

It came to a stop just over them and for some minutes, the driver looked down with a steady expressionless gaze to where they were sitting, and didn't speak. Then he turned his head and muttered something to the other two and they got out. One was a fat boy in black trousers and a red sweat shirt with a silver stallion embossed on the front of it. He moved around on the right side of them and stood staring, his mouth partly open in a kind of loose grin. The other had on khaki pants and a blue striped coat and a gray hat pulled down very low, hiding most of his face. He came around slowly on the left side. Neither spoke.

The driver got out of the car and stood by the side of it, looking down at them. He was an older man than the other two. His hair was just beginning to gray and he wore silver-rimmed spectacles that gave him a scholarly look. He had a long creased face and didn't have on any shirt or undershirt. He had on blue jeans that were too tight for him and was holding a black hat and a gun. The two boys also had guns.

"We've had an ACCIDENT!" the children screamed.

The grandmother had the peculiar feeling that the bespectacled man was someone she knew. His face was as familiar to her as if she had known him all her life but she could not recall who he was. He moved away from the car and began to come down the embankment, placing his feet carefully so that he wouldn't slip. He had on tan and white shoes and no socks, and his ankles were red and thin. "Good afternoon," he said. "I see you all had you a little spill."

75   "We turned over twice!" said the grandmother.

"Oncet," he corrected. "We seen it happen. Try their car and see will it run, Hiram," he said quietly to the boy with the gray hat.

"What you got that gun for?" John Wesley asked. "Whatcha gonna do with that gun?"

"Lady," the man said to the children's mother, "would you mind calling them children to sit down by you? Children make me nervous. I want all you all to sit down right together there where you're at."

"What are you telling US what to do for?" June Star asked.

Behind them the line of woods gaped like a dark open mouth. "Come here," said their mother.   80

"Look here now," Bailey began suddenly, "we're in a predicament! We're in . . ."

The grandmother shrieked. She scrambled to her feet and stood staring. "You're The Misfit!" she said. "I recognized you at once!"

"Yes'm," the man said, smiling slightly as if he were pleased in spite of himself to be known, "but it would have been better for all of you, lady, if you hadn't of reckernized me."

Bailey turned his head sharply and said something to his mother that shocked even the children. The old lady began to cry and The Misfit reddened.

"Lady," he said, "don't you get upset. Sometimes a man says things he don't mean. I don't reckon he meant to talk to you thataway."   85

"You wouldn't shoot a lady, would you?" the grandmother said and removed a clean handkerchief from her cuff and began to slap at her eyes with it.

The Misfit pointed the toe of his shoe into the ground and made a little hole and then covered it up again. "I would hate to have to," he said.

"Listen," the grandmother almost screamed, "I know you're a good man. You don't look a bit like you have common blood. I know you must come from nice people!"

"Yes ma'am," he said, "finest people in the world." When he smiled he showed a row of strong white teeth. "God never made a finer woman than my mother and my daddy's heart was pure gold," he said. The boy with the red sweat shirt had come around behind them and was standing with his gun at his hip. The Misfit squatted down on the ground. "Watch them children, Bobby Lee," he said. "You know they make me nervous." He looked at the six of them huddled together in front of him and he seemed to be embarrassed as if he couldn't think of anything to say. "Ain't a cloud in the sky," he remarked, looking up at it. "Don't see no sun but don't see no cloud neither."

"Yes, it's a beautiful day," said the grandmother. "Listen," she said,   90 "you shouldn't call yourself The Misfit because I know you're a good man at heart. I can just look at you and tell."

"Hush!" Bailey yelled. "Hush! Everybody shut up and let me handle this!" He was squatting in the position of a runner about to sprint forward but he didn't move.

"I pre-chate that, lady," The Misfit said and drew a little circle in the ground with the butt of his gun.

"It'll take a half a hour to fix this here car," Hiram called, looking over the raised hood of it.

"Well, first you and Bobby Lee get him and that little boy to step over yonder with you," The Misfit said, pointing to Bailey and John Wesley. "The boys want to ast you something," he said to Bailey. "Would you mind stepping back in them woods there with them?"

95   "Listen," Bailey began, "we're in a terrible predicament! Nobody realizes what this is," and his voice cracked. His eyes were as blue and intense as the parrots in his shirt and he remained perfectly still.

The grandmother reached up to adjust her hat brim as if she were going to the woods with him but it came off in her hand. She stood staring at it and after a second she let it fall on the ground. Hiram pulled Bailey up by the arm as if he were assisting an old man. John Wesley caught hold of his father's hand and Bobby Lee followed. They went off toward the woods and just as they reached the dark edge, Bailey turned and supporting himself against a gray naked pine trunk, he shouted, "I'll be back in a minute, Mamma, wait on me!"

"Come back this instant!" his mother shrilled but they all disappeared into the woods.

"Bailey Boy!" the grandmother called in a tragic voice but she found she was looking at The Misfit squatting on the ground in front of her. "I just know you're a good man," she said desperately. "You're not a bit common!"

"Nome, I ain't a good man," The Misfit said after a second as if he had considered her statement carefully, "but I ain't the worst in the world neither. My daddy said I was a different breed of dog from my brothers and sisters. 'You know,' Daddy said, 'it's some that can live their whole life out without asking about it and it's others has to know why it is, and this boy is one of the latters. He's going to be into everything!'" He put on his black hat and looked up suddenly and then away deep into the woods as if he were embarrassed again. "I'm sorry I don't have on a shirt before you ladies," he said, hunching his shoulders slightly. "We buried our clothes that we had on when we escaped and we're just making do until we can get better. We borrowed these from some folks we met," he explained.

100   "That's perfectly all right," the grandmother said. "Maybe Bailey has an extra shirt in his suitcase."

"I'll look and see terrectly," The Misfit said.

"Where are they taking him?" the children's mother screamed.

"Daddy was a card himself," The Misfit said. "You couldn't put anything over on him. He never got in trouble with the Authorities though. Just had the knack of handling them."

"You could be honest too if you'd only try," said the grandmother. "Think how wonderful it would be to settle down and live a comfortable life and not have to think about somebody chasing you all the time."

The Misfit kept scratching in the ground with the butt of his gun as if he were thinking about it. "Yes'm, somebody is always after you," he murmured. 105

The grandmother noticed how thin his shoulder blades were just behind his hat because she was standing up looking down on him. "Do you ever pray?" she asked.

He shook his head. All she saw was the black hat wiggle between his shoulder blades. "Nome," he said.

There was a pistol shot from the woods, followed closely by another. Then silence. The old lady's head jerked around. She could hear the wind move through the tree tops like a long satisfied insuck of breath. "Bailey Boy!" she called.

"I was a gospel singer for a while," The Misfit said. "I been most everything. Been in the arm service, both land and sea, at home and abroad, been twict married, been an undertaker, been with the railroads, plowed Mother Earth, been in a tornado, seen a man burnt alive oncet," and looked up at the children's mother and the little girl who were sitting close together, their faces white and their eyes glassy; "I even seen a woman flogged," he said.

"Pray, pray," the grandmother began, "pray, pray . . ." 110

"I never was a bad boy that I remember of," The Misfit said in an almost dreamy voice, "but somewheres along the line I done something wrong and got sent to the penitentiary. I was buried alive," and he looked up and held her attention to him by a steady stare.

"That's when you should have started to pray," she said. "What did you do to get sent to the penitentiary that first time?"

"Turn to the right, it was a wall," The Misfit said, looking up again at the cloudless sky. "Turn to the left, it was a wall. Look up it was a ceiling, look down it was a floor. I forget what I done, lady. I set there and set there, trying to remember what it was I done and I ain't recalled it to this day. Oncet in a while, I would think it was coming to me, but it never come."

"Maybe they put you in by mistake," the old lady said vaguely.

"Nome," he said. "It wasn't no mistake. They had the papers on me." 115

"You must have stolen something," she said.

The Misfit sneered slightly. "Nobody had nothing I wanted," he said. "It was a head-doctor at the penitentiary said what I had done was kill my daddy but I known that for a lie. My daddy died in nineteen ought nineteen of the epidemic flu and I never had a thing to do with it. He was buried in the Mount Hopewell Baptist churchyard and you can go there and see for yourself."

"If you would pray," the old lady said, "Jesus would help you."

"That's right," The Misfit said.

120 "Well then, why don't you pray?" she asked trembling with delight suddenly.

"I don't want no hep," he said. "I'm doing all right by myself."

Bobby Lee and Hiram came ambling back from the woods. Bobby Lee was dragging a yellow shirt with bright blue parrots in it.

"Thow me that shirt, Bobby Lee," The Misfit said. The shirt came flying at him and landed on his shoulder and he put it on. The grandmother couldn't name what the shirt reminded her of. "No, lady," The Misfit said while he was buttoning it up, "I found out the crime don't matter. You can do one thing or you can do another, kill a man or take a tire off his car, because sooner or later you're going to forget what it was you done and just be punished for it."

The children's mother had begun to make heaving noises as if she couldn't get her breath. "Lady," he asked, "would you and that little girl like to step off yonder with Bobby Lee and Hiram and join your husband?"

125 "Yes, thank you," the mother said faintly. Her left arm dangled helplessly and she was holding the baby, who had gone to sleep, in the other. "Hep that lady up, Hiram," The Misfit said as she struggled to climb out of the ditch, "and Bobby Lee, you hold onto that little girl's hand."

"I don't want to hold hands with him," June Star said. "He reminds me of a pig."

The fat boy blushed and laughed and caught her by the arm and pulled her off into the woods after Hiram and her mother.

Alone with The Misfit, the grandmother found that she had lost her voice. There was not a cloud in the sky nor any sun. There was nothing around her but woods. She wanted to tell him that he must pray. She opened and closed her mouth several times before anything came out. Finally she found herself saying, "Jesus, Jesus," meaning, Jesus will help you, but the way she was saying it, it sounded as if she might be cursing.

"Yes'm," The Misfit said as if he agreed. "Jesus thown everything off balance. It was the same case with Him as with me except He hadn't committed any crime and they could prove I had committed one because they had the papers on me. Of course," he said, "they never shown me my papers. That's why I sign myself now. I said long ago, you get you a signature and sign everything you do and keep a copy of it. Then you'll know what you done and you can hold up the crime to the punishment and see do they match and in the end you'll have something to prove you ain't been treated right. I call myself The Misfit," he said, "because I can't make what all I done wrong fit what all I gone through in punishment."

There was a piercing scream from the woods, followed closely by a   130
pistol report. "Does it seem right to you, lady, that one is punished a heap
and another ain't punished at all?"

"Jesus!" the old lady cried. "You've got good blood! I know you
wouldn't shoot a lady! I know you come from nice people! Pray! Jesus, you
ought not to shoot a lady. I'll give you all the money I've got!"

"Lady," The Misfit said, looking beyond her far into the woods, "there
never was a body that give the undertaker a tip."

There were two more pistol reports and the grandmother raised her
head like a parched old turkey hen crying for water and called, "Bailey Boy,
Bailey Boy!" as if her heart would break.

"Jesus was the only One that ever raised the dead." The Misfit continued, "and He shouldn't have done it. He thown everything off balance.
If He did what He said, then it's nothing for you to do but throw away
everything and follow Him, and if He didn't, then it's nothing for you to
do but enjoy the few minutes you got left the best way you can—by killing somebody or burning down his house or doing some other meanness to
him. No pleasure but meanness," he said and his voice had become almost
a snarl.

"Maybe He didn't raise the dead," the old lady mumbled, not knowing   135
what she was saying and feeling so dizzy that she sank down in the ditch
with her legs twisted under her.

"I wasn't there so I can't say He didn't," The Misfit said. "I wisht I
had of been there," he said, hitting the ground with his fist, "It ain't right
I wasn't there because if I had of been there I would of known. Listen
lady," he said in a high voice, "if I had of been there I would of known
and I wouldn't be like I am now." His voice seemed about to crack and the
grandmother's head cleared for an instant. She saw the man's face twisted
close to her own as if he were going to cry and she murmured, "Why
you're one of my babies. You're one of my own children!" She reached out
and touched him on the shoulder. The Misfit sprang back as if a snake had
bitten him and shot her three times through the chest. Then he put his
gun down on the ground and took off his glasses and began to clean them.

Hiram and Bobby Lee returned from the woods and stood over the
ditch, looking down at the grandmother who half sat and half lay in a
puddle of blood with her legs crossed under her like a child's and her face
smiling up at the cloudless sky.

Without his glasses, The Misfit's eyes were red-rimmed and pale and
defenseless-looking. "Take her off and thow her where you thown the
others," he said, picking up the cat that was rubbing itself against his leg.

"She was a talker, wasn't she?" Bobby Lee said, sliding down the ditch
with a yodel.

140   "She would of been a good woman," The Misfit said, "if it had been somebody there to shoot her every minute of her life."

"Some fun!" Bobby Lee said.

"Shut up, Bobby Lee," The Misfit said. "It's no real pleasure in life."

QUESTIONS

1. The family members surrounding the grandmother are carefully portrayed. Discuss their characterizations and the way they affect our perceptions of the grandmother.

2. Some readers have found the grandmother sympathetic and others have found her a figure of evil, portrayed with imagery often associated with witches. How can these conflicting responses be resolved? Is she more or less sympathetic than the other members of her family?

3. What is the function of the scene at Red Sammy's barbecue place? How does it advance the plot? the theme?

4. During the conversation between the grandmother and Red Sammy, they discuss the difficulty of finding a "good man" in the modern world. Is this a plain statement of the theme, or does the context of their conversation make the dialogue ironic? How does their discussion relate to the larger dramatization of good and evil in the story?

5. The story makes extensive use of animal symbolism. Find the many references to animals and discuss the overall significance of this motif.

6. Analyze The Misfit's motivation for killing the family and for his criminal behavior in general. Unlike his sidekicks, he has a philosophical temperament and carefully rationalizes his behavior. What do his remarks contribute to the theme of the story?

7. Why do the murders of the grandmother's family members take place "offstage," out in the woods? Could it be argued that this heightens the effect of the violence?

8. At the end of the story, what does The Misfit mean when he says of the grandmother, "She would of been a good woman . . . if it had been somebody there to shoot her every minute of her life" (paragraph 140)?

9. Reread the description of the grandmother after she has been murdered and is lying in the ditch (paragraph 137). Why is she described in this way?

10. In an essay, "A Reasonable Use of the Unreasonable," O'Connor argues that just before the grandmother's death "Her head clears for an instant and she realizes, even in her limited way, that she is responsible for the man before her and joined to him by ties of kinship. . . . And at this point she does the right thing, she makes the right gesture." Compare these comments with your own initial sense of the climactic scene. Does O'Connor's "reading" of this scene differ from your own? Does her commentary change your understanding of the story?

11. In the same essay, O'Connor argues that not only is The Misfit more intelligent than the grandmother but his "capacity for grace" is greater than hers. Do you agree with this remark? Why or why not?

FLANNERY O'CONNOR
Good Country People

Besides the neutral expression that she wore when she was alone, Mrs. Freeman had two others, forward and reverse, that she used for all her human dealings. Her forward expression was steady and driving like the advance of a heavy truck. Her eyes never swerved to left or right but turned as the story turned as if they followed a yellow line down the center of it. She seldom used the other expression because it was not often necessary for her to retract a statement, but when she did, her face came to a complete stop, there was an almost imperceptible movement of her black eyes, during which they seemed to be receding, and then the observer would see that Mrs. Freeman, though she might stand there as real as several grain sacks thrown on top of each other, was no longer there in spirit. As for getting anything across to her when this was the case, Mrs. Hopewell had given it up. She might talk her head off. Mrs. Freeman could never be brought to admit herself wrong on any point. She would stand there and if she could be brought to say anything, it was something like, "Well, I wouldn't of said it was and I wouldn't of said it wasn't," or letting her gaze range over the top kitchen shelf where there was an assortment of dusty bottles, she might remark, "I see you ain't ate many of them figs you put up last summer."

They carried on their most important business in the kitchen at breakfast. Every morning Mrs. Hopewell got up at seven o'clock and lit her gas heater and Joy's. Joy was her daughter, a large blonde girl who had an artificial leg. Mrs. Hopewell thought of her as a child though she was thirty-two years old and highly educated. Joy would get up while her mother was eating and lumber into the bathroom and slam the door, and before long, Mrs. Freeman would arrive at the back door. Joy would hear her mother call, "Come on in," and then they would talk for a while in low voices that were indistinguishable in the bathroom. By the time Joy came in, they had usually finished the weather report and were on one or the other of Mrs. Freeman's daughters, Glynese or Carramae; Joy called them Glycerin and Caramel. Glynese, a redhead, was eighteen and had many admirers; Carramae, a blonde, was only fifteen but already married and pregnant. She could not keep anything on her stomach. Every morning Mrs. Freeman told Mrs. Hopewell how many times she had vomited since the last report.

Mrs. Hopewell liked to tell people that Glynese and Carramae were two of the finest girls she knew and that Mrs. Freeman was a *lady* and that

GOOD COUNTRY PEOPLE   First published in 1955. See the footnote on page 445 for more information on O'Connor and her career.

she was never ashamed to take her anywhere or introduce her to anybody they might meet. Then she would tell how she had happened to hire the Freemans in the first place and how they were a godsend to her and how she had had them four years. The reason for her keeping them so long was that they were not trash. They were good country people. She had telephoned the man whose name they had given as a reference and he had told her that Mr. Freeman was a good farmer but that his wife was the nosiest woman ever to walk the earth. "She's got to be into everything," the man said. "If she don't get there before the dust settles, you can bet she's dead, that's all. She'll want to know all your business. I can stand him real good," he had said, "but me nor my wife neither could have stood that woman one more minute on this place." That had put Mrs. Hopewell off for a few days.

She had hired them in the end because there were no other applicants but she had made up her mind beforehand exactly how she would handle the woman. Since she was the type who had to be into everything, then, Mrs. Hopewell had decided, she would not only let her be into everything, she would *see to it* that she was into everything—she would give her the responsibility of everything, she would put her in charge. Mrs. Hopewell had no bad qualities of her own but she was able to use other people's in such a constructive way that she never felt the lack. She had hired the Freemans and she had kept them four years.

5   Nothing is perfect. This was one of Mrs. Hopewell's favorite sayings. Another was: that is life! And still another, the most important, was: well, other people have their opinions too. She would make these statements, usually at the table, in a tone of gentle insistence as if no one held them but her, and the large hulking Joy, whose constant outrage had obliterated every expression from her face, would stare just a little to the side of her, her eyes icy blue, with the look of someone who has achieved blindness by an act of will and means to keep it.

When Mrs. Hopewell said to Mrs. Freeman that life was like that, Mrs. Freeman would say, "I always said so myself." Nothing had been arrived at by anyone that had not first been arrived at by her. She was quicker than Mr. Freeman. When Mrs. Hopewell said to her after they had been on the place a while, "You know, you're the wheel behind the wheel," and winked, Mrs. Freeman had said, "I know it. I've always been quick. It's some that are quicker than others."

"Everybody is different," Mrs. Hopewell said.

"Yes, most people is," Mrs. Freeman said.

"It takes all kinds to make the world."

10   "I always said it did myself."

The girl was used to this kind of dialogue for breakfast and more of it for dinner; sometimes they had it for supper too. When they had no guest they ate in the kitchen because that was easier. Mrs. Freeman always managed to arrive at some point during the meal and to watch them finish it. She would stand in the doorway if it were summer but in the winter she would stand with one elbow on top of the refrigerator and look down on them, or she would stand by the gas heater, lifting the back of her skirt slightly. Occasionally she would stand against the wall and roll her head from side to side. At no time was she in any hurry to leave. All this was very trying on Mrs. Hopewell but she was a woman of great patience. She realized that nothing is perfect and that in the Freemans she had good country people and that if, in this day and age, you get good country people, you had better hang onto them.

She had had plenty of experience with trash. Before the Freemans she had averaged one tenant family a year. The wives of these farmers were not the kind you would want to be around you for very long. Mrs. Hopewell, who had divorced her husband long ago, needed someone to walk over the fields with her; and when Joy had to be impressed for these services, her remarks were usually so ugly and her face so glum that Mrs. Hopewell would say, "If you can't come pleasantly, I don't want you at all," to which the girl, standing square and rigid-shouldered with her neck thrust slightly forward, would reply, "If you want me, here I am—LIKE I AM."

Mrs. Hopewell excused this attitude because of the leg (which had been shot off in a hunting accident when Joy was ten). It was hard for Mrs. Hopewell to realize that her child was thirty-two now and that for more than twenty years she had had only one leg. She thought of her still as a child because it tore her heart to think instead of the poor stout girl in her thirties who had never danced a step or had any *normal* good times. Her name was really Joy but as soon as she was twenty-one and away from home, she had had it legally changed. Mrs. Hopewell was certain that she had thought and thought until she had hit upon the ugliest name in any language. Then she had gone and had the beautiful name, Joy, changed without telling her mother until after she had done it. Her legal name was Hulga.

When Mrs. Hopewell thought the name, Hulga, she thought of the broad blank hull of a battleship. She would not use it. She continued to call her Joy to which the girl responded but in a purely mechanical way.

Hulga had learned to tolerate Mrs. Freeman who saved her from taking walks with her mother. Even Glynese and Carramae were useful when they occupied attention that might otherwise have been directed at her. At first she had thought she could not stand Mrs. Freeman for she had found that it was not possible to be rude to her. Mrs. Freeman would take on strange resentments and for days together she would be sullen but the source of her displeasure was always obscure; a direct attack, a positive leer, blatant ugliness to her face—these never touched her. And without warning one day, she began calling her Hulga.

She did not call her that in front of Mrs. Hopewell who would have been incensed but when she and the girl happened to be out of the house together, she would say something and add the name Hulga to the end of it, and the big spectacled Joy-Hulga would scowl and redden as if her privacy had been intruded upon. She considered the name her personal affair. She had arrived at it first purely on the basis of its ugly sound and then the full genius of its fitness had struck her. She had a vision of the name working like the ugly sweating Vulcan who stayed in the furnace and to whom, presumably, the goddess had to come when called. She saw it as the name of her highest creative act. One of her major triumphs was that her mother had not been able to turn her dust into Joy, but the greater one was that she had been able to turn it herself into Hulga. However, Mrs. Freeman's relish for using the name only irritated her. It was as if Mrs. Freeman's beady steel-pointed eyes had penetrated far enough behind her face to reach some secret fact. Something about her seemed to fascinate Mrs. Freeman and then one day Hulga realized that it was the artificial leg. Mrs. Freeman had a special fondness for the details of secret infections, hidden deformities, assaults upon children. Of diseases, she preferred the lingering or incurable. Hulga had heard Mrs. Hopewell give her the details of the hunting accident, how the leg had been literally blasted off, how she had never lost consciousness. Mrs. Freeman could listen to it any time as if it had happened an hour ago.

When Hulga stumped into the kitchen in the morning (she could walk without making the awful noise but she made it—Mrs. Hopewell was certain—because it was ugly-sounding), she glanced at them and did not speak. Mrs. Hopewell would be in her red kimono with her hair tied around her head in rags. She would be sitting at the table, finishing her breakfast and Mrs. Freeman would be hanging by her elbow outward from the refrigerator, looking down at the table. Hulga always put her eggs on the stove to boil and then stood over them with her arms folded, and Mrs. Hopewell would look at her—a kind of indirect gaze divided between her and Mrs. Freeman—and would think that if she would only keep herself up a little, she wouldn't be so bad looking. There was nothing wrong with her face that a pleasant expression wouldn't help. Mrs. Hopewell said that people who looked on the bright side of things would be beautiful even if they were not.

Whenever she looked at Joy this way, she could not help but feel that it would have been better if the child had not taken the Ph.D. It had certainly not brought her out any and now that she had it, there was no more excuse for her to go to school again. Mrs. Hopewell thought it was nice for girls to go to school to have a good time but Joy had "gone through." Anyhow, she would not have been strong enough to go again. The doctors had told Mrs. Hopewell that with the best of care, Joy might see forty-five. She had a weak heart. Joy had made it plain that if it had not been for this condition, she would be far from these red hills and good country people. She would be in a university lecturing to people who knew what she was talking about. And Mrs. Hopewell could very well picture her there, looking like a scarecrow and lecturing to more of the same. Here she went about all day in a six-year-old skirt and a yellow sweat shirt with a faded cowboy on a horse embossed on it. She thought this was funny; Mrs. Hopewell thought it was idiotic and showed simply that she was still a child. She was brilliant but she didn't have a grain of sense. It seemed to Mrs. Hopewell that every year she grew less like other people and more like herself—bloated, rude, and squint-cyed. And she said such strange things! To her own mother she had said—without warning, without excuse, standing up in the middle of a meal with her face purple and her mouth half full—"Woman! Do you ever look inside? Do you ever look inside and see what you are *not*? God!" she had cried sinking down again and staring at her plate, "Malebranche was right: we are not our own light. We are not our own light!" Mrs. Hopewell had no idea to this day what brought that on. She had only made the remark, hoping Joy would take it in, that a smile never hurt anyone.

The girl had taken the Ph.D. in philosophy and this left Mrs. Hopewell at a complete loss. You could say, "My daughter is a nurse," or "My daughter is a schoolteacher," or even, "My daughter is a chemical engineer." You could not say, "My daughter is a philosopher." That was something that had ended with the Greeks and Romans. All day Joy sat on her neck in a deep chair, reading. Sometimes she went for walks but she didn't like dogs or cats or birds or flowers or nature or nice young men. She looked at nice young men as if she could smell their stupidity.

One day Mrs. Hopewell had picked up one of the books the girl had 20 just put down and opening it at random, she read, "Science, on the other hand, has to assert its soberness and seriousness afresh and declare that it is concerned solely with what-is. Nothing—how can it be for science anything but a horror and a phantasm? If science is right, then one thing stands firm: science wishes to know nothing of Nothing. Such is after all the strictly scientific approach to Nothing. We know it by wishing to know nothing of Nothing." These words had been underlined with a blue pencil and they worked on Mrs. Hopewell like some evil incantation in gibberish. She shut the book quickly and went out of the room as if she were having a chill.

This morning when the girl came in, Mrs. Freeman was on Carramae. "She thrown up four times after supper," she said, "and was up twict in the night after three o'clock. Yesterday she didn't do nothing but ramble in the bureau drawer. All she did. Stand up there and see what she could run up on."

"She's got to eat," Mrs. Hopewell muttered, sipping her coffee, while she watched Joy's back at the stove. She was wondering what the child had said to the Bible salesman. She could not imagine what kind of a conversation she could possibly have had with him.

He was a tall gaunt hatless youth who had called yesterday to sell them a Bible. He had appeared at the door, carrying a large black suitcase that weighted him so heavily on one side that he had to brace himself against the door facing. He seemed on the point of collapse but he said in a cheerful voice. "Good morning, Mrs. Cedars!" and set the suitcase down on the mat. He was not a bad-looking young man though he had on a bright blue suit and yellow socks that were not pulled up far enough. He had prominent face bones and a streak of sticky-looking brown hair falling across his forehead.

"I'm Mrs. Hopewell," she said.

25 "Oh!" he said, pretending to look puzzled but with his eyes sparkling, "I saw it said The Cedars' on the mailbox so I thought you was Mrs. Cedars!" and he burst out in a pleasant laugh. He picked up the satchel and under cover of a pant, he fell forward into her hall. It was rather as if the suitcase had moved first, jerking him after it. "Mrs. Hopewell!" he said and grabbed her hand. "I hope you are well!" and he laughed again and then all at once his face sobered completely. He paused and gave her a straight earnest look and said, "Lady, I've come to speak of serious things."

"Well, come in," she muttered, none too pleased because her dinner was almost ready. He came into the parlor and sat down on the edge of a straight chair and put the suitcase between his feet and glanced around the room as if he were sizing her up by it. Her silver gleamed on the two sideboards; she decided he had never been in a room as elegant as this.

"Mrs. Hopewell," he began, using her name in a way that sounded almost intimate, "I know you believe in Chrustian service."

"Well yes," she murmured.

"I know," he said and paused, looking very wise with his head cocked on one side, "that you're a good woman. Friends have told me."

30 Mrs. Hopewell never liked to be taken for a fool. "What are you selling?" she asked.

"Bibles," the young man said and his eye raced around the room before he added, "I see you have no family Bible in your parlor, I see that is the one lack you got!"

Mrs. Hopewell could not say, "My daughter is an atheist and won't let me keep the Bible in the parlor." She said, stiffening slightly, "I keep my Bible by my bedside." This was not the truth. It was in the attic somewhere.

"Lady," he said, "the word of God ought to be in the parlor."

"Well, I think that's a matter of taste," she began. "I think . . ."

"Lady," he said, "for a Christian, the word of God ought to be in every 35 room in the house besides in his heart. I know you're a Christian because I can see it in every line of your face."

She stood up and said, "Well, young man, I don't want to buy a Bible and I smell my dinner burning."

He didn't get up. He began to twist his hands and looking down at them, he said softly, "Well lady, I'll tell you the truth—not many people want to buy one nowadays and besides, I know I'm real simple. I don't know how to say a thing but to say it. I'm just a country boy." He glanced up into her unfriendly face. "People like you don't like to fool with country people like me!"

"Why!" she cried, "good country people are the salt of the earth! Besides, we all have different ways of doing, it takes all kinds to make the world go 'round. That's life!"

"You said a mouthful," he said.

"Why, I think there aren't enough good country people in the world!" 40 she said, stirred. "I think that's what's wrong with it!"

His face had brightened. "I didn't intraduce myself," he said. "I'm Manley Pointer from out in the country around Willohobie, not even from a place, just from near a place."

"You wait a minute," she said. "I have to see about my dinner." She went out to the kitchen and found Joy standing near the door where she had been listening.

"Get rid of the salt of the earth," she said, "and let's eat."

Mrs. Hopewell gave her a pained look and turned the heat down under the vegetables. "*I* can't be rude to anybody," she murmured and went back into the parlor.

He had opened the suitcase and was sitting with a Bible on each knee. 45

"You might as well put those up," she told him. "I don't want one."

"I appreciate your honesty," he said. "You don't see any more real honest people unless you go way out in the country."

"I know," she said, "real genuine folks!" Through the crack in the door she heard a groan.

"I guess a lot of boys come telling you they're working their way through college," he said, "but I'm not going to tell you that. Somehow," he said, "I don't want to go to college. I want to devote my life to Christian service. See," he said, lowering his voice, "I got this heart condition. I may not live long. When you know it's something wrong with you and you may not live long, well then, lady . . ." He paused, with his mouth open, and stared at her.

50   He and Joy had the same condition! She knew that her eyes were filling with tears but she collected herself quickly and murmured, "Won't you stay for dinner? We'd love to have you!" and was sorry the instant she heard herself say it.

"Yes mam," he said in an abashed voice, "I would sher love to do that!"

Joy had given him one look on being introduced to him and then throughout the meal had not glanced at him again. He had addressed several remarks to her, which she had pretended not to hear. Mrs. Hopewell could not understand deliberate rudeness, although she lived with it, and she felt she had always to overflow with hospitality to make up for Joy's lack of courtesy. She urged him to talk about himself and he did. He said he was the seventh child of twelve and that his father had been crushed under a tree when he himself was eight year old. He had been crushed very badly, in fact, almost cut in two and was practically not recognizable. His mother had got along the best she could by hard working and she had always seen that her children went to Sunday School and that they read the Bible every evening. He was now nineteen year old and he had been selling Bibles for four months. In that time he had sold seventy-seven Bibles and had the promise of two more sales. He wanted to become a missionary because he thought that was the way you could do most for people. "He who losest his life shall find it," he said simply and he was so sincere, so genuine and earnest that Mrs. Hopewell would not for the world have smiled. He prevented his peas from sliding onto the table by blocking them with a piece of bread which he later cleaned his plate with. She could see Joy observing side-wise how he handled his knife and fork and she saw too that every few minutes, the boy would dart a keen appraising glance at the girl as if he were trying to attract her attention.

After dinner Joy cleared the dishes off the table and disappeared and Mrs. Hopewell was left to talk with him. He told her again about his childhood and his father's accident and about various things that had happened to him. Every five minutes or so she would stifle a yawn. He sat for two hours until finally she told him she must go because she had an appointment in town. He packed his Bibles and thanked her and prepared to leave, but in the doorway he stopped and wrung her hand and said that not on any of his trips had he met a lady as nice as her and he asked if he could come again. She had said she would always be happy to see him.

Joy had been standing in the road, apparently looking at something in the distance, when he came down the steps toward her, bent to the side with his heavy valise. He stopped where she was standing and confronted her directly. Mrs. Hopewell could not hear what he said but she trembled to think what Joy would say to him. She could see that after a minute Joy said something and that then the boy began to speak again, making an excited gesture with his free hand. After a minute Joy said something else at which the boy began to speak once more. Then to her amazement, Mrs. Hopewell saw the two of them walk off together, toward the gate. Joy had walked all the way to the gate with him and Mrs. Hopewell could not imagine what they had said to each other, and she had not yet dared to ask.

Mrs. Freeman was insisting upon her attention. She had moved from the refrigerator to the heater so that Mrs. Hopewell had to turn and face her in order to seem to be listening. "Glynese gone out with Harvey Hill again last night," she said. "She had this sty." 55

"Hill," Mrs. Hopewell said absently, "is that the one who works in the garage?"

"Nome, he's the one that goes to chiropracter school," Mrs. Freeman said. "She had this sty. Been had it two days. So she says when he brought her in the other night he says, 'Lemme get rid of that sty for you,' and she says, 'How?' and he says, 'You just lay yourself down across the seat of that car and I'll show you.' So she done it and he popped her neck. Kept on a-popping it several times until she made him quit. This morning," Mrs. Freeman said, "she ain't got no sty. She ain't got no traces of a sty."

"I never heard of that before," Mrs. Hopewell said.

"He ast her to marry him before the Ordinary," Mrs. Freeman went on, "and she told him she wan't going to be married in no *office*."

"Well, Glynese is a fine girl," Mrs. Hopewell said. "Glynese and Carramae are both fine girls." 60

"Carramae said when her and Lyman was married Lyman said it sure felt sacred to him. She said he said he wouldn't take five hundred dollars for being married by a preacher."

"How much would he take?" the girl asked from the stove.

"He said he wouldn't take five hundred dollars," Mrs. Freeman repeated.

"Well we all have work to do," Mrs. Hopewell said.

"Lyman said it just felt more sacred to him," Mrs. Freeman said. 65

"The doctor wants Carramae to eat prunes. Says instead of medicine. Says them cramps is coming from pressure. You know where I think it is?"

"She'll be better in a few weeks," Mrs. Hopewell said.

"In the tube," Mrs. Freeman said. "Else she wouldn't be as sick as she is."

Hulga had cracked her two eggs into a saucer and was bringing them to the table along with a cup of coffee that she had filled too full. She sat down carefully and began to eat, meaning to keep Mrs. Freeman there by questions if for any reason she showed an inclination to leave. She could perceive her mother's eye on her. The first round-about question would be about the Bible salesman and she did not wish to bring it on. "How did he pop her neck?" she asked.

70   Mrs. Freeman went into a description of how he had popped her neck. She said he owned a '55 Mercury but that Glynese said she would rather marry a man with only a '36 Plymouth who would be married by a preacher. The girl asked what if he had a '32 Plymouth and Mrs.Freeman said what Glynese had said was a '36 Plymouth.

Mrs. Hopewell said there were not many girls with Glynese's common sense. She said what she admired in those girls was their common sense. She said that reminded her that they had had a nice visitor yesterday, a young man selling Bibles. "Lord," she said, "he bored me to death but he was so sincere and genuine I couldn't be rude to him. He was just good country people, you know," she said, "—just the salt of the earth."

"I seen him walk up," Mrs. Freeman said, "and then later—I seen him walk off," and Hulga could feel the slight shift in her voice, the slight insinuation, that he had not walked off alone, had he? Her face remained expressionless but the color rose into her neck and she seemed to swallow it down with the next spoonful of egg. Mrs. Freeman was looking at her as if they had a secret together.

"Well, it takes all kinds of people to make the world go 'round," Mrs. Hopewell said. "It's very good we aren't all alike."

"Some people are more alike than others," Mrs. Freeman said.

75   Hulga got up and stumped, with about twice the noise that was necessary, into her room and locked the door. She was to meet the Bible salesman at ten o'clock at the gate. She had thought about it half the night. She had started thinking of it as a great joke and then she had begun to see profound implications in it. She had lain in bed imagining dialogues for them that were insane on the surface but that reached below to depths that no Bible salesman would be aware of. Their conversation yesterday had been of this kind.

He had stopped in front of her and had simply stood there. His face was bony and sweaty and bright, with a little pointed nose in the center of it, and his look was different from what it had been at the dinner table. He was gazing at her with open curiosity, with fascination, like a child watching a new fantastic animal at the zoo, and he was breathing as if he had run a great distance to reach her. His gaze seemed somehow familiar but she could not think where she had been regarded with it before. For almost a minute he didn't say anything. Then on what seemed an insuck of breath, he whispered, "You ever ate a chicken that was two days old?"

The girl looked at him stonily. He might have just put this question up for consideration at the meeting of a philosophical association. "Yes," she presently replied as if she had considered it from all angles.

"It must have been mighty small!" he said triumphantly and shook all over with little nervous giggles, getting very red in the face, and subsiding finally into his gaze of complete admiration, while the girl's expression remained exactly the same.

"How old are you?" he asked softly.

She waited some time before she answered. Then in a flat voice   80 she said, "Seventeen."

His smiles came in succession like waves breaking on the surface of a little lake. "I see you got a wooden leg," he said. "I think you're brave. I think you're real sweet."

The girl stood blank and solid and silent.

"Walk to the gate with me," he said. "You're a brave sweet little thing and I liked you the minute I seen you walk in the door."

Hulga began to move forward.

"What's your name?" he asked, smiling down on the top of her head.   85

"Hulga," she said.

"Hulga," he murmured, "Hulga, Hulga. I never heard of anybody name Hulga before. You're shy, aren't you, Hulga?" he asked.

She nodded, watching his large red hand on the handle of the giant valise.

"I like girls that wear glasses," he said. "I think a lot. I'm not like these people that a serious thought don't ever enter their heads. It's because I may die."

"I may die too," she said suddenly and looked up at him. His eyes were   90 very small and brown, glittering feverishly.

"Listen," he said, "don't you think some people was meant to meet on account of what all they got in common and all? Like they both think serious thoughts and all?" He shifted the valise to his other hand so that the hand nearest her was free. He caught hold of her elbow and shook it a little. "I don't work on Saturday," he said. "I like to walk in the woods and see what Mother Nature is wearing. O'er the hills and far away. Pic-nics and things. Couldn't we go on a pic-nic tomorrow? Say yes, Hulga," he said and gave her a dying look as if he felt his insides about to drop out of him. He had even seemed to sway slightly toward her.

During the night she had imagined that she seduced him. She imagined that the two of them walked on the place until they came to the storage barn beyond the two back fields and there, she imagined, that things came to such a pass that she very easily seduced him and that then, of course, she had to reckon with his remorse. True genius can get an idea across even to an inferior mind. She imagined that she took his remorse in hand and changed it into a deeper understanding of life. She took all his shame away and turned it into something useful.

She set off for the gate at exactly ten o'clock, escaping without drawing Mrs. Hopewell's attention. She didn't take anything to eat, forgetting that food is usually taken on a picnic. She wore a pair of slacks and a dirty white shirt, and as an afterthought, she had put some Vapex on the collar of it since she did not own any perfume. When she reached the gate no one was there.

She looked up and down the empty highway and had the furious feeling that she had been tricked, that he had only meant to make her walk to the gate after the idea of him. Then suddenly he stood up, very tall, from behind a bush on the opposite embankment. Smiling, he lifted his hat which was new and wide-brimmed. He had not worn it yesterday and she wondered if he had bought it for the occasion. It was toast-colored with a red and white band around it and was slightly too large for him. He stepped from behind the bush still carrying the black valise. He had on the same suit and the same yellow socks sucked down in his shoes from walking. He crossed the highway and said, "I knew you'd come!"

95   The girl wondered acidly how he had known this. She pointed to the valise and asked, "Why did you bring your Bibles?"

He took her elbow, smiling down on her as if he could not stop. "You can never tell when you'll need the word of God, Hulga," he said. She had a moment in which she doubted that this was actually happening and then they began to climb the embankment. They went down into the pasture toward the woods. The boy walked lightly by her side, bouncing on his toes. The valise did not seem to be heavy today; he even swung it. They crossed half the pasture without saying anything and then, putting his hand easily on the small of her back, he asked softly, "Where does your wooden leg join on?"

She turned an ugly red and glared at him and for an instant the boy looked abashed. "I didn't mean you no harm," he said. "I only meant you're so brave and all. I guess God takes care of you."

"No," she said, looking forward and walking fast, "I don't even believe in God."

At this he stopped and whistled. "No!" he exclaimed as if he were too astonished to say anything else.

100   She walked on and in a second he was bouncing at her side, fanning with his hat. "That's very unusual for a girl," he remarked, watching her out of the corner of his eye. When they reached the edge of the wood, he put his hand on her back again and drew her against him without a word and kissed her heavily.

The kiss, which had more pressure than feeling behind it, produced that extra surge of adrenalin in the girl that enables one to carry a packed trunk out of a burning house, but in her, the power went at once to the brain. Even before he released her, her mind, clear and detached and ironic anyway, was regarding him from a great distance, with amusement but with pity. She had never been kissed before and she was pleased to discover that it was an unexceptional experience and all a matter of the mind's control. Some people might enjoy drain water if they were told it was vodka. When the boy, looking expectant but uncertain, pushed her gently away, she turned and walked on, saying nothing as if such business, for her, were common enough.

He came along panting at her side, trying to help her when he saw a root that she might trip over. He caught and held back the long swaying blades of thorn vine until she had passed beyond them. She led the way and he came breathing heavily behind her. Then they came out on a sunlit hillside, sloping softly into another one a little smaller. Beyond, they could see the rusted top of the old barn where the extra hay was stored.

The hill was sprinkled with small pink weeds. "Then you ain't saved?" he asked suddenly, stopping.

The girl smiled. It was the first time she had smiled at him at all. "In my economy," she said, "I'm saved and you are damned but I told you I didn't believe in God."

Nothing seemed to destroy the boy's look of admiration. He gazed at 105 her now as if the fantastic animal at the zoo had put its paw through the bars and given him a loving poke. She thought he looked as if he wanted to kiss her again and she walked on before he had the chance.

"Ain't there somewheres we can sit down sometime?" he murmured, his voice softening toward the end of the sentence.

"In that barn," she said.

They made for it rapidly as if it might slide away like a train. It was a large two-story barn, cool and dark inside. The boy pointed up the ladder that led into the loft and said, "It's too bad we can't go up there."

"Why can't we?" she asked.

"Yer leg," he said reverently.   110

The girl gave him a contemptuous look and putting both hands on the ladder, she climbed it while he stood below, apparently awestruck. She pulled herself expertly through the opening and then looked down at him and said, "Well, come on if you're coming," and he began to climb the ladder, awkwardly bringing the suitcase with him.

"We won't need the Bible," she observed.

"You never can tell," he said, panting. After he had got into the loft, he was a few seconds catching his breath. She had sat down in a pile of straw. A wide sheath of sunlight, filled with dust particles, slanted over her. She lay back against a bale, her face turned away, looking out the front opening of the barn where hay was thrown from a wagon into the loft. The two pink-speckled hillsides lay back against a dark ridge of woods. The sky was cloudless and cold blue. The boy dropped down by her side and put one arm under her and the other over her and began methodically kissing her face, making little noises like a fish. He did not remove his hat but it was pushed far enough back not to interfere. When her glasses got in his way, he took them off of her and slipped them into his pocket.

The girl at first did not return any of the kisses but presently she began to and after she had put several on his cheek, she reached his lips and remained there, kissing him again and again as if she were trying to draw all the breath out of him. His breath was clear and sweet like a child's and the kisses were sticky like a child's. He mumbled about loving her and about knowing when he first seen her that he loved her, but the mumbling was like the sleepy fretting of a child being put to sleep by his mother. Her mind, throughout this, never stopped or lost itself for a second to her feelings. "You ain't said you loved me none," he whispered finally, pulling back from her. "You got to say that."

115   She looked away from him off into the hollow sky and then down at a black ridge and then down farther into what appeared to be two green swelling lakes. She didn't realize he had taken her glasses but this landscape could not seem exceptional to her for she seldom paid any close attention to her surroundings.

"You got to say it," he repeated. "You got to say you love me."

She was always careful how she committed herself. "In a sense," she began, "if you use the word loosely, you might say that. But it's not a word I use. I don't have illusions. I'm one of those people who see *through* to nothing."

The boy was frowning. "You got to say it. I said it and you got to say it," he said.

The girl looked at him almost tenderly. "You poor baby," she murmured. "It's just as well you don't understand," and she pulled him by the neck, face-down, against her. "We are all damned," she said, "but some of us have taken off our blindfolds and see that there's nothing to see. It's a kind of salvation."

120   The boy's astonished eyes looked blankly through the ends of her hair. "Okay," he almost whined, "but do you love me or don'tcher?"

"Yes," she said and added, "in a sense. But I must tell you something. There mustn't be anything dishonest between us." She lifted his head and looked him in the eye. "I am thirty years old," she said. "I have a number of degrees."

The boy's look was irritated but dogged. "I don't care," he said. "I don't care a thing about what all you done. I just want to know if you love me or don'tcher?" and he caught her to him and wildly planted her face with kisses until she said, "Yes, yes."

"Okay then," he said, letting her go. "Prove it."

She smiled, looking dreamily out on the shifty landscape. She had seduced him without even making up her mind to try. "How?" she asked, feeling that he should be delayed a little.

He leaned over and put his lips to her ear. "Show me where your 125 wooden leg joins on," he whispered.

The girl uttered a sharp little cry and her face instantly drained of color. The obscenity of the suggestion was not what shocked her. As a child she had sometimes been subject to feelings of shame but education had removed the last traces of that as a good surgeon scrapes for cancer; she would no more have felt it over what he was asking than she would have believed in his Bible. But she was as sensitive about the artificial leg as a peacock about his tail. No one ever touched it but her. She took care of it as someone else would his soul, in private and almost with her own eyes turned away. "No," she said.

"I known it," he muttered, sitting up. "You're just playing me for a sucker."

"Oh no no!" she cried. "It joins on at the knee. Only at the knee. Why do you want to see it?"

The boy gave her a long penetrating look. "Because," he said, "it's what makes you different. You ain't like anybody else."

She sat staring at him. There was nothing about her face or her round 130 freezing-blue eyes to indicate that this had moved her; but she felt as if her heart had stopped and left her mind to pump her blood. She decided that for the first time in her life she was face to face with real innocence. This boy, with an instinct that came from beyond wisdom, had touched the truth about her. When after a minute, she said in a hoarse high voice, "All right," it was like surrendering to him completely. It was like losing her own life and finding it again, miraculously, in his.

Very gently he began to roll the slack leg up. The artificial limb, in a white sock and brown flat shoe, was bound in a heavy material like canvas and ended in an ugly jointure where it was attached to the stump. The boy's face and his voice were entirely reverent as he uncovered it and said, "Now show me how to take it off and on."

She took it off for him and put it back on again and then he took it off himself, handling it as tenderly as if it were a real one. "See!" he said with a delighted child's face. "Now I can do it myself!"

"Put it back on," she said. She was thinking that she would run away with him and that every night he would take the leg off and every morning put it back on again. "Put it back on," she said.

"Not yet," he murmured, setting it on its foot out of her reach. "Leave it off for a while. You got me instead."

135   She gave a little cry of alarm but he pushed her down and began to kiss her again. Without the leg she felt entirely dependent on him. Her brain seemed to have stopped thinking altogether and to be about some other function that it was not very good at. Different expressions raced back and forth over her face. Every now and then the boy, his eyes like two steel spikes, would glance behind him where the leg stood. Finally she pushed him off and said, "Put it back on me now."

       "Wait," he said. He leaned the other way and pulled the valise toward him and opened, it. It had a pale blue spotted lining and there were only two Bibles in it. He took one of these out and opened the cover of it. It was hollow and contained a pocket flask of whiskey, a pack of cards, and a small blue box with printing on it. He laid these out in front of her one at a time in an evenly-spaced row, like one presenting offerings at the shrine of a goddess. He put the blue box in her hand. THIS PRODUCT TO BE USED ONLY FOR THE PREVENTION OF DISEASE, she read, and dropped it. The boy was unscrewing the top of the flask. He stopped and pointed, with a smile, to the deck of cards. It was not an ordinary deck but one with an obscene picture on the back of each card. "Take a swig," he said, offering her the bottle first. He held it in front of her, but like one mesmerized, she did not move.

       Her voice when she spoke had an almost pleading sound. "Aren't you," she murmured, "aren't you just good country people?"

       The boy cocked his head. He looked as if he were just beginning to understand that she might be trying to insult him. "Yeah," he said, curling his lip slightly, "but it ain't held me back none. I'm as good as you any day in the week."

       "Give me my leg," she said.

140   He pushed it farther away with his foot. "Come on now, let's begin to have us a good time," he said coaxingly. "We ain't got to know one another good yet."

       "Give me my leg!" she screamed and tried to lunge for it but he pushed her down easily.

       "What's the matter with you all of a sudden?" he asked, frowning as he screwed the top on the flask and put it quickly back inside the Bible. "You just a while ago said you didn't believe in nothing. I thought you was some girl!"

       Her face was almost purple. "You're a Christian!" she hissed. "You're a fine Christian! You're just like them, all—say one thing and do another. You're a perfect Christian, you're . . ."

       The boy's mouth was set angrily. "I hope you don't think," he said in a lofty indignant tone, "that I believe in that crap! I may sell Bibles but I know which end is up and I wasn't born yesterday and I know where I'm going!"

"Give me my leg!" she screeched. He jumped up so quickly that she 145 barely saw him sweep the cards and the blue box into the Bible and throw the Bible into the valise. She saw him grab the leg and then she saw it for an instant slanted forlornly across the inside of the suitcase with a Bible at either side of its opposite ends. He slammed the lid shut and snatched up the valise and swung it down the hole and then stepped through himself.

When all of him had passed but his head, he turned and regarded her with a look that no longer had any admiration in it. "I've gotten a lot of interesting things," he said. "One time I got a woman's glass eye this way. And you needn't to think you'll catch me because Pointer ain't really my name. I use a different name at every house I call at and don't stay nowhere long. And I'll tell you another thing, Hulga," he said, using the name as if he didn't think much of it, "you ain't so smart. I been believing in nothing ever since I was born!" and then the toast-colored hat disappeared down the hole and the girl was left, sitting on the straw in the dusty sunlight. When she turned her churning face toward the opening, she saw his blue figure struggling successfully over the green speckled lake.

Mrs. Hopewell and Mrs. Freeman, who were in the back pasture, digging up onions, saw him emerge a little later from the woods and head across the meadow toward the highway. "Why, that looks like that nice dull young man that tried to sell me a Bible yesterday," Mrs. Hopewell said, squinting. "He must have been selling them to the Negroes back in there. He was so simple," she said, "but I guess the world would be better off if we were all that simple."

Mrs. Freeman's gaze drove forward and just touched him before he disappeared under the hill. Then she returned her attention to the evil-smelling onion shoot she was lifting from the ground. "Some can't be that simple," she said. "I know I never could."

QUESTIONS

1. Consider the use of irony in this story. What different types of irony does O'Connor employ?
2. The story features a "frame narrative" involving a minor character, Mrs. Freeman. How does this structure relate to the meaning? What does Mrs. Freeman add to the story?
3. Discuss the use of name symbolism. How do the names Mrs. Hopewell, Mrs. Freeman, Joy/Hulga, and Manley Pointer relate to their respective characterizations?
4. Why does Joy/Hulga take an interest in the Bible salesman? What does she hope to gain by interacting with him?
5. How would you describe the relationship between Joy/Hulga and her mother? Do you think the relationship will change after the story's conclusion?
6. What is the symbolic meaning of Joy/Hulga's wooden leg? How does her own view of it differ from the reader's as the story proceeds?

7. How is Mrs. Hopewell characterized? Is she a sympathetic character? Does the reader's view of her change during the story?
8. Does Joy/Hulga experience an epiphany by the end of the story? Why is her face described as "churning" in the final scene? Do you think she will undergo any permanent change?

FLANNERY O'CONNOR
Everything That Rises Must Converge

Her doctor had told Julian's mother that she must lose twenty pounds on account of her blood pressure, so on Wednesday nights Julian had to take her downtown on the bus for a reducing class at the Y. The reducing class was designed for working girls over fifty, who weighed from 165 to 200 pounds. His mother was one of the slimmer ones, but she said ladies did not tell their age or weight. She would not ride the buses by herself at night since they had been integrated, and because the reducing class was one of her few pleasures, necessary for her health, and *free,* she said Julian could at least put himself out to take her, considering all she did for him. Julian did not like to consider all she did for him, but every Wednesday night he braced himself and took her.

She was almost ready to go, standing before the hall mirror, putting on her hat, while he, his hands behind him, appeared pinned to the door frame, waiting like Saint Sebastian for the arrows to begin piercing him. The hat was new and had cost her seven dollars and a half. She kept saying, "Maybe I shouldn't have paid that for it. No, I shouldn't have. I'll take it off and return it tomorrow. I shouldn't have bought it."

Julian raised his eyes to heaven. "Yes, you should have bought it," he said. "Put it on and let's go." It was a hideous hat. A purple velvet flap came down on one side of it and stood up on the other; the rest of it was green and looked like a cushion with the stuffing out. He decided it was less comical than jaunty and pathetic. Everything that gave her pleasure was small and depressed him.

She lifted the hat one more time and set it down slowly on top of her head. Two wings of gray hair protruded on either side of her florid face, but her eyes, sky-blue, were as innocent and untouched by experience as they must have been when she was ten. Were it not that she was a widow who had struggled fiercely to feed and clothe and put him through school and who was supporting him still, "until he got on his feet," she might have been a little girl that he had to take to town.

EVERYTHING THAT RISES MUST CONVERGE   First published in 1965. See the footnote on page 445 for more information on O'Connor and her career.

"It's all right, it's all right," he said. "Let's go." He opened the door   5
himself and started down the walk to get her going. The sky was a dying
violet and the houses stood out darkly against it, bulbous liver-colored
monstrosities of a uniform ugliness though no two were alike. Since this
had been a fashionable neighborhood forty years ago, his mother persisted
in thinking they did well to have an apartment in it. Each house had a
narrow collar of dirt around it in which sat, usually, a grubby child. Julian
walked with his hands in his pockets, his head down and thrust forward
and his eyes glazed with the determination to make himself completely
numb during the time he would be sacrificed to her pleasure.

The door closed and he turned to find the dumpy figure, surmounted
by the atrocious hat, coming toward him. "Well," she said, "you only live
once and paying a little more for it, I at least won't meet myself coming
and going."

"Some day I'll start making money," Julian said gloomily—he knew
he never would—"and you can have one of those jokes whenever you take
the fit." But first they would move. He visualized a place where the nearest
neighbors would be three miles away on either side.

"I think you're doing fine," she said, drawing on her gloves. "You've
only been out of school a year. Rome wasn't built in a day."

She was one of the few members of the Y reducing class who arrived in
hat and gloves and who had a son who had been to college: "It takes time," she
said, "and the world is in such a mess. This hat looked better on me than any
of the others, though when she brought it out I said, 'Take that thing back. I
wouldn't have it on my head,' and she said, 'Now wait till you see it on,' and
when she put it on me, I said, 'We-ull,' and she said, 'If you ask me, that hat
does something for you and you do something for the hat, and besides,' she
said, 'with that hat, you won't meet yourself coming and going.'"

Julian thought he could have stood his lot better if she had been self-   10
ish, if she had been an old hag who drank and screamed at him. He walked
along, saturated in depression, as if in the midst of his martyrdom he
had lost his faith. Catching sight of his long, hopeless, irritated face, she
stopped suddenly with a grief-stricken look, and pulled back on his arm.
"Wait on me," she said. "I'm going back to the house and take this thing
off and tomorrow I'm going to return it. I was out of my head. I can pay
the gas bill with that seven-fifty."

He caught her arm in a vicious grip. "You are not going to take it
back," he said. "I like it."

"Well," she said, "I don't think I ought . . . ."

"Shut up and enjoy it," he muttered, more depressed than ever.

"With the world in the mess it's in," she said, "it's a wonder we can
enjoy anything. I tell you, the bottom rail is on the top."

15 Julian sighed.

"Of course," she said, "if you know who you are, you can go anywhere." She said this every time he took her to the reducing class. "Most of them in it are not our kind of people," she said, "but I can be gracious to anybody. I know who I am."

"They don't give a damn for your graciousness," Julian said savagely. "Knowing who you are is good for one generation only. You haven't the foggiest idea where you stand now or who you are."

She stopped and allowed her eyes to flash at him. "I most certainly do know who I am," she said, "and if you don't know who you are, I'm ashamed of you."

"Oh hell," Julian said.

20 "Your great-grandfather was a former governor of this state," she said. "Your grandfather was a prosperous landowner. Your grandmother was a Godhigh."

"Will you look around you," he said tensely, "and see where you are now?" and he swept his arm jerkily out to indicate the neighborhood, which the growing darkness at least made less dingy.

"You remain what you are," she said. "Your great-grandfather had a plantation and two hundred slaves."

"There are no more slaves," he said irritably.

"They were better off when they were," she said. He groaned to see that she was off on that topic. She rolled onto it every few days like a train on an open track. He knew every stop, every junction, every swamp along the way, and knew the exact point at which her conclusion would roll majestically into the station: "It's ridiculous. It's simply not realistic. They should rise, yes, but on their own side of the fence."

25 "Let's skip it," Julian said.

"The ones I feel sorry for," she said, "are the ones that are half white. They're tragic."

"Will you skip it?"

"Suppose we were half white. We would certainly have mixed feelings."

"I have mixed feelings now," he groaned.

30 "Well let's talk about something pleasant," she said. "I remember going to Grandpa's when I was a little girl. Then the house had double stairways that went up to what was really the second floor—all the cooking was done on the first. I used to like to stay down in the kitchen on account of the way the walls smelled. I would sit with my nose pressed against the plaster and take deep breaths. Actually the place belonged to the Godhighs but your grandfather Chestny paid the mortgage and saved it for them. They were in reduced circumstances," she said, "but reduced or not, they never forgot who they were."

"Doubtless that decayed mansion reminded them," Julian muttered. He never spoke of it without contempt or thought of it without longing. He had seen it once when he was a child before it had been sold. The double stairways had rotted and been torn down. Negroes were living in it. But it remained in his mind as his mother had known it. It appeared in his dreams regularly. He would stand on the wide porch, listening to the rustle of oak leaves, then wander through the high-ceilinged hall into the parlor that opened onto it and gaze at the worn rugs and faded draperies. It occurred to him that it was he, not she, who could have appreciated it. He preferred its threadbare elegance to anything he could name and it was because of it that all the neighborhoods they had lived in had been a torment to him—whereas she had hardly known the difference. She called her insensitivity "being adjustable."

"And I remember the old darky who was my nurse, Caroline. There was no better person in the world. I've always had a great respect for my colored friends," she said. "I'd do anything in the world for them and they'd . . ."

"Will you for God's sake get off that subject?" Julian said. When he got on a bus by himself, he made it a point to sit down beside a Negro, in reparation as it were for his mother's sins.

"You're mighty touchy tonight," she said. "Do you feel all right?"

"Yes I feel all right," he said. "Now lay off."   35

She pursed her lips. "Well, you certainly are in a vile humor," she observed. "I just won't speak to you at all."

They had reached the bus stop. There was no bus in sight and Julian, his hands still jammed in his pockets and his head thrust forward, scowled down the empty street. The frustration of having to wait on the bus as well as ride on it began to creep up his neck like a hot hand. The presence of his mother was borne in upon him as she gave a pained sigh. He looked at her bleakly. She was holding herself very erect under the preposterous hat, wearing it like a banner of her imaginary dignity. There was in him an evil urge to break her spirit. He suddenly unloosened his tie and pulled it off and put it in his pocket.

She stiffened. "Why must you look like *that* when you take me to town?" she said. "Why must you deliberately embarrass me?"

"If you'll never learn where you are," he said, "you can at least learn where I am."

"You look like a—thug," she said.   40

"Then I must be one," he murmured.

"I'll just go home," she said. "I will not bother you. If you can't do a little thing like that for me . . ."

Rolling his eyes upward, he put his tie back on. "Restored to my class," he muttered. He thrust his face toward her and hissed, "True culture is in the mind, the *mind*," he said, and tapped his head, "the mind."

"It's in the heart," she said, "and in how you do things and how you do things is because of who you *are*."

45   "Nobody in the damn bus cares who you are."

"I care who I am," she said icily.

The lighted bus appeared on top of the next hill and as it approached, they moved out into the street to meet it. He put his hand under her elbow and hoisted her up on the creaking step. She entered with a little smile, as if she were going into a drawing room where everyone had been waiting for her. While he put in the tokens, she sat down on one of the broad front seats for three which faced the aisle. A thin woman with protruding teeth and long yellow hair was sitting on the end of it. His mother moved up beside her and left room for Julian beside herself. He sat down and looked at the floor across the aisle where a pair of thin feet in red and white canvas sandals were planted.

His mother immediately began a general conversation meant to attract anyone who felt like talking. "Can it get any hotter?" she said and removed from her purse a folding fan, black with a Japanese scene on it, which she began to flutter before her.

"I reckon it might could," the woman with the protruding teeth said, "but I know for a fact my apartment couldn't get no hotter."

50   "It must get the afternoon sun," his mother said. She sat forward and looked up and down the bus. It was half filled. Everybody was white. "I see we have the bus to ourselves," she said. Julian cringed.

"For a change," said the woman across the aisle, the owner of the red and white canvas sandals. "I come on one the other day and they were thick as fleas—up front and all through."

"The world is in a mess everywhere," his mother said. "I don't know how we've let it get in this fix."

"What gets my goat is all those boys from good families stealing automobile tires," the woman with the protruding teeth said. "I told my boy, I said you may not be rich but you been raised right and if I ever catch you in any such mess, they can send you on to the reformatory. Be exactly where you belong."

"Training tells," his mother said. "Is your boy in high school?"

55   "Ninth grade," the woman said.

"My son just finished college last year. He wants to write but he's selling typewriters until he gets started," his mother said.

The woman leaned forward and peered at Julian. He threw her such a malevolent look that she subsided against the seat. On the floor across the aisle there was an abandoned newspaper. He got up and got it and opened it out in front of him. His mother discreetly continued the conversation in a lower tone but the woman across the aisle said in a loud voice, "Well that's nice. Selling typewriters is close to writing. He can go right from one to the other."

"I tell him," his mother said, "that Rome wasn't built in a day."

Behind the newspaper Julian was withdrawing into the inner compartment of his mind where he spent most of his time. This was a kind of mental bubble in which he established himself when he could not bear to be a part of what was going on around him. From it he could see out and judge but in it he was safe from any kind of penetration from without. It was the only place where he felt free of the general idiocy of his fellows. His mother had never entered it but from it he could see her with absolute clarity.

The old lady was clever enough and he thought that if she had started from any of the right premises, more might have been expected of her. She lived according to the laws of her own fantasy world, outside of which he had never seen her set foot. The law of it was to sacrifice herself for him after she had first created the necessity to do so by making a mess of things. If he had permitted her sacrifices, it was only because her lack of foresight had made them necessary. All of her life had been a struggle to act like a Chestny without the Chestny goods, and to give him everything she thought a Chestny ought to have; but since, said she, it was fun to struggle, why complain? And when you had won, as she had won, what fun to look back on the hard times! He could not forgive her that she had enjoyed the struggle and that she thought *she* had won.

What she meant when she said she had won was that she had brought him up successfully and had sent him to college and that he had turned out so well—good looking (her teeth had gone unfilled so that his could be straightened), intelligent (he realized he was too intelligent to be a success), and with a future ahead of him (there was of course no future ahead of him). She excused his gloominess on the grounds that he was still growing up and his radical ideas on his lack of practical experience. She said he didn't yet know a thing about "life," that he hadn't even entered the real world—when already he was as disenchanted with it as a man of fifty.

The further irony of all this was that in spite of her, he had turned out so well. In spite of going to only a third-rate college, he had, on his own initiative, come out with a first-rate education; in spite of growing up dominated by a small mind, he had ended up with a large one; in spite of all her foolish views, he was free of prejudice and unafraid to face facts. Most miraculous of all, instead of being blinded by love for her as she was for him, he had cut himself emotionally free of her and could see her with complete objectivity. He was not dominated by his mother.

The bus stopped with a sudden jerk and shook him from his meditation. A woman from the back lurched forward with little steps and barely escaped falling in his newspaper as she righted herself. She got off and a

60

large Negro got on. Julian kept his paper lowered to watch. It gave him a certain satisfaction to see injustice in daily operation. It confirmed his view that with a few exceptions there was no one worth knowing within a radius of three hundred miles. The Negro was well dressed and carried a briefcase. He looked around and then sat down on the other end of the seat where the woman with the red and white canvas sandals was sitting. He immediately unfolded a newspaper and obscured himself behind it. Julian's mother's elbow at once prodded insistently into his ribs. "Now you see why I won't ride on these buses by myself," she whispered.

The woman with the red and white canvas sandals had risen at the same time the Negro sat down and had gone further back in the bus and taken the seat of the woman who had got off. His mother leaned forward and cast her an approving look.

65   Julian rose, crossed the aisle, and sat down in the place of the woman with the canvas sandals. From this position, he looked serenely across at his mother. Her face had turned an angry red. He stared at her, making his eyes the eyes of a stranger. He felt his tension suddenly lift as if he had openly declared war on her.

He would have liked to get in conversation with the Negro and to talk with him about art or politics or any subject that would be above the comprehension of those around them, but the man remained entrenched behind his paper. He was either ignoring the change of seating or had never noticed it. There was no way for Julian to convey his sympathy.

His mother kept her eyes fixed reproachfully on his face. The woman with the protruding teeth was looking at him avidly as if he were a type of monster new to her.

"Do you have a light?" he asked the Negro.

Without looking away from his paper, the man reached in his pocket and handed him a packet of matches.

70   "Thanks," Julian said. For a moment he held the matches foolishly. A NO SMOKING sign looked down upon him from over the door. This alone would not have deterred him; he had no cigarettes. He had quit smoking some months before because he could not afford it. "Sorry," he muttered and handed back the matches. The Negro lowered the paper and gave him an annoyed look. He took the matches and raised the paper again.

His mother continued to gaze at him but she did not take advantage of his momentary discomfort. Her eyes retained their battered look. Her face seemed to be unnaturally red, as if her blood pressure had risen. Julian allowed no glimmer of sympathy to show on his face. Having got the advantage, he wanted desperately to keep it and carry it through. He would have liked to teach her a lesson that would last her a while, but there seemed no way to continue the point. The Negro refused to come out from behind his paper.

Julian folded his arms and looked stolidly before him, facing her but as if he did not see her, as if he had ceased to recognize her existence. He visualized a scene in which, the bus having reached their stop, he would remain in his seat and when she said, "Aren't you going to get off?" he would look at her as at a stranger who had rashly addressed him. The corner they got off on was usually deserted, but it was well lighted and it would not hurt her to walk by herself the four blocks to the Y. He decided to wait until the time came and then decide whether or not he would let her get off by herself. He would have to be at the Y at ten to bring her back, but he could leave her wondering if he was going to show up. There was no reason for her to think she could always depend on him.

He retired again into the high-ceilinged room sparsely settled with large pieces of antique furniture. His soul expanded momentarily but then he became aware of his mother across from him and the vision shriveled. He studied her coldly. Her feet in little pumps dangled like a child's and did not quite reach the floor. She was training on him an exaggerated look of reproach. He felt completely detached from her. At that moment he could with pleasure have slapped her as he would have slapped a particularly obnoxious child in his charge.

He began to imagine various unlikely ways by which he could teach her a lesson. He might make friends with some distinguished Negro professor or lawyer and bring him home to spend the evening. He would be entirely justified but her blood pressure would rise to 300. He could not push her to the extent of making her have a stroke, and moreover, he had never been successful at making any Negro friends. He had tried to strike up an acquaintance on the bus with some of the better types, with ones that looked like professors or ministers or lawyers. One morning he had sat down next to a distinguished-looking dark brown man who had answered his questions with a sonorous solemnity but who had turned out to be an undertaker. Another day he had sat down beside a cigar-smoking Negro with a diamond ring on his finger, but after a few stilted pleasantries, the Negro had rung the buzzer and risen, slipping two lottery tickets into Julian's hand as he climbed over him to leave.

He imagined his mother lying desperately ill and his being able to 75 secure only a Negro doctor for her. He toyed with that idea for a few minutes and then dropped it for a momentary vision of himself participating as a sympathizer in a sit-in demonstration. This was possible but he did not linger with it. Instead, he approached the ultimate horror. He brought home a beautiful suspiciously Negroid woman. Prepare yourself, he said. There is nothing you can do about it. This is the woman I've chosen. She's intelligent, dignified, even good, and she's suffered and she hasn't thought it *fun*. Now persecute us, go ahead and persecute us. Drive her out of here, but remember, you're driving me too. His eyes were narrowed and through the indignation he had generated, he saw his mother across the aisle, purple-faced, shrunken to the dwarf-like proportions of her moral nature, sitting like a mummy beneath the ridiculous banner of her hat.

He was tilted out of his fantasy again as the bus stopped. The door opened with a sucking hiss and out of the dark a large, gaily dressed, sullen-looking colored woman got on with a little boy. The child, who might have been four, had on a short plaid suit and a Tyrolean hat with a blue feather in it. Julian hoped that he would sit down beside him and that the woman would push in beside his mother. He could think of no better arrangement.

As she waited for her tokens, the woman was surveying the seating possibilities—he hoped with the idea of sitting where she was least wanted. There was something familiar-looking about her but Julian could not place what it was. She was a giant of a woman. Her face was set not only to meet opposition but to seek it out. The downward tilt of her large lower lip was like a warning sign: DON'T TAMPER WITH ME. Her bulging figure was encased in a green crepe dress and her feet overflowed in red shoes. She had on a hideous hat. A purple velvet flap came down on one side of it and stood up on the other; the rest of it was green and looked like a cushion with the stuffing out. She carried a mammoth red pocketbook that bulged throughout as if it were stuffed with rocks.

To Julian's disappointment, the little boy climbed up on the empty seat beside his mother. His mother lumped all children, black and white, into the common category, "cute," and she thought little Negroes were on the whole cuter than little white children. She smiled at the little boy as he climbed on the seat.

Meanwhile the woman was bearing down upon the empty seat beside Julian. To his annoyance, she squeezed herself into it. He saw his mother's face change as the woman settled herself next to him and he realized with satisfaction that this was more objectionable to her than it was to him. Her face seemed almost gray and there was a look of dull recognition in her eyes, as if suddenly she had sickened at some awful confrontation. Julian saw that it was because she and the woman had, in a sense, swapped sons. Though his mother would not realize the symbolic significance of this, she would feel it. His amusement showed plainly on his face.

The woman next to him muttered something unintelligible to herself. He was conscious of a kind of bristling next to him, a muted growling like that of an angry cat. He could not see anything but the red pocketbook upright on the bulging green thighs. He visualized the woman as she had stood waiting for her tokens—the ponderous figure, rising from the red shoes upward over the solid hips, the mammoth bosom, the haughty face, to the green and purple hat.

His eyes widened.

The vision of the two hats, identical, broke upon him with the radiance of a brilliant sunrise. His face was suddenly lit with joy. He could not believe that Fate had thrust upon his mother such a lesson. He gave a loud chuckle so that she would look at him and see that he saw. She turned her eyes on him slowly. The blue in them seemed to have turned a bruised purple. For a moment he had an uncomfortable sense of her innocence, but it lasted only a second before principle rescued him. Justice entitled him to laugh. His grin hardened until it said to her as plainly as if he were saying aloud: Your punishment exactly fits your pettiness. This should teach you a permanent lesson.

Her eyes shifted to the woman. She seemed unable to bear looking at him and to find the woman preferable. He became conscious again of the bristling presence at his side. The woman was rumbling like a volcano about to become active. His mother's mouth began to twitch slightly at one corner. With a sinking heart, he saw incipient signs of recovery on her face and realized that this was going to strike her suddenly as funny and was going to be no lesson at all. She kept her eyes on the woman and an amused smile came over her face as if the woman were a monkey that had stolen her hat. The little Negro was looking up at her with large fascinated eyes. He had been trying to attract her attention for some time.

"Carver!" the woman said suddenly. "Come heah!"

When he saw that the spotlight was on him at last, Carver drew his 85 feet up and turned himself toward Julian's mother and giggled.

"Carver!" the woman said. "You heah me? Come heah!"

Carver slid down from the seat but remained squatting with his back against the base of it, his head turned slyly around toward Julian's mother, who was smiling at him. The woman reached a hand across the aisle and snatched him to her. He righted himself and hung backwards on her knees, grinning at Julian's mother. "Isn't he cute?" Julian's mother said to the woman with the protruding teeth.

"I reckon he is," the woman said without conviction.

The Negress yanked him upright but he eased out of her grip and shot across the aisle and scrambled, giggling wildly, onto the seat beside his love.

"I think he likes me," Julian's mother said, and smiled at the woman. 90 It was the smile she used when she was being particularly gracious to an inferior. Julian saw everything lost. The lesson had rolled off her like rain on a roof.

The woman stood up and yanked the little boy off the seat as if she were snatching him from contagion. Julian could feel the rage in her at having no weapon like his mother's smile. She gave the child a sharp slap across his leg. He howled once and then thrust his head into her stomach and kicked his feet against her shins. "Be-have," she said vehemently.

The bus stopped and the Negro who had been reading the newspaper got off. The woman moved over and set the little boy down with a thump between herself and Julian. She held him firmly by the knee. In a moment he put his hands in front of his face and peeped at Julian's mother through his fingers.

"I see yoooooooo!" she said and put her hand in front of her face and peeped at him.

The woman slapped his hand down. "Quit yo' foolishness," she said, "before I knock the living Jesus out of you!"

95   Julian was thankful that the next stop was theirs. He reached up and pulled the cord. The woman reached up and pulled it at the same time. Oh my God, he thought. He had the terrible intuition that when they got off the bus together, his mother would open her purse and give the little boy a nickel. The gesture would be as natural to her as breathing. The bus stopped and the woman got up and lunged to the front, dragging the child, who wished to stay on, after her. Julian and his mother got up and followed. As they neared the door, Julian tried to relieve her of her pocketbook.

"No," she murmured. "I want to give the little boy a nickel."

"No!" Julian hissed. "No!"

She smiled down at the child and opened her bag. The bus door opened and the woman picked him up by the arm and descended with him, hanging at her hip. Once in the street she set him down and shook him.

Julian's mother had to close her purse while she got down the bus step but as soon as her feet were on the ground, she opened it again and began to rummage inside. "I can't find but a penny," she whispered, "but it looks like a new one."

100   "Don't do it!" Julian said fiercely between his teeth. There was a streetlight on the corner and she hurried to get under it so that she could better see into her pocketbook. The woman was heading off rapidly down the street with the child still hanging backward on her hand.

"Oh little boy!" Julian's mother called and took a few quick steps and caught up with them just beyond the lamppost. "Here's a bright new penny for you," and she held out the coin, which shone bronze in the dim light.

The huge woman turned and for a moment stood, her shoulders lifted and her face frozen with frustrated rage, and stared at Julian's mother. Then all at once she seemed to explode like a piece of machinery that had been given one ounce of pressure too much. Julian saw the black fist swing out with the red pocketbook. He shut his eyes and cringed as he heard the woman shout, "He don't take nobody's pennies!" When he opened his eyes, the woman was disappearing down the street with the little boy staring wide-eyed over her shoulder. Julian's mother was sitting on the sidewalk.

"I told you not to do that," Julian said angrily. "I told you not to do that!"

He stood over her for a minute, gritting his teeth. Her legs were stretched out in front of her and her hat was on her lap. He squatted down and looked her in the face. It was totally expressionless. "You got exactly what you deserved," he said. "Now get up."

He picked up her pocketbook and put what had fallen out back in it. 105
He picked the hat up off her lap. The penny caught his eye on the sidewalk and he picked that up and let it drop before her eyes into the purse. Then he stood up and leaned over and held his hands out to pull her up. She remained immobile. He sighed. Rising above them on either side were black apartment buildings, marked with irregular rectangles of light. At the end of the block a man came out of a door and walked off in the opposite direction. "All right," he said, "suppose somebody happens by and wants to know why you're sitting on the sidewalk?"

She took the hand and, breathing hard, pulled heavily up on it and then stood for a moment, swaying slightly as if the spots of light in the darkness were circling around her. Her eyes, shadowed and confused, finally settled on his face. He did not try to conceal his irritation. "I hope this teaches you a lesson," he said. She leaned forward and her eyes raked his face. She seemed trying to determine his identity. Then, as if she found nothing familiar about him, she started off with a headlong movement in the wrong direction.

"Aren't you going on to the Y?" he asked.

"Home," she muttered.

"Well, are we walking?"

For answer she kept going. Julian followed along, his hands behind 110
him. He saw no reason to let the lesson she had had go without backing it up with an explanation of its meaning. She might as well be made to understand what had happened to her. "Don't think that was just an uppity Negro woman," he said. "That was the whole colored race which will no longer take your condescending pennies. That was your black double. She can wear the same hat as you, and to be sure," he added gratuitously (because he thought it was funny), "it looked better on her than it did on you. What all this means," he said, "is that the old world is gone. The old manners are obsolete and your graciousness is not worth a damn." He thought bitterly of the house that had been lost for him. "You aren't who you think you are," he said.

She continued to plow ahead, paying no attention to him. Her hair had come undone on one side. She dropped her pocketbook and took no notice. He stooped and picked it up and handed it to her but she did not take it.

"You needn't act as if the world had come to an end," he said, "because it hasn't. From now on you've got to live in a new world and face a few realities for a change. Buck up," he said, "it won't kill you."

She was breathing fast.

"Let's wait on the bus," he said.

115   "Home," she said thickly.

"I hate to see you behave like this," he said. "Just like a child. I should be able to expect more of you." He decided to stop where he was and make her stop and wait for a bus. "I'm not going any farther," he said, stopping. "We're going on the bus."

She continued to go on as if she had not heard him. He took a few steps and caught her arm and stopped her. He looked into her face and caught his breath. He was looking into a face he had never seen before. "Tell Grandpa to come get me," she said.

He stared, stricken.

"Tell Caroline to come get me," she said.

120   Stunned, he let her go and she lurched forward again, walking as if one leg were shorter than the other. A tide of darkness seemed to be sweeping her from him. "Mother!" he cried. "Darling, sweetheart, wait!" Crumpling, she fell to the pavement. He dashed forward and fell at her side, crying, "Mamma, Mamma!" He turned her over. Her face was fiercely distorted. One eye, large and staring, moved slightly to the left as if it had become unmoored. The other remained fixed on him, raked his face again, found nothing and closed.

"Wait here, wait here!" he cried and jumped up and began to run for help toward a cluster of lights he saw in the distance ahead of him. "Help, help!" he shouted, but his voice was thin, scarcely a thread of sound. The lights drifted farther away the faster he ran and his feet moved numbly as if they carried him nowhere. The tide of darkness seemed to sweep him back to her, postponing from moment to moment his entry into the world of guilt and sorrow.

QUESTIONS

1. Discuss the mother-son relationship in the story. What values does each generation represent? Which character is more dependent on the other, the mother or Julian? Which character is more admirable, and why?

2. Roughly what historical time period in the American South does the story examine? How is the issue of race presented differently here than if the story were set in the present?

3. Why is it significant that Julian's mother and Carver's mother are wearing identical hats? How does this coincidence help elucidate the theme?

4. How does O'Connor use humor effectively in the story? Isolate the passages you found particularly humorous and consider the ways in which these passages represent a serious intention on the author's part.

5. In the concluding paragraphs, Julian undergoes a remarkable change. What is the nature of this change, or "epiphany," and what does it say about him? In what ways will he be a different person in his future life?
6. Compare the ending of this story to that of "A Good Man Is Hard to Find." How are the endings similar?

JOYCE CAROL OATES

Where Are You Going, Where Have You Been?

Her name was Connie. She was fifteen and she had a quick nervous giggling habit of craning her neck to glance into mirrors, or checking other people's faces to make sure her own was all right. Her mother, who noticed everything and knew everything and who hadn't much reason any longer to look at her own face, always scolded Connie about it. "Stop gawking at yourself, who are you? You think you're so pretty?" she would say. Connie would raise her eyebrows at these familiar complaints and look right through her mother, into a shadowy vision of herself as she was right at that moment: she knew she was pretty and that was everything. Her mother had been pretty once too, if you could believe those old snapshots in the album, but now her looks were gone and that was why she was always after Connie.

"Why don't you keep your room clean like your sister? How've you got your hair fixed—what the hell stinks? Hair spray? You don't see your sister using that junk."

Her sister June was twenty-four and still lived at home. She was a secretary in the high school Connie attended, and if that wasn't bad enough—with her in the same building—she was so plain and chunky and steady that Connie had to hear her praised all the time by her mother and her mother's sisters. June did this, June did that, she saved money and helped clean the house and cooked and Connie couldn't do a thing, her mind was all filled with trashy daydreams. Their father was away at work most of the time and when he came home he wanted supper and he read the newspaper at supper and after supper he went to bed. He didn't bother talking much to them, but around his bent head Connie's mother kept picking at her until Connie wished her mother was dead and she herself was dead and it was all over. "She makes me want to throw up sometimes," she complained to her friends. She had a high, breathless, amused voice which made everything she said sound a little forced, whether it was sincere or not.

WHERE ARE YOU GOING, WHERE HAVE YOU BEEN?   First published in 1966. Joyce Carol Oates (b. 1938), one of contemporary America's most prolific writers, is the author of more than ninety volumes of fiction, literary criticism, poetry, and drama. She grew up in rural New York and since 1978 has taught creative writing at Princeton University. Concerning "Where Are You Going, Where Have You Been?" Oates has written that "every third or fourth story of mine is probably in this mode—'realistic allegory,' it might be called. It is Hawthornean, romantic, shading into parable."

There was one good thing: June went places with girl friends of hers, girls who were just as plain and steady as she, and so when Connie wanted to do that her mother had no objections. The father of Connie's best girl friend drove the girls the three miles to town and left them off at a shopping plaza, so that they could walk through the stores or go to a movie, and when he came to pick them up again at eleven he never bothered to ask what they had done.

5   They must have been familiar sights, walking around that shopping plaza in their shorts and flat ballerina slippers that always scuffed the sidewalk, with charm bracelets jingling on their thin wrists; they would lean together to whisper and laugh secretly if someone passed by who amused or interested them. Connie had long dark blond hair that drew anyone's eye to it, and she wore part of it pulled up on her head and puffed out and the rest of it she let fall down her back. She wore a pullover jersey blouse that looked one way when she was at home and another way when she was away from home. Everything about her had two sides to it, one for home and one for anywhere that was not home: her walk that could be childlike and bobbing, or languid enough to make anyone think she was hearing music in her head, her mouth which was pale and smirking most of the time, but bright and pink on these evenings out, her laugh which was cynical and drawling at home—"Ha, ha, very funny"—but high-pitched and nervous anywhere else, like the jingling of the charms on her bracelet.

Sometimes they did go shopping or to a movie, but sometimes they went across the highway, ducking fast across the busy road, to a drive-in restaurant where older kids hung out. The restaurant was shaped like a big bottle, though squatter than a real bottle, and on its cap was a revolving figure of a grinning boy who held a hamburger aloft. One night in midsummer they ran across, breathless with daring, and right away someone leaned out a car window and invited them over, but it was just a boy from high school they didn't like. It made them feel good to be able to ignore him. They went up through the maze of parked and cruising cars to the bright-lit, fly-infested restaurant, their faces pleased and expectant as if they were entering a sacred building that loomed out of the night to give them what haven and what blessing they yearned for. They sat at the counter and crossed their legs at the ankles, their thin shoulders rigid with excitement, and listened to the music that made everything so good: the music was always in the background like music at a church service, it was something to depend upon.

A boy named Eddie came in to talk with them. He sat backwards on his stool, turning himself jerkily around in semi-circles and then stopping and turning again, and after a while he asked Connie if she would like something to eat. She said she did and so she tapped her friend's arm on her way out—her friend pulled her face up into a brave droll look—and Connie said she would meet her at eleven, across the way. "I just hate to leave her like that," Connie said earnestly, but the boy said that she wouldn't be alone for long. So they went out to his car and on the way Connie couldn't help but let her eyes wander over the windshields and faces all around her, her face gleaming with a joy that had nothing to do with Eddie or even this place; it might have been the music. She drew her shoulders up and sucked in her breath with the pure pleasure of being alive, and just at that moment she happened to glance at a face just a few feet from hers. It was a boy with shaggy black hair, in a convertible jalopy painted gold. He stared at her and then his lips widened into a grin. Connie slit her eyes at him and turned away, but she couldn't help glancing back and there he was still watching her. He wagged a finger and laughed and said, "Gonna get you, baby," and Connie turned away again without Eddie noticing anything.

She spent three hours with him, at the restaurant where they ate hamburgers and drank Cokes in wax cups that were always sweating, and then down an alley a mile or so away, and when he left her off at five to eleven only the movie house was still open at the plaza. Her girl friend was there, talking with a boy. When Connie came up the two girls smiled at each other and Connie said, "How was the movie?" and the girl said, "*You* should know." They rode off with the girl's father, sleepy and pleased, and Connie couldn't help but look at the darkened shopping plaza with its big empty parking lot and its signs that were faded and ghostly now, and over at the drive-in restaurant where cars were still circling tirelessly. She couldn't hear the music at this distance.

Next morning June asked her how the movie was and Connie said, "So-so."

She and that girl and occasionally another girl went out several times a   10
week that way, and the rest of the time Connie spent around the house—it was summer vacation—getting in her mother's way and thinking, dreaming, about the boys she met. But all the boys fell back and dissolved into a single face that was not even a face, but an idea, a feeling, mixed up with the urgent insistent pounding of the music and the humid night air of July. Connie's mother kept dragging her back to the daylight by finding things for her to do or saying, suddenly, "What's this about the Pettinger girl?"

And Connie would say nervously, "Oh, her. That dope." She always drew thick clear lines between herself and such girls, and her mother was simple and kindly enough to believe her. Her mother was so simple, Connie thought, that it was maybe cruel to fool her so much. Her mother went scuffling around the house in old bedroom slippers and complained over the telephone to one sister about the other, then the other called up and the two of them complained about the third one. If June's name was mentioned her mother's tone was approving, and if Connie's name was mentioned it was disapproving. This did not really mean she disliked Connie and actually Connie thought that her mother preferred her to June because she was prettier, but the two of them kept up a pretense of exasperation, a sense that they were tugging and struggling over something of little value to either of them. Sometimes, over coffee, they were almost friends, but something would come up—some vexation that was like a fly buzzing suddenly around their heads—and their faces went hard with contempt.

One Sunday Connie got up at eleven—none of them bothered with church—and washed her hair so that it could dry all day long, in the sun. Her parents and sister were going to a barbecue at an aunt's house and Connie said no, she wasn't interested, rolling her eyes to let her mother know just what she thought of it. "Stay home alone then," her mother said sharply. Connie sat out back in a lawn chair and watched them drive away, her father quiet and bald, hunched around so that he could back the car out, her mother with a look that was still angry and not at all softened through the windshield, and in the back seat poor old June all dressed up as if she didn't know what a barbecue was, with all the running yelling kids and the flies. Connie sat with her eyes closed in the sun, dreaming and dazed with the warmth about her as if this were a kind of love, the caresses of love, and her mind slipped over onto thoughts of the boy she had been with the night before and how nice he had been, how sweet it always was, not the way someone like June would suppose but sweet, gentle, the way it was in movies and promised in songs; and when she opened her eyes she hardly knew where she was, the back yard ran off into weeds and a fence-line of trees and behind it the sky was perfectly blue and still. The asbestos "ranch house" that was now three years old startled her—it looked small. She shook her head as if to get awake.

It was too hot. She went inside the house and turned on the radio to drown out the quiet. She sat on the edge of her bed, barefoot, and listened for an hour and a half to a program called XYZ Sunday Jamboree, record after record of hard, fast, shrieking songs she sang along with, interspersed by exclamations from "Bobby King": "An' look here you girls at Napoleon's—Son and Charley want you to pay real close attention to this song coming up!"

And Connie paid close attention herself, bathed in a glow of slow-pulsed joy that seemed to rise mysteriously out of the music itself and lay languidly about the airless little room, breathed in and breathed out with each gentle rise and fall of her chest.

15   After a while she heard a car coming up the drive. She sat up at once, startled, because it couldn't be her father so soon. The gravel kept crunching all the way in from the road—the driveway was long—and Connie

ran to the window. It was a car she didn't know. It was an open jalopy, painted a bright gold that caught the sunlight opaquely. Her heart began to pound and her fingers snatched at her hair, checking it, and she whispered "Christ. Christ," wondering how bad she looked. The car came to a stop at the side door and the horn sounded four short taps as if this were a signal Connie knew.

She went into the kitchen and approached the door slowly, then hung out the screen door, her bare toes curling down off the step. There were two boys in the car and now she recognized the driver: he had shaggy, shabby black hair that looked crazy as a wig and he was grinning at her.

"I ain't late, am I?" he said.

"Who the hell do you think you are?" Connie said.

"Toldja I'd be out, didn't I?"

"I don't even know who you are."   20

She spoke sullenly, careful to show no interest or pleasure, and he spoke in a fast bright monotone. Connie looked past him to the other boy, taking her time. He had fair brown hair, with a lock that fell onto his forehead. His sideburns gave him a fierce, embarrassed look, but so far he hadn't even bothered to glance at her. Both boys wore sunglasses. The driver's glasses were metallic and mirrored everything in miniature.

"You wanta come for a ride?" he said.

Connie smirked and let her hair fall loose over one shoulder.

"Don'tcha like my car? New paint job," he said. "Hey."

"What?"   25

"You're cute."

She pretended to fidget, chasing flies away from the door.

"Don'tcha believe me, or what?" he said.

"Look, I don't even know who you are," Connie said in disgust.

"Hey, Ellie's got a radio, see. Mine's broke down." He lifted his friend's   30
arm and showed her the little transistor the boy was holding, and now Connie began to hear the music. It was the same program that was playing inside the house.

"Bobby King?" she said.

"I listen to him all the time. I think he's great."

"He's kind of great," Connie said reluctantly.

"Listen, that guy's *great*. He knows where the action is."

Connie blushed a little, because the glasses made it impossible for   35
her to see just what this boy was looking at. She couldn't decide if she liked him or if he was just a jerk, and so she dawdled in the doorway and wouldn't come down or go back inside. She said, "What's all that stuff painted on your car?"

"Can'tcha read it?" He opened the door very carefully, as if he was afraid it might fall off. He slid out just as carefully, planting his feet firmly on the ground, the tiny metallic world in his glasses slowing down like gelatine hardening and in the midst of it Connie's bright green blouse. "This here is my name, to begin with," he said. ARNOLD FRIEND was written in tarlike black letters on the side, with a drawing of a round grinning face that reminded Connie of a pumpkin, except it wore sunglasses. "I wanta introduce myself, I'm Arnold Friend and that's my real name and I'm gonna be your friend, honey, and inside the car's Ellie Oscar, he's kinda shy." Ellie brought his transistor radio up to his shoulder and balanced it there. "Now these numbers are a secret code, honey," Arnold Friend explained. He read off the numbers 33, 19, 17 and raised his eyebrows at her to see what she thought of that, but she didn't think much of it. The left rear fender had been smashed and around it was written, on the gleaming gold background: DONE BY CRAZY WOMAN DRIVER. Connie had to laugh at that. Arnold Friend was pleased at her laughter and looked up at her. "Around the other side's a lot more—you wanta come and see them?"

"No."

"Why not?"

"Why should I?"

40   "Don'tcha wanta see what's on the car? Don'tcha wanta go a ride?"

"I don't know."

"Why not?"

"I got things to do."

"Like what?"

45   "Things."

He laughed as if she had said something funny. He slapped his thighs. He was standing in a strange way, leaning back against the car as if he were balancing himself. He wasn't tall, only an inch or so taller than she would be if she came down to him. Connie liked the way he was dressed, which was the way all of them dressed: tight faded jeans stuffed into black, scuffed boots, a belt that was a little soiled and showed how lean he was, and a white pull-over shirt that was a little soiled and showed the hard small muscles of his arms and shoulders. He looked as if he probably did hard work, lifting and carrying things. Even his neck looked muscular. And his face was a familiar face, somehow: the jaw and chin and cheeks slightly darkened, because he hadn't shaved for a day or two, and the nose long and hawk-like, sniffing as if she were a treat he was going to gobble up and it was all a joke.

"Connie, you ain't telling the truth. This is your day set aside for a ride with me and you know it," he said, still laughing. The way he straightened and recovered from his fit of laughing showed that it had been all fake.

"How do you know what my name is?" she said suspiciously.

"It's Connie."

"Maybe and maybe not." 50

"I know my Connie," he said, wagging his finger. Now she remembered him even better, back at the restaurant, and her cheeks warmed at the thought of how she sucked in her breath just at the moment she passed him—how she must have looked to him. And he had remembered her. "Ellie and I come out here especially for you," he said. "Ellie can sit in back. How about it?"

"Where?"

"Where what?"

"Where're we going?"

He looked at her. He took off the sunglasses and she saw how pale the 55 skin around his eyes was, like holes that were not in shadow but instead in light. His eyes were chips of broken glass that catch the light in an amiable way. He smiled. It was as if the idea of going for a ride somewhere, to some place, was a new idea to him.

"Just for a ride, Connie sweetheart."

"I never said my name was Connie," she said.

"But I know what it is. I know your name and all about you, lots of things," Arnold Friend said. He had not moved yet but stood still leaning back against the side of the jalopy. "I took a special interest in you, such a pretty girl, and found out all about you like I know your parents and sister are gone somewheres and I know where and how long they're going to be gone, and I know who you were with last night, and your best girl friend's name is Betty. Right?"

He spoke in a simple lilting voice, exactly as if he were reciting the words to a song. His smile assured her that everything was fine. In the car Ellie turned up the volume on his radio and did not bother to look around at them.

"Ellie can sit in the back seat," Arnold Friend said. He indicated his 60 friend with a casual jerk of his chin, as if Ellie did not count and she should not bother with him.

"How'd you find out all that stuff?" Connie said.

"Listen: Betty Schultz and Tony Fitch and Jimmy Pettinger and Nancy Pettinger," he said, in a chant. "Raymond Stanley and Bob Hutter—"

"Do you know all those kids?"

"I know everybody."

"Look, you're kidding. You're not from around here." 65

"Sure."

"But—how come we never saw you before?"

"Sure you saw me before," he said. He looked down at his boots, as if he were a little offended. "You just don't remember."

"I guess I'd remember you," Connie said.

70 "Yeah?" He looked up at this, beaming. He was pleased. He began to mark time with the music from Ellie's radio, tapping his fists lightly together. Connie looked away from his smile to the car, which was painted so bright it almost hurt her eyes to look at it. She looked at that name, ARNOLD FRIEND. And up at the front fender was an expression that was familiar—MAN THE FLYING SAUCERS. It was an expression kids had used the year before, but didn't use this year. She looked at it for a while as if the words meant something to her that she did not yet know.

"What're you thinking about? Huh?" Arnold Friend demanded. "Not worried about your hair blowing around in the car, are you?"

"No."

"Think I maybe can't drive good?"

"How do I know?"

75 "You're a hard girl to handle. How come?" he said. "Don't you know I'm your friend? Didn't you see me put my sign in the air when you walked by?"

"What sign?"

"My sign." And he drew an X in the air, leaning out toward her. They were maybe ten feet apart. After his hand fell back to his side the X was still in the air, almost visible. Connie let the screen door close and stood perfectly still inside it, listening to the music from her radio and the boy's blend together. She stared at Arnold Friend. He stood there so stiffly relaxed, pretending to be relaxed, with one hand idly on the door handle as if he were keeping himself up that way and had no intention of ever moving again. She recognized most things about him, the tight jeans that showed his thighs and buttocks and the greasy leather boots and the tight shirt, and even that slippery friendly smile of his, that sleepy dreamy smile that all the boys used to get across ideas they didn't want to put into words. She recognized all this and also the singsong way he talked, slightly mocking, kidding, but serious and a little melancholy, and she recognized the way he tapped one fist against the other in homage to the perpetual music behind him. But all these things did not come together.

She said suddenly, "Hey, how old are you?"

His smile faded. She could see then that he wasn't a kid, he was much older—thirty, maybe more. At this knowledge her heart began to pound faster.

80 "That's a crazy thing to ask. Can'tcha see I'm your own age?"

"Like hell you are."

"Or maybe a coupla years older, I'm eighteen."

"Eighteen?" she said doubtfully.

He grinned to reassure her and lines appeared at the corners of his mouth. His teeth were big and white. He grinned so broadly his eyes became slits and she saw how thick the lashes were, thick and black as if painted with a black tar-like material. Then he seemed to become embarrassed, abruptly, and looked over his shoulder at Ellie. "*Him,* he's crazy," he said. "Ain't he a riot, he's a nut, a real character." Ellie was still listening to the music. His sunglasses told nothing about what he was thinking. He wore a bright orange shirt unbuttoned halfway to show his chest, which was a pale, bluish chest and not muscular like Arnold Friend's. His shirt collar was turned up all around and the very tips of the collar pointed out past his chin as if they were protecting him. He was pressing the transistor radio up against his ear and sat there in a kind of daze, right in the sun.

"He's kinda strange," Connie said. 85

"Hey, she says you're kinda strange! Kinda strange!" Arnold Friend cried. He pounded on the car to get Ellie's attention. Ellie turned for the first time and Connie saw with shock that he wasn't a kid either—he had a fair, hairless face, cheeks reddened slightly as if the veins grew too close to the surface of his skin, the face of a forty-year-old baby. Connie felt a wave of dizziness rise in her at this sight and she stared at him as if waiting for something to change the shock of the moment, make it all right again. Ellie's lips kept shaping words, mumbling along with the words blasting in his ear.

"Maybe you two better go away," Connie said faintly.

"What? How come?" Arnold Friend cried. "We come out here to take you for a ride. It's Sunday." He had the voice of the man on the radio now. It was the same voice, Connie thought. "Don'tcha know it's Sunday all day and honey, no matter who you were with last night today you're with Arnold Friend and don't you forget it!—Maybe you better step out here," he said, and this last was in a different voice. It was a little flatter, as if the heat was finally getting to him.

"No. I got things to do."

"Hey." 90

"You two better leave."

"We ain't leaving until you come with us."

"Like hell I am—"

"Connie, don't fool around with me. I mean, I mean, don't fool *around,*" he said, shaking his head. He laughed incredulously. He placed his sunglasses on top of his head, carefully, as if he were indeed wearing a wig, and brought the stems down behind his ears. Connie stared at him, another wave of dizziness and fear rising in her so that for a moment he wasn't even in focus but was just a blur, standing there against his gold car, and she had the idea that he had driven up the driveway all right but had come from nowhere before that and belonged nowhere and that everything about him and even about the music that was so familiar to her was only half real.

95   "If my father comes and sees you—"

"He ain't coming. He's at a barbecue."

"How do you know that?"

"Aunt Tillie's. Right now they're—uh—they're drinking. Sitting around," he said vaguely, squinting as if he were staring all the way to town and over to Aunt Tillie's backyard. Then the vision seemed to get clear and he nodded energetically. "Yeah. Sitting around. There's your sister in a blue dress, huh? And high heels, the poor sad bitch—nothing like you sweetheart! And your mother's helping some fat woman with the corn, they're cleaning the corn—husking the corn—"

"What fat woman?" Connie cried.

100   "How do I know what fat woman. I don't know every goddam fat woman in the world!" Arnold Friend laughed.

"Oh, that's Mrs. Hornby. . . . Who invited her?" Connie said. She felt a little lightheaded. Her breath was coming quickly.

"She's too fat. I don't like them fat. I like them the way you are, honey," he said, smiling sleepily at her. They stared at each other for a while, through the screen door. He said softly, "Now what you're going to do is this: you're going to come out that door. You're going to sit up front with me and Ellie's going to sit in the back, the hell with Ellie, right? This isn't Ellie's date. You're my date. I'm your lover, honey."

"What? You're crazy—"

"Yes, I'm your lover. You don't know what that is but you will," he said. "I know that too. I know all about you. But look: it's real nice and you couldn't ask for nobody better than me, or more polite. I always keep my word. I'll tell you how it is, I'm always nice at first, the first time. I'll hold you so tight you won't think you have to try to get away or pretend anything because you'll know you can't. And I'll come inside you where it's all secret and you'll give in to me and you'll love me—"

105   "Shut up! You're crazy!" Connie said. She backed away from the door. She put her hands against her ears as if she'd heard something terrible, something not meant for her. "People don't talk like that, you're crazy," she muttered. Her heart was almost too big now for her chest and its pumping made sweat break out all over her. She looked out to see Arnold Friend pause and then take a step toward the porch lurching. He almost fell. But, like a clever drunken man, he managed to catch his balance. He wobbled in his high boots and grabbed hold of one of the porch posts.

"Honey?" he said. "You still listening?"

"Get the hell out of here!"

"Be nice, honey. Listen."

"I'm going to call the police——"

He wobbled again and out of the side of his mouth came a fast 110
spat curse, an aside not meant for her to hear. But even this "Christ!"
sounded forced. Then he began to smile again. She watched this smile
come, awkward as if he were smiling from inside a mask. His whole face
was a mask, she thought wildly, tanned down onto his throat but then
running out as if he had plastered makeup on his face but had forgotten
about his throat.

"Honey——? Listen, here's how it is. I always tell the truth and I
promise you this: I ain't coming in that house after you."

"You better not! I'm going to call the police if you—if you don't——"

"Honey," he said, talking right through her voice, "honey, I'm not
coming in there but you are coming out here. You know why?"

She was panting. The kitchen looked like a place she had never seen
before, some room she had run inside but which wasn't good enough,
wasn't going to help her. The kitchen window had never had a curtain,
after three years, and there were dishes in the sink for her to do—
probably—and if you ran your hand across the table you'd probably feel
something sticky there.

"You listening, honey? Hey?" 115

"——going to call the police——"

"Soon as you touch the phone I don't need to keep my promise and can
come inside. You won't want that."

She rushed forward and tried to lock the door. Her fingers were shaking. "But why lock it," Arnold Friend said gently, talking right into her
face. "It's just a screen door. It's just nothing." One of his boots was at a
strange angle, as if his foot wasn't in it. It pointed out to the left, bent at
the ankle. "I mean, anybody can break through a screen door and glass and
wood and iron or anything else if he needs to, anybody at all and specially
Arnold Friend. If the place got lit up with a fire honey you'd come running
out into my arms, right into my arms and safe at home—like you knew I
was your lover and'd stopped fooling around. I don't mind a nice shy girl
but I don't like no fooling around." Part of those words were spoken with
a slight rhythmic lilt, and Connie somehow recognized them—the echo of
a song from last year, about a girl rushing into her boyfriend's arms and
coming home again——

Connie stood barefoot on the linoleum floor, staring at him. "What do
you want?" she whispered.

"I want you," he said. 120

"What?"

"Seen you that night and thought, that's the one, yes sir. I never
needed to look any more."

"But my father's coming back. He's coming to get me. I had to wash my hair first—" She spoke in a dry, rapid voice, hardly raising it for him to hear.

"No, your daddy is not coming and yes, you had to wash your hair and you washed it for me. It's nice and shining and all for me, I thank you, sweetheart," he said, with a mock bow, but again he almost lost his balance. He had to bend and adjust his boots. Evidently his feet did not go all the way down; the boots must have been stuffed with something so that he would seem taller. Connie stared out at him and behind him Ellie in the car, who seemed to be looking off toward Connie's right, into nothing. This Ellie said, pulling the words out of the air one after another as if he were just discovering them, "You want me to pull out the phone?"

125   "Shut your mouth and keep it shut," Arnold Friend said, his face red from bending over or maybe from embarrassment because Connie had seen his boots. "This ain't none of your business."

"What—what are you doing? What do you want?" Connie said. "If I call the police they'll get you, they'll arrest you—"

"Promise was not to come in unless you touch that phone, and I'll keep that promise," he said. He resumed his erect position and tried to force his shoulders back. He sounded like a hero in a movie, declaring something important. He spoke too loudly and it was as if he were speaking to someone behind Connie. "I ain't made plans for coming in that house where I don't belong but just for you to come out to me, the way you should. Don't you know who I am?"

"You're crazy," she whispered. She backed away from the door but did not want to go into another part of the house, as if this would give him permission to come through the door. "What do you. . . . You're crazy, you . . ."

"Huh? What're you saying, honey?"

130   Her eyes darted everywhere in the kitchen. She could not remember what it was, this room.

"This is how it is, honey: you come out and we'll drive away, have a nice ride. But if you don't come out we're gonna wait till your people come home and then they're all going to get it."

"You want that telephone pulled out?" Ellie said. He held the radio away from his ear and grimaced, as if without the radio the air was too much for him.

"I toldja shut up, Ellie," Arnold Friend said, "you're deaf, get a hearing aid, right? Fix yourself up. This little girl's no trouble and's gonna be nice to me, so Ellie keep to yourself, this ain't your date—right? Don't hem in on me, don't hog, don't crush, don't bird dog, don't trail me," he said in a rapid meaningless voice, as if he were running through all the expressions he'd learned but was no longer sure which one of them was in style, then rushing on to new ones, making them up with his eyes closed, "Don't crawl under my fence, don't squeeze in my chipmunk hole, don't sniff my glue, suck my Popsicle, keep your own greasy fingers on yourself!" He shaded his eyes and peered in at Connie, who was backed against the kitchen table. "Don't mind him honey he's just a creep. He's a dope. Right? I'm the boy for you and like I said you come out here nice like a lady and give me your hand, and nobody else gets hurt, I mean, your nice old bald-headed daddy and your mummy and your sister in her high heels. Because listen: why bring them in this?"

"Leave me alone," Connie whispered.

"Hey, you know that old woman down the road, the one with the   135 chickens and stuff—you know her?"

"She's dead!"

"Dead? What? You know her?" Arnold Friend said.

"She's dead—"

"Don't you like her?"

"She's dead—she's—she isn't here any more—"   140

"But don't you like her, I mean, you got something against her? Some grudge or something?" Then his voice dipped as if he were conscious of a rudeness. He touched the sunglasses perched on top of his head as if to make sure they were still there. "Now you be a good girl."

"What are you going to do?"

"Just two things, or maybe three," Arnold Friend said. "But I promise it won't last long and you'll like me that way you get to like people you're close to. You will. It's all over for you here, so come on out. You don't want your people in any trouble, do you?"

She turned and bumped against a chair or something, hurting her leg, but she ran into the back room and picked up the telephone. Something roared in her ear, a tiny roaring, and she was so sick with fear that she could do nothing but listen to it—the telephone was clammy and very heavy and her fingers groped down to the dial but were too weak to touch it. She began to scream into the phone, into the roaring. She cried out, she cried for her mother, she felt her breath start jerking back and forth in her lungs as if it were something Arnold Friend were stabbing her with again and again with no tenderness. A noisy sorrowful wailing rose all about her and she was locked inside it the way she was locked inside the house.

After a while she could hear again. She was sitting on the floor with   145 her wet back against the wall.

Arnold Friend was saying from the door, "That's a good girl. Put the phone back."

She kicked the phone away from her.

"No, honey. Pick it up. Put it back right."

She picked it up and put it back. The dial tone stopped.

150 "That's a good girl. Now you come outside."

She was hollow with what had been fear, but what was now just an emptiness. All that screaming had blasted it out of her. She sat, one leg cramped under her, and deep inside her brain was something like a pinpoint of light that kept going and would not let her relax. She thought, I'm not going to see my mother again. She thought, I'm not going to sleep in my bed again. Her bright green blouse was all wet.

Arnold Friend said, in a gentle-loud voice that was like a stage voice, "The place where you came from ain't there any more, and where you had in mind to go is cancelled out. This place you are now—inside your daddy's house—is nothing but a cardboard box I can knock down any time. You know that and always did know it. You hear me?"

She thought, I have got to think. I have to know what to do.

"We'll go out to a nice field, out in the country here where it smells so nice and it's sunny," Arnold Friend said. "I'll have my arms around you so you won't need to try to get away and I'll show you what love is like, what it does. The hell with this house! It looks solid all right," he said. He ran a fingernail down the screen and the noise did not make Connie shiver, as it would have the day before. "Now put your hand on your heart, honey. Feel that? That feels solid too but we know better, be nice to me, be sweet like you can because what else is there for a girl like you but to be sweet and pretty and give in?—and get away before her people come back?"

155 She felt her pounding heart. Her hand seemed to enclose it. She thought for the first time in her life that it was nothing that was hers, that belonged to her, but just a pounding, living thing inside this body that wasn't really hers either.

"You don't want them to get hurt," Arnold Friend went on. "Now get up, honey. Get up all by yourself."

She stood.

"Now turn this way. That's right. Come over here to me—Ellie, put that away, didn't I tell you? You dope. You miserable creepy dope," Arnold Friend said. His words were not angry but only part of an incantation. The incantation was kindly. "Now come out through the kitchen to me honey and let's see a smile, try it, you're a brave sweet little girl and now they're eating corn and hotdogs cooked to bursting over an outdoor fire, and they don't know one thing about you and never did and honey you're better than them because not a one of them would have done this for you."

Connie felt the linoleum under her feet; it was cool. She brushed her hair back out of her eyes. Arnold Friend let go of the post tentatively and opened his arms for her, his elbows pointing in toward each other and his wrists limp, to show that this was an embarrassed embrace and a little mocking, he didn't want to make her self-conscious.

She put out her hand against the screen. She watched herself push the 160 door slowly open as if she were safe back somewhere in the other doorway, watching this body and this head of long hair moving out into the sunlight where Arnold Friend waited.

"My sweet little blue-eyed girl," he said, in a half-sung sigh that had nothing to do with her brown eyes but was taken up just the same by the vast sunlit reaches of the land behind him and on all sides of him, so much land that Connie had never seen before and did not recognize except to know that she was going to it.

QUESTIONS

1. Oates has called this story a "realistic allegory." What are the allegorical elements in the story?
2. Describe the characterization of Connie. Is she a typical teenage girl of her time and place? What techniques does Oates employ to make her an individual, three-dimensional character?
3. Why is Connie's sister June included in the story? How does her characterization serve to highlight Connie's own?
4. Do the descriptions of Arnold Friend—his face, his clothing, his dialogue—have symbolic meaning? Is his name symbolic?
5. Discuss the symbolic importance of music in the story. Why is music so important to Connie and to the story as a whole?
6. What is the significance of the title? Does it point to an allegorical interpretation?
7. Describe the ways in which the story generates suspense. At which points is an increase of suspense particularly noticeable?
8. Why does Connie agree to go with Arnold Friend? Is she motivated by altruism and a love for her family, or by simple fear and hysteria? What is her ultimate fate?

JOYCE CAROL OATES

Life After High School

"Sunny? Sun-ny?"

On that last night of March 1959, in soiled sheepskin parka, unbuckled overshoes, but bare-headed in the lightly falling snow, Zachary Graff, eighteen years old, six feet one and a half inches tall, weight 203 pounds, IQ 160, stood beneath Sunny Burhman's second-story bedroom window, calling her name softly, urgently, as if his very life depended upon it. It was nearly midnight: Sunny had been in bed for a half hour, and woke from a

LIFE AFTER HIGH SCHOOL First published in 1995. See the footnote on page 489 for more information on Oates and her career.

thin dissolving sleep to hear her name rising mysteriously out of the dark, low, gravelly, repetitive as the surf. "*Sun*-ny—?" She had not spoken with Zachary Graff since the previous week, when she'd told him, quietly, tears shining in her eyes, that she did not love him; she could not accept his engagement ring, still less marry him. This was the first time in the twelve weeks of Zachary's pursuit of her that he'd dared to come to the rear of the Burhmans' house, by day or night; the first time, as Sunny would say afterward, he'd ever appealed to her in such a way.

They would ask, In what way?

Sunny would hesitate, and say, So—emotionally. In a way that scared me.

5   So you sent him away?

She did: She'd sent him away.

* * *

It was much talked-of, at South Lebanon High School, how, in this spring of their senior year, Zachary Graff, who had never to anyone's recollection asked a girl out before, let alone pursued her so publicly and with such clumsy devotion, seemed to have fallen in love with Sunny Burhman.

Of all people—Sunny Burhman.

Odd too that Zachary should seem to have discovered Sunny, when the two had been classmates in the South Lebanon, New York, public schools since first grade, back in 1947.

10   Zachary, whose father was Homer Graff, the town's preeminent physician, had, since ninth grade, cultivated a clipped, mock-gallant manner when speaking with female classmates; his Clifton Webb style. He was unfailingly courteous, but unfailingly cool; measured; formal. He seemed impervious to the giddy rise and ebb of adolescent emotion, moving, clumsy but determined, like a grizzly bear on its hind legs, through the school corridors, rarely glancing to left or right: *his* gaze, its myopia corrected by lenses encased in chunky black plastic frames, was firmly fixed on the horizon. Dr. Graff's son was not unpopular so much as feared, thus disliked.

If Zachary's excellent academic record continued uninterrupted through final papers, final exams, and there was no reason to suspect it would not, Zachary would be valedictorian of the Class of 1959. Barbara ("Sunny") Burhman, later to distinguish herself at Cornell, would graduate only ninth, in a class of eighty-two.

Zachary's attentiveness to Sunny had begun, with no warning, immediately after Christmas recess, when classes resumed in January. Suddenly, a half-dozen times a day, in Sunny's vicinity, looming large, eyeglasses glittering, there Zachary *was*. His Clifton Webb pose had dissolved, he was shy, stammering, yet forceful, even bold, waiting for the advantageous moment (for Sunny was always surrounded by friends) to push forward and say, "Hi, Sunny!" The greeting, utterly commonplace in content, sounded, in Zachary's mouth, like a Latin phrase tortuously translated.

Sunny, so-named for her really quite astonishing smile, that dazzling white Sunny-smile that transformed a girl of conventional freckled snub-nosed prettiness to true beauty, might have been surprised, initially, but gave no sign, saying, "Hi, Zach!"

In those years, the corridors of South Lebanon High School were lyric crossfires of *Hi!* and *H'lo!* and *Good to see ya!* uttered hundreds of times daily by the golden girls, the popular, confident, good-looking girls, club officers, prom queens, cheerleaders like Sunny Burhman and her friends, tossed out indiscriminately, for that was the style.

Most of the students were in fact practicing Christians, of Lutheran, 15 Presbyterian, Methodist stock.

Like Sunny Burhman, who was, or seemed, even at the time of this story, too good to be true.

That's to say—*good*.

So, though Sunny soon wondered why on earth Zachary Graff was hanging around her, why, again, at her elbow, or lying in wait for her at the foot of a stairs, why, for the nth time that week, *him*, she was too *good* to indicate impatience, or exasperation; too *good* to tell him, as her friends advised, to get lost.

He telephoned her too. Poor Zachary. Stammering over the phone, his voice lowered as if he were in terror of being overheard, "Is S-Sunny there, Mrs. D-Burhman? May I speak with her, please?" And Mrs. Burhman, who knew Dr. Graff and his wife, of course, since everyone in South Lebanon, population 3,800, knew everyone else or knew of them, including frequently their family histories and facts about them of which their children were entirely unaware, hesitated, and said, "Yes, I'll put her on, but I hope you won't talk long—Sunny has homework tonight." Or, apologetically but firmly: "No, I'm afraid she isn't here. May I take a message?"

"N-no message," Zachary would murmur, and hurriedly hang up. 20

Sunny, standing close by, thumbnail between her just perceptibly gap-toothed front teeth, expression crinkled in dismay, would whisper, "Oh Mom. I feel so *bad*. I just feel so—*bad*."

Mrs. Burhman said briskly, "You don't have time for all of them, honey."

Still, Zachary was not discouraged, and with the swift passage of time it began to be observed that Sunny engaged in conversations with him—the two of them sitting, alone, in a corner of the cafeteria, or walking together after a meeting of the Debate Club, of which Zachary was president, and Sunny a member. They were both on the staff of the South Lebanon High Beacon, and the South Lebanon High Yearbook 1959, and the South Lebanon Torch (the literary magazine). They were both members of the National Honor Society and the Quill & Scroll Society. Though Zachary Graff in his aloofness and impatience with most of his peers would be remembered as antisocial, a "loner," in fact, as his record of activities suggested, printed beneath his photograph in the yearbook, he had time, or made time, for things that mattered to him.

He shunned sports, however. High school sports, at least.

25   His life's game, he informed Sunny Burhman, unaware of the solemn pomposity with which he spoke, would be *golf.* His father had been instructing him, informally, since his twelfth birthday.

Said Zachary, "I have no natural talent for it, and I find it profoundly boring, but golf will be my game." And he pushed his chunky black glasses roughly against the bridge of his nose, as he did countless times a day, as if they were in danger of sliding off.

Zachary Graff had such a physical presence, few of his contemporaries would have described him as unattractive, still less homely, ugly. His head appeared oversized, even for his massive body; his eyes were deep-set, with a look of watchfulness and secrecy; his skin was tallow-colored, and blemished, in wavering patches like topographical maps. His big teeth glinted with filaments of silver, and his breath, oddly for one whose father was a doctor, was stale, musty, cobwebby—not that Sunny Burhman ever alluded to this fact, to others.

Her friends began to ask of her, a bit jealously, reproachfully, "What do you two talk about so much?—you and *him?*" and Sunny replied, taking care not to hint, with the slightest movement of her eyebrows, or rolling of her eyes, that, yes, she found the situation peculiar too, "Oh—Zachary and I talk about all kinds of things. *He* talks, mainly. He's brilliant, He's—" pausing, her forehead delicately crinkling in thought, her lovely brown eyes for a moment clouded, "—well, *brilliant.*"

In fact, at first, Zachary spoke, in his intense, obsessive way, of impersonal subjects: the meaning of life, the future of Earth, whether science or art best satisfies the human hunger for self-expression. He said, laughing nervously, fixing Sunny with his shyly bold stare, "Just to pose certain questions is, I guess, to show your hope they can be answered."

30   Early on, Zachary seemed to have understood that, if he expressed doubt, for instance about "whether God exists" and so forth, Sunny Burhman would listen seriously; and would talk with him earnestly, with the air of a nurse giving a transfusion to a patient in danger of expiring for loss of blood. She was not a religious fanatic, but she *was* a devout Christian— the Burhmans were members of the First Presbyterian Church of South Lebanon, and Sunny was president of her youth group, and, among other good deeds, did YWCA volunteer work on Saturday afternoons; she had not the slightest doubt that Jesus Christ, that's to say His spirit, dwelled

in her heart, and that, simply by speaking the truth of what she believed, she could convince others.

Though one day, and soon, Sunny would examine her beliefs, and question the faith into which she'd been born; she had not done so by the age of seventeen and a half. She was a virgin, and virginal in all, or most, of her thoughts.

Sometimes, behind her back, even by friends, Sunny was laughed at, gently—never ridiculed, for no one would ridicule Sunny.

Once, when Sunny Burhman and her date and another couple were gazing up into the night sky, standing in the parking lot of the high school, following a prom, Sunny had said in a quavering voice, "It's so big it would be terrifying, wouldn't it?—except for Jesus, who makes us feel at home."

When popular Chuck Crueller, a quarterback for the South Lebanon varsity football team, was injured during a game, and carried off by ambulance to undergo emergency surgery, Sunny mobilized the other cheerleaders, tears fierce in her eyes. "We can do it for Chuck—we can pray." And so the eight girls in their short-skirted crimson jumpers and starched white cotton blouses had gripped one another's hands tight, weeping, on the verge of hysteria, had prayed, prayed, *prayed*—hidden away in the depths of the girls' locker room for hours. Sunny had led the prayers, and Chuck Crueller recovered.

So you wouldn't ridicule Sunny Burhman, somehow it wouldn't have 35 been appropriate.

As her classmate Tobias Shanks wrote of her, as one of his duties as literary editor of the 1959 South Lebanon yearbook: *"Sunny" Burhman!—an all American girl too good to be true who is nonetheless TRUE!*

If there was a slyly mocking tone to Tobias Shanks's praise, a hint that such goodness was predictable, and superficial, and of no genuine merit, the caption, mere print, beneath Sunny's dazzlingly beautiful photograph, conveyed nothing of this.

Surprisingly, for all his pose of skepticism and superiority, Zachary Graff too was a Christian. He'd been baptized Lutheran, and never failed to attend Sunday services with his parents at the First Lutheran Church. Amid the congregation of somber, somnambulant worshippers, Zachary Graff's frowning young face, the very set of his beefy shoulders, drew the minister's uneasy eye; it would be murmured of Dr. Graff's precocious son, in retrospect, that he'd been perhaps too *serious*.

Before falling in love with Sunny Burhman, and discussing his religious doubts with her, Zachary had often discussed them with Tobias Shanks, who'd been his friend, you might say his only friend, since seventh grade. (But only sporadically since seventh grade, since the boys, each highly intelligent, inclined to impatience and sarcasm, got on each other's nerves.) Once, Zachary confided in Tobias that he prayed every morning of his life—immediately upon waking he scrambled out of bed, knelt, hid his face in his hands, and prayed. For his sinful soul, for his sinful thoughts, deeds, desires. He lacerated his soul the way he'd been taught by his mother to tug a fine-toothed steel comb through his coarse, oily hair, never less than once a day.

40   Tobias Shanks, a self-professed agnostic since the age of fourteen, laughed, and asked derisively, "Yes, but what do you pray *for,* exactly?" and Zachary had thought a bit, and said, not ironically, but altogether seriously, "To get through the day. Doesn't everyone?"

This melancholy reply, Tobias was never to reveal.

Zachary's parents were urging him to go to Muhlenberg College, which was church-affiliated; Zachary hoped to go elsewhere. He said, humbly, to Sunny Burhman, "If you go to Cornell, Sunny, I—maybe I'll go there too?"

Sunny hesitated, then smiled. "Oh. That would be nice."

"You wouldn't mind, Sunny?"

45   "Why would I *mind,* Zachary?" Sunny laughed, to hide her impatience. They were headed for Zachary's car, parked just up the hill from the YM-YWCA building. It was a gusty Saturday afternoon in early March. Leaving the YWCA, Sunny had seen Zachary Graff standing at the curb, hands in the pockets of his sheepskin parka, head lowered, but eyes nervously alert. Standing there, as if accidentally.

It was impossible to avoid him, she had to allow him to drive her home. Though she was beginning to feel panic, like darting tongues of flame, at the prospect of Zachary Graff always *there.*

Tell the creep to get lost, her friends counseled. Even her nice friends were without sentiment regarding Zachary Graff.

Until sixth grade, Sunny had been plain little Barbara Burhman. Then, one day, her teacher had said, to all the class, in one of those moments of inspiration that can alter, by whim, the course of an entire life, "Tell you what, boys and girls—let's call Barbara 'Sunny' from now on—that's what she *is.*"

Ever afterward, in South Lebanon, she was "Sunny" Burhman. Plain little Barbara had been left behind, seemingly forever.

50   So, of course, Sunny could not tell Zachary Graff to get lost. Such words were not part of her vocabulary.

Zachary owned a plum-colored 1956 Plymouth which other boys envied—it seemed to them distinctly unfair that Zachary, of all people, had his own car, when so few of them, who loved cars, did. But Zachary was oblivious of their envy, as, in a way, he seemed oblivious of his own good fortune. He drove the car as if it were an adult duty, with middle-aged fussiness and worry. He drove the car as if he were its own chauffeur. Yet, driving Sunny home, he talked—chattered—continuously. Speaking of college, and of religious "obligations," and of his parents' expectations of him; speaking of medical school; the future; the life—"beyond South Lebanon."

He asked again, in that gravelly, irksomely humble voice, if Sunny would mind if he went to Cornell. And Sunny said, trying to sound merely reasonable, "Zachary, it's a *free world.*"

Zachary said, "Oh no it isn't, Sunny. For some of us, it isn't."

This enigmatic remark Sunny was determined not to follow up.

Braking to a careful stop in front of the Burhmans' house, Zachary 55 said, with an almost boyish enthusiasm, "So—Cornell? In the fall? We'll both go to Cornell?"

Sunny was quickly out of the car before Zachary could put on the emergency brake and come around, ceremoniously, to open her door. Gaily, recklessly, infinitely relieved to be out of his company, she called back over her shoulder, "Why not?"

Sunny's secret vanity must have been what linked them.

For several times, gravely, Zachary had said to her, "When I'm with you, Sunny, it's possible for me to believe."

He meant, she thought, in God. In Jesus. In the life hereafter.

The next time Zachary maneuvered Sunny into his car, under the 60 pretext of driving her home, it was to present the startled girl with an engagement ring.

He'd bought the ring at Stern's Jewelers, South Lebanon's single good jewelry store, with money secretly withdrawn from his savings account; that account to which, over a period of more than a decade, he'd deposited modest sums with a painstaking devotion. This was his "college fund," or had been—out of the $3,245 saved, only $1,090 remained. How astonished, upset, furious his parents would be when they learned— Zachary hadn't allowed himself to contemplate.

The Graffs knew nothing about Sunny Burhman. So far as they might have surmised, their son's frequent absences from home were nothing out of the ordinary—he'd always spent time at the public library, where his preferred reading was reference books. He'd begin with Volume One of an encyclopedia, and make his diligent way through each successive volume, like a horse grazing a field, rarely glancing up, uninterested in his surroundings.

"Please—will you accept it?"

Sunny was staring incredulously at the diamond ring, which was presented to her, not in Zachary's big clumsy fingers, with the dirt-edged nails, but in the plush-lined little box, as if it might be more attractive that way, more like a gift. The ring was 24-karat gold and the diamond was small but distinctive, and coldly glittering. A beautiful ring, but Sunny did not see it that way.

65   She whispered, "Oh. Zachary. Oh *no*—there must be some misunderstanding."

Zachary seemed prepared for her reaction, for he said, quickly, "Will you just try it on?—see if it fits?"

Sunny shook her head. No she couldn't.

"They'll take it back to adjust it, if it's too big," Zachary said. "They promised."

"Zachary, no," Sunny said gently. "I'm so sorry."

70   Tears flooded her eyes and spilled over onto her cheeks.

Zachary was saying, eagerly, his lips flecked with spittle, "I realize you don't l-love me, Sunny, at least not yet, but—you could wear the ring, couldn't you? Just—wear it?" He continued to hold the little box out to her, his hand visibly shaking. "On your right hand, if you don't want to wear it on your left? Please?"

"Zachary, no. That's impossible."

"Just, you know, as a, a gift—? Oh Sunny—"

They were sitting in the plum-colored Plymouth, parked, in an awkwardly public place, on Upchurch Avenue three blocks from Sunny's house. It was 4:25 P.M., March 26, a Thursday: Zachary had lingered after school in order to drive Sunny home after choir practice. Sunny would afterward recall, with an odd haltingness, as if her memory of the episode were blurred with tears, that, as usual, Zachary had done most of the talking. He had not argued with her, nor exactly begged, but spoke almost formally, as if setting out the basic points of his debating strategy: If Sunny did not love him, he could love enough for both; and, If Sunny did not want to be "officially" engaged, she could wear his ring anyway, couldn't she?

75   It would mean so much to him, Zachary said.

Life or death, Zachary said.

Sunny closed the lid of the little box, and pushed it from her, gently. She was crying, and her smooth pageboy was now disheveled. "Oh Zachary, I'm sorry. I *can't*."

Sunny knelt by her bed, hid her face in her hands, prayed.

Please help Zachary not to be in love with me. Please help me not to be cruel. Have mercy on us both O God.

80   O God help him to realize he doesn't love me—doesn't know *me*.

Days passed, and Zachary did not call. If he was absent from school, Sunny did not seem to notice.

Sunny Burhman and Zachary Graff had two classes together, English and physics; but, in the busyness of Sunny's high school life, surrounded by friends, mesmerized by her own rapid motion as if she were lashed to the prow of a boat bearing swiftly through the water, she did not seem to notice.

She was not a girl of secrets. She was not a girl of stealth. Still, though she had confided in her mother all her life, she did not tell her mother about Zachary's desperate proposal; perhaps, so flattered, she did not acknowledge it as desperate. She reasoned that if she told either of her parents they would have telephoned Zachary's parents immediately. *I can't betray him*, she thought.

Nor did she tell her closest girlfriends, or the boy she was seeing most frequently at the time, knowing that the account would turn comical in the telling, that she and her listeners would collapse into laughter, and this too would be a betrayal of Zachary.

She happened to see Tobias Shanks, one day, looking oddly at *her*. That 85 boy who might have been twelve years old, seen from a short distance. Sunny knew that he was, or had been, a friend of Zachary Graff's; she wondered if Zachary confided in him; yet made no effort to speak with him. He didn't like her, she sensed.

No, Sunny didn't tell anyone about Zachary and the engagement ring. Of all sins, she thought, betrayal is surely the worst.

"Sunny? Sun-ny?"

She did not believe she had been sleeping but the low, persistent, gravelly sound of Zachary's voice penetrated her consciousness like a dream-voice—felt, not heard.

Quickly, she got out of bed. Crouched at her window without turning on the light. Saw, to her horror, Zachary down below, standing in the shrubbery, his large head uplifted, face round like the moon, and shadowed like the moon's face. There was a light, damp snowfall; blossomlike clumps fell on the boy's broad shoulders, in his matted hair. Sighting her, he began to wave excitedly, like an impatient child.

"Oh. Zachary. My God." 90

In haste, fumbling, she put on a bulky-knit ski sweater over her flannel nightgown, kicked on bedroom slippers, hurried downstairs. The house was already darkened; the Burhmans were in the habit of going to bed early. Sunny's only concern was that she could send Zachary away without her parents knowing he was there. Even in her distress she was not thinking of the trouble Zachary might make for her: she was thinking of the trouble he might make for himself.

Yet, as soon as she saw him close up, she realized that something was gravely wrong. Here was Zachary Graff—yet not Zachary.

He told her he had to talk with her, and he had to talk with her now. His car was parked in the alley, he said.

He made a gesture as if to take her hand, but Sunny drew back. He loomed over her, his breath steaming. She could not see his eyes.

95 She said no she couldn't go with him. She said he must go home, at once, before her parents woke up.

He said he couldn't leave without her, he had to talk with her. There was a raw urgency, a forcefulness, in him, that Sunny had never seen before, and that frightened her.

She said no. He said yes.

He reached again for her hand, this time taking hold of her wrist. His fingers were strong.

100 "I told you—I can love enough for both!"

Sunny stared up at him, for an instant mute, paralyzed, seeing not Zachary Graff's eyes but the lenses of his glasses which appeared, in the semidark, opaque. Large snowflakes were falling languidly, there was no wind. Sunny saw Zachary Graff's face which was pale and clenched as a muscle, and she heard his voice which was the voice of a stranger, and she felt him tug at her so roughly her arm was strained in its very socket, and she cried, "No! no! go away! no!"—and the spell was broken, the boy gaped at her another moment, then released her, turned, and ran.

No more than two or three minutes had passed since Sunny unlocked the rear door and stepped outside, and Zachary fled. Yet, afterward, she would recall the encounter as if it had taken a very long time, like a scene in a protracted and repetitive nightmare.

It would be the last time Sunny Burhman saw Zachary Graff alive.

Next morning, all of South Lebanon talked of the death of Dr. Graff's son Zachary: he'd committed suicide by parking his car in a garage behind an unoccupied house on Upchurch Avenue, and letting the motor run until the gas tank was emptied. Death was diagnosed as the result of carbon monoxide poisoning, the time estimated at approximately 4:30 A.M. of April 1, 1959.

105 Was the date deliberate?—Zachary had left only a single note behind, printed in firm block letters and taped to the outside of the car windshield:

April Fool's Day 1959

To Whom It May (Or May Not) Concern:

I, Zachary A. Graff, being of sound mind & body, do hereby declare that I have taken my own life of my own free will & I hereby declare all others guiltless as they are ignorant of the death of the aforementioned & the life.

(signed)

ZACHARY A. GRAFF

Police officers, called to the scene at 7:45 A.M., reported finding Zachary, lifeless, stripped to his underwear, in the rear seat of the car; the sheepskin parka was oddly draped over the steering wheel, and the interior of the car was, again oddly, for a boy known for his fastidious habits, littered with numerous items: a Bible, several high school textbooks, a pizza carton and some uneaten crusts of pizza, several empty Pepsi bottles, an empty bag of M&M's candies, a pair of new, unlaced gym shoes (size eleven), a ten-foot length of clothesline (in the glove compartment), and the diamond ring in its plush-lined little box from Stern's Jewelers (in a pocket of the parka).

Sunny Burhman heard the news of Zachary's suicide before leaving for school that morning, when a friend telephoned. Within earshot of both her astonished parents, Sunny burst into tears, and sobbed, "Oh my God—it's my fault."

So the consensus in South Lebanon would be, following the police investigation, and much public speculation, not that it was Sunny Burhman's fault, exactly, not that the girl was to blame, exactly, but, yes, poor Zachary Graff, the doctor's son, had killed himself in despondency over her: her refusal of his engagement ring, her rejection of his love.

That was the final season of her life as "Sunny" Burhman.

She was out of school for a full week following Zachary's death, and, 110 when she returned, conspicuously paler, more subdued, in all ways less sunny, she did not speak, even with her closest friends, of the tragedy; nor did anyone bring up the subject with her. She withdrew her name from the balloting for the senior prom queen, she withdrew from her part in the senior play, she dropped out of the school choir, she did not participate in the annual statewide debating competition—in which, in previous years, Zachary Graff had excelled. Following her last class of the day she went home immediately, and rarely saw her friends on weekends. Was she in mourning?—or was she simply ashamed? Like the bearer of a deadly virus, herself unaffected, Sunny knew how, on all sides, her classmates and her teachers were regarding her: She was the girl for whose love a boy had thrown away his life, she was an unwitting agent of death.

Of course, her family told her that it wasn't her fault that Zachary Graff had been mentally unbalanced.

Even the Graffs did not blame her—or said they didn't.

Sunny said, "Yes. But it's my fault he's dead."

The Presbyterian minister, who counseled Sunny, and prayed with her, assured her that Jesus surely understood, and that there could be no sin in *her*—it wasn't her fault that Zachary Graff had been mentally unbalanced. And Sunny replied, not stubbornly, but matter-of-factly, sadly, as if stating a self-evident truth, "Yes. But it's my fault he's dead."

115   Her older sister, Helen, later that summer, meaning only well, said, in exasperation, "Sunny, when are you going to cheer *up?*" and Sunny turned on her with uncharacteristic fury, and said, "Don't call me that idiotic name ever again—I want it *gone!"*

     When in the fall she enrolled at Cornell University, she was " Barbara Burhman."

     She would remain "Barbara Burhman" for the rest of her life.

     Barbara Burhman excelled as an undergraduate, concentrating on academic work almost exclusively; she went on to graduate school at Harvard, in American studies; she taught at several prestigious universities, rising rapidly through administrative ranks before accepting a position, both highly paid and politically visible, with a well-known research foundation based in Manhattan. She was the author of numerous books and articles; she was married, and the mother of three children; she lectured widely, she was frequently interviewed in the popular press, she lent her name to good causes. She would not have wished to think of herself as extraordinary— in the world she now inhabited, she was surrounded by similarly active, energetic, professionally engaged men and women—except in recalling as she sometimes did, with a mild pang of nostalgia, her old, lost self, sweet "Sunny" Burhman of South Lebanon, New York.

     She hadn't been queen of the senior prom. She hadn't even continued to be a Christian.

120   The irony had not escaped Barbara Burhman that, in casting away his young life so recklessly, Zachary Graff had freed her for hers.

     With the passage of time, grief had lessened. Perhaps in fact it had disappeared. After twenty, and then twenty-five, and now thirty-one years, it was difficult for Barbara, known in her adult life as an exemplar of practical sense, to feel a kinship with the adolescent girl she'd been, or that claustrophobic high school world of the late 1950s. She'd never returned for a single reunion. If she thought of Zachary Graff—about whom, incidentally, she'd never told her husband of twenty-eight years—it was with the regret we think of remote acquaintances, lost to us by accidents of fate. Forever, Zachary Graff, the most brilliant member of the class of 1959 of South Lebanon High, would remain a high school boy, trapped, aged eighteen.

     Of that class, the only other person to have acquired what might be called a national reputation was Tobias Shanks, now known as T. R. Shanks, a playwright and director of experimental drama; Barbara Burhman had followed Tobias's career with interest, and had sent him a telegram congratulating him on his most recent play, which went on to win a number of awards, dealing, as it did, with the vicissitudes of gay life in the 1980s. In the winter of 1990 Barbara and Tobias began to encounter each other socially, when Tobias was playwright-in-residence at Bard College, close by Hazelton-on-Hudson where Barbara lived. At first they were strangely shy of each other; even guarded; as if, in even this neutral setting, their South Lebanon ghost-selves exerted a powerful influence. The golden girl, the loner. The splendidly normal, the defiantly "odd." One night Tobias Shanks, shaking Barbara Burhman's hand, had smiled wryly, and said, "It *is* Sunny, isn't it?" and Barbara Burhman, laughing nervously, hoping no one had overheard, said, "No, in fact it isn't. It's Barbara."

They looked at each other, mildly dazed. For one saw a small-boned but solidly built man of youthful middle-age, sweet-faced, yet with ironic, pouched eyes, thinning gray hair, and a close-trimmed gray beard; the other saw woman of youthful middle-age, striking in appearance, impeccably well-groomed, with fading hair of no distinctive color and faint, white, puckering lines at the edges of her eyes. Their ghost-selves *were* there—not aged, or not aged merely, but transformed, as the genes of a previous generation are transformed by the next.

Tobias stared at Barbara for a long moment, as if unable to speak. Finally he said, "I have something to tell you, Barbara. When can we meet?"

Tobias Shanks handed the much-folded letter across the table to 125
Barbara Burhman, and watched as she opened it, and read it, with an expression of increasing astonishment and wonder.

"*He* wrote this? Zachary? To you?"

"He did."

"And you—Did you—?"

Tobias shook his head.

His expression was carefully neutral, but his eyes swam suddenly with tears. 130

"We'd been friends, very close friends, for years. Each other's only friend, most of the time. The way kids that age can be, in certain restricted environments—kids who aren't what's called 'average' or 'normal.' We talked a good deal about religion—Zachary was afraid of hell. We both liked science fiction. We both had very strict parents. I suppose I might have been attracted to Zachary at times—I knew I was attracted to other guys—but of course I never acted upon it; I wouldn't have dared. Almost no one dared, in those days." He laughed, with a mild shudder. He passed a hand over his eyes. "I couldn't have *loved* Zachary Graff as he claimed he loved me, because—I couldn't. But I could have allowed him to know that he wasn't sick, crazy, 'perverted' as he called himself in that letter." He paused. For a long painful moment Barbara thought he wasn't going to continue. Then he said, with that same mirthless shuddering laugh, "I could have made him feel less lonely. But I didn't. I failed him. My only friend."

Barbara had taken out a tissue, and was dabbing at her eyes.

She felt as if she'd been dealt a blow so hard she could not gauge how she'd been hurt—if there was hurt at all.

She said, "Then it hadn't ever been 'Sunny'—she was an illusion."

135   Tobias said thoughtfully, "I don't know. I suppose so. There was the sense, at least as I saw it at the time, that, yes, he'd chosen you; decided upon you."

"As a symbol."

"Not just a symbol. We all adored you—we were all a little in love with you." Tobias laughed, embarrassed. "Even me."

"I wish you'd come to me and told me, back then. After—it happened."

"I was too cowardly. I was terrified of being exposed, and, maybe, doing to myself what he'd done to himself. Suicide is so very attractive to adolescents." Tobias paused, and reached over to touch Barbara's hand. His fingertips were cold. "I'm not proud of myself, Barbara, and I've tried to deal with it in my writing, but—that's how I was, back then." Again he paused. He pressed a little harder against Barbara's hand. "Another thing—after Zachary went to you, that night, he came to me."

140   "To you?"

"To me."

"And—?"

"And I refused to go with him too. I was furious with him for coming to the house like that, risking my parents discovering us. I guess I got a little hysterical. And he fled."

"He fled."

145   "Then, afterward, I just couldn't bring myself to come forward. Why I saved that letter, I don't know—I'd thrown away some others that were less incriminating. I suppose I figured—no one knew about me, everyone knew about you. 'Sunny' Burhman."

They were at lunch—they ordered two more drinks—they'd forgotten their surroundings—they talked.

After an hour or so Barbara Burhman leaned across the table, as at one of her professional meetings, to ask, in a tone of intellectual curiosity, "What do you think Zachary planned to do with the clothesline?"

QUESTIONS

1. Analyze the characterizations of the three principal figures: Sunny, Zachary, and Tobias. Which of them are developing characters?
2. This story is set in 1959. Today Zachary's behavior would be considered "stalking." Can it be argued that he is a sympathetic character nonetheless? Is he more sympathetic as a boy in 1959 than if the story were set in 2009?

3. What do you infer about the relationship between Zachary and Tobias? Cite evidence from the text for your opinion.
4. After learning the contents of Zachary's letter to Tobias, Barbara Burhman "felt as if she'd been dealt a blow." What is the reason for her discomfort?
5. Discuss the significance of the title. Does it have a different meaning by the end of the story than it has at first glance?
6. Discuss the adult Barbara Burhman's final question. How is this question an appropriate closure to the story?

JOYCE CAROL OATES

A Brutal Murder in a Public Place

At Gate C33 of Newark International Airport in a waiting area of seats facing curved glass windows and a heavily occluded sky beyond the windows, a sudden frantic chirping!

Everyone looks around—upward—the frantic chirping continues—the bird—(if it is a bird)—is hidden from view.

A bird? Is that a—bird? Here? How—*here?*

In these rows of seats, strangers. Directly in front of the curved-glass windows facing the runway outside and the overcast New Jersey sky are three sections of seats of ten seats each, with six plate-glass windows facing each section of seats: in all, eighteen windows.

On the other side of the walkway, which is not wide, no more than a 5 few yards, are rows of seats arranged in the usual utilitarian way: back to back and, across a narrow aisle, facing one another.

Barely, there is room for people to make their way through this narrow aisle, pulling suitcases.

You might guess fifteen seats in each row. Ten such rows of seats at Gate C33.

This place of utter anonymity, impersonality.

This place of *randomness.*

Emptiness. 10

And suddenly—the tiny bird-chirping!

An improbable and heartrending little musical trill like an old-fashioned music box!

A sound to make you glance upward, smiling—in expectation of seeing—what?

At the ceiling above the closest row of seats facing the window there appears to be a ledge of some kind, probably containing air vents—(from

A BRUTAL MURDER IN A PUBLIC PLACE   First published in 2012. See the footnote on page 489 for more information on Oates and her career.

my seat about fifteen feet from the outer row of seats by the window, I am not able to see the front of the ledge)—and very likely the trapped little bird—(if it is a bird, it must be "trapped" in this place, and if it is between the ledge and the ceiling, it must be little)—is perched there.

15   The seated travelers continue to look around, quizzical and bemused.

A white-haired woman in a wheelchair squints upward, with an expression of mild anxiety A contingent of soldiers—mostly young, mostly male—mostly dark-skinned—in casual-camouflage uniform like mud-splotched pajamas—squint upward frowning as if the bird's chirping might be a warning, or an alarm.

How is it possible, a bird *here*?

Though the chirping is fairly loud, rapid-fire and somewhere close by, yet no one has sighted the bird. A lanky young man with a backpack stands, to squint toward the ceiling, with the air of an alert birdwatcher, but the bird remains invisible.

Another possible place (I see now) in which the little bird might be hidden is in the leaves of a stunted little tree near the windows.

20   This is a melancholy tree of no discernible species in a plastic pot meant to resemble a clay pot. At first you assume that the tree must be artificial then, when you look more closely, you see to your surprise that the stunted little tree is a *living thing*.

The tree is a well-intentioned "decorative touch" in Newark International Airport. Intended to soften the harsh utilitarian anonymity of the place.

And the horror of *randomness*—of strangers gathered together to no purpose other than to depart from one another as swiftly and expeditiously as possible.

But the little tree has not fared well in this mostly fluorescent-lit environment. Coaxed out of a seed, nurtured into life, it is now a *thing* scarcely living: its large spade-shaped leaves are no longer green but threaded with what looks like rust. Still, the little bird might yet be hidden among these leaves . . .

I've noticed another tree of the same indistinct species in the same plastic pot about thirty feet away, at (unoccupied) Gate C34. Very likely at other gates in the terminal, in all the terminals of the airport, there are other trees similarly potted, of a near-identical type, height and condition, their once-glossy green leaves grown shabby, desiccated. You can tell that these trees are *not artificial* because they are *shabby, desiccated*.

25   The *artificial* endures. *Living* wears out.

Invisibly, almost teasingly, the tiny chirping continues,

Like tiny bits of glass being shaken together in a great fist.

The chirping is drowned out by an announcement—a particularly shrill-voiced woman—and when the announcement ends, the chirping has ceased.

Everyone has turned back to their preoccupations of a moment before—desultory conversations, laptops and books, the high-perched TV news of far-flung and domestic tragedies that never ceases whether anyone is watching or not.

Even the soldiers who'd appeared vigilant a moment before have 30 turned away. Even the lanky young man with the backpack, who is hunched in his seat speaking on a cell phone.

Am I the only traveler thinking—The little bird is still here somewhere, it could not have flown away without our seeing?

Stubbornly, I listen for the little bird. Scarcely daring to breathe I listen for the little bird. As if its tiny heartbeat had aligned itself with my heartbeat and acutely it is aware of me, as I am aware of it.

A living thing. Somewhere close by, invisible.

How loud and intrusive are the announcements—flights boarding, flights departing—flights delayed. How grating, the human voice.

For it seems that, at Gate C33, an incoming flight has been delayed 35 (weather, Chicago) and an outgoing flight has been delayed (weather, Minneapolis).

But at last, a few minutes later, the frantic little chirping resumes, with greater urgency.

Already I am on my feet, restless and alert. Where I'd been annoyed and mildly anxious that my flight has been delayed—(another forty minutes)—yet I am more intrigued by the mysterious little bird, that has drawn my attention. Pages of the *New York Times* lay scattered on the seat beside mine, and on the floor.

I know—you are advised not to leave your luggage unattended in this public place, but I intend only to walk—to stretch my legs—for a short distance.

Unlike the others who've turned their attentions away from the mysterious chirping overhead, I'm consumed with curiosity about the little bird in our midst who is not only hypothetical but also invisible. For the fact remains: *there is a bird here at Gate C33 of Newark International Airport*

It's probable that the bird entered the terminal through an opened 40 door in this area when passengers boarded one of the smaller, propeller planes. At such times passengers are not shunted directly onto the plane through a covered chute but are obliged to walk across the pavement— (invariably in windy, wet weather)—to steep metal steps ascending to the prop-plane that, when entered, exudes the cramped, airless, and claustrophobic air of a straining intestine.

And yet—think of the odds against this! A luckless bird blown by the wind, unable to prevent itself from being sucked into the terminal through the opened door . . . Unless, confused by plate-glass reflections, the poor bird had blundered into the opened doorway of its own volition.

Now there's a sudden blur of wings! Small wings! My vigilance has paid off since I am almost directly below the bird—it was hidden, as I'd surmised, between the ledge and the ceiling—it's a small sparrow—beating its wings madly, careening in the air—striking the rows of plate-glass windows looking out onto the runway—making its way dazed and confused into a high, windowless corner of the waiting area. By this time everyone has glanced up again and several people smile—(why does the panicked fluttering of a small bird, trapped in such a place, provoke people to smile?).

After a few minutes of wing-bearing, chirping, blundering along the row of windows, the little bird—(it's a beautifully patterned sparrow)—has positioned itself back on the ledge, but near the edge where it's visible. I have followed it here, in this relatively quiet space near the (unmanned, unlighted) Gate C34; beyond the window here is an empty runway, and close by is another stunted little potted tree—glamorous poster-ads for Costa Rica, Tampa Bay, Rio. Poor little bird! How did it get into this terrible place, and what can I do to help it?

Gazing up at the tiny damp eyes, the tiny beak moving soundlessly, as if its terror has made it mute—and my heart begins to beat rapidly, and my wings—(wings! suddenly 1 realize what is sprouting from my shoulders)—and now I see a fattish woman standing about twelve feet below me and peering up at me, quizzical and curious rather than concerned—I am crying *Oh please help me! I am one of you! I don't know what this terrible thing is, that has happened to me but—I am a living thing, I am one of you* . . .

Unable to stop the agitation of my wings, I am flying about in terror—striking the ugly, unyielding ceiling—ricocheting against the windows—and the ledge—there is a ventilator humming within, a ghastly grinding sound—in the midst of my terror another woman comes to observe, eating an apple—so acute is my eyesight, I can see saliva gleaming on this woman's lips—in her eyes a reflection of mild concern—so very mild, it's like a flickering candle seen at a distance; beyond this woman are rows of seats of which most are occupied—there are the U.S. soldiers in their bizarre jungle-uniforms—some glance up frowning, or smiling—faint distracted smiles; a few have seen me, or the blurred beating of wings that I have become. *Help me! I want to go home! I don't belong here, I live in—*but my tiny trilling voice can't accommodate multisyllabic words. *I am one of you—I am a living creature—help me out of this terrible place—I was* *a traveler like you—a human being like you—my flight to Chicago was delayed for forty minutes—and then for another forty minutes—and then—somehow—this has happened—this, to which I can give no name—this curse! Please hear me! Please help me! I have done nothing to deserve this punishment—I am innocent—I cannot even remember my "sins"—my "crimes"—I may have believed that I was an extraordinary individual but the fact is, I was utterly ordinary—I am utterly ordinary—I am blameless—it is a terrible injustice that I have been singled out like this—please, you must help me! Don't just smile inanely at me or look away, bored—help me! It is a mistake that I am here trapped against plate-glass windows—flinging myself against plate-glass windows—so yearning to escape into the open air, to freedom, my tiny heart is near to bursting! Take me to my home—when they see me, they will recognize me—there are those who love me—they will know who I am—I must consume food at once, I am starving—my little sparrow-wings, my tiny organs, my heart, my teaspoon of blood must be nourished—I am so very cold, I am shivering convulsively—if I don't consume food—just a few crumbs please, just a few crumbs—I will begin to die within a few minutes—my organs will begin to shut down—my panicked-darting eyes will begin to close over, and my vision will become occluded—my wings which I had believed would beat forever, will slow—not one of you is starving—not one of you is beginning to shut down, and die—you have no right to smile at the suffering of a bird in the final minutes of its life—you have no right to ignore me for I am a very beautiful white-crowned sparrow with elaborately patterned wings of white, brown, black and rust-colored curved feathers—*

—I am more beautiful than any of you crude, wingless, earthbound creatures—I am as deserving of life as you!—more deserving than you!—I deserve better than this nightmare-curse: a random death among strangers.

Except—am I going to be rescued? Has someone called for help, and help has come? Eagerly my eyes take in an unexpected sight below: two men in work-uniforms—quick-striding, efficient and seemingly well-practiced—are approaching, at last. One has a stepladder and a small net with a three-foot handle, the other a wicked-looking broom.

QUESTIONS

1. Does this very brief story have a plot? Does it have conflict and suspense?
2. How is the narrator characterized? Is she sympathetic or unsympathetic to the sparrow's plight?
3. Analyze the setting. What features of this "public place" are stressed.'
4. Near the end of the story, the narrator seems to give over the narration to the sparrow, and in a sense she becomes the sparrow. What is the purpose of this unexpected transformation?
5. What is happening in the last few lines of the story? What will happen to the sparrow?

SUGGESTIONS FOR WRITING

The following are suggestions for essays on the featured authors. Use of secondary sources, widely available for the three authors, should assist you in developing your ideas.

1. Compare the characterizations of Joy-Hulga in "Good Country People" and Connie in "Where Are You Going, Where Have You Been?" In what ways are they typical young women of their era? How do they differ?

2. Study the use of settings in "A Good Man Is Hard to Find" and in "Odour of Chrysanthemums." How do the authors employ the settings differently in each story? How are the characters related to the settings of each?

3. Analyze and compare the plot structures of each of the three O'Connor stories. How are the plots similar? How do the main characters' fates elucidate a common theme?

4. Discuss the depiction of the intergenerational relationships in the three O'Connor stories, focusing on Bailey and the grandmother, Mrs. Hopewell and Joy-Hulga, and Julian and his mother. What are the primary similarities and differences in these relationships in the three stories?

5. Write an essay on family dysfunction as dramatized in Lawrence's "The Rocking-Horse Winner" and O'Connor's "A Good Man Is Hard to Find." What do these stories say about family interaction and the relationship of the family to the larger world? What comparisons and contrasts can you identify between the depictions of family in the two stories?

6. Discuss the theme of romantic love in Lawrence's "The Horse-Dealer's Daughter" and Oates's "Life After High School." What do these stories say about the satisfactions and frustrations of romantic relationships? How are healthy and unhealthy forms of love contrasted and dramatized?

7. Write an essay on one of the following characters, elucidating his or her significance within the story.
   a. Walter Bates's mother in "Odour of Chrysanthemums"
   b. The Misfit in "A Good Man Is Hard to Find"
   c. Red Sammy in "A Good Man Is Hard to Find"
   d. The Bible salesman in "Good Country People"
   e. Mrs. Freeman in "Good Country People"
   f. Carver's mother in "Everything That Rises Must Converge"
   g. Arnold Friend in "Where Are You Going, Where Have You Been?"
   h. Zachary Graff in "Life After High School"
   i. The narrator in "A Brutal Murder in a Public Place"

8. Discuss the use of the following symbols: nature symbolism in "Odour of Chrysanthemums" or in "The Horse-Dealer's Daughter"; the purple hat in "Everything That Rises Must Converge"; animal symbolism in "A Good Man Is Hard to Find" and "A Brutal Murder in a Public Place"; the golden car in "Where Are You Going, Where Have You Been?"

PRACTICE AP WRITING PROMPTS

D. H. Lawrence, "The Rocking-Horse Winner" (p. 432)

40-minute prompt: Read "The Rocking-Horse Winner" carefully from the opening of the story (p. 432) through paragraph 5 (p. 433). Write a well-organized essay in which you analyze how Lawrence establishes the story's tone. In your analysis, pay close attention to literary elements such as setting, diction, sound devices, and personification.

Flannery O'Connor, "A Good Man Is Hard to Find" (pp. 445–458)

Read paragraphs 70 through 90, in "A Good Man Is Hard to Find." In this passage a family on an outing has had an auto accident. The driver of the other car involved in the accident is an escaped killer known as "The Misfit." Read the passage with care, and then write a well-supported essay analyzing how setting, dialogue, and narrative voice all give us information essential to understanding the different characters involved in the scene.

Flannery O' Connor, "Good Country People" (p. 459)

Flannery O'Connor stated that "spiritual isolation"—the inability to give and receive love—often typifies her physically limited characters. Read "Good Country People." Then, in a well-organized essay, analyze how Hulga's (Joy's) spiritual isolation and eventual redemption contribute to the story's meaning as a whole.

Flannery O'Connor, "Everything That Rises Must Converge" (p. 476)

Read "Everything That Rises Must Converge." Then, in a well-organized essay, analyze the conflicted relationship of Julian and his mother against the backdrop of the social changes of the early 1960s. Show how literary elements such as irony, point of view, and selection of detail help to portray this relationship.

Joyce Carol Oates, "Life after High School" (p. 503)

40-minute prompt: Read "Life after High School" carefully from paragraph 60 (p. 501) through paragraph 86 (p. 503). Then write an essay in which you analyze how Oates uses literary elements such as dialogue, point of view, and selection of detail to communicate Sonny's rejection of Zachary.

Stories for Further

Reading

RAYMOND CARVER
What We Talk about
When We Talk about Love

My friend Mel McGinnis was talking. Mel McGinnis is a cardiologist, and sometimes that gives him the right.

The four of us were sitting around his kitchen table drinking gin. Sunlight filled the kitchen from the big window behind the sink. There were Mel and me and his second wife, Teresa—Terri, we called her—and my wife, Laura. We lived in Albuquerque then. But we were all from somewhere else.

There was an ice bucket on the table. The gin and the tonic water kept going around, and we somehow got on the subject of love. Mel thought real love was nothing less than spiritual love. He said he'd spent five years in a seminary before quitting to go to medical school. He said he still looked back on those years in the seminary as the most important years in his life.

Terri said the man she lived with before she lived with Mel loved her so much he tried to kill her. Then Terri said, "He beat me up one night. He dragged me around the living room by my ankles. He kept saying, 'I love you, I love you, you bitch.' He went on dragging me around the living room. My head kept knocking on things." Terri looked around the table. "What do you do with love like that?"

5   She was a bone-thin woman with a pretty face, dark eyes, and brown hair that hung down her back. She liked necklaces made of turquoise, and long pendant earrings.

"My God, don't be silly. That's not love, and you know it," Mel said. "I don't know what you'd call it, but I sure know you wouldn't call it love."

"Say what you want to, but I know it was," Terri said. "It may sound crazy to you, but it's true just the same. People are different, Mel. Sure, sometimes he may have acted crazy. Okay. But he loved me. In his own way maybe, but he loved me. There was love there, Mel. Don't say there wasn't."

Mel let out his breath. He held his glass and turned to Laura and me. "The man threatened to kill me," Mel said. He finished his drink and

WHAT WE TALK ABOUT WHEN WE TALK ABOUT LOVE   First published in 1981. Raymond Carver (1938–1988) was born in Oregon, attended college in California, and earned an M.F.A. from the University of Iowa. During the 1970s and 1980s his spare, carefully crafted short stories brought him wide acclaim, and he is now considered one of the American masters of the short story in the twentieth century. During Carver's last months, before succumbing to lung cancer, he married his longtime companion, the poet Tess Gallagher.

reached for the gin bottle. "Terri's a romantic. Terri's of the kick-me-so-I'll-know-you-love-me school. Terri, hon, don't look that way." Mel reached across the table and touched Terri's cheek with his fingers. He grinned at her.

"Now he wants to make up," Terri said.

"Make up what?" Mel said. "What is there to make up? I know what   10
I know. That's all."

"How'd we get started on this subject, anyway?" Terri said. She raised her glass and drank from it. "Mel always has love on his mind," she said. "Don't you, honey?" She smiled, and I thought that was the last of it.

"I just wouldn't call Ed's behavior love. That's all I'm saying, honey," Mel said. "What about you guys?" Mel said to Laura and me. "Does that sound like love to you?"

"I'm the wrong person to ask," I said. "I didn't even know the man. I've only heard his name mentioned in passing. I wouldn't know. You'd have to know the particulars. But I think what you're saying is that love is an absolute."

Mel said, "The kind of love I'm talking about is. The kind of love I'm talking about, you don't try to kill people."

Laura said, "I don't know anything about Ed, or anything about the   15
situation. But who can judge anyone else's situation?"

I touched the back of Laura's hand. She gave me a quick smile. I picked up Laura's hand. It was warm, the nails polished, perfectly manicured. I encircled the broad wrist with my fingers, and I held her.

"When I left, he drank rat poison," Terri said. She clasped her arms with her hands. "They took him to the hospital in Sante Fe. That's where we lived then, about ten miles out. They saved his life. But his gums went crazy from it. I mean they pulled away from his teeth. After that, his teeth stood out like fangs. My God," Terri said. She waited a minute, then let go of her arms and picked up her glass.

"What people won't do!" Laura said.

"He's out of the action now," Mel said. "He's dead."

Mel handed me the saucer of limes. I took a section, squeezed it over   20
my drink, and stirred the ice cubes with my finger.

"It gets worse," Terri said. "He shot himself in the mouth. But he bungled that too. Poor Ed," she said. Terri shook her head.

"Poor Ed nothing," Mel said. "He was dangerous."

Mel was forty-five years old. He was tall and rangy with curly soft hair. His face and arms were brown from the tennis he played. When he was sober, his gestures, all his movements, were precise, very careful.

"He did love me though, Mel. Grant me that," Terri said. "That's all I'm asking. He didn't love me the way you love me. I'm not saying that. But he loved me. You can grant me that, can't you?"

25   "What do you mean, he bungled it?" I said.

Laura leaned forward with her glass. She put her elbows on the table and held her glass in both hands. She glanced from Mel to Terri and waited with a look of bewilderment on her open face, as if amazed that such things happened to people you were friendly with.

"How'd he bungle it when he killed himself?" I said.

"I'll tell you what happened," Mel said. "He took this twenty-two pistol he'd bought to threaten Terri and me with. Oh, I'm serious, the man was always threatening. You should have seen the way we lived in those days. Like fugitives. I even bought a gun myself. Can you believe it? A guy like me? But I did. I bought one for self-defense and carried it in the glove compartment. Sometimes I'd have to leave the apartment in the middle of the night. To go to the hospital, you know? Terri and I weren't married then, and my first wife had the house and kids, the dog, everything, and Terri and I were living in this apartment here. Sometimes, as I say, I'd get a call in the middle of the night and have to go in to the hospital at two or three in the morning. It'd be dark out there in the parking lot, and I'd break into a sweat before I could even get to my car. I never knew if he was going to come up out of the shrubbery or from behind a car and start shooting. I mean, the man was crazy. He was capable of wiring a bomb, anything. He used to call my service at all hours and say he needed to talk to the doctor, and when I'd return the call, he'd say, 'Son of a bitch, your days are numbered.' Little things like that. It was scary, I'm telling you."

"I still feel sorry for him," Terri said.

30   "It sounds like a nightmare," Laura said. "But what exactly happened after he shot himself?"

Laura is a legal secretary. We'd met in a professional capacity. Before we knew it, it was a courtship. She's thirty-five, three years younger than I am. In addition to being in love, we like each other and enjoy one another's company. She's easy to be with.

"What happened?" Laura said.

Mel said, "He shot himself in the mouth in his room. Someone heard the shot and told the manager. They came in with a passkey, saw what had happened, and called an ambulance. I happened to be there when they brought him in, alive but past recall. The man lived for three days. His head swelled up to twice the size of a normal head. I'd never seen anything like it, and I hope I never do again. Terri wanted to go in and sit with him when she found out about it. We had a fight over it. I didn't think she should see him like that. I didn't think she should see him, and I still don't."

"Who won the fight?" Laura said.

"I was in the room with him when he died," Terri said. "He never came 35 up out of it. But I sat with him. He didn't have anyone else."

"He was dangerous," Mel said. "If you call that love, you can have it."

"It was love," Terri said. "Sure, it's abnormal in most people's eyes. But he was willing to die for it. He did die for it."

"I sure as hell wouldn't call it love," Mel said. "I mean, no one knows what he did it for. I've seen a lot of suicides, and I couldn't say anyone ever knew what they did it for."

Mel put his hands behind his neck and tilted his chair back. "I'm not interested in that kind of love," he said. "If that's love, you can have it."

Terri said, "We were afraid. Mel even made a will out and wrote to his 40 brother in California who used to be a Green Beret. Mel told him who to look for if something happened to him."

Terri drank from her glass. She said, "But Mel's right—we lived like fugitives. We were afraid. Mel was, weren't you, honey? I even called the police at one point, but they were no help. They said they couldn't do anything until Ed actually did something. Isn't that a laugh?" Terri said.

She poured the last of the gin into her glass and waggled the bottle. Mel got up from the table and went to the cupboard. He took down another bottle.

"Well, Nick and I know what love is," Laura said. "For us, I mean," Laura said. She bumped my knee with her knee. "You're supposed to say something now," Laura said, and turned her smile on me.

For an answer, I took Laura's hand and raised it to my lips. I made a big production out of kissing her hand. Everyone was amused.

"We're lucky," I said. 45

"You guys," Terri said. "Stop that now. You're making me sick. You're still on the honeymoon, for God's sake. You're still gaga, for crying out loud. Just wait. How long have you been together now? How long has it been? A year? Longer than a year?"

"Going on a year and a half," Laura said, flushed and smiling.

"Oh, now," Terri said. "Wait a while."

She held her drink and gazed at Laura.

"I'm only kidding," Terri said. 50

Mel opened the gin and went around the table with the bottle.

"Here, you guys," he said. "Let's have a toast. I want to propose a toast. A toast to love. To true love," Mel said.

We touched glasses.

"To love," we said.

Outside in the backyard, one of the dogs began to bark. The leaves 55 of the aspen that leaned past the window ticked against the glass. The afternoon sun was like a presence in this room, the spacious light of ease and generosity. We could have been anywhere, somewhere enchanted. We raised our glasses again and grinned at each other like children who had agreed on something forbidden.

"I'll tell you what real love is," Mel said. "I mean, I'll give you a good example. And then you can draw your own conclusions." He poured more gin into his glass. He added an ice cube and a sliver of lime. We waited and sipped our drinks. Laura and I touched knees again. I put a hand on her warm thigh and left it there.

"What do any of us really know about love?" Mel said. "It seems to me we're just beginners at love. We say we love each other and we do, I don't doubt it. I love Terri and Terri loves me, and you guys love each other too. You know the kind of love I'm talking about now. Physical love, that impulse that drives you to someone special, as well as love of the other person's being, his or her essence, as it were. Carnal love and, well, call it sentimental love, the day-to-day caring about the other person. But sometimes I have a hard time accounting for the fact that I must have loved my first wife too. But I did, I know I did. So I suppose I am like Terri in that regard. Terri and Ed." He thought about it and then he went on. "There was a time when I thought I loved my first wife more than life itself. But now I hate her guts. I do. How do you explain that? What happened to that love? What happened to it, is what I'd like to know. I wish someone could tell me. Then there's Ed. Okay, we're back to Ed. He loves Terri so much he tries to kill her and he winds up killing himself." Mel stopped talking and swallowed from his glass. "You guys have been together eighteen months and you love each other. It shows all over you. You glow with it. But you both loved other people before you met each other. You've both been married before, just like us. And you probably loved other people before that too, even. Terri and I have been together five years, been married for four. And the terrible thing, the terrible thing is, but the good thing too, the saving grace, you might say, is that if something happened to one of us—excuse me for saying this— but if something happened to one of us tomorrow I think the other one, the other person, would grieve for a while, you know, but then the surviving party would go out and love again, have someone else soon enough. All this, all of this love we're talking about, it would just be a memory. Maybe not even a memory. Am I wrong? Am I way off base? Because I want you to set me straight if you think I'm wrong. I want to know. I mean, I don't know anything, and I'm the first one to admit it."

"Mel, for God's sake," Terri said. She reached out and took hold of his wrist. "Are you getting drunk? Honey? Are you drunk?"

"Honey, I'm just talking," Mel said. "All right? I don't have to be drunk to say what I think. I mean, we're all just talking, right?" Mel said. He fixed his eyes on her.

"Sweetie, I'm not criticizing," Terri said.   60
She picked up her glass.
"I'm not on call today," Mel said. "Let me remind you of that. I am
not on call," he said.
"Mel, we love you," Laura said.
Mel looked at Laura. He looked at her as if he could not place her, as
if she was not the woman she was.
"Love you too, Laura," Mel said. "And you, Nick, love you too. You   65
know something?" Mel said. "You guys are our pals," Mel said.
He picked up his glass.

Mel said, "I was going to tell you about something. I mean, I was
going to prove a point. You see, this happened a few months ago, but it's
still going on right now, and it ought to make us feel ashamed when we
talk like we know what we're talking about when we talk above love."
"Come on now," Terri said. "Don't talk like you're drunk if you're not
drunk."
"Just shut up for once in your life," Mel said very quietly. "Will you do
me a favor and do that for a minute? So as I was saying, there's this old couple
who had this car wreck out on the interstate. A kid hit them and they were
all torn to shit and nobody was giving them much chance to pull through."
Terri looked at us and then back at Mel. She seemed anxious, or maybe   70
that's too strong a word.
Mel was handling the bottle around the table.
"I was on call that night," Mel said. "It was May or maybe it was June.
Terri and I had just sat down to dinner when the hospital called. There'd
been this thing out on the interstate. Drunk kid, teenager, plowed his dad's
pickup into this camper with this old couple in it. They were up in their
mid-seventies, that couple. The kid—eighteen, nineteen, something—he
was DOA. Taken the steering wheel through his sternum. The old couple,
they were alive, you understand. I mean, just barely. But they had everything. Multiple fractures, internal injuries, hemorrhaging, contusions,
lacerations, the works, and they each of them had themselves concussions.
They were in a bad way, believe me. And, of course, their age was two strikes
against them. I'd say she was worse off than he was. Ruptured spleen along
with everything else. Both kneecaps broken. But they'd been wearing their
seatbelts and, God knows, that's what saved them for the time being."
"Folks, this is an advertisement for the National Safety Council,"
Terri said. "This is your spokesman, Dr. Melvin R. McGinnis, talking."
Terri laughed. "Mel," she said, "sometimes you're just too much. But
I love you, hon," she said.
"Honey, I love you," Mel said.

75 He leaned across the table. Terri met him halfway. They kissed.

"Terri's right," Mel said as he settled himself again. "Get those seat-belts on. But seriously, they were in some shape, those oldsters. By the time I got down there, the kid was dead, as I said. He was off in a corner, laid out on a gurney. I took one look at the old couple and told the ER nurse to get me a neurologist and an orthopedic man and a couple of surgeons down there right away."

He drank from his glass. "I'll try to keep this short," he said. "So we took the two of them up to the OR and worked like fuck on them most of the night. They had these incredible reserves, those two. You see that once in a while. So we did everything that could be done, and toward morning we're giving them a fifty-fifty chance, maybe less than that for her. So here they are, still alive the next morning. So, okay, we move them into the ICU, which is where they both kept plugging away at it for two weeks, hitting it better and better on all the scopes. So we transfer them out to their own room."

Mel stopped talking. "Here," he said, "let's drink this cheapo gin the hell up. Then we're going to dinner, right? Terri and I know a new place. That's where we'll go, to this new place we know about. But we're not going until we finish up this cut-rate, lousy gin."

Terri said, "We haven't actually eaten there yet. But it looks good. From the outside, you know."

80 "I like food," Mel said. "If I had it to do all over again, I'd be a chef, you know? Right, Terri?" Mel said.

He laughed. He fingered the ice in his glass.

"Terri knows," he said. "Terri can tell you. But let me say this. If I could come back again in a different life, a different time and all, you know what? I'd like to come back as a knight. You were pretty safe wearing all that armor. It was all right being a knight until gunpowder and muskets and pistols came along."

"Mel would like to ride a horse and carry a lance," Terri said.

"Carry a woman's scarf with you everywhere," Laura said.

85 "Or just a woman," Mel said.

"Shame on you," Laura said.

Terri said, "Suppose you came back as a serf. The serfs didn't have it so good in those days," Terri said.

"The serfs never had it good," Mel said. "But I guess even the knights were vessels to someone. Isn't that the way it worked? But then everyone is always a vessel to someone. Isn't that right? Terri? But what I liked about knights, besides their ladies, was that they had that suit of armor, you know, and they couldn't get hurt very easy. No cars in those days, you know? No drunk teenagers to tear into your ass."

"Vassals," Terri said.

"What?" Mel said.   90

"Vassals," Terri said. "They were called vassals, not vessels."

"Vassals, vessels," Mel said, "what the fuck's the difference? You knew what I meant anyway. All right," Mel said. "So I'm not educated. I learned my stuff. I'm a heart surgeon, sure, but I'm just a mechanic. I go in and I fuck around and I fix things. Shit," Mel said.

"Modesty doesn't become you," Terri said.

"He's just a humble sawbones," I said. "But sometimes they suffocated in all that armor, Mel. They'd even have heart attacks if it got too hot and they were too tired and worn out. I read somewhere that they'd fall off their horses and not be able to get up because they were too tired to stand with all that armor on them. They got trampled by their own horses sometimes."

"That's terrible," Mel said. "That's a terrible thing, Nicky. I guess   95
they'd just lay there and wait until somebody came along and made a shish kebab out of them."

"Some other vessel," Terri said.

"That's right," Mel said. "Some vassal would come along and spear the bastard in the name of love. Or whatever the fuck it was they fought over in those days."

"Same things we fight over these days," Terri said.

Laura said, "Nothing's changed."

The color was still high in Laura's cheeks. Her eyes were bright. She   100
brought her glass to her lips.

Mel poured himself another drink. He looked at the label closely as if studying a long row of numbers. Then he slowly put the bottle down on the table and slowly reached for the tonic water.

"What about the old couple?" Laura said. "You didn't finish that story you started."

Laura was having a hard time lighting her cigarette. Her matches kept going out.

The sunshine inside the room was different now, changing, getting thinner. But the leaves outside the window were still shimmering, and I stared at the pattern they made on the panes and on the Formica counter. They weren't the same patterns, of course.

"What about the old couple?" I said.   105

"Older but wiser," Terri said.

Mel stared at her.

Terri said, "Go on with your story, hon. I was only kidding. Then what happened?"

"Terri, sometimes," Mel said.

110   "Please, Mel," Terri said. "Don't always be so serious, sweetie. Can't you take a joke?"

"Where's the joke?" Mel said.

He held his glass and gazed steadily at his wife.

"What happened?" Laura said.

Mel fastened his eyes on Laura. He said, "Laura, if I didn't have Terri and if I didn't love her so much, and if Nick wasn't my best friend, I'd fall in love with you, I'd carry you off, honey," he said.

115   "Tell your story," Terri said. "Then we'll go to that new place, okay?"

"Okay," Mel said. "Where was I?" he said. He stared at the table and then he began again.

"I dropped in to see each of them every day, sometimes twice a day if I was up doing other calls anyway. Casts and bandages, head to foot, the both of them. You know, you've seen it in the movies. That's just the way they looked, just like in the movies. Little eye-holes and nose-holes and mouth-holes. And she had to have her legs slung up on top of it. Well, the husband was very depressed for the longest while. Even after he found out that his wife was going to pull through, he was still very depressed. Not about the accident, though. I mean, the accident was one thing, but it wasn't everything. I'd get up to his mouth-hole, you know, and he'd say no, it wasn't the accident exactly but it was because he couldn't see her through his eye-holes. He said that was what was making him feel so bad. Can you imagine? I'm telling you, the man's heart was breaking because he couldn't turn his goddamn head and *see* his goddamn wife."

Mel looked around the table and shook his head at what he was going to say.

"I mean, it was killing the old fart just because he couldn't *look* at the fucking woman."

120   We all looked at Mel.

"Do you see what I'm saying?" he said.

Maybe we were a little drunk by then. I know it was hard keeping things in focus. The light was draining out of the room, going back through the window where it had come from. Yet nobody made a move to get up from the table to turn on the overhead light.

"Listen," Mel said. "Let's finish this fucking gin. There's about enough left here for one shooter all around. Then let's go eat. Let's go to the new place."

"He's depressed," Terri said. "Mel, why don't you take a pill?"

125   Mel shook his head. "I've taken everything there is."

"We all need a pill now and then," I said.

"Some people are born needing them," Terri said.

She was using her finger to rub at something on the table. Then she stopped rubbing.

"I think I want to call my kids," Mel said. "Is that all right with everybody? I'll call my kids," he said.

Terri said, "What if Marjorie answers the phone? You guys, you've 130 heard us on the subject of Marjorie? Honey, you know you don't want to talk to Marjorie. It'll make you feel even worse."

"I don't want to talk to Marjorie," Mel said. "But I want to talk to my kids."

"There isn't a day goes by that Mel doesn't say he wishes she'd get married again. Or else die," Terri said. "For one thing," Terri said, "she's bankrupting us. Mel says it's just to spite him that she won't get married again. She has a boyfriend who lives with her and the kids, so Mel is supporting the boyfriend too."

"She's allergic to bees," Mel said. "If I'm not praying she'll get married again, I'm praying she'll get herself stung to death by a swarm of fucking bees."

"Shame on you," Laura said.

"Bzzzzzzz," Mel said, turning his fingers into bees and buzzing them 135 at Terri's throat. Then he let his hands drop all the way to his sides.

"She's vicious," Mel said. "Sometimes I think I'll go up there dressed like a beekeeper. You know, that hat that's like a helmet with the plate that comes down over your face, the big gloves, and the padded coat? I'll knock on the door and let loose a hive of bees in the house. But first I'd make sure the kids were out, of course."

He crossed one leg over the other. It seemed to take him a lot of time to do it. Then he put both feet on the floor and leaned forward, elbows on the table, his chin cupped in his hands.

"Maybe I won't call the kids, after all. Maybe it isn't such a hot idea. Maybe we'll just go eat. How does that sound?"

"Sounds fine to me," I said. "Eat or not eat. Or keep drinking. I could head right on out into the sunset."

"What does that mean, honey?" Laura said. 140

"It just means what I said," I said. "It means I could just keep going. That's all it means."

"I could eat something myself," Laura said. "I don't think I've ever been so hungry in my life. Is there something to nibble on?"

"I'll put out some cheese and crackers," Terri said.

But Terri just sat there. She did not get up to get anything.

Mel turned his glass over. He spilled it out on the table. 145

"Gin's gone," Mel said.

Terri said, "Now what?"

I could hear my heart beating. I could hear everyone's heart. I could hear the human noise we sat there making, not one of us moving, not even when the room went dark.

KATE CHOPIN

The Story of an Hour

Knowing that Mrs. Mallard was afflicted with a heart trouble, great care was taken to break to her as gently as possible the news of her husband's death.

It was her sister Josephine who told her, in broken sentences, veiled hints that revealed in half concealing. Her husband's friend Richards was there, too, near her. It was he who had been in the newspaper office when intelligence of the railroad disaster was received, with Brently Mallard's name leading the list of "killed." He had only taken the time to assure himself of its truth by a second telegram, and had hastened to forestall any less careful, less tender friend in bearing the sad message.

She did not hear the story as many women have heard the same, with a paralyzed inability to accept its significance. She wept at once, with sudden, wild abandonment, in her sister's arms. When the storm of grief had spent itself she went away to her room alone. She would have no one follow her.

There stood, facing the open window, a comfortable, roomy armchair. Into this she sank, pressed down by a physical exhaustion that haunted her body and seemed to reach into her soul.

5 She could see in the open square before her house the tops of trees that were all aquiver with the new spring life. The delicious breath of rain was in the air. In the street below a peddler was crying his wares. The notes of a distant song which some one was singing reached her faintly, and countless sparrows were twittering in the eaves.

There were patches of blue sky showing here and there through the clouds that had met and piled one above the other in the west facing her window.

She sat with her head thrown back upon the cushion of the chair, quite motionless, except when a sob came up into her throat and shook her, as a child who has cried itself to sleep continues to sob in its dreams.

She was young, with a fair, calm face, whose lines bespoke repression and even a certain strength. But now there was a dull stare in her eyes, whose gaze was fixed away off yonder on one of those patches of blue sky. It was not a glance of reflection, but rather indicated a suspension of intelligent thought.

THE STORY OF AN HOUR   First published in 1894. Kate Chopin (1851–1904) is best known for her novel *The Awakening* (1899), which scandalized nineteenth-century critics with its frank treatment of adultery and of a woman's sexual awakening. Chopin was also a prolific short-story writer who often wrote about women trapped in stifling, unhappy marriages.

There was something coming to her and she was waiting for it, fearfully. What was it? She did not know; it was too subtle and elusive to name. But she felt it, creeping out of the sky, reaching toward her through the sounds, the scents, the color that filled the air.

Now her bosom rose and fell tumultuously. She was beginning to 10 recognize this thing that was approaching to possess her, and she was striving to beat it back with her will—as powerless as her two white slender hands would have been.

When she abandoned herself a little whispered word escaped her slightly parted lips. She said it over and over under her breath: "Free, free, free!" The vacant stare and the look of terror that had followed it went from her eyes. They stayed keen and bright. Her pulses beat fast, and the coursing blood warmed and relaxed every inch of her body.

She did not stop to ask if it were not a monstrous joy that held her. A clear and exalted perception enabled her to dismiss the suggestion as trivial.

She knew that she would weep again when she saw the kind, tender hands folded in death; the face that had never looked save with love upon her, fixed and gray and dead. But she saw beyond that bitter moment a long procession of years to come that would belong to her absolutely. And she opened and spread her arms out to them in welcome.

There would be no one to live for during those coming years; she would live for herself. There would be no powerful will bending her in that blind persistence with which men and women believe they have a right to impose a private will upon a fellow creature. A kind intention or a cruel intention made the act seem no less a crime as she looked upon it in that brief moment of illumination.

And yet she had loved him—sometimes. Often she had not. What 15 did it matter! What could love, the unsolved mystery, count for in the face of this possession of self-assertion which she suddenly recognized as the strongest impulse of her being.

"Free! Body and soul free!" she kept whispering.

Josephine was kneeling before the closed door with her lips to the keyhole, imploring for admission. "Louise, open the door! I beg; open the door—you will make yourself ill. What are you doing, Louise? For heaven's sake open the door."

"Go away. I am not making myself ill." No; she was drinking in a very elixir of life through that open window.

Her fancy was running riot along those days ahead of her. Spring days, and summer days, and all sorts of days that would be her own. She breathed a quick prayer that life might be long. It was only yesterday she had thought with a shudder that life might be long.

20   She arose at length and opened the door to her sister's importunities. There was a feverish triumph in her eyes, and she carried herself unwittingly like a goddess of Victory. She clasped her sister's waist, and together they descended the stairs. Richards stood waiting for them at the bottom.

Some one was opening the front door with a latchkey. It was Brently Mallard who entered, a little travel-stained, composedly carrying his grip-sack and umbrella. He had been far from the scene of the accident, and did not even know there had been one. He stood amazed at Josephine's piercing cry; at Richards' quick motion to screen him from the view of his wife.

But Richards was too late.

When the doctors came they said she had died of heart disease—of joy that kills.

WILLIAM FAULKNER
A Rose for Emily

1

When Miss Emily Grierson died, our whole town went to her funeral: the men through a sort of respectful affection for a fallen monument, the women mostly out of curiosity to see the inside of her house, which no one save an old manservant—a combined gardener and cook—had seen in at least ten years.

It was a big, squarish frame house that had once been white, decorated with cupolas and spires and scrolled balconies in the heavily lightsome style of the seventies, set on what had once been our most select street. But garages and cotton gins had encroached and obliterated even the august names of that neighborhood; only Miss Emily's house was left, lifting its stubborn and coquettish decay above the cotton wagons and the gasoline pumps—an eyesore among eyesores. And now Miss Emily had gone to join the representatives of those august names where they lay in the cedar-bemused cemetery among the ranked and anonymous graves of Union and Confederate soldiers who fell at the battle of Jefferson.

Alive, Miss Emily had been a tradition, a duty, and a care; a sort of hereditary obligation upon the town, dating from that day in 1894 when Colonel Sartoris, the mayor—he who fathered the edict that no Negro woman should appear on the streets without an apron—remitted her taxes,

A ROSE FOR EMILY   First published in 1930. William Faulkner (1897–1962) spent most of his life in Oxford, Mississippi, the small town he mythologized as "Jefferson" in his fiction. Faulkner's novels and stories often portray small-town southerners isolated psychologically—sometimes to an extreme degree—from the modern world. He won the Nobel Prize for literature in 1950.

the dispensation dating from the death of her father on into perpetuity. Not that Miss Emily would have accepted charity. Colonel Sartoris invented an involved tale to the effect that Miss Emily's father had loaned money to the town, which the town, as a matter of business, preferred this way of repaying. Only a man of Colonel Sartoris' generation and thought could have invented it, and only a woman could have believed it.

When the next generation, with its more modern ideas, became mayors and aldermen, this arrangement created some little dissatisfaction. On the first of the year they mailed her a tax notice. February came, and there was no reply. They wrote her a formal letter, asking her to call at the sheriff's office at her convenience. A week later the mayor wrote her himself, offering to call or to send his car for her, and received in reply a note on paper of an archaic shape, in a thin, flowing calligraphy in faded ink, to the effect that she no longer went out at all. The tax notice was also enclosed, without comment.

They called a special meeting of the Board of Aldermen. A deputa- 5 tion waited upon her, knocked at the door through which no visitor had passed since she ceased giving china-painting lessons eight or ten years earlier. They were admitted by the old Negro into a dim hall from which a stairway mounted into still more shadow. It smelled of dust and disuse—a close, dank smell. The Negro led them into the parlor. It was furnished in heavy, leather-covered furniture. When the Negro opened the blinds of one window, a faint dust rose sluggishly about their thighs, spinning with slow motes in the single sun ray. On a tarnished gilt easel before the fireplace stood a crayon portrait of Miss Emily's father.

They rose when she entered—a small, fat woman in black, with a thin gold chain descending to her waist and vanishing into her belt, leaning on an ebony cane with a tarnished gold head. Her skeleton was small and spare; perhaps that was why what would have been merely plumpness in another was obesity in her. She looked bloated, like a body long submerged in motionless water, and of that pallid hue. Her eyes, lost in the fatty ridges of her face, looked like two small pieces of coal pressed into a lump of dough as they moved from one face to another while the visitors stated their errand.

She did not ask them to sit. She just stood in the door and listened quietly until the spokesman came to a stumbling halt. Then they could hear the invisible watch ticking at the end of the gold chain.

Her voice was dry and cold. "I have no taxes in Jefferson. Colonel Sartoris explained it to me. Perhaps one of you can gain access to the city records and satisfy yourselves."

"But we have. We are the city authorities, Miss Emily. Didn't you get a notice from the sheriff, signed by him?"

10   "I received a paper, yes," Miss Emily said. "Perhaps he considers himself the sheriff.... I have no taxes in Jefferson."

"But there is nothing on the books to show that, you see. We must go by the—"

"See Colonel Sartoris. I have no taxes in Jefferson."

"But, Miss Emily—"

"See Colonel Sartoris." (Colonel Sartoris had been dead almost ten years.) "I have no taxes in Jefferson. Tobe!" The Negro appeared. "Show these gentlemen out."

2

15   So she vanquished them, horse and foot, just as she had vanquished their fathers thirty years before about the smell. That was two years after her father's death and a short time after her sweetheart—the one we believed would marry her—had deserted her. After her father's death she went out very little; after her sweetheart went away, people hardly saw her at all. A few of the ladies had the temerity to call, but were not received, and the only sign of life about the place was the Negro man—a young man then—going in and out with a market basket.

"Just as if a man—any man—could keep a kitchen properly," the ladies said; so they were not surprised when the smell developed. It was another link between the gross, teeming world and the high and mighty Griersons.

A neighbor, a woman, complained to the mayor, Judge Stevens, eighty years old.

"But what will you have me do about it, madam?" he said.

"Why, send her word to stop it," the woman said. "Isn't there a law?"

20   "I'm sure that won't be necessary," Judge Stevens said. "It's probably just a snake or a rat that nigger of hers killed in the yard. I'll speak to him about it."

The next day he received two more complaints, one from a man who came in diffident deprecation. "We really must do something about it, Judge. I'd be the last one in the world to bother Miss Emily, but we've got to do something." That night the Board of Aldermen met—three gray-beards and one younger man, a member of the rising generation.

"It's simple enough," he said. "Send her word to have her place cleaned up. Give her a certain time to do it in, and if she don't . . ."

"Dammit, sir," Judge Stevens said, "will you accuse a lady to her face of smelling bad?"

So the next night, after midnight, four men crossed Miss Emily's lawn and slunk about the house like burglars, sniffing along the base of the brickwork and at the cellar openings while one of them performed a regular sowing motion with his hand out of a sack slung from his shoulder. They broke open the cellar door and sprinkled lime there, and in all the outbuildings. As they recrossed the lawn, a window that had been dark was lighted and Miss Emily sat in it, the light behind her, and her upright torso motionless as that of an idol. They crept quietly across the lawn and into the shadow of the locusts that lined the street. After a week or two the smell went away.

That was when people had begun to feel really sorry for her. People 25 in our town, remembering how old lady Wyatt, her great-aunt, had gone completely crazy at last, believed that the Griersons held themselves a little too high for what they really were. None of the young men were quite good enough for Miss Emily and such. We had long thought of them as a tableau; Miss Emily a slender figure in white in the background, her father a spraddled silhouette in the foreground, his back to her and clutching a horsewhip, the two of them framed by the back-flung front door. So when she got to be thirty and was still single, we were not pleased exactly, but vindicated; even with insanity in the family she wouldn't have turned down all of her chances if they had really materialized.

When her father died, it got about that the house was all that was left to her; and in a way, people were glad. At last they could pity Miss Emily. Being left alone, and a pauper, she had become humanized. Now she too would know the old thrill and the old despair of a penny more or less.

The day after his death all the ladies prepared to call at the house and offer condolence and aid, as is our custom. Miss Emily met them at the door, dressed as usual and with no trace of grief on her face. She told them that her father was not dead. She did that for three days, with the ministers calling on her, and the doctors, trying to persuade her to let them dispose of the body. Just as they were about to resort to law and force, she broke down, and they buried her father quickly.

We did not say she was crazy then. We believed she had to do that. We remembered all the young men her father had driven away, and we knew that with nothing left, she would have to cling to that which had robbed her, as people will.

3

She was sick for a long time. When we saw her again, her hair was cut short, making her look like a girl, with a vague resemblance to those angels in colored church windows—sort of tragic and serene.

The town had just let the contracts for paving the sidewalks, and in 30 the summer after her father's death they began to work. The construction company came with niggers and mules and machinery, and a foreman named Homer Barron, a Yankee—a big, dark, ready man, with a big voice and eyes lighter than his face. The little boys would follow in groups to hear him cuss the niggers, and the niggers singing in time to the rise and fall of picks. Pretty soon he knew everybody in town. Whenever you heard a lot of laughing anywhere about the square, Homer Barron would be in the center of the group. Presently we began to see him and Miss Emily on Sunday afternoons driving in the yellow-wheeled buggy and the matched team of bays from the livery stable.

At first we were glad that Miss Emily would have an interest, because the ladies all said, "Of course a Grierson would not think seriously of a Northerner, a day laborer." But there were still others, older people, who said that even grief could not cause a real lady to forget *noblesse oblige*— without calling it *noblesse oblige*. They just said, "Poor Emily. Her kinsfolk should come to her." She had some kin in Alabama; but years ago her father had fallen out with them over the estate of old lady Wyatt, the crazy woman, and there was no communication between the two families. They had not even been represented at the funeral.

And as soon as the old people said, "Poor Emily," the whispering began. "Do you suppose it's really so?" they said to one another. "Of course it is. What else could . . ." This behind their hands; rustling of craned silk and satin behind jalousies closed upon the sun of Sunday afternoon as the thin, swift clop-clop-clop of the matched team passed: "Poor Emily."

She carried her head high enough—even when we believed that she was fallen. It was as if she demanded more than ever the recognition of her dignity as the last Grierson; as if it had wanted that touch of earthiness to reaffirm her imperviousness. Like when she bought the rat poison, the arsenic. That was over a year after they had begun to say "Poor Emily," and while the two female cousins were visiting her.

"I want some poison," she said to the druggist. She was over thirty then, still a slight woman, though thinner than usual, with cold, haughty black eyes in a face the flesh of which was strained across the temples and about the eyesockets as you imagine a lighthouse-keeper's face ought to look. "I want some poison," she said.

35   "Yes, Miss Emily. What kind? For rats and such? I'd recom—"

"I want the best you have. I don't care what kind."

The druggist named several. "They'll kill anything up to an elephant. But what you want is—"

"Arsenic," Miss Emily said. "Is that a good one?"

"Is . . . arsenic? Yes ma'am. But what you want—"

40   "I want arsenic."

The druggist looked down at her. She looked back at him, erect, her face like a strained flag. "Why, of course," the druggist said. "If that's what you want. But the law requires you to tell what you are going to use it for."

Miss Emily just stared at him, her head tilted back in order to look him eye for eye, until he looked away and went and got the arsenic and wrapped it up. The Negro delivery boy brought her the package; the druggist didn't come back. When she opened the package at home there was written on the box, under the skull and bones: "For rats."

4

So the next day we all said, "She will kill herself"; and we said it would be the best thing. When she had first begun to be seen with Homer Barron, we had said, "She will marry him." Then we said, "She will persuade him yet," because Homer himself had remarked—he liked men, and it was known that he drank with the younger men in the Elk's Club—that he was not a marrying man. Later we said, "Poor Emily," behind the jalousies as they passed on Sunday afternoon in the glittering buggy, Miss Emily with her head high and Homer Barron with his hat cocked and a cigar in his teeth, reins and whip in a yellow glove.

Then some of the ladies began to say that it was a disgrace to the town and a bad example to the young people. The men did not want to interfere, but at last the ladies forced the Baptist minister—Miss Emily's people were Episcopal—to call upon her. He would never divulge what happened during that interview, but he refused to go back again. The next Sunday they again drove about the streets, and the following day the minister's wife wrote to Miss Emily's relations in Alabama.

So she had blood-kin under her roof again and we sat back to watch   45 developments. At first nothing happened. Then we were sure that they were to be married. We learned that Miss Emily had been to the jeweler's and ordered a man's toilet set in silver, with the letters H. B. on each piece. Two days later we learned that she had bought a complete outfit of men's clothing, including a nightshirt, and we said, "They are married." We were really glad. We were glad because the two female cousins were even more Grierson than Miss Emily had ever been.

So we were not surprised when Homer Barron—the streets had been finished some time since—was gone. We were a little disappointed that there was not a public blowing-off, but we believed that he had gone on to prepare for Miss Emily's coming, or to give her a chance to get rid of the cousins. (By that time it was a cabal, and we were all Miss Emily's allies to help circumvent the cousins.) Sure enough, after another week they departed. And, as we had expected all along, within three days Homer Barron was back in town. A neighbor saw the Negro man admit him at the kitchen door at dusk one evening.

And that was the last we saw of Homer Barron. And of Miss Emily for some time. The Negro man went in and out with the market basket, but the front door remained closed. Now and then we would see her at a window for a moment, as the men did that night when they sprinkled the lime, but for almost six months she did not appear on the streets. Then we knew that this was to be expected too; as if that quality of her father which had thwarted her woman's life so many times had been too virulent and too furious to die.

When we next saw Miss Emily, she had grown fat and her hair was turning gray. During the next few years it grew grayer and grayer until it attained an even pepper-and-salt iron-gray, when it ceased turning. Up to the day of her death at seventy-four it was still that vigorous iron-gray, like the hair of an active man.

From that time on her front door remained closed, save for a period of six or seven years, when she was about forty, during which she gave lessons in china-painting. She fitted up a studio in one of the downstairs rooms, where the daughters and grand-daughters of Colonel Sartoris' contemporaries were sent to her with the same regularity and in the same spirit that they were sent on Sundays with a twenty-five cent piece for the collection plate. Meanwhile her taxes had been remitted.

50   Then the newer generation became the backbone and the spirit of the town, and the painting pupils grew up and fell away and did not send their children to her with boxes of color and tedious brushes and pictures cut from the ladies' magazines. The front door closed upon the last one and remained closed for good. When the town got free postal delivery Miss Emily alone refused to let them fasten the metal numbers above her door and attach a mailbox to it. She would not listen to them.

Daily, monthly, yearly we watched the Negro grow grayer and more stooped, going in and out with the market basket. Each December we sent her a tax notice, which would be returned by the post office a week later, unclaimed. Now and then we would see her in one of the downstairs windows—she had evidently shut up the top floor of the house—like the carven torso of an idol in a niche, looking or not looking at us, we could never tell which. Thus she passed from generation to generation—dear, inescapable, impervious, tranquil, and perverse.

And so she died. Fell ill in the house filled with dust and shadows, with only a doddering Negro man to wait on her. We did not even know she was sick; we had long since given up trying to get any information from the Negro. He talked to no one, probably not even to her, for his voice had grown harsh and rusty, as if from disuse.

She died in one of the downstairs rooms, in a heavy walnut bed with a curtain, her gray head propped on a pillow yellow and moldy with age and lack of sunlight.

5

The Negro met the first of the ladies at the front door and let them in, with their hushed, sibilant voices and their quick, curious glances, and then he disappeared. He walked right through the house and out the back and was not seen again.

The two female cousins came at once. They held the funeral on the 55 second day, with the town coming to look at Miss Emily beneath a mass of bought flowers, with the crayon face of her father musing profoundly above the bier and the ladies sibilant and macabre; and the very old men—some in their brushed Confederate uniforms—on the porch and the lawn, talking of Miss Emily as if she had been a contemporary of theirs, believing that they had danced with her and courted her perhaps, confusing time with its mathematical progression, as the old do, to whom all the past is not a diminishing road, but, instead, a huge meadow which no winter ever quite touches, divided from them now by the narrow bottleneck of the most recent decade of years.

Already we knew that there was one room in that region above stairs which no one had seen in forty years, and which would have to be forced. They waited until Miss Emily was decently in the ground before they opened it.

The violence of breaking down the door seemed to fill this room with pervading dust. A thin, acrid pall as of the tomb seemed to lie everywhere upon this room decked and furnished as for a bridal: upon the valance curtains of faded rose color, upon the rose-shaded lights, upon the dressing table, upon the delicate array of crystal and the man's toilet things backed with tarnished silver, silver so tarnished that the monogram was obscured. Among them lay a collar and tie, as if they had just been removed, which, lifted, left upon the surface a pale crescent in the dust. Upon a chair hung the suit, carefully folded; beneath it the two mute shoes and the discarded socks.

The man himself lay in the bed.

For a long while we just stood there, looking down at the profound and fleshless grin. The body had apparently once lain in the attitude of an embrace, but now the long sleep that outlasts love, that conquers even the grimace of love, had cuckolded him. What was left of him, rotted beneath what was left of the nightshirt, had become inextricable from the bed in which he lay; and upon him and upon the pillow beside him lay that even coating of the patient and biding dust.

Then we noticed that in the second pillow was the indentation of a 60 head. One of us lifted something from it, and leaning forward, that faint and invisible dust dry and acrid in the nostrils, we saw a long strand of iron-gray hair.

SUSAN GLASPELL
A Jury of Her Peers

When Martha Hale opened the storm door and got a cut of the north wind, she ran back for her big woolen scarf. As she hurriedly wound that round her head her eye made a scandalized sweep of her kitchen. It was no ordinary thing that called her away—it was probably farther from ordinary than anything that had ever happened in Dickson County. But what her eye took in was that her kitchen was in no shape for leaving: her bread all ready for mixing, half the flour sifted and half unsifted.

She hated to see things half done; but she had been at that when the team from town stopped to get Mr. Hale, and then the sheriff came running in to say his wife wished Mrs. Hale would come too—adding, with a grin, that he guessed she was getting scarey and wanted another woman along. So she had dropped everything right where it was.

"Martha!" now came her husband's impatient voice. "Don't keep folks waiting out here in the cold."

She again opened the storm door, and this time joined the three men and the one woman waiting for her in the big two-seated buggy.

5   After she had the robes tucked around her she took another look at the woman who sat beside her on the back seat. She had met Mrs. Peters the year before at the county fair, and the thing she remembered about her was that she didn't seem like a sheriff's wife. She was small and thin and didn't have a strong voice. Mrs. Gorman, sheriff's wife before Gorman went out and Peters came in, had a voice that somehow seemed to be backing up the law with every word. But if Mrs. Peters didn't look like a sheriff's wife, Peters made it up in looking like a sheriff. He was to a dot the kind of man who could get himself elected sheriff—a heavy man with a big voice, who was particularly genial with the law-abiding, as if to make it plain that he knew the difference between criminals and non-criminals. And right there it came into Mrs. Hale's mind, with a stab, that this man who was so pleasant and lively with all of them was going to the Wrights' now as a sheriff.

"The country's not very pleasant this time of year," Mrs. Peters at last ventured, as if she felt they ought to be talking as well as the men.

Mrs. Hale scarcely finished her reply, for they had gone up a little hill and could see the Wright place now, and seeing it did not make her feel like talking. It looked very lonesome this cold March morning. It had

A JURY OF HER PEERS   First published in 1917, the story is based on the author's one-act play *Trifles*, written in 1916 for the Provincetown Players. Susan Glaspell (1882–1948) lived for the first thirty-two years of her life in Iowa. She said that *Trifles* (and hence this short story) was suggested to her by an experience she had while working for a Des Moines newspaper.

always been a lonesome-looking place. It was down in a hollow, and the poplar trees around it were lonesome-looking trees. The men were looking at it and talking about what had happened. The county attorney was bending to one side of the buggy, and kept looking steadily at the place as they drew up to it.

"I'm glad you came with me," Mrs. Peters said nervously, as the two women were about to follow the men in through the kitchen door.

Even after she had her foot on the doorstep, her hand on the knob, Martha Hale had a moment of feeling she could not cross the threshold. And the reason it seemed she couldn't cross it now was simply because she hadn't crossed it before. Time and time again it had been in her mind, "I ought to go over and see Minnie Foster"—she still thought of her as Minnie Foster, though for twenty years she had been Mrs. Wright. And then there was always something to do and Minnie Foster would go from her mind. But *now* she could come.

The men went over to the stove. The women stood close together by 10 the door. Young Henderson, the county attorney, turned around and said, "Come up to the fire, ladies."

Mrs. Peters took a step forward, then stopped. "I'm not—cold," she said.

And so the two women stood by the door, at first not even so much as looking around the kitchen.

The men talked for a minute about what a good thing it was the sheriff had sent his deputy out that morning to make a fire for them, and then Sheriff Peters stepped back from the stove, unbuttoned his outer coat, and leaned his hands on the kitchen table in a way that seemed to mark the beginning of official business. "Now, Mr. Hale," he said in a sort of semi-official voice, "before we move things about, you tell Mr. Henderson just what it was you saw when you came here yesterday morning."

The county attorney was looking around the kitchen,

"By the way," he said, "has anything been moved?" He turned to the 15 sheriff. "Are things just as you left them yesterday?"

Peters looked from cupboard to sink; from that to a small worn rocker a little to one side of the kitchen table.

"It's just the same."

"Somebody should have been left here yesterday," said the county attorney.

"Oh—yesterday," returned the sheriff, with a little gesture as of yesterday having been more than he could bear to think of. "When I had to send Frank to Morris Center for that man who went crazy—let me tell you, I had my hands full *yesterday*. I knew you could get back from Omaha by today, George, and as long as I went over everything here myself—"

20   "Well, Mr. Hale," said the county attorney, in a way of letting what was past and gone go, "tell just what happened when you came here yesterday morning."

Mrs. Hale, still leaning against the door, had that sinking feeling of the mother whose child is about to speak a piece. Lewis often wandered along and got things mixed up in a story. She hoped he would tell this straight and plain, and not say unnecessary things that would just make things harder for Minnie Foster. He didn't begin at once, and she noticed that he looked queer—as if standing in that kitchen and having to tell what he had seen there yesterday morning made him almost sick.

"Yes, Mr. Hale?" the county attorney reminded.

"Harry and I had started to town with a load of potatoes," Mrs. Hale's husband began.

Harry was Mrs. Hale's oldest boy. He wasn't with them now, for the very good reason that those potatoes never got to town yesterday and he was taking them this morning, so he hadn't been home when the sheriff stopped to say he wanted Mr. Hale to come over to the Wright place and tell the county attorney his story there, where he could point it all out. With all Mrs. Hale's other emotions came the fear that maybe Harry wasn't dressed warm enough—they hadn't any of them realized how that north wind did bite.

25   "We come along this road," Hale was going on, with a motion of his hand to the road over which they had just come, "and as we got in sight of the house I says to Harry, 'I'm goin' to see if I can't get John Wright to take a telephone.' You see," he explained to Henderson, "unless I can get somebody to go in with me they won't come out this branch road except for a price I can't pay. I'd spoke to Wright about it once before; but he put me off, saying folks talked too much anyway, and all he asked was peace and quiet—guess you know about how much he talked himself. But I thought maybe if I went to the house and talked about it before his wife, and said all the women-folks liked the telephones, and that in this lonesome stretch of road it would be a good thing—well, I said to Harry that that was what I was going to say—though I said at the same time that I didn't know as what his wife wanted made much difference to John—"

Now, there he was!—saying things he didn't need to say. Mrs. Hale tried to catch her husband's eye, but fortunately the county attorney interrupted with:

"Let's talk about that a little later, Mr. Hale. I do want to talk about that, but I'm anxious now to get along to just what happened when you got here."

When he began this time, it was very deliberately and carefully:

"I didn't see or hear anything. I knocked at the door. And still it was all quiet inside. I knew they must be up—it was past eight o'clock.

So I knocked again, louder, and I thought I heard somebody say 'Come in.' I wasn't sure—I'm not sure yet. But I opened the door—this door," jerking a hand toward the door by which the two women stood, "and there, in that rocker"—pointing to it—"sat Mrs. Wright."

Every one in the kitchen looked at the rocker. It came into Mrs. Hale's 30 mind that that rocker didn't look in the least like Minnie Foster—the Minnie Foster of twenty years before. It was a dingy red, with wooden rungs up the back, and the middle rung was gone, and the chair sagged to one side.

"How did she—look?" the county attorney was inquiring.

"Well," said Hale, "she looked—queer."

"How do you mean—queer?"

As he asked it he took out a notebook and pencil. Mrs. Hale did not like the sight of that pencil. She kept her eye fixed on her husband, as if to keep him from saying unnecessary things that would go into that notebook and make trouble.

Hale did speak guardedly, as if the pencil had affected him too.   35

"Well, as if she didn't know what she was going to do next. And kind of—done up."

"How did she seem to feel about your coming?"

"Why, I don't think she minded—one way or other. She didn't pay much attention. I said, 'Ho' do, Mrs. Wright? It's cold, ain't it?' And she said, 'Is it?'—and went on pleatin' at her apron.

"Well, I was surprised. She didn't ask me to come up to the stove, or to sit down, but just set there, not even lookin' at me. And so I said: 'I want to see John.'

"And then she—laughed. I guess you would call it a laugh.   40

"I thought of Harry and the team outside, so I said, a little sharp, 'Can I see John?' 'No,' says she—kind of dull like. 'Ain't he home?' says I. Then she looked at me. 'Yes,' says she, 'he's home.' 'Then why can't I see him?' I asked her, out of patience with her now. ''Cause he's dead,' says she, just as quiet and dull—and fell to pleatin' her apron. 'Dead?' says I, like you do when you can't take in what you've heard.

"She just nodded her head, not getting a bit excited, but rockin' back and forth.

" 'Why—where is he?' says I, not knowing *what* to say.

"She just pointed upstairs—like this"—pointing to the room above.

"I got up, with the idea of going up there myself. By this time I—   45 didn't know what to do. I walked from there to here; then I says: 'Why, what did he die of?'

" 'He died of a rope around his neck,' says she; and just went on pleatin' at her apron."

Hale stopped speaking, and stood staring at the rocker, as if he were still seeing the woman who had sat there the morning before. Nobody spoke; it was as if every one were seeing the woman who had sat there the morning before.

"And what did you do then?" the county attorney at last broke the silence.

"I went out and called Harry. I thought I might—need help. I got Harry in, and we went upstairs." His voice fell almost to a whisper. "There he was—lying over the—"

50 "I think I'd rather have you go into that upstairs," the county attorney interrupted, "where you can point it all out. Just go on now with the rest of the story."

"Well, my first thought was to get that rope off. It looked—"

He stopped, his face twitching.

"But Harry, he went up to him, and he said, 'No, he's dead all right, and we'd better not touch anything.' So we went downstairs.

"She was still sitting that same way. 'Has anybody been notified?' I asked. 'No,' says she, unconcerned."

55 "'Who did this, Mrs. Wright?' said Harry. He said it businesslike, and she stopped pleatin' at her apron. 'I don't know,' she says. 'You don't *know?*' says Harry. 'Weren't you sleepin' in the bed with him?' 'Yes,' says she, 'but I was on the inside.' 'Somebody slipped a rope round his neck and strangled him, and you didn't wake up?' says Harry. 'I didn't wake up,' she said after him.

"We may have looked as if we didn't see how that could be, for after a minute she said, 'I sleep sound.'

"Harry was going to ask her more questions, but I said maybe that weren't our business; maybe we ought to let her tell her story first to the coroner or the sheriff. So Harry went fast as he could over to High Road—the Rivers's place, where there's a telephone."

"And what did she do when she knew you had gone for the coroner?" The attorney got his pencil in his hand all ready for writing.

"She moved from that chair to this one over here"—Hale pointed to a small chair in the corner—"and just sat there with her hands held together and looking down. I got a feeling that I ought to make some conversation, so I said I had come in to see if John wanted to put in a telephone; and at that she started to laugh, and then she stopped and looked at me—scared."

60 At the sound of a moving pencil the man who was telling the story looked up.

"I dunno—maybe it wasn't scared," he hastened; "I wouldn't like to say it was. Soon Harry got back, and then Dr. Lloyd came, and you, Mr. Peters, and so I guess that's all I know that you don't."

He said that last with relief, and moved a little, as if relaxing. Every one moved a little. The county attorney walked toward the stair door.

"I guess we'll go upstairs first—then out to the barn and around there."

He paused and looked around the kitchen.

"You're convinced there was nothing important here?" he asked the 65 sheriff. "Nothing that would—point to any motive?"

The sheriff too looked all around, as if to re-convince himself.

"Nothing here but kitchen things," he said, with a little laugh for the insignificance of kitchen things.

The county attorney was looking at the cupboard—a peculiar, ungainly structure, half closet and half cupboard, the upper part of it being built in the wall, and the lower part just the old-fashioned kitchen cupboard. As if its queerness attracted him, he got a chair and opened the upper part and looked in. After a moment he drew his hand away sticky.

"Here's a nice mess," he said resentfully.

The two women had drawn nearer, and now the sheriff's wife spoke. 70

"Oh—her fruit," she said, looking to Mrs. Hale for sympathetic understanding. She turned back to the county attorney and explained: "She worried about that when it turned so cold last night. She said the fire would go out and her jars might burst."

Mrs. Peters's husband broke into a laugh.

"Well, can you beat the women! Held for murder, and worrying about her preserves!"

The young attorney set his lips.

"I guess before we're through with her she may have something more 75 serious than preserves to worry about."

"Oh, well," said Mrs. Hale's husband, with good-natured superiority, "women are used to worrying over trifles."

The two women moved a little closer together. Neither of them spoke. The county attorney seemed suddenly to remember his manners—and think of his future.

"And yet," said he, with the gallantry of a young politician, "for all their worries, what would we do without the ladies?"

The women did not speak, did not unbend. He went to the sink and began washing his hands. He turned to wipe them on the roller wheel— whirled it for a cleaner place.

"Dirty towels! Not much of a housekeeper, would you say, ladies?" 80

He kicked his foot against some dirty pans under the sink.

"There's a great deal of work to be done on a farm," said Mrs. Hale stiffly.

"To be sure. And yet"—with a little bow to her—"I know there are some Dickson County farmhouses that do not have such roller towels." He gave it a pull to expose its full length again.

"Those towels get dirty awful quick. Men's hands aren't always as clean as they might be."

85 "Ah, loyal to your sex, I see," he laughed. He stopped and gave her a keen look. "But you and Mrs. Wright were neighbors. I suppose you were friends, too."

Martha Hale shook her head.

"I've seen little enough of her of late years. I've not been in this house—it's more than a year."

"And why was that? You didn't like her?"

"I liked her well enough," she replied with spirit. "Farmers' wives have their hands full, Mr. Henderson. And then—" She looked around the kitchen.

90 "Yes?" he encouraged.

"It never seemed a very cheerful place," said she, more to herself than to him.

"No," he agreed; "I don't think any one would call it cheerful. I shouldn't say she had the homemaking instinct."

"Well, I don't know as Wright had, either," she muttered.

"You mean they didn't get on very well?" he was quick to ask.

95 "No; I don't mean anything," she answered, with decision. As she turned a little away from him, she added: "But I don't think a place would be any the cheerfuler for John Wright's bein' in it."

"I'd like to talk to you about that a little later, Mrs. Hale," he said. "I'm anxious to get the lay of things upstairs now."

He moved toward the stair door, followed by the two men.

"I suppose anything Mrs. Peters does'll be all right?" the sheriff inquired. "She was to take in some clothes for her, you know—and a few little things. We left in such a hurry yesterday."

The county attorney looked at the two women whom they were leaving alone there among the kitchen things.

100 "Yes—Mrs. Peters," he said, his glance resting on the woman who was not Mrs. Peters, the big farmer woman who stood behind the sheriff's wife. "Of course Mrs. Peters is one of us," he said, in a manner of entrusting responsibility. "And keep your eye out, Mrs. Peters, for anything that might be of use. No telling; you women might come upon a clue to the motive—and that's the thing we need."

Mr. Hale rubbed his face after the fashion of a show man getting ready for a pleasantry.

"But would the women know a clue if they did come upon it!" he said; and, having delivered himself of this, he followed the others through the stair door.

The women stood motionless and silent, listening to the footsteps, first upon the stairs, then in the room above them.

Then, as if releasing herself from something strange, Mrs. Hale began to arrange the dirty pans under the sink, which the county attorney's disdainful push of the foot had deranged.

"I'd hate to have men comin' into my kitchen," she said testily— 105 "snoopin' round and criticizin'."

"Of course it's no more than their duty," said the sheriff's wife, in her manner of timid acquiescence.

"Duty's all right," replied Mrs. Hale bluffly; "but I guess that deputy sheriff that come out to make the fire might have got a little of this on." She gave the roller towel a pull. "Wish I'd thought of that sooner! Seems mean to talk about her for not having things slicked up, when she had to come away in such a hurry."

She looked around the kitchen. Certainly it was not "slicked up." Her eye was held by a bucket of sugar on a low shelf. The cover was off the wooden bucket, and beside it was a paper bag—half full.

Mrs. Hale moved toward it.

"She was putting this in here," she said to herself—slowly. 110

She thought of the flour in her kitchen at home—half sifted, half not sifted. She had been interrupted, and had left things half done. What had interrupted Minnie Foster? Why had that work been left half done? She made a move as if to finish it,—unfinished things always bothered her,—and then she glanced around and saw that Mrs. Peters was watching her—and she didn't want Mrs. Peters to get that feeling she had got of work begun and then—for some reason—not finished.

"It's a shame about her fruit," she said, and walked toward the cupboard that the county attorney had opened, and got on the chair, murmuring: "I wonder if it's all gone."

It was a sorry enough looking sight, but "Here's one that's all right," she said at last. She held it toward the light. "This is cherries, too." She looked again. "I declare I believe that's the only one."

With a sigh, she got down from the chair, went to the sink, and wiped off the bottle.

"She'll feel awful bad, after all her hard work in the hot weather. I 115 remember the afternoon I put up my cherries last summer!"

She set the bottle on the table, and, with another sigh, started to sit down in the rocker. But she did not sit down. Something kept her from sitting down in that chair. She straightened—stepped back, and, half turned away, stood looking at it, seeing the woman who sat there "pleatin' at her apron."

The thin voice of the sheriff's wife broke in upon her: "I must be getting those things from the front room closet." She opened the door into the other room, started in, stepped back. "You coming with me, Mrs. Hale?" she asked nervously. "You—you could help me get them."

"I suppose maybe the cat got it," suggested Mrs. Hale, resuming her sewing.

"No, she didn't have a cat. She's got that feeling some people have about cats—being afraid of them. When they brought her to our house yesterday, my cat got in the room, and she was real upset and asked me to take it out."

"My sister Bessie was like that," laughed Mrs. Hale.

The sheriff's wife did not reply. The silence made Mrs. Hale turn around. Mrs. Peters was examining the birdcage.

190 "Look at this door," she said slowly. "It's broke. One hinge has been pulled apart."

Mrs. Hale came nearer.

"Looks as if some one must have been—rough with it."

Again their eyes met—startled, questioning, apprehensive. For a moment neither spoke nor stirred. Then Mrs. Hale, turning away, said brusquely:

"If they're going to find any evidence, I wish they'd be about it. I don't like this place."

195 "But I'm awful glad you came with me, Mrs. Hale." Mrs. Peters put the birdcage on the table and sat down. "It would be lonesome for me—sitting here alone."

"Yes, it would, wouldn't it?" agreed Mrs. Hale, a certain determined naturalness in her voice. She picked up the sewing, but now it dropped in her lap, and she murmured in a different voice: "But I tell you what I *do* wish, Mrs. Peters. I wish I had come over sometimes when she was here. I wish—I had."

"But of course you were awful busy, Mrs. Hale. Your house—and your children."

"I could've come," retorted Mrs. Hale shortly. "I stayed away because it weren't cheerful—and that's why I ought to have come. I"—she looked around—"I've never liked this place. Maybe because it's down in a hollow and you don't see the road. I don't know what it is, but it's a lonesome place, and always was. I wish I had come over to see Minnie Foster some-times. I can see now—" She did not put it into words.

"Well, you mustn't reproach yourself," counseled Mrs. Peters. "Somehow, we just don't see how it is with other folks till—something comes up."

200 "Not having children makes less work," mused Mrs. Hale, after a silence, "but it makes a quiet house—and Wright out to work all day—and no company when he did come in. Did you know John Wright, Mrs. Peters?"

"Not to know him. I've seen him in town. They say he was a good man."

"Yes—good," conceded John Wright's neighbor grimly. "He didn't drink, and kept his word as well as most, I guess, and paid his debts. But he was a hard man, Mrs. Peters. Just to pass the time of day with him——." She stopped, shivered a little. "Like a raw wind that gets to the bone." Her eye fell upon the cage on the table before her, and she added, almost bitterly: "1 should think she would've wanted a bird!"

Suddenly she leaned forward, looking intently at the cage. "But what do you s'pose went wrong with it?"

"I don't know," returned Mrs. Peters; "unless it got sick and died."

But after she said it she reached over and swung the broken door. Both 205 women watched it as if somehow held by it.

"You didn't know—her?" Mrs. Hale asked, a gentler note in her voice.

"Not till they brought her yesterday," said the sheriff's wife.

"She—come to think of it, she was kind of like a bird herself. Real sweet and pretty, but kind of timid and—fluttery. How—she—did—change."

That held her for a long time. Finally, as if struck with a happy thought and relieved to get back to everyday things, she exclaimed:

"Tell you what, Mrs. Peters, why don't you take the quilt in with you? 210 It might take up her mind."

"Why, I think that's a real nice idea, Mrs. Hale," agreed the sheriff's wife, as if she too were glad to come into the atmosphere of a simple kindness. "There couldn't possibly be any objection to that, could there? Now, just what will I take? I wonder if her patches are in here—and her things."

They turned to the sewing basket.

"Here's some red," said Mrs. Hale, bringing out a roll of cloth. Underneath that was a box. "Here, maybe her scissors are in here—and her things." She held it up. "What a pretty box! I'll warrant that was something she had a long time ago—when she was a girl."

She held it in her hand a moment; then, with a little sigh, opened it. Instantly her hand went to her nose. 215

"Why—!"

Mrs. Peters drew nearer—then turned away.

"There's something wrapped up in this piece of silk," faltered Mrs. Hale.

"This isn't her scissors," said Mrs. Peters in a shrinking voice.

Her hand not steady, Mrs. Hale raised the piece of silk. "Oh, 220 Mrs. Peters!" she cried. "It's——"

Mrs. Peters bent closer.

"It's the bird," she whispered.

"But, Mrs. Peters!" cried Mrs. Hale. "*Look* at it! Its neck—look at its neck! It's all—other side *to*."

She held the box away from her.

225   The sheriff's wife again bent closer.

"Somebody wrung its neck," said she, in a voice that was slow and deep.

And then again the eyes of the two women met—this time clung together in a look of dawning comprehension, of growing horror. Mrs. Peters looked from the dead bird to the broken door of the cage. Again their eyes met. And just then there was a sound at the outside door.

Mrs. Hale slipped the box under the quilt pieces in the basket, and sank into the chair before it. Mrs. Peters stood holding to the table. The county attorney and the sheriff came in from outside.

"Well, ladies," said the county attorney, as one turning from serious things to little pleasantries, "have you decided whether she was going to quilt it or knot it?"

230   "We think," began the sheriff's wife in a flurried voice, "that she was going to—knot it."

He was too preoccupied to notice the change that came in her voice on that last.

"Well, that's very interesting, I'm sure," he said tolerantly. He caught sight of the birdcage. "Has the bird flown?"

"We think the cat got it," said Mrs. Hale in a voice curiously even.

He was walking up and down, as if thinking something out.

235   "Is there a cat?" he asked absently.

Mrs. Hale shot a look up at the sheriff's wife.

"Well, not *now*," said Mrs. Peters. "They're superstitious, you know; they leave."

She sank into the chair.

The county attorney did not heed her. "No sign at all of any one having come in from the outside," he said to Peters, in the manner of continuing an interrupted conversation. "Their own rope. Now let's go upstairs again and go over it, piece by piece. It would have to have been some one who knew just the—"

240   The stair door closed behind them and their voices were lost.

The two women sat motionless, not looking at each other, but as if peering into something and at the same time holding back. When they spoke now it was as if they were afraid of what they were saying, but as if they could not help saying it.

"She liked the bird," said Martha Hale, low and slowly. "She was going to bury it in that pretty box."

"When I was a girl," said Mrs. Peters, under her breath, "my kitten—there was a boy took a hatchet, and before my eyes—before I could get there—" She covered her face an instant. "If they hadn't held me back I would have"—she caught herself, looked upstairs where footsteps were heard, and finished weakly—"hurt him."

Then they sat without speaking or moving.

"I wonder how it would seem," Mrs. Hale at last began, as if feeling   245
her way over strange ground—"never to have had any children around?"
Her eyes made a slow sweep of the kitchen, as if seeing what that kitchen
had meant through all the years. "No, Wright wouldn't like the bird," she
said after that—"a thing that sang. She used to sing. He killed that too."
Her voice tightened.

Mrs. Peters moved uneasily.

"Of course we don't know who killed the bird."

"I knew John Wright," was Mrs. Hale's answer.

"It was an awful thing was done in this house that night, Mrs. Hale,"
said the sheriff's wife. "Killing a man while he slept—slipping a thing
round his neck that choked the life out of him."

Mrs. Hale's hand went out to the birdcage.   250

"His neck. Choked the life out of him."

"We don't *know* who killed him," whispered Mrs. Peters wildly. "We
don't *know*."

Mrs. Hale had not moved. "If there had been years and years of—
nothing, then a bird to sing to you, it would be awful—still—after the
bird was still."

It was as if something within her not herself had spoken, and it found
in Mrs. Peters something she did not know as herself.

"I know what stillness is," she said, in a queer, monotonous voice.   255
"When we homesteaded in Dakota, and my first baby died—after he was
two years old—and me with no other then—"

Mrs. Hale stirred.

"How soon do you suppose they'll be through looking for evidence?"

"I know what stillness is," repeated Mrs. Peters, in just that same way.
Then she too pulled back. "The law has got to punish crime, Mrs. Hale,"
she said in her tight little way.

"I wish you'd seen Minnie Foster," was the answer, "when she wore a
white dress with blue ribbons, and stood up there in the choir and sang."

The picture of that girl, the fact that she had lived neighbor to that   260
girl for twenty years, and had let her die for lack of life, was suddenly more
than she could bear.

"Oh, I *wish* I'd come over here once in a while!" she cried. "That was
a crime! That was a crime! Who's going to punish that?"

"We mustn't take on," said Mrs. Peters, with a frightened look toward
the stairs.

"I might 'a' *known* she needed help! I tell you, it's *queer*, Mrs. Peters. We live close together, and we live far apart. We all go through the same things—it's all just a different kind of the same thing! If it weren't—why do you and I *understand?* Why do we *know*—what we know this minute?"

She dashed her hand across her eyes. Then, seeing the jar of fruit on the table, she reached for it and choked out:

265   "If I was you I wouldn't *tell* her her fruit was gone! Tell her it *ain't.* Tell her it's all right—all of it. Here—take this in to prove it to her! She—she may never know whether it was broke or not."

She turned away.

Mrs. Peters reached out for the bottle of fruit as if she were glad to take it—as if touching a familiar thing, having something to do, could keep her from something else. She got up, looked about for something to wrap the fruit in, took a petticoat from the pile of clothes she had brought from the front room, and nervously started winding that round the bottle.

"My!" she began, in a high, false voice, "it's a good thing the men couldn't hear us! Getting all stirred up over a little thing like a—dead canary." She hurried over that. "As if that could have anything to do with—with—My, wouldn't they *laugh?*"

Footsteps were heard on the stairs.

270   "Maybe they would," muttered Mrs. Hale—"maybe they wouldn't."

"No, Peters," said the county attorney incisively; "it's all perfectly clear, except the reason for doing it. But you know juries when it comes to women. If there was some definite thing—something to show. Something to make a story about. A thing that would connect up with this clumsy way of doing it!"

In a covert way Mrs. Hale looked at Mrs. Peters. Mrs. Peters was looking at her. Quickly they looked away from each other. The outer door opened and Mr. Hale came in.

"I've got the team round now," he said. "Pretty cold out there."

"I'm going to stay here awhile by myself," the county attorney suddenly announced. "You can send Frank out for me, can't you?" he asked the sheriff. "I want to go over everything. I'm not satisfied we can't do better."

275   Again, for one brief moment, the two women's eyes found one another.

The sheriff came up to the table.

"Did you want to see what Mrs. Peters was going to take in?"

The county attorney picked up the apron. He laughed.

"Oh, I guess they're not very dangerous things the ladies have picked out."

280   Mrs. Hale's hand was on the sewing basket in which the box was concealed. She felt that she ought to take her hand off the basket. She did not seem able to. He picked up one of the quilt blocks which she had piled on to cover the box. Her eyes felt like fire. She had a feeling that if he took up the basket she would snatch it from him.

But he did not take it up. With another little laugh, he turned away, saying:

"No; Mrs. Peters doesn't need supervising. For that matter, a sheriff's wife is married to the law. Ever think of it that way, Mrs. Peters?"

Mrs. Peters was standing beside the table. Mrs. Hale shot a look up at her; but she could not see her face. Mrs. Peters had turned away. When she spoke, her voice was muffled.

"Not—just that way," she said.

"Married to the law!" chuckled Mrs. Peters's husband. He moved 285 toward the door into the front room, and said to the county attorney:

"I just want you to come in here a minute, George. We ought to take a look at these windows."

"Oh—windows," said the county attorney scoffingly.

"We'll be right out, Mr. Hale," said the sheriff to the farmer, who was still waiting by the door.

Hale went to look after the horses. The sheriff followed the county attorney into the other room. Again—for one moment—the two women were alone in that kitchen.

Martha Hale sprang up, her hands tight together, looking at that other 290 woman, with whom it rested. At first she could not see her eyes, for the sheriff's wife had not turned back since she turned away at that suggestion of being married to the law. But now Mrs. Hale made her turn back. Her eyes made her turn back. Slowly, unwillingly, Mrs. Peters turned her head until her eyes met the eyes of the other woman. There was a moment when they held each other in a steady, burning look in which there was no evasion nor flinching. Then Martha Hale's eyes pointed the way to the basket in which was hidden the thing that would make certain the conviction of the other woman—that woman who was not there and yet who had been there with them all through the hour.

For a moment Mrs. Peters did not move. And then she did it. With a rush forward, she threw back the quilt pieces, got the box, tried to put it in her handbag. It was too big. Desperately she opened it, started to take the bird out. But there she broke—she could not touch the bird. She stood helpless, foolish.

There was the sound of a knob turning in the inner door. Martha Hale snatched the box from the sheriff's wife, and got it in the pocket of her big coat just as the sheriff and the county attorney came back into the kitchen.

"Well, Henry," said the county attorney facetiously, "at least we found out that she was not going to quilt it. She was going to—what is it you call it, ladies?"

Mrs. Hale's hand was against the pocket of her coat.

"We call it—knot it, Mr. Henderson."   295

Zora Neale Hurston
Spunk

1

A giant of a brown skinned man sauntered up the one street of the Village and out into the palmetto thickets with a small pretty woman clinging lovingly to his arm.

"Looka theah, folkses!" cried Elijah Mosley, slapping his leg gleefully. "Theah they go, big as life an' brassy as tacks."

All the loungers in the store tried to walk to the door with an air of nonchalance but with small success.

"Now pee-eople!" Walter Thomas gasped. "Will you look at 'em!"

5 "But that's one thing Ah likes about Spunk Banks—he ain't skeered of nothin' on God's green foot-stool—*nothin'!* He rides that log down at saw-mill jus' like he struts round wid another man's wife—jus' don't give a kitty. When Tes' Miller got cut to giblets on that circle-saw. Spunk steps right up and starts ridin'. The rest of us was skeered to go near it."

A round-shouldered figure in overalls much too large, came nervously in the door and the talking ceased. The men looked at each other and winked.

"Gimme some soda-water. Sass'prilla Ah reckon," the newcomer ordered, and stood far down the counter near the open pickled pig-feet tub to drink it.

Elijah nudged Walter and turned with mock gravity to the newcomer. "Say Joe, how's everything up yo' way? How's yo' wife?"

10 Joe started and all but dropped the bottle he held in his hands. He swallowed several times painfully and his lips trembled.

"Aw 'Lige, you oughtn't to do nothin' like that," Walter grumbled. Elijah ignored him.

"She jus' passed heah a few minutes ago goin' thata way," with a wave of his hand in the direction of the woods.

Now Joe knew his wife had passed that way. He knew that the men lounging in the general store had seen her, moreover, he knew that the men knew *he* knew. He stood there silent for a long moment staring blankly, with his Adam's apple twitching nervously up and down his throat. One

SPUNK   First published in 1925. Zora Neale Hurston (1891–1960), the daughter of a preacher and of a teacher who died when Hurston was thirteen, was raised in the African American community of Eatonville, Florida. Her schooling was repeatedly interrupted, but included a high school diploma in 1918 and college studies at Howard University in Washington, D.C., and Barnard College in New York. She did extensive field research in the folkways of African Americans in the south and in the Caribbean, an interest reflected in this story.

could actually *see* the pain he was suffering, his eyes, his face, his hands and even the dejected slump of his shoulders. He set the bottle down upon the counter. He didn't bang it, just eased it out of his hand silently and fiddled with his suspender buckle.

"Well, Ah'm goin' after her today. Ah'm goin' an' fetch her back. Spunk's done gone too fur."

He reached deep down into his trouser pocket and drew out a hollow 15 ground razor, large and shiny, and passed his moistened thumb back and forth over the edge.

"Talkin' like a man, Joe. Course that's *yo'* fambly affairs, but Ah like to see grit in anybody."

Joe Kanty laid down a nickel and stumbled out into the street.

Dusk crept in from the woods. Ike Clarke lit the swinging oil lamp that was almost immediately surrounded by candle-flies. The men laughed boisterously behind Joe's back as they watched him shamble woodward.

"You oughtn't to said whut you did to him, 'Lige,—look how it worked him up," Walter chided.

"And Ah hope it did work him up. Tain't even decent for a man to 20 take and take like he do."

"Spunk will sho' kill him."

"Aw, Ah doan't know. You never kin tell. He might turn him up an' spank him fur gettin' in the way, but Spunk wouldn't shoot no unarmed man. Dat razor he carried outa heah ain't gonna run Spunk down an' cut him, an' Joe ain't got the nerve to go up to Spunk with it knowing he totes that Army 45. He makes that break outa heah to bluff us. He's gonna hide that razor behind the first likely palmetto root an' sneak back home to bed. Don't tell me nothin' 'bout that rabbit-foot colored man. Didn't he meet Spunk an' Lena face to face one day las' week an' mumble sumthin' to Spunk 'bout lettin' his wife alone?"

"What did Spunk say?" Walter broke in—"Ah like him fine but tain't right the way he carries on wid Lena Kanty, jus' cause Joe's timid 'bout fightin.' "

"You wrong theah, Walter. 'Tain't cause Joe's timid at all, it's cause Spunk wants Lena. If Joe was a passel of wile cats Spunk would tackle the job just the same. He'd go after *anything* he wanted the same way. As Ah wuz sayin' a minute ago, he tole Joe right to his face that Lena was his. 'Call her,' he says to Joe. 'Call her and see if she'll come. A woman knows her boss an' she answers when he calls.' 'Lena, ain't I yo' husband?' Joe sorter whines out. Lena looked at him real disgusted but she don't answer and she don't move outa her tracks. Then Spunk reaches out an' takes hold of her arm an' says: 'Lena, youse mine. From now on Ah works for you an' fights for you an' Ah never wants you to look to nobody for a crumb of bread, a stitch of close or a shingle to go over yo' head, but *me* long as Ah live. Ah'll git the lumber foh owah house tomorrow. Go home an' git yo' things together!'

25   'Thass mah house,' Lena speaks up. 'Papa gimme that.'

'Well,' says Spunk, 'doan give up whut's yours, but when youse inside don't forgit youse mine, an' let no other man git outa his place wid you!'

Lena looked up at him with her eyes so full of love that they wuz runnin' over an' Spunk seen it an' Joe seen it too, and his lips started to tremblin' and his Adam's apple was galloping up and down his neck like a race horse. Ah bet he's wore out half a dozen Adam's apples since Spunk's been on the job with Lena. That's all he'll do. He'll be back heah after while swallowin' an' workin' his lips like he wants to say somethin' an' can't."

"But didn't he do *nothin'* to stop 'em?"

"Nope, not a frazzlin' thing—jus' stood there. Spunk took Lena's arm and walked off jus' like nothin' ain't happened and he stood there gazin' after them till they was outa sight. Now you know a woman don't want no man like that. I'm jus' waitin' to see whut he's goin' to say when he gits back."

2

30   But Joe Kanty never came back, never. The men in the store heard the sharp report of a pistol somewhere distant in the palmetto thicket and soon Spunk came walking leisurely, with his big black Stetson set at the same rakish angle and Lena clinging to his arm, came walking right into the general store. Lena wept in a frightened manner.

"Well," Spunk announced calmly, "Joe come out there wid a meatax an' made me kill him."

He sent Lena home and led the men back to Joe—Joe crumple and limp with his right hand still clutching his razor.

"See mah back? Mah close cut clear through. He sneaked up an' tried to kill me from the back, but Ah got him, an' got him good, first shot," Spunk said.

The men glared at Elijah, accusingly.

35   "Take him up an' plant him in 'Stoney lonesome,' "Spunk said in a careless voice. "Ah didn't wanna shoot him but he made me do it. He's a dirty coward, jumpin' on a man from behind."

Spunk turned on his heel and sauntered away to where he knew his love wept in fear for him and no man stopped him. At the general store later on, they all talked of locking him up until the sheriff should come from Orlando, but no one did anything but talk.

A clear case of self-defense, the trial was a short one, and Spunk walked out of the court house to freedom again. He could work again, ride the dangerous log-carriage that fed the singing, snarling, biting, circle-saw; he could stroll the soft dark lanes with his guitar. He was free to roam the woods again; he was free to return to Lena. He did all of these things.

3

"Whut you reckon, Walt?" Elijah asked one night later. "Spunk's gittin' ready to marry Lena!"

"Naw! Why Joe ain't had time to git cold yit. Nohow Ah didn't figger Spunk was the marryin' kind."

"Well, he is," rejoined Elijah. "He done moved most of Lena's things—and her along wid 'em—over to the Bradley hose. He's buying it. Jus' like Ah told yo' all right in heah the night Joe wuz kilt. Spunk's crazy 'bout Lena. He don't want folks to keep on talkin' 'bout her—thass reason he's rushin' so. Funny thing 'bout that bob-cat, wan't it?"

"Whut bob-cat, 'Lige? Ah ain't heered 'bout none."

"Ain't cher? Well, night befo' las' was the fust night Spunk an' Lena moved together an' jus' as they was goin' to bed, a big black bob-cat, black all over, you hear me, *black,* walked round and round that house and howled like forty, an' when Spunk got his gun an' went to the winder to shoot it, he says it stood right still an' looked him in the eye, an' howled right at him. The thing got Spunk so nervoused up he couldn't shoot. But Spunk says twan't no bob-cat nohow. He says it was Joe done sneaked back from Hell!"

"Humph!" sniffed Walter, "he oughter be nervous after what he done. Ah reckon Joe come back to dare him to marry Lena, or to come out an' fight. Ah bet he'll be back time and agin, too. Know what Ah think? Joe wuz a braver man than Spunk."

There was a general shout of derision from the group.

"Thass a fact," went on Walter. "Lookit whut he done; took a razor an' went out to fight a man he knowed toted a gun an' wuz a crack shot, too; 'nother thing Joe wuz skeered of Spunk, skeered plumb stiff! But he went jes' the same. It took him a long time to get his nerve up. 'Tain't nothin' for Spunk to fight when he ain't skeered of nothin'. Now, Joe's done come back to have it out wid the man that's got all he ever had. Y'all know Joe ain't never had nothin' nor wanted nothin' besides Lena. It musta been a h'ant° cause ain' nobody never seen no black bob-cat."

"'Nother thing," cut in one of the men, "Spunk wuz cussin' a blue streak today 'cause he 'lowed dat saw wuz wobblin'—almos' got 'im once. The machinist come, looked it over an' said it wuz alright. Spunk musta been leanin' t'wards it some. Den he claimed somebody pushed 'im but 'twant nobody close to 'im. Ah wuz glad when knockin' off time come. I'm skeered of dat man when he gits hot. He'd beat you full of button holes as quick as he's look atcher."

40

45

h'ant: "haint," a ghost

4

The men gathered the next evening in a different mood, no laughter. No badinage this time.

"Look 'Lige, you goin' to set up wid Spunk?"

"Naw, Ah reckon not, Walter. Tell yuh the truth, Ah'm a lil bit skittish. Spunk died too wicket—died cussin' he did. You know he thought he wuz done outa life."

50 "Good Lawd, who'd he think done it?"

"Joe."

"Joe Kanty? How come?"

"Walter, Ah b'leeve Ah will walk up thata way an' set. Lena would like it Ah reckon."

"But whut did he say, 'Lige?"

55 Elijah did not answer until they had left the lighted store and were strolling down the dark street.

"Ah wuz loadin' a wagon wid scantlin' right near the saw when Spunk fell on the carriage but 'fore Ah could git to him the saw got him in the body—awful sight. Me an' Skint Miller got him off but it was too late. Anybody could see that. The fust thing he said wuz: 'He pushed me, 'Lige—the dirty hound pushed me in the back!'—He was spittin' blood at ev'ry breath. We laid him on the sawdust pile with his face to the East so's he could die easy. He helt mah han' till the last, Walter, and said: 'It was Joe, 'Lige—the dirty sneak shoved me . . . he didn't dare come to mah face . . . but Ah'll git the son-of-a-wood louse soon's Ah get there an' make hell too hot for him.... Ah felt him shove me . . .!' Thass how he died."

"If spirits kin fight, there's a powerful tussle goin' on somewhere ovah Jordan 'cause Ah b'leeve Joe's ready for Spunk an' ain't skeered anymore—yas, Ah b'leeve Joe pushed 'im mahself."

They had arrived at the house. Lena's lamentations were deep and loud. She had filled the room with magnolia blossoms that gave off a heavy sweet odor. The keepers of the wake tipped about whispering in frightened tones. Everyone in the Village was there, even old Jeff Kanty, Joe's father, who a few hours before would have been afraid to come within ten feet of him, stood leering triumphantly down upon the fallen giant as if his fingers had been the teeth of steel that laid him low.

The cooling board consisted of three sixteen-inch boards on saw horses; a dingy sheet was his shroud.

60 The women ate heartily of the funeral baked meats and wondered who would be Lena's next. The men whispered coarse conjectures between guzzles of whiskey.

Henry James
The Real Thing

1

When the porter's wife, who used to answer the house-bell, announced "A gentleman and a lady, sir," I had, as I often had in those days—the wish being father to the thought—an immediate vision of sitters. Sitters my visitors in this case proved to be; but not in the sense I should have preferred. There was nothing at first however to indicate that they mightn't have come for a portrait. The gentleman, a man of fifty, very high and very straight, with a moustache slightly grizzled and a dark grey walking-coat admirably fitted, both of which I noted professionally—I don't mean as a barber or yet as a tailor—would have struck me as a celebrity if celebrities often were striking. It was a truth of which I had for some time been conscious that a figure with a good deal of frontage was, as one might say, almost never a public institution. A glance at the lady helped to remind me of this paradoxical law: she also looked too distinguished to be a "personality." Moreover one would scarcely come across two variations together.

Neither of the pair immediately spoke—they only prolonged the preliminary gaze suggesting that each wished to give the other a chance. They were visibly shy; they stood there letting me take them in—which, as I afterwards perceived, was the most practical thing they could have done. In this way their embarrassment served their cause. I had seen people painfully reluctant to mention that they desired anything so gross as to be represented on canvas; but the scruples of my new friends appeared almost insurmountable. Yet the gentleman might have said "I should like a portrait of my wife," and the lady might have said "I should like a portrait of my husband." Perhaps they weren't husband and wife—this naturally would make the matter more delicate. Perhaps they wished to be done together—in which case they ought to have brought a third person to break the news.

"We come from Mr. Rivet," the lady finally said with a dim smile that had the effect of a moist sponge passed over a "sunk"° piece of painting, as well as of a vague allusion to vanished beauty. She was as tall and straight,

THE REAL THING First published in 1891. Henry James (1843–1916) published numerous novels and short stories during his illustrious career, including such classics as *The Portrait of a Lady* (1881) and *The Ambassadors* (1903). Considered one of America's premier masters of the fictional art, James came from an intellectual family—his father was a religious philosopher, his brother William a brilliant psychologist and philosopher, and his sister Alice a talented diarist—and though born in New York, he spent most of his adult life in England. His fiction often dealt with the theme of the artist's place in society.

"sunk": faded

in her degree, as her companion, and with ten years less to carry. She looked as sad as a woman could look whose face was not charged with expression; that is her tinted oval mask showed waste as an exposed surface shows friction. The hand of time had played over her freely, but to an effect of elimination. She was slim and stiff, and so well-dressed, in dark blue cloth, with lappets and pockets and buttons, that it was clear she employed the same tailor as her husband. The couple had an indefinable air of prosperous thrift—they evidently got a good deal of luxury for their money. If I was to be one of their luxuries it would behoove me to consider my terms.

"Ah Claude Rivet recommended me?" I echoed; and I added that it was very kind of him, though I could reflect that, as he only painted landscape, this wasn't a sacrifice.

5   The lady looked very hard at the gentleman, and the gentleman looked round the room. Then staring at the floor a moment and stroking his moustache, he rested his pleasant eyes on me with the remark: "He said you were the right one."

"I try to be, when people want to sit."

"Yes, we should like to," said the lady anxiously.

"Do you mean together?"

My visitors exchanged a glance. "If you could do anything with *me* I suppose it would be double," the gentleman stammered.

10   "Oh yes, there's naturally a higher charge for two figures than for one."

"We should like to make it pay," the husband confessed.

"That's very good of you," I returned, appreciating so unwonted a sympathy—for I supposed he meant pay the artist.

A sense of strangeness seemed to dawn on the lady. "We mean for the illustrations—Mr. Rivet said you might put one in."

"Put in—an illustration?" I was equally confused.

15   "Sketch her off, you know," said the gentleman, coloring.

It was only then that I understood the service Claude Rivet had rendered me; he had told them how I worked in black-and-white, for magazines, for storybooks, for sketches of contemporary life, and consequently had copious employment for models. These things were true, but it was not less true—I may confess it now; whether because the aspiration was to lead to everything or to nothing I leave the reader to guess—that I couldn't get the honors, to say nothing of the emoluments, of a great painter of portraits out of my head. My "illustrations" were my pot-boilers; I looked to a different branch of art—far and away the most interesting it had always seemed to me—to perpetuate my fame. There was no shame in looking to it also to make my fortune; but that fortune was by so much further from being made from the moment my visitors wished to be "done" for nothing. I was disappointed; for in the pictorial sense I had immediately *seen* them. I had seized their type—I had already settled what I would do with it. Something that wouldn't absolutely have pleased them, I afterwards reflected.

"Ah you're—you're—a?" I began as soon as I had mastered my surprise. I couldn't bring out the dingy word "models": it seemed so little to fit the case.

"We haven't had much practice," said the lady.

"We've got to *do* something, and we've thought that an artist in your line might perhaps make something of us," her husband threw off. He further mentioned that they didn't know many artists and that they had gone first, on the off-chance—he painted views of course, but sometimes put in figures; perhaps I remembered—to Mr. Rivet, whom they had met a few years before at a place in Norfolk where he was sketching.

"We used to sketch a little ourselves," the lady hinted.   20

"It's very awkward, but we absolutely *must* do something," her husband went on.

"Of course we're not so *very* young," she admitted with a wan smile.

With the remark that I might as well know something more about them the husband had handed me a card extracted from a neat new pocket-book—their appurtenances were all of the freshest—and inscribed with the words "Major Monarch." Impressive as these words were they didn't carry my knowledge much further; but my visitor presently added: "I've left the army and we've had the misfortune to lose our money. In fact our means are dreadfully small."

"It's awfully trying—a regular strain," said Mrs. Monarch.

They evidently wished to be discreet—to take care not to swagger   25
because they were gentlefolk. I felt them willing to recognize this as something of a drawback, at the same time that I guessed at an underlying sense—their consolation in adversity—that they *had* their points. They certainly had; but these advantages struck me as preponderantly social; such for instance as would help to make a drawing-room look well. However, a drawing-room was always, or ought to be, a picture.

In consequence of his wife's allusion to their age Major Monarch observed: "Naturally, it's more for the figure that we thought of going in. We can still hold ourselves up." On the instant I saw that the figure was indeed their strong point. His "naturally" didn't sound vain, but it lighted up the question. "*She* has got the best," he continued, nodding at his wife, with a pleasant after-dinner absence of circumlocution. I could only reply, as if we were in fact sitting over our wine, that this didn't prevent his own from being very good; which led him in turn to rejoin: "We thought that if you ever have to do people like us, we might be something like it. *She*, particularly—for a lady in a book, you know."

I was so amused by them that, to get more of it, I did my best to take their point of view; and though it was an embarrassment to find myself appraising physically, as if they were animals on hire or useful blacks, a pair whom I should have expected to meet only in one of the relations in which criticism is tacit, I looked at Mrs. Monarch judicially enough to be able to exclaim, after a moment, with conviction: "Oh yes, a lady in a book!" She was singularly like a bad illustration.

"We'll stand up, if you like," said the Major; and he raised himself before me with a really grand air.

I could take his measure at a glance—he was six feet two and a perfect gentleman. It would have paid any club in process of formation and in want of a stamp to engage him at a salary to stand in the principal window. What struck me immediately was that in coming to me they had rather missed their vocation; they could surely have been turned to better account for advertising purposes. I couldn't of course see the thing in detail, but I could see them make someone's fortune—I don't mean their own. There was something in them for a waistcoat-maker, an hotel-keeper, or a soap-vendor. I could imagine "We always use it" pinned on their bosoms with the greatest effect; I had a vision of the promptitude with which they would launch a table d'hôte.°

30   Mrs. Monarch sat still, not from pride but from shyness, and presently her husband said to her: "Get up my dear and show how smart you are." She obeyed, but she had no need to get up to show it. She walked to the end of the studio, and then she came back blushing, with her fluttered eyes on her husband. I was reminded of an incident I had accidentally had a glimpse of in Paris—being with a friend there, a dramatist about to produce a play—when an actress came to him to ask to be intrusted with a part. She went through her paces before him, walked up and down as Mrs. Monarch was doing. Mrs. Monarch did it quite as well, but I abstained from applauding. It was very odd to see such people apply for such poor pay. She looked as if she had ten thousand a year. Her husband had used the word that described her: she was in the London current jargon essentially and typically "smart." Her figure was, in the same order of ideas, conspicuously and irreproachably "good." For a woman of her age her waist was surprisingly small; her elbow moreover had the orthodox crook. She held her head at the conventional angle, but why did she come to *me?* She ought to have tried on jackets at a big shop. I feared my visitors were not only destitute but "artistic"—which would be a great complication. When she sat down again I thanked her, observing that what a draughtsman most valued in his model was the faculty of keeping quiet.

a table d'hôte: a restaurant

"Oh *she* can keep quiet," said Major Monarch. Then he added jocosely: "I've always kept her quiet."

"I'm not a nasty fidget, am I?" It was going to wring tears from me, I felt, the way she hid her head, ostrich-like, in the other broad bosom.

The owner of this expanse addressed his answer to me. "Perhaps it isn't out of place to mention—because we ought to be quite businesslike, oughtn't we?—that when I married her she was known as the Beautiful Statue."

"Oh dear!" said Mrs. Monarch ruefully.

"Of course I should want a certain amount of expression," I rejoined.   35

"Of *course!*"—and I had never heard such unanimity.

"And then I suppose you know that you'll get awfully tired."

"Oh, we *never* get tired!" they eagerly cried.

"Have you had any kind of practice?"

They hesitated—they looked at each other. "We've been   40 photographed—*immensely*," said Mrs. Monarch.

"She means the fellows have asked us themselves," added the Major.

"I see—because you're so good-looking."

"I don't know what they thought, but they were always after us."

"We always got our photographs for nothing," smiled Mrs. Monarch.

"We might have brought some, my dear," her husband remarked.   45

"I'm not sure we have any left. We've given quantities away," she explained to me.

"With our autographs and that sort of thing," said the Major.

"Are they to be got in the shops?" I enquired as a harmless pleasantry.

"Oh yes, *hers*—they used to be."

"Not now," said Mrs. Monarch, with her eyes on the floor.   50

2

I could fancy the "sort of thing" they put on the presentation copies of their photographs, and I was sure they wrote a beautiful hand. It was odd how quickly I was sure of everything that concerned them. If they were now so poor as to have to earn shillings and pence they could never have had much of a margin. Their good looks had been their capital, and they had good-humoredly made the most of the career that this resource marked out for them. It was in their faces, the blankness, the deep intellectual repose of the twenty years of country-house visiting that had given them pleasant intonations. I could see the sunny drawing-rooms, sprinkled with periodicals she didn't read, in which Mrs. Monarch had continually sat; I could see the wet shrubberies in which she had walked, equipped to admiration for either exercise. I could see the rich covers the Major had helped to shoot and the wonderful garments in which, late at night, he repaired to the smoking-room to talk about them. I could imagine their leggings and waterproofs, their knowing tweeds and rugs, their rolls of sticks and cases of tackle and neat umbrellas; and I could evoke the exact appearance of their servants and the compact variety of their luggage on the platforms of country stations.

They gave small tips, but they were liked; they didn't do anything themselves, but they were welcome. They looked so well everywhere; they gratified the general relish for stature, complexion, and "form." They knew it without fatuity or vulgarity, and they respected themselves in consequence. They weren't superficial; they were thorough and kept themselves up—it had been their line. People with such a taste for activity had to have some line. I could feel how even in a dull house they could have been counted on for the joy of life. At present something had happened—it didn't matter what, their little income had grown less, it had grown least—and they had to do something for pocket-money. Their friends could like them, I made out, without liking to support them. There was something about them that represented credit—their clothes, their manners, their type; but if credit is a large empty pocket in which an occasional chink reverberates, the chink at least must be audible. What they wanted of me was to help to make it so. Fortunately they had no children—I soon divined that. They would also perhaps wish our relations to be kept secret: this was why it was "for the figure"—the reproduction of the face would betray them.

I liked them—I felt, quite as their friends must have done—they were so simple; and I had no objection to them if they would suit. But somehow with all their perfections I didn't easily believe in them. After all they were amateurs, and the ruling passion of my life was the detestation of the amateur. Combined with this was another perversity—an innate preference for the represented subject over the real one: the defect of the real one was so apt to be a lack of representation. I like things that appeared; then one was sure. Whether they *were* or not was a subordinate and almost always a profitless question. There were other considerations, the first of which was that I already had two or three recruits in use, notably a young person with big feet, in alpaca, from Kilburn, who for a couple of years had come to me regularly for my illustrations and with whom I was still—perhaps ignobly—satisfied. I frankly explained to my visitors how the case stood, but they had taken more precautions than I supposed. They had reasoned out their opportunity, for Claude Rivet had told them of the projected *édition de luxe* of one of the writers of our day—the rarest of the novelists—who, long neglected by the multitudinous vulgar and dearly prized by the attentive (need I mention Philip Vincent?), had had the happy fortune of seeing, late in life, the dawn and then the full light of a higher criticism; an estimate in which on the part of the public there was something really of expiation. The edition preparing, planned by a publisher of taste, was practically an act of high reparation; the woodcuts with which it was to be enriched were the homage of English art to one of the most independent representatives of English letters. Major and Mrs. Monarch confessed to me they had hoped I might be able to work *them* into my branch of the enterprise. They knew I was to do the first of the books, "Rutland Ramsay," but I had to make clear to them that my participation in the rest of the affair—this first book was to be a test—must depend on the satisfaction I should give. If this should be limited my employers would drop me with scarce common forms. It was therefore a crisis for me, and naturally I was making special preparations, looking about for new people, should they be necessary, and securing the best types. I admitted however that I should like to settle down to two or three good models who would do for everything.

"Should we have often to—a—put on special clothes?" Mrs. Monarch timidly demanded.

"Dear yes—that's half the business."   55

"And should we be expected to supply our own costumes?"

"Oh no; I've got a lot of things. A painter's models put on—or put off—anything he likes."

"And you mean—a—the same?"

"The same?"

Mrs. Monarch looked at her husband again.   60

"Oh she was just wondering," he explained, "if the costumes are in *general* use." I had to confess that they were, and I mentioned further that some of them—I had a lot of genuine greasy last-century things—had served their time, a hundred years ago, on living world-stained men and women; on figures not perhaps so far removed, in that vanished world, from *their* type, the Monarchs', *quoi!*° of a breeched and bewigged age. "We'll put on anything that *fits*," said the Major.

"Oh I arrange that—they fit in the pictures."

"I'm afraid I should do better for the modern books. I'd come as you like," said Mrs. Monarch.

"She has got a lot of clothes at home: they might do for contemporary life," her husband continued.

"Oh I can fancy scenes in which you'd be quite natural." And indeed   65
I could see the slipshod rearrangements of stale properties—the stories I tried to produce pictures for without the exasperation of reading them—whose sandy tracts the good lady might help to people. But I had to return

quoi!: French for "what!"

to the fact that for this sort of work—the daily mechanical grind—I was already equipped: the people I was working with were fully adequate.

"We only thought we might be more like *some* characters," said Mrs. Monarch mildly, getting up.

Her husband also rose; he stood looking at me with a dim wistfulness that was touching in so fine a man. "Wouldn't it be rather a pull sometimes to have—a—to have—?" He hung fire; he wanted me to help him by phrasing what he meant. But I couldn't—I didn't know. So he brought it out awkwardly: "The *real* thing; a gentleman, you know, or a lady." I was quite ready to give a general assent—I admitted that there was a great deal in that. This encouraged Major Monarch to say, following up his appeal with an unacted gulp: "It's awfully hard—we've tried everything." The gulp was communicative; it proved too much for his wife. Before I knew it Mrs. Monarch had dropped again upon a divan and burst into tears. Her husband sat down beside her, holding one of her hands; whereupon she quickly dried her eyes with the other, while I felt embarrassed as she looked up at me. "There isn't a confounded job I haven't applied for—waited for—prayed for. You can fancy we'd be pretty bad first. Secretaryships and that sort of thing? You might as well ask for a peerage. I'd be *anything*—I'm strong; a messenger or a coal-heaver. I'd put on a gold-laced cap and open carriage doors in front of the haberdasher's; I'd hang about a station to carry portmanteaux; I'd be a postman. But they won't *look* at you; there are thousands as good as yourself already on the ground. *Gentlemen*, poor beggars, who've drunk their wine, who've kept their hunters!"

I was as reassuring as I knew how to be, and my visitors were presently on their feet again while, for the experiment, we agreed on an hour. We were discussing it when the door opened and Miss Churm came in with a wet umbrella. Miss Churm had to take the omnibus to Maida Vale and then walk half a mile. She looked a trifle blowsy and slightly splashed. I scarcely ever saw her come in without thinking afresh how odd it was that, being so little in herself, she should yet be so much in others. She was a meagre little Miss Churm, but was such an ample heroine of romance. She was only a freckled cockney, but she could represent everything, from a fine lady to a shepherdess; she had the faculty as she might have had a fine voice or long hair. She couldn't spell and she loved beer, but she had two or three "points," and practice, and a knack, and mother-wit, and a whimsical sensibility, and a love of the theater, and seven sisters, and not an ounce of respect, especially for the *h*. The first thing my visitors saw was that her umbrella was wet, and in their spotless perfection they visibly winced at it. The rain had come on since their arrival.

"I'm all in a soak; there *was* a mess of people in the 'bus. I wish you lived near a stytion," said Miss Churm. I requested her to get ready as quickly as possible, and she passed into the room in which she always changed her dress. But before going out she asked me what she was to get into this time.

"It's the Russian princess, don't you know?" I answered; "the one with the 'golden eyes,' in black velvet, for the long thing in the *Cheapside*."°   70

"Golden eyes? I *say*!" cried Miss Churm, while my companions watched her with intensity as she withdrew. She always arranged herself, when she was late, before I could turn round; and I kept my visitors a little on purpose, so that they might get an idea, from seeing her, what would be expected of themselves. I mentioned that she was quite my notion of an excellent model—she was really very clever.

"Do you think she looks like a Russian princess?" Major Monarch asked with lurking alarm.

"When I make her, yes."

"Oh if you have to *make* her—!" he reasoned, not without point.

"That's the most you can ask. There are so many who are not makeable."   75

"Well now, *here's* a lady"—and with a persuasive smile he passed his arm into his wife's —"who's already made!"

"Oh I'm not a Russian princess," Mrs. Monarch protested a little coldly. I could see she had known some and didn't like them. There at once was a complication of a kind I never had to fear with Miss Churm.

This young lady came back in black velvet—the gown was rather rusty and very low on her lean shoulders—and with a Japanese fan in her red hands. I reminded her that in the scene I was doing she had to look over some one's head. "I forget whose it is; but it doesn't matter. Just look over a head."

"I'd rather look over a stove," said Miss Churm; and she took her station near the fire. She fell into position, settled herself into a tall attitude, gave a certain backward inclination to her head and a certain forward droop to her fan, and looked, at least to my prejudiced sense, distinguished and charming, foreign and dangerous. We left her looking so while I went downstairs with Major and Mrs. Monarch.

"I believe I could come about as near it as that," said Mrs. Monarch.   80

"Oh you think she's shabby, but you must allow for the alchemy of art."

However, they went off with an evident increase of comfort founded on their demonstrable advantage in being the real thing. I could fancy them shuddering over Miss Churm. She was very droll about them when I went back, for I told her what they wanted.

"Well, if *she* can sit I'll tyke to book-keeping," said my model.

"She's very ladylike," I replied as an innocent form of aggravation.

"So much the worse for *you*. That means she can't turn round."   85

the *Cheapside*: a London magazine

"She'll do for the fashionable novels."

"Oh yes, she'll *do* for them!" my model humorously declared. "Ain't they bad enough without her?" I had often sociably denounced them to Miss Churm.

3

It was for the elucidation of a mystery in one of these works that I first tried Mrs. Monarch. Her husband came with her, to be useful if necessary—it was sufficiently clear that as a general thing he would prefer to come with her. At first I wondered if this were for "propriety's" sake—if he were going to be jealous and meddling. The idea was too tiresome, and if it had been confirmed it would speedily have brought our acquaintance to a close. But I soon saw there was nothing in it and that if he accompanied Mrs. Monarch it was—in addition to the chance of being wanted—simply because he had nothing else to do. When they were separate his occupation was gone and they never *had* been separate. I judged rightly that in their awkward situation their close union was their main comfort and that this union had no weak spot. It was a real marriage, an encouragement to the hesitating, a nut for pessimists to crack. Their address was humble—I remember afterwards thinking it had been the only thing about them that was really professional—and I could fancy the lamentable lodgings in which the Major would have been left alone. He could sit there more or less grimly with his wife—he couldn't sit there anyhow without her.

He had too much tact to try and make himself agreeable when he couldn't be useful; so when I was too absorbed in my work to talk he simply sat and waited. But I liked to hear him talk—it made my work, when not interrupting it, less mechanical, less special. To listen to him was to combine the excitement of going out with the economy of staying at home. There was only one hindrance—that I seemed not to know any of the people this brilliant couple had known. I think he wondered extremely, during the term of our intercourse, whom the deuce I *did* know. He hadn't a stray sixpence of an idea to fumble for, so we didn't spin it very fine; we confined ourselves to questions of leather and even of liquor—saddlers and breeches-makers and how to get excellent claret cheap—and matters like "good trains" and the habits of small game. His lore on these last subjects was astonishing—he managed to interweave the station-master with the ornithologist. When he couldn't talk about greater things he could talk cheerfully about smaller, and since I couldn't accompany him into reminiscences of the fashionable world he could lower the conversation without a visible effort to my level.

90 So earnest a desire to please was touching in a man who could so easily have knocked one down. He looked after the fire and had an opinion on

the draught of the stove without my asking him, and I could see that he thought many of my arrangements not half knowing. I remember telling him that if I were only rich I'd offer him a salary to come and teach me how to live. Sometimes he gave a random sigh of which the essence might have been: "Give me even such a bare old barrack as *this*, and I'd do something with it!" When I wanted to use him he came alone; which was an illustration of the superior courage of women. His wife could bear her solitary second floor, and she was in general more discreet; showing by various small reserves that she was alive to the propriety of keeping our relations markedly professional—not letting them slide into sociability. She wished it to remain clear that she and the Major were employed, not cultivated, and if she approved of me as a superior, who could be kept in his place, she never thought me quite good enough for an equal.

She sat with great intensity, giving the whole of her mind to it, and was capable of remaining for an hour almost as motionless as before a photographer's lens. I could see she had been photographed often, but somehow the very habit that made her good for that purpose unfitted her for mine. At first I was extremely pleased with her ladylike air, and it was a satisfaction, on coming to follow her lines, to see how good they were and how far they could lead the pencil. But after a little skirmishing I began to find her too insurmountably stiff; do what I would with it my drawing looked like a photograph or a copy of a photograph. Her figure had no variety of expression—she herself had no sense of variety. You may say that this was my business and was only a question of placing her. Yet I placed her in every conceivable position and she managed to obliterate their differences. She was always a lady certainly, and into the bargain was always the same lady. She was the real thing, but always the same thing. There were moments when I rather writhed under the serenity of her confidence that she *was* the real thing. All her dealings with me and all her husband's were an implication that this was lucky for *me*. Meanwhile I found myself trying to invent types that approached her own, instead of making her own transform itself—in the clever way that was not impossible for instance to poor Miss Churm. Arrange as I would and take the precautions I would, she always came out, in my pictures, too tall—landing me in the dilemma of having represented a fascinating woman as seven feet high, which (out of respect perhaps to my own very much scantier inches) was far from my idea of such a personage.

The case was worse with the Major—nothing I could do would keep *him* down, so that he became useful only for the representation of brawny giants. I adored variety and range, I cherished human accidents, the illustrative note; I wanted to characterize closely, and the thing in the world I most hated was the danger of being ridden by a type. I had quarreled with some of my friends about it; I had parted company with them for maintaining that one *had* to be, and that if the type was beautiful—witness Raphael and Leonardo°—the servitude was only a gain. I was neither Leonardo nor Raphael—I might only be a presumptuous young modern searcher; but I held that everything was to be sacrificed sooner than character. When they claimed that the obsessional form could easily *be* character I retorted, perhaps superficially, "Whose?" It couldn't be everybody's—it might end in being nobody's.

After I had drawn Mrs. Monarch a dozen times I felt surer even than before that the value of such a model as Miss Churm resided precisely in the fact that she had no positive stamp, combined of course with the other fact that what she did have was a curious and inexplicable talent for imitation. Her usual appearance was like a curtain which she could draw up at request for a capital performance. This performance was simply suggestive; but it was a word to the wise—it was vivid and pretty. Sometimes even I thought it, though she was plain herself, too insipidly pretty; I made it a reproach to her that the figures drawn from her were monotonously (*bêtement*, as we used to say) graceful. Nothing made her more angry; it was so much her pride to feel she could sit for characters that had nothing in common with each other. She would accuse me at such moments of taking away her "reputytion."

It suffered a certain shrinkage, this queer quantity, from the repeated visits of my new friends. Miss Churm was greatly in demand, never in want of employment, so I had no scruple in putting her off occasionally, to try them more at my ease. It was certainly amusing at first to do the real thing—it was amusing to do Major Monarch's trousers. They *were* the real thing, even if he did come out colossal. It was amusing to do his wife's back hair—it was so mathematically neat—and the particular "smart" tension of her tight stays. She lent herself especially to positions in which the face was somewhat averted or blurred; she abounded in ladylike back views and *profils perdus*.° When she stood erect she took naturally one of the attitudes in which court-painters represent queens and princesses; so that I found myself wondering whether, to draw out this accomplishment, I couldn't get the editor of the *Cheapside* to publish a really royal romance, "A Tale of Buckingham Palace." Sometimes however the real thing and the make-believe came into contact; by which I mean that Miss Churm, keeping an appointment or coming to make one on days when I had much work in hand, encountered her invidious rivals. The encounter was not on their part, for they noticed her no more than if she had been the housemaid;

Raphael and Leonardo: Raphael Sanzio (1483–1520) and Leonardo da Vinci (1452–1519), Italian artists of the Renaissance period   *profils perdus*: French for, literally, "lost profiles," meaning profiles in which the face is averted and unseen

not from intentional loftiness, but simply because as yet, professionally, they didn't know how to fraternize, as I could imagine they would have liked—or at least that the Major would. They couldn't talk about the omnibus—they always walked; and they didn't know what else to try—she wasn't interested in good trains or cheap claret. Besides, they must have felt—in the air—that she was amused at them, secretly derisive of their ever knowing how. She wasn't a person to conceal the limits of her faith if she had had a chance to show them. On the other hand Mrs. Monarch didn't think her tidy; for why else did she take pains to say to me—it was going out of the way, for Mrs. Monarch—that she didn't like dirty women?

One day when my young lady happened to be present with my other 95 sitters—she even dropped in, when it was convenient, for a chat—I asked her to be so good as to lend a hand in getting tea, a service with which she was familiar and which was one of a class that, living as I did in a small way, with slender domestic resources, I often appealed to my models to render. They liked to lay hands on my property, to break the sitting, and sometimes the china—it made them feel Bohemian. The next time I saw Miss Churm after this incident she surprised me greatly by making a scene about it—she accused me of having wished to humiliate her. She hadn't resented the outrage at the time, but had seemed obliging and amused, enjoying the comedy of asking Mrs. Monarch, who sat vague and silent, whether she would have cream and sugar, and putting an exaggerated simper into the question. She had tried intonations—as if she too wished to pass for the real thing—till I was afraid my other visitors would take offense.

Oh they were determined not to do this, and their touching patience was the measure of their great need. They would sit by the hour, uncomplaining, till I was ready to use them; they would come back on the chance of being wanted and would walk away cheerfully if it failed. I used to go to the door with them to see in what magnificent order they retreated. I tried to find other employment for them—I introduced them to several artists. But they didn't "take," for reasons I could appreciate, and I became rather anxiously aware that after such disappointments they fell back upon me with a heavier weight. They did me the honor to think me most *their* form. They weren't romantic enough for the painters, and in those days there were few serious workers in black-and-white. Besides, they had an eye to the great job I had mentioned to them—they had secretly set their hearts on supplying the right essence for my pictorial vindication of our fine novelist. They knew that for this undertaking I should want no costume-effects, none of the frippery of past ages—that it was a case in which everything would be contemporary and satirical and presumably genteel. If I could work them into it their future would be assured, for the labor would of course be long and the occupation steady.

One day Mrs. Monarch came without her husband—she explained his absence by his having had to go to the City. While she sat there in her usual relaxed majesty there came at the door a knock which I immediately recognized as the subdued appeal of a model out of work. It was followed by the entrance of a young man whom I at once saw to be a foreigner and who proved in fact an Italian acquainted with no English word but my name, which he uttered in a way that made it seem to include all others. I hadn't then visited his country, nor was I proficient in his tongue; but as he was not so meanly constituted—what Italian is?—as to depend only on that member for expression he conveyed to me, in familiar but graceful mimicry, that he was in search of exactly the employment in which the lady before me was engaged. I was not struck with him at first, and while I continued to draw I dropped few signs of interest or encouragement. He stood his ground however—not importunately, but with a dumb dog-like fidelity in his eyes that amounted to innocent impudence, the manner of a devoted servant—he might have been in the house for years—unjustly suspected. Suddenly it struck me that this very attitude and expression made a picture; whereupon I told him to sit down and wait till I should be free. There was another picture in the way he obeyed me, and I observed as I worked that there were others still in the way he looked wonderingly, with his head thrown back, about the high studio. He might have been crossing himself in Saint Peter's. Before I finished I said to myself "The fellow's a bankrupt orange-monger, but a treasure."

When Mrs. Monarch withdrew he passed across the room like a flash to open the door for her, standing there with the rapt pure gaze of the young Dante spellbound by the young Beatrice.° As I never insisted, in such situations, on the blankness of the British domestic, I reflected that he had the making of a servant—and I needed one, but couldn't pay him to be only that—as well as of a model; in short I resolved to adopt my bright adventurer if he would agree to officiate in the double capacity. He jumped at my offer, and in the event my rashness—for I had really known nothing about him—wasn't brought home to me. He proved a sympathetic though a desultory ministrant, and had in a wonderful degree the *sentiment de la pose.*° It was uncultivated, instinctive, a part of the happy instinct that had guided him to my door and helped him to spell out my name on the card nailed to it. He had had no other introduction to me than a guess, from the shape of my high north window, seen outside, that my place was a studio and that as a studio it would contain an artist. He had wandered to England in search of fortune, like other itinerants, and had embarked, with a partner and a small green hand-cart, on the sale of penny ices. The ices had melted away and the partner had dissolved in their train. My young man wore tight yellow trousers with

---

Beatrice: Beatrice Portinari (1266–1290), a Florentine woman who served as an inspiration for the poet Dante   *sentiment de la pose:* an inborn knack for posing (French)

reddish stripes and his name was Oronte. He was sallow but fair, and when I put him into some old clothes of my own he looked like an Englishman. He was as good as Miss Churm, who could look, when requested, like an Italian.

4

I thought Mrs. Monarch's face slightly convulsed when, on her coming back with her husband, she found Oronte installed. It was strange to have to recognize in a scrap of a lazzarone° a competitor to her magnificent Major. It was she who scented danger first, for the Major was anecdotically unconscious. But Oronte gave us tea, with a hundred eager confusions—he had never been concerned in so queer a process—and I think she thought better of me for having at last an "establishment." They saw a couple of drawings that I had made of the establishment, and Mrs. Monarch hinted that it never would have struck her he had sat for them. "Now the drawings you make from *us*, they look exactly like us," she reminded me, smiling in triumph; and I recognized that this was indeed just their defect. When I drew the Monarchs I couldn't anyhow get away from them—get into the character I wanted to represent; and I hadn't the least desire my model should be discoverable in my picture. Miss Churm never was, and Mrs. Monarch thought I hid her, very properly, because she was vulgar; whereas if she was lost it was only as the dead who go to heaven are lost—in the gain of an angel the more.

By this time I had got a certain start with "Rutland Ramsay," the first 100 novel in the great projected series; that is I had produced a dozen drawings, several with the help of the Major and his wife, and I had sent them in for approval. My understanding with the publishers, as I have already hinted, had been that I was to be left to do my work, in this particular case, as I liked, with the whole book committed to me; but my connection with the rest of the series was only contingent. There were moments when, frankly, it *was* a comfort to have the real thing under one's hand; for there were characters in "Rutland Ramsay" that were very much like it. There were people presumably as erect as the Major and women of as good a fashion as Mrs. Monarch. There was a great deal of country-house life—treated, it is true, in a fine fanciful ironical generalized way—and there was a considerable implication of knickerbockers and kilts. There were certain things I had to settle at the outset; such things for instance as the exact appearance of the hero and the particular bloom and figure of the heroine. The author of course gave me a lead, but there was a margin for interpretation. I took the Monarchs into my confidence, I told them frankly what I was about, I mentioned my embarrassments and alternatives. "Oh take *him*!" Mrs. Monarch murmured sweetly, looking at her husband; and "What could you want better than my wife?" the Major enquired with the comfortable candor that now prevailed between us.

---

lazzarone: Italian for "beggar"

I wasn't obliged to answer these remarks—I was only obliged to place my sitters. I wasn't easy in mind, and I postponed a little timidly perhaps the solving of my question. The book was a large canvas, the other figures were numerous, and I worked off at first some of the episodes in which the hero and the heroine were not concerned. When once I had set *them* up I should have to stick to them—I couldn't make my young man seven feet high in one place and five feet nine in another. I inclined on the whole to the latter measurement, though the Major more than once reminded me that *he* looked about as young as any one. It was indeed quite possible to arrange him, for the figure, so that it would have been difficult to detect his age. After the spontaneous Oronte had been with me a month, and after I had given him to understand several times over that his native exuberance would presently constitute an insurmountable barrier to our further intercourse, I waked to a sense of his heroic capacity. He was only five feet seven, but the remaining inches were latent. I tried him almost secretly at first, for I was really rather afraid of the judgment my other models would pass on such a choice. If they regarded Miss Churm as little better than a snare what would they think of the representation by a person so little the real thing as an Italian street-vendor of a protagonist formed by a public school?

If I went a little in fear of them it wasn't because they bullied me, because they had got an oppressive foothold, but because in their really pathetic decorum and mysteriously permanent newness they counted on me so intensely. I was therefore very glad when Jack Hawley came home: he was always of such good counsel. He painted badly himself, but there was no one like him for putting his finger on the place. He had been absent from England for a year; he had been somewhere—I don't remember where—to get a fresh eye. I was in a good deal of dread of any such organ, but we were old friends; he had been away for months and a sense of emptiness was creeping into my life. I hadn't dodged a missile for a year.

He came back with a fresh eye, but with the same old black velvet blouse, and the first evening he spent in my studio we smoked cigarettes till the small hours. He had done no work himself, he had only got the eye; so the field was clear for the production of my little things. He wanted to see what I had produced for the *Cheapside*, but he was disappointed in the exhibition. That at least seemed the meaning of two or three comprehensive groans which, as he lounged on my big divan, his leg folded under him, looking at my latest drawings, issued from his lips with the smoke of the cigarette.

"What's the matter with you?" I asked.

105 "What's the matter with *you*?"

"Nothing save that I'm mystified."

"You are indeed. You're quite off the hinge. What's the meaning of this new fad?" And he tossed me, with visible irreverence, a drawing in which I happened to have depicted both my elegant models. I asked if he didn't think it good, and he replied that it struck him as execrable, given the sort of thing I had always represented myself to him as wishing to arrive at; but I let that pass—I was so anxious to see exactly what he meant. The two figures in the picture looked colossal, but I supposed this was *not* what he meant, inasmuch as, for aught he knew to the contrary, I might have been trying for some such effect. I maintained that I was working exactly in the same way as when he last had done me the honor to tell me I might do something some day. "Well, there's a screw loose somewhere," he answered; "wait a bit and I'll discover it." I depended upon him to do so: where else was the fresh eye? But he produced at last nothing more luminous than "I don't know—I don't like your types." This was lame for a critic who had never consented to discuss with me anything but the question of execution, the direction of strokes, and the mystery of values.

"In the drawings you've been looking at I think my types are very handsome."

"Oh they won't do!"

"I've been working with new models." 110

"I see you have. *They* won't do."

"Are you very sure of that?"

"Absolutely—they're stupid."

"You mean *I* am—for I ought to get round that."

"You *can't*—with such people. Who are they?" 115

I told him, so far as was necessary, and he concluded heartlessly: "*Ce sont des gens qu'il faut mettre à la porte.*"°

"You've never seen them; they're awfully good"—I flew to their defense.

"Not seen them? Why all this recent work of yours drops to pieces with them. It's all I want to see of them."

"No one else has said anything against it—the *Cheapside* people are pleased."

"Every one else is an ass, and the *Cheapside* people the biggest asses of 120 all. Come, don't pretend at this time of day to have pretty illusions about the public, especially about publishers and editors. It's not for *such* animals you work—it's for those you know, *coloro che sanno*;° so keep straight for *me* if you can't keep straight for yourself. There was a certain sort of thing you used to try for—and a very good thing it was. But this twaddle isn't *in* it."

Ce sont . . . la porte: French for "You'll have to show them to the door"   *coloro che sanno:* Italian for "the ones who know"

When I talked with Hawley later about "Rutland Ramsay" and its possible successors he declared that I must get back into my boat again or I should go to the bottom. His voice in short was the voice of warning.

I noted the warning, but I didn't turn my friends out of doors. They bored me a good deal; but the very fact that they bored me admonished me not to sacrifice them—if there was anything to be done with them— simply to irritation. As I look back at this phase they seem to me to have pervaded my life not a little. I have a vision of them as most of the time in my studio, seated against the wall on an old velvet bench to be out of the way, and resembling the while a pair of patient courtiers in a royal ante-chamber. I'm convinced that during the coldest weeks of the winter they held their ground because it saved them fire. Their newness was losing its gloss, and it was impossible not to feel them objects of charity. Whenever Miss Churm arrived they went away, and after I was fairly launched in "Rutland Ramsay" Miss Churm arrived pretty often. They managed to express to me tacitly that they supposed I wanted her for the low life of the book, and I let them suppose it, since they had attempted to study the work—it was lying about the studio—without discovering that it dealt only with the highest circles. They had dipped into the most brilliant of our novelists without deciphering many passages. I still took an hour from them, now and again, in spite of Jack Hawley's warning: it would be time enough to dismiss them, if dismissal should be necessary, when the rigor of the season was over. Hawley had made their acquaintance—he had met them at my fireside—and thought them a ridiculous pair. Learning that he was a painter they tried to approach him, to show him too that they were the real thing; but he looked at them, across the big room, as if they were miles away: they were a compendium of everything he most objected to in the social system of his country. Such people as that, all convention and patent-leather, with ejaculations that stopped conversation, had no business in a studio. A studio was a place to learn to see, and how could you see through a pair of featherbeds?

The main inconvenience I suffered at their hands was that at first I was shy of letting it break upon them that my artful little servant had begun to sit to me for "Rutland Ramsay." They knew I had been odd enough—they were prepared by this time to allow oddity to artists—to pick a foreign vagabond out of the streets when I might have had a person with whiskers and credentials; but it was some time before they learned how high I rated his accomplishments. They found him in an attitude more than once, but they never doubted I was doing him as an organ-grinder. There were several things they never guessed, and one of them was that for a striking scene in the novel, in which a footman briefly figured, it occurred to me to make use of Major Monarch as the menial. I kept putting this off, I didn't like to ask him to don the livery—besides the difficulty of finding a livery to fit him. At last, one day late in the winter, when I was at work on the despised Oronte, who caught one's idea on the wing, and was in the glow of feeling myself go very straight, they came in, the Major and his wife, with their society laugh about nothing (there was less and less to laugh at); came in like country-callers—they always reminded me of that—who have walked across the park after church and are presently persuaded to stay to luncheon. Luncheon was over, but they could stay to tea—I knew they wanted it. The fit was on me, however, and I couldn't let my ardor cool and my work wait, with the fading daylight, while my model prepared it. So I asked Mrs. Monarch if she would mind laying it out—a request which for an instant brought all the blood to her face. Her eyes were on her husband's for a second, and some mute telegraphy passed between them. Their folly was over the next instant; his cheerful shrewdness put an end to it. So far from pitying their wounded pride, I must add, I was moved to give it as complete a lesson as I could. They bustled about together and got out the cups and saucers and made the kettle boil. I know they felt as if they were waiting on my servant, and when the tea was prepared I said: "He'll have a cup, please—he's tired." Mrs. Monarch brought him one where he stood, and he took it from her as if he had been a gentleman at a party squeezing a crush-hat with an elbow.

Then it came over me that she had made a great effort for me—made it with a kind of nobleness—and that I owed her a compensation. Each time I saw her after this I wondered what the compensation could be. I couldn't go on doing the wrong thing to oblige them. Oh it *was* the wrong thing, the stamp of the work for which they sat—Hawley was not the only person to say it now. I sent in a large number of the drawings I had made for "Rutland Ramsay," and I received a warning that was more to the point than Hawley's. The artistic adviser of the house for which I was working was of opinion that many of my illustrations were not what had been looked for. Most of these illustrations were the subjects in which the Monarchs had figured. Without going into the question of what *had* been looked for, I had to face the fact that at this rate I shouldn't get the other books to do. I hurled myself in despair on Miss Churm—I put her through all her paces. I not only adopted Oronte publicly as my hero, but one morning when the Major looked in to see if I didn't require him to finish a *Cheapside* figure for which he had begun to sit the week before, I told him I had changed my mind—I'd do the drawing from my man. At this my visitor turned pale and stood looking at me. "Is *he* your idea of an English gentleman?" he asked.

I was disappointed, I was nervous, I wanted to get on with my work; so I replied with irritation: "Oh my dear Major—I can't be ruined for *you*!"

125 It was a horrid speech, but he stood another moment—after which, without a word, he quitted the studio. I drew a long breath, for I said to myself that I shouldn't see him again. I hadn't told him definitely that I was in danger of having my work rejected, but I was vexed at his not having felt the catastrophe in the air, read with me the moral of our fruitless collaboration, the lesson that in the deceptive atmosphere of art even the highest respectability may fail of being plastic.

I didn't owe my friends money, but I did see them again. They reappeared together three days later; and, given all the other facts, there was something tragic in that one. It was a clear proof they could find nothing else in life to do. They had threshed the matter out in a dismal conference—they had digested the bad news that they were not in for the series. If they weren't useful to me for the *Cheapside* their function seemed difficult to determine, and I could only judge at first that they had come, forgivingly, decorously, to take a last leave. This made me rejoice in secret that I had little leisure for a scene; for I had placed both my other models in position together and I was pegging away at a drawing from which I hoped to derive glory. It had been suggested by the passage in which Rutland Ramsay, drawing up a chair to Artemisia's piano-stool, says extraordinary things to her while she ostensibly fingers out a difficult piece of music. I had done Miss Churm at the piano before—it was an attitude in which she knew how to take on an absolutely poetic grace. I wished the two figures to "compose" together with intensity, and my little Italian had entered perfectly into my conception. The pair were vividly before me, the piano had been pulled out; it was a charming show of blended youth and murmured love, which I had only to catch and keep. My visitors stood and looked at it, and I was friendly to them over my shoulder.

They made no response, but I was used to silent company and went on with my work, only a little disconcerted—even though exhilarated by the sense that *this* was at least the ideal thing—at not having got rid of them after all. Presently I heard Mrs. Monarch's sweet voice beside or rather above me: "I wish her hair were a little better done." I looked up and she was staring with a strange fixedness at Miss Churm, whose back was turned to her. "Do you mind my just touching it?" she went on—a question which made me spring up for an instant as with the instinctive fear that she might do the young lady a harm. But she quieted me with a glance I shall never forget—I confess I should like to have been able to paint *that*—and went for a moment to my model. She spoke to her softly, laying a hand on her shoulder and bending over her; and as the girl, understanding, gratefully assented, she disposed her rough curls, with a few quick passes, in such a way as to make Miss Churm's head twice as charming. It was one of the most heroic personal services I've ever seen rendered. Then Mrs. Monarch turned away with a low sigh and, looking about her as if for something to do, stooped to the floor with a noble humility and picked up a dirty rag that had dropped out of my paint-box.

The Major meanwhile had also been looking for something to do, and, wandering to the other end of the studio, saw before him my breakfast-things neglected, unremoved. "I say, can't I be useful *here?*" he called out to me with an irrepressible quaver. I assented with a laugh that I fear was awkward, and for the next ten minutes, while I worked, I heard the light clatter of china and the tinkle of spoons and glass. Mrs. Monarch assisted her husband—they washed up my crockery, they put it away. They wandered off into my little scullery, and I afterwards found that they had cleaned my knives and that my slender stock of plate had an unprecedented surface. When it came over me, the latent eloquence of what they were doing, I confess that my drawing was blurred for a moment—the picture swam. They had accepted their failure, but they couldn't accept their fate. They had bowed their heads in bewilderment to the perverse and cruel law in virtue of which the real thing could be so much less precious than the unreal; but they didn't want to starve. If my servants were my models, then my models might be my servants. They would reverse the parts—the others would sit for the ladies and gentlemen and *they* would do the work. They would still be in the studio—it was an intense dumb appeal to me not to turn them out. "Take us on," they wanted to say, "we'll do *anything*."

My pencil dropped from my hand; my sitting was spoiled and I got rid of my sitters, who were also evidently rather mystified and awe-struck. Then, alone with the Major and his wife I had a most uncomfortable moment. He put their prayer into a single sentence: "I say, you know—just let *us* do for you, can't you?" I couldn't—it was dreadful to see them emptying my slops; but I pretended I could, to oblige them, for about a week. Then I gave them a sum of money to go away, and I never saw them again. I obtained the remaining books, but my friend Hawley repeats that Major and Mrs. Monarch did me a permanent harm, got me into false ways. If it be true I'm content to have paid the price—for the memory.

JHUMPA LAHIRI
Interpreter of Maladies

At the tea stall Mr. and Mrs. Das bickered about who should take Tina to the toilet. Eventually Mrs. Das relented when Mr. Das pointed out that he had given the girl her bath the night before. In the rearview mirror Mr. Kapasi watched as Mrs. Das emerged slowly from his bulky white Ambassador, dragging her shaved, largely bare legs across the back seat. She did not hold the little girl's hand as they walked to the rest room.

They were on their way to see the Sun Temple at Konarak. It was a dry, bright Saturday, the mid-July heat tempered by a steady ocean breeze, ideal weather for sightseeing. Ordinarily Mr. Kapasi would not have stopped so soon along the way, but less than five minutes after he'd picked up the family that morning in front of Hotel Sandy Villa, the little girl had complained. The first thing Mr. Kapasi had noticed when he saw Mr. and Mrs. Das, standing with their children under the portico of the hotel, was that they were very young, perhaps not even thirty. In addition to Tina they had two boys, Ronny and Bobby, who appeared very close in age and had teeth covered in a network of flashing silver wires. The family looked Indian but dressed as foreigners did, the children in stiff, brightly colored clothing and caps with translucent visors. Mr. Kapasi was accustomed to foreign tourists; he was assigned to them regularly because he could speak English. Yesterday he had driven an elderly couple from Scotland, both with spotted faces and fluffy white hair so thin it exposed their sunburnt scalps. In comparison, the tanned, youthful faces of Mr. and Mrs. Das were all the more striking. When he'd introduced himself, Mr. Kapasi had pressed his palms together in greeting, but Mr. Das squeezed hands like an American so that Mr. Kapasi felt it in his elbow. Mrs. Das, for her part, had flexed one side of her mouth, smiling dutifully at Mr. Kapasi, without displaying any interest in him.

As they waited at the tea stall, Ronny, who looked like the older of the two boys, clambered suddenly out of the back seat, intrigued by a goat tied to a stake in the ground.

INTERPRETER OF MALADIES   First published in her 1999 collection *Interpreter of Maladies*, which won the 2000 Pulitzer Prize for fiction. Lahiri's book conducts an incisive exploration of Indian culture, especially as it collides with the values of western Europe and the United States. This story takes place in the state of Orissa on the eastern coast of India; the "Sun Temple at Konarak" is located on the coast near the city of Puri, where the Das family is staying. Of Indian ancestry, Jhumpa Lahiri (b. 1967) was born in London, grew up in Rhode Island, and earned an M.A. in creative writing and a Ph.D. in Renaissance Studies from Boston University. She now lives in New York City.

"Don't touch it," Mr. Das said. He glanced up from his paperback tour book, which said "INDIA" in yellow letters and looked as if it had been published abroad. His voice, somehow tentative and a little shrill, sounded as though it had not yet settled into maturity.

"I want to give it a piece of gum," the boy called back as he trotted 5 ahead.

Mr. Das stepped out of the car and stretched his legs by squatting briefly to the ground. A clean-shaven man, he looked exactly like a magnified version of Ronny. He had a sapphire blue visor, and was dressed in shorts, sneakers, and a T-shirt. The camera slung around his neck, with an impressive telephoto lens and numerous buttons and markings, was the only complicated thing he wore. He frowned, watching as Ronny rushed toward the goat, but appeared to have no intention of intervening. "Bobby, make sure that your brother doesn't do anything stupid."

"I don't feel like it," Bobby said, not moving. He was sitting in the front seat beside Mr. Kapasi, studying a picture of the elephant god taped to the glove compartment.

"No need to worry," Mr. Kapasi said. "They are quite tame." Mr. Kapasi was forty-six years old, with receding hair that had gone completely silver, but his butterscotch complexion and his unlined brow, which he treated in spare moments to dabs of lotus-oil balm, made it easy to imagine what he must have looked like at an earlier age. He wore gray trousers and a matching jacket-style shirt, tapered at the waist, with short sleeves and a large pointed collar, made of a thin but durable synthetic material. He had specified both the cut and the fabric to his tailor—it was his preferred uniform for giving tours because it did not get crushed during his long hours behind the wheel. Through the windshield he watched as Ronny circled around the goat, touched it quickly on its side, then trotted back to the car.

"You left India as a child?" Mr. Kapasi asked when Mr. Das had settled once again into the passenger seat.

"Oh, Mina and I were both born in America," Mr. Das announced with 10 an air of sudden confidence. "Born and raised. Our parents live here now, in Assansol. They retired. We visit them every couple years." He turned to watch as the little girl ran toward the car, the wide purple bows of her sundress flopping on her narrow brown shoulders. She was holding to her chest a doll with yellow hair that looked as if it had been chopped, as a punitive measure, with a pair of dull scissors. "This is Tina's first trip to India, isn't it, Tina?"

"I don't have to go to the bathroom anymore," Tina announced.

"Where's Mina?" Mr. Das asked.

Mr. Kapasi found it strange that Mr. Das should refer to his wife by her first name when speaking to the little girl. Tina pointed to where

Mrs. Das was purchasing something from one of the shirtless men who worked at the tea stall. Mr. Kapasi heard one of the shirtless men sing a phrase from a popular Hindi love song as Mrs. Das walked back to the car, but she did not appear to understand the words of the song, for she did not express irritation, or embarrassment, or react in any other way to the man's declarations.

He observed her. She wore a red-and-white-checkered skirt that stopped above her knees, slip-on shoes with a square wooden heel, and a close-fitting blouse styled like a man's undershirt. The blouse was decorated at chest-level with a calico appliqué in the shape of a strawberry. She was a short woman, with small hands like paws, her frosty pink fingernails painted to match her lips, and was slightly plump in her figure. Her hair, shorn only a little longer than her husband's, was parted far to one side. She was wearing large dark brown sunglasses with a pinkish tint to them, and carried a big straw bag, almost as big as her torso, shaped like a bowl, with a water bottle poking out of it. She walked slowly, carrying some puffed rice tossed with peanuts and chili peppers in a large packet made from newspapers. Mr. Kapasi turned to Mr. Das.

15 "Where in America do you live?"

"New Brunswick, New Jersey."

"Next to New York?"

"Exactly. I teach middle school there."

"What subject?"

20 "Science. In fact, every year I take my students on a trip to the Museum of Natural History in New York City. In a way we have a lot in common, you could say, you and I. How long have you been a tour guide, Mr. Kapasi?"

"Five years."

Mrs. Das reached the car. "How long's the trip?" she asked, shutting the door.

"About two and a half hours," Mr. Kapasi replied.

At this Mrs. Das gave an impatient sigh, as if she had been traveling her whole life without pause. She fanned herself with a folded Bombay film magazine written in English.

25 "I thought that the Sun Temple is only eighteen miles north of Puri," Mr. Das said, tapping on the tour book.

"The roads to Konarak are poor. Actually it is a distance of fifty-two miles," Mr. Kapasi explained.

Mr. Das nodded, readjusting the camera strap where it had begun to chafe the back of his neck.

Before starting the ignition, Mr. Kapasi reached back to make sure the cranklike locks on the inside of each of the back doors were secured. As soon as the car began to move the little girl began to play with the lock on her side, clicking it with some effort forward and backward, but Mrs. Das said nothing to stop her. She sat a bit slouched at one end of the back seat, not offering her puffed rice to anyone. Ronny and Tina sat on either side of her, both snapping bright green gum.

"Look," Bobby said as the car began to gather speed. He pointed with his finger to the tall trees that lined the road. "Look."

"Monkeys!" Ronny shrieked. "Wow!"   30

They were seated in groups along the branches, with shining black faces, silver bodies, horizontal eyebrows, and crested heads. Their long gray tails dangled like a series of ropes among the leaves. A few scratched themselves with black leathery hands, or swung their feet, staring as the car passed.

"We call them the hanuman,"° Mr. Kapasi said. "They are quite common in the area."

As soon as he spoke, one of the monkeys leaped into the middle of the road, causing Mr. Kapasi to brake suddenly. Another bounced onto the hood of the car, then sprang away. Mr. Kapasi beeped his horn. The children began to get excited, sucking in their breath and covering their faces partly with their hands. They had never seen monkeys outside of a zoo, Mr. Das explained. He asked Mr. Kapasi to stop the car so that he could take a picture.

While Mr. Das adjusted his telephoto lens, Mrs. Das reached into her straw bag and pulled out a bottle of colorless nail polish, which she proceeded to stroke on the tip of her index finger.

The little girl stuck out a hand. "Mine too. Mommy, do mine too."   35

"Leave me alone," Mrs. Das said, blowing on her nail and turning her body slightly. "You're making me mess up."

The little girl occupied herself by buttoning and unbuttoning a pinafore on the doll's plastic body.

"All set," Mr. Das said, replacing the lens cap.

The car rattled considerably as it raced along the dusty road, causing them all to pop up from their seats every now and then, but Mrs. Das continued to polish her nails. Mr. Kapasi eased up on the accelerator, hoping to produce a smoother ride. When he reached for the gearshift the boy in front accommodated him by swinging his hairless knees out of the way. Mr. Kapasi noted that this boy was slightly paler than the other children. "Daddy, why is the driver sitting on the wrong side in this car, too?" the boy asked.

"They all do that here, dummy," Ronny said.   40

"Don't call your brother a dummy," Mr. Das said. He turned to Mr. Kapasi. "In America, you know . . . it confuses them."

---

hanuman: a gray monkey venerated by Hindus

"Oh yes, I am well aware," Mr. Kapasi said. As delicately as he could, he shifted gears again, accelerating as they approached a hill in the road. "I see it on *Dallas*, the steering wheels are on the left-hand side."

"What's *Dallas*?" Tina asked, banging her now naked doll on the seat behind Mr. Kapasi.

"It went off the air," Mr. Das explained. "It's a television show."

45 They were all like siblings, Mr. Kapasi thought as they passed a row of date trees. Mr. and Mrs. Das behaved like an older brother and sister, not parents. It seemed that they were in charge of the children only for the day; it was hard to believe they were regularly responsible for anything other than themselves. Mr. Das tapped on his lens cap, and his tour book, dragging his thumbnail occasionally across the pages so that they made a scraping sound. Mrs. Das continued to polish her nails. She had still not removed her sunglasses. Every now and then Tina renewed her plea that she wanted her nails done, too, and so at one point Mrs. Das flicked a drop of polish on the little girl's finger before depositing the bottle back inside her straw bag.

"Isn't this an air-conditioned car?" she asked, still blowing on her hand. The window on Tina's side was broken and could not be rolled down.

"Quit complaining," Mr. Das said. "It isn't so hot."

"I told you to get a car with air-conditioning," Mrs. Das continued. "Why do you do this, Raj, just to save a few stupid rupees. What are you saving us, fifty cents?"

Their accents sounded just like the ones Mr. Kapasi heard on American television programs, though not like the ones on *Dallas*.

50 "Doesn't it get tiresome, Mr. Kapasi, showing people the same thing every day?" Mr. Das asked, rolling down his own window all the way. "Hey, do you mind stopping the car. I just want to get a shot of this guy."

Mr. Kapasi pulled over to the side of the road as Mr. Das took a picture of a barefoot man, his head wrapped in a dirty turban, seated on top of a cart of grain sacks pulled by a pair of bullocks. Both the man and the bullocks were emaciated. In the back seat Mrs. Das gazed out another window, at the sky, where nearly transparent clouds passed quickly in front of one another.

"I look forward to it, actually," Mr. Kapasi said as they continued on their way. "The Sun Temple is one of my favorite places. In that way it is a reward for me. I give tours on Fridays and Saturdays only. I have another job during the week."

"Oh? Where?" Mr. Das asked.

"I work in a doctor's office."

55 "You're a doctor?"

"I am not a doctor. I work with one. As an interpreter."

"What does a doctor need an interpreter for?"

"He has a number of Gujarati° patients. My father was Gujarati, but many people do not speak Gujarati in this area, including the doctor. And so the doctor asked me to work in his office, interpreting what the patients say."

"Interesting. I've never heard of anything like that," Mr. Das said.

Mr. Kapasi shrugged. "It is a job like any other."   60

"But so romantic," Mrs. Das said dreamily, breaking her extended silence. She lifted her pinkish brown sunglasses and arranged them on top of her head like a tiara. For the first time, her eyes met Mr. Kapasi's in the rearview mirror: pale, a bit small, their gaze fixed but drowsy.

Mr. Das craned to look at her. "What's so romantic about it?"

"I don't know. Something." She shrugged, knitting her brows together for an instant. "Would you like a piece of gum, Mr. Kapasi?" she asked brightly. She reached into her straw bag and handed him a small square wrapped in green-and-white-striped paper. As soon as Mr. Kapasi put the gum in his mouth a thick sweet liquid burst onto his tongue.

"Tell us more about your job, Mr. Kapasi," Mrs. Das said.

"What would you like to know, madame?"   65

"I don't know," she shrugged, munching on some puffed rice and licking the mustard oil from the corners of her mouth. "Tell us a typical situation." She settled back in her seat, her head tilted in a patch of sun, and closed her eyes. "I want to picture what happens."

"Very well. The other day a man came in with a pain in his throat."

"Did he smoke cigarettes?"

"No. It was very curious. He complained that he felt as if there were long pieces of straw stuck in his throat. When I told the doctor he was able to prescribe the proper medication."

"That's so neat."   70

"Yes," Mr. Kapasi agreed after some hesitation.

"So these patients are totally dependent on you," Mrs. Das said. She spoke slowly, as if she were thinking aloud. "In a way, more dependent on you than the doctor."

"How do you mean? How could it be?"

"Well, for example, you could tell the doctor that the pain felt like a burning, not straw. The patient would never know what you had told the doctor, and the doctor wouldn't know that you had told the wrong thing. It's a big responsibility."

"Yes, a big responsibility you have there, Mr. Kapasi," Mr. Das agreed. 75

Mr. Kapasi had never thought of his job in such complimentary terms. To him it was a thankless occupation. He found nothing noble in

Gujarati: from Gujarat, a state in western India

interpreting people's maladies, assiduously translating the symptoms of so many swollen bones, countless cramps of bellies and bowels, spots on people's palms that changed color, shape, or size. The doctor, nearly half his age, had an affinity for bell-bottom trousers and made humorless jokes about the Congress party. Together they worked in a stale little infirmary where Mr. Kapasi's smartly tailored clothes clung to him in the heat, in spite of the blackened blades of a ceiling fan churning over their heads.

The job was a sign of his failings. In his youth he'd been a devoted scholar of foreign languages, the owner of an impressive collection of dictionaries. He had dreamed of being an interpreter for diplomats and dignitaries, resolving conflicts between people and nations, settling disputes of which he alone could understand both sides. He was a self-educated man. In a series of notebooks, in the evenings before his parents settled his marriage, he had listed the common etymologies of words, and at one point in his life he was confident that he could converse, if given the opportunity, in English, French, Russian, Portuguese, and Italian, not to mention Hindi, Bengali, Orissi, and Gujarati. Now only a handful of European phrases remained in his memory, scattered words for things like saucers and chairs. English was the only non-Indian language he spoke fluently anymore. Mr. Kapasi knew it was not a remarkable talent. Sometimes he feared that his children knew better English than he did, just from watching television. Still, it came in handy for the tours.

He had taken the job as an interpreter after his first son, at the age of seven, contracted typhoid—that was how he had first made the acquaintance of the doctor. At the time Mr. Kapasi had been teaching English in a grammar school, and he bartered his skills as an interpreter to pay the increasingly exorbitant medical bills. In the end the boy had died one evening in his mother's arms, his limbs burning with fever, but then there was the funeral to pay for, and the other children who were born soon enough, and the newer, bigger house, and the good schools and tutors, and the fine shoes and the television, and the countless other ways he tried to console his wife and to keep her from crying in her sleep, and so when the doctor offered to pay him twice as much as he earned at the grammar school, he accepted. Mr. Kapasi knew that his wife had little regard for his career as an interpreter. He knew it reminded her of the son she'd lost, and that she resented the other lives he helped, in his own small way, to save. If ever she referred to his position, she used the phrase "doctor's assistant," as if the process of interpretation were equal to taking someone's temperature, or changing a bedpan. She never asked him about the patients who came to the doctor's office, or said that his job was a big responsibility.

For this reason it flattered Mr. Kapasi that Mrs. Das was so intrigued by his job. Unlike his wife, she had reminded him of its intellectual challenges. She had also used the word "romantic." She did not behave in a romantic way toward her husband, and yet she had used the word to describe him. He wondered if Mr. and Mrs. Das were a bad match, just as he and his wife were. Perhaps they, too, had little in common apart from three children and a decade of their lives. The signs he recognized from his own marriage were there—the bickering, the indifference, the protracted silences. Her sudden interest in him, an interest she did not express in either her husband or her children, was mildly intoxicating. When Mr. Kapasi thought once again about how she had said "romantic," the feeling of intoxication grew.

He began to check his reflection in the rearview mirror as he drove, 80 feeling grateful that he had chosen the gray suit that morning and not the brown one, which tended to sag a little in the knees. From time to time he glanced through the mirror at Mrs. Das. In addition to glancing at her face he glanced at the strawberry between her breasts, and the golden brown hollow in her throat. He decided to tell Mrs. Das about another patient, and another: the young woman who had complained of a sensation of raindrops in her spine, the gentleman whose birthmark had begun to sprout hairs. Mrs. Das listened attentively, stroking her hair with a small plastic brush that resembled an oval bed of nails, asking more questions, for yet another example. The children were quiet, intent on spotting more monkeys in the trees, and Mr. Das was absorbed by his tour book, so it seemed like a private conversation between Mr. Kapasi and Mrs. Das. In this manner the next half hour passed, and when they stopped for lunch at a roadside restaurant that sold fritters and omelette sandwiches, usually something Mr. Kapasi looked forward to on his tours so that he could sit in peace and enjoy some hot tea, he was disappointed. As the Das family settled together under a magenta umbrella fringed with white and orange tassels, and placed their orders with one of the waiters who marched about in tricornered caps, Mr. Kapasi reluctantly headed toward a neighboring table.

"Mr. Kapasi, wait. There's room here," Mrs. Das called out. She gathered Tina onto her lap, insisting that he accompany them. And so, together, they had bottled mango juice and sandwiches and plates of onions and potatoes deep-fried in graham-flour batter. After finishing two omelette sandwiches Mr. Das took more pictures of the group as they ate.

"How much longer?" he asked Mr. Kapasi as he paused to load a new roll of film in the camera.

"About half an hour more."

By now the children had gotten up from the table to look at more monkeys perched in a nearby tree, so there was a considerable space between Mrs. Das and Mr. Kapasi. Mr. Das placed the camera to his face and squeezed one eye shut, his tongue exposed at one corner of his mouth. "This looks funny. Mina, you need to lean in closer to Mr. Kapasi."

85   She did. He could smell a scent on her skin, like a mixture of whiskey and rosewater. He worried suddenly that she could smell his perspiration, which he knew had collected beneath the synthetic material of his shirt. He polished off his mango juice in one gulp and smoothed his silver hair with his hands. A bit of the juice dripped onto his chin. He wondered if Mrs. Das had noticed.

She had not. "What's your address, Mr. Kapasi?" she inquired, fishing for something inside her straw bag.

"You would like my address?"

"So we can send you copies," she said. "Of the pictures." She handed him a scrap of paper which she had hastily ripped from a page of her film magazine. The blank portion was limited, for the narrow strip was crowded by lines of text and a tiny picture of a hero and heroine embracing under a eucalyptus tree.

The paper curled as Mr. Kapasi wrote his address in clear, careful letters. She would write to him, asking about his days interpreting at the doctor's office, and he would respond eloquently, choosing only the most entertaining anecdotes, ones that would make her laugh out loud as she read them in her house in New Jersey. In time she would reveal the disappointment of her marriage, and he his. In this way their friendship would grow, and flourish. He would possess a picture of the two of them, eating fried onions under a magenta umbrella, which he would keep, he decided, safely tucked between the pages of his Russian grammar. As his mind raced, Mr. Kapasi experienced a mild and pleasant shock. It was similar to a feeling he used to experience long ago when, after months of translating with the aid of a dictionary, he would finally read a passage from a French novel, or an Italian sonnet, and understand the words, one after another, unencumbered by his own efforts. In those moments Mr. Kapasi used to believe that all was right with the world, that all struggles were rewarded, that all of life's mistakes made sense in the end. The promise that he would hear from Mrs. Das now filled him with the same belief.

90   When he finished writing his address Mr. Kapasi handed her the paper, but as soon as he did so he worried that he had either misspelled his name, or accidentally reversed the numbers of his postal code. He dreaded the possibility of a lost letter, the photograph never reaching him, hovering somewhere in Orissa, close but ultimately unattainable. He thought of asking for the slip of paper again, just to make sure he had written his address accurately, but Mrs. Das had already dropped it into the jumble of her bag.

They reached Konarak at two-thirty. The temple, made of sandstone, was a massive pyramid-like structure in the shape of a chariot.

It was dedicated to the great master of life, the sun, which struck three sides of the edifice as it made its journey each day across the sky. Twenty-four giant wheels were carved on the north and south sides of the plinth. The whole thing was drawn by a team of seven horses, speeding as if through the heavens. As they approached, Mr. Kapasi explained that the temple had been built between A.D. 1243 and 1255, with the efforts of twelve hundred artisans, by the great ruler of the Ganga dynasty, King Narasimhadeva the First, to commemorate his victory against the Muslim army.

"It says the temple occupies about a hundred and seventy acres of land," Mr. Das said, reading from his book.

"It's like a desert," Ronny said, his eyes wandering across the sand that stretched on all sides beyond the temple.

"The Chandrabhaga River once flowed one mile north of here. It is dry now," Mr. Kapasi said, turning off the engine.

They got out and walked toward the temple, posing first for pictures by the pair of lions that flanked the steps. Mr. Kapasi led them next to one of the wheels of the chariot, higher than any human being, nine feet in diameter.

" 'The wheels are supposed to symbolize the wheel of life,' " Mr. Das read. " 'They depict the cycle of creation, preservation, and achievement of realization.' Cool." He turned the page of his book. ' "Each wheel is divided into eight thick and thin spokes, dividing the day into eight equal parts. The rims are carved with designs of birds and animals, whereas the medallions in the spokes are carved with women in luxurious poses, largely erotic in nature.' "

What he referred to were the countless friezes of entwined naked bodies, making love in various positions, women clinging to the necks of men, their knees wrapped eternally around their lovers' thighs. In addition to these were assorted scenes from daily life, of hunting and trading, of deer being killed with bows and arrows and marching warriors holding swords in their hands.

It was no longer possible to enter the temple, for it had filled with rubble years ago, but they admired the exterior, as did all the tourists Mr. Kapasi brought there, slowly strolling along each of its sides. Mr. Das trailed behind, taking pictures. The children ran ahead, pointing to figures of naked people, intrigued in particular by the Nagamithunas, the half-human, half-serpentine couples who were said, Mr. Kapasi told them, to live in the deepest waters of the sea. Mr. Kapasi was pleased that they liked the temple, pleased especially that it appealed to Mrs. Das. She stopped every three or four paces, staring silently at the carved lovers, and the processions of elephants, and the topless female musicians beating on two-sided drums.

Though Mr. Kapasi had been to the temple countless times, it occurred to him, as he, too, gazed at the topless women, that he had never seen his own wife fully naked. Even when they had made love she kept the panels of her blouse hooked together, the string of her petticoat knotted around her waist. He had never admired the backs of his wife's legs the way he now admired those of Mrs. Das, walking as if for his benefit alone. He had, of course, seen plenty of bare limbs before, belonging to the American and European ladies who took his tours. But Mrs. Das was different. Unlike the other women, who had an interest only in the temple, and kept their noses buried in a guidebook, or their eyes behind the lens of a camera, Mrs. Das had taken an interest in him.

100   Mr. Kapasi was anxious to be alone with her, to continue their private conversation, yet he felt nervous to walk at her side. She was lost behind her sunglasses, ignoring her husband's requests that she pose for another picture, walking past her children as if they were strangers. Worried that he might disturb her, Mr. Kapasi walked ahead, to admire, as he always did, the three life-sized bronze avatars of Surya, the sun god, each emerging from its own niche on the temple facade to greet the sun at dawn, noon, and evening. They wore elaborate headdresses, their languid, elongated eyes closed, their bare chests draped with carved chains and amulets. Hibiscus petals, offerings from previous visitors, were strewn at their gray-green feet. The last statue, on the northern wall of the temple, was Mr. Kapasi's favorite. This Surya had a tired expression, weary after a hard day of work, sitting astride a horse with folded legs. Even his horse's eyes were drowsy. Around his body were smaller sculptures of women in pairs, their hips thrust to one side.

"Who's that?" Mrs. Das asked. He was startled to see that she was standing beside him.

"He is the Astachala-Surya," Mr. Kapasi said. "The setting sun."

"So in a couple of hours the sun will set right here?" She slipped a foot out of one of her square-heeled shoes, rubbed her toes on the back of her other leg.

"That is correct."

105   She raised her sunglasses for a moment, then put them back on again. "Neat."

Mr. Kapasi was not certain exactly what the word suggested, but he had a feeling it was a favorable response. He hoped that Mrs. Das had understood Surya's beauty, his power. Perhaps they would discuss it further in their letters. He would explain things to her, things about India, and she would explain things to him about America. In its own way this correspondence would fulfill his dream, of serving as an interpreter between nations. He looked at her straw bag, delighted that his address lay nestled among its contents. When he pictured her so many thousands of miles away he plummeted, so much so that he had an overwhelming urge to wrap his arms around her, to freeze with her, even for an instant, in an embrace witnessed by his favorite Surya. But Mrs. Das had already started walking. "When do you return to America?" he asked, trying to sound placid. "In ten days."

He calculated: A week to settle in, a week to develop the pictures, a few days to compose her letter, two weeks to get to India by air. According to his schedule, allowing room for delays, he would hear from Mrs. Das in approximately six weeks' time.

The family was silent as Mr. Kapasi drove them back, a little past four-thirty, to Hotel Sandy Villa. The children had bought miniature granite versions of the chariot's wheels at a souvenir stand, and they turned them round in their hands. Mr. Das continued to read his book. Mrs. Das untangled Tina's hair with her brush and divided it into two little ponytails. 110

Mr. Kapasi was beginning to dread the thought of dropping them off. He was not prepared to begin his six-week wait to hear from Mrs. Das. As he stole glances at her in the rearview mirror, wrapping elastic bands around Tina's hair, he wondered how he might make the tour last a little longer. Ordinarily he sped back to Puri using a shortcut, eager to return home, scrub his feet and hands with sandalwood soap, and enjoy the evening newspaper and a cup of tea that his wife would serve him in silence. The thought of that silence, something to which he'd long been resigned, now oppressed him. It was then that he suggested visiting the hills at Udayagiri and Khandagiri, where a number of monastic dwellings were hewn out of the ground, facing one another across a defile. It was some miles away, but well worth seeing, Mr. Kapasi told them.

"Oh yeah, there's something mentioned about it in this book," Mr. Das said. "Built by a Jain king or something."

"Shall we go then?" Mr. Kapasi asked. He paused at a turn in the road. "It's to the left."

Mr. Das turned to look at Mrs. Das. Both of them shrugged.

"Left, left," the children chanted. 115

Mr. Kapasi turned the wheel, almost delirious with relief. He did not know what he would do or say to Mrs. Das once they arrived at the hills. Perhaps he would tell her what a pleasing smile she had. Perhaps he would compliment her strawberry shirt, which he found irresistibly becoming. Perhaps, when Mr. Das was busy taking a picture, he would take her hand.

He did not have to worry. When they got to the hills, divided by a steep path thick with trees, Mrs. Das refused to get out of the car. All along the path, dozens of monkeys were seated on stones, as well as on the branches of the trees. Their hind legs were stretched out in front and raised to shoulder level, their arms resting on their knees.

"My legs are tired," she said, sinking low in her seat. "I'll stay here."

"Why did you have to wear those stupid shoes?" Mr. Das said. "You won't be in the pictures."

120   "Pretend I'm there."

"But we could use one of these pictures for our Christmas card this year. We didn't get one of all five of us at the Sun Temple. Mr. Kapasi could take it."

"I'm not coming. Anyway, those monkeys give me the creeps."

"But they're harmless," Mr. Das said. He turned to Mr. Kapasi. "Aren't they?"

"They are more hungry than dangerous," Mr. Kapasi said. "Do not provoke them with food, and they will not bother you."

125   Mr. Das headed up the defile with the children, the boys at his side, the little girl on his shoulders. Mr. Kapasi watched as they crossed paths with a Japanese man and woman, the only other tourists there, who paused for a final photograph, then stepped into a nearby car and drove away. As the car disappeared out of view some of the monkeys called out, emitting soft whooping sounds, and then walked on their flat black hands and feet up the path. At one point a group of them formed a little ring around Mr. Das and the children. Tina screamed in delight. Ronny ran in circles around his father. Bobby bent down and picked up a fat stick on the ground. When he extended it, one of the monkeys approached him and snatched it, then briefly beat the ground.

"I'll join them," Mr. Kapasi said, unlocking the door on his side. "There is much to explain about the caves."

"No. Stay a minute," Mrs. Das said. She got out of the back seat and slipped in beside Mr. Kapasi. "Raj has his dumb book anyway." Together, through the windshield, Mrs. Das and Mr. Kapasi watched as Bobby and the monkey passed the stick back and forth between them.

"A brave little boy," Mr. Kapasi commented.

"It's not so surprising," Mrs. Das said.

130   "No?"

"He's not his."

"I beg your pardon?"

"Raj's. He's not Raj's son."

Mr. Kapasi felt a prickle on his skin. He reached into his shirt pocket for the small tin of lotus-oil balm he carried with him at all times, and applied it to three spots on his forehead. He knew that Mrs. Das was watching him, but he did not turn to face her. Instead he watched as the figures of Mr. Das and the children grew smaller, climbing up the steep path, pausing every now and then for a picture, surrounded by a growing number of monkeys.

"Are you surprised?" The way she put it made him choose his words 135
with care.

"It's not the type of thing one assumes," Mr. Kapasi replied slowly. He
put the tin of lotus-oil balm back in his pocket.

"No, of course not. And no one knows, of course. No one at all. I've
kept it a secret for eight whole years." She looked at Mr. Kapasi, tilting her
chin as if to gain a fresh perspective. "But now I've told you."

Mr. Kapasi nodded. He felt suddenly parched, and his forehead was
warm and slightly numb from the balm. He considered asking Mrs. Das
for a sip of water, then decided against it.

"We met when we were very young," she said. She reached into her
straw bag in search of something, then pulled out a packet of puffed rice.
"Want some?"

"No, thank you." 140

She put a fistful in her mouth, sank into the seat a little, and looked
away from Mr. Kapasi, out the window on her side of the car. "We married
when we were still in college. We were in high school when he proposed.
We went to the same college, of course. Back then we couldn't stand the
thought of being separated, not for a day, not for a minute. Our parents
were best friends who lived in the same town. My entire life I saw him
every weekend, either at our house or theirs. We were sent upstairs to play
together while our parents joked about our marriage. Imagine! They never
caught us at anything, though in a way I think it was all more or less a
setup. The things we did those Friday and Saturday nights, while our parents sat downstairs drinking tea . . . I could tell you stories, Mr. Kapasi."

As a result of spending all her time in college with Raj, she continued,
she did not make many close friends. There was no one to confide in about
him at the end of a difficult day, or to share a passing thought or a worry.
Her parents now lived on the other side of the world, but she had never
been very close to them, anyway. After marrying so young she was overwhelmed by it all, having a child so quickly, and nursing, and warming up
bottles of milk and testing their temperature against her wrist while Raj
was at work, dressed in sweaters and corduroy pants, teaching his students
about rocks and dinosaurs. Raj never looked cross or harried, or plump as
she had become after the first baby.

Always tired, she declined invitations from her one or two college
girlfriends, to have lunch or shop in Manhattan. Eventually the friends
stopped calling her, so that she was left at home all day with the baby,
surrounded by toys that made her trip when she walked or wince when she
sat, always cross and tired. Only occasionally did they go out after Ronny
was born, and even more rarely did they entertain. Raj didn't mind; he
looked forward to coming home from teaching and watching television

and bouncing Ronny on his knee. She had been outraged when Raj told her that a Punjabi friend, someone whom she had once met but did not remember, would be staying with them for a week for some job interviews in the New Brunswick area.

Bobby was conceived in the afternoon, on a sofa littered with rubber teething toys, after the friend learned that a London pharmaceutical company had hired him, while Ronny cried to be freed from his playpen. She made no protest when the friend touched the small of her back as she was about to make a pot of coffee, then pulled her against his crisp navy suit. He made love to her swiftly, in silence, with an expertise she had never known, without the meaningful expressions and smiles Raj always insisted on afterward. The next day Raj drove the friend to JFK. He was married now, to a Punjabi girl, and they lived in London still, and every year they exchanged Christmas cards with Raj and Mina, each couple tucking photos of their families into the envelopes. He did not know that he was Bobby's father. He never would.

145   "I beg your pardon, Mrs. Das, but why have you told me this information?" Mr. Kapasi asked when she had finally finished speaking, and had turned to face him once again.

"For God's sake, stop calling me Mrs. Das. I'm twenty-eight. You probably have children my age."

"Not quite." It disturbed Mr. Kapasi to learn that she thought of him as a parent. The feeling he had had toward her, that had made him check his reflection in the rearview mirror as they drove, evaporated a little.

"I told you because of your talents." She put the packet of puffed rice back into her bag without folding over the top.

"I don't understand," Mr. Kapasi said.

150   "Don't you see? For eight years I haven't been able to express this to anybody, not to friends, certainly not to Raj. He doesn't even suspect it. He thinks I'm still in love with him. Well, don't you have anything to say?"

"About what?"

"About what I've just told you. About my secret, and about how terrible it makes me feel. I feel terrible looking at my children, and at Raj, always terrible. I have terrible urges, Mr. Kapasi, to throw things away. One day I had the urge to throw everything I own out the window, the television, the children, everything. Don't you think it's unhealthy?"

He was silent.

"Mr. Kapasi, don't you have anything to say? I thought that was your job."

155   "My job is to give tours, Mrs. Das."

"Not that. Your other job. As an interpreter."

"But we do not face a language barrier. What need is there for an interpreter?"

"That's not what I mean. I would never have told you otherwise. Don't you realize what it means for me to tell you?"

"What does it mean?"

"It means that I'm tired of feeling so terrible all the time. Eight years, 160 Mr. Kapasi, I've been in pain eight years. I was hoping you could help me feel better, say the right thing. Suggest some kind of remedy."

He looked at her, in her red plaid skirt and strawberry T-shirt, a woman not yet thirty, who loved neither her husband nor her children, who had already fallen out of love with life. Her confession depressed him, depressed him all the more when he thought of Mr. Das at the top of the path, Tina clinging to his shoulders, taking pictures of ancient monastic cells cut into the hills to show his students in America, unsuspecting and unaware that one of his sons was not his own. Mr. Kapasi felt insulted that Mrs. Das should ask him to interpret her common, trivial little secret. She did not resemble the patients in the doctor's office, those who came glassy-eyed and desperate, unable to sleep or breathe or urinate with ease, unable, above all, to give words to their pains. Still, Mr. Kapasi believed it was his duty to assist Mrs. Das. Perhaps he ought to tell her to confess the truth to Mr. Das. He would explain that honesty was the best policy. Honesty, surely, would help her feel better, as she'd put it. Perhaps he would offer to preside over the discussion, as a mediator. He decided to begin with the most obvious question, to get to the heart of the matter, and so he asked, "Is it really pain you feel, Mrs. Das, or is it guilt?"

She turned to him and glared, mustard oil thick on her frosty pink lips. She opened her mouth to say something, but as she glared at Mr. Kapasi some certain knowledge seemed to pass before her eyes, and she stopped. It crushed him; he knew at that moment that he was not even important enough to be properly insulted. She opened the car door and began walking up the path, wobbling a little on her square wooden heels, reaching into her straw bag to eat handfuls of puffed rice. It fell through her fingers, leaving a zigzagging trail, causing a monkey to leap down from a tree and devour the little white grains. In search of more, the monkey began to follow Mrs. Das. Others joined him, so that she was soon being followed by about half a dozen of them, their velvety tails dragging behind.

Mr. Kapasi stepped out of the car. He wanted to holler, to alert her in some way, but he worried that if she knew they were behind her, she would grow nervous. Perhaps she would lose her balance. Perhaps they would pull at her bag or her hair. He began to jog up the path, taking a fallen branch in his hand to scare away the monkeys. Mrs. Das continued walking, oblivious, trailing grains of puffed rice. Near the top of the incline, before a group of cells fronted by a row of squat stone pillars, Mr. Das was kneeling on the ground, focusing the lens of his camera. The children stood under the arcade, now hiding, now emerging from view.

"Wait for me," Mrs. Das called out. "I'm coming."

165 Tina jumped up and down. "Here comes Mommy!"

"Great," Mr. Das said without looking up. "Just in time. We'll get Mr. Kapasi to take a picture of the five of us."

Mr. Kapasi quickened his pace, waving his branch so that the monkeys scampered away, distracted, in another direction.

"Where's Bobby?" Mrs. Das asked when she stopped.

Mr. Das looked up from the camera. "I don't know. Ronny, where's Bobby?"

170 Ronny shrugged. "I thought he was right here."

"Where is he?" Mrs. Das repeated sharply. "What's wrong with all of you?"

They began calling his name, wandering up and down the path a bit. Because they were calling, they did not initially hear the boy's screams. When they found him, a little farther down the path under a tree, he was surrounded by a group of monkeys, over a dozen of them, pulling at his T-shirt with their long black fingers. The puffed rice Mrs. Das had spilled was scattered at his feet, raked over by the monkeys' hands. The boy was silent, his body frozen, swift tears running down his startled face. His bare legs were dusty and red with welts from where one of the monkeys struck him repeatedly with the stick he had given to it earlier.

"Daddy, the monkey's hurting Bobby," Tina said.

Mr. Das wiped his palms on the front of his shorts. In his nervousness he accidentally pressed the shutter on his camera; the whirring noise of the advancing film excited the monkeys, and the one with the stick began to beat Bobby more intently. "What are we supposed to do? What if they start attacking?"

175 "Mr. Kapasi," Mrs. Das shrieked, noticing him standing to one side. "Do something, for God's sake, do something!"

Mr. Kapasi took his branch and shooed them away, hissing at the ones that remained, stomping his feet to scare them. The animals retreated slowly, with a measured gait, obedient but unintimidated. Mr. Kapasi gathered Bobby in his arms and brought him back to where his parents and siblings were standing. As he carried him he was tempted to whisper a secret into the boy's ear. But Bobby was stunned, and shivering with fright, his legs bleeding slightly where the stick had broken the skin. When Mr. Kapasi delivered him to his parents, Mr. Das brushed some dirt off the boy's T-shirt and put the visor on him the right way. Mrs. Das reached into her straw bag to find a bandage which she taped over the cut on his knee. Ronny offered his brother a fresh piece of gum. "He's fine. Just a little scared, right, Bobby?" Mr. Das said, patting the top of his head.

"God, let's get out of here," Mrs. Das said. She folded her arms across the strawberry on her chest. "This place gives me the creeps."

"Yeah. Back to the hotel, definitely," Mr. Das agreed.

"Poor Bobby," Mrs. Das said. "Come here a second. Let Mommy 180 fix your hair." Again she reached into her straw bag, this time for her hairbrush, and began to run it around the edges of the translucent visor. When she whipped out the hairbrush, the slip of paper with Mr. Kapasi's address on it fluttered away in the wind. No one but Mr. Kapasi noticed. He watched as it rose, carried higher and higher by the breeze, into the trees where the monkeys now sat, solemnly observing the scene below. Mr. Kapasi observed it too, knowing that this was the picture of the Das family he would preserve forever in his mind.

URSULA K. LE GUIN
The Ones Who Walk Away from Omelas

With a clamor of bells that set the swallows soaring, the Festival of Summer came to the city. Omelas, bright-towered by the sea. The rigging of the boats in harbor sparkled with flags. In the streets between houses with red roofs and painted walls, between old moss-grown gardens and under avenues of trees, past great parks and public buildings, processions moved. Some were decorous: old people in long stiff robes of mauve and grey, grave master workmen, quiet, merry women carrying their babies and chatting as they walked. In other streets the music beat faster, a shimmering of gong and tambourine, and the people went dancing, the procession was a dance. Children dodged in and out, their high calls rising like the swallows' crossing flights over the music and the singing. All the processions wound towards the north side of the city, where on the great water-meadow called the Green Fields boys and girls, naked in the bright air, with mud-stained feet and ankles and long, lithe arms, exercised their restive horses before the race. The horses wore no gear at all but a halter without bit. Their manes were braided with streamers of silver, gold, and green. They flared their nostrils and pranced and boasted to one another, they were vastly excited, the horse being the only animal who has adopted our ceremonies as his own. Far off to the north and west the mountains stood up half encircling Omelas on her bay. The air of morning was so clear that the snow still crowning the Eighteen Peaks burned with white-gold

THE ONES WHO WALK AWAY FROM OMELAS   First published in 1973. Ursula K. Le Guin (b. 1929) is a prolific author of science fiction and fantasy novels and short stories. Educated at Radcliffe College and Columbia University, she lives in Oregon. Her best-known works are the novels *The Left Hand of Darkness* (1969) and *The Dispossessed* (1974).

fire across the miles of sunlit air, under the dark blue of the sky. There was just enough wind to make the banners that marked the racecourse snap and flutter now and then. In the silence of the broad green meadows one could hear the music winding through the city streets, farther and nearer and ever approaching, a cheerful faint sweetness of the air that from time to time trembled and gathered together and broke out into the great joyous clanging of the bells.

Joyous! How is one to tell about joy? How describe the citizens of Omelas?

They were not simple folk, you see, though they were happy. But we do not say the words of cheer much any more. All smiles have become archaic. Given a description such as this one tends to make certain assumptions. Given a description such as this one tends to look next for the King, mounted on a splendid stallion and surrounded by his noble knights, or perhaps in a golden litter borne by great-muscled slaves. But there was no king. They did not use swords, or keep slaves. They were not barbarians. I do not know the rules and laws of their society, but I suspect that they were singularly few. As they did without monarchy and slavery, so they also got on without the stock exchange, the advertisement, the secret police, and the bomb. Yet I repeat that these were not simple folk, not dulcet shepherds, noble savages, bland utopians. They were not less complex than us. The trouble is that we have a bad habit, encouraged by pedants and sophisticates, of considering happiness as something rather stupid. Only pain is intellectual, only evil interesting. This is the treason of the artist: a refusal to admit the banality of evil and the terrible boredom of pain. If you can't lick 'em, join 'em. If it hurts, repeat it. But to praise despair is to condemn delight, to embrace violence is to lose hold of everything else. We have almost lost hold; we can no longer describe a happy man, nor make any celebration of joy. How can I tell you about the people of Omelas? They were not naïve and happy children—though their children were, in fact, happy. They were mature, intelligent, passionate adults whose lives were not wretched. O miracle! but I wish I could describe it better. I wish I could convince you. Omelas sounds in my words like a city in a fairy tale, long ago and far away, once upon a time. Perhaps it would be best if you imagined it as your own fancy bids, assuming it will rise to the occasion, for certainly I cannot suit you all. For instance, how about technology? I think that there would be no cars or helicopters in and above the streets; this follows from the fact that the people of Omelas are happy people. Happiness is based on a just discrimination of what is necessary, what is neither necessary nor destructive, and what is destructive. In the middle category, however—that of the unnecessary but undestructive, that of comfort, luxury, exuberance, etc.—they could perfectly well have central heating, subway trains, washing machines, and all kinds of marvelous devices not yet invented here, floating light-sources, fuel-less power, a cure for the common cold. Or they could have none of that: it doesn't matter. As you like it. I incline to think that people from towns up and down the coast have been coming in to Omelas during the last days before the Festival on very fast little trains and double-decked trams and that the train station of Omelas is actually the handsomest building in town, though plainer than the magnificent Farmers' Market. But even granted trains, I fear that Omelas so far strikes some of you as goody-goody. Smiles, bells, parades, horses, bleh. If so, please add an orgy. If an orgy would help, don't hesitate. Let us not, however, have temples from which issue beautiful nude priests and priestesses already half in ecstasy and ready to copulate with any man or woman, lover or stranger, who desires union with the deep godhead of the blood, although that was my first idea. But really it would be better not to have any temples in Omelas—at least, not manned temples. Religion yes, clergy no. Surely the beautiful nudes can just wander about, offering themselves like divine soufflés to the hunger of the needy and the rapture of the flesh. Let them join the processions. Let tambourines be struck above the copulations, and the glory of desire be proclaimed upon the gongs, and (a not unimportant point) let the offspring of these delightful rituals be beloved and looked after by all. One thing I know there is none of in Omelas is guilt. But what else should there be? I thought at first there were no drugs, but that is puritanical. For those who like it, the faint insistent sweetness of *drooz* may perfume the ways of the city, *drooz* which first brings a great lightness and brilliance to the mind and limbs, and then after some hours a dreamy languor, and wonderful visions at last of the very arcana and inmost secrets of the Universe, as well as exciting the pleasure of sex beyond all belief; and it is not habit-forming. For more modest tastes I think there ought to be beer. What else, what else belongs in the joyous city? The sense of victory, surely, the celebration of courage. But as we did without clergy, let us do without soldiers. The joy built upon successful slaughter is not the right kind of joy; it will not do; it is fearful and it is trivial. A boundless and generous contentment, a magnanimous triumph felt not against some outer enemy but in communion with the finest and fairest in the souls of all men everywhere and the splendor of the world's summer: this is what swells the hearts of the people of Omelas, and the victory they celebrate is that of life. I really don't think many of them need to take *drooz*.

Most of the processions have reached the Green Fields by now. A marvelous smell of cooking goes forth from the red and blue tents of the provisioners. The faces of small children are amiably sticky; in the benign grey beard of a man a couple of crumbs of rich pastry are entangled. The youths and girls have mounted their horses and are beginning to group around the starting line of the course. An old woman, small, fat, and laughing, is passing out flowers from a basket, and tall young men wear her flowers in their shining hair. A child of nine or ten sits at the edge of the crowd, alone, playing on a wooden flute. People pause to listen, and they smile, but they do not speak to him, for he never ceases playing and never sees them, his dark eyes wholly rapt in the sweet, thin magic of the tune.

5   He finishes, and slowly lowers his hands holding the wooden flute.

As if that little private silence were the signal, all at once a trumpet sounds from the pavillion near the starting line: imperious, melancholy, piercing. The horses rear on their slender legs, and some of them neigh in answer. Sober-faced, the young riders stroke the horses' necks and soothe them, whispering, "Quiet, quiet, there my beauty, my hope. . . ." They begin to form in rank along the starting line. The crowds along the racecourse are like a field of grass and flowers in the wind. The Festival of Summer has begun.

Do you believe? Do you accept the festival, the city, the joy? No? Then let me describe one more thing.

In a basement under one of the beautiful public buildings of Omelas, or perhaps in the cellar of one of its spacious private homes, there is a room. It has one locked door, and no window. A little light seeps in dustily between cracks in the boards, secondhand from a cobwebbed window somewhere across the cellar. In one corner of the little room a couple of mops, with stiff, clotted, foul-smelling heads, stand near a rusty bucket. The floor is dirt, a little damp to the touch, as cellar dirt usually is. The room is about three paces long and two wide: a mere broom closet or disused tool room. In the room a child is sitting. It could be a boy or a girl. It looks about six, but actually is nearly ten. It is feeble-minded. Perhaps it was born defective, or perhaps it has become imbecile through fear, malnutrition, and neglect. It picks its nose and occasionally fumbles vaguely with its toes or genitals, as it sits hunched in the corner farthest from the bucket and the two mops. It is afraid of the mops. It finds them horrible. It shuts its eyes, but it knows the mops are still standing there; and the door is locked; and nobody will come. The door is always locked; and nobody ever comes, except that sometimes—the child has no understanding of time or interval—sometimes the door rattles terribly and opens, and a person, or several people, are there. One of them may come in and kick the child to make it stand up. The others never come close, but peer in at it with frightened, disgusted eyes. The food bowl and the water jug are hastily filled, the door is locked, the eyes disappear. The people at the door never say anything, but the child, who has not always lived in the tool room, and can remember sunlight and its mother's voice, sometimes speaks. "I will be good," it says. "Please let me out. I will be good!" They never answer. The child used to scream for help at night, and cry a good deal, but now it only makes a kind of whining, "eh-haa, eh-haa," and it speaks less and less often. It is so thin there are no calves to its legs; its belly protrudes; it lives on a half-bowl of corn meal and grease a day. It is naked. Its buttocks and thighs are a mass of festered sores, as it sits in its own excrement continually.

They all know it is there, all the people of Omelas. Some of them have come to see it, others are content merely to know it is there. They all know that it has to be there. Some of them understand why, and some do not, but they all understand that their happiness, the beauty of their city, the tenderness of their friendships, the health of their children, the wisdom of their scholars, the skill of their makers, even the abundance of their harvest and the kindly weathers of their skies, depend wholly on this child's abominable misery.

This is usually explained to children when they are between eight and 10 twelve, whenever they seem capable of understanding; and most of those who come to see the child are young people, though often enough an adult comes, or comes back, to see the child. No matter how well the matter has been explained to them, these young spectators are always shocked and sickened at the sight. They feel disgust, which they had thought themselves superior to. They feel anger, outrage, impotence, despite all the explanations. They would like to do something for the child. But there is nothing they can do. If the child were brought up into the sunlight out of that vile place, if it were cleaned and fed and comforted, that would be a good thing, indeed; but if it were done, in that day and hour all the prosperity and beauty and delight of Omelas would wither and be destroyed. Those are the terms. To exchange all the goodness and grace of every life in Omelas for that single, small improvement: to throw away the happiness of thousands for the chance of the happiness of one: that would be to let guilt within the walls indeed.

The terms are strict and absolute; there may not even be a kind word spoken to the child.

Often the young people go home in tears, or in a tearless rage, when they have seen the child and faced this terrible paradox. They may brood over it for weeks or years. But as time goes on they begin to realize that even if the child could be released, it would not get much good of its freedom: a little vague pleasure of warmth and food, no doubt, but little more. It is too degraded and imbecile to know any real joy. It has been afraid too long ever to be free of fear. Its habits are too uncouth for it to respond to humane treatment. Indeed, after so long it would probably be wretched without walls about it to protect it, and darkness for its eyes, and its own excrement to sit in. Their tears at the bitter injustice dry when they begin to perceive the terrible justice of reality and to accept it. Yet it is their tears and anger, the trying of their generosity and the acceptance of their help-lessness, which are perhaps the true source of the splendor of their lives. Theirs is no vapid, irresponsible happiness. They know that they, like the child, are not free. They know compassion. It is the existence of the child, and their knowledge of its existence, that makes possible the nobility of their architecture, the poignancy of their music, the profundity of their science. It is because of the child that they are so gentle with children. They know that if the wretched one were not there snivelling in the dark, the other one, the flute-player, could make no joyful music as the young riders line up in their beauty for the race in the sunlight of the first morning of summer.

Now do you believe in them? Are they not more credible? But there is one more thing to tell, and this is quite incredible.

At times one of the adolescent girls or boys who go to see the child does not go home to weep or rage, does not, in fact, go home at all. Sometimes also a man or woman much older falls silent for a day or two, and then leaves home. These people go out into the street, and walk down the street alone. They keep walking, and walk straight out of the city of Omelas, through the beautiful gates. They keep walking across the farm-lands of Omelas. Each one goes alone, youth or girl, man or woman. Night falls; the traveler must pass down village streets, between the houses with yellow-lit windows, and on out into the darkness of the fields. Each alone, they go west or north, towards the mountains. They go on. They leave Omelas, they walk ahead into the darkness, and they do not come back. The place they go towards is a place even less imaginable to most of us than the city of happiness. I cannot describe it at all. It is possible that it does not exist. But they seem to know where they are going, the ones who walk away from Omelas.

BERNARD MALAMUD

The Magic Barrel

Not long ago there lived in uptown New York, in a small, almost mea-ger room, though crowded with books, Leo Finkle, a rabbinical student in the Yeshivah University. Finkle, after six years of study, was to be ordained in June and had been advised by an acquaintance that he might find it

---

THE MAGIC BARREL   First published in 1954. Bernard Malamud (1914–1986) grew up in New York City, where much of his fiction dealing with Jewish immigrant life is set. His novels include *The Natural* (1952), *The Assistant* (1957), and *The Fixer* (1966), which won the Pulitzer Prize for fiction.

easier to win himself a congregation if he were married. Since he had no present prospects of marriage, after two tormented days of turning it over in his mind, he called in Pinye Salzman, a marriage broker whose two-line advertisement he had read in the *Forward*.°

The matchmaker appeared one night out of the dark fourth-floor hallway of the graystone rooming house where Finkle lived, grasping a black, strapped portfolio that had been worn thin with use. Salzman, who had been long in the business, was of slight but dignified build, wearing an old hat, and an overcoat too short and tight for him. He smelled frankly of fish, which he loved to eat, and although he was missing a few teeth, his presence was not displeasing, because of an amiable manner curiously contrasted with mournful eyes. His voice, his lips, his wisp of beard, his bony fingers were animated, but give him a moment of repose and his mild blue eyes revealed a depth of sadness, a characteristic that put Leo a little at ease although the situation, for him, was inherently tense.

He at once informed Salzman why he had asked him to come, explaining that his home was in Cleveland, and that but for his parents, who had married comparatively late in life, he was alone in the world. He had for six years devoted himself almost entirely to his studies, as a result of which, understandably, he had found himself without time for a social life and the company of young women. Therefore he thought it the better part of trial and error—of embarrassing fumbling—to call in an experienced person to advise him on these matters. He remarked in passing that the function of the marriage broker was ancient and honorable, highly approved in the Jewish community, because it made practical the necessary without hindering joy. Moreover, his own parents had been brought together by a matchmaker. They had made, if not a financially profitable marriage— since neither had possessed any worldly goods to speak of—at least a successful one in the sense of their everlasting devotion to each other. Salzman listened in embarrassed surprise, sensing a sort of apology. Later, however, he experienced a glow of pride in his work, an emotion that had left him years ago, and he heartily approved of Finkle.

The two went to their business. Leo had led Salzman to the only clear place in the room, a table near a window that overlooked the lamp-lit city. He seated himself at the matchmaker's side but facing him, attempting by an act of will to suppress the unpleasant tickle in his throat. Salzman eagerly unstrapped his portfolio and removed a loose rubber band from a thin packet of much-handled cards. As he flipped through them, a gesture and sound that physically hurt Leo, the student

---

Forward: *The Jewish Daily Forward*, a newspaper published in New York for Yiddish-speaking Jewish immigrants

pretended not to see and gazed steadfastly out the window. Although it was still February, winter was on its last legs, signs of which he had for the first time in years begun to notice. He now observed the round white moon, moving high in the sky through a cloud menagerie, and watched with half-open mouth as it penetrated a huge hen, and dropped out of her like an egg laying itself. Salzman, though pretending through eyeglasses he had just slipped on, to be engaged in scanning the writing on the cards, stole occasional glances at the young man's distinguished face, noting with pleasure the long, severe scholar's nose, brown eyes heavy with learning, sensitive yet ascetic lips, and a certain, almost hollow quality of the dark cheeks. He gazed around at shelves upon shelves of books and let out a soft, contented sigh.

5　　When Leo's eyes fell upon the cards, he counted six spread out in Salzman's hand.

"So few?" he asked in disappointment.

"You wouldn't believe me how much cards I got in my office," Salzman replied. "The drawers are already filled to the top, so I keep them now in a barrel, but is every girl good for a new rabbi?"

Leo blushed at this, regretting all he had revealed of himself in a curriculum vitae he had sent to Salzman. He had thought it best to acquaint him with his strict standards and specifications, but in having done so, he felt he had told the marriage broker more than was absolutely necessary.

He hesitantly inquired, "Do you keep photographs of your clients on file?"

10　　"First comes family, amount of dowry, also what kind promises," Salzman replied, unbuttoning his tight coat and settling himself in the chair. "After comes pictures, rabbi."

"Call me Mr. Finkle. I'm not yet a rabbi."

Salzman said he would, but instead called him doctor, which he changed to rabbi when Leo was not listening too attentively.

Salzman adjusted his horn-rimmed spectacles, gently cleared his throat and read in an eager voice the contents of the top card:

"Sophie P. Twenty four years. Widow one year. No children. Educated high school and two years college. Father promises eight thousand dollars. Has wonderful wholesale business. Also real estate. On the mother's side comes teachers, also one actor. Well known on Second Avenue."

15　　Leo gazed up in surprise. "Did you say a widow?"

"A widow don't mean spoiled, rabbi. She lived with her husband maybe four months. He was a sick boy she made a mistake to marry him."

"Marrying a widow has never entered my mind."

"This is because you have no experience. A widow, especially if she is young and healthy like this girl, is a wonderful person to marry. She will be thankful to you the rest of her life. Believe me, if I was looking now for a bride, I would marry a widow."

Leo reflected, then shook his head.

Salzman hunched his shoulders in an almost imperceptible gesture of 20 disappointment. He placed the card down on the wooden table and began to read another:

"Lily H. High school teacher. Regular. Not a substitute. Has savings and new Dodge car. Lived in Paris one year. Father is successful dentist thirty-five years. Interested in professional man. Well Americanized family. Wonderful opportunity."

"I knew her personally," said Salzman. "I wish you could see this girl. She is a doll. Also very intelligent. All day you could talk to her about books and theyater and what not. She also knows current events."

"I don't believe you mentioned her age?"

"Her age?" Salzman said, raising his brows. "Her age is thirty-two years."

Leo said after a while, "I'm afraid that seems a little too old." 25

Salzman let out a laugh. "So how old are you, rabbi?"

"Twenty-seven."

"So what is the difference, tell me, between twenty-seven and thirty-two? My own wife is seven years older than me. So what did I suffer?— Nothing. If Rothschild's daughter wants to marry you, would you say on account her age, no?"

"Yes," Leo said dryly.

Salzman shook off the no in the yes. "Five years don't mean a thing. I 30 give you my word that when you will live with her for one week you will forget her age. What does it mean five years—that she lived more and knows more than somebody who is younger? On this girl, God bless her, years are not wasted. Each one that it comes makes better the bargain."

"What subject does she teach in high school?"

"Languages. If you heard the way she speaks French, you will think it is music. I am in the business twenty-five years, and I recommend her with my whole heart. Believe me, I know what I'm talking, rabbi."

"What's on the next card?" Leo said abruptly.

Salzman reluctantly turned up the third card:

"Ruth K. Nineteen years. Honor student. Father offers thirteen thousand 35 cash to the right bridegroom. He is a medical doctor. Stomach specialist with marvelous practice. Brother-in-law owns own garment business. Particular people."

Salzman looked as if he had read his trump card.

"Did you say nineteen?" Leo asked with interest.

"On the dot."

"Is she attractive?" He blushed. "Pretty?"

40   Salzman kissed his finger tips. "A little doll. On this I give my word. Let me call the father tonight and you will see what means pretty."

But Leo was troubled. "You're sure she's that young?"

"This I am positive. The father will show you the birth certificate."

"Are you positive there isn't something wrong with her?" Leo insisted.

"Who says there is wrong?"

45   "I don't understand why an American girl her age should go to a marriage broker."

A smile spread over Salzman's face.

"So for the same reason you went, she comes."

Leo flushed. "I am pressed for time."

Salzman, realizing he had been tactless, quickly explained. "The father came, not her. He wants she should have the best, so he looks around himself. When we will locate the right boy he will introduce him and encourage. This makes a better marriage than if a young girl without experience takes for herself. I don't have to tell you this."

50   "But don't you think this young girl believes in love?" Leo spoke uneasily.

Salzman was about to guffaw but caught himself and said soberly, "Love comes with the right person, not before."

Leo parted dry lips but did not speak. Noticing that Salzman had snatched a glance at the next card, he cleverly asked, "How is her health?"

"Perfect," Salzman said, breathing with difficulty. "Of course, she is a little lame on her right foot from an auto accident that it happened to her when she was twelve years, but nobody notices on account she is so brilliant and also beautiful."

Leo got up heavily and went to the window. He felt curiously bitter and upbraided himself for having called in the marriage broker. Finally, he shook his head.

55   "Why not?" Salzman persisted, the pitch of his voice rising.

"Because I detest stomach specialists."

"So what do you care what is his business? After you marry her do you need him? Who says he must come every Friday night in your house?"

Ashamed of the way the talk was going, Leo dismissed Salzman, who went home with heavy, melancholy eyes.

Though he had felt only relief at the marriage broker's departure, Leo was in low spirits the next day. He explained it as arising from Salzman's failure to produce a suitable bride for him. He did not care for his type of clientele. But when Leo found himself hesitating whether to seek out another matchmaker, one more polished than Pinye, he wondered if it could be—his protestations to the contrary, and although he honored his father and mother—that he did not, in essence, care for the match-making institution? This thought he quickly put out of mind yet found himself still upset. All day he ran around in the woods—missed an important appointment, forgot to give out his laundry, walked out of a Broadway cafeteria without paying and had to run back with the ticket in his hand; had even not recognized his landlady in the street when she passed with a friend and courteously called out, "A good evening to you, Doctor Finkle." By nightfall, however, he had regained sufficient calm to sink his nose into a book and there found peace from his thoughts.

Almost at once there came a knock on the door. Before Leo could say 60 enter, Salzman, commercial cupid, was standing in the room. His face was gray and meager, his expression hungry, and he looked as if he would expire on his feet. Yet the marriage broker managed, by some trick of the muscles, to display a broad smile.

"So good evening. I am invited?"

Leo nodded, disturbed to see him again, yet unwilling to ask the man to leave.

Beaming still, Salzman laid his portfolio on the table. "Rabbi, I got for you tonight good news."

"I've asked you not to call me rabbi. I'm still a student."

"Your worries are finished. I have for you a first-class bride." 65

"Leave me in peace concerning this subject." Leo pretended lack of interest.

"The world will dance at your wedding."

"Please, Mr. Salzman, no more."

"But first must come back my strength," Salzman said weakly. He fumbled with the portfolio straps and took out of the leather case an oily paper bag, from which he extracted a hard, seeded roll and a small, smoked whitefish. With a quick motion of his hand he stripped the fish out of its skin and began ravenously to chew. "All day in a rush," he muttered.

Leo watched him eat. 70

"A sliced tomato you have maybe?" Salzman hesitantly inquired.

"No."

The marriage broker shut his eyes and ate. When he had finished he carefully cleaned up the crumbs and rolled up the remains of the fish, in the paper bag. His spectacled eyes roamed the room until he discovered, amid some piles of books, a one-burner gas stove. Lifting his hat he humbly asked, "A glass tea you got, rabbi?"

Conscience-stricken, Leo rose and brewed the tea. He served it with a chunk of lemon and two cubes of lump sugar, delighting Salzman.

After he had drunk his tea, Salzman's strength and good spirits were 75 restored.

"Oh, did Mr. Salzman tell you, Rabbi Finkle?" Leo winced but she went on, "It was ages ago and almost forgotten. I remember I had to return for my sister's wedding."

And Lily would not be put off. "When," she asked in a trembly voice, "did you become enamored of God?"

110 He stared at her. Then it came to him that she was talking not about Leo Finkle, but of a total stranger, some mystical figure, perhaps even passionate prophet that Salzman had dreamed up for her—no relation to the living or dead. Leo trembled with rage and weakness. The trickster had obviously sold her a bill of goods, just as he had him, who'd expected to become acquainted with a young lady of twenty-nine, only to behold, the moment he laid eyes upon her strained and anxious face, a woman past thirty-five and aging rapidly. Only his self control had kept him this long in her presence.

"I am not," he said gravely, "a talented religious person," and in seeking words to go on, found himself possessed by shame and fear. "I think," he said in a strained manner, "that I came to God not because I loved Him, but because I did not."

This confession he spoke harshly because its unexpectedness shook him.

Lily wilted. Leo saw a profusion of loaves of bread go flying like ducks high over his head, not unlike the winged loaves by which he had counted himself to sleep last night. Mercifully, then, it snowed, which he would not put past Salzman's machinations.

He was infuriated with the marriage broker and swore he would throw him out of the room the minute he reappeared. But Salzman did not come that night, and when Leo's anger had subsided, an unaccountable despair grew in its place. At first he thought this was caused by his disappointment in Lily, but before long it became evident that he had involved himself with Salzman without a true knowledge of his own intent. He gradually realized—with an emptiness that seized him with six hands—that he had called in the broker to find him a bride because he was incapable of doing it himself. This terrifying insight he had derived as a result of his meeting and conversation with Lily Hirschorn. Her probing questions had somehow irritated him into revealing—to himself more than her—the true nature of his relationship to God, and from that it had come upon him, with shocking force, that apart from his parents, he had never loved anyone. Or perhaps it went the other way, that he did not love God so well as he might, because he had not loved man. It seemed to Leo that his whole life stood starkly revealed and he saw himself for the first time as he truly was—unloved and loveless. This bitter but somehow not fully unexpected revelation brought him to a point of panic controlled only by extraordinary effort. He covered his face with his hands and cried.

115 The week that followed was the worst of his life. He did not eat and lost weight. His beard darkened and grew ragged. He stopped attending

seminars and almost never opened a book. He seriously considered leaving the Yeshivah, although he was deeply troubled at the thought of the loss of all his years of study—saw them like pages torn from a book, strewn over the city—and at the devastating effect of this decision upon his parents. But he had lived without knowledge of himself, and never in the Five Books° and all the Commentaries—mea culpa°—had the truth been revealed to him. He did not know where to turn, and in all this desolating loneliness there was no *to whom*, although he often thought of Lily but not once could bring himself to go downstairs and make the call. He became touchy and irritable, especially with his landlady, who asked him all manner of personal questions; on the other hand, sensing his own disagreeableness, he waylaid her on the stairs and apologized abjectly, until mortified, she ran from him. Out of this, however, he drew the consolation that he was a Jew and that a Jew suffered. But gradually, as the long and terrible week drew to a close, he regained his composure and some idea of purpose in life: to go on as planned. Although he was imperfect, the ideal was not. As for his quest of a bride, the thought of continuing afflicted him with anxiety and heartburn; yet perhaps with this new knowledge of himself he would be more successful than in the past. Perhaps love would now come to him and a bride to that love. And for this sanctified seeking who needed a Salzman?

The marriage broker, a skeleton with haunted eyes, returned that very night. He looked, withal, the picture of frustrated expectancy—as if he had steadfastly waited the week at Miss Lily Hirschorn's side for a telephone call that never came.

Casually coughing, Salzman came immediately to the point: "So how did you like her?"

Leo's anger rose and he could not refrain from chiding the matchmaker: "Why did you lie to me, Salzman?"

Salzman's pale face went dead white, the world had snowed on him.

"Did you not state that she was twenty-nine?" Leo insisted.   120

"I gave you my word—"

"She was thirty-five, if a day. *At least* thirty-five."

"Of this don't be too sure. Her father told me—"

"Never mind. The worst of it was that you lied to her."

"How did I lie to her, tell me?"   125

"You told her things about me that weren't true. You made me out to be more, consequently less than I am. She had in mind a totally different person, a sort of semimystical Wonder Rabbi."

Five Books: first five books of the Old Testament, relating the history of the Jewish people
mea culpa: through my fault (Latin)

"All I said, you was a religious man."

"I can imagine."

Salzman sighed. "This is my weakness that I have," he confessed. "My wife says to me I shouldn't be a salesman, but when I have two fine people that they would be wonderful to be married, I am so happy that I talk too much." He smiled wanly. "This is why Salzman is a poor man."

130   Leo's anger left him. "Well, Salzman, I'm afraid that's all."

The marriage broker fastened hungry eyes on him.

"You don't want any more a bride?"

"I do," said Leo, "but I have decided to seek her in a different way. I am no longer interested in an arranged marriage. To be frank, I now admit the necessity of premarital love. That is, I want to be in love with the one I marry."

"Love?" said Salzman, astounded. After a moment he remarked, "For us, our love is our life, not for the ladies. In the ghetto they—"

135   "I know, I know," said Leo. "I've thought of it often. Love, I have said to myself, should be a by-product of living and worship rather than its own end. Yet for myself I find it necessary to establish the level of my need and fulfill it."

Salzman shrugged but answered, "Listen, rabbi, if you want love, this I can find for you also. I have such beautiful clients that you will love them the minute your eyes will see them."

Leo smiled unhappily. "I'm afraid you don't understand."

But Salzman hastily unstrapped his portfolio and withdrew a manila packet from it.

"Pictures," he said, quickly laying the envelope on the table.

140   Leo called after him to take the pictures away, but as if on the wings of the wind, Salzman had disappeared.

March came. Leo had returned to his regular routine. Although he felt not quite himself yet—-lacked energy—he was making plans for a more active social life. Of course it would cost something, but he was an expert in cutting corners; and when there were no corners left he would make circles rounder. All the while Salzman's pictures had lain on the table, gathering dust. Occasionally as Leo sat studying, or enjoying a cup of tea, his eyes fell on the manila envelope, but he never opened it.

The days went by and no social life to speak of developed with a member of the opposite sex—it was difficult, given the circumstances of his situation. One morning Leo toiled up the stairs to his room and stared out the window at the city. Although the day was bright his view of it was dark. For some time he watched the people in the street below hurrying along and then turned with a heavy heart to his little room. On the table was the packet. With a sudden relentless gesture he tore it open. For a half-hour he stood by the table in a state of excitement, examining the photographs of the ladies Salzman had included. Finally, with a deep sigh he put them down. There were six, of varying degrees of attractiveness, but look at them long enough and they all became Lily Hirschorn; all past their prime, all starved behind bright smiles, not a true personality in the lot. Life, despite their frantic yoohooings, had passed them by; they were pictures in a briefcase that stunk of fish. After a while, however, as Leo attempted to return the photographs into the envelope, he found in it another, a snapshot of the type taken by a machine for a quarter. He gazed at it a moment and let out a cry.

Her face deeply moved him. Why, he could at first not say. It gave him the impression of youth—spring flowers, yet age—a sense of having been used to the bone, wasted; this came from the eyes, which were hauntingly familiar, yet absolutely strange. He had a vivid impression that he had met her before, but try as he might he could not place her although he could almost recall her name, as if he had read it in her own handwriting. No, this couldn't be; he would have remembered her. It was not, he affirmed, that she had an extraordinary beauty—no, though her face was attractive enough; it was that *something* about her moved him. Feature for feature, even some of the ladies of the photographs could do better; but she leaped forth to his heart—had *lived*, or wanted to—more than just wanted, perhaps regretted how she had lived—had somehow deeply suffered: it could be seen in the depths of those reluctant eyes, and from the way the light enclosed and shone from her, and within her, opening realms of possibility: this was her own. Her he desired. His head ached and eyes narrowed with the intensity of his gazing, then as if an obscure fog had blown up in the mind, he experienced fear of her and was aware that he had received an impression, somehow, of evil. He shuddered, saying softly, it is thus with us all. Leo brewed some tea in a small pot and sat sipping it without sugar, to calm himself. But before he had finished drinking, again with excitement he examined the face and found it good: good for Leo Finkle. Only such a one could understand him and help him seek whatever he was seeking. She might, perhaps, love him. How she had happened to be among the discards in Salzman's barrel he could never guess, but he knew he must urgently go find her.

Leo rushed downstairs, grabbed up the Bronx telephone book, and searched for Salzman's home address. He was not listed, nor was his office. Neither was he in the Manhattan book. But Leo remembered having written down the address on a slip of paper after he had read Salzman's advertisement in the "personals" column of the *Forward*. He ran up to his room and tore through his papers, without luck. It was exasperating. Just when he needed the matchmaker he was nowhere to be found. Fortunately Leo remembered to look in his wallet. There on a card he found his name written and a Bronx address. No phone number was listed, the reason—Leo now recalled—he had originally communicated with Salzman by letter. He got on his coat, put a hat on over his skull cap and hurried to the subway station. All the way to the far end of the Bronx he sat on the edge of his seat. He was more than once tempted to take out the picture and see if the girl's face was as he remembered it, but he refrained, allowing the snapshot to remain in his coat pocket, content to have her so close. When the train pulled into the station he was waiting at the door and bolted out. He quickly located the street Salzman had advertised.

145   The building he sought was less than a block from the subway, but it was not an office building, nor even a loft, nor a store in which one could rent office space. It was a very old tenement house. Leo found Salzman's name in pencil on a soiled tag under the bell, and climbed three dark flights to his apartment. When he knocked, the door was opened by a thin, asthmatic, gray-haired woman, in felt slippers.

"Yes?" she said, expecting nothing. She listened without listening. He could have sworn he had seen her, too, before but knew it was an illusion.

"Salzman—does he live here? Pinye Salzman," he said, "the matchmaker?"

She stared at him a long minute. "Of course."

He felt embarrassed. "Is he in?"

150   "No." Her mouth, though left open, offered nothing more.

"The matter is urgent. Can you tell me where his office is?"

"In the air." She pointed upward.

"You mean he has no office?" Leo asked.

"In his socks."

155   He peered into the apartment. It was sunless and dingy, one large room divided by a half-open curtain, beyond which he could see a sagging metal bed. The near side of a room was crowded with rickety chairs, old bureaus, a three-legged table, racks of cooking utensils, and all the apparatus of a kitchen. But there was no sign of Salzman or his magic barrel, probably also a figment of the imagination. An odor of frying fish made Leo weak to the knees.

"Where is he?" he insisted. "I've got to see your husband."

At length she answered, "So who knows where he is? Every time he thinks a new thought he runs to a different place. Go home, he will find you."

"Tell him Leo Finkle."

She gave no sign she had heard.

He walked downstairs, depressed.

But Salzman, breathless, stood waiting at his door. Leo was astounded and overjoyed. "How did you get here before me?"

"I rushed."

"Come inside."

They entered. Leo fixed tea, and a sardine sandwich for Salzman. As they were drinking he reached behind him for the packet of pictures and handed them to the marriage broker.

Salzman put down his glass and said expectantly, "You found somebody you like?"

"Not among these."

The marriage broker turned away.

"Here is the one I want." Leo held forth the snapshot.

Salzman slipped on his glasses and took the picture into his trembling hand. He turned ghastly and let out a groan.

"What's the matter?" cried Leo.

"Excuse me. Was an accident this picture. She isn't for you."

Salzman frantically shoved the manila packet into his portfolio. He thrust the snapshot into his pocket and fled down the stairs.

Leo, after momentary paralysis, gave chase and cornered the marriage broker in the vestibule. The landlady made hysterical outcries but neither of them listened.

"Give me back the picture, Salzman."

"No." The pain in his eyes was terrible.

"Tell me who she is then."

"This I can't tell you. Excuse me."

He made to depart, but Leo, forgetting himself, seized the matchmaker by his tight coat and shook him frenziedly.

"Please," sighed Salzman. "*Please.*"

Leo ashamedly let him go. "Tell me who she is," he begged. "It's very important for me to know."

"She is not for you. She is a wild one—wild, without shame. This is not a bride for a rabbi."

"What do you mean wild?"

"Like an animal. Like a dog. For her to be poor was a sin. This is why to me she is dead now."

"In God's name, what do you mean?"

"Her I can't introduce to you," Salzman cried.

"Why are you so excited?"

"Why, he asks," Salzman said, bursting into tears. "This is my baby, my Stella, she should burn in hell."

Leo hurried up to bed and hid under the covers. Under the covers he thought his life through. Although he soon fell asleep he could not sleep her out of his mind. He woke, beating his breast. Though he prayed to be rid of her, his prayers went unanswered. Through days of torment he endlessly struggled not to love her; fearing success, he escaped it. He then concluded to convert her to goodness, himself to God. The idea alternately nauseated and exalted him.

190   He perhaps did not know that he had come to a final decision until he encountered Salzman in a Broadway cafeteria. He was sitting alone at a rear table, sucking the bony remains of a fish. The marriage broker appeared haggard, and transparent to the point of vanishing.

Salzman looked up at first without recognizing him. Leo had grown a pointed beard and his eyes were weighted with wisdom.

"Salzman," he said, "love has at last come to my heart."

"Who can love from a picture?" mocked the marriage broker.

"It is not impossible."

195   "If you can love her, then you can love anybody. Let me show you some new clients that they just sent me their photographs. One is a little doll."

"Just her I want," Leo murmured.

"Don't be a fool, doctor. Don't bother with her."

"Put me in touch with her, Salzman," Leo said humbly. "Perhaps I can be of service."

Salzman had stopped eating and Leo understood with emotion that it was now arranged.

200   Leaving the cafeteria, he was, however, afflicted by a tormenting suspicion that Salzman had planned it all to happen this way.

Leo was informed by letter that she would meet him on a certain corner, and she was there one spring night, waiting under a street lamp. He appeared, carrying a small bouquet of violets and rosebuds. Stella stood by the lamp post, smoking. She wore white with red shoes, which fitted his expectations, although in a troubled moment he had imagined the dress red, and only the shoes white. She waited uneasily and shyly. From afar he saw that her eyes—clearly her father's—were filled with desperate innocence. He pictured, in her, his own redemption. Violins and lit candles revolved in the sky. Leo ran forward with flowers outthrust.

Around the corner, Salzman, leaning against a wall, chanted prayers for the dead.

HERMAN MELVILLE
Bartleby the Scrivener
A Story of Wall Street

I am a rather elderly man. The nature of my avocations for the last thirty years has brought me into more than ordinary contact with what would seem an interesting and somewhat singular set of men of whom as yet nothing that I know of has ever been written—I mean the law-copyists or scriveners. I have known very many of them, professionally and privately, and if I pleased could relate diverse histories at which good-natured gentlemen might smile and sentimental souls might weep. But I waive the biographies of all other scriveners for a few passages in the life of Bartleby, who was a scrivener the strangest I ever saw or heard of. While of other law-copyists I might write the complete life, of Bartleby nothing of that sort can be done. I believe that no materials exist for a full and satisfactory biography of this man. It is an irreparable loss to literature. Bartleby was one of those beings of whom nothing is ascertainable except from the original sources, and in his case those are very small. What my own astonished eyes saw of Bartleby, *that* is all I know of him except, indeed, one vague report which will appear in the sequel.

Ere introducing the scrivener as he first appeared to me, it is fit I make some mention of myself, my employees, my business, my chambers, and general surroundings, because some such description is indispensable to an adequate understanding of the chief character about to be presented.

Imprimis: I am a man who from his youth upwards has been filled with a profound conviction that the easiest way of life is the best. Hence, though I belong to a profession proverbially energetic and nervous, even to turbulence at times, yet nothing of that sort have I ever suffered to invade my peace. I am one of those unambitious lawyers who never addresses a jury or in any way draws down public applause, but in the cool tranquility of a snug retreat do a snug business among rich men's bonds and mortgages and title-deeds. All who know me consider me an eminently *safe* man. The

BARTLEBY THE SCRIVENER   First published in 1853. Herman Melville (1819–1891) was born in New York City. After working as a farmhand, clerk, bookkeeper, and teacher, he went to sea in 1837, where his adventures and observations supplied him with the material for several novels of the sea including *Moby-Dick* (1851). The lack of financial success of that book and later works of fiction, including *Piazza Tales*, which reprinted "Bartleby the Scrivener," led Melville eventually to write poetry instead. By the time of the story, Wall Street had become the financial and business center of New York City. In the days before the invention of the typewriter, official documents and legal papers had to be copied by hand—the job of a "scrivener." "The Tombs" (paragraph 11 and thereafter) was the vivid nickname of the city prison, properly called the Halls of Justice.

late John Jacob Astor, a personage little given to poetic enthusiasm, had no hesitation in pronouncing my first grand point to be prudence; my next, method. I do not speak it in vanity but simply record the fact that I was not unemployed in my profession by the late John Jacob Astor, a name which, I admit, I love to repeat, for it hath a rounded and orbicular sound to it and rings like unto bullion. I will freely add that I was not insensible to the late John Jacob Astor's good opinion.

Sometime prior to the period at which this little history begins, my avocations had been largely increased. The good old office now extinct in the State of New York of a Master in Chancery had been conferred upon me. It was not a very arduous office but very pleasantly remunerative. I seldom lose my temper; much more seldom indulge in dangerous indignation at wrongs and outrages; but I must be permitted to be rash here and declare that I consider the sudden and violent abrogation of the office of Master in Chancery by the new Constitution as a—premature act, inasmuch as I had counted upon a life-lease of the profits, whereas I only received those of a few short years. But this is by the way.

5   My chambers were upstairs at No.—Wall Street. At one end they looked upon the white wall of the interior of a spacious skylight shaft penetrating the building from top to bottom. This view might have been considered rather tame than otherwise, deficient in what landscape painters call "life." But if so, the view from the other end of my chambers offered at least a contrast, if nothing more. In that direction my windows commanded an unobstructed view of a lofty brick wall, black by age and everlasting shade, which wall required no spy-glass to bring out its lurking beauties, but for the benefit of all near-sighted spectators was pushed up to within ten feet of my window panes. Owing to the great height of the surrounding buildings, and my chambers being on the second floor, the interval between this wall and mine not a little resembled a huge square cistern.

At the period just preceding the advent of Bartleby, I had two persons as copyists in my employment and a promising lad as an office boy. First, Turkey; second, Nippers; third, Ginger Nut. These may seem names the like of which are not usually found in the Directory. In truth they were nicknames mutually conferred upon each other by my three clerks, and were deemed expressive of their respective persons or characters. Turkey was a short, pursy Englishman of about my own age, that is, somewhere not far from sixty. In the morning, one might say, his face was of a fine florid hue, but after twelve o'clock, meridian—his dinner hour—it blazed like a grate full of Christmas coals, and continued blazing—but as it were with a gradual wane—till 6 o'clock P.M. or thereabouts, after which I saw no more of the proprietor of the face, which gaining its meridian with the sun, seemed to set with it, to rise, culminate, and decline the following day, with the like regularity and undiminished glory. There are many singular coincidences I have known in the course of my life, not the least among which was the fact that exactly when Turkey displayed his fullest beams from his red and radiant countenance, just then, too, at the critical moment began the daily period when I considered his business capacities as seriously disturbed for the remainder of the twenty-four hours. Not that he was absolutely idle or averse to business then; far from it. The difficulty was, he was apt to be altogether too energetic. There was a strange, inflamed, flurried, flighty recklessness of activity about him. He would be incautious in dipping his pen into his inkstand. All his blots upon my documents were dropped there after twelve o'clock, meridian. Indeed not only would he be reckless and sadly given to making blots in the afternoon, but some days he went further and was rather noisy. At such times, too, his face flamed with augmented blazonry, as if cannel coal had been heaped on anthracite. He made an unpleasant racket with his chair; spilled his sand-box;° in mending his pens, impatiently split them all to pieces, and threw them on the floor in a sudden passion; stood up and leaned over his table, box-ing his papers about in a most indecorous manner, very sad to behold in an elderly man like him. Nevertheless, as he was in many ways a most valuable person to me, and all the time before twelve o'clock, meridian, was the quickest, steadiest creature too, accomplishing a great deal of work in a style not easy to be matched—for these reasons, I was willing to overlook his eccentricities, though indeed occasionally I remonstrated with him. I did this very gently, however, because though the civilest, nay, the blandest and most reverential of men in the morning, yet in the afternoon he was disposed upon provocation to be slightly rash with his tongue, in fact insolent. Now valuing his morning services as I did, and resolved not to lose them; yet at the same time made uncomfortable by his inflamed ways after twelve o'clock; and being a man of peace, unwill-ing by my admonitions to call forth unseemly retorts from him, I took upon me one Saturday noon (he was always worse on Saturdays) to hint to him very kindly that perhaps now that he was growing old, it might be well to abridge his labors; in short, he need not come to my chambers after twelve o'clock but, dinner over, had best go home to his lodgings and rest himself till tea-time. But no; he insisted upon his afternoon devotions. His countenance became intolerably fervid as he oratorically assured me—gesticulating with a long ruler at the other end of the room—that if his services in the morning were useful, how indispens-able, then, in the afternoon?

sand-box: sand kept in a shaker and used for blotting wet ink

"With submission, sir," said Turkey on this occasion. "I consider myself your right-hand man. In the morning I but marshal and deploy my columns, but in the afternoon I put myself at their head and gallantly charge the foe, thus!"—and he made a violent thrust with the ruler.

"But the blots, Turkey," intimated I.

"True,—but, with submission, sir, behold these hairs! I am getting old. Surely, sir, a blot or two of a warm afternoon is not to be severely urged against gray hairs. Old age—even if it blot the page—is honorable. With submission, sir, we *both* are getting old."

10   This appeal to my fellow-feeling was hardly to be resisted. At all events, I saw that go he would not. So I made up my mind to let him stay, resolving nevertheless to see to it that during the afternoon he had to do with my less important papers.

Nippers, the second on my list, was a whiskered, sallow, and upon the whole rather piratical-looking young man of about five and twenty. I always deemed him the victim of two evil powers—ambition and indigestion. The ambition was evinced by a certain impatience of the duties of a mere copyist, an unwarrantable usurpation of strictly professional affairs such as the original drawing up of legal documents. The indigestion seemed betokened in an occasional nervous testiness and grinning irritability causing the teeth to audibly grind together over mistakes committed in copying; unnecessary maledictions hissed rather than spoken in the heat of business; and especially by a continual discontent with the height of the table where he worked. Though of a very ingenious mechanical turn, Nippers could never get this table to suit him. He put chips under it, blocks of various sorts, bits of paste-board, and at last went so far as to attempt an exquisite adjustment by final pieces of folded blotting-paper. But no invention would answer. If for the sake of easing his back he brought the table lid at a sharp angle well up towards his chin, and wrote there like a man using the steep roof of a Dutch house for his desk, then he declared that it stopped the circulation in his arms. If now he lowered the table to his waistbands and stooped over it in writing, then there was a sore aching in his back. In short, the truth of the matter was Nippers knew not what he wanted. Or if he wanted anything, it was to be rid of a scrivener's table altogether. Among the manifestations of his diseased ambition was a fondness he had for receiving visits from certain ambiguous-looking fellows in seedy coats, whom he called his clients. Indeed I was aware that not only was he at times considerable of a ward-politician, but he occasionally did a little business at the Justices' courts and was not unknown on the steps of the Tombs. I have good reason to believe however that one individual who called upon him at my chambers and who with a grand air he insisted was his client was no other than a dun, and the alleged title-deed, a bill. But with all his failings, and the annoyances he caused me, Nippers, like his compatriot Turkey, was a very useful man to me; wrote a neat, swift hand; and, when he chose, was not deficient in a gentlemanly sort of deportment. Added to this, he always dressed in a gentlemanly sort of way, and so incidentally reflected credit upon my chambers. Whereas with respect to Turkey, I had much ado to keep him from being a reproach to me. His clothes were apt to look oily and smell of eating-houses. He wore his pantaloons very loose and baggy in the summer. His coats were execrable, his hat not to be handled. But while the hat was a thing of indifference to me inasmuch as his natural civility and deference as a dependent Englishman always led him to doff it the moment he entered the room, yet his coat was another matter. Concerning his coats, I reasoned with him, but with no effect. The truth was I suppose that a man with so small an income could not afford to sport such a lustrous face and a lustrous coat at one and the same time. As Nippers once observed, Turkey's money went chiefly for red ink. One winter day I presented Turkey with a highly respectable looking coat of my own, a padded gray coat of a most comfortable warmth and which buttoned straight up from the knee to the neck. I thought Turkey would appreciate the favor and abate his rashness and obstreperousness of afternoons. But no. I verily believe that buttoning himself up in so downy and blanket-like a coat had a pernicious effect upon him, upon the same principle that too much oats are bad for horses. In fact, precisely as a rash, restive horse is said to feel his oats, so Turkey felt his coat. It made him insolent. He was a man whom prosperity harmed.

Though concerning the self-indulgent habits of Turkey I had my own private surmises, yet touching Nippers I was well persuaded that whatever might be his faults in other respects, he was at least a temperate young man. But indeed, nature herself seemed to have been his vintner and at his birth charged him so thoroughly with an irritable, brandy-like disposition that all subsequent potations were needless. When I consider how amid the stillness of my chambers Nippers would sometimes impatiently rise from his seat and stooping over his table spread his arms wide apart, seize the whole desk, and move it, and jerk it, with a grim, grinding motion on the floor, as if the table were a perverse voluntary agent intent on thwarting and vexing him, I plainly perceive that for Nippers, brandy and water were altogether superfluous.

It was fortunate for me that, owing to its peculiar cause—indigestion— the irritability and consequent nervousness of Nippers were mainly observable in the morning, while in the afternoon he was comparatively mild. So that Turkey's paroxysms only coming on about twelve o'clock, I never had to do with their eccentricities at one time. Their fits relieved each other like guards. When Nippers's was on, Turkey's was off, and vice versa. This was a good natural arrangement under the circumstances.

Ginger Nut, the third on my list, was a lad some twelve years old. His father was a carman,° ambitious of seeing his son on the bench instead of a cart before he died. So he sent him to my office as student at law, errand boy, and cleaner and sweeper, at the rate of one dollar a week. He had a little desk to himself but he did not use it much. Upon inspection, the drawer exhibited a great array of the shells of various sorts of nuts. Indeed, to this quick-witted youth the whole noble science of the law was contained in a nutshell. Not the least among the employments of Ginger Nut, as well as one which he discharged with the most alacrity, was his duty as cake and apple purveyor for Turkey and Nippers. Copying law papers being proverbially a dry, husky sort of business, my two scriveners were fain to moisten their mouths very often with Spitzenbergs° to be had at the numerous stalls nigh the Custom House and Post Office. Also, they sent Ginger Nut very frequently for that peculiar cake—small, flat, round, and very spicy—after which he had been named by them. Of a cold morning when business was but dull, Turkey would gobble up scores of these cakes as if they were mere wafers—indeed they sell them at the rate of six or eight for a penny—the scrape of his pen blending with the crunching of the crisp particles in his mouth. Of all the fiery afternoon blunders and flurried rashnesses of Turkey was his once moistening a ginger cake between his lips and clapping it on to a mortgage for a seal. I came within an ace of dismissing him then. But he mollified me by making an oriental bow and saying—"With submission, sir, it was generous of me to find you in stationery on my own account."

15   Now my original business—that of a conveyancer and title hunter, and drawer-up of recondite documents of all sorts—was considerably increased by receiving the master's office. There was now great work for scriveners. Not only must I push the clerks already with me, but I must have additional help. In answer to my advertisement, a motionless young man one morning stood upon my office threshold, the door being open, for it was summer. I can see that figure now—pallidly neat, pitiably respectable, incurably forlorn! It was Bartleby.

After a few words touching his qualifications I engaged him, glad to have among my corps of copyists a man of so singularly sedate an aspect, which I thought might operate beneficially upon the flighty temper of Turkey and the fiery one of Nippers.

---

carman: a cart driver   **Spitzenbergs:** a variety of apple

I should have stated before that ground glass folding doors divided my premises into two parts, one of which was occupied by my scriveners, the other by myself. According to my humor I threw open these doors, or closed them. I resolved to assign Bartleby a corner by the folding doors, but on my side of them so as to have this quiet man within easy call in case any trifling thing was to be done. I placed his desk close up to a small side window in that part of the room, a window which originally had afforded a lateral view of certain grimy backyards and bricks, but which owing to subsequent erections commanded at present no view at all, though it gave some light. Within three feet of the panes was a wall, and the light came down from far above between two lofty buildings as from a very small opening in a dome. Still further to a satisfactory arrangement, I procured a high green folding screen which might entirely isolate Bartleby from my sight though not remove him from my voice. And thus, in a manner privacy and society were conjoined.

At first Bartleby did an extraordinary quantity of writing. As if long famishing for something to copy, he seemed to gorge himself on my documents. There was no pause for digestion. He ran a day and night line, copying by sunlight and by candlelight. I should have been quite delighted with his application had he been cheerfully industrious. But he wrote on silently, palely, mechanically.

It is of course an indispensable part of a scrivener's business to verify the accuracy of his copy, word by word. Where there are two or more scriveners in an office, they assist each other in this examination, one reading from the copy, the other holding the original. It is a very dull, wearisome, and lethargic affair. I can readily imagine that to some sanguine temperaments it would be altogether intolerable. For example, I cannot credit that the mettlesome poet Byron would have contentedly sat down with Bartleby to examine a law document of, say, five hundred pages closely written in a crimpy hand.

Now and then in the haste of business, it had been my habit to assist in comparing some brief document myself, calling Turkey or Nippers for this purpose. One object I had in placing Bartleby so handy to me behind the screen was to avail myself of his services on such trivial occasions. It was on the third day, I think, of his being with me, and before any necessity had arisen for having his own writing examined, that being much hurried to complete a small affair I had in hand, I abruptly called to Bartleby. In my haste and natural expectancy of instant compliance, I sat with my head bent over the original on my desk and my right hand sideways and somewhat nervously extended with the copy, so that immediately upon emerging from his retreat Bartleby might snatch it and proceed to business without the least delay.

In this very attitude did I sit when I called to him, rapidly stating what it was I wanted him to do—namely, to examine a small paper with me. Imagine my surprise, nay my consternation, when without moving from his privacy Bartleby in a singularly mild, firm voice replied, "I would prefer not to."

I sat awhile in perfect silence, rallying my stunned faculties. Immediately it occurred to me that my ears had deceived me, or Bartleby had entirely misunderstood my meaning. I repeated my request in the clearest tone I could assume. But in quite as clear a one came the previous reply, "I would prefer not to."

"Prefer not to," echoed I, rising in high excitement and crossing the room with a stride. "What do you mean? Are you moonstruck? I want you to help me compare this sheet here—take it," and I thrust it towards him.

"I would prefer not to," said he.

25　　I looked at him steadfastly. His face was leanly composed, his gray eye dimly calm. Not a wrinkle of agitation rippled him. Had there been the least uneasiness, anger, impatience or impertinence in his manner, in other words had there been anything ordinarily human about him, doubtless I should have violently dismissed him from the premises. But as it was, I should have as soon thought of turning my pale plaster-of-paris bust of Cicero out of doors. I stood gazing at him awhile as he went on with his own writing, and then reseated myself at my desk. This is very strange, thought I. What had one best do? But my business hurried me. I concluded to forget the matter for the present, reserving it for my future leisure. So calling Nippers from the other room, the paper was speedily examined.

A few days after this Bartleby concluded four lengthy documents, being quadruplicates of a week's testimony taken before me in my High Court of Chancery. It became necessary to examine them. It was an important suit and great accuracy was imperative. Having all things arranged I called Turkey, Nippers and Ginger Nut from the next room, meaning to place the four copies in the hands of my four clerks while I should read from the original. Accordingly Turkey, Nippers and Ginger Nut had taken their seats in a row, each with his document in hand, when I called to Bartleby to join this interesting group.

"Bartleby! quick, I am waiting."

I heard a slow scrape of his chair legs on the unscraped floor, and soon he appeared standing at the entrance of his hermitage.

"What is wanted?" said he mildly.

30　　"The copies, the copies," said I hurriedly. "We are going to examine them. There"—and I held towards him the fourth quadruplicate.

"I would prefer not to," he said, and gently disappeared behind the screen.

For a few moments I was turned into a pillar of salt° standing at the head of my seated column of clerks. Recovering myself, I advanced towards the screen and demanded the reason for such extraordinary conduct.

"*Why* do you refuse?"

"I would prefer not to."

With any other man I should have flown outright into a dreadful pas- 35 sion, scorned all further words, and thrust him ignominiously from my presence. But there was something about Bartleby that not only strangely disarmed me, but in a wonderful manner touched and disconcerted me. I began to reason with him.

"These are your own copies we are about to examine. It is labor saving to you, because one examination will answer for your four papers. It is common usage. Every copyist is bound to help examine his copy. Is it not so? Will you not speak? Answer!"

"I prefer not to," he replied in a flute-like tone. It seemed to me that while I had been addressing him, he carefully revolved every statement that I made, fully comprehended the meaning, could not gainsay the irresistible conclusion, but at the same time some paramount consideration prevailed with him to reply as he did.

"You are decided, then, not to comply with my request—a request made according to common usage and common sense?"

He briefly gave me to understand that on that point my judgment was sound. Yes: his decision was irreversible.

It is not seldom the case that when a man is browbeaten in some 40 unprecedented and violently unreasonable way he begins to stagger in his own plainest faith. He begins, as it were, vaguely to surmise that wonderful as it may be, all the justice and all the reason is on the other side. Accordingly, if any disinterested persons are present he turns to them for some reinforcement for his own faltering mind.

"Turkey," said I, "what do you think of this? Am I not right?"

"With submission, sir," said Turkey with his blandest tone, "I think that you are."

"Nippers," said I, "what do *you* think of it?"

"I think I should kick him out of the office."

(The reader of nice perceptions will here perceive that, it being morn- 45 ing, Turkey's answer is couched in polite and tranquil terms, but Nippers replies in ill-tempered ones. Or, to repeat a previous sentence, Nippers's ugly mood was on duty, and Turkey's off.)

"Ginger Nut," said I, willing to enlist the smallest suffrage in my behalf, "what do *you* think of it?"

pillar of salt: See Genesis 19:26.

"I think, sir, he's a little *loony*," replied Ginger Nut, with a grin.

"You hear what they say," said I, turning towards the screen, "come forth and do your duty."

But he vouchsafed no reply. I pondered a moment in sore perplexity. But once more business hurried me. I determined again to postpone the consideration of this dilemma to my future leisure. With a little trouble we made out to examine the papers without Bartleby, though at every page or two, Turkey deferentially dropped his opinion that this proceeding was quite out of the common, while Nippers, twitching in his chair with a dyspeptic nervousness, ground out between his set teeth occasional hissing maledictions against the stubborn oaf behind the screen. And for his (Nippers's) part, this was the first and the last time he would do another man's business without pay.

50   Meanwhile Bartleby sat in his hermitage, oblivious to everything but his own peculiar business there.

Some days passed, the scrivener being employed upon another lengthy work. His late remarkable conduct led me to regard his way narrowly. I observed that he never went to dinner, indeed that he never went anywhere. As yet I had never of my personal knowledge known him to be outside of my office. He was a perpetual sentry in the corner. At about eleven o'clock though, in the morning, I noticed that Ginger Nut would advance toward the opening in Bartleby's screen as if silently beckoned thither by a gesture invisible to me where I sat. That boy would then leave the office jingling a few pence and reappear with a handful of ginger nuts which he delivered in the hermitage, receiving two of the cakes for his trouble.

He lives then on ginger nuts, thought I; never eats a dinner, properly speaking; he must be a vegetarian then, but no, he never eats even vegetables, he eats nothing but ginger nuts. My mind then ran on in reveries concerning the probable effects upon the human constitution of living entirely on ginger nuts. Ginger nuts are so called because they contain ginger as one of their peculiar constituents, and the final flavoring one. Now what was ginger? A hot, spicy thing. Was Bartleby hot and spicy? Not at all. Ginger, then, had no effect upon Bartleby. Probably he preferred it should have none.

Nothing so aggravates an earnest person as a passive resistance. If the individual so resisted be of a not inhumane temper, and the resisting one perfectly harmless in his passivity, then in the better moods of the former, he will endeavor charitably to construe to his imagination what proves impossible to be solved by his judgment. Even so for the most part I regarded Bartleby and his ways. Poor fellow! thought I, he means no mischief; it is plain he intends no insolence; his aspect sufficiently evinces that his eccentricities are involuntary. He is useful to me. I can get along with him. If I turn him away, the chances are he will fall in with some less indulgent employer, and then he will be rudely treated and perhaps driven forth miserably to starve. Yes. Here I can cheaply purchase a delicious self-approval. To befriend Bartleby, to humor him in his strange wilfulness, will cost me little or nothing, while I lay up in my soul what will eventually prove a sweet morsel for my conscience. But this mood was not invariable with me. The passiveness of Bartleby sometimes irritated me. I felt strangely goaded on to encounter him in new opposition, to elicit some angry spark from him answerable to my own. But indeed I might as well have essayed to strike fire with my knuckles against a bit of Windsor soap. But one afternoon the evil impulse in me mastered me, and the following little scene ensued:

"Bartleby," said I, "when those papers are all copied I will compare them with you."

"I would prefer not to."   55

"How? Surely you do not mean to persist in that mulish vagary?"

No answer.

I threw open the folding doors nearby, and turning upon Turkey and Nippers, exclaimed in an excited manner—

"He says, a second time, he won't examine his papers. What do you think of it, Turkey?"

It was afternoon, be it remembered. Turkey sat glowing like a brass   60 boiler, his bald head steaming, his hands reeling among his blotted papers.

"Think of it?" roared Turkey, "I think I'll just step behind his screen and black his eyes for him!"

So saying, Turkey rose to his feet and threw his arms into a pugilistic position. He was hurrying away to make good his promise when I detained him, alarmed at the effect of incautiously rousing Turkey's combativeness after dinner.

"Sit down, Turkey," said I, "and hear what Nippers has to say. What do you think of it, Nippers? Would I not be justified in immediately dismissing Bartleby?"

"Excuse me, that is for you to decide, sir. I think his conduct quite unusual, and indeed unjust as regards Turkey and myself. But it may only be a passing whim."

"Ah," exclaimed I, "you have strangely changed your mind then—you   65 speak very gently of him now."

"All beer," cried Turkey, "gentleness is effects of beer—Nippers and I dined together today. You see how gentle *I* am, sir. Shall I go and black his eyes?"

"You refer to Bartleby, I suppose. No, not today, Turkey," I replied, "pray, put up your fists."

I closed the doors, and again advanced towards Bartleby. I felt additional incentives tempting me to my fate. I burned to be rebelled against again. I remembered that Bartleby never left the office.

"Bartleby," said I, "Ginger Nut is away; just step round to the post office, won't you? (it was but a three minutes walk) and see if there is anything for me."

70   "I would prefer not to."

"You *will* not?"

"I *prefer* not."

I staggered to my desk and sat there in a deep study. My blind inveteracy returned. Was there any other thing in which I could procure myself to be ignominiously repulsed by this lean, penniless wight?—my hired clerk? What added thing is there, perfectly reasonable, that he will be sure to refuse to do?

"Bartleby!"

75   No answer.

"Bartleby," in a louder tone.

No answer.

"Bartleby," I roared.

Like a very ghost, agreeably to the laws of magical invocation, at the third summons he appeared at the entrance of his hermitage.

80   "Go to the next room, and tell Nippers to come to me."

"I prefer not to," he respectfully and slowly said, and mildly disappeared.

"Very good, Bartleby," said I, in a quiet sort of serenely severe self-possessed tone, intimating the unalterable purpose of some terrible retribution very close at hand. At the moment I half intended something of the kind. But upon the whole, as it was drawing towards my dinner hour, I thought it best to put on my hat and walk home for the day, suffering much from perplexity and distress of mind.

Shall I acknowledge it? The conclusion of this whole business was that it soon became a fixed fact of my chambers that a pale young scrivener by the name of Bartleby had a desk there; that he copied for me at the usual rate of four cents a folio (one hundred words); but he was permanently exempt from examining the work done by him, that duty being transferred to Turkey and Nippers, one of compliment doubtless to their superior acuteness; moreover, said Bartleby was never on any account to be dispatched on the most trivial errand of any sort, and that even if entreated to take upon him such a matter, it was generally understood that he would prefer not to—in other words, that he would refuse point-blank.

As days passed on, I became considerably reconciled to Bartleby. His steadiness, his freedom from all dissipation, his incessant industry (except when he chose to throw himself into a standing revery behind his screen), his great stillness, his unalterableness of demeanor under all circumstances, made him a valuable acquisition. One prime thing was this—*he was always there*—first in the morning, continually through the day, and the last at night. I had a singular confidence in his honesty. I felt my most precious papers perfectly safe in his hands. Sometimes to be sure I could not for the very soul of me avoid falling into sudden spasmodic passions with him. For it was exceeding difficult to bear in mind all the time those strange peculiarities, privileges, and unheard of exemptions forming the tacit stipulations on Bartleby's part under which he remained in my office. Now and then in the eagerness of dispatching pressing business, I would inadvertently summon Bartleby, in a short rapid tone, to put his finger, say, on the incipient tie of a bit of red tape with which I was about compressing some papers. Of course, from behind the screen the usual answer, "I prefer not to," was sure to come, and then how could a human creature with the common infirmities of our nature, refrain from bitterly exclaiming upon such perverseness—such unreasonableness? However, every added repulse of this sort which I received only tended to lessen the probability of my repeating the inadvertence.

Here it must be said that according to the custom of most legal gentle- 85 men occupying chambers in densely populated law buildings, there were several keys to my door. One was kept by a woman residing in the attic, which person weekly scrubbed and daily swept and dusted my apartments. Another was kept by Turkey for convenience sake. The third I sometimes carried in my own pocket. The fourth I knew not who had.

Now one Sunday morning I happened to go to Trinity Church° to hear a celebrated preacher, and finding myself rather early on the ground I thought I would walk round to my chambers for a while. Luckily I had my key with me, but upon applying it to the lock, I found it resisted by something inserted from the inside. Quite surprised, I called out, when to my consternation a key was turned from within, and thrusting his lean visage at me and holding the door ajar, the apparition of Bartleby appeared, in his shirt sleeves, and otherwise in a strangely tattered dishabille, saying quietly that he was sorry but he was deeply engaged just then and—preferred not admitting me at present. In a brief word or two, he moreover added that perhaps I had better walk round the block two or three times, and by that time he would probably have concluded his affairs.

Now, the utterly unsurmised appearance of Bartleby tenanting my law-chambers of a Sunday morning with his cadaverously gentlemanly nonchalance, yet withal firm and self-possessed, had such a strange effect

---

Trinity Church: located at the corner of Broadway and Wall Street

upon me that incontinently I slunk away from my own door and did as desired. But not without sundry twinges of impotent rebellion against the mild effrontery of this unaccountable scrivener. Indeed it was his wonderful mildness chiefly which not only disarmed me but unmanned me, as it were. For I consider that one, for the time, is sort of unmanned when he tranquilly permits his hired clerk to dictate to him and order him away from his own premises. Furthermore, I was full of uneasiness as to what Bartleby could possibly be doing in my office in his shirt sleeves and in an otherwise dismantled condition of a Sunday morning. Was anything amiss going on? Nay, that was out of the question. It was not to be thought of for a moment that Bartleby was an immoral person. But what could he be doing there?—copying? Nay again, whatever might be his eccentricities, Bartleby was an eminently decorous person. He would be the last man to sit down to his desk in any state approaching to nudity. Besides, it was Sunday, and there was something about Bartleby that forbade the supposition that he would by any secular occupation violate the proprieties of the day.

Nevertheless, my mind was not pacified; and full of a restless curiosity, at last I returned to the door. Without hindrance I inserted my key, opened it, and entered. Bartleby was not to be seen. I looked round anxiously, peeped behind his screen, but it was very plain that he was gone. Upon more closely examining the place, I surmised that for an indefinite period Bartleby must have ate, dressed, and slept in my office, and that too without plate, mirror, or bed. The cushioned seat of a rickety old sofa in one corner bore the faint impress of a lean, reclining form. Rolled away under his desk I found a blanket; under the empty grate, a blacking box and brush; on a chair, a tin basin with soap and a ragged towel; in a newspaper a few crumbs of ginger nuts and a morsel of cheese. Yes, thought I, it is evident enough that Bartleby has been making his home here, keeping bachelor's hall all by himself. Immediately then the thought came sweeping across me, what miserable friendlessness and loneliness are here revealed! His poverty is great; but his solitude, how horrible! Think of it. Of a Sunday, Wall Street is deserted as Petra, and every night of every day it is an emptiness. This building too which of weekdays hums with industry and life at nightfall echoes with sheer vacancy, and all through Sunday is forlorn. And here Bartleby makes his home, sole spectator of a solitude which he has seen all populous—a sort of innocent and transformed Marius brooding among the ruins of Carthage!

For the first time in my life a feeling of overpowering stinging melancholy seized me. Before I had never experienced aught but a not unpleasing sadness. The bond of a common humanity now drew me irresistibly to gloom. A fraternal melancholy! For both I and Bartleby were sons of Adam. I remembered the bright silks and sparkling faces I had seen that day in gala trim, swan-like sailing down the Mississippi of Broadway; and I contrasted them with the pallid copyist, and thought to myself, Ah, happiness courts the light, so we deem the world is gay; but misery hides aloof, so we deem that misery there is none. These sad fancyings—chimeras doubtless of a sick and silly brain—led on to other and more special thoughts concerning the eccentricities of Bartleby. Presentiments of strange discoveries hovered round me. The scrivener's pale form appeared to me laid out, among uncaring strangers, in its shivering winding sheet.

Suddenly I was attracted by Bartleby's closed desk, the key in open 90 sight left in the lock.

I mean no mischief, seek the gratification of no heartless curiosity, thought I; besides, the desk is mine, and its contents too, so I will make bold to look within. Everything was methodically arranged, the papers smoothly placed. The pigeon holes were deep, and removing the files of documents, I groped into their recesses. Presently I felt something there and dragged it out. It was an old bandanna handkerchief, heavy and knotted. I opened it, and saw it was a savings bank.

I now recalled all the quiet mysteries which I had noted in the man. I remembered that he never spoke but to answer; that though at intervals he had considerable time to himself, yet I had never seen him reading—no, not even a newspaper; that for long periods he would stand looking out, at his pale window behind the screen, upon the dead brick wall; I was quite sure he never visited any refectory or eating house, while his pale face clearly indicated that he never drank beer like Turkey, or tea and coffee even, like other men; that he never went anywhere in particular that I could learn, never went out for a walk, unless indeed that was the case at present; that he had declined telling who he was or whence he came or whether he had any relatives in the world; that though so thin and pale, he never complained of ill health. And more than all, I remembered a certain unconscious air of pallid—how shall I call it?—of pallid haughtiness, say, or rather an austere reserve about him, which had positively awed me into my tame compliance with his eccentricities when I had feared to ask him to do the slightest incidental thing for me, even though I might know from his long-continued motionlessness that behind his screen he must be standing in one of those dead-wall reveries of his.

Revolving all these things, and coupling them with the recently discovered fact that he made my office his constant abiding place and home, and not forgetful of his morbid moodiness; revolving all these things, a prudential feeling began to steal over me. My first emotions had been those of pure melancholy and sincerest pity; but just in proportion as the forlornness of Bartleby grew and grew to my imagination, did that same melancholy merge into fear, that pity into repulsion. So true it is, and so terrible too, that up to a certain point the thought or sight of misery enlists our best affections; but in certain special cases, beyond that point it does not. They err who would assert that invariably this is owing to the inherent selfishness of the human heart. It rather proceeds from a certain hopelessness of remedying excessive and organic ill. To a sensitive being, pity is not seldom pain. And when at last it is perceived that such pity cannot lead to effectual succor, common sense bids the soul be rid of it. What I saw that morning persuaded me that the scrivener was the victim of innate and incurable disorder. I might give alms to his body, but his body did not pain him; it was his soul that suffered, and his soul I could not reach.

I did not accomplish the purpose of going to Trinity Church that morning. Somehow, the things I had seen disqualified me for the time from church-going. I walked homeward, thinking what I would do with Bartleby. Finally I resolved upon this:—I would put certain calm questions to him the next morning, touching his history, &c., and if he declined to answer them openly and unreservedly (and I supposed he would prefer not), then to give him a twenty dollar bill over and above whatever I might owe him, and tell him his services were no longer required; but that if in any other way I could assist him, I would be happy to do so, especially if he desired to return to his native place, wherever that might be, I would willingly help to defray the expenses. Moreover, if after reaching home he found himself at any time in want of aid, a letter from him would be sure of a reply.

95   The next morning came.

"Bartleby," said I, gently calling to him behind his screen.

No reply.

"Bartleby," said I, in a still gentler tone, "come here; I am not going to ask you to do anything you would prefer not to do—I simply wish to speak to you."

Upon this he noiselessly slid into view.

100   "Will you tell me, Bartleby, where you were born?"

"I would prefer not to."

"Will you tell me *anything* about yourself?"

"I would prefer not to."

"But what reasonable objection can you have to speak to me? I feel friendly towards you."

105   He did not look at me while I spoke, but kept his glance fixed upon my bust of Cicero, which as I then sat was directly behind me, some six inches above my head.

"What is your answer, Bartleby?" said I, after waiting a considerable time for a reply, during which his countenance remained immovable, only there was the faintest conceivable tremor of the white attenuated mouth.

"At present I prefer to give no answer," he said, and retired into his hermitage.

It was rather weak in me I confess, but his manner on this occasion nettled me. Not only did there seem to lurk in it a certain disdain, but his perverseness seemed ungrateful, considering the undeniable good usage and indulgence he had received from me.

Again I sat ruminating what I should do. Mortified as I was at his behavior, and resolved as I had been to dismiss him when I entered my office, nevertheless I strangely felt something superstitious knocking at my heart, and forbidding me to carry out my purpose, and denouncing me for a villain if I dared to breathe one bitter word against this forlornest of mankind. At last, familiarly drawing my chair behind his screen, I sat down and said: "Bartleby, never mind then about revealing your history; but let me entreat you, as a friend, to comply as far as may be with the usages of this office. Say now you will help to examine papers tomorrow or next day: in short, say now that in a day or two you will begin to be a little reasonable:—say so, Bartleby."

"At present I would prefer not to be a little reasonable," was his mildly 110 cadaverous reply.

Just then the folding doors opened, and Nippers approached. He seemed suffering from an unusually bad night's rest, induced by severer indigestion than common. He overheard those final words of Bartleby.

"*Prefer not*, eh?" gritted Nippers—"I'd *prefer* him, if I were you, sir," addressing me—"I'd *prefer* him; I'd give him preferences, the stubborn mule! What is it, sir, pray, that he *prefers* not to do now?"

Bartleby moved not a limb.

"Mr. Nippers," said I, "I'd prefer that you would withdraw for the present."

Somehow, of late I had got into the way of involuntarily using this 115 word "prefer" upon all sorts of not exactly suitable occasions. And I trembled to think that my contact with the scrivener had already and seriously affected me in a mental way. And what further and deeper aberration might it not yet produce? This apprehension had not been without efficacy in determining me to summary means.

As Nippers, looking very sour and sulky, was departing, Turkey blandly and deferentially approached.

"With submission, sir," said he, "yesterday I was thinking about Bartleby here, and I think that if he would but prefer to take a quart of good ale every day, it would do much towards mending him and enabling him to assist in examining his papers."

"So you have got the word too," said I, slightly excited.

"With submission, what word, sir?" asked Turkey, respectfully crowding himself into the contracted space behind the screen, and by so doing making me jostle the scrivener. "What word, sir?"

120 "I would prefer to be left alone here," said Bartleby, as if offended at being mobbed in his privacy.

"*That's* the word, Turkey," said I—"*that's* it."

"Oh, *prefer?* oh yes—queer word. I never use it myself. But, sir, as I was saying, if he would but prefer—"

"Turkey," interrupted I, "you will please withdraw."

"Oh certainly, sir, if you prefer that I should."

125 As he opened the folding door to retire, Nippers at his desk caught a glimpse of me and asked whether I would prefer to have a certain paper copied on blue paper or white. He did not in the least roguishly accent the word prefer. It was plain that it involuntarily rolled from his tongue. I thought to myself, surely I must get rid of a demented man who already has in some degree turned the tongues if not the heads of myself and clerks. But I thought it prudent not to break the dismission at once.

The next day I noticed that Bartleby did nothing but stand at his window in his dead-wall revery. Upon my asking him why he did not write, he said that he had decided upon doing no more writing.

"Why, how now? what next?" exclaimed I, "do no more writing?"

"No more."

"And what is the reason?"

130 "Do you not see the reason for yourself?" he indifferently replied.

I looked steadfastly at him, and perceived that his eyes looked dull and glazed. Instantly it occurred to me that his unexampled diligence in copying by his dim window for the first few weeks of his stay with me might have temporarily impaired his vision.

I was touched. I said something in condolence with him. I hinted that of course he did wisely in abstaining from writing for a while, and urged him to embrace that opportunity of taking wholesome exercise in the open air. This, however, he did not do. A few days after this, my other clerks being absent, and being in a great hurry to dispatch certain letters by the mail, I thought that, having nothing else earthly to do, Bartleby would surely be less inflexible than usual and carry these letters to the post office. But he blankly declined. So, much to my inconvenience, I went myself.

Still added days went by. Whether Bartleby's eyes improved or not, I could not say. To all appearance, I thought they did. But when I asked him if they did, he vouchsafed no answer. At all events, he would do no copying. At last, in reply to my urgings, he informed me that he had permanently given up copying.

"What!" exclaimed I; "suppose your eyes should get entirely well—better than ever before—would you not copy then?"

"I have given up copying," he answered, and slid aside.   135

He remained as ever, a fixture in my chamber. Nay—if that were possible—he became still more of a fixture than before. What was to be done? He would do nothing in the office: why should he stay there? In plain fact, he had now become a millstone to me, not only useless as a necklace but afflictive to bear. Yet I was sorry for him. I speak less than truth when I say that on his own account, he occasioned me uneasiness. If he would but have named a single relative or friend, I would instantly have written and urged their taking the poor fellow away to some convenient retreat. But he seemed alone, absolutely alone in the universe. A bit of wreck in the mid-Atlantic. At length, necessities connected with my business tyrannized over all other considerations. Decently as I could, I told Bartleby that in six days' time he must unconditionally leave the office. I warned him to take measures, in the interval, for procuring some other abode. I offered to assist him in this endeavor, if he himself would but take the first step towards a removal. "And when you finally quit me, Bartleby," added I, "I shall see that you go not away entirely unprovided. Six days from this hour, remember."

At the expiration of that period I peeped behind the screen, and lo! Bartleby was there.

I buttoned up my coat, balanced myself, advanced slowly towards him, touched his shoulder, and said, "The time has come; you must quit this place; I am sorry for you; here is money; but you must go."

"I would prefer not," he replied, with his back still towards me.

"You *must*."   140

He remained silent.

Now I had an unbounded confidence in this man's common honesty. He had frequently restored to me six pences and shillings carelessly dropped upon the floor, for I am apt to be very reckless in such shirt-button affairs. The proceeding then which followed will not be deemed extraordinary.

"Bartleby," said I, "I owe you twelve dollars on account; here are thirty-two; the odd twenty are yours. Will you take it?" and I handed the bills towards him.

But he made no motion.

"I will leave them here then," putting them under a weight on the   145 table. Then taking my hat and cane and going to the door I tranquilly turned and added, "After you have removed your things from these offices, Bartleby, you will of course lock the door—since every one is now gone for the day but you—and if you please, slip your key underneath the mat so that I may have it in the morning. I shall not see you again, so good-bye to you. If hereafter in your new place of abode I can be of any service to you, do not fail to advise me by letter. Good-bye, Bartleby, and fare you well."

But he answered not a word; like the last column of some ruined temple, he remained standing mute and solitary in the middle of the otherwise deserted room.

As I walked home in a pensive mood, my vanity got the better of my pity. I could not but highly plume myself on my masterly management in getting rid of Bartleby. Masterly I call it, and such it must appear to any dispassionate thinker. The beauty of my procedure seemed to consist in its perfect quietness. There was no vulgar bullying, no bravado of any sort, no choleric hectoring and striding to and fro across the apartment, jerking out vehement commands for Bartleby to bundle himself off with his beggarly traps.° Nothing of the kind. Without loudly bidding Bartleby depart—as an inferior genius might have done—I *assumed* the ground that depart he must, and upon the assumption built all I had to say. The more I thought over my procedure, the more I was charmed with it. Nevertheless, next morning, upon awakening, I had my doubts—I had somehow slept off the fumes of vanity. One of the coolest and wisest hours a man has is just after he awakes in the morning. My procedure seemed as sagacious as ever—but only in theory. How it would prove in practice—there was the rub. It was truly a beautiful thought to have assumed Bartleby's departure; but after all, that assumption was simply my own, and none of Bartleby's. The great point was not whether I had assumed that he would quit me, but whether he would prefer so to do. He was more a man of preferences than assumptions.

After breakfast, I walked downtown, arguing the probabilities *pro* and *con.* One moment I thought it would prove a miserable failure, and Bartleby would be found all alive at my office as usual; the next moment it seemed certain that I should see his chair empty. And so I kept veering about. At the corner of Broadway and Canal Street, I saw quite an excited group of people standing in earnest conversation.

"I'll take odds he doesn't," said a voice as I passed.

150 "Doesn't go?—done!" said I, "put up your money."

I was instinctively putting my hand in my pocket to produce my own, when I remembered that this was an election day. The words I had overheard bore no reference to Bartleby, but to the success or non-success of some candidate for the mayoralty. In my intent frame of mind, I had, as it were, imagined that all Broadway shared in my excitement and were debating the same question with me. I passed on, very thankful that the uproar of the street screened my momentary absentmindedness.

traps: belongings

As I had intended, I was earlier than usual at my office door. I stood listening for a moment. All was still. He must be gone. I tried the knob. The door was locked. Yes, my procedure had worked to a charm; he indeed must be vanished. Yet a certain melancholy mixed with this: I was almost sorry for my brilliant success. I was fumbling under the door mat for the key which Bartleby was to have left there for me when accidentally my knee knocked against a panel, producing a summoning sound, and in response a voice came to me from within—"Not yet; I am occupied."

It was Bartleby.

I was thunderstruck. For an instant I stood like the man who, pipe in mouth, was killed one cloudless afternoon long ago in Virginia, by summer lightning; at his own warm open window he was killed, and remained leaning out there upon the dreamy afternoon till someone touched him, when he fell.

"Not gone!" I murmured at last. But again obeying that wondrous 155 ascendancy which the inscrutable scrivener had over me, and from which ascendancy, for all my chafing, I could not completely escape, I slowly went downstairs and out into the street, and while walking round the block, considered what I should next do in this unheard of perplexity. Turn the man out by an actual thrusting I could not; to drive him away by calling him hard names would not do; calling in the police was an unpleasant idea; and yet, permit him to enjoy his cadaverous triumph over me?—this too I could not think of. What was to be done? or if nothing could be done, was there anything further that I could *assume* in the matter? Yes, as before I had prospectively assumed that Bartleby would depart, so now I might retrospectively assume that departed he was. In the legitimate carrying out of this assumption, I might enter my office in a great hurry, and pretending not to see Bartleby at all, walk straight against him as if he were air. Such a proceeding would in a singular degree have the appearance of a home-thrust. It was hardly possible that Bartleby could withstand such an application of the doctrine of assumptions. But upon second thoughts the success of the plan seemed rather dubious. I resolved to argue the matter over with him again.

"Bartleby," said I, entering the office with a quietly severe expression, "I am seriously displeased. I am pained, Bartleby. I had thought better of you. I had imagined you of such a gentlemanly organization that in my delicate dilemma a slight hint would suffice—in short, an assumption. But it appears I am deceived. Why," I added, unaffectedly starting, "you have not even touched that money yet," pointing to it just where I had left it the evening previous.

He answered nothing.

"Will you, or will you not, quit me?" I now demanded in a sudden passion, advancing close to him.

"I would prefer *not* to quit you," he replied, gently emphasizing the not.
160 "What earthly right have you to stay here? Do you pay any rent? Do you pay my taxes? Or is this property yours?"

He answered nothing.

"Are you ready to go on and write now? Are your eyes recovered? Could you copy a small paper for me this morning? or help examine a few lines? or step round to the post office? In a word, will you do anything at all to give a coloring to your refusal to depart the premises?"

He silently retired into his hermitage.

I was now in such a state of nervous resentment that I thought it but prudent to check myself at present from further demonstrations. Bartleby and I were alone. I remembered the tragedy of the unfortunate Adams and the still more unfortunate Colt° in the solitary office of the latter; and how poor Colt, being dreadfully incensed by Adams, and imprudently permitting himself to get wildly excited, was at unawares hurried into his fatal act—an act which certainly no man could possibly deplore more than the actor himself. Often it had occurred to me in my ponderings upon the subject that had that altercation taken place in the public street, or at a private residence, it would not have terminated as it did. It was the circumstance of being alone in a solitary office, upstairs, of a building entirely unhallowed by humanizing domestic associations—an uncarpeted office, doubtless, of a dusty haggard sort of appearance—this it must have been which greatly helped to enhance the irritable desperation of the hapless Colt.

165 But when this old Adam of resentment rose in me and tempted me concerning Bartleby, I grappled him and threw him. How? Why, simply by recalling the divine injunction: "A new commandment° give I unto you, that ye love one another." Yes, this it was that saved me. Aside from higher considerations, charity often operates as a vastly wise and prudent principle—a great safeguard to its possessor. Men have committed murder for jealousy's sake, and anger's sake, and hatred's sake, and selfishness' sake, and spiritual pride's sake; but no man that ever I heard of ever committed a diabolical murder for sweet charity's sake. Mere self-interest, then, if no better motive can be enlisted, should, especially with high-tempered men, prompt all beings to charity and philanthropy. At any rate, upon the occasion in question, I strove to drown my exasperated feelings towards the scrivener by benevolently construing his conduct. Poor fellow, poor fellow! thought I, he don't mean anything; and besides, he has seen hard times, and ought to be indulged.

Colt: In a famous murder case in 1841, John Colt used a hatchet to kill Samuel Adams, who owed him money. **commandment:** See John 15:12.

I endeavored also immediately to occupy myself, and at the same time to comfort my despondency. I tried to fancy that in the course of the morning, at such time as might prove agreeable to him, Bartleby of his own free accord would emerge from his hermitage and take up some decided line of march in the direction of the door. But no. Half-past twelve o'clock came; Turkey began to glow in the face, overturn his inkstand, and become generally obstreperous; Nippers abated down into quietude and courtesy; Ginger Nut munched his noon apple; and Bartleby remained standing at his window in one of his profoundest dead-wall reveries. Will it be credited? Ought I to acknowledge it? That afternoon I left the office without saying one further word to him.

Some days now passed, during which at leisure intervals I looked a little into "Edwards on the Will," and "Priestly on Necessity."° Under the circumstances, those books induced a salutary feeling. Gradually I slid into the persuasion that these troubles of mine touching the scrivener had been all predestinated from eternity, and Bartleby was billeted upon me for some mysterious purpose of an all-wise Providence which it was not for a mere mortal like me to fathom. Yes, Bartleby, stay there behind your screen, thought I; I shall persecute you no more; you are harmless and noiseless as any of these old chairs; in short, I never feel so private as when I know you are here. At least I see it, I feel it; I penetrate to the predestinated purpose of my life. I am content. Others may have loftier parts to enact; but my mission in this world, Bartleby, is to furnish you with office-room for such period as you may see fit to remain.

I believe that this wise and blessed frame of mind would have continued with me had it not been for the unsolicited and uncharitable remarks obtruded upon me by my professional friends who visited the rooms. But thus it often is, that the constant friction of illiberal minds wears out at last the best resolves of the more generous. Though to be sure, when I reflected upon it, it was not strange that people entering my office should be struck by the peculiar aspect of the unaccountable Bartleby, and so be tempted to throw out some sinister observations concerning him. Sometimes an attorney having business with me, and calling at my office, and finding no one but the scrivener there, would undertake to obtain some sort of precise information from him touching my whereabouts; but without heeding his idle talk, Bartleby would remain standing immovable in the middle of the room. So after contemplating him in that position for a time, the attorney would depart, no wiser than he came.

"**Edwards . . . Necessity**": writings by eighteenth-century philosophers who took the position that free will does not exist

Also, when a reference was going on, and the room full of lawyers and witnesses and business was driving fast, some deeply occupied legal gentleman present seeing Bartleby wholly unemployed would request him to run round to his (the legal gentleman's) office and fetch some papers for him. Thereupon, Bartleby would tranquilly decline, and remain idle as before. Then the lawyer would give a great stare and turn to me. And what could I say? At last I was made aware that all through the circle of my professional acquaintance, a whisper of wonder was running round having reference to the strange creature I kept at my office. This worried me very much. And as the idea came upon me of his possibly turning out a long-lived man, and keep occupying my chambers, and denying my authority, and perplexing my visitors, and scandalizing my professional reputation, and casting a general gloom over the premises, keeping soul and body together to the last upon his savings (for doubtless he spent but half a dime a day), and in the end perhaps outliving me, and claiming possession of my office by right of his perpetual occupancy: as all these dark anticipations crowded upon me more and more, and my friends continually intruded their relentless remarks upon the apparition in my room, a great change was wrought in me. I resolved to gather all my faculties together, and forever rid me of this intolerable incubus.

170   Ere revolving any complicated project, however, adapted to this end, I first simply suggested to Bartleby the propriety of his permanent departure. In a calm and serious tone, I commended the idea to his careful and mature consideration. But having taken three days to meditate upon it, he apprised me that his original determination remained the same, in short, that he still preferred to abide with me.

What shall I do? I now said to myself, buttoning up my coat to the last button. What shall I do? what ought I do? what does conscience say I *should* do with this man, or rather ghost? Rid myself of him, I must; go, he shall. But how? You will not thrust him, the poor, pale, passive mortal— you will not thrust such a helpless creature out of your door? you will not dishonor yourself by such cruelty? No, I will not, I cannot do that. Rather would I let him live and die here, and then mason up his remains in the wall. What then will you do? For all your coaxing, he will not budge. Bribes he leaves under your own paperweight on your table; in short, it is quite plain that he prefers to cling to you.

Then something severe, something unusual must be done. What! surely you will not have him collared by a constable, and commit his innocent pallor to the common jail? And upon what ground could you procure such a thing to be done?—a vagrant, is he? What! he a vagrant, a wanderer, who refuses to budge? It is because he will *not* be a vagrant, then, that you seek to count him *as* a vagrant. That is too absurd. No visible means of support: there I have him. Wrong again: for indubitably he *does* support himself, and that is the only unanswerable proof that any man can show of his possessing the means so to do. No more then. Since he will not quit me, I must quit him. I will change my offices; I will move elsewhere, and give him fair notice that if I find him on my new premises I will then proceed against him as a common trespasser.

Acting accordingly, next day I thus addressed him: "I find these chambers too far from the City Hall; the air is unwholesome. In a word, I propose to remove my offices next week, and shall no longer require your services. I tell you this now, in order that you may seek another place."

He made no reply, and nothing more was said.

On the appointed day I engaged carts and men, proceeded to my 175 chambers, and having but little furniture, everything was removed in a few hours. Throughout, the scrivener remained standing behind the screen, which I directed to be removed the last thing. It was withdrawn, and being folded up like a huge folio, left him the motionless occupant of a naked room. I stood in the entry watching him a moment, while something from within me upbraided me.

I re-entered, with my hand in my pocket—and—and my heart in my mouth.

"Good-bye, Bartleby; I am going—good-bye, and God some way bless you; and take that," slipping something in his hand. But it dropped upon the floor, and then—strange to say—I tore myself from him whom I had so longed to be rid of.

Established in my new quarters, for a day or two I kept the door locked, and started at every footfall in the passages. When I returned to my rooms after any little absence, I would pause at the threshold for an instant, and attentively listen ere applying my key. But these fears were needless. Bartleby never came nigh me.

I thought all was going well, when a perturbed looking stranger visited me inquiring whether I was the person who had recently occupied rooms at No.—Wall Street.

Full of forebodings, I replied that I was. 180

"Then sir," said the stranger, who proved a lawyer, "you are responsible for the man you left there. He refuses to do any copying; he refuses to do anything; he says he prefers not to; and he refuses to quit the premises."

"I am very sorry, sir," said I, with assumed tranquility, but an inward tremor, "but, really, the man you allude to is nothing to me—he is no relation or apprentice of mine, that you should hold me responsible for him."

"In mercy's name, who is he?"

"I certainly cannot inform you. I know nothing about him. Formerly I employed him as a copyist, but he has done nothing for me now for some time past."

185   "I shall settle him then—good morning, sir."

Several days passed, and I heard nothing more; and though I often felt a charitable prompting to call at the place and see poor Bartleby, yet a certain squeamishness of I know not what withheld me.

All is over with him by this time, thought I at last, when through another week no further intelligence reached me. But coming to my room the day after, I found several persons waiting at my door in a high state of nervous excitement.

"That's the man—here he comes," cried the foremost one, whom I recognized as the lawyer who had previously called upon me alone.

"You must take him away, sir, at once," cried a portly person among them, advancing upon me, and whom I knew to be the landlord of No.— Wall Street. "These gentlemen, my tenants, cannot stand it any longer; Mr. B——" pointing to the lawyer, "has turned him out of his room, and he now persists in haunting the building generally, sitting upon the banisters of the stairs by day, and sleeping in the entry by night. Everybody is concerned; clients are leaving the offices; some fears are entertained of a mob; something you must do, and that without delay."

190   Aghast at this torrent; I fell back before it, and would fain have locked myself in my new quarters. In vain I persisted that Bartleby was nothing to me—no more than to anyone else. In vain—I was the last person known to have anything to do with him, and they held me to the terrible account. Fearful then of being exposed in the papers (as one person present obscurely threatened), I considered the matter, and at length said that if the lawyer would give me a confidential interview with the scrivener, in his (the lawyer's) own room, I would that afternoon strive my best to rid them of the nuisance they complained of.

Going upstairs to my old haunt, there was Bartleby silently sitting upon the banister at the landing.

"What are you doing here, Bartleby?" said I.

"Sitting upon the banister," he mildly replied.

I motioned him into the lawyer's room, who then left us.

195   "Bartleby," said I, "are you aware that you are the cause of great tribulation to me, by persisting in occupying the entry after being dismissed from the office?"

No answer.

"Now one of two things must take place. Either you must do something or something must be done to you. Now what sort of business would you like to engage in? Would you like to re-engage in copying for someone?"

"No; I would prefer not to make any change."

"Would you like a clerkship in a dry-goods store?"

"There is too much confinement about that. No, I would not like a   200
clerkship; but I am not particular."

"Too much confinement," I cried, "why you keep yourself confined all
the time!"

"I would prefer not to take a clerkship," he rejoined, as if to settle that
little item at once.

"How would a bar-tender's business° suit you? There is no trying of
the eyesight in that."

"I would not like it at all; though, as I said before, I am not particular."

His unwonted wordiness inspirited me. I returned to the charge.   205

"Well then, would you like to travel through the country collecting
bills for the merchants? That would improve your health."

"No, I would prefer to be doing something else."

"How then would going as a companion to Europe, to entertain some
young gentleman with your conversation—how would that suit you?"

"Not at all. It does not strike me that there is anything definite about
that. I like to be stationary. But I am not particular."

"Stationary you shall be then," I cried, now losing all patience, and for   210
the first time in all my exasperating connection with him fairly flying into
a passion. "If you do not go away from these premises before night, I shall
feel bound—indeed I *am* bound—to—to—to quit the premises myself!" I
rather absurdly concluded, knowing not with what possible threat to try to
frighten his immobility into compliance. Despairing of all further efforts,
I was precipitately leaving him, when a final thought occurred to me—one
which had not been wholly unindulged before.

"Bartleby," said I, in the kindest tone I could assume under such
exciting circumstances, "will you go home with me now—not to my
office, but my dwelling—and remain there till we can conclude upon some
convenient arrangement for you at our leisure? Come, let us start now,
right away."

"No: at present I would prefer not to make any change at all."

I answered nothing, but effectually dodging everyone by the suddenness and rapidity of my flight, rushed from the building, ran up Wall Street
towards Broadway, and jumping into the first omnibus was soon removed
from pursuit. As soon as tranquility returned I distinctly perceived that I
had now done all that I possibly could, both in respect to the demands of
the landlord and his tenants, and with regard to my own desire and sense
of duty, to benefit Bartleby and shield him from rude persecution. I now

---

bar-tender's business: work as an attendant in a courtroom

strove to be entirely carefree and quiescent; and my conscience justified me in the attempt though indeed it was not so successful as I could have wished. So fearful was I of being again hunted out by the incensed landlord and his exasperated tenants that, surrendering my business to Nippers, for a few days I drove about the upper part of the town and through the suburbs in my rockaway; crossed over to Jersey City and Hoboken, and paid fugitive visits to Manhattanville and Astoria. In fact I almost lived in my rockaway for the time.

When again I entered my office, lo, a note from the landlord lay upon the desk. I opened it with trembling hands. It informed me that the writer had sent to the police and had Bartleby removed to the Tombs as a vagrant. Moreover, since I knew more about him than anyone else, he wished me to appear at that place and make a suitable statement of the facts. These tidings had a conflicting effect upon me. At first I was indignant, but at last almost approved. The landlord's energetic, summary disposition had led him to adopt a procedure which I do not think I would have decided upon myself; and yet as a last resort, under such peculiar circumstances, it seemed the only plan.

215   As I afterwards learned, the poor scrivener, when told that he must be conducted to the Tombs, offered not the slightest obstacle, but in his pale unmoving way, silently acquiesced.

Some of the compassionate and curious bystanders joined the party; and headed by one of the constables arm in arm with Bartleby, the silent procession filed its way through all the noise, and heat, and joy of the roaring thoroughfares at noon.

The same day I received the note I went to the Tombs or, to speak more properly, the Halls of Justice. Seeking the right officer, I stated the purpose of my call, and was informed that the individual I described was indeed within. I then assured the functionary that Bartleby was a perfectly honest man, and greatly to be compassionated, however unaccountably eccentric. I narrated all I knew, and closed by suggesting the idea of letting him remain in as indulgent confinement as possible till something less harsh might be done—though indeed I hardly knew what. At all events, if nothing else could be decided upon, the alms-house must receive him. I then begged to have an interview.

Being under no disgraceful charge, and quite serene and harmless in all his ways, they had permitted him freely to wander about the prison, and especially in the inclosed grass-platted yards thereof. And so I found him there, standing all alone in the quietest of the yards, his face towards a high wall, while all around, from the narrow slits of the jail windows, I thought I saw peering out upon him the eyes of murderers and thieves.

"Bartleby!"

"I know you," he said, without looking around—"and I want nothing 220
to say to you."

"It was not I that brought you here, Bartleby," said I, keenly pained
at his implied suspicion. "And to you, this should not be so vile a place.
Nothing reproachful attaches to you by being here. And see, it is not so sad
a place as one might think. Look, there is the sky, and here is the grass."

"I know where I am," he replied, but would say nothing more, and so
I left him.

As I entered the corridor again, a broad meat-like man in an apron
accosted me, and jerking his thumb over his shoulder said—"Is that your
friend?"

"Yes."

"Does he want to starve? If he does, let him live on the prison fare, 225
that's all."

"Who are you?" asked I, not knowing what to make of such an unof-
ficially speaking person in such a place.

"I am the grub-man. Such gentlemen as have friends here, hire me to
provide them with something good to eat."

"Is this so?" said I, turning to the turnkey.

He said it was.

"Well, then," said I, slipping some silver into the grub-man's hands 230
(for so they called him), "I want you to give particular attention to my
friend there; let him have the best dinner you can get. And you must be as
polite to him as possible."

"Introduce me, will you?" said the grub-man, looking at me with an
expression which seemed to say he was all impatience for an opportunity
to give a specimen of his breeding.

Thinking it would prove of benefit to the scrivener, I acquiesced, and
asking the grub-man his name, went up with him to Bartleby.

"Bartleby, this is a friend; you will find him very useful to you."

"Your sarvant, sir, your sarvant," said the grub-man making a low
salutation behind his apron. "Hope you find it pleasant here, sir—spacious
grounds—cool apartments, sir—hope you'll stay with us some time—try
to make it agreeable. What will you have for dinner today?"

"I prefer not to dine today," said Bartleby, turning away. "It would dis- 235
agree with me; I am unused to dinners." So saying he slowly moved to the
other side of the enclosure, and took up a position fronting the dead wall.

"How's this?" said the grub-man, addressing me with a stare of astonishment. "He's odd, ain't he?"

"I think he is a little deranged," said I, sadly.

"Deranged? deranged is it? Well now, upon my word, I thought
that friend of yourn was a gentleman forger; they are always pale and

genteel-like, them forgers. I can't help pity 'em—can't help it, sir. Did you know Monroe Edwards?" he added touchingly, and paused. Then, laying his hand pityingly on my shoulder, sighed, "he died of consumption at Sing-Sing. So you weren't acquainted with Monroe?"

"No, I was never socially acquainted with any forgers. But I cannot stop longer. Look to my friend yonder. You will not lose by it. I will see you again."

240   Some few days after this, I again obtained admission to the Tombs, and went through the corridors in quest of Bartleby, but without finding him.

"I saw him coming from his cell not long ago," said a turnkey, "maybe he's gone to loiter in the yards."

So I went in that direction.

"Are you looking for the silent man?" said another turnkey passing me. "Yonder he lies—sleeping in the yard there. 'Tis not twenty minutes since I saw him lie down."

The yard was entirely quiet. It was not accessible to the common prisoners. The surrounding walls, of amazing thickness, kept off all sound behind them. The Egyptian character of the masonry weighed upon me with its gloom. But a soft imprisoned turf grew under foot. The heart of the eternal pyramids, it seemed, wherein, by some strange magic, through the clefts, grass-seed dropped by birds had sprung.

245   Strangely huddled at the base of the wall, his knees drawn up, and lying on his side, his head touching the cold stones, I saw the wasted Bartleby. But nothing stirred. I paused; then went close up to him; stooped over, and saw that his dim eyes were open; otherwise he seemed profoundly sleeping. Something prompted me to touch him. I felt his hand, when a tingling shiver ran up my arm and down my spine to my feet.

The round face of the grub-man peered upon me now. "His dinner is ready. Won't he dine today, either? Or does he live without dining?"

"Lives without dining," said I, and closed the eyes.

"Eh!—He's asleep, ain't he?"

"With kings and counselors,"° murmured I.

250   There would seem little need for proceeding further in this history. Imagination will readily supply the meager recital of poor Bartleby's interment. But ere parting with the reader, let me say that if this little narrative has sufficiently interested him to awaken curiosity as to who Bartleby was, and what manner of life he led prior to the present narrator's making his acquaintance, I can only reply that in such curiosity I fully share, but am wholly unable to gratify it. Yet here I hardly know whether I should divulge one little item of rumor which came to my ear a few months after the scrivener's decease. Upon what basis it rested, I could never ascertain; and hence

"With . . . counselors": Job 3:14

how true it is I cannot now tell. But inasmuch as this vague report has not been without a certain strange suggestive interest to me, however sad, it may prove the same with some others; and so I will briefly mention it. The report was this: that Bartleby had been a subordinate clerk in the Dead Letter Office at Washington, from which he had been suddenly removed by a change in the administration. When I think over this rumor, I cannot adequately express the emotions which seize me. Dead letters! does it not sound like dead men? Conceive a man by nature and misfortune prone to a pallid hopelessness, can any business seem more fitted to heighten it than that of continually handling these dead letters and assorting them for the flames? For by the cart-load they are annually burned. Sometimes from out the folded paper the pale clerk takes a ring—the finger it was meant for, perhaps, moulders in the grave; a bank note sent in swiftest charity—he whom it would relieve, nor eats nor hungers any more; pardon for those who died despairing; hope for those who died unhoping; good tidings for those who died stifled by unrelieved calamities. On errands of life, these letters speed to death.

Ah, Bartleby! Ah, humanity!

EDGAR ALLAN POE

The Cask of Amontillado

The thousand injuries of Fortunato I had borne as I best could, but when he ventured upon insult, I vowed revenge. You, who so well know the nature of my soul, will not suppose, however, that I gave utterance to a threat. At *length* I would be avenged; this was a point definitely settled—but the very definitiveness with which it was resolved precluded the idea of risk. I must not only punish, but punish with impunity. A wrong is unredressed when retribution overtakes its redresser. It is equally unredressed when the avenger fails to make himself felt as such to him who has done the wrong.

It must be understood that neither by word nor deed had I given Fortunato cause to doubt my good will. I continued, as was my wont, to smile in his face, and he did not perceive that my smile *now* was at the thought of his immolation.

He had a weak point—this Fortunato—although in other regards he was a man to be respected and even feared. He prided himself on his

---

THE CASK OF AMONTILLADO   First published in 1846. Edgar Allan Poe (1809–1849) was one of the first modern practitioners and theorists of the short story as a literary form, prescribing as the highest goal the creation of "a certain unique or single effect." His own achievement best matches his theory in his psychologically intense horror tales, of which this is an example. Poe was born in Boston, abandoned at the age of three by his father after the death of his mother, and raised by adoptive parents in Virginia. As a young man he failed in his educational endeavors at the University of Virginia and at West Point. Alcoholism combined with nervous sensitivity led to continuing health problems and perhaps to his early death.

connoisseurship in wine. Few Italians have the true virtuoso spirit. For the most part their enthusiasm is adopted to suit the time and opportunity to practise imposture upon the British and Austrian *millionaires*. In painting and gemmary Fortunato, like his countrymen, was a quack, but in the matter of old wines he was sincere. In this respect I did not differ from him materially;—I was skillful in the Italian vintages myself, and bought largely whenever I could.

It was about dusk, one evening during the supreme madness of the carnival season, that I encountered my friend. He accosted me with excessive warmth, for he had been drinking much. The man wore motley. He had on a tight-fitting parti-striped dress, and his head was surmounted by the conical cap and bells. I was so pleased to see him, that I thought I should never have done wringing his hand.

5   I said to him—"My dear Fortunato, you are luckily met. How remarkably well you are looking to-day! But I have received a pipe° of what passes for Amontillado, and I have my doubts."

"How?" said he, "Amontillado? A pipe? Impossible! And in the middle of the carnival!"

"I have my doubts," I replied; "and I was silly enough to pay the full Amontillado price without consulting you in the matter. You were not to be found, and I was fearful of losing a bargain."

"Amontillado!"

"I have my doubts."

10   "Amontillado!"

"And I must satisfy them."

"Amontillado!"

"As you are engaged, I am on my way to Luchesi. If any one has a critical turn, it is he. He will tell me—"

"Luchesi cannot tell Amontillado from Sherry."

15   "And yet some fools will have it that his taste is a match for your own."

"Come, let us go."

"Whither?"

"To your vaults."

"My friend, no; I will not impose upon your good nature. I perceive you have an engagement. Luchesi—"

20   "I have no engagement;—come."

"My friend, no. It is not the engagement, but the severe cold with which I perceive you are afflicted. The vaults are insufferably damp. They are encrusted with nitre."

"Let us go, nevertheless. The cold is merely nothing. Amontillado! You have been imposed upon; and as for Luchesi, he cannot distinguish Sherry from Amontillado."

pipe: a wine cask

Thus speaking, Fortunato possessed himself of my arm. Putting on a mask of black silk, and drawing a *roquelaure*° closely about my person, I suffered him to hurry me to my palazzo.

There were no attendants at home; they had absconded to make merry in honor of the time. I had told them that I should not return until the morning, and had given them explicit orders not to stir from the house. These orders were sufficient, I well knew, to insure their immediate disappearance, one and all, as soon as my back was turned.

I took from their sconces two flambeaux, and giving one to Fortunato, 25 bowed him through several suites of rooms to the archway that led into the vaults. I passed down a long and winding staircase, requesting him to be cautious as he followed. We came at length to the foot of the descent, and stood together on the damp ground of the catacombs of the Montresors.

The gait of my friend was unsteady, and the bells upon his cap jingled as he strode.

"The pipe," said he.

"It is farther on," said I; "but observe the white web-work which gleams from these cavern walls."

He turned towards me, and looked into my eyes with two filmy orbs that distilled the rheum of intoxication.

"Nitre?" he asked, at length. 30

"Nitre," I replied. "How long have you had that cough?"

"Ugh! ugh! ugh!—ugh! ugh! ugh!—ugh! ugh! ugh!—ugh! ugh! ugh!—ugh! ugh! ugh!"

My poor friend found it impossible to reply for many minutes.

"It is nothing," he said, at last.

"Come," I said, with decision, "we will go back; your health is pre- 35 cious. You are rich, respected, admired, beloved; you are happy, as once I was. You are a man to be missed. For me it is no matter. We will go back; you will be ill, and I cannot be responsible. Besides, there is Luchesi—"

"Enough," he said; "the cough is a mere nothing: it will not kill me. I shall not die of a cough."

"True—true," I replied; "and, indeed, I had no intention of alarming you unnecessarily—but you should use all proper caution. A draught of this Medoc will defend us from the damps."

Here I knocked off the neck of a bottle which I drew from a long row of its fellows that lay upon the mould.

"Drink," I said, presenting him the wine.

He raised it to his lips with a leer. He paused and nodded to me famil- 40 iarly, while his bells jingled.

"I drink," he said, "to the buried that repose around us."

"And I to your long life."

roquelaure: (French) a winter cloak

He again took my arm, and we proceeded.

"These vaults," he said, "are extensive."

45 "The Montresors," I replied, "were a great and numerous family."

"I forget your arms."

"A huge human foot d'or, in a field azure; the foot crushes a serpent rampant whose fangs are imbedded in the heel."

"And the motto?"

"*Nemo me impune lacessit.*"°

50 "Good!" he said.

The wine sparkled in his eyes and the bells jingled. My own fancy grew warm with the Medoc. We had passed through walls of piled bones, with casks and puncheons intermingling, into the inmost recesses of the catacombs. I paused again, and this time I made bold to seize Fortunato by an arm above the elbow.

"The nitre!" I said; "see, it increases. It hangs like moss upon the vaults. We are below the river's bed. The drops of moisture trickle among the bones. Come, we will go back ere it is too late. Your cough—"

"It is nothing," he said; "let us go on. But first, another draught of the Medoc."

I broke and reached him a flagon of De Grâve. He emptied it at a breath. His eyes flashed with a fierce light. He laughed and threw the bottle upwards with a gesticulation I did not understand.

55 I looked at him in surprise. He repeated the movement—a grotesque one.

"You do not comprehend?" he said.

"Not I," I replied.

"Then you are not of the brotherhood."

"How?"

60 "You are not of the masons."

"Yes, yes," I said; "yes, yes."

"You? Impossible! A mason?"

"A mason," I replied.

"A sign," he said.

65 "It is this," I answered, producing a trowel from beneath the folds of my *roquelaure*.

"You jest," he exclaimed, recoiling a few paces. "But let us proceed to the Amontillado."

"Be it so," I said, replacing the tool beneath the cloak, and again offering him my arm. He leaned upon it heavily. We continued our route in search of the Amontillado. We passed through a range of low arches, descended, passed on, and descending again, arrived at a deep crypt, in which the foulness of the air caused our flambeaux rather to glow than flame.

Nemo me impune lacessit: (Latin) No one will attack me with impunity

At the most remote end of the crypt there appeared another less spacious. Its walls had been lined with human remains piled to the vault overhead, in the fashion of the great catacombs of Paris. Three sides of this interior crypt were still ornamented in this manner. From the fourth the bones had been thrown down, and lay promiscuously upon the earth, forming at one point a mound of some size. Within the wall thus exposed by the displacing of the bones, we perceived a still interior recess, in depth about four feet, in width three, in height six or seven. It seemed to have been constructed for no especial use within itself, but formed merely the interval between two of the colossal supports of the roof of the catacombs, and was backed by one of their circumscribing walls of solid granite.

It was in vain that Fortunato, uplifting his dull torch, endeavored to pry into the depths of the recess. Its termination the feeble light did not enable us to see.

"Proceed," I said; "herein is the Amontillado. As for Luchesi—" 70

"He is an ignoramus," interrupted my friend, as he stepped unsteadily forward, while I followed immediately at his heels. In an instant he had reached the extremity of the niche, and finding his progress arrested by the rock, stood stupidly bewildered. A moment more and I had fettered him to the granite. In its surface were two iron staples, distant from each other about two feet, horizontally. From one of these depended a short chain, from the other a padlock. Throwing the links about his waist, it was but the work of a few seconds to secure it. He was too much astounded to resist. Withdrawing the key I stepped back from the recess.

"Pass your hand," I said, "over the wall; you cannot help feeling the nitre. Indeed it is *very* damp. Once more let me *implore* you to return. No? Then I must positively leave you. But I must first render you all the little attentions in my power."

"The Amontillado!" ejaculated my friend, not yet recovered from his astonishment.

"True," I replied; "the Amontillado."

As I said these words I busied myself among the pile of bones of which 75
I have before spoken. Throwing them aside, I soon uncovered a quantity of building-stone and mortar. With these materials and with the aid of my trowel, I began vigorously to wall up the entrance of the niche.

I had scarcely laid the first tier of the masonry when I discovered that the intoxication of Fortunato had in a great measure worn off. The earliest indication I had of this was a low moaning cry from the depth of the recess. It was *not* the cry of a drunken man. There was then a long and obstinate silence. I laid the second tier, and the third, and the fourth; and then I heard the furious vibrations of the chain. The noise lasted for several minutes, during which, that I might hearken to it with the more satisfaction, I ceased my labors and sat down upon the bones. When at last the clanking subsided, I resumed the trowel, and finished without interruption the fifth, the sixth, and the seventh tier. The wall was now nearly upon a level with my breast. I again paused, and holding the flambeaux over the masonwork, threw a few feeble rays upon the figure within.

A succession of loud and shrill screams, bursting suddenly from the throat of the chained form, seemed to thrust me violently back. For a brief moment I hesitated—I trembled. Unsheathing my rapier, I began to grope with it about the recess; but the thought of an instant reassured me. I placed my hand upon the solid fabric of the catacombs, and felt satisfied. I reapproached the wall. I replied to the yells of him who clamored. I re-echoed—I aided—I surpassed them in volume and in strength. I did this, and the clamorer grew still.

It was now midnight, and my task was drawing to a close. I had completed the eighth, the ninth, and the tenth tier. I had finished a portion of the last and the eleventh; there remained but a single stone to be fitted and plastered in. I struggled with its weight; I placed it partially in its destined position. But now there came from out the niche a low laugh that erected the hairs upon my head. It was succeeded by a sad voice, which I had difficulty in recognizing as that of the noble Fortunato. The voice said—

"Ha! ha! ha!—he! he! he!—a very good joke indeed—an excellent jest. We will have many a rich laugh about it at the palazzo—he! he! he!—over our wine—he! he! he!"

80   "The Amontillado!" I said.

"He! he! he!—he! he! he!—yes, the Amontillado. But is it not getting late? Will not they be awaiting us at the palazzo, the Lady Fortunato and the rest? Let us be gone."

"Yes," I said, "let us be gone."

"*For the love of God, Montresor!*"

"Yes," I said, "for the love of God!"

85   But to these words I hearkened in vain for a reply. I grew impatient. I called aloud;

"Fortunato!"

No answer. I called again;

"Fortunato!"

No answer still, I thrust a torch through the remaining aperture and let it fall within. There came forth in return only a jingling of the bells. My heart grew sick—on account of the dampness of the catacombs. I hastened to make an end of my labor. I forced the last stone into its position; I plastered it up. Against the new masonry I reerected the old rampart of bones. For the half of a century no mortal has disturbed them. *In pace requiescat!*°

In pace requiescat! (Latin) Rest in peace!

PRACTICE AP WRITING PROMPTS

Kate Chopin, "The Story of an Hour" (p. 536)

40-minute prompt: Read "The Story of an Hour" carefully, and write a well-organized essay in which you analyze Louise Mallard's complex response to the news she receives. Show how the story's irony, including the title, contributes to its impact on the reader.

William Faulkner, "A Rose for Emily" (p. 538)

The element of time plays an important role in many of Faulkner's works. Consider the author's use of time in narrating "A Rose for Emily": think about when events occur in relation to each other in the narrative, and at what points the reader learns important information that explains or predicts outcomes—foreshadowing. In a well-written essay, analyze the story's use of time, and show how it contributes to the story's unity and prepares the reader for its conclusion.

Zora Neale Hurston, "Spunk" (p. 564)

40-minute prompt: Carefully read the second and third sections (paragraphs 27 through 43, pp. 566–567) of "Spunk." In a well-organized essay, analyze how Hurston employs the traditions of folklore and storytelling to create her intended effect.

Edgar Allan Poe, "The Cask of Amontillado" (p. 657–662)

Read paragraphs 1 through 23 of "The Cask of Amontillado" several times. Then write an essay in which you analyze the steps by which the reader realizes that the narrator is both an astute observer of his fellow humans and a frightening psychopath. Avoid mere plot summary.

EXCERPT FROM "THE LOTTERY" BY SHIRLEY JACKSON

QUESTIONS 1–14. Carefully read the passage, the end of the short story, before choosing your answers.

Mr. Graves opened the slip of paper and there was a general sigh through the crowd as he held it up and everyone could see that it was blank. Nancy and Bill, Jr., opened theirs at the same time, and both beamed and laughed, turning around to
5   the crowd and holding their slips of paper above their heads.

"Tessie," Mr. Summers said. There was a pause, and then Mr. summers looked at Bill Hutchinson, and Bill unfolded his paper and showed it. It was blank.

"It's Tessie," Mr. Summers said, and his voice was hushed.
10   "Show us her paper, Bill."

Bill Hutchinson went over to his wife and forced the slip of paper out of her hand. It had a black spot on it, the black spot Mr. Summers had made the night before with the heavy pencil in the coal-company office. Bill Hutchinson held it up,
15   and there was a stir in the crowd.

"All right, folks," Mr. Summers said. "Let's finish quickly."

Although the villagers had forgotten the ritual and lost the original black box, they still remembered to use stones. The pile of stones the boys had made earlier was ready; there
20   were stones on the ground with the blowing scraps of paper that had come out of the box. Mrs. Delacroix selected a stone so large she had to pick it up with both hands and turned to Mrs. Dunbar. "Come on," she said. "Hurry up."

Mrs. Dunbar had small stones in both hands, and she said,
25   gasping for breath, "I can't run at all. You'll have to go ahead and I'll catch up with you."

The children had stones already, and someone gave little Davy Hutchinson a few pebbles.

Tessie Hutchinson was in the center of a cleared space by
30   now, and she held her hands out desperately as the villagers moved in on her. "It isn't fair," she said. A stone hit her on the side of the head.

Old Man Warner was saying, "Come on, come on, everyone." Steve Adams was in front of the crowd of villagers, with
35   Mrs. Graves beside him.

"It isn't fair, it isn't right," Mrs. Hutchinson screamed, and then they were upon her.

1. In the passage, ritualistic actions are shown in a manner that could best be described as
   (A) blind
   (B) opportunistic
   (C) clever
   (D) sagacious
   (E) entertaining

2. When little Davy Hutchinson is given a few pebbles, the reader feels
   (A) relieved
   (B) somewhat tricked
   (C) happily noninvolved
   (D) cautiously optimistic
   (E) blatantly misled

3. The fact that Mrs. Dunbar is gasping and out of breath shows
   (A) refusal
   (B) that the aphorism "with age goes wisdom" is often incorrect
   (C) cultural passivity
   (D) certain positive aspects
   (E) disobedience

4. At the end of the passage (line 36), Tessie says, "It isn't fair." This is a prime example of
   (A) understatement
   (B) hyperbole
   (C) kinesthesia
   (D) foreboding
   (E) futility

5. The tone of Jackson's story is best described as
   (A) contemplative
   (B) reflective
   (C) matter-of-fact
   (D) iconoclastic
   (E) facetious

6. An underlying theme of the story is
   (A) stoning is cruel and brutal
   (B) violence takes place anywhere all the people are uneducated
   (C) acts of irrationality can be committed by ordinary people
   (D) clear thinking always trumps mob rule
   (E) good wins over evil

7. The black box is symbolic of
   (A) hope for the future
   (B) happiness that results from change
   (C) the villagers' inability to change
   (D) a happy tradition
   (E) stasis

8. Mrs. Delacroix was friendly to Tessie at the beginning of the story. The fact that she rushes at her with a large stone "she had to pick up with both hands" (lines 21–22) shows
   (A) irony
   (B) resistance
   (C) hope
   (D) flattery
   (E) gluttony

9. Shirley Jackson highlights humankind's capacity to victimize even family and friends to explicate
   (A) the beneficial aspects of humankind
   (B) the value of ancient customs
   (C) the benefit of sacrifice
   (D) a symbol of victimization
   (E) the danger of adherence to norms

10. Because the men pick for their families and the women are treated as subservient, Tessie objects to the method of drawing. This
    (A) stresses the importance of women in society
    (B) reveals the true nature of society
    (C) highlights a negative aspect of patriarchal societies
    (D) shows that Tessie is loved
    (E) shows that Tessie is unloved

11. "The Lottery" is a
    (A) parable
    (B) fabliau
    (C) poem
    (D) tableau
    (E) novella

12. "Although the villagers had forgotten the ritual and lost the original black box, they still remembered to use stones" (lines 1718) is Jackson's commentary on
    (A) money in society
    (B) the rigors of society
    (C) hope in society

(D) death in society

(E) tradition in society

13. "The pile of stones the boys had made earlier was ready" (lines 18–19) shows that the people in Jackson's town want all of the following EXCEPT
    (A) the ritual to persist
    (B) blind adherence to the ritual
    (C) the younger generation to get on board with respect to the town's practices
    (D) the ritual to advance and prevail
    (E) a time when the ritual exists no longer

14. "Bill Hutchinson went over to his wife and forced the slip of paper out of her hand" (lines 11–12) shows
    (A) the unity of Hutchinson's family
    (B) the depth of the Hutchinson family's conviction
    (C) hope for the future
    (D) an utter disregard for human decency
    (E) the senselessness of nonrational adherence to patrimony

See page 1607 for the answers to this set of questions.

EXCERPT FROM "A VERY OLD MAN WITH ENORMOUS WINGS" BY GABRIEL GARCÍA MÀRQUEZ

QUESTIONS 15–28. Carefully read the following passage from the beginning of Gabriel García Márquez's short story "A Very Old Man with Enormous Wings" before choosing your answers.

On the third day of rain they had killed so many crabs inside the house that Pelayo had to cross his drenched courtyard and throw them into the sea, because the newborn child had a temperature all night and they thought it was due to the
5   stench. The world had been sad since Tuesday. Sea and sky were a single ash-gray thing and the sands of the beach, which on March nights glimmered like powdered light, had become a stew of mud and rotten shellfish. The light was so weak at noon that when Pelayo was coming back to the house after
10   throwing away the crabs, it was hard for him to see what it was that was moving and groaning in the rear of the courtyard. He had to go very close to see that it was an old man, a very old man, lying face down in the mud, who, in spite of his tremendous efforts, couldn't get up, impeded by his
15   enormous wings.

Frightened by that nightmare, Pelayo ran to get Elisenda, his wife, who was putting compresses on the sick child, and he took her to the rear of the courtyard. They both looked at the fallen body with mute stupor. He was dressed like a
20   ragpicker. There were only a few faded hairs left on his bald skull and very few teeth in his mouth, and his pitiful condition of a drenched greatgrandfather had taken away any sense of grandeur he might have had. His huge buzzard wings, dirty and half-plucked, were forever entangled in the mud. They
25   looked at him so long and so closely that Pelayo and Elisenda very soon overcame their surprise and in the end found him familiar. Then they dared speak to him, and he answered in an incomprehensible dialect with a strong sailor's voice. That was how they skipped over the inconvenience of the wings and
30   quite intelligently concluded that he was a lonely castaway from some foreign ship wrecked by the storm. And yet, they called in a neighbor woman who knew everything about life and death to see him, and all she needed was one look to show them their mistake.

"He's an angel," she told them. "He must have been com- 35
ing for the child, but the poor fellow is so old that the rain
knocked him down."

On the following day everyone knew that a flesh-and-blood
angel was held captive in Pelayo's house. Against the judgment
of the wise neighbor woman, for whom angels in those times 40
were the fugitive survivors of a celestial conspiracy, they did not
have the heart to club him to death. Pelayo watched over him
all afternoon from the kitchen, armed with his bailiff's club,
and before going to bed he dragged him out of the mud and
locked him up with the hens in the wire chicken coop. In the 45
middle of the night, when the rain stopped, Pelayo and Elisenda
were still killing crabs. A short time afterward the child woke
up without a fever and with a desire to eat. Then they felt
magnanimous and decided to put the angel on a raft with fresh
water and provisions for three days and leave him to his fate on 50
the high seas. But when they went out into the courtyard with
the first light of dawn, they found the whole neighborhood in
front of the chicken coop having fun with the angel, without
the slightest reverence, tossing him things to eat through the
openings in the wire as if he weren't a supernatural creature but 55
a circus animal.

Father Gonzaga arrived before seven o'clock, alarmed at
the strange news. By that time onlookers less frivolous than
those at dawn had already arrived and they were making all
kinds of conjectures concerning the captive's future. The sim- 60
plest among them thought that he should be named mayor of
the world. Others of sterner mind felt that he should be promoted to the rank of five-star general in order to win all wars.
Some visionaries hoped that he could be put to stud in order
to implant on earth a race of winged wise men who could take 65
charge of the universe. But Father Gonzaga, before becoming a
priest, had been a robust woodcutter. Standing by the wire, he
reviewed his catechism in an instant and asked them to open
the door so that he could take a close look at that pitiful man
who looked more like a huge decrepit hen among the fascinated 70
chickens. He was lying in a corner drying his open wings in
the sunlight among the fruit peels and breakfast leftovers that
the early risers had thrown him. Alien to the impertinences of
the world, he only lifted his antiquarian eyes and murmured
something in his dialect when Father Gonzaga went into the 75
chicken coop and said good morning to him in Latin. The par-

ish priest had his first suspicion of an imposter when he saw
that he did not understand the language of God or know how
to greet His ministers. Then he noticed that seen close up he
80 was much too human: he had an unbearable smell of the outdoors, the back side of his wings was strewn with parasites and
his main feathers had been mistreated by terrestrial winds, and
nothing about him measured up to the proud dignity of angels.
Then he came out of the chicken coop and in a brief sermon
85 warned the curious against the risks of being ingenuous. He
reminded them that the devil had the bad habit of making use
of carnival tricks in order to confuse the unwary. He argued
that if wings were not the essential element in determining the
difference between a hawk and an airplane, they were even less
90 so in the recognition of angels. Nevertheless, he promised to
write a letter to his bishop so that the latter would write to his
primate so that the latter would write to the Supreme Pontiff in
order to get the final verdict from the highest courts.

His prudence fell on sterile hearts. The news of the cap-
95 tive angel spread with such rapidity that after a few hours the
courtyard had the bustle of a marketplace and they had to call
in troops with fixed bayonets to disperse the mob that was
about to knock the house down. Elisenda, her spine all twisted
from sweeping up so much marketplace trash, then got the
100 idea of fencing in the yard and charging five cents admission
to see the angel.

15. The point of view of the narrator is
(A) omniscient
(B) first-person limited
(C) third-person limited
(D) unreliable
(E) naïve

16. The imagery of the setting described in the first paragraph
(A) presages a deluge
(B) heralds an epic
(C) signifies poverty
(D) implies contamination
(E) reveals a magical realm

17. All of the following roles are considered for the old man EXCEPT to
    (A) take the sick child to heaven
    (B) take over the world
    (C) reprimand the town sinners
    (D) defend the town
    (E) father a new race

18. In the second paragraph, the old man is described in terms that make him seem
    (A) celestial
    (B) pitiable
    (C) deceitful
    (D) puzzled
    (E) execrable

19. The phrase "quite intelligently concluded" (line 32) in the context of the sentence is
    (A) mystifying
    (B) understandable
    (C) overly simplistic
    (D) ironic
    (E) characteristic

20. The tone of the passage is
    (A) insinuating
    (B) skeptical
    (C) sardonic
    (D) detached
    (E) bemused

21. Pelayo's act of enclosing the old man in a chicken coop connotes
    (A) economic prowess
    (B) an unhealthy desire to control his environment
    (C) a misinterpretation of God's will
    (D) religious apostasy
    (E) spiritual impoverishment

22. Overall, the story is
    (A) serio-comic
    (B) blasphemous
    (C) juvenile
    (D) allegorical
    (E) sacrosanct

23. The second paragraph includes all of the following EXCEPT
    (A) imagery
    (B) analogy
    (C) hyperbole
    (D) understatement
    (E) an appositive

24. Pelayo's interest in the old man moves from
    (A) curiosity, to fear, to exploitation
    (B) disdain, to apathy, to confusion
    (C) fear, to reverence, to manipulation
    (D) obligation, to adulation, to revulsion
    (E) caution, to respect, to deference

25. At different times, the townspeople see the old man as all of the following EXCEPT a(n)
    (A) trickster
    (B) potential savior
    (C) alien
    (D) castaway sailor
    (E) angel

26. The theme of the excerpt is
    (A) greed
    (B) divine revelation
    (C) the bane of poverty
    (D) human folly
    (E) celestial inscrutability

27. Father Gonzaga's reaction after speaking Latin to the old man reveals his
    (A) reverence
    (B) erudition
    (C) ignorance
    (D) piety
    (E) sense of humor

28. The story exemplifies the statement
    (A) The poor cannot afford piety
    (B) The ignorant are easily tricked
    (C) The Church has lost credibility
    (D) God works in mysterious ways
    (E) Faith is trust without reservation

See page 1607 for the answers to this set of questions.

EXCERPT FROM "BARTLEBY THE SCRIVENER: A STORY OF WALL STREET" BY HERMAN MELVILLE

QUESTIONS 29–42. Carefully read the passage, from the beginning of the short story, before choosing your answers.

I am a rather elderly man. The nature of my avocations for the last thirty years has brought me into more than ordinary contact with what would seem an interesting and somewhat singular set of men of whom as yet nothing that I know of has ever been written—I mean the law-copyists or scriveners. 5
I have known very many of them, professionally and privately, and if I pleased could relate diverse histories at which good-natured gentlemen might smile and sentimental souls might weep. But I waive the biographies of all other scriveners for a few passages in the life of Bartleby, who was a scrivener of the 10
strangest I ever saw or heard of. While of other law-copyists I might write the complete life, of Bartleby nothing of that sort can be done. I believe that no materials exist for a full and satisfactory biography of this man. It is an irreparable loss to literature. Bartleby was one of those beings of whom nothing 15
is ascertainable except from the original sources, and in his case those are very small. What my own astonished eyes saw of Bartleby, *that* is all I know of him except, indeed, one vague report which will appear in the sequel.

Ere introducing the scrivener as he first appeared to me, it 20
is fit I make some mention of myself, my employees, my business, my chambers, and general surroundings, because some such description is indispensable to an adequate understanding of the chief character about to be presented.

Imprimis: I am a man who from his youth upwards has 25
been filled with a profound conviction that the easiest way of life is the best. Hence, though I belong to a profession proverbially energetic and nervous, even to turbulence at times, yet nothing of that sort have I ever suffered to invade my peace. I am one of those unambitious lawyers who never addresses a 30
jury or in any way draws down public applause, but in the cool tranquility of a snug retreat do a snug business among rich men's bonds and mortgages and title-deeds. All who know me consider me an eminently *safe* man. The late John Jacob Astor,

35　　a personage little given to poetic enthusiasm, had no hesitation
　　　in pronouncing my first grand point to be prudence; my next,
　　　method. I do not speak it in vanity but simply record the fact
　　　that I was not unemployed in my profession by the late John
　　　Jacob Astor, a name which, I admit, I love to repeat, for it hath
40　　a rounded and orbicular sound to it and rings like unto bullion.
　　　I will freely add that I was not insensible to the late John Jacob
　　　Astor's good opinion.

　　　　　Sometime prior to the period at which this little history
　　　begins, my avocations had been largely increased. The good
45　　old office now extinct in the State of New York of a Master in
　　　Chancery had been conferred upon me. It was not a very ardu-
　　　ous office but very pleasantly remunerative. I seldom lose my
　　　temper; much more seldom indulge in dangerous indignation
　　　at wrongs and outrages; but I must be permitted to 41 be rash
50　　here and declare that I consider the sudden and violent abroga-
　　　tion of the office of Master in Chancery by the new Constitu-
　　　tion as a ＿＿＿＿＿ premature act, inasmuch as I had counted
　　　upon a life-lease of the profits, whereas I only received those of
　　　a few short years. But this is by the way.

29.　From the context clues in this excerpt the reader knows that a
　　　person who is a scrivener does all of the following duties EXCEPT
　　　(A) copy manuscripts
　　　(B) act as a writer
　　　(C) is paid for exact transcription
　　　(D) is noted for penmanship
　　　(E) guard against a bully

30.　The storyteller is
　　　(A) an observer who is not omnipotent
　　　(B) a lawyer
　　　(C) a man named Bartleby
　　　(D) a man named Melville
　　　(E) an observer who is not an omnivore

31.　In line 25, the word "Imprimis" means
　　　(A) in conclusion
　　　(B) in the first place
　　　(C) in moderation
　　　(D) inconsequential
　　　(E) insipid and lethargic

32. "But I waive the biographies of all other scriveners for a few passages in the life of Bartleby" (lines 9–10) indicates that
    I. Bartleby is unique
    II. Bartleby is strange
    III. the boss admires Bartleby
    (A) I only
    (B) II only
    (C) I and II only
    (D) III only
    (E) II and III only

33. "I believe that no materials exist for a full and satisfactory biography of this man. It is an irreparable loss to literature" (lines 13–15) expresses the storyteller's
    (A) fear of Bartleby
    (B) admiration for Bartleby
    (C) hidden discontent with the Bartleby situation
    (D) veiled threat against Bartleby's life
    (E) love of corporate greed

34. "[A] profound conviction that the easiest way of life is the best" (lines 26–27) refers to the
    (A) occupation of scrivener in the way he works
    (B) legal profession in the manner the narrator works it
    (C) profession of journalists in the way it works
    (D) profession of John Jacob Astor and how he worked
    (E) profession of politics and the way it works

35. In line 44, the phrase "this little history" refers to the
    (A) historical account of the life of John Jacob Astor
    (B) historical account of the firm
    (C) historical account of all scriveners
    (D) story concerning Bartleby
    (E) life of Herman Melville

36. In lines 54, the "rash" behavior is directed at
    (A) the fact that Bartleby works there
    (B) the sudden and violent abolition of the office of Master in Chancery
    (C) the happy ending of the office of Master in Chancery
    (D) the fact that the scriveners are all overworked and underpaid
    (E) the fact that members of the legal profession are lazy

37. In the context of lines 30–33, the word "snug" refers to
    (A) the conformable aspects of the situation thus far
    (B) the black comedy of the piece
    (C) the lack of clarity in the situation
    (D) the tight fit between the storyteller and Bartleby
    (E) working hard for the money

38. The phrase "in pronouncing my first grand point to be prudence; my next, method" (lines 36–37) shows
    (A) the narrator's interpretation of John Jacob Astor's view of the narrator
    (B) that Bartleby was a great worker
    (C) that Melville is being humorous
    (D) that God does not seem to be on Bartleby's side
    (E) that God does not seem to be on the storyteller's side

39. "I will freely add that I was not insensible to the late John Jacob Astor's good opinion" (lines 41–43) stresses to the reader that the teller of the tale
    (A) is proud of all his scriveners
    (B) is being self-congratulatory due to the expressed opinion of a well-respected colleague
    (C) is proud of himself
    (D) is proud of Bartleby's work ethic
    (E) hates John Jacob Astor

40. An underlying theme for this selection is
    (A) legality trumps hard work
    (B) a revelation of class prejudice
    (C) cleanliness is next to godliness
    (D) hard work trumps legality
    (E) religion improves society

41. The narrator's mention of "a name which, I admit, I love to repeat, for it hath a rounded and orbicular sound to it" (lines 39–41) does all of the following EXCEPT
    (A) carry the weight of prominence and importance
    (B) evoke the idea of money
    (C) carry a hidden significance
    (D) indicate name dropping
    (E) testify to diminution

42. In the context of lines 44–45, the word "avocation" connotes
    (A) a full-time job or work
    (B) a profession
    (C) a part-time distraction or diversion
    (D) the task of a scribe
    (E) the position of one who cleans the office

See page 1607 for the answers to this set of questions.

The Elements

of Poetry

CHAPTER ONE

What Is Poetry?

Poetry is as universal as language and almost as ancient. The most primitive peoples have used it, and the most civilized have cultivated it. In all ages and in all countries, poetry has been written, and eagerly read or listened to, by all kinds and conditions of people—by soldiers, statesmen, lawyers, homemakers, farmers, doctors, scientists, clergy, philosophers, kings, and queens. In all ages, it has been especially the concern of the educated, the intelligent, and the sensitive, yet it has appealed, in its simpler forms, to the uneducated and to children. Why? First, because it has given pleasure. People have read it, listened to it, or recited it because they liked it—because it gave them enjoyment. But this is not the whole answer. Poetry in all ages has been regarded as important, not simply as one of several alternative forms of amusement, as one person might choose video games, another chess, and another poetry. Rather, it has been regarded as something central to existence, something having unique value to the fully realized life, something that we are better off for having and without which we are spiritually impoverished. To understand the reasons for this, we need to have at least a provisional understanding of what poetry is— provisional, because people have always been more successful at appreciating poetry than at defining it.

Initially, poetry might be defined as a kind of language that says *more* and says it *more intensely* than does ordinary language. To understand this fully, we need to understand what poetry "says." For language is employed on different occasions to say quite different kinds of things; in other words, language has different uses.

Perhaps the most common use of language is to communicate *information.* We say that it is nine o'clock, that we liked a certain movie, that George Washington was the first president of the United States, that bromine and iodine are members of the halogen group of chemical elements.

This we might call the *practical* use of language; it helps us with the ordinary business of living.

But it is not primarily to communicate information that novels, short stories, plays, and poems are written. These exist to bring us a sense and a perception of life, to widen and sharpen our contacts with existence. Their concern is with *experience*. We all have an inner need to live more deeply and fully and with greater awareness, to know the experience of others, and to understand our own experience better. Poets, from their own store of felt, observed, or imagined experiences, select, combine, and reorganize. They create significant new experiences for their readers—significant because focused and formed—in which readers can participate and from which they may gain a greater awareness and understanding of their world. Literature, in other words, can be used as a gear for stepping up the intensity and increasing the range of our experience, and as a glass for clarifying it. This is the *literary* use of language, for literature is not only an aid to living but a means of living.

In advertisements, sermons, political speeches, and even some poems we find a third use of language: as an instrument of *persuasion,* or argument. But the distinctions among these three uses—the practical, the literary, and the argumentative—are not always clear-cut, since some written language simultaneously performs two or even all three functions. For example, an excellent poem we consider "literary" may convey information, and may also try to persuade us to share a particular point of view. Effectiveness in communicating experience, however, is the one essential criterion for any poem aspiring to the condition of literature.

Suppose, for instance, that we are interested in eagles. If we want simply to acquire information about eagles, we may turn to an encyclopedia, a book of natural history, or Wikipedia. We would find that there are about fifty-five species of eagles and that most have hooked bills, curved claws, broad wings, and powerfully developed breast muscles. We would also learn that eagles vary in length from about sixteen inches to as long as forty inches; that most hunt while flying, though some await their prey on a high perch; that they nest in tall trees or on inaccessible cliffs; that they lay only one or two eggs; and that for human beings eagles "symbolize power, courage, freedom, and immortality and have long been used as national, military, and heraldic emblems and as symbols in religion."*

But unless we are interested in this information only for practical purposes, we are likely to feel a little disappointed, as though we had grasped the feathers of the eagle but not its soul. True, we have learned many facts

Encyclopedia Americana, International Edition, Vol. 9 (1995) 520–22.

about the eagle, but we have missed somehow its lonely majesty, its power, and the wild grandeur of its surroundings that would make the eagle a living creature rather than a mere museum specimen. For the living eagle we must turn to literature.

The Eagle

He clasps the crag with crooked hands;
Close to the sun in lonely lands,
Ringed with the azure world, he stands.

The wrinkled sea beneath him crawls;
He watches from his mountain walls,   5
And like a thunderbolt he falls.

—ALFRED, LORD TENNYSON (1809–1892)

QUESTIONS

1. What is peculiarly effective about the expressions "crooked hands," "Close to the sun," "Ringed with the azure world," "wrinkled," "crawls," and "like a thunderbolt"?
2. Notice the formal pattern of the poem, particularly the contrast of "he stands" in the first stanza and "he falls" in the second. Is there any other contrast between the two stanzas?

When "The Eagle" has been read well, readers will feel that they have enjoyed a significant experience and understand eagles better, though in a different way, than they did from the encyclopedia article alone. Although the article *analyzes* our experience of eagles, the poem in some sense *synthesizes* such an experience. Indeed, we may say the two approaches to experience—the scientific and the literary—complement each other, and we may contend that the kind of understanding we get from the second is at least as valuable as the kind we get from the first.

Literature, then, exists to communicate significant experience—significant because it is concentrated and organized. Its function is not to tell us *about* experience but to allow us imaginatively to *participate* in it. It is a means of allowing us, through the imagination, to live more fully, more deeply, more richly, and with greater awareness. It can do this in two ways: by *broadening* our experience—that is, by making us acquainted with a range of experience with which in the ordinary course of events we might have no contact, or by *deepening* our experience—that is, by making us feel more poignantly and more understandingly the everyday experiences all of us have. It enlarges our perspectives and breaks down some of the limits we may feel.

We can avoid two limiting approaches to poetry if we keep this conception of literature firmly in mind. The first approach always looks for a lesson or a bit of moral instruction. The second expects to find poetry always beautiful. Let us consider one of the songs from Shakespeare's *Love's Labor's Lost* (Act 5, scene 2).

Winter

When icicles hang by the wall,
And Dick the shepherd blows his nail,
And Tom bears logs into the hall,
And milk comes frozen home in pail,
When blood is nipped and ways be foul,   5
Then nightly sings the staring owl,
"Tu-whit, tu-who!"
    A merry note,
    While greasy Joan doth keel° the pot.   skim

When all aloud the wind doth blow,   10
And coughing drowns the parson's saw,
And birds sit brooding in the snow,
And Marian's nose looks red and raw,
When roasted crabs° hiss in the bowl,   crab apples
Then nightly sings the staring owl,   15
"Tu-whit, tu-who!"
    A merry note,
    While greasy Joan doth keel the pot.

—WILLIAM SHAKESPEARE (1564–1616)

QUESTIONS

1. Vocabulary: *saw* (11), *brooding* (12).
2. Is the owl's cry really a "merry" note? How are this adjective and the verb "sings" employed?
3. In what way does the owl's cry contrast with the other details of the poem?

In this poem, Shakespeare communicates the quality of winter life around a sixteenth-century English country house. But he does not do so by telling us flatly that winter in such surroundings is cold and in many respects unpleasant, though with some pleasant features too (the adjectives *cold, unpleasant,* and *pleasant* are not even used in the poem). Instead, he provides a series of concrete, homely details that suggest these qualities and enable us, imaginatively, to experience this winter life ourselves. The shepherd blows on his fingernails to warm his hands; the milk freezes in the pail between the cowshed and the kitchen; the cook is slovenly and unclean, "greasy" either from spattered cooking fat or from her own sweat as she leans over the hot fire; the roads are muddy; the folk listening to the parson have colds; the birds "sit brooding in the snow"; and the servant girl's nose is raw from cold. But pleasant things are in prospect. Tom is bringing in logs for the fire, the hot cider or ale with its roasted crab-apples is ready for drinking, and the soup or stew will soon be ready. In contrast to all these familiar details of country life is the mournful and eerie note of the owl.

Obviously the poem contains no moral. If we limit ourselves to looking in poetry for some lesson, message, or noble truth about life, we are bound to be disappointed. This limited approach sees poetry as a kind of sugarcoated pill—a wholesome truth or lesson made palatable by being put into pretty words. What this narrow approach really wants is a sermon—not a poem, but something inspirational. Yet "Winter," which has appealed to readers for more than four centuries, is not inspirational and contains no moral preachment.

Neither is the poem "Winter" beautiful. Though it is appealing in its way and contains elements of beauty, there is little that is really beautiful in red, raw noses, coughing in chapel, nipped blood, foul roads, and greasy cooks. Yet the second limiting approach may lead us to feel that poetry deals exclusively with beauty—with sunsets, flowers, butterflies, love, God—and that the one appropriate response to any poem is, after a moment of awed silence, "Isn't that beautiful!" But this narrow approach excludes a large proportion of poetry. The function of poetry is sometimes to be ugly rather than beautiful. And poetry may deal with common colds and greasy cooks as legitimately as with sunsets and flowers. Consider another example:

Dulce et Decorum Est

Bent double, like old beggars under sacks,
Knock-kneed, coughing like hags, we cursed through sludge,
Till on the haunting flares we turned our backs,
And towards our distant rest began to trudge.
Men marched asleep. Many had lost their boots,   5
But limped on, blood-shod. All went lame, all blind;
Drunk with fatigue; deaf even to the hoots
Of gas-shells dropping softly behind.

Gas! GAS! Quick, boys!—An ecstasy of fumbling,
Fitting the clumsy helmets just in time,   10
But someone still was yelling out and stumbling
And flound'ring like a man in fire or lime.—
Dim through the misty panes and thick green light,
As under a green sea, I saw him drowning.
In all my dreams before my helpless sight   15
He plunges at me, guttering, choking, drowning.

If in some smothering dreams, you too could pace
Behind the wagon that we flung him in,
And watch the white eyes writhing in his face,
His hanging face, like a devil's sick of sin,   20
If you could hear, at every jolt, the blood
Come gargling from the froth-corrupted lungs
Bitter as the cud
Of vile, incurable sores on innocent tongues,—
My friend, you would not tell with such high zest   25
To children ardent for some desperate glory,
The old lie: *Dulce et decorum est*
Pro patria mori.

—WILFRED OWEN (1893–1918)

QUESTIONS

1. The Latin quotation (27–28), from the Roman poet Horace, means "It is sweet
    and becoming to die for one's country." What is the poem's comment on this
    statement?
2. List the elements of the poem that seem not beautiful and therefore "unpoetic."
    Are there any elements of beauty in the poem?
3. How do the comparisons in lines 1, 14, 20, and 23–24 contribute to the
    effectiveness of the poem?
4. What does the poem gain by moving from plural pronouns and the past tense
    to singular pronouns and the present tense?

Poetry takes all life as its province. Its primary concern is not with
beauty, not with philosophical truth, not with persuasion, but with
experience. Beauty and philosophical truth are aspects of experience, and
the poet is often engaged with them. But poetry as a whole is concerned
with all kinds of experience—beautiful or ugly, strange or common,
noble or ignoble, actual or imaginary. Paradoxically, an artist can transform even the most unpleasant or painful experiences into works of great
beauty and emotional power. Encountered in real life, pain and death are

not pleasurable for most people; but we might read and reread poems about these subjects because of their ability to enlighten and move us. A real-life experience that makes us cry is usually an unhappy one; but if we cry while reading a great novel or poem it is because we are deeply moved, our humanity affirmed. Similarly, we do not ordinarily like to be frightened in real life, but we sometimes seek out books or movies that will terrify us. Works of art focus and organize experiences of all kinds, conveying the broad spectrum of human life and evoking a full range of emotional and intellectual responses. Even the most tragic literature, through its artistry of language, can help us to see and feel the significance of life, appealing to our essential humanity in a way that can be intensely pleasurable and affirming.

There is no sharp distinction between poetry and other forms of imaginative literature. Although some readers may believe that poetry can be recognized by the arrangement of its lines on the page or by its use of rhyme and meter, such superficial signs are of little worth. The Book of Job in the Bible and Melville's *Moby-Dick* are highly poetical, but the familiar verse that begins "Thirty days hath September, / April, June, and November ..." is not. The difference between poetry and other literature is one of degree. Poetry is the most condensed and concentrated form of literature. It is language whose individual lines, either because of their own brilliance or because they focus so powerfully on what has gone before, have a higher voltage than most language. It is language that grows frequently incandescent, giving off both light and heat.

Ultimately, therefore, poetry can be recognized only by the response made to it by a practiced reader, someone who has acquired some sensitivity to poetry. But there is a catch here. We are not all equally experienced readers. To some readers, poetry may often seem dull and boring, a fancy way of writing something that could be said more simply. So might a color-blind person deny that there is such a thing as color.

The act of communication involved in reading poetry is like the act of communication involved in receiving a message by radio. Two devices are required: a transmitting station and a receiving set. The completeness of the communication depends on both the power and clarity of the transmitter and the sensitivity and tuning of the receiver. When a person reads a poem and no experience is received, either the poem is not a good poem or the reader is not properly tuned. With new poetry, we cannot always be sure which is at fault. With older poetry, if it has acquired critical acceptance—has been enjoyed and admired by generations of readers—we may assume that the receiving set is at fault. Fortunately, the fault is not irremediable. Though we cannot all become expert readers, we can become good enough to find both pleasure and value in much good poetry, or we can increase the amount of pleasure we already find in poetry and the number of kinds of poetry in which we find it. The purpose of this book is to help you increase your sensitivity and range as a receiving set.

Poetry, finally, is a kind of multidimensional language. Ordinary language—the kind that we use to communicate information—is one-dimensional. It is directed at only part of the listener, the understanding. Its one dimension is intellectual. Poetry, which is language used to communicate experience, has at least four dimensions. If it is to communicate experience, it must be directed at the *whole* person, not just at your understanding. It must involve not only your intelligence but also your senses, emotions, and imagination. To the intellectual dimension, poetry adds a sensuous dimension, an emotional dimension, and an imaginative dimension.

Poetry achieves its extra dimensions—its greater pressure per word and its greater tension per poem—by drawing more fully and more consistently than does ordinary language on a number of language resources, none of which is peculiar to poetry. These various resources form the subjects of a number of the following chapters. Among them are connotation, imagery, metaphor, symbol, paradox, irony, allusion, sound repetition, rhythm, and pattern. Using these resources and the materials of life, the poet shapes and makes a poem. Successful poetry is never effusive language. If it is to come alive it must be as cunningly put together and as efficiently organized as a tree. It must be an organism whose every part serves a useful purpose and cooperates with every other part to preserve and express the life that is within it.

REVIEWING CHAPTER ONE

1. Differentiate between ordinary language and poetic language.
2. Describe the uses of language: information, experience, persuasion.
3. Consider how looking for moral instruction or beauty are limiting approaches.
4. Explain the distinctions between poetry and other imaginative literature.
5. Review the four dimensions of experience that poetry involves.
6. Determine which ideas in this chapter are exemplified in the following poems.

UNDERSTANDING AND EVALUATING POETRY

Most of the poems in this book are accompanied by study questions that are by no means exhaustive. The following is a list of questions that you may apply to any poem. You may be unable to answer many of them until you have read further into the book.

1. Who is the speaker? What kind of person is the speaker?
2. Is there an identifiable audience for the speaker? What can we know about it (her, him, or them)?
3. What is the occasion?
4. What is the setting in time (hour, season, century, and so on)?
5. What is the setting in place (indoors or out, city or country, land or sea, region, nation, hemisphere)?
6. What is the central purpose of the poem?
7. State the central idea or theme of the poem in a sentence.
8. a. Outline the poem to show its structure and development, or
   b. Summarize the events of the poem.
9. Paraphrase the poem.
10. Discuss the diction of the poem. Point out words that are particularly well chosen and explain why.
11. Discuss the imagery of the poem. What kinds of imagery are used? Is there a structure of imagery?
12. Point out examples of metaphor, simile, personification, and metonymy, and explain their appropriateness.
13. Point out and explain any symbols. If the poem is allegorical, explain the allegory.
14. Point out and explain examples of paradox, overstatement, understatement, and irony. What is their function?
15. Point out and explain any allusions. What is their function?
16. What is the tone of the poem? How is it achieved?
17. Point out significant examples of sound repetition and explain their function.
18. a. What is the meter of the poem?
    b. Copy the poem and mark its scansion.
19. Discuss the adaptation of sound to sense.
20. Describe the form or pattern of the poem.
21. Criticize and evaluate the poem.

Shall I compare thee to a summer's day?*

Shall I compare thee to a summer's day?
Thou art more lovely and more temperate:
Rough winds do shake the darling buds of May,
And summer's lease hath all too short a date.
Sometimes too hot the eye of heaven shines,   5
And often is his gold complexion dimmed;
And every fair° from fair sometimes declines   beauty
By chance of nature's changing course untrimmed°;   stripped bare
But thy eternal summer shall not fade
Nor lose possession of that fair thou ow'st°,   own 10
Nor shall death brag thou wand'rest in his shade
When in eternal lines to time thou grow'st.
So long as men can breathe or eyes can see,
So long lives this°, and this gives life to thee.   this poem

—WILLIAM SHAKESPEARE (1564–1616)

QUESTIONS

1. Vocabulary: temperate (2), shade (11). What different meanings does "temperate" have when used to describe a person or "a summer's day"?
2. What details show that "a summer's day" is lacking in loveliness and is intemperate?
3. What are "the eye of heaven" (5) and "his gold complexion" (6)?
4. The poem begins more or less literally comparing the person being addressed to "a summer's day," but at line 9 it departs from what is literally possible into what is impossible. What does the poem gain by this shift in meaning?
5. Explain the logic behind lines 13–14. Is this a valid proof? Why or why not?

The Whipping

The old woman across the way
    is whipping the boy again
and shouting to the neighborhood
    her goodness and his wrongs.

*Whenever a heading duplicates the first line of the poem or a substantial portion thereof, with typically only the first word capitalized, it is probable that the poet left the poem untitled and that the anthologist has substituted the first line or part of it as an editorial convenience. Such a heading is not referred to as the title of the poem.

Wildly he crashes through elephant-ears, 5
    pleads in dusty zinnias,
while she in spite of crippling fat
    pursues and corners him.

She strikes and strikes the shrilly circling
    boy till the stick breaks 10
in her hand. His tears are rainy weather
    to woundlike memories:

My head gripped in bony vise
    of knees, the writhing struggle
to wrench free, the blows, the fear 15
    worse than blows that hateful

Words could bring, the face that I
    no longer knew or loved ...
Well, it is over now, it is over,
    and the boy sobs in his room, 20

And the woman leans muttering against
    a tree, exhausted, purged—
avenged in part for lifelong hidings
    she has had to bear.

—ROBERT HAYDEN (1913–1980)

QUESTIONS

1. What similarities connect the old woman, the boy, and the speaker? Can you say that one of them is the main subject of the poem?
2. Does this poem express any beauty? What human truth does it embody? Could you argue against the claim that "it is over now, it is over" (19)?

I like a look of Agony

I like a look of Agony,
Because I know it's true—
Men do not sham Convulsion,
Nor simulate, a Throe—

The Eyes glaze once—and that is Death— 5
Impossible to feign

The Beads upon the Forehead
By homely Anguish strung.

—EMILY DICKINSON (1830–1886)

QUESTIONS

1. Vocabulary: *Throe* (4), *feign* (6).
2. Why does the speaker assert that an agonized expression is "true" (2)?
3. What are the "Beads upon the Forehead" (7)? Why does the speaker compare these figurative beads to decorative or ornamental beads? In what way are they "homely" (8) rather than attractive?

The Bean Eaters

They eat beans mostly, this old yellow pair.
Dinner is a casual affair.
Plain chipware on a plain and creaking wood,
Tin flatware.

Two who are Mostly Good.   5
Two who have lived their day,
But keep on putting on their clothes
And putting things away.

And remembering ...
Remembering, with twinklings and twinges,   10
As they lean over the beans in their rented back room that
     is full of beads and receipts and dolls and cloths, tobacco
     crumbs, vases and fringes.

—GWENDOLYN BROOKS (1917–2000)

QUESTIONS

1. What details in the poem suggest that these old people are poor?
2. What details suggest that they have overcome their poverty emotionally?
3. What is the poet's attitude toward them? Is it pity? Is it admiration?

The Red Wheelbarrow

so much depends
upon

a red wheel
barrow

glazed with rain   5
water

beside the white
chickens.

—WILLIAM CARLOS WILLIAMS (1883–1963)

QUESTIONS

1. The speaker asserts that "so much depends upon" the objects he refers to, leading the reader to ask: *How much* and *why?* This glimpse of a farm scene implies
   one kind of answer. What is the importance of the wheelbarrow, rain, and
   chicken to a farmer? To all of us?
2. What further importance can you infer from the references to color, shape,
   texture, and the juxtaposition of objects? Does the poem itself have a shape?
3. What two ways of observing and valuing the world does the poem imply?
4. What are the possible reasons for "experimental" qualities in this poem—for
   instance, its lack of capitalization, its very short lines, and its plain, even homely
   images? Do these qualities give the poem a greater emotional power than a more
   conventional and decorative poem on the same topic might have achieved?

Constantly risking absurdity

Constantly risking absurdity
                              and death
          whenever he performs
                    above the heads
                              of his audience   5
          the poet like an acrobat
                    climbs on rime
                              to a high wire of his own making
and balancing on eyebeams
                              above a sea of faces   10
          paces his way
                    to the other side of day
performing entrechats
                    and sleight-of-foot tricks
and other high theatrics   15
                    and all without mistaking
          any thing
                    for what it may not be
          For he's the super realist
                              who must perforce perceive   20

                    taut truth
                        before the taking of each stance or step
        in his supposed advance
                            toward that still higher perch
        where Beauty stands and waits   25
                            with gravity
                                to start her death-defying leap
            And he
                a little charleychaplin man
                                    who may or may not catch   30
                    her fair eternal form
                            spreadeagled in the empty air
                of existence

                                            —LAWRENCE FERLINGHETTI (B. 1919)

QUESTIONS

1. Vocabulary: *entrechats* (13). Explain the meanings of "above the heads" (4), "sleight-of-foot tricks" (14), "high theatrics" (15), and "with gravity" (26).
2. The poet "climbs on rime" (7), the poem asserts. To what extent does this poem utilize rhyme and other musical devices?
3. What statement does the poem make about poetry, truth, and beauty?
4. How do the rhythms created by the length and placement of lines reinforce the meanings of the poem? Does this poem take poets and poetry seriously? solemnly?

Filling Station

Oh, but it is dirty!
—this little filling station,
oil-soaked, oil-permeated
to a disturbing, over-all
black translucency.   5
Be careful with that match!

Father wears a dirty,
oil-soaked monkey suit
that cuts him under the arms,
and several quick and saucy   10
and greasy sons assist him
(it's a family filling station),
all quite thoroughly dirty.

Do they live in the station?
It has a cement porch   15
behind the pumps, and on it
a set of crushed and grease-
impregnated wickerwork;
on the wicker sofa
a dirty dog, quite comfy.   20

Some comic books provide
the only note of color—
of certain color. They lie
upon a big dim doily
draping a taboret   25
(part of the set), beside
a big hirsute begonia.

Why the extraneous plant?
Why the taboret?
Why, oh why, the doily?   30
(Embroidered in daisy stitch
with marguerites, I think,
and heavy with gray crochet.)

Somebody embroidered the doily.
Somebody waters the plant,   35
or oils it, maybe. Somebody
arranges the rows of cans
so that they softly say:
ESSO—SO—SO—SO
to high-strung automobiles.   40
Somebody loves us all.

—ELIZABETH BISHOP (1911–1979)

QUESTIONS

1. Vocabulary: *taboret* (25), *hirsute* (27), *marguerites* (32). The brand name "ESSO" (39) is the former name of the Exxon Mobil oil company.
2. What is the speaker's attitude toward the filling station? Is her physical description of the station affectionate or critical? Can it be both?
3. Discuss the rhetorical questions beginning in line 28. What are the implied answers to these questions?
4. Analyze the final stanza. Why does the speaker stress that somebody takes care of and decorates the filling station? What is the significance of the final line?

Suicide's Note

The calm,
Cool face of the river
Asked me for a kiss.

—LANGSTON HUGHES (1902–1967)

QUESTIONS

1. How is the speaker's desire for death like the desire expressed in the comparison of the river to a person? How are they unlike? Explore the frame of mind that would create this comparison.
2. Does the repeated "k" sound seem beautiful to you? Can you explain the repetition in terms that reflect the speaker's frame of mind?

Survival: A Guide

It's not easy living here, waiting to be charmed
by the first little scribble of green. Even in May
the crows want to own the place, and the heron, old bent thing,
spends hours looking like graying bark,
part of a dead trunk lying over opaque water.   5
She strikes the pose so long I begin to worry
she's determined to be something ordinary.
The small lakes continue their slide into bog and muck—
remember when they ran clear, an invisible spring
renewing the water? But the ducks stay longer, amusing   10
ruffle and chatter. I can be distracted.

If I do catch her move, the heron appears
to have no particular fear or hunger, her gaunt body
hinged haphazardly, a few gears unlocking
one wing, then another. More than a generation here   15
and every year more drab.
Once I called her blue heron, as in Great Blue,
true to a book—part myth, part childhood's color.
Older now, I see her plain: a mere surviving
against a weedy bank with fox dens   20
and the ruthless, overhead patrol.
Some blind clockwork keeps her going.

—CLEOPATRA MATHIS (B. 1947)

QUESTIONS

1. Consider the poem's title. In what sense is the poem a "guide" to survival?
2. What do we know about the speaker?
3. What are the major characteristics of the heron? Are they admirable? What is the "blind clockwork" (22) that helps assure her survival?

Introduction to Poetry

I ask them to take a poem
and hold it up to the light
like a color slide

or press an ear against its hive.

I say drop a mouse into a poem   5
and watch him probe his way out,
or walk inside the poem's room
and feel the walls for a light switch.

I want them to water-ski
across the surface of a poem   10
waving at the author's name on the shore.

But all they want to do
is tie the poem to a chair with rope
and torture a confession out of it.

They begin beating it with a hose   15
to find out what it really means.

—BILLY COLLINS (B. 1941)

QUESTIONS

1. What is the basic situation of the poem? Who are "I" (1) and "them" (1)?
2. Explain the simile in line 3. From that point onward through line 11, the speaker invents a series of metaphors. For each of them, define what a poem is being compared to and how the metaphor expresses some characteristic quality of poetry. For example, how is a poem like a "hive" (4) full of buzzing bees?
3. The last five lines present a single extended metaphor to express what "they want to do" when they encounter a poem. What are "they" and "the poem" compared to, and how do these comparisons reflect a different attitude toward poetry from the ones expressed in the first 11 lines? What, ultimately, does this poem express about poetry and its readers?

Prosody 101

When they taught me that what mattered most
was not the strict iambic line goose-stepping
over the page but the variations
in that line and the tension produced
on the ear by the surprise of difference,   5
I understood yet didn't understand
exactly, until just now, years later
in spring, with the trees already lacy
and camellias blowsy with middle age
I looked out and saw what a cold front had done   10
to the garden, sweeping in like common language,
unexpected in the sensuous
extravagance of a Maryland spring.
There was a dark edge around each flower
as if it had been outlined in ink   15
instead of frost, and the tension I felt
between the expected and actual
was like that time I came to you, ready
to say goodbye for good, for you had been
a cold front yourself lately, and as I walked in   20
you laughed and lifted me up in your arms
as if I too were lacy with spring
instead of middle-aged like the camellias,
and I thought: So this is Poetry.

—LINDA PASTAN (B. 1932)

QUESTIONS

1. Vocabulary: *iambic* (2), *blowsy* (9).
2. Explain the phrase "surprise of difference" (5). How does this surprise help create poetic effects?
3. Does the speaker strike you as an experienced reader of poetry? Why or why not?
4. In the last few lines, the speaker compares a romantic experience of a middle-aged couple to poetry. Why is this an effective closure to the poem?

SUGGESTIONS FOR WRITING

"Writing about Literature," the first section of this book, offers practical advice about the formal requirements and style that are usually expected in student papers. Although many of the suggestions presented there may be familiar to you, reviewing them when you prepare to complete these writing assignments should help you to write more effectively.

1. The following pairs of poems deal with similar subject matter treated in very different ways. Yet in each case the two poems employ the multidimensional language that is one criterion of poetic excellence. Choose one pair and discuss the ways in which both poems qualify as poetry, even though they take different approaches to similar topics.
   a. Tennyson, "The Eagle" (page 682) and Hughes, "Hawk Roosting" (page 710).
   b. Owen, "Dulce et Decorum Est" (page 684) and Whitman, "A Sight in Camp in the Daybreak Gray and Dim" (page 1046).
   c. Hopkins, "Spring" (page 735) and Williams, "Spring and All" (page 1047).
   d. Olds, "35/10" (page 729) and Lorde, "Black Mother Woman" (page 1022).
   e. Hayden, "The Whipping" (page 689) and Roethke, "My Papa's Waltz" (page 1035).
   f. Hughes, "Suicide's Note" (page 695) and Robinson, "Richard Cory" (page 1034).

2. According to "Ars Poetica" by Archibald MacLeish (page 1023), "A poem should not mean / But be" (23–24). Relate this assertion to one or more of the following:
   a. Williams, "The Red Wheelbarrow" (page 691).
   b. Keats, "Ode on a Grecian Urn" (page 949).
   c. Blake, "The Tiger" (page 835).
   d. cummings, "Buffalo Bill's defunct" (page 989).
   e. Stevens, "Disillusionment of Ten O'Clock" (page 1042).
   f. Bishop, "Electrical Storm" (page 742).
   g. Wordsworth, "I wandered lonely as a cloud" (page 1048).

PRACTICE AP WRITING PROMPTS

Langston Hughes, "Suicide's Note" (p. 695) and Edwin Arlington Robinson, "Richard Cory" (p. 1034)

Read both "Suicide's Note" and "Richard Cory" carefully. Write an essay in which you compare and contrast the two speakers' perspectives on suicide. In your analysis, refer to such poetic elements as tone, point of view, and structure.

....

William Shakespeare, "My mistress' eyes are nothing like the sun" (p. 845) and "Shall I compare thee to a summer's day" (p. 689)

In both "My mistress' eyes are nothing like the sun" and "Shall I compare thee to a summer's day," The speaker tries to draw analogies between aspects of nature and the attributes of his beloved. Focusing on imagery, figurative language, and the plain prose sense of the two poems' statements, compare the strategies the speakers use to achieve their poetic and emotional purposes.

....

CHAPTER TWO

Reading the Poem

How can you develop your understanding and appreciation of poetry? Here are some preliminary suggestions:

1. Read a poem more than once. A good poem will no more yield its full meaning on a single reading than will a Beethoven symphony on a single hearing. Two readings may be necessary simply to let you get your bearings. And if the poem is a work of art, it will repay repeated and prolonged examination. One does not listen to a good piece of music once and forget it; one does not look at a good painting once and throw it away. A poem is not like a website, to be hastily read and forgotten. It is to be hung on the wall of one's mind.

2. Keep a dictionary by you and use it. It is futile to try to understand poetry without knowing the meanings of the words of which it is composed. You might as well attempt to play tennis without a ball. One of the benefits of studying literature is an enlarged vocabulary, and the study of poetry offers an excellent opportunity. A few other reference books also will be invaluable, particularly a good book on mythology (your instructor may recommend one) and a Bible.

3. Read so as to hear the sounds of the words in your mind. Poetry is written to be heard: its meanings are conveyed through sound as well as through print. Every word is therefore important. The best way to read a poem may be just the opposite of the best way to read a newspaper. One might read a website article rapidly, and probably only once; but a poem should be read slowly, and most poems must be read many times before their full complexity and meaning can be experienced. When you cannot read a poem aloud so as to hear its sounds, lip-read it: form the words with your tongue and mouth even though you do not utter sounds. With ordinary reading material, lip-reading is a bad habit; with poetry, it is a good habit.

4. Always pay careful attention to what the poem is saying. Though you should be conscious of the sounds of the poem, you should never be so exclusively conscious of them that you pay no attention to what the poem means. For some readers, reading a poem is like getting on board a rhythmical roller coaster. The car starts and off they go, up and down, paying no attention to the landscape flashing past them, arriving at the end of the poem breathless, with no idea of what it has been about. This is the wrong way to read a poem. One should make the utmost effort to follow the thought continuously and to grasp the full implications and suggestions. Because a poem says so much, several readings may be necessary, but on the very first reading you should determine the subjects of the verbs, the antecedents of the pronouns, and other normal grammatical facts.

5. Practice reading poems aloud. When you find one you especially like, have friends listen to your reading of it. Try to read it to them in such a way that they will like it too. (a) Read it affectionately, but not affectedly. The two extremes that oral readers often fall into are equally deadly: One is to read as if one were reading a tax report or a railroad timetable, unexpressively, in a monotone; the other is to elocute, with artificial flourishes and vocal histrionics. It is not necessary to put emotion into reading a poem. The emotion is already there. It wants only a fair chance to get out. It will express *itself* if the poem is read naturally and sensitively. (b) Of the two extremes, reading too fast offers greater danger than reading too slow. Read slowly enough that each word is clear and distinct and that the meaning has time to sink in. Remember that your friends do not have the advantage, as you do, of having the text before them. Your ordinary rate of reading will probably be too fast. (c) Read the poem so that the rhythmical pattern is felt but not exaggerated. Remember that poetry, with few exceptions, is written in sentences, just as prose is, and that punctuation is a signal as to how it should be read. Give all grammatical pauses their full due. Do not distort the natural pronunciation of words or a normal accentuation of the sentence to fit into what you have decided is its metrical pattern. One of the worst ways to read a poem is to read it ta-DUM ta-DUM ta-DUM, with an exaggerated emphasis on every other syllable. On the other hand, it should not be read as if it were prose. An important test of your reading will be how you handle the end of a line that lacks line-ending punctuation. A frequent mistake of the beginning reader is to treat each line as if it were a complete thought, whether grammatically complete or not, and to drop the voice at the end of it. A frequent mistake of the sophisticated reader is to take a running start upon approaching the end of a line and fly over it as if it were not there. The line is a rhythmical unit, and its end should be observed whether there is punctuation or not. If there is no punctuation, you ordinarily should observe the end of the line by the

slightest of pauses or by holding on to the last word in the line just a little longer than usual, without dropping your voice. In line 12 of the following poem, you should hold on to the word "although" longer than if it occurred elsewhere in the line. But do not lower your voice on it: it is part of the clause that follows in the next stanza.

The Man He Killed

Had he and I but met
By some old ancient inn,
We should have sat us down to wet
Right many a nipperkin!°   half-pint cup

But ranged as infantry,   5
And staring face to face,
I shot at him as he at me,
And killed him in his place.

I shot him dead because—
Because he was my foe,   10
Just so: my foe of course he was;
That's clear enough; although

He thought he'd 'list, perhaps,
Off-hand-like—just as I—
Was out of work—had sold his traps—°   belongings 15
No other reason why.

Yes; quaint and curious war is!
You shoot a fellow down
You'd treat, if met where any bar is,
Or help to half-a-crown.   20

—THOMAS HARDY (1840–1928)

QUESTIONS

1. Vocabulary: *half-a-crown* (20).
2. In informational prose, the repetition of a word like "because" (9–10) would be an error. What purpose does the repetition serve here? Why does the speaker repeat to himself his "clear" reason for killing a man (10–11)? The word "although" (12) gets more emphasis than it would ordinarily because it comes not only at the

end of a line but at the end of a stanza. What purpose does this emphasis serve? Can the redundancy of "old ancient" (2) be poetically justified?

3. Poetry has been defined as "the expression of elevated thought in elevated language." Comment on the adequacy of this definition in the light of Hardy's poem.

One starting point for understanding a poem at the simplest level, and for clearing up misunderstanding, is to paraphrase its content or part of its content. To **paraphrase** a poem means to restate it in different language, so as to make its prose sense as plain as possible. The paraphrase may be longer or shorter than the poem, but it should contain all the ideas in the poem in such a way as to make them clear and to make the central idea, or **theme**, of the poem more accessible.

A Study of Reading Habits

When getting my nose in a book
Cured most things short of school,
It was worth ruining my eyes
To know I could still keep cool,
And deal out the old right hook   5
To dirty dogs twice my size.

Later, with inch-thick specs,
Evil was just my lark:
Me and my cloak and fangs
Had ripping times in the dark.   10
The women I clubbed with sex!
I broke them up like meringues.

Don't read much now: the dude
Who lets the girl down before
The hero arrives, the chap   15
Who's yellow and keeps the store,
Seem far too familiar. Get stewed:
Books are a load of crap.

—PHILIP LARKIN (1922–1985)

QUESTIONS

1. The three stanzas delineate three stages in the speaker's life. Describe each.
2. What kind of person is the speaker? What kinds of books does he read? May we identify him with the poet?

Larkin's poem may be paraphrased as follows:

There was a time when reading was one way I could avoid almost all my troubles—except for school. It seemed worth the danger of ruining my eyes to read stories in which I could imagine myself maintaining my poise in the face of threats and having the boxing skill and experience needed to defeat bullies who were twice my size.

Later, already having to wear thick glasses because my eyesight had become so poor, I found my delight in stories of sex and evil: imagining myself with Dracula cloak and fangs, I relished vicious nocturnal adventures. I identified myself with sexual marauders whose inexhaustible potency was like a weapon wielded against women who were sweet and fragile.

I don't read much anymore because now I can identify myself only with the flawed secondary characters, such as the flashy dresser who wins the heroine's confidence and then betrays her in a moment of crisis before the cowboy hero comes to her rescue, or the cowardly storekeeper who cringes behind the counter at the first sign of danger. Getting drunk is better than reading—books are just full of useless lies.

Notice that in a paraphrase, figurative language gives way to literal language (similes replace metaphors) and normal word order supplants inverted syntax. But a paraphrase retains the speaker's use of first, second, and third person, and the tenses of verbs. Though it is neither necessary nor possible to avoid using some of the words found in the original, a paraphrase should strive for plain, direct diction. And since a paraphrase is prose, it does not maintain the length and position of poetic lines.

A paraphrase is useful only if you understand that it is the barest, most inadequate approximation of what the poem really "says" and is no more equivalent to the poem than a corpse is to a person. After you have paraphrased a poem, you should endeavor to see how far short of the poem it falls, and why. In what respects does Larkin's poem say more, and say it more memorably, than the paraphrase? Does the phrase "full of useless lies" capture the impact of "a load of crap"? Furthermore, a paraphrase may fall far short of revealing the theme of a poem. "A Study of Reading Habits" represents a man summing up his reading experience and evaluating it— but in turn the poem itself evaluates *him* and his defects. A statement of the theme of the poem might be this:

A person who turns to books as a source of self-gratifying fantasies may, in the course of time, discover that escapist reading no longer protects him from his awareness of his own reality, and he may out of habit have to find other, more potent, and perhaps more self-destructive means of escaping.

Notice that in stating a theme, we should be careful not to phrase it as a moral or lesson—not "you shouldn't" but "a person may."

To aid us in the understanding of a poem, we may ask ourselves a number of questions about it. Two of the most important are *Who is the speaker?* and *What is the occasion?* A cardinal error of some readers is to assume that a speaker who uses the first-person pronouns (*I, my, mine, me*) is always the poet. A less risky course would be to assume always that the speaker is someone other than the poet. Poems, like short stories, novels, and plays, belong to the world of fiction, an imaginatively conceived world that at its best is "truer" than the factually "real" world that it reflects. When poets put themselves or their thoughts into a poem, they present a *version* of themselves; that is, they present a person who in many ways is *like* themselves but who, consciously or unconsciously, is shaped to fit the needs of the poem. We must be very careful, therefore, about identifying anything in a poem with the biography of the poet.

However, caution is not prohibition. Sometimes events or ideas in a poem will help us to understand some episodes in the poet's life. More importantly for us, knowledge of the poet's life may help us understand a poem. There can be little doubt, when all the evidence is in, that "Terence, this is stupid stuff" (page 1007) is Housman's defense of the kind of poetry he writes, and that the six lines in which Terence sums up his beliefs about life and the function of poetry closely echo Housman's own beliefs. On the other hand, it would be folly to suppose that Housman ever got drunk at "Ludlow fair" and once lay down in "lovely muck" and slept all night in a roadside ditch. It may seem paradoxical that Philip Larkin, a poet and novelist and for many years the chief administrator of a university library, would end a poem with the line, "Books are a load of crap." But poems often feature a persona, or speaker, who expresses a viewpoint the poet presumably does not share.

We may well think of every poem, therefore, as being to some degree *dramatic*—that is, the utterance not of the person who wrote the poem but of a fictional character in a particular situation that may be inferred. Many poems are expressly dramatic.

In "The Man He Killed" the speaker is a soldier; the occasion is his having been in battle and killed a man—obviously for the first time in his life. We can tell a good deal about him. He is not a career soldier: he enlisted only because he was out of work. He is a workingman: he speaks a simple and colloquial language ("nipperkin," "list," "off-hand-like," "traps"). He is a friendly, kindly sort who enjoys a neighborly drink of ale in a bar and will gladly lend a friend a half-a-crown when he has it. He has known what it is to be poor. In any other circumstances he would have been horrified at taking a human life. It gives him pause even now. He is trying to figure it out. But he is not a deep thinker and thinks he has supplied a reason when he has only supplied a name: "I killed the man . . . because he was my foe." The critical question, of course, is *why* was the man his "foe"? Even the speaker is left unsatisfied by his answer, though he is not analytical enough to know what is wrong with it. Obviously this poem is expressly dramatic. We need know nothing about Thomas Hardy's life (he was never a soldier and never killed a man) to realize that the poem is dramatic. The internal evidence of the poem tells us so.

A third important question that we should ask ourselves upon reading any poem is *What is the central purpose of the poem?** The purpose may be to tell a story, to reveal human character, to impart a vivid impression of a scene, to express a mood or an emotion, or to convey vividly some idea or attitude. Whatever the purpose is, we must determine it for ourselves and define it mentally as precisely as possible. Only by relating the various details in the poem to the central purpose or theme can we fully understand their function and meaning. Only then can we begin to assess the value of the poem and determine whether it is a good one or a poor one. In "The Man He Killed" the central purpose is quite clear: it is to make us realize more keenly the irrationality of war. The puzzlement of the speaker may be our puzzlement. But even if we are able to give a more sophisticated answer than his as to why men kill each other, we ought still to have a greater awareness, after reading the poem, of the fundamental irrationality in war that makes men kill who have no grudge against each other and who might under different circumstances show each other considerable kindness.

Is my team plowing

"Is my team plowing,
    That I was used to drive
And hear the harness jingle
    When I was man alive?"

---

*Our only reliable evidence of the poem's purpose, of course, is the poem itself. External evidence, when it exists, though often helpful, may also be misleading. Some critics have objected to the use of such terms as "purpose" and "intention" altogether; we cannot know, they maintain, what was *attempted* in the poem; we can only know what was *done*. We are concerned, however, not with the *poet's* purpose, but with the *poem's* purpose; that is, with the theme (if it has one), and this is determinable from the poem itself.

Aye, the horses trample,   5
The harness jingles now;
No change though you lie under
The land you used to plow.

"Is football playing
Along the river shore,   10
With lads to chase the leather,
Now I stand up no more?"

Aye, the ball is flying,
The lads play heart and soul;
The goal stands up, the keeper   15
Stands up to keep the goal.

"Is my girl happy,
That I thought hard to leave,
And has she tired of weeping
As she lies down at eve?"   20

Aye, she lies down lightly,
She lies not down to weep:
Your girl is well contented.
Be still, my lad, and sleep.

"Is my friend hearty,   25
Now I am thin and pine;
And has he found to sleep in
A better bed than mine?"

Yes, lad, I lie easy,
I lie as lads would choose;   30
I cheer a dead man's sweetheart,
Never ask me whose.

—A. E. HOUSMAN (1859–1936)

QUESTIONS

1. How many actual speakers are there in this poem? What is meant by "whose" in line 32?
2. Is this poem cynical in its observation of human nature?
3. The word "sleep" (24, 27) in the concluding stanzas suggests three different meanings. What are they? How many meanings are suggested by the word *bed*?

Once we have answered the question *What is the central purpose of the poem?* we can consider another question, equally important to full understanding: *By what means is that purpose achieved?* It is important to distinguish means from ends. A student on an examination once used the poem "Is my team plowing" as evidence that A. E. Housman believed in immortality because in it a man speaks from the grave. This is as much a misconstruction as to say that Thomas Hardy joined the army because he was out of work. The purpose of Housman's poem is to communicate poignantly a certain truth about human life: life goes on after our deaths pretty much as it did before—our dying does not disturb the universe. Further, it dramatizes that irrational sense of betrayal and guilt that may follow the death of a friend. The poem achieves this purpose by means of a fanciful dramatic framework in which a dead man converses with his still-living friend. The framework tells us nothing about whether Housman believed in immortality (as a matter of fact, he did not). It is simply an effective means by which we *can* learn how Housman felt a man's death affected the life he left behind. The question *By what means is that purpose achieved?* is partially answered by describing the poem's dramatic framework, if it has any. The complete answer requires an accounting of various resources of communication that we will discuss in this book.

The most important preliminary advice we can give for reading poetry is to maintain always, while reading it, the utmost mental alertness. The most harmful idea one can get about poetry is that its purpose is to soothe and relax and that the best place to read it is lying in a hammock with a cool drink while low music plays in the background. You *can* read poetry lying in a hammock, but only if you refuse to put your mind in the same attitude as your body. Its purpose is not to soothe and relax but to arouse and awake, to shock us into life, to make us more alive.

An analogy can be drawn between reading poetry and playing tennis. Both offer great enjoyment if the game is played hard. Good tennis players must be constantly on the tips of their toes, concentrating on their opponent's every move. They must be ready for a drive to the right or left, a lob overhead, or a drop shot barely over the net. They must be ready for topspin or underspin, a ball that bounces crazily to the left or right. They must jump for the high ones and run for the long ones. And they will enjoy the game almost exactly in proportion to the effort they put into it. The same is true of reading poetry. Great enjoyment is there, but this enjoyment demands a mental effort equivalent to the physical effort one puts into tennis.

The reader of poetry has one advantage over the tennis player: poets are not trying to win matches. They may expect the reader to stretch for their shots, but they *want* the reader to return them.

REVIEWING CHAPTER TWO

....

1. Review the five preliminary suggestions for reading poems.
2. List steps in paraphrasing, and create paraphrases of several poems, showing how paraphrase helps to clarify the theme.
3. Explain how identifying the speaker and the occasion of the poem shows the dramatic quality of poetry.
4. Explore the concept of a "central purpose" of a poem.
5. Consider the difference between the means and the ends in determining the central purpose of a poem.
6. Determine which ideas in this chapter are exemplified in the following poems.

Break of Day

'Tis true, 'tis day; what though it be?
Oh, wilt thou therefore rise from me?
Why should we rise because 'tis light?
Did we lie down because 'twas night?
Love which in spite of darkness brought us hither   5
Should, in despite of light, keep us together.

Light hath no tongue, but is all eye;
If it could speak as well as spy,
This were the worst that it could say:
That, being well, I fain would stay,   10
And that I loved my heart and honor so,
That I would not from him that had them go.
Must business thee from hence remove?
Oh, that's the worst disease of love;
The poor, the foul, the false, love can   15
Admit, but not the busied man.
He which hath business and makes love, doth do
Such wrong as when a married man doth woo.

—JOHN DONNE (1572–1631)

QUESTIONS

1. Who is the speaker? Who is addressed? What is the situation? Can the speaker be identified with the poet?
2. Explain the comparison in line 7. To whom does "I" (10–12) refer? Is "love" (15–16) the subject or object of "can admit"?
3. Summarize the arguments used by the speaker to keep the person addressed from leaving. What does the speaker value most?
4. Are the two persons married or unmarried? Justify your answer.

There's been a Death, in the Opposite House

There's been a Death, in the Opposite House,
As lately as Today—
I know it, by the numb look
Such Houses have—alway—

The Neighbors rustle in and out—   5
The Doctor—drives away—
A Window opens like a Pod—
Abrupt—mechanically—

Somebody flings a Mattress out—
The Children hurry by—   10
They wonder if it died—on that—
I used to—when a Boy—

The Minister—goes stiffly in—
As if the House were His—
And He owned all the Mourners—now—   15
And little Boys—besides—

And then the Milliner—and the Man
Of the Appalling Trade—
To take the measure of the House—

There'll be that Dark Parade—   20

Of Tassels—and of Coaches—soon—
It's easy as a Sign—

The Intuition of the News—
In just a Country Town—

—EMILY DICKINSON (1830–1886)

QUESTIONS

1. What can we know about the speaker in the poem?
2. By what signs does the speaker "intuit" that a death has occurred? Explain them stanza by stanza. What does it mean that the speaker must intuit rather than simply *know* that death has taken place?
3. Comment on the words "Appalling" (18) and "Dark" (20).
4. What shift in the poem is signaled by the separation of line 20 from the end of stanza 5?
5. What is the speaker's attitude toward death?

Hawk Roosting

I sit in the top of the wood, my eyes closed.
Inaction, no falsifying dream
Between my hooked head and hooked feet:
Or in sleep rehearse perfect kills and eat.

The convenience of the high trees!   5
The air's buoyancy and the sun's ray
Are of advantage to me;
And the earth's face upward for my inspection.

My feet are locked upon the rough bark.
It took the whole of Creation   10
To produce my foot, my each feather:
Now I hold Creation in my foot

Or fly up, and revolve it all slowly—
I kill where I please because it is all mine.
There is no sophistry in my body: 15
My manners are tearing off heads—

The allotment of death.
For the one path of my flight is direct
Through the bones of the living.
No arguments assert my right: 20

The sun is behind me.
Nothing has changed since I began.
My eye has permitted no change.
I am going to keep things like this.

—TED HUGHES (1930–1998)

QUESTIONS

1. Vocabulary: *sophistry* (15).
2. Who is the speaker of this poem? Characterize his "personality." What do his errors in summing up his situation contribute to your characterization?
3. What are the similarities and differences between this poem and "The Eagle" (page 682)?

Ode on Melancholy

No, no, go not to Lethe, neither twist
    Wolf's-bane, tight-rooted, for its poisonous wine;
Nor suffer thy pale forehead to be kissed
    By nightshade, ruby grape of Proserpine;
Make not your rosary of yew-berries,   5
    Nor let the beetle, nor the death-moth be
Your mournful Psyche, nor the downy owl
    A partner in your sorrow's mysteries;
For shade to shade will come too drowsily,
    And drown the wakeful anguish of the soul.   10

But when the melancholy fit shall fall
    Sudden from heaven like a weeping cloud,
That fosters the droop-headed flowers all,
    And hides the green hill in an April shroud;
Then glut thy sorrow on a morning rose,   15
    Or on the rainbow of the salt sand-wave,
    Or on the wealth of globed peonies;
Or if thy mistress some rich anger shows,
    Emprison her soft hand, and let her rave,
    And feed deep, deep upon her peerless eyes.   20

She dwells with Beauty—Beauty that must die;
    And Joy, whose hand is ever at his lips
Bidding adieu; and aching Pleasure nigh,
    Turning to Poison while the bee-mouth sips:

> Ay, in the very temple of delight   25
>   Veiled Melancholy has her sovereign shrine,
>   Though seen of none save him whose strenuous tongue
> Can burst Joy's grape against his palate fine;
>   His soul shall taste the sadness of her might,
>   And be among her cloudy trophies hung.   30

—JOHN KEATS (1795–1821)

QUESTIONS

1. Using a good book on Greek mythology or an Internet search, find out the meaning of the following mythical references: *Lethe* (1); *Wolf's-bane* (2); *nightshade, Proserpine* (4); *Psyche* (7).
2. In the second stanza, the speaker gives advice on how to endure a "fit" (11) of melancholy. What is the essence of his advice?
3. According to the third stanza, what is the root cause of human melancholy (today we would simply call it "depression")? What kind of person is most susceptible to experiencing melancholy?

In the Waiting Room

> In Worcester, Massachusetts,
> I went with Aunt Consuelo
> to keep her dentist's appointment
> and sat and waited for her
> in the dentist's waiting room.   5
> It was winter. It got dark
> early. The waiting room
> was full of grown-up people,
> arctics and overcoats,
> lamps and magazines.   10
> My aunt was inside
> what seemed like a long time
> and while I waited I read
> the *National Geographic*
> (I could read) and carefully   15
> studied the photographs:
> the inside of a volcano,
> black, and full of ashes;
> then it was spilling over
> in rivulets of fire.   20
> Osa and Martin Johnson

dressed in riding breeches,
laced boots, and pith helmets.
A dead man slung on a pole
—"Long Pig," the caption said.
Babies with pointed heads   25
wound round and round with string;
black, naked women with necks
wound round and round with wire
like the necks of light bulbs.
Their breasts were horrifying.   30
I read it right straight through.
I was too shy to stop.
And then I looked at the cover:
the yellow margins, the date.
Suddenly, from inside,   35
came an *oh!* of pain
—Aunt Consuelo's voice—
not very loud or long.
I wasn't at all surprised;
even then I knew she was   40
a foolish, timid woman.
I might have been embarrassed,
but wasn't. What took me
completely by surprise
was that it was *me:*   45
my voice, in my mouth.
Without thinking at all
I was my foolish aunt,
I—we—were falling, falling,
our eyes glued to the cover   50
of the *National Geographic,*
February, 1918.

I said to myself: three days
and you'll be seven years old.
I was saying it to stop   55
the sensation of falling off
the round, turning world
into cold, blue-black space.
But I felt: you are an *I,*
you are an *Elizabeth,*   60
you are one of *them.*

Why should you be one, too?
I scarcely dared to look
to see what it was I was.   65
I gave a sidelong glance
—I couldn't look any higher—
at shadowy gray knees,
trousers and skirts and boots
and different pairs of hands   70
lying under the lamps.
I knew that nothing stranger
had ever happened, that nothing
stranger could ever happen.

Why should I be my aunt,   75
or me, or anyone?
What similarities—
boots, hands, the family voice
I felt in my throat, or even
the *National Geographic*   80
and those awful hanging breasts—
held us all together
or made us all just one?
How—I didn't know any
word for it—how "unlikely". . .   85
How had I come to be here,
like them, and overhear
a cry of pain that could have
got loud and worse but hadn't?

The waiting room was bright   90
and too hot. It was sliding
beneath a big black wave,
another, and another.

Then I was back in it.
The War was on. Outside,   95
in Worcester, Massachusetts,
were night and slush and cold,
and it was still the fifth
of February, 1918.

—ELIZABETH BISHOP (1911–1979)

QUESTIONS

1. Vocabulary: *arctics* (9); *pith helmets* (23). Osa and Martin Johnson (21) were early twentieth-century explorers and documentary filmmakers.
2. The poem situates the speaker very specifically in time and place. Why is this important, given the theme of the poem?
3. The speaker, almost seven years old, is in a dentist's waiting room. In what sense is this setting a metaphor for a different kind of waiting?
4. Reread lines 60–74. In what sense had "nothing stranger" ever happened to the speaker before? What *has* happened to her?
5. Discuss the significance of the final stanza, with its reiteration of the poem's time and place. Why is this an effective ending to the poem?

Mirror

I am silver and exact. I have no preconceptions.
Whatever I see I swallow immediately
Just as it is, unmisted by love or dislike.
I am not cruel, only truthful—
The eye of a little god, four-cornered.   5
Most of the time I meditate on the opposite wall.
It is pink, with speckles. I have looked at it so long
I think it is a part of my heart. But it flickers.
Faces and darkness separate us over and over.

Now I am a lake. A woman bends over me,   10
Searching my reaches for what she really is.
Then she turns to those liars, the candles or the moon.
I see her back, and reflect it faithfully.
She rewards me with tears and an agitation of hands.
I am important to her. She comes and goes.   15
Each morning it is her face that replaces the darkness.
In me she has drowned a young girl, and in me an old woman
Rises toward her day after day, like a terrible fish.

—SYLVIA PLATH (1932–1963)

QUESTIONS

1. Who is the speaker? What is the central purpose of the poem, and by what means is it achieved?
2. In what ways is the mirror like and unlike a person (stanza 1)? In what ways is it like a lake (stanza 2)?
3. What is the meaning of the last two lines?

Collection Day

Saturday morning, Motown
forty-fives and thick seventy-eights
on the phonograph, window fans
turning light into our rooms,
we clean house to a spiral groove,   5
sorting through our dailiness—
washtubs of boiled-white linens,
lima beans soaking, green as luck,
trash heaped out back for burning—
everything we can't keep,   10
make new with thread or glue.

Beside the stove, a picture calendar
of the seasons, daily scripture,
compliments of the Everlast Interment
Company, one day each month marked   15
in red—PREMIUM DUE—collection visit
from the insurance man, his black suits
worn to a shine. In our living room
he'll pull out photos of our tiny plot,
show us the slight eastward slope,   20
all the flowers in bloom now, how neat
the shrubs are trimmed, and *See here,*
the trees we planted are coming up fine.

We look out for him all day, listen
for the turn-stop of wheels   25
and rocks crunching underfoot.
Mama leafs through the Bible
for our payment card—June 1969,
the month he'll stamp PAID
in bright green letters, putting us   30
one step closer to what we'll own,
something to last: patch of earth,
view of sky.

—NATASHA TRETHEWEY (B. 1966)

QUESTIONS

1. The poem recounts a fact of life for poor African American families early in the twentieth century: they were sold insurance, often at usurious rates, to assure

themselves a burial plot. What is the speaker's attitude toward her memory of the insurance man's visits and her mother's participation in the insurance program? Is she bitter, angry, resigned, or a combination of all these?

2. Find details in the poem that help clarify the time and place being described.
3. Focus on the last few lines. What do the images tell us about the speaker's mother's motivation for continuing to pay the monthly fee for her insurance?

Ethics

In ethics class so many years ago
our teacher asked this question every fall:
if there were a fire in a museum
which would you save, a Rembrandt painting
or an old woman who hadn't many   5
years left anyhow? Restless on hard chairs
caring little for pictures or old age
we'd opt one year for life, the next for art
and always half-heartedly. Sometimes
the woman borrowed my grandmother's face   10
leaving her usual kitchen to wander
some drafty, half-imagined museum.
One year, feeling clever, I replied
why not let the woman decide herself?
Linda, the teacher would report, eschews   15
the burdens of responsibility.
This fall in a real museum I stand
before a real Rembrandt, old woman,
or nearly so, myself. The colors
within this frame are darker than autumn,   20
darker even than winter—the browns of earth,
though earth's most radiant elements burn
through the canvas. I know now that woman
and painting and season are almost one
and all beyond saving by children.   25

—LINDA PASTAN (B. 1932)

QUESTIONS

1. Explore the fictitious time frame the poem creates—how often a girl takes the same class with the same teacher. What does this element of fantasy add to the poem?
2. Does the poem answer its central ethical question? If so, what is that answer; if not, what is the value of asking? What is the central purpose of the poem?

Storm Warnings

The glass has been falling all the afternoon,
And knowing better than the instrument
What winds are walking overhead, what zone
Of gray unrest is moving across the land,
I leave the book upon a pillowed chair   5
And walk from window to closed window, watching
Boughs strain against the sky

And think again, as often when the air
Moves inward toward a silent core of waiting,
How with a single purpose time has traveled   10
By secret currents of the undiscerned
Into this polar realm. Weather abroad
And weather in the heart alike come on
Regardless of prediction.

Between foreseeing and averting change   15
Lies all the mastery of elements
Which clocks and weatherglasses cannot alter.
Time in the hand is not control of time,
Nor shattered fragments of an instrument
A proof against the wind; the wind will rise,   20
We can only close the shutters.

I draw the curtains as the sky goes black
And set a match to candles sheathed in glass
Against the keyhole draught, the insistent whine
Of weather through the unsealed aperture.   25
This is our sole defense against the season;
These are the things that we have learned to do
Who live in troubled regions.

—ADRIENNE RICH (1929–2012)

SUGGESTIONS FOR WRITING

1. Here are four definitions of poetry, all framed by poets themselves. Which defini-
    tion best fits the poems you have so far read?
    a. I wish our clever young poets would remember my homely definitions of
        prose and poetry: that is, prose = words in their best order; poetry = the
        best words in the best order.   *Samuel Taylor Coleridge*

b. It is not meters, but a meter-making argument, that makes a poem—a thought so passionate and alive that, like the spirit of a plant or an animal, it has an architecture of its own, and adorns nature with a new thing.

Ralph Waldo Emerson

c. If I read a book and it makes my whole body so cold no fire can warm me, I know that is poetry. If I feel physically as if the top of my head were taken off, I know that is poetry. These are the only ways I know it. Is there any other way?

Emily Dickinson

d. A poem begins in delight, it inclines to the impulse, it assumes a direction with the first line laid down, it runs a course of lucky events, and ends in a clarification of life—not necessarily a great clarification, such as sects and cults are founded on, but in a momentary stay against confusion.

Robert Frost

2. Using two or three poems from this chapter, or poems from the following list, write an essay that supports the definition you have chosen.

a. Atwood, "Siren Song" (page 818).
b. Clifton, "good times" (page 982).
c. Dickinson, "A narrow Fellow in the Grass" (page 840).
d. Donne, "Song: Go and catch a falling star" (page 992).
e. Keats, "Ode on Melancholy" (page 711).
f. Olds, "The Victims" (page 1029).

PRACTICE AP WRITING PROMPTS ▰▰▰▰

Thomas Hardy, "The Man He Killed" (p. 701) and Stephen Crane, "War Is Kind" (p. 988)

Read "The Man He Killed" by Thomas Hardy and "War Is Kind" by Stephen Crane carefully. Then write a well-organized essay in which you compare and contrast the way each poem illustrates the futility and devastation of war. In your analysis, explain how both poets use literary techniques such as irony, point of view, and diction.

···

A.E. Housman, "Is my team plowing" (p. 705)

Read "Is my team plowing" carefully. Then write a well-organized essay in which you explain how the speakers in the poem convey a nuanced perspective on life, death, and human nature. Refer to specific elements such as point of view, tone, and diction in your analysis.

···

CHAPTER THREE

Denotation
and Connotation

A primary distinction between the practical use of language and the literary use is that in literature, especially in poetry, a *fuller* use is made of individual words. To understand this, we need to examine the composition of a word.

The average word has three component parts: sound, denotation, and connotation. It begins as a combination of tones and noises, uttered by the lips, tongue, and throat, for which the written word is a notation. But it differs from a musical tone or a noise in that it has a meaning attached to it. The basic part of this meaning is its **denotation** or denotations; that is, the dictionary meaning or meanings of the word. Beyond its denotations, a word may also have connotations. The **connotations** are what it suggests beyond what it expresses: its overtones of meaning. It acquires these connotations from its past history and associations, from the way and the circumstances in which it has been used. The word *home,* for instance, by denotation means only a place where one lives, but by connotation it suggests security, love, comfort, and family. The words *childlike* and *childish* both mean "characteristic of a child," but *childlike* suggests meekness, innocence, and wide-eyed wonder, whereas *childish* suggests pettiness, willfulness, and temper tantrums. If we list the names of different coins—nickel, peso, euro, sen, doubloon—the word *doubloon,* to four out of five readers, immediately will suggest pirates, though a dictionary definition includes nothing about pirates. Pirates are part of its connotation.

Connotation is very important in poetry, for it is one of the means by which the poet can concentrate or enrich meaning—say more in fewer words. Consider, for instance, the following short poem:

There is no Frigate like a Book

There is no Frigate like a Book
To take us Lands away
Nor any Coursers like a Page
Of prancing Poetry—
This Traverse may the poorest take   5
Without oppress of Toll—
How frugal is the Chariot
That bears the Human soul.

—EMILY DICKINSON (1830–1886)

This poem considers the power of a book or of poetry to carry us away, to take us from our immediate surroundings into a world of the imagination. To do this it compares literature to various means of transportation: a boat, a team of horses, a wheeled land vehicle. But the poet has been careful to choose kinds of transportation and names for them that have romantic connotations. "Frigate" suggests exploration and adventure; "coursers," beauty, spirit, and speed; "chariot," speed and the ability to go through the air as well as on land. (Compare "Swing Low, Sweet Chariot" and the myth of Phaëthon, who tried to drive the chariot of Apollo, and the famous painting of Aurora with her horses, once hung in almost every school.) How much of the meaning of the poem comes from this selection of vehicles and words is apparent if we substitute *cruise ship* for "frigate," *horses* for "coursers," and *bus* for "chariot."

QUESTIONS

1. What is lost if *miles* is substituted for "Lands" (2) or *cheap* for "frugal" (7)?
2. How is "prancing" (4) peculiarly appropriate to poetry as well as to coursers? Could the poet without loss have compared a book to coursers and poetry to a frigate?
3. Is this account appropriate to all kinds of poetry or just to certain kinds? That is, was the poet thinking of poems like Wilfred Owen's "Dulce et Decorum Est" (page 684) or of poems like Coleridge's "Kubla Khan" (page 984) and Keats's "La Belle Dame sans Merci" (page 1014)?

Just as a word has a variety of connotations, so may it have more than one denotation. If we look up the word *spring* in the dictionary, for instance, we will find that it has between twenty-five and thirty distinguishable meanings: it may mean (1) a pounce or leap, (2) a season of the year, (3) a natural source of water, (4) a coiled elastic wire, and so forth. This variety of denotation, complicated by additional tones of connotation, makes language confusing and difficult to use. Any person using words must be careful to define precisely by context the denotation that is intended. But the difference between the writer using language to communicate and the poet is this: the practical writer will usually attempt to confine words to one denotation at a time; the poet will often take advantage of the fact that the word has more than one meaning by using it to mean more than one thing at the same time. Thus, when Edith Sitwell in one of her poems writes, "this is the time of the wild spring and the mating of the tigers,"* she uses the word "spring" to denote both a season of the year and a sudden leap (and she uses the word "tigers" rather than *deer* or *birds* because it has a connotation of fierceness and wildness that the others lack). The two denotations of "spring" are also appropriately possessed of contrasting connotations: the season is positive in its implications, whereas a sudden leap in a line that includes "tigers" may connote the pouncing of a beast of prey. Similarly, in "Mirror" (page 715), the word "swallow" in line 2 denotes both accepting without question and consuming or devouring, and so connotes both an inability to think and an obliteration or destruction.

When my love swears that she is made of truth

When my love swears that she is made of truth,
I do believe her, though I know she lies,
That she might think me some untutored youth,
Unlearnèd in the world's false subtleties.
Thus vainly thinking that she thinks me young,   5
Although she knows my days are past the best,
Simply I credit her false-speaking tongue;
On both sides thus is simple truth supprest.
But wherefore says she not she is unjust?°   unfaithful
And wherefore say not I that I am old?   10
Oh, love's best habit is in seeming trust,
And age in love loves not to have years told:
Therefore I lie with her and she with me,
And in our faults by lies we flattered be.

—WILLIAM SHAKESPEARE (1564–1616)

* *Collected Poems* (New York: Vanguard, 1968) 392.

QUESTIONS

1. How old is the speaker? How old is his beloved? What is the nature of their relationship?
2. How is the contradiction in line 2 to be resolved? In lines 5–6? Who is lying to whom?
3. How do "simply" (7) and "simple" (8) differ in meaning? The words "vainly" (5), "habit" (11), "told" (12), and "lie" (13) all have double denotative meanings. What are they?
4. What is the tone of the poem—that is, the attitude of the speaker toward his situation? Should line 11 be taken as an expression of (a) wisdom, (b) conscious rationalization, or (c) self-deception? In answering these questions, consider both the situation and the connotations of all the important words beginning with "swears" (1) and ending with "flattered" (14).

A frequent misconception of poetic language is that poets seek always the most beautiful or noble-sounding words. What they really seek are the most *meaningful* words, and these vary from one context to another. Language has many levels and varieties, and poets may choose from all of them. Their words may be grandiose or humble, fanciful or matter-of-fact, romantic or realistic, archaic or modern, technical or everyday, monosyllabic or polysyllabic. Usually a poem will be pitched pretty much in one key: the words in Emily Dickinson's "There is no Frigate like a Book" (page 721) and those in Thomas Hardy's "The Man He Killed" (page 701) are chosen from quite different areas of language, but both poets have chosen the words most meaningful for their own poetic context. It is always important to determine the level of diction employed in a poem, for it may provide clear insight into the purpose of the poem by helping to characterize the speaker. Sometimes a poet may import a word from one level or area of language into a poem composed mostly of words from a different level or area. If this is done clumsily, the result will be incongruous and sloppy; if it is done skillfully, the result will be a shock of surprise and an increment of meaning for the reader. In fact, the many varieties of language open to poets provide their richest resource. Their task is one of constant exploration and discovery. They search always for the secret affinities of words that allow them to be brought together with soft explosions of meaning.

Spring in the Classroom

Elbows on dry books, we dreamed
Past Miss Willow Bangs, and lessons, and windows,
To catch all day glimpses and guesses of the greening
    woodlot,

Its secrets and increases,
Its hidden nests and kind.   5
And what warmed in us was no book-learning,
But the old mud blood murmuring,
Loosening like petals from bone sleep.
So spring surrounded the classroom, and we suffered to be
    kept indoors,
Droned through lessons, carved when we could with
    jackknives   10
Our pulsing initials into the desks, and grew
Angry to be held so, without pity and beyond reason,
By Miss Willow Bangs, her eyes two stones behind glass,
Her legs thick, her heart
In love with pencils and arithmetic.   15

So it went—one gorgeous day lost after another
While we sat like captives and breathed the chalky air
And the leaves thickened and birds called
From the edge of the world—till it grew easy to hate,
To plot mutiny, even murder. Oh, we had her in chains,   20
We had her hanged and cold, in our longing to be gone!
And then one day, Miss Willow Bangs, we saw you
As we ran wild in our three o'clock escape
Past the abandoned swings; you were leaning
All furry and blooming against the old brick wall   25
In the Art Teacher's arms.

—MARY OLIVER (B. 1935)

QUESTIONS

1. The poem juxtaposes two contrasted concepts, "Spring" and "Classroom." What
   are the connotations of the two words?
2. Based on their connotations, show how the following words support one or
   the other of those concepts: "dry" (1), "greening" (3), "petals" and "bone"
   (8), "droned" (10), "pulsing" (11), "chalky" (17), "wild" (23), "furry," "blooming,"
   and "brick" (25).
3. How does the surprise ending contribute to the characterization of the speaker?

People using language only to convey information are usually indifferent to the sounds of the words and may feel frustrated by their connotations and multiple denotations. They would rather confine each word to a
single, exact meaning. They use, one might say, a fraction of the word and
throw away the rest. Poets, on the other hand, use as much of the word as

possible. They are interested in connotation and use it to enrich and convey meaning. And they may rely on more than one denotation.

Perhaps the purest form of practical language is scientific language. Scientists need a precise language to convey information precisely. The existence of multiple denotations and various overtones of meaning may interfere with this purpose. As a result of this, scientists have even devised special "languages" such as the following:

$$SO_2 + H_2O = H_2SO_3$$

In such a statement the symbols are entirely unambiguous; they have been stripped of all connotation and of all denotations but one. The word *sulfurous,* if it occurred in poetry, might have all kinds of connotations: fire, smoke, brimstone, hell, damnation. But H_2SO_3 means one thing and one thing only: sulfurous acid.

The ambiguity and multiplicity of meanings possessed by words might be an obstacle to the scientist, but they are an advantage for the poet who seeks richness of meaning. One resource for that is a multidimensional language using a multidimensional vocabulary, in which the dimensions of connotation and sound are added to the dimension of denotation.

The poet, we may say, plays on a many-stringed instrument and sounds more than one note at a time.

The first task in reading poetry, therefore, as in reading any kind of literature, is to develop a sense of language, a feeling for words. One needs to become acquainted with their shape, their color, and their flavor. Two of the ways of doing this are extensive use of the dictionary and extensive reading.

EXERCISES

1. Which word in each group has the most "romantic" connotations: (a) horse, steed, nag; (b) king, ruler, tyrant, autocrat; (c) Chicago, Pittsburgh, Samarkand, Detroit?
2. Which word in each group is the most emotionally connotative: (a) female parent, mother, dam; (b) offspring, children, progeny; (c) brother, sibling?
3. Arrange the words in each of the following groups from most positive to most negative in connotation: (a) skinny, thin, gaunt, slender; (b) prosperous, loaded, moneyed, affluent; (c) brainy, intelligent, eggheaded, smart.
4. Of the following, which should you be less offended at being accused of: (a) having acted foolishly, (b) having acted like a fool?
5. In any competent piece of writing, the possible multiple denotations and connotations of the words used are controlled by context. The context screens out irrelevant meanings while allowing the relevant meanings to pass through. What denotation has the word *fast* in the following contexts: fast runner, fast color, fast living, fast day? What are the varying connotations of these four denotations of *fast?*

6. Explain how in the following examples the denotation of the word *white* remains the same, but the connotations differ: (a) The young princess had blue eyes, golden hair, and a breast as white as snow; (b) Confronted with the evidence, the false princess turned as white as a sheet.

REVIEWING CHAPTER THREE

1. Distinguish between connotation and denotation as components of words.
2. Explain how words accumulate their connotations.
3. Explore the ways in which a word may have multiple denotations, and multiple connotations, showing that different denotations may have different connotations.
4. Explore the ways in which the context will determine which denotations and which connotations are relevant in a poem.
5. Show how levels of diction may characterize the speaker in a poem.

Cross

My old man's a white old man
And my old mother's black.
If ever I cursed my white old man
I take my curses back.

If ever I cursed my black old mother   5
And wished she were in hell,
I'm sorry for that evil wish
And now I wish her well.

My old man died in a fine big house.
My ma died in a shack.   10
I wonder where I'm gonna die,
Being neither white nor black?

—LANGSTON HUGHES (1902–1967)

QUESTIONS

1. What different denotations does the title have? What connotations are linked to each of them?

2. The language in this poem, such as "old man" (1, 3, 9), "ma" (10), and "gonna" (11),
is plain, and even colloquial. Is it appropriate to the subject? Why or why not?

The world is too much with us

The world is too much with us; late and soon,
Getting and spending, we lay waste our powers:
Little we see in nature that is ours;
We have given our hearts away, a sordid boon!
This sea that bares her bosom to the moon,   5
The winds that will be howling at all hours,
And are up-gathered now like sleeping flowers,
For this, for everything, we are out of tune;
It moves us not. —Great God! I'd rather be
A pagan suckled in a creed outworn;   10
So might I, standing on this pleasant lea,
Have glimpses that would make me less forlorn;
Have sight of Proteus rising from the sea;
Or hear old Triton blow his wreathèd horn.

—WILLIAM WORDSWORTH (1770–1850)

QUESTIONS

1. Vocabulary: *boon* (4), *Proteus* (13), *Triton* (14). What two relevant denotations has
   "wreathèd" (14)?
2. Explain why the poet's words are more effective than these possible alternatives:
   earth for "world" (1); *selling and buying* for "getting and spending" (2); *exposes*
   for "bares" (5); *dozing* for "sleeping" (7); *posies* for "flowers" (7); *nourished* for
   "suckled" (10); *visions* for "glimpses" (12); *sound* for "blow" (14).
3. Is "Great God!" (9) a vocative (term of address) or an expletive (exclamation)?
   Or something of both?
4. State the theme (central idea) of the poem in a sentence.

Desert Places

Snow falling and night falling fast, oh, fast
In a field I looked into going past,
And the ground almost covered smooth in snow,
But a few weeds and stubble showing last.

The woods around it have it—it is theirs.   5
All animals are smothered in their lairs.

I am too absent-spirited to count;
The loneliness includes me unawares.

And lonely as it is that loneliness
Will be more lonely ere it will be less—   10
A blanker whiteness of benighted snow
With no expression, nothing to express.

They cannot scare me with their empty spaces
Between stars—on stars where no human race is.
I have it in me so much nearer home   15
To scare myself with my own desert places.

—ROBERT FROST (1874–1963)

QUESTIONS

1. Examine the poem for examples of words or phrases with negative or positive connotations. Which stanza is most negative? Considering its possible synonyms, how emotionally powerful is the word "scare" (13 and 16)?
2. What multiple denotations of the word "benighted" (11) are functional in the poem? How does the etymology of "blanker" add to its force in this context?
3. "Absent-spirited" (7) is coined from the common word *absent-minded*. What denotations of "spirit" are relevant here?
4. Who are "They" (13) who can create fear by talking about the emptiness of space? Fear of what? What are the "desert places" (16) within the speaker that may be compared to literal emptiness of space?
5. In the first publication of the poem, line 14 concluded "on stars void of human races." Frost's final version calls attention to the potentially comic effect of rhyming *spaces/race is/places,* a device called feminine rhyme often used in humorous verse (see pages 859, 863). Is the speaker feeling comical? Can you relate this effect to what you determined about the word "scare" in question 1?

Accounting

Nights too warm for TV
we're flung outdoors to the porch,
citronella candles scenting the space
between us, our faces aglow
in gold light. She crowds the card table   5
with coin banks, an abacus,
five and ten dollar rolling paper,
our tidy ledger.

I count, line the coins in neat rows,
the abacus clicking out our worth,   10
how much we can save, stack up
against the seasons—winter coming,
her tightly braided hair turning white;
her hands quick, filling the paper casings
like homemade sausage.   15

There's money in the bank downtown,
but this we'll keep at home
buried in jars beneath the house,
the crawl space filling up, packed solid
as any foundation.   20

—NATASHA TRETHEWEY (B. 1966)

QUESTIONS

1. Vocabulary: *citronella* (3), *abacus* (6).
2. Discuss the connotations of "worth" in the phrase "the abacus clicking out our worth" (10). Is the speaker referring only to financial worth, or to something more as well?
3. Why do the speaker and her mother keep money "buried in jars beneath the house" (18) when, as she says, they have money in a downtown bank? Is there an emotional or psychological reason for hoarding the coins at home?
4. Consider the connotations of the word "foundation" (20), which concludes the poem.

35/10

Brushing out our daughter's brown
silken hair before the mirror
I see the grey gleaming on my head,
the silver-haired servant behind her. Why is it
just as we begin to go   5
they begin to arrive, the fold in my neck
clarifying as the fine bones of her
hips sharpen? As my skin shows
its dry pitting, she opens like a moist
precise flower on the tip of a cactus;   10
as my last chances to bear a child
are falling through my body, the duds among them,
her full purse of eggs, round and
firm as hard-boiled yolks, is about
to snap its clasp. I brush her tangled   15

fragrant hair at bedtime. It's an old
story—the oldest we have on our planet—
the story of replacement.

—SHARON OLDS (B. 1942)

QUESTIONS

1. What does the title mean?
2. Much of the poem consists of contrasts between physical characteristics of the mother and daughter. What connotations give emotional weight to these contrasts?
3. Is the last sentence (16–18) regretful or resigned, or can it be seen to be positive?

Tree Heart/True Heart

The hearts of trees
are serially displaced
pressed annually
outward to a ring.
They aren't really   5
what we mean
by hearts, they so
easily acquiesce,
willing to thin and
stretch around some   10
upstart green. A
real heart does not
give way to spring.
A heart is true.
I say no more springs   15
without you.

—KAY RYAN (B. 1945)

QUESTIONS

1. Discuss the implied comparison between the hearts of trees and those of human beings. How are they similar? How are they different?
2. The title implies a distinction between a "tree heart" and a "true heart." What is the major distinction between them?
3. The poem concludes with an unexpected assertion, "I say no more springs / without you" (15–16). Why is this an appropriate conclusion to the poem?

SUGGESTIONS FOR WRITING

Consider the denotative meaning(s) of the following titles. Then read each poem carefully and note the multiple connotations that attach to the title phrase as the poem progresses. Choose two or three titles, then write a short essay comparing the denotative and connotative meanings of each.

1. Williams, "The Red Wheelbarrow" (page 691).
2. Frost, "Fire and Ice" (page 781).
3. Piercy, "Barbie Doll" (page 796).
4. Pastan, "To a Daughter Leaving Home" (page 893).
5. Baca, "Main Character" (page 975).
6. Donne, "The Good-Morrow" (page 993).
7. Roethke, "My Papa's Waltz" (page 1035).
8. Soto, "Small Town with One Road" (page 1040).

PRACTICE AP WRITING PROMPTS

Mary Oliver, "Spring in the Classroom" (p. 723)

Read "Spring in the Classroom" carefully, paying close attention to Mary Oliver's characterization of the teacher and her students. Write an essay in which you analyze these character portraits, showing how such literary elements as figurative language, tone, and hyperbole contribute to meaning.

Sharon Olds, "35/10" (p. 729) and "My Son the Man" (p. 818)

Contemporary poet Sharon Olds has written many poems about her feelings and experiences as a parent. Read carefully "35/10" and "My Son the Man." In a well-organized essay, compare and contrast the two poems as responses to seeing one's children grow up. Show how literary devices such as figurative language and allusion contribute to each poem's meaning.

CHAPTER FOUR

Imagery

Experience comes to us largely through the senses. Our experiences of a spring day, for instance, may consist partly of certain emotions we feel and partly of certain thoughts we think, but most of it will be a cluster of sense impressions. It will consist of *seeing* blue sky and white clouds, budding leaves and daffodils; of *hearing* robins and bluebirds singing in the early morning; of *smelling* damp earth and blossoming hyacinths; and of *feeling* a fresh wind against one's cheek. A poet seeking to express the experience of a spring day therefore provides a selection of sense impressions. Similarly, to present a winter day (page 683), Shakespeare gives us hanging "icicles," milk "frozen," blood "nipped," and Marian's "red and raw" nose as well as the melancholy "'Tu-whit, tu-who'" of the owl. Had he not done so, he might have failed to evoke the emotions that accompany these sensations. The poet's language, then, is more *sensuous* than ordinary language. It is richer in imagery.

Imagery may be defined as the representation through language of sense experience. Poetry appeals directly to our senses, of course, through its music and rhythms, which we actually hear when it is read aloud. But indirectly it appeals to our senses through imagery, the representation to the imagination of sense experience. The word *image* perhaps most often suggests a mental picture, something seen in the mind's eye—and *visual* imagery is the kind of imagery that occurs most frequently in poetry. But an image may also represent a sound (*auditory imagery*); a smell (*olfactory imagery*); a taste (*gustatory imagery*); touch, such as hardness, softness, wetness, or heat and cold (*tactile imagery*); an internal sensation, such as hunger, thirst, fatigue, or nausea (*organic imagery*); or movement or tension in the muscles or joints (*kinesthetic imagery*). If we wish to be scientific, we could extend this list further, for psychologists no longer confine themselves to five or even six senses, but for purposes of discussing poetry the preceding classification should ordinarily be sufficient.

Meeting at Night

The gray sea and the long black land;
And the yellow half-moon large and low;
And the startled little waves that leap
In fiery ringlets from their sleep,
As I gain the cove with pushing prow,   5
And quench its speed i' the slushy sand.

Then a mile of warm sea-scented beach;
Three fields to cross till a farm appears;
A tap at the pane, the quick sharp scratch
And blue spurt of a lighted match,   10
And a voice less loud, through its joys and fears,
Than the two hearts beating each to each!

—ROBERT BROWNING (1812–1889)

"Meeting at Night" is a poem about love. It makes, one might say, a number of statements about love: being in love is a sweet and exciting experience; when one is in love everything seems beautiful, and the most trivial things become significant; when one is in love one's beloved seems the most important thing in the world. But the poet actually *tells* us none of these things directly. He does not even use the word *love* in his poem. His business is to communicate experience, not information. He does this largely in two ways. First, he presents us with a specific situation, in which a lover goes to meet his love. Second, he describes the lover's journey so vividly in terms of sense impressions that the reader virtually sees and hears what the lover saw and heard and seems to share his anticipation and excitement.

Every line in the poem contains some image, some appeal to the senses: the gray sea, the long black land, the yellow half-moon, the startled little waves with their fiery ringlets, the blue spurt of the lighted match—all appeal to our sense of sight and convey not only shape but also color and motion. The warm sea-scented beach appeals to the senses of both smell and touch. The pushing prow of the boat on the slushy sand, the tap at the pane, the quick scratch of the match, the low speech of the lovers, and the sound of their hearts beating—all appeal to the sense of hearing.

Parting at Morning

Round the cape of a sudden came the sea,
And the sun looked over the mountain's rim:
And straight was a path of gold for him,
And the need of a world of men for me.

—ROBERT BROWNING (1812–1889)

QUESTIONS

1. This poem is a sequel to "Meeting at Night." "[H]im" (3) refers to the sun. Does the last line mean that the lover needs the world of men or that the world of men needs the lover? Or both?

2. Does the sea *actually* come suddenly around the cape or *appear* to? Why does Browning mention the *effect* before its *cause* (the sun looking over the mountain's rim)?

3. Do these two poems, taken together, suggest any larger truths about love? Browning, in answer to a question, said that the second poem is the man's confession of "how fleeting is the belief (implied in the first part) that such raptures are self-sufficient and enduring—as for the time they appear."

The sharpness and vividness of any image will ordinarily depend on how specific it is and on the poet's use of effective detail. The word *hummingbird,* for instance, conveys a more definite image than does *bird,* and *ruby-throated hummingbird* is sharper and more specific still. However, to represent something vividly a poet need not describe it completely. One or two especially sharp and representative details will often serve, inviting the reader's imagination to fill in the rest. Tennyson in "The Eagle" (page 682) gives only one visual detail about the eagle itself—that he clasps the crag with "crooked hands"—but this detail is an effective and memorable one. Oliver in "Spring in the Classroom" (page 723) does not state why the students grow to hate their teacher but through the series of contrasted images leads us to feel their frustration and desire. Browning, in "Meeting at Night," calls up a whole scene with "A tap at the pane, the quick sharp scratch / And blue spurt of a lighted match."

Since imagery is a peculiarly effective way of evoking vivid experience, and since it may be used to convey emotion and suggest ideas as well as to cause a mental reproduction of sensations, it is an invaluable resource for the poet. In general, the poet will seek concrete or image-bearing words in preference to abstract or non-image-bearing words. We cannot evaluate a poem, however, by the amount or quality of its imagery alone. Sense impression is only one of the elements of experience. Poetry may attain its ends by other means. We should never judge any single element of a poem except in reference to the total intent of that poem.

EXERCISES

In the following images, what sense is being evoked, and what does the image contribute to its context?

1. "Dulce et Decorum Est" (page 684): "deaf even to the hoots / Of gas-shells" (7–8); "He plunges at me, guttering, choking, drowning" (16); "gargling from the froth-corrupted lungs" (22).

2. "Shall I compare thee to a summer's day?" (page 689): "Rough winds do shake the darling buds of May" (3); "Sometimes too hot the eye of heaven shines" (5); "often is his gold complexion dimmed" (6).

3. "Spring in the Classroom" (page 723): "mud blood murmuring" (7); "Droned through lessons" (10); "the chalky air" (18); "All furry and blooming" (25).

REVIEWING CHAPTER FOUR

1. State the definition of poetic imagery.

2. Relate imagery to its uses in conveying emotion, suggesting ideas, and mentally evoking sense experience.

3. Select individual images that demonstrate these three uses of imagery, and explain how they work.

4. Show that specificity in an image contributes to its sharpness and vividness.

5. Draw the distinction between abstract statements and concrete, image-bearing statements, providing examples.

6. Demonstrate that ambiguity and multiplicity of meanings contribute to the richness of poetic language.

Spring

Nothing is so beautiful as spring—
    When weeds, in wheels, shoot long and lovely and lush;
    Thrush's eggs look little low heavens, and thrush
Through the echoing timber does so rinse and wring
The ear, it strikes like lightnings to hear him sing;   5
    The glassy peartree leaves and blooms, they brush
    The descending blue; that blue is all in a rush
With richness; the racing lambs too have fair their fling.

What is all this juice and all this joy?
    A strain of the earth's sweet being in the beginning   10
In Eden garden.——Have, get, before it cloy,

    Before it cloud, Christ, lord, and sour with sinning,
Innocent mind and Mayday in girl and boy,
    Most, O maid's child, thy choice and worthy the winning.

—GERARD MANLEY HOPKINS (1844–1889)

QUESTIONS

1. The first line makes an abstract statement. How is this statement brought to carry conviction?
2. The sky is described as being "all in a rush / With richness" (7–8). In what other respects is the poem "rich"?
3. To what two things does the speaker compare the spring in lines 9–14? In what ways are the comparisons appropriate?
4. Lines 11–14 might be made clearer by paraphrasing them thus: "Christ, lord, child of the Virgin: save the innocent mind of girl and boy before sin taints it, since it is most like yours and worth saving." Why are Hopkins's lines more effective, both in imagery and in syntax?

The Widow's Lament in Springtime

Sorrow is my own yard
where the new grass
flames as it has flamed
often before but not
with the cold fire   5
that closes round me this year.
Thirtyfive years
I lived with my husband.
The plumtree is white today
with masses of flowers.   10
Masses of flowers
load the cherry branches
and color some bushes
yellow and some red
but the grief in my heart   15
is stronger than they
for though they were my joy

formerly, today I notice them
and turned away forgetting.
Today my son told me   20
that in the meadows,
at the edge of the heavy woods
in the distance, he saw
trees of white flowers.
I feel that I would like   25
to go there
and fall into those flowers
and sink into the marsh near them.

—WILLIAM CARLOS WILLIAMS (1883–1963)

QUESTIONS

1. Why is springtime so poignant a time for this lament? What has been the speaker's previous experience at this time of year?
2. Why does the speaker's son tell her of the flowering trees "in the distance" (23)? What does he want her to do? Contrast the two locations in the poem— "yard" versus "meadows" (21), "woods" (22), and "marsh" (28). What does the widow desire?
3. Imagery may have degrees of vividness, depending on its particularity, concreteness, and specific detail. What is the result of the contrast between the vividness of lines 2–3 and the relative flatness of lines 13–14? How does the fact that "masses" (10, 11) appeals to two senses relate to the speaker's emotional condition?

I felt a Funeral, in my Brain

I felt a Funeral, in my Brain,
And Mourners to and fro
Kept treading—treading—till it seemed
That Sense was breaking through—

And when they all were seated,   5
A Service, like a Drum—
Kept beating—beating—till I thought
My Mind was going numb—

And then I heard them lift a Box
And creak across my Soul   10

With those same Boots of Lead, again,
Then Space—began to toll,

As all the Heavens were a Bell,
And Being, but an Ear,
And I, and Silence, some strange Race   15
Wrecked, solitary, here—

And then a Plank in Reason, broke,
And I dropped down, and down—
And hit a World, at every plunge,
And Finished knowing—then—   20

—EMILY DICKINSON (1830–1886)

QUESTIONS

1. What senses are being evoked by the imagery? Can you account for the fact that one important sense is absent from the poem?
2. In sequence, what aspects of a funeral and burial are represented in the poem? Is it possible to define the sequence of mental events that are being compared to them?
3. With respect to the funeral activities in stanzas 1–3, where is the speaker imaginatively located?
4. What finally happens to the speaker?

Living in Sin

She had thought the studio would keep itself,
no dust upon the furniture of love.
Half heresy, to wish the taps less vocal,
the panes relieved of grime. A plate of pears,
a piano with a Persian shawl, a cat   5
stalking the picturesque amusing mouse
had risen at his urging.
Not that at five each separate stair would writhe
under the milkman's tramp; that morning light
so coldly would delineate the scraps   10
of last night's cheese and three sepulchral bottles;
that on the kitchen shelf among the saucers
a pair of beetle-eyes would fix her own—
envoy from some village in the moldings . . .

Meanwhile, he, with a yawn,   15
sounded a dozen notes upon the keyboard,
declared it out of tune, shrugged at the mirror,
rubbed at his beard, went out for cigarettes;
while she, jeered by the minor demons,
pulled back the sheets and made the bed and found   20
a towel to dust the table-top,
and let the coffee-pot boil over on the stove.
By evening she was back in love again,
though not so wholly but throughout the night
she woke sometimes to feel the daylight coming   25
like a relentless milkman up the stairs.

—ADRIENNE RICH (1929–2012)

The Forge

All I know is a door into the dark.
Outside, old axles and iron hoops rusting;
Inside, the hammered anvil's short-pitched ring,
The unpredictable fantail of sparks
Or hiss when a new shoe toughens in water.   5
The anvil must be somewhere in the center,
Horned as a unicorn, at one end square,
Set there immovable: an altar
Where he expends himself in shape and music.
Sometimes, leather-aproned, hairs in his nose,   10
He leans out on the jamb, recalls a clatter
Of hoofs where traffic is flashing in rows;
Then grunts and goes in, with a slam and flick
To beat real iron out, to work the bellows.

—SEAMUS HEANEY (1939–2013)

QUESTIONS

1. What does the speaker mean when he says that "all" he knows is "a door into the dark" (1)? What more does he know, and how does he make his knowledge evident?
2. How do the images describing the blacksmith (10–11) relate to his attitude toward his work and toward the changing times?
3. The speaker summarizes the smith's world as "shape and music" (9), terms that suggest visual and auditory imagery. What do the contrasts between visual images contribute? The contrasts between auditory images?

After Apple-Picking

My long two-pointed ladder's sticking through a tree
Toward heaven still,
And there's a barrel that I didn't fill
Beside it, and there may be two or three
Apples I didn't pick upon some bough.   5
But I am done with apple-picking now.
Essence of winter sleep is on the night,
The scent of apples: I am drowsing off.
I cannot rub the strangeness from my sight
I got from looking through a pane of glass   10
I skimmed this morning from the drinking trough
And held against the world of hoary grass.
It melted, and I let it fall and break.
But I was well
Upon my way to sleep before it fell,   15
And I could tell
What form my dreaming was about to take.
Magnified apples appear and disappear,
Stem end and blossom end,
And every fleck of russet showing clear.   20
My instep arch not only keeps the ache,
It keeps the pressure of a ladder-round.
I feel the ladder sway as the boughs bend.
And I keep hearing from the cellar bin
The rumbling sound   25
Of load on load of apples coming in.
For I have had too much
Of apple-picking: I am overtired
Of the great harvest I myself desired.
There were ten thousand thousand fruit to touch,   30
Cherish in hand, lift down, and not let fall.
For all
That struck the earth,
No matter if not bruised or spiked with stubble,
Went surely to the cider-apple heap   35
As of no worth.
One can see what will trouble
This sleep of mine, whatever sleep it is.
Were he not gone,
The woodchuck could say whether it's like his   40

Long sleep, as I describe its coming on,
Or just some human sleep.

—ROBERT FROST (1874–1963)

QUESTIONS

1. How does the poet convey so vividly the experience of "apple-picking"? Point out effective examples of each kind of imagery used. What emotional responses do the images evoke?
2. How does the speaker regard his work? Has he done it well or poorly? Does he find it enjoyable or tedious? Is he dissatisfied with its results?
3. The speaker predicts what he will dream about in his sleep. Why does he shift to the present tense (18) when he begins describing a dream he has not yet had? How sharply are real experience and dream experience differentiated in the poem?
4. The poem uses the word *sleep* six times. Does it, through repetition, come to suggest a meaning beyond the purely literal? If so, what attitude does the speaker take toward this second signification? Does he fear it? Does he look forward to it? What does he expect of it?
5. If sleep is symbolic (both literal and metaphorical), other details also may take on additional meaning. If so, how would you interpret (a) the ladder, (b) the season of the year, (c) the harvesting, (d) the "pane of glass" (10)? What denotations has the word "Essence" (7)?
6. How does the woodchuck's sleep differ from "just some human sleep" (42)?

Those Winter Sundays

Sundays too my father got up early
and put his clothes on in the blueblack cold,
then with cracked hands that ached
from labor in the weekday weather made
banked fires blaze. No one ever thanked him.   5

I'd wake and hear the cold splintering, breaking.
When the rooms were warm, he'd call,
and slowly I would rise and dress,
fearing the chronic angers of that house,

Speaking indifferently to him,   10
who had driven out the cold
and polished my good shoes as well.
What did I know, what did I know
of love's austere and lonely offices?

—ROBERT HAYDEN (1913–1980)

QUESTIONS

1. Vocabulary: *offices* (14).
2. What kind of imagery is central to the poem? How is this imagery related to the emotional concerns of the poem?
3. How do the subsidiary images relate to the central images?
4. From what point in time does the speaker view the subject matter of the poem? What has happened to him in the interval?

Electrical Storm

Dawn an unsympathetic yellow.
Cra-aack!—dry and light.
The house was really struck.
Crack! A tinny sound, like a dropped tumbler.
Tobias jumped in the window, got in bed—   5
silent, his eyes bleached white, his fur on end.
Personal and spiteful as a neighbor's child,
thunder began to bang and bump the roof.
One pink flash;
then hail, the biggest size of artificial pearls.   10
Dead-white, wax-white, cold—
diplomats' wives' favors
from an old moon party—
they lay in melting windrows
on the red ground until well after sunrise.   15
We got up to find the wiring fused,
no lights, a smell of saltpetre,
and the telephone dead.

The cat stayed in the warm sheets.
The Lent trees had shed all their petals: 20
wet, stuck, purple, among the dead-eye pearls.

—ELIZABETH BISHOP (1911–1979)

QUESTIONS

1. Vocabulary: *favors* (12); *windrows* (14); *saltpetre* (17).
2. Which images work to convey the experience of an "electrical storm"?
3. Discuss the way the language evokes the senses of sight, hearing, and smell.

The Snow Man

One must have a mind of winter
To regard the frost and the boughs
Of the pine-trees crusted with snow;

And have been cold a long time
To behold the junipers shagged with ice,   5
The spruces rough in the distant glitter

Of the January sun; and not to think
Of any misery in the sound of the wind,
In the sound of a few leaves,

Which is the sound of the land   10
Full of the same wind
That is blowing in the same bare place

For the listener, who listens in the snow,
And, nothing himself, beholds
Nothing that is not there and the nothing that is.   15

—WALLACE STEVENS (1879–1955)

QUESTIONS

1. The poem presents two kinds of "mind"—one that is cold and unmoved, the
   other emotional and responsive. What advantages does each of them have?
   Does the poem promote one or the other?
2. What emotional meanings are presented in the visual imagery in lines 2–3
   and 5–7?
3. What emotional meanings are presented in the auditory imagery in lines 8–11?
4. How is the snow man "nothing himself" (14)? What is the meaning of what he
   "beholds" (14–15)? Paraphrase the poem.

To Autumn

Season of mists and mellow fruitfulness,
    Close bosom-friend of the maturing sun;
Conspiring with him how to load and bless
    With fruit the vines that round the thatch-eaves run;

To bend with apples the mossed cottage-trees, 5
    And fill all fruit with ripeness to the core;
        To swell the gourd, and plump the hazel shells
With a sweet kernel; to set budding more,
    And still more, later flowers for the bees,
Until they think warm days will never cease, 10
    For summer has o'er-brimmed their clammy cells.

Who hath not seen thee oft amid thy store?
    Sometimes whoever seeks abroad may find
Thee sitting careless on a granary floor,
    Thy hair soft-lifted by the winnowing wind; 15
Or on a half-reaped furrow sound asleep,
    Drowsed with the fume of poppies, while thy hook
        Spares the next swath and all its twinèd flowers:
And sometimes like a gleaner thou dost keep
    Steady thy laden head across a brook; 20
Or by a cider-press, with patient look,
    Thou watchest the last oozings hours by hours.

Where are the songs of spring? Ay, where are they?
    Think not of them, thou hast thy music too,—
While barred clouds bloom the soft-dying day, 25
    And touch the stubble-plains with rosy hue;
Then in a wailful choir the small gnats mourn
    Among the river sallows, borne aloft
        Or sinking as the light wind lives or dies;
And full-grown lambs loud bleat from hilly bourn; 30
    Hedge-crickets sing; and now with treble soft
    The red-breast whistles from a garden-croft;
        And gathering swallows twitter in the skies.

—JOHN KEATS (1795–1821)

QUESTIONS

1. Vocabulary: *hook* (17), *barred* (25), *sallows* (28), *bourn* (30), *croft* (32).
2. How many kinds of imagery do you find in the poem? Give examples of each.
3. Are the images arranged haphazardly or are they carefully organized? In answering this question, consider (a) what aspect of autumn each stanza particularly concerns, (b) what kind of imagery dominates each stanza, and (c) what time of the season each stanza presents. Is there any progression in time of day?

4. What is autumn personified as in stanza 2? Is there any suggestion of personification in the other two stanzas?
5. Although the poem is primarily descriptive, what attitude toward transience and passing beauty is implicit in it?

SUGGESTIONS FOR WRITING

Analyze the imagery in one of the following poems, drawing some conclusions as to whether individual images function primarily to evoke vivid experience, convey emotion, or suggest ideas (see page 734). Be sure in each case to identify the sense reference of the imagery—visual, auditory, and so forth.

1. Dickinson, "A narrow Fellow in the Grass" (page 840).
2. Forché, "The Colonel" (page 997).
3. Kumin, "The Sound of Night" (page 913).
4. Plath, "Lady Lazarus" (page 781).
5. Roethke, "My Papa's Waltz" (page 1035).
6. Rogers, "Night and the Creation of Geography" (page 912).
7. Stevens, "Sunday Morning" (page 963).
8. Yeats, "The Wild Swans at Coole" (page 1051).

PRACTICE AP WRITING PROMPTS

Robert Browning, "Meeting at Night" (p. 733) and "Parting at Morning" (p. 734)

Robert Browning's "Parting at Morning" was written as a sequel to "Meeting at Night." Read both poems carefully, and write an essay in which you explain how the two poems, taken together, suggest the roles of love and "the world of men" in the speaker's life. Explain how literary devices such as imagery, personification, and point of view convey Browning's theme.

....

William Carlos Williams, "The Widow's Lament in Springtime" (p. 736)

"The Widow's Lament in Springtime" juxtaposes a widow's grief against the vividness of spring. Read the poem carefully. Then write an essay in which you show how poetic techniques such as imagery, metaphor, and concrete detail combine to illustrate the speaker's response to the coming of spring.

....

Adrienne Rich, "Living in Sin" (p. 738)

The expression "Living in Sin," a common euphemism when Adrienne Rich wrote this poem in 1955, denotes an unmarried couple living together. Rich's poem describes the routine of a woman in such a relationship. In a well-organized essay, analyze the writer's selection of details and choices of language, showing how they contribute to an understanding of the woman's complex feelings about her situation.

....

Robert Frost, "After Apple-Picking" (p. 740)

Read "After Apple-Picking" carefully, paying close attention to Robert Frost's imagery and to the intensity of the experience described in the poem. Then write a well-organized essay in which you show how the speaker conveys the literal experience of picking apples as well as deeper meanings.

....

Theodore Roethke, "My Papa's Waltz" (p. 1035) and Robert Hayden, "Those Winter Sundays" (p. 741)

Read "My Papa's Waltz" and "Those Winter Sundays." Then write an essay in which you compare the way each poet combines childhood memory and adult reflection to arrive at a moment of deep feeling. Consider literary elements such as imagery, rhythm, and detail.

....

CHAPTER FIVE

Figurative Language I

Simile, Metaphor, Personification, Apostrophe, Metonymy

> *Poetry provides the one permissible way of saying one thing and meaning another.*
>
> Robert Frost

Let us assume that your brother has just come in out of a rainstorm and you say to him, "Well, you're a pretty sight! Got slightly wet, didn't you?" And he replies, "Wet? I'm drowned! It's raining cats and dogs, and my raincoat's like a sieve!"

You and your brother probably understand each other well enough; yet if you examine this conversation literally, that is to say unimaginatively, you will find that you have been speaking nonsense. Actually you have been speaking figuratively. You have been saying less than what you mean, or more than what you mean, or the opposite of what you mean, or something other than what you mean. You did not mean that your brother was a pretty sight but that he was a wretched sight. You did not mean that he got slightly wet but that he got very wet. Your brother did not mean that he got drowned but that he got drenched. It was not raining cats and dogs; it was raining water. And your brother's raincoat is so unlike a sieve that not even a child would confuse them.

If you are familiar with Molière's play *Le Bourgeois Gentilhomme*, you will remember how delighted M. Jourdain is to discover that he has been speaking prose all his life. Many people might be equally surprised to learn that they have been speaking a kind of subpoetry all their lives. The difference between their figures of speech and the poet's is that theirs are probably worn and trite, the poet's fresh and original.

On first examination, it might seem absurd to say one thing and mean another. But we all do it—and with good reason. We do it because we can say what we want to say more vividly and forcefully by figures of speech than we can by saying it directly. And we can say more by figurative statement than we can by literal statement. Figures of speech offer another way of adding extra dimensions to language.

Broadly defined, a **figure of speech** is any way of saying something other than the ordinary way, and some rhetoricians have classified as many as 250 separate figures. For our purposes, however, a figure of speech is more narrowly definable as a way of saying one thing and meaning another, and we need to be concerned with no more than a dozen. **Figurative language**—language using figures of speech—is language that cannot be taken literally (or should not be taken literally only).

Simile and **metaphor** are both used as a means of comparing things that are essentially unlike. The only distinction between them is that in simile the comparison is *expressed* by the use of some word or phrase, such as *like, as, than, similar to, resembles,* or *seems*; in metaphor, the comparison is not expressed but is created when a figurative term is *substituted for* or *identified with* the literal term.

Harlem

What happens to a dream deferred?

Does it dry up
like a raisin in the sun?
Or fester like a sore—
And then run?   5
Does it stink like rotten meat?
Or crust and sugar over—
like a syrupy sweet?

Maybe it just sags
like a heavy load.   10

Or does it explode?

—LANGSTON HUGHES (1902–1967)

QUESTIONS

1. Of the six images, five are similes. Which is a metaphor? Comment on its position and effectiveness.
2. What specific denotation has the word "dream"? Since the poem does not reveal the contents of the dream, the poem is general in its implication. What happens to your understanding of it on learning that the poet was an African American?

Metaphors may take one of four forms, depending on whether the literal and figurative terms are respectively *named* or *implied*. In the first form of metaphor, as in simile, *both* the literal and figurative terms are *named*. In Williams's "The Widow's Lament in Springtime" (page 736), for example, the literal term is "sorrow" and the figurative term is "yard." In the second form, shown in Hughes's "Harlem," the literal term "dream" is *named* and the figurative term, bomb, is *implied*.

In the third form of metaphor, the literal term is *implied* and the figurative term is *named*. In the fourth form, *both* the literal *and* figurative terms are *implied*. The following poem exemplifies both forms:

It sifts from Leaden Sieves

It sifts from Leaden Sieves—
It powders all the Wood.
It fills with Alabaster Wool
The Wrinkles of the Road—

It makes an Even Face   5
Of Mountain, and of Plain—
Unbroken Forehead from the East
Unto the East again—

It reaches to the Fence—
It wraps it Rail by Rail   10
Till it is lost in Fleeces—
It deals Celestial Veil

To Stump, and Stack—and Stem—
A Summer's empty Room—
Acres of Joints, where Harvests were,   15
Recordless,° but for them—   unrecorded

It Ruffles Wrists of Posts
As Ankles of a Queen—
Then stills its Artisans—like Ghosts—
Denying they have been—   20

—EMILY DICKINSON (1830–1886)

QUESTIONS

1. This poem consists essentially of a series of metaphors with the same literal term identified only as "It." What is "It"?
2. In several of these metaphors the figurative term is named—"Alabaster Wool" (3), "Fleeces" (11), "Celestial Veil" (12). In two of them, however, the figurative term as well as the literal term is left unnamed. To what is "It" compared in lines 1–2? In lines 17–18?
3. Comment on the additional metaphorical expressions or complications contained in "Leaden Sieves" (1), "Alabaster Wool" (3), "Even Face" (5), "Unbroken Forehead" (7), "A Summer's empty Room" (14), "Artisans" (19).

Metaphors of the fourth form, as one might guess, are comparatively rare.

Using some examples from the poems discussed in this and the preceding chapters, the chart below provides a visual demonstration of the figures of comparison (simile and the four forms of metaphor).

		Poet	Literal Term	Figurative Term
Similes (*like, as, seems,* etc.)		Hughes	named dream	named raisin
Metaphors (*is, are,* etc.)	**Form 1**	Williams	named sorrow	named yard
	Form 2	Hughes	named dream	implied bomb
	Form 3	Dickinson	implied it [snow]	named wool
	Form 4	Dickinson	implied it [snow]	implied [flour] sifts

Personification consists of giving the attributes of a human being to an animal, an object, or a concept. It is really a subtype of metaphor, an implied comparison in which the figurative term of the comparison is always a human being. When Sylvia Plath makes a mirror speak and think (page 915), she is personifying an object. When Keats describes autumn as a harvester "sitting careless on a granary floor" or "on a half-reaped furrow sound asleep" (page 743), he is personifying a season. Personifications differ in the degree to which they ask the reader actually to visualize the literal term in human form. In Keats's comparison, we are asked to make a complete identification of autumn with a human being. In Sylvia Plath's, though the mirror speaks and thinks, we continue to visualize it as a mirror. In Browning's reference to "the startled little waves" (page 733), a personification is barely suggested; we would make a mistake if we tried to visualize the waves in human form or even, really, to think of them as having human emotions.

The Author to Her Book

Thou ill-formed offspring of my feeble brain,
Who after birth did'st by my side remain,
Till snatched from thence by friends, less wise than true,
Who thee abroad exposed to public view;
Made thee in rags, halting, to the press to trudge,   5
Where errors were not lessened, all may judge.
At thy return my blushing was not small,
My rambling brat (in print) should mother call;
I cast thee by as one unfit for light,
Thy visage was so irksome in my sight;   10
Yet being mine own, at length affection would
Thy blemishes amend, if so I could:
I washed thy face, but more defects I saw,
And rubbing off a spot, still made a flaw.
I stretched thy joints to make thee even feet,   15
Yet still thou run'st more hobbling than is meet;
In better dress to trim thee was my mind,
But nought save homespun cloth in the house I find.
In this array, 'mongst vulgars may'st thou roam;
In critics' hands beware thou dost not come;   20
And take thy way where yet thou are not known.
If for thy Father asked, say thou had'st none;
And for thy Mother, she alas is poor,
Which caused her thus to send thee out of door.

—ANNE BRADSTREET (1612?–1672)

QUESTIONS

1. Vocabulary: *halting* (5), *feet* (15), *meet* (16), *vulgars* (19). Lines 3–4 refer to the fact that Bradstreet's book *The Tenth Muse* was published in 1650 without her permission.

2. The poem is an extended personification addressing her book as a child. What similarities does the speaker find between a child and a book of poems? What does she plan to do now that her child has been put on public display?
3. Trace the developing attitudes of the speaker toward the child/book. Why does she instruct the child to deny it has a father (22)?

The various figures of speech blend into each other, and it is sometimes difficult to classify a specific example as definitely metaphor or simile, symbol or allegory, understatement or irony, irony or paradox (some of these topics will be examined in the next two chapters). Often, a given example may exemplify two or more figures at once. In Wordsworth's "The world is too much with us" (page 727), when the winds are described as calm, "like sleeping flowers," the flowers function as part of a simile and are also personified as something that can sleep. The important consideration in reading poetry is not that we classify figures but that we construe them correctly.

Closely related to personification is **apostrophe,** which consists of addressing someone absent or dead or something nonhuman as if that person or thing were present and alive and could reply to what is being said. The speaker in A. E. Housman's "To an Athlete Dying Young" (page 1009) apostrophizes a dead runner. William Blake apostrophizes a tiger throughout his famous poem (page 835) but does not otherwise personify it. In the poem printed below, Keats apostrophizes *and* personifies a star, as he does with autumn in "To Autumn" (page 743).

Personification and apostrophe are both ways of giving life and immediacy to one's language, but since neither requires great imaginative power on the part of the poet—apostrophe especially does not—they may degenerate into mere mannerisms and occur as often in bad and mediocre poetry as in good, a fact that Shakespeare parodies in Bottom's apostrophe to night in *A Midsummer Night's Dream* (Act 5, scene 1):

O grim-looked night! O night with hue so black!
O night, which ever art when day is not!
O night, O night! Alack, alack, alack.

We need to distinguish between their effective use and their merely conventional use.

Bright Star

Bright star, would I were steadfast as thou art—
    Not in lone splendor hung aloft the night,
And watching, with eternal lids apart,
    Like nature's patient, sleepless Eremite,°   hermit

The moving waters at their priestlike task 5
    Of pure ablution° round earth's human shores,   cleansing
Or gazing on the new soft fallen mask
    Of snow upon the mountains and the moors—
No—yet still steadfast, still unchangeable,
    Pillowed upon my fair love's ripening breast, 10
To feel forever its soft fall and swell,
    Awake forever in a sweet unrest,
Still, still to hear her tender-taken breath,
And so live ever—or else swoon to death.

—JOHN KEATS (1795–1821)

QUESTIONS

1. The speaker longs to be as "steadfast" (1) as the star, yet lines 2–8 express his wish to be unlike the star in important ways. What are the qualities of the star that he would not want to emulate? Why would these be wrong for him in his situation?
2. Explore the apparent contradictions in the phrase "sweet unrest" (12). How do they anticipate the final line?
3. The speaker repeats "still" (13). What relevant denotations does the word evoke, and how does the repetition add intensity and meaning to this apostrophe?
4. Why is an apostrophe more effective here than a description of the star that does not address it?

In contrast to the preceding figures that compare *unlike* things are two figures that rest on congruences or correspondences. **Synecdoche** (the use of the part for the whole) and **metonymy** (the use of something closely related for the thing actually meant) are alike in that both substitute some signifi cant detail or quality of an experience for the experience itself. Housman's Terence uses synecdoche when he declares that "malt does more than Milton can/To justify God's ways to man" (page 1007), for "malt" means beer or ale, of which malt is an essential ingredient. On the other hand, when Terence advises "fellows whom it hurts to think" to "Look into the pewter pot/To see the world as the world's not," he is using metonymy, for by "pew ter pot" he means the ale *in* the pot, not the pot itself, and by "world" he means human life and the conditions under which it is lived. Robert Frost uses metonymy in "'Out, Out—'" (page 811) when he describes an injured boy holding up his cut hand "as if to keep/The life from spilling," for liter ally he means to keep the blood from spilling. In each case, however, the poem gains in compactness, vividness, or meaning. Frost tells us both that the boy's hand is bleeding and that his life is in danger.

Many synecdoches and metonymies, of course, like many metaphors, have become so much a part of the language that they no longer strike us as figurative; this is the case with *redhead* for a red-haired person, *hands* for manual workers, *highbrow* for a sophisticate, *tongues* for languages, and a boiling *kettle* for the water *in* the kettle. Such figures are often called *dead metaphors* (where the word *metaphor* is itself a metonymy for all figurative speech). Synecdoche and metonymy are so much alike that it is hardly worthwhile to distinguish between them, and the latter term is increasingly used for both. In this book, *metonymy* will be used for both figures—that is, for any figure in which a part or something closely related is substituted for the thing literally meant.

We said at the beginning of this chapter that figurative language often provides a more effective means of saying what we mean than does direct statement. What are some of the reasons for that effectiveness?

First, figurative language affords us imaginative pleasure. Imagination might be described in one sense as that faculty or ability of the mind that proceeds by sudden leaps from one point to another, that goes up a stair by leaping in one jump from the bottom to the top rather than by climbing up one step at a time.* The mind takes delight in these sudden leaps, in seeing likenesses between unlike things. We have all probably taken pleasure in staring into a fire and seeing castles and cities and armies in it, or in looking into the clouds and shaping them into animals or faces, or in seeing a man in the moon. We name our plants and flowers after fancied resemblances: jack-in-the-pulpit, baby's breath, Queen Anne's lace. Figures of speech are therefore satisfying in themselves, providing us with a source of pleasure in the exercise of the imagination.

Second, figures of speech are a way of bringing additional imagery into verse, of making the abstract concrete, of making poetry more sensuous. When Tennyson's eagle falls "like a thunderbolt" (page 682), his swooping down for his prey is charged with energy, speed, and power; the simile also recalls that the Greek god Zeus was accompanied by an eagle and armed with lightning. When Emily Dickinson compares poetry to prancing coursers (page 721), she objectifies imaginative and rhythmical qualities by presenting them in visual terms. When Robert Browning compares the crisping waves to "fiery ringlets" (page 733), he starts with one image and transforms it into three. Figurative language is a way of augmenting the sense appeal of poetry.

Third, figures of speech are a way of adding emotional intensity to otherwise merely informative statements and of conveying attitudes along with information. If we say, "So-and-so is a rat" or "My feet are killing me," our meaning is as much emotional as informative. When Philip Larkin's pathetic escapist metaphorically compares books to "a load of crap"

---

*It is also the faculty of mind that is able to "picture" or "image" absent objects as if they were present. It was with imagination in this sense that we were concerned in the chapter on imagery.

(page 702), the vulgar language not only expresses his distaste for reading, but intensifies the characterization of him as a man whose intellectual growth was stunted. As this example shows, the use of figures may be a poet's means of revealing the characteristics of a speaker—*how* he or she expresses a thought will define the attitudes or qualities as much as *what* that thought is. When Wilfred Owen compares a soldier caught in a gas attack to a man drowning under a green sea (page 684), he conveys a feeling of despair and suffocation as well as a visual image.

Fourth, figures of speech are an effective means of concentration, a way of saying much in brief compass. Like words, they may be multidimensional. Consider, for instance, the merits of comparing life to a candle, as Shakespeare does in a passage from *Macbeth* (pages 812–813). Life is like a candle in that it begins and ends in darkness; in that while it burns, it gives off light and energy, is active and colorful; in that it gradually consumes itself, gets shorter and shorter; in that it can be snuffed out at any moment; in that it is brief at best, burning only for a short duration. Possibly your imagination can suggest other similarities. But at any rate, Macbeth's compact, metaphorical description of life as a "brief candle" suggests certain truths about life that would require dozens of words to state in literal language. At the same time it makes the abstract concrete, provides imaginative pleasure, and adds a degree of emotional intensity.

It is as important, when analyzing and discussing a poem, to decide what it is that the figures accomplish as it is to identify them. Seeing a personification or a simile should lead to analytical questions: *What use is being made of this figure? How does it contribute to the experience of the poem?*

If we are to read poetry well, we must be able to respond to figurative language. Every use of figurative language involves a risk of misinterpretation, though the risk is well worth taking. For the person who can interpret the figure, the dividends are immense. Fortunately all people have imagination to some degree, and imagination can be cultivated. Through practice, one's ability to interpret figures of speech can be enhanced.

EXERCISE

Decide whether the following quotations are literal or figurative. If figurative, identify the figure, explain what is being compared to what, and explain the appropriateness of the comparison. EXAMPLE:"Talent is a cistern; genius is a fountain." ANSWER: Metaphor. Talent = cistern; genius = fountain. Talent exists in finite supply, and can be used up. Genius is inexhaustible, ever renewing.

1. O tenderly the haughty day
   Fills his blue urn with fire.   —*Ralph Waldo Emerson*
2. It is with words as with sunbeams—the more
   they are condensed, the deeper they burn.   —*Robert Southey*

3. Joy and Temperance and Repose
   Slam the door on the doctor's nose.   —*Anonymous*
4. The pen is mightier than the sword.   —*Edward Bulwer-Lytton*
5. The strongest oaths are straw
   To the fire i' the blood.   —*William Shakespeare*
6. The Cambridge ladies ... live in furnished souls.   —*E. E. Cummings*
7. Dorothy's eyes, with their long brown lashes,
   looked very much like her mother's.   —*Laetitia Johnson*
8. The tawny-hided desert crouches watching her.   —*Francis Thompson*
9. Let us eat and drink, for tomorrow we shall die.   —*Isaiah 22.13*
10. Let us eat and drink, for tomorrow
    we may die.   —*Common misquotation of the above*

REVIEWING CHAPTER FIVE

1. Distinguish between language used literally and language used figuratively, and consider why poetry is often figurative.
2. Define the figures of comparison (simile and metaphor, personification and apostrophe), and rank them in order of their emotional effectiveness.
3. Define the figures of congruence or correspondence (synecdoche and metonymy).
4. Review the four major contributions of figurative language.

Traveling Light

I'm only leaving you
for a handful of days,
but it feels as though
I'll be gone forever—
the way the door closes   5

behind me with such solidity,
the way my suitcase

carries everything
I'd need for an eternity
of traveling light.   10

I've left my hotel number
on your desk, instructions
about the dog
and heating dinner. But
like the weather front   15

they warn is on its way
with its switchblades
of wind and ice,
our lives have minds
of their own.   20

—LINDA PASTAN (B. 1932)

QUESTIONS

1. To whom does the speaker address the poem?
2. Does the title, "Traveling Light," introduce an extended metaphor? Why or why not?
3. Discuss the function of the term "switchblades" (17). Is this an example of figurative language?

I taste a liquor never brewed

I taste a liquor never brewed—
From Tankards scooped in Pearl—
Not all the Vats upon the Rhine
Yield such an Alcohol!

Inebriate of Air—am I—   5
And Debauchee of Dew—
Reeling—thro endless summer days—
From inns of Molten Blue—

When "Landlords" turn the drunken Bee
Out of the Foxglove's door—   10
When Butterflies—renounce their "drams"—
I shall but drink the more!

Till Seraphs swing their snowy Hats—
And Saints—to windows run—
To see the little Tippler   15
Leaning against the—Sun—

—EMILY DICKINSON (1830–1886)

QUESTIONS

1. Vocabulary: *debauchee* (6), *foxglove* (10).
2. In this **extended metaphor,** what is being compared to alcoholic intoxication? The clues are given in the variety of "liquors" named or implied—"Air" (5), "Dew" (6), and the nectar upon which birds and butterflies feed.
3. What figurative meanings have the following details: "Tankards scooped in Pearl" (2), "inns of Molten Blue" (8), "snowy Hats" (13)?
4. The last stanza creates a stereotypical street scene in which neighbors observe the behavior of a drunkard. What do comic drunks lean against in the street? What unexpected attitude do the seraphs and saints display?

Metaphors

I'm a riddle in nine syllables,
An elephant, a ponderous house,
A melon strolling on two tendrils.
O red fruit, ivory, fine timbers!
This loaf's big with its yeasty rising.   5
Money's new-minted in this fat purse.
I'm a means, a stage, a cow in calf.
I've eaten a bag of green apples,
Boarded the train there's no getting off.

—SYLVIA PLATH (1932–1963)

QUESTIONS

1. Like its first metaphor, this poem is a riddle to be solved by identifying the literal terms of its metaphors. After you have identified the speaker ("riddle," "elephant," "house," "melon," "stage," "cow"), identify the literal meanings of the related metaphors ("syllables," "tendrils," "fruit," "ivory," "timbers," "loaf," "yeasty rising," "money," "purse," "train"). How do you interpret line 8?
2. How does the form of the poem relate to its content? Is this poem a complaint?

Toads

Why should I let the toad *work*
        Squat on my life?
Can't I use my wit as a pitchfork
        And drive the brute off?

Six days of the week it soils   5
        With its sickening poison—
Just for paying a few bills!
        That's out of proportion.

Lots of folk live on their wits:
    Lecturers, lispers,   10
Losels,° loblolly-men,° louts—   scoundrels; bumpkins
    They don't end as paupers;

Lots of folk live up lanes
    With fires in a bucket,
Eat windfalls and tinned sardines—   15
    They seem to like it.

Their nippers° have got bare feet,   children
    Their unspeakable wives
Are skinny as whippets—and yet
    No one actually *starves.*   20

Ah, were I courageous enough
    To shout *Stuff your pension!*
But I know, all too well, that's the stuff
    That dreams are made on;

For something sufficiently toad-like   25
    Squats in me, too;
Its hunkers° are heavy as hard luck,   haunches
    And cold as snow,

And will never allow me to blarney
    My way to getting   30
The fame and the girl and the money
    All at one sitting.

I don't say, one bodies the other
    One's spiritual truth;
But I do say it's hard to lose either,   35
    When you have both.

—PHILIP LARKIN (1922–1985)

QUESTIONS

1. The poem describes two "toads." Where is each located? How are they described? What are the antecedents of the pronouns "one" and "the other/One's" (33–34) respectively?
2. What characteristics in common have the people mentioned in lines 9–12? Those mentioned in lines 13–20?

3. Explain the pun in lines 22–23 and the literary allusion it leads into. (If you don't recognize the allusion, check Shakespeare's *The Tempest*, Act 4, scene 1, lines 156–58.)
4. The first "toad" is explicitly identified as *"work"* (1). The literal term for the second "toad" is not named. Why not? What do you take it to be?
5. What kind of person is the speaker? What are his attitudes toward work?

A Valediction: Forbidding Mourning

As virtuous men pass mildly away,
    And whisper to their souls to go,
While some of their sad friends do say,
    The breath goes now, and some say, no:

So let us melt, and make no noise,   5
    No tear-floods, nor sigh-tempests move;
'Twere profanation of our joys
    To tell the laity our love.

Moving of th' earth brings harms and fears,
    Men reckon what it did and meant,   10
But trepidation of the spheres,
    Though greater far, is innocent.

Dull sublunary lovers' love
    (Whose soul is sense) cannot admit
Absence, because it doth remove   15
    Those things which elemented it.

But we by a love so much refined,
    That ourselves know not what it is,
Inter-assurèd of the mind,
    Care less, eyes, lips, and hands to miss.   20

Our two souls therefore, which are one,
    Though I must go, endure not yet
A breach, but an expansion,
    Like gold to airy thinness beat.

If they be two, they are two so   25
    As stiff twin compasses are two;
Thy soul, the fixed foot, makes no show
    To move, but doth, if th' other do.

And though it in the center sit,
    Yet when the other far doth roam,   30
It leans, and hearkens after it,
    And grows erect, as that comes home.

Such wilt thou be to me, who must
    Like th' other foot, obliquely run;
Thy firmness makes my circle just,   35
    And makes me end, where I begun.

— JOHN DONNE (1572–1631)

QUESTIONS

1. Vocabulary: *valediction* (title), *mourning* (title), *profanation* (7), *laity* (8), *trepidation* (11), *innocent* (12), *sublunary* (13), *elemented* (16). Line 11 is a reference to the spheres of the Ptolemaic cosmology, whose movements caused no such disturbance as does a movement of the earth—that is, an earthquake.
2. Is the speaker in the poem about to die? Or about to leave on a journey? (The answer may be found in a careful analysis of the simile in the last three stanzas and by noticing that the idea of dying in stanza 1 is introduced in a simile.)
3. The poem is organized around a contrast of two kinds of lovers: the "laity" (8) and, as their implied opposite, the priesthood. Are these terms literal or meta-phorical? What is the essential difference between their two kinds of love? How, according to the speaker, does their behavior differ when they must separate from each other? What is the motivation of the speaker in this "valediction"?
4. Find and explain three similes and one metaphor used to describe the parting of true lovers. The figure in the last three stanzas is one of the most famous in English literature. Demonstrate its appropriateness by obtaining a drawing com-pass or by using two pencils to imitate the two legs.

To His Coy Mistress

    Had we but world enough, and time,
This coyness, lady, were no crime.
We would sit down, and think which way
To walk, and pass our long love's day.
Thou by the Indian Ganges' side   5
Shouldst rubies find; I by the tide
Of Humber would complain. I would
Love you ten years before the Flood,
And you should, if you please, refuse
Till the conversion of the Jews.   10
My vegetable love should grow

Vaster than empires, and more slow;
An hundred years should go to praise
Thine eyes, and on thy forehead gaze;
Two hundred to adore each breast,   15
But thirty thousand to the rest;
An age at least to every part,
And the last age should show your heart.
For, lady, you deserve this state,
Nor would I love at lower rate.   20
    But at my back I always hear
Time's wingèd chariot hurrying near;
And yonder all before us lie
Deserts of vast eternity.
Thy beauty shall no more be found,   25
Nor, in thy marble vault, shall sound
My echoing song; then worms shall try
That long-preserved virginity,
And your quaint honor turn to dust,
And into ashes all my lust: 30
The grave's a fine and private place,
But none, I think, do there embrace.
    Now therefore, while the youthful hue
Sits on thy skin like morning dew,
And while thy willing soul transpires   35
At every pore with instant fires,
Now let us sport us while we may,
And now, like amorous birds of prey,
Rather at once our time devour
Than languish in his slow-chapped power.   40
Let us roll all our strength and all
Our sweetness up into one ball,
And tear our pleasures with rough strife
Thorough° the iron gates of life.   *through*
Thus, though we cannot make our sun   45
Stand still, yet we will make him run.

—ANDREW MARVELL (1621–1678)

QUESTIONS

1. Vocabulary: *coy* (title), *Humber* (7), *transpires* (35). "Mistress" (title) has the now archaic meaning of *sweetheart;* "slow-chapped" (40) derives from *chap,* meaning *jaw.*
2. What is the speaker urging his sweetheart to do? Why is she being "coy"?

3. Outline the speaker's argument in three sentences that begin with the words *If*, *But*, and *Therefore*. Is the argument valid?
4. Explain the appropriateness of "vegetable love" (11). What simile in the third section contrasts with it and how? What image in the third section contrasts with the distance between the Ganges and the Humber? Of what would the speaker be "complaining" by the Humber (7)?
5. Explain the figures in lines 22, 24, and 40 and their implications.
6. Explain the last two lines. For what is "sun" a metonymy?
7. Is this poem principally about love or about time? If the latter, what might making love represent? What philosophy is the poet advancing here?

SUGGESTIONS FOR WRITING

1. Robert Frost has said that "poetry is what evaporates from all translations." Why might this be true? How much of a word can be translated?

2. Ezra Pound has defined great literature as "simply language charged with meaning to the utmost possible degree." Would this be a good definition of poetry? The word "charged" is roughly equivalent to *filled*. Why is "charged" a better word in Pound's definition?

3. In each of the following, the title announces a metaphor that dominates the poem. Write an essay describing the pair of objects and/or concepts compared in one of these poems. How does the figurative language help to communicate an idea with greater vividness or force than an ordinary, prosaic description could have achieved?
   a. Stevens, "The Snow Man" (page 743).
   b. Larkin, "Toads" (page 758).
   c. Atwood, "Landcrab" (page 910).
   d. Herbert, "The Pulley" (page 918).
   e. Collins, "Weighing the Dog" (page 987).
   f. Dickinson, "A Clock stopped" (page 990).

PRACTICE AP WRITING PROMPTS ▬▬▬▬

John Donne, "A Valediction: Forbidding Mourning" (p. 760) and William Shakespeare, "Let me not to the marriage of true minds" (p. 1037)

John Donne's "A Valediction: Forbidding Mourning" and William Shakespeare's Sonnet 116, "Let me not to the marriage of true minds," both try to define true love. Read the two poems with care. Then write an essay in which you compare the way both poets use poetry itself to develop their ideas about love. You may wish to focus on such elements as figurative language, poetic form, and word choice.

Andrew Marvell, "To His Coy Mistress" (p. 761)

Andrew Marvell's "To His Coy mistress" is a well-known carpe diem ("seize the day") poem in which the speaker tries to seduce a woman to whom the poem is addressed. Read the poem carefully. Then write a well-organized essay in which you analyze the speaker's argument, showing how such literary elements as simile, allusion, and hyperbole help support his case.

CHAPTER SIX

Figurative Language 2

Symbol, Allegory

The Road Not Taken

Two roads diverged in a yellow wood,
And sorry I could not travel both
And be one traveler, long I stood
And looked down one as far as I could
To where it bent in the undergrowth;   5

Then took the other, as just as fair,
And having perhaps the better claim,
Because it was grassy and wanted wear;
Though as for that the passing there
Had worn them really about the same,   10

And both that morning equally lay
In leaves no step had trodden black.
Oh, I kept the first for another day!
Yet knowing how way leads on to way,
I doubted if I should ever come back.   15

I shall be telling this with a sigh
Somewhere ages and ages hence:
Two roads diverged in a wood, and I—

I took the one less traveled by,
And that has made all the difference.   20

—ROBERT FROST (1874–1963)

QUESTIONS

1. Does the speaker feel that he has made the wrong choice in taking the road "less traveled by" (19)? If not, why will he "sigh" (16)? What does he regret?
2. Why will the choice between two roads that seem very much alike make such a big difference many years later?

A **symbol** may be roughly defined as something that means *more* than what it is. "The Road Not Taken," for instance, concerns a choice made between two roads by a person out walking in the woods. He would like to explore both roads. He tells himself that he will explore one and then come back and explore the other, but he knows that he will probably be unable to do so. By the last stanza, however, we realize that the poem is about something more than the choice of paths in a wood, for that choice would be relatively unimportant, whereas this choice, the speaker believes, is one that will make a great difference in his life and is one that he will remember "with a sigh ... ages and ages hence." We must interpret his choice of a road as a symbol for any choice in life between alternatives that appear almost equally attractive but will result through the years in a large difference in the kind of experience one knows.

Image, metaphor, and symbol shade into each other and are sometimes difficult to distinguish. In general, however, an image means only what it is; the figurative term in a metaphor means something other than what it is; and a symbol means what it is and something more, too. A symbol, that is, functions literally and figuratively at the same time.* If I say that a shaggy brown dog was rubbing its back against a white picket fence, I am talking about nothing but a dog (and a picket fence) and am therefore presenting an image. If I say, "Some dirty dog stole my wallet at the party," I am not talking about a dog at all and am therefore using a metaphor. But if I say, "You can't teach an old dog new tricks," I am talking not only about dogs but about living creatures of any species and am therefore speaking symbolically. Images, of course, do not cease to be images when they become incorporated in metaphors or symbols. If we are discussing

---

* This account does not hold for nonliterary symbols such as the letters of the alphabet and algebraic signs (the symbol ∞ for infinity or = for equals). With these, the symbol is meaningless except as it stands for something else, and the connection between the sign and what it stands for is purely arbitrary.

the sensuous qualities of "The Road Not Taken," we should refer to the two leaf-strewn roads in the yellow wood as an image; if we are discussing the significance of the poem, we talk about the roads as symbols.

The symbol is the richest and, at the same time, the most difficult of the poetic figures. Both its richness and its difficulty result from its imprecision. Although the poet may pin down the meaning of a symbol to something fairly definite and precise, more often the symbol is so general in its meaning that it can suggest a great variety of specific meanings. It is like an opal that flashes out different colors when slowly turned in the light. "The Road Not Taken," for instance, concerns some choice in life, but what choice? Was it a choice of profession? A choice of residence? A choice of mate? It might be any, all, or none of these. We cannot determine what particular choice the poet had in mind, if any, and it is not important that we do so. It is enough if we see in the poem an expression of regret that the possibilities of life experience are so sharply limited. The speaker in the poem would have liked to explore both roads, but he could explore only one. The person with a craving for life, whether satisfied or dissatisfied with the choices he has made, will always long for the realms of experience that he had to forgo. Because the symbol is a rich one, the poem suggests other meanings too. It affirms a belief in the possibility of choice and says something about the nature of choice—how each choice narrows the range of possible future choices, so that we make our lives as we go, both freely choosing and being determined by past choices. Though not a philosophical poem, it obliquely comments on the issue of free will and determinism and indicates the poet's own position. It can do all these things, concretely and compactly, by its use of an effective symbol.

Symbols vary in the degree of identification and definition given them by their authors. In this poem Frost forces us to interpret the choice of roads symbolically by the degree of importance he gives it in the last stanza. Sometimes poets are much more specific in identifying their symbols. Sometimes they do not identify them at all. Consider, for instance, the next two poems.

A Noiseless Patient Spider

A noiseless patient spider,
I marked where on a little promontory it stood isolated,
Marked how to explore the vacant vast surrounding,
It launched forth filament, filament, filament, out of itself,
Ever unreeling them, ever tirelessly speeding them.   5
And you, O my soul where you stand,

Surrounded, detached, in measureless oceans of space,
Ceaselessly musing, venturing, throwing, seeking the spheres
    to connect them,
Till the bridge you will need be formed, till the ductile
    anchor hold,
Till the gossamer thread you fling catch somewhere,
    O my soul.   10

—WALT WHITMAN (1819–1892)

In the first stanza, the speaker describes a spider's apparently tireless effort to attach its thread to some substantial support so that it can begin constructing a web. The speaker reveals his attentive interest by the hinted personification of the spider, and his sympathy with it is expressed in the overstatement of size and distance—he is trying to perceive the world as a spider sees it from a "promontory" surrounded by vast space. He even attributes a human motive to the spider: exploration, rather than instinctive web-building. Nevertheless, the first stanza is essentially literal—the close observation of an actual spider at its task. In the second stanza the speaker explicitly interprets the symbolic meaning of what he has observed: his soul (personified by apostrophe and by the capabilities assigned to it) is like the spider in its constant striving. But the soul's purpose is to find spiritual or intellectual certainties in the vast universe it inhabits. The symbolic meaning is richer than a mere comparison; although a spider's actual purpose is limited to its instinctive drives, the human soul strives for much more, in a much more complex "surrounding." And, of course, the result of the soul's symbolized striving is much more open-ended than is the attempt of a spider to spin a web, as the paradoxical language ("Surrounded, detached," "ductile anchor") implies. *Can* the human soul connect the celestial spheres?

QUESTIONS

1. In "Harlem" (page 748) Langston Hughes compares a frustrated dream to a bomb. Whitman compares the striving human soul to a spider. Why is Hughes's comparison a metaphor and Whitman's a symbol? What additional comparison does Whitman make to the soul's quest? What figure of speech is it?
2. In what ways are the spider and the soul contrasted? What do the contrasts contribute to the meaning of the symbol?
3. Can the questing soul represent human actions other than the search for spiritual certainties?

The Sick Rose

O Rose, thou art sick!
The invisible worm
That flies in the night,
In the howling storm,
Has found out thy bed
Of crimson joy,
And his dark secret love
Does thy life destroy.

—WILLIAM BLAKE (1757–1827)

QUESTIONS

1. What figures of speech do you find in the poem in addition to symbol? How do they contribute to its force or meaning?
2. Several symbolic interpretations of this poem are given below. Can you think of others?
3. Should symbolic meanings be sought for the night and the storm? If so, what meanings would you suggest?

In "A Noiseless Patient Spider" the symbolic meaning of the spider is identified and named. By contrast, in "The Sick Rose" no meanings are explicitly indicated for the rose and the worm. Indeed, we are not *compelled* to assign them specific meanings. The poem might literally be read as being about a rose that has been attacked on a stormy night by a cankerworm.

The organization of "The Sick Rose" is so rich, however, and its language so powerful that the rose and the worm refuse to remain *merely* a flower and an insect. The rose, apostrophized and personified in the first line, has traditionally been a symbol of feminine beauty and love, as well as of sensual pleasures. "Bed" can refer to a woman's bed as well as to a flower bed. "Crimson joy" suggests the intense pleasure of passionate lovemaking as well as the brilliant beauty of a red flower. The "dark secret love" of the "invisible worm" is more strongly suggestive of a concealed or illicit love affair than of the feeding of a cankerworm on a plant, though it fits that too. For all these reasons the rose almost immediately suggests a woman and the worm her secret lover—and the poem suggests the corruption of innocent but physical love by concealment and deceit. But the possibilities do not stop there. The worm is a common symbol or metonymy for death; and for readers steeped in Milton (as Blake was) it recalls the "undying worm" of *Paradise Lost*, Milton's metaphor for the snake (or Satan in the form of a snake) that tempted Eve. Meanings multiply also for the reader who is familiar with Blake's other writings. Thus, "The Sick Rose" has been variously interpreted as referring to the destruction of joyous physical love by jealousy, deceit, concealment, or the possessive instinct; of innocence by experience; of humanity by Satan; of imagination and joy by analytic reason; of life by death. We cannot say what specifically the poet had in mind, nor need we do so. A symbol defines an *area* of meaning, and any interpretation that falls within that area is permissible. In Blake's poem the rose stands for something beautiful, or desirable, or good. The worm stands for some corrupting agent. Within these limits, the meaning is largely "open." And because the meaning is open, the reader is justified in bringing personal experience to its interpretation. Blake's poem, for instance, might remind someone of a gifted friend whose promise has been destroyed by drug addiction.

Between the extremes exemplified by "A Noiseless Patient Spider" and "The Sick Rose," a poem may exercise all degrees of control over the range and meaning of its symbolism. Consider another example:

Digging

Between my finger and my thumb
The squat pen rests; snug as a gun.

Under my window, a clean rasping sound
When the spade sinks into gravelly ground:
My father, digging. I look down   5

Till his straining rump among the flowerbeds
Bends low, comes up twenty years away
Stooping in rhythm through potato drills
Where he was digging.

The coarse boot nestled on the lug, the shaft   10
Against the inside knee was levered firmly.
He rooted out tall tops, buried the bright edge deep
To scatter new potatoes that we picked
Loving their cool hardness in our hands.

By God, the old man could handle a spade.   15
Just like his old man.

My grandfather cut more turf in a day
Than any other man on Toner's bog.

Once I carried him milk in a bottle
Corked sloppily with paper. He straightened up   20
To drink it, then fell to right away
Nicking and slicing neatly, heaving sods
Over his shoulder, going down and down
For the good turf. Digging.

The cold smell of potato mould, the squelch and slap   25
Of soggy peat, the curt cuts of an edge
Through living roots awaken in my head.
But I've no spade to follow men like them.

Between my finger and my thumb
The squat pen rests.   30
I'll dig with it.

—SEAMUS HEANEY (1939–2013)

QUESTIONS

1. Vocabulary: *drills* (8), *fell to* (21). In Ireland, "turf" (17) is a block of peat dug from a bog; when dried, it is used as fuel.
2. What emotional responses are evoked by the imagery?

On the literal level, this poem presents a writer who interrupts himself to have a look at his father digging in a flower garden below his window. He is reminded of his father twenty years earlier digging potatoes for harvesting, and by that memory he is drawn farther back to his grandfather digging peat from a bog for fuel. The memories are vivid and appealing and rich in imagery, but the writer is not like his forebears; he has "no spade to follow" their examples. And so, with a trace of regret, he decides that his writing will have to be his substitute for their manual tasks.

But the title and the emphasis on varieties of the same task carried out in several different ways over a span of generations alert the reader to the need to discover the further significance of this literal statement. The last line is metaphorical, comparing digging to writing (and thus is itself not symbolic, for on a literal level one cannot dig with a pen). The metaphor, however, suggesting that the writer will commit himself to exploring the kinds of memories in this poem, invites an interpretation of the literal forms of digging. We notice then that the father has been involved in two sorts— the practical, backbreaking task of digging up potatoes to be gathered by the children, and twenty years later the relatively easy chore of digging in flowerbeds so as to encourage the growth of ornamental plants. There is a progression represented in the father's activities, from the necessary and arduous earlier life to the leisurely growing of flowers. Farther back in time, the grandfather's labors were deeper, heavier, and more essential, cutting and digging the material that would be used for heating and cooking—cooking potatoes, we should assume. The grandfather digs deeper and deeper, always in quest of the best peat, "the good turf."

Symbolically, then, digging has meanings that relate to basic needs—for warmth, for sustenance, for beauty, and for the personal satisfaction of doing a job well. In the concluding metaphor, another basic need is implied, the need to remember and confront one's origins, to find oneself in a continuum of meaningful activities, to assert the relevance and importance of one's vocation. And it is not coincidental that an Irish poet should find symbolic meanings in a confluence of Irish materials—from peat bogs to potatoes to poets and writers, that long-beleaguered island has asserted its special and distinct identity. Nor is it coincidental that Heaney selected this to be the opening poem in his first book of poetry: "Digging" is what his poetry does.

Meanings ray out from a symbol, like the corona around the sun or like connotations around a richly suggestive word. But the very fact that a symbol may be so rich in meanings requires that we use the greatest tact in its interpretation. Although Blake's "The Sick Rose" might, because of personal association, remind us of a friend destroyed by drug addiction, it would be unwise to say that Blake uses the rose to symbolize a gifted person succumbing to drug addiction, for this interpretation is private, idiosyncratic, and narrow. The poem allows it, but does not itself suggest it.

Moreover, we should never assume that because the meaning of a symbol is more or less open, we may make it mean anything we choose. We would be wrong, for instance, in interpreting the choice in "The Road Not Taken" as some choice between good and evil, for the poem tells us that the two roads are much alike and that both lie "In leaves no step had trodden black." Whatever the choice is, it is a choice between two goods. Whatever our interpretation of a symbolic poem, it must be tied firmly to the facts of the poem. We must not let loose of the string and let our imaginations go ballooning up among the clouds. Because the symbol is capable of adding so many dimensions to a poem, it is a peculiarly effective resource for the poet, but it is also peculiarly susceptible to misinterpretation by the incautious reader.

Accurate interpretation of the symbol requires delicacy, tact, and good sense. The reader must maintain balance while walking a tightrope between too little and too much—between underinterpretation and overinterpretation. If the reader falls off, however, it is much more desirable to fall off on the side of too little. Someone who reads "The Road Not

Taken" as being only about a choice between two roads in a wood has at least understood part of the experience that the poem communicates, but the reader who reads into it anything imaginable might as well discard the poem and simply daydream.

Above all, we should avoid the tendency to indulge in symbol-hunting and to see virtually anything in a poem as symbolic. It is preferable to miss a symbol than to try to find one in every line of a poem.

To the Virgins, to Make Much of Time

Gather ye rosebuds while ye may,
    Old Time is still a-flying;
And this same flower that smiles today
    Tomorrow will be dying.

The glorious lamp of heaven, the Sun,   5
    The higher he's a-getting,
The sooner will his race be run,
    And nearer he's to setting.

That age is best which is the first,
    When youth and blood are warmer;   10
But being spent, the worse, and worst
    Times still succeed the former.

Then be not coy, but use your time;
    And while ye may, go marry;
For having lost but once your prime,   15
    You may forever tarry.

—ROBERT HERRICK (1591–1674)

QUESTIONS

1. The first two stanzas might be interpreted literally if the third and fourth stanzas did not force us to interpret them symbolically. What do the "rosebuds" symbolize (stanza 1)? What does the course of a day symbolize (stanza 2)? Does the poet narrow the meaning of the rosebud symbol in the last stanza or merely name *one* of its specific meanings?

2. How does the title help us interpret the meaning of the symbol? Why is "virgins" a more meaningful word than, for example, *maidens*?

3. Why is such haste necessary in gathering the rosebuds? True, the blossoms die quickly, but others will replace them. Who *really* is dying?

4. What are "the worse, and worst" times (11)? Why?
5. Why is the wording of the poem better than these possible alternatives: *blooms* for "smiles" (3); *course* for "race" (7); *used* for "spent" (11); *spend* for "use" (13)?

Allegory is a narrative or description that has a second meaning beneath the surface. Although the surface story or description may have its own interest, the author's major interest is in the ulterior meaning. When Pharoah in the Bible, for instance, has a dream in which seven fat kine (cattle) are devoured by seven lean kine, the story does not really become significant until Joseph interprets its allegorical meaning: that Egypt is to enjoy seven years of fruitfulness and prosperity followed by seven years of famine. Allegory has been defined sometimes as an extended metaphor and sometimes as a series of related symbols. But it is usually distinguishable from both of these. It is unlike extended metaphor in that it involves a *system* of related comparisons rather than one comparison drawn out. It differs from symbolism in that it puts less emphasis on the images for their own sake and more on their ulterior meanings. Also, these meanings are more fixed. In allegory there is usually a one-to-one correspondence between the details and a single set of ulterior meanings. In complex allegories the details may have more than one meaning, but these meanings tend to be definite. Meanings do not ray out from allegory as they do from a symbol.

Allegory is less popular in modern literature than it was in medieval and Renaissance writing, and it is much less often found in short poems than in long narrative works such as *The Faerie Queene*, *Everyman*, and *Pilgrim's Progress*. It has sometimes, especially with political allegory, been used to disguise meaning rather than reveal it (or, rather, to disguise it from some people while revealing it to others). Though less rich than the symbol, allegory is an effective way of making the abstract concrete and has occasionally been used effectively even in fairly short poems.

Peace

Sweet Peace, where dost thou dwell? I humbly crave,
　　　Let me once know.
　　I sought thee in a secret cave,
　　　And asked if Peace were there.
A hollow wind did seem to answer, "No, 　　　　　　　5
　　Go seek elsewhere."

I did, and going did a rainbow note.
　　　"Surely," thought I,

"This is the lace of Peace's coat;
    I will search out the matter."   10
But while I looked, the clouds immediately
    Did break and scatter.

Then went I to a garden, and did spy
    A gallant flower,
The Crown Imperial. "Sure," said I,   15
    "Peace at the root must dwell."
But when I digged, I saw a worm devour
    What showed so well.

At length I met a reverend good old man,
    Whom when for Peace   20
I did demand, he thus began:
    "There was a prince of old
At Salem dwelt, who lived with good increase
    Of flock and fold.

"He sweetly lived; yet sweetness did not save   25
    His life from foes.
But after death out of his grave
    There sprang twelve stalks of wheat;
Which many wondering at, got some of those
    To plant and set.   30

"It prospered strangely, and did soon disperse
    Through all the earth,
For they that taste it do rehearse°   declare
    That virtue lies therein,
A secret virtue, bringing peace and mirth   35
    By flight of sin.

"Take of this grain, which in my garden grows,
    And grows for you;
Make bread of it; and that repose
    And peace, which everywhere
With so much earnestness you do pursue,   40
    Is only there."

          —GEORGE HERBERT (1593–1633)

QUESTIONS

1. Vocabulary: *gallant* (14), *virtue* (34). "Crown Imperial" (15) is a garden flower, fritillary; "Salem" (23) is Jerusalem.
2. Identify the "prince" (22), his "flock and fold" (24), the "twelve stalks of wheat" (28), the "grain" (37), and the "bread" (39).
3. Should the "secret cave" (stanza 1), the "rainbow" (stanza 2), and the flower "garden" (stanza 3) be understood merely as places where the speaker searched or do they have more precise meanings?
4. Who is the "reverend good old man" (19), and what is *his* garden (37)?

EXERCISES

1. Determine whether "sleep" in the following poems is literal, a symbol, or a metaphor (or simile).
   a. "Stopping by Woods on a Snowy Evening" (page 826).
   b. "The Chimney Sweeper" (page 798).
   c. "Is my team plowing" (page 705).
   d. "The Second Coming" (page 1050).
2. Donne's "The Flea" (page 848) and Dickinson's "I heard a Fly buzz—when I died" (page 906) deal with common insect pests. Which of them is symbolic? Explain your choice.
3. What do Blake's lamb and tiger symbolize (page 835)?
4. Determine whether the following poems are predominantly symbolic or literal.
   a. "Because I could not stop for Death" (page 784).
   b. "The Snow Man" (page 743).
   c. "Song: Go and catch a falling star" (page 992).
   d. "Blackberry Eating" (page 914).
   e. "Musée des Beaux Arts" (page 975).
   f. "Richard Cory" (page 1034).
   g. "The Wild Swans at Coole" (page 1051).
   h. "Desert Places" (page 727).
   i. "Constantly risking absurdity" (page 692).

REVIEWING CHAPTER SIX

1. Using examples from the poems that follow, explore how symbols must read both literally and figuratively.
2. Show that the context of a poem determines the limits of its symbolic meanings (as an exercise, you might want to examine the multiple possible meanings of a particular symbol, and eliminate those that are ruled out by the context).
3. Discuss the difference between symbol and allegory, if possible accounting for the fact that allegory is no longer as popular a figure as it once was.

Pink Dog

[Rio de Janeiro]

The sun is blazing and the sky is blue.
Umbrellas clothe the beach in every hue.
Naked, you trot across the avenue.

Oh, never have I seen a dog so bare!
Naked and pink, without a single hair ...   5
Startled, the passersby draw back and stare.

Of course they're mortally afraid of rabies.
You are not mad; you have a case of scabies
but look intelligent. Where are your babies?

(A nursing mother, by those hanging teats.)   10
In what slum have you hidden them, poor bitch,
while you go begging, living by your wits?

Didn't you know? It's been in all the papers,
to solve this problem, how they deal with beggars?
They take and throw them in the tidal rivers.   15

Yes, idiots, paralytics, parasites
go bobbing in the ebbing sewage, nights
out in the suburbs, where there are no lights.

If they do this to anyone who begs,
drugged, drunk, or sober, with or without legs,   20
what would they do to sick, four-leggèd dogs?

In the cafés and on the sidewalk corners
the joke is going round that all the beggars
who can afford them now wear life preservers.

In your condition you would not be able   25
even to float, much less to dog-paddle.
Now look, the practical, the sensible

solution is to wear a *fantasía*.
Tonight you simply can't afford to be
an eyesore. But no one will ever see a   30

dog in *máscara* this time of year.
Ash Wednesday'll come but Carnival is here.
What sambas can you dance? What will you wear?

They say that Carnival's degenerating
—radios, Americans, or something,   35
have ruined it completely. They're just talking.

Carnival is always wonderful!
A depilated dog would not look well.
Dress up! Dress up and dance at Carnival!

—ELIZABETH BISHOP (1911–1979)

QUESTIONS

1. Vocabulary: *scabies* (8), *sambas* (33), *depilated* (38). Rio de Janeiro (subtitle) is famous for its uninhibited Carnival celebration leading up to Ash Wednesday and the beginning of Lent in the Christian calendar, as well as for its beaches and its beggars. The following are associated with Carnival: *fantasía* (28), "carnival costume," according to a note written by the poet; *máscara* (31), a mask.
2. In what tone of voice does the speaker address the pink dog? How do the rhymes help to define that tone? In what ways is the speaker's attitude toward the dog more complex than it seems at first?
3. How does the personifying effect of apostrophe suggest a more serious meaning for the poem? What does the speaker finally suggest about the dog's "naked" (3) condition and about the possible ways of compensating for its identity as an outcast or object of ridicule? In what ways is the dog's condition related to the human condition, especially in a setting like Rio de Janeiro?

The Writer

In her room at the prow of the house
Where light breaks, and the windows are tossed with linden,
My daughter is writing a story.

I pause in the stairwell, hearing
From her shut door a commotion of typewriter-keys   5
Like a chain hauled over a gunwale.

Young as she is, the stuff
Of her life is a great cargo, and some of it heavy:
I wish her a lucky passage.

But now it is she who pauses,   10
As if to reject my thought and its easy figure.
A stillness greatens, in which

The whole house seems to be thinking,
And then she is at it again with a bunched clamor
Of strokes, and again is silent.   15

I remember the dazed starling
Which was trapped in that very room, two years ago;
How we stole in, lifted a sash

And retreated, not to affright it;
And how for a helpless hour, through the crack of the door,   20
We watched the sleek, wild, dark

And iridescent creature
Batter against the brilliance, drop like a glove
To the hard floor, or the desk-top,

And wait then, humped and bloody,   25
For the wits to try it again; and how our spirits
Rose when, suddenly sure,

It lifted off from a chair-back,
Beating a smooth course for the right window
And clearing the sill of the world.   30

It is always a matter, my darling,
Of life or death, as I had forgotten. I wish
What I wished you before, but harder.

—RICHARD WILBUR (B. 1921)

QUESTIONS

1. What "easy figure" (11) of speech is presented by such language as "prow" (1), "chain hauled over a gunwale" (6), "cargo" (8), and "passage" (9)? What is being compared to what? Why would "the writer"—either the daughter or the speaker—be justified in rejecting that figure?
2. The daughter seems to be rejecting both the figure of speech and the thought that it represents (11). Why might the thought be as unacceptable as the figure that expresses it?

3. Lines 16 through 30 develop the image of the trapped starling. Why should it be interpreted as a symbol? How is its meaning more complex than that of the figure developed in lines 1–15?
4. The poem symmetrically divides into two 15-line units, each developing a different figure of speech. What is the function of the additional three lines with which the poem ends?

Whitman and the Moth

Van Wyck Brooks tells us Whitman in old age
Sat by a pond in nothing but his hat,
Crowding his final notebooks page by page
With names of trees, birds, bugs, and things like that.

The war could never break him, though he'd seen   5
Horrors in hospitals to chill the soul.
But now, preserved, the Union had turned mean:
Evangelizing greed was in control.

Good reason to despair, yet grief was purged
By tracing how creation reigned supreme.   10
A pupa cracked, a butterfly emerged:
America, still unfolding from its dream.

Sometimes he rose and waded in the pond,
Soothing his aching feet in the sweet mud.
A moth he knew, of which he had grown fond,   15
Perched on his hand as if to draw his blood.

But they were joined by what each couldn't do,
The meeting point where great art comes to pass—
Whitman, who danced and sang but never flew,
The moth, which had not written "Leaves of Grass,"   20

Composed a picture of the interchange
Between the mind and all that it transcends
Yet must stay near. No, there was nothing strange
In how he put his hand out to make friends

With such a fragile creature, soft as dust.   25
Feeling the pond cool as the light grew dim,

He blessed new life, though it had only just
Arrived in time to see the end of him.

—CLIVE JAMES (B. 1939)

QUESTIONS

1. Van Wyck Brooks (1886–1963) was a biographer of Walt Whitman and other American writers. Vocabulary: *pupa* (11).
2. Analyze the symbol of the moth. What connotations are attached to this particular insect?
3. What contrast does the poem highlight between Walt Whitman, a human being, and a mere moth? What is the significance of their "meeting point" in line 18?

Fire and Ice

Some say the world will end in fire,
Some say in ice.
From what I've tasted of desire
I hold with those who favor fire.
But if it had to perish twice,   5
I think I know enough of hate
To say that for destruction ice
Is also great
And would suffice.

—ROBERT FROST (1874–1963)

QUESTIONS

1. Who are "Some" (1–2)? To which two theories do lines 1–2 refer? (In answering, it might help you to know that the poem was published in 1920.)
2. What do "fire" and "ice," respectively, symbolize? What two meanings has "the world"?
3. The poem ends with an *understatement* (see Chapter 7). How does it affect the tone of the poem?

Lady Lazarus

I have done it again.
One year in every ten
I manage it——

A sort of walking miracle, my skin
Bright as a Nazi lampshade,   5
My right foot

A paperweight,
My face a featureless, fine
Jew linen.

Peel off the napkin   10
O my enemy.
Do I terrify?——

The nose, the eye pits, the full set of teeth?
The sour breath
Will vanish in a day.   15

Soon, soon the flesh
The grave cave ate will be
At home on me

And I a smiling woman.
I am only thirty.   20
And like the cat I have nine times to die.

This is Number Three.
What a trash
To annihilate each decade.

What a million filaments.   25
The peanut-crunching crowd
Shoves in to see

Them unwrap me hand and foot——
The big strip tease.
Gentlemen, ladies   30

These are my hands
My knees.
I may be skin and bone,

Nevertheless, I am the same, identical woman.
The first time it happened I was ten.   35
It was an accident.

The second time I meant
To last it out and not come back at all.
I rocked shut

As a seashell.   40
They had to call and call
And pick the worms off me like sticky pearls.

Dying
Is an art, like everything else.
I do it exceptionally well.   45

I do it so it feels like hell.
I do it so it feels real.
I guess you could say I've a call.

It's easy enough to do it in a cell.
It's easy enough to do it and stay put.   50
It's the theatrical

Comeback in broad day
To the same place, the same face, the same brute
Amused shout:

'A miracle!'   55
That knocks me out.
There is a charge

For the eyeing of my scars, there is a charge
For the hearing of my heart——
It really goes.   60

And there is a charge, a very large charge
For a word or a touch
Or a bit of blood

Or a piece of my hair or my clothes.
So, so, Herr Doktor.   65
So, Herr Enemy.

I am your opus,
I am your valuable,
The pure gold baby

That melts to a shriek.   70
I turn and burn.
Do not think I underestimate your great concern.

Ash, ash——
You poke and stir.
Flesh, bone, there is nothing there——   75

A cake of soap,
A wedding ring,
A gold filling.

Herr God, Herr Lucifer
Beware   80
Beware.

Out of the ash
I rise with my red hair
And I eat men like air.

—SYLVIA PLATH (1932–1963)

QUESTIONS

1. Explore the Biblical reference to Lazarus (title) as a symbol for one who survives a suicide attempt. Sylvia Plath attempted suicide at least twice during her short life; this poem was written four months before she finally succeeded in 1963 at the age of thirty.
2. In the speaker's allegory, she identifies herself with the Jews during the Holocaust and with a striptease artist. Compare these references to the psychodrama of a suicidal poet. Who is "the peanut-crunching crowd" (26)? How can dying be said to constitute "an art" (44)?
3. Find a biographical essay on Plath either in the library or on the Internet. Can this poem be understood without knowing details of Plath's relationship to her father and her estranged husband, Ted Hughes?

Because I could not stop for Death

Because I could not stop for Death—
He kindly stopped for me—
The Carriage held but just Ourselves—
And Immortality.

We slowly drove—He knew no haste   5
And I had put away
My labor and my leisure too,
For His Civility—

We passed the School, where Children strove
At Recess—in the Ring—   10
We passed the Fields of Gazing Grain—
We passed the Setting Sun—

Or rather—He passed Us—
The Dews drew quivering and chill—
For only Gossamer, my Gown—   15
My Tippet   only Tulle—

We paused before a House that seemed
A Swelling of the Ground—
The Roof was scarcely visible—
The Cornice—in the Ground—   20

Since then—'tis Centuries—and yet
Feels shorter than the Day
I first surmised the Horses' Heads
Were toward Eternity—

—EMILY DICKINSON (1830–1886)

QUESTIONS

1. Vocabulary: *Gossamer* (15); *Tippet, Tulle* (16); *surmised* (23).
2. Define the stages of this journey—where it begins, what events occur on the way, and its destination. Where is the speaker *now*? What is her present emotional condition?
3. To what is "Death" (1) being compared?
4. Identify the allegorical implications of the events. For example, what aspects of human life are implied by the three items that are "passed" in stanza 3? What is the "House" (17) before which the carriage pauses, and why does it pause there?
5. Explore the three time references in the concluding stanza. Can you explain why the passage of "Centuries ... Feels shorter than the Day" the speaker guessed that her journey was proceeding "toward Eternity"? For what is "Eternity" a metonymy? Has the carriage reached that destination yet?

Hymn to God My God, in My Sickness

Since I am coming to that holy room
    Where, with thy choir of saints for evermore,
I shall be made thy music, as I come
    I tune the instrument here at the door,
    And what I must do then, think now before.　　　　5

Whilst my physicians by their love are grown
    Cosmographers, and I their map, who lie
Flat on this bed, that by them may be shown
    That this is my southwest discovery,
    Per fretum febris,° by these straits to die,　　*through the* 10
                                 raging of fever

I joy that in these straits I see my west;
    For though those currents yield return to none,
What shall my west hurt me? As west and east
    In all flat maps (and I am one) are one,
    So death doth touch the resurrection.　　　　15

Is the Pacific Sea my home? Or are
    The eastern riches? Is Jerusalem?
Anyan° and Magellan and Gibraltar,　　*Bering Strait*
    All straits, and none but straits, are ways to them,
    Whether where Japhet dwelt, or Cham, or Shem.　　20

We think that Paradise and Calvary,
    Christ's cross and Adam's tree, stood in one place;
Look, Lord, and find both Adams met in me;
    As the first Adam's sweat surrounds my face,
    May the last Adam's blood my soul embrace.　　　　25

So, in his purple wrapped receive me, Lord;
    By these his thorns give me his other crown;
And as to others' souls I preached thy word,
    Be this my text, my sermon to mine own:
    Therefore that he may raise, the Lord throws down.　　30

—JOHN DONNE (1572–1631)

QUESTIONS

1. Vocabulary: *Cosmographers* (7).
2. What is the speaker doing in stanza 1? What are "that holy room" (1) and "the instrument" (4)? For what is the speaker preparing himself?

3. In Donne's time explorers were seeking a Northwest Passage to Asia to match discovery of a southwest passage, the Straits of Magellan. Why is "southwest" more appropriate to the speaker's condition than "northwest"? In what ways is his fever like a strait? What denotations of "straits" (10) are relevant? What do the straits symbolize?

4. In what ways does the speaker's body resemble a map? Although the map is metaphorical, its parts are symbolic. What do west and east symbolize? Explain how the west and east "are one" (14).

5. Japhet, Cham (or Ham), and Shem (20)—sons of Noah—were in Christian legend the ancestors of the races of man, roughly identified as European, African, and Asian. In what ways are the Pacific Ocean, the East Indies, and Jerusalem (16–17) fitting symbols for the speaker's destination?

6. According to early Christian thinking, the Garden of Eden and Calvary were located in the same place. How does this tie in with the poem's geographical symbolism? Because Adam is said to prefigure Christ (Romans 5.12–21), Christ is called the second Adam. What connection is there between Adam's "sweat" (24) and Christ's "blood" (25)? How do the two Adams meet in the speaker? What do blood and sweat (together and separately) symbolize?

7. For what are "eastern riches" (17), "his purple" (26), and "his thorns" (27) metonymies? What do "purple" and "thorns" symbolize? What is Christ's "other crown" (27)?

8. How does this poem explain human suffering and give it meaning?

Ulysses

It little profits that an idle king,
By this still hearth, among these barren crags,
Matched with an agèd wife, I mete and dole
Unequal laws unto a savage race,
That hoard, and sleep, and feed, and know not me.   5
I cannot rest from travel; I will drink
Life to the lees. All times I have enjoyed
Greatly, have suffered greatly, both with those
That loved me, and alone; on shore, and when
Through scudding drifts the rainy Hyades   10
Vext the dim sea. I am become a name;
For always roaming with a hungry heart
Much have I seen and known,—cities of men,
And manners, climates, councils, governments,
Myself not least, but honored of them all;   15
And drunk delight of battle with my peers,
Far on the ringing plains of windy Troy.
I am a part of all that I have met;
Yet all experience is an arch wherethrough

Gleams that untraveled world, whose margin fades   20
For ever and for ever when I move.
How dull it is to pause, to make an end,
To rust unburnished, not to shine in use!
As though to breathe were life! Life piled on life
Were all too little, and of one to me   25
Little remains; but every hour is saved
From that eternal silence, something more,
A bringer of new things; and vile it were
For some three suns to store and hoard myself,
And this gray spirit yearning in desire   30
To follow knowledge like a sinking star,
Beyond the utmost bound of human thought.

This is my son, mine own Telemachus,
To whom I leave the scepter and the isle—
Well-loved of me, discerning to fulfill   35
This labor, by slow prudence to make mild
A rugged people, and through soft degrees
Subdue them to the useful and the good.
Most blameless is he, centered in the sphere
Of common duties, decent not to fail   40
In offices of tenderness, and pay
Meet adoration to my household gods,
When I am gone. He works his work, I mine.

There lies the port; the vessel puffs her sail:
There gloom the dark, broad seas. My mariners,   45
Souls that have toiled, and wrought, and thought with me—
That ever with a frolic welcome took
The thunder and the sunshine, and opposed
Free hearts, free foreheads—you and I are old;
Old age hath yet his honor and his toil.   50
Death closes all; but something ere the end,
Some work of noble note, may yet be done,
Not unbecoming men that strove with Gods.
The lights begin to twinkle from the rocks;
The long day wanes; the slow moon climbs; the deep   55
Moans round with many voices. Come, my friends,
'Tis not too late to seek a newer world.

Push off, and sitting well in order smite
The sounding furrows; for my purpose holds
To sail beyond the sunset, and the baths   60
Of all the western stars, until I die.
It may be that the gulfs will wash us down;
It may be we shall touch the Happy Isles,
And see the great Achilles, whom we knew.
Though much is taken, much abides; and though   65
We are not now that strength which in old days
Moved earth and heaven, that which we are, we are:
One equal temper of heroic hearts,
Made weak by time and fate, but strong in will
To strive, to seek, to find, and not to yield.   70

—ALFRED, LORD TENNYSON (1809–1892)

QUESTIONS

1. Vocabulary: *lees* (7), *Hyades* (10), *meet* (42).
2. Ulysses, king of Ithaca, is a legendary Greek hero, a major figure in Homer's *Iliad*, the hero of Homer's *Odyssey*, and a minor figure in Dante's *Divine Comedy*. After ten years at the siege of Troy, Ulysses set sail for home but, having incurred the wrath of the god of the sea, he was subjected to storms and vicissitudes and was forced to wander for another ten years, having many adventures and seeing most of the Mediterranean world before again reaching Ithaca, his wife, and his son. Once back home, according to Dante, he still wished to travel and "to follow virtue and knowledge." In Tennyson's poem, Ulysses is represented as about to set sail on a final voyage from which he will not return. Locate Ithaca on a map. Where exactly, in geographical terms, does Ulysses intend to sail (59–64)? (The Happy Isles were the Elysian fields, or Greek paradise; Achilles was another Greek prince, the hero of the *Iliad*, who was killed at the siege of Troy.)
3. Ulysses's speech is divided into three sections, beginning at lines 1, 33, and 44. What is the topic or purpose of each section? To whom, specifically, is the third section addressed? To whom, would you infer, are sections 1 and 2 addressed? Where do you visualize Ulysses as standing during his speech?
4. Characterize Ulysses. What kind of person is he as Tennyson represents him?
5. What way of life is symbolized by Ulysses? Find as many evidences as you can that Ulysses's desire for travel represents something more than mere wanderlust and wish for adventure.
6. Give two symbolic implications of the westward direction of Ulysses's journey.
7. Interpret lines 18–21 and 26–29. What metaphor is implied in line 23? What is symbolized by "The thunder and the sunshine" (48)? What do the two metonymies in line 49 stand for?

SUGGESTIONS FOR WRITING

The following poems may be regarded as character sketches, but in each case the richness and suggestiveness of the presentation point to the symbolic nature of the sketch. Of what are the characters symbolic, and what clues does the poem present that make a symbolic interpretation valid?

1. Oliver, "Spring in the Classroom" (page 723).
2. Frost, "After Apple-Picking" (page 740).
3. Collins, "The History Teacher" (page 986).
4. Dickinson, "I died for Beauty—but was scarce" (page 991).
5. Hardy, "The Ruined Maid" (page 1003).
6. Robinson, "Richard Cory" (page 1034).
7. Updike, "Ex-Basketball Player" (page 1045).

PRACTICE AP WRITING PROMPTS ▬▬▬▬▬

Robert Frost, "The Road Not Taken" (p. 765)

In his poem "Directive," Robert Frost likens himself to a mischievous guide "Who only has at heart your getting lost." Writing to his friend Louis Untermeyer in 1915, Frost made the unguarded remark, "I'll bet not half a dozen people can tell who was hit and where he was hit by my road not taken," perhaps the most authoritative evidence that this poem holds some intentional misdirection, a gesture that Frost often referred to broadly as his "kind of fooling." Carefully examine "The Road Not Taken," and write an essay in which you analyze the author's "fooling," showing how such tricks of language contribute to the overall meaning of the poem.

....

Walt Whitman, "A Noiseless Patient Spider" (p. 767)

Read "A Noiseless Patient Spider" carefully. In a well-organized essay, demonstrate how Whitman's diction and concrete details develop the literal and symbolic meanings of the spider's activity.

....

Richard Wilbur, "The Writer" (p. 778)

Read "The Writer" carefully. Then, with close attention to poetic devices, write an essay in which you show how the speaker's extended analogy in lines 16–30 supports his nuanced reflections about his daughter throughout the poem.

....

CHAPTER SEVEN

Figurative Language 3

Paradox, Overstatement,
Understatement, Irony

Aesop tells the tale of a traveler who sought refuge with a Satyr on a bitter winter night. On entering the Satyr's lodging, he blew on his fingers, and was asked by the Satyr why he did it. "To warm them up," he explained. Later, on being served a piping-hot bowl of porridge, he blew also on it, and again was asked why he did it. "To cool it off," he explained. The Satyr thereupon thrust him out of doors, for he would have nothing to do with a man who could blow hot and cold with the same breath.

A **paradox** is an apparent contradiction that is nevertheless somehow true. It may be either a situation or a statement. Aesop's tale of the traveler illustrates a **paradoxical situation.** As a figure of speech, paradox is a statement. When Alexander Pope wrote that a literary critic of his time would "damn with faint praise," he was using a **verbal paradox,** for how can a man damn by praising?

When we understand all the conditions and circumstances involved in a paradox, we find that what at first seemed impossible is actually entirely plausible and not strange at all. The paradox of the cold hands and hot porridge is not strange to anyone who knows that a stream of air directed upon an object of different temperature will tend to bring that object closer to its own temperature. And Pope's paradox is not strange when we realize that *damn* is being used figuratively, and that Pope means only that a too reserved praise may damage an author with the public almost as much as adverse criticism. In a **paradoxical statement** the contradiction usually stems from one of the words being used figuratively or with more than one denotation.

The value of paradox is its shock value. Its seeming impossibility startles the reader into attention and, by the fact of its apparent absurdity, underscores the truth of what is being said.

Much Madness is divinest Sense

Much Madness is divinest Sense—
To a discerning Eye—
Much Sense—the starkest Madness—
'Tis the Majority
In this, as All, prevail—
Assent—and you are sane—
Demur—you're straightway dangerous—
And handled with a Chain—

—EMILY DICKINSON (1830–1886)

QUESTIONS

1. This poem presents the two sides of a paradoxical proposition: that insanity is good sense, and that good sense is insane. How do the concepts implied by the words "discerning" (2) and "Majority" (4) provide the resolution of this paradox?
2. How do we know that the speaker does not believe that the majority is correct? How do the last five lines extend the subject beyond a contrast between sanity and insanity?

Overstatement, understatement, and verbal irony form a continuous series, for they consist, respectively, of saying more, saying less, and saying the opposite of what one really means.

Overstatement, or *hyperbole,* is simply exaggeration, but exaggeration in the service of truth. It is not the same as a fish story. If you say, "I'm starved!" or "You could have knocked me over with a feather!" or "I'll die if I don't pass this course!" you do not expect to be taken literally; you are merely adding emphasis to what you really mean. (And if you say, "There were literally millions of people at the beach!" you are merely piling one overstatement on top of another, for you really mean, "There were figuratively millions of people at the beach," or, literally, "The beach was very crowded.") Like all figures of speech, overstatement may be used with a variety of effects. It may be humorous or grave, fanciful or restrained, convincing or unconvincing. When Tennyson says of his eagle (page 682) that it is *"Close* to the sun in lonely lands," he says what appears to be literally true, though we know from our study of astronomy that it is not. When Frost says, at the conclusion of "The Road Not Taken" (page 765),

> I shall be telling this with a sigh
> Somewhere *ages and ages hence*

we are scarcely aware of the overstatement, so quietly is the assertion made. Unskillfully used, however, overstatement may seem strained and ridiculous, leading us to react as Gertrude does to the player-queen's speeches in *Hamlet:* "The lady doth protest too much."

It is paradoxical that one can emphasize a truth either by overstating it or by understating it. **Understatement,** or saying less than one means, may exist in what one says or merely in how one says it. If, for instance, upon sitting down to a loaded dinner plate, you say, "This looks like a nice snack," you are actually stating less than the truth; but if you say, with the humorist Artemus Ward, that a man who holds his hand for half an hour in a lighted fire will experience "a sensation of excessive and disagreeable warmth," you are stating what is literally true but with a good deal less force than the situation warrants.

The Sun Rising

Busy old fool, unruly sun,
    Why dost thou thus
Through windows and through curtains call on us?
Must to thy motions lovers' seasons run?
    Saucy pedantic wretch, go chide   5
    Late schoolboys and sour 'prentices,
Go tell court-huntsmen that the king will ride,
Call country ants to harvest offices;
Love, all alike, no season knows, nor clime,
Nor hours, days, months, which are the rags of time.   10

Thy beams so reverend and strong
    Why shouldst thou think?
I could eclipse and cloud them with a wink,
But that I would not lose her sight so long;
    If her eyes have not blinded thine,   15
    Look, and tomorrow late tell me
Whether both th' Indias of spice and mine
Be where thou left'st them, or lie here with me.

Ask for those kings whom thou saw'st yesterday,
And thou shalt hear, "All here in one bed lay."   20

      She's all states, and all princes I;
      Nothing else is.
Princes do but play us; compared to this,
All honor's mimic, all wealth alchemy.
      Thou, sun, art half as happy as we,   25
      In that the world's contracted thus;
Thine age asks ease, and since thy duties be
To warm the world, that's done in warming us.
Shine here to us, and thou art everywhere;
This bed thy center is, these walls thy sphere.   30

—JOHN DONNE (1572–1631)

QUESTIONS

1. Vocabulary: *offices* (8), *alchemy* (24).
2. As precisely as possible, identify the time of day and the locale. What three "persons" does the poem involve?
3. What is the speaker's attitude toward the sun in stanzas 1 and 2? How and why does it change in stanza 3?
4. Does the speaker understate or overstate the actual qualities of the sun? Point out specific examples. Identify the overstatements in lines 9–10, 13, 15, 16–20, 21–24, 29–30. What do these overstatements achieve?
5. Line 17 introduces a geographical image referring to the East and West Indies, sources respectively of spices and gold. What relationship between the lovers and the rest of the world is expressed in lines 15–22?
6. Who is actually the intended listener for this extended apostrophe? What is the speaker's purpose? What is the poem's purpose?

Incident

Once riding in old Baltimore
    Heart-filled, head-filled with glee,
I saw a Baltimorean
    Keep looking straight at me.

Now I was eight and very small,   5
    And he was no whit bigger,
And so I smiled, but he poked out
    His tongue, and called me, "Nigger."

I saw the whole of Baltimore
   From May until December;   10
Of all the things that happened there
   That's all that I remember.

—COUNTEE CULLEN (1903–1946)

QUESTION

What accounts for the effectiveness of the last stanza? Comment on the title. Is it in keeping with the meaning of the poem?

Like paradox, **irony** has meanings that extend beyond its use merely as a figure of speech.

Verbal irony, saying the opposite of what one means, is often confused with sarcasm and with satire, and for that reason it may be well to look at the meanings of all three terms. Sarcasm and satire both imply ridicule, one on the colloquial level, the other on the literary level. **Sarcasm** is simply bitter or cutting speech, intended to wound the feelings (it comes from a Greek word meaning to tear flesh). **Satire** is a more formal term, usually applied to written literature rather than to speech and ordinarily implying a higher motive: it is ridicule (either bitter or gentle) of human folly or vice, with the purpose of bringing about reform or at least of keeping other people from falling into similar folly or vice. Irony, on the other hand, is a literary device or figure that may be used in the service of sarcasm or ridicule or may not. It is popularly confused with sarcasm and satire because it is so often used as their tool; but irony may be used without either sarcastic or satirical intent, and sarcasm and satire may exist (though they do not usually) without irony. If, for instance, one of the members of your class raises his hand on the discussion of this point and says, "I don't understand," and your instructor replies, with a tone of heavy disgust in his voice, "Well, I wouldn't expect *you* to," he is being sarcastic but not ironic; he means exactly what he says. But if, after you have done particularly well on an examination, your instructor brings your test papers into the classroom saying, "Here's some *bad* news for you: you all got A's and B's!" he is being ironic but not sarcastic. Sarcasm, we may say, is cruel, as a bully is cruel: it intends to give hurt. Satire is both cruel and kind, as a surgeon is cruel and kind: it gives hurt in the interest of the patient or of society. Irony is neither cruel nor kind: it is simply a device, like a surgeon's scalpel, for performing any operation more skillfully.

Though verbal irony always implies the opposite of what is said, it has many gradations, and only in its simplest forms does it mean *only* the opposite of what is said. In more complex forms it means both what is said and the opposite of what is said, at once, though in different ways and with different degrees of emphasis. When Terence's critic, in Housman's "Terence, this is stupid stuff" (page 1007) says, "'*Pretty* friendship 'tis to rhyme/ Your friends to death before their time'" (11–12), we may substitute the literal *sorry* for the ironic "pretty" with little or no loss of meaning. When Terence speaks in reply, however, of the pleasure of drunkenness—"And down in *lovely* muck I've lain, / Happy till I woke again" (35–36)—we cannot substitute *loathsome* for "lovely" without considerable loss of meaning, for while muck is actually extremely unpleasant to lie in, it may *seem* lovely to an intoxicated person. Thus two meanings—one the opposite of the other—operate at once.

Like all figures of speech, verbal irony runs the danger of being misunderstood. With irony, the risks are perhaps greater than with other figures, for if metaphor is misunderstood, the result may be simply bewilderment; but if irony is misunderstood, the reader goes away with an idea exactly the opposite of what the user meant to convey. The results of misunderstanding if, for instance, you ironically called someone a numbskull might be calamitous. For this reason the user of irony must be very skillful in its use, conveying by an altered tone, or by a wink of the eye or pen, that irony is intended; and the reader of literature must be always alert to recognize the subtle signs of irony.

No matter how broad or obvious the irony, a number of people in any large audience always will misunderstand. Artemus Ward used to protect himself against these people by writing at the bottom of his newspaper column, "This is writ ironical." But irony is most delightful and most effective when it is subtlest. It sets up a special understanding between writer and reader that may add either grace or force. If irony is too obvious, it sometimes seems merely crude. But if effectively used, like all figurative language it is capable of adding extra dimensions to meaning.

Barbie Doll

This girlchild was born as usual
and presented dolls that did pee-pee
and miniature GE stoves and irons
and wee lipsticks the color of cherry candy.
Then in the magic of puberty, a classmate said: 5
You have a great big nose and fat legs.

She was healthy, tested intelligent,
possessed strong arms and back,

abundant sexual drive and manual dexterity.
She went to and fro apologizing.   10
Everyone saw a fat nose on thick legs.

She was advised to play coy,
exhorted to come on hearty,
exercise, diet, smile and wheedle.
Her good nature wore out   15
like a fan belt.
So she cut off her nose and her legs
and offered them up.

In the casket displayed on satin she lay
with the undertaker's cosmetics painted on,   20
a turned-up putty nose,
dressed in a pink and white nightie.
Doesn't she look pretty? everyone said.
Consummation at last.
To every woman a happy ending.   25

—MARGE PIERCY (B. 1936)

QUESTIONS

1. In what ways is the girl described in this poem different from a Barbie doll? Discuss the poem's contrast of the living girl, a human being with intelligence and
   healthy appetites, and the doll, an inanimate object.
2. The poem contains a surprising but apt simile: "Her good nature wore out /
   like a fan belt" (15–16). Why is the image of the fan belt appropriate here?
3. Why does the speaker mention the girl's "strong arms and back" (8) and her
   "manual dexterity" (9)? How do these qualities contribute to her fate?
4. Discuss the verbal irony in the phrase "the magic of puberty" (5) and in the last
   three lines. What is the target of this satire?

The term *irony* always implies some sort of discrepancy or incongruity.
In verbal irony the discrepancy is between what is said and what is meant.
In other forms the discrepancy may be between appearance and reality or
between expectation and fulfillment. These other forms of irony are, on
the whole, more important resources for the poet than is verbal irony. Two
types are especially important.

In **dramatic irony** the discrepancy is not between what the speaker
says and what the speaker means but between what the speaker says and
what the poem means. The speaker's words may be perfectly straightforward, but the author, by putting these words in a particular speaker's

mouth, may be indicating to the reader ideas or attitudes quite opposed to those the speaker is voicing. This form of irony is more complex than verbal irony and demands a more complex response from the reader. It may be used not only to convey attitudes but also to illuminate character, for the author who uses it is indirectly commenting not only upon the value of the ideas uttered but also upon the nature of the person who utters them. Such comment may be harsh, gently mocking, or sympathetic.

The Chimney Sweeper

When my mother died I was very young,
And my father sold me while yet my tongue
Could scarcely cry "'weep! 'weep! 'weep! 'weep!"
So your chimneys I sweep, and in soot I sleep.

There's little Tom Dacre, who cried when his head,   5
That curled like a lamb's back, was shaved; so I said,
"Hush, Tom! never mind it, for, when your head's bare,
You know that the soot cannot spoil your white hair."

And so he was quiet, and that very night,
As Tom was asleeping, he had such a sight!   10
That thousands of sweepers, Dick, Joe, Ned, and Jack,
Were all of them locked up in coffins of black.

And by came an Angel who had a bright key,
And he opened the coffins and set them all free;
Then down a green plain leaping, laughing, they run,   15
And wash in a river, and shine in the sun.

Then naked and white, all their bags left behind,
They rise upon clouds and sport in the wind;
And the Angel told Tom, if he'd be a good boy,
He'd have God for his father, and never want joy.   20

And so Tom awoke, and we rose in the dark,
And got with our bags and our brushes to work.
Though the morning was cold, Tom was happy and warm;
So if all do their duty they need not fear harm.

—WILLIAM BLAKE (1757–1827)

QUESTIONS

1. In the eighteenth century small boys, sometimes no more than four or five years old, were employed to climb up the narrow chimney flues and clean them, collecting the soot in bags. Such boys, sometimes sold to the master sweepers by their parents, were miserably treated by their masters and often suffered disease and physical deformity. Characterize the boy who speaks in this poem. How do his and the poet's attitudes toward his lot in life differ? How, especially, are the meanings of the poet and the speaker different in lines 3, 7–8, and 24?

2. The dream in lines 11–20, besides being a happy dream, can be interpreted allegorically. Point out possible significances of the sweepers' being "locked up in coffins of black" (12) and the Angel's releasing them with a bright key to play upon green plains.

A third type of irony, **irony of situation,** occurs when a discrepancy exists between the actual circumstances and those that would seem appropriate or between what one anticipates and what actually comes to pass. If a man and his second wife, on the first night of their honeymoon, are accidentally seated at the theater next to the man's first wife, we should call the situation ironic. When, in O. Henry's famous short story "The Gift of the Magi," a poor young husband pawns his gold watch, in order to buy his wife a set of combs for her hair for Christmas, and his wife sells her long brown hair, in order to buy a fob for her husband's watch, the situation is ironic. When King Midas in the famous fable is granted his wish that anything he touch turn to gold, and then finds that he cannot eat because even his food turns to gold, the situation is ironic. When Coleridge's Ancient Mariner finds himself in the middle of the ocean with "Water, water, everywhere" but not a "drop to drink," the situation is ironic. In each case the circumstances are not what would seem appropriate or what we would expect.

Dramatic irony and irony of situation are powerful devices for poetry, for, like symbol, they enable a poem to suggest meanings without stating them—to communicate a great deal more than is said. We have seen one effective use of irony of situation in "The Widow's Lament in Springtime" (page 736). Another is in "Ozymandias," which follows.

Ozymandias

I met a traveler from an antique land
Who said: Two vast and trunkless legs of stone
Stand in the desert ... Near them, on the sand,
Half sunk, a shattered visage lies, whose frown,
And wrinkled lip, and sneer of cold command,   5

Tell that its sculptor well those passions read
Which yet survive, stamped on these lifeless things,
The hand that mocked them, and the heart that fed;
And on the pedestal these words appear:
"My name is Ozymandias, king of kings;   10
Look on my works, ye Mighty, and despair!"
Nothing beside remains. Round the decay
Of that colossal wreck, boundless and bare
The lone and level sands stretch far away.

—PERCY BYSSHE SHELLEY (1792–1822)

QUESTIONS

1. "[S]urvive" (7) is a transitive verb with "hand" and "heart" as direct objects. Whose hand? Whose heart? What figure of speech is exemplified in "hand" and "heart"?
2. Characterize Ozymandias.
3. Ozymandias was an ancient Egyptian tyrant. This poem was first published in 1817. Of what is Ozymandias a symbol? What contemporary reference might the poem have had in Shelley's time?
4. What is the theme of the poem and how is it "stated"?

Irony and paradox may be trivial or powerful devices, depending on their use. At their worst they may degenerate into mere mannerism and mental habit. At their best they may greatly extend the dimensions of meaning in a work of literature. Because irony and paradox demand an exercise of critical intelligence, they are particularly valuable as safeguards against sentimentality.

EXERCISE

Identify the figure in each of the following quotations as paradox, overstatement, understatement, or irony—and explain the use to which the figure is put (emotional emphasis, humor, satire, etc.).

1. Poetry is a language that tells us, through a more or less emotional reaction, something that cannot be said.   —Edwin Arlington Robinson
2. Christians have burnt each other, quite persuaded / That all the Apostles would have done as they did.   —Lord Byron
3. A man who could make so vile a pun would not scruple to pick a pocket.
—John Dennis
4. Last week I saw a woman flayed, and you will hardly believe how much it altered her person for the worse.   —Jonathan Swift
5. Where ignorance is bliss, / 'Tis folly to be wise.   —Thomas Gray
6. All night I made my bed to swim; with my tears
   I dissolved my couch.   —Psalms 6.6

7. Believe him, he has known the world too long / And seen the death of much
immortal song.   —*Alexander Pope*
8. Cowards die many times before their deaths;
The valiant never taste of death but once.   —*William Shakespeare*
9. ... all men would be cowards if they durst.   —*John Wilmot, Earl Of Rochester*

REVIEWING CHAPTER SEVEN

1. Distinguish between paradoxical actions and paradoxical statements, and explain how paradoxical statements may usually be resolved—that is, how their underlying validity is determined.
2. Define overstatement and understatement, and draw the distinction between stating what is less than is true and underemphasizing what is true.
3. Review the definitions of sarcasm and satire.
4. Using examples from the poems that follow in this chapter, define the three principal forms of irony and demonstrate how the ironies contribute meaning or forcefulness to the poems.

A slumber did my spirit seal

A slumber did my spirit seal;
    I had no human fears:
She seemed a thing that could not feel
    The touch of earthly years.

No motion has she now, no force;   5
    She neither hears nor sees;
Rolled round in earth's diurnal course,
    With rocks, and stones, and trees.

—WILLIAM WORDSWORTH (1770–1850)

QUESTIONS

1. Vocabulary: *diurnal* (7).
2. What frame of mind does the first line exhibit? How does it justify the second line?
3. Explain the situational irony. How is the phrase "could not feel" (3) an example of dramatic irony?

Batter my heart, three-personed God

Batter my heart, three-personed God; for you
As yet but knock, breathe, shine, and seek to mend;
That I may rise and stand, o'erthrow me, and bend
Your force to break, blow, burn, and make me new.
I, like an usurped town, to another due,   5
Labor to admit you, but oh, to no end;
Reason, your viceroy in me, me should defend,
But is captived, and proves weak or untrue.
Yet dearly I love you and would be lovèd fain,°   gladly
But am betrothed unto your enemy;   10
Divorce me, untie or break that knot again,
Take me to you, imprison me, for I,
Except° you enthrall me, never shall be free,   unless
Nor ever chaste, except you ravish me.

—JOHN DONNE (1572–1631)

QUESTIONS

1. In this sonnet (one in a group called "Holy Sonnets") the speaker addresses God in a series of metaphors and paradoxes. What is the paradox in the first quatrain? To what is the "three-personed God" metaphorically compared? To what is the speaker compared? Can the first three verbs of the parallel lines 2 and 4 be taken as addressed to specific "persons" of the Trinity (Father, Son, Holy Spirit)? If so, to which are "knock" and "break" addressed? "breathe" and "blow"? "shine" and "burn"? (What concealed pun helps in the attribution of the last pair? What etymological pun in the attribution of the second pair?)

2. To what does the speaker compare himself in the second quatrain? To what is God compared? Who is the usurper? What role does "Reason" (7) play in this political metaphor, and why is it a weak one?

3. To what does the speaker compare himself in the sestet (lines 9–14)? To what does he compare God? Who is the "enemy" (10)? Resolve the paradox in lines 12–13 by explaining the double meaning of "enthrall." Resolve the paradox in line 14 by explaining the double meaning of "ravish."

Mid-Term Break

I sat all morning in the college sick bay
Counting bells knelling classes to a close.
At two o'clock our neighbors drove me home.

In the porch I met my father crying—
He had always taken funerals in stride—   5
And Big Jim Evans saying it was a hard blow.

The baby cooed and laughed and rocked the pram
When I came in, and I was embarrassed
By old men standing up to shake my hand

And tell me they were 'sorry for my trouble.'   10
Whispers informed strangers I was the eldest,
Away at school, as my mother held my hand

In hers and coughed out angry tearless sighs.
At ten o'clock the ambulance arrived
With the corpse, stanched and bandaged by the nurses.   15

Next morning I went up into the room. Snowdrops
And candles soothed the bedside; I saw him
For the first time in six weeks. Paler now,

Wearing a poppy bruise on his left temple,
He lay in the four-foot box as in his cot.   20
No gaudy scars, the bumper knocked him clear.

A four-foot box, a foot for every year.

—SEAMUS HEANEY (1939–2013)

QUESTIONS

1. Vocabulary: *knelling* (2), *stanched* (15), *Snowdrops* (16).
2. Describe in your own words the "story" being told in this narrative poem. Who is the speaker, and what is his attitude toward this event of his distant past?
3. How would you describe the general tone of the poem? Is the speaker making use of understatement or overstatement in conveying his emotion?
4. Discuss the impact of the final line. Why is the line set off in a separate stanza by itself?

The Unknown Citizen

(To JS/07/M/378 This Marble Monument Is Erected by the State)

He was found by the Bureau of Statistics to be
One against whom there was no official complaint,

And all the reports on his conduct agree
That, in the modern sense of an old-fashioned word, he was
    a saint,
For in everything he did he served the Greater Community.   5
Except for the War till the day he retired
He worked in a factory and never got fired,
But satisfied his employers, Fudge Motors Inc.
Yet he wasn't a scab or odd in his views,
For his Union reports that he paid his dues   10
(Our report on his Union shows it was sound),
And our Social Psychology workers found
That he was popular with his mates and liked a drink.
The Press are convinced that he bought a paper every day
And that his reactions to advertisements were normal in
    every way.   15
Policies taken out in his name prove that he was fully
    insured,
And his Health-card shows he was once in hospital but left it
    cured.
Both Producers Research and High-Grade Living declare
He was fully sensible to the advantages of the Installment
    Plan
And had everything necessary to the Modern Man,   20
A phonograph, a radio, a car and a frigidaire.
Our researchers into Public Opinion are content
That he held the proper opinions for the time of year;
When there was peace, he was for peace; when there was
    war, he went.
He was married and added five children to the population,   25
Which our Eugenist says was the right number for a parent
    of his generation,
And our teachers report that he never interfered with their
    education.
Was he free? Was he happy? The question is absurd:
Had anything been wrong, we should certainly have heard.

                            —W. H. AUDEN (1907–1973)

QUESTIONS

1. Vocabulary: *scab* (9), *Eugenist* (26).
2. Explain the allusion and the irony in the title. Why was the citizen "unknown"?

3. This obituary of an unknown state "hero" was apparently prepared by a functionary of the state. Give an account of the citizen's life and character from Auden's own point of view.
4. What trends in modern life and social organization does the poem satirize?

in the inner city

in the inner city
or
like we call it
home
we think a lot about uptown   5
and the silent nights
and the houses straight as
dead men
and the pastel lights
and we hang on to our no place   10
happy to be alive
and in the inner city
or
like we call it
home   15

—Lucille Clifton (1936–2010)

QUESTIONS

1. In what contexts is the term "inner city" most often used, and what is it usually meant to imply?
2. What are the connotations of "silent nights" (6), "straight as / dead men" (7–8), and "pastel lights" (9)? By implication, what contrasting qualities might be found in the life of the inner city?
3. Is the irony in this poem verbal or dramatic?

The Gardener

He's out rescuing his fallen hollies
after the renegade snowstorm,

sawing their wounded limbs off
quite mercilessly (I think of the scene

in "Kings Row," the young soldier waking   5
to find his legs gone).

He's tying up young bamboo—
their delicate tresses litter the driveway—

shovelling a door through the snow
to free the imprisoned azaleas.   10

I half expect him to tend his trees
with aspirin and soup, the gardener

who finds in destruction
the very reason to carry on;

who would look at the ruins   15
of Eden and tell the hovering angel

to put down his sword,
there was work to be done.

—LINDA PASTAN (B. 1932)

QUESTIONS

1. *Kings Row* (1942) is a Hollywood film starring Ronald Reagan. In the film, Reagan's character has both his legs amputated.
2. Normally a gardener is associated with nurturing and tenderness, but in this poem gardening is associated with images of violence. Explain why these images are appropriate and effective.
3. Identify and discuss the Biblical image in the penultimate stanza. How do the garden of Eden and the "hovering angel" (16) relate to the poem as a whole?

My Last Duchess

Ferrara

That's my last duchess painted on the wall,
Looking as if she were alive. I call
That piece a wonder, now; Fra Pandolf's hands
Worked busily a day, and there she stands.
Will 't please you sit and look at her? I said   5
"Fra Pandolf" by design, for never read

Strangers like you that pictured countenance,
The depth and passion of its earnest glance,
But to myself they turned (since none puts by
The curtain I have drawn for you, but I)   10
And seemed as they would ask me, if they durst,
How such a glance came there; so, not the first
Are you to turn and ask thus. Sir, 'twas not
Her husband's presence only, called that spot
Of joy into the Duchess' cheek; perhaps   15
Fra Pandolf chanced to say, "Her mantle laps
Over my lady's wrist too much," or, "Paint
Must never hope to reproduce the faint
Half-flush that dies along her throat." Such stuff
Was courtesy, she thought, and cause enough   20
For calling up that spot of joy. She had
A heart—how shall I say?—too soon made glad,
Too easily impressed; she liked whate'er
She looked on, and her looks went everywhere.
Sir, 'twas all one! My favor at her breast,   25
The dropping of the daylight in the West,
The bough of cherries some officious fool
Broke in the orchard for her, the white mule
She rode with round the terrace—all and each
Would draw from her alike the approving speech,   30
Or blush, at least. She thanked men—good! but thanked
Somehow—I know not how—as if she ranked
My gift of a nine-hundred-years-old name
With anybody's gift. Who'd stoop to blame
This sort of trifling? Even had you skill   35
In speech—which I have not—to make your will
Quite clear to such an one, and say, "Just this
Or that in you disgusts me; here you miss,
Or there exceed the mark"—and if she let
Herself be lessoned so, nor plainly set   40
Her wits to yours, forsooth, and made excuse,
—E'en then would be some stooping; and I choose
Never to stoop. Oh, sir, she smiled, no doubt,
Whene'er I passed her; but who passed without
Much the same smile? This grew; I gave commands;   45
Then all smiles stopped together. There she stands
As if alive. Will 't please you rise? We'll meet
The company below, then. I repeat,

The Count your master's known munificence
Is ample warrant that no just pretense   50
Of mine for dowry will be disallowed;
Though his fair daughter's self, as I avowed
At starting, is my object. Nay, we'll go
Together down, sir. Notice Neptune, though,
Taming a sea-horse, thought a rarity,   55
Which Claus of Innsbruck cast in bronze for me!

—ROBERT BROWNING (1812–1889)

QUESTIONS

1. Vocabulary: *favor* (25), *officious* (27), *munificence* (49).
2. Ferrara is in Italy. The time is during the Renaissance, probably the sixteenth century. To whom is the Duke speaking? What is the occasion? Are the Duke's remarks about his last Duchess a digression, or do they have some relation to the business at hand?
3. Characterize the Duke as fully as you can. How does your characterization differ from the Duke's opinion of himself? What kind of irony is this?
4. Why was the Duke dissatisfied with his last Duchess? Was it sexual jealousy? What opinion do you get of the Duchess's personality, and how does it differ from the Duke's opinion?
5. What characteristics of the Italian Renaissance appear in the poem (marriage customs, social classes, art)? What is the Duke's attitude toward art? Is it insincere?
6. What happened to the Duchess? Should Browning have told us?

SUGGESTIONS FOR WRITING

1. Discuss the irony in one of the following poems. Does the poem employ verbal irony, dramatic irony, or irony of situation? How does the ironic content of the poem heighten its impact?
   a. Byron, "Stanzas" (page 891).
   b. Jonson, "Still to be neat" (page 933).
   c. Crane, "War Is Kind" (page 988).
   d. Dickinson, "I died for Beauty—but was scarce" (page 991).
   e. Larkin, "Aubade" (page 1020).

2. Each of the following poems deals, at least in part, with the relationship between the individual human being and a society that imposes a dehumanizing conformity. Choose any two of the poems and compare their use(s) of irony in conveying this theme.
   a. Dickinson, "Much Madness is divinest Sense" (page 792).
   b. Piercy, "Barbie Doll" (page 796).
   c. Auden, "The Unknown Citizen" (page 803).
   d. Atwood, "Siren Song" (page 818).
   e. Hughes, "Theme for English B" (page 1012).

PRACTICE AP WRITING PROMPTS ▮▮▮▮▮▮▮

Countee Cullen, "Incident" (p. 794) and Natasha Trethewey, "Southern History" (p. 833)

Read both "Incident" by Countee Cullen and "Southern History" by Natasha Trethewey carefully. Each poem captures a moment when the speaker is made sharply aware of his or her racial identity. In a comparison-contrast essay, show how elements such as tone, irony, and point of view help to convey the significance of these moments of recognition.

....

Percy Bysshe Shelley, "Ozymandias" (p. 799)

The sonnet "Ozymandias" turns on the words inscribed on the base of the ruined statue. If we examine the poem closely, we can identify as many as five distinct voices in the narrative, five separate persons who may have some stake in the language of the inscription: the ancient king, the unknown sculptor, the "traveler from an antique land," the narrative "I," and perhaps Shelley himself. Write an essay in which you describe the differences among these distinct voices, focusing especially on the quoted words in lines 10 and 11. Explore the motivation and attitude that might be ascribed to each voice, and show how the voices interact to produce the poem's ironic effect.

....

John Donne, "Batter my heart, three-personed God" (p. 802)

Carefully read John Donne's "Batter my heart, three-personed god." Write an essay in which you examine the speaker's ambivalent feelings and attitudes toward God. In your analysis, refer to such elements as metaphor, paradox, and poetic form.

....

Robert Browning, "My Last Duchess" (p. 806)

Robert Browning's poem "My Last Duchess" is a dramatic monologue in which the Duke of Ferrara speaks to the representative of a count whose daughter the duke wishes to marry. In the poem, he is speaking about his previous wife, his "last duchess." Read the poem with care, and then write an essay in which you show how Browning uses word choice, conversational rhythms, and implied tone of voice to create a discrepancy between what the speaker believes he is communicating and what he is actually revealing about himself.

....

CHAPTER EIGHT

Allusion

The famous English diplomat and letter writer Lord Chesterfield once was invited to a great dinner given by the Spanish ambassador. At the conclusion of the meal the host rose and proposed a toast to his master, the king of Spain, whom he compared to the sun. The French ambassador followed with a health to the king of France, whom he likened to the moon. It was then Lord Chesterfield's turn. "Your excellencies have taken from me," he said, "all the greatest luminaries of heaven, and the stars are too small for me to make a comparison of my royal master; I therefore beg leave to give your excellencies—Joshua!"*

A reader familiar with the Bible—that is, one who recognizes the biblical allusion—will recognize the witty point of Lord Chesterfield's story. For an **allusion**—a reference to something in history or previous literature—is, like a richly connotative word or a symbol, a means of suggesting far more than it says. The one word "Joshua," in the context of Chesterfield's toast, calls up in the reader's mind the whole biblical story of how the Israelite captain stopped the sun and the moon in order that the Israelites might finish a battle and conquer their enemies before nightfall (Josh. 10.12–14). The force of the toast lies in its extreme economy; it says so much in so little, and it exercises the mind of the reader to make the connection for himself.

The effect of Chesterfield's allusion is chiefly humorous or witty, but allusions also may have a powerful emotional effect. The essayist William Hazlitt writes of addressing a fashionable audience about the lexicographer Samuel Johnson. Speaking of Johnson's great heart and of his charity to the unfortunate, Hazlitt recounted how, finding a drunken prostitute lying in Fleet Street late at night, Johnson carried her on his broad back to the

*Samuel Shellabarger, *Lord Chesterfield and His World* (Boston: Little, Brown, 1951) 132.

address she managed to give him. The audience, unable to face the picture of the famous dictionary-maker doing such a thing, broke out in titters and expostulations, whereupon Hazlitt simply said: "I remind you, ladies and gentlemen, of the parable of the Good Samaritan." The audience was promptly silenced.*

Allusions are a means of reinforcing the emotion or the ideas of one's own work with the emotion or ideas of another work or occasion. Because they may compact so much meaning in so small a space, they are extremely useful to the poet.

"Out, Out—"

The buzz-saw snarled and rattled in the yard
And made dust and dropped stove-length sticks of wood,
Sweet-scented stuff when the breeze drew across it.
And from there those that lifted eyes could count
Five mountain ranges one behind the other   5
Under the sunset far into Vermont.
And the saw snarled and rattled, snarled and rattled,
As it ran light, or had to bear a load.
And nothing happened: day was all but done.
Call it a day, I wish they might have said   10
To please the boy by giving him the half hour
That a boy counts so much when saved from work.
His sister stood beside them in her apron
To tell them "Supper." At the word, the saw,
As if to prove saws knew what supper meant,   15
Leaped out at the boy's hand, or seemed to leap—
He must have given the hand. However it was,
Neither refused the meeting. But the hand!
The boy's first outcry was a rueful laugh,
As he swung toward them holding up the hand   20
Half in appeal, but half as if to keep
The life from spilling. Then the boy saw all—
Since he was old enough to know, big boy
Doing a man's work, though a child at heart—
He saw all spoiled. "Don't let him cut my hand off—   25
The doctor, when he comes. Don't let him, sister!"
So. But the hand was gone already.

*Jacques Barzun, *Teacher in America* (Boston: Little, Brown, 1945) 160.

The doctor put him in the dark of ether.
He lay and puffed his lips out with his breath.
And then—the watcher at his pulse took fright.   30
No one believed. They listened at his heart.
Little—less—nothing!—and that ended it.
No more to build on there. And they, since they
Were not the one dead, turned to their affairs.

—ROBERT FROST (1874–1963)

QUESTIONS

1. How does this poem differ from a newspaper account that might have dealt with the same incident?
2. To whom does "they" (33) refer? The boy's family? The doctor and medical attendants? Casual onlookers? Need we assume that all these people—whoever they are—turned immediately "to their affairs" (34)? Does the ending of this poem seem to you callous or merely realistic? Would a more tearful and sentimental ending have made the poem better or worse?
3. What is the figure of speech in lines 21–22?

Allusions vary widely in the burden put on them by the poet to convey meaning. Lord Chesterfield risked his whole meaning on his hearers' recognizing his allusion. Robert Frost in " 'Out, Out—' " makes his meaning entirely clear even for the reader who does not recognize the allusion contained in the poem's title. His theme is the uncertainty and unpredictability of life, which may end accidentally at any moment, and the tragic waste of human potentiality that takes place when such premature deaths occur. A boy who is already "Doing a man's work" and gives every promise of having a useful life ahead of him is suddenly wiped out. There seems no rational explanation for either the accident or the death. The only comment to be made is, "No more to build on there."

Frost's title, however, is an allusion to one of the most famous passages in all English literature, and it offers a good illustration of how a poet may use allusion not only to reinforce emotion but also to help define his theme. The passage is that in *Macbeth* in which Macbeth has just been informed of his wife's death. A good many readers will recall the key phrase, "Out, out, brief candle!" with its underscoring of the tragic brevity and uncertainty of life. For some readers, however, the allusion will summon up the whole passage in Act 5, scene 5, in which Macbeth uses this phrase:

She should have died hereafter;
There would have been a time for such a word.
Tomorrow, and tomorrow, and tomorrow

Creeps in this petty pace from day to day
To the last syllable of recorded time;   5
And all our yesterdays have lighted fools
The way to dusty death. Out, out, brief candle!
Life's but a walking shadow, a poor player,
That struts and frets his hour upon the stage
And then is heard no more. It is a tale   10
Told by an idiot, full of sound and fury,
Signifying nothing.

—WILLIAM SHAKESPEARE (1564–1616)

QUESTION

Examine Macbeth's speech for examples of personification, apostrophe, and metonymy.
How many metaphors for an individual human life does it present?

Macbeth's first words underscore the theme of premature death. The
boy also "should have died hereafter." The rest of the passage, with its marvelous evocation of the vanity and meaninglessness of life, expresses neither Shakespeare's philosophy nor, ultimately, Frost's, but it is Macbeth's
philosophy at the time of his bereavement, and it is likely to express the
feelings of us all when such tragic accidents occur. Life does indeed seem
cruel and meaningless, "a tale / Told by an idiot, ... / Signifying nothing,"
when human life and potentiality are thus without explanation so suddenly
ended.

Allusions also vary widely in the number of readers to whom they
will be familiar. Poets, in using an allusion, as in using a figure of speech,
are always in danger of being misunderstood. What appeals powerfully to
one reader may lose another reader altogether. But poets must assume a
certain fund of common experience in readers. They could not even write
about the ocean unless they could assume that readers have seen the ocean
or pictures of it. In the same way poets assume a certain common fund of
literary experience, most frequently of classical mythology, Shakespeare, or
the Bible—particularly the King James Version. Poets are often justified
in expecting a rather wide range of literary experience in readers, for the
people who read poetry for pleasure are generally intelligent and well-read.
But, obviously, beginning readers will not have this range, just as they will
not know the meanings of as many words as will more experienced readers.
Students should therefore be prepared to look up certain allusions, just as
they should look up in their dictionaries the meanings of unfamiliar words.
They will find that every increase in knowledge broadens their base for
understanding both literature and life.

REVIEWING CHAPTER EIGHT

....

1. Show how allusion is similar in its effect to connotative language as well as to symbolism.
2. Using examples from the poems that follow in this chapter, draw clear distinctions between allusions that reinforce the ideas in a poem and allusions that intensify the emotions being expressed—and note those allusions that carry both intellectual and emotional meanings.

The Maypole

—after Wallace Stevens

One must have a mind of spring
to regard the cherry tree burdened
with blossom;

and have been warm for days
to behold the boughs of the redbud   5
prickly with color in the glint

of the April sun; and not to think
of any cruelty in the difficult birthing
of so many leaves, to feel only pure

elation at the sound of the undulant breeze   10
which is the sound of every garden
with a breeze blowing among its flowers,

the sound the listener hears, watching the buds
which were not quite here a week ago
pushing up from oblivion now.   15

—LINDA PASTAN (B. 1932)

QUESTIONS

1. Read Wallace Stevens's "The Snow Man" (page 743) and compare "The Maypole" with that poem. How are they similar? How are they different?
2. Can you discern the attitude of the speaker in "The Maypole" toward the Stevens poem? Is it respectful? Ironic? Or a mixture of both?
3. Is Pastan's poem finally more optimistic or more pessimistic than Stevens's?

in Just—

in Just—
spring   when the world is mud-
luscious the little
lame balloonman

whistles   far   and wee   5

and eddieandbill come
running from marbles and
piracies and it's
spring

when the world is puddle-wonderful   10

the queer
old balloonman whistles
far   and   wee
and bettyandisbel come dancing

from hop-scotch and jump-rope and   15

it's
spring
and
    the
       goat-footed   20

balloonMan   whistles
far
and
wee

—E. E. CUMMINGS (1894–1962)

QUESTION

Why is the balloonman called "goat-footed" (20)? How does the identification made
by this mythological allusion enrich the meaning of the poem?

On His Blindness

When I consider how my light is spent
    Ere half my days in this dark world and wide,
    And that one talent which is death to hide
    Lodged with me useless, though my soul more bent
To serve therewith my Maker, and present   5
    My true account, lest he returning chide,
    "Doth God exact day-labor, light denied?"
    I fondly ask. But Patience, to prevent
That murmur, soon replies, "God doth not need
    Either man's work or his own gifts. Who best   10
    Bear his mild yoke, they serve him best. His state
Is kingly: thousands at his bidding speed,
    And post o'er land and ocean without rest;
    They also serve who only stand and wait."

—JOHN MILTON (1608–1674)

QUESTIONS

1. Vocabulary: *spent* (1), *fondly* (8), *prevent* (8), *post* (13).
2. What two meanings has "talent" (3)? What is Milton's "one talent"?
3. The poem is unified and expanded in its dimensions by a biblical allusion that Milton's original readers would have recognized immediately. What is it? If you do not know, look up Matthew 25.14–30. In what ways is the situation in the poem similar to that in the parable? In what ways is it different?
4. What is the point of the poem?

Miniver Cheevy

Miniver Cheevy, child of scorn,
    Grew lean while he assailed the seasons;
He wept that he was ever born,
    And he had reasons.

Miniver loved the days of old   5
    When swords were bright and steeds were prancing;
The vision of a warrior bold
    Would set him dancing.

Miniver sighed for what was not,
    And dreamed, and rested from his labors;   10
He dreamed of Thebes and Camelot,
    And Priam's neighbors.

Miniver mourned the ripe renown
    That made so many a name so fragrant;
He mourned Romance, now on the town,   15
    And Art, a vagrant.

Miniver loved the Medici,
    Albeit he had never seen one;
He would have sinned incessantly
    Could he have been one.   20

Miniver cursed the commonplace
    And eyed a khaki suit with loathing;
He missed the medieval grace
    Of iron clothing.

Miniver scorned the gold he sought,   25
    But sore annoyed was he without it;
Miniver thought, and thought, and thought,
    And thought about it.

Miniver Cheevy, born too late,
    Scratched his head and kept on thinking;   30
Miniver coughed, and called it fate,
    And kept on drinking.

—EDWIN ARLINGTON ROBINSON (1869–1935)

QUESTIONS

1. Vocabulary: *khaki* (22). The phrase "on the town" (15) means "on charity" or "down and out."
2. Identify Thebes (11), Camelot (11), Priam (12), and the Medici (17). What names and what sort of life does each call up? What does Miniver's love of these names tell about him?
3. Discuss the phrase "child of scorn" (1). What does it mean? In how many ways is it applicable to Miniver?
4. What is Miniver's attitude toward material wealth?
5. The phrase "rested from his labors" (10) alludes to the Bible *and* to Greek mythology. Explore the ironic effect of comparing Miniver to the Creator (Genesis 2.2) and to Hercules. Point out other examples of irony in the poem and discuss their importance.
6. Can we call this a poem about a man whose "fate" was to be "born too late"? Explain your answer.

My Son the Man

Suddenly his shoulders get a lot wider,
the way Houdini would expand his body
while people were putting him in chains. It seems
no time since I would help him put on his sleeper,
guide his calves into the shadowy interior,   5
zip him up and toss him up and
catch his weight. I cannot imagine him
no longer a child, and I know I must get ready,
get over my fear of men now my son
is going to be one. This was not   10
what I had in mind when he pressed up through me like a
sealed trunk through the ice of the Hudson,
snapped the padlock, unsnaked the chains,
appeared in my arms. Now he looks at me
the way Houdini studied a box   15
to learn the way out, then smiled and let himself be
     manacled.

—SHARON OLDS (B. 1942)

QUESTIONS

1. "Harry Houdini" was the stage name of Erich Weiss (1874–1926), an escape
   artist whose most famous stunt was freeing himself after being chained, sealed
   in a padlocked trunk, and dropped into deep water.
2. To what event does the speaker compare Houdini's escape?
3. How does this allusion express the speaker's feelings about her son? Are they
   mixed feelings?

Siren Song

This is the one song everyone
would like to learn: the song
that is irresistible:

the song that forces men
to leap overboard in squadrons   5
even though they see the beached skulls

the song nobody knows
because anyone who has heard it
is dead, and the others can't remember.

Shall I tell you the secret 10
and if I do, will you get me
out of this bird suit?

I don't enjoy it here
squatting on this island
looking picturesque and mythical 15

with these two feathery maniacs,
I don't enjoy singing
this trio, fatal and valuable.

I will tell the secret to you,
to you, only to you. 20
Come closer. This song

is a cry for help: Help me!
Only you, only you can,
you are unique

at last. Alas 25
it is a boring song
but it works every time.

—MARGARET ATWOOD (B. 1939)

QUESTIONS

1. Vocabulary: *Siren* (title).
2. What weakness in men does the siren exploit? How is this allusive poem about
   relations between women and men?

Journey of the Magi

"A cold coming we had of it,
Just the worst time of the year
For a journey, and such a long journey:
The ways deep and the weather sharp,
The very dead of winter." 5
And the camels galled, sore-footed, refractory,
Lying down in the melting snow.
There were times we regretted
The summer palaces on slopes, the terraces,

And the silken girls bringing sherbet.   10
Then the camel men cursing and grumbling
And running away, and wanting their liquor and women,
And the night-fires going out, and the lack of shelters,
And the cities hostile and the towns unfriendly
And the villages dirty and charging high prices: 15
A hard time we had of it.
At the end we preferred to travel all night,
Sleeping in snatches,
With the voices singing in our ears, saying
That this was all folly.   20

Then at dawn we came down to a temperate valley,
Wet, below the snow line, smelling of vegetation;
With a running stream and a water-mill beating the darkness,
And three trees on the low sky,
And an old white horse galloped away in the meadow.   25
Then we came to a tavern with vine-leaves over the lintel,
Six hands at an open door dicing for pieces of silver,
And feet kicking the empty wine-skins.
But there was no information, and so we continued
And arrived at evening, not a moment too soon   30
Finding the place; it was (you may say) satisfactory.

All this was a long time ago, I remember,
And I would do it again, but set down
This set down
This: were we led all that way for   35
Birth or Death? There was a Birth, certainly,
We had evidence and no doubt. I had seen birth and death,
But had thought they were different; this Birth was
Hard and bitter agony for us, like Death, our death.
We returned to our places, these Kingdoms,   40
But no longer at ease here, in the old dispensation,
With an alien people clutching their gods.
I should be glad of another death.

—T. S. ELIOT (1888–1965)

QUESTIONS

1. The biblical account of the journey of the Magi, or wise men, to Bethlehem is given in Matthew 2.1–12 and has since been elaborated by numerous legendary

accretions. It has been made familiar through countless pageants and Christmas cards. How does this account differ from the familiar one? Compare it with the biblical account. What has been added? What has been left out? What is the poet doing? (Lines 1–5 are in quotation marks because they are taken, with very slight modification, from a Christmas sermon [1622] by the Anglican bishop Lancelot Andrewes.)

2. Who is the speaker? Where and when is he speaking? What is the "old dispensation" (41) to which he refers, and why are the people "alien" (42)? Why does he speak of the "Birth" (38) as being "like Death" (39)? Of whose "Birth" and "Death" is he speaking? How does his life differ from the life he lived before his journey? What does he mean by saying that he would be "glad of another death" (43)?

3. This poem was written while the poet was undergoing religious conversion. (Eliot published it in 1927, the year he was confirmed in the Anglican Church.) Could the poem be considered a parable of the conversion experience? If so, how does this account differ from popular conceptions of this experience?

4. How do the images in the second section differ from those of the first? Do any of them suggest connections with the life of Christ?

Leda and the Swan

A sudden blow: the great wings beating still
Above the staggering girl, her thighs caressed
By the dark webs, her nape caught in his bill,
He holds her helpless breast upon his breast.

How can those terrified vague fingers push   5
The feathered glory from her loosening thighs?
And how can body, laid in that white rush,
But feel the strange heart beating where it lies?

A shudder in the loins engenders there
The broken wall, the burning roof and tower   10
And Agamemnon dead.

                    Being so caught up,
So mastered by the brute blood of the air,
Did she put on his knowledge with his power
Before the indifferent beak could let her drop?

—WILLIAM BUTLER YEATS (1865–1939)

QUESTIONS

1. What is the connection between Leda and "The broken wall, the burning roof and tower / And Agamemnon dead" (10–11)? If you do not know, look up the myth of Leda and the story of Agamemnon.
2. How does this poem do more than evoke an episode out of mythology? What is the significance of the question asked in the last two lines? How would you answer it?

On the Inevitable Decline into Mediocrity of the Popular Musician Who Attains a Comfortable Middle Age

O Sting, where is thy death?

—David Musgrave (b. 1965)

QUESTIONS

1. Read the Biblical passage to which this poem alludes: First Corinthians, 15.54–55. Discuss the contrast between the allusion and the topic of this poem.
2. Why is it appropriate that the title of the poem is longer than the poem itself?

SUGGESTIONS FOR WRITING

An allusion may present a comparison or parallel, or it may create an ironic contrast. Choosing one or more of the following examples, write an essay demonstrating that the poem(s) use allusion positively, to enrich the theme, or ironically, to undercut the speaker's ideas.

1. Larkin, "A Study of Reading Habits" (page 702; allusions to types of cheap fiction).
2. Keats, "On the Sonnet" (page 831; allusions to Andromeda and Midas).
3. Collins, "Sonnet" (page 832; allusions to Petrarch and Laura).
4. Ferlinghetti, "Constantly risking absurdity" (page 692, line 29; allusion to Charlie Chaplin).
5. Atwood, "Siren Song" (page 818; allusion to Greek mythology).
6. Dove, "Persephone, Falling" (page 994; allusion to Greek mythology).
7. Keats, "Ode to a Nightingale" (page 1015, line 66; allusion to the Book of Ruth).

PRACTICE AP WRITING PROMPTS

Sharon Olds, "35/10" (p. 818) and "My Son the Man" (p. 818)

See the comparison prompt for "My Son the Man" paired with "35/10" in Chapter Three of the Poetry section.

....

T. S. Eliot, "Journey of the Magi" (p. 819)

Read "The Journey of the Magi," paying close attention to the footnotes explaining some of the poem's allusions. Then write an essay in which you analyze how repetition, allusion, and detail enable the speaker to express his complex attitude toward Christ's nativity.

....

CHAPTER NINE

Meaning and Idea

The meaning of a poem is the experience it expresses—nothing less. But readers who, baffled by a particular poem, ask perplexedly, "What does it *mean?*" are usually after something more specific than this. They want something they can grasp entirely with their minds. We may therefore find it useful to distinguish the **total meaning** of a poem—the experience it communicates (and which can be communicated in no other way)—from its **prose meaning**—the ingredient that can be separated out in the form of a prose paraphrase (see Chapter 2). If we make this distinction, however, we must be careful not to confuse the two kinds of meaning. The prose meaning is no more the poem than a plum is a pie or a prune is a plum.

The prose meaning will not necessarily or perhaps even usually be an idea. It may be a story, a description, a statement of emotion, a presentation of human character, or some combination of these. "Porphyria's Lover" (page 894) tells a story; "The Eagle" (page 682) is primarily descriptive; "The Widow's Lament in Springtime" (page 736) is an expression of emotion; "My Last Duchess" (page 806) is an account of human character. None of these poems is directly concerned with ideas. Message-hunters will be baffled and disappointed by poetry of this kind because they will not find what they are looking for, and they may attempt to read some idea into the poem that is really not there. Yet ideas are also part of human experience, and therefore many poems are concerned, at least partially, with presenting ideas. But with these poems message-hunting is an even more dangerous activity, for the message-hunters are likely to think that the whole object of reading the poem is to find the message—that the idea is really the only important thing in it. Like Little Jack Horner, they will reach in and pluck out the idea and say, "What a good boy am I!" as if the pie existed for the plum.

The idea in a poem is only part of the total experience that it communicates. The value and worth of the poem are determined by the value of the total experience, not by the truth or the nobility of the idea itself. This is not to say that the truth of the idea is unimportant, or that its validity should not be examined and appraised. But a good idea alone will not make a good poem, nor need an idea with which the reader does not agree ruin one. Readers of poetry are receptive to all kinds of experience. They are able to make that "willing suspension of disbelief" that Coleridge characterized as constituting poetic faith. When one attends a performance of *Hamlet,* one is willing to forget for the time being that such a person as Hamlet never existed and that the events on the stage are fictions. Likewise, poetry readers should be willing to entertain imaginatively, for the time being, ideas they objectively regard as untrue. It is one way of better understanding these ideas and of enlarging the reader's own experience. The person who believes in God should be able to enjoy a good poem expressing atheistic ideas, just as the atheist should be able to appreciate a good poem in praise of God. The optimist should be able to find pleasure in pessimistic poetry, and the pessimist in optimistic poetry. The teetotaler should be able to enjoy *The Rubáiyát of Omar Khayyám,* and the winebibber a good poem in praise of abstinence. The primary value of a poem depends not so much on the truth of the idea presented as on the power with which it is communicated and on its being made a convincing part of a meaningful total experience. We must feel that the idea has been truly and deeply *felt* by the poet, and that the poet is doing something more than merely moralizing. The plum must be made part of a pie. If the plum is properly combined with other ingredients and if the pie is well baked, it should be enjoyable even for persons who do not care for the type of plums from which it is made. Consider, for instance, the following two poems.

Loveliest of Trees

Loveliest of trees, the cherry now
Is hung with bloom along the bough,
And stands about the woodland ride
Wearing white for Eastertide.

Now, of my threescore years and ten,   5
Twenty will not come again,
And take from seventy springs a score,
It only leaves me fifty more.

And since to look at things in bloom
Fifty springs are little room,   10

About the woodlands I will go
To see the cherry hung with snow.

—A. E. HOUSMAN (1859–1936)

QUESTIONS

1. Very briefly, this poem presents a philosophy of life. In a sentence, what is it?
2. How old is the speaker? Why does he assume that his life will be seventy years in length? What is surprising about the words "only" (8) and "little" (10)?
3. A good deal of ink has been spilt over whether "snow" (12) is literal or figurative. What do you say? Justify your answer.

Stopping by Woods on a Snowy Evening

Whose woods these are I think I know.
His house is in the village though;
He will not see me stopping here
To watch his woods fill up with snow.

My little horse must think it queer   5
To stop without a farmhouse near
Between the woods and frozen lake
The darkest evening of the year.

He gives his harness bells a shake
To ask if there is some mistake.   10
The only other sound's the sweep
Of easy wind and downy flake.

The woods are lovely, dark and deep,
But I have promises to keep,
And miles to go before I sleep,   15
And miles to go before I sleep.

—ROBERT FROST (1874–1963)

QUESTIONS

1. How do these two poems differ in idea?
2. What contrasts are suggested between the speaker in the second poem and (a) his horse and (b) the owner of the woods?

Both of these poems present ideas, the first more or less explicitly, the second symbolically. Perhaps the best way to get at the idea of the second poem is to ask two questions. First, why does the speaker stop? Second, why does he go on? He stops, we answer, to watch the woods fill up with snow—to observe a scene of natural beauty. He goes on, we answer, because he has "promises to keep"—that is, he has obligations to fulfill. He is momentarily torn between his love of beauty and these other various and complex claims that life has upon him. The small conflict in the poem is symbolic of a larger conflict in life. One part of the sensitive, thinking person would like to give up his life to the enjoyment of beauty and art. But another part is aware of larger duties and responsibilities—responsibilities owed, at least in part, to other human beings. The speaker in the poem would like to satisfy both impulses. But when the two conflict, he seems to suggest, the "promises" must take precedence.

The first poem also presents a philosophy but it is an opposing one. For the twenty-year-old speaker, the appreciation of beauty is of such importance that he will make it his lifelong dedication, filling his time with enjoying whatever the seasons bring. The metaphor comparing white cherry blossoms to snow suggests that each season has its own special beauty, though the immediate season is spring. In a limited life, one should seek out and delight in whatever beauty is present. Thoughtful readers will have to choose between these two philosophies—to commit themselves to one or the other—but this commitment should not destroy for them their enjoyment of either poem. If it does, they are reading for plums and not for pies.

Nothing we have said so far in this chapter should be construed as meaning that the truth or falsity of the idea in a poem is a matter of no importance. *Other things being equal,* good readers naturally will, and properly should, value more highly the poem whose idea they feel to be more mature and nearer to the heart of human experience. Some ideas, moreover, may seem so vicious or so foolish or so beyond the pale of normal human decency as to discredit *by themselves* the poems in which they are found. A rotten plum may spoil a pie. But good readers strive for intellectual flexibility and tolerance, and are able to entertain sympathetically ideas other than their own. They often will like a poem whose idea they disagree with better than one with an idea they accept. And, above all, they will not confuse the prose meaning of any poem with its total meaning. They will not mistake plums for pies.

REVIEWING CHAPTER NINE

....

1. The second paragraph of this chapter identifies four poems as not being "directly concerned with ideas"; examine those poems and demonstrate that although that statement is true of the prose meaning of each, the total meaning does in fact express an idea.

2. Explain how a poem that expresses an idea with which you do not agree may, nevertheless, be a source of appreciation and enjoyment.

3. The poems that follow in this chapter are paired in terms of their contrasted ideas; as you read them, practice discriminating between their ideas as we have done with the pair of poems by Housman and Frost, and determine which of the contrasted ideas more closely reflects your own beliefs.

4. Having determined where your beliefs are reflected, explain how the contrasting poem nevertheless has qualities you can admire.

Cootchie

Cootchie, Miss Lula's servant, lies in marl,
black into white she went
    below the surface of the coral-reef.
Her life was spent
    in caring for Miss Lula, who is deaf,   5
eating her dinner off the kitchen sink
while Lula ate hers off the kitchen table.
The skies were egg-white for the funeral
    and the faces sable.

Tonight the moonlight will alleviate   10
the melting of the pink wax roses
    planted in tin cans filled with sand
placed in a line to mark Miss Lula's losses;
    but who will shout and make her understand?
Searching the land and sea for someone else,   15
the lighthouse will discover Cootchie's grave
and dismiss all as trivial; the sea, desperate,
    will proffer wave after wave.

—Elizabeth Bishop (1911–1979)

QUESTIONS

1. Vocabulary: *marl* (1); *proffer* (18).
2. What does the poem tell us about the principal characters Cootchie and Miss Lula?
3. What is the speaker's attitude toward Cootchie? Toward Miss Lula?
4. How does the symbol of the ocean, near the end of the poem, help to clarify the significance of Cootchie's life?

Design

I found a dimpled spider, fat and white,
On a white heal-all, holding up a moth
Like a white piece of rigid satin cloth—
Assorted characters of death and blight
Mixed ready to begin the morning right,   5
Like the ingredients of a witches' broth—
A snow-drop spider, a flower like a froth,
And dead wings carried like a paper kite.

What had that flower to do with being white,
The wayside blue and innocent heal-all?   10
What brought the kindred spider to that height,
Then steered the white moth thither in the night?
What but design of darkness to appall?—
If design govern in a thing so small.

—ROBERT FROST (1874–1963)

QUESTIONS

1. Vocabulary: *characters* (4), *snow-drop* (7).
2. The heal-all is a wildflower, usually blue or violet but occasionally white, found blooming along roadsides in the summer. It was once supposed to have healing qualities, hence its name. Of what significance, scientific and poetic, is the fact that the spider, the heal-all, and the moth are all white? Of what poetic significance is the fact that the spider is "dimpled" and "fat" and like a "snow-drop," and that the flower is "innocent" and named "heal-all"?
3. The "argument from design"—that the manifest existence of design in the universe implies the existence of a Great Designer—was a favorite eighteenth-century argument for the existence of God. What twist does Frost give the argument? What answer does he suggest to the question in lines 11–12? How comforting is the apparent concession in line 14?

O sweet spontaneous

O sweet spontaneous
earth how often have
the
doting

    fingers of   5
prurient philosophers pinched
and
poked

thee
,has the naughty thumb   10
of science prodded
thy

beauty   .how
often have religions taken
thee upon their scraggy knees   15
squeezing and

buffeting thee that thou mightest conceive
gods
    (but
true   20

to the incomparable
couch of death thy
rhythmic
lover

    thou answerest   25

them only with

       spring)

—E. E. CUMMINGS (1894–1962)

QUESTIONS

1. What metaphorical context is created by such words as *doting, prurient, naughty, conceive* (4, 6, 10, 17) and others? What have the philosophers attempted to do, and to what purpose?

2. Explain "the incomparable / couch of death" (21–22) and the "rhythmic / lover" (23–24).
3. How is "spring" (27) a response to the philosophers' attempts?

When I Heard the Learn'd Astronomer

When I heard the learn'd astronomer,
When the proofs, the figures, were ranged in columns
   before me,
When I was shown the charts and diagrams, to add, divide,
   and measure them,
When I sitting heard the astronomer where he lectured
   with much applause in the lecture-room,
How soon unaccountable I became tired and sick,   5
Till rising and gliding out I wandered off by myself,
In the mystical moist night-air, and from time to time,
Looked up in perfect silence at the stars.

—WALT WHITMAN (1819–1892)

QUESTIONS

1. What is it that makes the speaker "tired and sick" (5)?
2. Explain how "gliding" and "wandered off" (6) are contrasted to the astronomer's lecture. How is the phrase "from time to time" (7) a denial of the validity of the scientific approach to the universe? What attitude is expressed by the speaker's "perfect silence" (8)?
3. Both Whitman and cummings present emotional objections to science and scientific attempts to explain nature. How are these poems different in tone (see page 838)?

On the Sonnet

If by dull rhymes our English must be chained,
And like Andromeda, the sonnet sweet
Fettered, in spite of painéd loveliness,
Let us find, if we must be constrained,
Sandals more interwoven and complete   5
To fit the naked foot of Poesy:
Let us inspect the lyre, and weigh the stress
Of every chord, and see what may be gained
By ear industrious, and attention meet;

Misers of sound and syllable, no less 10
Than Midas of his coinage, let us be
Jealous of dead leaves in the bay-wreath crown;
So, if we may not let the Muse be free,
She will be bound with garlands of her own.

—JOHN KEATS (1795–1821)

QUESTIONS

1. Vocabulary: Andromeda (2), meet (9), Midas (11).
2. The poem prescribes a specific approach to writing sonnets. What qualities does the speaker suggest a good sonnet should have?
3. The speaker compares poetry to a foot and the sonnet form to a sandal. What does he mean by suggesting that the sonnet-sandals should be "more interwoven and complete" (5)?
4. What negative qualities does the poem imply that bad sonnets display?

Sonnet

All we need is fourteen lines, well, thirteen now,
and after this one just a dozen
to launch a little ship on love's storm-tossed seas,
then only ten more left like rows of beans.
How easily it goes unless you get Elizabethan 5
and insist the iambic bongos must be played
and rhymes positioned at the ends of lines,
one for every station of the cross.
But hang on here while we make the turn
into the final six where all will be resolved, 10
where longing and heartache will find an end,
where Laura will tell Petrarch to put down his pen,
take off those crazy medieval tights,
blow out the lights, and come at last to bed.

—BILLY COLLINS (B. 1941)

QUESTIONS

1. In line 12, "Laura will tell Petrarch to put down his pen," the poem alludes to the Italian poet Francesco Petrarch (1304–1374), who wrote a sequence of sonnets to his idealized lady-love, Laura. What attitude does the speaker take toward Petrarch and the Petrarchan sonnet?

2. The phrase "love's storm-tossed seas" (3) is a deliberate cliché. Why is the cliché appropriate here?
3. What is the effect of images such as "rows of beans" (4) and "iambic bongos" (6)? How do they help create the speaker's distinctive voice?
4. While this and the preceding poem differ greatly in language and emotion, they may be compared as statements about the sonnet. What are their essential ideas about this poetic form?

Southern History

Before the war, they were happy, he said,
quoting our textbook. (This was senior-year

history class.) *The slaves were clothed, fed,*
and better off under a master's care.

I watched the words blur on the page. No one   5
raised a hand, disagreed. Not even me.

It was late; we still had Reconstruction
to cover before the test, and—luckily

three hours of watching *Gone with the Wind.*
History, the teacher said, *of the old South—*   10

a true account of how things were back then.
On screen a slave stood big as life: big mouth,

bucked eyes, our textbook's grinning proof—a lie
my teacher guarded. Silent, so did I.

—NATASHA TRETHEWEY (B. 1966)

QUESTIONS

1. Is the history teacher African American? Is he presenting his own attitudes or those he is expected to teach? If the speaker can detect a lie in the lesson, can the teacher?
2. Why do none of the students disagree with the lesson? How does the speaker feel about herself? How does she feel about the teacher?

Kentucky, 1833

It is Sunday, day of roughhousing. We are let out in the woods. The
young boys wrestle and butt their heads together like sheep—a circle
forms; claps and shouts fill the air. The women, brown and glossy,
gather round the banjo player, or simply lie in the sun, legs and aprons
folded. The weather's an odd monkey—any other day he's on our backs,   5
his cotton eye everywhere; today the light sifts down like the finest
cornmeal, coating our hands and arms with a dust. God's dust, old
woman Acker says. She's the only one who could read to us from the
Bible, before Massa forbade it. On Sundays, something hangs in the
air, a hallelujah, a skitter of brass, but we can't call it by name and it   10
disappears.

Then Massa and his gentlemen friends come to bet on the boys. They
guffaw and shout, taking sides, red-faced on the edge of the boxing ring.
There is more kicking, butting, and scuffling—the winner gets a dram   15
of whiskey if he can drink it all in one swig without choking.

Jason is bucking and prancing about—Massa said his name reminded
him of some sailor, a hero who crossed an ocean, looking for a golden
cotton field. Jason thinks he's been born to great things—a suit with
gold threads, vest and all. Now the winner is sprawled out under a tree   20
and the sun, that weary tambourine, hesitates at the rim of the sky's
green light. It's a crazy feeling that carries through the night; as if the
sky were an omen we could not understand, the book that, if we could
read, would change our lives.

—RITA DOVE (B. 1953)

QUESTIONS

1. In this **prose poem** (see page 876) the speaker is remembering an experience
   of a group of slaves. Is the experience good or bad? Find details that support
   both impressions.
2. Examine the poem for its imagery and figurative language. Do these justify calling
   it a poem?
3. Does Dove's poem present a more or less moving condemnation of slavery than
   Trethewey's?

The Lamb

Little Lamb, who made thee?
Dost thou know who made thee?
Gave thee life and bid thee feed
By the stream and o'er the mead;
Gave thee clothing of delight,   5
Softest clothing wooly bright;
Gave thee such a tender voice,
Making all the vales rejoice!
Little Lamb, who made thee?
Dost thou know who made thee?   10

Little Lamb, I'll tell thee,
Little Lamb, I'll tell thee!
He is callèd by thy name,
For he calls himself a Lamb;
He is meek and he is mild,   15
He became a little child;
I a child and thou a lamb,
We are callèd by his name.
Little Lamb, God bless thee.
Little Lamb, God bless thee.   20

—WILLIAM BLAKE (1757–1827)

QUESTIONS

1. Why does the speaker address the "Little Lamb" (1) directly? What effects does the poem gain from this use of apostrophe?
2. What is the relationship between the two stanzas? Why is the poem constructed in this way?
3. What is the significance of the "lamb" imagery? What connotations does it have?

The Tiger

Tiger! Tiger! burning bright
In the forests of the night,
What immortal hand or eye
Could frame thy fearful symmetry?

In what distant deeps or skies   5
Burnt the fire of thine eyes?

On what wings dare he aspire?
What the hand dare seize the fire?

And what shoulder, and what art,
Could twist the sinews of thy heart?   10
And when thy heart began to beat,
What dread hand forged thy dread feet?

What the hammer? what the chain?
In what furnace was thy brain?
What the anvil? what dread grasp   15
Dare its deadly terrors clasp?

When the stars threw down their spears,
And watered heaven with their tears,
Did he smile his work to see?
Did he who made the Lamb make thee?   20

Tiger! Tiger! burning bright
In the forests of the night,
What immortal hand or eye
Dare frame thy fearful symmetry?

—WILLIAM BLAKE (1757–1827)

QUESTIONS

1. Discuss the relationship of this poem to Blake's "The Lamb." How do the poems make a distinctive and meaningful pairing?
2. What is the meaning of the various questions the speaker asks of the tiger? What are the implications of these questions?
3. What is the symbolic meaning of the tiger? What connotations are associated with this symbol?

SUGGESTIONS FOR WRITING

Explore the contrasting ideas in the following pairs or groups of poems:

1. Brooks, "The Bean Eaters" (page 691) and Clifton, "good times" (page 982).
2. Hayden, "Those Winter Sundays" (page 741) and Roethke, "My Papa's Waltz" (page 1035).
3. Hopkins, "Spring" (page 735); Housman, "Loveliest of Trees" (page 825); and Williams, "Spring and All" (page 1047).
4. Pastan, "To a Daughter Leaving Home" (page 893) and Wilbur, "The Writer" (page 778).
5. Clifton, "in the inner city" (page 805) and Brooks, "a song in the front yard" (page 980).
6. Collins, "The History Teacher" (page 986) and Trethewey, "Southern History" (page 833).

PRACTICE AP WRITING PROMPTS ▅▅▅▅▅▅▅▅▅

A. E. Housman, "Loveliest of Trees" (p. 825) and Robert Frost, "Stopping by Woods on a Snowy Evening" (p. 826)

"Loveliest of Trees" by A. E. Housman and "Stopping by Woods on a Snowy Evening" by Robert Frost are both set amidst the beauty of the woods. Write an essay in which you compare and contrast the speakers' contrary moods, indicating how each employs a season to frame his particular response to beauty. In your essay, refer to such poetic techniques as metaphor, imagery, and understatement.

....

e. e. cummings, "O sweet spontaneous" (p. 830) and Walt Whitman, "When I Heard the Learn'd Astronomer" (p. 831)

"O sweet spontaneous" and "When I Heard the Learn'd Astronomer" both praise the mystery and wonders of the universe that continue to inspire awe amidst scientific advancement and rationality. Read each poem carefully. Then, in a well-organized analysis, compare and contrast the poems, showing how each poem's form, tone, or other literary elements convey the speaker's awe and wonder in the face of these enduring natural mysteries.

....

Countee Cullen, "Incident" (p. 794) and Natasha Trethewey, "Southern History" (p. 833)

See the comparison prompt for "Southern History" paired with "Incident" in Chapter Seven of the Poetry section.

....

CHAPTER TEN

Tone

Tone, in literature, may be defined as the writer's or speaker's attitude toward the subject, the reader, or herself or himself. It is the emotional coloring, or the emotional meaning, of the work and is an extremely important part of the full meaning. In spoken language it is indicated by the inflections of the speaker's voice. If, for instance, a friend tells you, "I'm going to get married today," the facts of the statement are entirely clear. But the emotional meaning of the statement may vary widely according to the tone of voice with which it is uttered. The tone may be ecstatic ("Hooray! I'm going to get married today!"); it may be incredulous ("I can't believe it! I'm going to get married today"); it may be despairing ("Horrors! I'm going to get married today"); it may be resigned ("Might as well face it. I'm going to get married today"). Obviously, a correct interpretation of the tone will be an important part of understanding the full meaning. It may even have rather important consequences. If someone calls you a fool, your interpretation of the tone may determine whether you take it as an insult or as playful banter. If a person says "No" to your proposal of marriage, your interpretation of the tone may determine whether you ask again or start dating someone else.

In poetry, tone is likewise important. We have not really understood a poem unless we have accurately sensed whether the attitude it manifests is playful or solemn, mocking or reverent, calm or excited. But the correct determination of tone in literature is a much more delicate matter than it is in spoken language, for we do not have the speaker's voice to guide us. We must learn to recognize tone by other means. Almost all of the elements of poetry help to indicate its tone: connotation, imagery, and metaphor; irony and understatement; rhythm, sentence construction, and formal pattern. There is therefore no simple formula for recognizing tone. It is an end product of all the elements in a poem. The best we can do is illustrate.

Robert Frost's "Stopping by Woods on a Snowy Evening" (page 826) seems a simple poem, but it has always afforded trouble to beginning readers. A very good student, asked to interpret it, once wrote this: "The poem means that we are forever passing up pleasures to go onward to what we wrongly consider our obligations. We would like to watch the snow fall on the peaceful countryside, but we always have to rush home to supper and other engagements. Frost feels that the average person considers life too short to stop and take time to appreciate true pleasures." This student did a good job in recognizing the central conflict of the poem but went astray in recognizing its tone. Let's examine why.

In the first place, the fact that the speaker in the poem *does* stop to watch the snow fall in the woods immediately establishes him as a human being with more sensitivity and feeling for beauty than most. He is not one of the people of Wordsworth's sonnet (page 727) who, "Getting and spending," have laid waste their imaginative powers and lost the capacity to be stirred by nature. Frost's speaker is contrasted with his horse, who, as a creature of habit and an animal without esthetic perception, cannot understand the speaker's reason for stopping. There is also a suggestion of contrast with the "owner" of the woods, who, if he saw the speaker stopping, might be as puzzled as the horse. (Who most truly "profits" from the woods—its absentee owner or the person who can enjoy its beauty?) The speaker goes on because he has "promises to keep." But the word "promises," though it may here have a wry ironic undertone of regret, has a favorable connotation: people almost universally agree that promises ought to be kept. If the poet had used a different term, say, "things to do," or "business to attend to," or "financial affairs to take care of," or "money to make," the connotations would have been quite different. As it is, the tone of the poem tells us that the poet is sympathetic to the speaker; Frost is endorsing rather than censuring the speaker's action. Perhaps we may go even further. In the concluding two lines, because of their climactic position, because they are repeated, and because "sleep" in poetry often figuratively refers to death, there is a suggestion of symbolic interpretation: "and many years to live before I die." If we accept this interpretation, it poses a parallel between giving oneself up to contemplation of the woods and dying. The poet's total implication would seem to be that beauty is a distinctively human value that deserves its place in a full life, but to devote one's life to its pursuit, at the expense of other obligations and duties, is tantamount to one's death as a responsible being. The poet therefore accepts the choice the speaker makes, though not without a touch of regret.

Differences in tone, and their importance, are most apparent in poems with similar content. Consider, for instance, the following pair.

To the Snake

Green Snake, when I hung you round my neck
and stroked your cold, pulsing throat
   as you hissed to me, glinting
arrowy gold scales, and I felt
   the weight of you on my shoulders,   5
and the whispering silver of your dryness
   sounded close at my ears—

Green Snake—I swore to my companions that certainly
   you were harmless! But truly
I had no certainty, and no hope, only desiring   10
   to hold you, for that joy,
                which left
a long wake of pleasure, as the leaves moved
and you faded into the pattern
of grass and shadows, and I returned   15
smiling and haunted, to a dark morning.

—Denise Levertov (1923–1977)

QUESTIONS

1. What figure of speech dominates in the poem? How does that reinforce the closeness the speaker is reporting?
2. Comment on these word pairs: "cold, pulsing" (2), "arrowy gold" (4), "smiling and haunted" (16), and "dark morning" (16). How do they contribute to the emotional meaning?
3. Is the experience of the speaker positive, or negative, or a combination?

A narrow Fellow in the Grass

A narrow Fellow in the Grass
Occasionally rides—
You may have met him? Did you not
His notice sudden is—

The Grass divides as with a Comb—   5
A spotted shaft is seen—
And then it closes at your feet
And opens further on—

He likes a Boggy Acre
A Floor too cool for Corn—
Yet when a Boy, and Barefoot—
I more than once at Noon

10

Have passed, I thought, a Whip lash—
Unbraiding in the Sun
When stooping to secure it
It wrinkled, and was gone—

15

Several of Nature's People
I know, and they know me—
I feel for them a transport
Of cordiality—

20

But never met this Fellow
Attended, or alone
Without a tighter breathing
And Zero at the Bone.

—EMILY DICKINSON (1830–1886)

QUESTIONS

1. Vocabulary: *Whip lash* (whiplash) (13), *transport* (19), *cordiality* (20).
2. Explain the simile in line 5.
3. Characterize the speaker.

Both poems exhibit a fascination with snakes, both relate a personal experience with them, and both focus on the emotional aftermath of that experience. But in tone the two poems are sharply different. The first is ecstatically engaged from the outset, not only emotional but even physical in its presentation of the experience. The second is detached, descriptive, and analytical, revealing its emotional response only in the last stanza. Let us examine the difference.

The first begins with an apostrophe, addressing the snake directly and thus bringing the reader into a close relationship with it as the speaker handles it, hangs it about her neck, strokes it, listens to its hissing, feels its weight, and stares at its beauty. At line 8 she turns to her "companions" to witness her closeness, but dismisses them to focus again on the snake itself. The intense moment of "joy" passes, leaving an intense memory of pleasure and the double response of "smiling" to her companions while being "haunted" by the whole encounter.

The second poem begins descriptively (and in typical Dickinson fashion, mysteriously, because the subject is not named). The snake is a familiar "fellow" who rides through the grass, startling the observer by his sudden appearance and disappearance. At line 11 the speaker reveals himself as a mature man recalling his boyhood experience and his acquired knowledge of the snake's preferred environment. The action then is focused on one particular encounter when the boy mistook the snake for a leather whip lying in the sun and—as boys will—attempted to pick up this exciting implement. The snake disappeared as suddenly as it can appear. The consequence of that moment is then generalized: the adult man has found throughout his life a "cordiality" for natural creatures, but not for snakes. They terrify him, and by implication he would much rather avoid them altogether. That momentary deceptiveness in his young life, when the snake seemed an attractive object, has resulted in continuing animosity.

In understanding the tone of these two poems we might explore the implicit allusion to the story of Eve in the garden of Eden, enticed by the serpent into disobeying God and thus to the punishments that resulted (Genesis: 1–24). There we are told that Eve and the serpent will be eternal enemies, and that Adam will share in the miseries that ensued. Levertov's poem invites the reader to equate her story of seduction, pleasure, and loss with Eve's experience, focusing chiefly on the seduction in language that implies physical sexuality. Dickinson's poem, by deliberately choosing a male speaker and appealing to the stereotype that makes little boys more curious and aggressive, plays against the feminine stereotype of squeamishness about bugs, worms, snakes, and the like. The boy is attracted to the snake because it resembles an object of boyish self-expression, a weapon to be wielded.

Both poems conclude with a sense of separation from the snake, but with opposite effect: for Dickinson's speaker, a lifelong terror; for Levertov's, a lifelong loss.

We have been discussing tone as if every poem could be distinguished by a single tone. But varying or shifting tones in a single poem are often a valuable means for achieving the poet's purpose, and indeed may create the dramatic structure of a poem. Consider the following:

Since there's no help

Since there's no help, come let us kiss and part;
Nay, I have done, you get no more of me,
And I am glad, yea, glad with all my heart
That thus so cleanly I myself can free;
Shake hands forever, cancel all our vows,   5

And when we meet at any time again,
Be it not seen in either of our brows
That we one jot of former love retain.
Now, at the last gasp of Love's latest breath,
When, his pulse failing, Passion speechless lies,   10
When Faith is kneeling by his bed of death,
And Innocence is closing up his eyes,
Now, if thou wouldst, when all have given him over,
From death to life thou mightst him yet recover.

—MICHAEL DRAYTON (1563–1631)

QUESTIONS

1. What difference in tone do you find between the first eight lines and the last six? In which part is the speaker more sincere? What differences in rhythm and language help to establish the difference in tone?
2. How many figures are there in the allegorical scene in lines 9–12? What do the pronouns "his" and "him" in lines 10–14 refer to? What is dying? Why? How might the person addressed still restore it from death to life?
3. Define the dramatic situation as precisely as possible, taking into consideration both the man's attitude and the woman's.

Accurately determining tone, whether it be the tone of a rejected marriage proposal or of an insulting remark, is extremely important when interpreting language in poetry as well as in everyday conversations. For the experienced reader it will be instinctive and automatic. For the inexperienced reader it will require study. But beyond the general suggestions for reading that we already have made, there are no specific instructions we can give. Recognition of tone requires an increasing familiarity with the meanings and connotations of words, alertness to the presence of irony and other figures, and, above all, careful reading.

Picnic, Lightning

My very photogenic mother died in a freak accident
(picnic, lightning) when I was three.

Lolita

It is possible to be struck by a meteor
or a single-engine plane
while reading in a chair at home.

Safes drop from rooftops
and flatten the odd pedestrian   5
mostly within the panels of the comics,
but still, we know it is possible,
as well as the flash of summer lightning,
the thermos toppling over,
spilling out on the grass.   10

And we know the message
can be delivered from within.
The heart, no valentine,
decides to quit after lunch,
the power shut off like a switch,   15
or a tiny dark ship is unmoored
into the flow of the body's rivers,
the brain a monastery,
defenseless on the shore.

This is what I think about   20
when I shovel compost
into a wheelbarrow,
and when I fill the long flower boxes,
then press into rows
the limp roots of red impatiens—   25
the instant hand of Death
always ready to burst forth
from the sleeve of his voluminous cloak.

Then the soil is full of marvels,
bits of leaf like flakes off a fresco,   30
red-brown pine needles, a beetle quick
to burrow back under the loam.
Then the wheelbarrow is a wider blue,
the clouds a brighter white,
and all I hear is the rasp of the steel edge   35
against a round stone,
the small plants singing
with lifted faces, and the click
of the sundial
as one hour sweeps into the next.   40

—BILLY COLLINS (B. 1941)

QUESTIONS

1. Vocabulary: *unmoored* (16), *voluminous* (28).
2. What is the meaning of the epigraph taken from Vladimir Nabokov's *Lolita*? How does the epigraph help us to focus and understand the poem?
3. Various kinds of accidents are discussed in the poem, both external and internal. What is the poem saying about the perilous and provisional nature of life's experiences? What tone does the speaker adopt in writing about this topic?
4. Why does the speaker use gardening metaphors from line 21 to the end of the poem? How do these metaphors enrich the poem's meaning?

REVIEWING CHAPTER TEN

1. Consider the ways in which tone is part of the total meaning of a poem (you might think of the total meaning as a compound of the intellectual and the emotional).
2. The second paragraph of this chapter lists many of the elements of poetry that contribute to tone; as you examine the first two poems presented in the chapter, try to identify which of the elements are particularly significant in each of them.
3. Tone is customarily identified by an adjective (*wistful, pessimistic, horrified* in the discussion of the first two poems). Choose adjectives to identify the two contrasting tones in "Since there's no help." (Do not settle for the first adjective that pops into mind—this is a good opportunity to exercise your vocabulary and strive for precision.)

My mistress' eyes

My mistress' eyes are nothing like the sun;
Coral is far more red than her lips' red;
If snow be white, why then her breasts are dun;
If hairs be wires, black wires grow on her head.
I have seen roses damasked,° red and white,   of different colors
But no such roses see I in her cheeks;   6
And in some perfumes is there more delight
Than in the breath that from my mistress reeks.°   exhales
I love to hear her speak, yet well I know
That music hath a far more pleasing sound;   10
I grant I never saw a goddess go,—

My mistress, when she walks, treads on the ground.
And yet, by heaven, I think my love as rare
As any she belied with false compare.

—WILLIAM SHAKESPEARE (1564–1616)

QUESTIONS

1. The speaker draws a contrast between the qualities often praised in exaggerated love poetry and the reality of his mistress' physical attributes. Construct the series of "false compar[isons]" that this poem implies that other poets have used (eyes as bright as the sun, hair like spun gold, etc.).
2. What is the speaker's tone in lines 1–12? Is there anything about those lines that his mistress might find pleasing? (In Shakespeare's time the word "reeks" did not have its modern denotation of "stinks.")
3. The tone clearly shifts with line 13—signaled by the simple phrase "And yet." What is the tone of the last two lines? The last line might be paraphrased "as any woman who has been lied to with false comparisons." How important are truth and lies as subjects in the poem?

Crossing the Bar

Sunset and evening star,
   And one clear call for me!
And may there be no moaning of the bar
   When I put out to sea,

But such a tide as moving seems asleep,   5
   Too full for sound and foam,
When that which drew from out the boundless deep
   Turns again home.

Twilight and evening bell,
   And after that the dark!   10
And may there be no sadness of farewell
   When I embark;

For though from out our bourne of Time and Place
   The flood may bear me far,
I hope to see my Pilot face to face   15
   When I have crossed the bar.

—ALFRED, LORD TENNYSON (1809–1892)

QUESTIONS

1. Vocabulary: *bourne* (13).
2. What two sets of figures does Tennyson use for approaching death? What is the precise moment of death in each set?
3. In troubled weather the wind and waves above the sandbar across a harbor's mouth make a moaning sound. What metaphorical meaning has the "moaning of the bar" (3) here? For what kind of death is the speaker wishing? Why does he want "no sadness of farewell" (11)?
4. What is "that which drew from out the boundless deep" (7)? What is "the boundless deep"? To what is it opposed in the poem? Why is "Pilot" (15) capitalized?

The Oxen

Christmas Eve, and twelve of the clock.
   "Now they are all on their knees,"
An elder said as we sat in a flock
   By the embers in hearthside ease.

We pictured the meek mild creatures where   5
   They dwelt in their strawy pen,
Nor did it occur to one of us there
   To doubt they were kneeling then.

So fair a fancy few would weave
   In these years! Yet, I feel,   10
If someone said on Christmas Eve,
   "Come; see the oxen kneel

"In the lonely barton° by yonder coomb°   farm; valley
   Our childhood used to know,"
I should go with him in the gloom,   15
   Hoping it might be so.

—THOMAS HARDY (1840–1928)

QUESTIONS

1. Is the simple superstition referred to in this poem opposed to, or identified with, religious faith? With what implications for the meaning of the poem?
2. What are "these years" (10), and how do they contrast with the years of the poet's boyhood? What event in intellectual history between 1840 and 1915 (the date Hardy composed this poem) was most responsible for the change?

3. Both "Crossing the Bar" and "The Oxen" in their last lines use a form of the verb *hope*. By fully discussing tone, establish the precise meaning of hope in each poem. What degree of expectation does it imply? How should the word be handled in reading Tennyson's poem aloud?

The Flea

Mark but this flea, and mark in this
How little that which thou deny'st me is;
It sucked me first, and now sucks thee,
And in this flea our two bloods mingled be;
Thou know'st that this cannot be said   5
A sin, nor shame, nor loss of maidenhead;
    Yet this enjoys before it woo,
      And pampered swells with one blood made of two,
    And this, alas, is more than we would do.

Oh stay, three lives in one flea spare,   10
Where we almost, yea more than married are.
This flea is you and I, and this
Our marriage bed and marriage temple is;
Though parents grudge, and you, we are met
And cloistered in these living walls of jet.   15
    Though use° make you apt to kill me,   habit
      Let not to that, self-murder added be,
    And sacrilege, three sins in killing three.

Cruel and sudden, hast thou since
Purpled° thy nail in blood of innocence?   crimsoned   20
Wherein could this flea guilty be,
Except in that drop which it sucked from thee?
Yet thou triumph'st and say'st that thou
Find'st not thyself, nor me, the weaker now.
    'Tis true. Then learn how false fears be: 25
      Just so much honor, when thou yield'st to me,
    Will waste, as this flea's death took life from thee.

—JOHN DONNE (1572–1631)

QUESTIONS

1. In many respects this poem is like a miniature play: it has two characters, dramatic conflict, dialogue (though we hear only one speaker), and stage action. The action

is indicated by stage directions embodied in the dialogue. What has happened just *preceding* the first line of the poem? What happens *between* the first and second stanzas? What happens *between* the second and third? How does the female character behave and what does she say *during* the third stanza?

2. What has been the past relationship of the speaker and the woman? What has she denied him (2)? How has she habitually "kill[ed]" him (16)? Why has she done so? How does it happen that he is still alive? What is his objective in the poem?

3. According to a traditional Renaissance belief, the blood of lovers "mingled" during sexual intercourse. What is the speaker's argument in stanza 1? Reduce it to paraphrase. How logical is it?

4. What do "parents grudge, and you" in stanza 2? What are the "living walls of jet" (15)? What three things will the woman kill by crushing the flea? What three sins will she commit (18)?

5. Why and how does the woman "triumph" in stanza 3? What is the speaker's response? How logical is his concluding argument?

Exchanging Hats

Unfunny uncles who insist
in trying on a lady's hat,
—oh, even if the joke falls flat,
we share your slight transvestite twist

in spite of our embarrassment.   5
Costume and custom are complex.
The headgear of the other sex
inspires us to experiment.

Anandrous aunts who, at the beach
with paper plates upon your laps,   10
keep putting on the yachtsmen's caps
with exhibitionistic screech,

the visors hanging o'er the ear
so that the golden anchors drag,
—the tides of fashion never lag.   15
Such caps may not be worn next year.

Or you who don the paper plate
itself, and put some grapes upon it,
or sport the Indian's feather bonnet,
—perversities may aggravate   20

the natural madness of the hatter.
And if the opera hats collapse
and crowns grow draughty, then, perhaps,
he thinks what might a miter matter?

Unfunny uncle, you who wore a   25
hat too big, or one too many,
tell us, can't you, are there any
stars inside your black fedora?

Aunt exemplary and slim,
with avernal eyes, we wonder   30
what slow changes they see under
their vast, shady, turned-down brim.

—ELIZABETH BISHOP (1911–1979)

QUESTIONS

1. Vocabulary: *anandrous* (9); *miter* (24); *avernal* (30).
2. What point is the poem making about gender roles and expectations?
3. How would you describe the tone of the poem?

History Lesson

I am four in this photograph, standing
on a wide strip of Mississippi beach,
my hands on the flowered hips

of a bright bikini. My toes dig in,
curl around wet sand. The sun cuts   5
the rippling Gulf in flashes with each

tidal rush. Minnows dart at my feet
glinting like switchblades. I am alone
except for my grandmother, other side

of the camera, telling me how to pose.   10
It is 1970, two years after they opened
the rest of this beach to us,

forty years since the photograph
where she stood on a narrow plot
of sand marked *colored*, smiling,   15

her hands on the flowered hips
of a cotton meal-sack dress.

— NATASHA TRETHEWEY (B. 1966)

QUESTIONS

1. Analyze the tone of this poem. Is it nostalgic? Angry? Bitter? Point to specific passages and images that support your argument.
2. Discuss the significance of the following images: "wide strip" (2) and "narrow plot" (14); "flowered hips / of a bright bikini" (3–4) and "flowered hips / of a cotton meal-sack dress" (16–17); "glinting like switchblades" (8).
3. In what sense does this photograph represent a "History Lesson" (title)?

Dover Beach

The sea is calm tonight,
The tide is full, the moon lies fair
Upon the straits;—on the French coast the light
Gleams and is gone; the cliffs of England stand,
Glimmering and vast, out in the tranquil bay.   5
Come to the window, sweet is the night-air!
Only, from the long line of spray
Where the sea meets the moon-blanched land,
Listen! you hear the grating roar
Of pebbles which the waves draw back, and fling,   10
At their return, up the high strand,
Begin, and cease, and then again begin,
With tremulous cadence slow, and bring
The eternal note of sadness in.

Sophocles long ago   15
Heard it on the Aegean, and it brought
Into his mind the turbid ebb and flow
Of human misery; we
Find also in the sound a thought,
Hearing it by this distant northern sea.   20

The Sea of Faith
Was once, too, at the full, and round earth's shore
Lay like the folds of a bright girdle furled.
But now I only hear

Its melancholy, long, withdrawing roar,   25
Retreating, to the breath
Of the night-wind, down the vast edges drear
And naked shingles° of the world.   *pebbled beaches*

Ah, love, let us be true
To one another! for the world, which seems   30
To lie before us like a land of dreams,
So various, so beautiful, so new,
Hath really neither joy, nor love, nor light,
Nor certitude, nor peace, nor help for pain;
And we are here as on a darkling plain   35
Swept with confused alarms of struggle and flight,
Where ignorant armies clash by night.

—MATTHEW ARNOLD (1822–1888)

QUESTIONS

1. Vocabulary: *strand* (11), *girdle* (23), *darkling* (35). Identify the physical locale of the cliffs of Dover and their relation to the French coast; identify Sophocles and the Aegean.
2. As precisely as possible, define the implied scene: What is the speaker's physical location? Whom is he addressing? What is the time of day and the state of the weather?
3. Discuss the visual and auditory images of the poem and their relation to illusion and reality.
4. The speaker is lamenting the decline of religious faith in his time. Is he himself a believer? Does he see any medicine for the world's maladies?
5. Discuss in detail the imagery in the last three lines. Are the "armies" figurative or literal? What makes these lines so effective?
6. What term or terms would you choose to describe the overall tone of the poem?

Church Going

Once I am sure there's nothing going on
I step inside, letting the door thud shut.
Another church: matting, seats, and stone,
And little books; sprawlings of flowers, cut
For Sunday, brownish now; some brass and stuff   5
Up at the holy end; the small neat organ;
And a tense, musty, unignorable silence,
Brewed God knows how long. Hatless, I take off
My cycle-clips in awkward reverence,

Move forward, run my hand around the font.   10
From where I stand, the roof looks almost new—
Cleaned, or restored? Someone would know: I don't.
Mounting the lectern, I peruse a few
Hectoring large-scale verses, and pronounce
"Here endeth" much more loudly than I'd meant.   15
The echoes snigger briefly. Back at the door
I sign the book, donate an Irish sixpence,
Reflect the place was not worth stopping for.

Yet stop I did: in fact I often do,
And always end much at a loss like this,   20
Wondering what to look for, wondering, too,
When churches fall completely out of use
What we shall turn them into, if we shall keep
A few cathedrals chronically on show,
Their parchment, plate and pyx in locked cases,   25
And let the rest rent-free to rain and sheep.
Shall we avoid them as unlucky places?

Or, after dark, will dubious women come
To make their children touch a particular stone;
Pick simples for a cancer; or on some   30
Advised night see walking a dead one?
Power of some sort or other will go on
In games, in riddles, seemingly at random;
But superstition, like belief, must die,
And what remains when disbelief has gone?   35
Grass, weedy pavement, brambles, buttress, sky,

A shape less recognizable each week,
A purpose more obscure. I wonder who
Will be the last, the very last, to seek
This place for what it was; one of the crew   40
That tap and jot and know what rood-lofts were?
Some ruin-bibber, randy for antique,
Or Christmas-addict, counting on a whiff
Of gown-and-bands and organ-pipes and myrrh?
Or will he be my representative,   45

Bored, uninformed, knowing the ghostly silt
Dispersed, yet tending to this cross of ground

Through suburb scrub because it held unspilt
So long and equably what since is found
Only in separation—marriage, and birth,   50
And death, and thoughts of these—for whom was built
This special shell? For though I've no idea
What this accoutered frowsty barn is worth,
It pleases me to stand in silence here;

A serious house on serious earth it is,   55
In whose blent air all our compulsions meet,
Are recognized, and robed as destinies.
And that much never can be obsolete,
Since someone will forever be surprising
A hunger in himself to be more serious,   60
And gravitating with it to this ground,
Which, he once heard, was proper to grow wise in,
If only that so many dead lie round.

—PHILIP LARKIN (1922–1985)

QUESTIONS

1. Vocabulary: Hectoring (14), pyx (25), dubious (28), simples (30), accoutered (53), frowsty (53), blent (56). Large-scale (14) indicates a print size suited to oral reading; an Irish sixpence (17) was a small coin not legal tender in England, the scene of the poem; rood-lofts (41) are architectural features found in many early Christian churches; bibber and randy (42) are figurative, literally meaning "drunkard" and "lustful"; gown-and-bands (44) are ornate robes worn by church officials in religious ceremonies.
2. Like "Dover Beach" (first published in 1867), "Church Going" (1954) is concerned with belief and disbelief. In modern England the landscape is dotted with small churches, often charming in their combination of stone (outside) and intricately carved wood (inside). Some are in ruins, some are badly in need of repair, and some are well tended by parishioners who keep them dusted and provide fresh flowers for the diminishing attendance at Sunday services. These churches often have by the entrance a book that visitors can sign as a record of their having been there and a collection box with a sign urging them to drop in a few coins for upkeep, repair, or restoration. In small towns and villages the church is often the chief or only building of architectural or historical interest, and tourist visitors may outnumber parishioners. To which of the three categories of churches mentioned here does Larkin's poem refer?
3. What different denotations does the title contain?
4. In what activity has the speaker been engaging when he stops to see the church? How is it revealed? Why does he stop? Is he a believer? How involved is he in inspecting this church building?

5. Compare the language used by the speakers in "Dover Beach" and "Church Going." Which speaker is more eloquent? Which is more informal and conversational? Without looking back at the texts, try to assign the following words to one poem or the other: *moon-blanched, cycle-clips, darkling, hath, snigger, whiff, drear, brownish, tremulous, glimmering, frowsty, stuff.* Then go back and check your success.
6. Define the tone of "Church Going" as precisely as possible. Compare this tone with that of "Dover Beach."

SUGGESTIONS FOR WRITING

1. Marvell's "To His Coy Mistress" (page 761), Herrick's "To the Virgins, to Make Much of Time" (page 773), and Housman's "Loveliest of Trees" (page 825) all treat a traditional poetic theme known as *carpe diem* ("seize the day"). They differ sharply in tone. Pointing out the differences in poetic technique among them, characterize the tone of each.
2. Describe and account for the differences in tone between the following pairs:
   a. Hopkins, "Spring" (page 735) and Williams, "The Widow's Lament in Springtime" (page 736).
   b. Tennyson, "The Eagle" (page 682) and Mathis, "Survival: A Guide" (page 695).
   c. Owen, "Dulce et Decorum Est" (page 684) and Whitman, "A Sight in Camp in the Daybreak Gray and Dim" (page 1046).
   d. Drayton, "Since there's no help" (page 842) and Addonizio, "Sonnenizio" (page 974).
   e. Blake, "The Lamb" (page 835) and Blake, "The Tiger" (page 835).
   f. Shakespeare, "Winter" (page 683) and Stevens, "The Snow Man" (page 743).
   g. Hayden, "The Whipping" (page 689) and Roethke, "My Papa's Waltz" (page 1035).

PRACTICE AP WRITING PROMPTS

William Shakespeare, "My mistress' eyes are nothing like the sun" (p. 845) and "Shall I compare thee to a summer's day" (p. 689)

See the comparison prompt for "My mistress' eyes are nothing like the sun" paired with "Shall I compare thee to a summer's day" in Chapter One of the Poetry section.

Alfred, Lord Tennyson, "Crossing the Bar" (p. 846)

Read "Crossing the Bar" carefully. Then, in a well-organized essay, analyze how structure, diction, and the poem's two complementary metaphors convey the speaker's attitude toward his own death.

CHAPTER ELEVEN

Musical Devices

Poetry obviously makes a greater use of the "music" of language than does language that is not poetry. The poet, unlike the person who uses language to convey only information, chooses words for sound as well as for meaning, and uses the sound as a means of reinforcing meaning. So prominent is this musical quality of poetry that some writers have made it the distinguishing term in their definitions of poetry. Edgar Allan Poe, for instance, describes poetry as "music ... combined with a pleasurable idea." Whether or not it deserves this much importance, verbal music, like connotation, imagery, and figurative language, is one of the important resources that enable the poet to do more than communicate mere information. The poet may indeed sometimes pursue verbal music for its own sake; more often, at least in first-rate poetry, it is an adjunct to the total meaning or communication of the poem.

The poet achieves musical quality in two broad ways: by the choice and arrangement of sounds and by the arrangement of accents. In this chapter we will consider the first of these.

An essential element in all music is repetition. In fact, we might say that all art consists of giving structure to two elements: repetition and variation. All things we enjoy greatly and lastingly have these two elements. We enjoy the sea endlessly because it is always the same yet always different. We enjoy a baseball game because it contains the same complex combination of pattern and variation. Our love of art, then, is rooted in human psychology. We like the familiar, we like variety, but we like them combined. If we get too much sameness, the result is monotony and tedium; if we get too much variety, the result is bewilderment and confusion. The composer of music, therefore, repeats certain musical tones; repeats them in certain combinations, or chords; and repeats them in certain patterns, or melodies. The poet likewise repeats certain sounds in certain combinations and arrangements, and thus adds musical meaning to verse. Consider the following short example.

The Turtle

The turtle lives 'twixt plated decks
Which practically conceal its sex.
I think it clever of the turtle
In such a fix to be so fertile.

—OGDEN NASH (1902–1971)

Here is a little joke, a paradox of animal life to which the author has cleverly drawn our attention. An experiment will show us, however, that much of its appeal lies not so much in what it says as in the manner in which it says it. If, for instance, we recast the verse as prose: "The turtle lives in a shell that almost conceals its sex. It is ingenious of the turtle, in such a situation, to be so prolific," the joke falls flat. Some of its appeal must lie in its metrical form. So now we cast it in unrhymed verse:

Because he lives between two decks,
It's hard to tell a turtle's gender.
The turtle is a clever beast
In such a plight to be so fertile.

Here, perhaps, is *some* improvement over the prose version, but still the piquancy of the original is missing. Much of that appeal must have consisted in the use of rhyme—the repetition of sound in "decks" and "sex," "turtle" and "fertile." So we try once more.

The turtle lives 'twixt plated decks
Which practically conceal its sex.
I think it clever of the turtle
In such a plight to be so fertile.

But for perceptive readers there is still something missing—they may not at first see what—but some little touch that makes the difference between a good piece of verse and a little masterpiece of its kind. And then they see it: "plight" has been substituted for "fix."

But why should "fix" make such a difference? Its meaning is little different from that of "plight"; its only important difference is in sound. But there we are. The final x in "fix" catches up the concluding consonant sound in "sex," and its initial *f* is repeated in the initial consonant sound of "fertile." Not only do these sound recurrences provide a subtle gratification to the ear, but they also give the verse structure; they emphasize and draw together the key words of the piece: "sex," "fix," and "fertile."

Poets may repeat any unit of sound from the smallest to the largest. They may repeat individual vowel and consonant sounds, whole syllables, words, phrases, lines, or groups of lines. In each instance, in a good poem, the repetition will serve several purposes: it will please the ear, it will emphasize the words in which the repetition occurs, and it will give structure to the poem. The popularity and initial impressiveness of such repetitions are evidenced by their becoming in many instances embedded in the language as clichés like "wild and woolly," "first and foremost," "footloose and fancy-free," "penny-wise, pound-foolish," "dead as a doornail," "might and main," "sink or swim," "do or die," "pell-mell," "helter-skelter," "harum-scarum," "hocus-pocus." Some of these kinds of repetition have names, as we will see.

A syllable consists of a vowel sound that may be preceded or followed by consonant sounds. Any of these sounds may be repeated. The repetition of initial consonant sounds, as in "tried and true," "safe and sound," "fish or fowl," "rhyme or reason," is **alliteration**. The repetition of vowel sounds, as in "mad as a hatter," "time out of mind," "free and easy," or "slapdash," is **assonance**. The repetition of final consonant sounds, as in "first and last," "odds and ends," "short and sweet," "a stroke of luck," or Shakespeare's "struts and frets" (page 813) is **consonance**.*

Repetitions may be used alone or in combination. Alliteration and assonance are combined in such phrases as "time and tide," "thick and thin," "kith and kin," "alas and alack," "fit as a fiddle," and Edgar Allan Poe's famous line, "The viol, the violet, and the vine." Alliteration and consonance are combined in such phrases as "crisscross," "last but not least," "lone and lorn," "good as gold," and Housman's "malt does more than Milton can" (page 1007).

Rhyme is the repetition of the accented vowel sound and any succeeding consonant sounds. It is called **masculine** when the rhyme sounds involve

---

*Different writers have defined these repetitions in various ways. *Alliteration* is used by some writers to mean any repetition of consonant sounds. *Assonance* has been used to mean the similarity as well as the identity of vowel sounds, or even the similarity of any sounds whatever. *Consonance* has often been reserved for words in which both the initial *and* final consonant sounds correspond, as in *green* and *groan*, *moon* and *mine*. *Rhyme* has been used to mean any sound repetition, including alliteration, assonance, and consonance. In the absence of clear agreement on the meanings of these terms, the terminology chosen here has appeared most useful, with support in usage. Labels are useful in analysis. However, the student should learn to recognize the devices and, more important, should learn to see their function, without worrying too much over nomenclature.

only one syllable, as in *decks* and *sex* or *support* and *retort*. It is **feminine** when the rhyme sounds involve two or more syllables, as in *turtle* and *fertile* or *spitefully* and *delightfully*. It is referred to as **internal rhyme** when one or more rhyming words are *within* the line and as **end rhyme** when the rhyming words are at the *ends* of lines. End rhyme is probably the most frequently used and most consciously sought sound repetition in English poetry. Because it comes at the end of the line, it receives emphasis as a musical effect and perhaps contributes more than any other musical resource except rhythm to give poetry its musical effect as well as its structure. There exists, however, a large body of poetry that does not employ rhyme and for which rhyme would not be appropriate. Also, there has always been a tendency, especially noticeable in modern poetry, to substitute approximate rhymes for perfect rhymes at the ends of lines. **Approximate rhymes** (also called slant rhymes) include words with any kind of sound similarity, from close to fairly remote. Under approximate rhyme we include alliteration, assonance, and consonance or their combinations when used at the end of the line; half-rhyme (feminine rhymes in which only half of the word rhymes—the accented half, as in *lightly* and *frightful*, or the unaccented half, as in *yellow* and *willow*); and other similarities too elusive to name. "Because I could not stop for Death" (page 784), "Toads" (page 758), and "Mid-Term Break" (page 802), to different degrees, all employ various kinds of approximate end rhyme. Many contemporary song lyrics, especially in rap music, depend almost entirely on approximate rhyme or assonance for their rhyme schemes.

That night when joy began

That night when joy began
Our narrowest veins to flush,
We waited for the flash
Of morning's leveled gun.

But morning let us pass,   5
And day by day relief
Outgrows his nervous laugh,
Grown credulous of peace,

As mile by mile is seen
No trespasser's reproach,   10
And love's best glasses reach
No fields but are his own.

—W. H. AUDEN (1907–1973)

QUESTIONS

1. What has been the past experience with love of the two people in the poem? What is their present experience? What precisely is the tone of the poem?
2. What basic metaphor underlies the poem? Work it out stanza by stanza. What is "the flash / Of morning's leveled gun" (3–4)? Does line 10 mean that no trespasser reproaches the lovers or that no one reproaches the lovers for being trespassers? Does "glasses" (11) refer to spectacles, drinking glasses, mirrors, or field glasses? Point out three personifications.
3. The rhyme pattern in the poem is intricate and exact. Work it out, considering alliteration, assonance, and consonance.

In addition to the repetition of individual sounds and syllables, the poet may repeat whole words, phrases, lines, or groups of lines. When such repetition is done according to some fixed pattern, it is called a **refrain**. The refrain is especially common in songlike poetry. Shakespeare's "Winter" (page 683) furnishes an example of a refrain.

The Waking

I wake to sleep, and take my waking slow.
I feel my fate in what I cannot fear.
I learn by going where I have to go.

We think by feeling. What is there to know?
I hear my being dance from ear to ear.　　　　　5
I wake to sleep, and take my waking slow.

Of those so close beside me, which are you?
God bless the Ground! I shall walk softly there,
And learn by going where I have to go.

Light takes the Tree; but who can tell us how?　　　10
The lowly worm climbs up a winding stair;
I wake to sleep, and take my waking slow.

Great Nature has another thing to do
To you and me; so take the lively air,
And, lovely, learn by going where to go.　　　　15

This shaking keeps me steady. I should know.
What falls away is always. And is near.

I wake to sleep, and take my waking slow.
I learn by going where I have to go.

—THEODORE ROETHKE (1908–1963)

QUESTIONS

1. The refrains in lines 1 and 3 occur at patterned intervals in this example of the form called "villanelle" (see page 922 for a definition of the form). Even without the definition, you can work out the repetitive pattern—but the key question is, what do these two lines *mean,* as statements both within the first stanza and in each subsequent repetition? Starting with line 1, for what is "sleep" a common metaphor? What would be the meaning if the first phrase were "I was born to die"?

2. Paraphrase the third line, in light of the idea that the first line presents an attitude toward the fact that all living things must die. Where does the speaker "have to go" ultimately? What is the process of his present "going"?

3. Explain the clear-cut attitude toward emotive experience versus intellectual knowledge expressed in line 4. How is that attitude a basis for the ideas in the refrain lines? How does it support line 10?

4. What is it that "Great Nature has ... to do" (13) to people? How should they live their lives, according to the speaker?

5. Explain the paradox that "shaking keeps [the speaker] steady" (16). Consider the possibility that the speaker is personifying "the Tree" (10) as himself—what then is "fall[ing] away," and how near is it (17)?

6. Is the tone of this poem melancholy? resigned? joyous? Explain

We have not nearly exhausted the possibilities of sound repetition by giving names to a few of the more prominent kinds. The complete study of possible kinds of sound repetition in poetry would be so complex, however, that it would exceed the scope of this introductory text.

Some of the subtlest and loveliest effects escape our net of names. In as short a phrase as this from the prose of John Ruskin—"ivy as light and lovely as the vine"—we notice alliteration in *light* and *lovely*; assonance in *ivy, light,* and *vine*; and consonance in *ivy* and *lovely.* But we have no name to connect the *v* in *vine* with the *v*s in *ivy* and *lovely,* or the second *l* in *lovely* with the first *l,* or the final syllables of *ivy* and *lovely* with each other; yet these are all an effective part of the music of the line. Also contributing to the music of poetry is the linking of related rather than identical sounds, such as *m* and *n,* or *p* and *b,* or the vowel sounds in *boat, boot,* and *book.*

These various musical repetitions, for trained readers, will ordinarily make an almost subconscious contribution to their reading of the poem: readers will feel their effect without necessarily being aware of what has caused it. There is value, however, in occasionally analyzing a poem for these devices in order to increase awareness of them. A few words of caution are necessary. First, the repetitions are entirely a matter of sound; spelling is irrelevant. *Bear* and *pair* are rhymes, but *through* and *rough* are not. *Cell* and *sin, folly* and *philosophy* alliterate, but *sin* and *sugar, gun* and *gem* do not. Second, alliteration, assonance, consonance, and masculine rhyme are matters that ordinarily involve only stressed or accented syllables; for only such syllables ordinarily make enough impression on the ear to be significant in the sound pattern of the poem. For instance, we should hardly consider *which* and *its* in the second line of "The Turtle" an example of assonance, for neither word is stressed enough in the reading to make it significant as a sound. Third, the words involved in these repetitions must be close enough together that the ear retains the sound, consciously or subconsciously, from its first occurrence to its second. This distance varies according to circumstances, but for alliteration, assonance, and consonance the words ordinarily have to be in the same line or adjacent lines. End rhyme bridges a longer gap.

God's Grandeur

The world is charged with the grandeur of God.
   It will flame out, like shining from shook foil;
   It gathers to a greatness, like the ooze of oil
Crushed. Why do men then now not reck his rod?
Generations have trod, have trod, have trod;   5
   And all is seared with trade; bleared, smeared with toil;
   And wears man's smudge and shares man's smell: the soil
Is bare now, nor can foot feel, being shod.

And for all this, nature is never spent;
   There lives the dearest freshness deep down things;   10
And though the last lights off the black West went
   Oh, morning, at the brown brink eastward, springs—
Because the Holy Ghost over the bent
   World broods with warm breast and with ah! bright wings.

—GERARD MANLEY HOPKINS (1844–1889)

QUESTIONS

1. What is the theme of this sonnet?
2. The image in lines 3–4 possibly refers to olive oil being collected in great vats from crushed olives, but the image is much disputed. Explain the simile in line 2 and the symbols in lines 7–8 and 11–12.
3. Explain "reck his rod" (4), "spent" (9), "bent" (13).
4. Using different-colored pencils, encircle and connect examples of alliteration, assonance, consonance, and internal rhyme. Do these help to carry the meaning?

We should not leave the impression that the use of these musical devices is necessarily or always valuable. Like the other resources of poetry, they can be judged only in the light of the poem's total intention. Many of the greatest works of English poetry—for instance, *Hamlet* and *King Lear* and *Paradise Lost*—do not employ end rhyme. Both alliteration and rhyme, especially feminine rhyme, become humorous or silly if used excessively or unskillfully. If the intention is humorous, the result is delightful; if not, fatal. Shakespeare, who knew how to use all these devices to the utmost advantage, parodied their unskillful use in lines like "The preyful princess pierced and pricked a pretty pleasing prickett" in *Love's Labor's Lost* and

> Whereat with blade, with bloody, blameful blade,
> He bravely broached his boiling bloody breast

in *A Midsummer Night's Dream.* Swinburne parodied his own highly alliterative style in "Nephelidia" with lines like "Life is the lust of a lamp for the light that is dark till the dawn of the day when we die." Used skillfully and judiciously, however, musical devices provide a palpable and delicate pleasure to the ear and, even more important, add dimension to meaning.

EXERCISE

Discuss the various ways in which the following poems make use of refrain.
1. Shakespeare, "Winter" (page 683).
2. Shakespeare, "Blow, blow, thou winter wind" (page 861).
3. cummings, "in Just—" (page 815).
4. Blake, "The Lamb" (page 835).
5. Crane, "War Is Kind" (page 988).
6. Dunbar, "Sympathy" (page 995).
7. Clifton, "good times" (page 982).

REVIEWING CHAPTER ELEVEN

1. Review the terms printed in boldface, and as you read on in this chapter take note of the examples that you find (that is, make a conscious search for the materials that normally would not rise above the subconscious in their effects).

2. Musical devices do not convey meaning but reinforce meanings that are established by the other aspects of language; as you explore these musical devices, identify the ways in which emotional and intellectual meanings are conveyed so as to make it clear what the music is reinforcing and supporting.

Blow, blow, thou winter wind

Blow, blow, thou winter wind.
Thou art not so unkind
    As man's ingratitude.
Thy tooth is not so keen,
Because thou art not seen,   5
    Although thy breath be rude.°   rough
Heigh-ho, sing heigh-ho, unto the green holly.
Most friendship is feigning, most loving mere folly.
    Then heigh-ho, the holly!
        This life is most jolly.   10

Freeze, freeze, thou bitter sky,
That dost not bite so nigh°   near the heart
    As benefits forgot.
Though thou the waters warp,
Thy sting is not so sharp   15
    As friend remembered not.
Heigh-ho, sing heigh-ho, unto the green holly.
Most friendship is feigning, most loving mere folly.
    Then heigh-ho, the holly!
        This life is most jolly.   20

—WILLIAM SHAKESPEARE (1564–1616)

QUESTIONS

1. Vocabulary: *Heigh-ho* (7) is an expression of melancholy or disappointment; *holly* (7) is an emblem of cheerfulness (as at Christmas); *warp* (14) implies freezing into ridges.
2. This song from *As You Like It* (Act 2, scene 7), contrasts the social and natural worlds and is sung to celebrate living freely in the forest. What essential qualities does it ascribe to the two environments displayed in the behavior of people and the actions of nature? What paradox does the poem create by presenting the expression "heigh-ho" linked with "the holly"? Are we to take "heigh-ho" at its literal meaning?
3. What musical devices help to create the songlike quality of this poem?

We Real Cool

The Pool Players.
Seven At The Golden Shovel.

We real cool. We
Left school. We

Lurk late. We
Strike straight. We

Sing sin. We   5
Thin gin. We

Jazz June. We
Die soon.

—GWENDOLYN BROOKS (1917–2000)

QUESTIONS

1. In addition to end rhyme, what other musical devices does this poem employ?
2. Try reading this poem with the pronouns at the beginning of the lines instead of at the end. What is lost?
3. English teachers in a certain urban school were once criticized for having their students read this poem: it was said to be immoral. What essential poetic device did the critics misunderstand?

Woman Work

I've got the children to tend
The clothes to mend
The floor to mop
The food to shop
Then the chicken to fry   5
The baby to dry
I got company to feed
The garden to weed
I've got the shirts to press
The tots to dress   10
The cane to be cut
I gotta clean up this hut
Then see about the sick
And the cotton to pick.

Shine on me, sunshine   15
Rain on me, rain
Fall softly, dewdrops
And cool my brow again.

Storm, blow me from here
With your fiercest wind   20
Let me float across the sky
'Til I can rest again.

Fall gently, snowflakes
Cover me with white
Cold icy kisses and   25
Let me rest tonight.

Sun, rain, curving sky
Mountain, oceans, leaf and stone
Star shine, moon glow
You're all that I can call my own.   30

—MAYA ANGELOU (B. 1928)

QUESTIONS

1. What is the pattern of rhymes in lines 1–14? What does it shift to in lines 15–30? Whom is the speaker addressing in the first 14 lines? What figurative address characterizes the rest of the poem?
2. The phrases "I've got … gotta" (1–12) produce a type of refrain called **anaphora,** the repetition of an opening word or phrase in a series of lines. What feeling is expressed by this repetition here? How do the varying forms of the phrase characterize the speaker?
3. Most of the chores in the first 14 lines are associated popularly with "woman['s] work," but two are not. What do these exceptions reveal about the situation of the speaker?
4. What kinds of release from "work" are presented in lines 15–30? Metaphorically, what does the speaker desire in lines 19–26?
5. Explain the statement in the last four lines.

The Bells

I

Hear the sledges with the bells—
    Silver bells!
What a world of merriment their melody foretells!
How they tinkle, tinkle, tinkle,
    In the icy air of night!   5
While the stars that oversprinkle
All the heavens, seem to twinkle
    With a crystalline delight;

Keeping time, time, time,
    In a sort of Runic rhyme,   10
To the tintinnabulation that so musically wells
    From the bells, bells, bells, bells,
        Bells, bells, bells—
From the jingling and the tinkling of the bells.

                          II
Hear the mellow wedding bells—   15
    Golden bells!
What a world of happiness their harmony foretells!
    Through the balmy air of night
    How they ring out their delight!—
        From the molten-golden notes,   20
        And all in tune,
    What a liquid ditty floats
To the turtle-dove that listens, while she gloats
        On the moon!
        Oh, from out the sounding cells,   25
What a gush of euphony voluminously wells!
        How is swells!
        How it dwells
        On the Future!—how it tells
        Of the rapture that impels   30
    To the swinging and the ringing
        Of the bells, bells, bells—
Of the bells, bells, bells, bells,
        Bells, bells, bells—
To the rhyming and the chiming of the bells!   35

                          III
Hear the loud alarum bells—
    Brazen bells!
What a tale of terror, now, their turbulency tells!
    In the startled ear of night
    How they scream out their affright!   40
        Too much horrified to speak,
        They can only shriek, shriek,
            Out of tune,
In a clamorous appealing to the mercy of the fire,
In a mad expostulation with the deaf and frantic fire,   45
        Leaping higher, higher, higher,

With a desperate desire,
And a resolute endeavor
Now—now to sit, or never,
By the side of the pale-faced moon,   50
Oh, the bells, bells, bells!
What a tale their terror tells
Of Despair!
How they clang, and clash, and roar!
What a horror they outpour   55
On the bosom of the palpitating air!
Yet the ear, it fully knows,
By the twanging
And the clanging,
How the danger ebbs and flows;   60
Yet the ear distinctly tells,
In the jangling
And the wrangling,
How the danger sinks and swells,
By the sinking or the swelling in the anger of the bells—   65
Of the bells,—
Of the bells, bells, bells, bells,
Bells, bells, bells—
In the clamor and the clangor of the bells!

IV
Hear the tolling of the bells—   70
Iron bells!
What a world of solemn thought their monody compels!
In the silence of the night,
How we shiver with affright
At the melancholy menace of their tone!   75
For every sound that floats
From the rust within their throats
Is a groan.
And the people—ah, the people—
They that dwell up in the steeple,   80
All alone,
And who tolling, tolling, tolling,
In that muffled monotone,
Feel a glory in so rolling
On the human heart a stone—   85
They are neither man nor woman—

They are neither brute nor human—
    They are Ghouls:—
    And their king it is who tolls:—
    And he rolls, rolls, rolls,   90
    Rolls
       A paean from the bells!
  And his merry bosom swells
    With the paean of the bells!
And he dances, and he yells;   95
Keeping time, time, time,
In a sort of Runic rhyme,
    To the paean of the bells—
    Of the bells:
Keeping time, time, time,   100
In a sort of Runic rhyme,
    To the throbbing of the bells—
  Of the bells, bells, bells—
    To the sobbing of the bells;
Keeping time, time, time,   105
  As he knells, knells, knells,
In a happy Runic rhyme,
    To the rolling of the bells—
  Of the bells, bells, bells:—
    To the tolling of the bells—   110
Of the bells, bells, bells, bells,
    Bells, bells, bells—
To the moaning and the groaning of the bells.

—EDGAR ALLAN POE (1809–1849)

QUESTIONS

1. Vocabulary: *sledges* (1); *tintinnabulation* (11); *euphony* (26); *expostulation* (45); *paean* (92); *Runic* (101).
2. What different kinds of bells are described in the poem? How does the sound of the various stanzas comport with the type of bells being described?
3. How would you describe the tone of the poem? Besides his attitude toward the bells, what can we infer about the speaker?
4. What effects do the rhyme scheme and the punctuation have on the way you experience the poem?

Rite of Passage

As the guests arrive at my son's party
they gather in the living room—
short men, men in first grade
with smooth jaws and chins.
Hands in pockets, they stand around   5
jostling, jockeying for place, small fights
breaking out and calming. One says to another
How old are you? Six. I'm seven. So?
They eye each other, seeing themselves
tiny in the other's pupils. They clear their   10
throats a lot, a room of small bankers,
they fold their arms and frown. *I could beat you
up*, a seven says to a six,
the dark cake, round and heavy as a
turret, behind them on the table. My son,   15
freckles like specks of nutmeg on his cheeks,
chest narrow as the balsa keel of a
model boat, long hands
cool and thin as the day they guided him
out of me, speaks up as a host   20
for the sake of the group.
We could easily kill a two-year-old,
he says in his clear voice. The other
men agree, they clear their throats
like Generals, they relax and get down to   25
playing war, celebrating my son's life.

—SHARON OLDS (B. 1942)

QUESTIONS

1. Vocabulary: *Rite of Passage* (title).
2. What is the implication of the metaphor comparing the boys to "bankers" (11) clearing their throats? of that comparing them to "Generals" (25) doing the same thing? Is there a "rite of passage" implied in the shift from one comparison to the other?
3. What tones of voice would be appropriate for the phrase *"I'm seven"* and the reply *"So?"* (8)? Explain the image in the next sentence.
4. How are the similes in lines 14–15 and 16–17 linked? How do they function in the progress from bankers to Generals?
5. What is the speaker's tone as she describes the children's violent impulses?
6. The poem displays a considerable amount of musicality—alliteration, assonance, and consonance—through line 21. Identify these devices, and discuss the implication of their absence in the remainder of the poem.

Music Lessons

Sometimes, in the middle of the lesson,
we exchanged places. She would gaze a moment at her hands
spread over the keys; then the small house with its knickknacks,
its shut windows,

its photographs of her sons and the serious husband,   5
vanished as new shapes formed. Sound
became music, and music a white
scarp for the listener to climb

alone. I leaped rock over rock to the top
and found myself waiting, transformed,   10
and still she played, her eyes luminous and willful,
her pinned hair falling down—

forgetting me, the house, the neat green yard,
she fled in that lick of flame all tedious bonds:
supper, the duties of flesh and home,   15
the knife at the throat, the death in the metronome.

—MARY OLIVER (B. 1935)

QUESTIONS

1. Vocabulary: *scarp* (8), *metronome* (16).
2. What musical qualities do you see in the poem? How are they appropriate?
3. Discuss the characterization of the piano teacher. What kind of woman is she? What does the speaker, now a mature adult, see in her that she didn't see when she actually knew the teacher?
4. Why does the speaker use imagery of violence and death in the final line? What poetic effect does this imagery have on the reader?

Traveling through the dark

Traveling through the dark I found a deer
dead on the edge of the Wilson River road.
It is usually best to roll them into the canyon:
that road is narrow; to swerve might make more dead.

By glow of the tail-light I stumbled back of the car   5
and stood by the heap, a doe, a recent killing;
she had stiffened already, almost cold.
I dragged her off; she was large in the belly.

My fingers touching her side brought me the reason—
her side was warm; her fawn lay there waiting,   10
alive, still, never to be born.
Beside that mountain road I hesitated.

The car aimed ahead its lowered parking lights;
under the hood purred the steady engine.
I stood in the glare of the warm exhaust turning red;   15
around our group I could hear the wilderness listen.

I thought hard for us all — my only swerving —,
then pushed her over the edge into the river.

—WILLIAM STAFFORD (1914–1993)

QUESTIONS

1. State precisely the speaker's dilemma. What kind of person is he? Does he make the right decision? Why does he call his hesitation "my only swerving" (17), and how does this connect with the word "swerve" in line 4?

2. What different kinds of imagery and of image contrasts give life to the poem? Do any of the images have symbolic overtones?

3. At first glance this poem may appear to be without end rhyme. Looking closer, do you find any correspondences between lines 2 and 4 in each four-line stanza? between lines 1 and 3 of stanzas 2 and 3? between the final words of the concluding couplet? What one line end in the poem has no connection in sound to another line end in its stanza?

SUGGESTIONS FOR WRITING

1. Write an essay analyzing the use and effectiveness of alliteration and/or assonance in one of the following:
   a. Shakespeare, "Shall I compare thee to a summer's day?" (page 689).
   b. Dickinson, "There's a certain Slant of light" (page 951).
   c. Donne, "The Good-Morrow" (page 993).
   d. Hopkins, "God's Grandeur" (page 862).
   e. Robinson, "Richard Cory" (page 1034).

2. Discuss the rhymes in one of the following. Does the poem employ exact rhymes or approximate rhymes? How do the kind and pattern of rhyme contribute to the poem's effect?
   a. MacLeish, "Ars Poetica" (page 1023).
   b. Browning, "My Last Duchess" (page 806).
   c. Dickinson, "A narrow Fellow in the Grass" (page 840).
   d. Plath, "Lady Lazarus" (page 781).
   e. Heaney, "Follower" (page 1004).

PRACTICE AP WRITING PROMPTS ▰▰▰▰

Gerard Manley Hopkins, "God's Grandeur" (p. 862) and William Shakespeare, "Blow, blow, thou winter wind" (p. 864)

"God's Grandeur" and "Blow, blow, thou winter wind" both suggest ways in which nature is better than humankind. Read each poem carefully. Then write a comparison-contrast essay in which you analyze the poetic techniques through which each poem considers what nature can teach us.

CHAPTER TWELVE

Rhythm and Meter

Our love of rhythm is rooted even more deeply in us than our love of musical repetition. It is related to the beat of our hearts, the pulse of our blood, the intake and outflow of air from our lungs. Everything that we do naturally and gracefully we do rhythmically. There is rhythm in the way we walk, the way we swim, the way we ride a horse, the way we swing a golf club or a baseball bat. So native is rhythm to us that we read it, when we can, into the mechanical world around us. Our clocks go tick-tick-tick, but we hear tick-tock, tick-tock. The click of railway wheels beneath us patterns itself into a tune in our heads. There is a strong appeal for us in language that is rhythmic.

The term **rhythm** refers to any wavelike recurrence of motion or sound. In speech it is the natural rise and fall of language. All language is to some degree rhythmic, for all language involves alternations between accented and unaccented syllables. Language varies considerably, however, in the degree to which it exhibits rhythm. Sometimes in speech the rhythm is so unobtrusive or so unpatterned that we are scarcely aware of it. Sometimes, as in rap or in oratory, the rhythm is so pronounced that we may be tempted to tap our feet to it.

In every word of more than one syllable, one or more syllables are **accented** or **stressed**; that is, given more prominence in pronunciation than the rest.* We say toDAY, toMORrow, YESterday, interVENE. These accents within individual words are indicated by stress marks in

---

*Though the words *accent* and *stress* generally are used interchangeably, as here, a distinction is sometimes made between them in technical discussions. **Accent**, the relative prominence given a syllable in relation to its neighbors, is then said to result from one or more of four causes: *stress*, or force of utterance, producing loudness; *duration; pitch*; and *juncture*, the manner of transition between successive sounds. Of these, *stress*, in verse written in English, is the most important.

dictionaries, and with many words of more than two syllables primary and secondary stresses are shown (in'-ter-vene"). When words are arranged into a sentence, we give certain words or syllables more prominence in pronunciation than the rest. We say: "He WENT to the STORE" or "ANN is DRIVing her CAR." There is nothing mysterious about this; it is the normal process of language. The major difference between prose and verse is that in prose these accents occur more or less haphazardly; in verse the poet may arrange them to occur at regular intervals.

In poetry as in prose, the rhythmic effects depend almost entirely on what a statement means, and different intended meanings will produce different rhythms even in identical statements. If I say "I don't believe YOU," I mean something different from "*I* don't believe you" or from "I don't beLIEVE you." In speech, these are **rhetorical stresses**, which we use to make our intentions clear. Stressing "I" separates me from others who *do* believe you; stressing "you" separates you from others whom I believe; stressing "believe" intensifies my statement of disbelief. Such rhetorical stressing comes as naturally to us as language itself, and is at least as important in poetry as it is in expressive speaking. It is also basic to understanding the rhythm of poetry, for poetic rhythm depends on the plain, rhetorical stresses to communicate its meaning. We must be able to recognize the meaning of a line of poetry before we can determine its rhythm.

In addition to accent or stress, rhythm is based on pauses. In poetry, as in prose or speech, pauses are the result of natural speech rhythms and the structure of sentences. Periods and commas create pauses, but so does the normal flow of phrases and clauses. Poetry, however, adds another kind of pause arising from the fact that poetry is written in lines. The poetic line is a unit that creates pauses in the flow of speech, sometimes slight and sometimes large. Poets have at their disposal a variety of possibilities when ending a line. An **end-stopped line** is one in which the end of the line corresponds with a natural speech pause; a **run-on line** is one in which the sense of the line moves on without pause into the next line. (There are of course all degrees of end-stop and run-on. A line ending with a period or semicolon is heavily end-stopped. A line without punctuation at the end is normally considered a run-on line, but it is less forcibly run-on if it ends at a natural speech pause—as between subject and predicate—than if it ends, say, between an article and its noun, between an auxiliary and its verb, or between a preposition and its object.) In addition there are pauses that occur within lines, either grammatical or rhetorical. These are called **caesuras**, and they are another resource for varying the rhythm of lines.

The poetic line is the basic rhythmic unit in **free verse,** the predominating type of poetry now being written. Except for its line arrangement there are no necessary differences between the rhythms of free verse and the rhythms of prose, so our awareness of the line as a rhythmic unit is essential. Consider the rhythmic contrast between end-stopped lines and run-on lines in these two excerpts from poems presented earlier, and notice how the caesuras (marked ||) help to vary the rhythms:

> A noiseless patient spider,
> I marked where on a little promontory it stood isolated,
> Marked how to explore the vacant vast surrounding,
> It launched forth filament, || filament, || filament, || out of
>   itself,
> Ever unreeling them, || ever tirelessly speeding them.
>
> (page 767)

> Sorrow is my own yard
> where the new grass
> flames || as it has flamed
> often before || but not
> with the cold fire
> that closes round me this year.
>
> (page 736)

There is another sort of poetry that depends entirely on ordinary prose rhythms—the **prose poem,** exemplified by Carolyn Forché's "The Colonel" (page 997) and Rita Dove's "Kentucky, 1833" (page 834). Having dispensed even with the line as a unit of rhythm, the prose poem lays its claim to being poetry by its attention to many of the poetic elements presented earlier in this book: connotation, imagery, figurative language, and the concentration of meaning in evocative language.

But most often, when people think of poetry they think of the two broad branches, free verse and metrical verse, which are distinguished mainly by the absence or presence of meter. **Meter** is the identifying characteristic of rhythmic language that we can tap our feet to. When verse is metrical, the accents of language are so arranged as to occur at apparently equal intervals of time, and it is this interval we mark off with the tap of a foot.

The study of meter is fascinating but highly complex. It is by no means an absolute prerequisite to an enjoyment, even a rich enjoyment, of poetry, any more than is the ability to identify by name the multiplicity of figures of speech. But a knowledge of the fundamentals of meter does have value. It can make the beginning reader more aware of the rhythmic effects of poetry and of how poetry should be read. It can enable the more advanced reader to analyze how certain effects are achieved, to see how rhythm interacts with meaning, and to explain what makes one poem (in this respect) better than another. The beginning student ought to have at least an elementary knowledge of the subject. And it is not so difficult as its traditional terminology might suggest.

Even for the beginner, one essential distinction must be understood: although the terms *rhythm* and *meter* are sometimes used interchangeably, they mean different things. Rhythm designates the flow of actual, pronounced sound (or sound heard in the mind's ear), whereas meter refers to the patterns that sounds follow when a poet has arranged them into metrical verse. This may be illustrated by an analogy of a well-designed building and the architect's blueprint for its construction. The building, like rhythmic sound, is actual and real; the blueprint for it is an abstract, idealized pattern, like metrical form. When we look at a building, we see the actuality, but we also recognize that it is based on a pattern. The actuality of the building goes beyond the idealized blueprint in a number of ways—it presents us with texture, with color, with varying effects depending on light and shade, with contrasts of building materials. In poetry, the actuality is language arranged in sentences, with a progression through time, with varying emotions, dramatic contrasts of meaning and tone, the revelation of the speaker's situation, and so forth. All these are expressed through the sounds of language, which are constantly shifting to create meanings and implications.

The word *meter* comes from a word meaning "measure" (the word *rhythm* from a word meaning "flow," as in waves). To measure something we must have a unit of measurement. For measuring length we use the inch, foot, yard; for measuring time we use the second, minute, hour. For measuring verse we use the foot, the line, and (sometimes) the stanza.

One basic unit of meter, the foot, consists normally of one accented syllable plus one or two unaccented syllables, though occasionally there may be no unaccented syllables. To determine which syllable in a foot is accented, we compare its sound with that of the other syllables *within the foot,* not with the sounds of syllables in other feet within a line. In fact, because of the varying stresses on syllables in a spoken sentence, it is very unusual for all of the stressed syllables in a line to be equally stressed.

For diagramming the metrical form of verse, various systems of visual symbols have been devised. In this book we shall use a breve (˘) to indicate an unstressed syllable, an ictus (′) to indicate a stressed syllable, and a vertical bar to indicate the division between feet. The basic kinds of feet are as follows:

Examples	Name of Foot	Adjectival Form	
˘ ´ ˘ ´ to-day, the sun	Iamb	Iambic	⎤
			⎬ Duple meters
´ ˘ ´ ˘ dai-ly, went to	Trochee	Trochaic	⎦
˘ ˘ ´ ˘ ˘ ´ in-ter-vene, in the dark	Anapest	Anapestic	⎤
			⎬ Triple meters
´ ˘ ˘ ´ ˘ ˘ mul-ti-ple, col-or of	Dactyl	Dactylic	⎦
´ ´ true-blue	Spondee*	Spondaic	

Two kinds of examples are given here, whole words and phrases, to indicate the fact that one must not assume that every individual word will be a foot, nor that divisions between feet necessarily fall between words. In actual lines, one might for example find the word *intervene* constituting parts of two different feet:

˘ ´ | ˘ ´ | ˘ ´
I want | to in- | ter-vene.

As this example demonstrates, in diagramming meters we must sometimes acknowledge the primary and secondary stresses provided by dictionaries: the word *intervene* provides the stresses for two consecutive feet.

The other basic unit of measurement in metrical verse is the line, which has the same properties as in free verse—it may be end-stopped or run-on, and its phrasing and punctuation will create caesuras. The difference between metrical and free-verse lines is that metrical lines are

---

*In the spondee the accent is thought of as being distributed equally or almost equally over the two syllables and is sometimes referred to as a hovering accent. No whole poems are written in spondees. Hence, there are only four basic meters: iambic, trochaic, anapestic, and dactylic. Iambic and trochaic are called duple because they employ two-syllable feet, anapestic and dactylic triple because they employ three-syllable feet. Of the four standard meters, iambic is by far the most common, followed by anapestic. Trochaic occurs relatively infrequently as the meter of poems, and dactylic is so rare as to be almost a museum specimen.

measured by naming the number of feet in them. The following names indicate number:

Monometer	one foot	Tetrameter	four feet
Dimeter	two feet	Pentameter	five feet
Trimeter	three feet	Hexameter	six feet

The third unit of measurement, the **stanza**, consists of a group of lines whose metrical pattern is repeated throughout the poem. Since much verse is not written in stanzas, we shall save our discussion of this unit till a later chapter.

Although metrical form is potentially uniform in its regularity, the poet may introduce **metrical variations**, which call attention to some of the sounds because they depart from what is regular. Three means for varying meter are **substitution** (replacing the regular foot with another one), **extrametrical syllables** added at the beginnings or endings of lines, and **truncation** (the omission of an unaccented syllable at either end of a line). Because these represent clear changes in the pattern, they are usually obvious and striking. But even metrical regularity rarely creates a monotonous rhythm because rhythm is the actuality in sound, not the pattern or blueprint of meter. The rhythm of a line of poetry, like the actuality of a building, depends on the components of sound mentioned previously—stress, duration, pitch, and juncture—as these are presented in rhetorically stressed sentences. We may diagram the metrical form of a line, but because no two sentences in English are identical in sound, there can be no formulas or mechanical systems for indicating rhythm. Rhythm must be described rather than formulated.

The process of defining the metrical form of a poem is called **scansion**. To *scan* any specimen of verse, we do three things: (1) we identify the prevailing foot; (2) we name the number of feet in a line—if this length follows any regular pattern; and (3) we describe the stanzaic pattern—if there is one. We may try out our skill on the following poem:

Virtue

Sweet day, so cool, so calm, so bright,
    The bridal of the earth and sky;
The dew shall weep thy fall to night,
    For thou must die.

Sweet rose, whose hue, angry and brave,
    Bids the rash gazer wipe his eye;

5

Thy root is ever in its grave,
    And thou must die.

Sweet spring, full of sweet days and roses,
    A box where sweets compacted lie;   10
My music shows ye have your closes,
    And all must die.

Only a sweet and virtuous soul,
    Like seasoned timber, never gives;
But though the whole world turn to coal,   15
    Then chiefly lives.

—GEORGE HERBERT (1593–1633)

QUESTIONS

1. Vocabulary: *bridal* (2), *brave* (5), *closes* (11), *coal* (15).
2. How are the four stanzas interconnected? How do they build to a climax? How does the fourth contrast with the first three?

The first step in scanning a poem is to read it normally, according to its prose meaning, listening to where the accents fall naturally, and perhaps beating time with the hand. If we have any doubt about how a line should be marked, we should skip it temporarily and go on to lines where we feel greater confidence; that is, to those lines that seem most regular, with accents that fall unmistakably at regular intervals—for we are seeking the poem's pattern, which will be revealed by what is regular in it. In "Virtue" lines 3, 10, and 14 clearly fall into this category, as do the short lines 4, 8, and 12. Lines 3, 10, and 14 may be marked as follows:

The dew | shall weep | thy fall | to night,   3

A box | where sweets | com-pact- | ed lie;   10

Like sea- | soned tim- | ber, nev- | er gives   14

Lines 4, 8, and 12 are so nearly identical that we may use line 4 to represent all three.

For thou | must die.   4

Surveying what we have done so far, we may with some confidence say that the prevailing metrical foot of the poem is iambic; and we may reasonably hypothesize that the second and third lines of each stanza are tetrameter (four-foot) lines and the fourth line dimeter. What about the first lines? Line 1 contains eight syllables, and since the poem is iambic, we may mark them into four feet. The last six syllables clearly constitute three iambic feet (as a general rule, the last few feet in a line tend to reflect the prevailing meter of a poem).

Sweet day, | so cool, | so calm, | so bright | 1

This too, then, is a tetrameter line, and the only question is whether to mark the first foot as another iamb or as a spondee—that is, whether it conforms to the norm established by the iambic meter, or is a substituted foot. The adjective "Sweet" is certainly more important in the line than the repeated adverb "so," and ought to receive more stress than the adverbs on the principle of *rhetorical stress,* by which the plain prose sense governs the pronunciation. But we must remember that in marking metrical stresses, we are only comparing the syllables *within a foot,* so the comparison with the repeated "so" is irrelevant. The real question is whether "Sweet" receives as much emphasis as "day."

As another general rule (but by no means an absolute one), a noun usually receives more stress than an adjective that modifies it, a verb more than its adverbs, and an adjective more than an adverb that modifies it—except when the modifying word points to an unusual or unexpected condition. If the phrase were "fat day" or "red day," we would probably feel that those adjectives were odd enough to warrant stressing them. "Sweet day" does not strike us as particularly unusual, so the noun ought to receive stress. Further, as we notice that each of the first three stanzas begins with "Sweet" modifying different nouns, we recognize that the statement of the poem is drawing attention to the similarities (and differences) of three things that can be called *sweet*—"day," "rose," and "spring." By its repetition before those three nouns, the word *sweet* may come to seem formulaic, and the nouns the object of attention. On the other hand, the repetition of "Sweet" may seem emphatic, and lead us to give approximately equal stress to both the noun and its adjective. As our purpose is to detect the *pattern* of sounds in the poem, the most likely result of this study will be to mark it iambic. However, judging it to be spondaic would not be incorrect, for ultimately we are reporting what we *hear,* and there is room for subjective differences.

The first feet of lines 5 and 9 raise the same problem as line 1 and should be marked in the same way. Choices of a similar sort occur in other lines (15 and 16). Many readers will quite legitimately perceive line 16 as parallel to lines 4, 8, and 12. Others, however, may argue that the word "Then"—emphasizing what happens to the virtuous soul when everything else has perished—has an importance that should be reflected in both the reading and the scansion, and will therefore mark the first foot of this line as a spondee:

Then chief- | ly lives. | 16

These readers also will hear the third foot in line 15 as a spondee:

                                         15
But though | the whole | world turn | to coal |

Lines 2 and 7 introduce a different problem. Most readers, if they encountered these lines in a paragraph of prose, would read them thus:

The BRIdal of the EARTH and SKY   2
Thy ROOT is EVer in its GRAVE   7

But this reading leaves us with an anomalous situation. First, we have only three stresses where our pattern calls for four. Second, we have three unaccented syllables occurring together, which is almost never found in verse of duple meter. From this situation we may learn an important principle. Though normal reading of the sentences in a poem establishes its metrical pattern, the metrical pattern so established in turn influences the reading. An interactive process is at work. In this poem the pressure of the pattern will cause most practiced readers to stress the second of the three unaccented syllables in both lines slightly more than those on either side of it. In scansion, comparing the syllables within the individual foot, we acknowledge that slight increase of stress by marking those syllables as stressed (remember, the marking of the accent does not indicate a *degree* of stress in comparison with other accents in the line). We mark them thus:

The bri- | dal of | the earth | and sky | 2

Thy root | is ev- | er in | its grave | 7

Line 5 presents a situation about which there can be no dispute. The word "angry," though it occurs in a position where we would expect an iamb, by virtue of its normal pronunciation *must* be accented on the first syllable, and thus must be marked a trochee:

> Sweet rose, whose hue, an-gry and brave   5

There is little question also that the following line begins with a trochee, but the second foot ("rash gaz-") must be examined, for we may wonder whether the adjective *rash* presents an unexpected modification for the noun *gazer*. Since the possibilities seem about equal, we prefer to let the pattern again take precedence, although a spondee would be acceptable:

> Bids the rash gaz- er wipe his eye   6

Similarly, the word "Only," beginning line 13, must be accented on the first syllable, thus introducing a trochaic substitution in the first foot of the line. Line 13 also presents another problem. A modern reader perceives the word "virtuous" as a three-syllable word, but the poet writing in the seventeenth century, when metrical requirements were stricter than they are today, would probably have meant the word to be pronounced as two syllables: *ver-tyus*. Following the tastes of this century, we mark it as three syllables, so introducing an anapest instead of the expected iamb in the last foot:

> On-ly a sweet and vir- tu-ous soul   13

In doing this, however, we are consciously modernizing—altering the probable practice of the poet for the sake of a contemporary audience.

One problem of scansion remains: in the third stanza, lines 9 and 11 differ from the other lines of the poem in two respects—(a) they contain an uneven number of syllables (nine rather than the expected eight); (b) they end on unaccented syllables:

> Sweet spring, full of sweet days and ros- es,   9

> My mu- sic shows ye have your clos- es   11

Such leftover unaccented syllables at line ends are examples of extra-metrical syllables and are not counted in identifying and naming the meter. These lines are both tetrameter, and if we tap our feet when reading them, we shall tap four times. Metrical verse will often have one and sometimes two leftover unaccented syllables. In iambic and anapestic verse they will come at the end of the lines; in trochaic and dactylic, at the beginning. They never occur in the middle of a line.

Our metrical analysis of "Virtue" is completed. Though (mainly for ease of discussion) we have skipped about, we have indicated a scansion for all its lines. "Virtue" is written in iambic meter (meaning that most of its feet are iambs), and is composed of four-line stanzas, the first three lines tetrameter, the final line dimeter. We are now ready to make a few generalizations about scansion.

1. Most readers will not ordinarily stop to scan a poem they are reading, and they certainly will not read a poem aloud with the exaggerated emphasis on accented syllables that we sometimes give them in order to make the metrical pattern more apparent. However, occasional scansion of a poem has value, as will be indicated in the next chapter, which discusses the relation of sound and meter to sense. Just one example here. The structure of meaning of "Virtue" is unmistakable; three parallel stanzas concerning things that die are followed by a contrasting fourth stanza concerning the one thing that does not die. The first three stanzas all begin with the word "Sweet" preceding a noun, and the first metrical foot in these stanzas is either an iamb or a spondee. The contrasting fourth stanza, however, begins with a trochee, thus departing both from the previous pattern and from the basic meter of the poem. This departure is significant, for the word *only* is the hinge upon which the structure of the poem turns, and the metrical reversal gives it emphasis. Thus meter serves meaning.

2. Scansion only begins to reveal the rhythmic quality of a poem. It simply involves classifying all syllables as either accented or unaccented and ignores the sometimes considerable differences between degrees of accent. Whether we call a syllable accented or unaccented depends only on its degree of accent relative to the other syllable(s) in its foot. In lines 2 and 7 of "Virtue," the accents on "of" and "in" are obviously much lighter than on the other accented syllables in the line. Further, unaccented syllables also vary in weight. In line 5 "whose" is clearly heavier than "-gry" or "and," and is arguably even heavier than the accented "of" and "in" of lines 2 and 7. It is not unusual, either, to find the unaccented syllable of a foot receiving more stress than the accented syllable immediately preceding it in another foot, as in this line by Gerard Manley Hopkins (page 862):

It will ˈflame out ˈlike shin- ˈing from ˈshook foil

The last four syllables of the line, two perfectly regular iambs, are actually spoken as a sequence of four increasingly stressed accents. A similar sequence of increasing accents occurs in lines 4, 8, and 12 of "Virtue,"

$$\breve{\ } \quad \acute{\ } \mid \breve{\ } \quad \acute{\ }$$

For thou |must die| 4

since the necessity expressed in the word "must" makes it more heavily stressed than the pronoun "thou." The point is that metrical scansion is incapable of describing subtle rhythmic effects in poetry. It is nevertheless a useful and serviceable tool, for by showing us the metrical *pattern,* it draws attention to the way in which the actuality of sound follows the pattern even while departing from it; that is, recognizing the meter, we can more clearly hear rhythms. The *idea* of regularity helps us be aware of the *actuality* of sounds.

3. Notice that the divisions between feet have no meaning except to help us identify the meter. They do not correspond to the speech rhythms in the line. In the third foot of line 14 of "Virtue," a syntactical pause occurs *within* the foot; and, indeed, feet divisions often fall in the middle of a word. It is sometimes a mistake of beginners to expect the word and the foot to be identical units. We mark the feet divisions only to reveal regularity or pattern, not to indicate rhythm. But in "Virtue," if we examine all of the two-syllable words, we find that all eleven of them as isolated words removed from their lines would be called *trochaic.* Yet only two of them— "angry" (5) and "only" (13)—actually occur as trochaic feet. All the rest are divided in the middle between two iambic feet. This calls for two observations: (a) the rhythm of the poem, the *heard* sound, often runs counter to the meter—iambic feet have what is called a "rising" pattern, yet these words individually and as they are spoken have a "falling" rhythm; and (b) the trochaic hinge word "only" thus has rhythmic echoes throughout the poem, those preceding it yielding a kind of predictive power, and those following it reinforcing the fact that the sense of the poem turns at that word. This rhythmic effect is especially pronounced in the simile of line 14:

$$\breve{\ } \quad \acute{\ } \mid \breve{\ } \quad \acute{\ } \mid \breve{\ } \quad \acute{\ } \mid \breve{\ } \quad \acute{\ }$$

Like sea- |soned tim- |ber, nev- |er gives| 14

Echoing the key word "only," this line contains three disyllabic words, each of them having a falling rhythm running counter to the iambic meter.

4. Finally—and this is the most important generalization of all— perfect regularity of meter is no criterion of merit. Inexperienced readers

sometimes get the notion that it is. If the meter is regular and the rhythm mirrors that regularity in sound, they may feel that the poet has handled the meter successfully and deserves all credit for it. Actually there is nothing easier for any moderately talented versifier than to make language go ta-DUM ta-DUM ta-DUM. But there are two reasons why this is not generally desirable. The first is that, as we have said, all art consists essentially of repetition and variation. If a rhythm alternates too regularly between light and heavy beats, the result is to banish variation; the rhythm mechanically follows the meter and becomes monotonous. But used occasionally or emphatically, a monotonous rhythm can be very effective, as in the triumphant last line of Tennyson's "Ulysses" (page 787):

To strive, to seek, to find, and not to yield.

The second reason is that once a basic meter has been established, deviations from it become highly significant and are a means by which the poet can reinforce meaning. If a meter is too regular and the rhythm shows little deviation from it, the probability is that the poet, instead of adapting rhythm to meaning, has simply forced the meaning into a metrical straitjacket.

Actually what gives the skillful use of meter its greatest effectiveness is to be found in the distinction between meter and rhythm. Once we have determined the basic meter of a poem, say iambic tetrameter, we have an expectation that the rhythm will coincide with it—that the pattern will be identical to the actual sound. Thus, a silent drumbeat is set up in our minds, and this drumbeat constitutes an **expected rhythm**. But the actual rhythm of the words—the **heard rhythm**—will sometimes confirm this expected rhythm and sometimes not. Thus, the two— meter and rhythm—are counterpointed, and the appeal of the verse is magnified, just as when two melodies are counterpointed in music, or when we see two swallows flying together and around each other, following the same general course but with individual variations and so making a more eye-catching pattern than one swallow flying alone. If the heard rhythm conforms too closely to the expected rhythm (meter), the poem becomes dull and uninteresting rhythmically. If it departs too far from the meter, there ceases to be an expected rhythm and the result is likely to be a muddle.

There are several ways by which variation can be introduced into a poem's rhythm. The most obvious way, as we have said, is by the substitution of other kinds of feet for the basic foot. Such metrical variation will always be reflected as a rhythmic variation. In our scansion of line 13 of "Virtue," for instance, we found a trochee and an anapest substituted for the expected iambs in the first and last feet. A less obvious but equally important means of variation is through varying degrees of accent arising from the prose meaning of phrases—from the rhetorical stressing. Though we began our scansion of "Virtue" by marking lines 3, 10, and 14 as perfectly regular metrically, there is actually a considerable rhythmic difference among them. Line 3 is quite regular because the rhythmic phrasing corresponds to the metrical pattern, and the line can be read: ta DUM ta DUM ta DUM ta DUM (The DEW shall WEEP thy FALL to NIGHT). Line 10 is less regular, for the three-syllable word "compacted" cuts across the division between two feet. This should be read: ta DUM ta DUM ta-DUM-ta DUM (a BOX where SWEETS comPACTed LIE). Line 14 is the least regular of these three because here there is no correspondence between rhythmic phrasing and metrical division. This should be read: ta DUM-ta DUM-ta DUM-ta DUM (Like SEAsoned TIMber, NEVer GIVES). Finally, variation can be introduced by **grammatical and rhetorical pauses,** whether or not signaled by punctuation (punctuated pauses are usually of longer duration than those occasioned only by syntax and rhetoric, and pauses for periods are longer than those for commas). The comma in line 14, by introducing a grammatical pause (in the middle of a foot), provides an additional variation from its perfect regularity. Probably the most violently irregular line in the poem is line 5,

Sweet rose, | whose hue, | an-gry | and brave, | 5

for here the unusual trochaic substitution in the second from last foot of an iambic line (a rare occurrence) is set off and emphasized by the grammatical pause; and also, as we have noted, the unaccented "whose" is considerably heavier than the other unaccented syllables in the line. This trochee "angry" is the first unquestionable metrical substitution in the poem. It occurs in a line which, because it opens a stanza, is subconsciously compared to the first line of the first stanza—an example of regularity with its grammatical pauses separating all four of its feet. Once we have noticed that the first line of the second stanza contains a metrical variation, our attention is called to the fact that after the first, each stanza opens with a line containing a trochee—and that these trochees are moved forward one foot in each of the successive stanzas, from the third position in stanza two, to the second in four, and finally to the first in the concluding stanza. This pattern itself tends to add even more emphasis to the climactic change signaled by the final trochee, "only." Again, meter and rhythm serve meaning.

The effects of rhythm and meter are several. Like the musical repetitions of sound, the musical repetitions of accent can be pleasing for their own sake. In addition, rhythm works as an emotional stimulus and heightens our awareness of what is going on in a poem. Finally, a poet can adapt the sound of the verse to its content and thus make meter a powerful reinforcement of meaning. We should avoid, however, the notion that there is any mystical correspondence between certain meters or rhythms and certain emotions. There are no "happy" meters and no "melancholy" meters. The "falling" rhythm of line 14 of "Virtue," counterpointed against its "rising" meter, does not indicate a depression of mood or feeling—the line has quite the opposite emotional tone. Poets' choice of meter is probably less important than how they handle it after they have chosen it. In most great poetry, meter and rhythm work intimately with the other elements of the poem to produce the total effect.

And because of the importance of free verse today, we must not forget that poetry need not be metrical at all. Like alliteration and rhyme, like metaphor and irony, like even imagery, meter is simply *one* resource poets may or may not use. Their job is to employ their resources to the best advantage for the object they have in mind—the kind of experience they wish to express. And on no other basis should they be judged.

EXERCISES

1. A term that every student of poetry should know (and should be careful not to confuse with *free verse*) is blank verse. **Blank verse** has a very specific meter: it is *iambic pentameter, unrhymed.* It has a special name because it is the principal English meter; that is, the meter that has been used for a large proportion of the greatest English poetry, including the plays of Shakespeare and the epics of Milton. Iambic pentameter in English seems especially suitable for the serious treatment of serious themes. The natural movement of the English language tends to be iambic. Lines shorter than pentameter tend to be songlike, or at least less suited to sustained treatment of serious material. Lines longer than pentameter tend to break up into shorter units, the hexameter line being read as two three-foot units. Rhyme, while highly appropriate to many short poems, often proves a handicap for a long and lofty work. (The word *blank* indicates that the end of the line is bare of rhyme.)

   Of the following poems, four are in blank verse, two are in other meters, and four are in free verse. Determine in which category each belongs.
   a. Frost, "Birches" (page 998).
   b. Donne, "Break of Day" (page 708).
   c. Stafford, "Traveling through the dark" (page 871).
   d. Plath, "Mirror" (page 715).
   e. Tennyson, "Ulysses" (page 787).
   f. Arnold, "Dover Beach" (page 851).

g. Auden, "The Unknown Citizen" (page 803).
h. Yeats, "The Second Coming" (page 1050).
i. Frost, "'Out, Out—'" (page 811).
j. Atwood, "Siren Song" (page 818).
2. Examine Browning, "My Last Duchess" (page 806) and Pope, "Sound and Sense" (page 902). Both are in the same meter, iambic pentameter rhymed in couplets, but their general rhythmic effect is markedly different. What accounts for the difference? How does the contrast support our statement that the way poets handle meter is more important than their choice of a meter?
3. Examine Williams, "The Widow's Lament in Springtime" (page 736) and Williams, "The Dance" (page 915). Which is the most forcibly run-on in the majority of its lines? Describe the differences in effect.

REVIEWING CHAPTER TWELVE

1. Review the terms printed in boldface, and as you read on in this chapter take note of the examples that you find; identify the poems as free verse or metrical, and write out scansions of the metrical verse.
2. Using examples from the poems that follow in this chapter, draw clear distinctions between rhythm and meter; and using appropriate adjectives, describe the rhythmic effects (jolly, somber, playful, etc.).
3. When possible, explain how the rhythms of a poem reinforce emotional or intellectual meanings.

"Introduction" to *Songs of Innocence*

Piping down the valleys wild,
Piping songs of pleasant glee,
On a cloud I saw a child,
And he laughing said to me:

"Pipe a song about a Lamb." 5
So I piped with merry cheer.
"Piper, pipe that song again."
So I piped; he wept to hear.

"Drop thy pipe, thy happy pipe;
Sing thy songs of happy cheer." 10

So I sung the same again
While he wept with joy to hear.

"Piper, sit thee down and write
In a book that all may read."
So he vanished from my sight,   15
And I plucked a hollow reed,

And I made a rural pen,
And I stained the water clear,
And I wrote my happy songs
Every child may joy to hear.   20

—WILLIAM BLAKE (1757–1827)

QUESTIONS

1. Poets have traditionally been thought of as inspired by one of the Muses (Greek female divinities whose duties were to nurture the arts). Blake's *Songs of Innocence,* a book of poems about childhood and the state of innocence, includes "The Chimney Sweeper" (page 798) and "The Lamb" (page 835). In this introductory poem to the book, what function is performed by the child upon a cloud?
2. What is symbolized by "a Lamb" (5)?
3. What three stages of poetic composition are suggested in stanzas 1–2, 3, and 4–5 respectively?
4. What features of the poems in his book does Blake hint at in this "Introduction"? Name at least four.
5. Mark the stressed and unstressed syllables in lines 1–2 and 9–10. Do they establish the basic meter of the poem? If so, is that meter iambic or trochaic? Or could it be either? Some metrists have discarded the distinction between iambic and trochaic, and between anapestic and dactylic, as being artificial. The important distinction, they feel, is between duple and triple meters. Does this poem support their claim?

Had I the Choice

Had I the choice to tally greatest bards,
To limn their portraits, stately, beautiful, and emulate at will,
Homer with all his wars and warriors—Hector, Achilles, Ajax,
Or Shakespeare's woe-entangled Hamlet, Lear, Othello—Tennyson's
    fair ladies,
Meter or wit the best, or choice conceit to wield in perfect rhyme,
    delight of singers;   5
These, these, O sea, all these I'd gladly barter,

Would you the undulation of one wave, its trick to me transfer,
Or breathe one breath of yours upon my verse,
And leave its odor there.

—WALT WHITMAN (1819–1892)

QUESTIONS

1. Vocabulary: *tally* (1), *limn* (2), *conceit* (5).
2. What poetic qualities does the speaker propose to barter in exchange for what? What qualities do the sea and its waves symbolize?
3. Is this free verse, or metrical verse in duple meter? In what way might this be taken as an imitation of the rhythms of the sea?

Stanzas

When a man hath no freedom to fight for at home,
   Let him combat for that of his neighbors;
Let him think of the glories of Greece and of Rome,
   And get knocked on his head for his labors.

To do good to mankind is the chivalrous plan,   5
   And is always as nobly requited:
Then battle for freedom wherever you can,
   And, if not shot or hanged, you'll get knighted.

—GEORGE GORDON, LORD BYRON (1788–1824)

QUESTIONS

1. Vocabulary: *chivalrous* (5), *requited* (6).
2. Scan the poem. How would you describe its rhythmical effects? How do these effects relate to the poem's tone and general meaning?
3. This poem makes use of feminine rhyme. Does this particular kind of rhyme affect the way you read and understand the poem?
4. How is irony effectively used in this poem, particularly in the final line?

Insomnia

The moon in the bureau mirror
looks out a million miles
(and perhaps with pride, at herself,
but she never, never smiles)
far and away beyond sleep, or   5
perhaps she's a daytime sleeper.

By the Universe deserted,
she'd tell it to go to hell,
and she'd find a body of water,
or a mirror, on which to dwell.   10
So wrap up care in a cobweb
and drop it down the well

into that world inverted
where left is always right,
where the shadows are really the body,   15
where we stay awake all night,
where the heavens are shallow as the sea
is now deep, and you love me.

—ELIZABETH BISHOP (1911–1979)

QUESTIONS

1. Discuss the symbolism of the moon. What are its connotations? What is the situation in which the moon is being observed in the bureau mirror?
2. Explain the title and how it relates to the poem. Can we infer from the poem the reason for the speaker's insomnia?
3. Can this be called a love poem? Why or why not?

Old Ladies' Home

Sharded in black, like beetles,
Frail as antique earthenware
One breath might shiver to bits,
The old women creep out here
To sun on the rocks or prop   5
Themselves up against the wall
Whose stones keep a little heat.

Needles knit in a bird-beaked
Counterpoint to their voices:
Sons, daughters, daughters and sons,   10
Distant and cold as photos,
Grandchildren nobody knows.
Age wears the best black fabric
Rust-red or green as lichens.

At owl-call the old ghosts flock   15
To hustle them off the lawn.

From beds boxed-in like coffins
The bonneted ladies grin.
And Death, that bald-head buzzard,
Stalls in halls where the lamp wick   20
Shortens with each breath drawn.

—SYLVIA PLATH (1932–1963)

QUESTIONS

1. Vocabulary: *Sharded* (1), *Stalls* (20).
2. Discuss the significance of these natural images: "beetles" (1), "bird-beaked /
   Counterpoint" (8–9), "Rust-red or green as lichens" (14), "owl-call" (15), "bald-
   head buzzard" (19). These are all metaphors or similes; in each case, what is being
   compared to what?
3. What is the speaker's tone?
4. This poem is an example of **syllabic verse,** which counts only the number of
   syllables per line, regardless of accents. (Plath's "Metaphors" [page 758] is another
   example.) In this case, the poem is constructed of seven-syllable lines in seven-
   line stanzas—but there is one line that contains only six syllables. What is the
   significance of the shortening of that line?
5. The poem contains some rhyme (particularly slant rhyme), and some of the lines
   contain duple metrical feet. Are these musical effects regular enough to call this
   a metrical poem?

To a Daughter Leaving Home

When I taught you
at eight to ride
a bicycle, loping along
beside you
as you wobbled away   5
on two round wheels,
my own mouth rounding
in surprise when you pulled
ahead down the curved
path of the park,   10
I kept waiting
for the thud
of your crash as I
sprinted to catch up,
while you grew   15
smaller, more breakable
with distance,
pumping, pumping

for your life, screaming
with laughter,   20
the hair flapping
behind you like a
handkerchief waving
goodbye.

—LINDA PASTAN (B. 1932)

QUESTIONS

1. How does the discrepancy between the title and the event create meaning? Which details of the poem take on symbolic meaning?
2. Write out this poem as prose, ignoring line ends. What poetic effect has been lost? Which of the original line ends are particularly important to meaning and feeling?

Porphyria's Lover

The rain set early in tonight,
    The sullen wind was soon awake,
It tore the elm-tops down for spite,
    And did its worst to vex the lake:
    I listened with heart fit to break.   5
When glided in Porphyria; straight
    She shut the cold out and the storm,
And kneeled and made the cheerless grate
    Blaze up, and all the cottage warm;
    Which done, she rose, and from her form   10
Withdrew the dripping cloak and shawl,
    And laid her soiled gloves by, untied
Her hat and let the damp hair fall,
    And, last, she sat down by my side
    And called me. When no voice replied,   15
She put my arm about her waist,
    And made her smooth white shoulder bare,
And all her yellow hair displaced,
    And, stooping, made my cheek lie there,
    And spread, o'er all, her yellow hair,   20
Murmuring how she loved me—she
    Too weak, for all her heart's endeavor,
To set its struggling passion free
    From pride, and vainer ties dissever,
    And give herself to me forever.   25

But passion sometimes would prevail,
   Nor could tonight's gay feast restrain
A sudden thought of one so pale
   For love of her, and all in vain:
   So, she was come through wind and rain.   30
Be sure I looked up at her eyes
   Happy and proud; at last I knew
Porphyria worshipped me: surprise
   Made my heart swell, and still it grew
   While I debated what to do.   35
That moment she was mine, mine, fair,
   Perfectly pure and good: I found
A thing to do, and all her hair
   In one long yellow string I wound
   Three times her little throat around,   40
And strangled her. No pain felt she;
   I am quite sure she felt no pain.
As a shut bud that holds a bee,
   I warily oped her lids: again
   Laughed the blue eyes without a stain.   45
And I untightened next the tress
   About her neck; her cheek once more
Blushed bright beneath my burning kiss:
   I propped her head up as before,
   Only, this time my shoulder bore   50
Her head, which droops upon it still:
   The smiling rosy little head,
So glad it has its utmost will,
   That all it scorned at once is fled,
   And I, its love, am gained instead!   55
Porphyria's love: she guessed not how
   Her darling one wish would be heard.
And thus we sit together now,
   And all night long we have not stirred
   And yet God has not said a word!   60

—ROBERT BROWNING (1812–1889)

QUESTIONS

1. Why can Porphyria and the speaker not be together in a normal romantic relationship? What has kept them apart?
2. What is the "gay feast" mentioned in line 27?

3. The poem deals, in part, with abnormal human psychology. What kind of a person is the speaker? What does he reveal about himself as the poem proceeds? Why does he take such drastic action?
4. The final line has been read in a variety of ways. Why has God "not said a word"? Does this mean that God has countenanced the murder?
5. How would you describe the metrical pattern in this poem? How does the pattern help reinforce the poem's meaning?

Break, break, break

Break, break, break,
   On thy cold gray stones, O sea!
And I would that my tongue could utter
   The thoughts that arise in me.

O, well for the fisherman's boy,   5
   That he shouts with his sister at play!
O, well for the sailor lad,
   That he sings in his boat on the bay!

And the stately ships go on
   To their haven under the hill;   10
But O for the touch of a vanished hand,
   And the sound of a voice that is still!

Break, break, break,
   At the foot of thy crags, O sea!
But the tender grace of a day that is dead   15
   Will never come back to me.

—ALFRED, LORD TENNYSON (1809–1892)

QUESTIONS

1. In lines 3–4 the speaker wishes he could put his thoughts into words. Does he make those thoughts explicit in the course of the poem?
2. What aspects of life are symbolized by the two images in stanza 2? By the image in lines 9–10? How do lines 11–12 contrast with those images?
3. The basic meter of this poem is anapestic, and all but two lines are trimeter. Which two? What other variations from a strict anapestic trimeter do you find? How many lines (and which ones) display a strict anapestic pattern? With this much variation, would you be justified in calling the poem free verse? Do the departures from a strict metrical norm contribute to the meaning?

Her Kind

I have gone out, a possessed witch,
haunting the black air, braver at night;
dreaming evil, I have done my hitch
over the plain houses, light by light:
lonely thing, twelve-fingered, out of mind.   5
A woman like that is not a woman, quite.
I have been her kind.

I have found the warm caves in the woods,
filled them with skillets, carvings, shelves,
closets, silks, innumerable goods;   10
fixed the suppers for the worms and the elves:
whining, rearranging the disaligned.
A woman like that is misunderstood.
I have been her kind.

I have ridden in your cart, driver,   15
waved my nude arms at villages going by,
learning the last bright routes, survivor
where your flames still bite my thigh
and my ribs crack where your wheels wind.
A woman like that is not ashamed to die.   20
I have been her kind.

—ANNE SEXTON (1928–1974)

QUESTIONS

1. What "kind" of woman is being described here? Why does she compare herself to a "possessed witch" (1)?
2. In the third stanza, where is the woman going in the "cart" (15)? Is the image the speaker creates in this stanza comic or tragic?
3. How does the refrain work to make the poem more effective?
4. Compare the speaker here to that in Plath's "Lady Lazarus" (page 781). In what ways are they similar?

SUGGESTIONS FOR WRITING

The following suggestions are for brief writing exercises, not for full critical essays. The suggestions here could constitute a part of a full essay that includes some discussion of the contribution of rhythm and meter to the total meaning of a poem.

1. Scan one of the following metrical poems, and indicate how the rhythmic effects (including substitutions and variations from the metrical norm) contribute to meaning:

   a. Dickinson, "Because I could not stop for Death" (page 784).

   b. Shelley, "Ozymandias" (page 799); consider regular and irregular meters in lines 10–14.

   c. Blake, "Introduction" to *Songs of Innocence* (page 889; see question 5).

   d. Tennyson, "Break, break, break" (page 896; see question 3).

2. In the following free-verse poems, discuss how the line forms a rhythmic unit, paying particular attention to run-on and end-stopped lines:

   a. Williams, "The Widow's Lament in Springtime" (page 736; particularly examine lines 20–24).

   b. Pastan, "To a Daughter Leaving Home" (page 893; see question 2, and particularly examine lines 12–14, 15–16, 19–20, 21–24).

   c. Ferlinghetti, "Constantly risking absurdity" (page 692; see question 4).

   d. Hughes, "Theme for English B" (page 1012).

PRACTICE AP WRITING PROMPTS ▬▬▬▬▬

Walt Whitman, "Had I the Choice" (p. 890)

In Whitman's brief free-verse statement "Had I the Choice," the speaker wishes he could create the sort of sensual delight with words that nature makes using its ability to appeal to all our senses. Read "Had I the Choice" several times. Then write an essay in which you discuss Whitman's attempts to use words as musical instruments.

Linda Pastan, "To a Daughter Leaving Home" (p. 893)

Read "To a Daughter Leaving Home" carefully. Then, taking into consideration the poem's title, explain how the rite of passage described in the poem reflects the speaker's feelings as she learns to let her child go. In your essay, consider such elements as simile, sound devices, and rhythm.

Alfred, Lord Tennyson, "Break, break, break" (p. 896)

Read "Break, break, break" carefully. Then write a well-organized essay in which you show how imagery, rhythm, and diction convey the speaker's experience and mood of loss.

CHAPTER THIRTEEN

Sound and Meaning

Rhythm and sound cooperate to produce what we call the music of poetry. This music, as we have pointed out, may serve two general functions: it may be enjoyable in itself, or it may reinforce meaning and intensify the communication.

Pure pleasure in sound and rhythm exists from a very early age in the human being—probably from the age the baby first starts cooing in its cradle, certainly from the age that children begin chanting nursery rhymes and skipping rope. The appeal of the following verse, for instance, depends almost entirely on its "music":

> Pease porridge hot,
>> Pease porridge cold,
> Pease porridge in the pot
>> Nine days old.

> —Anonymous

There is very little sense here; the attraction comes from the emphatic rhythm, the emphatic rhymes (with a strong contrast between the short vowel and short final consonant of *hot–pot* and the long vowel and long final consonant combination of *cold–old*), and the heavy alliteration (exactly half the words begin with *p*). From nonsense rhymes such as this, many of us graduate to a love of more meaningful poems whose appeal resides largely in the sounds they make. Much of the pleasure that we find in poems like Vachel Lindsay's "The Congo" and Edgar Allan Poe's "The Bells" (page 866) derives from their musical qualities.

The peculiar function of poetry as distinguished from music, however, is to convey not sounds but meaning or experience *through* sounds. In first-rate poetry, sound exists neither for its own sake nor for mere decoration, but to enhance the meaning. Its function is to support the leading player, not to steal the scene.

The poet may reinforce meaning through sound in numerous ways. Without claiming to exhaust them, we can include most of the chief means under four general headings.

First, the poet can choose words whose sound in some degree suggests their meaning. In its narrowest sense this is called onomatopoeia. **Onomatopoeia,** strictly defined, means the use of words that, at least supposedly, sound like what they mean, such as *hiss, snap,* and *bang.* Animal noises offer many examples—*bow-wow, cock-a-doodle-do, oink*—and sometimes poets may even invent words to represent them, as Shakespeare does in "Winter" (page 683) when the owl sings "Tu-whit, tu-who!" Poetry, of course, does not usually present the vocalized sounds made by animals, but onomatopoeia often expresses the sounds of movements or actions, as in the following examples: "The harness *jingles*" in Housman's "Is my team plowing" (page 705); "Neighbors *rustle* in and out" in Dickinson's "There's been a Death, in the Opposite House" (page 709); the mourners "*creak* across" in Dickinson's "I felt a Funeral, in my Brain" (page 737); and in Heaney's "The Forge" (page 739) we hear *ring, hiss, clatter, grunts,* and *slam.* Generally, we can detect the presence of onomatopoetic words simply by sounding them, but you can also use your dictionary to verify your discovery: most have the term "imitative" as part of the information about word origins.

The usefulness of onomatopoeia, of course, is strictly limited, because it occurs only where the poet is describing sound, and most poems do not describe sound. But by combining onomatopoeia with other devices that help convey meaning, the poet can achieve subtle or bold emotional effects.

In addition to onomatopoetic words there is another group of words, sometimes called **phonetic intensives,** whose sound, by a process as yet obscure, to some degree connects with their meaning. An initial *fl* sound, for instance, is often associated with the idea of moving light, as in *flame, flare, flash, flicker, flimmer.* An initial *gl* also frequently accompanies the idea of light, usually unmoving, as in *glare, gleam, glint, glow, glisten.* An initial *sl* often introduces words meaning "smoothly wet," as in *slippery, slick, slide, slime, slop, slosh, slobber, slushy.* An initial *st* often suggests strength, as in *staunch, stalwart, stout, sturdy, stable, steady, stocky, stern, strong, stubborn, steel.* Short *i* often goes with the idea of smallness, as in *inch, imp, thin, slim, little, bit, chip, sliver, chink, slit, sip, whit, tittle, snip, wink, glint, glimmer, flicker, pigmy, midge, chick, kid, kitten, minikin, miniature.* Long *o* or *oo* may suggest melancholy or sorrow, as in *moan, groan, woe, mourn, forlorn, toll, doom, gloom, moody.* Final *are* sometimes goes with the idea of a big light or noise, as *flare, glare, stare, blare.* Medial *att* suggests some kind of particled movement as in *spatter, scatter, shatter, chatter, rattle, prattle, clatter, batter*. Final *er* and *le* indicate repetition, as in *glitter, flutter, shimmer, whisper, jabber, chatter, clatter, sputter, flicker, twitter, mutter,* and *ripple, bubble, twinkle, sparkle, rattle, rumble, jingle*.

None of these various sounds is invariably associated with the idea that it seems to suggest and, in fact, a short *i* is found in *thick* as well as *thin,* in *big* as well as *little.* Language is a complex phenomenon. But there is enough association between these sounds and ideas to suggest some sort of intrinsic if obscure relationship. A word like *flicker,* though not onomatopoetic (because it does not refer to sound) would seem somehow to suggest its sense, with the *fl* suggesting moving light, the *i* suggesting smallness, the *ck* suggesting sudden cessation of movement (as in *crack, peck, pick, hack,* and *flick*), and the *er* suggesting repetition. The preceding list of sound-idea correspondences is only a very partial one. A complete list, though it would involve only a small proportion of words in the language, would probably be longer than that of the more strictly onomatopoetic words, to which they are related.

Eight O'Clock

He stood, and heard the steeple
   Sprinkle the quarters on the morning town.
One, two, three, four, to market-place and people
   It tossed them down.

Strapped, noosed, nighing his hour,   5
   He stood and counted them and cursed his luck;
And then the clock collected in the tower
   Its strength, and struck.

                          —A. E. HOUSMAN (1859–1936)

QUESTIONS

1. Vocabulary: *quarters* (2).
2. Eight A.M. was the traditional hour in England for putting condemned criminals to death. Discuss the force of "morning" (2) and "struck" (8). Discuss the appropriateness of the image of the clock collecting its strength. Can you suggest any reason for the use of "nighing" (5) rather than *nearing?*
3. Consider the contribution to meaning of the following phonetic intensives: "steeple" and "Sprinkle" (1, 2), "stood" (1, 6), "Strapped" (5), "strength" and "struck" (8). Comment on the frequent *k* sounds leading up to "struck" in the second stanza.

A second and far more important way that the poet can reinforce meaning through sound is to choose sounds and group them so that the effect is smooth and pleasant sounding (*euphonious*) or rough and harsh sounding (*cacophonous*). Vowels are in general more pleasing than consonants, for vowels are musical tones, whereas consonants are merely noises. A line with a high percentage of vowel sounds in proportion to consonant sounds will therefore tend to be more melodious than one in which the proportion is low. The vowels and consonants themselves differ considerably in quality. The "long" vowels, such as those in *fate, reed, rhyme, coat, food,* and *dune* are fuller and more resonant than the "short" vowels, as in *fat, red, rim, cot, foot,* and *dun.* Of the consonants, some are fairly mellifluous, such as the "liquids," *l, m, n,* and *r*; the soft *v* and *f* sounds; the semivowels *w* and *y*; and such combinations as *th* and *wh*. Others, such as the "plosives," *b, d, g, k, p,* and *t,* are harsher and sharper in their effect. These differences in sound are the poet's materials. Good poets, however, will not necessarily seek out the sounds that are pleasing and attempt to combine them in melodious combinations. Rather, they will use **euphony** and **cacophony** as they are appropriate to content. Consider, for instance, the following lines.

Sound and Sense

True ease in writing comes from art, not chance,
As those move easiest who have learned to dance.
'Tis not enough no harshness gives offense,
The sound must seem an echo to the sense:
Soft is the strain when Zephyr gently blows,   5
And the smooth stream in smoother numbers flows;
But when loud surges lash the sounding shore,
The hoarse, rough verse should like the torrent roar;
When Ajax strives some rock's vast weight to throw,
The line too labors, and the words move slow;   10
Not so, when swift Camilla scours the plain,
Flies o'er the unbending corn, and skims along the main.
Hear how Timotheus' varied lays surprise,
And bid alternate passions fall and rise!

—ALEXANDER POPE (1688–1744)

QUESTIONS

1. Vocabulary: *numbers* (6), *lays* (13).
2. This excerpt is from a long poem (called *An Essay on Criticism*) on the arts of writing and judging poetry. Which line states the thesis of the passage?

3. There are four classical allusions: Zephyr (5) was god of the west wind; Ajax (9), a Greek warrior noted for his strength; Camilla (11), a legendary queen reputedly so fleet of foot that she could run over a field of grain without bending the blades or over the sea without wetting her feet; Timotheus (13), a famous Greek rhapsodic poet. How do these allusions enable Pope to achieve greater economy?
4. Copy the passage and scan it. Then, considering both meter and sounds, show how Pope practices what he preaches. (Incidentally, on which syllable should "alternate" in line 14 be accented? Does the meter help you to know the pronunciation of "Timotheus" in line 13?)

There are no strictly onomatopoetic words in this passage, and yet the sound seems marvelously adapted to the sense. When the poem is about soft, smooth effects (lines 5–6), there is an abundance of alliteration (*s* in *soft, strain, smooth stream, smoother*) and consonance (the voiced *s* or *z* sound in *Zephyr, blows, numbers flows;* the voiced *th* of *smooth* and *smoother*). When harshness and loudness are the subject, the lines become cacophonous and even the pleasant smoothness of *s*-alliteration when coupled with *sh* evokes angry hissing: "*s*urges la*sh* the *s*ounding *sh*ore, / The hoar*s*e, rough ver*s*e *sh*ould. . . ." Heavy labor is expressed in cacophony ("Ajax strives some rock's vast weight to throw"), while lightness and speed are expressed with euphonious short *i* sounds ("sw*i*ft Cam*i*lla . . . sk*i*ms"). Throughout the passage there is a remarkable correspondence between the pleasant-sounding and the pleasant in idea, the unpleasant-sounding and the unpleasant in idea.

As the excerpt from Alexander Pope also demonstrates, a third way in which a poet can reinforce meaning through sound is by controlling the speed and movement of the lines by the choice and use of meter, by the choice and arrangement of vowel and consonant sounds, and by the disposition of pauses. In meter, the unaccented syllables usually go faster than the accented syllables; hence, the triple meters are swifter than the duple. But the poet can vary the tempo of any meter by the use of substitute feet. Generally, whenever two or more unaccented syllables come together, the effect will be to speed up the pace of the line; when two or more accented syllables come together, the effect will be to slow it down. This pace will also be affected by the vowel lengths and by whether the sounds are easily run together. The long vowels take longer to pronounce than the short ones. Some words are easily run together, while others demand that the position of the mouth be re-formed before the next word is uttered. It takes much longer, for instance, to say "Watch dogs catch much meat" than to say "My aunt is away," though the number of syllables is the same. And finally the poet can slow down the speed of a line through the introduction of grammatical and rhetorical pauses. Consider lines 54–56 from Tennyson's "Ulysses" (page 787):

The lights | be-gín | to twin- | kle from | the rocks;

The long day wanes; the slow moon climbs; the deep   55

Moans round with man-y voi-ces. . . .

In these lines Tennyson wished the movement to be slow, in accordance with the slow waning of the long day and the slow climbing of the moon. His meter is iambic pentameter. This is not a swift meter, but in lines 55–56 he slows it down further, by (a) introducing three spondaic feet, thus bringing three accented syllables together in two separate places; (b) choosing for his accented syllables words that have long vowel sounds or dipthongs that the voice hangs onto: "long," "day," "wanes," "slow," "moon," "climbs," "deep," "Moans," "round"; (c) choosing words that are not easily run together (except for "day" and "slow," each of these words begins and ends with consonant sounds that require varying degrees of readjustment of the mouth before pronunciation can continue); and (d) introducing two grammatical pauses, after "wanes" and "climbs," and a rhetorical pause after "deep." The result is an extremely effective use of the movement of the verse to accord with the movement suggested by the words.

A fourth way for a poet to fit sound to sense is to control both sound and meter in such a way as to emphasize words that are important in meaning. This can be done by highlighting such words through alliteration, assonance, consonance, or rhyme; by placing them before a pause; or by skillfully placing or displacing them in the metrical scheme. We have already seen how Ogden Nash uses alliteration and consonance to emphasize and link the three major words ("sex," "fix," and "fertile") in his little verse "The Turtle" (page 857), and how George Herbert pivots the structure of meaning in "Virtue" (page 879) on a trochaic substitution in the initial foot of his final stanza. For an additional example, let us look again at Drayton's "Since there's no help" (page 842). This poem is a sonnet—fourteen lines of iambic pentameter—in which a lover threatens to abandon his courtship if the woman he desires will not go to bed with him. In the first eight lines he pretends to be *glad* that they are parting so cleanly. In the last six lines, however, he paints a vivid picture of the death of his personified Love/ Passion for her but intimates that even at this last moment ("Now") she could restore it to life—by satisfying his sexual desires:

Now, at the last gasp of Love's la-test breath,

When, his pulse failing, Passion speechless lies,   10

When Faith is kneeling by his bed of death,

And In-|no-cence|is clos-|ing up|his eyes,|

Now, if|thou wouldst,|when all|have given|him o-|ver,*

From death|to life|thou mightst|him yet|re-cov-|er.

The emphasis is on *Now*. In a matter of seconds, the speaker indicates, it will be too late: his Love/Passion will be dead, and he himself will be gone. The word "Now" begins line 9. It also begins a new sentence and a new direction in the poem. It is separated from what has gone before by a period at the end of the preceding line. Metrically it initiates a trochee, thus breaking away from the poem's basic iambic meter (line 8 is perfectly regular). In all these ways—its initial position in line, sentence, and thought, and its metrical irregularity—the word "Now" is given extraordinary emphasis appropriate to its importance in the context. Its repetition in line 13 reaffirms this importance, and there again it is given emphasis by its positional and metrical situation. It begins both a line and the final rhyming couplet, is separated by punctuation from the line before, and participates in a metrical inversion. (The lines before and after are metrically regular.)

While Herbert and Drayton use metrical deviation to give emphasis to important words, Tennyson, in the concluding line of "Ulysses," uses marked regularity, plus skillful use of grammatical pauses, to achieve the same effect.

We are|not now|that strength|which in|old days|

Moved earth|and heav-|en, that|which we are,|we are:|

One e-|qual tem-|per of|he-ro-|ic hearts,|

Made weak|by time|and fate,|but strong|in will|

To strive,|to seek,|to find,|and not|to yield.| 70

The blank-verse rhythm throughout "Ulysses" is remarkably subtle and varied, but the last line is not only regular in its scansion but heavily regular, for a number of reasons. First, all the words are monosyllables. Second, the unaccented syllables are all very small and unimportant words—four

*Drayton probably intended "given" to be pronounced as one syllable (*giv'n*), and most sixteenth-century readers would have pronounced it thus in this poem.

*to*s and one *and*—whereas the accented syllables consist of four important verbs and a very important *not*. Third, each of the verbs is followed by a grammatical pause pointed off by a mark of punctuation. The result is to cause a pronounced alternation between light and heavy syllables that brings the accent down on the four verbs and the *not* with sledgehammer blows. The line rings out like a challenge, which it is.

I heard a Fly buzz—when I died

I heard a Fly buzz—when I died—
The Stillness in the Room
Was like the Stillness in the Air—
Between the Heaves of Storm—

The Eyes around—had wrung them dry—   5
And Breaths were gathering firm
For that last Onset—when the King
Be witnessed—in the Room—

I willed my Keepsakes—Signed away
What portion of me be   10
Assignable—and then it was
There interposed a Fly—

With Blue—uncertain stumbling Buzz—
Between the light—and me—
And then the Windows failed—and then   15
I could not see to see—

—EMILY DICKINSON (1830–1886)

QUESTIONS

1. It is important to understand the sequence of events in this deathbed scene. Arrange the following events in correct chronological order: (a) the willing of keepsakes, (b) the weeping of mourners, (c) the appearance of the fly, (d) the preternatural stillness in the room.

2. What or who are the "Eyes" and the "Breaths" in lines 5–6? What figures of speech are involved in these lines? Is the speaker making out her will in lines 9–11? What *is* she doing?

3. What sort of expectation is set up by phrases like "last Onset" (7), "the King" (7), and "Be witnessed" (8)?

4. Explain "the Windows failed" (15) and "I could not see to see" (16).

We may well conclude our discussion of the adaptation of sound to sense by analyzing this poem. It consists of 4 four-line stanzas of alternating iambic tetrameter (first and third lines) and iambic trimeter (second and fourth); the first and third lines are unrhymed, the second and fourth display approximate rhymes in the first three stanzas. The fourth stanza uses an exact rhyme that echoes the last word in line 3 of the preceding stanza. The poem depicts a speaker's recollection of her own deathbed scene, focusing on the suspenseful interval during which she and her loved ones await the arrival of death—ironically symbolized in the closing lines as a common housefly. But the poem does not move chronologically. Surprisingly, it begins with its conclusion, the apparently trivial fact that the last conscious perception was hearing the buzzing fly; then it proceeds to summarize the events leading up to that moment.

How is the poem's sound fitted to its sense? In the opening stanzas, the pace is slow and even solemn, the rhythm perfectly matching the meter, as befits this apparently momentous occasion with its "Stillness," its quiet, breathless awaiting of "the King"—death itself. The approximate rhymes provide a formal unity even as they convey an atmosphere of unease, an uncertainty and fear in the face of imminent death; and the dashes contribute to the poem's measured, stately rhythm. Then the poem returns to the insignificant topic of its opening line and invests it with enormous meaning.

The one onomatopoetic word in the poem is *Buzz*, introduced abruptly in line 1 without capitalization and then reintroduced with intensity in line 13. In line 11, the final word, *was*, though unrhymed in its own stanza and unrhymed in the formal rhyme scheme, nevertheless is an exact rhyme for *Buzz* in the first line of the final stanza. In line 12, the word *interposed* continues the buzzing into the final stanza. In line 13 the vowel sound of *Buzz* is preceded by the identical vowel sounds in "*u*ncertain" and "st*u*mbling," making three *u* sounds in close succession. Finally, the *b* sound in *Buzz* is preceded in line 13 by the *b*s in "*B*lue" and "stum*b*ling." Thus, *all* the sounds in *Buzz*—its initial and final consonants and its vowel—are heard at least three times in lines 11–13. This outburst of onomatopoetic effect consummates the aural imagery promised in the opening line, "I *heard* a Fly buzz."

But line 13 combines images of color and motion as well as sound. Though the sound imagery is the most important, the poem concludes with a reference to the speaker's dimming eyesight, and we may infer that she *saw* a blur of the bluebottle's deep metallic blue as well as hearing its buzz. This image is an example of **synesthesia,** the stimulation of two or more senses simultaneously, especially as here, where one sense perception is described in terms of another (as in a "Blue ... Buzz"). The images of motion between "Blue" and "Buzz" also belong to both the visual and aural modes of sensing. The speaker hears and imperfectly sees the "uncertain" flight of the fly as it bumbles from one pane of glass to another, its buzzing now louder, now softer. Furthermore, the exact rhymes in the last stanza that pick up on "was" in the preceding one underscore the abrupt finality of the speaker's confrontation with death, and thus the sudden end of her human perception.

In analyzing verse for correspondence between sound and sense, we need to be very cautious not to make exaggerated claims. A great deal of nonsense has been written about the moods of certain meters and the effects of certain sounds, and it is easy to suggest correspondences that exist only in our imaginations. Nevertheless, the first-rate poet has nearly always an instinctive tact about handling sound so that it in some degree supports meaning. One of the few absolute rules that applies to the judgment of poetry is that the form should be adequate to the content. This rule does not mean that there must always be a close and easily demonstrable correspondence. It does mean that there will be no glaring discrepancies.

The selection that introduces this chapter ("Pease porridge hot") illustrates the use of sound in verse almost purely for its own sake, and it is, as significant poetry, among the most trivial passages in the whole book. But beyond this there is an abundant range of poetic possibilities where sound is pleasurable for itself without violating meaning and where sound to varying degrees corresponds with and corroborates meaning; and in this rich middle range lie many of the great pleasures of reading poetry.

EXERCISE

In each of the following paired quotations, the named poet wrote the version that more successfully adapts sound to sense. As specifically as possible, account for the superiority of the better version.

1. a. Go forth—and Virtue, ever in your sight,
   Shall be your guide by day, your guard by night.
   b. Go forth—and Virtue, ever in your sight,
   Shall point your way by day, and keep you safe at night. —CHARLES CHURCHILL
2. a. How charming is divine philosophy!
   Not harsh and rough as foolish men suppose
   But musical as is the lute of Phoebus.
   b. How charming is divine philosophy!
   Not harsh and crabbed as dull fools suppose
   But musical as is Apollo's lute. —JOHN MILTON
3. a. All day the fleeing crows croak hoarsely over the snow.
   b. All day the out-cast crows croak hoarsely across the whiteness.
   —ELIZABETH COATSWORTH
4. a. Your talk attests how bells of singing gold Would sound at evening over silent water.
   b. Your low voice tells how bells of singing gold
   Would sound at twilight over silent water. —EDWIN ARLINGTON ROBINSON

5. a. A thousand streamlets flowing through the lawn,
   The moan of doves in gnarled ancient oaks,
   And quiet murmuring of countless bees.

   b. Myriads of rivulets hurrying through the lawn,
   The moan of doves in immemorial elms,
   And murmuring of innumerable bees. —ALFRED, LORD TENNYSON

6. a. It is the lark that sings so out of tune,
   Straining harsh discords and unpleasing sharps.

   b. It is the lark that warbles out of tune
   In harsh discordant tones with doleful flats. —WILLIAM SHAKESPEARE

7. a. "Artillery" and "armaments" and "implements of war"
   Are phrases too severe to please the gentle Muse.

   b. Bombs, drums, guns, bastions, batteries, bayonets, bullets,—
   Hard words, which stick in the soft Muses' gullets. —LORD BYRON

8. a. The hands of the sisters Death and Night incessantly softly
   wash again, and ever again, this soiled world.

   b. The hands of the soft twins Death and Night repeatedly
   wash again, and ever again, this dirty world. —WALT WHITMAN

9. a. The curfew sounds the knell of parting day,
   The lowing cattle slowly cross the lea,
   The plowman goes wearily plodding his homeward way,
   Leaving the world to the darkening night and me.

   b. The curfew tolls the knell of parting day,
   The lowing herd wind slowly o'er the lea,
   The plowman homeward plods his weary way,
   And leaves the world to darkness and to me. —THOMAS GRAY

10. a. Let me chastise this odious, gilded bug,
    This painted son of dirt, that smells and bites.

    b. Yet let me flap this bug with gilded wings,
    This painted child of dirt, that stinks and stings. —ALEXANDER POPE

REVIEWING CHAPTER THIRTEEN

1. Review the terms in the chapter presented in boldface.

2. The chapter presents four important means by which sound reinforces meaning; in reviewing them, decide whether the meaning being reinforced is intellectual or emotional, or both.

3. In the following poems, identify any of the devices by which sound reinforces meaning, being sure to define the meaning that is being reinforced—and identifying any elements of poetry that are employed in creating that meaning.

Anthem for Doomed Youth

What passing-bells for these who die as cattle?
Only the monstrous anger of the guns.
Only the stuttering rifles' rapid rattle
Can patter out their hasty orisons.
No mockeries now for them; no prayers nor bells,   5
Nor any voice of mourning save the choirs—
The shrill, demented choirs of wailing shells;
And bugles calling for them from sad shires.

What candles may be held to speed them all?
Not in the hands of boys, but in their eyes   10
Shall shine the holy glimmers of good-byes.
The pallor of girls' brows shall be their pall;
Their flowers the tenderness of patient minds,
And each slow dusk a drawing-down of blinds.

—WILFRED OWEN (1893–1918)

QUESTIONS

1. Vocabulary: *passing-bells* (1), *orisons* (4), *shires* (8), *pall* (12). It was the custom during World War I to draw down the blinds in homes where a son had been lost (14).
2. How do lines 1–8 and 9–14 of this sonnet differ in (a) geographical setting, (b) subject matter, (c) kind of imagery used, and (d) tone? Who are the "boys" (10) and "girls" (12) referred to in the sestet?
3. What central metaphorical image runs throughout the poem? What secondary metaphors build up the central one?
4. Why are the "doomed youth" said to die "as cattle" (1)? Why would prayers, bells, and so on, be "mockeries" for them (5)?
5. Show how sound is adapted to sense throughout the poem.

Landcrab

A lie, that we come from water.
The truth is we were born
from stones, dragons, the sea's
teeth, as you testify,
with your crust and jagged scissors.   5

Hermit, hard socket
for a timid eye

you're a soft gut scuttling
sideways, a bone skull,
round bone on the prowl.   10
Wolf of treeroots and gravelly holes,
a mount on stilts,
the husk of a small demon.

Attack, voracious
eating, and flight: 15
it's a sound routine
for staying alive on edges.
Then there's the tide, and that dance
you do for the moon
on wet sand, claws raised   20
to fend off your mate,
your coupling a quick
dry clatter of rocks.
For mammals
with their lobes and bulbs,   25
scruples and warm milk,
you've nothing but contempt.

Here you are, a frozen scowl
targeted in flashlight,
then gone: a piece of what   30
we are, not all,
my stunted child, my momentary
face in the mirror,
my tiny nightmare.

—MARGARET ATWOOD (B. 1939)

QUESTIONS

1. What theory of the origin of human life is alluded to in line 1? Line 3 alludes to
   two Greek myths, of Deucalion strewing stones and Cadmus sowing dragon's
   teeth. If these are unfamiliar, look them up. What do theories about the origins
   of humankind have to do with the speaker's description of the landcrab? How
   do lines 30–34 return to that subject?
2. What do the free-verse rhythms contribute to the experience of the poem?
   Discuss the cacophony and euphony in lines 22–25. Where do you find other
   examples?

Night and the Creation of Geography

The screeching cries
of the killdeer in the night create
their own narrow channels through the blades
of broken grasses and sharp-edged
dunes lining the shore.   Likewise,   5
the nightjar's whistle cuts a passage,
like a stream, across the open desert.
Only the nightjar knows the stars
of that passage, just as the limpkin's
wail is a direction only the limpkin forges   10
through the marshlands.   The furrows
of the field cricket's triplet chirps and shrill
courtship trills transform the sorrels
and doveweeds in the ditch, fashioning
needle ways and grids of space by the run   15
of their own notes.   And the thin cough-bark
of the bobcat establishes another sparse and arid
stalk among the rocks and brushy land where
it roots and withers.   No one can fully explore
the corridor made through the dark by the coyote's   20
jagged shrieks and clacking yaps, those yelping
howls like sheer descending cliffs, a noise
jumbled like rock-filled gulches and gulleys.
None but the coyote.   On icy plains, the snowy
owl occupies the cavern of its own silence,   25
a cavern formed by its quest for sweet blood
of lemming or hare. Within the polished,
black-and-white crystals of the freezing
night air, the owl watches from the warm
hollow of its stillness.   30

—PATTIANN ROGERS (B. 1940)

QUESTIONS

1. Vocabulary: *killdeer* (2), *nightjar's* (6), *limpkin's* (9), *sorrels* (13), *lemming* (27).
2. Through many examples of birds and other animals that are said to create geography with their sounds, the poem fashions a myth. What figure of speech is chiefly used? What is the meaning of that myth? Which animal creates its world with silence?
3. Find examples of onomatopoeia and phonetic intensives. Does the poem tend to be cacaphonous or euphonious? What do these sound effects contribute to meaning?

The Sound of Night

And now the dark comes on, all full of chitter noise.
Birds huggermugger crowd the trees,
the air thick with their vesper cries,
and bats, snub seven-pointed kites,
skitter across the lake, swing out,   5
squeak, chirp, dip, and skim on skates
of air, and the fat frogs wake and prink
wide-lipped, noisy as ducks, drunk
on the boozy black, gloating chink-chunk.

And now on the narrow beach we defend ourselves from
    dark.   10
The cooking done, we build our firework
bright and hot and less for outlook
than for magic, and lie in our blankets
while night nickers around us. Crickets
chorus hallelujahs; paws, quiet   15
and quick as raindrops, play on the stones
expertly soft, run past and are gone;
fish pulse in the lake; the frogs hoarsen.

Now every voice of the hour—the known, the supposed, the
    strange,
the mindless, the witted, the never seen—   20
sing, thrum, impinge, and rearrange
endlessly; and debarred from sleep we wait
for the birds, importantly silent,
for the crease of first eye-licking light,
for the sun, lost long ago and sweet.   25
By the lake, locked black away and tight,
we lie, day creatures, overhearing night.

—MAXINE KUMIN (B. 1925)

QUESTIONS

1. Vocabulary: the poem contains a wealth of words that seem chosen for their sounds rather than their denotations—but, from *chitter* (1) through *thrum* (21), the "sound effect" words do in fact have meanings. Be sure to look up any whose precise meanings are not clear to you.
2. Describe the rhyme scheme of the poem, taking into account both approximate and exact rhymes.
3. The title identifies the general subject. In addition to presenting and imitating the sounds, what does the poem say about them—and about the speaker?

Aunt Jennifer's Tigers

Aunt Jennifer's tigers prance across a screen,
Bright topaz denizens of a world of green.
They do not fear the men beneath the tree;
They pace in sleek chivalric certainty.

Aunt Jennifer's fingers fluttering through her wool   5
Find even the ivory needle hard to pull.
The massive weight of Uncle's wedding band
Sits heavily upon Aunt Jennifer's hand.

When Aunt is dead, her terrified hands will lie
Still ringed with ordeals she was mastered by.   10
The tigers in the panel that she made
Will go on prancing, proud and unafraid.

—ADRIENNE RICH (1929–2012)

Blackberry Eating

I love to go out in late September
among fat, overripe, icy, black blackberries
to eat blackberries for breakfast,
the stalks very prickly, a penalty
they earn for knowing the black art   5
of blackberry-making; and as I stand among them
lifting the stalks to my mouth, the ripest berries
fall almost unbidden to my tongue,
as words sometimes do, certain peculiar words

like *strengths* or *squinched,*   10
many-lettered, one-syllabled lumps,
which I squeeze, squinch open, and splurge well
in the silent, startled, icy, black language
of blackberry-eating in late September.

—GALWAY KINNELL (B. 1927)

QUESTIONS

1. Vocabulary: *black art* (5), *squinched* (10).
2. What comparison does the poet find between "certain peculiar words" (9) and blackberries? How appropriate is it?
3. Is the poem free verse or metrical? How do various musical devices reinforce its meaning?

The Dance

In Breughel's great picture, The Kermess,
the dancers go round, they go round and
around, the squeal and the blare and the
tweedle of bagpipes, a bugle and fiddles
tipping their bellies (round as the thick-   5
sided glasses whose wash they impound)
their hips and their bellies off balance
to turn them. Kicking and rolling about
the Fair Grounds, swinging their butts, those
shanks must be sound to bear up under such   10
rollicking measures, prance as they dance
in Breughel's great picture, The Kermess.

—WILLIAM CARLOS WILLIAMS (1883–1963)

QUESTIONS

1. Peter Breughel the Elder was a sixteenth-century Flemish painter of peasant life. A *kermess* is an annual outdoor festival or fair. How would you characterize the mood of the people depicted in this poem?
2. Examine the poem for alliteration, consonance, assonance, and onomatopoeia. When you pronounce the syllable *ound* (lines 2, 3, 5, 6, 9, 10), how does the shape your mouth makes seem to intensify the effect?
3. Scan the poem. (Notice that the initial syllable in lines 2, 3, and 8 has the effect of completing the rhythm of the preceding line.) What one word in the poem echoes

the prevailing metrical foot, describes the rhythm of the poem, and defines the mood of the picture?

4. How does sound reinforce content in this poem? What is the attitude of the speaker to the activities shown in the picture?

SUGGESTIONS FOR WRITING

Write a short essay discussing the relationship of the poem's sound to its meaning in one of the following.

1. Dickinson, "I felt a Funeral, in my Brain" (page 737).
2. Atwood, "Landcrab" (page 910).
3. Hopkins, "Spring" (page 735).
4. Keats, "Ode on a Grecian Urn" (page 949).
5. Hardy, "The Ruined Maid" (page 1003).
6. Owen, "Dulce et Decorum Est" (page 684).
7. Stevens, "The Snow Man" (page 743).
8. Yeats, "Sailing to Byzantium" (page 961).

PRACTICE AP WRITING PROMPTS ▰▰▰▰▰

Emily Dickinson, "I heard a Fly buzz—when I died" (p. 906)

Emily Dickinson wrote more than 500 poems on the subject of death (out of more than 1,700 in all). "I heard a Fly buzz—when I died" imagines the actual moment of death being recalled. Read the poem carefully, and write a well-organized essay on the speaker's perceptions of death—as anticipated and as experienced. Show how such devices as onomatopoeia, repetition, and point of view contribute to the meaning of the poem.

CHAPTER FOURTEEN

Pattern

Art, ultimately, is organization. It is a searching after order and significance. Most artists seek to transform the chaotic nature of experience into a meaningful and coherent pattern, largely by means of selection and arrangement. For this reason we evaluate a poem partially by the same criteria that an English instructor uses to evaluate a student's essay—by its unity, its coherence, and its proper placing of emphasis. A well-constructed poem contains neither too little nor too much; every part of the poem belongs where it is and could be placed nowhere else; any interchanging of two stanzas, two lines, or even two words, would to some extent damage the poem and make it less effective. We come to feel, with a truly first-rate poem, that the choice and placement of every word are inevitable, that they could not be otherwise.

In addition to the internal ordering of the materials—the arrangement of ideas, images, thoughts, sentences, which we refer to as the poem's **structure**—the poet may impose some external pattern on a poem, may give it not only its internal order of materials but an external shape or **form**. Such formality appeals to the human instinct for design, the instinct that has prompted people, at various times, to tattoo and paint their bodies, to decorate their swords and armor with beautiful and complex tracery, and to choose patterned fabrics for their clothing, carpets, and curtains. The poet appeals to our love of the shapely.

In general, a poem may be cast in one of the three broad kinds of form: continuous form, stanzaic form, and fixed form. In **continuous form**, as illustrated by "The Widow's Lament in Springtime" (page 736), "After Apple-Picking" (page 740), "Ulysses" (page 787), and "My Last Duchess" (page 806), the element of design is slight. The lines follow each other without formal grouping, the only breaks being dictated by units of meaning, as paragraphs are in prose. But even here there are degrees of pattern. "The Widow's Lament in Springtime" has neither regular meter nor rhyme. "After Apple-Picking," on the other hand, is metrical; it has no regularity of length of line, but the meter is predominantly iambic; in addition, every line rhymes with another, though not according to any fixed pattern. "Ulysses" is regular in both meter and length of line: it is unrhymed iambic pentameter, or blank verse. And to these regularities "My Last Duchess" adds regularity of rhyme, for it is written in rhyming pentameter couplets. Thus, in increasing degrees, the authors of "After Apple-Picking," "Ulysses," and "My Last Duchess" have chosen a predetermined pattern in which to cast their work.

In **stanzaic form** the poet writes in a series of **stanzas**; that is, repeated units having the same number of lines, usually the same metrical pattern, and often the same **rhyme scheme**. The poet may choose some traditional stanza pattern or invent an original one. The traditional stanza patterns (for example, terza rima, ballad meter, rhyme royal, Spenserian stanza) are many, and the student specializing in literature will wish to become familiar with some of them; the general student should know that they exist. Often the use of one of these traditional stanza forms constitutes a kind of literary allusion. When we are aware of the traditional use of a stanza form, or of its previous use by a great poet for a particular subject or experience, we may find additional subtleties of meaning in its later use. Robert Frost employs the same verse form for his poem about a moral quest as Dante uses for his great poem about moral truth, *The Divine Comedy,* with meaningful results (see "Acquainted with the Night," page 931).

Stanzaic form, like continuous form, exhibits degrees of formal pattern. The poem "in Just—" (page 815) is divided into alternating stanzas of four lines and one line, but the four-line stanzas have no formal resemblance to each other except for the number of lines, and the one-line stanzas are similarly disparate. In "Winter" (page 683) and "Blow, blow, thou winter wind" (page 864) Shakespeare employs a refrain in addition to the patterns of meter and rhyme. The following poem illustrates additional elements of design.

The Pulley

When God at first made man,
Having a glass of blessings standing by,
"Let us," said he, "pour on him all we can:
Let the world's riches, which dispersèd lie,
    Contract into a span."   5

So Strength first made a way;
Then Beauty flowed; then Wisdom, Honor, Pleasure.
When almost all was out, God made a stay,
Perceiving that alone of all his treasure
Rest in the bottom lay. 10

"For if I should," said he,
"Bestow this jewel also on my creature,
He would adore my gifts instead of me,
And rest in Nature, not the God of Nature;
So both should losers be. 15

"Yet let him keep the rest,
But keep them with repining restlessness:
Let him be rich and weary, that at least,
If goodness lead him not, yet weariness
May toss him to my breast." 20

—GEORGE HERBERT (1593–1633)

QUESTIONS

1. Vocabulary: *span* (5, archaic meaning).
2. The words "riches" (4), "treasure" (9), "jewel" (12), and "gifts" (13) create an extended metaphor. What is being compared to things of material value? Does the word "rich" in line 18 refer to the same thing as "riches" in line 4?
3. The title "The Pulley" refers to a simple mechanical device for lifting weights. How does a pulley work? How does it metaphorically express the meaning of the last stanza?
4. To what does "both" (15) refer? What are God's final intentions?

A stanza form may be described by designating four things: the rhyme scheme (if there is one), the position of the refrain (if there is one), the prevailing metrical foot, and the number of feet in each line. Rhyme scheme is traditionally designated by using letters of the alphabet to indicate the rhyming lines, and *x* for unrhymed lines. Refrain lines may be indicated by a capital letter, and the number of feet in the line by a numerical exponent after the letter. Thus, the stanza pattern of Browning's "Meeting at Night" (page 733) is iambic tetrameter *abccba* (or iambic *abccba⁴*); that of "The Pulley" is iambic $a^3bab^5a^3$.

A **fixed form** is a traditional pattern that applies to a whole poem. In French poetry many fixed forms have been widely used: rondeaus, rondels, villanelles, triolets, sestinas, ballades, double ballades, and others. In English poetry, though most of the fixed forms have been experimented with, perhaps only two—the sonnet and the villanelle—have really taken hold.

Although it is classified as a fixed form, through centuries of practice the **sonnet** has attained a degree of flexibility. It must be fourteen lines in length, and it almost always is iambic pentameter, but in structure and rhyme scheme there may be considerable leeway. Most sonnets, however, conform more or less closely to one of two general models or types: the Italian and the English.

The **Italian** or *Petrarchan* **sonnet** (so-called because the Italian poet Petrarch practiced it so extensively) is divided usually between eight lines called the **octave,** using two rhymes arranged *abbaabba,* and six lines called the **sestet,** using any arrangement of either two or three rhymes: *cdcdcd* and *cdecde* are common patterns. The division between octave and sestet in the Italian sonnet (indicated by the rhyme scheme and sometimes marked off in printing by a space) usually corresponds to a division of thought. The octave may, for instance, present a situation and the sestet a comment, or the octave an idea and the sestet an example, or the octave a question and the sestet an answer. Thus, the form reflects the structure.

On First Looking into Chapman's Homer

Much have I traveled in the realms of gold,
    And many goodly states and kingdoms seen;
    Round many western islands have I been
Which bards in fealty to Apollo hold.
Oft of one wide expanse had I been told   5
    That deep-browed Homer ruled as his demesne;
    Yet did I never breathe its pure serene
Till I heard Chapman speak out loud and bold:
Then felt I like some watcher of the skies
    When a new planet swims into his ken;   10
Or like stout Cortez when with eagle eyes
    He stared at the Pacific—and all his men
Looked at each other with a wild surmise—
    Silent, upon a peak in Darien.

—JOHN KEATS (1795–1821)

QUESTIONS

1. Vocabulary: *fealty* (4), *Apollo* (4), *demesne* (6), *ken* (10). *Darien* (14) is an ancient name for the Isthmus of Panama.
2. John Keats, at twenty-one, could not read Greek and was probably acquainted with Homer's *Iliad* and *Odyssey* only through the translations of Alexander Pope, which to him very likely seemed prosy and stilted. Then one day he and a friend found a vigorous poetic translation by the Elizabethan poet George Chapman.

Keats and his friend, enthralled, sat up late at night excitedly reading aloud to each other from Chapman's book. Toward morning Keats walked home and, before going to bed, wrote the above sonnet and sent it to his friend. What common ideas underlie the three major figures of speech in the poem?

3. What is the rhyme scheme? What division of thought corresponds to the division between octave and sestet?

4. Balboa, not Cortez, discovered the Pacific. How seriously does this mistake detract from the value of the poem?

The **English** or *Shakespearean* **sonnet** (invented by the English poet Surrey and made famous by Shakespeare) consists of three **quatrains** and a concluding **couplet**, rhyming *abab cdcd efef gg*. Again, the units marked off by the rhymes and the development of the thought often correspond. The three quatrains, for instance, may present three examples and the couplet a conclusion, or (as in the following example) the quatrains three metaphorical statements of one idea and the couplet an application.

That time of year

That time of year thou mayst in me behold
When yellow leaves, or none, or few, do hang
Upon those boughs which shake against the cold,
Bare ruined choirs where late the sweet birds sang.
In me thou see'st the twilight of such day   5
As after sunset fadeth in the west,
Which by and by black night doth take away,
Death's second self, that seals up all in rest.
In me thou see'st the glowing of such fire,
That on the ashes of his youth doth lie   10
As the deathbed whereon it must expire,
Consumed with that which it was nourished by.
This thou perceivest, which makes thy love more strong,
To love that well which thou must leave ere long.

—WILLIAM SHAKESPEARE (1564–1616)

QUESTIONS

1. What are the three major images introduced by the three quatrains? What do they have in common? Can you see any reason for presenting them in this particular order, or might they be rearranged without loss?

2. Each of the images is to some degree complicated rather than simple. For instance, what additional image is introduced by "Bare ruined choirs" (4)? Explain its appropriateness.

3. What additional comparisons are introduced in the second and third quatrains? Explain line 12.
4. Whom does the speaker address? What assertion does he make in the concluding couplet, and with what degree of confidence? Paraphrase these lines so as to state their meaning as clearly as possible.

The tradition of the sonnet has proved useful because it seems effective or appropriate for certain types of subject matter and treatment. By its history as the vehicle for love poetry in the sixteenth century, the sonnet is particularly effective when used for the serious treatment of love. But it has also been used for the discussion of death, religion, political situations, and various other serious subjects. There is, of course, no magical or mysterious identity between certain forms and certain types of content, but there may be more or less correspondence. A form may seem appropriate or inappropriate. Excellent sonnets have been written outside the traditional areas.

The **villanelle**, with its complex pattern of repetition and rhyme, has become a significant form in English only in the past hundred years or so, but of the fixed forms it probably now ranks second to the sonnet. The form requires only two rhyme sounds, and its nineteen lines are divided into five 3-line stanzas (**tercets**) and a four-line concluding quatrain. The first and third lines of the first stanza serve as refrain lines entwined with the rhyme pattern—the first line repeated at the ends of the second and fourth stanzas, and the third repeated at the ends of the third and fifth stanzas. In the concluding stanza, the refrains are repeated as lines 18 and 19. We can express the pattern thus: $A^1bA^2 \ abA^1 \ abA^2 \ abA^1 \ abA^2 \ abA^1A^2$ (in this case, the numerical exponent identifies which of the refrain lines is being used).

Poets have been attracted to villanelles partly because they are notoriously difficult to compose effectively, thus posing a challenge to a poet's technical skill, and partly because the varying emphases given to repeated lines, along with the repetition itself, can achieve haunting, unforgettable effects. The original French models were usually lighthearted and witty, exploiting the potential for cleverness and humor inherent in the form, but modern poets often have employed the villanelle for serious subject matter. The following example, composed when the poet's father was near death, is perhaps the most famous villanelle in English.

Do Not Go Gentle into That Good Night

Do not go gentle into that good night,
Old age should burn and rave at close of day;
Rage, rage against the dying of the light.

Though wise men at their end know dark is right,
Because their words had forked no lightning they   5
Do not go gentle into that good night.

Good men, the last wave by, crying how bright
Their frail deeds might have danced in a green bay,
Rage, rage against the dying of the light.

Wild men who caught and sang the sun in flight,   10
And learn, too late, they grieved it on its way,
Do not go gentle into that good night.

Grave men, near death, who see with blinding sight
Blind eyes could blaze like meteors and be gay,
Rage, rage against the dying of the light.   15

And you, my father, there on the sad height,
Curse, bless, me now with your fierce tears, I pray.
Do not go gentle into that good night.
Rage, rage against the dying of the light.

—DYLAN THOMAS (1914–1953)

QUESTIONS

1. Discuss the various meanings in this poem of the common phrase "good night."
2. Apart from the fixed form, the poem creates another structural principle in stanzas two through six by describing in turn "wise men" (4), "Good men" (7), "Wild men" (10), and "Grave men" (13). How does the speaker view these various types of men in their differing stances toward both life and death?
3. There are several paradoxical expressions in the poem: "dark is right" (4), "blinding sight" (13), "the sad height" (16), and "Curse, bless, me now" (17). How do these contribute to the poem's meaning?

A good villanelle avoids the potentially monotonous effects of repetition by varying the stress patterns and the meaning of the repeated lines. In Thomas's poem, for example, the third line is a direct address by the speaker to his father, while the repetition in line 9 describes the rage "Good men" feel just before their deaths. Similarly, the poem deftly alternates lines containing grammatical pauses, such as line 7, with lines having no pauses, such as line 8; the blend of run-on and end-stopped lines likewise helps to vary the rhythm. The fixed form also serves the poem's meaning, since the repetition and circular quality of the villanelle, its continued reiteration of the same two lines, emphasizes the speaker's emotional treadmill, his desperate and perhaps hopeless prayer that his father might rage against death. As in all good poetry, a fixed form like the villanelle does not merely display the poet's technical ability but appropriately supports the tone and meaning of the poem.

Initially, it may seem absurd that poets should choose to confine themselves in an arbitrary formal mold with prescribed meter and rhyme scheme. They do so partly from the desire to carry on a tradition, as all of us carry out certain traditions for their own sake, else why should we bring a tree indoors at Christmas time? Traditional forms are also useful because they have provided a challenge to the poet, and good poets are inspired by the challenge: it will call forth ideas and images that might not otherwise have come. They will subdue the form rather than be subdued by it; they will make it do what they require. There is no doubt that the presence of a net makes good tennis players more precise in their shots than they otherwise might be. And finally, for the poet and for the reader, there is the pleasure of form itself.

EXERCISES

The typographical shape of a poem on the page (whether, for example, printed with a straight left-hand margin or with a system of indentations) is determined sometimes by the poet, sometimes by the printer, sometimes by an editor. Examine each of the following poems and try to deduce what *principle* (if any) determined its typographical design:

1. Shakespeare, "Winter" (page 683).
2. Marvell, "To His Coy Mistress" (page 761).
3. Hughes, "Harlem" (page 748).
4. Plath, "Lady Lazarus" (page 781).
5. cummings, "in Just—" (page 815).
6. Wilbur, "The Writer" (page 778).
7. Yeats, "Leda and the Swan" (page 821).
8. Donne, "The Flea" (page 848).
9. Ferlinghetti, "Constantly risking absurdity" (page 692).
10. Blake, "The Lamb" (page 835).

REVIEWING CHAPTER FOURTEEN

1. Distinguish between structure and form, and review the definitions of the three broad types of form in poetry; using examples from the following poems in the chapter, define both the form and the structure of the poem.
2. Examine the definitions of the two types of sonnet, and explore the way in which the form of each seems to promote the structure of materials in the poem.

3. The villanelle also suggests the structure of the poem's materials; using examples from the following poems, define that implied structure.

4. Poetic forms may rely on the reader's familiarity with the subjects customarily presented in such forms—and poets may employ a form either to fulfill a reader's expectations or ironically to play against them. Find examples of both uses of the forms of the sonnet and the villanelle.

One Art

The art of losing isn't hard to master;
so many things seem filled with the intent
to be lost that their loss is no disaster.

Lose something every day. Accept the fluster
of lost door keys, the hour badly spent.   5
The art of losing isn't hard to master.

Then practice losing farther, losing faster:
places, and names, and where it was you meant
to travel. None of these will bring disaster.

I lost my mother's watch. And look! my last, or   10
next-to-last, of three loved houses went.
The art of losing isn't hard to master.

I lost two cities, lovely ones. And, vaster,
some realms I owned, two rivers, a continent.
I miss them, but it wasn't a disaster.   15

—Even losing you (the joking voice, a gesture
I love) I shan't have lied. It's evident
the art of losing's not too hard to master
though it may look like (*Write* it!) like disaster.

—ELIZABETH BISHOP (1911–1979)

QUESTIONS

1. What various denotations of "lose" and its derivative forms are relevant to the context? What connotations are attached to the separate denotative meanings?

2. Explain how "owned" (14) and "lost" (13) shift the meanings of possessing and losing.
3. What seems to be the purpose of the speaker in the first three tercets (three-line units)? How is the advice given there supported by the personal experiences related in the next two tercets?
4. The concluding quatrain (four-line unit) contains direct address to a person, as well as a command the speaker addresses to herself. How do these details reveal the real purpose of the poem? *Can* all kinds of losses be mastered with one "art of losing"?

Mad Girl's Love Song

I shut my eyes and all the world drops dead;
I lift my lids and all is born again.
(I think I made you up inside my head.)

The stars go waltzing out in blue and red,
And arbitrary blackness gallops in: 5
I shut my eyes and all the world drops dead.

I dreamed that you bewitched me into bed
And sung me moon-struck, kissed me quite insane.
(I think I made you up inside my head.)

God topples from the sky, hell's fires fade: 10
Exit seraphim and Satan's men:
I shut my eyes and all the world drops dead.

I fancied you'd return the way you said,
But I grow old and I forget your name.
(I think I made you up inside my head.)   15

I should have loved a thunderbird instead;
At least when spring comes they roar back again.
I shut my eyes and all the world drops dead.
(I think I made you up inside my head.)

—SYLVIA PLATH (1932–1963)

QUESTIONS

1. Discuss the relationship of form to content in the poem. Why is it appropriate than this particular poem is written in the villanelle form?

2. The spaker calls herself "Mad" (title) and "insane" (8). Compare the use of these terms with that in Dickinson's "Much Madness is divinest Sense" (page 792). What different forms of "madness" are being discussed?
3. Discuss the rhythmic effects of the poem. How do they reinforce the meaning?

From *Romeo and Juliet*

ROMEO	If I profane with my unworthiest hand
	This holy shrine, the gentle sin is this:
	My lips, two blushing pilgrims, ready stand
	To smooth that rough touch with a tender kiss.
JULIET	Good pilgrim, you do wrong your hand too much,
	Which mannerly devotion shows in this;
	For saints have hands that pilgrims' hands do touch,
	And palm to palm is holy palmers' kiss.
ROMEO	Have not saints lips, and holy palmers too?
JULIET	Ay, pilgrim, lips that they must use in prayer.
ROMEO	O! then, dear saint, let lips do what hands do;
	They pray, "Grant thou, lest faith turn to despair."
JULIET	Saints do not move,° though grant for prayer's sake.
ROMEO	Then move not, while my prayer's effect I take.

5

10

propose, instigate

—WILLIAM SHAKESPEARE (1564–1616)

QUESTIONS

1. These fourteen lines occur in Act 1, scene 5, of Shakespeare's play. They are the first words exchanged between Romeo and Juliet, who are meeting, for the first time, at a masquerade ball given by her father. Struck by Juliet's beauty, Romeo has come up to greet her. What stage action accompanies this passage?
2. What is the basic metaphor created by such religious terms as "profane" (1), "shrine" (2), "pilgrims" (3), and "holy palmers" (8)? How does this metaphor affect the tone of the relationship between Romeo and Juliet?
3. What play on words do you find in lines 8 and 13–14? What two meanings has line 11?
4. By meter and rhyme scheme, these lines form a sonnet. Do you think this was coincidental or intentional on Shakespeare's part? Discuss.

Death, be not proud

Death, be not proud, though some have callèd thee
Mighty and dreadful, for thou art not so;
For those whom thou think'st thou dost overthrow

Die not, poor death, nor yet canst thou kill me.
From rest and sleep, which but thy pictures be,   5
Much pleasure—then, from thee much more must flow;
And soonest° our best men with thee do go,   readiest
Rest of their bones and soul's delivery.
Thou art slave to fate, chance, kings, and desperate men,
And dost with poison, war, and sickness dwell;   10
And poppy or charms can make us sleep as well,
And better than thy stroke. Why swell'st thou then?
One short sleep passed, we wake eternally,
And death shall be no more; death, thou shalt die.

—JOHN DONNE (1572–1631)

QUESTIONS

1. What two figures of speech dominate the poem?
2. Why should death not be proud? List the speaker's major reasons. Are they consistent? Logical? Persuasive?
3. Discuss the tone of the poem. Is the speaker (a) a man of assured faith with a firm conviction that death is not to be feared or (b) a man desperately trying to convince himself that there is nothing to fear in death?
4. In form, this sonnet blends the English and Italian models. Explain. Is its organization of thought closer to the Italian or the English sonnet?

The Folly of Being Comforted

One that is ever kind said yesterday:
'Your well-belovèd's hair has threads of grey,
And little shadows come about her eyes;
Time can but make it easier to be wise
Though now it seem impossible, and so   5
All that you need is patience.'
                                        Heart cries, 'No,
I have not a crumb of comfort, not a grain.
Time can but make her beauty over again:
Because of that great nobleness of hers
The fire that stirs about her, when she stirs,   10
Burns but more clearly. O she had not these ways
When all the wild summer was in her gaze.'

O heart! O heart! if she'd but turn her head,
You'd know the folly of being comforted.

—WILLIAM BUTLER YEATS (1865–1939)

QUESTIONS

1. How can the friend's pointing out that the woman shows signs of aging be considered an attempt to "comfort" the speaker? What does that imply about the relationship between the speaker and his "well-belovèd" (2)?
2. The personification of "Heart" (6, 13) is contrasted to the friend's attempt to make the speaker "wise." Explain what the outburst from "Heart" means, and how it is an answer to the friend's reasonable advice.
3. The poem is 14 lines of iambic pentameter. Is it a sonnet?

The White City

I will not toy with it nor bend an inch.
Deep in the secret chambers of my heart
I muse my life-long hate, and without flinch
I bear it nobly as I live my part.
My being would be a skeleton, a shell,   5
If this dark Passion that fills my every mood,
And makes my heaven in the white world's hell,
Did not forever feed me vital blood.
I see the mighty city through a mist—
The strident trains that speed the goaded mass,   10
The poles and spires and towers vapor-kissed,
The fortressed port through which the great ships pass,
The tides, the wharves, the dens I contemplate,
Are sweet like wanton loves because I hate.

—CLAUDE MCKAY (1890–1948)

QUESTIONS

1. Claude McKay was a native black Jamaican who as an adult lived in New York. Why does the speaker "hate" (3) the city?
2. Traditionally, sonnets originated as love poems. Why might McKay have cast this poem in sonnet form?
3. How does the city feed the speaker with "vital blood" (8)?
4. Why are the elements of the New York landscape described in the last line as "sweet like wanton loves" (14)?

My Great-Grandmother's Bible

Faux-leather bound and thick as an onion, it flakes—
an heirloom from Iowa my dead often read.
I open the black flap to speak the "spake"s

and quickly lose track of who wed, who bred.
She taped our family register as it tore,   5
her hand stuttering like a sewing machine,
darning the blanks with farmers gone before—
Inez, Alvah, Delbert, Ermadean.
Our undistinguished line she pressed in the heft
between the Testaments, with spaces to spare,   10
smudged with mistakes or tears; her fingers left
a mounting watchfulness I find hard to bear.
When I saw the AIDS quilt, spread out in acres,
it was stitched with similar scripts by similar makers.

—Spencer Reece (b. 1963)

QUESTIONS

1. What similarities does the speaker find between his great-grandmother's bible and the AIDS quilt?
2. Why is it appropriate that this is a poem written in a pattern—i.e., as a sonnet?
3. After twelve lines describing the bible, the poem makes a surprising shift. Is the shift effective? Why or why not? Does it still allow the poem to remain unified in theme and tone?

We Wear the Mask

We wear the mask that grins and lies,
It hides our cheeks and shades our eyes,—
This debt we pay to human guile;
With torn and bleeding hearts we smile,
And mouth with myriad subtleties.   5
Why should the world be over-wise,
In counting all our tears and sighs?
Nay, let them only see us, while
      We wear the mask.

We smile, but, O great Christ, our cries   10
To thee from tortured souls arise.
We sing, but oh the clay is vile
Beneath our feet, and long the mile;
But let the world dream otherwise,
      We wear the mask!   15

—Paul Laurence Dunbar (1872–1906)

QUESTIONS

1. The poet was African American. What racial theme is implied in the poem? What kind of "mask" is the speaker describing?
2. How would you define the tone of this poem? Is the speaker angry? Who are the "tortured souls" (11)?
3. How do the departures from the strict sonnet form contribute to the effect of the poem?

Acquainted with the Night

I have been one acquainted with the night.
I have walked out in rain—and back in rain.
I have outwalked the furthest city light.

I have looked down the saddest city lane.
I have passed by the watchman on his beat   5
And dropped my eyes, unwilling to explain.

I have stood still and stopped the sound of feet
When far away an interrupted cry
Came over houses from another street,

But not to call me back or say good-by;   10
And further still at an unearthly height,
One luminary clock against the sky

Proclaimed the time was neither wrong nor right.
I have been one acquainted with the night.

—ROBERT FROST (1874–1963)

QUESTIONS

1. How does the speaker reveal the strength of his purpose in his night-walking? Can you specify what that purpose is? What symbolic meanings does the night hold?
2. How is the poem structured into sentences? What is the effect of repeating the phrase "I have"? of repeating line 1 at the conclusion? How do these repetitions affect the tone of the poem?
3. Some critics have interpreted the "luminary clock" (12) literally—as the illuminated dial of a tower clock; others have interpreted it figuratively as the full moon. Of what, in either case, is it a symbol? Does the clock tell accurate chronometric time? What kind of "time" is it proclaiming in line 13? Is knowing *that* kind of time the speaker's quest?
4. The poem contains 14 lines—like a sonnet. But its rhyme scheme is **terza rima**, an interlocking scheme with the pattern *aba bcb cdc*, etc., a formal arrangement

that implies continual progression. How does Frost bring the progression to an end? Terza rima was the form memorably employed by Dante for his *Divine Comedy*, of which the *Inferno* is the best-known section. In what ways does Frost's poem allude to the subject and framework of that poem?

Villanelle for an Anniversary

A spirit moved, John Harvard walked the yard,
The atom lay unsplit, the west unwon,
The books stood open and the gates unbarred.

The maps dreamt on like moondust. Nothing stirred.
The future was a verb in hibernation.   5
A spirit moved, John Harvard walked the yard.

Before the classic style, before the clapboard,
All through the small hours on an origin,
The books stood open and the gates unbarred.

Night passage of a migratory bird.   10
Wingflap. Gownflap. Like a homing pigeon
A spirit moved, John Harvard walked the yard.

Was that his soul (look) sped to its reward
By grace or works? A shooting star? An omen?
The books stood open and the gates unbarred.   15

Begin again where frosts and tests were hard.
Find yourself or founder. Here, imagine
A spirit moved, John Harvard walked the yard,
The books stand open and the gates unbarred.

—SEAMUS HEANEY (1939–2013)

QUESTIONS

1. John Harvard (1607–1638), an English clergyman who arrived in Massachusetts in 1637, bequeathed his library and a sum of money to the new college at Cambridge, which was then named in his honor.
2. How do the refrain lines of this villanelle help to reinforce its meaning?
3. How do you interpret line 3, "The book stood open and the gates unbarred"? In line 14, what is the meaning of the phrase "grace or works"? How is this an important distinction?
4. What is the impact of the final stanza? What additional meanings have the refrain lines gathered by the end of the poem?

Delight in Disorder

A sweet disorder in the dress
Kindles in clothes a wantonness.
A lawn° about the shoulders thrown   linen scarf
Into a fine distraction;
An erring lace, which here and there   5
Enthralls the crimson stomacher;
A cuff neglected, and thereby
Ribbons to flow confusedly;
A winning wave, deserving note,
In the tempestuous petticoat;   10
A careless shoestring, in whose tie
I see a wild civility;
Do more bewitch me than when art
Is too precise in every part.

—ROBERT HERRICK (1591–1674)

QUESTIONS

1. Vocabulary: *wantonness* (2), *stomacher* (6).
2. The phrase "wild civility" (12) is another example of oxymoron. Discuss the effectiveness of this device in this phrase and examine the poem for other examples.
3. Consider the relationship of form to structure in this poem. How does this contribute to the meaning?

Still to be neat

Still° to be neat, still to be dressed,   always
As you were going to a feast;
Still to be powdered, still perfumed;
Lady, it is to be presumed,
Though art's hid causes are not found,   5
All is not sweet, all is not sound.
Give me a look, give me a face
That makes simplicity a grace;
Robes loosely flowing, hair as free;
Such sweet neglect more taketh me   10
Then all th' adulteries of art.
They strike mine eyes, but not my heart.

—BEN JONSON (1572–1637)

QUESTIONS

1. Does the speaker admire the woman he is addressing in this poem? What lines provide clues to his attitude?
2. What contrast is defined by the separation of the poem into two stanzas? What does the speaker prefer to the "adulteries of art"?
3. How does the oxymoron "sweet neglect" (10) help to elucidate the poem's theme?
4. What are the similarities and differences in theme between this poem and Herrick's "Delight in Disorder"? How are they structured differently?

SUGGESTIONS FOR WRITING

Following are two lists: one of sonnets and the other of villanelles. Using one or two examples of either form, explore the effectiveness of the relationship of structure to form. In particular, be alert for variations or departures from the form and what these contribute to meaning and emotional effect.

Sonnets
Wordsworth, "The world is too much with us" (page 727).
Shelley, "Ozymandias" (page 799).
Donne, "Batter my heart, three-personed God" (page 802).
Yeats, "Leda and the Swan" (page 821).
Frost, "Design" (page 829).
Drayton, "Since there's no help" (page 842).
Shakespeare, "My mistress' eyes" (page 845).
Owen, "Anthem for Doomed Youth" (page 910).

Villanelles
Bishop, "One Art" (page 925).
Roethke, "The Waking" (page 860).
Plath, "Mad Girl's Love Song" (page 926).

PRACTICE AP WRITING PROMPTS ▆▆▆▆▆▆

Paul Laurence Dunbar, "We Wear the Mask" (p. 930)

African American poet Paul Laurence Dunbar was the son of slaves. Read Dunbar's "We Wear the mask" carefully. Then write an essay in which you show how the speaker's language effectively demonstrates the contradiction between the façade he presents to the world and the emotions he truly feels.

CHAPTER FIFTEEN

Evaluating Poetry 1

Sentimental, Rhetorical, Didactic Verse

The attempt to evaluate a poem should never be made before the poem is understood; and, unless one has developed the capacity to experience poetry intellectually and emotionally, any judgments one makes will be of little worth. A person who likes no wines can hardly be a judge of them. But the ability to make judgments, to discriminate between good and bad, great and good, good and half-good, is surely a primary object of all liberal education, and one's appreciation of poetry is incomplete unless it includes discrimination.

In judging a poem, as in judging any work of art, we need to ask three basic questions: (1) *What is its central purpose?* (2) *How fully has this purpose been accomplished?* (3) *How important is this purpose?* We need to answer the first question in order to understand the poem. Questions 2 and 3 are those by which we evaluate it. Question 2 judges the poem on a scale of perfection. Question 3 judges it on a scale of significance.

For answering the first of our evaluative questions, *How fully has the poem's purpose been accomplished?*, there are no easy yardsticks that we can apply. We cannot ask: Is the poem melodious? Does it have smooth rhythm? Does it use good grammar? Does it contain figures of speech? Are the rhymes perfect? Excellent poems exist without any of these attributes. We can judge any element in a poem only as it contributes or fails to contribute to the achievement of the central purpose; and we can judge the total poem only as these elements work together to form an integrated whole. But we can at least attempt a few generalizations. A wholly successful poem contains no excess words, no words that do not bear their full weight in contributing to the total experience, and no words that are used just to fill out the meter. Each word is the best word for expressing the total meaning: there are no inexact words forced by the rhyme scheme or the metrical pattern. The word order is the best order for expressing the author's total meaning; distortions or departures from normal order are for emphasis or some other meaningful purpose. The diction, the images, and the figures of speech are fresh, not trite (except, of course, when the poet uses trite language deliberately for purposes of irony). The sound of the poem does not clash with its sense, or the form with its content; and in general both sound and pattern are used to support meaning. The organization of the poem is the best possible organization: images and ideas are so effectively arranged that any rearrangement would be harmful to the poem. Always remember, however, that a good poem may have flaws. We should never damn a poem for its flaws if these flaws are amply compensated for by positive excellence.

What constitutes excellence in poetry? One criterion is that its combination of thought, emotion, language, and sound must be fresh and original. As the poet and critic Ezra Pound insisted, good writing must "make it new." An excellent poem will neither be merely imitative of previous literature nor appeal to stock, preestablished ways of thinking and feeling. The following discussion highlights three particular ways in which a poem can fail to achieve excellence: if a poem is sentimental, excessively rhetorical, or purely didactic, in fact, we would probably call it "verse" rather than true poetry.

Sentimentality is indulgence in emotion for its own sake, or expression of more emotion than an occasion warrants. Sentimentalists are gushy, stirred to tears by trivial or inappropriate causes; they weep at all weddings and all funerals; they are made ecstatic by manifestations of young love; they clip locks of hair, gild baby shoes, and talk baby talk. Sentimental *literature* is "tear-jerking" literature. It aims primarily at stimulating the emotions directly rather than at communicating experience truly and freshly; it depends on trite and well-tried formulas for exciting emotion; it revels in old oaken buckets, rocking chairs, mother love, and the pitter-patter of little feet; it oversimplifies; it is unfaithful to the full complexity of human experience.

Rhetorical poetry uses a language more glittering and high-flown than its substance warrants. It offers a spurious vehemence of language— language without a corresponding reality of emotion or thought underneath. It is oratorical, overelegant, artificially eloquent. It is superficial and, again, often basically trite. It loves rolling phrases like "from the rocky coast of Maine to the sun-washed shores of California" and "our heroic dead" and "Old Glory." It deals in generalities. At its worst it is bombast. In this book an example is offered by the two lines quoted from the play within a play in the fifth act of Shakespeare's *A Midsummer Night's Dream:*

> Whereat with blade, with bloody, blameful blade,
> He bravely broached his boiling bloody breast.

Another example may be found in the player's recitation in *Hamlet* (in Act 2, scene 2):

> Out, out, thou strumpet Fortune! All you gods,
> In general synod take away her power,
> Break all the spokes and fellies from her wheel,
> And bowl the round nave down the hill of heaven
> As low as to the fiends!

Didactic poetry has as a primary purpose to teach or preach. It is probable that all the very greatest poetry teaches in subtle ways, without being expressly didactic; and much expressly didactic poetry ranks high in poetic excellence: that is, it accomplishes its teaching without ceasing to be poetry. But when the didactic purpose supersedes the poetic purpose, when the poem communicates information or moral instruction only, then it ceases to be didactic poetry and becomes didactic verse. Such verse appeals to people who read poetry primarily for noble thoughts or inspiring lessons and like them prettily expressed. It is recognizable often by its lack of any specific situation, the flatness of its diction, the poverty of its imagery and figurative language, its emphasis on moral platitudes, its lack of poetic freshness. It is either very trite or has little to distinguish it from informational prose except rhyme or meter. Donne's "Hymn to God My God, in My Sickness (page 786) is an example of didactic *poetry*. The familiar couplet

> Early to bed and early to rise,
> Makes a man healthy, wealthy, and wise

is aptly characterized as didactic *verse*.

Undoubtedly, so far in this chapter, we have spoken too categorically, have made our distinctions too sharp and definite. All poetic excellence is a matter of degree. There are no absolute lines between sentimentality and true emotion, artificial and genuine eloquence, didactic verse and didactic poetry. Though the difference between extreme examples is easy to recognize, subtler discriminations are harder to make.

A final caution to students: when making judgments on literature, always be honest. Do not pretend to like what you do not like. Do not be afraid to admit a liking for what you do like. A genuine enthusiasm for the second-rate is much better than false enthusiasm or no enthusiasm at all. Be neither hasty nor timorous in making your judgments. When you have attentively read a poem and thoroughly considered it, decide what you think. Do not hedge, equivocate, or try to find out others' opinions before forming your own. But, having formed an opinion and expressed it, do not allow it to harden into a narrow-minded bias. Compare your opinion *then* with the opinions of others; allow yourself to change it when convinced of its error: in this way you learn.

In the pairs of poems for comparison that follow in this chapter, the distinction to be made is not always between bad and good; it may be between varying degrees of poetic merit.

REVIEWING CHAPTER FIFTEEN

1. Review the three basic questions to be answered in evaluating a poem.
2. Explore the three weaknesses that may lead us to judge a poem less than excellent, finding examples of each in the poems that follow in this chapter.

God's Will for You and Me

Just to be tender, just to be true,
Just to be glad the whole day through,
Just to be merciful, just to be mild,
Just to be trustful as a child,
Just to be gentle and kind and sweet,   5
Just to be helpful with willing feet,
Just to be cheery when things go wrong,
Just to drive sadness away with a song,
Whether the hour is dark or bright,
Just to be loyal to God and right,   10
Just to believe that God knows best,
Just in his promises ever to rest—

Just to let love be our daily key,
That is God's will for you and me.

Pied Beauty

Glory be to God for dappled things—
    For skies of couple-color as a brinded cow;
      For rose-moles all in stipple upon trout that swim;
Fresh-firecoal chestnut-falls; finches' wings;
    Landscape plotted and pieced—fold, fallow and plow;   5
      And all trades, their gear and tackle and trim.
All things counter, original, spare, strange;
    Whatever is fickle, freckled (who knows how?)
      With swift, slow; sweet, sour; adazzle, dim;
He fathers-forth whose beauty is past change: 10
      Praise him.

QUESTION

Which is the superior poem? Explain in full.

A Poison Tree

I was angry with my friend:
I told my wrath, my wrath did end.
I was angry with my foe:
I told it not, my wrath did grow.

And I watered it in fears,   5
Night and morning with my tears;
And I sunnèd it with smiles,
And with soft deceitful wiles.

And it grew both day and night
Till it bore an apple bright;   10
And my foe beheld it shine,
And he knew that it was mine,

And into my garden stole
When the night had veiled the pole:°   sky
In the morning glad I see   15
My foe outstretched beneath the tree.

The Most Vital Thing in Life

When you feel like saying something
    That you know you will regret,
Or keenly feel an insult
    Not quite easy to forget,
That's the time to curb resentment   5
    And maintain a mental peace,
For when your mind is tranquil
    All your ill-thoughts simply cease.

It is easy to be angry
    When defrauded or defied,   10
To be peeved and disappointed
    If your wishes are denied;
But to win a worthwhile battle
    Over selfishness and spite,
You must learn to keep strict silence   15
    Though you know you're in the right.

So keep your mental balance
    When confronted by a foe,
Be it enemy in ambush
    Or some danger that you know.   20
If you are poised and tranquil
    When all around is strife,
Be assured that you have mastered
    The most vital thing in life.

QUESTION

Which poem has more poetic merit? Explain.

Lower New York: At Dawn

Here is the dawn a hopeless thing to see:
    Sordid and pale as is the face of one
    Who sinks exhausted in oblivion
    After a night of deep debauchery.
Here, as the light reveals relentlessly   5
    All that the soul has lost and greed has won,
    Scarce we believe that somewhere now the sun

Dawns overseas in stainless majesty.
Yet the day comes!—ghastly and harsh and thin
    Down the cold street; and now, from far away,   10
    We hear a vast and sullen rumor run,
As of the tides of ocean turning in ...
    And know, for yet another human day,
    The world's dull, dreadful labor is begun!

Composed upon Westminster Bridge, September 3, 1802

Earth has not anything to show more fair:
Dull would he be of soul who could pass by
A sight so touching in its majesty:
This City now doth, like a garment, wear
The beauty of the morning; silent, bare,   5
Ships, towers, domes, theaters, and temples lie
Open unto the fields, and to the sky,
All bright and glittering in the smokeless air.
Never did sun more beautifully steep
In his first splendor, valley, rock, or hill;   10
Ne'er saw I, never felt, a calm so deep!
The river glideth at his own sweet will:
Dear God! the very houses seem asleep,
And all that mighty heart is lying still!

QUESTION

Which poem has more freshness of language?

Piano

Softly, in the dusk, a woman is singing to me;
Taking me back down the vista of years, till I see
A child sitting under the piano, in the boom of the tingling
    strings
And pressing the small, poised feet of a mother who smiles as
    she sings.

In spite of myself, the insidious mastery of song   5
Betrays me back, till the heart of me weeps to belong
To the old Sunday evenings at home, with winter outside
And hymns in the cozy parlor, the tinkling piano our guide.

So now it is vain for the singer to burst into clamor
With the great black piano appassionato. The glamour   10
Of childish days is upon me, my manhood is cast
Down in the flood of remembrance, I weep like a child for
    the past.

The Days Gone By

O the days gone by! O the days gone by!
The apples in the orchard, and the pathway through the rye;
The chirrup of the robin, and the whistle of the quail
As he piped across the meadows sweet as any nightingale;
When the bloom was on the clover, and the blue was in
    the sky,   5
And my happy heart brimmed over in the days gone by.

In the days gone by, when my naked feet were tripped
By the honey-suckle's tangles where the water-lilies dipped,
And the ripples of the river lipped the moss along the brink
Where the placid-eyed and lazy-footed cattle came to
    drink,   10
And the tilting snipe stood fearless of the truant's wayward
    cry
And the splashing of the swimmer, in the days gone by.

O the days gone by! O the days gone by!
The music of the laughing lip, the luster of the eye;
The childish faith in fairies, and Aladdin's magic ring—   15
The simple, soul-reposing, glad belief in everything,—
When life was like a story, holding neither sob nor sigh,
In the golden olden glory of the days gone by.

QUESTION

Which poem is more rhetorical in treating the subject?

We play at Paste—

We play at Paste —
Till qualified, for Pearl —
Then, drop the Paste —
And deem ourself a fool —

The Shapes — though — were similar —   5
And our new Hands
Learned *Gem*-Tactics —
Practicing *Sands* —

If I can stop one Heart from breaking

If I can stop one Heart from breaking
I shall not live in vain
If I can ease one Life the Aching
Or cool one Pain

Or help one fainting Robin   5
Unto his Nest again
I shall not live in Vain.

QUESTION

These two poems by Emily Dickinson both deal with the art of writing poetry, but
they deal with the topic in very different ways. Which of the two poems is the more
fresh and original?

When I have fears that I may cease to be

When I have fears that I may cease to be
    Before my pen has gleaned my teeming brain,
Before high-pilèd books, in charactery,°   written symbols
    Hold like rich garners the full-ripened grain;
When I behold, upon the night's starred face,   5
    Huge cloudy symbols of a high romance,
And think that I may never live to trace
    Their shadows, with the magic hand of chance;
And when I feel, fair creature of an hour,
    That I shall never look upon thee more,   10

Never have relish in the faery power
    Of unreflecting love—then on the shore
Of the wide world I stand alone, and think
    Till love and fame to nothingness do sink.

O Solitude!

O Solitude! if I must with thee dwell,
    Let it not be among the jumbled heap
    Of murky buildings; climb with me the steep—
Nature's observatory—whence the dell,
Its flowery slopes, its river's crystal swell,   5
    May seem a span; let me thy vigils keep
    'Mongst boughs pavilioned, where the deer's swift leap
Startles the wild bee from the fox-glove bell.
But though I'll gladly trace these scenes with thee,
    Yet the sweet converse of an innocent mind,   10
    Whose words are images of thoughts refined,
Is my soul's pleasure; and it sure must be
    Almost the highest bliss of human-kind,
When to thy haunts two kindred spirits flee.

QUESTION

Both poems are by John Keats (1795–1821). Which of them displays true excellence? Explain.

SUGGESTIONS FOR WRITING

In each of the following pairs, both poems have literary merit, but one is clearly a more ambitious and more successful poem. Choose one pair and write a short essay in which you argue which is the better of the two poems, and why.

1. Owen, "Dulce et Decorum Est" (page 684) and Crane, "War Is Kind" (page 988).
2. Ryan, "Tree Heart, True Heart" (page 730) and Donne, "A Valediction: Forbidding Mourning" (page 760).
3. Dickinson, "I felt a Funeral, in my Brain" (page 737) and Plath, "Mad Girl's Love Song" (page 926).
4. Clifton, "good times" (page 982) and Hughes, "Theme for English B" (page 1012).
5. Yeats, "The Folly of Being Comforted" (page 928) and Bishop, "Insomnia" (page 891).
6. Roethke, "My Papa's Waltz" (page 1035) and Hayden's, "The Whipping" (page 689).

PRACTICE AP WRITING PROMPTS

"Pied Beauty" (p. 939) and "Composed upon Westminster Bridge, September 3, 1802" (p. 941)

In "Pied Beauty" and "Composed upon Westminster Bridge, September 3, 1802," the speakers express strikingly different ideas about the world's beauty. Write an essay in which you compare and contrast these conceptions of beauty. Include in your analysis how poetic elements such as rhythm, form, diction, and figurative language convey the poets' concepts.

CHAPTER SIXTEEN

Evaluating Poetry 2
Poetic Excellence

If a poem has successfully met the test of the question, *How fully has it accomplished its purpose?* we are ready to subject it to our second evaluative question: *How important is its purpose?*

Great poetry must, of course, be good poetry. Noble intent alone cannot redeem a work that does not measure high on the scale of accomplishment; otherwise the sentimental and purely didactic verse of much of the preceding chapter would stand with the world's masterpieces. But once a work has been judged as successful on the scale of execution, its final standing will depend on its significance of purpose.

Suppose, for instance, we consider three examples in our text: the anonymous verse "Pease Porridge Hot" (page 899); the poem "It sifts from Leaden Sieves" by Emily Dickinson (page 749); and Shakespeare's sonnet "That time of year" (page 921). Each of these would probably be judged by critics as successful in what it sets out to do. "Pease Porridge Hot" is a charming nursery rhyme that makes clever use of rhyme and alliteration. But what is this verse *about?* Virtually nothing. Dickinson's poem, in contrast, *is* poetry, and very good poetry. It appeals richly to our senses and to our imaginations, and it succeeds excellently in its purpose: to convey the appearance and the quality of falling and newly fallen snow as well as a sense of the magic and the mystery of nature. Yet when we compare this excellent poem with Shakespeare's, we again see important differences. Although Dickinson's poem engages the senses and the imagination and may affect us with wonder and cause us to meditate on nature, it does not deeply engage the emotions or the intellect. It does not come as close to the core of human living and suffering as does Shakespeare's sonnet. In fact, it is concerned primarily with that staple of small talk, the weather. On the other hand, Shakespeare's sonnet evokes the universal human concerns of growing old, approaching death, and love. Of these three selections, then, Shakespeare's is the greatest. It "says" more than Dickinson's poem or the nursery rhyme; it communicates a richer experience; it successfully accomplishes a more significant purpose. The reader will get from it a deeper enjoyment because it is nourishing as well as delightful.

Great poetry engages the whole person—senses, imagination, emotion, intellect; it does not touch us merely on one or two sides of our nature. Great poetry seeks not merely to entertain us but to bring us—along with pure pleasure—fresh insights, or renewed insights, and important insights, into the nature of human experience. Great poetry, we might say, gives us a broader and deeper understanding of life, of other people, and of ourselves, always with the qualification, of course, that the kind of insight literature gives is not necessarily the kind that can be summed up in a simple "lesson" or "moral." It is *knowledge*—*felt* knowledge, *new* knowledge—of the complexities of human nature and of the tragedies and sufferings, the excitements and joys, that characterize human experience.

Yet, after all, we have provided no easy yardsticks or rule-of-thumb measures for literary judgment. There are no mechanical tests. The final measuring rod can be only the responsiveness, the taste, and the discernment of the reader. Such taste and discernment are partly a native endowment, partly the product of experience, partly the achievement of conscious study, training, and intellectual effort. They cannot be achieved suddenly or quickly; they can never be achieved in perfection. The pull is a long and a hard one. But success, even relative success, brings enormous personal and aesthetic rewards.

The Canonization

For God's sake, hold your tongue, and let me love!
   Or chide my palsy or my gout,
My five gray hairs or ruined fortune flout;
With wealth your state, your mind with arts improve,
    Take you a course,° get you a place,   career 5
      Observe his honor° or his grace,°   judge; bishop
Or the king's real or his stamped face°   on a coin
    Contemplate; what you will, approve,°   try out
      So you will let me love.

Alas, alas, who's injured by my love?   10
   What merchant ships have my sighs drowned?

Who says my tears have overflowed his ground?
When did my colds a forward° spring remove?   early
    When did the heats which my veins fill
    Add one more to the plaguy bill?   15
Soldiers find wars, and lawyers find out still
    Litigious men which quarrels move,
        Though she and I do love.

Call us what you will, we are made such by love.
    Call her one, me another fly;°   moth 20
We are tapers too, and at our own cost die;
And we in us find the eagle and the dove;
    The phoenix riddle hath more wit°   meaning
    By us; we two, being one, are it.
So to one neutral thing both sexes fit.   25
    We die and rise the same, and prove
        Mysterious by this love.

We can die by it, if not live by love,
    And if unfit for tombs and hearse
Our legend be, it will be fit for verse;
And if no piece of chronicle° we prove,   30 history
    We'll build in sonnets pretty rooms:
    As well a well-wrought urn becomes
The greatest ashes as half-acre tombs,
    And by these hymns all shall approve°   confirm 35
        Us canonized for love,

And thus invoke us: "You whom reverend love
    Made one another's hermitage,
You to whom love was peace, that now is rage,
Who did the whole world's soul contract, and drove   40
    Into the glasses of your eyes
    (So made such mirrors and such spies
That they did all to you epitomize)
    Countries, towns, courts: beg from above
        A pattern of your love!"   45

—JOHN DONNE (1572–1631)

QUESTIONS

1. Vocabulary: *Canonization* (title), *tapers* (21), *phoenix* (23), *invoke* (37), *epitomize* (43). "[R]eal" (7), pronounced as two syllables, puns on *royal*. The "plaguy bill" (15) is a list of plague victims. The word "die" (21, 26, 28) in seventeenth-century slang

meant to experience the sexual climax. To understand lines 21 and 28, one also needs to be familiar with the Renaissance superstition that every act of sexual intercourse shortened one's life by one day. The "eagle" and the "dove" (22) are symbols for strength and mildness. "[P]attern" (45) is a model that one can copy.

2. Who is the speaker and what is his condition? How old is he? To whom is he speaking? What has his auditor been saying to him before the opening of the poem? What sort of values can we ascribe to the auditor by inference from the first stanza? What value does the speaker oppose to these? How does the stanzaic pattern of the poem emphasize this value?

3. The sighs, tears, fevers, and chills in the second stanza were commonplace in the love poetry of Donne's time. How does Donne make them fresh? What is the speaker's argument in this stanza? How does it begin to turn from pure defense to offense in the last three lines of the stanza?

4. How are the things to which the lovers are compared in the third stanza *arranged*? Does their ordering reflect in any way the arrangement of the whole poem? Elucidate line 21. Interpret or paraphrase lines 23–27.

5. Explain the first line of the fourth stanza. What status does the speaker claim for himself and his beloved in the last line of this stanza?

6. In what sense is the last stanza an invocation? Who speaks in it? To whom? What powers are ascribed to the lovers in it?

7. What do the following words from the poem have in common: "Mysterious" (27), "hymns" (35), "canonized" (36), "reverend" (37), "hermitage" (38)? What judgment about love does the speaker make by the use of these words?

Ode on a Grecian Urn

Thou still unravished bride of quietness,
    Thou foster-child of silence and slow time,
Sylvan historian, who canst thus express
    A flowery tale more sweetly than our rhyme:
What leaf-fringed legend haunts about thy shape   5
    Of deities or mortals, or of both,
        In Tempe or the dales of Arcady?
What men or gods are these? What maidens loth?
What mad pursuit? What struggle to escape?
    What pipes and timbrels? What wild ecstasy?   10

Heard melodies are sweet, but those unheard
    Are sweeter; therefore, ye soft pipes, play on;
Not to the sensual ear, but, more endeared,
    Pipe to the spirit ditties of no tone:
Fair youth, beneath the trees, thou canst not leave   15
    Thy song, nor ever can those trees be bare;
        Bold lover, never, never canst thou kiss,

Though winning near the goal—yet, do not grieve;
    She cannot fade, though thou hast not thy bliss,
For ever wilt thou love, and she be fair!   20

Ah, happy, happy boughs! that cannot shed
    Your leaves, nor ever bid the spring adieu;
And, happy melodist, unwearièd,
    For ever piping songs for ever new;
More happy love! more happy, happy love!   25
    For ever warm and still to be enjoyed,
    For ever panting and for ever young;
All breathing human passion far above,
    That leaves a heart high-sorrowful and cloyed,
        A burning forehead, and a parching tongue.   30

Who are these coming to the sacrifice?
    To what green altar, O mysterious priest,
Lead'st thou that heifer lowing at the skies,
    And all her silken flanks with garlands drest?
What little town by river or sea shore,   35
    Or mountain-built with peaceful citadel,
    Is emptied of its folk, this pious morn?
And, little town, thy streets for evermore
    Will silent be; and not a soul to tell
        Why thou are desolate, can e'er return.   40

O Attic shape! Fair attitude! with brede
    Of marble men and maidens overwrought,
With forest branches and the trodden weed;
    Thou, silent form, dost tease us out of thought
As doth eternity: Cold Pastoral!   45
    When old age shall this generation waste,
    Thou shalt remain, in midst of other woe
    Than ours, a friend to man, to whom thou say'st,
Beauty is truth, truth beauty,—that is all
    Ye know on earth, and all ye need to know.*   50

—JOHN KEATS (1795–1821)

---

*(49–50) In the 1820 edition of Keats's poems the words "Beauty is truth, truth beauty" were
enclosed in quotation marks, and the poem is often reprinted that way. It is now generally agreed,
however, on the basis of contemporary transcripts of Keats's poem, that Keats intended the entire
last two lines to be spoken by the urn.

QUESTIONS

1. The poem is an extended apostrophe addressed to a painted vase from ancient Greece. There are two separate scenes on the urn; the speaker summarizes their subjects in lines 5–10, and then specifically addresses them in 11–30 and 31–40. As completely as you can, describe what each of the scenes depicts.
2. What three denotations of "still" (1) are appropriate to the metaphorical identities ascribed to the urn in lines 1–4? What modes of sensory experience and of knowledge are evoked in those lines?
3. The structure of the poem includes the speaker's shifting motivations in the spaces *between* the stanzas. For example, lines 5–10 request information about the actions depicted on the urn, but lines 11–14 dismiss the need for answers. What do you suppose motivates that change?
4. Lines 15–28 celebrate the scene because it has captured in a still moment the intensity of pursuit and desire. Explain. How is that permanence contrasted to the reality of "breathing human passion" (28)?
5. In the fourth stanza the speaker turns to the second scene, again with a series of questions requesting specific information. How do the concluding lines of the third stanza motivate this shift of subject? Lines 31–34 are questions about what the speaker sees on the urn; lines 35–40 refer to something he cannot see—and are expressed in a tone of desolation. What is it that leads the speaker to that tone? What has he done to cause it?
6. In the final stanza, the speaker does not engage himself with the subjects of the scenes but with "shape" (41), "form" (44), and "attitude" (41—in its older meaning, the posture of a painted figure). What at the end of the preceding stanza might cause the speaker to withdraw his imagination from the scenes and to comment in general on the "form" of the urn? Explain lines 44–45 and the culminating oxymoron "Cold Pastoral."
7. The footnote bases its deduction—that the last two lines in their entirety are claimed by the speaker to be the urn's advice to "man" (48)—on external evidence. Can you find internal support for this in the obsolete grammatical usage in line 50? How is the urn's message suited to the experience that the speaker has undergone?

There's a certain Slant of light

There's a certain Slant of light,
Winter Afternoons—
That oppresses, like the Heft
Of Cathedral Tunes—

Heavenly Hurt, it gives us—   5
We can find no scar,
But internal difference,
Where the Meanings, are—

None may teach it—Any—
'Tis the Seal Despair—   10
An imperial affliction
Sent us of the Air—

When it comes, the Landscape listens—
Shadows—hold their breath—
When it goes, 'tis like the Distance   15
On the look of Death—

—EMILY DICKINSON (1830–1886)

QUESTIONS

1. This is one of Dickinson's most famous poems dealing with human psychological states. Here the speaker calls her state of mind "Despair" (10), but many today would consider it "clinical depression." What particular images help convey the speaker's depressed state of mind?

2. The scene is carefully set: a winter afternoon, a speaker attempting to describe what she feels. How does the poem relate a possibly fleeting psychological state to such issues as religious faith, self-examination, and death?

3. Could it be argued that this experience, however painful, is ultimately a positive one for the speaker? What is the significance of the oxymorons "Heavenly Hurt" (5) and "imperial affliction" (11)?

4. Discuss the use of abstractions in this poem: "Hurt" (5), "Meanings" (8), "Despair" (10), "Death" (16). How do these abstractions work to enlarge the poem's meaning beyond a mere depiction of a specific person's temporary mood?

5. The final stanza describes the moment of great tension when the "Seal" (10) of despair falls upon the speaker. Why does she imagine that the entire landscape participates in this personal crisis? Does this suggest a self-absorbed projection onto the landscape or an honest attempt to understand and describe her mental state?

6. Discuss the concluding simile, "like the Distance / On the look of Death—". Do any specific visual images come to mind as you ponder this abstract phrase? Could "Death" here be interpreted as meaning "a dead person"?

Home Burial

He saw her from the bottom of the stairs
Before she saw him. She was starting down,
Looking back over her shoulder at some fear.
She took a doubtful step and then undid it
To raise herself and look again. He spoke   5
Advancing toward her: "What is it you see

From up there always—for I want to know."
She turned and sank upon her skirts at that,
And her face changed from terrified to dull.
He said to gain time: "What is it you see,"   10
Mounting until she cowered under him.
"I will find out now—you must tell me, dear."
She, in her place, refused him any help
With the least stiffening of her neck and silence.
She let him look, sure that he wouldn't see,   15
Blind creature; and awhile he didn't see.
But at last he murmured, "Oh," and again, "Oh."

"What is it—what?" she said.

                     "Just that I see."

"You don't," she challenged. "Tell me what it is."

"The wonder is I didn't see at once.   20
I never noticed it from here before.
I must be wonted to it—that's the reason.
The little graveyard where my people are!
So small the window frames the whole of it.
Not so much larger than a bedroom, is it?   25
There are three stones of slate and one of marble,
Broad-shouldered little slabs there in the sunlight
On the sidehill. We haven't to mind *those*.
But I understand: it is not the stones,
But the child's mound—"

                    "Don't, don't, don't, don't,"
she cried.   30

She withdrew, shrinking from beneath his arm
That rested on the banister, and slid downstairs;
And turned on him with such a daunting look,
He said twice over before he knew himself:
"Can't a man speak of his own child he's lost?"   35

"Not you! Oh, where's my hat? Oh, I don't need it!
I must get out of here. I must get air.
I don't know rightly whether any man can."

"Amy! Don't go to someone else this time.
Listen to me. I won't come down the stairs."   40
He sat and fixed his chin between his fists.
"There's something I should like to ask you, dear."

"You don't know how to ask it."

                                        "Help me, then."

Her fingers moved the latch for all reply.

"My words are nearly always an offense.   45
I don't know how to speak of anything
So as to please you. But I might be taught,
I should suppose. I can't say I see how.
A man must partly give up being a man
With women-folk. We could have some arrangement   50
By which I'd bind myself to keep hands off
Anything special you're a-mind to name.
Though I don't like such things 'twixt those that love.
Two that don't love can't live together without them.
But two that do can't live together with them."   55
She moved the latch a little. "Don't—don't go.
Don't carry it to someone else this time.
Tell me about it if it's something human.
Let me into your grief. I'm not so much
Unlike other folks as your standing there   60
Apart would make me out. Give me my chance.
I do think, though, you overdo it a little.
What was it brought you up to think it the thing
To take your mother-loss of a first child
So inconsolably—in the face of love.   65
You'd think his memory might be satisfied—"

"There you go sneering now!"

                                        "I'm not, I'm not!
You make me angry. I'll come down to you.
God, what a woman! And it's come to this,
A man can't speak of his own child that's dead."   70

"You can't because you don't know how to speak.
If you had any feelings, you that dug

With your own hand—how could you?—his little grave;
I saw you from that very window there,
Making the gravel leap and leap in air, 75
Leap up, like that, like that, and land so lightly
And roll back down the mound beside the hole.
I thought, Who is that man? I didn't know you.
And I crept down the stairs and up the stairs
To look again, and still your spade kept lifting. 80
Then you came in. I heard your rumbling voice
Out in the kitchen, and I don't know why,
But I went near to see with my own eyes.
You could sit there with the stains on your shoes
Of the fresh earth from your own baby's grave 85
And talk about your everyday concerns.
You had stood the spade up against the wall
Outside there in the entry, for I saw it."

"I shall laugh the worst laugh I ever laughed.
I'm cursed. God, if I don't believe I'm cursed." 90
"I can repeat the very words you were saying:
'Three foggy mornings and one rainy day
Will rot the best birch fence a man can build.'
Think of it, talk like that at such a time!
What had how long it takes a birch to rot 95
To do with what was in the darkened parlor?
You *couldn't* care! The nearest friends can go
With anyone to death, comes so far short
They might as well not try to go at all.
No, from the time when one is sick to death, 100
One is alone, and he dies more alone.
Friends make pretense of following to the grave,
But before one is in it, their minds are turned
And making the best of their way back to life
And living people, and things they understand. 105
But the world's evil. I won't have grief so
If I can change it. Oh, I won't, I won't!"

"There, you have said it all and you feel better.
You won't go now. You're crying. Close the door.
The heart's gone out of it: why keep it up? 110
Amy! There's someone coming down the road!"

"*You*—oh, you think the talk is all. I must go—
Somewhere out of this house. How can I make you—"

"If—you—do!" She was opening the door wider.
"Where do you mean to go? First tell me that.   115
I'll follow and bring you back by force. I *will!*—"

—ROBERT FROST (1874–1963)

QUESTIONS

1. Vocabulary: *wonted* (22).
2. The poem centers on a conflict between husband and wife. What causes the conflict? Why does Amy resent her husband? What is *his* dissatisfaction with Amy?
3. Characterize the husband and wife respectively. What is the chief difference between them? Does the poem take sides? Is either presented more sympathetically than the other?
4. The poem does not say how long the couple have been married or how long the child has been buried. Does it contain suggestions from which we may make rough inferences?
5. The husband and wife both generalize on the other's faults during the course of the poem, attributing them to all men or to all women or to people in general. Point out these generalizations. Are they valid?
6. Finish the unfinished sentences in lines 30, 66, 113, 114.
7. Comment on the function of lines 25, 39, 92–93.
8. Following are three paraphrased and abbreviated versions of statements made in published discussions of the poem. Which would you support? Why?
   a. The young wife is gradually persuaded by her husband's kind yet firm reasonableness to express her feelings in words and to recognize that human nature is limited and cannot sacrifice everything to sorrow. Though she still suffers from excess grief, the crisis is past, and she will eventually be brought back to life.
   b. At the end, the whole poem is epitomized by the door that is neither open nor shut. The wife cannot really leave; the husband cannot really make her stay. Neither husband nor wife is capable of decisive action, of either self-liberation or liberation of the other.
   c. Her husband's attempt to talk, since it is the wrong kind of talk, only leads to her departure at the poem's end.

The Love Song of J. Alfred Prufrock

S'io credesse che mia risposta fosse
A persona che mai tornasse al mondo,
Questa fiamma staria senza piu scosse.

Ma perciocche giammai di questo fondo
Non torno vivo alcun, s'i'odo il vero,
Senza tema d'infamia ti rispondo.

Let us go then, you and I,
When the evening is spread out against the sky
Like a patient etherized upon a table;
Let us go, through certain half-deserted streets,
The muttering retreats   5
Of restless nights in one-night cheap hotels
And sawdust restaurants with oyster-shells:
Streets that follow like a tedious argument
Of insidious intent
To lead you to an overwhelming question. . . .   10
Oh, do not ask, "What is it?"
Let us go and make our visit.

In the room the women come and go
Talking of Michelangelo.

The yellow fog that rubs its back upon the window-panes,   15
The yellow smoke that rubs its muzzle on the window panes
Licked its tongue into the corners of the evening,
Lingered upon the pools that stand in drains,
Let fall upon its back the soot that falls from chimneys,
Slipped by the terrace, made a sudden leap,   20
And seeing that it was a soft October night,
Curled once about the house, and fell asleep.

And indeed there will be time
For the yellow smoke that slides along the street,
Rubbing its back upon the window-panes;   25
There will be time, there will be time
To prepare a face to meet the faces that you meet;
There will be time to murder and create,
And time for all the works and days of hands
That lift and drop a question on your plate;   30
Time for you and time for me,
And time yet for a hundred indecisions,
And for a hundred visions and revisions,
Before the taking of a toast and tea.

In the room the women come and go   35
Talking of Michelangelo.

And indeed there will be time
To wonder, "Do I dare?" and "Do I dare?"
Time to turn back and descend the stair,
With a bald spot in the middle of my hair—   40
(They will say: "How his hair is growing thin!")
My morning coat, my collar mounting firmly to the chin,
My necktie rich and modest, but asserted by a simple pin—
(They will say: "But how his arms and legs are thin!")
Do I dare   45
Disturb the universe?
In a minute there is time
For decisions and revisions which a minute will reverse.

For I have known them all already, known them all—
Have known the evenings, mornings, afternoons,   50
I have measured out my life with coffee spoons;
I know the voices dying with a dying fall
Beneath the music from a farther room.
         So how should I presume?

And I have known the eyes already, known them all—   55
The eyes that fix you in a formulated phrase,
And when I am formulated, sprawling on a pin,
When I am pinned and wriggling on the wall,
Then how should I begin
To spit out all the butt-ends of my days and ways?   60
         And how should I presume?

And I have known the arms already, known them all—
Arms that are braceleted and white and bare
(But in the lamplight, downed with light brown hair!)
Is it perfume from a dress   65
That makes me so digress?
Arms that lie along a table, or wrap about a shawl.
         And should I then presume?
         And how should I begin?

                    *   *   *

Shall I say, I have gone at dusk through narrow streets   70
And watched the smoke that rises from the pipes
Of lonely men in shirt-sleeves, leaning out of windows? ...

I should have been a pair of ragged claws
Scuttling across the floors of silent seas.

*   *   *

And the afternoon, the evening, sleeps so peacefully!   75
Smoothed by long fingers,
Asleep ... tired ... or it malingers,
Stretched on the floor, here beside you and me.
Should I, after tea and cakes and ices,
Have the strength to force the moment to its crisis?   80
But though I have wept and fasted, wept and prayed,
Though I have seen my head (grown slightly bald)
      brought in upon a platter,
I am no prophet—and here's no great matter;
I have seen the moment of my greatness flicker,
And I have seen the eternal Footman hold my coat, and
      snicker,   85
And in short, I was afraid.

And would it have been worth it, after all,
After the cups, the marmalade, the tea,
Among the porcelain, among some talk of you and me,
Would it have been worth while,   90
To have bitten off the matter with a smile,
To have squeezed the universe into a ball
To roll it toward some overwhelming question,
To say: "I am Lazarus, come from the dead,
Come back to tell you all, I shall tell you all"—   95
If one, settling a pillow by her head,
      Should say: "That is not what I meant at all.
      That is not it, at all."

And would it have been worth it, after all,
Would it have been worth while,   100
After the sunsets and the dooryards and the sprinkled streets,
After the novels, after the teacups, after the skirts that trail
      along the floor—
And this, and so much more?—
It is impossible to say just what I mean!

But as if a magic lantern threw the nerves in patterns   105
    on a screen:
Would it have been worth while
If one, settling a pillow or throwing off a shawl,
And turning toward the window, should say:
    "That is not it at all,
    That is not what I meant, at all."   110

*　　　*　　　*

No! I am not Prince Hamlet, nor was meant to be;
Am an attendant lord, one that will do
To swell a progress, start a scene or two,
Advise the prince; no doubt, an easy tool,
Deferential, glad to be of use,   115
Politic, cautious, and meticulous;
Full of high sentence, but a bit obtuse;
At times, indeed, almost ridiculous—
Almost, at times, the Fool.

I grow old . . . I grow old . . .   120
I shall wear the bottoms of my trousers rolled.°   cuffed

Shall I part my hair behind? Do I dare to eat a peach?
I shall wear white flannel trousers, and walk upon the beach.
I have heard the mermaids singing, each to each.

I do not think that they will sing to me.   125

I have seen them riding seaward on the waves
Combing the white hair of the waves blown back
When the wind blows the water white and black.

We have lingered in the chambers of the sea
By sea-girls wreathed with seaweed red and brown   130
Till human voices wake us, and we drown.

—T. S. ELIOT (1888–1965)

QUESTIONS

1. Vocabulary: *insidious* (9), *Michelangelo* (14, 36), *muzzle* (16), *malingers* (77), *progress* (113), *Deferential* (115), *Politic* (116), *meticulous* (116), *sentence* (117).
2. This poem may be for some readers the most difficult in the book because it uses a "stream of consciousness" technique (that is, it presents the apparently

random thoughts going through a person's head within a certain time interval), in which the transitional links are psychological rather than logical, and also because it uses allusions you may be unfamiliar with. Even if you do not at first understand the poem in detail, you should be able to get from it a quite accurate picture of Prufrock's character and personality. What kind of person is he (answer this as fully as possible)? From what class of society does he come? What one line especially well sums up the nature of his past life? A brief initial orientation may be helpful: Prufrock is apparently on his way, at the beginning of the poem, to a late afternoon tea, at which he wishes (or does he?) to make a declaration of love to some lady who will be present. The "you and I" of the first line are divided parts of Prufrock's own nature, for he is experiencing internal conflict. Does he or does he not make the declaration? Where does the climax of the poem come? If the portion leading up to the climax is devoted to Prufrock's effort to prepare himself psychologically to make the declaration (or to postpone such effort), what is the portion after the climax devoted to?

3. The poem contains a number of striking or unusual figures of speech. Most of them in some way reflect Prufrock's own nature or his desires or fears. From this point of view discuss lines 2–3; 15–22 and 75–78; 57–58; 73–74; and 124–131. What figure of speech is lines 73–74? In what respect is the title ironic?

4. The poem makes extensive use of literary allusion. The Italian epigraph is a passage from Dante's *Inferno* in which a man in Hell tells a visitor that he would never tell his story if there were a chance that it would get back to living ears. In line 29 the phrase "works and days" is the title of a long poem—a description of agricultural life and a call to toil—by the early Greek poet Hesiod. Line 52 echoes the opening speech of Shakespeare's *Twelfth Night*. The prophet of lines 81–83 is John the Baptist, whose head was delivered to Salome by Herod as a reward for her dancing (Matthew 14.1–11, and Oscar Wilde's play *Salome*). Line 92 echoes the closing six lines of Marvell's "To His Coy Mistress" (page 761). Lazarus (94–95) may be either the beggar Lazarus (of Luke 16) who was not permitted to return from the dead to warn a rich man's brothers about Hell, the Lazarus (of John 11) whom Christ raised from death, or both. Lines 111–119 allude to a number of characters from Shakespeare's *Hamlet*: Hamlet himself, the chamberlain Polonius, and various minor characters including probably Rosencrantz, Guildenstern, and Osric. "Full of high sentence" (117) echoes Chaucer's description of the Clerk of Oxford in the Prologue to *The Canterbury Tales*. Relate as many of these allusions as you can to the character of Prufrock. How is Prufrock particularly like Hamlet, and how is he unlike him? Contrast Prufrock with the speaker in "To His Coy Mistress."

Sailing to Byzantium

That is no country for old men. The young
In one another's arms, birds in the trees
—Those dying generations—at their song,

The salmon-falls, the mackerel-crowded seas,
Fish, flesh, or fowl, commend all summer long   5
Whatever is begotten, born, and dies.
Caught in that sensual music all neglect
Monuments of unaging intellect.

An aged man is but a paltry thing,
A tattered coat upon a stick, unless   10
Soul clap its hands and sing, and louder sing
For every tatter in its mortal dress,
Nor is there singing school but studying
Monuments of its own magnificence;
And therefore I have sailed the seas and come   15
To the holy city of Byzantium.

O sages standing in God's holy fire
As in the gold mosaic of a wall,
Come from the holy fire, perne° in a gyre,   spin
And be the singing-masters of my soul.   20
Consume my heart away; sick with desire
And fastened to a dying animal
It knows not what it is; and gather me
Into the artifice of eternity.

Once out of nature I shall never take   25
My bodily form from any natural thing,
But such a form as Grecian goldsmiths make
Of hammered gold and gold enameling
To keep a drowsy Emperor awake;
Or set upon a golden bough to sing   30
To lords and ladies of Byzantium
Of what is past, or passing, or to come.

—WILLIAM BUTLER YEATS (1865–1939)

(Title) *Byzantium:* Ancient eastern capital of the Roman Empire; in this poem symbolically a holy city of the imagination. (1) *That:* Ireland, or the ordinary sensual world. (27–31) *such ... Byzantium:* The Byzantine emperor Theophilus had made for himself mechanical golden birds that sang upon the branches of a golden tree.

QUESTIONS

1. Vocabulary: *gyre* (19).
2. What kind of "country" is being described in the first line? Why does a learned old man not belong in that country?
3. Contrast the speaker's native country, Ireland, with Byzantium. What are the characteristics of each? Which does the speaker prefer, and why?
4. Why does the speaker want his heart to be consumed so that he can be gathered "Into the artifice of eternity" (24)? Is he longing simply for death, or for something else?
5. Normally we think of "artificial" as a pejorative term, and "natural" as a positive attribute. But in the last stanza, especially, the speaker reverses the usual connotations of these concepts. Explain why, and describe the kind of world in which the speaker wishes to dwell.

Sunday Morning

1

Complacencies of the peignoir, and late
Coffee and oranges in a sunny chair,
And the green freedom of a cockatoo
Upon a rug mingle to dissipate
The holy hush of ancient sacrifice.   5
She dreams a little, and she feels the dark
Encroachment of that old catastrophe,
As a calm darkens among water-lights.
The pungent oranges and bright, green wings
Seem things in some procession of the dead,   10
Winding across wide water, without sound.
The day is like wide water, without sound,
Stilled for the passing of her dreaming feet
Over the seas, to silent Palestine,
Dominion of the blood and sepulchre.   15

2

Why should she give her bounty to the dead?
What is divinity if it can come
Only in silent shadows and in dreams?
Shall she not find in comforts of the sun,
In pungent fruit and bright, green wings, or else   20
In any balm or beauty of the earth,
Things to be cherished like the thought of heaven?
Divinity must live within herself:

Passions of rain, or moods in falling snow;
Grievings in loneliness, or unsubdued   25
Elations when the forest blooms; gusty
Emotions on wet roads on autumn nights;
All pleasures and all pains, remembering
The bough of summer and the winter branch.
These are the measures destined for her soul.   30

                              3
Jove in the clouds had his inhuman birth.
No mother suckled him, no sweet land gave
Large-mannered motions to his mythy mind.
He moved among us, as a muttering king,
Magnificent, would move among his hinds,   35
Until our blood, commingling, virginal,
With heaven, brought such requital to desire
The very hinds discerned it, in a star.
Shall our blood fail? Or shall it come to be
The blood of paradise? And shall the earth   40
Seem all of paradise that we shall know?
The sky will be much friendlier then than now,
A part of labor and a part of pain,
And next in glory to enduring love,
Not this dividing and indifferent blue.   45

                              4
She says, "I am content when wakened birds,
Before they fly, test the reality
Of misty fields, by their sweet questionings;
But when the birds are gone, and their warm fields
Return no more, where, then, is paradise?"   50
There is not any haunt of prophecy,
Nor any old chimera of the grave,
Neither the golden underground, nor isle
Melodious, where spirits gat them home,
Nor visionary south, nor cloudy palm   55
Remote on heaven's hill, that has endured
As April's green endures; or will endure
Like her remembrance of awakened birds,
Or her desire for June and evening, tipped
By the consummation of the swallow's wings.   60

5

She says, "But in contentment I still feel
The need of some imperishable bliss."
Death is the mother of beauty; hence from her,
Alone, shall come fulfillment to our dreams
And our desires. Although she strews the leaves   65
Of sure obliteration on our paths,
The path sick sorrow took, the many paths
Where triumph rang its brassy phrase, or love
Whispered a little out of tenderness,
She makes the willow shiver in the sun   70
For maidens who were wont to sit and gaze
Upon the grass, relinquished to their feet.
She causes boys to pile new plums and pears
On disregarded plate. The maidens taste
And stray impassioned in the littering leaves.   75

6

Is there no change of death in paradise?
Does ripe fruit never fall? Or do the boughs
Hang always heavy in that perfect sky,
Unchanging, yet so like our perishing earth,
With rivers like our own that seek for seas   80
They never find, the same receding shores
That never touch with inarticulate pang?
Why set the pear upon those river-banks
Or spice the shores with odors of the plum?
Alas, that they should wear our colors there,   85
The silken weavings of our afternoons,
And pick the strings of our insipid lutes!
Death is the mother of beauty, mystical,
Within whose burning bosom we devise
Our earthly mothers waiting, sleeplessly.   90

7

Supple and turbulent, a ring of men
Shall chant in orgy on a summer morn
Their boisterous devotion to the sun,
Not as a god, but as a god might be,
Naked among them, like a savage source.   95
Their chant shall be a chant of paradise,
Out of their blood, returning to the sky;

And in their chant shall enter, voice by voice,
The windy lake wherein their lord delights,
The trees, like serafin, and echoing hills,   100
That choir among themselves long afterward.
They shall know well the heavenly fellowship
Of men that perish and of summer morn.
And whence they came and whither they shall go
The dew upon their feet shall manifest.   105

                          8
She hears, upon that water without sound,
A voice that cries, "The tomb in Palestine
Is not the porch of spirits lingering.
It is the grave of Jesus, where he lay."
We live in an old chaos of the sun,   110
Or old dependency of day and night,
Or island solitude, unsponsored, free,
Of that wide water, inescapable.
Deer walk upon our mountains, and the quail
Whistle about us their spontaneous cries;   115
Sweet berries ripen in the wilderness;
And, in the isolation of the sky,
At evening, casual flocks of pigeons make
Ambiguous undulations as they sink,
Downward to darkness, on extended wings.   120

—WALLACE STEVENS (1879–1955)

QUESTIONS

1. Vocabulary: *peignoir* (1), *hinds* (35, 38), *requital* (37), *chimera* (52), *consummation* (60), *obliteration* (66), *serafin* (seraphim) (100). "[G]at" (54) is an obsolete past tense of "get."

2. The poem presents a woman meditating on questions of death, mutability, and permanence, beginning with a stanza that sets the stage and shows her being drawn to these questions beyond her conscious will. The meditation proper is structured as a series of questions and answers stated in direct or indirect quotations, with the answer to a preceding question suggesting a further question, and so forth. In reading through the poem, paraphrase the sequence of implied or stated questions, and the answers to them.

3. The opening scene (stanza 1), in a collection of images and details, indicates the means the woman has chosen to avoid thinking of the typical "Sunday morning" topic, the Christian religion. Define the means she employs. Trace the further references to fruits and birds throughout the poem, and

explain the ordering principle that ties them together (for example, what development of idea or attitude is implied in the sequence oranges/plums and pears/wild berries?).

4. What symbolic meanings are implied by the images of (a) water, (b) the sun, and (c) birds and other animals?

5. Why does the woman give up her desire for unchanging permanence? With what does she replace it? What is her final attitude toward a world that includes change and death? What is meant by "Death is the mother of beauty" (63, 88)?

6. The poet wrote, "This is not essentially a woman's meditation on religion and the meaning of life. It is anybody's meditation" (*Letters of Wallace Stevens,* ed. Holly Stevens [New York: Knopf, 1966], 250). Can you justify that claim?

The Weary Blues

Droning a drowsy syncopated tune,
Rocking back and forth to a mellow croon,
    I heard a Negro play.
Down on Lenox Avenue the other night
By the pale dull pallor of an old gas light   5
    He did a lazy sway. . . .
    He did a lazy sway . . .
To the tune o' those Weary Blues.
With his ebony hands on each ivory key
He made that poor piano moan with melody.   10
    O Blues!
Swaying to and fro on his rickety stool
He played that sad raggy tune like a musical fool.
    Sweet Blues!
Coming from a black man's soul.   15
    O Blues!
In a deep song voice with a melancholy tone
I heard that Negro sing, that old piano moan—
    "Ain't got nobody in all this world,
    Ain't got nobody but ma self.   20
    I's gwine to quit ma frownin'
    And put ma troubles on the shelf."
Thump, thump, thump, went his foot on the floor.
He played a few chords then he sang some more—
    "I got the Weary Blues   25
    And I can't be satisfied.
    Got the Weary Blues

And can't be satisfied—
I ain't happy no mo'
And I wish that I had died."   30
And far into the night he crooned that tune.
The stars went out and so did the moon.
The singer stopped playing and went to bed
While the Weary Blues echoed through his head.
He slept like a rock or a man that's dead.   35

—LANGSTON HUGHES (1902–1967)

QUESTIONS

1. Vocabulary: *syncopated* (1), *raggy* (13).
2. What kind of music is the blues? Why is the form of "The Weary Blues" appropriate to a poem about this music?
3. The poem makes frequent use of repetition. What effect does this have on the reader?
4. Who is the speaker, and why does he respond so intensely to the piano player's "sad raggy tune" (13)?
5. The two quoted lyrics from the piano player's song (19–22 and 25–30) convey quite different messages and emotions. Describe these contrasting lyrics. What is the effect of this contrast on the reader's understanding of the song?
6. The piano player sings and plays "far into the night" (31). How is the music beneficial to him? Does the speaker derive a similar benefit?
7. Analyze the final line. How does the simile form an appropriate closure to the poem?

The Fish

I caught a tremendous fish
and held him beside the boat
half out of water, with my hook
fast in a corner of his mouth.
He didn't fight.   5
He hadn't fought at all.
He hung a grunting weight,
battered and venerable
and homely. Here and there
his brown skin hung in strips   10
like ancient wallpaper,
and its pattern of darker brown
was like wallpaper:

shapes like full-blown roses
stained and lost through age.
He was speckled with barnacles,
fine rosettes of lime,
and infested
with tiny white sea-lice,
and underneath two or three
rags of green weed hung down.
While his gills were breathing in
the terrible oxygen
—the frightening gills,
fresh and crisp with blood,
that can cut so badly—
I thought of the coarse white flesh
packed in like feathers,
the big bones and the little bones,
the dramatic reds and blacks
of his shiny entrails,
and the pink swim-bladder
like a big peony.
I looked into his eyes
which were far larger than mine
but shallower, and yellowed,
the irises backed and packed
with tarnished tinfoil
seen through the lenses
of old scratched isinglass.
They shifted a little, but not
to return my stare.
—It was more like the tipping
of an object toward the light.
I admired his sullen face,
the mechanism of his jaw,
and then I saw
that from his lower lip
—if you could call it a lip—
grim, wet, and weaponlike,
hung five old pieces of fish-line,
or four and a wire leader
with the swivel still attached,
with all their five big hooks
grown firmly in his mouth.

15

20

25

30

35

40

45

50

55

A green line, frayed at the end
where he broke it, two heavier lines,
and a fine black thread
still crimped from the strain and snap
when it broke and he got away.   60
Like medals with their ribbons
frayed and wavering,
a five-haired beard of wisdom
trailing from his aching jaw.
I stared and stared   65
and victory filled up
the little rented boat,
from the pool of bilge
where oil had spread a rainbow
around the rusted engine   70
to the bailer rusted orange,
the sun-cracked thwarts,
the oarlocks on their strings,
the gunnels—until everything
was rainbow, rainbow, rainbow!   75
And I let the fish go.

—ELIZABETH BISHOP (1911–1979)

QUESTIONS

1. Explore the multiple denotations of "tremendous" (1) and the connotations attached to them. How does the richness of that word prepare you for the complexity of the poem?

2. In what ways are many of the images paradoxical in their emotional evocations? Where does the poem create imagery out of the speaker's imagination rather than her present observation?

3. Much of the imagery is elucidated by figurative comparisons or is itself figurative. Find examples of both uses of figures, and trace what they convey in the way of ideas and/or emotions.

4. Whose "victory" fills the boat (66–67)? What is the nature of that victory? Might the term apply to more than one kind of victory?

5. What literally is the "rainbow" (69)? To what is it transformed in lines 74–75? What accounts for the transformation?

6. Explain how the tone of the poem shifts and develops. What is happening to the speaker as she observes and comments upon the physical aspects of the fish?

7. Why does the speaker "let the fish go" (76)? Is the fish symbolic?

PRACTICE AP WRITING PROMPTS ▬▬▬

Elizabeth Bishop, "The Fish" (p. 968)

Read "The Fish" carefully, paying close attention to the speaker's conflicted attitude toward the fish. Then write a well-organized essay in which you describe the speaker's shifting perspective. Show how such elements as imagery, paradox, diction, and tone support the poem's meaning.

Poems for Further
Reading

Sonnenizio on a Line from Drayton

Since there's no help, come let us kiss and part;
or kiss anyway, let's start with that, with the kissing part,
because it's better than the parting part, isn't it—
we're good at kissing, we like how that part goes:
we part our lips, our mouths get near and nearer,   5
then we're close, my breasts, your chest, our bodies partway
to making love, so we might as well, part of me thinks—
the wrong part, I know, the bad part, but still
let's pretend we're at that party where we met
and scandalized everyone, remember that part? Hold me   10
like that again, unbutton my shirt, part of you
wants to I can tell, I'm touching that part and it says
yes, the ardent partisan, let it win you over,
it's hopeless, come, we'll kiss and part forever.

—KIM ADDONIZIO (B. 1954)

The Facebook Sonnet

Welcome to the endless high-school
Reunion. Welcome to past friends
And lovers, however kind or cruel.
Let's undervalue and unmend

The present. Why can't we pretend   5
Every stage of life is the same?
Let's exhume, resume, and extend
Childhood. Let's all play the games

That occupy the young. Let fame
And shame intertwine. Let one's search   10
For God become public domain.
Let church.com become our church.

Let's sign up, sign in, and confess
Here at the altar of loneliness.

—SHERMAN ALEXIE (B. 1966)

Musée des Beaux Arts

About suffering they were never wrong,
The Old Masters: how well they understood
Its human position; how it takes place
While someone else is eating or opening a window or just
    walking dully along;
How, when the aged are reverently, passionately waiting   5
For the miraculous birth, there always must be
Children who did not specially want it to happen, skating
On a pond at the edge of the wood:
They never forgot
That even the dreadful martyrdom must run its course   10
Anyhow in a corner, some untidy spot
Where the dogs go on with their doggy life and the
    torturer's horse
Scratches its innocent behind on a tree.

In Brueghel's *Icarus*, for instance: how everything
    turns away
Quite leisurely from the disaster; the plowman may   15
Have heard the splash, the forsaken cry,
But for him it was not an important failure; the sun shone
As it had to on the white legs disappearing into the green
Water; and the expensive delicate ship that must have seen
Something amazing, a boy falling out of the sky,   20
Had somewhere to get to and sailed calmly on.

—W. H. AUDEN (1907–1973)

Main Character

I went to see
How the West Was Won
at the Sunshine Theater.
Five years old,
deep in a plush seat,   5
light turned off,
bright screen lit up
with MGM roaring lion—
    in front of me
    a drunk Indian rose,   10

      cursed
      the western violins
      and hurled his uncapped bagged bottle
      of wine
      at the rocket roaring to the moon.   15
His dark angry body
convulsed with his obscene gestures
at the screen,
and then ushers escorted him
up the aisle,   20
and as he staggered past me,
I heard his grieving sobs.
      Red wine streaked
      blue sky and take-off smoke,
      sizzled cowboys' campfires,   25
      dripped down barbwire,
      slogged the brave, daring scouts
      who galloped off to mesa buttes
      to speak peace with Apaches,
      and made the prairie   30
      lush with wine streams.
When the movie
was over,
I squinted at the bright
sunny street outside,   35
looking for the main character.

—JIMMY SANTIAGO BACA (B. 1952)

On Her Loving Two Equally

I

How strong does my passion flow,
Divided equally twixt two?
Damon had ne'er subdued my heart
Had not Alexis took his part;
Nor could Alexis powerful prove,   5
Without my Damon's aid, to gain my love.

II

When my Alexis present is,
Then I for Damon sigh and mourn;
But when Alexis I do miss,
Damon gains nothing but my scorn.   10
But if it chance they both are by,
For both alike I languish, sigh, and die.

III

Cure then, thou mighty wingéd god,
This restless fever in my blood;
One golden-pointed dart take back: 15
But which, O Cupid, wilt thou take?
If Damon's, all my hopes are crossed;
Or that of my Alexis, I am lost.

—APHRA BEHN (1640–1689)

First Death in Nova Scotia

In the cold, cold parlor
my mother laid out Arthur
beneath the chromographs:
Edward, Prince of Wales,
with Princess Alexandra,   5
and King George with Queen Mary.
Below them on the table
stood a stuffed loon
shot and stuffed by Uncle
Arthur, Arthur's father.   10

Since Uncle Arthur fired
a bullet into him,
he hadn't said a word.
He kept his own counsel
on his white, frozen lake,   15
the marble-topped table.
His breast was deep and white,
cold and caressable;
his eyes were red glass,
much to be desired.   20

"Come," said my mother,
"Come and say good-bye
to your little cousin Arthur."
I was lifted up and given
one lily of the valley   25
to put in Arthur's hand.
Arthur's coffin was
a little frosted cake,
and the red-eyed loon eyed it
from his white, frozen lake.   30

Arthur was very small.
He was all white, like a doll
that hadn't been painted yet.
Jack Frost had started to paint him
the way he always painted   35
the Maple Leaf (Forever).
He had just begun on his hair,
a few red strokes, and then
Jack Frost had dropped the brush
and left him white, forever.   40

The gracious royal couples
were warm in red and ermine;
their feet were well wrapped up
in the ladies' ermine trains.
They invited Arthur to be   45
the smallest page at court.
But how could Arthur go,
clutching his tiny lily,
with his eyes shut up so tight
and the roads deep in snow?   50

—ELIZABETH BISHOP (1911–1979)

Manners

for a Child of 1918

My grandfather said to me
as we sat on the wagon seat,

"Be sure to remember to always
speak to everyone you meet."

We met a stranger on foot.   5
My grandfather's whip tapped his hat.
"Good day, sir. Good day. A fine day."
And I said it and bowed where I sat.

Then we overtook a boy we knew
with his big pet crow on his shoulder.   10
"Always offer everyone a ride;
don't forget that when you get older,"

my grandfather said. So Willy
climbed up with us, but the crow
gave a "Caw!" and flew off. I was worried.   15
How would he know where to go?

But he flew a little way at a time
from fence post to fence post, ahead;
and when Willy whistled he answered.
"A fine bird," my grandfather said,   20

"and he's well brought up. See, he answers
nicely when he's spoken to.
Man or beast, that's good manners.
Be sure that you both always do."

When automobiles went by,   25
the dust hid the people's faces,
but we shouted "Good day! Good day!
Fine day!" at the top of our voices.

When we came to Hustler Hill,
he said that the mare was tired,   30
so we all got down and walked,
as our good manners required.

—ELIZABETH BISHOP (1911–1979)

Seascape

This celestial seascape, with white herons got up as angels,
flying as high as they want and as far as they want sidewise
in tiers and tiers of immaculate reflections;
the whole region, from the highest heron
down to the weightless mangrove island   5
with bright green leaves edged neatly with bird-droppings
like illumination in silver,
and down to the suggestively Gothic arches of the mangrove roots
and the beautiful pea-green back-pasture
where occasionally a fish jumps, like a wild-flower   10
in an ornamental spray of spray;
this cartoon by Raphael for a tapestry for a Pope:
it does look like heaven.
But a skeletal lighthouse standing there
in black and white clerical dress,   15
who lives on his nerves, thinks he knows better.
He thinks that hell rages below his iron feet,
that that is why the shallow water is so warm,
and he knows that heaven is not like this.
Heaven is not like flying or swimming,   20
but has something to do with blackness and a strong glare
and when it gets dark he will remember something
strongly worded to say on the subject.

—ELIZABETH BISHOP (1911–1979)

a song in the front yard

I've stayed in the front yard all my life.
I want a peek at the back
Where it's rough and untended and hungry weed grows.
A girl gets sick of a rose.

I want to go in the back yard now   5
And maybe down the alley,
To where the charity children play.
I want a good time today.

They do some wonderful things.
They have some wonderful fun.   10

My mother sneers, but I say it's fine
How they don't have to go in at quarter to nine.
My mother, she tells me that Johnnie Mae
Will grow up to be a bad woman.
That George'll be taken to Jail soon or late   15
(On account of last winter he sold our back gate).

But I say it's fine. Honest, I do.
And I'd like to be a bad woman, too,
And wear the brave stockings of night-black lace
And strut down the streets with paint on my face.   20

—GWENDOLYN BROOKS (1917–2000)

She Walks in Beauty

She walks in beauty, like the night
   Of cloudless climes and starry skies,
And all that's best of dark and bright
   Meet in her aspect and her eyes,
Thus mellowed to that tender light   5
   Which heaven to gaudy day denies.

One shade the more, one ray the less,
   Had half impaired the nameless grace
Which waves in every raven tress
   Or softly lightens o'er her face,   10
Where thoughts serenely sweet express
   How pure, how dear their dwelling-place.

And on that cheek and o'er that brow
   So soft, so calm, yet eloquent,
The smiles that win, the tints that glow,   15
   But tell of days in goodness spent,—
A mind at peace with all below,
   A heart whose love is innocent.

—GEORGE GORDON, LORD BYRON (1788–1824)

Witness

An ordinary evening in Wisconsin
seen from a Greyhound bus—mute aisles
of merchandise the sole inhabitants
of the half-darkened Five and Ten,

the tables of the single lit café awash   5
with unarticulated pathos, the surface membrane
of the inadvertently transparent instant
when no one is looking: outside town

the barns, their red gone dark with sundown,
withhold the shudder of a warped terrain—   10
the castle rocks above, tree-clogged ravines
already submarine with nightfall, flocks

(like dark sheep) of toehold junipers,
the lucent arms of birches: purity
without a mirror, other than a mind bound   15
elsewhere, to tell it how it looks

—AMY CLAMPITT (1920–1994)

good times

My Daddy has paid the rent
and the insurance man is gone
and the lights is back on
and my uncle Brud has hit
for one dollar straight   5
and they is good times
good times
good times

My Mama has made bread
and Grampaw has come   10
and everybody is drunk
and dancing in the kitchen
and singing in the kitchen
oh these is good times

good times   15
good times

oh children think about the
good times

—LUCILLE CLIFTON (1936–2010)

Mask

I tied a paper mask onto my face,
my lips almost inside its small red mouth.
Turning my head to the left, to the right,
I looked like someone I once knew, or was,
with straight white teeth and boyish bangs.   5
My ordinary life had come as far as it would,
like a silver arrow hitting cypress.
Know your place or you'll rue it, I sighed
to the mirror. To succeed, I'd done things
I hated; to be loved, I'd competed promiscuously: 10
my essence seemed to boil down to only this.
Then I saw my own hazel irises float up,
like eggs clinging to a water plant,
seamless and clear, in an empty, pondlike face.

—HENRI COLE (B. 1956)

My Weed

On the path to the water, I found an ugly weed
growing between rocks. The wind was stroking it,
saying, "My weed, my weed." Its solid,
hairy body rose up, with big silver leaves
that rubbed off on me, like sex. At first,   5
I thought it was a lamb's ear, but it wasn't.
I'm not a member of the ugly school,
but I circled around it and looked a lot,
which is to say, I was just being, and it seemed to me—
in a higher sense—to represent the sanity of living.   10

It was twilight. Planets were gathering.
"Mr. Weed," I said, "I'm competitive,
I'm afraid, I'm isolated, I'm bright.
Can you tell me how to survive?"

—HENRI COLE (B. 1956)

Kubla Khan

In Xanadu did Kubla Khan
A stately pleasure-dome decree:
Where Alph, the sacred river, ran
Through caverns measureless to man
    Down to a sunless sea.   5
So twice five miles of fertile ground
With walls and towers were girdled round:
And here were gardens bright with sinuous rills,
Where blossomed many an incense-bearing tree;
And here were forests ancient as the hills,   10
Enfolding sunny spots of greenery.

But oh! that deep romantic chasm which slanted
Down the green hill athwart a cedarn cover!
A savage place! as holy and enchanted
As e'er beneath a waning moon was haunted   15
By woman wailing for her demon-lover!
And from this chasm, with ceaseless turmoil seething,
As if this earth in fast thick pants were breathing,
A mighty fountain momently was forced:
Amid whose swift half-intermitted burst   20
Huge fragments vaulted like rebounding hail,
Or chaffy grain beneath the thresher's flail:
And 'mid these dancing rocks at once and ever
It flung up momently the sacred river.
Five miles meandering with a mazy motion   25
Through wood and dale the sacred river ran,
Then reached the caverns measureless to man,
And sank in tumult to a lifeless ocean:
And 'mid this tumult Kubla heard from far
Ancestral voices prophesying war!   30

    The shadow of the dome of pleasure
    Floated midway on the waves;

Where was heard the mingled measure
From the fountain and the caves.
It was a miracle of rare device,   35
A sunny pleasure-dome with caves of ice!

A damsel with a dulcimer
In a vision once I saw:
It was an Abyssinian maid,
And on her dulcimer she played,   40
Singing of Mount Abora.
Could I revive within me
Her symphony and song,
To such a deep delight, 'twould win me,
That with music loud and long,   45
I would build that dome in air,
That sunny dome! those caves of ice!
And all who heard should see them there,
And all should cry, Beware! Beware!
His flashing eyes, his floating hair!   50
Weave a circle round him thrice,
And close your eyes with holy dread,
For he on honey dew hath fed,
And drunk the milk of Paradise.

—SAMUEL TAYLOR COLERIDGE (1772–1834)

The Dead

The dead are always looking down on us, they say,
while we are putting on our shoes or making a sandwich,
they are looking down through the glass-bottom boats of heaven
as they row themselves slowly through eternity.

They watch the tops of our heads moving below on earth,   5
and when we lie down in a field or on a couch,
drugged perhaps by the hum of a warm afternoon,
they think we are looking back at them,

which makes them lift their oars and fall silent
and wait, like parents, for us to close our eyes.   10

—BILLY COLLINS (B. 1941)

The Golden Years

All I do these drawn-out days
is sit in my kitchen at Pheasant Ridge
where there are no pheasants to be seen
and last time I looked, no ridge.

I could drive over to Quail Falls   5
and spend the day there playing bridge,
but the lack of a falls and the absence of quail
would only remind me of Pheasant Ridge.

I know a widow at Fox Run
and another with a condo at Smokey Ledge.   10
One of them smokes, and neither can run,
so I'll stick to the pledge I made to Midge.

Who frightened the fox and bulldozed the ledge?
I ask in my kitchen at Pheasant Ridge.

—BILLY COLLINS (B. 1941)

The History Teacher

Trying to protect his students' innocence
he told them the Ice Age was really just
the Chilly Age, a period of a million years
when everyone had to wear sweaters.

And the Stone Age became the Gravel Age,   5
named after the long driveways of the time.

The Spanish Inquisition was nothing more
than an outbreak of questions such as
"How far is it from here to Madrid?"
"What do you call the matador's hat?"   10

The War of the Roses took place in a garden,
and the Enola Gay dropped one tiny atom
on Japan.

The children would leave his classroom
for the playground to torment the weak   15
and the smart,
mussing up their hair and breaking their glasses,

while he gathered up his notes and walked home
past flower beds and white picket fences,
wondering if they would believe that soldiers   20
in the Boer War told long, rambling stories
designed to make the enemy nod off.

—BILLY COLLINS (B. 1941)

Weighing the Dog

It is awkward for me and bewildering for him
as I hold him in my arms in the small bathroom,
balancing our weight on the shaky blue scale,

but this is the way to weigh a dog and easier
than training him to sit obediently on one spot   5
with his tongue out, waiting for the cookie.

With pencil and paper I subtract my weight
from our total to find out the remainder that is his,
and I start to wonder if there is an analogy here.

It could not have to do with my leaving you   10
though I never figured out what you amounted to
until I subtracted myself from our combination.

You held me in your arms more than I held you
through all those awkward and bewildering months
and now we are both lost in strange and distant
     neighborhoods.   15

—BILLY COLLINS (B. 1941)

War Is Kind

Do not weep, maiden, for war is kind.
Because your lover threw wild hands toward the sky
And the affrighted steed ran on alone,
Do not weep.
War is kind.   5

    Hoarse, booming drums of the regiment,
    Little souls who thirst for fight,
    These men were born to drill and die.
    The unexplained glory flies above them,
    Great is the battle god, great, and his kingdom   10
    A field where a thousand corpses lie.

Do not weep, babe, for war is kind.
Because your father tumbled in the yellow trenches,
Raged at his breast, gulped and died,
Do not weep.   15
War is kind.

    Swift blazing flag of the regiment,
    Eagle with crest of red and gold,
    These men were born to drill and die.
    Point for them the virtue of slaughter,   20
    Make plain for them the excellence of killing
    And a field where a thousand corpses lie.

Mother whose heart hung humble as a button
On the bright splendid shroud of your son,
Do not weep.   25
War is kind.

—STEPHEN CRANE (1871–1900)

Tableau

Locked arm in arm they cross the way
The black boy and the white,
The golden splendor of the day
The sable pride of night.

From lowered blinds the dark folk stare 5
And here the fair folk talk,
Indignant that these two should dare
In unison to walk.

Oblivious to look and word
They pass, and see no wonder 10
That lightning brilliant as a sword
Should blaze the path of thunder.

—COUNTEE CULLEN (1903–1946)

Yet Do I Marvel

I doubt not God is good, well-meaning, kind,
And did He stoop to quibble could tell why
The little buried mole continues blind,
Why flesh that mirrors Him must some day die,
Make plain the reason tortured Tantalus 5
Is baited by the fickle fruit, declare
If merely brute caprice dooms Sisyphus
To struggle up a never-ending stair.
Inscrutable His ways are, and immune
To catechism by a mind too strewn 10
With petty cares to slightly understand
What awful brain compels His awful hand.
Yet do I marvel at this curious thing:
To make a poet black, and bid him sing!

—COUNTEE CULLEN (1903–1946)

Buffalo Bill's defunct

Buffalo Bill's
defunct
         who used to
         ride a watersmooth-silver
                              stallion 5
and break onetwothreefourfive pigeonsjustlikethat
                                        Jesus

he was a handsome man

              and what i want to know is

how do you like your blueeyed boy
Mister Death   10

—e. e. cummings (1894–1962)

the Cambridge ladies who live in furnished souls

the Cambridge ladies who live in furnished souls
are unbeautiful and have comfortable minds
(also, with the church's protestant blessings
daughters, unscented shapeless spirited)
they believe in Christ and Longfellow, both dead,   5
are invariably interested in so many things—
at the present writing one still finds
delighted fingers knitting for the is it Poles?
perhaps. While permanent faces coyly bandy
scandal of Mrs. N and Professor D   10
. . . .the Cambridge ladies do not care, above
Cambridge if sometimes in its box of
sky lavender and cornerless, the
moon rattles like a fragment of angry candy

—e. e. cummings(1894–1962)

A Clock stopped

A Clock stopped—
Not the Mantel's—
Geneva's farthest skill
Can't put the puppet bowing—
That just now dangled still—   5

An awe came on the Trinket!
The Figures hunched, with pain—
Then quivered out of Decimals—
Into Degreeless Noon—

It will not stir for Doctors— 10
This Pendulum of snow—
This Shopman importunes it—
While cool—concernless No—

Nods from the Gilded pointers—
Nods from the Seconds slim— 15
Decades of Arrogance between
The Dial life—
And Him—

—EMILY DICKINSON (1830–1886)

"Faith" is a fine invention

"Faith" is a fine invention
When Gentlemen can *see*—
But *Microscopes* are prudent
In an Emergency.

—EMILY DICKINSON (1830–1886)

I died for Beauty—but was scarce

I died for Beauty—but was scarce
Adjusted in the Tomb
When One who died for Truth, was lain
In an adjoining Room—

He questioned softly "Why I failed"? 5
"For Beauty", I replied—
"And I—for Truth—Themself are One—
We Brethren, are", He said—

And so, as Kinsmen, met a Night—
We talked between the Rooms— 10
Until the Moss had reached our lips—
And covered up—our names—

—EMILY DICKINSON (1830–1886)

Song: Go and catch a falling star

Go and catch a falling star,
    Get with child a mandrake root,
Tell me where all past years are,
    Or who cleft the devil's foot,
Teach me to hear mermaids singing,   5
    Or to keep off envy's stinging,
        And find
        What wind
Serves to advance an honest mind.

If thou be'st born to strange sights,   10
    Things invisible to see,
Ride ten thousand days and nights,
    Till age snow white hairs on thee;
Thou, when thou return'st, wilt tell me
    All strange wonders that befell thee,   15
        And swear
        No where
Lives a woman true and fair.

If thou find'st one, let me know;
    Such a pilgrimage were sweet.   20
Yet do not; I would not go,
    Though at next door we might meet.
Though she were true when you met her,
    And last till you write your letter,
        Yet she   25
        Will be
False, ere I come, to two or three.

—JOHN DONNE (1572–1631)

(2) *mandrake:* supposed to resemble a human being because of its forked root.

The Apparition

When by thy scorn, O murderess, I am dead,
    And that thou thinkst thee free
From all solicitation from me,

Then shall my ghost come to thy bed,
And thee, feigned vestal, in worse arms shall see;   5
Then thy sick taper° will begin to wink,   candle
And he, whose thou art then, being tired before,
Will, if thou' stir, or pinch to wake him, think
    Thou call'st for more,
And in false sleep will from thee shrink.   10
And then, poor aspen wretch, neglected, thou,
Bathed in a cold quicksilver sweat, wilt lie
    A verier° ghost than I.   truer
What I will say, I will not tell thee now,
Lest that preserve thee; and since my love is spent,   15
I had rather thou shouldst painfully repent,
Than by my threatenings rest still innocent.

—JOHN DONNE (1572–1631)

The Good-Morrow

I wonder, by my troth, what thou and I
Did till we loved? were we not weaned till then,
But sucked on country pleasures childishly?
Or snorted we in the seven sleepers' den?
'Twas so; but this, all pleasures fancies be.   5
If ever any beauty I did see,
Which I desired, and got, 'twas but a dream of thee.

And now good-morrow to our waking souls,
Which watch not one another out of fear;
For love all love of other sights controls,   10
And makes one little room an everywhere.
Let sea-discoverers to new worlds have gone;
Let maps to other,° worlds on worlds have shown;   others
Let us possess one world; each hath one, and is one.

My face in thine eye, thine in mine appears,   15
And true plain hearts do in the faces rest;
Where can we find two better hemispheres
Without sharp north, without declining west?
Whatever dies was not mixed equally;

If our two loves be one, or thou and I   20
Love so alike that none can slacken, none can die.

—JOHN DONNE (1572–1631)

(4) *seven sleepers' den:* a cave where, according to Christian legend, seven youths escaped persecution
and slept for two centuries.

Pescadero

The little goats like my mouth and fingers,

and one stands up against the wire fence, and taps on the fence board
a hoof made blacker by the dirt of the field,

pushes her mouth forward to my mouth,
so that I can see the smallish squared seeds of her teeth,   5
and the bristle-whiskers,

and then she kisses me, though I know it doesn't mean "kiss,"

then leans her head way back, arcing her spine, goat yoga,
all pleasure and greeting and then good-natured indifference: she loves me,

she likes me a lot, she takes interest in me, she doesn't know me at all   10
or need to, having thus acknowledged me. Though I am all happiness,

since I have been welcomed by the field's small envoy, and the splayed hoof,
fragrant with soil, has rested on the fence board beside my hand.

—MARK DOTY (B. 1953)

Persephone, Falling

One narcissus among the ordinary beautiful
flowers, one unlike all the others! She pulled,
stooped to pull harder—
when, sprung out of the earth
on his glittering terrible   5
carriage, he claimed his due.

It is finished. No one heard her.
No one! She had strayed from the herd.

(Remember: go straight to school.
This is important, stop fooling around!   10
Don't answer to strangers. Stick
with your playmates. Keep your eyes down.)
This is how easily the pit
is waiting. This is how one foot sinks into the ground.

—RITA DOVE (B. 1952)

Sympathy

I know what the caged bird feels, alas!
 When the sun is bright on the upland slopes;
When the wind stirs soft through the springing grass,
And the river flows like a stream of glass;
 When the first bird sings and the first bud opes,   5
And the faint perfume from its chalice steals—
I know what the caged bird feels!

I know why the caged bird beats his wing
 Till its blood is red on the cruel bars;
For he must fly back to his perch and cling   10
When he fain would be on the bough a-swing;
 And a pain still throbs in the old, old scars
And they pulse again with a keener sting—
I know why he beats his wing!

I know why the caged bird sings, ah me,   15
 When his wing is bruised and his bosom sore;—
When he beats his bars and he would be free;
It is not a carol of joy or glee,
 But a prayer that he sends from his heart's deep core,
But a plea, that upward to Heaven he flings—   20
I know why the caged bird sings!

—PAUL LAURENCE DUNBAR (1872–1906)

I Sit and Sew

I sit and sew—a useless task it seems,
My hands grown tired, my head weighed down with dreams—
The panoply of war, the martial tred of men,
Grim-faced, stern-eyed, gazing beyond the ken
Of lesser souls, whose eyes have not seen Death,   5
Nor learned to hold their lives but as a breath—
But—I must sit and sew.

I sit and sew—my heart aches with desire—
That pageant terrible, that fiercely pouring fire
On wasted fields, and writhing grotesque things   10
Once men. My soul in pity flings
Appealing cries, yearning only to go
There in that holocaust of hell, those fields of woe—
But—I must sit and sew.

The little useless seam, the idle patch;   15
Why dream I here beneath my homely thatch,
When there they lie in sodden mud and rain,
Pitifully calling me, the quick ones and the slain?
You need me, Christ! It is no roseate dream
That beckons me—this pretty futile seam,   20
It stifles me—God, must I sit and sew?

—ALICE MOORE DUNBAR-NELSON (1875–1935)

Don't Do That

It was bring-your-own if you wanted anything
hard, so I brought Johnnie Walker Red
along with some resentment I'd held in
for a few weeks, which was not helped
by the sight of little nameless things   5
pierced with toothpicks on the tables,
or by talk that promised to be nothing
if not small. But I'd consented to come,
and I knew what part of the house
their animals would be sequestered,   10
whose company I loved. What else can I say,

except that old retainer of slights and wrongs,
that bad boy I hadn't quite outgrown—
I'd brought him along, too. I was out
to cultivate a mood. My hosts greeted me,   15
but did not ask about my soul, which was when
I was invited by Johnnie Walker Red
to find the right kind of glass, and pour.
I toasted the air. I said hello to the wall,
then walked past a group of women   20
dressed to be seen, undressing them
one by one, and went up the stairs to where

the Rottweilers were, Rosie and Tom,
and got down with them on all fours.
They licked the face I offered them,   25
and I proceeded to slick back my hair
with their saliva, and before long
I felt like a wild thing, ready to mess up
the party, scarf the hors d'œuvres.
But the dogs said, No, don't do that,   30
calm down, after awhile they open the door
and let you out, they pet your head, and everything
you might have held against them is gone,
and you're good friends again. Stay, they said.

—STEPHEN DUNN (B. 1939)

The Colonel

What you have heard is true. I was in his house. His wife carried a tray of
coffee and sugar. His daughter filed her nails, his son went out for the night.
There were daily papers, pet dogs, a pistol on the cushion beside him. The
moon swung bare on its black cord over the house. On the television was
a cop show. It was in English. Broken bottles were embedded in the walls
around the house to scoop the kneecaps from a man's legs or cut his hands
to lace. On the windows there were gratings like those in liquor stores. We
had dinner, rack of lamb, good wine, a gold bell was on the table for calling
the maid. The maid brought green mangoes, salt, a type of bread. I was
asked how I enjoyed the country. There was a brief commercial in Spanish.
His wife took everything away. There was some talk then of how difficult
it had become to govern. The parrot said hello on the terrace. The colonel
told it to shut up, and pushed himself from the table. My friend said to me

with his eyes: say nothing. The colonel returned with a sack used to bring groceries home. He spilled many human ears on the table. They were like dried peach halves. There is no other way to say this. He took one of them in his hands, shook it in our faces, dropped it into a water glass. It came alive there. I am tired of fooling around he said. As for the rights of anyone, tell your people they can go fuck themselves. He swept the ears to the floor with his arm and held the last of his wine in the air. Something for your poetry, no? he said. Some of the ears on the floor caught this scrap of his voice. Some of the ears on the floor were pressed to the ground.

May 1978

—CAROLYN FORCHÉ (B. 1950)

Birches

When I see birches bend to left and right
Across the lines of straighter darker trees,
I like to think some boy's been swinging them.
But swinging doesn't bend them down to stay
As ice-storms do. Often you must have seen them   5
Loaded with ice a sunny winter morning
After a rain. They click upon themselves
As the breeze rises, and turn many-colored
As the stir cracks and crazes their enamel.
Soon the sun's warmth makes them shed crystal shells   10
Shattering and avalanching on the snow-crust—
Such heaps of broken glass to sweep away
You'd think the inner dome of heaven had fallen.
They are dragged to the withered bracken by the load,
And they seem not to break; though once they are bowed   15
So low for long, they never right themselves:
You may see their trunks arching in the woods
Years afterwards, trailing their leaves on the ground
Like girls on hands and knees that throw their hair
Before them over their heads to dry in the sun.   20
But I was going to say when Truth broke in
With all her matter-of-fact about the ice-storm
I should prefer to have some boy bend them
As he went out and in to fetch the cows—
Some boy too far from town to learn baseball,   25
Whose only play was what he found himself,

Summer or winter, and could play alone.
One by one he subdued his father's trees
By riding them down over and over again
Until he took the stiffness out of them,   30
And not one but hung limp, not one was left
For him to conquer. He learned all there was
To learn about not launching out too soon
And so not carrying the tree away
Clear to the ground. He always kept his poise   35
To the top branches, climbing carefully
With the same pains you use to fill a cup
Up to the brim, and even above the brim.
Then he flung outward, feet first, with a swish,
Kicking his way down through the air to the ground.   40
So was I once myself a swinger of birches.
And so I dream of going back to be.
It's when I'm weary of considerations,
And life is too much like a pathless wood
Where your face burns and tickles with the cobwebs   45
Broken across it, and one eye is weeping
From a twig's having lashed across it open.
I'd like to get away from earth awhile
And then come back to it and begin over.
May no fate willfully misunderstand me   50
And half grant what I wish and snatch me away
Not to return. Earth's the right place for love:
I don't know where it's likely to go better.
I'd like to go by climbing a birch tree,
And climb black branches up a snow-white trunk   55
Toward heaven, till the tree could bear no more,
But dipped its top and set me down again.
That would be good both going and coming back.
One could do worse than be a swinger of birches.

—ROBERT FROST (1874–1963)

Mending Wall

Something there is that doesn't love a wall,
That sends the frozen-ground-swell under it,
And spills the upper boulders in the sun;
And makes gaps even two can pass abreast.

The work of hunters is another thing: 5
I have come after them and made repair
Where they have left not one stone on a stone,
But they would have the rabbit out of hiding,
To please the yelping dogs. The gaps I mean,
No one has seen them made or heard them made, 10
But at spring mending-time we find them there.
I let my neighbor know beyond the hill;
And on a day we meet to walk the line
And set the wall between us once again.
We keep the wall between us as we go. 15
To each the boulders that have fallen to each.
And some are loaves and some so nearly balls
We have to use a spell to make them balance:
"Stay where you are until our backs are turned!"
We wear our fingers rough with handling them. 20
Oh, just another kind of outdoor game,
One on a side. It comes to little more:
There where it is we do not need the wall:
He is all pine and I am apple orchard.
My apple trees will never get across 25
And eat the cones under his pines, I tell him.
He only says, "Good fences make good neighbors."
Spring is the mischief in me, and I wonder
If I could put a notion in his head:
"*Why* do they make good neighbors? Isn't it 30
Where there are cows? But here there are no cows.
Before I built a wall I'd ask to know
What I was walling in or walling out,
And to whom I was like to give offense.
Something there is that doesn't love a wall, 35
That wants it down." I could say "Elves" to him,
But it's not elves exactly, and I'd rather
He said it for himself. I see him there,
Bringing a stone grasped firmly by the top
In each hand, like an old-stone savage armed. 40
He moves in darkness as it seems to me,
Not of woods only and the shade of trees.
He will not go behind his father's saying,
And he likes having thought of it so well
He says again, "Good fences make good neighbors." 45

—ROBERT FROST (1874–1963)

A Supermarket in California

What thoughts I have of you tonight, Walt Whitman,
for I walked down the sidestreets under the trees with a
headache self-conscious looking at the full moon.

In my hungry fatigue, and shopping for images, I went into
the neon fruit supermarket, dreaming of your enumerations!   5

What peaches and what penumbras? Whole families
shopping at night! Aisles full of husbands! Wives in the
avocados, babies in the tomatoes!—and you, García Lorca,
what were you doing down by the watermelons?

I saw you, Walt Whitman, childless, lonely old grubber,   10
poking among the meats in the refrigerator and eyeing the
grocery boys.

I heard you asking questions of each: Who killed the
pork chops? What price bananas? Are you my Angel?

I wandered in and out of the brilliant stacks of cans
following you, and followed in my imagination by the store
detective.   15

We strode down the open corridors together in our
solitary fancy tasting artichokes, possessing every frozen
delicacy, and never passing the cashier.

Where are we going, Walt Whitman? The doors close in
an hour. Which way does your beard point tonight?   20

(I touch your book and dream of our odyssey in the
supermarket and feel absurd.)

Will we walk all night through solitary streets? The trees
add shade to shade, lights out in the houses, we'll both be
lonely.

Will we stroll dreaming of the lost America of love
past blue automobiles in driveways, home to our silent   25
cottage?

Ah, dear father, graybeard, lonely old courage-teacher,
what America did you have when Charon quit poling his
ferry and you got out on a smoking bank and stood watching
the boat disappear on the black waters of Lethe?   30

—ALLEN GINSBERG (1926–1997)

My Son, My Executioner

My son, my executioner,
    I take you in my arms,
Quiet and small and just astir
    And whom my body warms.

Sweet death, small son, our instrument   5
    Of immortality,
Your cries and hungers document
    Our bodily decay.

We twenty-five and twenty-two,
    Who seemed to live forever,   10
Observe enduring life in you
    And start to die together.

—DONALD HALL (B. 1928)

"Ah, Are You Digging on My Grave?"

"Ah, are you digging on my grave
    My loved one?—planting rue?"
—"No: yesterday he went to wed
One of the brightest wealth has bred.
'It cannot hurt her now,' he said,   5
    'That I should not be true.'"

"Then who is digging on my grave?
    My nearest dearest kin?"
—"Ah, no: they sit and think, 'What use!
'What good will planting flowers produce?   10
No tendance of her mound can loose
    Her spirit from Death's gin.'"°   snare

"But some one digs upon my grave?
    My enemy?—prodding sly?"
—"Nay: when she heard you had passed the Gate   15
That shuts on all flesh soon or late,
She thought you no more worth her hate,
    And cares not where you lie."

"Then, who is digging on my grave?
    Say—since I have not guessed!"   20
—"O it is I, my mistress dear,
Your little dog, who still lives near,
And much I hope my movements here
    Have not disturbed your rest?"

"Ah, yes! *You* dig upon my grave . . .   25
    Why flashed it not on me
That one true heart was left behind!
What feeling do we ever find
To equal among human kind
    A dog's fidelity!"   30

"Mistress, I dug upon your grave
    To bury a bone, in case
I should be hungry near this spot
When passing on my daily trot.
I am sorry, but I quite forgot   35
    It was your resting-place."

—THOMAS HARDY (1840–1928)

The Ruined Maid

"O 'Melia, my dear, this does everything crown!
Who could have supposed I should meet you in Town?°   London
And whence such fair garments, such prosperi-ty?"
"O didn't you know I'd been ruined?" said she.

"You left us in tatters, without shoes or socks,   5
Tired of digging potatoes, and spudding up docks;
And now you've gay bracelets and bright feathers three!"
"Yes: that's how we dress when we we're ruined," said she.

"At home in the barton you said 'thee' and 'thou,'
And 'thik oon,' and 'theäs oon,' and 't'other'; but now   10
Your talking quite fits 'ee for high compa-ny!"
"Some polish is gained with one's ruin," said she.

"Your hands were like paws then, your face blue and bleak
But now I'm bewitched by your delicate cheek,

And your little gloves fit as on any la-dy!"   15
"We never do work when we're ruined," said she.

"You used to call home-life a hag-ridden dream,
And you'd sigh, and you'd sock; but at present you seem
To know not of megrims or melancho-ly!"
"True. One's pretty lively when ruined," said she.   20

"I wish I had feathers, a fine sweeping gown,
And a delicate face, and could strut about Town!"
"My dear—a raw country girl, such as you be,
Cannot quite expect that. You ain't ruined," said she.

—THOMAS HARDY (1840–1928)

Follower

My father worked with a horse-plow,
His shoulders globed like a full sail strung
Between the shafts and the furrow.
The horses strained at his clicking tongue.

As expert. He would set the wing   5
And fit the bright steel-pointed sock.
The sod rolled over without breaking.
At the headrig, with a single pluck

Of reins, the sweating team turned round
And back into the land. His eye   10
Narrowed and angled at the ground,
Mapping the furrow exactly.

I stumbled in his hobnailed wake,
Fell sometimes on the polished sod;
Sometimes he rode me on his back   15
Dipping and rising to his plod.

I wanted to grow up and plow,
To close one eye, stiffen my arm.
All I ever did was follow
In his broad shadow round the farm.   20

I was a nuisance, tripping, falling,
Yapping always. But today
It is my father who keeps stumbling
Behind me, and will not go away.

—SEAMUS HEANEY (1939–2013)

Human Chain

Seeing the bags of meal passed hand to hand
In close-up by the aid workers, and soldiers
Firing over the mob, I was braced again

With a grip on two sack corners,
Two packed wads of grain I'd worked to lugs   5
To give me purchase, ready for the heave—

The eye-to-eye, one-two, one-two upswing
On to the trailer, then the stoop and drag and drain
Of the next lift. Nothing surpassed

That quick unburdening, backbreak's truest payback,   10
A letting go which will not come again.
Or it will, once. And for all.

—SEAMUS HEANEY (1939–2013)

The Skunk

Up, black, striped and damasked like the chasuble
At a funeral Mass, the skunk's tail
Paraded the skunk. Night after night
I expected her like a visitor.

The refrigerator whinnied into silence.   5
My desk light softened beyond the verandah.
Small oranges loomed in the orange tree.
I began to be tense as a voyeur.

After eleven years I was composing
Love-letters again, broaching the word 'wife'   10

Like a stored cask, as if its slender vowel
Had mutated into the night earth and air

Of California. The beautiful, useless
Tang of eucalyptus spelt your absence.
The aftermath of a mouthful of wine   15
Was like inhaling you off a cold pillow.

And there she was, the intent and glamorous,
Ordinary, mysterious skunk,
Mythologized, demythologized,
Snuffing the boards five feet beyond me.   20

It all came back to me last night, stirred
By the sootfall of your things at bedtime,
Your head-down, tail-up hunt in a bottom drawer
For the black plunge-line nightdress.

—SEAMUS HEANEY (1939–2013)

Love

Love bade me welcome; yet my soul drew back,
      Guilty of dust and sin.
But quick-eyed Love, observing me grow slack
      From my first entrance in,
Drew nearer to me, sweetly questioning   5
      If I lacked anything.

"A guest," I answered, "worthy to be here."
      Love said, "You shall be he."
"I, the unkind, ungrateful? Ah my dear,
      I cannot look on Thee."   10
Love took my hand, and smiling, did reply,
      "Who made the eyes but I?"

"Truth, Lord, but I have marred them; let my shame
      Go where it doth deserve."
"And know you not," says Love, "who bore the blame?"   15
      "My dear, then I will serve."
"You must sit down," says Love, "and taste my meat."
      So I did sit and eat.

—GEORGE HERBERT (1593–1633)

Terence, this is stupid stuff

"Terence, this is stupid stuff:
You eat your victuals fast enough;
There can't be much amiss, 'tis clear,
To see the rate you drink your beer.
But oh, good Lord, the verse you make,   5
It gives a chap the belly-ache.
The cow, the old cow, she is dead;
It sleeps well, the horned head:
We poor lads, 'tis our turn now
To hear such tunes as killed the cow.   10
Pretty friendship 'tis to rhyme
Your friends to death before their time
Moping melancholy mad:
Come, pipe a tune to dance to, lad."

Why, if 'tis dancing you would be,   15
There's brisker pipes than poetry.
Say, for what were hop-yards meant,
Or why was Burton built on Trent?
Oh many a peer of England brews
Livelier liquor than the Muse,   20
And malt does more than Milton can
To justify God's ways to man.
Ale, man, ale's the stuff to drink
For fellows whom it hurts to think:
Look into the pewter pot   25
To see the world as the world's not.
And faith, 'tis pleasant till 'tis past:
The mischief is that 'twill not last.
Oh I have been to Ludlow fair
And left my necktie God knows where,   30
And carried half-way home, or near,
Pints and quarts of Ludlow beer:
Then the world seemed none so bad,
And I myself a sterling lad;
And down in lovely muck I've lain,   35
Happy till I woke again.
Then I saw the morning sky:
Heigho, the tale was all a lie;
The world, it was the old world yet,

I was I, my things were wet,   40
And nothing now remained to do
But begin the game anew.

Therefore, since the world has still
Much good, but much less good than ill,
And while the sun and moon endure   45
Luck's a chance, but trouble's sure,
I'd face it as a wise man would,
And train for ill and not for good.
'Tis true, the stuff I bring for sale
Is not so brisk a brew as ale: 50
Out of a stem that scored the hand
I wrung it in a weary land.
But take it: if the smack is sour,
The better for the embittered hour;
It should do good to heart and head   55
When your soul is in my soul's stead;
And I will friend you, if I may,
In the dark and cloudy day.

There was a king reigned in the East:
There, when kings will sit to feast,   60
They get their fill before they think
With poisoned meat and poisoned drink.
He gathered all that springs to birth
From the many-venomed earth;
First a little, thence to more,   65
He sampled all her killing store;
And easy, smiling, seasoned sound,
Sate the king when healths went round.
They put arsenic in his meat
And stared aghast to watch him eat;   70
They poured strychnine in his cup
And shook to see him drink it up:
They shook, they stared as white's their shirt:
Them it was their poison hurt.
—I tell the tale that I heard told.   75
Mithridates, he died old.

—A. E. HOUSMAN (1859–1936)

To an Athlete Dying Young

The time you won your town the race
We chaired you through the market-place;
Man and boy stood cheering by,
And home we brought you shoulder-high.

Today, the road all runners come,   5
Shoulder-high, we bring you home,
And set you at your threshold down,
Townsman of a stiller town.

Smart lad, to slip betimes away
From fields where glory does not stay   10
And early though the laurel grows
It withers quicker than the rose.

Eyes the shady night has shut
Cannot see the record cut,
And silence sounds no worse than cheers   15
After earth has stopped the ears:

Now you will not swell the rout
Of lads that wore their honors out,
Runners whom renown outran
And the name died before the man.   20

So set, before its echoes fade,
The fleet foot on the sill of shade,
And hold to the low lintel up
The still-defended challenge-cup.

And round that early-laureled head   25
Will flock to gaze the strengthless dead,
And find unwithered on its curls
The garland briefer than a girl's.

—A. E. HOUSMAN (1859–1936)

Aunt Sue's Stories

Aunt Sue has a head full of stories.
Aunt Sue has a whole heart full of stories.
Summer nights on the front porch
Aunt Sue cuddles a brown-faced child to her bosom
And tells him stories.   5

Black slaves
Working in the hot sun,
And black slaves
Walking in the dewy night,
And black slaves   10
Singing sorrow songs on the banks of a mighty river
Mingle themselves softly
In the flow of old Aunt Sue's voice,
Mingle themselves softly
In the dark shadows that cross and recross   15
Aunt Sue's stories.

And the dark-faced child, listening,
Knows that Aunt Sue's stories are real stories.
He knows that Aunt Sue
Never got her stories out of any book at all,   20
But that they came
Right out of her own life.

And the dark-faced child is quiet
Of a summer night
Listening to Aunt Sue's stories.   25

—LANGSTON HUGHES (1902–1967)

Mother to Son

Well, son, I'll tell you:
Life for me ain't been no crystal stair.
It's had tacks in it,
And splinters,
And boards torn up,   5

And places with no carpet on the floor—
Bare.
But all the time
I'se been a-climbin' on,
And reachin' landin's,   10
And turnin' corners,
And sometimes goin' in the dark
Where there ain't been no light.
So boy, don't you turn back.
Don't you set down on the steps   15
'Cause you finds it's kinder hard.
Don't you fall now—
For I'se still goin', honey,
I'se still climbin',
And life for me ain't been no crystal stair.   20

—LANGSTON HUGHES (1902–1967)

Negro Servant

All day subdued, polite,
Kind, thoughtful to the faces that are white.
    O, tribal dance!
    O, drums!
    O, veldt at night!   5
Forgotten watch-fires on a hill somewhere!
    O, songs that do not care!
At six o'clock, or seven, or eight,
    You're through.
    You've worked all day.   10
    Dark Harlem waits for you.
    The bus, the sub—
    Pay-nights a taxi
    Through the park.
O, drums of life in Harlem after dark!   15
    O, dreams!
    O, songs!
    O, saxophones at night!
O, sweet relief from faces that are white!

—LANGSTON HUGHES (1902–1967)

Theme for English B

The instructor said,

> *Go home, and write*
> *a page tonight.*
> *And let that page come out of you—*
> *Then, it will be true.*   5

I wonder if it's that simple?
I am twenty-two, colored, born in Winston-Salem.
I went to school there, then Durham, then here
to this college on the hill above Harlem.
I am the only colored student in my class.   10
The steps from the hill lead down into Harlem,
through a park, then I cross St. Nicholas,
Eighth Avenue, Seventh, and I come to the Y,
the Harlem Branch Y, where I take the elevator
up to my room, sit down, and write this page: 15

It's not easy to know what is true for you or me
at twenty-two, my age. But I guess I'm what
I feel and see and hear, Harlem, I hear you:
hear you, hear me—we two—you, me, talk on this page.
(I hear New York, too.) Me—who?   20
Well, I like to eat, sleep, drink, and be in love.
I like to work, read, learn, and understand life.
I like a pipe for a Christmas present,
or records—Bessie, bop, or Bach.
I guess being colored doesn't make me *not* like   25
the same things other folks like who are other races.
So will my page be colored that I write?
Being me, it will not be white.
But it will be
a part of you, instructor.   30
You are white—
yet a part of me, as I am a part of you.
That's American.
Sometimes perhaps you don't want to be a part of me.
Nor do I often want to be a part of you.   35
But we are, that's true!

As I learn from you,
I guess you learn from me—
although you're older—and white—
and somewhat more free.   40

This is my page for English B.

—LANGSTON HUGHES (1902–1967)

(24) Bessie Smith: African American blues singer (1898?–1937).

The Death of the Ball Turret Gunner

From my mother's sleep I fell into the State,
And I hunched in its belly till my wet fur froze.
Six miles from earth, loosed from its dream of life,
I woke to black flak and the nightmare fighters.
When I died they washed me out of the turret with a hose.   5

—RANDALL JARRELL (1914–1965)

(Title) *Ball Turret:* the poet wrote, "A ball turret was a plexiglass sphere set into the belly of a B-17 or B-24 [bomber during World War II], and inhabited by two .50 caliber machine-guns and one man, a short small man. When this gunner tracked with his machine-guns a fighter [plane] attacking from below, he revolved with the turret; hunched in his little sphere, he looked like the fetus in the womb."

To Celia

Drink to me only with thine eyes,
    And I will pledge with mine;
Or leave a kiss but in the cup,
    And I'll not ask for wine.
The thirst that from the soul doth rise   5
    Doth ask a drink divine;
But might I of Jove's nectar sup,
    I would not change for thine.

I sent thee late a rosy wreath,
    Not so much honoring thee   10
As giving it a hope that there
    It could not withered be.

But thou thereon didst only breathe,
    And sent'st it back to me;
Since when it grows, and smells, I swear,   15
    Not of itself but thee.

—BEN JONSON (1572–1637)

La Belle Dame sans Merci

A Ballad

O, what can ail thee, knight-at-arms,
    Alone and palely loitering?
The sedge has withered from the lake,
    And no birds sing.

O, what can ail thee, knight-at-arms,   5
    So haggard and so woe-begone?
The squirrel's granary is full,
    And the harvest's done.

I see a lily on thy brow,
    With anguish moist and fever dew;   10
And on thy cheeks a fading rose
    Fast withereth too.

I met a lady in the meads,
    Full beautiful—a faery's child,
Her hair was long, her foot was light,   15
    And her eyes were wild.

I made a garland for her head,
    And bracelets too, and fragrant zone;
She looked at me as she did love,
    And made sweet moan.   20

I set her on my pacing steed,
    And nothing else saw all day long;
For sidelong would she bend, and sing
    A faery's song.

She found me roots of relish sweet,
    And honey wild, and manna dew,   25

And sure in language strange she said—
   "I love thee true."

She took me to her elfin grot,
   And there she wept and sighed full sore,   30
And there I shut her wild wild eyes
   With kisses four.

And there she lullèd me asleep
   And there I dreamed—Ah! woe betide!
The latest dream I ever dreamed   35
   On the cold hill side.

I saw pale kings and princes too,
   Pale warriors, death-pale were they all;
They cried—"La Belle Dame sans Merci
   Hath thee in thrall!"   40

I saw their starved lips in the gloam
   With horrid warning gapèd wide,
And I awoke and found me here
   On the cold hill's side.

And this is why I sojourn here   45
   Alone and palely loitering,
Though the sedge has withered from the lake,
   And no birds sing.

—JOHN KEATS (1795–1821)

The title means "The beautiful lady without pity."

Ode to a Nightingale

My heart aches, and a drowsy numbness pains
   My sense, as though of hemlock° I had drunk,   a poison
Or emptied some dull opiate to the drains
   One minute past, and Lethe-wards had sunk:
'Tis not through envy of thy happy lot,   5
   But being too happy in thine happiness,—
      That thou, light-wingèd Dryad° of the trees,   wood nymph
         In some melodious plot

Of beechen green, and shadows numberless,
    Singest of summer in full-throated ease.   10

O for a draught of vintage! that hath been
    Cooled a long age in the deep-delved earth,
Tasting of Flora° and the country green,   goddess of flowers
    Dance, and Provençal song, and sunburnt mirth!
O for a beaker full of the warm South,   15
    Full of the true, the blushful Hippocrene,
        With beaded bubbles winking at the brim,
           And purple-stainèd mouth;
        That I might drink, and leave the world unseen,
        And with thee fade away into the forest dim: 20

Fade far away, dissolve, and quite forget
    What thou among the leaves hast never known,
The weariness, the fever, and the fret
    Here, where men sit and hear each other groan;
Where palsy shakes a few, sad, last gray hairs,   25
    Where youth grows pale, and specter-thin, and dies,
        Where but to think is to be full of sorrow
           And leaden-eyed despairs,
        Where Beauty cannot keep her lustrous eyes,
        Or new Love pine at them beyond tomorrow.   30

Away! away! for I will fly to thee,
    Not charioted by Bacchus and his pards,
But on the viewless° wings of Poesy,   invisible
    Though the dull brain perplexes and retards:
Already with thee! tender is the night,   35
    And haply the Queen-Moon is on her throne,
        Clustered around by all her starry Fays;
           But here there is no light,
        Save what from heaven is with the breezes blown
        Through verdurous glooms and winding mossy ways.   40

I cannot see what flowers are at my feet,
    Nor what soft incense hangs upon the boughs,
But, in embalmèd° darkness, guess each sweet   perfumed
    Wherewith the seasonable month endows
The grass, the thicket, and the fruit-tree wild;   45
    White hawthorn, and the pastoral eglantine;

Fast fading violets covered up in leaves;
   And mid-May's eldest child,
The coming musk-rose, full of dewy wine,
   The murmurous haunt of flies on summer eves.   50

Darkling° I listen; and, for many a time   in darkness
   I have been half in love with easeful Death,
Called him soft names in many a musèd rhyme,
   To take into the air my quiet breath;
Now more than ever seems it rich to die,   55
   To cease upon the midnight with no pain,
      While thou art pouring forth thy soul abroad
         In such an ecstasy!
   Still wouldst thou sing, and I have ears in vain—
      To thy high requiem become a sod.   60

Thou wast not born for death, immortal Bird!
   No hungry generations tread thee down;
The voice I hear this passing night was heard
   In ancient days by emperor and clown:
Perhaps the self-same song that found a path   65
   Through the sad heart of Ruth, when, sick for home,
      She stood in tears amid the alien corn;
         The same that oft-times hath
   Charmed magic casements, opening on the foam
      Of perilous seas, in faery lands forlorn.   70

Forlorn! the very word is like a bell
   To toll me back from thee to my sole self!
Adieu! the fancy cannot cheat so well
   As she is famed to do, deceiving elf.
Adieu! adieu! thy plaintive anthem fades   75
   Past the near meadows, over the still stream,
      Up the hill-side; and now 'tis buried deep
         In the next valley-glades:
   Was it a vision, or a waking dream?
      Fled is that music:—Do I wake or sleep?   80

—JOHN KEATS (1795–1821)

(4) *Lethe:* river of forgetfulness in the Greek underworld. (14) *Provençal:* Provence, a wine-growing region in southern France famous, in the Middle Ages, for troubadours. (16) *Hippocrene:* fountain of the Muses on Mt. Helicon in Greece. (32) *Bacchus . . . pards:* Bacchus, god of wine, had a chariot drawn by leopards. (66) *Ruth:* see Bible, Ruth 2.

This living hand

This living hand, now warm and capable
Of earnest grasping, would, if it were cold
And in the icy silence of the tomb,
So haunt thy days and chill thy dreaming nights
That thou wouldst wish thine own heart dry of blood   5
So in my veins red life might stream again,
And thou be conscience-calmed—see here it is—
I hold it towards you.

—JOHN KEATS (1795–1821)

After Making Love We Hear Footsteps

For I can snore like a bullhorn
or play loud music
or sit up talking with any reasonably sober Irishman
and Fergus will only sink deeper
into his dreamless sleep, which goes by all in one flash,   5
but let there be that heavy breathing
or a stifled come-cry anywhere in the house
and he will wrench himself awake
and make for it on the run—as now, we lie together,
after making love, quiet, touching along the length of our bodies,   10
familiar touch of the long-married,
and he appears—in his baseball pajamas, it happens,
the neck opening so small he has to screw them on—
and flops down between us and hugs us and snuggles himself to
    sleep,
his face gleaming with satisfaction at being this very child.   15

In the half darkness we look at each other
and smile
and touch arms across this little, startlingly muscled body—
this one whom habit of memory propels to the ground of his making,
sleeper only the mortal sounds can sing awake,   20
this blessing love gives again into our arms.

—GALWAY KINNELL (B. 1927)

Facing It

My black face fades,
hiding inside the black granite.
I said I wouldn't
dammit: No tears.
I'm stone. I'm flesh.   5
My clouded reflection eyes me
like a bird of prey, the profile of night
slanted against morning. I turn
this way—the stone lets me go.
I turn that way—I'm inside   10
the Vietnam Veterans Memorial
again, depending on the light
to make a difference.
I go down the 58,022 names,
half-expecting to find   15
my own in letters like smoke.
I touch the name Andrew Johnson;
I see the booby trap's white flash.
Names shimmer on a woman's blouse
but when she walks away   20
the names stay on the wall.
Brushstrokes flash, a red bird's
wings cutting across my stare.
The sky. A plane in the sky.
A white vet's image floats   25
closer to me, then his pale eyes
look through mine. I'm a window.
He's lost his right arm
inside the stone. In the black mirror
a woman's trying to erase names: 30
No, she's brushing a boy's hair.

—YUSEF KOMUNYAKAA (B. 1947)

The Portrait

My mother never forgave my father
for killing himself,
especially at such an awkward time
and in a public park,

that spring 5
when I was waiting to be born.
She locked his name
in her deepest cabinet
and would not let him out,
though I could hear him thumping. 10
When I came down from the attic
with the pastel portrait in my hand
of a long-lipped stranger
with a brave moustache
and deep brown level eyes, 15
she ripped it into shreds
without a single word
and slapped me hard.
In my sixty-fourth year
I can feel my cheek 20
still burning.

—STANLEY KUNITZ (1905–2006)

Aubade

I work all day, and get half drunk at night.
Waking at four to soundless dark, I stare.
In time the curtain-edges will grow light.
Till then I see what's really always there:
Unresting death, a whole day nearer now, 5
Making all thought impossible but how
And where and when I shall myself die.
Arid interrogation: yet the dread
Of dying, and being dead,
Flashes afresh to hold and horrify. 10

The mind blanks at the glare. Not in remorse
—The good not done, the love not given, time
Torn off unused—nor wretchedly because
An only life can take so long to climb
Clear of its wrong beginnings, and may never; 15
But at the total emptiness for ever,
The sure extinction that we travel to

And shall be lost in always. Not to be here,
Not to be anywhere,
And soon; nothing more terrible, nothing more true.   20

This is a special way of being afraid
No trick dispels. Religion used to try,
That vast moth-eaten musical brocade
Created to pretend we never die,
And specious stuff that says *No rational being*   25
Can fear a thing it will not feel, not seeing
That this is what we fear—no sight, no sound,
No touch or taste or smell, nothing to think with,
Nothing to love or link with,
The anaesthetic from which none come round.   30

And so it stays just on the edge of vision,
A small unfocused blur, a standing chill
That slows each impulse down to indecision.
Most things may never happen: this one will,
And realization of it rages out   35
In furnace-fear when we are caught without
People or drink. Courage is no good:
It means not scaring others. Being brave
Lets no one off the grave.
Death is no different whined at than withstood.   40

Slowly light strengthens, and the room takes shape.
It stands plain as a wardrobe, what we know,
Have always known, know that we can't escape,
Yet can't accept. One side will have to go.
Meanwhile telephones crouch, getting ready to ring   45
In locked-up offices, and all the uncaring
Intricate rented world begins to rouse.
The sky is white as clay, with no sun.
Work has to be done.
Postmen like doctors go from house to house.   50

—PHILIP LARKIN (1922–1985)

Bald Sentiment

Older children grown and gone, one daughter
Remains at home. Her potions line the rim
Of the upstairs tub; small vials containing mixtures
Of baffling application. Or so it seems
To him. Exotic teas and leaves and herbs.   5
He steps into the shower to wash his hair.
A grayish bar of soap will have to serve.
He doesn't object. It's vanished into air,
His hair—or rather water; it clots the drain.
Farewell, old locks, he declaims, you who have given   10
Not a moment's pleasure. (O adolescent pain!)
Tart pleasure harrows him as he scents his turbaned
Teenage girl, with all her creams and balms—
The sorry, baffled gladness of affection

Mixed with her father's feckless fool intention   15
To keep his child forever clean of harm.

—SYDNEY LEA (B. 1942)

Black Mother Woman

I cannot recall you gentle
yet through your heavy love
I have become
an image of your once delicate flesh
split with deceitful longings.   5

When strangers come and compliment me
your aged spirit takes a bow
jingling with pride
but once you hid that secret
in the center of furies   10
hanging me
with deep breasts and wiry hair
with your own split flesh
and long suffering eyes
buried in myths of little worth.   15

But I have peeled away your anger
down to the core of love
and look mother
I Am
a dark temple where your true spirit rises   20
beautiful
and tough as chestnut
stanchion against your nightmare of weakness
and if my eyes conceal
a squadron of conflicting rebellions   25
I learned from you
to define myself
through your denials.

—AUDRE LORDE (1934–1992)

Ars Poetica

A poem should be palpable and mute
As a globed fruit,

Dumb
As old medallions to the thumb,

Silent as the sleeve-worn stone   5
Of casement ledges where the moss has grown—

A poem should be wordless
As the flight of birds.

                    *

A poem should be motionless in time
As the moon climbs,   10

Leaving, as the moon releases
Twig by twig the night-entangled trees,

Leaving, as the moon behind the winter leaves,
Memory by memory the mind—

A poem should be motionless in time   15
As the moon climbs.

*

A poem should be equal to:
Not true.

For all the history of grief
An empty doorway and a maple leaf.   20

For love
The leaning grasses and two lights above the sea—

A poem should not mean
But be.

—ARCHIBALD MACLEISH (1892–1982)

The Passionate Shepherd to His Love

Come live with me and be my Love,
And we will all the pleasures prove
That hills and valleys, dales and fields,
Or woods or steepy mountain yields.

And we will sit upon the rocks,   5
And see the shepherds feed their flocks
By shallow rivers, to whose falls
Melodious birds sing madrigals.

And I will make thee beds of roses
And a thousand fragrant posies;   10
A cap of flowers, and a kirtle
Embroider'd all with leaves of myrtle.

A gown made of the finest wool
Which from our pretty lambs we pull;
Fair-linèd slippers for the cold,   15
With buckles of the purest gold.

A belt of straw and ivy-buds
With coral clasps and amber studs:
And if these pleasures may thee move,
Come live with me and be my Love.   20

The shepherd swains shall dance and sing
For thy delight each May morning:
If these delights thy mind may move,
Then live with me and be my Love.

—CHRISTOPHER MARLOWE (1564–1593)

Stroke

The starry night will still look good in black,
but the arteries will thicken with luck,
the noon sky will darken in the lake,
the crow will drop the nickel from its beak,

the graveyard will crack its hilarious book,   5
the sun will feel cool on the farmer's neck,
the talkers will capsize in the little creek,
the rock star will step on his rake,

and the kitten will rip through the croker sack,
and the crucifix will throw off its yoke,   10
and the hospital will be beautiful with shock,
and the lame joke will work,

and the ghost, at last, will let go of the wreck,
and God will pick up that rock.

—JUDSON MITCHAM (B. 1948)

Silence

My father used to say,
"Superior people never make long visits,
have to be shown Longfellow's grave
or the glass flowers at Harvard.
Self-reliant like the cat—   5

that takes its prey to privacy,
the mouse's limp tail hanging like a shoelace from its mouth—
they sometimes enjoy solitude
and can be robbed of speech
by speech which has delighted them.   10
The deepest feeling always shows itself in silence;
not in silence, but restraint."
Nor was he insincere in saying, "Make my house your inn."
Inns are not residences.

—MARIANNE MOORE (1887–1972)

Immigrants

wrap their babies in the American flag,
feed them mashed hot dogs and apple pie,
name them Bill and Daisy,
buy them blonde dolls that blink blue
eyes or a football and tiny cleats   5
before the baby can even walk,
speak to them in thick English,
        hallo, babee, hallo.
whisper in Spanish or Polish
when the babies sleep, whisper   10
in a dark parent bed, that dark
parent fear, "Will they like
our boy, our girl, our fine american
boy, our fine american girl?"

—PAT MORA (B. 1942)

Apartment Living

So those despotic loves have become known to you,
rubbing cold hands up your thighs, leaving oily trails,
whispering, *Just how you like it, right?*
Upstairs the sorority girls are playing charades
again, smoking cigarettes, wearing shifts, burning   5
pain into their synapses.
Life is a needle. And now it pricks you:
the silver light in which you realize
your attempts at decadence

tire the earth and tire you. The etymology   10
of "flag" as in "to signal to stop"
is unknown. It is time to sit and watch. Don't
call that one again, he's pitiless in his self-certainty.
You used to be so.
You laid your black dress on the bed.   15
You stepped in your heels over sidewalk cracks.
You licked mint and sugar from the cocktail mixer,
singing nonsense songs,
and the strangers, they sang along.

—MEGHAN O'ROURKE (B. 1976)

Undefeated Heavyweight, 20 Years Old

I

Never been hurt! never
knocked down! or staggered or
stunned or made to know there's a blow
to kill not his own!—therefore the soul
glittering like jewels worn   5
on the outside of the body.

II

A boy with a death's-head mask dealing hurt
in an arc of six short inches. Unlike ours
his flesh recalls its godhead, if dimly. Unlike
us he knows he will live forever.   10

The walloping sounds of his body blows are iron
striking bone.
The joy he promises is of a fist breaking bone.
For whose soul is so bright, so burnished,
so naked in display?   15

All insult, says this death's-head—ancient, tribal,
last week's on the street—is redeemed in the taste
of another's blood.

You don't know. But you know.

—JOYCE CAROL OATES (B. 1938)

I Go Back to May 1937

I see them standing at the formal gates of their colleges,
I see my father strolling out
under the ochre sandstone arch, the
red tiles glinting like bent
plates of blood behind his head, I   5
see my mother with a few light books at her hip
standing at the pillar made of tiny bricks with the
wrought-iron gate still open behind her, its
sword-tips black in the May air,
they are about to graduate, they are about to get married,   10
they are kids, they are dumb, all they know is they are
innocent, they would never hurt anybody.
I want to go up to them and say Stop,
don't do it—she's the wrong woman,
he's the wrong man, you are going to do things   15
you cannot imagine you would ever do,
you are going to do bad things to children,
you are going to suffer in ways you never heard of,
you are going to want to die. I want to go
up to them there in the late May sunlight and say it,   20
her hungry pretty blank face turning to me,
her pitiful beautiful untouched body,
his arrogant handsome blind face turning to me,
his pitiful beautiful untouched body,
but I don't do it. I want to live. I   25
take them up like the male and female
paper dolls and bang them together
at the hips like chips of flint as if to
strike sparks from them, I say
Do what you are going to do, and I will tell about it.   30

—SHARON OLDS (B. 1942)

The Planned Child

I hated the fact that they had planned me, she had taken
a cardboard out of his shirt from the laundry
as if sliding the backbone up out of his body,
and made a chart of the month and put
her temperature on it, rising and falling,   5

to know the day to make me—I would have
liked to have been conceived in heat,
in haste, by mistake, in love, in sex,
not on cardboard, the little x on the
rising line that did not fall again.   10

But when a friend was pouring wine
and said that I seem to have been a child who had been wanted,
I took the wine against my lips
as if my mouth were moving along
that valved wall in my mother's body, she was   15
bearing down, and then breathing from the mask, and then
bearing down, pressing me out into
the world that was not enough for her without me in it,
not the moon, the sun, Orion
cartwheeling across the dark, nor   20
the earth, the sea—none of it
was enough, for her, without me.

SHARON OLDS (B. 1942)

The Victims

When Mother divorced you, we were glad. She took it and
took it, in silence, all those years and then
kicked you out, suddenly, and her
kids loved it. Then you were fired, and we
grinned inside, the way people grinned when   5
Nixon's helicopter lifted off the South
Lawn for the last time. We were tickled
to think of your office taken away,
your secretaries taken away,
your luncheons with three double bourbons,   10
your pencils, your reams of paper. Would they take your
suits back, too, those dark
carcasses hung in your closet, and the black
noses of your shoes with their large pores?
She had taught us to take it, to hate you and take it   15
until we pricked with her for your
annihilation, Father. Now I
pass the bums in doorways, the white
slugs of their bodies gleaming through slits in their

suits of compressed silt, the stained   20
flippers of their hands, the underwater
fire of their eyes, ships gone down with the
lanterns lit, and I wonder who took it and
took it from them in silence until they had
given it all away and had nothing   25
left but this.

—SHARON OLDS (B. 1942)

The Black Snake

When the black snake
flashed onto the morning road,
and the truck could not swerve—
death, that is how it happens.

Now he lies looped and useless   5
as an old bicycle tire.
I stop the car
and carry him into the bushes.

He is as cool and gleaming
as a braided whip, he is as beautiful and quiet   10
as a dead brother.
I leave him under the leaves

and drive on, thinking
about *death,* its suddenness,
its terrible weight,   15
its certain coming. Yet under

reason burns a brighter fire, which the bones
have always preferred.
It is the story of endless good fortune.
It says to oblivion: not me!   20

It is the light at the center of every cell.
It is what sent the snake coiling and flowing forward
happily all spring through the green leaves before
he came to the road.

—MARY OLIVER (B. 1935)

Résumé

Razors pain you;
Rivers are damp;
Acids stain you;
And drugs cause cramp.
Guns aren't lawful;   5
Nooses give;
Gas smells awful;
You might as well live.

—DOROTHY PARKER (1893–1967)

The Burglary

They stole my mother's silver,
melting it down, perhaps,

into pure mineral, worth
only its own weight.

We must eat with our hands now,   5
grab for food

in this new place of greed,
our table set

only with memories, tarnishing
even as we speak: 10

my mother holding a shining ladle
in her hand,

serving the broth
to children who will forget

to polish her silver, forget even   15
to lock the house.

While forks and spoons are divided
from all purpose,

patterns are lost like friezes
after centuries of rain,   20

and every knife is robbed
of its cutting edge.

                                                    —LINDA PASTAN (B. 1932)

Moth

Matthew 6:19

Come bumble-footed ones,
dust squigglers, furry ripplers,

inchers and squirmers
humble in gray and brown,

find out our secret places,   5
devour our hearts,

measure us, geometer, with your curved teeth!
Leaves lick at the window, clouds

stream away,
yet we lie here,   10

perfect,
locked in our dark chambers

when we could rise in you
brief, splendid

twenty-plume, gold   15
spotted ghost, pink scavenger,

luna whose pale-green wings
glow with moons and planets

at one with the burning world
whose one desire is to escape itself.   20

                                                    —KATHA POLLITT (B. 1949)

Salutation

O generation of the thoroughly smug
   and thoroughly uncomfortable,
I have seen fishermen picnicking in the sun,
I have seen them with untidy families,
I have seen their smiles full of teeth   5
   and heard ungainly laughter.
And I am happier than you are,
And they were happier than I am;
And the fish swim in the lake
   and do not even own clothing.   10

—EZRA POUND (1885–1972)

Poetry: I

Someone at a table under a brown metal lamp
is studying the history of poetry.
Someone in the library at closing-time
has learned to say *modernism,*
trope, vatic, text.   5
She is listening for shreds of music.
He is searching for his name
back in the old country.
They cannot learn without teachers.
They are like us   what we were   10
if you remember.

In a corner of night a voice
is crying in a kind of whisper:
More!

Can you remember?   when we thought   15
the poets taught   how to live?
That is not the voice of a critic
nor a common reader
it is someone young   in anger
hardly knowing what to ask   20
who finds our lines   our glosses
wanting   in this world.

—ADRIENNE RICH (1929–2012)

Richard Cory

Whenever Richard Cory went down town,
We people on the pavement looked at him:
He was a gentleman from sole to crown,
Clean favored, and imperially slim.

And he was always quietly arrayed,   5
And he was always human when he talked;
But still he fluttered pulses when he said,
"Good-morning," and he glittered when he walked.

And he was rich—yes, richer than a king—
And admirably schooled in every grace: 10
In fine, we thought that he was everything
To make us wish that we were in his place.

So on we worked, and waited for the light,
And went without the meat, and cursed the bread;
And Richard Cory, one calm summer night,   15
Went home and put a bullet through his head.

—EDWIN ARLINGTON ROBINSON (1869–1935)

I knew a woman

I knew a woman, lovely in her bones,
When small birds sighed, she would sigh back at them;
Ah, when she moved, she moved more ways than one:
The shapes a bright container can contain!
Of her choice virtues only gods should speak,   5
Or English poets who grew up on Greek
(I'd have them sing in chorus, cheek to cheek).

How well her wishes went! She stroked my chin,
She taught me Turn, and Counter-turn, and Stand;
She taught me Touch, that undulant white skin;   10
I nibbled meekly from her proffered hand;
She was the sickle; I, poor I, the rake,
Coming behind her for her pretty sake
(But what prodigious mowing we did make).

Love likes a gander, and adores a goose: 15
Her full lips pursed, the errant note to seize;
She played it quick, she played it light and loose;
My eyes, they dazzled at her flowing knees;
Her several parts could keep a pure repose,
Or one hip quiver with a mobile nose   20
(She moved in circles, and those circles moved).

Let seed be grass, and grass turn into hay:
I'm martyr to a motion not my own;
What's freedom for? To know eternity.
I swear she cast a shadow white as stone.   25
But who would count eternity in days?
These old bones live to learn her wanton ways:
(I measure time by how a body sways).

—THEODORE ROETHKE (1908–1963)

My Papa's Waltz

The whiskey on your breath
Could make a small boy dizzy;
But I hung on like death:
Such waltzing was not easy.

We romped until the pans   5
Slid from the kitchen shelf;
My mother's countenance
Could not unfrown itself.

The hand that held my wrist
Was battered on one knuckle;   10
At every step you missed
My right ear scraped a buckle.

You beat time on my head
With a palm caked hard by dirt,
Then waltzed me off to bed   15
Still clinging to your shirt.

—THEODORE ROETHKE (1908–1963)

Song

When I am dead, my dearest,
    Sing no sad songs for me;
Plant thou no roses at my head,
    Nor shady cypress tree;
Be the green grass above me   5
    With showers and dewdrops wet;
And if thou wilt, remember,
    And if thou wilt, forget.

I shall not see the shadows,
    I shall not feel the rain;   10
I shall not hear the nightingale
    Sing on, as if in pain;
And dreaming through the twilight
    That doth not rise nor set,
Haply I may remember,   15
    And haply may forget.

—Christina Rossetti (1830–1894)

Up-Hill

Does the road wind up-hill all the way?
    Yes, to the very end.
Will the day's journey take the whole long day?
    From morn to night, my friend.

But is there for the night a resting-place?   5
    A roof for when the slow dark hours begin.
May not the darkness hide it from my face?
    You cannot miss that inn.

Shall I meet other wayfarers at night?
    Those who have gone before.   10
Then must I knock, or call when just in sight?
    They will not keep you waiting at that door.

Shall I find comfort, travel-sore and weak?
    Of labor you shall find the sum.

Will there be beds for me and all who seek? 15
    Yea, beds for all who come.

—CHRISTINA ROSSETTI (1830–1894)

Young

A thousand doors ago
when I was a lonely kid
in a big house with four
garages and it was summer
as long as I could remember, 5
I lay on the lawn at night,
clover wrinkling under me,
the wise stars bedding over me,
my mother's window a funnel
of yellow heat running out, 10
my father's window, half shut,
an eye where sleepers pass,
and the boards of the house
were smooth and white as wax
and probably a million leaves 15
sailed on their strange stalks
as the crickets ticked together
and I, in my brand new body,
which was not a woman's yet,
told the stars my questions 20
and thought God could really see
the heat and the painted light,
elbows, knees, dreams, goodnight.

—ANNE SEXTON (1928–1974)

Let me not to the marriage of true minds

Let me not to the marriage of true minds
Admit impediments. Love is not love
Which alters when it alteration finds,
Or bends with the remover to remove.
O no! it is an ever-fixèd mark 5
That looks on tempests and is never shaken;

It is the star to every wandering bark,
Whose worth's unknown, although his height be taken.
Love's not Time's fool, though rosy lips and cheeks
Within his bending sickle's compass come;   10
Love alters not with his brief hours and weeks,
But bears it out even to the edge of doom.
If this be error and upon me proved,
I never writ, nor no man ever loved.

—WILLIAM SHAKESPEARE (1564–1616)

Evening Walk

You give the appearance of listening
To my thoughts, O trees,
Bent over the road I am walking
On a late summer evening
When every one of you is a steep staircase   5
The night is slowly descending.

The high leaves like my mother's lips
Forever trembling, unable to decide,
For there's a bit of wind,
And it's like hearing voices,   10
Or a mouth full of muffled laughter,
A huge dark mouth we can all fit in
Suddenly covered by a hand.

Everything quiet. Light
Of some other evening strolling ahead,   15
Long-ago evening of silk dresses,
Bare feet, hair unpinned and falling.
Happy heart, what heavy steps you take
As you follow after them in the shadows.

The sky at the road's end cloudless and blue.   20
The night birds like children
Who won't come to dinner.
Lost children in the darkening woods.

—CHARLES SIMIC (B. 1938)

Grayheaded Schoolchildren

Old men have bad dreams,
So they sleep little.
They walk on bare feet
Without turning on the light,
Or they stand leaning   5
On gloomy furniture
listening to their hearts beat.

The one window across the room
Is black like a blackboard.
Every old man is alone   10
In this classroom, squinting
At that fine chalk line
That divides being-here
From being-here-no-more.

No matter. It was a glass of water   15
They were going to get,
But not just yet.
They listen for mice in the walls,
A car passing on the street,
Their dead fathers shuffling past them   20
On their way to the kitchen.

—CHARLES SIMIC (B. 1938)

Not Waving But Drowning

Nobody heard him, the dead man,
But still he lay moaning:
I was much further out than you thought
And not waving but drowning.

Poor chap, he always loved larking   5
And now he's dead
It must have been too cold for him his heart gave way,
They said.

Oh, no no no, it was too cold always
(Still the dead one lay moaning)   10

I was much too far out all my life
And not waving but drowning.

—STEVIE SMITH (1902–1971)

Small Town with One Road

We could be here. This is the valley
And its black strip of highway, big-eyed
With rabbits that won't get across.
Kids could make it, though.
They leap barefoot to the store—   5
Sweetness on their tongues, red stain of laughter.
They are the spectators of fun.
Hot dimes fall from their palms,
Chinks of light, and they eat
Candies all the way home   10
Where there's a dog for each hand,
Cats, chickens in the yard.
A pot bangs and water runs in the kitchen.
Beans, they think, and beans it will be,
Brown soup that's muscle for the field   15
And crippled steps to a ladder.
Okie or Mexican, Jew that got lost,
It's a hard life where the sun looks.
The cotton gin stands tall in the money dream
And the mill is a paycheck for   20
A wife—and perhaps my wife
Who, when she was a girl,
Boxed peaches and plums, hoed
Papa's field that wavered like a mirage
That wouldn't leave. We could go back.   25
I could lose my job, this easy one
That's only words, and pick up a shovel,
Hoe, broom that takes it away.
Worry is my daughter's story.
She touches my hand. We suck roadside   30
Snowcones in the shade
And look about. Behind sunglasses
I see where I stood: a brown kid
Getting across. "He's like me,"

I tell my daughter, and she stops her mouth.   35
He looks both ways and then leaps
Across the road where riches
Happen on a red tongue.

—GARY SOTO (B. 1952)

One day I wrote her name upon the strand

One day I wrote her name upon the strand,°   beach
But came the waves and washèd it away:
Again I wrote it with a second hand,
But came the tide, and made my pains his prey.
"Vain man," said she, "that dost in vain assay°   attempt   5
A mortal thing so to immortalize.
For I myself shall, like to this, decay,
And eek° my name be wipèd out likewise."   also
"Not so," quoth I, "let baser things devise
To die in dust, but you shall live by fame: 10
My verse your virtues rare shall eternize,
And in the heavens write your glorious name,
Where whenas death shall all the world subdue
Our love shall live, and later life renew."

—EDMUND SPENSER (1552–1599)

Anecdote of the Jar

I placed a jar in Tennessee,
And round it was, upon a hill.
It made the slovenly wilderness
Surround that hill.

The wilderness rose up to it,   5
And sprawled around, no longer wild.
The jar was round upon the ground
And tall and of a port in air.

It took dominion everywhere.
The jar was gray and bare.   10

It did not give of bird or bush,
Like nothing else in Tennessee.

—WALLACE STEVENS (1879–1955)

Disillusionment of Ten O'Clock

The houses are haunted
By white night-gowns.
None are green,
Or purple with green rings,
Or green with yellow rings,   5
Or yellow with blue rings.
None of them are strange,
With socks of lace
And beaded ceintures.°   sashes
People are not going   10
To dream of baboons and periwinkles.
Only, here and there, an old sailor,
Drunk and asleep in his boots,
Catches tigers
In red weather.   15

—WALLACE STEVENS (1879–1955)

Fern Hill

Now as I was young and easy under the apple boughs
About the lilting house and happy as the grass was green,
   The night above the dingle starry,
    Time let me hail and climb
    Golden in the heydays of his eyes,   5
And honored among wagons I was prince of the apple towns
And once below a time I lordly had the trees and leaves
   Trail with daisies and barley
   Down the rivers of the windfall light.

And as I was green and carefree, famous among the barns   10
About the happy yard and singing as the farm was home,
   In the sun that is young once only,
    Time let me play and be
    Golden in the mercy of his means,

And green and golden I was huntsman and herdsman,
   the calves   15
Sang to my horn, the foxes on the hills barked clear and cold,
    And the sabbath rang slowly
      In the pebbles of the holy streams.

All the sun long it was running, it was lovely, the hay
Fields high as the house, the tunes from the chimneys,
   it was air   20
    And playing, lovely and watery
      And fire green as grass.
    And nightly under the simple stars
As I rode to sleep the owls were bearing the farm away,
All the moon long I heard, blessed among stables,
   the nightjars   25
    Flying with the ricks, and the horses
      Flashing into the dark.

And then to awake, and the farm, like a wanderer white
With the dew, come back, the cock on his shoulder: it was all
    Shining, it was Adam and maiden,   30
      The sky gathered again
    And the sun grew round that very day.
So it must have been after the birth of the simple light
In the first, spinning place, the spellbound horses
  walking warm
      Out of the whinnying green stable   35
      On to the fields of praise.

And honored among foxes and pheasants by the gay house
Under the new made clouds and happy as the heart was long,
    In the sun born over and over,
      I ran my heedless ways,   40
    My wishes raced through the house high hay
And nothing I cared, at my sky blue trades, that time allows
In all his tuneful turning so few and such morning songs
    Before the children green and golden
      Follow him out of grace,   45

Nothing I cared, in the lamb white days, that time would
  take me
Up to the swallow thronged loft by the shadow of my hand,

In the moon that is always rising,
  Nor that riding to sleep
I should hear him fly with the high fields   50
And wake to the farm forever fled from the childless land.
Oh as I was young and easy in the mercy of his means,
    Time held me green and dying
  Though I sang in my chains like the sea.

—DYLAN THOMAS (1914–1953)

Blond

Certainly it was possible—somewhere
in my parents' genes the recessive traits
that might have given me a different look:
not attached earlobes or my father's green eyes,
but another hair color—gentleman-preferred,   5
have-more-fun blond. And with my skin color,
like a good tan—an even mix of my parents'—
I could have passed for white.

When on Christmas day I woke to find
a blond wig, a pink sequined tutu,   10
and a blond ballerina doll, nearly tall as me,
I didn't know to ask, nor that it mattered,
if there'd been a brown version. This was years before
my grandmother nestled the dark baby
into our crèche, years before I'd understand it   15
as primer for a Mississippi childhood.

Instead, I pranced around our living room
in a whirl of possibility, my parents looking on
at their suddenly strange child. In the photograph
my mother took, my father—almost   20
out of the frame—looks on as Joseph must have
at the miraculous birth: I'm in the foreground—
my blond wig a shining halo, a newborn likeness
to the child that chance, the long odds,
might have brought.   25

—NATASHA TRETHEWEY (B. 1966)

Miscegenation

In 1965 my parents broke two laws of Mississippi;
they went to Ohio to marry, returned to Mississippi.

They crossed the river into Cincinnati, a city whose name
begins with a sound like *sin*, the sound of wrong—*mis* in Mississippi.

A year later they moved to Canada, followed a route the same   5
as slaves, the train slicing the white glaze of winter, leaving
    Mississippi.

Faulkner's Joe Christmas was born in winter, like Jesus, given his
    name
for the day he was left at the orphanage, his race unknown in
    Mississippi.

My father was reading *War and Peace* when he gave me my name.
I was born near Easter, 1966, in Mississippi.   10

When I turned 33 my father said, *It's your Jesus year—you're the same
age he was when he died.* It was spring, the hills green in Mississippi.

I know more than Joe Christmas did. Natasha is a Russian name—
though I'm not; it means *Christmas child,* even in Mississippi.

—NATASHA TRETHEWEY (B. 1966)

Ex-Basketball Player

Pearl Avenue runs past the high-school lot,
Bends with the trolley tracks, and stops, cut off
Before it has a chance to go two blocks,
At Colonel McComsky Plaza. Berth's Garage
Is on the corner facing west, and there,   5
Most days, you'll find Flick Webb, who helps Berth out.

Flick stands tall among the idiot pumps—
Five on a side, the old bubble-head style,
Their rubber elbows hanging loose and low.
One's nostrils are two S's, and his eyes   10

An E and O. And one is squat, without
A head at all—more of a football type.

Once Flick played for the high-school team, the Wizards.
He was good: in fact, the best. In '46
He bucketed three hundred ninety points,   15
A county record still. The ball loved Flick.
I saw him rack up thirty-eight or forty
In one home game. His hands were like wild birds.

He never learned a trade, he just sells gas,
Checks oil, and changes flats. Once in a while,   20
As a gag, he dribbles an inner tube,
But most of us remember anyway.
His hands are fine and nervous on the lug wrench.
It makes no difference to the lug wrench, though.

Off work, he hangs around Mae's luncheonette.   25
Grease-gray and kind of coiled, he plays pinball,
Smokes those thin cigars, nurses lemon phosphates.
Flick seldom says a word to Mae, just nods
Beyond her face toward bright applauding tiers
Of Necco Wafers, Nibs, and Juju Beads.   30

—JOHN UPDIKE (1932–2009)

(10–11) *two S's* . . . *E and O:* The brand of gasoline now called EXXON was called
ESSO prior to 1972. (27) *lemon phosphates:* soft drinks. (29–30) *tiers* . . . *Juju beads:*
display rack of candies.

A Sight in Camp in the Daybreak Gray and Dim

A sight in camp in the daybreak gray and dim,
As from my tent I emerge so early sleepless,
As slow I walk in the cool fresh air the path near by the
    hospital tent,
Three forms I see on stretchers lying, brought out there
    untended lying,
Over each the blanket spread, ample brownish woolen
    blanket,
Gray and heavy blanket, folding, covering all.   5

Curious I halt and silent stand,
Then with light fingers I from the face of the nearest the first
    just lift the blanket;
Who are you elderly man so gaunt and grim, with well-gray'd
    hair, and flesh all sunken about the eyes?
Who are you my dear comrade?   10

Then to the second I step—and who are you my child and
    darling?
Who are you sweet boy with cheeks yet blooming?
Then to the third—a face nor child nor old, very calm, as of
    beautiful yellow-white ivory;
Young man I think I know you—I think this face is the face
    of the Christ himself,
Dead and divine and brother of all, and here again he lies.   15

                                —WALT WHITMAN (1819–1892)

Spring and All

By the road to the contagious hospital
under the surge of the blue
mottled clouds driven from the
northeast—a cold wind. Beyond, the
waste of broad, muddy fields   5
brown with dried weeds, standing and fallen

patches of standing water
the scattering of tall trees

All along the road the reddish
purplish, forked, upstanding, twiggy   10
stuff of bushes and small trees
with dead, brown leaves under them
leafless vines—

Lifeless in appearance, sluggish
dazed spring approaches—   15

They enter the new world naked,
cold, uncertain of all
save that they enter. All about them
the cold, familiar wind—

Now the grass, tomorrow 20
the stiff curl of wildcarrot leaf
One by one objects are defined—
It quickens: clarity, outline of leaf

But now the stark dignity of
entrance—Still, the profound change 25
has come upon them: rooted they
grip down and begin to awaken

—WILLIAM CARLOS WILLIAMS (1883–1963)

I wandered lonely as a cloud

I wandered lonely as a cloud
That floats on high o'er vales and hills,
When all at once I saw a crowd,
A host, of golden daffodils;
Beside the lake, beneath the trees, 5
Fluttering and dancing in the breeze.

Continuous as the stars that shine
And twinkle on the milky way,
They stretched in never-ending line
Along the margin of a bay: 10
Ten thousand saw I at a glance,
Tossing their heads in sprightly dance.

The waves beside them danced; but they
Outdid the sparkling waves in glee;
A poet could not but be gay, 15
In such a jocund company;
I gazed—and gazed—but little thought
What wealth the show to me had brought:

For oft, when on my couch I lie
In vacant or in pensive mood, 20
They flash upon that inward eye
Which is the bliss of solitude;
And then my heart with pleasure fills,
And dances with the daffodils.

—WILLIAM WORDSWORTH (1770–1850)

My heart leaps up when I behold

My heart leaps up when I behold
   A rainbow in the sky:
So was it when my life began;
So is it now I am a man;
So be it when I shall grow old,   5
   Or let me die!
The Child is father of the Man;
And I could wish my days to be
Bound each to each by natural piety.

—WILLIAM WORDSWORTH (1770–1850)

Lying in a Hammock at William Duffy's Farm in Pine Island, Minnesota

Over my head, I see the bronze butterfly,
Asleep on the black trunk,
Blowing like a leaf in green shadow.
Down the ravine behind the empty house,
The cowbells follow one another   5
Into the distances of the afternoon.
To my right,
In a field of sunlight between two pines,
The droppings of last year's horses
Blaze up into golden stones.   10
I lean back, as the evening darkens and comes on.
A chicken hawk floats over, looking for home.
I have wasted my life.

—JAMES WRIGHT (1927–1980)

The Lake Isle of Innisfree

I will arise and go now, and go to Innisfree,
And a small cabin build there, of clay and wattles made:
Nine bean-rows will I have there, a hive for the honey-bee,
And live alone in the bee-loud glade.

And I shall have some peace there, for peace comes
   dropping slow,   5

Dropping from the veils of the morning to where the
    cricket sings;
There midnight's all a glimmer, and noon a purple glow,
And evening full of the linnet's wings.

I will arise and go now, for always night and day
I hear lake water lapping with low sounds by the shore;   10
While I stand on the roadway, or on the pavements gray,
I hear it in the deep heart's core.

—WILLIAM BUTLER YEATS (1865–1939)

The Second Coming

Turning and turning in the widening gyre
The falcon cannot hear the falconer;
Things fall apart; the center cannot hold;
Mere anarchy is loosed upon the world,
The blood-dimmed tide is loosed, and everywhere   5
The ceremony of innocence is drowned;
The best lack all conviction, while the worst
Are full of passionate intensity.

Surely some revelation is at hand;
Surely the Second Coming is at hand.   10
The Second Coming! Hardly are those words out
When a vast image out of *Spiritus Mundi*
Troubles my sight: somewhere in sands of the desert
A shape with lion body and the head of a man,
A gaze blank and pitiless as the sun,   15
Is moving its slow thighs, while all about it
Reel shadows of the indignant desert birds.
The darkness drops again; but now I know
That twenty centuries of stony sleep
Were vexed to nightmare by a rocking cradle,   20
And what rough beast, its hour come round at last,
Slouches towards Bethlehem to be born?

—WILLIAM BUTLER YEATS (1865–1939)

(Title) In Christian legend the prophesied Second Coming may refer either to Christ or to the
Antichrist. Yeats believed in a cyclical theory of history in which one historical era would be
replaced by an opposite kind of era every two thousand years. Here, the anarchy in the world following World War I (the poem was written in 1919) heralds the end of the Christian era. (12) *Spiritus
Mundi:* the racial memory or collective unconscious mind of mankind (literally, world spirit).

The Song of Wandering Aengus

I went out to the hazel wood,
Because a fire was in my head,
And cut and peeled a hazel wand,
And hooked a berry to a thread;
And when white moths were on the wing,⁵ 5
And moth-like stars were flickering out,
I dropped the berry in a stream
And caught a little silver trout.

When I had laid it on the floor
I went to blow the fire aflame, 10
But something rustled on the floor,
And some one called me by my name:
It had become a glimmering girl
With apple blossom in her hair
Who called me by my name and ran 15
And faded through the brightening air.

Though I am old with wandering
Through hollow lands and hilly lands,
I will find out where she has gone,
And kiss her lips and take her hands; 20
And walk among long dappled grass,
And pluck till time and times are done
The silver apples of the moon,
The golden apples of the sun.

—WILLIAM BUTLER YEATS (1865–1939)

The Wild Swans at Coole

The trees are in their autumn beauty,
The woodland paths are dry,
Under the October twilight the water
Mirrors a still sky;
Upon the brimming water among the stones 5
Are nine-and-fifty swans.

The nineteenth autumn has come upon me
Since I first made my count;
I saw, before I had well finished,
All suddenly mount 10

And scatter wheeling in great broken rings
Upon their clamorous wings.

I have looked upon those brilliant creatures,
And now my heart is sore,
All's changed since I, hearing at twilight,   15
The first time on this shore,
The bell-beat of their wings above my head,
Trod with a lighter tread.

Unwearied still, lover by lover,
They paddle in the cold   20
Companionable streams or climb the air;
Their hearts have not grown old;
Passion or conquest, wander where they will,
Attend upon them still.

But now they drift on the still water,   25
Mysterious, beautiful;
Among what rushes will they build,
By what lake's edge or pool
Delight men's eyes when I awake some day
To find they have flown away?   30

—WILLIAM BUTLER YEATS (1865–1939)

(Title) Coole Park, in County Galway, Ireland, was the estate of Lady Augusta Gregory, Yeats's
patroness and friend. Beginning in 1897, Yeats regularly summered there.

PRACTICE AP WRITING PROMPTS ▬▬▬▬

W. H. Auden, "Musée des Beaux Arts" (p. 975)

W. H. Auden's "Musée des Beaux arts" alludes to paintings by Peter Brueghel the
Elder and describes one in detail. Read the poem carefully; then write an essay
in which you discuss the speaker's response to the paintings, focusing especially
on why he believes the Old Masters "were never wrong." In your analysis,
explain how poetic elements such as diction, imagery, and allusion contribute
to Auden's meaning.

Jimmy Santiago Baca, "Main Character" (pp. 975–976)

Jimmy Santiago Baca is a contemporary Native American poet. Read his poem "Main Character" carefully. Then write an essay in which you describe the speaker's boyhood experience at the movie theater and its lasting impact on him. Show how elements such as imagery, diction, and tone convey the speaker's insights.

Elizabeth Bishop, "Manners" (pp. 978–979)

Read Elizabeth Bishop's "Manners" carefully, including the epigraphic note immediately preceding the poem. Then write an essay in which you explore what the child in the poem learns about civility among humans as well as harmony between humankind and nature. In your essay, discuss how such elements as structure, selective details, and tone contribute to the poem's overall effect.

Amy Clampitt, "Witness" (p. 982)

Amy Clampitt's "Witness" captures a speaker's impressions of scenes that normally go unnoticed, viewed from a greyhound bus on an "ordinary evening in Wisconsin." Read the poem carefully. Then, in a well-organized essay, analyze the poetic language that conveys the speaker's observations and insights as she recounts these moments.

Samuel Taylor Coleridge, "Kubla Khan" (pp. 984–985)

Literary critic Harold Bloom said of "Kubla Khan" that it is "a vision of creation and destruction, each complete." Read the poem carefully, paying close attention to its language and to the balancing of opposites. Then write a well-organized essay in which you show how poetic elements such as imagery, diction, and sound devices contribute to Coleridge's creation of this enchanted land.

Billy Collins, "Weighing the Dog" (p. 987)

Read "Weighing the Dog," paying careful attention to the significance of determining the dog's weight. Write an essay in which you analyze the poet's analogy and symbolism.

Thomas Hardy, "The Man He Killed" (p. 701) and Stephen Crane, "War Is Kind" (p. 988)

See the comparison prompt for "War is Kind" paired with "The Man He Killed" in Chapter Two of the Poetry section.

Langston Hughes, "Aunt Sue's Stories" (p. 1010) and "Mother to Son" (pp. 1010–1011)

Langston Hughes's "Aunt Sue's Stories" and "Mother to Son" both examine the importance of lessons and stories passed from the older generation to the younger. Compare and contrast these poems in a well-written essay in which you show how each poem conveys the significance and value of such lessons or stories. Cite such literary techniques as diction, point of view, metaphor, and imagery in your analysis.

John Keats, "Ode to a Nightingale" (pp. 1015–1017)

In lines 1–30 of "Ode to a Nightingale" the poet contrasts the "ease" of the nightingale with the "weariness" of human life. Read these first three verses several times; then write an essay showing how Keats exploits both the sound and the sense of English words to help make his case that it's better to be a nightingale than a person.

Audre Lorde, "Black Mother Woman" (pp. 1022–1023)

Read "Black Mother Woman" carefully. Then write an essay in which you examine the ambivalent feelings between the speaker and her mother. Explain how literary devices contribute to the poem's overall effect.

Archibald MacLeish, "Ars Poetica" (pp. 1023–1024)

Read "Ars Poetica" by Archibald MacLeish carefully. Then write an essay in which you show how the speaker develops a philosophy of poetry. Explain how such elements as figurative language, paradox, and sound devices support MacLeish's meaning.

Sharon Olds, "I Go Back to May 1937" (p. 1028)

Read Sharon Olds's poem "I Go Back to May 1937" carefully. Then write an essay in which you discuss the impact of the speaker's complex perspective as both witness to and product of her parents' marriage. In your essay, analyze how literary elements such as paradox, diction, and imagery contribute to the poem's overall effect.

Langston Hughes, "Suicide's Note" (p. 695) and Edwin Arlington Robinson, "Richard Cory" (p. 1034)

See the comparison prompt for "Richard Cory" paired with "Suicide's Note" in Chapter One of the Poetry section.

Christina Rossetti, "Up-Hill" (pp. 1036–1037)

Read "Uphill" carefully, paying close attention to the journey described. Then write an essay in which you analyze the conversation between the two speakers and explore the poem's allegorical significance. Support your essay with specific references to the poem's language and poetic techniques.

John Donne, "A Valediction: Forbidding Mourning" (pp. 1057–1059) and William Shakespeare, "Let me not to the marriage of true minds" (p. 1037)

See the comparison prompt for "Let me not to the marriage of true minds" paired with "A Valediction: Forbidding Mourning" in Chapter Five of the Poetry section.

Edmund Spenser, "One day I wrote her name upon the strand" (p. 1041)

The sonnet form often encourages ironic contrasts. In the sonnet "One day I wrote her name upon the strand," Spenser repeats a word in line 5 both to emphasize its importance to his theme and to play different shades of the word's meaning against each other. Write a carefully detailed essay showing how the contrasting yet resonant senses of the word contribute to the complex meaning of the poem as a whole.

"A VALEDICTION: FORBIDDING MOURNING" BY JOHN DONNE

QUESTIONS 1–15. Carefully read the poem before choosing your answers.

As virtuous men pass mildly away,
   And whisper to their souls to go,
Whilst some of their sad friends do say,
   The breath goes now, and some say no:

So let us melt, and make no noise,   5
   No tear-floods, nor sigh-tempests move;
'Twere profanation of our joys
   To tell the laity our love.

Moving of th' earth brings harms and fears;
   Men reckon what it did and meant;   10
But trepidation of the spheres,
   Though greater far, is innocent.

Dull sublunary lovers' love
   (Whose soul is sense) cannot admit
Absence, because it doth remove   15
   Those things which elemented it.

But we, by a love so much refined
   That ourselves know not what it is,
Inter-assurèd of the mind,
   Care less, eyes, lips, and hands to miss.   20

Our two souls, therefore, which are one,
   Though I must go, endure not yet
A breach, but an expansion,
   Like gold to airy thinness beat.

If they be two, they are two so   25
   As stiff twin compasses are two;
Thy soul, the fixed foot, makes no show
   To move, but doth, if th' other do.

And though it in the center sit,
Yet when the other far doth roam,   30
   It leans and harkens after it,
   And grows erect as that comes home.

Such wilt thou be to me, who must,
   Like th' other foot, obliquely run;
Thy firmness makes my circle just,   35
   And makes me end where I begun.

1. The poem shows the precise rhyme scheme knows as
   - (A) blank verse
   - (B) ballad
   - (C) terza rima
   - (D) rhyme royal
   - (E) ode

2. The poem suggests that Donne's love for his wife and hers for him is
   - (A) purely sensual and sexual
   - (B) physical, not spiritual
   - (C) a love of the mind as well as the body
   - (D) about to end
   - (E) fated to end

3. The entire poem exemplifies
   - (A) the Petrarchan sonnet
   - (B) the poetic parable
   - (C) the Elizabethan pastoral
   - (D) the metaphysical conceit
   - (E) stream of consciousness

4. The lovers are likened to moving planetary bodies that are
   - (A) chaotic
   - (B) natural disasters
   - (C) peaceful and calm
   - (D) out of order
   - (E) irrelevant

5. The poem suggests that the two lovers are their own self-sustaining universe because
   - (A) they have no need of anyone else
   - (B) they are made imperfect by their love
   - (C) they know how to use a compass
   - (D) they look at the moon together
   - (E) they will soon divorce

6. In lines 22–23, "endure not yet / A breach," the word "yet" hints that
   (A) there will never be a breach, not even with death
   (B) with death eventually there will be a breach
   (C) love will find a way
   (D) hope springs eternal
   (E) love will never rupture

7. The theme of this poem is best expressed as a separation that
   (A) must cause grief
   (B) does not need consolation or fortitude
   (C) is part of the nature and completeness of the lovers' world
   (D) is not sacred
   (E) is not a mystical force

8. Line 24, "Like gold to airy thinness beat," is an example of
   (A) metaphor
   (B) simile
   (C) oxymoron
   (D) alliteration
   (E) paradox

9. In the opening, "As virtuous men pass mildly away, / And whisper to their souls to go" (lines 1–2), Donne is describing
   (A) a love that eventually ends
   (B) a hope that eventually stops
   (C) a journey that eventually ends
   (D) a death that happens peacefully
   (E) a rage against death

10. In line 16, "Those things which elemented it," Donne uses the verb "elemented" to mean
    (A) separated
    (B) removed
    (C) composed
    (D) expunged
    (E) eliminated

11. In using the "twin compasses" (line 26), Donne does not compare the perfection of his love to a traditional object, but to two things so different that we feel an anomaly. This image is an example of
    (A) screed
    (B) malediction

(C) arrogance
(D) conceit
(E) voracity

12. The use of the pronoun "it" in the eighth stanza, in lines 29 and 31, refers metaphorically to
    (A) the poet
    (B) the poet's wife
    (C) the compass that always points north
    (D) the dead preacher
    (E) the part of the compass that moves

13. Lines 33–34, "Such wilt thou be to me, who must, / Like th' other foot, obliquely run," suggest that Donne is asking his wife
    (A) to remain at the center
    (B) to go with him
    (C) for a divorce
    (D) to learn how to use a compass
    (E) to realize that separation ends things

14. The poem's ending, "Thy firmness makes my circle just, / And makes me end where I begun" (lines 35–36), means that a compass
    (A) must always point north
    (B) works only if one foot remains centered firmly
    (C) is not a good item to compare to love
    (D) helps in understanding divorce
    (E) symbolizes hatred

15. In lines 7–8, "'Twere profanation of our joys / To tell the laity our love," Donne says that the love he and his wife have
    (A) can never really be understood by others
    (B) can never be understood because it is only spiritual
    (C) can never be understood because it is purely physical
    (D) cannot exist
    (E) can exist because it is only platonic

See page 1607 for the answers to this set of questions.

"A SUPERMARKET IN CALIFORNIA" BY ALLEN GINSBERG

QUESTIONS 16–26. Carefully read the poem before choosing your answers.

What thoughts I have of you tonight, Walt Whitman, for I walked down the sidestreets under the trees with a headache self-conscious looking at the full moon.

In my hungry fatigue, and shopping for images, I went into   5
the neon fruit supermarket, dreaming of your enumerations!

What peaches and what penumbras? Whole families shopping at night! Aisles full of husbands! Wives in the avocados, babies in the tomatoes!—and you, García Lorca, what were   10
you doing down by the watermelons?

LI I saw you, Walt Whitman, childless, lonely old grubber, poking among the meats in the refrigerator and eyeing the grocery boys.   15

I heard you asking questions of each: Who killed the pork chops? What price bananas? Are you my Angel?

I wandered in and out of the brilliant stacks of cans following you, and followed in my imagination by the store   20
detective.

We strode down the open corridors together in our solitary fancy tasting artichokes, possessing every frozen delicacy, and never passing the cashier.

Where are we going, Walt Whitman? The doors close in an   25
hour. Which way does your beard point tonight?

(I touch your book and dream of our odyssey in the supermarket and feel absurd.)

Will we walk all night through solitary streets? The trees   30
add shade to shade, lights out in the houses, we'll both be lonely.

Will we stroll dreaming of the lost America of love past blue automobiles in driveways, home to our silent cottage?   35

Ah, dear father, graybeard, lonely old courage-teacher, what America did you have when Charon quit poling his ferry and you got out on a smoking bank and stood watching the boat disappear on the black waters of Lethe?   40

16. The adjective "neon" (line 6) used in the context of a fruit
    market most significantly connotes
    (A) menace
    (B) sophistication
    (C) vitality
    (D) gaudiness
    (E) bricolage

17. The imagery of the third stanza raises the notion of
    (A) consumerism
    (B) economic colonialism
    (C) religion
    (D) aesthetic influence
    (E) sustenance

18. The poem uses all of the following rhetorical devices EXCEPT
    (A) rhetorical question
    (B) parenthetical aside
    (C) apostrophe
    (D) innuendo
    (E) invective

19. In the second stanza, "tasting artichokes," "possessing every
    frozen delicacy," and "never passing the cashier" are all
    (A) gerund phrases
    (B) participial phrases
    (C) adjectival clauses
    (D) noun clauses
    (E) prepositional phrases

20. The phrase "dreaming of your enumerations" in the first
    stanza most closely means
    (A) reflecting on your classification systems
    (B) feeling the loss of your presence
    (C) feeling inspired by your poetic images
    (D) computing a system of numerology
    (E) feeling envious of your metaphors

21. By using the word "odyssey" (line 28), the narrator
    indicates his feeling that
    (A) life is a challenge
    (B) his journey is coming to an end
    (C) his relationship with Whitman is only imaginary
    (D) he cannot achieve greatness as a poet
    (E) his supermarket experience is of epic proportions

22. The tone of the poem is one of
    (A) lyric nostalgia
    (B) aching loneliness
    (C) bitter reproof
    (D) elevated absurdity
    (E) spent enthusiasm

23. In the final stanza, the poem shifts from
    (A) criticism to homage
    (B) exultant living to death
    (C) melancholy to hope
    (D) sterility to vision
    (E) fantasy to nostalgia

24. The setting of a supermarket
    (A) expresses a distaste for materialism
    (B) bemoans the difficulty of making artistic choices
    (C) equates the artistic world with a marketplace
    (D) honors the entrepreneurial spirit
    (E) mourns the erosion of American democracy

25. In the final stanza, "Charon" (line 37) refers to
    (A) a character from Greek mythology
    (B) a contemporary ferryman
    (C) Walt Whitman
    (D) the poet himself
    (E) another Beat poet

26. The reader can detect Ginsberg's dominant feeling toward
    Whitman in the phrase
    (A) "lonely old grubber" (lines 13–14)
    (B) "eyeing the grocery boys" (line 15)
    (C) "Are you my Angel?" (lines 17–18)
    (D) "lonely old courage-teacher" (lines 36–37)
    (E) "watching the boat disappear on the black waters of
        Lethe" (lines 39–40)

See page 1607 for the answers to this set of questions.

"MID-TERM BREAK" BY SEAMUS HEANEY

QUESTIONS 27–39. Carefully read the poem before choosing your answers.

I sat all morning in the college sick bay
Counting bells knelling classes to a close.
At two o'clock our neighbors drove me home.

In the porch I met my father crying—
He had always taken funerals in his stride—   5
And Big Jim Evans saying it was a hard blow.

The baby cooed and laughed and rocked the pram
When I came in, and I was embarrassed
By old men standing up to shake my hand

And tell me they were "sorry for my trouble."   10
Whispers informed strangers I was the eldest,
Away at school, as my mother held my hand

In hers and coughed out angry tearless sighs.
At ten o'clock the ambulance arrived
With the corpse, stanched and bandaged by the nurses.   15

Next morning I went up into the room. Snowdrops
And candles soothed the bedside; I saw him
For the first time in six weeks. Paler now,

Wearing a poppy bruise on his left temple,
He lay in the four foot box as in his cot.   20
No gaudy scars, the bumper knocked him clear.

A four foot box, a foot for every year.

27. The title of this poem is
    (A) definitely epic
    (B) somewhat ironic
    (C) extremely realistic
    (D) recklessly naturalistic
    (E) clandestinely romantic

28. The subject of this poem is the memory of
    (A) a numbing bereavement
    (B) an ostentatious mourning
    (C) an agreeable event
    (D) an unambiguous reminiscence
    (E) a happy time, much to Heaney's chagrin

29. In the phrase "Counting bells knelling classes to a close" (line 2), the word "knelling" conjures up a sound that is all of the following EXCEPT
    (A) vividly and stridently staccato
    (B) slowly and solemnly tolling
    (C) strangely upbeat and fanciful
    (D) a deliberate and somber tempo
    (E) accompanied by sounds of keening

30. The entire poem is an example of
    (A) terza rima
    (B) enjambment
    (C) sonnet
    (D) deus ex machina
    (E) simple tercet schematics

31. Lines 12 and 13, "as my mother held my hand / In hers and coughed out angry tearless sighs," are an example of
    (A) terza rima
    (B) sonnet
    (C) enjambment
    (D) simile
    (E) onomatopoeia

32. Saying "By old men standing up to shake my hand / And tell me they were 'sorry for my trouble'" (lines 9–10) draws attention to the
    (A) awkwardness and evasion at such events
    (B) cacophony at such events
    (C) stealth at such events
    (D) rapture at such events
    (E) church's views of events such as this

33. The word "pram" (line 7) refers to
    (A) the baby
    (B) the ambulance
    (C) the baby's crib
    (D) a baby carriage
    (E) the hospital bed

34. The poet's emphases on specific words as he moves from
"the <u>corpse</u>, stanched and bandaged," (line 15) to "I saw
<u>him</u> (line 17) . . . <u>his</u> left temple (line 19) . . . <u>he</u> lay (line
20) . . . <u>his</u> cot. / No gaudy scars," (lines 20–21) suggests
a change from
(A) noninvolvement to involvement
(B) a universal reserve to a specific commitment
(C) nonparticipation to active participation
(D) detached and aloof sharing to active caring
(E) a scientific view to a religious view

35. The poem has a clearly defined formal structure that is
composed of
(A) unrhymed couplets
(B) three-line stanzas with loose iambic meter
(C) three-line stanzas with no meter
(D) three-line stanzas with strict dactylic hexameter
(E) three-line stanzas with strict anapestic trimeter

36. The lines "I saw him / For the first time in six weeks. Paler
now, / Wearing a poppy bruise on his left temple" (17–19)
show a memory of the death of
(A) the speaker's father
(B) the speaker's mother
(C) the speaker's brother
(D) Big Jim Evans
(E) the baby

37. "He lay in the four foot box as in his cot" (line 20) is an
example of
(A) scansion
(B) hamartia
(C) simile
(D) metaphor
(E) hubris

38. It can be inferred from the description in line 7, "The baby
cooed and laughed and rocked the pram," that the sounds are
(A) not valued by the speaker because they are out of place
(B) not valued by the speaker because they are not out of
place
(C) valued as a picture of the end of life with no affirmation
(D) valued as the antithesis to life with affirmation
(E) valued because they show a sharp contrast, an affirma-
tion of life

39. The final line, "A four foot box, a foot for every year" (line 22), emphasizes
   (A) candidly the great feeling of sadness at last transmitted to the reader
   (B) the grief that the author still hides from the reader
   (C) a faded unimportant memory
   (D) an adult embellishment of a recollection of sadness
   (E) an arithmetic equation

See page 1607 for the answers to this set of questions.

The Elements

of Drama

The Nature of Drama

Drama, like prose fiction, makes use of plot and characters, develops themes, arouses emotional responses, and may be either literary or commercial in its representation of reality.* Like poetry, it may draw upon all the resources of language, including verse. Much drama *is* poetry. But drama has one characteristic peculiar to itself. It is written primarily to be *performed*, not read. It normally presents its action (a) *through* actors, (b) *on* a stage, and (c) *before* an audience. Each of these conditions has important consequences for the nature of drama. Each presents an author with a potentially enormous source of power, and each imposes limitations on the directions a work may take.

Because a play presents its action *through* actors, its impact is direct, immediate, and heightened by the actors' skills. Instead of responding to words on a printed page, spectators see what is done and hear what is said. The experience of the play is registered directly upon their senses. It may therefore be both fuller and more compact. Where the work of prose fiction may tell us what a man looks like in one paragraph, how he moves or speaks in a second, what he says in a third, and how his auditors respond in a fourth, the acted play presents this material all at once. Simultaneous impressions are not temporally separated. Moreover, this experience is interpreted by actors who may be highly skilled in rendering nuances of meaning and strong emotion. Through facial expression, gesture, speech rhythm, and intonation, they may be able to make a speaker's words more expressive than can the reader's unaided imagination. Thus, the performance of a play by skilled actors expertly directed gives the playwright† a tremendous source of power.

---

*Plot, character, theme, symbol, irony, and other elements of literature have been discussed in the Fiction section and the Poetry section

†The word *wright*—as in *playwright, shipwright, wheelwright, cartwright,* and the common surname *Wright*—comes from an Anglo-Saxon word meaning a workman or craftsman. It is related to the verb *wrought* (a past-tense form of *work*) and has nothing whatever to do with the verb *write*.

But playwrights pay a price for this increased power. Of the four major points of view open to the fiction writer, dramatists are practically limited to one—the *objective*, or *dramatic*. They cannot directly comment on the action or the characters. They cannot enter the minds of their characters and tell us what is going on there. Although there are ways around these limitations, each way has its own limitations. Authorial commentary may be placed in the mouth of a character, but only at the risk of distorting characterization and of leaving the character's reliability uncertain. (Does the character speak for the author or only for herself or himself?) Entry can be made into a character's mind through the conventions of the **soliloquy** and the **aside**. In soliloquies, characters are presented as speaking to themselves—that is, they think out loud. In asides, characters turn from the persons with whom they are conversing to speak directly to (or for the benefit of) the audience, thus letting the audience know what they are really thinking or feeling as opposed to what they pretend to be thinking or feeling. Characters speaking in soliloquy or in asides are always presumed to be telling the truth, to the extent that they know the truth. Both devices can be used very effectively in the theater, but they interrupt the action and are therefore used sparingly. Also, they are inappropriate if the playwright is working in a strictly realistic mode.

Because a play presents its action *on* a stage, it can forcefully command the spectator's attention. The stage is lighted; the theater is dark; extraneous noises are shut out; spectators are almost literally pinned to their seats; there is nowhere they can go; there is nothing else to look at; there is nothing to distract. The playwright has extraordinary means by which to command the undivided attention of the audience. Unlike the fiction writer or the poet, the playwright is not dependent on the power of words alone.

But the necessity to confine the action to a stage, rather than to the imagination's vast arena, limits the kind of materials playwrights can easily and effectively present. For the most part, they must present human beings in spoken interaction with each other. They cannot easily use materials in which the main interest is in unspoken thoughts and reflections. They cannot present complex actions that involve nonhuman creatures such as attacking lions or charging bulls. They find it more difficult to shift scenes rapidly than writers of prose fiction do. The latter may whisk their readers from heaven to earth and back again in the twinkling of an eye, but playwrights must usually stick to one setting for an extended period of time and may feel constrained to do so for the whole play. Moreover, the events they depict must be of a magnitude appropriate to the stage. They cannot present the movements of armies and warfare on the vast scale that Tolstoy uses in *War and Peace*. They cannot easily present adventures at sea or action on a ski slope. Conversely, they cannot depict a fly crawling around the rim of a saucer or falling into a cup of milk. At best they can present a general on a hilltop reporting the movements of a battle, or two persons bending over a cup of milk reacting to a fly that the members of the audience cannot see.

The ease, and therefore the rapidity, with which a playwright can change from one scene to another depends, first, on the elaborateness of the stage setting and, second, on the means by which one scene is separated from another. In ancient plays and in many modern ones, stage settings have been extremely simple, depending only on a few easily moved proper-ties or even entirely on the actors' words and the spectators' imaginations. In such cases, change of scenes is made fairly easily, especially if the actors themselves are allowed to carry on and off any properties that may be needed. Various means have been used to separate scenes from each other. In Greek plays, dancing and chanting by a chorus served as a scene divider. More recently, the closing and opening or dropping and raising of a cur-tain has been the means used. In contemporary theater, with its command of electrical technology, increased reliance has been placed on darkening and illuminating the stage or on darkening one part of it while lighting up another. But even where there is no stage scenery and where the shift of scene is made only by a change in lighting, the playwright can seldom change the setting as rapidly as the writer of prose fiction. On the stage, too-frequent shifts of scene make a play seem jerky. A reader's imagination, on the other hand, can change from one setting to another without even shifting gears.

Because a play presents its action *before* an audience, the experience it creates is communal, and its impact is intensified. Reading a short story or a novel is a private transaction between the reader and a book, but the perfor-mance of a play is public. The spectator's response is affected by the presence of other spectators. A comedy becomes funnier when one hears others laugh-ing, a tragedy more moving when others are present to carry the current of feeling. A dramatic experience, in fact, becomes more intense almost exactly to the extent that it is shared and the individual spectator becomes aware that others are having the same experience. This intensification is partly depen-dent on the size of the audience, but more on their sense of community with each other. A play will be more successful performed before a small audience in a packed auditorium than before a large audience in a half-filled hall.

But, again, the advantage given playwrights by the fact of theatrical performance is paid for by limitations on the material they can present. A play must be able to hold the attention of a group audience. A higher premium than in prose fiction is placed on a well-defined plot, swift exposition, strong conflict, dramatic confrontations. Unless the play is very brief, it is usually divided into parts separated by an intermission or intermissions, and each part works up to its own climax or point of suspense. It is written so that its central meanings may be grasped in a single performance. Spectators at a play cannot back up and rerun a passage whose import they have missed; they cannot, in one night, sit through the whole performance a second time. In addition, playwrights usually avoid extensive use of materials that are purely narrative or lyrical. Long narrative passages are usually interrupted, descriptive passages kept short or eliminated altogether. Primarily, human beings are presented in spoken interaction with each other. Clearly, many of the world's literary masterpieces—stories and poems that enthrall the reader of a book—would not hold the attention of a group audience in a theater.

Drama, then, imposes sharp limitations on its writer but holds out the opportunity for extraordinary force. The successful playwright combines the power of words, the power of fiction, and the power of dramatic technique to make possible the achievement of that force.

REVIEWING CHAPTER ONE

1. Identify the three unique qualities that drama possesses (in contrast to literature written to be read).
2. Explore the advantages and disadvantages of having actors as the medium for the presentation of the dramatic experience.
3. Review the gains and losses imposed by having a drama acted on a stage rather than being presented on the page.
4. Explain how sharing the experience of drama with other audience members is an advantage over viewing it alone, and how the presence of an audience also can impose limitations on what the dramatist can include.

UNDERSTANDING AND EVALUATING DRAMA

As drama may combine the literary resources of both prose fiction and poetry, many of the "Understanding and Evaluating" exercises provided for those two genres (pages 94–96 and 688) may be applicable to drama—except for those directed toward the study of point of view in fiction, since drama always employs the objective or dramatic point of view. Even if a drama is not written in verse, the general questions about diction and figurative language supplied for the elements of poetry may be applicable to drama.

In addition, the variety of dramatic forms and the special nature of drama as a theatrical as well as a literary experience require a set of supplementary questions. Many of these questions will become more meaningful as you read further in the drama section of this book. (Some terms printed in boldface are not defined in this section but are included in the Glossary and Index of Literary Terms, page 1609.)

1. Does the play employ **realistic** or **nonrealistic** conventions? On the spectrum from literalistic imitation of reality to stylized or surrealistic representation, where is the play situated? Are there breaks from the conventions established as a norm in the play? If so, what is the dramatic effect of these departures? Are they meaningful?

2. Is the play a **tragedy** or a **comedy**, a **melodrama** or a **farce?** If a comedy, is it primarily **romantic** or **satiric?** Does it mingle aspects of these types of drama? How important to experiencing the drama is the audience's awareness of the classification of the play?

3. Identify the **protagonist(s)** and **antagonist(s)**. Are there any **foil characters?** What dramatic functions are served by the various minor characters? Do they shed light on the actions or motives of the major characters? Do they advance the **plot** by eliciting actions by others? Do they embody ideas or feelings that illuminate the major characters or the movement of the plot?

4. How is dramatic **suspense** created? Contrast the amount of information possessed by the audience as the play proceeds with the knowledge that various individual characters have: what is the effect of such a contrast?

5. What **themes** does the play present? To what extent do the thematic materials of the play have an effect on the dramatic experience?

Does the power of the ideas increase or decrease the pleasure of the theatrical experience? Does the play seem either too **didactic** or insufficient in its presentation of important human concerns?

6. How do the various physical effects—theatrical components such as sets, lights, costuming, makeup, gestures, stage movements, musical effects of song or dance, and so forth—reinforce the meanings and contribute to the emotional effects? By what means does the playwright indicate the nature of these physical effects—explicitly, through stage directions and set descriptions, or implicitly, through dialogue between characters?

7. What amount of time is covered in the action? How much of the action is presented as a report rather than dramatized on stage? Is there a meaning behind the selection of events to be dramatized and those to be reported? Does the play feel loose or tight in its construction? Is that feeling appropriate to the themes and dramatic effects of the play?

8. To what extent does the play employ narration as a means of **dramatic exposition?** What other expository methods does it use? Does the exposition have a function beyond communicating information about prior events? What effects on the audience do the expository methods have?

SUSAN GLASPELL

Trifles

Characters

GEORGE HENDERSON, *the county attorney*
HENRY PETERS, *the sheriff*
MRS. PETERS, *the sheriff's wife*
MRS. HALE, *a neighbor*
MR. HALE, *her husband, a farmer*

The kitchen in the now abandoned farmhouse of John Wright, a gloomy kitchen, and left without having been put in order—unwashed pans under the sink, a loaf of bread outside the bread-box, a dish-towel on the table—other signs of incompleted work. At the rear the outer door opens *and the* SHERIFF *comes in followed by the* COUNTY ATTORNEY *and* HALE. *The* SHERIFF *and* HALE *are men in middle life, the* COUNTY ATTORNEY *is a young man; all are much bundled up and go at once to the stove. They are followed by the two women—the* SHERIFF'*s wife first; she is a slight wiry woman, with a thin nervous face.* MRS. HALE *is larger and would ordinarily be called more comfortable looking, but she is disturbed now and looks fearfully about as she enters. The women have come in slowly, and stand close together near the door.*

COUNTY ATTORNEY (*rubbing his hands*). This feels good. Come up to the fire, ladies.

MRS. PETERS (*after taking a step forward*). I'm not—cold.

SHERIFF (*unbuttoning his overcoat and stepping away from the stove as if to mark the beginning of official business*). Now, Mr. Hale, before we move things about, you explain to Mr. Henderson just what you saw when you came here yesterday morning.

COUNTY ATTORNEY. By the way, has anything been moved? Are things just as you left them yesterday?

SHERIFF (*looking about*). It's just the same. When it dropped below zero last night I thought I'd send Frank out this morning to make a fire for us—no use getting pneumonia with a big case on, but I told him not to touch anything except the stove—and you know Frank.

TRIFLES   First performed in 1916. Susan Glaspell (1882–1948) was born and lived in Davenport, Iowa, earned a degree from Drake University, and worked as a reporter on a newspaper in Des Moines. In that capacity, she had occasion once to visit the kitchen of a woman who was in jail awaiting trial in a murder case. In her early thirties Glaspell moved to the East Coast to concentrate on writing fiction and plays. *Trifles* was produced at Provincetown on Cape Cod, Massachusetts, and a year later Glaspell adapted it as the short story "A Jury of Her Peers" (page 546).

COUNTY ATTORNEY. Somebody should have been left here yesterday.

SHERIFF. Oh—yesterday. When I had to send Frank to Morris Center for that man who went crazy—I want you to know I had my hands full yesterday. I knew you could get back from Omaha by today and as long as I went over everything here myself—

COUNTY ATTORNEY. Well, Mr. Hale, tell just what happened when you came here yesterday morning.

HALE. Harry and I had started to town with a load of potatoes. We came along the road from my place and as I got here I said, "I'm going to see if I can't get John Wright to go in with me on a party telephone." I spoke to Wright about it once before and he put me off, saying folks talked too much anyway, and all he asked was peace and quiet—I guess you know about how much he talked himself; but I thought maybe if I went to the house and talked about it before his wife, though I said to Harry that I didn't know as what his wife wanted made much difference to John—

COUNTY ATTORNEY. Let's talk about that later, Mr. Hale. I do want to talk about that, but tell now just what happened when you got to the house.

HALE. I didn't hear or see anything; I knocked at the door, and still it was all quiet inside. I knew they must be up, it was past eight o'clock. So I knocked again, and I thought I heard somebody say "Come in." I wasn't sure, I'm not sure yet, but I opened the door—this door (*indicating the door by which the two women are still standing*) and there in that rocker—(*pointing to it*) sat Mrs. Wright. (*They all look at the rocker.*)

COUNTY ATTORNEY. What—was she doing?

HALE. She was rockin' back and forth. She had her apron in her hand and was kind of—pleating it.

COUNTY ATTORNEY. And how did she—look?

HALE. Well, she looked queer.

COUNTY ATTORNEY. How do you mean—queer?

HALE. Well, as if she didn't know what she was going to do next. And kind of done up.

COUNTY ATTORNEY. How did she seem to feel about your coming?

HALE. Why, I don't think she minded—one way or other. She didn't pay much attention. I said, "How do, Mrs. Wright, it's cold, ain't it?" And she said "Is it?"—and went on kind of pleating at her apron. Well, I was surprised; she didn't ask me to come up to the stove, or to set down, but just sat there, not even looking at me, so I said, "I want to see John." And then she—laughed. I guess you would call it a laugh. I thought of Harry and the team outside, so I said a little sharp: "Can't I see John?" "No," she says, kind o' dull like. "Ain't he home?" says I. "Yes," says she, "he's home." "Then why can't I see him?" I asked her out of patience. "'Cause he's dead," says she. *"Dead?"* says I. She just nodded her head, not getting a bit excited, but rockin' back and forth. "Why—where is he?" says I, not knowing what to say. She just pointed upstairs—like that (*himself pointing to the room above*). I got up, with the idea of going up there. I walked from there to here—then I says, "Why, what did he die of?" "He died of a rope round his neck," says she, and just went on pleatin' at her apron. Well, I went out and called Harry. I thought I might—need help. We went upstairs and there he was lyin'—

COUNTY ATTORNEY. I think I'd rather have you go into that upstairs, where you can point it all out. Just go on now with the rest of the story.

HALE. Well, my first thought was to get that rope off. It looked . . . (*Stops, his face twitches.*) . . . but Harry, he went up to him, and he said, "No, he's dead all right, and we'd better not touch anything." So we went back downstairs. She was still sitting that same way. "Has anybody been notified?" I asked. "No," says she, unconcerned. "Who did this, Mrs. Wright?" said Harry. He said it business-like—and she stopped pleatin' of her apron. "I don't know," she says. "You don't *know?*" says Harry. "No," says she. "Weren't you sleepin' in the bed with him?" says Harry. "Yes," says she, "but I was on the inside." "Somebody slipped a rope round his neck and strangled him and you didn't wake up?" says Harry. "I didn't wake up," she said after him. We must 'a looked as if we didn't see how that could be, for after a minute she said, "I sleep sound." Harry was going to ask her more questions, but I said maybe we ought to let her tell her story first to the coroner, or the sheriff, so Harry went fast as he could to Rivers's place, where there's a telephone.

COUNTY ATTORNEY. And what did Mrs. Wright do when she knew that you had gone for the coroner?

HALE. She moved from that chair to this over here . . . (*pointing to a small chair in the corner*) . . . and just sat there with her hands held together and looking down. I got a feeling that I ought to make some conversation, so I said I had come in to see if John wanted to put in a telephone, and at that she started to laugh, and then she stopped and looked at me— scared. (*The* COUNTY ATTORNEY, *who has had his notebook out, makes a note.*) I dunno; maybe it wasn't scared. I wouldn't like to say it was. Soon Harry got back, and then Dr. Lloyd came and you, Mr. Peters, and so I guess that's all I know that you don't.

COUNTY ATTORNEY (*looking around*). I guess we'll go upstairs first—and then out to the barn and around there. (*To the* SHERIFF) You're convinced that there was nothing important here—nothing that would point to any motive?

SHERIFF. Nothing here but kitchen things. (*The* COUNTY ATTORNEY, *after again looking around the kitchen, opens the door of a cupboard closet. He gets up on a chair and looks on a shelf. Pulls his hand away, sticky.*)

COUNTY ATTORNEY. Here's a nice mess. (*The women draw nearer.*)

MRS. PETERS (*to the other woman*). Oh, her fruit; it did freeze. (*To the* ATTORNEY) She worried about that when it turned so cold. She said the fire'd go out and her jars would break.

SHERIFF. Well, can you beat the woman! Held for murder and worryin' about her preserves.

COUNTY ATTORNEY. I guess before we're through she may have something more serious than preserves to worry about.

HALE. Well, women are used to worrying over trifles. (*The two women move a little closer together.*)

COUNTY ATTORNEY (*with the gallantry of a young politician*). And yet, for all their worries, what would we do without the ladies? (*The women do not unbend. He goes to the sink, takes a dipperful of water from the pail and, pouring it into a basin, washes his hands. Starts to wipe them on the roller-towel, turns it for a cleaner place.*) Dirty towels! (*Kicks his foot against the pans under the sink.*) Not much of a housekeeper, would you say, ladies?

MRS. HALE (*stiffly*). There's a great deal of work to be done on a farm.

COUNTY ATTORNEY. To be sure. And yet . . . (*with a little bow to her*) . . . I know there are some Dickson County farmhouses which do not have such roller towels. (*He gives it a pull to expose its full length again.*)

MRS. HALE. Those towels get dirty awful quick. Men's hands aren't always as clean as they might be.

COUNTY ATTORNEY. Ah, loyal to your sex, I see. But you and Mrs. Wright were neighbors. I suppose you were friends, too.

MRS. HALE (*shaking her head*). I've not seen much of her of late years. I've not been in this house—it's more than a year.

COUNTY ATTORNEY. And why was that? You didn't like her?

MRS. HALE (*shaking her head*). I liked her all well enough. Farmers' wives have their hands full, Mr. Henderson. And then—

COUNTY ATTORNEY. Yes—?

MRS. HALE (*looking about*). It never seemed a very cheerful place.

COUNTY ATTORNEY. No—it's not cheerful. I shouldn't say she had the homemaking instinct.

MRS. HALE. Well, I don't know as Wright had, either.

COUNTY ATTORNEY. You mean that they didn't get on very well?

MRS. HALE. No, I don't mean anything. But I don't think a place'd be any cheerfuler for John Wright's being in it.

COUNTY ATTORNEY. I'd like to talk more of that a little later. I want to get the lay of things upstairs now. (*He goes to the left, where three steps lead to a stair door.*)

SHERIFF. I suppose anything Mrs. Peters does'll be all right. She was to take in some clothes for her, you know, and a few little things. We left in such a hurry yesterday.

COUNTY ATTORNEY. Yes, but I would like to see what you take, Mrs. Peters, and keep an eye out for anything that might be of use to us.

MRS. PETERS. Yes, Mr. Henderson. (*The women listen to the men's steps on the stairs, then look about the kitchen.*)

MRS. HALE. I'd hate to have men coming into my kitchen, snooping around and criticizing. (*She arranges the pans under the sink which the* ATTORNEY *had shoved out of place.*)

MRS. PETERS. Of course it's no more than their duty.

MRS. HALE. Duty's all right, but I guess that deputy sheriff that came out to make the fire might have got a little of this on. (*Gives the roller towel a pull.*) Wish I'd thought of that sooner. Seems mean to talk about her for not having things slicked up when she had to come away in such a hurry.

MRS. PETERS (*who has gone to a small table in the left corner of the room, and lifted one end of a towel that covers a pan*). She had bread set. (*Stands still.*)

MRS. HALE (*eyes fixed on a loaf of bread beside the bread-box, which is on a low shelf at the other side of the room. Moves slowly toward it*). She was going to put this in there. (*Picks up loaf, then abruptly drops it. In a manner of returning to familiar things.*) It's a shame about her fruit. I wonder if it's all gone. (*Gets up on the chair and looks.*) I think there's some here that's all right, Mrs. Peters. Yes—here; (*holding it toward the window*) this is cherries, too. (*Looking again*) I declare I believe that's the only one. (*Gets down, bottle in her hand. Goes to the sink and wipes it off on the outside.*) She'll feel awful bad after all her hard work in the hot weather. I remember the afternoon I put up my cherries last summer. (*She puts the bottle on the big kitchen table, center of the room, front table. With a sigh, is about to sit down in the rocking chair. Before she is seated realizes what chair it is: with a slow look at it, steps back. The chair which she has touched rocks back and forth.*)

MRS. PETERS. Well, I must get those things from the front room closet. (*She goes to the door at the right, but after looking into the other room, steps back.*) You coming with me, Mrs. Hale? You could help me carry them. (*They go in the other room; reappear;* MRS. PETERS *carrying a dress and skirt,* MRS. HALE *following with a pair of shoes.*)

MRS. PETERS. My, it's cold in there. (*She puts the clothes on the big table and hurries to the stove.*)

MRS. HALE (*examining the skirt*). Wright was close. I think maybe that's why she kept so much to herself. She didn't even belong to the Ladies' Aid. I suppose she felt she couldn't do her part, and then you don't enjoy things when you feel shabby. She used to wear pretty clothes and be lively, when she was Minnie Foster, one of the town girls singing in the choir. But that—oh, that was thirty years ago. This all you was to take in?

MRS. PETERS. She said she wanted an apron. Funny thing to want, for there isn't much to get you dirty in jail, goodness knows. But I suppose just to make her feel more natural. She said they was in the top drawer in this cupboard. Yes, here. And then her little shawl that always hung behind the door. (*Opens stair door and looks.*) Yes, here it is. (*Quickly shuts door leading upstairs.*)

MRS. HALE (*abruptly moving toward her*). Mrs. Peters?

MRS. PETERS. Yes, Mrs. Hale?

MRS. HALE. Do you think she did it?

MRS. PETERS (*in a frightened voice*). Oh, I don't know.

MRS. HALE. Well, I don't think she did. Asking for an apron and her little shawl. Worrying about her fruit.

MRS. PETERS (*starts to speak, glances up, where footsteps are heard in the room above. In a low voice*). Mr. Peters says it looks bad for her. Mr. Henderson is awful sarcastic in a speech and he'll make fun of her sayin' she didn't wake up.

MRS. HALE. Well, I guess John Wright didn't wake up when they was slipping that rope under his neck.

MRS. PETERS. No, it's strange. It must have been done awful crafty and still. They say it was such a—funny way to kill a man, rigging it all up like that.

MRS. HALE. That's just what Mr. Hale said. There was a gun in the house. He says that's what he can't understand.

MRS. PETERS. Mr. Henderson said coming out that what was needed for the case was a motive; something to show anger, or—sudden feeling.

MRS. HALE (*who is standing by the table*). Well, I don't see any signs of anger around here. (*She puts her hand on the dish towel which lies on the table, stands looking down at table, one half of which is clean, the other half messy.*) It's wiped here. (*Makes a move as if to finish work, then turns and looks at loaf of bread outside the bread-box. Drops towel. In that voice of coming back to familiar things*) Wonder how they are finding things upstairs? I hope she had it a little more red-up° up there. You know, it seems kind of *sneaking*. Locking her up in town and then coming out here and trying to get her own house to turn against her!

MRS. PETERS. But, Mrs. Hale, the law is the law.

MRS. HALE. I s'pose 'tis. (*Unbuttoning her coat.*) Better loosen up your things, Mrs. Peters. You won't feel them when you go out. (MRS. PETERS *takes off her fur tippet, goes to hang it on hook at back of room, stands looking at the under part of the small corner table.*)

MRS. PETERS. She was piecing a quilt. (*She brings the large sewing basket and they look at the bright pieces.*)

---

red-up: neatened, readied (dialectal)

MRS. HALE. It's log cabin pattern. Pretty, isn't it? I wonder if she was goin' to quilt it or just knot it? (*Footsteps have been heard coming down the stairs. The* SHERIFF *enters, followed by* HALE *and the* COUNTY ATTORNEY.)

SHERIFF. They wonder if she was going to quilt it or just knot it. (*The men laugh, the women look abashed.*)

COUNTY ATTORNEY (*rubbing his hands over the stove*). Frank's fire didn't do much up there, did it? Well, let's go out to the barn and get that cleared up. (*The men go outside.*)

MRS. HALE (*resentfully*). I don't know as there's anything so strange, our takin' up our time with little things while we're waiting for them to get the evidence. (*She sits down at the big table smoothing out a block with decision.*) I don't see as it's anything to laugh about.

MRS. PETERS (*apologetically*). Of course they've got awful important things on their minds. (*Pulls up a chair and joins* MRS. HALE *at the table.*)

MRS. HALE (*examining another block*). Mrs. Peters, look at this one. Here, this is the one she was working on, and look at the sewing! All the rest of it has been so nice and even. And look at this! It's all over the place! Why, it looks as if she didn't know what she was about! (*After she has said this they look at each other, then start to glance at the door. After an instant* MRS. HALE *has pulled at a knot and ripped the sewing.*)

MRS. PETERS. Oh, what are you doing, Mrs. Hale?

MRS. HALE (*mildly*). Just pulling out a stitch or two that's not sewed very good. (*Threading a needle.*) Bad sewing always made me fidgety.

MRS. PETERS (*nervously*). I don't think we ought to touch things.

MRS. HALE. I'll just finish up this end. (*Suddenly stopping and leaning forward*) Mrs. Peters?

MRS. PETERS. Yes, Mrs. Hale?

MRS. HALE. What do you suppose she was so nervous about?

MRS. PETERS. Oh—I don't know. I don't know as she was nervous. I sometimes sew awful queer when I'm just tired. (MRS. HALE *starts to say something, looks at* MRS. PETERS, *then goes on sewing.*) Well, I must get these things wrapped up. They may be through sooner than we think. (*Putting apron and other things together.*) I wonder where I can find a piece of paper, and string.

MRS. HALE. In that cupboard, maybe.

MRS. PETERS (*looking in cupboard*). Why, here's a bird-cage. (*Holds it up.*) Did she have a bird, Mrs. Hale?

MRS. HALE. Why, I don't know whether she did or not—I've not been here for so long. There was a man around last year selling canaries cheap, but I don't know as she took one; maybe she did. She used to sing real pretty herself.

MRS. PETERS (*glancing around*). Seems funny to think of a bird here. But she must have had one, or why should she have a cage? I wonder what happened to it?

MRS. HALE. I s'pose maybe the cat got it.

MRS. PETERS. No, she didn't have a cat. She's got that feeling some people have about cats—being afraid of them. My cat got in her room and she was real upset and asked me to take it out.

MRS. HALE. My sister Bessie was like that. Queer, ain't it?

MRS. PETERS (*examining the cage*). Why, look at this door. It's broke. One hinge is pulled apart.

MRS. HALE (*looking too*). Looks as if some one must have been rough with it.

MRS. PETERS. Why, yes. (*She brings the cage forward and puts it on the table.*)

MRS. HALE. I wish if they're going to find any evidence they'd be about it. I don't like this place.

MRS. PETERS. But I'm awful glad you came with me, Mrs. Hale. It would be lonesome for me sitting here alone.

MRS. HALE. It would, wouldn't it? (*Dropping her sewing.*) But I tell you what I do wish, Mrs. Peters. I wish I had come over sometimes when *she* was here. I—(*Looking around the room*)—wish I had.

MRS. PETERS. But of course you were awful busy, Mrs. Hale—your house and your children.

MRS. HALE. I could've come. I stayed away because it weren't cheerful—and that's why I ought to have come. I—I've never liked this place. Maybe because it's down in a hollow and you don't see the road. I dunno what it is, but it's a lonesome place and always was. I wish I had come over to see Minnie Foster sometimes. I can see now—(*Shakes her head.*)

MRS. PETERS. Well, you mustn't reproach yourself, Mrs. Hale. Somehow we just don't see how it is with other folks until—something comes up.

MRS. HALE. Not having children makes less work—but it makes a quiet house, and Wright out to work all day, and no company when he did come in. Did you know John Wright, Mrs. Peters?

MRS. PETERS. Not to know him; I've seen him in town. They say he was a good man.

MRS. HALE. Yes—good; he didn't drink, and kept his word as well as most, I guess, and paid his debts. But he was a hard man, Mrs. Peters. Just to pass the time of day with him. (*Shivers.*) Like a raw wind that gets to the bone. (*Pauses, her eye falling on the cage.*) I should think she would'a wanted a bird. But what do you suppose went wrong with it?

MRS. PETERS. I don't know, unless it got sick and died. (*She reaches over and swings the broken door, swings it again, both women watch it.*)

MRS. HALE. You weren't raised round here, were you? (MRS. PETERS *shakes her head.*) You didn't know—her?

MRS. PETERS. Not till they brought her yesterday.

MRS. HALE. She—come to think of it, she was kind of like a bird herself—real sweet and pretty, but kind of timid and—fluttery. How—she—did—change.

(*Silence; then as if struck by a happy thought and relieved to get back to everyday things.*) Tell you what, Mrs. Peters, why don't you take the quilt in with you? It might take up her mind.

MRS. PETERS. Why, I think that's a real nice idea, Mrs. Hale. There couldn't possibly be any objection to it, could there? Now, just what would I take? I wonder if her patches are in here—and her things. (*They look in the sewing basket.*)

MRS. HALE. Here's some red. I expect this has got sewing things in it. (*Brings out a fancy box.*) What a pretty box. Looks like something somebody would give you. Maybe her scissors are in here. (*Opens box. Suddenly puts her hand to her nose.*) Why—(MRS. PETERS *bends nearer, then turns her face away.*) There's something wrapped up in this piece of silk.

MRS. PETERS. Why, this isn't her scissors.

MRS. HALE (*lifting the silk*). Oh, Mrs. Peters—it's—(MRS. PETERS *bends closer.*)

MRS. PETERS. It's the bird.

MRS. HALE (*jumping up*). But, Mrs. Peters—look at it. Its neck! Look at its neck! It's all—other side *to.*

MRS. PETERS. Somebody—wrung—its neck. (*Their eyes meet. A look of growing comprehension, of horror. Steps are heard outside. MRS. HALE slips box under quilt pieces, and sinks into her chair. Enter SHERIFF and COUNTY ATTORNEY. MRS. PETERS rises.*)

COUNTY ATTORNEY (*as one turning from serious things to little pleasantries*). Well, ladies, have you decided whether she was going to quilt it or knot it?

MRS. PETERS. We think she was going to—knot it.

COUNTY ATTORNEY. Well, that's interesting, I'm sure. (*Seeing the bird-cage*) Has the bird flown?

MRS. HALE (*putting more quilt pieces over the box*). We think the—cat got it.

COUNTY ATTORNEY (*preoccupied*). Is there a cat? (MRS. HALE *glances in a quick covert way at* MRS. PETERS.)

MRS. PETERS. Well, not now. They're superstitious, you know. They leave.

COUNTY ATTORNEY (*to* SHERIFF PETERS, *continuing an interrupted conversation*). No sign at all of anyone having come in from the outside. Their own rope. Now let's go up again and go over it piece by piece. (*They start upstairs.*) It would have to have been some one who knew just the— (MRS. PETERS *sits down. The two women sit there not looking at one another, but as if peering into something and at the same time holding back. When they talk now it is in the manner of feeling their way over strange ground, as if afraid of what they are saying, but as if they cannot help saying it.*)

MRS. HALE. She liked the bird. She was going to bury it in that pretty box.

MRS. PETERS (*in a whisper*). When I was a girl—my kitten—there was a boy took a hatchet, and before my eyes—and before I could get there—(*Covers her face an instant.*) If they hadn't held me back I would have—(*Catches herself, looks upstairs where steps are heard, falters weakly*)—hurt him.

MRS. HALE (*with a slow look around her*). I wonder how it would seem never to have any children around. (*Pause*) No, Wright wouldn't like the bird—a thing that sang. She used to sing. He killed that, too.

MRS. PETERS (*moving uneasily*). We don't know who killed the bird.

MRS. HALE. I knew John Wright.

MRS. PETERS. It was an awful thing was done in this house that night, Mrs. Hale. Killing a man while he slept, slipping a rope around his neck that choked the life out of him.

MRS. HALE. His neck. Choked the life out of him. (*Her hand goes out and rests on the bird-cage.*)

MRS. PETERS (*with rising voice*). We don't know who killed him. We don't *know.*

MRS. HALE (*her own feeling not interrupted*). If there'd been years and years of nothing, then a bird to sing to you, it would be awful—still, after the bird was still.

MRS. PETERS (*something within her speaking*). I know what stillness is. When we homesteaded in Dakota, and my first baby died—after he was two years old, and me with no other then—

MRS. HALE (*moving*). How soon do you suppose they'll be through, looking for the evidence?

MRS. PETERS. I know what stillness is. (*Pulling herself back*) The law has got to punish crime, Mrs. Hale.

MRS. HALE (*not as if answering that*). I wish you'd seen Minnie Foster when she wore a white dress with blue ribbons and stood up there in the choir and sang. (*A look around the room.*) Oh, I *wish* I'd come over here once in a while. That was a crime! That was a crime! Who's going to punish that?

MRS. PETERS (*looking upstairs*). We mustn't—take on.

MRS. HALE. I might have known she needed help! I know how things can be—for women. I tell you, it's queer, Mrs. Peters. We live close together and we live far apart. We all go through the same things—it's all just a different kind of the same thing. (*Brushes her eyes, noticing the bottle of fruit, reaches out for it.*) If I was you I wouldn't tell her her fruit was gone. Tell her it *ain't.* Tell her it's all right. Take this in to prove it to her. She—she may never know whether it was broke or not.

MRS. PETERS (*takes the bottle, looks about for something to wrap it in; takes petticoat from the clothes brought from the other room, very nervously begins winding this around the bottle. In a false voice*). My, it's a good thing the men couldn't hear us. Wouldn't they just laugh. Getting all stirred up over a little thing like a—dead canary. As if that could have anything to do with—with—wouldn't they *laugh!* (*The men are heard coming downstairs.*)

MRS. HALE (*under her breath*). Maybe they would—maybe they wouldn't.

COUNTY ATTORNEY. No, Peters, it's all perfectly clear except a reason for doing it. But you know juries when it comes to women. If there was some definite thing. Something to show—something to make a story about—a thing that would connect up with this strange way of doing it. (*The women's eyes meet for an instant. Enter* HALE *from outer door.*)

HALE. Well, I've got the team around. Pretty cold out there.

COUNTY ATTORNEY. I'm going to stay here a while by myself. (*To the* SHERIFF) You can send Frank out for me, can't you? I want to go over everything. I'm not satisfied that we can't do better.

SHERIFF. Do you want to see what Mrs. Peters is going to take in? (*The* ATTORNEY *goes to the table, picks up the apron, laughs.*)

COUNTY ATTORNEY. Oh, I guess they're not very dangerous things the ladies have picked out. (*Moves a few things about, disturbing the quilt pieces which cover the box. Steps back.*) No, Mrs. Peters doesn't need supervising. For that matter, a sheriff's wife is married to the law. Ever think of it that way, Mrs. Peters?

MRS. PETERS. Not—just that way.

SHERIFF (*chuckling*). Married to the law. (*Moves toward the other room.*) I just want you to come in here a minute, George. We ought to take a look at these windows.

COUNTY ATTORNEY (*scoffingly*). Oh, windows!

SHERIFF. We'll be right out, Mr. Hale. (HALE *goes outside. The* SHERIFF *follows the* COUNTY ATTORNEY *into the other room. Then* MRS. HALE *rises, hands tight together, looking intensely at* MRS. PETERS, *whose eyes make a slow turn, finally meeting* MRS. HALE'S. *A moment* MRS. HALE *holds her, then her own eyes point the way to where the box is concealed. Suddenly* MRS. PETERS *throws back quilt pieces and tries to put the box in the handbag she is carrying. It is too big. She opens box, starts to take bird out, cannot touch it, goes to pieces, stands there helpless. Sound of a knob turning in the other room.* MRS. HALE *snatches the box and puts it in the pocket of her big coat. Enter* COUNTY ATTORNEY *and* SHERIFF.)

COUNTY ATTORNEY (*facetiously*). Well, Henry, at least we found out that she was not going to quilt it. She was going to—what is it you call it, ladies?

MRS. HALE (*her hand against her pocket*). We call it—knot it, Mr. Henderson.

QUESTIONS

1. What individualizing characteristics do you find in the five people in the play? What contrasts are drawn between the men as a group, and the women? In what sense does the title contribute to these contrasts?
2. What contrasts exist between the two women? Is one of them clearly the protagonist? Identify the antagonist.

3. Describe the life that Mrs. Wright must have lived. What is the importance of her having been a singer?
4. Was the murder in any way justified? Why do the women conceal the evidence?
5. It is a common practice for plays to be made out of novels or stories, but unusual for the play to precede the story. Compare this play with the story "A Jury of Her Peers" (page 546). Which is clearer in its presentation of action and feelings? Which has a more direct emotional impact on the audience or reader? Discuss the differences between hearing the short story read aloud by an experienced performer and seeing the play acted by experienced actors.

JANE MARTIN

Rodeo

A young woman in her late twenties sits working on a piece of tack. Beside her is a Lone Star beer in the can. As the lights come up we hear the last verse of a Tanya Tucker song or some other female country-western vocalist. She is wearing old worn jeans and boots plus a long-sleeved workshirt with the sleeves rolled up. She works until the song is over and then speaks.

BIG EIGHT. Shoot—Rodeo's just goin' to hell in a hand-basket. Rodeo used to be somethin'. I loved it. I did. Once Daddy an' a bunch of 'em was foolin' around with some old bronc over to our place and this ol' red nose named Cinch got bucked off and my Daddy hooted and said he had him a nine-year-old girl, namely me, wouldn't have no damn trouble cowboyin' that horse. Well, he put me on up there, stuck that ridin' rein in my hand, gimme a kiss, and said, "Now there's only one thing t' remember Honey Love, if ya fall off you jest don't come home." Well I stayed up. You gotta stay on a bronc eight seconds. Otherwise the ride don't count. So from that day on my daddy called me Big Eight. Heck! That's all the name I got anymore . . . Big Eight.

Used to be fer cowboys, the rodeo did. Do it in some open field, folks would pull their cars and pick-ups round it, sit on the hoods, some ranch hand'd bulldog him some rank steer and everybody'd wave their hats and call him by name. Ride us some buckin' stock, rope a few calves, git throwed off a bull, and then we'd jest git us to a bar and tell each other lies about how good we were.

RODEO   First produced in 1981. Jane Martin is the pen name of a writer who has chosen to remain anonymous, and refuses to make a public appearance, to be interviewed, or to have a photograph published. All of her plays were first produced by the Actors Theatre of Louisville at the annual Humana Festival of New American Plays. "Rodeo" is published by Samuel French, Inc., in a volume of Martin's monologues titled *Talking With* . . .

Used to be a family thing. Wooly Billy Tilson and Tammy Lee had them five kids on the circuit. Three boys, two girls and Wooly and Tammy. Wasn't no two-beer rodeo in Oklahoma didn't have a Tilson entered. Used to call the oldest girl Tits. Tits Tilson. Never seen a girl that top-heavy could ride so well. Said she only fell off when the gravity got her. Cowboys used to say if she landed face down you could plant two young trees in the holes she'd leave. Ha! Tits Tilson.

Used to be people, came to a rodeo had a horse of their own back home. Farm people, ranch people—lord, they *knew* what they were lookin' at. Knew a good ride from a bad ride, knew hard from easy. You broke some bones er spent the day eatin' dirt, at least ya got appreciated.

Now they bought the rodeo. Them. Coca-Cola, Pepsi Cola, Marlboro damn cigarettes. You know the ones I mean. Them. Hire some New York faggot t' sit on some ol' stuffed horse in front of a sagebrush photo n' smoke that junk. Hell, tobacco wasn't made to smoke, honey, it was made to chew. Lord wanted ya filled up with smoke he would've set ya on fire. Damn it gets me!

There's some guy in a banker's suit runs the rodeo now. Got him a pinky ring and a digital watch, honey. Told us we oughta have a watcha-macallit, choriographus or somethin', some ol' ballbuster used to be with the Ice damn Capades. Wants us to ride around dressed up like Mickey Mouse, Pluto, crap like that. Told me I had to haul my butt through the barrel race done up like Minnie damn Mouse in a tu-tu. Huh uh, honey! Them people is so screwed-up they probably eat what they run over in the road.

Listen, they got the clowns wearin' Astronaut suits! I ain't lyin'. You know what a rodeo clown does! You go down, fall off whatever—the clown runs in front of the bull so's ya don't git stomped. Pin-stripes he got 'em in space suits tellin' jokes on a microphone. First horse see 'em, done up like the Star Wars went crazy. Best buckin' horse on the circuit, name of Piss 'N' Vinegar, took one look at them clowns, had him a heart attack and died. Cowboy was ridin' him got hisself squashed. Twelve hundred pounds of coronary arrest jes fell right through 'em. Blam! Vio con dios. Crowd thought that was funnier than the astronauts. I swear it won't be long before they're strappin' ice-skates on the ponies. Big crowds now. Ain't hardly no ranch people, no farm people, nobody I know. Buncha disco babies and dee-vorce lawyers—designer jeans and day-glo Stetsons. Hell, the whole bunch of 'em wears French perfume. Oh it smells like money now! Got it on the cable T and V—hey, you know what, when ya rodeo yer just bound to kick yerself up some dust—well now, seems like that fogs up the ol' TV camera, so they told us a while back that from now on we was gonna ride on some new stuff called Astro-dirt. Dust free. Artificial damn dirt, honey. Lord have mercy.

Banker Suit called me in the other day said. "Lurlene . . ." "Hold it," I said, "Who's this Lurlene? Round here they call me Big Eight." "Well, Big Eight," he said, "My name's Wallace." "Well that's a real surprise t' me," I said, "Cause aroun' here everybody jes calls you Dumb-ass." My, he laughed real big, slapped his big ol' desk, an' then he said I wasn't suitable for the rodeo no more. Said they was lookin' fer another type, somethin' a little more in the show-girl line, like the Dallas Cowgirls maybe. Said the ridin' and ropin' wasn't the thing no more. Talked on about floats, costumes, dancin' choreogaphy. If I was a man I woulda pissed on his shoe. Said he'd give me a lifetime pass though. Said I could come to his rodeo any time I wanted.

Rodeo used to be people ridin' horses for the pleasure of people who rode horses—made you feel good about what you could do. Rodeo wasn't worth no money to nobody. Money didn't have nothing to do with it! Used to be seven Tilsons riding in the rodeo. Wouldn't none of 'em dress up like Donald damn Duck so they quit. That there's the law of gravity!

There's a bunch of assholes in this country sneak around until they see ya havin' fun and then they buy the fun and start in sellin' it. See, they figure if ya love it, they can sell it. Well you look out, honey! They want to make them a dollar out of what you love. Dress you up like Minnie Mouse. Sell your rodeo. Turn yer pleasure into Ice damn Capades. You hear what I'm sayin'? You're jus' merchandise to them, sweetie. You're jus' merchandise to them.

Blackout.

QUESTIONS

1. Characterize the speaker Lurlene (Big Eight). What is her background? What has she done for a living? Although her use of language suggests ignorance or a lack of education, what kind of intelligence does she display?

2. What are her values? What does she think has been lost in the transformation of rodeos? Select examples to support your answer, and show how they reveal her standards.

3. What do we learn about Big Eight from her digressions on Tits Tilson and Marlboro cigarettes?

4. Big Eight refers to her listener(s) as "honey" and "sweetie." Is this monologue addressed to a particular person, or is it spoken to the audience of a play? What can you deduce about the character of the listener from Big Eight's speech?

5. What are the sources of humor in the play? How do they contribute to the overall effect? Is this play sad or comic?

6. State the theme exemplified by the subject of the rodeo and its history. Where does Big Eight recognize that she is talking about more than the rodeo?

Lynn Nottage

POOF!

Characters

SAMUEL, *Loureen's husband*
LOUREEN, *a demure housewife, early thirties*
FLORENCE, *Loureen's best friend, early thirties*

SCENE. The present; a kitchen.

SAMUEL (*in the darkness*). WHEN I COUNT TO TEN I DON' WANT
TO SEE YA! I DON' WANT TO HEAR YA! ONE, TWO, THREE,
FOUR—
LOUREEN (*in the darkness*). DAMN YOU TO HELL, SAMUEL!
(*A bright flash. Lights rise. A huge pile of smoking ashes rests in the middle of
the kitchen.* LOUREEN, *a demure housewife in her early thirties, stares down at
the ashes incredulously. She bends and lifts a pair of spectacles from the remains.
She ever so slowly backs away.*)
Samuel? Uh! (*Places the spectacles on the kitchen table.*) Uh! . . . Samuel?
(*Looks around.*) Don't fool with me now. I'm not in the mood. (*Whispers.*)
Samuel? I didn't mean it really. I'll be good if you come back . . .
Come on now, dinner's waiting. (*Chuckles, then stops abruptly.*) Now stop
your foolishness . . . And let's sit down. (*Examines the spectacles.*) Uh!
(*Softly.*) Don't be cross with me. Sure I forgot to pick up your shirt for
tomorrow. I can wash another, I'll do it right now. Right now! Sam? . . .
(*Cautiously.*) You hear me! (*Awaits a response.*) Maybe I didn't ever intend
to wash your shirt. (*Pulls back as though about to receive a blow; a moment.*)
Uh! (*Sits down and dials the telephone.*) Florence, honey, could you come on
down for a moment. There's been a . . . little . . . accident . . . Quickly
please. Uh! (LOUREEN *hangs up the phone. She gets a broom and a dust pan.
She hesitantly approaches the pile of ashes. She gets down on her hands and knees
and takes a closer look. A fatuous grin spreads across her face. She is startled
by a sudden knock on the door. She slowly walks across the room like a possessed
child.* LOUREEN *lets in* FLORENCE, *her best friend and upstairs neighbor.*
FLORENCE, *also a housewife in her early thirties, wears a floral housecoat and*

POOF!   First performed in 1993 as part of the Humana Festival of New American Plays produced by Actors Theatre of Louisville. Lynn Nottage was born in 1964 in Brooklyn, New York,
and attended Brown University and the Yale School of Drama. She has received numerous awards
for her plays, including an Obie, the NY Drama Critics' Circle Award, a Guggenheim Fellowship,
and a Pulitzer Prize for Drama. Most recently she has taught writing at the Yale School of Drama.

a pair of oversized slippers. Without acknowledgment LOUREEN *proceeds to saunter back across the room.*)

FLORENCE. HEY!

LOUREEN (*pointing at the ashes*). Uh! . . . (*She struggles to formulate words, which press at the inside of her mouth, not quite realized.*) Uh! . . .

FLORENCE. You all right? What happened? (*Sniffs the air.*) Smells like you burned something? (*Stares at the huge pile of ashes.*) What the devil is that?

LOUREEN (*hushed*). Samuel . . . It's Samuel, I think.

FLORENCE. What's he done now?

LOUREEN. It's him. It's him. (*Nods her head repeatedly.*)

FLORENCE. Chile, what's wrong with you? Did he finally drive you out your mind? I knew something was going to happen sooner or later.

LOUREEN. Dial 911, Florence!

FLORENCE. Why? You're scaring me!

LOUREEN. Dial 911! (FLORENCE *picks up the telephone and quickly dials.*) I think I killed him. (FLORENCE *hangs up the telephone.*)

FLORENCE. What?

LOUREEN (*whimpers*). I killed him! I killed Samuel!

FLORENCE. Come again? . . . He's dead dead? (LOUREEN *wrings her hands and nods her head twice, mouthing "dead dead."* FLORENCE *backs away.*) No, stop it, I don't have time for this. I'm going back upstairs. You know how Samuel hates to find me here when he gets home. You're not going to get me this time. (*Louder.*) Y'all can have your little joke; I'm not part of it! (*A moment. She takes a hard look into* LOUREEN's *eyes; she squints.*) Did you really do it this time?

LOUREEN (*hushed*). I don't know how or why it happened, it just did.

FLORENCE. Why you whispering?

LOUREEN. I don't want to talk too loud—something else is liable to disappear.

FLORENCE. Where's his body?

LOUREEN. (*points to the pile of ashes*). There! . . .

FLORENCE. You burned him?

LOUREEN. I DON'T KNOW! (*Covers her mouth as if to muffle her words; hushed.*) I think so.

FLORENCE. Either you did or you didn't, what you mean you don't know? We're talking murder, Loureen, not oven settings.

LOUREEN. You think I'm playing?

FLORENCE. How many times have I heard you talk about being rid of him. How many times have we sat at this very table and laughed about the many ways we could do it and how many times have you done it? None.

LOUREEN (*lifting the spectacles*). A pair of cheap spectacles, that's all that's left. And you know how much I hate these. You ever seen him without them, no! . . . He counted to four and disappeared. I swear to God!

FLORENCE. Don't bring the Lord into this just yet! Sit down now . . . What you got to sip on?

LOUREEN. I don't know whether to have a stiff shot of scotch or a glass of champagne. (FLORENCE *takes a bottle of sherry out of the cupboard and pours them each a glass.* LOUREEN *downs hers, then holds out her glass for more.*) He was . . .

FLORENCE. Take your time.

LOUREEN. Standing there.

FLORENCE. And?

LOUREEN. He exploded.

FLORENCE. Did that muthafucka hit you again?

LOUREEN. No . . . he exploded. Boom! Right in front of me. He was shouting like he does, being all colored, then he raised up that big crusty hand to hit me, and poof, he was gone . . . I barely got words out and I'm looking down at a pile of ash. (FLORENCE *belts back her sherry. She wipes her forehead and pours them both another.*)

FLORENCE. Chile, I'll give you this, in terms of color you've matched my husband Edgar, the story king. He came in at six Sunday morning, talking about he'd hit someone with his car, and had spent all night trying to outrun the police. I felt sorry for him. It turns out he was playing poker with his paycheck no less. You don't want to know how I found out . . . But I did.

LOUREEN. You think I'm lying?

FLORENCE. I certainly hope so, Loureen. For your sake and my heart's.

LOUREEN. Samuel always said if I raised my voice something horrible would happen. And it did. I'm a witch . . . the devil spawn!

FLORENCE. You've been watching too much television.

LOUREEN. Never seen anything like this on television. Wish I had, then I'd know what to do . . . There's no question, I'm a witch. (*Looks at her hands with disgust.*)

FLORENCE. Chile, don't tell me you've been messing with them mojo women again? What did I tell ya? (LOUREEN, *agitated, stands and sits back down.*)

LOUREEN. He's not coming back. Oh no, how could he? It would be a miracle! Two in one day . . . I could be canonized. Worse yet, he could be . . . All that needs to happen now is for my palms to bleed and I'll be eternally remembered as Saint Loureen, the patron of battered wives. Women from across the country will make pilgrimages to me, laying pies and pot roast at my feet and asking the good saint to make their husbands turn to dust. How often does a man like Samuel get damned to hell, and go? (*She breaks down.* FLORENCE *moves to console her friend, then realizes that* LOUREEN *is actually laughing hysterically.*)

FLORENCE. You smoking crack?

LOUREEN. Do I look like I am?

FLORENCE. Hell, I've seen old biddies creeping out of crack houses, talking about they were doing church work.

FLORENCE. Florence, please be helpful, I'm very close to the edge! . . . I don't know what to do next! Do I sweep him up? Do I call the police? Do I . . . (*The phone rings*) Oh God.

FLORENCE. You gonna let it ring? (LOUREEN *reaches for the telephone slowly.*)

LOUREEN. NO! (*holds the receiver without picking it up, paralyzed*). What if it's his mother? . . . She knows! (*The phone continues to ring. They sit until it stops. They both breathe a sigh of relief.*) I should be mourning, I should be praying, I should be thinking of the burial, but all that keeps popping into my mind is what will I wear on television when I share my horrible and wonderful story with a studio audience . . . (*Whimpers.*) He's made me a killer, Florence, and you remember what a gentle child I was. (*Whispers.*) I'm a killer, I'm a killer, I'm a killer.

FLORENCE. I wouldn't throw that word about too lightly even in jest. Talk like that gets around.

LOUREEN. You think they'll lock me up? A few misplaced words and I'll probably get the death penalty, isn't that what they do with women like me, murderesses?

FLORENCE. Folks have done time for less.

LOUREEN. Thank you, just what I needed to hear!

FLORENCE. What did you expect, that I was going to throw up my arms and congratulate you? Why'd you have to go and lose your mind at this time of day, while I got a pot of rice on the stove and Edgar's about to walk in the door and wonder where his goddamn food is. (*Losing her cool.*) And he's going to start in on me about all the nothing I've been doing during the day and why I can't work and then he'll mention how clean you keep your home. And I don't know how I'm going to look him in the eye without . . .

LOUREEN. I'm sorry, Florence. Really. It's out of my hands now. (*She takes* FLORENCE'S *hand and squeezes it.*)

FLORENCE (*regaining her composure*). You swear on your right tit?

LOUREEN (*clutching both breasts*). I swear on both of them!

FLORENCE. Both your breasts, Loureen! You know what will happen if you're lying. (LOUREEN *nods; hushed.*) Both your breasts, Loureen?

LOUREEN. Yeah!

FLORENCE (*examines the pile of ashes, then shakes her head*). Oh sweet, sweet Jesus. He must have done something truly terrible.

LOUREEN. No more than usual. I just couldn't take being hit one more time.

FLORENCE. You've taken a thousand blows from that man, couldn't you've turned the cheek and waited. I'd have helped you pack. Like we talked about. (*A moment.*)

LOUREEN. Uh! . . . I could blow on him and he'd disappear across the linoleum. (*Snaps her fingers.*) Just like that. Should I be feeling remorse or regret or some other "R" word? I'm strangely jubilant, like on prom night when Samuel and I first made love. That's the feeling! (*The women lock eyes.*) Uh!

FLORENCE. Is it . . .

LOUREEN. Like a ton of bricks been lifted from my shoulders, yeah.

FLORENCE. Really?

LOUREEN. Yeah! (FLORENCE *walks to the other side of the room.*)

FLORENCE. You bitch!

LOUREEN. What?

FLORENCE. We made a pact.

LOUREEN. I know.

FLORENCE. You've broken it . . . We agreed that when things got real bad for both of us we'd . . . you know . . . together . . . Do I have to go back upstairs to that? . . . What next?

LOUREEN. I thought you'd tell me! . . . I don't know!

FLORENCE. I don't know!

LOUREEN. I don't know! (FLORENCE *begins to walk around the room, nervously touching objects.* LOUREEN *sits, wringing her hands and mumbling softly to herself.*)

FLORENCE. Now you got me, Loureen, I'm truly at a loss for words.

LOUREEN. Everybody always told me, "Keep your place, Loureen." My place, the silent spot on the couch with a wine cooler in my hand and a pleasant smile that warmed the heart. All this time I didn't know why he was so afraid for me to say anything, to speak up. Poof! . . . I've never been by myself, except for them two weeks when he won the office pool and went to Reno with his cousin Mitchell. He wouldn't tell me where he was going until I got that postcard with the cowboy smoking a hundred cigarettes . . . Didn't Sonny Larkin look good last week at Caroline's? He looked good, didn't he . . . (FLORENCE *nods. She nervously picks up Samuel's jacket, which is hanging on the back of the chair. She clutches it unconsciously.*) NO! No! Don't wrinkle that, that's his favorite jacket. He'll kill me. Put it back! (FLORENCE *returns the jacket to its perch.* LOUREEN *begins to quiver.*) I'm sorry. (*She grabs the jacket and wrinkles it up.*) There!

(*She then digs into the coat pockets and pulls out his wallet and a movie stub.*) Look at that, he said he didn't go to the movies last night. Working late. (*Frantically thumbs through his wallet.*) Picture of his motorcycle, Social Security card, driver's license, and look at that from our wedding. (*Smiling.*) I looked good, didn't I? (*She puts the pictures back in the wallet and holds the jacket up to her face.*) There were some good things. (*She then sweeps her hand over the jacket to remove the wrinkles, and folds it ever so carefully, and finally throws it in the garbage.*) And out of my mouth those words made him disappear. All these years and just words, Florence. That's all they were.

FLORENCE. I'm afraid I won't ever get those words out. I'll start resenting you, honey. I'm afraid won't anything change for me.

LOUREEN. I been to that place.

FLORENCE. Yeah? But now I wish I could relax these old lines (*touches her forehead*) for a minute maybe. Edgar has never done me the way Samuel did you, but he sure did take the better part of my life.

LOUREEN. Not yet, Florence.

FLORENCE (*nods*). I have the children to think of . . . right?

LOUREEN. You can think up a hundred things before . . .

FLORENCE. Then come upstairs with me . . . we'll wait together for Edgar and then you can spit out your words and . . .

LOUREEN. I can't do that.

FLORENCE. Yes you can. Come on now. (LOUREEN *shakes her head no.*) Well, I guess my mornings are not going to be any different.

LOUREEN. If you can say for certain, then I guess they won't be. I couldn't say that.

FLORENCE. But you got a broom and a dust pan, you don't need anything more than that . . . He was a bastard and nobody will care that he's gone.

LOUREEN. Phone's gonna start ringing soon, people are gonna start asking soon, and they'll care.

FLORENCE. What's your crime? Speaking your mind?

LOUREEN. Maybe I should mail him to his mother. I owe her that. I feel bad for her, she didn't understand how it was. I can't just throw him away and pretend like it didn't happen. Can I?

FLORENCE. I didn't see anything but a pile of ash. As far as I know you got a little careless and burned a chicken.

LOUREEN. He was always threatening not to come back.

FLORENCE. I heard him.

LOUREEN. It would've been me eventually.

FLORENCE. Yes.

LOUREEN. I should call the police, or someone.

FLORENCE. Why? What are you gonna tell them? About all those times they refused to help, about all those nights you slept in my bed 'cause you were afraid to stay down here? About the time he nearly took out your eye 'cause you flipped the television channel?

LOUREEN. No.

FLORENCE. You've got it, girl!

LOUREEN. Good-bye to the fatty meats and the salty food. Good-bye to the bourbon and the bologna sandwiches. Good-bye to the smell of his feet, his breath and his bowel movements . . . (*A moment. She closes her eyes and, reliving a horrible memory, she shudders.*) Good-bye. (*Walks over to the pile of ashes.*) Samuel? . . . Just checking.

FLORENCE. Good-bye Samuel. (*They both smile.*)

LOUREEN. I'll let the police know that he's missing tomorrow . . .

FLORENCE. Why not the next day?

LOUREEN. Chicken's warming in the oven, you're welcome to stay.

FLORENCE. Chile, I got a pot of rice on the stove, kids are probably acting out . . . and Edgar, well . . . Listen, I'll stop in tomorrow.

LOUREEN. For dinner?

FLORENCE. Edgar wouldn't stand for that. Cards maybe.

LOUREEN. Cards. (*The women hug for a long moment.* FLORENCE *exits.* LOUREEN *stands over the ashes for a few moments contemplating what to do. She finally decides to sweep them under the carpet, and then proceeds to set the table and sit down to eat her dinner.*)

END OF PLAY

QUESTIONS

1. What do Loureen and Florence have in common, and what differentiates them?
2. Citing specific reported events, describe Loureen's life with Samuel.
3. What are Loureen's various emotional states as the play progresses? In particular, what do you learn about her and Samuel in the incident involving Samuel's jacket?
4. What have Loureen and Florence been planning to do if their husbands become too abusive?
5. Explore the ironic situation that leads a woman to continue to live with an abusive husband.

EDWARD ALBEE

The Sandbox

A Brief Play, in Memory of My Grandmother (1876–1959)

Players

THE YOUNG MAN, *25, a good-looking, well-built boy in a bathing suit*
MOMMY, *55, a well-dressed, imposing woman*
DADDY, *60, a small man; gray, thin*
GRANDMA, *86, a tiny, wizened woman with bright eyes*
THE MUSICIAN, *no particular age, but young would be nice*

> NOTE. *When, in the course of the play,* MOMMY *and* DADDY *call each other by these names, there should be no suggestion of regionalism. These names are of empty affection and point up the pre-senility and vacuity of their characters.*
>
> *The Scene. A bare stage, with only the following: Near the footlights, far stage-right, two simple chairs set side by side, facing the audience; near the footlights, far stage-left, a chair facing stage-right with a music stand before it; farther back, and stage-center, slightly elevated and raked, a large child's sandbox with a toy pail and shovel; the background is the sky, which alters from brightest day to deepest night.*
>
> *At the beginning, it is brightest day; the* YOUNG MAN *is alone on stage to the rear of the sandbox, and to one side. He is doing calisthenics; he does calisthenics until quite at the very end of the play. These calisthenics, employing the arms only, should suggest the beating and fluttering of wings. The* YOUNG MAN *is, after all, the Angel of Death.*

MOMMY *and* DADDY *enter from stage-left,* MOMMY *first.*
MOMMY *(motioning to* DADDY*).* Well, here we are; this is the beach.
DADDY *(whining).* I'm cold.

THE SANDBOX   Written in 1959. Edward Albee, abandoned by his natural parents, was adopted two weeks after birth in 1928 by a wealthy couple in Westchester Country, New York, and named after his adoptive grandfather, part owner of the Keith-Albee string of movie-and-vaudeville theatres. His early schooling frequently interrupted by family vacations, Albee attended a variety of private schools. Dismissed from Trinity College (Connecticut) after three semesters, he went to Greenwich Village, against his foster parents' wishes, determined to write. For about ten years he tried poetry and fiction while working at various odd jobs to supplement a weekly allowance from a trust fund established by his grandmother. After the success of his first play, *Zoo Story* (1959), and the completion of a second, Albee interrupted work on *The American Dream* when commissioned to do a short play for an international theatrical festival. For this play (*The Sandbox*) he used characters from the work in progress placed in a different situation and setting. Despite its overlap of characters and themes with *The American Dream* (1961), it is a separate play, and Albee in 1966 declared it his favorite among his plays.

MOMMY (*dismissing him with a little laugh*). Don't be silly; it's as warm as toast. Look at that nice young man over there: *he* doesn't think it's cold. (*Waves to the* YOUNG MAN.) Hello.

YOUNG MAN (*with an endearing smile*). Hi!

MOMMY (*looking about*). This will do perfectly . . . don't you think so, Daddy? There's sand there . . . and the water beyond. What do you think, Daddy?

DADDY (*vaguely*). Whatever you say, Mommy.

MOMMY (*with the same little laugh*). Well, of course . . . whatever I say. Then, it's settled, is it?

DADDY (*shrugs*). She's *your* mother, not mine.

MOMMY. *I* know she's my mother. What do you take me for? (*A pause.*) All right, now; let's get on with it. (*She shouts into the wings, stage-left.*) You! Out there! You can come in now. (*The* MUSICIAN *enters, seats himself in the chair, stage-left, places music on the music stand, is ready to play.* MOMMY *nods approvingly.*) Very nice; very nice. Are you ready, Daddy? Let's go get Grandma.

DADDY. Whatever you say, Mommy.

MOMMY (*leading the way out, stage-left*). Of course, whatever I say. (*To the* MUSICIAN) You can begin now. (*The* MUSICIAN *begins playing;* MOMMY *and* DADDY *exit; the* MUSICIAN, *all the while playing, nods to the* YOUNG MAN.)

YOUNG MAN (*with the same endearing smile*). Hi! (*After a moment,* MOMMY *and* DADDY *re-enter, carrying* GRANDMA. *She is borne in by their hands under her armpits; she is quite rigid; her legs are drawn up; her feet do not touch the ground; the expression on her ancient face is that of puzzlement and fear.*)

DADDY. Where do we put her?

MOMMY (*with the same little laugh*). Wherever I say, of course. Let me see . . . well . . . all right, over there . . . in the sandbox. (*Pause.*) Well, what are you waiting for, Daddy? . . . The sandbox! (*Together they carry* GRANDMA *over to the sandbox and more or less dump her in.*)

GRANDMA (*righting herself to a sitting position; her voice a cross between a baby's laugh and cry*). Ahhhhh! Graaaaa!

DADDY (*dusting himself*). What do we do now?

MOMMY (*to the* MUSICIAN). You can stop now. (*The* MUSICIAN *stops.*) (*Back to* DADDY) What do you mean, what do we do now? We go over there and sit down, of course. (*To the* YOUNG MAN) Hello there.

YOUNG MAN (*again smiling*). Hi! (MOMMY *and* DADDY *move to the chairs, stage-right, and sit down. A pause.*)

GRANDMA (*same as before*). Ahhhhhh! Ah-haaaaaa! Graaaaaa!

DADDY. Do you think . . . do you think she's . . . comfortable?

MOMMY (*impatiently*). How would I know?

DADDY (*pause*). What do we do now?

MOMMY (*as if remembering*). We . . . wait. We . . . sit here . . . and we wait . . . that's what we do.

DADDY (*after a pause*). Shall we talk to each other?

MOMMY (*with that little laugh; picking something off her dress*). Well, *you* can talk, if you want to . . . if you can think of anything to say . . . if you can think of anything *new.*

DADDY (*thinks*). No . . . I suppose not.

MOMMY (*with a triumphant laugh*). Of course not!

GRANDMA (*banging the toy shovel against the pail*). Haaaaaa! Ah-haaaaaa!

MOMMY (*out over the audience*). Be quiet, Grandma . . . just be quiet, and wait. (GRANDMA *throws a shovelful of sand at* MOMMY. *Still out over the audience*) She's throwing sand at me! You stop that, Grandma; you stop throwing sand at Mommy! (*To* DADDY) She's throwing sand at me. (DADDY *looks around at* GRANDMA, *who screams at him.*)

GRANDMA. GRAAAAA!

MOMMY. Don't look at her. Just . . . sit here . . . be very still . . . and wait. (*To the* MUSICIAN) You . . . uh . . . you go ahead and do whatever it is you do. (*The* MUSICIAN *plays.* MOMMY *and* DADDY *are fixed, staring out beyond the audience.* GRANDMA *looks at them, looks at the* MUSICIAN, *looks at the sandbox, throws down the shovel.*)

GRANDMA. Ah-haaaaaa! Graaaaaa! (*Looks for reaction; gets none. Now . . . directly to the audience*) Honestly! What a way to treat an old woman! Drag her out of the house . . . stick her in a car . . . bring her out here from the city . . . dump her in a pile of sand . . . and leave her here to set. I'm eighty-six years old! I was married when I was seventeen. To a farmer. He died when I was thirty. (*To the* MUSICIAN) Will you stop that, please? (*The* MUSICIAN *stops playing.*) I'm a feeble old woman . . . how do you expect anybody to hear me over that peep! peep! peep! (*To herself*) There's no respect around here. (*To the* YOUNG MAN) There's no respect around here!

YOUNG MAN (*same smile*). Hi!

GRANDMA (*after a pause, a mild double-take, continues, to the audience*). My husband died when I was thirty (*indicates* MOMMY), and I had to raise that big cow over there all by my lonesome. You can imagine what *that* was like. Lordy! (*To the* YOUNG MAN) Where'd they get *you?*

YOUNG MAN. Oh . . . I've been around for a while.

GRANDMA. I'll bet you have! Heh, heh, heh. Will you look at you!

YOUNG MAN (*flexing his muscles*). Isn't that something? (*Continues his calisthenics.*)

GRANDMA. Boy, oh boy; I'll say. Pretty good.

YOUNG MAN (*sweetly*). I'll say.

GRANDMA. Where ya from?

YOUNG MAN. Southern California.

GRANDMA (*nodding*). Figgers; figgers. What's your name, honey?

YOUNG MAN. I don't know . . .

GRANDMA (*to the audience*). Bright, too!

YOUNG MAN. I mean . . . I mean, they haven't given me one yet . . . the studio . . .

GRANDMA (*giving him the once-over*). You don't say . . . you don't say. Well . . . uh, I've got to talk some more . . . don't you go 'way.

YOUNG MAN. Oh, no.

GRANDMA (*turning her attention back to the audience*). Fine; fine. (*Then, once more, back to the* YOUNG MAN) You're . . . you're an actor, hunh?

YOUNG MAN (*beaming*). Yes. I am.

GRANDMA (*to the audience again; shrugs*). I'm smart that way. *Anyhow,* I had to raise . . . *that* over there all by my lonesome; and what's next to her there . . . that's what she married. Rich? I tell you . . . money, money, money. They took me off the *farm* . . . which was real decent of them . . . fixed a nice place for me under the stove . . . gave me an army blanket . . . and my own dish . . . my very own dish! So, what have I got to complain about? Nothing, of course. I'm not complaining. (*She looks up at the sky, shouts to someone off stage.*) Shouldn't it be getting dark now, dear? (*The lights dim; night comes on. The* MUSICIAN *begins to play; it becomes deepest night. There are spots on all the players, including the* YOUNG MAN, *who is, of course, continuing his calisthenics.*)

DADDY (*stirring*). It's nighttime.

MOMMY. Shhhh. Be still . . . wait.

DADDY (*whining*). It's so hot.

MOMMY. Shhhhhh. Be still . . . wait.

GRANDMA (*to herself*). That's better. Night. (*To the* MUSICIAN) Honey, do you play all through this part? (*The* MUSICIAN *nods.*) Well, keep it nice and soft; that's a good boy. (*The* MUSICIAN *nods again; plays softly.*) That's nice. (*There is an off-stage rumble.*)

DADDY (*starting*). What was that?

MOMMY (*beginning to weep*). It was nothing.

DADDY. It was . . . it was . . . thunder . . . or a wave breaking . . . or something.

MOMMY (*whispering, through her tears*). It was an off-stage rumble . . . and you know what *that* means . . .

DADDY. I forget . . .

MOMMY (*barely able to talk*). It means the time has come for poor Grandma . . . and I can't bear it!

DADDY (*vacantly*). I . . . I suppose you've got to be brave.

GRANDMA (*mocking*). That's right, kid; be brave. You'll bear up, you'll get over it. (*Another off-stage rumble . . . louder.*)

MOMMY. Ohhhhhhhhhh . . . poor Grandma . . . poor Grandma . . .

GRANDMA (*To* MOMMY). I'm fine! I'm all right! It hasn't happened yet! (*A violent off-stage rumble. All the lights go out, save the spot on the* YOUNG MAN; *the* MUSICIAN *stops playing.*)

MOMMY. Ohhhhhhhh . . . Ohhhhhhhh . . . (*Silence.*)

GRANDMA. Don't put the lights up yet . . . I'm not ready; I'm not quite ready. (*Silence.*) All right, dear . . . I'm about done. (*The lights come up again, to brightest day; the* MUSICIAN *begins to play.* GRANDMA *is discovered, still in the sandbox, lying on her side, propped up on an elbow, half covered, busily shoveling sand over herself.*)

GRANDMA (*muttering*). I don't know how I'm supposed to do anything with this goddam toy shovel . . .

DADDY. Mommy! It's daylight!

MOMMY (*brightly*). So it is! Well! Our long night is over. We must put away our tears, take off our mourning . . . and face the future. It's our duty.

GRANDMA (*still shoveling; mimicking*). . . . take off our mourning . . . face the future . . . Lordy! (MOMMY *and* DADDY *rise, stretch.* MOMMY *waves to the* YOUNG MAN.)

YOUNG MAN (*with that smile*). Hi! (GRANDMA *plays dead.* [!] MOMMY *and* DADDY *go over to look at her; she is a little more than half buried in the sand; the toy shovel is in her hands, which are crossed on her breast.*)

MOMMY (*before the sandbox; shaking her head*). Lovely! It's . . . it's hard to be sad . . . she looks . . . so happy. (*With pride and conviction*) It pays to do things well. (*To the* MUSICIAN) All right, you can stop now, if you want to. I mean, stay around for a swim, or something; it's all right with us. (*She sighs heavily*) Well, Daddy . . . off we go.

DADDY. Brave Mommy!

MOMMY. Brave Daddy! (*They exit, stage left.*)

GRANDMA (*after they leave; lying quite still*). It pays to do things well . . . Boy, oh boy! (*She tries to sit up.*) . . . well, kids . . . (*But she finds she can't.*) . . . I . . . I can't get up. I . . . I can't move . . . (*The* YOUNG MAN *stops his calisthenics, nods to the* MUSICIAN, *walks over to* GRANDMA, *kneels down by the sandbox.*)

GRANDMA. I . . . can't move . . .

YOUNG MAN. Shhhhh . . . be very still . . .

GRANDMA. I . . . I can't move . . .

YOUNG MAN. Uh . . . ma'am; I . . . I have a line here.

GRANDMA. Oh, I'm sorry, sweetie; you go right ahead.

YOUNG MAN. I am . . . uh . . .

GRANDMA. Take your time, dear.

YOUNG MAN (*prepares; delivers the line like a real amateur*). I am the Angel of Death. I am . . . uh . . . I am come for you.

GRANDMA. What . . . wha . . . (*then, with resignation*) . . . ohhhh . . . ohhhh, I see. (*The* YOUNG MAN *bends over, kisses* GRANDMA *gently on the forehead.*)

GRANDMA (*her eyes closed, her hands folded on her breast again, the shovel between her hands, a sweet smile on her face*). Well . . . that was very nice, dear . . .

YOUNG MAN (*still kneeling*). Shhhhh . . . be still . . .

GRANDMA. What I meant was . . . you did that very well, dear . . .

YOUNG MAN (*blushing*). . . . oh . . .

GRANDMA. No; I mean it. You've got that . . . you've got a quality.

YOUNG MAN (*with his endearing smile*). Oh . . . thank you; thank you very much . . . ma'am.

GRANDMA (*slowly; softly—as the* YOUNG MAN *puts his hands on top of* GRANDMA's). You're . . . you're welcome . . . dear.

(*Tableau. The* MUSICIAN *continues to play as the curtain slowly comes down.*)

QUESTIONS

1. On the face of it, this little play is absurd—absurd both in the way it is presented and in what happens in it. Is it therefore simply horseplay, or does it have a serious subject? What is its subject?

2. The word **absurd**, used in question 1, itself demands attention, since it has been much used with reference to modern drama. The word suggests two different meanings: (a) funny, (b) meaningless. Do both meanings function here? Does either meaning predominate?

3. Characterize Mommy and Daddy. In what ways are they alike? In what ways are they foils? Two of Daddy's speeches are repeated. What do they tell us about his relationship to Mommy?

4. Discuss the treatment by Mommy and Daddy, especially Mommy, of Grandma and her death and burial. What discrepancy exists between appearance and reality? Is their treatment of her in death similar to or different from their treatment of her in life? What metaphor is submerged in Grandma's account of their fixing her a place under the stove with an army blanket and her own dish? What is the function of the Musician?

5. How does the treatment accorded the Young Man by most of the characters (Mommy, the Musician, Grandma) contrast with their treatment of Grandma? What accounts for the difference? What kind of person is the Young Man?

6. What aspects of modern American life are presented in the play? In answering this question, consider your answers to Questions 3, 4, and 5. What judgment does the play make on American life?

7. Contrast Grandma with the Young Man and with Mommy and Daddy. What admirable qualities does she have? What disagreeable qualities does she have? Why? On the whole, is she presented as more, or less, worthy of respect than the other characters in the play? Why?

8. Both in the notes and in the dialogue, the Young Man is identified as the Angel of Death. How is he a very unusual Angel of Death? Is he a simple or a multiple symbol? What other meanings does he suggest?

9. What symbolic meanings are suggested by the following: (a) the bareness of the stage, (b) the sandbox, (c) the toy pail and shovel, (d) the dimming and extinguishing of the lights, (e) Grandma's burying herself with sand, (f) the fact that Grandma is buried before she is dead, (g) the Young Man's kissing Grandma? Which of them, like the Young Man, are multiple symbols?

10. At various points in the action the characters seem aware that they are performers in a play. What effect does this have on the audience's response?

DAVID IVES
Time Flies

Characters

HORACE
MAY
DAVID ATTENBOROUGH
A FROG

SCENE: *Evening. A pond. The chirr of treetoads, and the buzz of a huge swarm of insects. Upstage, a thicket of tall cattails. Downstage, a deep green loveseat. Overhead, an enormous full moon.*
A loud cuckoo sounds, like the mechanical "cuckoo" of a clock.
Lights come up on two mayflies: HORACE *and* MAY, *buzzing as they "fly" in. They are dressed like singles on an evening out, he in a jacket and tie, she in a party dress—but they have insect-like antennae; long tube-like tails; and on their backs, translucent wings. Outsized hornrim glasses give the impression of very large eyes.* MAY *has distinctly hairy legs.*

HORACE and MAY. Bzzzzzzzzzzzzzzzzzz . . . (*Their wings stop fluttering, as they "settle."*)
MAY. Well here we are. This is my place.
HORACE. Already? That was fast.
MAY. Swell party, huh.
HORACE. Yeah. Quite a swarm.
MAY. Thank you for flying me home.
HORACE. No. Sure. I'm happy to. Absolutely. My pleasure. I mean—you're very, very, very welcome. (*Their eyes lock and they near each other as if for a kiss, their wings fluttering a little.*) Bzzzzzzzz . . .
MAY. Bzzzzzzzz . . . (*Before their jaws can meet:* "CUCKOO!"—*and* HORACE *breaks away.*)
HORACE. It's that late, is it. Anyway, it was very nice meeting you—I'm sorry, is it April?
MAY. May.
HORACE. May. Yes. Later than I thought, huh. (*They laugh politely.*)

TIME FLIES One of three one-act plays presented together as *Mere Mortals*, the play was first performed Off-Broadway in New York in 1998. David Ives was born in Chicago in 1951 and educated at Northwestern University and the Yale School of Drama, and in 1995 received a Guggenheim Fellowship for play writing. David Attenborough is the host of nature programs created for British television and broadcast in the United States. The phrase *carpe diem*, used several times in the play, is Latin for "seize the day," an admonition to live life fully because it is so brief—or, paraphrased, "time flies."

MAY. That's very funny, Vergil.

HORACE. It's Horace, actually.

MAY. I'm sorry. The buzz at that party was so loud.

HORACE. So you're "May the mayfly."

MAY. Yeah. Guess my parents didn't have much imagination. May, mayfly.

HORACE. You don't, ah, live with your parents, do you, May?

MAY. No, my parents died around dawn this morning.

HORACE. Isn't that funny. Mine died around dawn too.

MAY. Maybe it's fate.

HORACE. Is that what it izzzzzzzz . . . ?

MAY. Bzzzzzzzz . . .

HORACE. Bzzzzzzzzzzzz . . . (*They near for a kiss, but* HORACE *breaks away.*) Well I'd better be going now. Good night.

MAY. Do you want a drink?

HORACE. I'd love a drink, actually . . .

MAY. Let me just turn on a couple of fireflies. (MAY *tickles the underside of a couple of two foot-long fireflies hanging like a chandelier, and the fireflies light up.*)

HORACE. Wow. Great pond! (*Indicating the loveseat.*) I love the lilypad.

MAY. The lilypad was here. It kinda grew on me. (*Polite laugh.*) Care to take the load off your wings?

HORACE. That's all right. I'll just—you know—hover. But will you look at that . . . ! (*Turning,* HORACE *bats* MAY *with his wings.*)

MAY. Oof!

HORACE. I'm sorry. Did we collide?

MAY. No. No. It's fine.

HORACE. I've only had my wings about six hours.

MAY. Really! So have I . . . ! Wasn't molting disgusting?

HORACE. Eugh. I'm glad that's over.

MAY. Care for some music? I've got The Beatles, The Byrds, The Crickets . . .

HORACE. I love the Crickets.

MAY. Well so do I . . . (*She kicks a large, insect-shaped coffee table, and we hear the buzz of crickets.*)

HORACE (*as they boogie to that*). So are you going out with any—I mean, are there any other mayflies in the neighborhood?

MAY. No, it's mostly wasps.

HORACE. So, you live here by your, um, all by yourself? Alone?

MAY. All by my lonesome.

HORACE. And will you look at that moon.

MAY. You know that's the first moon I've ever seen?

HORACE. That's the first moon *I've* ever seen . . . !

MAY. Isn't that funny.

HORACE. When were you born?

MAY. About 7:30 this morning.

HORACE. So was I! Seven thirty-three!

MAY. Isn't that funny.

HORACE. Or maybe it's fate. (*They near each other again, as if for a kiss.*)
Bzzzzzz . . .

MAY. Bzzzzzzzzz . . . I think that moon is having a very emotional effect on me.

HORACE. Me too.

MAY. It must be nature.

HORACE. Me too.

MAY. Or maybe it's fate.

HORACE. Me too . . .

MAY. Bzzzzzzzzzz . . .

HORACE. Bzzzzzzzzzzzzz . . . (*They draw their tails very close. Suddenly*)

A FROG (*amplified, over loudspeaker*) Ribbit, ribbit!

HORACE. A frog!

MAY. A frog!

HORACE and MAY. The frogs are coming, the frogs are coming! (*They "fly"
around the stage in a panic. Ad lib*) A frog, a frog! The frogs are coming,
the frogs are coming! (*They finally stop, breathless.*)

MAY. It's okay. It's okay.

HORACE. Oh my goodness.

MAY. I think he's gone now.

HORACE. Oh my goodness, that scared me.

MAY. That is the only drawback to living here. The frogs.

HORACE. You know I like frog films and frog literature. I just don't like frogs.

MAY. And they're so rude if you're not a frog yourself.

HORACE. Look at me. I'm shaking.

MAY. Why don't I fix you something. Would you like a grasshopper? Or a
stinger?

HORACE. Just some stagnant water would be fine.

MAY. A little duckweed in that? Some algae?

HORACE. Straight up is fine.

MAY (*as she pours his drink*). Sure I couldn't tempt you to try the lily pad?

HORACE. Well, maybe for just a second. (*HORACE flutters down onto the love
seat.*) Zzzzzzz . . .

MAY (*handing him a glass*). Here you go. Cheers, Horace.

HORACE. Long life, May. (*They clink glasses.*)

MAY. Do you want to watch some tube?

HORACE. Sure. What's on?

MAY. Let's see. (*She checks a green TV Guide.*) There is . . . *The Love Bug*,
M. Butterfly, *The Spider's Stratagem*, *Travels With My Ant*, *Angels and
Insects*, *The Fly* . . .

HORACE. The original, or Jeff Goldblum?

MAY. Jeff Goldblum.

HORACE. Euch. Too gruesome.

MAY. *Born Yesterday* and *Life on Earth.*

HORACE. What's on that?

MAY. "Swamp Life," with Sir David Attenborough.

HORACE. That sounds good.

MAY. Shall we try it?

HORACE. Carpe diem.

MAY. Carpe diem? What's that?

HORACE. I don't know. It's Latin.

MAY. What's Latin?

HORACE. I don't know. I'm just a mayfly. (*"Cuckoo!"*) And we're right on time for it. (MAY *presses a remote control and* DAVID ATTENBOROUGH *appears, wearing a safari jacket.*)

DAVID ATTENBOROUGH. Hello, I'm David Attenborough. Welcome to "Swamp Life."

MAY. Isn't this comfy.

HORACE. Is my wing in your way?

MAY. No. It's fine.

DAVID ATTENBOROUGH. You may not believe it, but within this seemingly lifeless puddle, there thrives a teeming world of vibrant life.

HORACE. May, look—isn't that your pond?

MAY. I think that is my pond!

HORACE. He said "puddle."

DAVID ATTENBOROUGH. This puddle is only several inches across, but its stagnant water plays host to over 14 gazillion different species.

MAY. It is my pond!

DAVID ATTENBOROUGH. Every species here is engaged in a constant, desperate battle for survival. Feeding—meeting—mating—breeding—dying. And mating. And meeting. And mating. And feeding. And dying. Mating. Mating. Meeting. Breeding. Brooding. Braiding—those that can braid. Feeding. Mating.

MAY. All right, Sir Dave!

DAVID ATTENBOROUGH. Mating, mating, mating, and mating.

HORACE. Only one thing on his mind.

MAY. The filth on television these days.

DAVID ATTENBOROUGH. Tonight we start off with one of the saddest creatures of this environment.

HORACE. The dung beetle.

MAY. The toad.

DAVID ATTENBOROUGH. The lowly mayfly.

HORACE. Did he say "the mayfly?"

MAY. I think he said the lowly mayfly.

DAVID ATTENBOROUGH. Yes. The lowly mayfly. Like these two mayflies, for instance.

HORACE. May—I think that's us!

MAY. Oh my God . . .

HORACE and MAY (*together*). We're on television!

HORACE. I don't believe it!

MAY. I wish my mother was here to see this!

HORACE. This is amazing!

MAY. Oh God, I look terrible!

HORACE. You look very good.

MAY. I can't look at this.

DAVID ATTENBOROUGH. As you can see, the lowly mayfly is not one of nature's most attractive creatures.

MAY. At least we don't wear safari jackets.

HORACE. I wish he'd stop saying "lowly mayfly."

DAVID ATTENBOROUGH. The lowly mayfly has a very distinctive khkhkhkhkhkhkhkhkhkkh . . . (*the sound of TV static*)

MAY. I think there's something wrong with my antenna . . . (*She adjusts the antenna on her head.*)

HORACE. You don't have cable?

MAY. Not on this pond.

DAVID ATTENBOROUGH (*stops the static sound*). . . . and sixty tons of droppings.

HORACE. That fixed it.

MAY. Can I offer you some food? I've got some plankton in the pond. And some very nice gnat.

HORACE. I do love good gnat.

MAY. I'll set it out, you can pick. (*She rises and gets some food.*)

DAVID ATTENBOROUGH. The lowly mayfly first appeared some 350 million years ago . . .

MAY. That's impressive.

DAVID ATTENBOROUGH. . . . and is of the order Ephemeroptera, meaning, "living for a single day."

MAY. I did not know that!

HORACE. "Living for a single day." Huh . . .

MAY (*setting out a tray on the coffee table*). There you go.

HORACE. Gosh, May. That's beautiful.

MAY. There's curried gnat, salted gnat, Scottish smoked gnat . . .

HORACE. I love that.

MAY. . . . gnat with pesto, gnat au naturelle, and Gnat King Cole.

HORACE. I don't think I could finish a whole one.

MAY. "Gnat" to worry. (*They laugh politely.*) That's larva dip there in the center. Just dig in.

DAVID ATTENBOROUGH. As for the life of the common mayfly . . .

HORACE. Oh. We're "common" now.

DAVID ATTENBOROUGH. . . . it is a simple round of meeting, mating, meeting, mating—

MAY. Here we go again.

DAVID ATTENBOROUGH. —breeding, feeding, feeding . . .

HORACE. This dip is fabulous.

DAVID ATTENBOROUGH. . . . and dying.

MAY. Leaf?

HORACE. Thank you. (MAY *breaks a leaf off a plant and hands it to* HORACE.)

DAVID ATTENBOROUGH. Mayflies are a major food source for trout and salmon.

MAY. Will you look at that savagery?

HORACE. That poor, poor mayfly.

DAVID ATTENBOROUGH. Fishermen like to bait hooks with mayfly look-alikes.

MAY. Bastards!—Excuse me.

DAVID ATTENBOROUGH. And then there is the giant bullfrog.

FROG (*amplified, over loudspeaker*). Ribbit, ribbit!

HORACE and MAY. The frogs are coming, the frogs are coming! (*They "fly" around the stage in a panic—and end up "flying" right into each other's arms.*)

HORACE. Well there.

MAY. Hello.

DAVID ATTENBOROUGH. Welcome to "Swamp Life." (*Exits.*)

MAY (*hypnotized by* HORACE). Funny how we flew right into each other's wings.

HORACE. It is funny.

MAY. Or fate.

HORACE. Do you think he's gone?

MAY. David Attenborough?

HORACE. The frog.

MAY. What frog? Bzzzz . . .

HORACE. Bzzzzz . . .

DAVID ATTENBOROUGH'S VOICE. As you see, mayflies can be quite affectionate . . .

HORACE and MAY. Bzzzzzzzzzzzz . . .

DAVID ATTENBOROUGH'S VOICE. . . . mutually palpating their proboscises.

HORACE. You know I've been wanting to palpate your proboscis all evening?

MAY. I think it was larva at first sight.

HORACE and MAY (*rubbing proboscises together*). Zzzzzzzzzzzzzzzzzzzzzzzzzzzzz . . .

MAY (*very British, "Brief Encounter"*). Oh darling, darling.

HORACE. Oh do darling do let's always be good to each other, shall we?

MAY. Let's do do that, darling, always, always.

HORACE. Always?

MAY. Always.

HORACE and MAY. Zzzzzzzzzzzzzzzzzzzzzzzzzzzzzz!

MAY. Rub my antennae. Rub my antennae. (HORACE *rubs* MAY'*s antennae with his hands.*)

DAVID ATTENBOROUGH'S VOICE. Sometimes mayflies rub antennae together.

MAY. Oh yes. Yes. Just like that. Yes. Keep going. Harder. Rub harder.

HORACE. Rub mine now. Rub my antennae. Oh yes. Yes. Yes. Yes. There's the rub. There's the rub. Go. Go. Go!

DAVID ATTENBOROUGH'S VOICE. Isn't that a picture. Now get a load of mating. (HORACE *gets into mounting position, behind* MAY. *He rubs her antennae while she wolfs down the gnat-food in front of her.*)

HORACE and MAY. Bzzzzzzzzzzzzzzzzzzzzzzzzzzzzzzzzzzzzzz!

DAVID ATTENBOROUGH'S VOICE. Unfortunately for this insect, the may-fly has a lifespan of only one day. (HORACE *and* MAY *stop buzzing, abruptly.*)

HORACE. What was that . . . ?

DAVID ATTENBOROUGH'S VOICE. The mayfly has a lifespan of only one day—living just long enough to meet, mate, have offspring, and die.

MAY. Did he say "meet, mate, have offspring, and DIE"—?

DAVID ATTENBOROUGH'S VOICE. I did. In fact, mayflies born at 7:30 in the morning will die by the next dawn. (HORACE *whimpers softly at the thought*) But so much for the lowly mayfly. Let's move on to the newt. (*"Cuckoo!"*)

HORACE and MAY. We're going to die . . . We're going to die! Mayday, mayday! We're going to die, we're going to die! (*Weeping and wailing, they kneel, beat their breasts, cross themselves, and tear their hair: "Cuckoo!"*)

HORACE. What time is it? What time is it?

MAY. I don't wear a watch. I'm a lowly mayfly!

HORACE (*weeping*). Wah-ha-ha-ha!

MAY (*suddenly sober*). Well isn't this beautiful.

HORACE (*gasping for breath*). Oh my goodness. I think I'm having an asthma attack. Can mayflies have asthma?

MAY. I don't know. Ask Mr. Safari Jacket.

HORACE. Maybe if I put a paper bag over my head . . .

MAY. So this is my sex life?

HORACE. Do you have a paper bag?

MAY. One bang, a bambino, and boom—that's it?

HORACE. Do you have a paper bag?

MAY. For the common mayfly, foreplay segues right into funeral.

HORACE. Do you have a paper bag?

MAY. I don't have time to look for a paper bag, I'm going to be dead very shortly, all right? (*"Cuckoo!"*)

HORACE. Oh come on! That wasn't a whole hour! (*"Cuckoo!"*) Time is moving so fast now. (*"Cuckoo!"*)

HORACE and MAY. Shut up! (*"Cuckoo!"*)

HORACE (*suddenly sober*). This explains everything. We were born this morning, we hit puberty in mid-afternoon, our biological clocks went BONG, and here we are. Hot to copulate.

MAY. For the one brief miserable time we get to do it.

HORACE. Yeah.

MAY. Talk about a quickie.

HORACE. Wait a minute, wait a minute.

MAY. Talk fast.

HORACE. What makes you think it would be so brief?

MAY. Oh, I'm sorry. Did I insult your vast sexual experience?

HORACE. Are you more experienced than I am, Dr. Ruth? Luring me here to your pad?

MAY. I see. I see. Blame me!

HORACE. Can I remind you we only get one shot at this?

MAY. So I can rule out multiple orgasms, is that it?

HORACE. I'm just saying there's not a lot of time to hone one's erotic technique, okay?

MAY. Hmp!

HORACE. And I'm trying to sort out some very big entomontological questions here rather quickly, do you mind?

MAY. And I'm just the babe here, is that it? I'm just a piece of tail.

HORACE. I'm not the one who suggested TV.

MAY. I'm not the one who wanted to watch *Life on Earth*. "Oh—Swamp Life. That sounds interesting."

FROG. Ribbit, ribbit.

HORACE (*calmly*). There's a frog up there.

MAY. Oh, I'm really scared. I'm terrified.

FROG. Ribbit, ribbit!

HORACE (*calling to the frog*). We're right down here! Come and get us!

MAY. Breeding. Dying. Breeding. Dying. So this is the whole purpose of mayflies? To make more mayflies?

HORACE. Does the world *need* more mayflies?

MAY. We're a major food source for trout and salmon.

HORACE. How nice for the salmon.

MAY. Do you want more food?

HORACE. I've lost a bit of my appetite, all right?

MAY. Oh. Excuse me.

HORACE. I'm sorry. Really, May.

MAY (*starts to cry*). Males!

HORACE. Leaf? (*He plucks another leaf and hands it to her.*)

MAY. Thank you.

HORACE. Really. I didn't mean to snap at you.

MAY. Oh, you've been very nice. ("*CUCKOO!*" *They jump.*) Under the circumstances.

HORACE. I'm sorry.

MAY. No, I'm sorry.

HORACE. No, I'm sorry.

MAY. No, I'm sorry.

HORACE. No, I'm sorry.

MAY. We'd better stop apologizing, we're going to be dead soon.

HORACE. I'm sorry.

MAY. Oh Horace, I had such plans. I had such wonderful plans. I wanted to see Paris.

HORACE. What's Paris?

MAY. I have no fucking idea.

HORACE. Maybe we'll come back as caviar and find out. (*They laugh a little at that.*) I was just hoping to live till Tuesday.

MAY (*making a small joke*) What's a Tuesday? (*They laugh a little more at that.*) The sun's going to be up soon. I'm scared, Horace. I'm so scared.

HORACE. You know, May, we don't have much time, and really, we hardly know each other—but I'm going to say it. I think you're swell. I think you're divine. From your buggy eyes to the thick raspy hair on your legs to the intoxicating scent of your secretions.

MAY. Eeeuw.

HORACE. Eeeuw? No. I say *woof.* And I say who cares if life is a swamp and we're just a couple of small bugs in a very small pond. I say live, May! I say . . . darn it . . . live!

MAY. But how?

HORACE. Well I don't honestly know that . . . (ATTENBOROUGH *appears.*)

DAVID ATTENBOROUGH. You could fly to Paris.

MAY. We could fly to Paris!

HORACE. Do we have time to fly to Paris?

MAY. Carpe diem!

HORACE. What is carpe diem?

DAVID ATTENBOROUGH. It means "bon voyage."

HORACE and MAY. And we're outta here!

(*They fly off to Paris as . . . Blackout.*)

QUESTIONS

1. Although Horace and May are insects, the dialogue is distinctly human. Point out examples of contemporary social conversation. To what are these mayflies being compared?
2. Mayflies do live only one day. How does that fact become symbolic of some human relationships?
3. What is the function of the voice of David Attenborough? At what points does it shift away from what you expect of the TV host of a nature program? Why?
4. Much of the humor of the play arises from insects behaving like people. In addition, there are many puns and verbal jokes. Make a list of these, and show how they distance the audience from involvement in the emotions felt by the characters. For example, "frog" is a derogatory term for the French, and May and Horace have a bit of conversation about what they do and don't like about frogs. Translate that into trite comments on the French—and juxtapose it to the conclusion of the play. Does it matter that the audience cannot empathize with the serious emotions that the characters share?
5. Explain the pun in the title of the play. Would "carpe diem" have been as suitable as this title?

SUGGESTIONS FOR WRITING

1. Works written as short stories, novels, or poems have sometimes been dramatized for stage production. In light of the advantages and limitations discussed in this chapter, however, some are clearly more easily adapted for the stage than others. Select one or two from the following list, and explain the relative ease or difficulty—or impossibility—of a stage adaptation: "Araby" (page 186), "Miss Brill" (page 155), "The Lottery" (page 260), "A Very Old Man with Enormous Wings" (page 318), "To Autumn" (page 743), "Home Burial" (page 952), "The Love Song of J. Alfred Prufrock" (page 956).
2. Movie and broadcast (TV and radio) productions are in many ways more flexible than stage productions and are more easily brought to a mass audience. What limitations of stage performance discussed in this chapter can be minimized or eliminated in a movie or broadcast production? Conversely, what advantages of stage performances are unavailable to media productions?
3. In view of the greater flexibility of movies and broadcasting media in dramatic representation, what accounts for the continuing popularity of stage plays?
4. If plays are written to be *performed*, what justification is there for reading them?

PRACTICE AP WRITING PROMPTS ▬▬▬▬▬

Jane Martin, *Rodeo* (pp. 1085–1087)

Rodeo is approximately the length of many AP Literature Question 2 passages. Read the play and respond to this essay prompt in a 40-minute timed writing.

Read carefully the very brief one-woman play *Rodeo* (1981). Then, in a well-written essay, analyze how the diction in Lurlene's monologue conveys her attitude toward change and contributes to the playwright's intended effect.

....

Edward Albee, *The Sandbox* (pp. 1095–1100)

Chapter One consists solely of one-act plays. Although a one-act play is not a suitable choice for the AP Literature Exam Question 3, use the essay prompt below to analyze *The Sandbox* as you practice AP writing, or choose another novel or play in which characters step outside the bounds of strict realism.

Many works of imaginative literature contain characters who seem to recognize that they are, in fact, fictitious. They may step outside their roles within the narrative, or, in drama, they may break the fourth wall and speak to the audience. Choose a novel or play with such a character, and explain how this break from realism contributes to the development of the character and to the meaning of the work as a whole. Avoid merely providing a plot summary.

....

CHAPTER TWO

Realistic and Nonrealistic Drama

Literary truth in drama (as in fiction and in poetry) is not the same as fidelity to fact. Fantasy is as much the property of the theater as of poetry or the prose tale. In *A Midsummer Night's Dream* and *The Tempest,* Shakespeare has fairies and spirits and monsters as characters, and in *Hamlet* and *Macbeth* he introduces ghosts and witches. These supernatural characters, nevertheless, serve as a vehicle for truth. When Bottom, in *A Midsummer Night's Dream,* is given an ass's head, the enchantment is a visual metaphor. The witches in *Macbeth* truthfully prefigure a tragic destiny.

Because it is written to be performed, however, drama adds still another dimension of possible unreality. It may be **realistic** or **nonrealistic** in mode of production as well as in content. Staging, makeup, costuming, and acting may all be handled in such a way as to emphasize the realistic or the fanciful.

It must be recognized, however, that all stage production, no matter how realistic, involves a certain necessary artificiality. If an indoor scene is presented on a picture-frame proscenium stage, the spectator is asked to imagine that a room with only three walls is actually a room with four walls. In a thrust-stage or arena theater, in which audiences are in a semicircle around the playing area, the spectator must imagine three of the four walls, while theater-in-the-round has the audience seated on all sides of the action and spectators have to imagine all four walls—while imaginatively shutting their minds to the presence of spectators facing them from the other side of the action. All of these types of stage presentation, moreover, require adjustments in the acting. In a proscenium theater the actors must be facing the missing fourth wall most of the time. In arena or round stagings, they must not turn their backs too long on any "wall." Both types of staging, in the interests of effective presentation, require the actors to depart from an absolute realism.

Beyond these basic requirements of artificiality in stagecraft, the departure from the appearance of reality may be slight or considerable. In many late-nineteenth- and early-twentieth-century productions, an effort was made to make stage sets as realistic as possible. If the play called for a setting in a study, there had to be real bookshelves on the wall and real books on the shelves. If the room contained a sink, real water had to flow from the faucets. On the other hand, plays have been performed on bare stages with little more than platforms and a few props.

In between these two extremes, all degrees of realism are possible. The scenery may consist of painted flats, with painted bookshelves and painted books and painted pictures on the wall, and these paintings may strive for photographic faithfulness or for an impressionistic effect. Or, instead of scenery, a play may use only a few movable properties to suggest the required setting. Thornton Wilder's *Our Town* (1938) utilized a bare stage, without curtain, with exposed ropes and backstage equipment, and with a few chairs, two ladders, and a couple of trellises as the only properties. For a scene at a soda fountain counter, a plank was laid across the backs of two chairs. In fact, provision of elaborately realistic stage sets has been the exception rather than the rule in the long history of the theater. Neither in Greek nor in Shakespearean theater was setting much more than suggested.

The choice of realistic or nonrealistic stage sets, costuming, and makeup may, in fact, lie with the producer rather than the playwright, and a producer may choose to disregard a playwright's directions for the sake of novelty or emphasis. When we move to the realm of language and the management of dialogue, the choice is entirely the playwright's. Here again all degrees of realism and nonrealism are possible. In the realistic theater of the last hundred years, some playwrights have made an elaborate effort to reproduce the flat quality of ordinary speech, with all its stumblings and inarticulateness, its slang and its mispronunciations. Others go even further in imitating reality, even at the risk of offending some members of the audience, and reproduce the vulgarities of the language of the streets and the contemporary habit of using obscene terms simply to add force to a statement. In real life, of course, few lovers speak with the eloquence of Romeo and Juliet, and many people, in daily conversation, have difficulty getting through a grammatically correct sentence of any length or complexity. They break off, they begin again, they repeat themselves, and sometimes, like the Young Man in "The Sandbox," they are barely articulate ("I am . . . uh . . . I am the Angel of Death. I am . . . uh . . . I am come for you." [page 1095]). Such unimaginative and inadequate speech, skillfully used by the playwright, may faithfully render the quality of human life at some levels, yet its limitations for expressing the heights and depths of human experience are obvious. Most dramatic dialogue, even at its most realistic, is more coherent and expressive than speech in actual life. Art is always a heightening or an intensification of reality; else it would have little value. The heightening may be little or great. It is greatest in poetic drama. The love exchanges of Romeo and Juliet, spoken in rhymed iambic pentameter and at one point taking the form of a perfect sonnet (see page 927), are absurdly nonrealistic if judged as an imitation of actual speech, but they vividly express the emotional truth of passionate, idealistic young love. It is no criticism of Shakespearean tragedy, therefore, to say that in real life people do not speak in blank verse. The deepest purpose of the playwright is not to imitate actual human speech but to give accurate and powerful expression to human thought and emotion.

The term **nonrealistic** used in the previous paragraph to describe the dialogue of Romeo and Juliet should not be confused with the term "unrealistic." Nonrealistic and **realistic** describe qualities of dramatic presentation; "unrealistic" is a term that judges people's actions on a scale of good sense, practicality, and insight. It is useful in discussing drama only when you are considering a character's grasp on reality—for example, a drama (whether realistic or nonrealistic) might portray a character who is unrealistic in outlook, such as a hopeless optimist or an incorrigible sentimentalist. In drama, realism is the attempt to reproduce or imitate the sights and sounds of real life, insofar as these can be represented on a stage. In life, realism is looking at the world with good judgment and clear vision.

All drama asks us to accept certain departures from reality—certain **dramatic conventions**. That a room with three walls or fewer may represent one with four walls, that the actors speak in the language of the audience whatever the nationality of the persons they play, that the actors stand or sit so as to face the audience most of the time—these are all necessary conventions. Other conventions are optional—for example, that the characters may reveal their inner thoughts through soliloquies and asides or may speak in the heightened language of poetry. Playwrights working in a strictly realistic mode will avoid the optional conventions, for these conflict with the realistic method that they have chosen to achieve their purposes. Playwrights working in a freer mode may choose to use any or all of them, for they make possible the revelation of dimensions of reality unreachable by a strictly realistic method. The famous speech of Hamlet that begins "To be, or not to be," in which he debates the merits of onerous life and untimely death, is nonrealistic on two counts: (1) it is spoken as a soliloquy, and (2) it is in blank verse. But despite the nonrealistic conventions, it presents Hamlet's introspective mind, his clear rationality, and his profound emotions in a powerful way. The characteristic device of Greek drama, a chorus—a group of actors speaking in unison, often in a chant, while going through the steps of an elaborate formalized dance—is another nonrealistic device but a useful one for conveying communal or group emotion. It has been revived, in different forms, in many modern plays. The use of a narrator, as in *The Glass Menagerie* (page 1177), is a related nonrealistic device that has served playwrights as a vehicle for dramatic truth.

The history of drama might be told in a history of conventions that have arisen, flourished, and been replaced; and those readers and audiences who experience plays most fully are those who have learned to understand the main conventions of its various periods and major dramatists. The less experienced reader or spectator may judge a play defective because it makes use of conventions other than those in common current acceptance (whether or not consciously recognized as such). Most contemporary audiences, for example, have been trained by their experience with movies and television, two media based on the realistic conventions of photography. Few people pause to consider that looking at a photograph, whether filmed by a still camera or a movie camera, requires the acceptance of the simple convention that three-dimensional reality is being represented two-dimensionally, or that the full spectrum of color may be represented by shades of white, gray, or black. We accept these conventions without question, as we also accept in cinema and television the emotional reinforcement that comes with a musical background even though there is no justification for the presence of an orchestra in a living room or on a beach. The study of drama requires the purposeful learning of its conventions, both realistic and nonrealistic.

In most plays, the world into which we are taken—however unreal it may be—is treated as self-contained, and we are asked to regard it temporarily as a real world. Thus David Ives's puddle of mayflies in "Time Flies" is real to us while we watch the play. We quite willingly make that "temporary suspension of disbelief" that, according to Coleridge, "constitutes poetic faith." And the step from accepting May and Horace as real insects, though we know in fact that they are only costumed actors, is an easy one because they think and talk like human beings in a fleeting romance as they erotically rub antennae and enjoy gnat snacks. But some playwrights abandon even this much attempt to give their work an illusion of reality. They deliberately violate the self-containment of the fictional world and keep reminding us that we are only seeing a play. Thus Edward Albee, in "The Sandbox," not only presents as his main character a Grandma who buries herself alive and speaks after she is presumably dead, but he also systematically breaks down the barriers between his fictional world and the real one. The Musician, instead of being concealed in an orchestra pit, is summoned onstage and told by Mommy and Grandma when to play and when not to play. Grandma addresses herself much of the time directly to the audience and at one time shouts to the electricians offstage, instructing them to dim the lights. The Young Man reminds us that he is an actor by telling Grandma that he has "a line here" and by delivering the line "like a real amateur." When Mommy and Daddy hear a noise offstage, Daddy thinks it may be thunder or a breaking wave, but Mommy says, with literal accuracy, "It was an off-stage rumble." In short, Albee keeps reminding us that this is a play—not reality—and not even an imitation of reality, but a symbolic representation of it. The effects he gains thereby are various: partly comic, partly antisentimental, partly intellectual; and the play that results is both theatrically effective and dramatically significant.

The adjective *realistic,* then, as applied to literature, must be regarded as a descriptive, not an evaluative, term. When we call a play realistic, we are saying something about its mode of presentation, not praising nor dispraising it. Realism indicates fidelity to the outer appearances of life. Serious dramatists are interested in life's inner meanings, which they may approach through either realistic or nonrealistic presentation. Great plays have been written in both the realistic and nonrealistic modes. It is not without significance, however, that the greatest plays in this book are probably *Oedipus Rex, The Misanthrope,* and *Othello*—originally written in quantitative Greek verse, rhymed French hexameters, and English blank verse, respectively. Human truth, rather than fidelity to superficial fact, is the highest achievement of literary art.

REVIEWING CHAPTER TWO

1. Distinguish between realistic and nonrealistic conventions, and between the terms "nonrealistic" and "unrealistic."
2. List the important realistic conventions that may be reflected in physical appearances and in language, and consider what they may contribute to an audience's experience of a play.
3. Define the advantages gained by playwrights who employ nonrealistic conventions, both in production values and in spoken dialogue, and consider any disadvantages that may result from them.

HENRIK IBSEN
A Doll House

Characters

TORVALD HELMER, *a lawyer*
NORA, *his wife*
DR. RANK
MRS. LINDE
KROGSTAD
THE HELMERS' THREE SMALL CHILDREN
ANNE-MARIE, *the children's nurse*
A HOUSEMAID
A PORTER

SCENE. *The Helmers' living room.*

ACT I

A pleasant, tastefully but not expensively furnished, living room. A door on the rear wall, right, leads to the front hall, another door, left, to HELMER'S *study. Between the two doors a piano. A third door in the middle of the left wall; further front a window. Near the window a round table and a small couch. Towards the rear of the right wall a fourth door; further front a tile stove with a rocking chair and a couple of armchairs in front of it. Between the stove and the door a small table. Copperplate etchings on the walls. A whatnot with porcelain figurines and other small objects. A small bookcase with deluxe editions. A rug on the floor; fire in the stove. Winter day.*

The doorbell rings, then the sound of the front door opening. NORA *dressed for outdoors, enters, humming cheerfully. She carries several packages, which she puts down on the table, right. She leaves the door to the front hall open; there a* PORTER *is seen holding a Christmas tree and a basket. He gives them to the* MAID *who has let them in.*

A DOLL HOUSE   First published and then performed in 1879. English translation by Otto Reinert. Henrik Ibsen (1828–1906), widely regarded as one of the founders of modern drama, was born in Norway. Between 1851 and 1864, while employed at theaters in Bergen and Christiana (now Oslo), Ibsen gained experience but little financial success (he had known little but poverty since his early childhood, when his extravagant father went bankrupt). As a consequence of his promising achievement as a poet and playwright, a traveling grant and then a small annual stipend from the Norwegian government permitted him to move with his family to Rome, where he took up permanent residence in 1864. By the time he wrote this play, Ibsen had long been interested in women's rights.

NORA. Be sure to hide the Christmas tree, Helene. The children mustn't see it before tonight when we've trimmed it. (*Opens her purse; to the* PORTER) How much?

PORTER. Fifty øre.

NORA. Here's a crown.° No, keep the change. (*The* PORTER *thanks her, leaves.* NORA *closes the door. She keeps laughing quietly to herself as she takes off her coat, etc. She takes a bag of macaroons from her pocket and eats a couple. She walks cautiously over to the door to the study and listens.*) Yes, he's home. (*Resumes her humming, walks over to the table, right.*)

HELMER (*in his study*). Is that my little lark twittering out there?

NORA (*opening some packages*). That's right.

HELMER. My squirrel bustling about?

NORA. Yes.

HELMER. When did squirrel come home?

NORA. Just now. (*Puts the bag of macaroons back in her pocket, wipes her mouth.*) Come out here, Torvald. I want to show you what I've bought.

HELMER. I'm busy! (*After a little while he opens the door and looks in, pen in hand.*) Bought, eh? All that? So little wastrel has been throwing money around again?

NORA. Oh but Torvald, this Christmas we can be a little extravagant, can't we? It's the first Christmas we don't have to scrimp.

HELMER. I don't know about that. We certainly don't have money to waste.

NORA. Yes, Torvald, we do. A little, anyway. Just a tiny little bit? Now that you're going to get that big salary and make lots and lots of money.

HELMER. Starting at New Year's, yes. But payday isn't till the end of the quarter.

NORA. That doesn't matter. We can always borrow.

HELMER. Nora! (*Goes over to her and playfully pulls her ear.*) There you go being irresponsible again. Suppose I borrowed a thousand crowns today and you spent it all for Christmas and on New Year's Eve a tile hit me in the head and laid me out cold?

NORA (*putting her hand over his mouth*). I won't have you say such horrid things.

HELMER. But suppose it happened. Then what?

NORA. If it did, I wouldn't care whether we owed money or not.

HELMER. But what about the people I had borrowed from?

NORA. Who cares about them! They are strangers.

HELMER. Nora, Nora, you *are* a woman! No, really! You know how I feel about that. No debts! A home in debt isn't a free home, and if it isn't

---

Fifty øre . . . a crown: A crown was 100 øre.

free it isn't beautiful. We've managed nicely so far, you and I, and that's the way we'll go on. It won't be for much longer.

NORA (*walks over toward the stove*). All right, Torvald. Whatever you say.

HELMER (*follows her*). Come, come, my little songbird mustn't droop her wings. What's this? Can't have a pouty squirrel in the house, you know. (*Takes out his wallet.*) Nora, what do you think I have here?

NORA (*turns around quickly*). Money!

HELMER. Here. (*Gives her some bills.*) Don't you think I know Christmas is expensive?

NORA (*counting*). Ten—twenty—thirty—forty. Thank you, thank you, Torvald. This helps a lot.

HELMER. I certainly hope so.

NORA. It does, it does. But I want to show you what I got. It was cheap, too. Look. New clothes for Ivar. And a sword. And a horse and trumpet for Bob. And a doll and a little bed for Emmy. It isn't any good, but it wouldn't last, anyway. And here's some dress material and scarves for the maids. I feel bad about old Anne-Marie, though. She really should be getting much more.

HELMER. And what's in here?

NORA (*cries*). Not till tonight!

HELMER. I see. But now what does my little prodigal have in mind for herself?

NORA. Oh, nothing. I really don't care.

HELMER. Of course you do. Tell me what you'd like. Within reason.

NORA. Oh, I don't know. Really, I don't. The only thing—

HELMER. Well?

NORA (*fiddling with his buttons, without looking at him*). If you really want to give me something, you might—you could—

HELMER. All right, let's have it.

NORA (*quickly*). Some money, Torvald. Just as much as you think you can spare. Then I'll buy myself something one of these days.

HELMER. No, really Nora—

NORA. Oh yes, please, Torvald. Please? I'll wrap the money in pretty gold paper and hang it on the tree. Won't that be nice?

HELMER. What's the name for little birds that are always spending money?

NORA. Wastrels, I know. But please let's do it my way, Torvald. Then I'll have time to decide what I need most. Now that's sensible, isn't it?

HELMER (*smiling*). Oh, very sensible. That is, if you really bought yourself something you could use. But it all disappears in the household expenses or you buy things you don't need. And then you come back to me for more.

NORA. Oh, but Torvald—

HELMER. That's the truth, dear little Nora, and you know it. (*Puts his arm around her.*) My wastrel is a little sweetheart, but she *does* go through an awful lot of money awfully fast. You've no idea how expensive it is for a man to keep a wastrel.

NORA. That's not fair, Torvald. I really save all I can.

HELMER (*laughs*). Oh, I believe that. All you can. Meaning, exactly nothing!

NORA (*hums, smiles mysteriously*). You don't know all the things we songbirds and squirrels need money for, Torvald.

HELMER. You know, you're funny. Just like your father. You're always looking for ways to get money, but as soon as you do it runs through your fingers and you can never say what you spent it for. Well, I guess I'll just have to take you the way you are. It's in your blood. Yes, that sort of thing is hereditary, Nora.

NORA. In that case, I wish I had inherited many of Daddy's qualities.

HELMER. And I don't want you any different from just what you are—my own sweet little songbird. Hey!—I think I just noticed something. Aren't you looking—what's the word?—a little—sly—?

NORA. I am?

HELMER. You definitely are. Look at me.

NORA (*looks at him*). Well?

HELMER (*wagging a finger*). Little sweet-tooth hasn't by any chance been on a rampage today, has she?

NORA. Of course not. Whatever makes you think that?

HELMER. A little detour by the pastry shop maybe?

NORA. No, I assure you, Torvald—

HELMER. Nibbled a little jam?

NORA. Certainly not!

HELMER. Munched a macaroon or two?

NORA. No, really, Torvald, I honestly—

HELMER. All right. Of course I was only joking.

NORA (*walks toward the table, right*). You know I wouldn't do anything to displease you.

HELMER. I know. And I have your promise. (*Over to her.*) All right, keep your little Christmas secrets to yourself, Nora darling. They'll all come out tonight, I suppose, when we light the tree.

NORA. Did you remember to invite Rank?

HELMER. No, but there's no need to. He knows he'll have dinner with us. Anyway, I'll see him later this morning. I'll ask him then. I did order some good wine. Oh Nora, you've no idea how much I'm looking forward to tonight!

NORA. Me, too. And the children, Torvald! They'll have such a good time!

HELMER. You know it *is* nice to have a good, safe job and a comfortable income. Feels good just thinking about it. Don't you agree?

NORA. Oh, it's wonderful.

HELMER. Remember last Christmas? For three whole weeks you shut yourself up every evening till long after midnight making ornaments for the Christmas tree and I don't know what else. Some big surprise for all of us, anyway. I'll be damned if I've ever been so bored in my whole life!

NORA. I wasn't bored at all!

HELMER (*smiling*). But you've got to admit you didn't have much to show for it in the end.

NORA. Oh, don't tease me again about that! Could I help it that the cat got in and tore up everything?

HELMER. Of course you couldn't, my poor little Nora. You just wanted to please the rest of us, and that's the important thing. But I *am* glad the hard times are behind us. Aren't you?

NORA. Oh yes. I think it's just wonderful.

HELMER. This year, I won't be bored and lonely. And you won't have to strain your dear eyes and your delicate little hands—

NORA (*claps her hands*). No I won't, will I Torvald? Oh, how wonderful, how lovely, to hear you say that! (*Puts her arm under his.*) Let me tell you how I think we should arrange things, Torvald. Soon as Christmas is over— (*The doorbell rings.*) Someone's at the door. (*Straightens things up a bit.*) A caller, I suppose. Bother!

HELMER. Remember, I'm not home for visitors.

MAID (*in the door to the front hall*). Ma'am, there's a lady here—

NORA. All right. Ask her to come in.

MAID (*to* HELMER). And the Doctor just arrived.

HELMER. Is he in the study?

MAID. Yes, sir. (HELMER *exits into his study. The* MAID *shows* MRS. LINDE *in and closes the door behind her as she leaves.* MRS. LINDE *is in travel dress.*)

MRS. LINDE (*timid and a little hesitant*). Good morning, Nora.

NORA (*uncertainly*). Good morning.

MRS. LINDE. I don't believe you know who I am.

NORA. No—I'm not sure—Though I know I should—Of course! Kristine! It's you!

MRS. LINDE. Yes, it's me.

NORA. And I didn't even recognize you! I had no idea! (*In a lower voice.*) You've changed, Kristine.

MRS. LINDE. I'm sure I have. It's been nine or ten long years.

NORA. Has it really been that long? Yes, you're right. I've been so happy these last eight years. And now you're here. Such a long trip in the middle of winter. How brave!

MRS. LINDE. I got in on the steamer this morning.

NORA. To have some fun over the holidays, of course. That's lovely. For we are going to have fun. But take off your coat! You aren't cold, are you? (*Helps her.*) There, now! Let's sit down here by the fire and just relax and talk. No, you sit there. I want the rocking chair. (*Takes her hands.*) And now you've got your old face back. It was just for a minute, right at first—Though you are a little more pale, Kristine. And maybe a little thinner.

MRS. LINDE. And much, much older, Nora.

NORA. Maybe a little older. Just a teeny-weeny bit, not much. (*Interrupts herself, serious.*) Oh, but how thoughtless of me, chatting away like this! Sweet, good Kristine, can you forgive me?

MRS. LINDE. Forgive you what, Nora?

NORA (*in a low voice*). You poor dear, you lost your husband, didn't you?

MRS. LINDE. Three years ago, yes.

NORA. I know. I saw it in the paper. Oh please believe me, Kristine, I really meant to write you, but I never got around to it. Something was always coming up.

MRS. LINDE. Of course, Nora. I understand.

NORA. No, that wasn't very nice of me. You poor thing, all you must have been through. And he didn't leave you much, either, did he?

MRS. LINDE. No.

NORA. And no children?

MRS. LINDE. No.

NORA. Nothing at all, in other words?

MRS. LINDE. Not so much as a sense of loss—a grief to live on—

NORA (*incredulous*). But Kristine, how can that be?

MRS. LINDE (*with a sad smile, strokes* NORA's *hair*). That's the way it sometimes is, Nora.

NORA. All alone. How awful for you. I have three darling children. You can't see them right now, though; they're out with their nurse. But now you must tell me everything—

MRS. LINDE. No, no; I'd rather listen to you.

NORA. No, you begin. Today I won't be selfish. Today I'll think only of you. Except there's one thing I've just got to tell you first. Something marvelous that's happened to us just these last few days. You haven't heard, have you?

MRS. LINDE. No; tell me.

NORA. Just think. My husband's been made manager of the Mutual Bank.

MRS. LINDE. Your husband—! Oh, I'm so glad!

NORA. Yes, isn't that great? You see, private law practice is so uncertain, especially when you won't have anything to do with cases that aren't—you know—quite nice. And of course Torvald won't do that and I quite agree with him. Oh, you've no idea how delighted we are! He takes over at New Year's, and he'll be getting a big salary and all sorts of extras. From now on we'll be able to live in quite a different way—exactly as we like. Oh, Kristine! I feel so carefree and happy! It's lovely to have lots and lots of money and not have to worry about a thing! Don't you agree?

MRS. LINDE. It would be nice to have enough at any rate.

NORA. No, I don't mean just enough. I mean lots and lots!

MRS. LINDE (*smiles*). Nora, Nora, when are you going to be sensible? In school you spent a great deal of money.

NORA (*quietly laughing*). Yes, and Torvald says I still do. (*Raising her finger at* MRS. LINDE.) But "Nora, Nora" isn't so crazy as you all think. Believe me, we've had nothing to be extravagant with. We've both had to work.

MRS. LINDE. You too?

NORA. Yes. Oh, it's been little things, mostly—sewing, crocheting, embroidery—that sort of thing. (*Casually*) And other things too. You know of course, that Torvald left government service when we got married? There was no chance of promotion in his department, and of course he had to make more money than he had been making. So for the first few years he worked altogether too hard. He had to take jobs on the side and work night and day. It turned out to be too much for him. He became seriously ill. The doctors told him he needed to go south.

MRS. LINDE. That's right, you spent a year in Italy, didn't you?

NORA. Yes, we did. But you won't believe how hard it was to get away. Ivar had just been born. But of course we had to go. Oh, it was a wonderful trip. And it saved Torvald's life. But it took a lot of money, Kristine.

MRS. LINDE. I'm sure it did.

NORA. Twelve hundred specie dollars. Four thousand eight hundred crowns. That's a lot of money.

MRS. LINDE. Yes. So it's lucky you have it when something like that happens.

NORA. Well, actually we got the money from Daddy.

MRS. LINDE. I see. That was about the time your father died, I believe.

NORA. Yes, just about then. And I couldn't even go and take care of him. I was expecting little Ivar any day. And I had poor Torvald to look after, desperately sick and all. My dear, good Daddy! I never saw him again, Kristine. That's the saddest thing that's happened to me since I got married.

MRS. LINDE. I know you were very fond of him. But then you went to Italy?

NORA. Yes, for now we had the money and the doctors urged us to go. So we left about a month later.

MRS. LINDE. And when you came back your husband was well again?

NORA. Healthy as a horse!

MRS. LINDE. But——the doctor?

NORA. What do you mean?

MRS. LINDE. I thought the maid said it was the doctor, that gentleman who came the same time I did.

NORA. Oh, that's Dr. Rank. He doesn't come as a doctor. He's our closest friend. He looks in at least once every day. No, Torvald hasn't been sick once since then. And the children are strong and healthy, too, and so am I. (*Jumps up and claps her hands.*) Oh God, Kristine! Isn't it wonderful to be alive and happy! Isn't it just lovely!——But now I'm being mean again, talking only about myself and my things. (*Sits down on a footstool close to* MRS. LINDE *and puts her arms on her lap.*) Please don't be angry with me! Tell me, is it really true that you didn't care for your husband? Then why did you marry him?

MRS. LINDE. Mother was still alive then, but she was bedridden and helpless. And I had my two younger brothers to look after. I didn't think I had the right to turn him down.

NORA. No, I suppose not. So he had money then?

MRS. LINDE. He was quite well off, I think. But it was an uncertain business, Nora. When he died, the whole thing collapsed and there was nothing left.

NORA. And then——?

MRS. LINDE. Well, I had to manage as best I could. With a little store and a little school and anything else I could think of. The last three years have been one long workday for me, Nora, without any rest. But now it's over. My poor mother doesn't need me any more. She's passed away. And the boys are on their own too. They've both got jobs and support themselves.

NORA. What a relief for you—

MRS. LINDE. No, not relief. Just a great emptiness. Nobody to live for any more. (*Gets up restlessly.*) That's why I couldn't stand it any longer in that little hole. Here in town it has to be easier to find something to keep me busy and occupy my thoughts. With a little luck I should be able to find a permanent job, something in an office—

NORA. Oh but Kristine, that's exhausting work, and you look worn out already. It would be much better for you to go to a resort.

MRS. LINDE (*walks over to the window*). I don't have a Daddy who can give me the money, Nora.

NORA (*getting up*). Oh, don't be angry with me.

MRS. LINDE (*over to her*). Dear Nora, don't *you* be angry with *me*. That's the worst thing about my kind of situation: you become so bitter. You've nobody to work for, and yet you have to look out for yourself, somehow.

You've got to keep on living, and so you become selfish. Do you know—when you told me about your husband's new position I was delighted not so much for your sake as for my own.

NORA. Why was that? Oh, I see. You think maybe Torvald can give you a job?

MRS. LINDE. That's what I had in mind.

NORA. And he will too, Kristine. Just leave it to me. I'll be ever so subtle about it. I'll think of something nice to tell him, something he'll like. Oh I so much want to help you.

MRS. LINDE. That's very good of you, Nora—making an effort like that for me. Especially since you've known so little trouble and hardship in your own life.

NORA. I—?—have known so little—?

MRS. LINDE (smiling). Oh well, a little sewing or whatever it was. You're still a child, Nora.

NORA (with a toss of her head, walks away). You shouldn't sound so superior.

MRS. LINDE. I shouldn't?

NORA. You're just like all the others. None of you think I'm good for anything really serious.

MRS. LINDE. Well, now—

NORA. That I've never been through anything difficult.

MRS. LINDE. But Nora! You just told me all your troubles!

NORA. That's nothing! (Lowers her voice) I haven't told you about it.

MRS. LINDE. It? What's that? What do you mean?

NORA. You patronize me, Kristine, and that's not fair. You're proud that you worked so long and so hard for your mother.

MRS. LINDE. I don't think I patronize anyone. But it is true that I'm both proud and happy that I could make mother's last years comparatively easy.

NORA. And you're proud of all you did for your brothers.

MRS. LINDE. I think I have a right to be.

NORA. And so do I. But now I want to tell you something, Kristine. I have something to be proud and happy about too.

MRS. LINDE. I don't doubt that for a moment. But what exactly do you mean?

NORA. Not so loud! Torvald mustn't hear—not for anything in the world. Nobody must know about this, Kristine. Nobody but you.

MRS. LINDE. But what is it?

NORA. Come here. (Pulls her down on the couch beside her.) You see, I do have something to be proud and happy about. I've saved Torvald's life.

MRS. LINDE. Saved—? How do you mean—"saved"?

NORA. I told you about our trip to Italy. Torvald would have died if he hadn't gone.

MRS. LINDE. I understand that. And so your father gave you the money you needed.

NORA (*smiles*). Yes, that's what Torvald and all the others think. But—

MRS. LINDE. But what?

NORA. Daddy didn't give us a penny. *I* raised that money.

MRS. LINDE. *You* did? That whole big amount?

NORA. Twelve hundred specie dollars. Four thousand eight hundred crowns. *Now* what do you say?

MRS. LINDE. But Nora, how could you? Did you win in the state lottery?

NORA (*contemptuously*). State lottery! (*Snorts.*) What is so great about that?

MRS. LINDE. Where did it come from then?

NORA (*humming and smiling, enjoying her secret*). Hmmm. Tra-la-la-la-la!

MRS. LINDE. You certainly couldn't have borrowed it.

NORA. Oh? And why not?

MRS. LINDE. A wife can't borrow money without her husband's consent.

NORA (*with a toss of her head*). Oh, I don't know—take a wife with a little bit of a head for business—a wife who knows how to manage things—

MRS. LINDE. But Nora, I don't understand at all—

NORA. You don't have to. I didn't say I borrowed the money, did I? I could have gotten it some other way. (*Leans back.*) An admirer may have given it to me. When you're as tolerably good-looking as I am—

MRS. LINDE. Oh, you're crazy.

NORA. I think you're dying from curiosity, Kristine.

MRS. LINDE. I'm beginning to think you've done something very foolish, Nora.

NORA (*sits up*). Is it foolish to save your husband's life?

MRS. LINDE. I say it's foolish to act behind his back.

NORA. But don't you see: he couldn't be told! You're missing the whole point, Kristine. We couldn't even let him know how seriously ill he was. The doctors came to *me* and told me his life was in danger, that nothing could save him but a stay in the south. Don't you think I tried to work on him? I told him how lovely it would be if I could go abroad like other young wives. I cried and begged. I said he'd better remember what condition I was in, that he had to be nice to me and do what I wanted. I even hinted he could borrow the money. But that almost made him angry with me. He told me I was being irresponsible and that it was his duty as my husband not to give in to my moods and whims—I think that's what he called it. All right, I said to myself, you've got to be saved somehow, and so I found a way—

MRS. LINDE. And your husband never learned from your father that the money didn't come from him?

NORA. Never. Daddy died that same week. I thought of telling him all about it and asking him not to say anything. But since he was so sick—It turned out I didn't have to—

MRS. LINDE. And you've never told your husband?

NORA. Of course not! Good heavens, how could I? He, with his strict principles! Besides, you know how men are. Torvald would find it embarrassing and humiliating to learn that he owed me anything. It would upset our whole relationship. Our happy, beautiful home would no longer be what it is.

MRS. LINDE. Aren't you ever going to tell him?

NORA (*reflectively, half smiling*). Yes—one day, maybe. Many, many years from now, when I'm no longer young and pretty. Don't laugh! I mean when Torvald no longer feels about me the way he does now, when he no longer thinks it's fun when I dance for him and put on costumes and recite for him. Then it will be good to have something in reserve—(*Interrupts herself.*) Oh, I'm just being silly! That day will never come.—Well, now, Kristine, what do you think of my great secret? Don't you think I'm good for something too?—By the way, you wouldn't believe all the worry I've had because of it. It's been very hard to meet my obligations on schedule. You see, in business there's something called quarterly interest and something called installments on the principal, and those are terribly hard to come up with. I've had to save a little here and a little there, whenever I could. I couldn't use much of the housekeeping money, for Torvald has to eat well. And I couldn't use what I got for clothes for the children. They have to look nice, and I didn't think it would be right to spend less than I got—the sweet little things!

MRS. LINDE. Poor Nora! So you had to take it from your allowance!

NORA. Yes, of course. After all, it was my affair. Every time Torvald gave me money for a new dress and things like that, I never used more than half of it. I always bought the cheapest, simplest things for myself. Thank God, everything looks good on me, so Torvald never noticed. But it was hard many times, Kristine, for it's fun to have pretty clothes. Don't you think?

MRS. LINDE. Certainly.

NORA. Anyway, I had other ways of making money too. Last winter I was lucky enough to get some copying work. So I locked the door and sat up writing every night till quite late. God! I often got so tired—! But it was great fun, too, working and making money. It was almost like being a man.

MRS. LINDE. But how much have you been able to pay off this way?

NORA. I couldn't tell you exactly. You see, it's very difficult to keep track of business like that. All I know is I have been paying off as much as

I've been able to scrape together. Many times I just didn't know what to do. (*Smiles.*) Then I used to imagine a rich old gentleman had fallen in love with me—

MRS. LINDE. What! What old gentleman?

NORA. Phooey! And now he was dead and they were reading his will, and there it said in big letters, "All my money is to be paid in cash immediately to the charming Mrs. Nora Helmer."

MRS. LINDE. But dearest Nora—who *was* this old gentleman?

NORA. For heaven's sake, Kristine, don't you see? There *was* no old gentleman. He was just somebody I made up when I couldn't think of any way to raise the money. But never mind him. The old bore can be anyone he likes to for all I care. I have no use for him or his last will, for now I don't have a single worry in the world. (*Jumps up.*) Dear God, what a lovely thought this is! To be able to play and have fun with the children, to have everything nice and pretty in the house, just the way Torvald likes it! Not a care! And soon spring will be here, and the air will be blue and high. Maybe we can travel again. Maybe I'll see the ocean again! Oh, yes, yes!—it's wonderful to be alive and happy! (*The doorbell rings.*)

MRS. LINDE (*getting up*). There's the doorbell. Maybe I better be going.

NORA. No, please stay. I'm sure it's just someone for Torvald—

MAID (*in the hall door*). Excuse me, ma'am. There's a gentleman here who'd like to see Mr. Helmer.

NORA. You mean the bank manager.

MAID. Sorry, ma'am; the bank manager. But I didn't know—since the Doctor is with him—

NORA. Who is the gentleman?

KROGSTAD (*appearing in the door*). It's just me, Mrs. Helmer. (MRS. LINDE *starts, looks, turns away toward the window.*)

NORA (*takes a step toward him, tense, in a low voice*). You? What do you want? What do you want with my husband?

KROGSTAD. Bank business—in a way. I have a small job in the Mutual, and I understand your husband is going to be our new boss—

NORA. So it's just—

KROGSTAD. Just routine business, ma'am. Nothing else.

NORA. All right. In that case, why don't you go through the door to the office. (*Dismisses him casually as she closes the door. Walks over to the stove and tends the fire.*)

MRS. LINDE. Nora—who was that man?

NORA. His name is Krogstad. He's a lawyer.

MRS. LINDE. So it *was* him.

NORA. Do you know him?

MRS. LINDE. I used to—many years ago. For a while he clerked in our part of the country.

NORA. Right. He did.

MRS. LINDE. He has changed a great deal.

NORA. I believe he had a very unhappy marriage.

MRS. LINDE. And now he's a widower, isn't he?

NORA. With many children. There now; it's burning nicely again. (*Closes the stove and moves the rocking chair a little to the side.*)

MRS. LINDE. They say he's into all sorts of business.

NORA. Really? Maybe so. I wouldn't know. But let's not think about business. It's such a bore.

DR. RANK (*appears in the door to* HELMER's *study*). No, I don't want to be in the way. I'd rather talk to your wife a bit. (*Closes the door and notices* MRS. LINDE.) Oh, I beg your pardon. I believe I'm in the way here, too.

NORA. No, not at all. (*Introduces them.*) Dr. Rank, Mrs. Linde.

RANK. Aha. A name often heard in this house. I believe I passed you on the stairs coming up.

MRS. LINDE. Yes. I'm afraid I climb stairs very slowly. They aren't good for me.

RANK. I see. A slight case of inner decay, perhaps?

MRS. LINDE. Overwork, rather.

RANK. Oh, is that all? And now you've come to town to relax at all the parties?

MRS. LINDE. I have come to look for a job.

RANK. A proven cure for overwork, I take it?

MRS. LINDE. One has to live, Doctor.

RANK. Yes, that seems to be the common opinion.

NORA. Come on, Dr. Rank—you want to live just as much as the rest of us.

RANK. Of course I do. Miserable as I am, I prefer to go on being tortured as long as possible. All my patients feel the same way. And that's true of the moral invalids too. Helmer is talking with a specimen right this minute.

MRS. LINDE (*in a low voice*). Ah!

NORA. What do you mean?

RANK. Oh, this lawyer, Krogstad. You don't know him. The roots of his character are decayed. But even he began by saying something about having *to live*—as if it were a matter of the highest importance.

NORA. Oh? What did he want with Torvald?

RANK. I don't really know. All I heard was something about the bank.

NORA. I didn't know that Krog—that this Krogstad had anything to do with the Mutual Bank.

RANK. Yes, he seems to have some kind of job there. (*To* MRS. LINDE) I don't know if you are familiar in your part of the country with the kind of person who is always running around trying to sniff out cases of moral decrepitude and as soon as he finds one puts the individual under observation in some excellent position or other. All the healthy ones are left out in the cold.

MRS. LINDE. I should think it's the sick who need looking after the most.

RANK (*shrugs his shoulders*). There we are. That's the attitude that turns society into a hospital. (NORA, *absorbed in her own thoughts, suddenly starts giggling and clapping her hands.*) What's so funny about that? Do you even know what society is?

NORA. What do I care about your stupid society! I laughed at something entirely different—something terribly amusing. Tell me, Dr. Rank— all the employees in the Mutual Bank, from now on they'll all be dependent on Torvald, right?

RANK. Is that what you find so enormously amusing?

NORA (*smiles and hums*). That's my business, that's my business! (*Walks around.*) Yes, I do think it's fun that we—that Torvald is going to have so much influence on so many people's lives. (*Brings out the bag of macaroons.*) Have a macaroon, Dr. Rank.

RANK. Well, well—macaroons. I thought they were banned around here.

NORA. Yes, but these were some Kristine gave me.

MRS. LINDE. What! I?

NORA. That's all right. Don't look so scared. You couldn't know that Torvald won't let me have them. He's afraid they'll ruin my teeth. But who cares! Just once in a while—! Right, Dr. Rank? Have one! (*Puts a macaroon into his mouth.*) You too, Kristine. And one for me. A very small one. Or at most two. (*Walks around again.*) Yes, I really feel very, very happy. Now there's just one thing I'm dying to do.

RANK. Oh? And what's that?

NORA. Something I'm dying to say so Torvald could hear.

RANK. And why can't you?

NORA. I don't dare to, for it's not nice.

MRS. LINDE. Not nice?

RANK. In that case, I guess you'd better not. But surely to the two of us—? What is it you'd like to say for Helmer to hear?

NORA. I want to say, "Goddammit!"

RANK. Are you out of your mind!

MRS. LINDE. For heaven's sakes, Nora!

RANK. Say it. Here he comes.

NORA (*hiding the macaroons*). Shhh! (HELMER *enters from his study, carrying his hat and overcoat.* NORA *goes to him.*) Well, dear, did you get rid of him?

HELMER. Yes, he just left.

NORA. Torvald, I want you to meet Kristine. She's just come to town.

HELMER. Kristine——? I'm sorry; I don't think——

NORA. Mrs. Linde, Torvald dear. Mrs. Kristine Linde.

HELMER. Ah, yes. A childhood friend of my wife's, I suppose.

MRS. LINDE. Yes, we've known each other for a long time.

NORA. Just think; she has come all this way just to see you.

HELMER. I'm not sure I understand——

MRS. LINDE. Well, not really——

NORA. You see, Kristine is an absolutely fantastic secretary, and she would so much like to work for a competent executive and learn more than she knows already——

HELMER. Very sensible, I'm sure, Mrs. Linde.

NORA. So when she heard about your appointment—there was a wire—she came here as fast as she could. How about it, Torvald? Couldn't you do something for Kristine? For my sake. Please?

HELMER. Quite possibly. I take it you're a widow, Mrs. Linde?

MRS. LINDE. Yes.

HELMER. And you've had office experience?

MRS. LINDE. Some—yes.

HELMER. In that case I think it's quite likely that I'll be able to find you a position.

NORA (*claps her hands*). I knew it! I knew it!

HELMER. You've arrived at a most opportune time, Mrs. Linde.

MRS. LINDE. Oh, how can I ever thank you——

HELMER. Not at all, not at all. (*Puts his coat on.*) But today you'll have to excuse me——

RANK. Wait a minute; I'll come with you. (*Gets his fur coat from the front hall, warms it by the stove.*)

NORA. Don't be long, Torvald.

HELMER. An hour or so; no more.

NORA. Are you leaving, too, Kristine?

MRS. LINDE (*putting on her things*). Yes, I'd better go and find a place to stay.

HELMER. Good. Then we'll be going the same way.

NORA (*helping her*). I'm sorry this place is so small, but I don't think we very well could——

MRS. LINDE. Of course! Don't be silly, Nora. Goodbye, and thank you for everything.

NORA. Goodbye. We'll see you soon. You'll be back this evening, of course. And you too, Dr. Rank; right? If you feel well enough? Of course you will. Just wrap yourself up. (*General small talk as all exit into the hall.* CHILDREN'S *voices are heard on the stairs.*) There they are! There they are! (*She runs and opens the door. The nurse* ANNE-MARIE *enters with the* CHILDREN.)

NORA. Come in! Come in! (*Bends over and kisses them.*) Oh, you sweet, sweet darlings! Look at them, Kristine! Aren't they beautiful?

RANK. No standing around in the draft!

HELMER. Come along, Mrs. Linde. This place isn't fit for anyone but mothers right now. (DR. RANK, HELMER, *and* MRS. LINDE *go down the stairs. The* NURSE *enters the living room with the children.* NORA *follows, closing the door behind her.*)

NORA. My, how nice you all look! Such red cheeks! Like apples and roses. (*The* CHILDREN *all talk at the same time.*) You've had so much fun? I bet you have. Oh, isn't that nice! You pulled both Emmy and Bob on your sleigh? Both at the same time? That's very good, Ivar. Oh, let me hold her for a minute, Anne-Marie. My sweet little doll baby! (*Takes the smallest of the children from the* NURSE *and dances with her.*) Yes, yes, of course; Mama'll dance with you too, Bob. What? You threw snowballs? Oh, I wish I'd been there! No, no; *I* want to take their clothes off, Anne-Marie. Please let me; I think it's so much fun. You go on in. You look frozen. There's hot coffee on the stove. (*The* NURSE *exits into the room to the left.* NORA *takes the* CHILDREN'S *wraps off and throws them all around. They all keep telling her things at the same time.*)

NORA. Oh, really? A big dog ran after you? But it didn't bite you. Of course not. Dogs don't bite sweet little doll babies. Don't peek at the packages, Ivar! What's in them? Wouldn't you like to know! No, no; that's something terrible! Play? You want to play? What do you want to play? Okay, let's play hide-and-seek. Bob hides first. You want *me* to? All right. I'll go first. (*Laughing and shouting,* NORA *and the* CHILDREN *play in the living room and in the adjacent room, right. Finally,* NORA *hides herself under the table; the* CHILDREN *rush in, look for her, can't find her. They hear her low giggle, run to the table, lift the rug that covers it, see her. General hilarity. She crawls out, pretends to scare them. New delight. In the meantime there has been a knock on the door between the living room and the front hall, but nobody has noticed. Now the door is opened halfway;* KROGSTAD *appears. He waits a little. The play goes on.*)

KROGSTAD. Pardon me, Mrs. Helmer—

NORA (*with a muted cry turns around, jumps up*). Ah! What do you want?

KROGSTAD. I'm sorry. The front door was open. Somebody must have forgotten to close it—

NORA (*standing up*). My husband isn't here, Mr. Krogstad.

KROGSTAD. I know.

NORA. So what do you want?

KROGSTAD. I'd like a word with you.

NORA. With——? (*To the* CHILDREN) Go in to Anne-Marie. What? No, the strange man won't do anything bad to Mama. When he's gone we'll play some more. (*She takes the* CHILDREN *into the room to the left and closes the door. She turns—tense, troubled.*) You want to speak with me?

KROGSTAD. Yes I do.

NORA. Today——? It isn't the first of the month yet.

KROGSTAD. No, it's Christmas Eve. It's up to you what kind of holiday you'll have.

NORA. What do you want? I can't possibly——

KROGSTAD. Let's not talk about that just yet. There's something else. You do have a few minutes, don't you?

NORA. Yes. Yes, of course. That is,——

KROGSTAD. Good. I was sitting in Olsen's restaurant when I saw your husband go by.

NORA. Yes——?

KROGSTAD.—with a lady.

NORA. What of it?

KROGSTAD. May I be so free as to ask: wasn't that lady Mrs. Linde?

NORA. Yes.

KROGSTAD. Just arrived in town?

NORA. Yes, today.

KROGSTAD. She's a good friend of yours, I understand?

NORA. Yes, she is. But I fail to see——

KROGSTAD. I used to know her myself.

NORA. I know that.

KROGSTAD. So you know about that. I thought as much. In that case, let me ask you a simple question. Is Mrs. Linde going to be employed in the bank?

NORA. What makes you think you have the right to cross-examine me like this, Mr. Krogstad—you, one of my husband's employees? But since you ask, I'll tell you. Yes, Mrs. Linde is going to be working in the bank. And it was I who recommended her, Mr. Krogstad. Now you know.

KROGSTAD. So I was right.

NORA (*walks up and down*). After all, one does have a little influence, you know. Just because you're a woman, it doesn't mean that—Really, Mr. Krogstad, people in a subordinate position should be careful not to offend someone who—oh well——

KROGSTAD.—has influence?

NORA. Exactly.

KROGSTAD (*changing his tone*). Mrs. Helmer, I must ask you to be good enough to use your influence on my behalf.

NORA. What do you mean?

KROGSTAD. I want you to make sure that I am going to keep my subordinate position in the bank.

NORA. I don't understand. Who is going to take your position away from you?

KROGSTAD. There's no point in playing ignorant with me, Mrs. Helmer. I can very well appreciate that your friend will find it unpleasant to run into me. So now I know who I can thank for my dismissal.

NORA. But I assure you—

KROGSTAD. Never mind. Just want to say you still have time. I advise you to use your influence to prevent it.

NORA. But Mr. Krogstad, I don't have any influence—none at all.

KROGSTAD. No? I thought you just said—

NORA. Of course I didn't mean it that way. I! Whatever makes you think that I have any influence of that kind on my husband?

KROGSTAD. I went to law school with your husband. I have no reason to think that the bank manager is less susceptible than other husbands.

NORA. If you're going to insult my husband, I'll ask you to leave.

KROGSTAD. You're brave, Mrs. Helmer.

NORA. I'm not afraid of you any more. After New Year's I'll be out of this thing with you.

KROGSTAD (*more controlled*). Listen, Mrs. Helmer. If necessary I'll fight as for my life to keep my little job in the bank.

NORA. So it seems.

KROGSTAD. It isn't just the money; that's really the smallest part of it. There is something else—Well, I guess I might as well tell you. It's like this. I'm sure you know, like everybody else, that some years ago I committed—an impropriety.

NORA. I believe I've heard it mentioned.

KROGSTAD. The case never came to court, but from that moment all doors were closed to me. So I took up the kind of business you know about. I had to do something, and I think I can say about myself that I have not been among the worst. But now I want to get out of all that. My sons are growing up. For their sake I must get back as much of my good name as I can. This job in the bank was like the first rung on the ladder. And now your husband wants to kick me down and leave me back in the mud again.

NORA. But I swear to you, Mr. Krogstad; it's not at all in my power to help you.

KROGSTAD. That's because you don't want to. But I have the means to force you.

NORA. You don't mean you're going to tell my husband I owe you money?

KROGSTAD. And if I did?

NORA. That would be a mean thing to do. (*Almost crying.*) That secret, which is my joy and my pride—for him to learn about it in such a coarse and ugly manner—to learn it from *you*—! It would be terribly unpleasant for me.

KROGSTAD. Just unpleasant?

NORA (*heatedly*). But go ahead! Do it! It will be worse for you than for me. When my husband realizes what a bad person you are you'll be sure to lose your job.

KROGSTAD. I asked you if it was just domestic unpleasantness you were afraid of?

NORA. When my husband finds out, of course he'll pay off the loan, and then we won't have anything more to do with you.

KROGSTAD (*stepping closer*). Listen, Mrs. Helmer—either you have a very bad memory, or you don't know much about business. I think I had better straighten you out on a few things.

NORA. What do you mean?

KROGSTAD. When your husband was ill, you came to me to borrow twelve hundred dollars.

NORA. I knew nobody else.

KROGSTAD. I promised to get you the money on certain conditions. At the time you were so anxious about your husband's health and so set on getting him away that I doubt very much that you paid much attention to the details of our transaction. That's why I remind you of them now. Anyway, I promised to get you the money if you would sign an I.O.U., which I drafted.

NORA. And which I signed.

KROGSTAD. Good. But below your signature I added a few lines making your father security for the loan. Your father was supposed to put his signature to those lines.

NORA. Supposed to—? He did.

KROGSTAD. I had left the date blank. That is, your father was to date his own signature. You recall that, don't you, Mrs. Helmer?

NORA. I guess so—

KROGSTAD. I gave the note to you. You were to mail it to your father. Am I correct?

NORA. Yes.

KROGSTAD. And of course you did so right away, for no more than five or six days later you brought the paper back to me, signed by your father. Then I paid you the money.

NORA. Well? And haven't I been keeping up with the payments?

KROGSTAD. Fairly well, yes. But to get back to what we were talking about—those were difficult days for you, weren't they, Mrs. Helmer?

NORA. Yes, they were.

KROGSTAD. Your father was quite ill, I believe.

NORA. He was dying.

KROGSTAD. And died shortly afterwards?

NORA. That's right.

KROGSTAD. Tell me, Mrs. Helmer; do you happen to remember the date of your father's death? I mean the exact day of the month?

NORA. Daddy died on September 29.

KROGSTAD. Quite correct. I have ascertained that fact. That's why there is something peculiar about this (*takes out a piece of paper*), which I can't account for.

NORA. Peculiar? How? I don't understand—

KROGSTAD. It seems very peculiar, Mrs. Helmer, that your father signed this promissory note three days after his death.

NORA. How so? I don't see what—

KROGSTAD. Your father died on September 29. Now look. He has dated his signature October 2. Isn't that odd? (NORA *remains silent.*) Can you explain it? (NORA *is still silent.*) I also find it striking that the date and the month and the year are not in your father's handwriting but in a hand I think I recognize. Well, that might be explained. Your father may have forgotten to date his signature and somebody else may have done it here, guessing at the date before he had learned of your father's death. That's all right. It's only the signature itself that matters. And that is genuine, isn't it, Mrs. Helmer? Your father *did* put his name to this note?

NORA (*after a brief silence tosses her head back and looks defiantly at him*). No, he didn't. *I* wrote Daddy's name.

KROGSTAD. Mrs. Helmer—do you realize what a dangerous admission you just made?

NORA. Why? You'll get your money soon.

KROGSTAD. Let me ask you something. Why didn't you mail this note to your father?

NORA. Because it was impossible. Daddy was sick—you know that. If I had asked him to sign it, I would have had to tell him what the money was for. But I couldn't tell him, as sick as he was, that my husband's life was in danger. That was impossible. Surely you can see that.

KROGSTAD. Then it would have been better for you if you had given up your trip abroad.

NORA. No, that was impossible! That trip was to save my husband's life. I couldn't give it up.

KROGSTAD. But didn't you realize that what you did amounted to fraud against me?

NORA. I couldn't let that make any difference. I didn't care about you at all. I hated the way you made all those difficulties for me, even though you knew the danger my husband was in. I thought you were cold and unfeeling.

KROGSTAD. Mrs. Helmer, obviously you have no clear idea of what you have done. Let me tell you that what I did that time was no more and no worse. And it ruined my name and reputation.

NORA. You! Are you trying to tell me that you did something brave once in order to save your wife's life?

KROGSTAD. The law doesn't ask motives.

NORA. Then it's a bad law.

KROGSTAD. Bad or not—if I produce this note in court you'll be judged according to the law.

NORA. I refuse to believe you. A daughter shouldn't have the right to spare her dying old father worry and anxiety? A wife shouldn't have the right to save her husband's life? I don't know the laws very well, but I'm sure that somewhere they make allowances for cases like that. And you, a lawyer, don't know that? I think you must be a bad lawyer, Mr. Krogstad.

KROGSTAD. That may be. But business—the kind of business you and I have with one another—don't you think I know something about that? Very well. Do what you like. But let me tell you this: if I'm going to be kicked out again, you'll keep me company. (*He bows and exits through the front hall.*)

NORA (*pauses thoughtfully; then, with a defiant toss of her head*). Oh, nonsense! Trying to scare me like that! I'm not all that silly. (*Starts picking up the* CHILDREN's *clothes; soon stops.*) But—? No! That's impossible! I did it for love!

THE CHILDREN (*in the door to the left*). Mama, the strange man just left. We saw him.

NORA. Yes, yes; I know. But don't tell anybody about the strange man. Do you hear? Not even Daddy.

CHILDREN. We won't. But now you'll play with us again, won't you, mama?

NORA. No, not right now.

CHILDREN. But Mama—you promised.

NORA. I know, but I can't just now. Go to your own room. I've so much to do. Be nice now, my little darlings. Do as I say. (*She nudges them gently into the other room and closes the door. She sits down on the couch, picks up a piece of embroidery, makes a few stitches, then stops.*) No! (*Throws the embroidery down, goes to the hall door and calls out.*) Helene! Bring the Christmas tree in here, please! (*Goes to the table, left, opens the drawer, halts.*) No—that's impossible!

MAID (*with the Christmas tree*). Where do you want it, ma'am?

NORA. There. The middle of the floor.

MAID. You want anything else?

NORA. No, thanks. I have everything I need. (*The* MAID *goes out.* NORA *starts trimming the tree.*) I want candles—and flowers—. That awful man! Oh nonsense! There's nothing wrong. This will be a lovely tree. I'll do everything you want me to, Torvald. I'll sing for you—dance for you—

(HELMER, *a bundle of papers under his arm, enters from outside.*) Ah—you're back already?

HELMER. Yes. Has anybody been here?

NORA. Here? No.

HELMER. That's funny. I saw Krogstad leaving just now.

NORA. Oh? Oh yes, that's right. Krogstad was here for just a moment.

HELMER. I can tell from your face that he came to ask you to put in a word for him.

NORA. Yes.

HELMER. And it was supposed to be your own idea, wasn't it? You were not to tell me he'd been here. He asked you that too, didn't he?

NORA. Yes, Torvald, but—

HELMER. Nora, Nora, how could you! Talk to a man like that and make him promises! And lying to me about it afterward—!

NORA. Lying—?

HELMER. Didn't you say nobody had been here? (*Shakes his finger at her.*) My little songbird must never do that again. Songbirds are supposed to have clean beaks to chirp with—no false notes. (*Puts his arm around her waist.*) Isn't that so? Of course it is. (*Lets her go.*) And that's enough about that. (*Sits down in front of the fireplace.*) Ah, it's nice and warm in here. (*Begins to leaf through his papers.*)

NORA (*busy with the tree; after a brief pause*). Torvald.

HELMER. Yes.

NORA. I'm looking forward so much to the Stenborgs' costume party day after tomorrow.

HELMER. And I can't wait to find out what you're going to surprise me with.

NORA. Oh, that silly idea!

HELMER. Oh?

NORA. I can't think of anything. It all seems so foolish and pointless.

HELMER. Ah, my little Nora admits that?

NORA (*behind his chair, her arms on the back of the chair*). Are you very busy, Torvald?

HELMER. Well—

NORA. What are all those papers?

HELMER. Bank business.

NORA. Already?

HELMER. I've asked the board to give me the authority to make certain changes in organization and personnel. That's what I'll be doing over the holidays. I want it all settled before New Year's.

NORA. So that's why this poor Krogstad—

HELMER. Hm.

NORA (*leisurely playing with the hair on his neck*). If you weren't so busy, Torvald, I'd ask you for a great big favor.

HELMER. Let's hear it, anyway.

NORA. I don't know anyone with better taste than you, and I want so much to look nice at the party. Couldn't you sort of take charge of me, Torvald, and decide what I'll wear—Help me with my costume?

HELMER. Aha! Little Lady Obstinate is looking for someone to rescue her?

NORA. Yes, Torvald. I won't get anywhere without your help.

HELMER. All right. I'll think about it. We'll come up with something.

NORA. Oh, you *are* nice! (*Goes back to the Christmas tree. A pause.*) Those red flowers look so pretty.—Tell me, was it really all that bad what this Krogstad fellow did?

HELMER. He forged signatures. Do you have any idea what that means?

NORA. Couldn't it have been because he felt he had to?

HELMER. Yes, or like so many others he may simply have been thoughtless. I'm not so heartless as to condemn a man absolutely because of a single imprudent act.

NORA. Of course not, Torvald!

HELMER. People like him can redeem themselves morally by openly confessing their crime and taking their punishment.

NORA. Punishment—?

HELMER. But that was not the way Krogstad chose. He got out of it with tricks and evasions. That's what has corrupted him.

NORA. So you think that if—?

HELMER. Can't you imagine how a guilty person like that has to lie and fake and dissemble wherever he goes—putting on a mask before everybody he's close to, even his own wife and children. It's the thing with the children that's the worst part of it, Nora.

NORA. Why is that?

HELMER. Because when a man lives inside such a circle of stinking lies he brings infection into his own home and contaminates his whole family. With every breath of air his children inhale the germs of something ugly.

NORA (*moving closer behind him*). Are you so sure of that?

HELMER. Of course I am. I have seen enough examples of that in my work. Nearly all young criminals have had mothers who lied.

NORA. Why mothers—particularly?

HELMER. Most often mothers. But of course fathers tend to have the same influence. Every lawyer knows that. And yet, for years this Krogstad has been poisoning his own children in an atmosphere of lies and deceit. That's why I call him a lost soul morally. (*Reaches out for her hands.*) And that's why my sweet little Nora must promise me never to take his side again. Let's shake on that.—What? What's this? Give me your hand. There! Now that's settled. I assure you, I would find it impossible to work in the same room with that man. I feel literally sick when I'm around people like that.

NORA (*withdraws her hand and goes to the other side of the Christmas tree*). It's so hot in here. And I have so much to do.

HELMER (*gets up and collects his papers*). Yes, and I really should try to get some of this reading done before dinner. I must think about your costume too. And maybe just possibly I'll have something to wrap in gilt paper and hang on the Christmas tree. (*Puts his hand on her head.*) Oh my adorable little songbird! (*Enters his study and closes the door.*)

NORA (*after a pause, in a low voice*). It's all a lot of nonsense. It's not that way at all. It's impossible. It has to be impossible.

NURSE (*in the door, left*). The little ones are asking ever so nicely if they can't come in and be with their mamma.

NORA. No, no, no! Don't let them in here! You stay with them, Anne-Marie.

NURSE. If you say so, ma'am. (*Closes the door.*)

NORA (*pale with terror*). Corrupt my little children——! Poison my home——? (*Brief pause; she lifts her head.*) That's not true. Never. Never in a million years.

ACT 2

The same room. The Christmas tree is in the corner by the piano, stripped shabby-looking, with burnt-down candles. NORA's outside clothes are on the couch. NORA is alone. She walks around restlessly. She stops by the couch and picks up her coat.

NORA (*drops the coat again*). There's somebody now! (*Goes to the door, listens.*) No. Nobody. Of course not—not on Christmas. And not tomorrow either.*—But perhaps—(*Opens the door and looks.*) No, nothing in the mailbox. All empty. (*Comes forward.*) How silly I am! Of course he isn't serious. Nothing like that could happen. After all, I have three small children. (*The NURSE enters from the room, left, carrying a big carton.*)

NURSE. Well, at last I found it—the box with your costume.

NORA. Thanks. Just put it on the table.

NURSE (*does so*). But it's all a big mess, I'm afraid.

NORA. Oh, I wish I could tear the whole thing to little pieces!

NURSE. Heavens! It's not as bad as all that. It can be fixed all right. All it takes is a little patience.

NORA. I'll go over and get Mrs. Linde to help me.

NURSE. Going out again? In this awful weather? You'll catch a cold.

NORA. That might not be such a bad thing. How are the children?

NURSE. The poor little dears are playing with their presents, but——

---

*In Norway both Christmas and the day after are legal holidays.

NORA. Do they keep asking for me?

NURSE. Well, you know, they're used to being with their mamma.

NORA. I know. But Anne-Marie, from now on I can't be with them as much as before.

NURSE. Oh well. Little children get used to everything.

NORA. You think so? Do you think they'd forget their mamma if I were gone altogether?

NURSE. Goodness me—gone altogether?

NORA. Listen, Anne-Marie—something I've wondered about. How could you bring yourself to leave your child with strangers?

NURSE. But I had to, if I were to nurse you.

NORA. Yes, but how could you *want* to?

NURSE. When I could get such a nice place? When something like that happens to a poor young girl, she'd better be grateful for whatever she gets. For *he* didn't do a thing for me—the louse!

NORA. But your daughter has forgotten all about you, hasn't she?

NURSE. Oh no! Not at all! She wrote to me both when she was confirmed and when she got married.

NORA (*putting her arms around her neck*). You dear old thing—you were a good mother to me when I was little.

NURSE. Poor little Nora had no one else, you know.

NORA. And if my little ones didn't, I know you'd—oh, I'm being silly! (*Opens the carton.*) Go in to them, please. I really should—. Tomorrow you'll see how pretty I'll be.

NURSE. I know. There won't be anybody at that party half as pretty as you, ma'am. (*Goes out, left.*)

NORA (*begins to take clothes out of the carton; in a moment she throws it all down*). If only I dared to go out. If only I knew nobody would come. That nothing would happen while I was gone.—How silly! Nobody'll come. Just don't think about it. Brush the muff. Beautiful gloves. Beautiful gloves. Forget it. Forget it. One, two, three, four, five, six— (*Cries out.*) There they are! (NORA *moves toward the door, stops irresolutely.* MRS. LINDE *enters from the hall. She has already taken off her coat.*) Oh, it's you, Kristine. There's no one else out there, is there? I'm so glad you're here.

MRS. LINDE. They told me you'd asked for me.

NORA. I just happened to walk by. I need your help with something—badly. Let's sit here on the couch. Look. Torvald and I are going to a costume party tomorrow night—at Consul Stenborg's upstairs—and Torvald wants me to go as a Neapolitan fisher girl and dance the tarantella. I learned it when we were on Capri.

MRS. LINDE. Well, well! So you'll be putting on a whole show?

NORA. Yes. Torvald thinks I should. Look, here's the costume. Torvald had it made for me while we were there. But it's all torn and everything. I just don't know—

MRS. LINDE. Oh, that can be fixed. It's not that much. The trimmings have come loose in a few places. Do you have needle and thread? Ah, here we are. All set.

NORA. I really appreciate it, Kristine.

MRS. LINDE (*sewing*). So you'll be in disguise tomorrow night, eh? You know—I may come by for just a moment, just to look at you.—Oh dear. I haven't even thanked you for the nice evening last night.

NORA (*gets up, moves around*). Oh, I don't know. I don't think last night was as nice as it usually is.—You should have come to town a little earlier, Kristine.—Yes, Torvald knows how to make it nice and pretty around here.

MRS. LINDE. You too, I should think. After all, you're your father's daughter. By the way, is Dr. Rank always as depressed as he was last night?

NORA. No, last night was unusual. He's a very sick man, you know—very sick. Poor Rank, his spine is rotting away. Tuberculosis, I think. You see, his father was a nasty old man with mistresses and all that sort of thing. Rank has been sickly ever since he was a little boy.

MRS. LINDE (*dropping her sewing to her lap*). But dearest Nora, where have you learned about things like that?

NORA (*still walking about*). Oh, you know—with three children you sometimes get to talk with—other wives. Some of them know quite a bit about medicine. So you pick up a few things.

MRS. LINDE (*resumes her sewing; after a brief pause*). Does Dr. Rank come here every day?

NORA. Every single day. He's Torvald's oldest and best friend, after all. And my friend too, for that matter. He's part of the family, almost.

MRS. LINDE. But tell me, is he quite sincere? I mean, isn't he the kind of man who likes to say nice things to people?

NORA. No, not at all. Rather the opposite, in fact. What makes you say that?

MRS. LINDE. When you introduced me yesterday, he told me he'd often heard my name mentioned in the house. But later on it was quite obvious your husband really had no idea who I was. So how could Dr. Rank—?

NORA. You're right, Kristine, but I can explain that. You see, Torvald loves me so very much that he wants me all to himself. That's what he says. When we were first married he got almost jealous when I as much as mentioned anybody from back home that I was fond of. So of course I soon stopped doing that. But with Dr. Rank I often talk about home. You see, he likes to listen to me.

MRS. LINDE. Look here, Nora. In many ways you're still a child. After all, I'm quite a bit older than you and have had more experience. I want to give you a piece of advice. I think you should get out of this thing with Dr. Rank.

NORA. Get out of what thing?

MRS. LINDE. Several things in fact, if you want my opinion. Yesterday you said something about a rich admirer who was going to give you money—

NORA. One who doesn't exist, unfortunately. What of it?

MRS. LINDE. Does Dr. Rank have money?

NORA. Yes, he does.

MRS. LINDE. And no dependents?

NORA. No. But—?

MRS. LINDE. And he comes here every day?

NORA. Yes, I told you that already.

MRS. LINDE. But how can that sensitive man be so tactless?

NORA. I haven't the slightest idea what you're talking about.

MRS. LINDE. Don't play games with me, Nora. Don't you think I know who you borrowed the twelve hundred dollars from?

NORA. Are you out of your mind! The very idea—! A friend of both of us who sees us every day—! What a dreadfully uncomfortable position that would be!

MRS. LINDE. So it really isn't Dr. Rank?

NORA. Most certainly not! I would never have dreamed of asking him—not for a moment. Anyway, he didn't have any money then. He inherited it afterwards.

MRS. LINDE. Well, I still think it may have been lucky for you, Nora dear.

NORA. The idea! It would never have occurred to me to ask Dr. Rank—. Though I'm sure that if I *did* ask him—

MRS. LINDE. But of course you wouldn't.

NORA. Of course not. I can't imagine that that would ever be necessary. But I am quite sure that if I told Dr. Rank—

MRS. LINDE. Behind your husband's back?

NORA. I must get out of—this other thing. That's also behind his back. I *must* get out of it.

MRS. LINDE. That's what I told you yesterday. But—

NORA (*walking up and down*). A man manages these things so much better than a woman—

MRS. LINDE. One's husband, yes.

NORA. Silly, silly! (*Stops.*) When you've paid off all you owe, you get your I.O.U. back; right?

MRS. LINDE. Yes, of course.

NORA. And you can tear it into a hundred thousand little pieces and burn it—that dirty, filthy, paper!

MRS. LINDE (*looks hard at her, puts down her sewing, rising slowly*). Nora—you're hiding something from me.

NORA. Can you tell?

MRS. LINDE. Something's happened to you, Nora, since yesterday morning. What is it?

NORA (*going to her*). Kristine! (*Listens.*) Shhh. Torvald just came back. Listen. Why don't you go in to the children for a while. Torvald can't stand having sewing around. Get Anne-Marie to help you.

MRS. LINDE (*gathers some of the sewing things together*). All right, but I'm not leaving here till you and I have talked. (*She goes out left, just as* HELMER *enters from the front hall.*)

NORA (*towards him*). I have been waiting and waiting for you, Torvald.

HELMER. Was that the dressmaker?

NORA. No, it was Kristine. She's helping me with my costume. Oh Torvald, just wait till you see how nice I'll look!

HELMER. I told you. Pretty good idea I had, wasn't it?

NORA. Lovely! And wasn't it nice of me to go along with it?

HELMER (*his hand under her chin*). Nice? To do what your husband tells you? All right, you little rascal; I know you didn't mean it that way. But don't let me interrupt you. I suppose you want to try it on.

NORA. And you'll be working?

HELMER. Yes. (*Shows her a pile of papers.*) Look. I've been down to the bank. (*Is about to enter his study.*)

NORA. Torvald.

HELMER (*halts*). Yes?

NORA. What if your little squirrel asked you ever so nicely—

HELMER. For what?

NORA. Would you do it?

HELMER. Depends on what it is.

NORA. Squirrel would run around and do all sorts of fun tricks if you'd be nice and agreeable.

HELMER. All right. What is it?

NORA. Lark would chirp and twitter in all the rooms, up and down—

HELMER. So what? Lark does that anyway.

NORA. I'll be your elfmaid and dance for you in the moonlight, Torvald.

HELMER. Nora, don't tell me it's the same thing you mentioned this morning?

NORA (*closer to him*). Yes, Torvald. I beg you!

HELMER. You really have the nerve to bring that up again?

NORA. Yes. You've just got to do as I say. You *must* let Krogstad keep his job.

HELMER. My dear Nora. It's his job I intend to give to Mrs. Linde.

NORA. I know. And that's ever so nice of you. But can't you just fire someone else?

HELMER. This is incredible! You just don't give up do you? Because you make some foolish promise, I am supposed to—!

NORA. That's not the reason, Torvald. It's for your own sake. That man writes for the worst newspapers. You've said so yourself. There's no telling what he may do to you. I'm scared to death of him.

HELMER. Ah, I understand. You're afraid because of what happened before.

NORA. What do you mean?

HELMER. You're thinking of your father, of course.

NORA. Yes. You're right. Remember the awful things they wrote about Daddy in the newspapers. I really think they might have forced him to resign if the ministry hadn't sent you to look into the charges and if you hadn't been so helpful and understanding.

HELMER. My dear little Nora, there is a world of difference between your father and me. Your father's official conduct was not above reproach. Mine is, and I intend for it to remain that way as long as I hold my position.

NORA. Oh, but you don't know what vicious people like that may think of. Oh, Torvald! Now all of us could be so happy together here in our own home, peaceful and carefree. Such a good life, Torvald, for you and me and the children! That's why I implore you—

HELMER. And it's exactly because you plead for him that you make it impossible for me to keep him. It's already common knowledge in the bank that I intend to let Krogstad go. If it gets out that the new manager has changed his mind because of his wife—

NORA. Yes? What then?

HELMER. No, of course, that wouldn't matter at all as long as little Mrs. Pighead here got her way! Do you want me to make myself look ridiculous before my whole staff—make people think I can be swayed by just anybody—by outsiders? Believe me, I would soon enough find out what the consequences would be! Besides, there's another thing that makes it absolutely impossible for Krogstad to stay on in the bank now that I'm in charge.

NORA. What's that?

HELMER. I suppose in a pinch I could overlook his moral shortcomings—

NORA. Yes, you could; couldn't you, Torvald?

HELMER. And I understand he's quite a good worker, too. But we've known each other for a long time. It's one of those imprudent relationships you get into when you're young that embarrass you for the rest of your life. I guess I might as well be frank with you: he and I are on a first-name basis. And that tactless fellow never hides the fact even when other people are around. Rather, he seems to think it entitles him to be familiar with me. Every chance he gets he comes out with his damn "Torvald, Torvald." I'm telling you, I find it most awkward. He would make my position in the bank intolerable.

NORA. You don't really mean any of this, Torvald.

HELMER. Oh? I don't? And why not?

NORA. No, for it's all so petty.

HELMER. What! Petty? You think I'm being petty!

NORA. No, I *don't* think you are petty, Torvald dear. That's exactly why I—

HELMER. Never mind. You think my reasons are petty, so it follows that I must be petty too. Petty! Indeed! By God, I'll put an end to this right now! (*Opens the door to the front hall and calls out.*) Helene!

NORA. What are you doing?

HELMER (*searching among his papers*). Making a decision. (*The* MAID *enters.*) Here. Take this letter. Go out with it right away. Find somebody to deliver it. But quick. The address is on the envelope. Wait. Here's money.

MAID. Very good sir. (*She takes the letter and goes out.*)

HELMER (*collecting his papers*). There now, little Mrs. Obstinate!

NORA (*breathless*). Torvald—what was that letter?

HELMER. Krogstad's dismissal.

NORA. Call it back, Torvald! There's still time! Oh Torvald, please—call it back! For my sake, for your own sake, for the sake of the children! Listen to me, Torvald! Do it! You don't know what you're doing to all of us!

HELMER. Too late.

NORA. Yes. Too late.

HELMER. Dear Nora, I forgive you this fear you're in, although it really is an insult to me. Yes, it is! It's an insult to think that I am scared of a shabby scrivener's revenge. But I forgive you, for it's such a beautiful proof of how much you love me. (*Takes her in his arms.*) And that's the way it should be, my sweet darling. Whatever happens you'll see that when things get really rough I have both strength and courage. You'll find out that I am man enough to shoulder the whole burden.

NORA (*terrified*). What do you mean by that?

HELMER. All of it, I tell you—

NORA (*composed*). You'll never have to do that.

HELMER. Good. Then we'll share the burden, Nora—like husband and wife, the way it ought to be. (*Caresses her.*) Now are you satisfied? There, there, there. Not that look in your eyes—like a frightened dove. It's all your own foolish imagination.—Why don't you practice the tarantella—and your tambourine, too. I'll be in the inner office and close both doors, so

I won't hear you. You can make as much noise as you like. (*Turning in the doorway.*) And when Rank comes, tell him where to find me. (*He nods to her, enters his study carrying his papers, and closes the door.*)

NORA (*transfixed by terror, whispers*). He would do it. He'll do it. He'll do it in spite of the whole world.—No, this mustn't happen. Anything rather than that! There must be a way—! (*The doorbell rings.*) Dr. Rank! Anything rather than that! Anything—anything at all! (*She passes her hand over her face, pulls herself together, and opens the door to the hall. Dr. Rank is out there, hanging up his coat. Darkness begins to fall during the following scene.*) Hello there, Dr. Rank. I recognized your ringing. Don't go in to Torvald yet. I think he's busy.

RANK. And you?

NORA (*as he enters and she closes the door behind him*). You know I always have time for you.

RANK. Thanks. I'll make use of that as long as I can.

NORA. What do you mean by that—As long as you can?

RANK. Does that frighten you?

NORA. Well, it's a funny expression. As if something was going to happen.

RANK. Something is going to happen that I've long been expecting. But I admit I hadn't thought it would come quite so soon.

NORA (*seizes his arm*). What is it you've found out? Dr. Rank—tell me!

RANK (*sits down by the stove*). I'm going downhill fast. There's nothing to do about that.

NORA (*with audible relief*). So it's *you*—

RANK. Who else? No point in lying to myself. I'm in worse shape than any of my other patients, Mrs. Helmer. These last few days I've been making up my inner status. Bankrupt. Chances are that within a month I'll be rotting up in the cemetery.

NORA. Shame on you! Talking that horrid way!

RANK. The thing itself is horrid—damn horrid. The worst of it, though, is all that other horror that comes first. There is only one more test I need to make. After that I'll have a pretty good idea when I'll start coming apart. There is something I want to say to you. Helmer's refined nature can't stand anything hideous. I don't want him in my sick room.

NORA. Oh, but Dr. Rank—

RANK. I don't want him there. Under no circumstance. I'll close my door to him. As soon as I have full certainty that the worst is about to begin I'll give you my card with a black cross on it. Then you'll know the last horror of destruction has started.

NORA. Today you're really quite impossible. And I had hoped you'd be in a particularly good mood.

RANK. With death on my hands? Paying for someone else's sins? Is there justice in that? And yet there isn't a single family that isn't ruled by the same law of ruthless retribution, in one way or another.

NORA (*puts her hands over her ears*). Poppycock! Be fun! Be fun!

RANK. Well, yes. You may just as well laugh at the whole thing. My poor, innocent spine is suffering from my father's frolics as a young lieutenant.

NORA (*over by the table, left*). Right. He was addicted to asparagus and goose liver paté, wasn't he?

RANK. And truffles.

NORA. Of course. Truffles. And oysters too, I think.

RANK. And oysters. Obviously.

NORA. And all the port and champagne that go with it. It's really too bad that goodies like that ruin your backbone.

RANK. Particularly an unfortunate backbone that never enjoyed any of it.

NORA. Ah yes, that's the saddest part of all.

RANK (*looks searchingly at her*). Hm—

NORA (*after a brief pause*). Why did you smile just then?

RANK. No, it was you that laughed.

NORA. No, it was you that smiled, Dr. Rank!

RANK (*gets up*). You're more of a mischief-maker than I thought.

NORA. I feel in the mood for mischief today.

RANK. So it seems.

NORA (*with both her hands on his shoulders*). Dear, dear Dr. Rank, don't you go and die and leave Torvald and me.

RANK. Oh, you won't miss me for very long. Those who go away are soon forgotten.

NORA (*with an anxious look*). Do you believe that?

RANK. You'll make new friends, and then—

NORA. Who'll make new friends?

RANK. Both you and Helmer, once I'm gone. You yourself seem to have made a good start already. What was this Mrs. Linde doing here last night?

NORA. Aha—Don't tell me you're jealous of poor Kristine?

RANK. Yes, I am. She'll be my successor in this house. As soon as I have made my excuses, that woman is likely to—

NORA. Shh—not so loud. She's in there.

RANK. Today too? There you are!

NORA. She's mending my costume. My God, you really *are* unreasonable. (*Sits down on the couch.*) Now be nice, Dr. Rank. Tomorrow you'll see how beautifully I'll dance, and then you are to pretend I'm dancing just for you—and for Torvald too, of course. (*Takes several items out of the carton.*) Sit down, Dr. Rank; I want to show you something.

RANK (*sitting down*). What?

NORA. Look.

RANK. Silk stockings.

NORA. Flesh-colored. Aren't they lovely? Now it's getting dark in here, but tomorrow—No, no. You only get to see the foot. Oh well, you might as well see all of it.

RANK. Hmm.

NORA. Why do you look so critical? Don't you think they'll fit?

RANK. That's something I can't possibly have a reasoned opinion about.

NORA (*looks at him for a moment*). Shame on you. (*Slaps his ear lightly with the stocking.*) That's what you get. (*Puts the things back in the carton.*)

RANK. And what other treasures are you going to show me?

NORA. Nothing at all, because you're naughty. (*She hums a little and rummages in the carton.*)

RANK (*after a brief silence*). When I sit here like this, talking confidently with you, I can't imagine—I can't possibly imagine what would have become of me if I hadn't had you and Helmer.

NORA (*smiles*). Well, yes—I do believe you like being with us.

RANK (*in a lower voice, lost in thought*). And then to have to go away from it all—

NORA. Nonsense. You are not going anywhere.

RANK (*as before*).—and not to leave behind as much as a poor little token of gratitude, hardly a brief memory of someone missed, nothing but a vacant place that anyone can fill.

NORA. And what if I were to ask you—? No—

RANK. Ask me what?

NORA. For a great proof of your friendship—

RANK. Yes, yes—?

NORA. No, I mean—for an enormous favor—

RANK. Would you really for once make me as happy as all that?

NORA. But you don't even know what it is.

RANK. Well, then; tell me.

NORA. Oh, but I can't, Dr. Rank. It's altogether too much to ask—It's advice and help and a favor—

RANK. So much the better. I can't even begin to guess what it is you have in mind. So for heaven's sake tell me! Don't you trust me?

NORA. Yes, I trust you more than anyone else I know. You are my best and most faithful friend. I know that. So I will tell you. All right, Dr. Rank. There is something you can help me prevent. You know how much Torvald loves me—beyond all words. Never for a moment would he hesitate to give his life for me.

RANK (*leaning over to her*). Nora—do you really think he's the only one?

NORA (*with a slight start*). Who—?

RANK.—would gladly give his life for you.

NORA (*heavily*). I see.

RANK. I have sworn an oath to myself to tell you before I go. I'll never find a better occasion.—All right, Nora; now you know. And now you also know that you can confide in me more than in anyone else.

NORA (*gets up; in a calm, steady voice*). Let me get by.

RANK (*makes room for her but remains seated*). Nora—

NORA (*in the door to the front hall*). Helene, bring the lamp in here, please. (*Walks over to the stove.*) Oh, dear Dr. Rank. That really wasn't very nice of you.

RANK (*gets up*). That I have loved you as much as anybody—was that not nice?

NORA. No; not that. But that you told me. There was no need for that.

RANK. What do you mean? Have you known—? (*The* MAID *enters with the lamp, puts it on the table, and goes out.*) Nora—Mrs. Helmer—I'm asking you: did you know?

NORA. Oh, how can I tell what I knew and didn't know! I really can't say— But that you could be so awkward, Dr. Rank! Just when everything was so comfortable.

RANK. Well, anyway, now you know that I'm at your service with my life and soul. And now you must speak.

NORA (*looks at him*). After what just happened?

RANK. I beg of you—let me know what it is.

NORA. There is nothing I can tell you now.

RANK. Yes, yes. You mustn't punish me this way. Please let me do for you whatever anyone *can* do.

NORA. Now there is nothing you can do. Besides, I don't think I really need any help, anyway. It's probably just my imagination. Of course that's all it is. I'm sure of it! (*Sits down in the rocking chair, looks at him, smiles.*) Well, well, well, Dr. Rank! What a fine gentleman you turned out to be! Aren't you ashamed of yourself, now that we have light?

RANK. No, not really. But perhaps I ought to leave—and not come back?

NORA. Don't be silly; of course not! You'll come here exactly as you have been doing. You know perfectly well that Torvald can't do without you.

RANK. Yes, but what about you?

NORA. Oh, I always think it's perfectly delightful when you come.

RANK. That's the very thing that misled me. You are a riddle to me. It has often seemed to me that you'd just as soon be with me as with Helmer.

NORA. Well, you see, there are people you love, and then there are other people you'd almost rather be with.

RANK. Yes, there is something in that.

NORA. When I lived at home with Daddy, of course I loved him most. But I always thought it was so much fun to sneak off down to the maids' room, for they never gave me advice and they always talked about such fun things.

RANK. Aha! So it's *their* place I have taken.

NORA (*jumps up and goes over to him*). Oh dear, kind Dr. Rank, you know very well I didn't mean it that way. Can't you see that with Torvald it is the way it used to be with Daddy? (*The* MAID *enters from the front hall.*)

MAID. Ma'am! (*Whispers to her and gives her a caller's card.*)

NORA (*glances at the card*). Ah! (*Puts it in her pocket.*)

RANK. Anything wrong?

NORA. No, no; not at all. It's nothing—just my new costume—

RANK. But your costume is lying right there!

NORA. Oh yes, that one. But this is another one. I ordered it. Torvald mustn't know—

RANK. Aha. So that's the great secret.

NORA. That's it. Why don't you go in to him, please. He's in the inner office. And keep him there for a while—

RANK. Don't worry. He won't get away. (*Enters* HELMER'S *study.*)

NORA (*to the* MAID). You say he's waiting in the kitchen?

MAID. Yes. He came up the back stairs.

NORA. But didn't you tell him there was somebody with me?

MAID. Yes, but he wouldn't listen.

NORA. He won't leave?

MAID. No, not till he's had a word with you, ma'am.

NORA. All right. But try not to make any noise. And, Helene—don't tell anyone he's here. It's supposed to be a surprise for my husband.

MAID. I understand ma'am—(*She leaves.*)

NORA. The terrible is happening. It's happening after all. No, no, no. It can't happen. It won't happen. (*She bolts the study door. The* MAID *opens the front hall door for* KROGSTAD *and closes the door behind him. He wears a fur coat for traveling, boots, and a fur hat.* NORA *goes toward him.*) Keep your voice down. My husband's home.

KROGSTAD. That's all right.

NORA. What do you want?

KROGSTAD. To find out something.

NORA. Be quick, then. What is it?

KROGSTAD. I expect you know I've been fired.

NORA. I couldn't prevent it, Mr. Krogstad. I fought for you as long and as hard as I could but it didn't do any good.

KROGSTAD. Your husband doesn't love you any more than that? He knows what I can do to you, and yet he runs the risk—

NORA. Surely you didn't think I'd tell him?

KROGSTAD. No, I really didn't. It wouldn't be like Torvald Helmer to show that kind of guts—

NORA. Mr. Krogstad, I insist that you show respect for my husband.

KROGSTAD. By all means. All due respect. But since you're so anxious to keep this a secret, may I assume that you are a little better informed than yesterday about exactly what you have done?

NORA. Better than *you* could ever teach me.

KROGSTAD. Of course. Such a bad lawyer as I am—

NORA. What do you want of me?

KROGSTAD. I just wanted to find out how you are, Mrs. Helmer. I've been thinking about you all day. You see, even a bill collector, a pen pusher, a— anyway, someone like me—even he has a little of what they call a heart.

NORA. Then show it. Think of my little children.

KROGSTAD. Have you and your husband thought of mine? Never mind. All I want to tell you is that you don't need to take this business too seriously. I have no intentions of bringing charges right away.

NORA. Oh no, you wouldn't; would you? I knew you wouldn't.

KROGSTAD. The whole thing can be settled quite amiably. Nobody else needs to know anything. It will be between the three of us.

NORA. My husband must never find out about this.

KROGSTAD. How are you going to prevent that? Maybe you can pay me the balance of your loan?

NORA. No, not right now.

KROGSTAD. Or do you have a way of raising the money one of these next few days?

NORA. None I intend to make use of.

KROGSTAD. It wouldn't do you any good anyway. Even if you had the cash in your hand right this minute, I wouldn't give you your note back. It wouldn't make any difference *how* much money you offered me.

NORA. Then you'll have to tell what you plan to use the note *for*.

KROGSTAD. Just keep it; that's all. Have it on hand, so to speak. I won't say a word to anybody else. So if you've been thinking about doing something desperate—

NORA. I have.

KROGSTAD.—like leaving house and home—

NORA. I have.

KROGSTAD.—or even something worse—

NORA. How did you know?

KROGSTAD.—then: don't.

NORA. How did you know I was thinking of *that*?

KROGSTAD. Most of us do, right at first. I did, too, but when it came down to it I didn't have the courage—

NORA (*tonelessly*). Nor do I.

KROGSTAD (*relieved*). See what I mean? I thought so. You don't either.

NORA. I don't. I don't.

KROGSTAD. Besides, it would be very silly of you. Once that first domestic blowup is behind you——. Here in my pocket is a letter for your husband.

NORA. Telling him everything?

KROGSTAD. As delicately as possible.

NORA (*quickly*). He mustn't get that letter. Tear it up. I'll get you the money somehow.

KROGSTAD. Excuse me, Mrs. Helmer, I thought I just told you——

NORA. I'm not talking about the money I owe you. Just let me know how much money you want from my husband, and I'll get it for you.

KROGSTAD. I want no money from your husband.

NORA. Then, what *do* you want?

KROGSTAD. I'll tell you, Mrs. Helmer. I want to rehabilitate myself; I want to get up in the world; and your husband is going to help me. For a year and a half I haven't done anything disreputable. All that time I have been struggling with the most miserable circumstances. I was content to work my way up step by step. Now I've been kicked out, and I'm no longer satisfied just getting my old job back. I want more than that; I want to get to the top. I'm being quite serious. I want the bank to take me back but in a higher position. I want your husband to create a new job for me——

NORA. He'll never do that!

KROGSTAD. He will. I know him. He won't dare not to. And once I'm back inside and he and I are working together, you'll see! Within a year I'll be the manager's right hand. It will be Nils Krogstad and not Torvald Helmer who'll be running the Mutual Bank!

NORA. You'll never see that happen!

KROGSTAD. Are you thinking of——?

NORA. Now I *do* have the courage

KROGSTAD. You can't scare me. A fine, spoiled lady like you——

NORA. You'll see, you'll see!

KROGSTAD. Under the ice, perhaps? Down into that cold, black water? Then spring comes and you float up again——hideous, can't be identified, hair all gone——

NORA. You don't frighten me.

KROGSTAD. Nor you me. One doesn't do that sort of thing, Mrs. Helmer. Besides, what good would it do? He'd still be in my power.

NORA. Afterwards? When I'm no longer——?

KROGSTAD. Aren't you forgetting that your reputation would be in my hands? (NORA *stares at him, speechless.*) All right; now I've told you what to expect. So don't do anything foolish. When Helmer gets my letter I expect to hear from him. And don't you forget that it's your husband himself who forces me to use such means again. That I'll never forgive him. Goodbye, Mrs. Helmer. (*Goes out through the hall.*)

NORA (*at the door, opens it a little, listens*). He's going. And no letter. Of course not! That would be impossible! (*Opens the door more.*) What's he doing? He's still there. Doesn't go down. Having second thoughts—? Will he—? (*The sound of a letter dropping into the mailbox. Then* KROGSTAD'S *steps are heard going down the stairs, gradually dying away. With a muted cry* NORA *runs forward to the table by the couch; brief pause.*) In the mailbox. (*Tiptoes back to the door to the front hall.*) There it is. Torvald, Torvald— now we're lost!

MRS. LINDE (*enters from the left, carrying* NORA'S *Capri costume*). There now. I think it's all fixed. Why don't we try it on you—

NORA (*in a low, hoarse voice*). Kristine, come here.

MRS. LINDE. What's wrong with you? You look quite beside yourself.

NORA. Come over here. Do you see that letter? There, look—through the glass in the mailbox.

MRS. LINDE. Yes, yes; I see it.

NORA. That letter is from Krogstad.

MRS. LINDE. Nora—it was Krogstad who lent you the money!

NORA. Yes, and now Torvald will find out about it.

MRS. LINDE. Oh believe me, Nora. That's the best thing for both of you.

NORA. There's more to it than you know. I forged a signature—

MRS. LINDE. Oh my God—!

NORA. I just want to tell you this, Kristine, that you must be my witness.

MRS. LINDE. Witness? How? Witness to what?

NORA. If I lose my mind—and that could very well happen—

MRS. LINDE. Nora!

NORA.—or if something were to happen to me—something that made it impossible for me to be here—

MRS. LINDE. Nora, Nora! You're not yourself!

NORA.—and if someone were to take all the blame, assume the whole responsibility—Do you understand—?

MRS. LINDE. Yes, yes; but how can you think—!

NORA. Then you are to witness that that's not so, Kristine. I am not beside myself. I am perfectly rational, and what I'm telling you is that nobody else has known about this. I've done it all by myself, the whole thing. Just remember that.

MRS. LINDE. I will. But I don't understand any of it.

NORA. Oh, how could you! For it's the wonderful that's about to happen.

MRS. LINDE. The wonderful?

NORA. Yes, the wonderful. But it's so terrible, Kristine. It mustn't happen for anything in the whole world.

MRS. LINDE. I'm going over to talk to Krogstad right now.

NORA. No, don't. Don't go to him. He'll do something bad to you.

MRS. LINDE. There was a time when he would have done anything for me.

NORA. He!

MRS. LINDE. Where does he live?

NORA. Oh, I don't know—Yes, wait a minute—(*Reaches into her pocket.*) Here's his card.—But the letter, the letter—!

HELMER (*in his study, knocks on the door*). Nora!

NORA (*cries out in fear*). Oh, what is it? What do you want?

HELMER. That's all right. Nothing to be scared about. We're not coming in. For one thing, you've bolted the door, you know. Are you modeling your costume?

NORA. Yes, yes; I am. I'm going to be so pretty, Torvald!

MRS. LINDE (*having looked at the card*). He lives just around the corner.

NORA. Yes, but it's no use. Nothing can save us now. The letter is in the mailbox.

MRS. LINDE. And your husband has the key?

NORA. Yes. He always keeps it with him.

MRS. LINDE. Krogstad must ask for his letter back, unread. He's got to think up some pretext or other—

NORA. But this is just the time of day when Torvald—

MRS. LINDE. Delay him. Go in to him. I'll be back as soon as I can. (*She hurries out through the hall door.*)

NORA (*walks over to* HELMER's *door, opens it, and peeks in*). Torvald.

HELMER (*still offstage*). Well, well! So now one's allowed in one's own living room again. Come on, Rank. Now we'll see—(*In the doorway.*) But what's this?

NORA. What, Torvald dear?

HELMER. Rank prepared me for a splendid metamorphosis.

RANK (*in the doorway*). That's how I understood it. Evidently I was mistaken.

NORA. Nobody gets to admire me in my costume before tomorrow.

HELMER. But, dearest Nora—you look all done in. Have you been practicing too hard?

NORA. No, I haven't practiced at all.

HELMER. But you'll have to, you know.

NORA. I know it, Torvald. I simply must. But I can't do a thing unless you help me. I have forgotten everything.

HELMER. Oh it will all come back. We'll work on it.

NORA. Oh yes, please, Torvald. You just have to help me. Promise? I am so nervous. That big party—. You mustn't do anything else tonight. Not a bit of business. Don't even touch a pen. Will you promise, Torvald?

HELMER. I promise. Tonight I'll be entirely at your service—you helpless little thing.—Just a moment, though. First I want to—. (*Goes to the door to the front hall.*)

NORA. What are you doing out there?

HELMER. Just looking to see if there's any mail.

NORA. No, no! Don't, Torvald!

HELMER. Why not?

NORA. Torvald, I beg you. There is no mail.

HELMER. Let me just look, anyway. (*Is about to go out.* NORA *by the piano, plays the first bars of the tarantella dance.* HELMER *halts at the door.*) Aha!

NORA. I won't be able to dance tomorrow if I don't get to practice with you.

HELMER (*goes to her*). Are you really all that scared, Nora dear?

NORA. Yes, so terribly scared. Let's try it right now. There's still time before we eat. Oh please sit down and play for me, Torvald. Teach me, coach me, the way you always do.

HELMER. Of course I will, my darling, if that's what you want. (*Sits down at the piano.* NORA *takes the tambourine out of the carton, as well as a long, many-colored shawl. She quickly drapes the shawl around herself, then leaps into the middle of the floor.*)

NORA. Play for me! I want to dance! (HELMER *plays and* NORA *dances.* DR. RANK *stands by the piano behind* HELMER *and watches.*)

HELMER (*playing*). Slow down, slow down!

NORA. Can't!

HELMER. Not so violent, Nora!

NORA. It has to be this way.

HELMER (*stops playing*). No, no. This won't do at all.

NORA (*laughing, swinging her tambourine*). What did I tell you?

RANK. Why don't you let me play?

HELMER (*getting up*). Good idea. Then I can direct her better. (RANK *sits down at the piano and starts playing.* NORA *dances more and more wildly.* HELMER *stands over by the stove, repeatedly correcting her. She doesn't seem to hear. Her hair comes loose and falls down over her shoulders. She doesn't notice but keeps on dancing.* MRS. LINDE *enters.*)

MRS. LINDE (*stops by the door, dumbfounded*). Ah—!

NORA (*dancing*). We're having such fun, Kristine!

HELMER. My dearest Nora, you're dancing as if it were a matter of life and death!

NORA. It is! It is!

HELMER. Rank, stop. This is sheer madness. Stop I say! (RANK *stops playing;* NORA *suddenly stops dancing.* HELMER *goes over to her.*) If I hadn't seen it I wouldn't have believed it. You've forgotten every single thing I ever taught you.

NORA (*tosses away the tambourine*). See? I told you.

HELMER. Well! You certainly need coaching.

NORA. Didn't I tell you I did? Now you've seen for yourself. I'll need your help till the very minute we're leaving for the party. Will you promise, Torvald?

HELMER. You can count on it.

NORA. You're not to think of anything except me—not tonight and not tomorrow. You're not to read any letters—not to look in the mailbox—

HELMER. Ah, I see. You're still afraid of that man.

NORA. Yes—yes, that too.

HELMER. Nora, I can tell from looking at you. There's a letter from him out there.

NORA. I don't know. I think so. But you're not to read it now. I don't want anything ugly to come between us before it's all over.

RANK (*to* HELMER *in a low voice*). Better not argue with her.

HELMER (*throws his arm around her*). The child shall have her way. But tomorrow night, when you've done your dance—

NORA. Then you'll be free.

MAID (*in the door, right*). Dinner can be served any time, ma'am.

NORA. We want champagne, Helene.

MAID. Very good, ma'am. (*Goes out.*)

HELMER. Aha! Having a party, eh?

NORA. Champagne from now till sunrise! (*Calls out.*) And some macaroons, Helene. Lots!—just this once.

HELMER (*taking her hands*). There, there—I don't like this wild—frenzy—Be my own sweet little lark again, the way you always are.

NORA. Oh, I will. But you go on in. You too, Dr. Rank. Kristine, please help me put up my hair.

RANK (*in a low voice to* HELMER *as they go out*). You don't think she is—you know—expecting—?

HELMER. Oh no. Nothing like that. It's just this childish fear I was telling you about. (*They go out, right.*)

NORA. Well?

MRS. LINDE. Left town.

NORA. I saw it in your face.

MRS. LINDE. He'll be back tomorrow night. I left him a note.

NORA. You shouldn't have. I don't want you to try to stop anything. You see, it's kind of ecstasy, too, this waiting for the wonderful.

MRS. LINDE. But what is it you're waiting *for*?

NORA. You wouldn't understand. Why don't you go in to the others. I'll be there in a minute. (MRS. LINDE *enters the dining room, right.* NORA *stands still for a little while, as if collecting herself; she looks at her watch.*) Five o'clock. Seven hours till midnight. Twenty-four more hours till next midnight. Then the tarantella is over. Twenty-four plus seven—thirty-one more hours to live.

HELMER (*in the door, right*). What's happening to my little lark?

NORA (*to him, with open arms*). Here's your lark!

ACT 3

The same room. The table by the couch and the chairs around it have been moved to the middle of the floor. A lighted lamp is on the table. The door to the front hall is open. Dance music is heard from upstairs.

MRS. LINDE *is seated by the table, idly leafing through the pages of a book. She tries to read but seems unable to concentrate. Once or twice she turns her head in the direction of the door, anxiously listening.*

MRS. LINDE (*looks at her watch*). Not yet. It's almost too late. If only he hasn't— (*Listens again.*) Ah! There he is. (*She goes to the hall and opens the front door carefully. Quiet footsteps on the stairs. She whispers.*) Come in. There's nobody here.

KROGSTAD (*in the door*). I found your note when I got home. What's this all about?

MRS. LINDE. I've got to talk to you.

KROGSTAD. Oh? And it has to be here?

MRS. LINDE. It couldn't be at my place. My room doesn't have a separate entrance. Come in. We're quite alone. The maid is asleep and the Helmers are at a party upstairs.

KROGSTAD (*entering*). Really? The Helmers are dancing tonight, are they?

MRS. LINDE. And why not?

KROGSTAD. You're right. Why not, indeed.

MRS. LINDE. All right, Krogstad. Let's talk, you and I.

KROGSTAD. I didn't know we had anything to talk about.

MRS. LINDE. We have much to talk about.

KROGSTAD. I didn't think so.

MRS. LINDE. No, because you've never really understood me.

KROGSTAD. What was there to understand? What happened was perfectly commonplace. A heartless woman jilts a man when she gets a more attractive offer.

MRS. LINDE. Do you think I'm all that heartless? And do you think it was easy for me to break with you?

KROGSTAD. No?

MRS. LINDE. You really thought it was?

KROGSTAD. If it wasn't, why did you write the way you did that time?

MRS. LINDE. What else could I do? If I had to make a break, I also had the duty to destroy whatever feelings you had for me.

KROGSTAD (*clenching his hands*). So that's the way it was. And you did—
that—just for money!

MRS. LINDE. Don't forget I had a helpless mother and two small brothers. We couldn't wait for you, Krogstad. You know yourself how uncertain your prospects were then.

KROGSTAD. All right. But you still didn't have the right to throw me over for somebody else.

MRS. LINDE. I don't know. I have asked myself that question many times. Did I have that right?

KROGSTAD (*in a lower voice*). When I lost you I lost my footing. Look at me now. A shipwrecked man on a raft.

MRS. LINDE. Rescue may be near.

KROGSTAD. It *was* near. Then you came between.

MRS. LINDE. I didn't know that, Krogstad. Only today did I find out it's your job I'm taking over in the bank.

KROGSTAD. I believe you when you say so. But now that you *do* know, aren't you going to step aside?

MRS. LINDE. No, for it wouldn't do you any good.

KROGSTAD. Whether it would or not—*I* would do it.

MRS. LINDE. I have learned common sense. Life and hard necessity have taught me that.

KROGSTAD. And life has taught me not to believe in pretty speeches.

MRS. LINDE. Then life has taught you a very sensible thing. But you do believe in actions, don't you?

KROGSTAD. How do you mean?

MRS. LINDE. You referred to yourself just now as a shipwrecked man.

KROGSTAD. It seems to me I had every reason to do so.

MRS. LINDE. And I am a shipwrecked woman. No one to grieve for, no one to care for.

KROGSTAD. You made your choice.

MRS. LINDE. I had no other choice that time.

KROGSTAD. Let's say you didn't. What then?

MRS. LINDE. Krogstad, how would it be if we two shipwrecked people got together?

KROGSTAD. What's this!

MRS. LINDE. Two on one wreck are better off than each on his own.

KROGSTAD. Kristine!

MRS. LINDE. Why do you think I came to town?

KROGSTAD. Surely not because of me?

MRS. LINDE. If I'm going to live at all I must work. All my life, for as long as I can remember, I have worked. That's been my one and only pleasure.

But now that I'm all alone in the world I feel nothing but this terrible emptiness and desolation. There is no joy in working just for yourself. Krogstad—give me someone and something to work for.

KROGSTAD. I don't believe this. Only hysterical females go in for that kind of high-minded self-sacrifice.

MRS. LINDE. Did you ever know me to be hysterical?

KROGSTAD. You really could do this? Listen—do you know about my past? All of it?

MRS. LINDE. Yes, I do.

KROGSTAD. Do you also know what people think of me around here?

MRS. LINDE. A little while ago you sounded as if you thought that together with me you might have become a different person.

KROGSTAD. I'm sure of it.

MRS. LINDE. Couldn't that still be?

KROGSTAD. Kristine—do you know what you are doing? Yes, I see you do. And you think you have the courage—?

MRS. LINDE. I need someone to be a mother to, and your children need a mother. You and I need one another. Nils, I believe in you—in the real you. Together with you I dare to do anything.

KROGSTAD (*seizes her hands*). Thanks, thanks, Kristine—now I know I'll raise myself in the eyes of others—Ah, but I forget—!

MRS. LINDE (*listening*). Shhh!—There's the tarantella. You must go; hurry!

KROGSTAD. Why? What is it?

MRS. LINDE. Do you hear what they're playing up there? When that dance is over they'll be down.

KROGSTAD. All right. I'm leaving. The whole thing is pointless, anyway. Of course you don't know what I'm doing to the Helmers.

MRS. LINDE. Yes, Krogstad; I do know.

KROGSTAD. Still, you're brave enough—?

MRS. LINDE. I very well understand to what extremes despair can drive a man like you.

KROGSTAD. If only it could be undone!

MRS. LINDE. It could, for your letter is still out there in the mailbox.

KROGSTAD. Are you sure?

MRS. LINDE. Quite sure. But—

KROGSTAD (*looks searchingly at her*). Maybe I'm beginning to understand. You want to save your friend at any cost. Be honest with me. That's it, isn't it.

MRS. LINDE. Krogstad, you may sell yourself once for somebody else's sake, but you don't do it twice.

KROGSTAD. I'll demand my letter back.

MRS. LINDE. No, no.

KROGSTAD. Yes, of course. I'll wait here till Helmer comes down. Then I'll ask him for my letter. I'll tell him it's just about my dismissal—that he shouldn't read it.

MRS. LINDE. No, Krogstad. You are not to ask for that letter back.

KROGSTAD. But tell me—wasn't that the real reason you wanted to meet me here?

MRS. LINDE. At first it was, because I was so frightened. But that was yesterday. Since then I have seen the most incredible things going on in this house. Helmer must learn the whole truth. This miserable secret must come out in the open; those two must come to a full understanding. They simply can't continue with all this concealment and evasion.

KROGSTAD. All right; if you want to take that chance. But there is one thing I *can* do, and I'll do that right now.

MRS. LINDE (*listening*). But hurry! Go! The dance is over. We aren't safe another minute.

KROGSTAD. I'll be waiting for you downstairs.

MRS. LINDE. Yes, do. You must see me home.

KROGSTAD. I've never been so happy in my whole life. (*He leaves through the front door. The door between the living room and the front hall remains open.*)

MRS. LINDE (*straightens up the room a little and gets her things ready*). What a change! Oh yes!—what a change! People to work for—to live for—a home to bring happiness to. I can't wait to get to work—! If only they'd come soon—(*Listens.*) Ah, there they are. Get my coat on—(*Puts on her coat and hat.* HELMER'S *and* NORA'S *voices are heard outside. A key is turned in the lock, and* HELMER *almost forces* NORA *into the hall. She is dressed in her Italian costume, with a big black shawl over her shoulders. He is in evening dress under an open black cloak.*)

NORA (*in the door, still resisting*). No, no, no! I don't want to! I want to go back upstairs. I don't want to leave so early.

HELMER. But dearest Nora—

NORA. Oh please, Torvald—please! I'm asking you as nicely as I can—just another hour!

HELMER. Not another minute, sweet. You know we agreed. There now. Get inside. You'll catch a cold out here. (*She still resists, but he guides her gently into the room.*)

MRS. LINDE. Good evening.

NORA. Kristine!

HELMER. Ah, Mrs. Linde. Still here?

MRS. LINDE. I know. I really should apologize, but I so much wanted to see Nora in her costume.

NORA. You've been waiting up for me?

MRS. LINDE. Yes, unfortunately I didn't get here in time. You were already upstairs, but I just didn't feel like leaving till I had seen you.

HELMER (*removing* NORA's *shawl*). Yes, do take a good look at her, Mrs. Linde. I think I may say she's worth looking at. Isn't she lovely?

MRS. LINDE. She certainly is—

HELMER. Isn't she a miracle of loveliness, though? That was the general opinion at the party, too. But dreadfully obstinate—that she is, the sweet little thing. What can we do about that? Will you believe it—I practically had to use force to get her away.

NORA. Oh Torvald, you're going to be sorry you didn't give me even half an hour more.

HELMER. See what I mean, Mrs. Linde? She dances the tarantella—she is a tremendous success—quite deservedly so, though perhaps her performance was a little too natural—I mean, more than could be reconciled with the rules of art. But all right! The point is: she's a success, a tremendous success. So should I let her stay after that? Weaken the effect? Of course not. So I take my lovely little Capri girl—I might say, my capricious little Capri girl—under my arm—a quick turn around the room—a graceful bow in all directions, and— as they say in the novels—the beautiful apparition is gone. A finale should always be done for effect, Mrs. Linde, but there doesn't seem to be any way of getting that into Nora's head. Poooh—! It's hot in here. (*Throws his cloak down on a chair and opens the door to his room.*) Why, it's dark in here! Of course. Excuse me—(*Goes inside and lights a couple of candles.*)

NORA (*in a hurried, breathless whisper*). Well?

MRS. LINDE (*in a low voice*). I have talked to him.

NORA. And—?

MRS. LINDE. Nora—you've got to tell your husband everything.

NORA (*no expression in her voice*). I knew it.

MRS. LINDE. You have nothing to fear from Krogstad. But you must speak.

NORA. I'll say nothing.

MRS. LINDE. Then the letter will.

NORA. Thank you, Kristine. Now I know what I have to do. Shh!

HELMER (*returning*). Well, Mrs. Linde, have you looked your fill?

MRS. LINDE. Yes. And now I'll say goodnight.

HELMER. So soon? Is that your knitting?

MRS. LINDE (*takes it*). Yes, thank you. I almost forgot.

HELMER. So you knit, do you?

MRS. LINDE. Oh yes.

HELMER. You know—you ought to take up embroidery instead.

MRS. LINDE. Oh? Why?

HELMER. Because it's so much more beautiful. Look. You hold the embroidery so—in your left hand. Then with your right you move the needle—like this—in an easy, elongated arc—you see?

MRS. LINDE. Maybe you're right—

HELMER. Knitting, on the other hand, can never be anything but ugly. Look here: arms pressed close to the sides—the needles going up and down—there's something Chinese about it somehow—. That really was an excellent champagne they served us tonight.

MRS. LINDE. Well, goodnight, Nora. And don't be obstinate any more.

HELMER. Well said, Mrs. Linde!

MRS. LINDE. Goodnight, sir.

HELMER (*sees her to the front door*). Goodnight, goodnight. I hope you'll get home all right? I'd be very glad to—but of course you don't have far to walk, do you? Goodnight, goodnight. (*She leaves. He closes the door behind her and returns to the living room.*) There! At last we got rid of her. She really is an incredible bore, that woman.

NORA. Aren't you very tired, Torvald?

HELMER. No, not in the least.

NORA. Not sleepy either?

HELMER. Not at all. Quite the opposite. I feel enormously—animated. How about you? Yes, you do look tired and sleepy.

NORA. Yes, I am very tired. Soon I'll be asleep.

HELMER. What did I tell you? I was right, wasn't I? Good thing I didn't let you stay any longer.

NORA. Everything you do is right.

HELMER (*kissing her forehead*). Now my little lark is talking like a human being. But did you notice what splendid spirits Rank was in tonight?

NORA. Was he? I didn't notice. I didn't get to talk with him.

HELMER. Nor did I—hardly. But I haven't seen him in such a good mood for a long time. (*Looks at her, comes closer to her.*) Ah! It does feel good to be back in our own home again, to be quite alone with you—my young, lovely, ravishing woman!

NORA. Don't look at me like that, Torvald!

HELMER. Am I not to look at my most precious possession? All that loveliness that is mine, nobody's but mine, all of it mine.

NORA (*walks to the other side of the table*). I won't have you talk to me like that tonight.

HELMER (*follows her*). The tarantella is still in your blood. I can tell. That only makes you all the more alluring. Listen! The guests are beginning to leave. (*Softly.*) Nora—soon the whole house will be quiet.

NORA. Yes, I hope so.

HELMER. Yes, don't you, my darling? Do you know—when I'm at a party with you, like tonight—do you know why I hardly ever talk to you, why I keep away from you, only look at you once in a while—a few stolen glances—do you know why I do that? It's because I pretend that you are my secret love, my young, secret bride-to-be, and nobody has the slightest suspicion that there is anything between us.

NORA. Yes, I know. All your thoughts are with me.

HELMER. Then when we're leaving and I lay your shawl around your delicate young shoulders—around that wonderful curve of your neck—then I imagine you're my young bride, that we're coming away from the wedding, that I am taking you to my home for the first time—that I am alone with you for the first time—quite alone with you, you young, trembling beauty! I have desired you all evening—there hasn't been a longing in me that hasn't been for you. When you were dancing the tarantella, chasing, inviting—my blood was on fire; I couldn't stand it any longer—that's why I brought you down so early—

NORA. Leave me now, Torvald. Please! I don't want all this.

HELMER. What do you mean? You're only playing your little teasing bird game with me; aren't you, Nora? Don't want to? I'm your husband, aren't I? (*There is a knock on the front door.*)

NORA (*with a start*). Did you hear that—?

HELMER (*on his way to the hall*). Who is it?

RANK (*outside*). It's me. May I come in for a moment?

HELMER (*in a low voice, annoyed*). Oh, what does he want now? (*Aloud*) Just a minute. (*Opens the door.*) Well! How good of you not to pass by our door.

RANK. I thought I heard your voice, so I felt like saying hello. (*Looks around.*) Ah yes—this dear, familiar room. What a cozy, comfortable place you have here, you two.

HELMER. Looked to me as if you were quite comfortable upstairs too.

RANK. I certainly was. Why not? Why not enjoy all you can in this world? As much as you can for as long as you can, anyway. Excellent wine.

HELMER. The champagne, particularly.

RANK. You noticed that too? Incredible how much I managed to put away.

NORA. Torvald drank a lot of champagne tonight, too.

RANK. Did he?

NORA. Yes, he did, and then he's always so much fun afterwards.

RANK. Well, why not have some fun in the evening after a well spent day?

HELMER. Well spent? I'm afraid I can't claim that.

RANK (*slapping him lightly on the shoulder*). But you see, I can!

NORA. Dr. Rank, I believe you must have been conducting a scientific test today.

RANK. Exactly.

HELMER. What do you know—little Nora talking about scientific tests.

NORA. May I congratulate you on the result?

RANK. You may indeed.

NORA. It was a good one?

RANK. The best possible for both doctor and patient—certainty.

NORA (*a quick query*). Certainty?

RANK. Absolute certainty. So why shouldn't I have myself an enjoyable evening afterwards?

NORA. I quite agree with you, Dr. Rank. You should.

HELMER. And so do I. If only you don't pay for it tomorrow.

RANK. Oh well—you get nothing for nothing in this world.

NORA. Dr. Rank—you are fond of costume parties, aren't you?

RANK. Yes, particularly when there is a reasonable number of amusing disguises.

NORA. Listen—what are the two of us going to be the next time?

HELMER. You frivolous little thing! Already thinking about the next party!

RANK. You and I? That's easy. You'll be Fortune's Child.

HELMER. Yes, but what is a fitting costume for that?

RANK. Let your wife appear just the way she always is.

HELMER. Beautiful. Very good indeed. But how about yourself? Don't you know what you'll go as?

RANK. Yes, my friend. I know precisely what I'll be.

HELMER. Yes?

RANK. At the next masquerade I'll be invisible.

HELMER. That's a funny idea.

RANK. There's a certain black hat—you've heard about the hat that makes you invisible, haven't you? You put that on, and nobody can see you.

HELMER (*suppressing a smile*). I guess that's right.

RANK. But, I'm forgetting what I came for. Helmer, give me a cigar—one of your dark Havanas.

HELMER. With the greatest pleasure. (*Offers him his case.*)

RANK (*takes one and cuts off the tip*). Thanks.

NORA (*striking a match*). Let me give you a light.

RANK. Thanks. (*She holds the match; he lights his cigar.*) And now goodbye!

HELMER. Goodbye, goodbye, my friend.

NORA. Sleep well, Dr. Rank.

RANK. I thank you.

NORA. Wish me the same.

RANK. You? Well, if you really want me to—. Sleep well. And thanks for the light. (*He nods to both of them and goes out.*)

HELMER (*in a low voice*). He had had quite a bit to drink.

NORA (*absently*). Maybe so. (HELMER *takes out his keys and goes out into the hall.*) Torvald—what are you doing out there?

HELMER. Emptying the mailbox. It is quite full. There wouldn't be room for the newspapers in the morning—

NORA. Are you going to work tonight?

HELMER. You know very well I won't—Say! What's this? Somebody's been at the lock.

NORA. The lock—?

HELMER. Yes. Why, I wonder. I hate to think that any of the maids—. Here's a broken hairpin. It's one of yours, Nora.

NORA (*quickly*). Then it must be one of the children.

HELMER. You better make damn sure they stop that. Hm, hm.—There! I got it open, finally. (*Gathers up the mail, calls out to the kitchen.*) Helene—Oh Helene—turn out the light here in the hall, will you? (*He comes back into the living room and closes the door.*) Look how it's been piling up. (*Shows her the bundle of letters. Starts leafing through it.*) What's this?

NORA (*by the window*). The letter! Oh no, no, Torvald!

HELMER. Two calling cards—from Rank.

NORA. From Dr. Rank?

HELMER (*looking at them*). "Doctor medicinae Rank." They were on top. He must have put them there when he left just now.

NORA. Anything written on them?

HELMER. A black cross above the name. What a macabre idea. Like announcing his own death.

NORA. That's what it is.

HELMER. Hm? You know about this? Has he said anything to you?

NORA. That card means he has said goodbye to us. He'll lock himself up to die.

HELMER. My poor friend. I knew of course he wouldn't be with me very long. But so soon—. And hiding himself away like a wounded animal—

NORA. When it has to be, it's better it happens without words. Don't you think so, Torvald?

HELMER (*walking up and down*). He'd grown so close to us. I find it hard to think of him as gone. With his suffering and loneliness he was like a clouded background for our happy sunshine. Well, it may be better this way. For him, at any rate. (*Stops.*) And perhaps for us, too, Nora. For now we have nobody but each other. (*Embraces her.*) Oh you—my beloved wife! I feel I just can't hold you close enough. Do you know, Nora— many times I have wished some great danger threatened you, so I could risk my life and blood and everything—everything, for your sake.

NORA (*frees herself and says in a strong and firm voice*). I think you should go and read your letters now, Torvald.

HELMER. No, no—not tonight. I want to be with you, my darling.

NORA. With the thought of your dying friend—?

HELMER. You are right. This has shaken both of us. Something not beautiful has come between us. Thoughts of death and dissolution. We must try to get over it—out of it. Till then—we'll each go to our own room.

NORA (*her arms around his neck*). Torvald—goodnight! Goodnight!

HELMER (*kisses her forehead*). Goodnight, my little songbird. Sleep well, Nora. Now I'll read my letters. (*He goes into his room, carrying the mail. Closes the door.*)

NORA (*her eyes desperate, her hands groping, finds* HELMER's *black cloak and throws it around her; she whispers, quickly, brokenly, hoarsely*). Never see him again. Never. Never. Never. (*Puts her shawl over her head.*) And never see the children again, either. Never; never.—The black, icy water—fathomless—this—! If only it was all over.—Now he has it. Now he's reading it. No, no; not yet. Torvald—goodbye—you—the children—(*She is about to hurry through the hall, when* HELMER *flings open the door to his room and stands there with an open letter in his hand.*)

HELMER. Nora!

NORA (*cries out*). Ah—!

HELMER. What is it? You know what's in this letter?

NORA. Yes, I do! Let me go! Let me out!

HELMER (*holds her back*). Where do you think you're going?

NORA (*trying to tear herself loose from him*). I won't let you save me, Torvald!

HELMER (*tumbles back*). True! Is it true what he writes? Oh my God! No, no—this can't possibly be true.

NORA. It is true. I have loved you more than anything else in the whole world.

HELMER. Oh, don't give me any silly excuses.

NORA (*taking a step towards him*). Torvald—!

HELMER. You wretch! What have you done!

NORA. Let me go. You are not to sacrifice yourself for me. You are not to take the blame.

HELMER. No more playacting. (*Locks the door to the front hall.*) You'll stay here and answer me. Do you understand what you have done? Answer me! Do you understand?

NORA (*gazes steadily at him with an increasingly frozen expression*). Yes. Now I'm beginning to understand.

HELMER (*walking up and down*). What a dreadful awakening. All these years—all these eight years—she, my pride and my joy—a hypocrite, a liar—oh worse! worse!—a criminal! Oh, the bottomless ugliness in all this! Damn! Damn! Damn! (*NORA, silent, keeps gazing at him.* HELMER *stops in front of her.*) I ought to have guessed that something like this would happen. I should have expected it. All your father's loose principles—Silence! You have inherited every one of your father's loose principles. No religion, no morals, no sense of duty——. Now I am being punished for my leniency with him. I did it for your sake, and this is how you pay me back.

NORA. Yes. This is how.

HELMER. You have ruined all my happiness. My whole future—that's what you have destroyed. Oh, it's terrible to think about. I am at the mercy of an unscrupulous man. He can do with me whatever he likes, demand anything of me, command me and dispose of me just as he pleases—I dare not say a word! To go down so miserably, to be destroyed—all because of an irresponsible woman!

NORA. When I am gone from the world, you'll be free.

HELMER. No noble gestures, please. Your father was always full of such phrases too. What good would it do me if you were gone from the world, as you put it? Not the slightest good at all. He could still make the whole thing public, and if he did, people would be likely to think I had been your accomplice. They might even think it was my idea— that it was I who urged you to do it! And for all this I have you to thank—you, whom I've borne on my hands through all the years of our marriage. *Now* do you understand what you've done to me?

NORA (*with cold calm*). Yes.

HELMER. I just can't get it into my head that this is happening; it's all so incredible. But we have to come to terms with it somehow. Take your shawl off. Take it off, I say! I have to satisfy him one way or another. The whole affair must be kept quiet at whatever cost.—And as far as you and I are concerned, nothing must seem to have changed. I'm talking about appearances, of course. You'll go on living here; that goes without saying. But I won't let you bring up the children; I dare not trust you with them.—Oh! Having to say this to one I have loved so much, and whom I still—! But all that is past. It's not a question of happiness any more but of hanging on to what can be salvaged—pieces, appearances—(*The doorbell rings.* HELMER *jumps.*) What's that? So late. Is the worst—? Has he—! Hide, Nora! Say you're sick. (NORA *doesn't move.* HELMER *opens the door to the hall.*)

MAID (*half dressed, out in the hall*). A letter for your wife, sir.

HELMER. Give it to me. (*Takes the letter and closes the door.*) Yes, it's from him. But I won't let you have it. I'll read it myself.

NORA. Yes—you read it.

HELMER (*by the lamp*). I hardly dare. Perhaps we're lost, both you and I. No; I've got to know. (*Tears the letter open, glances through it, looks at an enclosure; a cry of joy.*) Nora! (NORA *looks at him with a question in her eyes.*) Nora!—No, I must read it again.—Yes, yes; it is so! I'm saved! Nora, I'm saved!

NORA. And I?

HELMER. You too, of course; we're both saved, both you and I. Look! He's
returning your note. He writes that he's sorry, he regrets, a happy turn
in his life—oh, it doesn't matter what he writes. We're saved, Nora!
Nobody can do anything to you now. Oh Nora, Nora—. No, I want to
get rid of this disgusting thing first. Let me see—(*Looks at the signature.*)
No, I don't want to see it. I don't want it to be more than a bad dream,
the whole thing. (*Tears up the note and both letters, throws the pieces in the
stove, and watches them burn.*) There! Now it's gone.—He wrote that ever
since Christmas Eve—. Good God, Nora, these must have been three
terrible days for you.

NORA. I have fought a hard fight these last three days.

HELMER. And been in agony and seen no other way out than—. No, we
won't think of all that ugliness. We'll just rejoice and tell ourselves it's
over, it's all over! Oh, listen to me, Nora. You don't seem to understand.
It's over. What *is* it? Why do you look like that—that frozen expression
on your face? Oh my poor little Nora, don't you think I know what it
is? You can't make yourself believe that I have forgiven you. But I have,
Nora; I swear to you, I have forgiven you for everything. Of course I
know that what you did was for love of me.

NORA. That is true.

HELMER. You have loved me the way a wife ought to love her husband. You
just didn't have the wisdom to judge the means. But do you think I love
you any less because you don't know how to act on your own? Of course
not. Just lean on me. I'll advise you; I'll guide you. I wouldn't be a man
if I didn't find you twice as attractive because of your womanly help-
lessness. You mustn't pay any attention to the hard words I said to you
right at first. It was just that first shock when I thought everything was
collapsing all around me. I have forgiven you, Nora. I swear to you—I
really have forgiven you.

NORA. I thank you for your forgiveness. (*She goes out through the door, right.*)

HELMER. No, stay—(*Looks into the room she entered.*) What are you doing in there?

NORA (*within*). Getting out of my costume.

HELMER (*by the open door*). Good, good. Try to calm down and compose
yourself, my poor little frightened songbird. Rest safely; I have broad
wings to cover you with. (*Walks around near the door.*) What a nice and
cozy home we have, Nora. Here's shelter for you. Here I'll keep you safe
like a hunted dove I have rescued from the hawk's talons. Believe me:
I'll know how to quiet your beating heart. It will happen by and by,
Nora; you'll see. Why, tomorrow you'll look at all this in quite a different light. And soon everything will be just the way it was before. I
won't need to keep reassuring you that I have forgiven you; you'll feel

it yourself. Did you really think I could have abandoned you, or even reproached you? Oh, you don't know a real man's heart, Nora. There is something unspeakably sweet and satisfactory for a man to know deep in himself that he has forgiven his wife—forgiven her in all the fullness of his honest heart. You see, that way she becomes his very own all over again—in a double sense, you might say. He has, so to speak, given her a second birth; it is as if she had become his wife and his child, both. From now on that's what you'll be to me, you lost and helpless creature. Don't worry about a thing, Nora. Only be frank with me, and I'll be your will and your conscience.—What's this? You're not in bed? You've changed your dress—!

NORA (*in everyday dress*). Yes, Torvald. I have changed my dress.

HELMER. But why—now—this late?

NORA. I'm not going to sleep tonight.

HELMER. But my dear Nora—

NORA (*looks at her watch*). It isn't all that late. Sit down here with me, Torvald. You and I have much to talk about. (*Sits down at the table.*)

HELMER. Nora—what is this all about? That rigid face—

NORA. Sit down. This will take a while. I have much to say to you.

HELMER (*sits down, facing her across the table*). You worry me, Nora. I don't understand you.

NORA. No, that's just it. You don't understand me. And I have never understood you—not till tonight. No, don't interrupt me. Just listen to what I have to say.—This is a settling of accounts, Torvald.

HELMER. What do you mean by that?

NORA (*after a brief silence*). Doesn't one thing strike you, now that we are sitting together like this?

HELMER. What would that be?

NORA. We have been married for eight years. Doesn't it occur to you that this is the first time that you and I, husband and wife, are having a serious talk?

HELMER. Well—serious—. What do you mean by that?

NORA. For eight whole years—longer, in fact—ever since we first met we have never talked seriously to each other about a single serious thing.

HELMER. You mean I should forever have been telling you about worries you couldn't have helped me with anyway?

NORA. I am not talking about worries. I'm saying we have never tried seriously to get to the bottom of anything together.

HELMER. But dearest Nora, I hardly think that would have been something you—

NORA. That's the whole point. You have never understood me. Great wrong has been done to me, Torvald. First by Daddy and then by you.

HELMER. What! By us two? We who have loved you more deeply than anyone else?

NORA (*shakes her head*). You never loved me—neither Daddy nor you. You only thought it was fun to be in love with me.

HELMER. But, Nora—what an expression to use!

NORA. That's the way it has been, Torvald. When I was home with Daddy, he told me all his opinions, and so they became my opinions too. If I disagreed with him I kept it to myself, for he wouldn't have liked that. He called me his little doll baby, and he played with me the way I played with my dolls. Then I came to your house—

HELMER. What a way to talk about our marriage!

NORA (*imperturbably*). I mean that I passed from Daddy's hands into yours. You arranged everything according to your taste, and so I came to share it—or I pretended to; I'm not sure which. I think it was a little of both, now one and now the other. When I look back on it now, it seems to me I've been living here like a pauper—just a hand-to-mouth kind of existence. I have earned my keep by doing tricks for you, Torvald. But that's the way you wanted it. You have great sins against me to answer for, Daddy and you. It's your fault that nothing has become of me.

HELMER. Nora, you're being both unreasonable and ungrateful. Haven't you been happy here?

NORA. No, never. I thought I was, but I wasn't.

HELMER. Not—not happy!

NORA. No; just having fun. And you have always been very good to me. But our home has never been more than a playroom. I have been your doll wife here, just the way I used to be Daddy's doll child. And the children have been my dolls. I thought it was fun when you played with me, just as they thought it was fun when I played with them. That's been our marriage, Torvald.

HELMER. There is something in what you are saying—exaggerated and hysterical though it is. But from now on things will be different. Playtime is over; it's time for growing up.

NORA. Whose growing up—mine or the children's?

HELMER. Both yours and the children's, Nora darling.

NORA. Oh Torvald, you're not the man to bring me up to be the right kind of wife for you.

HELMER. How can you say that?

NORA. And I—? What qualifications do I have for bringing up the children?

HELMER. Nora!

NORA. You said so yourself a minute ago—that you didn't dare to trust me with them.

HELMER. In the first flush of anger, yes. Surely, you're not going to count that.

NORA. But you were quite right. I am *not* qualified. Something else has to come first. Somehow I have to grow up myself. And you are not the man to help me do that. That's a job I have to do by myself. And that's why I'm leaving you.

HELMER (*jumps up*). What did you say!

NORA. I have to be by myself if I am to find out about myself and about all the other things too. So I can't stay here with you any longer.

HELMER. Nora, Nora!

NORA. I'm leaving now. I'm sure Kristine will put me up for tonight.

HELMER. You're out of your mind! I won't let you! I forbid you!

NORA. You can't forbid me anything any more; it won't do any good. I'm taking my own things with me. I won't accept anything from you, either now or later.

HELMER. But this is madness!

NORA. Tomorrow I'm going home—I mean back to my old home town. It will be easier for me to find some kind of job there.

HELMER. Oh, you blind, inexperienced creature—!

NORA. I must see to it that I get experience, Torvald.

HELMER. Leaving your home, your husband, your children! Not a thought of what people will say!

NORA. I can't worry about that. All I know is that I have to leave.

HELMER. Oh, this is shocking! Betraying your most sacred duties like this!

NORA. And what do you consider my most sacred duties?

HELMER. Do I need to tell you that? They are your duties to your husband and your children.

NORA. I have other duties equally sacred.

HELMER. You do not. What duties would they be?

NORA. My duties to myself.

HELMER. You are a wife and a mother before you are anything else.

NORA. I don't believe that any more. I believe I am first of all a human being, just as much as you—or at any rate that I must try to become one. Oh, I know very well that most people agree with you, Torvald, and that it says something like that in all the books. But what people say and what the books say is no longer enough for me. I have to think about these things myself and see if I can't find the answers.

HELMER. You mean to tell me you don't know what your proper place in your own home is? Don't you have a reliable guide in such matters? Don't you have religion?

NORA. Oh but Torvald—I don't really know what religion is.

HELMER. What are you saying!

NORA. All I know is what the Reverend Hansen told me when he prepared me for confirmation. He said that religion was *this* and it was *that*.

When I get by myself, away from here, I'll have to look into that, too.
I have to decide if what the Reverend Hansen said was right, or anyway
if it is right for *me*.

HELMER. Oh, this is unheard of in a young woman! If religion can't guide
you, let me appeal to your conscience. For surely you have moral feelings? Or—answer me—maybe you don't?

NORA. Well, you see, Torvald, I don't really know what to say. I just don't
know. I am confused about these things. All I know is that my ideas are
quite different from yours. I have just found out that the laws are different from what I thought they were, but in no way can I get it into my
head that those laws are right. A woman shouldn't have the right to spare
her dying old father or save her husband's life! I just can't believe that.

HELMER. You speak like a child. You don't understand the society you live in.

NORA. No, I don't. But I want to find out about it. I have to make up my
mind who is right, society or I.

HELMER. You are sick, Nora; you have a fever. I really don't think you are in
your right mind.

NORA. I have never felt so clearheaded and sure of myself as I do tonight.

HELMER. And clearheaded and sure of yourself you're leaving your husband
and children?

NORA. Yes.

HELMER. Then there is only one possible explanation.

NORA. What?

HELMER. You don't love me any more.

NORA. No, that's just it.

HELMER. Nora! Can you say that?

NORA. I am sorry, Torvald, for you have always been so good to me. But I
can't help it. I don't love you any more.

HELMER (*with forced composure*). And this too is a clear and sure conviction?

NORA. Completely clear and sure. That's why I don't want to stay here any
more.

HELMER. And are you ready to explain to me how I came to forfeit your love?

NORA. Certainly I am. It was tonight, when the wonderful didn't happen.
That was when I realized you were not the man I thought you were.

HELMER. You have to explain. I don't understand.

NORA. I have waited patiently for eight years, for I wasn't such a fool that
I thought the wonderful is something that happens any old day. Then
this—thing—came crashing in on me, and then there wasn't a doubt in
my mind that now—now comes the wonderful. When Krogstad's letter
was in that mailbox, never for a moment did it even occur to me that
you would submit to his conditions. I was so absolutely certain that you
would say to him: make the whole thing public—tell everybody. And
when that had happened—

HELMER. Yes, then what? When I surrendered my wife to shame and disgrace—!

NORA. When that had happened, I was absolutely certain that you would stand up and take the blame and say, "I'm the guilty one."

HELMER. Nora!

NORA. You mean I never would have accepted such a sacrifice from you? Of course not. But what would my protests have counted against yours? *That* was the wonderful I was hoping for in terror. And to prevent that I was going to kill myself.

HELMER. I'd gladly work nights and days for you, Nora—endure sorrow and want for your sake. But nobody sacrifices his *honor* for his love.

NORA. A hundred thousand women have done so.

HELMER. Oh, you think and talk like a silly child.

NORA. All right. But you don't think and talk like the man I can live with. When you had gotten over your fright—not because of what threatened *me* but because of the risk to *you*—and the whole danger was past, then you acted as if nothing at all had happened. Once again I was your little songbird, your doll, just as before, only now you had to handle her even more carefully, because she was so frail and weak. (*Rises.*) Torvald—that moment I realized that I had been living here for eight years with a stranger and had borne him three children—Oh, I can't stand thinking about it! I feel like tearing myself to pieces!

HELMER (*heavily*). I see it, I see it. An abyss has opened up between us.—Oh but Nora—surely it can be filled?

NORA. The way I am now I am no wife for you.

HELMER. I have it in me to change.

NORA. Perhaps—if your doll is taken from you.

HELMER. To part—to part from you! No, no, Nora! I can't grasp that thought!

NORA (*goes out, right*). All the more reason why it has to be. (*She returns with her outdoor clothes and a small bag, which she sets down on the chair by the table.*)

HELMER. Nora, Nora! Not now! Wait till tomorrow.

NORA (*putting on her coat*). I can't spend the night in a stranger's rooms.

HELMER. But couldn't we live here together like brother and sister—?

NORA (*tying on her hat*). You know very well that wouldn't last long—. (*Wraps her shawl around her.*) Goodbye, Torvald. I don't want to see the children. I know I leave them in better hands than mine. The way I am now I can't be anything to them.

HELMER. But some day, Nora—some day—?

NORA. How can I tell? I have no idea what's going to become of me.

HELMER. But you're still my wife, both as you are now and as you will be.

NORA. Listen, Torvald—when a wife leaves her husband's house, the way I am doing now, I have heard he has no more legal responsibilities for her. At any rate, I now release you from all responsibility. You are not to feel yourself obligated to me for anything, and I have no obligations to you. There has to be full freedom on both sides. Here is your ring back. Now give me mine.

HELMER. Even this?

NORA. Even this.

HELMER. Here it is.

NORA. There. So now it's over. I'm putting the keys here. The maids know everything about the house—better than I. Tomorrow, after I'm gone, Kristine will come over and pack my things from home. I want them sent after me.

HELMER. Over! It's all over! Nora, will you never think of me?

NORA. I'm sure I'll often think of you and the children and this house.

HELMER. May I write to you, Nora?

NORA. No—never. I won't have that.

HELMER. But send you things——? You must let me—

NORA. Nothing, nothing.

HELMER.—help you, when you need help—

NORA. I told you, no; I won't have it. I'll accept nothing from strangers.

HELMER. Nora—can I never again be more to you than a stranger?

NORA (picks up her bag). Oh Torvald—then the most wonderful of all would have to happen—

HELMER. Tell me what that would be—!

NORA. For that to happen, both you and I would have to change so that Oh Torvald, I no longer believe in the wonderful.

HELMER. But I will believe. Tell me! Change, so that—?

NORA. So that our living together would become a true marriage. Goodbye. (She goes out through the hall.)

HELMER (sinks down on a chair near the door and covers his face with his hands). Nora! Nora! (Looks around him and gets up.) All empty. She's gone. (With sudden hope.) The most wonderful—?!

(From downstairs comes the sound of a heavy door slamming shut.)

QUESTIONS

1. How do the following contribute to the characterizations of Nora at the beginning of the play: (a) her husband's nicknames for her, (b) her fondness for sweets, (c) her games with her children, (d) her prodigality with money, and (e) her deceptions? What evidence is there that these characteristics may reflect both her own nature and her conformity to her husband's expectations of her? What definition of marriage does she imply in her remarks to Mrs. Linde about how she may continue to act as long as she remains "young and pretty" (page 1127)? It was socially proper at the time of the play for Norwegian wives to address their husbands by their last names; what does Nora's use of Helmer's first name suggest about their relationship?

2. What are the various functions of Nora's conversation with Mrs. Linde in Act 1? Consider it from these perspectives: (a) the exposition of prior events and the definition of Nora's dilemma; (b) further revelations of Nora's character, both in the past and during the conversation; (c) the insight into herself that Nora gains from Mrs. Linde's history; (d) definitions of legal and moral standards of the time indicated by the prior actions of both women.

3. What are the symbolic meanings of the title? Why is it more appropriate than *A Doll's House?* Is Nora the only "doll" in the play?

4. How much time passes during the present action of the play, from the opening of Act 1 to the final curtain? What events that occurred before the first act may be considered causes for the present action? What events that take place during the present are reported rather than dramatized on the stage?

5. What is the significance of Mrs. Linde's former and present relationship to Krogstad? To what extent can Krogstad be labeled "villain"? Compare his motives and actions (in the past and in the present) with those of Helmer; with those of Dr. Rank.

6. Characterize Dr. Rank. What are his strengths? his weaknesses? Structurally and morally he may be contrasted to Krogstad—but is he a model of virtue?

7. The major characters can be described thus: Nora and Helmer are protagonist and antagonist; Mrs. Linde is a foil to Nora; and both Krogstad and Dr. Rank are foils to Helmer. By evaluating the actions and motives of the foil characters, locate Nora and Helmer on a scale of human value. To what extent do the foil characters offer models for the central characters? To what extent do they offer them examples of actions to be avoided?

8. What positive gains does Nora make in the course of the action? What must she learn in order to perform her final act? Is that act a triumph, or a failure, or some of both? (For the play's first performance in Berlin, Ibsen was pressured into creating a conventionally "happy ending"—Nora is persuaded by Helmer not to leave him for the sake of their children, and so sacrifices herself to their need for a mother. Why is the present ending truer to the themes Ibsen presents?)

9. Compare Nora and Helmer as developing characters. What opportunities for change does Helmer have? How does he respond to them? Consider the extent to which Nora and Helmer share the responsibility for having created "a doll house" of their marriage. Evaluate Nora's leaving him as an opportunity for Helmer.

10. From the first moments of the play, money is a recurring topic. Consider the importance it has in the motivations and actions of the five major characters. Can you establish a rank-order of more or less admirable attitudes toward it? Can you separate examples of genuine need from examples of desire for gain? Is the influence of money on the lives of these characters limited to the time and society in which they lived, or are there parallels to our time?

11. Consider the ways in which the marriage of Nora and Helmer is typical rather than uniquely theirs.

12. Assess the thematic importance of deception and honesty, of self-deception and self-discovery.

13. Explore the implications of this interpretation: *"A Doll House* represents a woman imbued with the idea of becoming a person, but it proposes nothing categorical about women becoming people; in fact, its real theme has nothing

to do with the sexes. It is the irrepressible conflict of two different personalities which have founded themselves on two radically different estimates of reality" (Robert M. Adams, "Ibsen on the Contrary," in *Modern Drama*, ed. Anthony Caputi [New York: Norton, 1966], 345).

TENNESSEE WILLIAMS
The Glass Menagerie

Characters

AMANDA WINGFIELD, *the mother, a little woman of great but confused vitality clinging frantically to another time and place. Her characterization must be carefully created, not copied from type. She is not paranoiac, but her life is paranoia. There is much to admire in* AMANDA, *and as much to love and pity as there is to laugh at. Certainly she has endurance and a kind of heroism, and though her foolishness makes her unwittingly cruel at times, there is tenderness in her slight person.*

LAURA WINGFIELD, *her daughter.* AMANDA, *having failed to establish contact with reality, continues to live vitally in her illusions, but* LAURA's *situation is even graver. A childhood illness has left her crippled, one leg slightly shorter than the other, and held in a brace. This defect need not be more than suggested on the stage. Stemming from this,* LAURA's *separation increases till she is like a piece of her own glass collection, too exquisitely fragile to move from the shelf.*

TOM WINGFIELD, *her son and the narrator of the play. A poet with a job in a warehouse. His nature is not remorseless, but to escape from a trap he has to act without pity.*

JIM O'CONNOR, *the gentleman caller, a nice, ordinary, young man.*

THE GLASS MENAGERIE   First performed in 1944; developed from a short story, "Portrait of a Girl in Glass" (published later in *One Arm and Other Stories*). Tennessee Williams (1911–1983) was born Thomas Lanier Williams in Mississippi, the son of a traveling salesman. In 1918 the family moved to St. Louis when the father was made a sales manager of International Shoe Company. Here, while the family lived in a succession of rented apartments, Tom published his first story at sixteen, graduated from high school, attended the University of Missouri for three years, worked at a menial job in the shoe company (1932–1935), had a nervous breakdown, and finished his education at Washington University and the University of Iowa. Adopting "Tennessee" as his writing name, he then embarked on a life that took him to Chicago, New Orleans, Los Angeles, Mexico City, New York, Key West, and other cities while he wrote steadily, supporting himself with odd jobs. *The Glass Menagerie*, his first commercial success, rescued him from penury. The play reflects his St. Louis years, although his real father (given to alcoholic excess) never disappeared from home; his sister (two years his elder) did have dates, was not handicapped, and did not have a glass collection; a younger brother (eight years Tom's junior) does not appear; and "Miss Edwina" (Williams's mother and his guest at the first performance) has written, "The only resemblance I have to Amanda is that we both like jonquils."

SCENE. An Alley in St. Louis.

Part 1. Preparation for a gentleman caller.
Part 2. The gentleman calls.

Time: Now and the Past.

SCENE I

The *Wingfield apartment is in the rear of the building, one of those vast hive-like conglomerations of cellular living-units that flower as warty growths in overcrowded urban centers of lower middle-class population and are symptomatic of the impulse of this largest and fundamentally enslaved section of American society to avoid fluidity and differentiation and to exist and function as one interfused mass of automatism.*

The *apartment faces an alley and is entered by a fire-escape, a structure whose name is a touch of accidental poetic truth, for all of these huge buildings are always burning with the slow and implacable fires of human desperation. The fire-escape is part of what we see—that is, the landing of it and steps descending from it.*

The *scene is memory and is therefore nonrealistic. Memory takes a lot of poetic license. It omits some details; others are exaggerated, according to the emotional value of the articles it touches, for memory is seated predominantly in the heart. The interior is therefore rather dim and poetic.*

At *the rise of the curtain, the audience is faced with the dark, grim rear wall of the Wingfield tenement. This building is flanked on both sides by dark, narrow alleys which run into murky canyons of tangled clotheslines, garbage cans and the sinister latticework of neighboring fire-escapes. It is up and down these side alleys that exterior entrances and exits are made, during the play. At the end of* **TOM's** *opening commentary, the dark tenement wall slowly becomes transparent and reveals the interior of the ground floor Wingfield apartment.*

Nearest *the audience is the living room, which also serves as a sleeping room for* **LAURA***, the sofa unfolding to make her bed. Just beyond, separated from the living room by a wide arch or second proscenium with transparent faded portieres (or second curtain), is the dining room. In an old-fashioned what-not in the living room are seen scores of transparent glass animals. A blown-up photograph of the father hangs on the wall of the living room to the left of the archway. It is the face of a very handsome young man in a doughboy's First World War cap. He is gallantly smiling, ineluctably smiling, as if to say, "I will be smiling forever."*

Also *hanging on the wall, near the photograph, are a typewriter keyboard chart and a Gregg shorthand diagram. An upright typewriter on a small table stands beneath the charts.*

The *audience hears and sees the opening scene in the dining room through both the transparent fourth wall of the building and the transparent gauze portieres of the dining-room arch. It is during this revealing scene that the fourth wall slowly ascends, out of sight. This transparent exterior wall is not brought down again until the very end of the play, during* TOM's *final speech.*

The narrator is an undisguised convention of the play. He takes whatever license with dramatic convention as is convenient to his purposes.

TOM *enters, dressed as a merchant sailor, and strolls across the front of the stage to the fire-escape. There he stops and lights a cigarette. He addresses the audience.*

TOM. Yes, I have tricks in my pocket, I have things up my sleeve. But I am the opposite of a stage magician. He gives you illusion that has the appearance of truth. I give you truth in the pleasant disguise of illusion.

To begin with, I turn back time. I reverse it to that quaint period, the thirties, when the huge middle class of America was matriculating in a school for the blind. Their eyes had failed them, or they had failed their eyes, and so they were having their fingers pressed forcibly down on the fiery Braille alphabet of a dissolving economy.

In Spain there was revolution. Here there was only shouting and confusion. In Spain there was Guernica.° Here there were disturbances of labor, sometimes pretty violent, in otherwise peaceful cities such as Chicago, Cleveland, Saint Louis . . . This is the social background of the play. (*Music.*)

The play is memory. Being a memory play, it is dimly lighted, it is sentimental, it is not realistic. In memory everything seems to happen to music. That explains the fiddle in the wings.

I am the narrator of the play, and also a character in it. The other characters are my mother, Amanda, my sister, Laura, and a gentleman caller who appears in the final scenes. He is the most realistic character in the play, being an emissary from a world of reality that we were somehow set apart from. But since I have a poet's weakness for symbols, I am using this character also as a symbol; he is the long delayed but always expected something that we live for.

There is a fifth character in the play who doesn't appear except in this larger-than-life-size photograph over the mantel. This is our father who left us a long time ago. He was a telephone man who fell in love with long distances; he gave up his job with the telephone company and skipped the light fantastic out of town . . .

The last we heard of him was a picture post-card from Mazatlán, on the Pacific coast of Mexico, containing a message of two words—"Hello— Good-bye!" and no address.

Guernica: A town in northern Spain destroyed in 1937 during the Spanish Civil War by German bombers, in the first mass air attack on an urban community.

I think the rest of the play will explain itself . . . (AMANDA's *voice becomes audible through the portieres.* TOM *divides the portieres and enters the upstage area.* AMANDA *and* LAURA *are seated at a drop-leaf table. Eating is indicated by gestures without food or utensils.* AMANDA *faces the audience.* TOM *and* LAURA *are seated in profile. The interior has lit up softly and through the scrim we see* AMANDA *and* LAURA *seated at the table in the upstage area.*)

AMANDA (*calling*). Tom?

TOM. Yes, Mother.

AMANDA. We can't say grace until you come to the table!

TOM. Coming, Mother. (*He bows slightly and withdraws, reappearing a few moments later in his place at the table.*)

AMANDA (*to her son*). Honey, don't *push* with your *fingers.* If you have to push with something, the thing to push with is a crust of bread. And chew—chew! Animals have sections in their stomachs which enable them to digest food without mastication, but human beings are supposed to chew their food before they swallow it down. Eat food leisurely, son, and really enjoy it. A well-cooked meal has lots of delicate flavors that have to be held in the mouth for appreciation. So chew your food and give your salivary glands a chance to function!

TOM (*deliberately lays his imaginary fork down and pushes his chair back from the table*). I haven't enjoyed one bite of this dinner because of your constant directions on how to eat it. It's you that makes me rush through meals with your hawk-like attention to every bite I take. Sickening—spoils my appetite—all this discussion of—animals' secretion—salivary glands—mastication!

AMANDA (*lightly*). Temperament like a Metropolitan star! (*He rises and crosses downstage.*) You're not excused from the table.

TOM. I'm getting a cigarette.

AMANDA. You smoke too much.

LAURA (*rises*). I'll bring in the blancmange. (TOM *remains standing with his cigarette by the portieres during the following.*)

AMANDA (*rising*). No, sister, no, sister—you be the lady this time and I'll be the darky.

LAURA. I'm already up.

AMANDA. Resume your seat, little sister—I want you fresh and pretty—for gentlemen callers!

LAURA. I'm not expecting any gentlemen callers.

AMANDA (*crossing out to kitchenette. Airily*). Sometimes they come when they are least expected! Why, I remember one Sunday afternoon in Blue Mountain—(*enters kitchenette*).

TOM. I know what's coming!

LAURA. Yes. But let her tell it.

TOM. Again?

LAURA. She loves to tell it.

AMANDA (*returning with a bowl of dessert*). One Sunday afternoon in Blue Mountain—your mother received—*seventeen!*—gentlemen callers! Why, sometimes there weren't chairs enough to accommodate them all. We had to send a servant over to bring in folding chairs from the parish house.

TOM (*remaining at portieres*). How did you entertain those gentlemen callers?

AMANDA. I understood the art of conversation!

TOM. I bet you could talk.

AMANDA. Girls in those days *knew* how to talk, I can tell you.

TOM. Yes?

AMANDA. They knew how to entertain their gentlemen callers. It wasn't enough for a girl to be possessed of a pretty face and a graceful figure—although I wasn't slighted in either respect. She also needed to have a nimble wit and a tongue to meet all occasions.

TOM. What did you talk about?

AMANDA. Things of importance going on in the world! Never anything coarse or common or vulgar. (*She addresses* TOM *as though he were seated in the vacant chair at the table though he remains by the portieres. He plays this scene as though he held the book.*) My callers were gentlemen—all! Among my callers were some of the most prominent young planters of the Mississippi Delta—planters and sons of planters! (TOM *motions for music and a spot of light on* AMANDA. *Her eyes lift, her face glows, her voice becomes rich and elegiac.*)

There was young Champ Laughlin who later became vice-president of the Delta Planters Bank. Hadley Stevenson who was drowned in Moon Lake and left his widow one hundred and fifty thousand in Government bonds. There were the Cutrere brothers, Wesley and Bates. Bates was one of my bright particular beaux! He got in a quarrel with that wild Wainwright boy. They shot it out on the floor of Moon Lake Casino. Bates was shot through the stomach. Died in the ambulance on his way to Memphis. His widow was so well provided for, came into eight or ten thousand acres, that's all. She married him on the rebound—never loved her—carried my picture on him the night he died! And there was that boy that every girl in the Delta had set her cap for! That beautiful, brilliant young Fitzhugh boy from Greene County!

TOM. What did he leave his widow?

AMANDA. He never married! Gracious, you talk as though all of my old admirers had turned up their toes to the daisies!

TOM. Isn't this the first you've mentioned that still survives?

AMANDA. That Fitzhugh boy went North and made a fortune—came to be known as the Wolf of Wall Street! He had the Midas touch, whatever he touched turned to gold! And I could have been Mrs. Duncan J. Fitzhugh, mind you! But—I picked your *father!*

LAURA (*rising*). Mother, let me clear the table.

AMANDA. No, dear, you go in front and study your typewriter chart. Or practice your shorthand a little. Stay fresh and pretty!—It's almost time for our gentlemen callers to start arriving. (*She flounces girlishly toward the kitchenette.*) How many do you suppose we're going to entertain this afternoon? (TOM *throws down the paper and jumps up with a groan.*)

LAURA (*alone in the dining room*). I don't believe we're going to receive any, Mother.

AMANDA (*reappearing, airily*). What? No one—not one? You must be joking! (LAURA *nervously echoes her laugh. She slips in a fugitive manner through the half-open portieres and draws them gently behind her. A shaft of very clear light is thrown on her face against the faded tapestry of the curtains. Music: "The Glass Menagerie"° under faintly. Lightly*) Not one gentleman caller? It can't be true! There must be a flood, there must have been a tornado!

LAURA. It isn't a flood, it's not a tornado, Mother. I'm just not popular like you were in Blue Mountain . . . (TOM *utters another groan.* LAURA *glances at him with a faint, apologetic smile. Her voice catching a little.*) Mother's afraid I'm going to be an old maid. (*The scene dims out with "Glass Menagerie" music.*)

SCENE 2

LAURA *is seated in the delicate ivory chair at the small claw-foot table. She wears a dress of soft violet material for a kimono—her hair tied back from her forehead with a ribbon. She is washing and polishing her collection of glass.* AMANDA *appears on the fire-escape steps. At the sound of her ascent,* LAURA *catches her breath, thrusts the bowl of ornaments away and seats herself stiffly before the diagram of the typewriter keyboard as though it held her spellbound. Something has happened to* AMANDA. *It is written in her face as she climbs to the landing: a look that is grim and hopeless and a little absurd. She has on one of those cheap or imitation velvety-looking cloth coats with imitation fur collar. Her hat is five or six years old, one of those dreadful cloche hats that were worn in the late twenties, and she is clasping an enormous black patent-leather pocketbook with nickel clasps and initials. This is her full-dress outfit, the one she usually wears to the D.A.R. Before entering she looks through the door. She purses her lips, opens her eyes very wide, rolls them upward and shakes her head. Then she slowly lets herself in the door. Seeing her mother's expression* LAURA *touches her lips with a nervous gesture.*

Music . . . Menagerie": Music for the play, including "The Glass Menagerie" theme, was composed by Paul Bowles (1910–1999), American composer, novelist, and short story writer.

LAURA. Hello, Mother, I was—(*She makes a nervous gesture toward the chart on the wall.* AMANDA *leans against the shut door and stares at* LAURA *with a martyred look.*)

AMANDA. Deception? Deception? (*She slowly removes her hat and gloves, continuing the sweet suffering stare. She lets the hat and gloves fall on the floor—a bit of acting.*)

LAURA (*shakily*). How was the D.A.R. meeting? (AMANDA *slowly opens her purse and removes a dainty white handkerchief which she shakes out delicately and delicately touches to her lips and nostrils.*) Didn't you go to the D.A.R. meeting, Mother?

AMANDA (*faintly, almost inaudibly*).—No.—No. (*Then more forcibly*) I did not have the strength—to go to the D.A.R. In fact, I did not have the courage! I wanted to find a hole in the ground and hide myself in it forever! (*She crosses slowly to the wall and removes the diagram of the typewriter keyboard. She holds it in front of her for a second, staring at it sweetly and sorrowfully—then bites her lips and tears it in two pieces.*)

LAURA (*faintly*). Why did you do that, Mother? (AMANDA *repeats the same procedure with the chart of the Gregg Alphabet.*) Why are you—

AMANDA. Why? Why? How old are you, Laura?

LAURA. Mother, you know my age.

AMANDA. I thought you were an adult; it seems that I was mistaken. (*She crosses slowly to the sofa and sinks down and stares at* LAURA.)

LAURA. Please don't stare at me, Mother. (AMANDA *closes her eyes and lowers her head. There is a ten-second pause.*)

AMANDA. What are we going to do, what is going to become of us, what is the future? (*There is another pause.*)

LAURA. Has something happened, Mother? (AMANDA *draws a long breath and takes out the handkerchief again. Dabbing process.*) Mother, has—something happened?

AMANDA. I'll be all right in a minute, I'm just bewildered—(*she hesitates*)—by life.

LAURA. Mother, I wish that you would tell me what's happened!

AMANDA. As you know, I was supposed to be inducted into my office at the D.A.R. this afternoon. But I stopped off at Rubicam's Business College to speak to your teachers about your having a cold and ask them what progress they thought were you making down there.

LAURA. Oh . . .

AMANDA. I went to the typing instructor and introduced myself as your mother. She didn't know who you were. "Wingfield," she said. "We don't have any such student enrolled at the school!"

I assured her she did, that you had been going to classes since early in January.

"I wonder," she said, "if you could be talking about that terribly shy little girl who dropped out of school after only a few days' attendance?"

"No," I said, "Laura, my daughter, has been going to school every day for the past six weeks!"

"Excuse me," she said. She took the attendance book out and there was your name, unmistakably printed, and all the dates you were absent until they decided that you had dropped out of school.

I still said, "No, there must have been some mistake! There must have been some mix-up in the records!"

And she said, "No—I remember her perfectly now. Her hands shook so that she couldn't hit the right keys! The first time we gave a speed-test, she broke down completely—was sick at the stomach and almost had to be carried into the wash-room! After that morning she never showed up any more. We phoned the house but never got any answer"—While I was working at Famous and Barr, I suppose, demonstrating those—

Oh! (*She indicates a brassiere with her hands.*) I felt so weak I could barely keep on my feet! I had to sit down while they got me a glass of water! Fifty dollars' tuition, all of our plans—my hopes and ambitions for you—just gone up the spout, just gone up the spout like that. (LAURA *draws a long breath and gets awkwardly to her feet. She crosses to the victrola and winds it up.*) What are you doing?

LAURA. Oh! (*She releases the handle and returns to her seat.*)

AMANDA. Laura, where have you been going when you've gone out pretending that you were going to business college?

LAURA. I've just been going out walking.

AMANDA. That's not true.

LAURA. It is. I just went walking.

AMANDA. Walking? Walking? In winter? Deliberately courting pneumonia in that light coat? Where did you walk to, Laura?

LAURA. All sorts of places—mostly in the park.

AMANDA. Even after you'd started catching that cold?

LAURA. It was the lesser of two evils, Mother. I couldn't go back up. I—threw up—on the floor!

AMANDA. From half past seven till after five every day you mean to tell me you walked around in the park, because you wanted me to think that you were still going to Rubicam's Business College?

LAURA. It wasn't as bad as it sounds. I went inside places to get warmed up.

AMANDA. Inside where?

LAURA. I went in the art museum and the bird-houses at the Zoo. I visited the penguins every day! Sometimes I did without lunch and went to the movies. Lately I've been spending most of my afternoons in the Jewel-box, that big glass house where they raise the tropical flowers.

AMANDA. You did all this to deceive me, just for deception? (LAURA *looks down.*) Why?

LAURA. Mother, when you're disappointed, you get that awful suffering look on your face, like the picture of Jesus's mother in the museum!

AMANDA. Hush!

LAURA. I couldn't face it. (*Pause. A whisper of strings.*)

AMANDA (*hopelessly fingering the huge pocketbook*). So what are we going to do the rest of our lives? Stay home and watch the parades go by? Amuse ourselves with the glass menagerie, darling? Eternally play those worn-out phonograph records your father left as a painful reminder of him? We won't have a business career—we've given that up because it gave us nervous indigestion! (*Laughs wearily.*) What is there left but dependency all our lives? I know so well what becomes of unmarried women who aren't prepared to occupy a position. I've seen such pitiful cases in the South—barely tolerated spinsters living upon the grudging patronage of sister's husband or brother's wife!—stuck away in some little mouse-trap of a room—encouraged by one in-law to visit another—little birdlike women without any nest—eating the crust of humility all their life!

Is that the future that we've mapped out for ourselves? I swear it's the only alternative I can think of! (*She pauses.*) It isn't a very pleasant alternative, is it? (*She pauses again.*) Of course—some girls *do* marry. (LAURA *twists her hands nervously.*) Haven't you ever liked some boy?

LAURA. Yes. I liked one once. (*Rises.*) I came across his picture a while ago.

AMANDA (*with some interest*). He gave you his picture?

LAURA. No, it's in the year-book.

AMANDA (*disappointed*). Oh—a high-school boy.

LAURA. Yes. His name was Jim. (LAURA *lifts the heavy annual from the claw-foot table.*) Here he is in *The Pirates of Penzance.*°

AMANDA (*absently*). The what?

LAURA. The operetta the senior class put on. He had a wonderful voice and we sat across the aisle from each other Mondays, Wednesdays and Fridays in the Aud. Here he is with the silver cup for debating! See his grin?

AMANDA (*absently*). He must have had a jolly disposition.

LAURA. He used to call me—Blue Roses.

AMANDA. Why did he call you such a name as that?

LAURA. When I had that attack of pleurosis—he asked me what was the matter when I came back. I said pleurosis—he thought that I said Blue Roses! So that's what he always called me after that. Whenever he saw

---

The . . . Penzance: comic operetta (1880) by Gilbert and Sullivan

me, he'd holler, "Hello, Blue Roses!" I didn't care for the girl he went out with. Emily Meisenbach. Emily was the best-dressed girl at Soldan. She never struck me, though, as being sincere . . . It says in the Personal Section—they're engaged. That's—six years ago! They must be married by now.

AMANDA. Girls that aren't cut out for business careers usually wind up married to some nice man. (*Gets up with a spark of revival.*) Sister, that's what you'll do! (LAURA *utters a startled, doubtful laugh. She reaches quickly for a piece of glass.*)

LAURA. But, Mother—

AMANDA. Yes? (*Crossing to photograph.*)

LAURA (*in a tone of frightened apology*). I'm—crippled!

AMANDA. Nonsense! Laura, I've told you never, never to use that word. Why, you're not crippled, you just have a little defect—hardly noticeable, even! When people have some slight disadvantage like that, they cultivate other things to make up for it—develop charm—and vivacity—and—*charm!* That's all you have to do! (*She turns again to the photograph.*) One thing your father had *plenty of*—was *charm!* (TOM *motions to the fiddle in the wings. The scene fades out with music.*)

SCENE 3

TOM *speaks from the fire-escape landing.*

TOM. After the fiasco at Rubicam's Business College, the idea of getting a gentleman caller for Laura began to play a more and more important part in Mother's calculations. It became an obsession. Like some archetype of the universal unconscious, the image of the gentleman caller haunted our small apartment . . .

An evening at home rarely passed without some allusion to this image, this specter, this hope . . . Even when he wasn't mentioned, his presence hung in Mother's preoccupied look and in my sister's frightened, apologetic manner—hung like a sentence passed upon the Wingfields!

Mother was a woman of action as well as words. She began to take logical steps in the planned direction. Late that winter and in the early spring—realizing that extra money would be needed to properly feather the nest and plume the bird—she conducted a vigorous campaign on the telephone, roping in subscribers to one of those magazines for matrons called *The Home-maker's Companion,* the type of journal that features the serialized sublimations of ladies of letters who think in terms of delicate cup-like breasts, slim, tapering waists, rich, creamy thighs, eyes like woodsmoke in autumn, fingers that soothe and caress like strains of music, bodies as powerful as Etruscan sculpture. (AMANDA *enters with phone on long extension cord. She is spotted in the dim stage.*)

AMANDA. Ida Scott? This is Amanda Wingfield! We *missed* you at the D.A.R. last Monday! I said to myself: She's probably suffering with that sinus condition! How is the sinus condition?

Horrors! Heaven have mercy!—You're a Christian martyr, yes, that's what you are, a Christian martyr!

Well, I just now happened to notice that your subscription to the *Companion*'s about to expire! Yes, it expires with the next issue, honey!—just when that wonderful new serial by Bessie Mae Hopper is getting off to such an exciting start. Oh, honey, it's something that you can't miss! You remember how *Gone with the Wind* took everybody by storm? You simply couldn't go out if you hadn't read it. All everybody *talked* was Scarlett O'Hara. Well, this is a book that critics already compare to *Gone with the Wind.* It's the *Gone with the Wind* of the post–World War generation—What?—Burning?—Oh, honey, don't let them burn, go take a look in the oven and I'll hold the wire! Heavens—I think she's hung up!

(*Before the stage is lighted, the violent voices of* TOM *and* AMANDA *are heard. They are quarreling behind the portieres. In front of them stands* LAURA *with clenched hands and panicky expression. A clear pool of light on her figure throughout this scene.*)

TOM. What in Christ's name am I—

AMANDA (*shrilly*). Don't you use that—

TOM. Supposed to do!

AMANDA. Expression! Not in my—

TOM. Ohhh!

AMANDA. Presence! Have you gone out of your senses?

TOM. I have, that's true, *driven* out!

AMANDA. What is the matter with you, you—big—big—IDIOT!

TOM. Look!—I've got *no thing,* no single thing—

AMANDA. Lower your voice!

TOM. In my life here that I can call my own! Everything is—

AMANDA. Stop that shouting!

TOM. Yesterday you confiscated my books! You have the nerve to—

AMANDA. I took that horrible novel back to the library—yes! That hideous book by that insane Mr. Lawrence.° (TOM *laughs wildly.*) I cannot control the output of diseased minds or people who cater to them—(TOM *laughs still more wildly.*) BUT I WON'T ALLOW SUCH FILTH BROUGHT INTO MY HOUSE! No, no, no, no, no!

TOM. House, house! Who pays rent on it, who makes a slave of himself to—

Mr. Lawrence: D. H. Lawrence, author of three stories printed in this anthology (pages 402, 418, 432), emphasized in his novels the force and importance of sexuality in human life.

AMANDA (*fairly screeching*). Don't you DARE to—

TOM. No, no, *I* mustn't say things. *I've* got to just—

AMANDA. Let me tell you—

TOM. I don't want to hear any more! (*He tears the portieres open. The upstage area is lit with a turgid smoky red glow. AMANDA's hair is in metal curlers and she wears a very old bathrobe, much too large for her slight figure, a relic of the faithless Mr. Wingfield. An upright typewriter and a wild disarray of manuscripts is on the drop-leaf table. The quarrel was probably precipitated by AMANDA's interruption of his creative labor. A chair lies overthrown on the floor. Their gesticulating shadows are cast on the ceiling by the fiery glow.*)

AMANDA. You *will* hear more, you—

TOM. No, I won't hear more, I'm going out!

AMANDA. You come right back in—

TOM. Out, out, out! Because I'm—

AMANDA. Come back here, Tom Wingfield! I'm not through talking to you!

TOM. Oh, go—

LAURA (*desperately*).—Tom!

AMANDA. You're going to listen, and no more insolence from you! I'm at the end of my patience!

TOM (*comes back toward her*). What do you think I'm at? Aren't I supposed to have any patience to reach the end of, Mother? I know, I know. It seems unimportant to you, what I'm *doing*—what I *want* to do—having a little *difference* between them! You don't think that—

AMANDA. I think you've been doing things that you're ashamed of. That's why you act like this. I don't believe that you go every night to the movies. Nobody goes to the movies night after night. Nobody in their right minds goes to the movies as often as you pretend to. People don't go to the movies at nearly midnight, and movies don't let out at two A.M. Come in stumbling. Muttering to yourself like a maniac! You get three hours' sleep and then go to work. Oh, I can picture the way you're doing down there. Moping, doping, because you're in no condition.

TOM (*wildly*). No, I'm in no condition!

AMANDA. What right have you got to jeopardize your job? Jeopardize the security of all of us? How do you think we'd manage if you were—

TOM. Listen! You think I'm crazy *about the warehouse?* (*He bends fiercely toward her slight figure.*) You think I'm in love with the Continental Shoemakers? You think I want to spend fifty-five *years* down there in that—*celotex interior!* with—*fluorescent—tubes!* Look! I'd rather somebody picked up a crowbar and battered out my brains—than go back mornings! I *go!* Every time you come in yelling that God damn *"Rise and Shine!" "Rise and Shine!"* I say to myself, "How *lucky dead* people are!" But I get up.

I *go!* For sixty-five dollars a month I give up all that I dream of doing and being *ever!* And you say self—*self's* all I ever think of. Why, listen, if self is what I thought of, Mother, I'd be where he is—GONE! (*Pointing to father's picture.*) As far as the system of transportation reaches! (*He starts past her. She grabs his arm.*) Don't grab at me, Mother!

AMANDA. Where are you going?

TOM. I'm going to the *movies!*

AMANDA. I don't believe that lie!

TOM (*crouching toward her, overtowering her tiny figure. She backs away, gasping*). I'm going to opium dens! Yes, opium dens, dens of vice and criminals' hang-outs, Mother. I've joined the Hogan gang, I'm a hired assassin, I carry a tommy-gun in a violin case! I run a string of cat-houses in the Valley! They call me Killer, Killer Wingfield, I'm leading a double-life, a simple, honest warehouse worker by day, by night a dynamic *czar* of the *underworld, Mother.* I go to gambling casinos, I spin away fortunes on the roulette table! I wear a patch over one eye and a false mustache, sometimes I put on green whiskers. On those occasions they call me—*El Diablo!* Oh, I could tell you things to make you sleepless! My enemies plan to dynamite this place. They're going to blow us all sky-high some night! I'll be glad, very happy, and so will you! You'll go up, up on a broomstick, over Blue Mountain with seventeen gentlemen callers! You ugly—babbling old—*witch* . . . (*He goes through a series of violent, clumsy movements, seizing his overcoat, lunging to the door, pulling it fiercely open. The women watch him, aghast. His arm catches in the sleeve of the coat as he struggles to pull it on. For a moment he is pinioned by the bulky garment. With an outraged groan he tears the coat off again, splitting the shoulder of it, and hurls it across the room. It strikes against the shelf of* LAURA's *glass collection, there is a tinkle of shattering glass.* LAURA *cries out as if wounded. Music: "The Glass Menagerie."*)

LAURA (*shrilly*). My glass!—menagerie . . . (*She covers her face and turns away. But* AMANDA *is still stunned and stupefied by the "ugly witch" so that she barely notices this occurrence. Now she recovers her speech.*)

AMANDA (*in an awful voice*). I won't speak to you—until you apologize!

(*She crosses through the portieres and draws them together behind her.* TOM *is left with* LAURA. LAURA *clings weakly to the mantel with her face averted.* TOM *stares at her stupidly for a moment. Then he crosses to shelf. Drops awkwardly on knees to collect the fallen glass, glancing at* LAURA *as if he would speak but couldn't. "The Glass Menagerie" steals in as the scene dims out.*)

SCENE 4

The interior of the apartment is dark. There is a faint light in the alley. A deep-voiced bell in a church is tolling the hour of five as the scene commences.

TOM *appears at the top of the alley. After each solemn boom of the bell in the tower, he shakes a little noise-maker or rattle as if to express the tiny spasm of man in contrast to the sustained power and dignity of the Almighty. This and the unsteadiness of his advance make it evident that he has been drinking. As he climbs the few steps to the fire-escape landing, light steals up inside.* LAURA *appears in night-dress, observing* TOM's *empty bed in the front room.* TOM *fishes in his pockets for his door-key, removing a motley assortment of articles in the search, including a perfect shower of movie-ticket stubs and an empty bottle. At last he finds the key, but just as he is about to insert it, it slips from his fingers. He strikes a match and crouches below the door.*

TOM (*bitterly*). One crack—and it falls through!

LAURA (*opens the door*). Tom! Tom, what are you doing?

TOM. Looking for a door-key.

LAURA. Where have you been all this time?

TOM. I have been to the movies.

LAURA. All this time at the movies?

TOM. There was a very long program. There was a Garbo picture and a Mickey Mouse and a travelogue and a newsreel and a preview of coming attractions. And there was an organ solo and a collection for the milk-fund—simultaneously—which ended up in a terrible fight between a fat lady and an usher!

LAURA (*innocently*). Did you have to stay through everything?

TOM. Of course! And, oh, I forgot! There was a big stage show! The head-liner on this stage show was Malvolio the Magician. He performed wonderful tricks, many of them, such as pouring water back and forth between pitchers. First it turned to wine and then it turned to beer and then it turned to whiskey. I know it was whiskey it finally turned into because he needed somebody to come up out of the audience to help him, and I came up—both shows! It was Kentucky Straight Bourbon. A very generous fellow, he gave souvenirs. (*He pulls from his back pocket a shimmering rainbow-colored scarf.*) He gave me this. This is his magic scarf. You can have it, Laura. You wave it over a canary cage and you get a bowl of goldfish. You wave it over the goldfish bowl and they fly away canaries . . . But the wonderfullest trick of all was the coffin trick. We nailed him into a coffin and he got out of the coffin without removing one nail. (*He has come inside.*) There is a trick that would come in handy for me—get me out of this 2 by 4 situation! (*Flops onto bed and starts removing shoes.*)

LAURA. Tom—Shhh!

TOM. What're you shushing me for?

LAURA. You'll wake up Mother.

TOM. Goody, goody! Pay 'er back for all those "Rise an' Shines." (*Lies down, groaning.*) You know it don't take much intelligence to get yourself into a nailed-up coffin, Laura. But who in hell ever got himself out of one without removing one nail? (*As if in answer, the father's grinning photograph lights up. Scene dims out. Immediately following the church bell is heard striking six. At the sixth stroke the alarm clock goes off in* AMANDA's *room, and after a few moments we hear her calling:* "Rise and Shine! Rise and Shine! Laura, go tell your brother to rise and shine!")

TOM (*sitting up slowly*). I'll rise—but I won't shine. (*The light increases.*)

AMANDA. Laura, tell your brother his coffee is ready.

LAURA (*slips into front room*). Tom!—It's nearly seven. Don't make Mother nervous. (*He stares at her stupidly. Beseechingly*) Tom, speak to Mother this morning. Make up with her, apologize, speak to her!

TOM. She won't to me. It's her that started not speaking.

LAURA. If you just say you're sorry she'll start speaking.

TOM. Her not speaking—is that such a tragedy?

LAURA. Please—please!

AMANDA (*calling from kitchenette*). Laura, are you going to do what I asked you to do, or do I have to get dressed and go out myself?

LAURA. Going, going—soon as I get on my coat! (*She pulls on a shapeless felt hat with nervous, jerky movement, pleadingly glancing at* TOM. *Rushes awkwardly for coat. The coat is one of* AMANDA's, *inaccurately made-over, the sleeves too short for* LAURA.) Butter and what else?

AMANDA (*entering upstage*). Just butter. Tell them to charge it.

LAURA. Mother, they make such faces when I do that.

AMANDA. Sticks and stones can break our bones, but the expression on Mr. Garfinkel's face won't harm us! Tell your brother his coffee is getting cold.

LAURA (*at door*). Do what I asked you, will you, will you, Tom? (*He looks sullenly away.*)

AMANDA. Laura, go now or just don't go at all!

LAURA (*rushing out*). Going—going! (*A second later she cries out.* TOM *springs up and crosses to door.* AMANDA *rushes anxiously in.* TOM *opens the door.*)

TOM. Laura?

LAURA. I'm all right. I slipped, but I'm all right.

AMANDA (*peering anxiously after her*). If anyone breaks a leg on those fire-escape steps, the landlord ought to be sued for every cent he possesses! (*She shuts door. Remembers she isn't speaking and returns to the other room.*)

(*As* TOM *enters listlessly for his coffee, she turns her back to him and stands rigidly facing the window on the gloomy gray vault of the areaway. Its light on her face with its aged but childish features is cruelly sharp, satirical as a Daumier print.*)

(*Music under:* "Ave Maria.")

(TOM *glances sheepishly but sullenly at her averted figure and slumps at the table. The coffee is scalding hot; he sips it and gasps and spits it back in the cup. At his gasp,* AMANDA *catches her breath and half turns. Then catches herself and turns back to window.* TOM *blows on his coffee, glancing sidewise at his mother. She clears her throat.* TOM *clears his. He starts to rise. Sinks back down again, scratches his head, clears his throat again.* AMANDA *coughs.* TOM *raises his cup in both hands to blow on it, his eyes staring over the rim of it at his mother for several moments. Then he slowly sets the cup down and awkwardly and hesitantly rises from the chair.*)

TOM (*hoarsely*). Mother. I—I apologize, Mother. (AMANDA *draws a quick, shuddering breath. Her face works grotesquely. She breaks into childlike tears.*) I'm sorry for what I said, for everything that I said, I didn't mean it.

AMANDA (*sobbingly*). My devotion has made me a witch and so I make myself hateful to my children!

TOM. *No,* you *don't.*

AMANDA. I worry so much, don't sleep, it makes me nervous!

TOM (*gently*). I understand that.

AMANDA. I've had to put up a solitary battle all these years. But you're my right-hand bower! Don't fall down, don't fail!

TOM (*gently*). I try, Mother.

AMANDA (*with great enthusiasm*). Try and you will succeed! (*The notion makes her breathless.*) Why, you—you're just *full* of natural endowments! Both of my children—they're *unusual* children! Don't you think I know it? I'm so—*proud!* Happy and—feel I've—so much to be thankful for but—Promise me one thing, son!

TOM. What, Mother?

AMANDA. Promise, son, you'll—never be a drunkard!

TOM (*turns to her grinning*). I will never be a drunkard, Mother.

AMANDA. That's what frightened me so, that you'd been drinking. Eat a bowl of Purina!

TOM. Just coffee, Mother.

AMANDA. Shredded wheat biscuit?

TOM. No. No, Mother, just coffee.

AMANDA. You can't put in a day's work on an empty stomach. You've got ten minutes—don't gulp! Drinking too-hot liquids makes cancer of the stomach . . . Put cream in.

TOM. No, thank you.

AMANDA. To cool it.

TOM. No! No, thank you, I want it black.

AMANDA. I know, but it's not good for you. We have to do all that we can to build ourselves up. In these trying times we live in, all that we have to cling to is—each other . . . That's why it's so important to—Tom, I—I sent out your sister so I could discuss something with you. If you hadn't spoken I would have spoken to you. (*Sits down.*)

TOM (*gently*). What is it, Mother, that you want to discuss?

AMANDA. *Laura!*

TOM (*puts his cup down slowly. Music: "The Glass Menagerie"*). Oh.—Laura . . .

AMANDA (*touching his sleeve*). You know how Laura is. So quiet but—still water runs deep! She notices things and I think she—broods about them. (TOM *looks up.*) A few days ago I came in and she was crying.

TOM. What about?

AMANDA. You.

TOM. Me?

AMANDA. She has an idea that you're not happy here.

TOM. What gave her that idea?

AMANDA. What gives her any idea? However, you do act strangely. I—I'm not criticizing, understand *that!* I know your ambitions do not lie in the warehouse, that like everybody in the whole wide world—you've had to—make sacrifices, but—Tom—Tom—life's not easy, it calls for—Spartan endurance! There's so many things in my heart that I cannot describe to you! I've never told you but I—*loved* your father . . .

TOM (*gently*). I know that, Mother.

AMANDA. And you—when I see you taking after his ways! Staying out late—and—well, you *had* been drinking the night you were in that—terrifying condition! Laura says that you hate the apartment and that you go out nights to get away from it! Is that true, Tom?

TOM. No. You say there's so much in your heart that you can't describe to me. That's true of me, too. There's so much in my heart that I can't describe to *you!* So let's respect each other's—

AMANDA. But, why—*why*, Tom—are you always so *restless?* Where do you go to, nights?

TOM. I—go to the movies.

AMANDA. Why do you go to the movies so much, Tom?

TOM. I go to the movies because—I like adventure. Adventure is something I don't have much of at work, so I go to the movies.

AMANDA. But, Tom, you go to the movies *entirely* too *much!*

TOM. I like a lot of adventure. (AMANDA *looks baffled, then hurt. As the familiar inquisition resumes he becomes hard and impatient again.* AMANDA *slips back to her querulous attitude toward him.*)

AMANDA. Most young men find adventure in their careers.

TOM. Then most young men are not employed in a warehouse.

AMANDA. The world is full of young men employed in warehouses and offices and factories.

TOM. Do all of them find adventure in their careers?

AMANDA. They do or they do without it! Not everybody has a craze for adventure.

TOM. Man is by instinct a lover, a hunter, a fighter, and none of those instincts are given much play at the warehouse!

AMANDA. Man is by instinct! Don't quote instincts to me! Instinct is something that people have got away from! It belongs to animals! Christian adults don't want it!

TOM. What do Christian adults want, then, Mother?

AMANDA. Superior things! Things of the mind and the spirit! Only animals have to satisfy instincts! Surely your aims are somewhat higher than theirs! Than monkeys—pigs—

TOM. I reckon they're not.

AMANDA. You're joking. However, that isn't what I wanted to discuss.

TOM (*rising*). I haven't much time.

AMANDA (*pushing his shoulders*). Sit down.

TOM. You want me to punch in red at the warehouse, Mother?

AMANDA. You have five minutes. I want to talk about Laura.

TOM. All right! What about Laura?

AMANDA. We have to be making some plans and provisions for her. She's older than you, two years, and nothing has happened. She just drifts along doing nothing. It frightens me terribly how she just drifts along.

TOM. I guess she's the type that people call home girls.

AMANDA. There's no such type, and if there is, it's a pity! That is unless the home is hers, with a husband!

TOM. What?

AMANDA. Oh, I can see the handwriting on the wall as plain as I see the nose in front of my face! It's terrifying! More and more you remind me of your father! He was out all hours without explanation!—Then *left!* *Goodbye!* And me with the bag to hold. I saw that letter you got from the Merchant Marine. I know what you're dreaming of. I'm not standing here blindfolded. (*She pauses.*) Very well, then. Then *do* it! But not till there's somebody to take your place.

TOM. What do you mean?

AMANDA. I mean that as soon as Laura has got somebody to take care of her, married, a home of her own, independent—why, then you'll be free to go wherever you please, on land, on sea, whichever way the wind blows you! But until that time you've got to look out for your sister. I don't say me because I'm old and don't matter! I say your sister because she's young and dependent.

I put her in business college—a dismal failure! Frightened her so it made her sick at the stomach. I took her over to the Young People's League at the church. Another fiasco. She spoke to nobody, nobody spoke to her. Now all she does is fool with those pieces of glass and play those worn-out records. What kind of a life is that for a girl to lead?

TOM. What can I do about it?

AMANDA. Overcome selfishness! Self, self, self is all that you ever think of! (TOM *springs up and crosses to get his coat. It is ugly and bulky. He pulls on a cap with earmuffs.*) Where is your muffler? Put your wool muffler on! (*He snatches it angrily from the closet and tosses it about his neck and pulls both ends tight.*) Tom! I haven't said what I had in mind to ask you.

TOM. I'm too late to—

AMANDA (*catching his arm—very importunately. Then shyly*). Down at the warehouse, aren't there some—nice young men?

TOM. No!

AMANDA. There *must* be—*some* . . .

TOM. Mother—(*Gesture.*)

AMANDA. Find out one that's clean-living—doesn't drink and—ask him out for sister!

TOM. What?

AMANDA. For *sister!* To *meet!* Get *acquainted!*

TOM (*stamping to door*). Oh, my *go-osh!*

AMANDA. Will you? (*He opens door. Imploringly*) Will you? (*He starts down.*) Will you? Will you, dear?

TOM (*calling back*). YES! (AMANDA *closes the door hesitantly and with a troubled but faintly hopeful expression.*)

AMANDA (*moves into spotlight at the phone*). Ella Cartwright? This is Amanda Wingfield!

How are you, honey?

How is that kidney condition? (*There is a five-second pause.*)

Horrors! (*There is another pause.*)

You're a Christian martyr, yes, honey, that's what you are, a Christian martyr! Well, I just now happened to notice in my little red book that your subscription to the *Companion* has just run out! I knew that you wouldn't want to miss out on the wonderful serial starting in this new issue. It's by Bessie Mae Hopper, the first thing she's written since *Honeymoon for Three.* Wasn't that a strange and interesting story? Well, this one is even lovelier, I believe. It has a sophisticated, society background. It's all about the horsey set on Long Island!

SCENE 5

It is early dusk of a spring evening. Supper has just been finished in the Wingfield apartment. AMANDA *and* LAURA *in light-colored dresses are removing dishes from the table, in the upstage area, which is shadowy, their movements formalized almost as a dance or ritual, their moving forms as pale and silent as moths.* TOM, *in white shirt and trousers, rises from the table and crosses toward the fire-escape.*

AMANDA (*as he passes her*). Son, will you do me a favor?

TOM. What?

AMANDA. Comb your hair! You look so pretty when your hair is combed! (TOM *slouches on sofa with evening paper. Enormous caption "Franco Triumphs."*) There is only one respect in which I would like you to emulate your father.

TOM. What respect is that?

AMANDA. The care he always took of his appearance. He never allowed himself to look untidy. (*He throws down the paper and crosses to fire-escape.*) Where are you going?

TOM. I'm going out to smoke.

AMANDA. You smoke too much. A pack a day at fifteen cents a pack. How much would that amount to in a month? Thirty times fifteen is how much, Tom? Figure it out and you will be astounded at what you could save. Enough to give you a night-school course in accounting at Washington U! Just think what a wonderful thing that would be for you, Son!

TOM. I'd rather smoke. (*He steps out on landing, letting the screen door slam.*)

AMANDA (*sharply*). I know! That's the tragedy of it . . . (*Alone, she turns to look at her husband's picture. Dance music: "All the World Is Waiting for the Sunrise!"*)

TOM (*to the audience*). Across the alley from us was the Paradise Dance Hall. On evenings in spring the windows and doors were open and the music came outdoors. Sometimes the lights were turned out except for a large glass sphere that hung from the ceiling. It would turn slowly about and filter the dusk with delicate rainbow colors. Then the orchestra played a waltz or a tango, something that had a slow and sensuous rhythm. Couples would come outside, to the relative privacy of the alley. You could see them kissing behind ash-pits and telephone poles. This was the compensation for lives that passed like mine, without any change or adventure. Adventure and change were imminent in this year. They were waiting around the corner for all these kids. Suspended in the mist over Berchtesgaden,° caught in the folds of Chamberlain's umbrella—.° In Spain there was Guernica! But here there was only hot swing music and liquor, dance halls, bars, and movies, and sex that hung in the

---

Berchtesgaden: Hitler's Bavarian summer retreat **Chamberlain's umbrella:** Neville Chamberlain, British prime minister (1937–1940), who always carried a furled umbrella, and whose name has become a symbol for appeasement, returned from a conference with Hitler in Munich in 1938 with a signed agreement that he proclaimed meant "Peace in our time." One year later, German troops invaded Poland, beginning World War II.

gloom like a chandelier and flooded the world with brief, deceptive rainbows . . . All the world was waiting for bombardments! (AMANDA *turns from the picture and comes outside.*)

AMANDA (*sighing*). A fire-escape landing's a poor excuse for a porch. (*She spreads a newspaper on a step and sits down, gracefully and demurely as if she were settling into a swing on a Mississippi veranda.*) What are you looking at?

TOM. The moon.

AMANDA. Is there a moon this evening?

TOM. It's rising over Garfinkel's Delicatessen.

AMANDA. So it is! A little silver slipper of a moon. Have you made a wish on it yet?

TOM. Um-hum.

AMANDA. What did you wish for?

TOM. That's a secret.

AMANDA. A secret, huh? Well, I won't tell mine either. I will be just as mysterious as you.

TOM. I bet I can guess what yours is.

AMANDA. Is my head so transparent?

TOM. You're not a sphinx.

AMANDA. No, I don't have secrets. I'll tell you what I wished for on the moon. Success and happiness for my precious children! I wish for that whenever there's a moon, and when there isn't a moon, I wish for it, too.

TOM. I thought perhaps you wished for a gentleman caller.

AMANDA. Why do you say that?

TOM. Don't you remember asking me to fetch one?

AMANDA. I remember suggesting that it would be nice for your sister if you brought home some nice young man from the warehouse. I think that I've made that suggestion more than once.

TOM. Yes, you have made it repeatedly.

AMANDA. Well?

TOM. We are going to have one.

AMANDA. *What?*

TOM. A gentleman caller! (*The annunciation is celebrated with music.* AMANDA *rises.*)

AMANDA. You mean you have asked some nice young man to come over?

TOM. Yep. I've asked him to dinner.

AMANDA. You really did?

TOM. I did!

AMANDA. You did, and did he—*accept?*

TOM. He did!

AMANDA. Well, well—well, well! That's—lovely!

TOM. I thought that you would be pleased.

AMANDA. It's definite, then?

TOM. Very definite.

AMANDA. Soon?

TOM. Very soon.

AMANDA. For heaven's sake, stop putting on and tell me some things, will you?

TOM. What things do you want me to tell you?

AMANDA. *Naturally* I would like to know when he's *coming!*

TOM. He's coming tomorrow.

AMANDA. *Tomorrow?*

TOM. Yep. Tomorrow.

AMANDA. But, Tom!

TOM. Yes, Mother?

AMANDA. Tomorrow gives me no time!

TOM. Time for what?

AMANDA. Preparations! Why didn't you phone me at once, as soon as you asked him, the minute that he accepted? Then, don't you see, I could have been getting ready!

TOM. You don't have to make any fuss.

AMANDA. Oh, Tom, Tom, Tom, of course I have to make a fuss! I want things nice, not sloppy! Not thrown together. I'll certainly have to do some fast thinking, won't I?

TOM. I don't see why you have to think at all.

AMANDA. You just don't know. We can't have a gentleman caller in a pig-sty! All my wedding silver has to be polished, the monogrammed table linen ought to be laundered! The windows have to be washed and fresh curtains put up. And how about clothes? We have to *wear* something, don't we?

TOM. Mother, this boy is no one to make a fuss over!

AMANDA. Do you realize he's the first young man we've introduced to your sister? It's terrible, dreadful, disgraceful that poor little sister has never received a single gentleman caller! Tom, come inside! (*She opens the screen door.*)

TOM. What for?

AMANDA. I want to ask you some things.

TOM. If you're going to make such a fuss, I'll call it off, I'll tell him not to come!

AMANDA. You certainly won't do anything of the kind. Nothing offends people worse than broken engagements. It simply means I'll have to work like a Turk! We won't be brilliant, but we'll pass inspection. Come on inside. (TOM *follows, groaning.*) Sit down.

TOM. Any particular place you would like me to sit?

AMANDA. Thank heavens I've got the new sofa! I'm also making payments on a floor lamp I'll have sent out! And put the chintz covers on, they'll

brighten things up! Of course I'd hoped to have these walls repapered
. . . What is the young man's name?

TOM. His name is O'Connor.

AMANDA. That, of course, means fish—tomorrow is Friday! I'll have that
salmon loaf—with Durkee's dressing! What does he do? He works at
the warehouse?

TOM. Of course! How else would I—

AMANDA. Tom, he—doesn't drink?

TOM. Why do you ask me that?

AMANDA. Your father *did!*

TOM. Don't get started on that!

AMANDA. He *does* drink, then?

TOM. Not that I know of!

AMANDA. Make sure, be certain! The last thing I want for my daughter's a
boy who drinks!

TOM. Aren't you being a little bit premature? Mr. O'Connor has not yet
appeared on the scene!

AMANDA. But will tomorrow. To meet your sister, and what do I know
about his character? Nothing! Old maids are better off than wives of
drunkards!

TOM. Oh, my God!

AMANDA. Be still!

TOM (*leaning forward to whisper*). Lots of fellows meet girls whom they don't
marry!

AMANDA. Oh, talk sensibly, Tom—and don't be sarcastic! (*She has gotten a
hairbrush.*)

TOM. What are you doing?

AMANDA. I'm brushing that cow-lick down! What is this young man's
position at the warehouse?

TOM (*submitting grimly to the brush and the interrogation*). This young man's
position is that of a shipping clerk, Mother.

AMANDA. Sounds to me like a fairly responsible job, the sort of a job *you*
would be in if you just had more *get-up.* What is his salary? Have you
any idea?

TOM. I would judge it to be approximately eighty-five dollars a month.

AMANDA. Well—not princely, but—

TOM. Twenty more than I make.

AMANDA. Yes, how well I know! But for a family man, eighty-five dollars a
month is not much more than you can just get by on . . .

TOM. Yes, but Mr. O'Connor is not a family man.

AMANDA. He might be, mightn't he? Some time in the future?

TOM. I see. Plans and provisions.

AMANDA. You are the only young man that I know of who ignores the fact that the future becomes the present, the present the past, and the past turns into everlasting regret if you don't plan for it!

TOM. I will think that over and see what I can make of it.

AMANDA. Don't be supercilious with your mother! Tell me some more about this—what do you call him?

TOM. James D. O'Connor. The D. is for Delaney.

AMANDA. Irish on *both* sides! *Gracious!* And doesn't drink?

TOM. Shall I call him up and ask him right this minute?

AMANDA. The only way to find out about these things is to make discreet inquiries at the proper moment. When I was a girl in Blue Mountain and it was suspected that a young man drank, the girl whose attentions he had been receiving, if any girl *was*, would sometimes speak to the minister of his church, or rather her father would if her father was living, and sort of feel him out on the young man's character. That is the way such things are discreetly handled to keep a young woman from making a tragic mistake!

TOM. Then how did you happen to make a tragic mistake?

AMANDA. That innocent look of your father's had everyone fooled! He *smiled*—the world was *enchanted!* No girl can do worse than put herself at the mercy of a handsome appearance! I hope that Mr. O'Connor is not too good-looking.

TOM. No, he's not too good-looking. He's covered with freckles and hasn't too much of a nose.

AMANDA. He's not right-down homely, though?

TOM. Not right-down homely. Just medium homely, I'd say.

AMANDA. Character's what to look for in a man.

TOM. That's what I've always said, Mother.

AMANDA. You've never said anything of the kind and I suspect you would never give it a thought.

TOM. Don't be so suspicious of me.

AMANDA. At least I hope he's the type that's up and coming.

TOM. I think he really goes in for self-improvement.

AMANDA. What reason have you to think so?

TOM. He goes to night school.

AMANDA (*beaming*). Splendid! What does he do, I mean study?

TOM. Radio engineering and public speaking!

AMANDA. Then he has visions of being advanced in the world! Any young man who studies public speaking is aiming to have an executive job some day! And radio engineering? A thing for the future! Both of these facts are very illuminating. Those are the sort of things that a mother should know concerning any young man who comes to call on her daughter. Seriously or—not.

TOM. One little warning. He doesn't know about Laura. I didn't let on that we had dark ulterior motives. I just said, why don't you come and have dinner with us? He said okay and that was the whole conversation.

AMANDA. I bet it was! You're eloquent as an oyster. However, he'll know about Laura when he gets here. When he sees how lovely and sweet and pretty she is, he'll thank his lucky stars he was asked to dinner.

TOM. Mother, you mustn't expect too much of Laura.

AMANDA. What do you mean?

TOM. Laura seems all those things to you and me because she's ours and we love her. We don't even notice she's crippled any more.

AMANDA. Don't say crippled! You know that I never allow that word to be used!

TOM. But face facts, Mother. She is and—that's not all—

AMANDA. What do you mean "not all"?

TOM. Laura is very different from other girls.

AMANDA. I think the difference is all to her advantage.

TOM. Not quite all—in the eyes of others—strangers—she's terribly shy and lives in a world of her own and those things make her seem a little peculiar to people outside the house.

AMANDA. Don't say peculiar.

TOM. Face the facts. She is. (*The dance-hall music changes to a tango that has a minor and somewhat ominous tone.*)

AMANDA. In what way is she peculiar—may I ask?

TOM (*gently*). She lives in a world of her own—a world of—little glass ornaments, Mother . . . (*Gets up.* AMANDA *remains holding the brush, looking at him, troubled.*) She plays old phonograph records and—that's about all—(*He glances at himself in the mirror and crosses to door.*)

AMANDA (*sharply*). Where are you going?

TOM. I'm going to the movies. (*Out screen door.*)

AMANDA. Not to the movies, every night to the movies! (*Follows quickly to screen door.*) I don't believe you always go to the movies! (*He is gone.* AMANDA *looks worriedly after him for a moment. Then vitality and optimism return and she turns from the door, crossing to portieres.*) Laura! Laura!

LAURA (*answers from kitchenette*). Yes, Mother.

AMANDA. Let those dishes go and come in front! (LAURA *appears with dish towel.* AMANDA *speaks to her gaily.*) Laura, come here and make a wish on the moon!

LAURA (*entering*). Moon—moon?

AMANDA. A little silver slipper of a moon. Look over your left shoulder, Laura, and make a wish! (LAURA *looks faintly puzzled as if called out of sleep.* AMANDA *seizes her shoulders and turns her at an angle by the door.*)

LAURA. What shall I wish for, Mother?

AMANDA (*her voice trembling and her eyes suddenly filled with tears*). Happiness!
Good fortune! (*The sound of the violin rises and the stage dims out.*)

SCENE 6

TOM. And so the following evening I brought Jim home to dinner. I
had known Jim slightly in high school. In high school Jim was a hero.
He had tremendous Irish good nature and vitality with the scrubbed and
polished look of white chinaware. He seemed to move in a continual spotlight. He was a star in basketball, captain of the debating club, president of
the senior class and the glee club and he sang the male lead in the annual
light operas. He was always running or bounding, never just walking. He
seemed always at the point of defeating the law of gravity. He was shooting
with such velocity through his adolescence that you would logically expect
him to arrive at nothing short of the White House by the time he was
thirty. But Jim apparently ran into more interference after his graduation
from Soldan. His speed had definitely slowed. Six years after he left high
school he was holding a job that wasn't much better than mine.

He was the only one at the warehouse with whom I was on friendly
terms. I was valuable to him as someone who could remember his former
glory, who had seen him win basketball games and the silver cup in debating. He knew of my secret practice of retiring to a cabinet of the washroom
to work on poems when business was slack in the warehouse. He called me
Shakespeare. And while the other boys in the warehouse regarded me with
suspicious hostility, Jim took a humorous attitude toward me. Gradually
his attitude affected the others, their hostility wore off and they also began
to smile at me as people smile at an oddly fashioned dog who trots across
their paths at some distance.

I knew that Jim and Laura had known each other at Soldan, and I had
heard Laura speak admiringly of his voice. I didn't know if Jim remembered her or not. In high school Laura had been as unobtrusive as Jim had
been astonishing. If he did remember Laura, it was not as my sister, for
when I asked him to dinner, he grinned and said, "You know, Shakespeare,
I never thought of you as having folks!"

He was about to discover that I did . . .

(*The light dims out on* TOM *and comes up in the Wingfield living room—a
delicate lemony light. It is about five on a Friday evening of late spring which comes
"scattering poems in the sky."*)

(AMANDA *has worked like a Turk in preparation for the gentleman caller.
The results are astonishing. The new floor lamp with its rose-silk shade is in place,
a colored paper lantern conceals the broken light fixture in the ceiling, new billow-
ing white curtains are at the windows, chintz covers are on chairs and sofa, a pair*

of new sofa pillows make their initial appearance. Open boxes and tissue paper are scattered on the floor.)

(LAURA *stands in the middle with lifted arms while* AMANDA *crouches before her, adjusting the hem of a new dress, devout and ritualistic. The dress is colored and designed by memory. The arrangement of* LAURA'*s hair is changed; it is softer and more becoming. A fragile, unearthly prettiness has come out in* LAURA: *she is like a piece of translucent glass touched by light, given a momentary radiance, not actual, not lasting.*)

AMANDA (*impatiently*). Why are you trembling?

LAURA. Mother, you've made me nervous!

AMANDA. How have I made you nervous?

LAURA. By all this fuss! You make it seem so important!

AMANDA. I don't understand you, Laura. You couldn't be satisfied with just sitting home, and yet whenever I try to arrange something for you, you seem to resist it. (*She gets up.*) Now take a look at yourself. No, wait! Wait just a moment—I have an idea!

LAURA. What is it now? (AMANDA *produces two powder puffs which she wraps in handkerchiefs and stuffs in* LAURA'*s bosom.*)

LAURA. Mother, what are you doing?

AMANDA. They call them "Gay Deceivers"!

LAURA. I won't wear them.

AMANDA. You will!

LAURA. Why should I?

AMANDA. Because, to be painfully honest, your chest is flat.

LAURA. You make it seem like we were setting a trap.

AMANDA. All pretty girls are a trap, a pretty trap, and men expect them to be. Now look at yourself, young lady. This is the prettiest you will ever be! (*She stands back to admire* LAURA.) I've got to fix myself now! You're going to be surprised by your mother's appearance! (*She crosses through portieres, humming gaily.* LAURA *moves slowly to the long mirror and stares solemnly at herself. A wind blows the white curtain inward in a slow, graceful motion and with a faint, sorrowful sighing.* AMANDA *speaks from somewhere behind the portieres.*) It isn't dark enough yet. (LAURA *turns slowly before the mirror with a troubled look.*)

AMANDA (*laughing, still not visible*). I'm going to show you something. I'm going to make a spectacular appearance!

LAURA. What is it, Mother?

AMANDA. Possess your soul in patience—you will see! Something I've resurrected from that old trunk! Styles haven't changed so terribly much after all . . . (*She parts the portieres.*) Now just look at your mother! (*She wears a girlish frock of yellow voile with a blue silk sash. She carries a bunch of*

jonquils—the legend of her youth is nearly revived. Now she speaks feverishly.)
This is the dress in which I led the cotillion. Won the cakewalk twice
at Sunset Hill, wore one spring to the Governor's ball in Jackson! See
how I sashayed around the ballroom, Laura? (*She raises her skirt and does
a mincing step around the room.*) I wore it on Sundays for my gentlemen
callers! I had it on the day I met your father—I had malaria fever all
that spring. The change of climate from East Tennessee to the Delta—
weakened resistance—I had a little temperature all the time—not
enough to be serious—just enough to make me restless and giddy!—
Invitations poured in—parties all over the Delta!—"Stay in bed," said
Mother, "you have fever!"—but I just wouldn't.—I took quinine but
kept on going, going!—Evenings, dances!—Afternoons, long, long
rides! Picnics—lovely!—So lovely, that country in May.—All lacy with
dogwood, literally flooded with jonquils!—That was the spring I had
the craze for jonquils. Jonquils became an absolute obsession. Mother
said, "Honey, there's no more room for jonquils." And still I kept on
bringing in more jonquils. Whenever, wherever I saw them, I'd say,
"Stop! Stop! I see jonquils!" I made the young men help me gather the
jonquils! It was a joke, Amanda and her jonquils! Finally there were no
more vases to hold them, every available space was filled with jonquils.
No vases to hold them? All right, I'll hold them myself! And then
I—(*She stops in front of the picture. Music.*) met your father! Malaria and
jonquils and then—this—boy . . . (*She switches on the rose-colored lamp.*)
I hope they get here before it starts to rain. (*She crosses upstage and places
the jonquils in bowl on table.*) I gave your brother a little extra change so
he and Mr. O'Connor could take the service car home.

LAURA (*with altered look*). What did you say his name was?

AMANDA. O'Connor.

LAURA. What is his first name?

AMANDA. I don't remember. Oh, yes, I do. It was—Jim! (LAURA *sways
slightly and catches hold of a chair.*)

LAURA (*faintly*). Not—Jim!

AMANDA. Yes, that was it, it was Jim! I've never known a Jim that wasn't
nice! (*The music becomes ominous.*)

LAURA. Are you sure his name is Jim O'Connor?

AMANDA. Yes. Why?

LAURA. Is he the one that Tom used to know in high school?

AMANDA. He didn't say so. I think he just got to know him at the warehouse.

LAURA. There was a Jim O'Connor we both knew in high school—(*Then,
with effort*) If that is the one that Tom is bringing to dinner—you'll have
to excuse me, I won't come to the table.

AMANDA. What sort of nonsense is this?

LAURA. You asked me once if I'd ever liked a boy. Don't you remember I showed you this boy's picture?

AMANDA. You mean the boy you showed me in the year-book?

LAURA. Yes, that boy.

AMANDA. Laura, Laura, were you in love with that boy?

LAURA. I don't know, Mother. All I know is I couldn't sit at the table if it was him!

AMANDA. It won't be him! It isn't the least bit likely. But whether it is or not, you will come to the table. You will not be excused.

LAURA. I'll have to be, Mother.

AMANDA. I don't intend to humor your silliness, Laura. I've had too much from you and your brother, both! So just sit down and compose yourself till they come. Tom has forgotten his key so you'll have to let them in, when they arrive.

LAURA (*panicky*). Oh, Mother—*you* answer the door!

AMANDA (*lightly*). I'll be in the kitchen—busy!

LAURA. Oh, Mother, please answer the door, don't make me do it!

AMANDA (*crossing into kitchenette*). I've got to fix the dressing for the salmon. Fuss, fuss—silliness!—over a gentleman caller! (*Door swings shut.* LAURA *is left alone. She utters a low moan and turns off the lamp—sits stiffly on the edge of the sofa, knotting her fingers together.* TOM *and* JIM *appear on the fire-escape steps and climb to landing. Hearing their approach,* LAURA *rises with a panicky gesture. She retreats to the portieres. The doorbell rings.* LAURA *catches her breath and touches her throat. Low drums sound.* AMANDA *calls.*) Laura, sweetheart! The door! (LAURA *stares at it without moving.*)

JIM. I think we just beat the rain.

TOM. Uh-huh. (*He rings again, nervously.* JIM *whistles and fishes for a cigarette.*)

AMANDA (*very, very gaily*). Laura, that is your brother and Mr. O'Connor! Will you let them in, darling? (LAURA *crosses toward kitchenette door.*)

LAURA (*breathlessly*). Mother—you go to the door! (AMANDA *steps out of the kitchenette and stares furiously at* LAURA. *She points imperiously at the door.*) Please, please!

AMANDA (*in a fierce whisper*). What is the matter with you, you silly thing?

LAURA (*desperately*). Please, you answer it, *please!*

AMANDA. I told you I wasn't going to humor you, Laura. Why have you chosen this moment to lose your mind?

LAURA. Please, please, please, you go!

AMANDA. You'll have to go to the door because I can't!

LAURA (*despairingly*). I can't either!

AMANDA. *Why?*

LAURA. I'm *sick!*

AMANDA. I'm sick too—of your nonsense! Why can't you and your brother be normal people? Fantastic whims and behavior. (TOM *gives a long ring.*) Preposterous goings on! Can you give me one reason—(*She calls out lyrically.*) *Coming! Just one second!*—why you should be afraid to open a door? Now you answer it, Laura!

LAURA. Oh, oh, oh . . . (*She returns through the portieres, darts to the victrola, winds it frantically and turns it on.*)

AMANDA. Laura Wingfield, you march right to that door!

LAURA. Yes—yes, Mother! (*A faraway, scratchy rendition of "Dardanella" softens the air and gives her strength to move through it. She slips to the door and draws it cautiously open. TOM enters with the caller, JIM O'CONNOR.*)

TOM. Laura, this is Jim. Jim, this is my sister, Laura.

JIM (*stepping inside*). I didn't know that Shakespeare had a sister!

LAURA (*retreating stiff and trembling from the door*). How—how do you do?

JIM (*heartily extending his hand*). Okay! (LAURA *touches it hesitantly with hers.*) Your hand's *cold*, Laura!

LAURA. Yes, well—I've been playing the victrola . . .

JIM. Must have been playing classical music on it! You ought to play a little hot swing music to warm you up!

LAURA. Excuse me—I haven't finished playing the victrola . . . (*She turns awkwardly and hurries into the front room. She pauses a second by the victrola. Then she catches her breath and darts through the portieres like a frightened deer.*)

JIM (*grinning*). What was the matter?

TOM. Oh—with Laura? Laura is—terribly shy.

JIM. Shy, huh? It's unusual to meet a shy girl nowadays. I don't believe you ever mentioned you had a sister.

TOM. Well, now you know. I have one. Here is the *Post Dispatch.* You want a piece of it?

JIM. Uh-huh.

TOM. What piece? The comics?

JIM. Sports! (*Glances at it.*) Ole Dizzy Dean is on his bad behavior.

TOM (*uninterested*). Yeah? (*Lights a cigarette and crosses back to fire-escape door.*)

JIM. Where are *you* going?

TOM. I'm going out on the terrace.

JIM (*goes after him*). You know, Shakespeare—I'm going to sell you a bill of goods!

TOM. What goods?

JIM. A course I'm taking.

TOM. Huh.

JIM. In public speaking! You and me, we're not the warehouse type.

TOM. Thanks—that's good news. But what has public speaking got to do with it?

JIM. It fits you for—executive positions!

TOM. Awww.

JIM. I tell you it's done a helluva lot for me.

TOM. In what respect?

JIM. In every! Ask yourself what is the difference between you an' me and men in the office down front? Brains?—No!—Ability?—No! Then what? Just one little thing—

TOM. What is that one little thing?

JIM. Primarily it amounts to—social poise! Being able to square up to people and hold your own on any social level!

AMANDA (*from the kitchenette*). Tom?

TOM. Yes, Mother?

AMANDA. Is that you and Mr. O'Connor?

TOM. Yes, Mother.

AMANDA. Well, you just make yourselves comfortable in there.

TOM. Yes, Mother.

AMANDA. Ask Mr. O'Connor if he would like to wash his hands.

JIM. Aw, no—no—thank you—I took care of that at the warehouse. Tom—

TOM. Yes?

JIM. Mr. Mendoza was speaking to me about you.

TOM. Favorably?

JIM. What do you think?

TOM. Well—

JIM. You're going to be out of a job if you don't wake up.

TOM. I am waking up—

JIM. You show no signs.

TOM. The signs are interior. I'm planning to change. (*He leans over the rail speaking with quiet exhilaration. The incandescent marquees and signs of the first-run movie houses light his face from across the alley. He looks like a voyager.*) I'm right at the point of committing myself to a future that doesn't include the warehouse and Mr. Mendoza or even a night-school course in public speaking.

JIM. What are you gassing about?

TOM. I'm tired of the movies.

JIM. Movies!

TOM. Yes, movies! Look at them—(*a wave toward the marvels of Grand Avenue*) all of those glamorous people—having adventures—hogging it all, gobbling the whole thing up! You know what happens? People go to the *movies* instead of *moving!* Hollywood characters are supposed to have all the adventures for everybody in America, while everybody in America sits in a dark room and watches them have them! Yes, until there's a war. That's when adventure becomes available to the masses! *Everyone's* dish, not only Gable's! Then the people in the dark room come out of the dark room to have some adventures themselves—Goody, goody!—It's our turn now, to go to the South Sea Island—to make a safari—to be exotic, far-off!—But I'm not patient. I don't want to wait till then. I'm tired of the *movies* and I am *about* to *move!*

JIM (*incredulously*). Move?

TOM. Yes.

JIM. When?

TOM. Soon!

JIM. Where? Where? (*The music seems to answer the question, while* TOM *thinks it over. He searches in his pockets.*)

TOM. I'm starting to boil inside. I know I seem dreamy, but inside—well, I'm boiling!—Whenever I pick up a shoe, I shudder a little thinking how short life is and what I am doing!—Whatever that means, I know it doesn't mean shoes—except as something to wear on a traveler's feet! (*Finds paper.*) Look—

JIM. What?

TOM. I'm a member.

JIM (*reading*). The Union of Merchant Seamen.

TOM. I paid my dues this month, instead of the light bill.

JIM. You will regret it when they turn the lights off.

TOM. I won't be here.

JIM. How about your mother?

TOM. I'm like my father. The bastard son of a bastard! See how he grins? And he's been absent going on sixteen years!

JIM. You're just talking, you drip. How does your mother feel about it?

TOM. Shh!—Here comes Mother! Mother is not acquainted with my plans!

AMANDA (*coming through the portieres*). Where are you all?

TOM. On the terrace, Mother. (*They start inside. She advances to them.* TOM *is distinctly shocked at her appearance. Even* JIM *blinks a little. He is making his first contact with girlish Southern vivacity and in spite of the night-school course in public speaking is somewhat thrown off the beam by the unexpected outlay of social charm. Certain responses are attempted by* JIM *but are swept aside by* AMANDA's *gay laughter and chatter.* TOM *is embarrassed but after the first shock* JIM *reacts very warmly. He grins and chuckles, is altogether won over.*)

AMANDA (*coyly smiling, shaking her girlish ringlets*). Well, well, well, so this is Mr. O'Connor. Introductions entirely unnecessary. I've heard so much about you from my boy. I finally said to him, Tom—good gracious!—why don't you bring this paragon to supper? I'd like to meet this nice young man at the warehouse!—Instead of just hearing him sing your praises so much! I don't know why my son is so stand-offish—that's not

Southern behavior! Let's sit down and—I think we could stand a little more air in here! Tom, leave the door open. I felt a nice fresh breeze a moment ago. Where has it gone? Mmm, so warm already! And not quite summer, even. We're going to burn up when summer really gets started. However, we're having—we're having a very light supper. I think light things are better fo' this time of year. The same as light clothes are. Light clothes an' light food are what warm weather calls fo'. You know our blood gets so thick during th' winter—it takes a while fo' us to *adjust* ou'selves!—when the season changes . . . It's come so quick this year. I wasn't prepared. All of a sudden—heavens! Already summer!—I ran to the trunk an' pulled out this light dress—Terribly old! Historical almost! But feels so good—so good an' co-ol, y' know . . .

TOM. Mother—

AMANDA. Yes, honey?

TOM. How about—supper?

AMANDA. Honey, you go ask Sister if supper is ready! You know that Sister is in full charge of supper! Tell her you hungry boys are waiting for it. (*To* JIM) Have you met Laura?

JIM. She—

AMANDA. Let you in? Oh, good, you've met already! It's rare for a girl as sweet an' pretty as Laura to be domestic! But Laura is, thank heavens, not only pretty but very domestic. I'm not at all. I never was a bit. I never could make a thing but angel-food cake. Well, in the south we had so many servants. Gone, gone, gone. All vestige of gracious living! Gone completely! I wasn't prepared for what the future brought me. All of my gentlemen callers were sons of planters and so of course I assumed that I would be married to one and raise my family on a large piece of land with plenty of servants. But man proposes—and woman accepts the proposal!—to vary that old, old saying° a little bit—I married no planter! I married a man who worked for the telephone company!— That gallantly smiling gentleman over there! (*Points to the picture.*) A telephone man who—fell in love with long-distance!—Now he travels and I don't even know where!—But what am I going on for about my— tribulations? Tell me yours—I hope you don't have any! Tom?

TOM (*returning*). Yes, Mother.

AMANDA. Is supper nearly ready?

TOM. It looks to me like supper is on the table.

AMANDA. Let me look—(*She rises prettily and looks through portieres.*) Oh, lovely!—But where is Sister?

---

old . . . **saying:** "Man proposes, but God disposes" (Thomas à Kempis [1380–1471], *Imitation of Christ*)

TOM. Laura is not feeling well and she says that she thinks she'd better not come to the table.

AMANDA. What?—Nonsense!—Laura? Oh, Laura!

LAURA (*off stage, faintly*). Yes, Mother.

AMANDA. You really must come to the table. We won't be seated until you come to the table! Come in, Mr. O'Connor. You sit over there, and I'll— Laura? Laura Wingfield! You're keeping us waiting, honey! We can't say grace until you come to the table! (*The kitchenette door is pushed weakly open and* LAURA *comes in. She is obviously quite faint, her lips trembling, her eyes wide and staring. She moves unsteadily toward the table. Outside a summer storm is coming abruptly. The white curtains billow inward at the windows and there is a sorrowful murmur and deep blue dusk.* LAURA *suddenly stumbles—she catches at a chair with a faint moan.*)

TOM. Laura!

AMANDA. Laura! (*There is a clap of thunder. Despairingly*) Why, Laura, you *are* sick, darling! Tom, help your sister into the living room, dear! Sit in the living room, Laura—rest on the sofa. Well! (*To* JIM *as* TOM *helps his sister to the sofa in the living room*) Standing over the hot stove made her ill!—I told her that it was just too warm this evening, but—(TOM *comes back to the table.*) Is Laura all right now?

TOM. Yes.

AMANDA. What *is* that? Rain? A nice cool rain has come up! (*She gives the gentleman caller a frightened look.*) I think we may—have grace—now . . . (TOM *looks at her stupidly.*) Tom, honey—you say grace!

TOM. Oh . . . . "For these and all thy mercies—" (*They bow their heads,* AMANDA *stealing a nervous glance at* JIM. *In the living room,* LAURA, *stretched on the sofa, clenches her hand to her lips, to hold back a shuddering sob.*) God's Holy Name be praised—(*The scene dims out.*)

SCENE 7

 Half an hour later. Dinner is just being finished in the dining room. LAURA *is still huddled upon the sofa, her feet drawn under her, her head resting on a pale blue pillow, her eyes wide and mysteriously watchful. The new floor lamp with its shade of rose-colored silk gives a soft, becoming light to her face, bringing out the fragile, unearthly prettiness which usually escapes attention. There is a steady murmur of rain, but it is slackening and soon stops; the air outside becomes pale and luminous as the moon breaks out. A moment after the curtain rises, the lights in both rooms flicker and go out.*

JIM. Hey, there, Mr. Light Bulb!

AMANDA (*laughs nervously*). Where was Moses when the lights went out? Ha-ha. Do you know the answer to that one, Mr. O'Connor?

JIM. No, Ma'am, what's the answer?

AMANDA. In the dark! (JIM *laughs appreciatively.*) Everybody sit still. I'll light the candles. Isn't it lucky we have them on the table? Where's a match? Which of you gentlemen can provide a match?

JIM. Here.

AMANDA. Thank you, sir.

JIM. Not at all, Ma'am!

AMANDA. I guess the fuse has burnt out. Mr. O'Connor, can you tell a burnt-out fuse? I know I can't and Tom is a total loss when it comes to mechanics. (*They rise from the table and go into the kitchenette, from where their voices are heard.*) Oh, be careful you don't bump into something. We don't want our gentleman caller to break his neck. Now wouldn't that be a fine howdy-do?

JIM. Ha-ha! Where is the fuse box?

AMANDA. Right here next to the stove. Can you see anything?

JIM. Just a minute.

AMANDA. Isn't electricity a mysterious thing? Wasn't it Benjamin Franklin who tied a key to a kite? We live in such a mysterious universe, don't we? Some people say that science clears up all the mysteries for us. In my opinion it only creates more! Have you found it yet?

JIM. No, Ma'am. All these fuses look okay to me.

AMANDA. Tom!

TOM. Yes, Mother?

AMANDA. That light bill I gave you several days ago. The one I told you we got the notices about?

TOM. Oh—Yeah.

AMANDA. You didn't neglect to pay it by chance?

TOM. Why, I—

AMANDA. Didn't! I might have known it!

JIM. Shakespeare probably wrote a poem on that light bill, Mrs. Wingfield.

AMANDA. I might have known better than to trust him with it! There's such a high price for negligence in this world!

JIM. Maybe the poem will win a ten-dollar prize.

AMANDA. We'll just have to spend the remainder of the evening in the nineteenth century, before Mr. Edison made the Mazda lamp!

JIM. Candlelight is my favorite kind of light.

AMANDA. That shows you're romantic! But that's no excuse for Tom. Well, we got through dinner. Very considerate of them to let us get through dinner before they plunged us into everlasting darkness, wasn't it, Mr. O'Connor?

JIM. Ha-ha!

AMANDA. Tom, as a penalty for your carelessness you can help me with the dishes.

JIM. Let me give you a hand.

AMANDA. Indeed you will not!

JIM. I ought to be good for something.

AMANDA. Good for something? (*Her tone is rhapsodic.*) You? Why, Mr. O'Connor nobody, *nobody's* given me this much entertainment in years—as you have!

JIM. Aw, now, Mrs. Wingfield!

AMANDA. I'm not exaggerating, not one bit! But Sister is all by her lonesome. You go keep her company in the parlor! I'll give you this lovely old candelabrum that used to be on the altar at the church of the Heavenly Rest. It was melted a little out of shape when the church burnt down. Lightning struck it one spring. Gypsy Jones was holding a revival at the time and he intimated that the church was destroyed because the Episcopalians gave card parties.

JIM. Ha-ha.

AMANDA. And how about you coaxing Sister to drink a little wine? I think it would be good for her! Can you carry both at once?

JIM. Sure. I'm Superman!

AMANDA. Now, Thomas, get into this apron! (JIM *comes into the dining room, carrying the candelabrum, its candles lighted, in one hand and a glass of wine in the other. The door of the kitchenette swings closed on* AMANDA'S *gay laughter; the flickering light approaches the portieres.* LAURA *sits up nervously as he enters. Her speech at first is low and breathless from the almost intolerable strain of being alone with a stranger. At first, before* JIM'S *warmth overcomes her paralyzing shyness,* LAURA'S *voice is thin and breathless, as though she had just run up a steep flight of stairs.* JIM'S *attitude is gently humorous. While the incident is apparently unimportant, it is to* LAURA *the climax of her secret life.*)

JIM. Hello, there, Laura.

LAURA (*faintly*). Hello. (*She clears her throat.*)

JIM. How are you feeling now? Better?

LAURA. Yes. Yes, thank you.

JIM. This is for you. A little dandelion wine. (*He extends it toward her with extravagant gallantry.*)

LAURA. Thank you.

JIM. Drink it—but don't get drunk! (*He laughs heartily.* LAURA *takes the glass uncertainly, laughs shyly.*) Where shall I set the candles?

LAURA. Oh—oh, anywhere . . .

JIM. How about here on the floor? Any objections?

LAURA. No.

JIM. I'll spread a newspaper to catch the drippings. I like to sit on the floor. Mind if I do?

LAURA. Oh, no.

JIM. Give me a pillow?

LAURA. What?

JIM. A pillow!

LAURA. Oh . . . (*Hands him one quickly.*)

JIM. How about you? Don't you like to sit on the floor?

LAURA. Oh—yes.

JIM. Why don't you, then?

LAURA. I—will.

JIM. Take a pillow! (LAURA *does. Sits on the other side of the candelabrum.* JIM *crosses his legs and smiles engagingly at her.*) I can't hardly see you sitting way over there.

LAURA. I can—see you.

JIM. I know, but that's not fair. I'm in the limelight. (LAURA *moves her pillow closer.*) Good! Now I can see you! Comfortable?

LAURA. Yes.

JIM. So am I. Comfortable as a cow! Will you have some gum?

LAURA. No, thank you.

JIM. I think I will indulge, with your permission. (*He musingly unwraps it and holds it up.*) Think of the fortune made by the guy that invented the first piece of chewing gum. Amazing, huh? The Wrigley Building is one of the sights of Chicago.—I saw it summer before last when I went up to the Century of Progress.° Did you take in the Century of Progress?

LAURA. No, I didn't.

JIM. Well, it was quite a wonderful exposition. What impressed me most was the Hall of Science. Gives you an idea of what the future will be in America, even more wonderful than the present time is! (*There is a pause.* JIM *smiles at her.*) Your brother tells me you're shy. Is that right, Laura?

LAURA. I—don't know.

JIM. I judge you to be an old-fashioned type of girl. Well, I think that's a pretty good type to be. Hope you don't think I'm being too personal—do you?

LAURA (*hastily, out of embarrassment*). I believe I *will* take a piece of gum, if you—don't mind. (*Clearing her throat.*) Mr. O'Connor, have you—kept up with your singing?

JIM. Singing? Me?

LAURA. Yes. I remember what a beautiful voice you had.

JIM. When did you hear me sing?

(*Voice off stage in the pause:*

> O blow, ye winds, heigh-ho,
> A-roving I will go!

Century of Progress: World's Fair in Chicago, 1933–1934

       I'm off to my love
       With a boxing glove—
       Ten thousand miles away!)

JIM. You say you've heard me sing?

LAURA. Oh, yes! Yes, very often . . . I—don't suppose—you remember me—at all?

JIM (*smiling doubtfully*). You know I have an idea I've seen you before. I had that idea soon as you opened the door. It seems almost like I was about to remember your name. But the name that I started to call you—wasn't a name! And so I stopped myself before I said it.

LAURA. Wasn't it—Blue Roses?

JIM (*springs up. Grinning*). Blue Roses!—My gosh, yes—Blue Roses! That's what I had on my tongue when you opened the door! Isn't it funny what tricks your memory plays? I didn't connect you with high school somehow or other. But that's where it was; it was high school. I didn't even know you were Shakespeare's sister! Gosh, I'm sorry.

LAURA. I didn't expect you to. You—barely knew me!

JIM. But we did have a speaking acquaintance, huh?

LAURA. Yes, we—spoke to each other.

JIM. When did you recognize me?

LAURA. Oh, right away!

JIM. Soon as I came in the door?

LAURA. When I heard your name I thought it was probably you. I knew that Tom used to know you a little in high school. So when you came in the door—well, then I was—sure.

JIM. Why didn't you *say* something, then?

LAURA (*breathlessly*). I didn't know what to say, I was—too surprised!

JIM. For goodness sakes! You know, this sure is funny!

LAURA. Yes! Yes, isn't it, though . . .

JIM. Didn't we have a class in something together?

LAURA. Yes, we did.

JIM. What class was that?

LAURA. It was—singing—chorus!

JIM. Aw!

LAURA. I sat across the aisle from you in the Aud.

JIM. Aw.

LAURA. Mondays, Wednesdays and Fridays.

JIM. Now I remember—you always came in late.

LAURA. Yes, it was so hard for me getting upstairs. I had that brace on my leg—it clumped so loud!

JIM. I never heard any clumping.

LAURA (*wincing at the recollection*). To me it sounded like—thunder!

JIM. Well, well, well, I never even noticed.

LAURA. And everybody was seated before I came in. I had to walk in front of all those people. My seat was in the back row. I had to go clumping all the way up the aisle with everyone watching!

JIM. You shouldn't have been self-conscious.

LAURA. I know, but I was. It was always such a relief when the singing started.

JIM. Aw, yes, I've placed you now! I used to call you Blue Roses. How was it that I got started calling you that?

LAURA. I was out of school a little while with pleurosis. When I came back you asked me what was the matter. I said I had pleurosis—you thought I said Blue Roses. That's what you always called me after that!

JIM. I hope you didn't mind.

LAURA. Oh, no—I liked it. You see, I wasn't acquainted with many—people . . .

JIM. As I remember you sort of stuck by yourself.

LAURA. I—I—never have had much luck at—making friends.

JIM. I don't see why you wouldn't.

LAURA. Well, I—started out badly.

JIM. You mean being—

LAURA. Yes, it sort of—stood between me—

JIM. You shouldn't have let it!

LAURA. I know, but it did, and—

JIM. You were shy with people!

LAURA. I tried not to be but never could—

JIM. Overcome it?

LAURA. No, I—I never could!

JIM. I guess being shy is something you have to work out of kind of gradually.

LAURA (*sorrowfully*). Yes—I guess it—

JIM. Takes time!

LAURA. Yes—

JIM. People are not so dreadful when you know them. That's what you have to remember! And everybody has problems, not just you, but practically everybody has got some problems. You think of yourself as having the only problems, as being the only one who is disappointed. But just look around you and you will see lots of people as disappointed as you are. For instance, I hoped when I was going to high school that I would be further along at this time, six years later, than I am now—You remember that wonderful write-up I had in *The Torch?*

LAURA. Yes! (*She rises and crosses to table.*)

JIM. It said I was bound to succeed in anything I went into! (LAURA *returns with the annual.*) Holy Jeez! *The Torch!* (*He accepts it reverently. They smile across it with mutual wonder.* LAURA *crouches beside him and they begin to turn through it.* LAURA's *shyness is dissolving in his warmth.*)

LAURA. Here you are in *The Pirates of Penzance!*

JIM (*wistfully*). I sang the baritone lead in that operetta.

LAURA (*raptly*). So—*beautifully!*

JIM (*protesting*). Aw—

LAURA. Yes, yes—beautifully—beautifully!

JIM. You heard me?

LAURA. All three times!

JIM. No!

LAURA. Yes!

JIM. All three performances?

LAURA (*looking down*). Yes.

JIM. Why?

LAURA. I—wanted to ask you to—autograph my program.

JIM. Why didn't you ask me to?

LAURA. You were always surrounded by your own friends so much that I never had a chance to.

JIM. You should have just—

LAURA. Well, I—thought you might think I was—

JIM. Thought I might think you was—what?

LAURA. Oh—

JIM (*with reflective relish*). I was beleaguered by females in those days.

LAURA. You were terribly popular!

JIM. Yeah—

LAURA. You had such a—friendly way—

JIM. I was spoiled in high school.

LAURA. Everybody—liked you!

JIM. Including you?

LAURA. I—yes, I—I did, too—(*She gently closes the book in her lap.*)

JIM. Well, well, well!—Give me that program, Laura. (*She hands it to him. He signs it with a flourish.*) There you are—better late than never!

LAURA. Oh, I—what a—surprise!

JIM. My signature isn't worth very much right now. But some day— maybe—it will increase in value! Being disappointed is one thing and being discouraged is something else. I am disappointed but I am not discouraged. I'm twenty-three years old. How old are you?

LAURA. I'll be twenty-four in June.

JIM. That's not old age!

LAURA. No, but—

JIM. You finished high school?

LAURA (*with difficulty*). I didn't go back.

JIM. You mean you dropped out?

LAURA. I made bad grades in my final examinations. (*She rises and replaces the book and the program. Her voice is strained.*) How is—Emily Meisenbach getting along?

JIM. Oh, that kraut-head!

LAURA. Why do you call her that?

JIM. That's what she was.

LAURA. You're not still—going with her?

JIM. I never see her.

LAURA. It said in the Personal Section that you were—engaged!

JIM. I know, but I wasn't impressed by that—propaganda!

LAURA. It wasn't—the truth?

JIM. Only in Emily's optimistic opinion!

LAURA. Oh—(JIM *lights a cigarette and leans indolently back on his elbows smiling at* LAURA *with a warmth and charm which lights her inwardly with altar candles. She remains by the table and turns in her hands a piece of glass to cover her tumult.*)

JIM (*after several reflective puffs on a cigarette*). What have you done since high school? (*She seems not to hear him.*) Huh? (LAURA *looks up.*) I said what have you done since high school, Laura?

LAURA. Nothing much.

JIM. You must have been doing something these six long years.

LAURA. Yes.

JIM. Well, then, such as what?

LAURA. I took a business course at business college—

JIM. How did that work out?

LAURA. Well, not very—well—I had to drop out, it gave me—indigestion—

JIM (*laughs gently*). What are you doing now?

LAURA. I don't do anything—much. Oh, please don't think I sit around doing nothing! My glass collection takes up a good deal of time. Glass is something you have to take good care of.

JIM. What did you say—about glass?

LAURA. Collection I said—I have one—(*She clears her throat and turns away again, acutely shy.*)

JIM (*abruptly*). You know what I judge to be the trouble with you? Inferiority complex! Know what that is? That's what they call it when someone low-rates himself! I understand it because I had it, too. Although my case was not so aggravated as yours seems to be. I had it until I took up public speaking, developed my voice, and learned that I had an aptitude for science. Before that time I never thought of myself as being outstanding in any way whatsoever! Now I've never made a regular study of it, but I have a friend who says I can analyze people better than doctors that make a profession of it. I don't claim that to be necessarily true, but I can sure guess a person's psychology, Laura! (*Takes out his gum.*) Excuse me, Laura. I always take it out when the flavor is gone. I'll use this scrap of paper to wrap it in. I know how it is to get it stuck on a shoe. Yep—that's what I judge to be your principal trouble. A lack of confidence in yourself as a person. You don't have the proper amount of faith in yourself. I'm basing that fact on a number of your remarks and also on certain observations I've made. For instance that clumping you thought was so awful in high school. You say that you even dreaded to walk into class. You see what you did? You dropped out of school, you gave up an education because of a clump, which as far as I know was practically non-existent! A little physical defect is what you have. Hardly noticeable even! Magnified thousands of times by imagination! You know what my strong advice to you is? Think of yourself as *superior* in some way!

LAURA. In what way would I think?

JIM. Why, man alive, Laura! Just look about you a little. What do you see? A world full of common people! All of 'em born and all of 'em going to die! Which of them has one-tenth of your good points! Or mine! Or anyone else's, as far as that goes—Gosh! Everybody excels in some one thing. Some in many! (*Unconsciously glances at himself in the mirror.*) All you've got to do is discover in *what!* Take me, for instance. (*He adjusts his tie at the mirror.*) My interest happens to lie in electrodynamics. I'm taking a course in radio engineering at night school, Laura, on top of a fairly responsible job at the warehouse. I'm taking that course and studying public speaking.

LAURA. Ohhhh.

JIM. Because I believe in the future of television! (*Turning back to her.*) I wish to be ready to go up right along with it. Therefore I'm planning to get in on the ground floor. In fact I've already made the right connections and all that remains is for the industry itself to get under way! Full steam—(*His eyes are starry.*) Knowledge—Zzzzzp! *Money*—Zzzzzzp!—*Power!* That's the cycle democracy is built on! (*His attitude is convincingly dynamic.* LAURA *stares at him, even her shyness eclipsed in her absolute wonder. He suddenly grins.*) I guess you think I think a lot of myself?

LAURA. No—o-o-o, I—

JIM. Now how about you? Isn't there something you take more interest in than anything else?

LAURA. Well, I do—as I said—have my—glass collection—(*A peal of girlish laughter from the kitchenette.*)

JIM. I'm not right sure I know what you're talking about. What kind of glass is it?

LAURA. Little articles of it, they're ornaments mostly! Most of them are little animals made out of glass, the tiniest little animals in the world. Mother calls them a glass menagerie! Here's an example of one, if you'd like to see it! This one is one of the oldest. It's nearly thirteen. (*Music: "The Glass Menagerie."* JIM *stretches out his hand.*) Oh, be careful—if you breathe, it breaks!

JIM. I'd better not take it. I'm pretty clumsy with things.

LAURA. Go on, I trust you with him! (*Places it in his palm.*) There now— you're holding him gently! Hold him over the light, he loves the light! You see how the light shines through him?

JIM. It sure does shine!

LAURA. I shouldn't be partial, but he is my favorite one.

JIM. What kind of thing is this one supposed to be?

LAURA. Haven't you noticed the single horn on his forehead?

JIM. A unicorn, huh?

LAURA. Mmm-hmmm!

JIM. Unicorns, aren't they extinct in the modern world?

LAURA. I know!

JIM. Poor little fellow, he must feel sort of lonesome.

LAURA (*smiling*). Well, if he does he doesn't complain about it. He stays on a shelf with some horses that don't have horns and all of them seem to get along nicely together.

JIM. How do you know?

LAURA (*lightly*). I haven't heard any arguments among them!

JIM (*grinning*). No arguments, huh? Well, that's a pretty good sign! Where shall I set him?

LAURA. Put him on the table. They all like a change of scenery once in a while!

JIM (*stretching*). Well, well, well, well—Look how big my shadow is when I stretch!

LAURA. Oh, oh, yes—it stretches across the ceiling!

JIM (*crossing to door*). I think it's stopped raining. (*Opens fire-escape door.*) Where does the music come from?

LAURA. From the Paradise Dance Hall across the alley.

JIM. How about cutting the rug a little, Miss Wingfield?

LAURA. Oh, I—

JIM. Or is your program filled up? Let me have a look at it. (*Grasps imaginary card.*) Why, every dance is taken! I'll just have to scratch some out. (*Waltz music: "La Golondrina."*) Ahhh, a waltz! (*He executes some sweeping turns by himself then holds his arms toward* LAURA.)

LAURA (*breathlessly*). I—can't dance!

JIM. There you go, that inferiority stuff!

LAURA. I've never danced in my life!

JIM. Come on, try!

LAURA. Oh, but I'd step on you!

JIM. I'm not made out of glass.

LAURA. How—how—how do we start?

JIM. Just leave it to me. You hold your arms out a little.

LAURA. Like this?

JIM. A bit higher. Right. Now don't tighten up, that's the main thing about it—relax.

LAURA (*laughing breathlessly*). It's hard not to.

JIM. Okay.

LAURA. I'm afraid you can't budge me.

JIM. What do you bet I can't? (*He swings her into motion.*)

LAURA. Goodness, yes, you can!

JIM. Let yourself go, now, Laura, just let yourself go.

LAURA. I'm—

JIM. Come on!

LAURA. Trying!

JIM. Not so stiff—Easy does it!

LAURA. I know but I'm—

JIM. Loosen th' backbone! There now, that's a lot better.

LAURA. Am I?

JIM. Lots, lots better! (*He moves her about the room in a clumsy waltz.*)

LAURA. Oh, my!

JIM. Ha-ha!

LAURA. Oh, my goodness!

JIM. Ha-ha-ha! (*They suddenly bump into the table.* JIM *stops.*) What did we hit on?

LAURA. Table.

JIM. Did something fall off it? I think—

LAURA. Yes.

JIM. I hope it wasn't the little glass horse with the horn!

LAURA. Yes.

JIM. Aw, aw, aw. Is it broken?

LAURA. Now it is just like all the other horses.

JIM. It's lost its—

LAURA. Horn! It doesn't matter. Maybe it's a blessing in disguise.

JIM. You'll never forgive me. I bet that was your favorite piece of glass.

LAURA. I don't have favorites much. It's no tragedy, Freckles. Glass breaks so easily. No matter how careful you are. The traffic jars the shelves and things fall off them.

JIM. Still I'm awfully sorry that I was the cause.

LAURA (*smiling*). I'll just imagine he had an operation. The horn was removed to make him feel less—freakish! (*They both laugh.*) Now he will feel more at home with the other horses, the ones that don't have horns . . .

JIM. Ha-ha, that's very funny! (*Suddenly serious.*) I'm glad to see that you have a sense of humor. You know—you're—well—very different! Surprisingly different from anyone else I know! (*His voice becomes soft and hesitant with a genuine feeling.*) Do you mind me telling you that? (LAURA *is abashed beyond speech.*) I mean it in a nice way . . . (LAURA *nods shyly, looking away.*) You make me feel sort of—I don't know how to put it! I'm usually pretty good at expressing things, but—this is something that I don't know how to say! (LAURA *touches her throat and clears it— turns the broken unicorn in her hands. His voice becomes softer.*) Has anyone ever told you that you were pretty? (*Pause: music.* LAURA *looks up slowly, with wonder, and shakes her head.*)

Well, you are! In a very different way from anyone else. And all the nicer because of the difference, too. (*His voice becomes low and husky.* LAURA *turns away, nearly faint with the novelty of her emotions.*) I wish that you were my sister. I'd teach you to have some confidence in yourself. The different people are not like other people, but being different is nothing to be ashamed of. Because other people are not such wonderful people. They're one hundred times one thousand. You're one times one! They walk all over the earth. You just stay here. They're common as—weeds, but—you—well, you're—*Blue Roses!* (*Music changes.*)

LAURA. But blue is wrong for—roses . . .

JIM. It's right for you!—You're—pretty!

LAURA. In what respect am I pretty?

JIM. In all respects—believe me! Your eyes—your hair—are pretty! Your hands are pretty! (*He catches hold of her hand.*) You think I'm making this up because I'm invited to dinner and have to be nice. Oh, I could do that! I could put on an act for you, Laura, and say lots of things without being very sincere. But this time I am. I'm talking to you sincerely. I happened to notice you had this inferiority complex that keeps you from feeling comfortable with people. Somebody needs to build your confidence up and make you proud instead of shy and turning away and—blushing—Somebody—ought to—ought to—*kiss* you, Laura! (*His hand slips slowly up her arm to her shoulder. Music swells tumultuously. He suddenly turns her about and kisses her on the lips. When he releases her,* LAURA *sinks on the sofa with a bright, dazed look.* JIM *backs away and fishes in his pocket for a cigarette.*) Stumble-john! (*He lights a cigarette, avoiding her look. There is a peal of girlish laughter from* AMANDA *in the kitchenette.*

LAURA *slowly raises and opens her hand. It still contains the little broken glass animal. She looks at it with a tender, bewildered expression.*)
    Stumble-john! I shouldn't have done that—That was way off beam. You don't smoke, do you? (*She looks up, smiling, not hearing the question. He sits beside her a little gingerly. She looks at him speechlessly—waiting. He coughs decorously and moves a little farther aside as he considers the situation and senses her feelings, dimly, with perturbation. He speaks gently.*) Would you—care for a—mint? (*She doesn't seem to hear him but her look grows brighter even.*) Peppermint—Life-Saver? My pocket's a regular drug store—wherever I go . . . (*He pops a mint in his mouth. Then gulps and decides to make a clean breast of it. He speaks slowly and gingerly.*) Laura, you know, if I had a sister like you, I'd do the same thing as Tom. I'd bring out fellows and—introduce her to them. The right type of boys of a type to—appreciate her. Only—well—he made a mistake with me. Maybe I've got no call to be saying this. That may not have been the idea in having me over. But what if it was? There's nothing wrong about that. The only trouble is that in my case—I'm not in a situation to—do the right thing. I can't take down your number and say I'll phone. I can't call up next week and—ask for a date. I thought I had better explain the situation in case you—misunderstood it and—hurt your feelings . . . (*Pause. Slowly, very slowly,* LAURA'S *look changes, her eyes returning slowly from his to the ornament in her palm.* AMANDA *utters another gay laugh in the kitchenette.*)

LAURA (*faintly*). You—won't—call again?

JIM. No, Laura, I can't. (*He rises from the sofa.*) As I was just explaining. I've—got strings on me. Laura, I've—been going steady! I go out all of the time with a girl named Betty. She's a home-girl like you, and Catholic, and Irish, and in a great many ways we—get along fine. I met her last summer on a moonlight boat trip up the river to Alton, on the *Majestic.* Well—right away from the start it was—love! (LAURA *sways slightly forward and grips the arm of the sofa. He fails to notice, now enrapt in his own comfortable being.*) Being in love has made a new man of me! (*Leaning stiffly forward, clutching the arm of the sofa,* LAURA *struggles visibly with her storm. But* JIM *is oblivious; she is a long way off.*) The power of love is really pretty tremendous! Love is something that—changes the whole world, Laura! (*The storm abates a little and* LAURA *leans back. He notices her again.*) It happened that Betty's aunt took sick, she got a wire and had to go to Centralia. So Tom—when he asked me to dinner—I naturally just accepted the invitation, not knowing that you—that he—that I—(*He stops awkwardly.*) Huh—I'm a stumble-john! (*He flops back on the sofa. The holy candles in the altar of* LAURA'S *face have been snuffed out. There is a look of almost infinite desolation.* JIM *glances at her uneasily.*) I wish that you would—say something. (*She bites her lip which was trembling and then bravely smiles. She opens her hand again on the broken glass ornament. Then she gently takes his hand and raises it level with her own. She carefully places the unicorn in the palm of his hand, then pushes his fingers closed upon it.*) What are you—doing that for? You want me to have him—Laura? (*She nods.*) What for?

LAURA. A—souvenir . . . (*She rises unsteadily and crouches beside the victrola to wind it up. At this moment* AMANDA *rushes brightly back into the living room. She bears a pitcher of fruit punch in an old-fashioned cut-glass pitcher and a plate of macaroons. The plate has a gold border and poppies painted on it.*)

AMANDA. Well, well, well! Isn't the air delightful after the shower? I've made you children a little liquid refreshment. (*She turns gaily to* JIM.) Jim, do you know that song about lemonade?

"Lemonade, lemonade,
Made in the shade and stirred with a spade—
Good enough for any old maid!"

JIM (*uneasily*). Ha-ha! No—I never heard it.

AMANDA. Why, Laura! You look so serious!

JIM. We were having a serious conversation.

AMANDA. Good! Now you're better acquainted!

JIM (*uncertainly*). Ha-ha! Yes.

AMANDA. You modern young people are much more serious-minded than my generation. I was so gay as a girl!

JIM. You haven't changed, Mrs. Wingfield.

AMANDA. Tonight I'm rejuvenated! The gaiety of the occasion, Mr. O'Connor! (*She tosses her head with a peal of laughter. Spills lemonade.*) Oooo! I'm baptizing myself!

JIM. Here—let me—

AMANDA (*setting the pitcher down*). There now. I discovered we had some maraschino cherries. I dumped them in, juice and all!

JIM. You shouldn't have gone to that trouble, Mrs. Wingfield.

AMANDA. Trouble, trouble? Why, it was loads of fun! Didn't you hear me cutting up in the kitchen? I bet your ears were burning! I told Tom how outdone with him I was for keeping you to himself so long a time! He should have brought you over much, much sooner! Well, now that you've found your way, I want you to be a frequent caller! Not just occasional but all the time. Oh, we're going to have a lot of gay times together! I see them coming! Mmm, just breathe that air! So fresh, and the moon's so pretty! I'll skip back out—I know where my place is when young folks are having a—serious conversation!

JIM. Oh, don't go out, Mrs. Wingfield. The fact of the matter is I've got to be going.

AMANDA. Going, now? You're joking! Why, it's only the shank of the evening, Mr. O'Connor!

JIM. Well, you know how it is.

AMANDA. You mean you're a young workingman and have to keep workingmen's hours. We'll let you off early tonight. But only on the condition that next time you stay later.

What's the best night for you? Isn't Saturday night the best night for you workingmen?

JIM. I have a couple of time-clocks to punch, Mrs. Wingfield. One at morning, another at night!

AMANDA. My, but you *are* ambitious! You work at night, too?

JIM. No, Ma'am, not work but—Betty! (*He crosses deliberately to pick up his hat. The band at the Paradise Dance Hall goes into a tender waltz.*)

AMANDA. Betty? Betty? Who's—Betty! (*There is an ominous cracking sound in the sky.*)

JIM. Oh, just a girl. The girl I go steady with! (*He smiles charmingly. The sky falls.*)

AMANDA (*a long-drawn exhalation*). Ohhhh. . . . Is it a serious romance, Mr. O'Connor?

JIM. We're going to be married the second Sunday in June.

AMANDA. Ohhhh—how nice! Tom didn't mention that you were engaged to be married.

JIM. The cat's not out of the bag at the warehouse yet. You know how they are. They call you Romeo and stuff like that. (*He stops at the oval mirror to put on his hat. He carefully shapes the brim and the crown to give a discreetly dashing effect.*) It's been a wonderful evening, Mrs. Wingfield. I guess this is what they mean by Southern hospitality.

AMANDA. It really wasn't anything at all.

JIM. I hope it don't seem like I'm rushing off. But I promised Betty I'd pick her up at the Wabash depot, an' by the time I get my jalopy down there her train'll be in. Some women are pretty upset if you keep 'em waiting.

AMANDA. Yes, I know—The tyranny of women! (*Extends her hand.*) Good-bye, Mr. O'Connor. I wish you luck—and happiness—and success! All three of them, and so does Laura—Don't you Laura?

LAURA. Yes!

JIM (*taking her hand*). Good-bye Laura. I'm certainly going to treasure that souvenir. And don't you forget the good advice I gave you. (*Raises his voice to a cheery shout.*) So long, Shakespeare! Thanks again, ladies—Good night! (*He grins and ducks jauntily out. Still bravely grimacing,* AMANDA *closes the door on the gentleman caller. Then she turns back to the room with a puzzled expression. She and* LAURA *don't dare to face each other.* LAURA *crouches beside the victrola to wind it.*)

AMANDA (*faintly*). Things have a way of turning out so badly. I don't believe that I would play the victrola. Well, well—well—Our gentleman caller was engaged to be married! (*She raises her voice.*) Tom!

TOM (*from the kitchenette*). Yes, Mother?

AMANDA. Come in here a minute. I want to tell you something awfully funny.

TOM (*enters with a macaroon and a glass of lemonade*). Has the gentleman caller gotten away already?

AMANDA. The gentleman caller has made an early departure. What a wonderful joke you played on us!

TOM. How do you mean?

AMANDA. You didn't mention that he was engaged to be married.

TOM. Jim? Engaged?

AMANDA. That's what he just informed us.

TOM. I'll be jiggered! I didn't know about that.

AMANDA. That seems very peculiar.

TOM. What's peculiar about it?

AMANDA. Didn't you call him your best friend down at the warehouse?

TOM. He is, but how did I know?

AMANDA. It seems extremely peculiar that you wouldn't know your best friend was going to be married!

TOM. The warehouse is where I work, not where I know things about people!

AMANDA. You don't know things anywhere! You live in a dream; you manufacture illusions! (*He crosses to the door.*) Where are you going?

TOM. I'm going to the movies.

AMANDA. That's right, now that you've had us make such fools of ourselves. The effort, the preparations, all the expense! The new floor lamp, the rug, the clothes for Laura! All for what? To entertain some other girl's fiancé! Go to the movies, go! Don't think about us, a mother deserted, an unmarried sister who's crippled and has no job! Don't let anything interfere with your selfish pleasure! Just go, go, go—to the movies!

TOM. All right, I will! The more you shout about my selfishness to me the quicker I'll go, and I won't go to the movies!

AMANDA. Go, then! Then go to the moon—you selfish dreamer!

(TOM *smashes his glass on the floor. He plunges out of the fire-escape, slamming the door.* LAURA *screams in fright. The dance-hall music becomes louder.* TOM *goes to the rail and grips it desperately, lifting his face in the chill white moonlight penetrating the narrow abyss of the alley.*

(TOM'*s closing speech is timed with what is happening inside the house. The interior scene is played as though viewed through soundproof glass.* AMANDA *appears to be making a comforting speech to* LAURA *who is huddled upon the sofa. Now that we cannot hear the mother's speech, her silliness is gone and she has dignity and tragic beauty.* LAURA'*s dark hair hides her face until at the end of the speech she lifts it to smile at her mother.* AMANDA'*s gestures are slow and graceful, almost dance-like, as she comforts her daughter. At the end of her speech she glances a moment at the father's picture—then withdraws through the portieres. At the close of* TOM'*s speech,* LAURA *blows out the candles, ending the play.*)

TOM. I didn't go to the moon, I went much further—for time is the longest distance between two places—Not long after that I was fired for writing a poem on the lid of a shoe-box. I left Saint Louis. I descended the steps of this fire-escape for a last time and followed, from then on, in my father's footsteps, attempting to find in motion what was lost in space—I traveled around a great deal. The cities swept about me like dead leaves, leaves that were brightly colored but torn away from the branches. I would have stopped, but I was pursued by something. It always came upon me unawares, taking me altogether by surprise. Perhaps it was a familiar bit of music. Perhaps it was only a piece of transparent glass—Perhaps I am walking along a street at night, in some strange city, before I have found companions. I pass the lighted window of a shop where perfume is sold. The window is filled with pieces of colored glass, tiny transparent bottles in delicate colors, like bits of a shattered rainbow. Then all at once my sister touches my shoulder. I turn around and look into her eyes . . . Oh, Laura, Laura, I tried to leave you behind me, but I am more faithful than I intended to be! I reach for a cigarette, I cross the street, I run into the movies or a bar, I buy a drink, I speak to the nearest stranger—anything that can blow your candles out! (LAURA *bends over the candles.*) For nowadays the world is lit by lightning! Blow out your candles, Laura—and so goodbye . . . (*She blows the candles out.*)

QUESTIONS

1. In presenting Scene 1, the author says:"The scene is memory and is therefore nonrealistic." To whose memory does he refer? Why should memory be nonrealistic? List the different ways in which the play is nonrealistic. What, according to Tom in his opening speech, is the ultimate aim of this nonrealistic method of presentation?

2. How does the kind of language Tom uses as a narrator differ from that he uses as a character? What would happen to the play if Tom used the first kind of language throughout?

3. What is Tom's dilemma? Why is he always quarreling with his mother? What is his attitude toward Laura? Why does he finally leave? Does he ever resolve his dilemma?

4. What qualities possessed by Tom, and by him alone, make him the proper narrator of the play?

5. LAURA is the pivotal character in the play, as evidenced by its title and by the fact that the main actions of the play revolve around her. What are the symptoms and causes of her mental condition? Can they all be traced to her physical defect? What qualities make her a sympathetic character? How does her relationship with her mother differ from Tom's?

6. What symbolic meanings has Laura's glass menagerie? What, especially, is symbolized by the unicorn? How and why does her reaction to Jim's breaking the unicorn differ from her reaction to Tom's breaking several pieces at the end of Scene 3? Why does she give the broken unicorn to Jim as a souvenir? What future do you predict for her? What symbolism has her blowing out the candles at the end of the play?

7. The author tells us (page 1177) that "Amanda, having failed to establish contact with reality, continues to live vitally in her illusions." What part of this statement could be applied to Laura as well? What part could not? What are the chief instances in the play of Amanda's having lost "contact with reality"? What are her chief illusions? What are her strengths? How is she both cruel and tender with her children? What qualities has she in common with Jim, the gentleman caller? Why do you suppose her husband left her?

8. The author describes Jim O'Connor as "a nice, ordinary, young man" (page 1177). Tom (in Scene 1) describes him as "the most realistic character, being an emissary from that world of reality that we were set apart from." In what ways is Jim "nice"? In what ways is he "ordinary"? In what ways and in what sense is he more "realistic" than the Wingfields? Does this mean that he is without delusions? What would you predict for his future? Of what is he symbolic?

9. Account for Jim's treatment of Laura in Scene 7.

10. What trait do Laura, Amanda, and Tom all share, which makes Jim more realistic than they? Explain the dramatic irony in Amanda's remark to Tom, in their final dialogue, "You don't know things anywhere! You live in a dream; you manufacture illusions!"

11. What respective claims have Tom, Laura, and Amanda for being considered the protagonist of the play? For which character would it be most crucial to the success or failure of a production to obtain a highly accomplished actor or actress? Why?

12. The play is set in the 1930s. Of what significance are the many references throughout the play to its social and historical background? How are these larger events and the Wingfields' domestic lives related?

13. The play is divided into seven scenes. If you were to produce it with one intermission, where would you put the intermission? For what reasons?

LUIS VALDEZ
Los Vendidos

Characters

HONEST SANCHO	JOHNNY PACHUCO
SECRETARY	REVOLUCIONARIO
FARMWORKER	MEXICAN-AMERICAN

SCENE: HONEST SANCHO's *Used Mexican Lot and Mexican Curio Shop. Three models are on display in* HONEST SANCHO's *shop. To the right, there is a* REVOLUCIONARIO, *complete with sombrero, carrilleras and carabina 30-30.° At center, on the floor, there is the* FARMWORKER, *under a broad straw sombrero. At stage left is the* PACHUCO, *filero° in hand.* HONEST SANCHO *is moving among his models, dusting them off and preparing for another day of business.*

SANCHO. Bueno, bueno, mis monos, vamos a ver a quién vendemos ahora, ¿no? (*To audience*) ¡Quihubo!° I'm Honest Sancho and this is my shop. Antes fui contratista, pero ahora logré mi negocito.° All I need now is a customer. (*A bell rings offstage.*) Ay, a customer!

SECRETARY (*entering*). Good morning, I'm Miss Jimenez from . . .

SANCHO. Ah, una chicana! Welcome, welcome Señorita Jiménez.

SECRETARY (*Anglo pronunciation*). JIM-enez.

SANCHO. ¿Qué?

SECRETARY. My name is Miss JIM-enez. Don't you speak English? What's wrong with you?

SANCHO. Oh, nothing, Señorita JIM-enez. I'm here to help you.

SECRETARY. That's better. As I was starting to say, I'm a secretary from Governor Reagan's office, and we're looking for a Mexican type for the administration.

LOS VENDIDOS First performed in 1967. The title may be translated both "men who are sold" and "the sellouts," i.e., traitors to the cause. Luis Valdez was born in 1940 in Delano, California, the son of migrant farmworkers (*campesinos*). Although his early education was interrupted by the need to work in the fields, he earned a B.A. in English from San Jose State College in 1964 and then joined the San Francisco Mime Troupe performing political and satirical plays in public parks. In 1965 he founded El Teatro Campesino in Delano to present satirical skits (called "Actos") in support of the farmworkers' cause and as a means of political protest. Like others of the Actos, "Los Vendidos" was presented free to an audience in a park. Subsequently, in 1972, it won an Emmy in a television production for the Corporation for Public Broadcasting. At the time of its writing, Ronald Reagan was governor of California and another former film actor, George Murphy, was a U.S. senator.

---

carrilleras . . . 30-30: cartridge belts and 30-30 rifle   **filero:** switchblade   **Bueno . . . Quihubo!:** Good, good, my cuties, let's see who we can sell now. What's going on?   **Antes fui . . . negocito:** I used to be a contractor, but now I run my little business.

SANCHO. Well, you come to the right place, lady. This is Honest Sancho's Used Mexican Lot, and we got all types here. Any particular type you want?

SECRETARY. Yes, we were looking for somebody suave . . .

SANCHO. Suave.

SECRETARY. Debonaire.

SANCHO. De buen aire.

SECRETARY. Dark.

SANCHO. Prieto.

SECRETARY. But of course, not too dark.

SANCHO. No muy prieto.

SECRETARY. Perhaps, beige.

SANCHO. Beige, just the tone. Así como cafecito con leche,° ¿no?

SECRETARY. One more thing. He must be hard-working.

SANCHO. That could only be one model. Step right over here to the center of the shop, lady. (*They cross to the* FARMWORKER.) This is our standard farm worker model. As you can see, in the words of our beloved Senator George Murphy, he is "built close to the ground." Also, take special notice of his 4-ply Goodyear huaraches,° made from the rain tire. This wide-brimmed sombrero is an extra added feature; keeps off the sun, rain and dust.

SECRETARY. Yes, it does look durable.

SANCHO. And our farmworker model is friendly, Muy amable.° Watch. (*Snaps his fingers.*)

FARMWORKER (*lifts up head*). Buenos días, señorita. (*His head drops.*)

SECRETARY. My, he is friendly.

SANCHO. Didn't I tell you? Loves his patrones!° But his most attractive feature is that he's hard-working. Let me show you. (*Snaps fingers.* FARM-WORKER *stands.*)

FARMWORKER. ¡El jale!° (*He begins to work.*)

SANCHO. As you can see he is cutting grapes.

SECRETARY. Oh, I wouldn't know.

SANCHO. He also picks cotton. (*Snaps.* FARMWORKER *begins to pick cotton.*)

SECRETARY. Versatile, isn't he?

SANCHO. He also picks melons. (*Snaps.* FARMWORKER *picks melons.*) That's his slow speed for late in the season. Here's his fast speed. (*Snap.* FARM-WORKER *picks faster.*)

SECRETARY. Chihuahua.° . . . I mean, goodness, he sure is a hard-worker.

Así . . . leche: Like coffee with milk huaraches: sandals Muy amable: Very friendly
patrones: bosses El jale: The job Chihuahua: Hot damn!

SANCHO (*pulls the* FARMWORKER *to his feet*). And that isn't the half of it. Do you see these little holes on his arms that appear to be pores? During those hot sluggish days in the field when the vines or the branches get so entangled, it's almost impossible to move, these holes emit a certain grease that allows our model to slip and slide right through the crop with no trouble at all.

SECRETARY. Wonderful. But is he economical?

SANCHO. Economical? Señorita, you are looking at the Volkswagen of Mexicans. Pennies a day is all it takes. One plate of beans and tortillas will keep him going all day. That, and chile. Plenty of chile. Chile jalapeños, chile verde, chile colorado. But, of course, if you do give him chile (*Snap.* FARMWORKER *turns left face. Snap.* FARMWORKER *bends over.*), then you have to change his oil filter once a week.

SECRETARY. What about storage?

SANCHO. No problem. You know these new farm labor camps our Honorable Governor Reagan has built out by Parlier or Raisin City? They were designed with our model in mind. Five, six, seven, even ten in one of those shacks will give you no trouble at all. You can also put him in old barns, old cars, riverbanks. You can even leave him out in the field overnight with no worry!

SECRETARY. Remarkable.

SANCHO. And here's an added feature: every year at the end of the season, this model goes back to Mexico and doesn't return, automatically, until next spring.

SECRETARY. How about that. But tell me, does he speak English?

SANCHO. Another outstanding feature is that last year this model was programmed to go out on STRIKE! (*Snap.*)

FARMWORKER. ¡Huelga! ¡Huelga! Hermanos, sálganse de esos files.° (*Snap. He stops.*)

SECRETARY. No! Oh no, we can't strike in the State Capitol.

SANCHO. Well, he also scabs. (*Snap.*)

FARMWORKER. Me vendo barato, ¿y qué?° (*Snap.*)

SECRETARY. That's much better, but you didn't answer my question. Does he speak English?

SANCHO. Bueno . . . no, pero° he has other . . .

SECRETARY. No.

SANCHO. Other features.

SECRETARY. No! He just won't do!

SANCHO. Okay, okay, pues.° We have other models.

¡Huelga! . . . files: Strike! Strike! Brothers, leave those rows. Me vendo . . . qué?: My price is cheap, so what? Bueno . . . pero: Well, no, but pues: then

SECRETARY. I hope so. What we need is something a little more sophisticated.

SANCHO. Sophisti-qué?

SECRETARY. An urban model.

SANCHO. Ah, from the city! Step right back. Over here in this corner of the shop is exactly what you're looking for. Introducing our new 1969 JOHNNY PACHUCO° model! This is our fast-back model. Streamlined. Built for speed, low-riding, city life. Take a look at some of these features. Mag shoes, dual exhausts, green chartreuse paint-job, dark-tint windshield, a little poof on top. Let me just turn him on. (*Snap.* JOHNNY *walks to stage center with a* PACHUCO *bounce.*)

SECRETARY. What was that?

SANCHO. That, señorita, was the Chicano shuffle.

SECRETARY. Okay, what does he do?

SANCHO. Anything and everything necessary for city life. For instance, survival: he knife fights. (*Snaps.* JOHNNY *pulls out a switchblade and swings at* SECRETARY. SECRETARY *screams.*) He dances. (*Snap.*)

JOHNNY (*singing*). "Angel Baby, my Angel Baby . . ." (*Snap.*)

SANCHO. And here's a feature no city model can be without. He gets arrested, but not without resisting, of course. (*Snap.*)

JOHNNY. En la madre, la placa.° I didn't do it! I didn't do it!

(JOHNNY *turns and stands up against an imaginary wall, legs spread out, arms behind his back.*)

SECRETARY. Oh no, we can't have arrests! We must maintain law and order.

SANCHO. But he's bilingual.

SECRETARY. Bilingual?

SANCHO. Simón que yes. He speaks English! Johnny, give us some English. (*Snap.*)

JOHNNY (*comes downstage*). Fuck-you!

SECRETARY (*gasps*). Oh! I've never been so insulted in my whole life!

SANCHO. Well, he learned it in your school.

SECRETARY. I don't care where he learned it.

SANCHO. But he's economical.

SECRETARY. Economical?

SANCHO. Nickels and dimes. You can keep Johnny running on hamburgers, Taco Bell tacos, Lucky Lager beer, Thunderbird wine, yesca . . .

SECRETARY. Yesca?

SANCHO. Mota.

SECRETARY. Mota?

SANCHO. Leños° . . . marijuana. (*Snap.* JOHNNY *inhales on an imaginary joint.*)

SECRETARY. That's against the law!

JOHNNY (*big smile, holding his breath*). Yeah.

Pachuco: a slang term for an urban tough   **En la . . . placa:** Oh, oh, the cops   **Leños:** Joints

SANCHO. He also sniffs glue. (*Snap.* JOHNNY *inhales glue, big smile.*)

JOHNNY. Tha's too much, man, ése.°

SECRETARY. No, Mr. Sancho, I don't think this . . .

SANCHO. Wait a minute, he has other qualities I know you'll love. For example, an inferiority complex. (*Snap.*)

JOHNNY (*to* SANCHO). You think you're better than me, huh, ése? (*Swings switchblade.*)

SANCHO. He can also be beaten and he bruises. Cut him and he bleeds, kick him and he . . . . (*He beats, bruises and kicks* PACHUCO.) Would you like to try it?

SECRETARY. Oh, I couldn't.

SANCHO. Be my guest. He's a great scapegoat.

SECRETARY. No really.

SANCHO. Please.

SECRETARY. Well, all right. Just once. (*She kicks* PACHUCO.) Oh, he's so soft.

SANCHO. Wasn't that good? Try again.

SECRETARY (*kicks* PACHUCO). Oh, he's wonderful! (*She kicks him again.*)

SANCHO. Okay, that's enough, lady. You'll ruin the merchandise. Yes, our Johnny Pachuco model can give you many hours of pleasure. Why, the LAPD just bought twenty of these to train their rookie cops on. And talk about maintenance. Señorita, you are looking at an entirely self-supporting machine. You're never going to find our Johnny Pachuco model on the relief rolls. No, sir, this model knows how to liberate.

SECRETARY. Liberate?

SANCHO. He steals. (*Snap.* JOHNNY *rushes to* SECRETARY *and steals her purse.*)

JOHNNY. ¡Dame esa bolsa, vieja!° (*He grabs the purse and runs. Snap by* SANCHO, *he stops.* SECRETARY *runs after* JOHNNY *and grabs purse away from him, kicking him as she goes.*)

SECRETARY. No, no, no! We can't have any more thieves in the State Administration. Put him back.

SANCHO. Okay, we still got other models. Come on, Johnny, we'll sell you to some old lady. (SANCHO *takes* JOHNNY *back to his place.*)

SECRETARY. Mr. Sancho, I don't think you quite understand what we need. What we need is something that will attract the women voters. Something more traditional, more romantic.

SANCHO. Ah, a lover. (*He smiles meaningfully.*) Step right over here, señorita. Introducing our standard REVOLUCIONARIO and/or Early California Bandit type. As you can see, he is well-built, sturdy, durable. This is the International Harvester of Mexicans.

ése: man   ¡Dame . . . vieja!: Give me that purse, old lady!

SECRETARY. What does he do?

SANCHO. You name it, he does it. He rides horses, stays in the mountains, crosses deserts, plains, rivers, leads revolutions, follows revolutions, kills, can be killed, serves as a martyr, hero, movie star. Did I say movie star? Did you ever see *Viva Zapata? Viva Villa, Villa Rides, Pancho Villa Returns, Pancho Villa Goes Back, Pancho Villa Meets Abbott and Costello?*

SECRETARY. I've never seen any of those.

SANCHO. Well, he was in all of them. Listen to this. (*Snap.*)

REVOLUCIONARIO (*scream*). ¡Viva Villaaaaa!

SECRETARY. That's awfully loud.

SANCHO. He has a volume control. (*He adjusts volume. Snap.*)

REVOLUCIONARIO (*mousey voice*). Viva Villa.

SECRETARY. That's better.

SANCHO. And even if you didn't see him in the movies, perhaps you saw him on TV. He makes commercials. (*Snap.*)

REVOLUCIONARIO. Is there a Frito Bandito in your house?

SECRETARY. Oh, yes, I've seen that one!

SANCHO. Another feature about this one is that he is economical. He runs on raw horsemeat and tequila!

SECRETARY. Isn't that rather savage?

SANCHO. Al contrario,° it makes him a lover. (*Snap.*)

REVOLUCIONARIO (*to* SECRETARY). Ay, mamasota, cochota, ven pa 'ca!° (*He grabs* SECRETARY *and folds her back, Latin-lover style.*)

SANCHO (*Snap.* REVOLUCIONARIO *goes back upright*). Now wasn't that nice?

SECRETARY. Well, it was rather nice.

SANCHO. And finally, there is one outstanding feature about this model I know the ladies are going to love: he's a genuine antique! He was made in Mexico in 1910!

SECRETARY. Made in Mexico?

SANCHO. That's right. Once in Tijuana, twice in Guadalajara, three times in Cuernavaca.

SECRETARY. Mr. Sancho, I thought he was an American product.

SANCHO. No, but . . .

SECRETARY. No, I'm sorry. We can't buy anything but American made products. He just won't do.

SANCHO. But he's an antique!

SECRETARY. I don't care. You still don't understand what we need. It's true we need Mexican models, such as these, but it's more important that he be American.

Al contrario: On the contrary   **Ay . . . pa 'ca:** Hey, c'mere, big mama!

SANCHO. American?

SECRETARY. That's right, and judging from what you've shown me, I don't think you have what we want. Well, my lunch hour's almost over, I better . . .

SANCHO. Wait a minute! Mexican but American?

SECRETARY. That's correct.

SANCHO. Mexican but . . . (*A sudden flash.*) American! Yeah, I think we've got exactly what you want. He just came in today! Give me a minute. (*He exits. Talks from backstage.*) Here he is in the shop. Let me just get some papers off. There. Introducing our new 1970 Mexican-American! Ta-ra-ra-raaaa! (SANCHO *brings out the* MEXICAN-AMERICAN *model, a clean-shaven middle-class type in a business suit, with glasses.*)

SECRETARY (*impressed*). Where have you been hiding this one?

SANCHO. He just came in this morning. Ain't he a beauty? Feast your eyes on him! Sturdy U.S. Steel frame, streamlined, modern. As a matter of fact, he is built exactly like our Anglo models, except that he comes in a variety of darker shades: naugahyde, leather or leatherette.

SECRETARY. Naugahyde.

SANCHO. Well, we'll just write that down. Yes, señorita, this model represents the apex of American engineering! He is bilingual, college educated, ambitious! Say the word "acculturate" and he accelerates. He is intelligent, well-mannered, clean. Did I say clean? (*Snap.* MEXICAN-AMERICAN *raises his arm.*) Smell.

SECRETARY (*smells*). Old Sobaco, my favorite.

SANCHO (*Snap.* MEXICAN-AMERICAN *turns toward* SANCHO). Eric? (*To* SECRETARY) We call him Eric García. (*To* ERIC) I want you to meet Miss JIM-enez, Eric.

MEXICAN-AMERICAN. Miss JIM-enez, I am delighted to make your acquaintance. (*He kisses her hand.*)

SECRETARY. Oh, my, how charming!

SANCHO. Did you feel the suction? He has seven especially engineered suction cups right behind his lips. He's a charmer all right!

SECRETARY. How about boards, does he function on boards?

SANCHO. You name them, he is on them. Parole boards, draft boards, school boards, taco quality control boards, surf boards, two by fours.

SECRETARY. Does he function in politics?

SANCHO. Señorita, you are looking at a political machine. Have you ever heard of the OEO, EOC, COD, WAR ON POVERTY? That's our model! Not only that, he makes political speeches.

SECRETARY. May I hear one?

SANCHO. With pleasure. (*Snap.*) Eric, give us a speech.

MEXICAN-AMERICAN. Mr. Congressman, Mr. Chairman, members of the board, honored guests, ladies and gentlemen. (SANCHO *and* SECRETARY *applaud.*) Please, please. I come before you as a Mexican-American to tell you about the problems of the Mexican. The problems of the Mexican stem from one thing and one thing only: he's stupid. He's uneducated. He needs to stay in school. He needs to be ambitious, forward-looking, harder-working. He needs to think American, American, American, American, American! God bless America! God bless America! God bless America! (*He goes out of control.* SANCHO *snaps frantically and the* MEXICAN-AMERICAN *finally slumps forward, bending at the waist.*)

SECRETARY. Oh my, he's patriotic too!

SANCHO. Sí, señorita, he loves his country. Let me just make a little adjustment here. (*Stands* MEXICAN-AMERICAN *up.*)

SECRETARY. What about upkeep? Is he economical?

SANCHO. Well, no, I won't lie to you. The Mexican-American costs a little bit more, but you get what you pay for. He's worth every extra cent. You can keep him running on dry Martinis, Langendorf bread . . .

SECRETARY. Apple pie?

SANCHO. Only Mom's. Of course, he's also programmed to eat Mexican food at ceremonial functions, but I must warn you, an overdose of beans will plug up his exhaust.

SECRETARY. Fine! There's just one more question. How much do you want for him?

SANCHO. Well, I tell you what I'm gonna do. Today and today only, because you've been so sweet, I'm gonna let you steal this model from me! I'm gonna let you drive him off the lot for the simple price of, let's see, taxes and license included, $15,000.

SECRETARY. Fifteen thousand dollars? For a Mexican!!!!

SANCHO. Mexican? What are you talking about? This is a Mexican-American! We had to melt down two pachucos, a farmworker and three gabachos° to make this model! You want quality, but you gotta pay for it! This is no cheap run-about. He's got class!

SECRETARY. Okay, I'll take him.

SANCHO. You will?

SECRETARY. Here's your money.

SANCHO. You mind if I count it?

SECRETARY. Go right ahead.

SANCHO. Well, you'll get your pink slip in the mail. Oh, do you want me to wrap him up for you? We have a box in the back.

SECRETARY. No, thank you. The Governor is having a luncheon this afternoon, and we need a brown face in the crowd. How do I drive him?

gabachos: whites

SANCHO. Just snap your fingers. He'll do anything you want. (SECRETARY *snaps.* MEXICAN-AMERICAN *steps forward.*)

MEXICAN-AMERICAN. ¡Raza querida, vamos levantando armas para liberarnos de estos desgraciados gabachos que nos explotan! Vamos . . .°

SECRETARY. What did he say?

SANCHO. Something about taking up arms, killing white people, etc.

SECRETARY. But he's not supposed to say that!

SANCHO. Look, lady, don't blame me for bugs from the factory. He's your Mexican-American, you bought him, now drive him off the lot!

SECRETARY. But he's broken!

SANCHO. Try snapping another finger. (SECRETARY *snaps.* MEXICAN-AMERICAN *comes to life again.*)

MEXICAN-AMERICAN. Esta gran humanidad ha dicho basta! ¡Y se ha puesto en marcha! ¡Basta! ¡Basta! ¡Viva la raza! ¡Viva la causa! ¡Viva la huelga! ¡Vivan los brown berets! ¡Vivan los estudiantes!° ¡Chicano power! (*The* MEXICAN-AMERICAN *turns toward the* SECRETARY, *who gasps and backs up. He keeps turning toward the* PACHUCO, FARMWORKER *and* REVOLUCIONARIO, *snapping his fingers and turning each of them on, one by one.*)

PACHUCO (*Snap. To* SECRETARY). I'm going to get you, baby! ¡Viva la raza!

FARMWORKER (*Snap. To* SECRETARY). ¡Viva la huelga! ¡Viva la huelga! ¡Viva la huelga!

REVOLUCIONARIO (*Snap. To* SECRETARY). ¡Viva la revolución! (*The three models join together and advance toward the* SECRETARY, *who backs up and runs out of the shop screaming.* SANCHO *is at the other end of the shop holding his money in his hand. All freeze. After a few seconds of silence, the* PACHUCO *moves and stretches, shaking his arms and loosening up. The* FARMWORKER *and* REVOLUCIONARIO *do the same.* SANCHO *stays where he is, frozen to his spot.*)

JOHNNY. Man, that was a long one, ése. (*Others agree with him.*)

FARMWORKER. How did we do?

JOHNNY. Pretty good, look at all that lana,° man! (*He goes over to* SANCHO *and removes the money from his hand.* SANCHO *stays where he is.*)

REVOLUCIONARIO. En la madre, look at all the money.

JOHNNY. We keep this up, we're going to be rich.

FARMWORKER. They think we're machines.

REVOLUCIONARIO. Burros.

¡Raza querida . . . Vamos: Beloved members of our Mexican race, let's take up arms to free ourselves from those damned whites who exploit us! Let's go . . .   Esta . . . estudiantes!: This great mass of humanity has done enough talking! It has begun to march! Enough! Enough! Long live our race! Long live our cause! Long live the strike! Long live the brown berets! Long live the students!   lana: money

JOHNNY. Puppets.

MEXICAN-AMERICAN. The only thing I don't like is how come I always get to play the goddamn Mexican-American?

JOHNNY. That's what you get for finishing high school.

FARMWORKER. How about our wages, ése?

JOHNNY. Here it comes right now, $3,000 for you, $3,000 for you, $3,000 for you and $3,000 for me. The rest we put back into the business.

MEXICAN-AMERICAN. Too much, man. Hey, where you vatos° going tonight?

FARMWORKER. I'm going over to Concha's. There's a party.

JOHNNY. Wait a minute, vatos. What about our salesman? I think he needs an oil job.

REVOLUCIONARIO. Leave him to me. (*The* PACHUCO, FARMWORKER *and* MEXICAN-AMERICAN *exit, talking loudly about their plans for the night. The* REVOLUCIONARIO *goes over to* SANCHO, *removes his derby hat and cigar, lifts him up and throws him over his shoulder.* SANCHO *hangs loose, lifeless. To audience*) He's the best model we got! ¡Ajúa!° (*Exit.*)

QUESTIONS

1. "Honest Sancho" runs his "Used Mexican Lot" like a used car lot. How is this metaphorical context developed in the play? How is the satire directed at both used car salesmen and a Mexican who has sold out his race?

2. Explore the stereotyping that characterizes the "models" that Honest Sancho offers for sale. At whom is the satire directed—the four "models," or people who stereotype others? What is the implication of these men being presented as if they were machines?

3. Of the characters in the play, only Miss Jimenez escapes being portrayed as a machine. Is she therefore treated sympathetically by the play?

4. How effective is the surprise ending?

5. How do you think an audience composed entirely of Mexican Americans would respond to this play? an audience of Anglos? a mixed audience? Would there be differences among these audiences as to how comic the play is?

SUGGESTIONS FOR WRITING

1. Review the chapter on "Characterization" in the Fiction section of this book, paying particular attention to the qualities that contribute to a convincing character. Write an essay demonstrating that one or more characters in one of the plays in chapter 1 displays those qualities. If you are permitted the space to write a longer essay, extend the essay to include two of these plays, one more realistic than the other.

2. After reviewing the chapter on "Plot" in the Fiction section of this book, write an analysis of the plot of one of the plays in chapter 1. To what extent does plot help to determine whether a play is realistic or nonrealistic?

vatos: guys   ¡Ajúa!: Wow!

3. The three plays in this chapter represent a range from realistic to nonrealistic conventions. Using the materials in the opening discussion of those conventions, write an essay on realistic elements in *A Doll House* or *The Glass Menagerie;* or an essay on nonrealistic elements in *The Glass Menagerie* or "Los Vendidos." In each case, consider the way in which the conventions are used to represent human realities and themes.

4. In any classification of the plays in chapter 1, Glaspell's *Trifles* would undoubtedly be called realistic, Ives's *Time Flies* nonrealistic. Write an essay in which you classify any of the other plays in chapter 1 based on the criterion of faithfulness "to the outer appearances of life."

5. In some plays, the audience only gradually realizes that the incidents are not literally possible. In others (such as Albee's "The Sandbox" or Ives's "Time Flies"), the play establishes its unreality early on. Using two or three of the plays presented so far, discuss the advantages and disadvantages of either approach.

6. Write an essay ranking the plays in chapter 1 in terms of their presentation of "life's inner meanings"—their revelation of "human truth."

7. You have had the opportunity to read eight plays thus far. Write an essay in which you use some or all of them to create a hypothesis about the correlation between realistic conventions and significant insights into human behavior.

8. Through the centuries, theatrical producers and writers have sometimes sought to modernize older plays, chiefly by recasting them in the conventions of contemporary theater. Considering the plays you have read so far, and considering the remainder of the plays as you read on in this book, write an essay in which you explore what would be necessary to modernize one of them. Would you find it always appropriate to remove the nonrealistic elements in the play so as to appeal to today's audience—or might you want to adapt the play for that part of the audience that prefers musical dramas?

PRACTICE AP WRITING PROMPTS ▩▩▩▩▩

Henrik Ibsen, *A Doll House* (pp. 1117–1177)

Answer the following prompt using *A Doll House* or another literary work that presents a conflict with society.

Many works of literature include characters who experience troubling conflicts with the accepted norms of their society. Choose such a character from a novel or play and write a well-organized essay in which you analyze the character's divergence from these societal norms. Include in your essay the significance of this conflict to the work as a whole. Avoid merely providing a plot summary.

Tennessee Williams, *The Glass Menagerie* (pp. 1177–1227)

American author John Updike stated, "In memory's telephoto lens, far objects are magnified." Choose a character from a novel or play whose memories are "magnified" as if through such a lens. Write an essay in which you analyze how these magnified or distorted memories drive the character's emotions and behavior, and discuss the impact of these memories on the meaning of the work as a whole.

....

CHAPTER THREE

Tragedy and Comedy

The two masks of drama—one with the corners of its mouth turned down expressing agony or suffering, the other with the corners of its mouth turned up expressing joy or laughter—are familiar everywhere. Derived from masks actually worn by the actors in ancient Greek plays, they symbolize two principal modes of drama. Indeed, just as life gravitates between tears and laughter, they seem to imply that all drama is divided between **tragedy** and **comedy**.

But drama is an ancient literary form; in its development from the beginnings to the present it has produced a rich variety of plays. Can all these plays be classified under two terms? If our answer to this question is Yes, we must define the terms very broadly. If our answer is No, then how many terms do we need, and where do we stop? Polonius, in *Hamlet*, says of a visiting troupe of players that they can act "tragedy, comedy, history, pastoral, pastoral-comical, historical-pastoral, tragical-historical, tragical-comical-historical-pastoral, scene individable, or poem unlimited." Like Polonius himself, his list seems ridiculous. Moreover, even if we adopted these terms, and more, could we be sure that they would accurately classify all plays or that a new play, written tomorrow, would not demand a totally new category?

The discussion that follows proceeds on four assumptions. First, perfect definitions and an airtight system of classification are impossible. There exist no views of tragedy and comedy that have not been challenged and no classification system that unequivocally provides for all examples. Second, it is quite unnecessary that we classify each play we read or see. The most important questions to ask about a play are not "Is this a tragedy?" or "Is this a comedy?" but "Does this play furnish an enjoyable, valid, and significant experience?" Third, the quality of experience furnished by a play may be partially dependent on our perception of its relationship to earlier literary forms, and therefore familiarity with traditional notions of tragedy and comedy is important for our understanding and appreciation of plays. Many of the conventions used in specific plays have been determined by the kind of play the author intended to write. Other plays have been written in deliberate defiance of these conventions. Fourth, whether or not tragedy and comedy be taken as the two all-inclusive dramatic modes, they are certainly, as symbolized by the masks, the two principal ones, and useful points, therefore, from which to begin discussion.

The popular distinctions between comedy and tragedy are fairly simple: comedy is funny; tragedy is sad. Comedy has a happy ending; tragedy an unhappy one. The typical ending for comedy is a marriage; the typical ending for tragedy is a death. There is some truth in these notions, but only some. Some plays called comedies make no attempt to be funny. Successful tragedies, though they involve suffering and sadness, do not leave the spectator depressed. Some funny plays have sad endings: they send the viewer away with a lump in the throat. A few plays usually classified as tragedies do not have unhappy endings but conclude with the protagonist's triumph. In short, the popular distinctions are unreliable. Though we need not abandon them entirely, we must take a more complex view. Let us begin with tragedy.

The first great theorist of dramatic art was Aristotle (384–322 B.C.), whose discussion of tragedy in *Poetics* has dominated critical thought ever since. A very brief summary of Aristotle's view will be helpful.

A tragedy, so Aristotle wrote, is the imitation in dramatic form of an action that is serious and complete, with incidents arousing pity and fear with which it effects a **catharsis** of such emotions. The language used is pleasurable and appropriate throughout to the situation. The chief characters are noble personages ("better than ourselves," says Aristotle), and the actions they perform are noble actions. The plot involves a change in the protagonist's fortune, in which he usually, but not always, falls from happiness to misery. The protagonist, though not perfect, is hardly a bad person; his misfortunes result not from character deficiencies but rather from what Aristotle calls **hamartia**, a criminal act committed in ignorance of some material fact or even for the sake of a greater good. A tragic plot has organic unity: the events follow not just *after* one another but *because* of one another. The best tragic plots involve a reversal (a change from one state of things within the play to its opposite) or a discovery (a change from ignorance to knowledge) or both.

In the more extensive account that follows, we will not attempt to delineate the boundaries of tragedy or necessarily describe it at its greatest. Instead, we will describe a common understanding of tragedy as a point of departure for further discussion. Nor shall we enter into the endless controversies over what Aristotle meant by "catharsis" or over which of his statements are meant to apply to all tragedies and which only to the best ones. The important thing is that Aristotle had important insights into the nature of some of the greatest tragedies and that, rightly or wrongly interpreted, his conceptions are the basis for a kind of archetypal notion of tragedy that has dominated critical thought. What are the central features of that archetype? (The following summary retains Aristotle's reference to the tragic protagonist in masculine terms; however, the definitions apply equally to female protagonists such as Sophocles's Antigone and Shakespeare's Cleopatra.)

1. The tragic hero is a man of noble stature. He has a greatness about him. He is not an ordinary man but one of outstanding quality. In Greek and in Shakespearean tragedy, he is usually a prince or a king. We may, if we wish, set down this predilection of former times for kings as tragic heroes as an undemocratic prejudice that regarded some men to be of nobler "blood" than others—preeminent by virtue of their aristocratic birth. But it is only partially that. We may with equal validity regard the hero's kingship as the symbol rather than as the cause of his greatness. He is great not primarily by virtue of his kingship but by his possession of extraordinary powers, by qualities of passion or aspiration or nobility of mind. The tragic hero's kingship is also a symbol of his initial good fortune, the mark of his high position. If the hero's fall is to arouse in us the emotions of pity and fear, it must be a fall from a height. A clumsy man tripping over his shoelace is comic, not tragic—even if it could cause him serious physical pain.

2. The tragic hero is good, though not perfect, and his fall results from his committing what Aristotle calls "an act of injustice" (*hamartia*) either through ignorance or from a conviction that some greater good will be served. This act is, nevertheless, a criminal one, and the good hero is still responsible for it, even if he is totally unaware of its criminality and is acting out of the best intentions. Some later critics ignore Aristotle's insistence on the hero's commission of a guilty act and choose instead to blame the hero's fall on a flaw in his character or personality. Such a notion misrepresents Aristotle's view both of tragedy and of a basically just natural order. It implies a world in which personality alone, not one's actions, can bring on catastrophe.

Aristotle notwithstanding, there is a critical tradition that attributes the fall of the hero to a so-called "tragic flaw"—some fault of character such as inordinate ambition, quickness to anger, a tendency to jealousy, or overweening pride. Conversely, the protagonist's vulnerability has been attributed to some excess of virtue—a nobility of character that unfits him for life among ordinary mortals. But whatever it be—a criminal act, a fault of character, or excessive virtue—the protagonist is personally responsible for his downfall.

3. The hero's downfall, therefore, is his own fault, the result of his own free choice—not the result of pure accident or someone else's villainy or some overriding malignant fate. Accident, villainy, or fate may contribute to the downfall but only as cooperating agents: they are not alone responsible. The combination of the hero's greatness and his responsibility for his own downfall is what entitles us to describe his downfall as tragic rather than as merely pathetic. In common speech these two adjectives are often confused. If a father of ten children is accidentally killed at a street corner, the event, strictly speaking, is pathetic, not tragic. When a weak man succumbs to his weakness and comes to a bad end, the event should be called pathetic, not tragic. The tragic event involves a fall from greatness, brought about, at least partially, by the agent's free action.

4. Nevertheless, the hero's misfortune is not wholly deserved. The punishment exceeds the crime. We do not come away from tragedy with the feeling that "he got what he had coming to him" but rather with the sad sense of a waste of human potential. For what most impresses us about the tragic hero is not his weakness but his greatness. He is, in a sense, "larger than life," or, as Aristotle said, "better than ourselves." He reveals to us the dimensions of human possibility. He is a person mainly admirable, and his fall therefore fills us with pity and fear.

5. Yet the tragic fall is not pure loss. Though it may result in the protagonist's death, it involves, before his death, some increase in awareness, some gain in self-knowledge—as Aristotle puts it, some "discovery"—a change from ignorance to knowledge. On the level of plot, the discovery may be merely learning the truth about some fact or situation of which the protagonist was ignorant, but on the level of character it is accompanied or followed by a significant insight, a fuller self-knowledge, an increase not only in knowledge but in wisdom. Often this increase in wisdom involves some sort of reconciliation with the universe or with the protagonist's situation. He exits not cursing his fate but accepting it and acknowledging that it is to some degree just.

6. Though it arouses solemn emotions—pity and fear, says Aristotle, but compassion and awe might be better terms—tragedy, when well performed, does not leave its audience in a state of depression. Though we cannot be sure what Aristotle meant by his term "catharsis," some sort of emotional release at the end is a common experience of those who witness great tragedies on the stage. They have been greatly moved by pity, fear, and associated emotions, but they are not left emotionally beaten down or dejected. Instead, there may be a feeling almost of exhilaration. This feeling is a response to the tragic action. With the fall of the hero and his

gain in wisdom or self-knowledge, there is, besides the appalling sense of human waste, a fresh recognition of human greatness, a sense that human life has unrealized potentialities. Though the hero may be defeated, he at least has dared greatly, and he gains understanding from his defeat.

Is the comic mask laughing or smiling? The question is more important than it may at first appear, for usually we laugh *at* something but smile *with* someone. The laugh expresses recognition of some absurdity in human behavior; the smile expresses pleasure in someone's company or good fortune.

The comic mask may be interpreted both ways. Historically, there have been two chief kinds of comedy—**scornful comedy** and **romantic comedy**, laughing comedy and smiling comedy. Of the two, scornful or satiric comedy is the older and probably still the more dominant.

The most essential difference between tragedy and comedy, particularly scornful comedy, is in their depiction of human nature. Where tragedy emphasizes human greatness, comedy delineates human weakness. Where tragedy celebrates human freedom, comedy points up human limitations. Wherever human beings fail to measure up to their own resolutions or to their own self-conceptions, wherever they are guilty of hypocrisy, vanity, or folly, wherever they fly in the face of good sense and rational behavior, comedy exhibits their absurdity and invites us to laugh at them. Where tragedy tends to say, with Shakespeare's Hamlet, "What a piece of work is a man! how noble in reason! how infinite in faculty! in form and moving how express and admirable! in action how like an angel! in apprehension how like a god!" comedy says, with Shakespeare's Puck, "Lord, what fools these mortals be!"

Because comedy exposes human folly, its function is partly critical and corrective. Where tragedy challenges us with a vision of human possibility, comedy reveals to us a spectacle of human ridiculousness that it makes us want to avoid. No doubt, we should not exaggerate this function of comedy. We go to the theater primarily for enjoyment, not to receive lessons in personality or character development. Nevertheless, laughter may be educative at the same time that it is enjoyable. The comedies of Aristophanes and Molière, of Ben Jonson and Congreve, are, first of all, good fun, but, secondly, they are antidotes for human folly.

Romantic or smiling comedy, as opposed to scornful comedy, and as exemplified by many plays of Shakespeare—*A Midsummer Night's Dream, As You Like It, Twelfth Night, Much Ado About Nothing, The Tempest*, for instance—puts its emphasis upon sympathetic rather than ridiculous characters. These characters—likable, not given up to folly or vanity—are placed in various kinds of difficulties from which, at the end of the play, they are rescued, attaining their ends or having their good fortunes restored.

Though different from the protagonists of scornful comedy, however, these characters are not the commanding or lofty figures that tragic protagonists are. They are sensible and good rather than noble, aspiring, and grand. They do not strike us with awe as the tragic protagonist does. They do not so challengingly test the limits of human possibility. In short, they move in a smaller world. Romantic comedies, therefore, do not occupy a different universe from satiric comedies; they simply lie at opposite sides of the same territory. The romantic comedy, moreover, though its protagonists are sympathetic, has usually a number of lesser characters whose folly is held up to ridicule. The satiric comedy, on the other hand, frequently has minor characters—often a pair of young lovers—who are sympathetic and likable. The difference between the two kinds of comedy may be only a matter of whether we laugh at the primary or at the secondary characters.

There are other differences between comedy and tragedy. The norms of comedy are primarily social. Where tragedies tend to isolate their protagonists to emphasize their uniqueness, comedies put their protagonists in the midst of a group to emphasize their commonness. Where tragic protagonists possess overpowering individuality, so that plays are often named after them (for example, *Oedipus Rex, Othello*), comic protagonists tend to be types of individuals, and the plays in which they appear are often named for the type (for example, Molière's *The Misanthrope*, Congreve's *The Double Dealer*). We judge tragic protagonists by absolute moral standards, by how far they soar above society. We judge comic protagonists by social standards, by how well they adjust to society and conform to the expectations of the group.

Finally, comic plots are less likely than tragic plots to exhibit the high degree of organic unity—of logical cause-and-effect progression—that Aristotle required of tragedy. Plausibility, in fact, is not usually the central characteristic of a comic plot. Unlikely coincidences, improbable disguises, mistaken identities—these are the stuff of which comedy is made; and, as long as they make us laugh and, at the same time, help to illuminate human nature and human folly, we need not greatly care. Not that plausibility is no longer important—only that other things are more important, and these other things are often achieved by the most outrageous violations of probability.

This is particularly true regarding the comic ending. *Conventionally*, comedies have a happy ending. The happy ending is, indeed, a *convention* of comedy, which is to say that a comedy ends happily because comedies end happily—that is the nature of the form—not necessarily because a happy ending is a plausible outcome of the events that have preceded it. The greatest masters of comedy—Aristophanes, Shakespeare, Molière—have often been extremely arbitrary in the manner in which they achieved their endings. The accidental discovery of a lost will, rescue by an act of divine intervention (*deus ex machina*), the sudden reform of a mean-spirited person into a friendly person—such devices have been used by the greatest comic writers. And, even where the ending is achieved more plausibly, comedy asks us to forget for the time being that in actuality life has no endings except for death. Marriage, which provides the ending for so many comedies, is really a beginning.

And now, though we do not wish to imitate the folly of Polonius, it is well that we define two additional terms: melodrama and farce. In the two-part classification suggested by the two symbolic masks, melodrama belongs with tragedy, and farce with comedy; but the differences are sufficient to make the two new terms useful.

Melodrama, like tragedy, attempts to arouse feelings of fear and pity, but it does so ordinarily through cruder means. The conflict is an oversimplified one between good and evil depicted in absolute terms. Plot is emphasized at the expense of characterization. Sensational incidents provide the staple of the plot. The young mother and her baby are evicted into a howling storm by the villain holding the mortgage; the heroine is tied to the railroad tracks as the express train approaches. Most important, good finally triumphs over evil, and the ending is happy. Typically, at the end, the hero marries the heroine; villainy is foiled or crushed. Melodrama may, of course, have different degrees of power and subtlety; it is not always as crude as its crudest examples. But in it, moral issues are typically oversimplified, and good is finally triumphant. Melodrama does not provide the complex insights of tragedy. It is usually commercial rather than literary. Much of what television and films present as science fiction, police or medical dramas, and thrillers are examples of melodrama.

Farce, more consistently than comedy, is aimed at rousing explosive laughter. But again the means are cruder. The conflicts are violent and usually at the physical level. Plot is emphasized at the expense of characterization, improbable situations and coincidence at the expense of articulated plot. Comic implausibility is raised to heights of absurd impossibility. Coarse wit, practical jokes, and physical action are staples. Characters trip over benches, insult each other, run into walls, knock each other down, get into brawls. Performed with gusto, farce may be hilariously funny. Psychologically, it may boost our spirits and purge us of hostility and aggression. In content, however, like melodrama, it is usually commercial rather than literary. Contemporary farces are a staple of the movies.

Now we have four classifications—tragedy, comedy, melodrama, farce—the latter two as appendages of the former. But none of these classifications is rigid. They blend into each other and defy exact definition. If we take them too seriously, the tragic mask may laugh, and the comic mask weep.

REVIEWING CHAPTER THREE
....

1. Summarize the main points of Aristotle's definition of tragedy, indicating where possible how these characteristics arouse responses from the audience.
2. Define the two major types of comedy, satiric and romantic, in terms of their materials and their effects on audiences.
3. Explain how melodrama and farce are related to the major genres of tragedy and comedy.
4. As you read the plays in this chapter, identify any melodramatic events in the tragedies and any farcical elements in the comedies.

SOPHOCLES

Oedipus Rex

The plots of Greek tragedies were based on legends with which Greek audiences were more or less familiar (as American audiences, for example, would be familiar with the major events in a historical play based on the life of Lincoln). These plays often owed much of their impact to the audience's previous knowledge of the characters and their fate, for it enabled the playwright to make powerful use of dramatic irony and allusion. Much of the audience's delight, in addition, came from seeing how the playwright worked out the details of the familiar story. The purpose of this introductory note is therefore to supply such information as the play's first audiences might be presumed to have had.

Because of a prophecy that their new son would kill his father, Laius and Jocasta, King and Queen of Thebes, gave their infant to a shepherd with orders that he be left on a mountainside to die. The shepherd, however, after having pinned the babe's ankles together, took pity on him and gave him instead to a Corinthian shepherd. This shepherd in turn presented him to Polybus and Merope, King and Queen of Corinth, who, childless, adopted him as their own. The child was given the name Oedipus ("Swollen-foot") because of the injury to his ankles.

When grown to manhood at Polybus's court, Oedipus was accused by a drunken guest of not being his father's son. Though reassured by Polybus and Merope, he was still disturbed and traveled to consult the Delphic oracle. The oracle, without answering the question about his parentage, prophesied that Oedipus would kill his father and beget children by his mother. Horrified, resolved to avert this fate, Oedipus determined never to return to Corinth. Traveling from Delphi, he came to a place where three roads met and was ordered off the road by a man in a chariot. Blows were exchanged, and Oedipus killed the man and four of his attendants. Later, on the outskirts of Thebes, he encountered the Sphinx, a monster with the head of a woman, wings of an eagle, and body of a lion, which was terrorizing Thebes by slaying all who failed to answer her riddle ("What goes on four legs in the morning, two legs at noon, and three legs in the evening?"). When Oedipus correctly answered the riddle ("man, for he crawls as an infant, walks erect as a man, and uses a staff in old age"), the Sphinx destroyed herself. As a reward, Oedipus was named King of Thebes to replace the recently slain Laius and was given the hand of Jocasta in marriage. With her, he ruled Thebes successfully for some years and had four children—two sons and two daughters. Then the city was afflicted by a plague. It is at this point that the action of Sophocles's play begins.

The play was first performed in Athens about 430 B.C. In the present version, prepared by Dudley Fitts and Robert Fitzgerald, the translators use spellings for the proper names that are closer to the original Greek than the more familiar Anglicized spellings used in this note. Sophocles (496?–406 B.C.), an active and devoted citizen of Athens during its democratic period, served as an elected general in an Athenian military expedition and held other posts of civic responsibility, but was most importantly its leading and most prolific tragic playwright.

Characters

OEDIPUS, *King of Thebes, supposed son of Polybus and Meropê, King and Queen of Corinth*
IOKASTÊ, *wife of Oedipus and widow of the late King Laïos*
KREON, *brother of Iokastê, a prince of Thebes*
TEIRESIAS, *a blind seer who serves Apollo*
PRIEST
MESSENGER, *from Corinth*
SHEPHERD, *former servant of Laïos*
SECOND MESSENGER, *from the palace*
CHORUS OF THEBAN ELDERS
CHORAGOS, *leader of the Chorus*
ANTIGONE *and* ISMENE, *young daughters of Oedipus and Iokastê. They appear in the Exodus but do not speak.*
SUPPLIANTS, GUARDS, SERVANTS

THE SCENE. *Before the palace of* OEDIPUS, *King of Thebes. A central door and two lateral doors open onto a platform which runs the length of the façade. On*

*the platform, right and left, are altars; and three steps lead down into the orchêstra,
or chorus-ground. At the beginning of the action these steps are crowded by suppliants who have brought branches and chaplets of olive leaves and who sit in various
attitudes of despair.* OEDIPUS *enters.*

PROLOGUE

OEDIPUS. My children, generations of the living
   In the line of Kadmos,° nursed at his ancient hearth:
   Why have you strewn yourselves before these altars
   In supplication, with your boughs and garlands?
   The breath of incense rises from the city   5
   With a sound of prayer and lamentation.
                     Children,
   I would not have you speak through messengers,
   And therefore I have come myself to hear you—
   I, Oedipus, who bear the famous name.
   (*To a* PRIEST) You, there, since you are eldest in the company,   10
   Speak for them all, tell me what preys upon you,
   Whether you come in dread, or crave some blessing:
   Tell me, and never doubt that I will help you
   In every way I can; I should be heartless
   Were I not moved to find you suppliant here.   15
PRIEST. Great Oedipus, O powerful king of Thebes!
   You see how all the ages of our people
   Cling to your altar steps: here are boys
   Who can barely stand alone, and here are priests
   By weight of age, as I am a priest of God,   20
   And young men chosen from those yet unmarried;
   As for the others, all that multitude,
   They wait with olive chaplets in the squares,
   At the two shrines of Pallas, and where Apollo
   Speaks in the glowing embers.
                 Your own eyes   25
   Must tell you: Thebes is tossed on a murdering sea
   And can not lift her head from the death surge.
   A rust consumes the buds and fruits of the earth;
   The herds are sick; children die unborn,
   And labor is vain. The god of plague and pyre   30
   Raids like detestable lightning through the city,

2. **Kadmos:** Founder of Thebes

And all the house of Kadmos is laid waste,
All emptied, and all darkened: Death alone
Battens upon the misery of Thebes.
You are not one of the immortal gods, we know;   35
Yet we have come to you to make our prayer
As to the man surest in mortal ways
And wisest in the ways of God. You saved us
From the Sphinx, that flinty singer, and the tribute
We paid to her so long; yet you were never   40
Better informed than we, nor could we teach you:
A god's touch, it seems, enabled you to help us.

Therefore, O mighty power, we turn to you:
Find us our safety, find us a remedy,
Whether by counsel of the gods or of men.   45
A king of wisdom tested in the past
Can act in a time of troubles, and act well.
Noblest of men, restore
Life to your city! Think how all men call you
Liberator for your boldness long ago;   50
Ah, when your years of kingship are remembered,
Let them not say *We rose, but later fell*—
Keep the State from going down in the storm!
Once, years ago, with happy augury,
You brought us fortune; be the same again!   55
No man questions your power to rule the land:
But rule over men, not over a dead city!
Ships are only hulls, high walls are nothing,
When no life moves in the empty passageways.

OEDIPUS. Poor children! You may be sure I know   60
All that you longed for in your coming here.
I know that you are deathly sick; and yet,
Sick as you are, not one is as sick as I.
Each of you suffers in himself alone
His anguish, not another's; but my spirit   65
Groans for the city, for myself, for you.

I was not sleeping, you are not waking me.
No, I have been in tears for a long while
And in my restless thought walked many ways.
In all my search I found one remedy,   70
And I have adopted it: I have sent Kreon,

Son of Menoikeus, brother of the queen,
To Delphi, Apollo's place of revelation,
To learn there, if he can,
What act or pledge of mine may save the city. 75
I have counted the days, and now, this very day,
I am troubled, for he has overstayed his time.
What is he doing? He has been gone too long.
Yet whenever he comes back, I should do ill
Not to take any action the god orders. 80

PRIEST. It is a timely promise. At this instant
They tell me Kreon is here.

OEDIPUS.   O Lord Apollo!
May his news be fair as his face is radiant!

PRIEST. Good news, I gather! he is crowned with bay,
The chaplet is thick with berries.

OEDIPUS.   We shall soon know; 85
He is near enough to hear us now. (*Enter* KREON.) O prince:
Brother: son of Menoikeus:
What answer do you bring us from the god?

KREON. A strong one. I can tell you, great afflictions
Will turn out well, if they are taken well. 90

OEDIPUS. What was the oracle? These vague words
Leave me still hanging between hope and fear.

KREON. Is it your pleasure to hear me with all these
Gathered around us? I am prepared to speak,
But should we not go in?

OEDIPUS.   Speak to them all, 95
It is for them I suffer, more than for myself.

KREON. Then I will tell you what I heard at Delphi.
In plain words
The god commands us to expel from the land of Thebes
An old defilement we are sheltering. 100
It is a deathly thing, beyond cure;
We must not let it feed upon us longer.

OEDIPUS. What defilement? How shall we rid ourselves of it?

KREON. By exile or death, blood for blood. It was
Murder that brought the plague-wind on the city. 105

OEDIPUS. Murder of whom? Surely the god has named him?

KREON. My lord: Laïos once ruled this land,
Before you came to govern us.

OEDIPUS.   I know;
I learned of him from others; I never saw him.

KREON. He was murdered; and Apollo commands us now   110
   To take revenge upon whoever killed him.
OEDIPUS. Upon whom? Where are they? Where shall we find a clue
   To solve that crime after so many years?
KREON. Here in this land, he said. Search reveals
   Things that escape an inattentive man.   115
OEDIPUS. Tell me: Was Laïos murdered in his house,
   Or in the fields, or in some foreign country?
KREON. He said he planned to make a pilgrimage.
   He did not come home again.
OEDIPUS.   And was there no one,
   No witness, no companion, to tell what happened?   120
KREON. They were all killed but one, and he got away,
   So frightened that he could remember one thing only.
OEDIPUS. What was that one thing? One may be the key
   To everything, if we resolve to use it.
KREON. He said that a band of highwaymen attacked them,   125
   Outnumbered them, and overwhelmed the king.
OEDIPUS. Strange, that a highwayman should be so daring—
   Unless some faction here bribed him to do it.
KREON. We thought of that. But after Laïos's death
   New troubles arose and we had no avenger.   130
OEDIPUS. What troubles could prevent your hunting
   down the killers?
KREON. The riddling Sphinx's song
   Made us deaf to all mysteries but her own.
OEDIPUS. Then once more I must bring what is dark
   to light.
   It is most fitting that Apollo shows,   135
   As you do, this compunction for the dead.
   You shall see how I stand by you, as I should,
   Avenging this country and the god as well,
   And not as though it were for some distant friend,
   But for my own sake, to be rid of evil.   140
   Whoever killed King Laïos might—who knows?—
   Lay violent hands even on me—and soon.
   I act for the murdered king in my own interest.

   Come, then, my children: leave the altar steps,
   Lift up your olive boughs!
                    One of you go   145
   And summon the people of Kadmos to gather here.

I will do all that I can; you may tell them that. (*Exit a* PAGE.)
So, with the help of God,
We shall be saved—or else indeed we are lost.

PRIEST. Let us rise, children. It was for this we came,   150
And now the king has promised it.
Phoibus° has sent us an oracle; may he descend
Himself to save us and drive out the plague. (*Exeunt* OEDIPUS *and*
KREON *into the palace by the central door. The* PRIEST *and the* SUPPLIANTS
disperse right and left. After a short pause the CHORUS *enters the orchêstra.*)

PÁRODOS°

STROPHE I

CHORUS. What is God singing in his profound
Delphi of gold and shadow?   155
What oracle for Thebes, the sunwhipped city?
Fear unjoints me, the roots of my heart tremble.
Now I remember, O Healer, your power, and wonder:
Will you send doom like a sudden cloud, or weave it
Like nightfall of the past?   160
Speak to me, tell me, O
Child of golden Hope, immortal Voice.

ANTISTROPHE I

Let me pray to Athenê, the immortal daughter of Zeus,
And to Artemis her sister
Who keeps her famous throne in the market ring,   165
And to Apollo, archer from distant heaven—
O gods, descend! Like three streams leap against
The fires of our grief, the fires of darkness;
Be swift to bring us rest!
As in the old time from the brilliant house   170
Of air you stepped to save us, come again!

152. **Phoibus:** Apollo, god of light and truth
Párodos: The song or ode chanted by the chorus on their entry. It is accompanied by dancing
and music played on a flute. The chorus, in this play, represents elders of the city of Thebes. They
remain on stage (on a level lower than the principal actors) for the remainder of the play. The choral
odes and dances serve to separate one scene from another (there was no curtain in Greek theater) as
well as to comment on the action, reinforce the emotion, and interpret the situation. The chorus
also performs dance movements during certain portions of the scenes themselves. *Strophe* and
antistrophe are terms denoting the movement and countermovement of the chorus from one side of
their playing area to the other. When the chorus participates in dialogue with the other characters,
their lines are spoken by the Choragos, their leader.

STROPHE 2

Now our afflictions have no end,
Now all our stricken host lies down
And no man fights off death with his mind;
The noble plowland bears no grain,   175
And groaning mothers can not bear—
See, how our lives like birds take wing,
Like sparks that fly when a fire soars,
To the shore of the god of evening.

ANTISTROPHE 2

The plague burns on, it is pitiless,   180
Though pallid children laden with death
Lie unwept in the stony ways,
And old gray women by every path
Flock to the strand about the altars
There to strike their breasts and cry   185
Worship of Phoibus in wailing prayers:
Be kind, God's golden child!

STROPHE 3

There are no swords in this attack by fire,
No shields, but we are ringed with cries.
Send the besieger plunging from our homes   190
Into the vast sea-room of the Atlantic
Or into the waves that foam eastward of Thrace—
For the day ravages what the night spares—
Destroy our enemy, lord of the thunder!
Let him be riven by lightning from heaven!   195

ANTISTROPHE 3

Phoibus Apollo, stretch the sun's bowstring,
That golden cord, until it sing for us,
Flashing arrows in heaven!
                              Artemis, Huntress,
Race with flaring lights upon our mountains!
O scarlet god,° O golden-banded brow,   200
O Theban Bacchos in a storm of Maenads, (*Enter* OEDIPUS, *center.*)

---

200. **scarlet god:** Bacchos, god of wine and revelry; the Maenads were his female attendants.

Whirl upon Death, that all the Undying hate!
Come with blinding torches, come in joy!

SCENE I

OEDIPUS. Is this your prayer? It may be answered. Come,
    Listen to me, act as the crisis demands,   205
    And you shall have relief from all these evils.

    Until now I was a stranger to this tale,
    As I had been a stranger to the crime.
    Could I track down the murderer without a clue?
    But now, friends,   210
    As one who became a citizen after the murder,
    I make this proclamation to all Thebans:
    If any man knows by whose hand Laïos, son of Labdakos,
    Met his death, I direct that man to tell me everything,
    No matter what he fears for having so long withheld it.   215
    Let it stand as promised that no further trouble
    Will come to him, but he may leave the land in safety.
    Moreover: If anyone knows the murderer to be foreign,
    Let him not keep silent: he shall have his reward from me.
    However, if he does conceal it; if any man   220
    Fearing for his friend or for himself disobeys this edict,
    Hear what I propose to do:

    I solemnly forbid the people of this country,
    Where power and throne are mine, ever to receive that man
    Or speak to him, no matter who he is, or let him   225
    Join in sacrifice, lustration, or in prayer.
    I decree that he be driven from every house,
    Being, as he is, corruption itself to us: the Delphic
    Voice of Apollo has pronounced this revelation.
    Thus I associate myself with the oracle   230
    And take the side of the murdered king.
    As for the criminal, I pray to God—
    Whether it be a lurking thief, or one of a number—
    I pray that that man's life be consumed in evil and wretchedness.
    And as for me, this curse applies no less   235
    If it should turn out that the culprit is my guest here,
    Sharing my hearth.
                You have heard the penalty.

I lay it on you now to attend to this
For my sake, for Apollo's, for the sick
Sterile city that heaven has abandoned. 240
Suppose the oracle had given you no command:
Should this defilement go uncleansed for ever?
You should have found the murderer: your king,
A noble king, had been destroyed!

                 Now I,
Having the power that he held before me, 245
Having his bed, begetting children there
Upon his wife, as he would have, had he lived—
Their son would have been my children's brother,
If Laïos had had luck in fatherhood!
(And now his bad fortune has struck him down)— 250
I say I take the son's part, just as though
I were his son, to press the fight for him
And see it won! I'll find the hand that brought
Death to Labdakos's and Polydoros's child,
Heir of Kadmos's and Agenor's line.° 255
And as for those who fail me,
May the gods deny them the fruit of the earth,
Fruit of the womb, and may they rot utterly!
Let them be wretched as we are wretched, and worse!

For you, for loyal Thebans, and for all 260
Who find my actions right, I pray the favor
Of justice, and of all the immortal gods.
CHORAGOS. Since I am under oath, my lord, I swear
I did not do the murder, I can not name
The murderer. Phoibus ordained the search; 265
Why did he not say who the culprit was?
OEDIPUS. An honest question. But no man in the world
Can make the gods do more than the gods will.
CHORAGOS. There is an alternative, I think—
OEDIPUS.   Tell me. 270
Any or all, you must not fail to tell me.
CHORAGOS. A lord clairvoyant to the lord Apollo,
As we all know, is the skilled Teiresias.
One might learn much about this from him, Oedipus.

254–55. **Labdakos, Polydoros, Kadmos, and Agenor:** father, grandfather, great-grandfather, and great-great-grandfather of Laïos

OEDIPUS. I am not wasting time:
    Kreon spoke of this, and I have sent for him—   275
    Twice, in fact; it is strange that he is not here.
CHORAGOS. The other matter—that old report—seems useless.
OEDIPUS. What was that? I am interested in all reports.
CHORAGOS. The king was said to have been killed by highwaymen.
OEDIPUS. I know. But we have no witness to that.   280
CHORAGOS. If the killer can feel a particle of dread,
    Your curse will bring him out of hiding!
OEDIPUS.   No,
    The man who dared that act will fear no curse.
    (*Enter the blind seer* TEIRESIAS, *led by a* PAGE.)
CHORAGOS. But there is one man who may detect the criminal.
    This is Teiresias, this is the holy prophet   285
    In whom, alone of all men, truth was born.
OEDIPUS. Teiresias: seer: student of mysteries,
    Of all that's taught and all that no man tells,
    Secrets of Heaven and secrets of the earth:
    Blind though you are, you know the city lies   290
    Sick with plague; and from this plague, my lord,
    We find that you alone can guard or save us.

    Possibly you did not hear the messengers?
    Apollo, when we sent to him,
    Sent us back word that this great pestilence   295
    Would lift, but only if we established clearly
    The identity of those who murdered Laïos.
    They must be killed or exiled.
                                Can you use
    Birdflight° or any art of divination
    To purify yourself, and Thebes, and me   300
    From this contagion? We are in your hands.
    There is no fairer duty
    Than that of helping others in distress.
TEIRESIAS. How dreadful knowledge of the truth can be
    When there's no help in truth! I knew this well,   305
    But did not act on it: else I should not have come.
OEDIPUS. What is troubling you? Why are your eyes so cold?
TEIRESIAS. Let me go home. Bear your own fate, and I'll

---

299. Birdflight: Prophets predicted the future or divined the unknown by observing the flight of birds.

Bear mine. It is better so: trust what I say.

OEDIPUS. What you say is ungracious and unhelpful   310
To your native country. Do not refuse to speak.

TEIRESIAS. When it comes to speech, your own is neither temperate
Nor opportune. I wish to be more prudent.

OEDIPUS. In God's name, we all beg you—

TEIRESIAS.   You are all ignorant.
No; I will never tell you what I know.   315
Now it is my misery; then, it would be yours.

OEDIPUS. What! You do know something, and will not tell us?
You would betray us all and wreck the State?

TEIRESIAS. I do not intend to torture myself, or you.
Why persist in asking? You will not persuade me.   320

OEDIPUS. What a wicked old man you are! You'd try a stone's
Patience! Out with it! Have you no feeling at all?

TEIRESIAS. You call me unfeeling. If you could only see
The nature of your own feelings . . .

OEDIPUS.   Why,
Who would not feel as I do? Who could endure   325
Your arrogance toward the city?

TEIRESIAS.   What does it matter?
Whether I speak or not, it is bound to come.

OEDIPUS. Then, if "it" is bound to come, you are bound to tell me.

TEIRESIAS. No, I will not go on. Rage as you please.

OEDIPUS. Rage? Why not!
                         And I'll tell you what I think: 330
You planned it, you had it done, you all but
Killed him with your own hands: if you had eyes,
I'd say the crime was yours, and yours alone.

TEIRESIAS. So? I charge you, then,
Abide by the proclamation you have made: 335
From this day forth
Never speak again to these men or me;
You yourself are the pollution of this country.

OEDIPUS. You dare say that! Can you possibly think you have
Some way of going free, after such insolence?   340

TEIRESIAS. I have gone free. It is the truth sustains me.

OEDIPUS. Who taught you shamelessness? It was not your craft.

TEIRESIAS. You did. You made me speak. I did not want to.

OEDIPUS. Speak what? Let me hear it again more clearly.

TEIRESIAS. Was it not clear before? Are you tempting me?   345

OEDIPUS. I did not understand it. Say it again.

TEIRESIAS. I say that you are the murderer whom you seek.

OEDIPUS. Now twice you have spat out infamy. You'll pay for it!

TEIRESIAS. Would you care for more? Do you wish to be really angry?

OEDIPUS. Say what you will. Whatever you say is worthless. 350

TEIRESIAS. I say you live in hideous shame with those

    Most dear to you. You can not see the evil.

OEDIPUS. Can you go on babbling like this for ever?

TEIRESIAS. I can, if there is power in truth.

OEDIPUS.   There is:

    But not for you, not for you, 355

    You sightless, witless, senseless, mad old man!

TEIRESIAS. You are the madman. There is no one here

    Who will not curse you soon, as you curse me.

OEDIPUS. You child of total night! I would not touch you;

    Neither would any man who sees the sun. 360

TEIRESIAS. True: it is not from you my fate will come.

    That lies within Apollo's competence,

    As it is his concern.

OEDIPUS.   Tell me, who made

    These fine discoveries? Kreon? or someone else?

TEIRESIAS. Kreon is no threat. You weave your own doom. 365

OEDIPUS. Wealth, power, craft of statesmanship!

    Kingly position, everywhere admired!

    What savage envy is stored up against these,

    If Kreon, whom I trusted, Kreon my friend,

    For this great office which the city once 370

    Put in my hands unsought—if for this power

    Kreon desires in secret to destroy me!

    He has bought this decrepit fortune-teller, this

    Collector of dirty pennies, this prophet fraud—

    Why, he is no more clairvoyant than I am!

                        Tell us: 375

    Has your mystic mummery ever approached the truth?

    When that hellcat the Sphinx was performing here,

    What help were you to these people?

    Her magic was not for the first man who came along:

    It demanded a real exorcist. Your birds— 380

    What good were they? or the gods, for the matter of that?

    But I came by,

    Oedipus, the simple man, who knows nothing—

    I thought it out for myself, no birds helped me!

And this is the man you think you can destroy,   385
That you may be close to Kreon when he's king!
Well, you and your friend Kreon, it seems to me,
Will suffer most. If you were not an old man,
You would have paid already for your plot.

CHORAGOS. We can not see that his words or yours   390
Have been spoken except in anger, Oedipus,
And of anger we have no need. How to accomplish
The god's will best: that is what most concerns us.

TEIRESIAS. You are a king. But where argument's concerned
I am your man, as much a king as you.   395
I am not your servant, but Apollo's.
I have no need of Kreon or Kreon's name.
Listen to me. You mock my blindness, do you?
But I say that you, with both your eyes, are blind:
You can not see the wretchedness of your life,   400
Nor in whose house you live, no, nor with whom.
Who are your father and mother? Can you tell me?
You do not even know the blind wrongs
That you have done them, on earth and in the world below.
But the double lash of your parents' curse will whip you   405
Out of this land some day, with only night
Upon your precious eyes.
Your cries then—where will they not be heard?
What fastness of Kithairon° will not echo them?
And that bridal-descant of yours—you'll know it then,   410
The song they sang when you came here to Thebes
And found your misguided berthing.
All this, and more, that you can not guess at now,
Will bring you to yourself among your children.

Be angry, then. Curse Kreon. Curse my words.   415
I tell you, no man that walks upon the earth
Shall be rooted out more horribly than you.

OEDIPUS. Am I to bear this from him?—Damnation
Take you! Out of this place! Out of my sight!

TEIRESIAS. I would not have come at all if you had not asked me.   420

OEDIPUS. Could I have told that you'd talk nonsense, that
You'd come here to make a fool of yourself, and of me?

TEIRESIAS. A fool? Your parents thought me sane enough.

---

409. Kithairon: the mountain where Oedipus was taken to be exposed as an infant

OEDIPUS. My parents again!—Wait: who were my parents?

TEIRESIAS. This day will give you a father, and break your heart.   425

OEDIPUS. Your infantile riddles! Your damned abracadabra!

TEIRESIAS. You were a great man once at solving riddles.

OEDIPUS. Mock me with that if you like; you will find it true.

TEIRESIAS. It was true enough. It brought about your ruin.

OEDIPUS. But if it saved the town?

TEIRESIAS (*to the* PAGE).   Boy, give me your hand.   430

OEDIPUS. Yes, boy; lead him away.

             —While you are here
We can do nothing. Go; leave us in peace.

TEIRESIAS. I will go when I have said what I have to say.
How can you hurt me? And I tell you again:
The man you have been looking for all this time,   435
The damned man, the murderer of Laïos,
That man is in Thebes. To your mind he is foreign-born,
But it will soon be shown that he is a Theban,
A revelation that will fail to please.

               A blind man,
Who has his eyes now; a penniless man, who is rich now;   440
And he will go tapping the strange earth with his staff.
To the children with whom he lives now he will be
Brother and father—the very same; to her
Who bore him, son and husband—the very same
Who came to his father's bed, wet with his father's blood.   445
Enough. Go think that over.
If later you find error in what I have said,
You may say that I have no skill in prophecy.

(*Exit* TEIRESIAS, *led by his* PAGE. OEDIPUS *goes into the palace.*)

ODE I

STROPHE 1

CHORUS. The Delphic stone of prophecies
Remembers ancient regicide   450
And a still bloody hand.
That killer's hour of flight has come.
He must be stronger than riderless
Coursers of untiring wind,
For the son° of Zeus armed with his father's thunder   455
Leaps in lightning after him;
And the Furies hold his track, the sad Furies.

455. son: Apollo

ANTISTROPHE 1

Holy Parnassos'° peak of snow
Flashes and blinds that secret man,
That all shall hunt him down: 460
Though he may roam the forest shade
Like a bull gone wild from pasture
To rage through glooms of stone,
Doom comes down on him; flight will not avail him;
For the world's heart calls him desolate,   465
And the immortal voices follow, for ever follow.

STROPHE 2

But now a wilder thing is heard
From the old man skilled at hearing Fate in the wing-beat of a bird.
Bewildered as a blown bird, my soul hovers and can not find
Foothold in this debate, or any reason or rest of mind.   470
But no man ever brought—none can bring
Proof of strife between Thebes' royal house,
Labdakos's line, and the son of Polybos;
And never until now has any man brought word
Of Laïos's dark death staining Oedipus the King.   475

ANTISTROPHE 2

Divine Zeus and Apollo hold
Perfect intelligence alone of all tales ever told;
And well though this diviner works, he works in his own night;
No man can judge that rough unknown or trust in second sight,
For wisdom changes hands among the wise.   480
Shall I believe my great lord criminal
At a raging word that a blind old man let fall?
I saw him, when the carrion woman° faced him of old,
Prove his heroic mind. These evil words are lies.

SCENE 2

KREON. Men of Thebes:
I am told that heavy accusations   485
Have been brought against me by King Oedipus.

I am not the kind of man to bear this tamely.

---

458. **Parnassos:** mountain sacred to Apollo   483. **carrion woman:** the Sphinx

If in these present difficulties
He holds me accountable for any harm to him   490
Through anything I have said or done—why, then,
I do not value life in this dishonor.
It is not as though this rumor touched upon
Some private indiscretion. The matter is grave.
The fact is that I am being called disloyal   495
To the State, to my fellow citizens, to my friends.

CHORAGOS. He may have spoken in anger, not from his mind.

KREON. But did you not hear him say I was the one
Who seduced the old prophet into lying?

CHORAGOS. The thing was said; I do not know how seriously.   500

KREON. But you were watching him! Were his eyes steady?
Did he look like a man in his right mind?

CHORAGOS.   I do not know.
I can not judge the behavior of great men.
But here is the king himself. (*Enter* OEDIPUS.)

OEDIPUS.   So you dared come back.
Why? How brazen of you to come to my house,   505
You murderer!
                Do you think I do not know
That you plotted to kill me, plotted to steal my throne?
Tell me, in God's name: am I coward, a fool,
That you should dream you could accomplish this?
A fool who could not see your slippery game?   510
A coward, not to fight back when I saw it?
You are the fool, Kreon, are you not? hoping
Without support or friends to get a throne?
Thrones may be won or bought: you could do neither.

KREON. Now listen to me. You have talked; let me talk, too.   515
You can not judge unless you know the facts.

OEDIPUS. You speak well: there is one fact; but I find it hard
To learn from the deadliest enemy I have.

KREON. That above all I must dispute with you.

OEDIPUS. That above all I will not hear you deny.   520

KREON. If you think there is anything good in being stubborn
Against all reason, then I say you are wrong.

OEDIPUS. If you think a man can sin against his own kind
And not be punished for it, I say you are mad.

KREON. I agree. But tell me: what have I done to you?   525

OEDIPUS. You advised me to send for that wizard, did you not?

KREON. I did. I should do it again.

OEDIPUS.   Very well. Now tell me:

How long has it been since Laïos—

KREON.   What of Laïos?

OEDIPUS. Since he vanished in that onset by the road?

KREON. It was long ago, a long time.

OEDIPUS.   And this prophet,   530
Was he practicing here then?

KREON.   He was; and with honor, as now.

OEDIPUS. Did he speak of me at that time?

KREON.   He never did,
At least, not when I was present.

OEDIPUS.   But . . . the enquiry?
I suppose you held one?

KREON.   We did, but we learned nothing.

OEDIPUS. Why did the prophet not speak against me then?   535

KREON. I do not know; and I am the kind of man
Who holds his tongue when he has no facts to go on.

OEDIPUS. There's one fact that you know, and you could tell it.

KREON. What fact is that? If I know it, you shall have it.

OEDIPUS. If he were not involved with you, he could not say   540
That it was I who murdered Laïos.

KREON. If he says that, you are the one that knows it!—
But now it is my turn to question you.

OEDIPUS. Put your questions. I am no murderer.

KREON. First, then: You married my sister?

OEDIPUS.   I married your sister.   545

KREON. And you rule the kingdom equally with her?

OEDIPUS. Everything that she wants she has from me.

KREON. And I am the third, equal to both of you?

OEDIPUS. That is why I call you a bad friend.

KREON. No. Reason it out, as I have done.   550
Think of this first: Would any sane man prefer
Power, with all a king's anxieties,
To that same power and the grace of sleep?
Certainly not I.
I have never longed for the king's power—only his rights.   555
Would any wise man differ from me in this?
As the matters stand, I have my way in everything
With your consent, and no responsibilities.
If I were king, I should be a slave to policy.
How could I desire a scepter more   560
Than what is now mine—untroubled influence?

No, I have not gone mad; I need no honors,
Except those with the perquisites I have now.
I am welcome everywhere; every man salutes me,
And those who want your favor seek my ear,   565
Since I know how to manage what they ask.
Should I exchange this ease for that anxiety?
Besides, no sober mind is treasonable.
I hate anarchy
And never would deal with any man who likes it.   570
Test what I have said. Go to the priestess
At Delphi, ask if I quoted her correctly.
And as for this other thing: if I am found
Guilty of treason with Teiresias,
Then sentence me to death. You have my word   575
It is a sentence I should cast my vote for—
But not without evidence!
                               You do wrong
When you take good men for bad, bad men for good.
A true friend thrown aside—why, life itself
Is not more precious!
                               In time you will know this well: 580
For time, and time alone, will show the just man,
Though scoundrels are discovered in a day.
CHORAGOS. This is well said, and a prudent man would ponder it.
     Judgments too quickly formed are dangerous.
OEDIPUS. But is he not quick in his duplicity?   585
     And shall I not be quick to parry him?
     Would you have me stand still, hold my peace, and let
     This man win everything, through my inaction?
KREON. And you want—what is it, then? To banish me?
OEDIPUS. No, not exile. It is your death I want,   590
     So that all the world may see what treason means.
KREON. You will persist, then? You will not believe me?
OEDIPUS. How can I believe you?
KREON.   Then you are a fool.
OEDIPUS. To save myself?
KREON.   In justice, think of me.
OEDIPUS. You are evil incarnate.
KREON.   But suppose that you are wrong? 595
OEDIPUS. Still I must rule.
KREON.   But not if you rule badly.

OEDIPUS. O city, city!

KREON.   It is my city, too!

CHORAGOS. Now, my lords, be still. I see the queen,
    Iokastê, coming from her palace chambers;
    And it is time she came, for the sake of you both.   600
    This dreadful quarrel can be resolved through her. (*Enter* IOKASTÊ.)

IOKASTÊ. Poor foolish men, what wicked din is this?
    With Thebes sick to death, is it not shameful
    That you should rake some private quarrel up?
    (*To* OEDIPUS) Come into the house.

                            —And you, Kreon, go now: 605
    Let us have no more of this tumult over nothing.

KREON. Nothing? No, sister: what your husband plans for me
    Is one of two great evils: exile or death.

OEDIPUS. He is right.

              Why, woman I have caught him squarely
    Plotting against my life.

KREON.   No! Let me die   610
    Accurst if ever I have wished you harm!

IOKASTÊ. Ah, believe it, Oedipus!
    In the name of the gods, respect this oath of his
    For my sake, for the sake of these people here!

STROPHE 1

CHORAGOS. Open your mind to her, my lord. Be ruled by her, I beg you!

OEDIPUS. What would you have me do?   616

CHORAGOS. Respect Kreon's word. He has never spoken like a fool,
    And now he has sworn an oath.

OEDIPUS.   You know what you ask?

CHORAGOS.   I do.

OEDIPUS.   Speak on, then.

CHORAGOS. A friend so sworn should not be baited so,
    In blind malice, and without final proof.   620

OEDIPUS. You are aware, I hope, that what you say
    Means death for me, or exile at the least.

STROPHE 2

CHORAGOS. No, I swear by Helios, first in heaven!
            May I die friendless and accurst,
                The worst of deaths, if ever I meant that!   625
            It is the withering fields
            That hurt my sick heart:

> Must we bear all these ills,
> And now your blood as well?

OEDIPUS. Then let him go. And let me die, if I must,   630
Or be driven by him in shame from the land of Thebes.
It is your unhappiness, and not his talk,
That touches me.
> As for him—
Wherever he goes, hatred will follow him.

KREON. Ugly in yielding, as you were ugly in rage!   635
Natures like yours chiefly torment themselves.

OEDIPUS. Can you not go? Can you not leave me?

KREON.   I can.
You do not know me; but the city knows me,
And in its eyes I am just, if not in yours. (*Exit* KREON.)

ANTISTROPHE I

CHORAGOS. Lady Iokastê, did you not ask the King to go to his
chambers?   640

IOKASTÊ. First tell me what has happened.

CHORAGOS. There was suspicion without evidence; yet it rankled
As even false charges will.

IOKASTÊ.   On both sides?

CHORAGOS.   On both.

IOKASTÊ.   But what was said?

CHORAGOS. Oh let it rest, let it be done with!
Have we not suffered enough?   645

OEDIPUS. You see to what your decency has brought you:
You have made difficulties where my heart saw none.

ANTISTROPHE 2

CHORAGOS. Oedipus, it is not once only I have told you—
> You must know I should count myself unwise
> To the point of madness, should I now forsake you—   650
> You, under whose hand,
> In the storm of another time,
> Our dear land sailed out free.
> But now stand fast at the helm!

IOKASTÊ. In God's name, Oedipus, inform your wife as well: 655
Why are you so set in this hard anger?

OEDIPUS. I will tell you, for none of these men deserves
My confidence as you do. It is Kreon's work,

His treachery, his plotting against me.

IOKASTÊ. Go on, if you can make this clear to me. 660

OEDIPUS. He charges me with the murder of Laïos.

IOKASTÊ. Has he some knowledge? Or does he speak from
hearsay?

OEDIPUS. He would not commit himself to such a charge,
But he has brought in that damnable soothsayer
To tell his story.

IOKASTÊ.   Set your mind at rest. 665
If it is a question of soothsayers, I tell you
That you will find no man whose craft gives knowledge
Of the unknowable.

             Here is my proof:
An oracle was reported to Laïos once
(I will not say from Phoibos himself, but from 670
His appointed ministers, at any rate)
That his doom would be death at the hands of his own son—
His son, born of his flesh and of mine!

Now, you remember the story: Laïos was killed
By marauding strangers where three highways meet; 675
But his child had not been three days in this world
Before the king had pierced the baby's ankles
And left him to die on a lonely mountainside.

Thus, Apollo never caused that child
To kill his father, and it was not Laïos's fate 680
To die at the hands of his son, as he had feared.
This is what prophets and prophecies are worth!
Have no dread of them.

             It is God himself
Who can show us what he wills, in his own way.

OEDIPUS. How strange a shadowy memory crossed my mind, 685
Just now while you were speaking; it chilled my heart.

IOKASTÊ. What do you mean? What memory do you speak of?

OEDIPUS. If I understand you, Laïos was killed
At a place where three roads meet.

IOKASTÊ.   So it was said;
We have no later story.

OEDIPUS.   Where did it happen? 690

IOKASTÊ. Phokis, it is called: at a place where the Theban Way
Divides into the roads toward Delphi and Daulia.

OEDIPUS. When?

IOKASTÊ.   We had the news not long before you came
And proved the right to your succession here.

OEDIPUS. Ah, what net has God been weaving for me?   695

IOKASTÊ. Oedipus! Why does this trouble you?

OEDIPUS.   Do not ask me yet.
First, tell me how Laïos looked, and tell me
How old he was.

IOKASTÊ.   He was tall, his hair just touched
With white; his form was not unlike your own.

OEDIPUS. I think that I myself may be accurst   700
By my own ignorant edict.

IOKASTÊ.   You speak strangely.
It makes me tremble to look at you, my king.

OEDIPUS. I am not sure that the blind man can not see.
But I should know better if you were to tell me—

IOKASTÊ. Anything—though I dread to hear you ask it.   705

OEDIPUS. Was the king lightly escorted, or did he ride
With a large company, as a ruler should?

IOKASTÊ. There were five men with him in all: one was a herald;
And a single chariot, which he was driving.

OEDIPUS. Alas, that makes it plain enough!
                                   But who—   710
Who told you how it happened?

IOKASTÊ.   A household servant,
The only one to escape.

OEDIPUS.   And is he still
A servant of ours?

IOKASTÊ.   No; for when he came back at last
And found you enthroned in the place of the dead king,
He came to me, touched my hand with his, and begged   715
That I would send him away to the frontier district
Where only the shepherds go—
As far away from the city as I could send him.
I granted his prayer; for although the man was a slave,
He had earned more than this favor at my hands.   720

OEDIPUS. Can he be called back quickly?

IOKASTÊ.   Easily.
But why?

OEDIPUS. I have taken too much upon myself
Without enquiry; therefore I wish to consult him.

IOKASTÊ. Then he shall come.

                        But am I not one also
To whom you might confide these fears of yours?   725
OEDIPUS. That is your right; it will not be denied you,
    Now least of all; for I have reached a pitch
    Of wild foreboding. Is there anyone
    To whom I should sooner speak?

    Polybos of Corinth is my father.   730
    My mother is a Dorian: Meropê.
    I grew up chief among the men of Corinth
    Until a strange thing happened—
    Not worth my passion, it may be, but strange.
    At a feast, a drunken man maundering in his cups   735
    Cries out that I am not my father's son!

    I contained myself that night, though I felt anger
    And a sinking heart. The next day I visited
    My father and mother, and questioned them. They stormed,
    Calling it all the slanderous rant of a fool;   740
    And this relieved me. Yet the suspicion
    Remained always aching in my mind;
    I knew there was talk; I could not rest;
    And finally, saying nothing to my parents,
    I went to the shrine at Delphi.   745

    The god dismissed my question without reply;
    He spoke of other things.
                        Some were clear,
    Full of wretchedness, dreadful, unbearable:
    As, that I should lie with my own mother, breed
    Children from whom all men would turn their eyes;   750
    And that I should be my father's murderer.

    I heard all this, and fled. And from that day
    Corinth to me was only in the stars
    Descending in that quarter of the sky,
    As I wandered farther and farther on my way   755
    To a land where I should never see the evil
    Sung by the oracle. And I came to this country
    Where, so you say, King Laïos was killed.

    I will tell you all that happened there, my lady.
    There were three highways   760

Coming together at a place I passed;
And there a herald came towards me, and a chariot
Drawn by horses, with a man such as you describe
Seated in it. The groom leading the horses
Forced me off the road at his lord's command;   765
But as this charioteer lurched over towards me
I struck him in my rage. The old man saw me
And brought his double goad down upon my head
As I came abreast.
               He was paid back, and more!
Swinging my club in this right hand I knocked him   770
Out of his car, and he rolled on the ground.
                    I killed him.

I killed them all.
Now if that stranger and Laïos were—kin,
Where is a man more miserable than I?
More hated by the gods? Citizen and alien alike   775
Must never shelter me or speak to me—
I must be shunned by all.
                 And I myself
Pronounced this malediction upon myself!

Think of it: I have touched you with these hands,
These hands that killed your husband. What defilement!   780
Am I all evil, then? It must be so,
Since I must flee from Thebes, yet never again
See my own countrymen, my own country,
For fear of joining my mother in marriage
And killing Polybos, my father.
                   Ah,   785
If I was created so, born to this fate,
Who could deny the savagery of God?

O holy majesty of heavenly powers!
May I never see that day! Never!
Rather let me vanish from the race of men   790
Than know the abomination destined me!
CHORAGOS. We too, my lord, have felt dismay at this.
   But there is hope: you have yet to hear the shepherd.
OEDIPUS. Indeed, I fear no other hope is left me.
IOKASTÊ. What do you hope from him when he comes?
OEDIPUS.   This much: 795

If his account of the murder tallies with yours,
Then I am cleared.

IOKASTĒ.   What was it that I said
Of such importance?

OEDIPUS.   Why, "marauders," you said,
Killed the king, according to this man's story.
If he maintains that still, if there were several,   800
Clearly the guilt is not mine: I was alone.
But if he says one man, singlehanded, did it,
Then the evidence all points to me.

IOKASTĒ. You may be sure that he said there were several;
And can he call back that story now? He can not.   805
The whole city heard it as plainly as I.
But suppose he alters some detail of it:
He can not ever show that Laïos's death
Fulfilled the oracle: for Apollo said
My child was doomed to kill him; and my child—   810
Poor baby!—it was my child that died first.

No. From now on, where oracles are concerned,
I would not waste a second thought on any.

OEDIPUS. You may be right.
                         But come: let someone go
For the shepherd at once. This matter must be settled.   815

IOKASTĒ. I will send for him.
I would not wish to cross you in anything.
And surely not in this.—Let us go in. (*Exeunt into the palace.*)

ODE 2

STROPHE I

CHORUS. Let me be reverent in the ways of right,
Lowly the paths I journey on;   820
Let all my words and actions keep
The laws of the pure universe
From highest Heaven handed down
For Heaven is their bright nurse,
Those generations of the realms of light;   825
Ah, never of mortal kind were they begot,
Nor are they slaves of memory, lost in sleep:
Their Father is greater than Time, and ages not.

ANTISTROPHE 1

The tyrant is a child of Pride
Who drinks from his great sickening cup   830
Recklessness and vanity,
Until from his high crest headlong
He plummets to the dust of hope.
That strong man is not strong.
But let no fair ambition be denied;   835
May God protect the wrestler for the State
In government, in comely policy,
Who will fear God, and on His ordinance wait.

STROPHE 2

Haughtiness and the high hand of disdain
Tempt and outrage God's holy law;   840
And any mortal who dares hold
No immortal Power in awe
Will be caught up in a net of pain:
The price for which his levity is sold.
Let each man take due earnings, then,   845
And keep his hands from holy things,
And from blasphemy stand apart—
Else the crackling blast of heaven
Blows on his head, and on his desperate heart.
Though fools will honor impious men,   850
In their cities no tragic poet sings.

ANTISTROPHE 2

Shall we lose faith in Delphi's obscurities,
We who have heard the world's core
Discredited, and the sacred wood
Of Zeus at Elis praised no more?   855
The deeds and the strange prophecies
Must make a pattern yet to be understood.
Zeus, if indeed you are lord of all,
Throned in light over night and day,
Mirror this in your endless mind: 860
Our masters call the oracle
Words on the wind, and the Delphic vision blind!
Their hearts no longer know Apollo,
And reverence for the gods has died away.

SCENE 3

Enter IOKASTÊ.

IOKASTÊ. Princes of Thebes, it has occurred to me   865
    To visit the altars of the gods, bearing
    These branches as a suppliant, and this incense.
    Our king is not himself: his noble soul
    Is overwrought with fantasies of dread,
    Else he would consider   870
    The new prophecies in the light of the old.
    He will listen to any voice that speaks disaster,
    And my advice goes for nothing. (*She approaches the altar, right.*)
                       To you, then, Apollo,
    Lycéan lord, since you are nearest, I turn in prayer.
    Receive these offerings, and grant us deliverance   875
    From defilement. Our hearts are heavy with fear
    When we see our leader distracted, as helpless sailors
    Are terrified by the confusion of their helmsman. (*Enter* MESSENGER.)

MESSENGER. Friends, no doubt you can direct me:
    Where shall I find the house of Oedipus,   880
    Or, better still, where is the king himself?

CHORAGOS. It is this very place, stranger; he is inside.
    This is his wife and mother of his children.

MESSENGER. I wish her happiness in a happy house,
    Blest in all the fulfillment of her marriage.   885

IOKASTÊ. I wish as much for you: your courtesy
    Deserves a like good fortune. But now, tell me:
    Why have you come? What have you to say to us?

MESSENGER. Good news, my lady, for your house and your husband.

IOKASTÊ. What news? Who sent you here?

MESSENGER.   I am from Corinth.   890
    The news I bring ought to mean joy for you,
    Though it may be you will find some grief in it.

IOKASTÊ. What is it? How can it touch us in both ways?

MESSENGER. The word is that the people of the Isthmus
    Intend to call Oedipus to be their king.   895

IOKASTÊ. But old King Polybos—is he not reigning still?

MESSENGER. No. Death holds him in his sepulcher.

IOKASTÊ. What are you saying? Polybos is dead?

MESSENGER. If I am not telling the truth, may I die myself.

IOKASTÊ (*to a* MAIDSERVANT). Go in, go quickly; tell this to your
    master.   900
    O riddlers of God's will, where are you now!
    This was the man whom Oedipus, long ago,

Feared so, fled so, in dread of destroying him—
But it was another fate by which he died. (*Enter* OEDIPUS, *center.*)

OEDIPUS. Dearest Iokastê, why have you sent for me?   905

IOKASTÊ. Listen to what this man says, and then tell me
What has become of the solemn prophecies.

OEDIPUS. Who is this man? What is his news for me?

IOKASTÊ. He has come from Corinth to announce your father's death!

OEDIPUS. Is it true, stranger? Tell me in your own words.   910

MESSENGER. I can not say it more clearly: the king is dead.

OEDIPUS. Was it by treason? Or by an attack of illness?

MESSENGER. A little thing brings old men to their rest.

OEDIPUS. It was sickness, then?

MESSENGER.   Yes, and his many years.

OEDIPUS. Ah!   915
Why should a man respect the Pythian hearth,° or
Give heed to the birds that jangle above his head?
They prophesied that I should kill Polybos,
Kill my own father; but he is dead and buried,
And I am here—I never touched him, never,   920
Unless he died of grief for my departure,
And thus, in a sense, through me. No. Polybos
Has packed the oracles off with him underground.
They are empty words.

IOKASTÊ.   Had I not told you so?

OEDIPUS. You had; it was my faint heart that betrayed me.   925

IOKASTÊ. From now on never think of those things again.

OEDIPUS. And yet—must I not fear my mother's bed?

IOKASTÊ. Why should anyone in this world be afraid,
Since Fate rules us and nothing can be foreseen?
A man should live only for the present day.   930

Have no more fear of sleeping with your mother:
How many men, in dreams, have lain with their mothers!
No reasonable man is troubled by such things.

OEDIPUS. That is true; only—
If only my mother were not still alive!   935
But she is alive. I can not help my dread.

IOKASTÊ. Yet this news of your father's death is wonderful.

OEDIPUS. Wonderful. But I fear the living woman.

MESSENGER. Tell me who is this woman that you fear?

OEDIPUS. It is Meropê, man; the wife of King Polybos.   940

916. **Pythian hearth:** Delphi

MESSENGER. Meropê? Why should you be afraid of her?

OEDIPUS. An oracle of the gods, a dreadful saying.

MESSENGER. Can you tell me about it or are you sworn to silence?

OEDIPUS. I can tell you, and I will.

 Apollo said through his prophet that I was the man   945

 Who should marry his own mother, shed his father's blood

 With his own hands. And so, for all these years

 I have kept clear of Corinth, and no harm has come—

 Though it would have been sweet to see my parents again.

MESSENGER. And is this the fear that drove you out of Corinth? 950

OEDIPUS. Would you have me kill my father?

MESSENGER.   As for that

 You must be reassured by the news I gave you.

OEDIPUS. If you could reassure me, I would reward you.

MESSENGER. I had that in mind, I will confess; I thought

 I could count on you when you returned to Corinth. 955

OEDIPUS. No: I will never go near my parents again.

MESSENGER. Ah, son, you still do not know what you are doing—

OEDIPUS. What do you mean? In the name of God tell me!

MESSENGER. —If these are your reasons for not going home.

OEDIPUS. I tell you, I fear the oracle may come true. 960

MESSENGER. And guilt may come upon you through your parents?

OEDIPUS. That is the dread that is always in my heart.

MESSENGER. Can you not see that all your fears are groundless?

OEDIPUS. Groundless? Am I not my parents' son?

MESSENGER. Polybos was not your father.

OEDIPUS.   Not my father? 965

MESSENGER. No more your father than the man speaking to you.

OEDIPUS. But you are nothing to me!

MESSENGER.   Neither was he.

OEDIPUS. Then why did he call me son?

MESSENGER.   I will tell you:

 Long ago he had you from my hands, as a gift.

OEDIPUS. Then how could he love me so, if I was not his? 970

MESSENGER. He had no children, and his heart turned to you.

OEDIPUS. What of you? Did you buy me? Did you find me by chance?

MESSENGER. I came upon you in the woody vales of Kithairon.

OEDIPUS. And what were you doing there?

MESSENGER.   Tending my flocks.

OEDIPUS. A wandering shepherd?

MESSENGER. But your savior, son, that day. 975

OEDIPUS. From what did you save me?

MESSENGER. Your ankles should tell you that.

OEDIPUS. Ah, stranger, why do you speak of that childhood pain?

MESSENGER. I pulled the skewer that pinned your feet together.

OEDIPUS. I have had the mark as long as I can remember.

MESSENGER. That was why you were given the name you bear. 980

OEDIPUS. God! Was it my father or my mother who did it?
　Tell me!

MESSENGER. I do not know. The man who gave you to me
　Can tell you better than I.

OEDIPUS. It was not you that found me, but another?

MESSENGER. It was another shepherd gave you to me. 985

OEDIPUS. Who was he? Can you tell me who he was?

MESSENGER. I think he was said to be one of Laïos's people.

OEDIPUS. You mean the Laïos who was king here years ago?

MESSENGER. Yes; King Laïos; and the man was one of his herdsmen.

OEDIPUS. Is he still alive? Can I see him?

MESSENGER. These men here 990
　Know best about such things.

OEDIPUS. Does anyone here
　Know this shepherd that he is talking about?
　Have you seen him in the fields, or in the town?
　If you have, tell me. It is time things were made plain.

CHORAGOS. I think the man he means is that same shepherd 995
　You have already asked to see. Iokastê perhaps
　Could tell you something.

OEDIPUS. Do you know anything
　About him, Lady? Is he the man we have summoned?
　Is that the man this shepherd means?

IOKASTÊ. Why think of him?
　Forget this herdsman. Forget it all. 1000
　This talk is a waste of time.

OEDIPUS. How can you say that,
　When the clues to my true birth are in my hands?

IOKASTÊ. For God's love, let us have no more questioning!
　Is your life nothing to you?
　My own is pain enough for me to bear. 1005

OEDIPUS. You need not worry. Suppose my mother a slave,
　And born of slaves: no baseness can touch you.

IOKASTÊ. Listen to me, I beg you: do not do this thing!

OEDIPUS. I will not listen; the truth must be made known.

IOKASTÊ. Everything that I say is for your own good!

OEDIPUS.   My own good   1010
  Snaps my patience, then; I want none of it.

IOKASTÊ. You are fatally wrong! May you never learn who you are!

OEDIPUS. Go, one of you, and bring the shepherd here.
  Let us leave this woman to brag of her royal name.

IOKASTÊ. Ah, miserable!   1015
  That is the only word I have for you now.
  That is the only word I can ever have. (*Exit into the palace.*)

CHORAGOS. Why has she left us, Oedipus? Why has she gone
  In such a passion of sorrow? I fear this silence:
  Something dreadful may come of it.

OEDIPUS.   Let it come!   1020
  However base my birth, I must know about it.
  The Queen, like a woman, is perhaps ashamed
  To think of my low origin. But I
  Am a child of Luck; I can not be dishonored.
  Luck is my mother; the passing months, my brothers,   1025
  Have seen me rich and poor.
                            If this is so,
  How could I wish that I were someone else?
  How could I not be glad to know my birth?

ODE 3

STROPHE

CHORUS. If ever the coming time were known
  To my heart's pondering,   1030
  Kithairon, now by Heaven I see the torches
  At the festival of the next full moon,
  And see the dance, and hear the choir sing
  A grace to your gentle shade:
  Mountain where Oedipus was found,   1035
  O mountain guard of a noble race!
  May the god° who heals us lend his aid,
  And let that glory come to pass
  For our king's cradling-ground.

1037. god: Apollo

ANTISTROPHE

> Of the nymphs that flower beyond the years,   1040
> Who bore you,° royal child,
> To Pan of the hills or the timberline Apollo,
> Cold in delight where the upland clears,
> Or Hermês for whom Kyllenê's heights° are piled?
> Or flushed as evening cloud,   1045
> Great Dionysis, roamer of mountains,
> He—was it he who found you there,
> And caught you up in his own proud
> Arms from the sweet god-ravisher
> Who laughed by the Muses' fountains?   1050

SCENE 4

OEDIPUS. Sirs: though I do not know the man,
  I think I see him coming, this shepherd we want:
  He is old, like our friend here, and the men
  Bringing him seem to be servants of my house.
  But you can tell, if you have ever seen him.   1055
  (*Enter* SHEPHERD *escorted by* SERVANTS.)
CHORAGOS. I know him, he was Laïos's man. You can trust him.
OEDIPUS. Tell me first, you from Corinth: is this the shepherd
  We were discussing?
MESSENGER.   This is the very man.
OEDIPUS (*to* SHEPHERD). Come here. No, look at me. You must answer
  Everything I ask.—You belonged to Laïos?   1060
SHEPHERD. Yes: born his slave, brought up in his house.
OEDIPUS. Tell me: what kind of work did you do for him?
SHEPHERD. I was a shepherd of his, most of my life.
OEDIPUS. Where mainly did you go for pasturage?
SHEPHERD. Sometimes Kithairon, sometimes the hills near-by.   1065
OEDIPUS. Do you remember ever seeing this man out there?
SHEPHERD. What would he be doing there? This man?
OEDIPUS. This man standing here. Have you ever seen him before?
SHEPHERD. No. At least, not to my recollection.
MESSENGER. And that is not strange, my lord. But I'll refresh   1070
  His memory: he must remember when we two

1041. **Who bore you:** The chorus is suggesting that perhaps Oedipus is the son of one of the
immortal nymphs and of a god—Pan, Apollo, Hermes, or Dionysis. The "sweet god-ravisher" (line
1049) is the presumed mother.   1044. **Kyllenê's heights:** the mountain where Hermes was born

Spent three whole seasons together, March to September,
On Kithairon or thereabouts. He had two flocks;
I had one. Each autumn I'd drive mine home
And he would go back with his to Laïos's sheepfold.— 1075
Is this not true, just as I have described it?

SHEPHERD. True, yes; but it was all so long ago.

MESSENGER. Well, then: do you remember, back in those days,
That you gave me a baby boy to bring up as my own?

SHEPHERD. What if I did? What are you trying to say? 1080

MESSENGER. King Oedipus was once that little child.

SHEPHERD. Damn you, hold your tongue!

OEDIPUS.   No more of that!
It is your tongue needs watching, not this man's.

SHEPHERD. My king, my master, what is it I have done wrong?

OEDIPUS. You have not answered his question about the boy. 1085

SHEPHERD. He does not know . . . He is only making trouble . . .

OEDIPUS. Come, speak plainly, or it will go hard with you.

SHEPHERD. In God's name, do not torture an old man!

OEDIPUS. Come here, one of you; bind his arms behind him.

SHEPHERD. Unhappy king! What more do you wish to learn? 1090

OEDIPUS. Did you give this man the child he speaks of?

SHEPHERD.   I did.
And I would to God I had died that very day.

OEDIPUS. You will die now unless you speak the truth.

SHEPHERD. Yet if I speak the truth, I am worse than dead.

OEDIPUS (*to* ATTENDANT). He intends to draw it out, apparently— 1095

SHEPHERD. No! I have told you already that I gave him the boy.

OEDIPUS. Where did you get him? From your house? From somewhere
    else?

SHEPHERD. Not from mine, no. A man gave him to me.

OEDIPUS. Is that man here? Whose house did he belong to?

SHEPHERD. For God's love, my king, do not ask me any more! 1100

OEDIPUS. You are a dead man if I have to ask you again.

SHEPHERD. Then . . . Then the child was from the palace of Laïos.

OEDIPUS. A slave child? or a child of his own line?

SHEPHERD. Ah, I am on the brink of dreadful speech!

OEDIPUS. And I of dreadful hearing. Yet I must hear. 1105

SHEPHERD. If you must be told, then . . .
                                     They said it was Laïos's child;
But it is your wife who can tell you about that.

OEDIPUS. My wife—Did she give it to you?

SHEPHERD.   My lord, she did.

OEDIPUS. Do you know why?

SHEPHERD.   I was told to get rid of it.

OEDIPUS. Oh heartless mother!

SHEPHERD.   But in dread of prophecies . . .   1110

OEDIPUS. Tell me.

SHEPHERD.   It was said that the boy would kill his own father.

OEDIPUS. Then why did you give him over to this old man?

SHEPHERD. I pitied the baby, my king,
    And I thought that this man would take him far away
    To his own country.

                    He saved him—but for what a fate!   1115
    For if you are what this man says you are,
    No man living is more wretched than Oedipus.

OEDIPUS. Ah God!
    It was true!

            All the prophecies!

                    —Now,
    O Light, may I look on you for the last time!   1120
    I, Oedipus,
    Oedipus, damned in his birth, in his marriage damned,
    Damned in the blood he shed with his own hand!
    (*He rushes into the palace.*)

ODE 4

STROPHE 1

CHORUS. Alas for the seed of men.
    What measure shall I give these generations   1125
    That breathe on the void and are void
    And exist and do not exist?
    Who bears more weight of joy
    Than mass of sunlight shifting in images,
    Or who shall make his thought stay on   1130
    That down time drifts away?
    Your splendor is all fallen.
    O naked brow of wrath and tears,
    O change of Oedipus!
    I who saw your days call no man blest—   1135
    Your great days like ghósts góne.

ANTISTROPHE 1

    That mind was a strong bow.
    Deep, how deep you drew it then, hard archer,

At a dim fearful range,
And brought dear glory down!
You overcame the stranger°—   1140
The virgin with her hooking lion claws—
And though death sang, stood like a tower
To make pale Thebes take heart.
Fortress against our sorrow!   1145
True king, giver of laws,
Majestic Oedipus!
No prince in Thebes had ever such renown,
No prince won such grace of power.

STROPHE 2

And now of all men ever known   1150
Most pitiful is this man's story:
His fortunes are most changed; his state
Fallen to a low slave's
Ground under bitter fate.
O Oedipus, most royal one!   1155
The great door° that expelled you to the light
Gave at night—ah, gave night to your glory:
As to the father, to the fathering son.
All understood too late.
How could that queen whom Laïos won,   1160
The garden that he harrowed at his height,
Be silent when that act was done?

ANTISTROPHE 2

But all eyes fail before time's eye,
All actions come to justice there.
Though never willed, though far down the deep past,   1165
Your bed, your dread sirings,
Are brought to book at last.
Child by Laïos doomed to die,
Then doomed to lose that fortunate little death,
Would God you never took breath in this air   1170
That with my wailing lips I take to cry:
For I weep the world's outcast.
I was blind, and now I can tell why:

1141. **stranger:** the Sphinx   1156. **door:** Iokastê's womb

Asleep, for you had given ease of breath
To Thebes, while the false years went by.   1175

EXODOS°

Enter, from the palace, SECOND MESSENGER.

SECOND MESSENGER. Elders of Thebes, most honored in this land,
What horrors are yours to see and hear, what weight
Of sorrow to be endured, if, true to your birth,
You venerate the line of Labdakos!
I think neither Istros nor Phasis, those great rivers,   1180
Could purify this place of all the evil
It shelters now, or soon must bring to light—
Evil not done unconsciously, but willed.

The greatest griefs are those we cause ourselves.

CHORAGOS. Surely, friend, we have grief enough already;   1185
What new sorrow do you mean?
SECOND MESSENGER.   The queen is dead.
CHORAGOS. O miserable queen! But at whose hand?
SECOND MESSENGER.   Her own.
The full horror of what happened you can not know,
For you did not see it; but I, who did, will tell you
As clearly as I can how she met her death.   1190

When she had left us,
In passionate silence, passing through the court,
She ran to her apartment in the house,
Her hair clutched by the fingers of both hands.
She closed the doors behind her; then, by that bed   1195
Where long ago the fatal son was conceived—
That son who should bring about his father's death—
We heard her call upon Laïos, dead so many years,
And heard her wail for the double fruit of her marriage,
A husband by her husband, children by her child.   1200

Exactly how she died I do not know:
For Oedipus burst in moaning and would not let us
Keep vigil to the end: it was by him
As he stormed about the room that our eyes were caught.
From one to another of us he went, begging a sword,   1205

Exodos: final scene

Hunting the wife who was not his wife, the mother
Whose womb had carried his own children and himself.
I do not know: it was none of us aided him,
But surely one of the gods was in control!
For with a dreadful cry   1210
He hurled his weight, as though wrenched out of himself,
At the twin doors: the bolts gave, and he rushed in.
And there we saw her hanging, her body swaying
From the cruel cord she had noosed about her neck.
A great sob broke from him, heartbreaking to hear,   1215
As he loosened the rope and lowered her to the ground.

I would blot out from my mind what happened next!
For the king ripped from her gown the golden brooches
That were her ornament, and raised them, and plunged them down
Straight into his own eyeballs, crying, "No more,   1220
No more shall you look on the misery about me,
The horrors of my own doing! Too long you have known
The faces of those whom I should never have seen,
Too long been blind to those for whom I was searching!
From this hour, go in darkness!" And as he spoke,   1225
He struck his eyes—not once, but many times;
And the blood spattered his beard,
Bursting from his ruined sockets like red hail.
So from the unhappiness of two this evil has sprung,
A curse on the man and woman alike. The old   1230
Happiness of the house of Labdakos
Was happiness enough: where is it today?
It is all wailing and ruin, disgrace, death—all
The misery of mankind that has a name—
And it is wholly and for ever theirs.   1235
CHORAGOS. Is he in agony still? Is there no rest for him?
SECOND MESSENGER. He is calling for someone to open the doors wide
    So that all the children of Kadmos may look upon
    His father's murderer, his mother's—no,
    I can not say it!
                        And then he will leave Thebes,   1240
    Self-exiled, in order that the curse
    Which he himself pronounced may depart from the house.
    He is weak, and there is none to lead him,
    So terrible is his suffering.
                        But you will see:

Look, the doors are opening; in a moment 1245
You will see a thing that would crush a heart of stone.
(*The central door is opened;* OEDIPUS, *blinded, is led in.*)
CHORAGOS. Dreadful indeed for me to see.
Never have my own eyes
Looked on a sight so full of fear.

Oedipus! 1250
What madness came upon you, what daemon
Leaped on your life with heavier
Punishment than a mortal man can bear?
No: I can not even
Look at you, poor ruined one. 1255
And I would speak, question, ponder,
If I were able. No.
You make me shudder.
OEDIPUS. God. God.
Is there a sorrow greater? 1260
Where shall I find harbor in this world?
My voice is hurled far on a dark wind.
What has God done to me?
CHORAGOS. Too terrible to think of, or to see.

STROPHE 1

OEDIPUS. O cloud of night, 1265
    Never to be turned away: night coming on,
    I can not tell how: night like a shroud!
    My fair winds brought me here.
                                    O God. Again
    The pain of the spikes where I had sight,
    The flooding pain 1270
    Of memory, never to be gouged out.
CHORAGOS. This is not strange.
    You suffer it all twice over, remorse in pain,
    Pain in remorse.

ANTISTROPHE 1

OEDIPUS. Ah dear friend 1275
    Are you faithful even yet, you alone?
    Are you still standing near me, will you stay here,
    Patient, to care for the blind?
                                    The blind man!

Yet even blind I know who it is attends me,
By the voice's tone—   1280
Though my new darkness hide the comforter.
CHORAGOS. Oh fearful act!
What god was it drove you to rake black
Night across your eyes?

STROPHE 2

OEDIPUS. Apollo. Apollo. Dear   1285
Children, the god was Apollo.
He brought my sick, sick fate upon me.
But the blinding hand was my own!
How could I bear to see
When all my sight was horror everywhere?   1290
CHORAGOS. Everywhere; that is true.
OEDIPUS. And now what is left?
Images? Love? A greeting even,
Sweet to the senses? Is there anything?
Ah, no, friends: lead me away.   1295
Lead me away from Thebes.
                              Lead the great wreck
And hell of Oedipus, whom the gods hate.
CHORAGOS. Your misery, you are not blind to that.
Would God you had never found it out!

ANTISTROPHE 2

OEDIPUS. Death take the man who unbound   1300
My feet on that hillside
And delivered me from death to life! What life?
If only I had died,
This weight of monstrous doom
Could not have dragged me and my darlings down.   1305
CHORAGOS. I would have wished the same.
OEDIPUS. Oh never to have come here
With my father's blood upon me! Never
To have been the man they call his mother's husband!
Oh accurst! Oh child of evil,   1310
To have entered that wretched bed—
                              the selfsame one!
More primal than sin itself, this fell to me.
CHORAGOS. I do not know what words to offer you.
You were better dead than alive and blind.

OEDIPUS. Do not counsel me any more. This punishment   1315
    That I have laid upon myself is just.
    If I had eyes,
    I do not know how I could bear the sight
    Of my father, when I came to the house of Death,
    Or my mother: for I have sinned against them both   1320
    So vilely that I could not make my peace
    By strangling my own life.
                              Or do you think my children,
    Born as they were born, would be sweet to my eyes?
    Ah never, never! Nor this town with its high walls,
    Nor the holy images of the gods.
                              For I,   1325
    Thrice miserable!—Oedipus, noblest of all the line
    Of Kadmos, have condemned myself to enjoy
    These things no more, by my own malediction
    Expelling that man whom the gods declared
    To be a defilement in the house of Laïos.   1330
    After exposing the rankness of my own guilt,
    How could I look men frankly in the eyes?
    No, I swear it.
    If I could have stifled my hearing at its source,
    I would have done it and made all this body   1335
    A tight cell of misery, blank to light and sound:
    So I should have been safe in my dark mind
    Beyond external evil.
                              Ah Kithairon!
    Why did you shelter me? When I was cast upon you,
    Why did I not die? Then I should never   1340
    Have shown the world my execrable birth.

    Ah Polybos! Corinth, city that I believed
    The ancient seat of my ancestors: how fair
    I seemed, your child! And all the while this evil
    Was cancerous within me!
                              For I am sick,   1345
    In my own being, sick in my origin.

    O three roads, dark ravine, woodland and way
    Where three roads met: you, drinking my father's blood,
    My own blood, spilled by my own hand: can you remember
    The unspeakable things I did there, and the things   1350
    I went on from there to do?

O marriage, marriage!
The act that engendered me, and again the act
Performed by the son in the same bed—

Ah, the net
Of incest, mingling fathers, brothers, sons,
With brides, wives, mothers: the last evil   1355
That can be known by men: no tongue can say
How evil!

No. For the love of God, conceal me
Somewhere far from Thebes; or kill me; or hurl me
Into the sea, away from men's eyes for ever.

Come, lead me. You need not fear to touch me.   1360
Of all men, I alone can bear this guilt. (*Enter* KREON.)

CHORAGOS. Kreon is here now. As to what you ask,
He may decide the course to take. He only
Is left to protect the city in your place.

OEDIPUS. Alas, how can I speak to him? What right have I   1365
To beg his courtesy whom I have deeply wronged?

KREON. I have not come to mock you, Oedipus,
Or to reproach you, either.

(*To* ATTENDANTS)   —You, standing there:
If you have lost all respect for man's dignity,
At least respect the flame of Lord Helios: 1370
Do not allow this pollution to show itself
Openly here, an affront to the earth
And Heaven's rain and the light of day. No, take him
Into the house as quickly as you can.
For it is proper   1375
That only the close kindred see his grief.

OEDIPUS. I pray you in God's name, since your courtesy
Ignores my dark expectation, visiting
With mercy this man of all men most execrable:
Give me what I ask for—for your good, not for mine.   1380

KREON. And what is it that you turn to me begging for?

OEDIPUS. Drive me out of this country as quickly as may be
To a place where no human voice can ever greet me.

KREON. I should have done that before now—only,
God's will had not been wholly revealed to me.   1385

OEDIPUS. But his command is plain: the parricide
Must be destroyed. I am that evil man.

KREON. That is the sense of it, yes; but as things are,

We had best discover clearly what is to be done.

OEDIPUS. You would learn more about a man like me?　　　　1390

KREON. You are ready now to listen to the god.

OEDIPUS. I will listen. But it is to you
That I must turn for help. I beg you, hear me.

The woman in there—
Give her whatever funeral you think proper:　　　　1395
She is your sister.
　　　　　　—But let me go, Kreon!
Let me purge my father's Thebes of the pollution
Of my living here, and go out to the wild hills,
To Kithairon, that has won such fame with me,
The tomb my mother and father appointed for me,　　　　1400
And let me die there, as they willed I should.
And yet I know
Death will not ever come to me through sickness
Or in any natural way: I have been preserved
For some unthinkable fate. But let that be.　　　　1405

As for my sons, you need not care for them.
They are men, they will find some way to live.
But my poor daughters, who have shared my table,
Who never before have been parted from their father—
Take care of them, Kreon; do this for me.　　　　1410

And will you let me touch them with my hands
A last time, and let us weep together?
Be kind, my lord,
Great prince, be kind!
　　　　　　Could I but touch them,
They would be mine again, as when I had my eyes.　　　　1415
(*Enter* ANTIGONE *and* ISMENE, *attended.*)
Ah, God!
Is it my dearest children I hear weeping?
Has Kreon pitied me and sent my daughters?

KREON. Yes, Oedipus: I knew that they were dear to you
In the old days, and know you must love them still.　　　　1420

OEDIPUS. May God bless you for this—and be a friendlier
Guardian to you than he has been to me!

Children, where are you?
Come quickly to my hands: they are your brother's—
Hands that have brought your father's once clear eyes   1425
To this way of seeing—
              Ah dearest ones,
I had neither sight nor knowledge then, your father
By the woman who was the source of his own life!
And I weep for you—having no strength to see you—
I weep for you when I think of the bitterness   1430
That men will visit upon you all your lives.
What homes, what festivals can you attend
Without being forced to depart again in tears?
And when you come to marriageable age,
Where is the man, my daughters, who would dare   1435
Risk the bane that lies on all my children?
Is there any evil wanting? Your father killed
His father; sowed the womb of her who bore him;
Engendered you at the fount of his own existence!
That is what they will say of you.

                        Then, whom   1440
Can you ever marry? There are no bridegrooms for you,
And your lives must wither away in sterile dreaming.
O Kreon, son of Menoikeus!
You are the only father my daughters have,
Since we, their parents, are both of us gone for ever.   1445
They are your own blood: you will not let them
Fall into beggary and loneliness;
You will keep them from the miseries that are mine!
Take pity on them; see, they are only children,
Friendless except for you. Promise me this,   1450
Great prince, and give me your hand in token of it.
(KREON *clasps his right hand.*)
Children:
I could say much, if you could understand me,
But as it is, I have only this prayer for you:
Live where you can, be as happy as you can—   1455
Happier, please God, than God has made your father.
KREON. Enough. You have wept enough. Now go within.
OEDIPUS. I must; but it is hard.
KREON.   Time eases all things.

OEDIPUS. You know my mind, then?

KREON. Say what you desire.

OEDIPUS. Send me from Thebes!

KREON. God grant that I may! 1460

OEDIPUS. But since God hates me . . .

KREON. No, he will grant your wish.

OEDIPUS. You promise?

KREON. I can not speak beyond my knowledge.

OEDIPUS. Then lead me in.

KREON. Come now, and leave your children.

OEDIPUS. No! Do not take them from me!

KREON. Think no longer

That you are in command here, but rather think 1465

How, when you were, you served your own destruction. (*Exeunt into the house all but the* CHORUS; *the* CHORAGOS *chants directly to the audience.*)

CHORAGOS. Men of Thebes: look upon Oedipus.

This is the king who solved the famous riddle

And towered up, most powerful of men.

No mortal eyes but looked on him with envy, 1470

Yet in the end ruin swept over him.

Let every man in mankind's frailty

Consider his last day; and let none

Presume on his good fortune until he find

Life, at his death, a memory without pain. 1475

QUESTIONS

1. The oracles had prophesied that Oedipus would kill his father and beget children by his mother. Is Oedipus therefore *made* to do these things? Is the play premised on the notion that Oedipus is bound or free—the puppet of fate or the creator of his own fate? Or some of each?

2. Outline the actions presented on the stage: begin where the play begins, with the people turning to their king for relief from the plague, and disregard for the moment the revelation of incidents that preceded the play. Then summarize the antecedent actions as they are gradually revealed. In what ways are Oedipus's stage actions consistent with his prior actions? In what ways are they different? How do these two sets of actions reveal him to be a person of extraordinary stature?

3. What is Oedipus's primary motivation throughout the action of the play? What were his motives in actions prior to the play? What characters try to dissuade him from pursuing his purpose, and why do they do so? How do his subjects regard him?

4. Is any common pattern of behavior exhibited in Oedipus's encounters with Laïos, with Teiresias, and with Kreon? Is there any justification for his anger with Teiresias? For his suspicion of Kreon? Why?

5. Oedipus's original question, "Who killed Laïos?" soon turns into the question "Who am I?" On the level of plot, the answer is "Son of Laïos and Iokastê, father's murderer, mother's husband." What is the answer at the level of character—that is, in a psychological or philosophical sense?

6. What philosophical issues are raised by Iokastê's judgment on the oracles (Scene 2)? How does the chorus respond to her judgment? How does the play resolve these issues?

7. Why does Oedipus blind himself? Is this an act of weakness or of strength? Why does he ask Kreon to drive him from Thebes? Does he feel that his fate has been just or unjust? Is his suffering, in fact, deserved? Partially deserved? Undeserved?

8. There is a good deal in the play about seeing and blindness. What purpose does this serve? How is Oedipus contrasted with Teiresias? How does Oedipus at the beginning of the play contrast with Oedipus at the end? Why is his blinding himself dramatically appropriate?

9. In what sense may Oedipus be regarded as a better man, though a less fortunate one, at the end of the play than at the beginning? What has he gained from his experience?

10. Some critics have suggested that Oedipus's answer to the Sphinx's riddle was incomplete—that the answer should have been not just man but Oedipus himself—and that Oedipus was as ignorant of the whole truth here as he is when he lays his curse in Scene 1 on the murderer of Laïos. Does this suggestion make sense? On how many legs does Oedipus walk at the end of the play?

11. If the answer to the Sphinx's riddle is not just man but Oedipus himself, may the answer to Oedipus's question "Who am I?" pertain not only to Oedipus but also to man, or at least to civilized Western man? What characteristics of Oedipus as an individual are also characteristics of man in the Western world? Is Sophocles writing only about Oedipus the king, or is he saying something about man's presumed place and his real place in the universe?

12. What purposes are served by the appearance of Antigone and Ismene in the Exodos?

13. What purposes does the chorus serve in the play? Whom does it speak for? Comment on the function of each of the four Odes.

14. What does the final speech of the Choragos tell us about human life?

15. A central formal feature of the play is its use of dramatic irony. Point out speeches by Oedipus, especially in the Prologue and Scene 1, that have a different or a larger meaning for the audience than for Oedipus himself. Sophocles's title literally translates "Oedipus the Tyrant," but the word *tyrant* denoted a ruler who had earned his position through his own intelligence and strength rather than by inheritance—it was not a negative term. Given that, what ironies are suggested by Sophocles's title?

16. The plot of *Oedipus Rex* has been called one of the most perfect dramatic plots ever devised. Why is it admired? What are its outstanding characteristics?

WILLIAM SHAKESPEARE

Othello, the Moor of Venice

Characters

DUKE OF VENICE

BRABANTIO, *a Senator*

OTHER SENATORS

GRATIANO, *Brabantio's brother*

LODOVICO, *Brabantio's kinsman*

OTHELLO, *a noble Moor in the service of the Venetian state*

CASSIO, *his lieutenant*

IAGO, *his ensign*

MONTANO, *Othello's predecessor in the government of Cyprus*

RODERIGO, *a Venetian gentleman*

CLOWN, *Othello's servant*

DESDEMONA, *Brabantio's daughter and Othello's wife*

EMILIA, *Iago's wife*

BIANCA, *Cassio's mistress*

SAILOR, MESSENGER, HERALD, OFFICERS, GENTLEMEN,

    MUSICIANS, *and* ATTENDANTS

SCENE: *Venice, and a seaport in Cyprus*

OTHELLO, THE MOOR OF VENICE First performed in 1604. The general historical background of the action is probably sometime between 1470 and 1522, a period when Venice, an independent city-state headed by a duke (or doge) elected by the heads of the noble families, was the strongest sea power of the Christian world and included Cyprus and Rhodes among its dominions. Its chief rival for power in the Mediterranean was the Turkish or Ottomite empire. Venetian law required that the commander-in-chief of its forces be an alien, not a Venetian citizen, to prevent political ambition from interfering with his duties. Othello, a black African of royal blood and a soldier of great experience, fulfills the qualifications. The events and characters of the play are fictional, and in any case Shakespeare was not overly concerned with historical accuracy.

    William Shakespeare (1564–1616) was born in Stratford-upon-Avon but went to London as a young man and made his fortune as an actor, playwright, and part-owner of the Globe Theatre. He did not supervise the publication of his plays, and the two earliest printings of *Othello*—the quarto of 1622 and the folio of 1623—differ in various ways. Modern editors must rely on judgment and scholarship in reconciling the two to arrive at their texts. The version presented here is that of G. B. Harrison, from *Shakespeare: The Complete Works* (New York: Harcourt, 1952). The editors of this book have selected some notes from Harrison's text and supplemented them with newly created notes.

ACT I

SCENE I. Venice. A street.

Enter RODERIGO *and* IAGO.

RODERIGO. Tush, never tell me! I take it much unkindly
  That thou, Iago, who hast had my purse
  As if the strings were thine, shouldst know of this.
IAGO. 'Sblood, but you will not hear me.
  If ever I did dream of such a matter,   5
  Abhor me.
RODERIGO. Thou told'st me thou didst hold him in thy hate.
IAGO. Despise me if I do not. Three great ones of the city,
  In personal suit to make me his Lieutenant,
  Off-capped to him. And, by the faith of man,   10
  I know my price, I am worth no worse a place.
  But he, as loving his own pride and purposes,
  Evades them, with a bombast circumstance
  Horribly stuffed with epithets of war.
  And, in conclusion,   15
  Nonsuits° my mediators, for, "Certes," says he,
  "I have already chose my officer."
  And what was he?
  Forsooth, a great arithmetician,°
  One Michael Cassio, a Florentine,   20
  A fellow almost damned in a fair wife,°
  That never set a squadron in the field,
  Nor the division of a battle knows
  More than a spinster, unless the bookish theoric,
  Wherein the toged Consuls° can propose   25
  As masterly as he—mere prattle without practice
  Is all his soldiership. But he, sir, had the election.
  And I, of whom his° eyes had seen the proof
  At Rhodes, at Cyprus, and on other grounds
  Christian and heathen, must be beleed° and calmed   30
  By debitor and creditor. This countercaster,°
  He, in good time,° must his Lieutenant be,

---

16. **Nonsuits:** Rejects the petition of   19. **arithmetician:** Contemporary books on military tactics
are full of elaborate diagrams and numerals to explain military formations. Cassio is a student of such
books.   21. **almost . . . wife:** A much-disputed phrase. There is an Italian proverb, "You have married a fair wife? You are damned." If Iago has this in mind, he means by *almost* that Cassio is about to
marry.   25. **toged Consuls:** senators in togas [Eds.]   28. **his:** Othello's [Eds.]   30. **beleed:** placed
on the lee (or unfavorable) side   31. **countercaster:** calculator (repeating the idea of arithmetician).
Counters were used in making calculations.   32. **in good time:** a phrase expressing indignation

And I—God bless the mark!—his Moorship's Ancient.°

RODERIGO. By Heaven, I rather would have been his hangman.

IAGO. Why, there's no remedy. 'Tis the curse of service,   35
  Preferment goes by letter and affection,
  And not by old gradation,° where each second
  Stood heir to the first. Now, sir, be judge yourself
  Whether I in any just term am affined°
  To love the Moor.

RODERIGO.   I would not follow him, then.   40

IAGO. Oh, sir, content you,
  I follow him to serve my turn upon him.
  We cannot all be masters, nor all masters
  Cannot be truly followed. You shall mark
  Many a duteous and knee-crooking knave   45
  That doting on his own obsequious bondage
  Wears out his time, much like his master's ass,
  For naught but provender, and when he's old, cashiered.
  Whip me such honest knaves. Others there are
  Who, trimmed in forms and visages of duty,   50
  Keep yet their hearts attending on themselves,
  And throwing but shows of service on their lords
  Do well thrive by them, and when they have lined their coats
  Do themselves homage. These fellows have some soul,
  And such a one do I profess myself. For, sir,   55
  It is as sure as you are Roderigo,
  Were I the Moor, I would not be Iago.
  In following him, I follow but myself.
  Heaven is my judge, not I for love and duty,
  But seeming so, for my peculiar° end.   60
  For when my outward action doth demonstrate
  The native act and figure of my heart
  In compliment extern, 'tis not long after
  But I will wear my heart upon my sleeve
  For daws to peck at. I am not what I am.   65

RODERIGO. What a full fortune does the thick-lips owe°
  If he can carry 't thus!°

IAGO.   Call up her father,

---

33. **Ancient:** Ensign, the third officer in the company of which Othello is Captain and Cassio
Lieutenant 36–37.   **Preferment . . . gradation:** Promotion comes through private recommenda-
tion and favoritism and not by order of seniority.   39. **affined:** tied by affection   60. **peculiar:**
personal [Eds.]   66. **owe:** own   67. **carry't thus:** i.e., bring off this marriage

Rouse him. Make after him, poison his delight,
Proclaim him in the streets. Incense her kinsmen,
And though he in a fertile climate dwell,   70
Plague him with flies. Though that his joy be joy,
Yet throw such changes of vexation on 't
As it may lose some color.
RODERIGO. Here is her father's house, I'll call aloud.
IAGO. Do, with like timorous° accent and dire yell   75
As when, by night and negligence, the fire
Is spied in populous cities.
RODERIGO. What ho, Brabantio! Signior Brabantio, ho!
IAGO. Awake! What ho, Brabantio! Thieves! Thieves! Thieves!
Look to your house, your daughter and your bags!°   80
Thieves! Thieves! (BRABANTIO *appears above, at a window.*)
BRABANTIO. What is the reason of this terrible summons?
What is the matter there?
RODERIGO. Signior, is all your family within?
IAGO. Are your doors locked?
BRABANTIO.   Why, wherefore ask you this?   85
IAGO. 'Zounds, sir, you're robbed. For shame, put on your gown,
Your heart is burst, you have lost half your soul.
Even now, now, very now, an old black ram
Is tupping your white ewe. Arise, arise,
Awake the snorting° citizens with the bell,   90
Or else the Devil° will make a grandsire of you.
Arise, I say.
BRABANTIO. What, have you lost your wits?
RODERIGO. Most reverend signior, do you know my voice?
BRABANTIO. Not I. What are you?
RODERIGO. My name is Roderigo.
BRABANTIO.   The worser welcome.   95
I have charged thee not to haunt about my doors.
In honest plainness thou hast heard me say
My daughter is not for thee, and now, in madness,
Being full of supper and distempering draughts,
Upon malicious bravery° dost thou come   100
To start° my quiet.
RODERIGO. Sir, sir, sir—

---

75. **timorous:** terrifying   80. **bags:** moneybags   90. **snorting:** snoring   91. **Devil:** The Devil in old pictures and woodcuts was represented as black.   100. **bravery:** defiance   101. **start:** startle

BRABANTIO. But thou must needs be sure
My spirit and my place have in them power
To make this bitter to thee.
RODERIGO. Patience, good sir.
BRABANTIO. What tell'st thou me of robbing? This is Venice, 105
My house is not a grange.°
RODERIGO. Most grave Brabantio,
In simple and pure soul I come to you.
IAGO. 'Zounds, sir, you are one of those that will not serve God if the
Devil bid you. Because we come to do you service and you think
we are ruffians, you'll have your daughter covered with a Barbary°
horse, you'll have your nephews° neigh to you, you'll have coursers for
cousins,° and jennets° for germans.° 112
BRABANTIO. What profane wretch art thou?
IAGO. I am one, sir, that comes to tell you your daughter and the Moor are
now making the beast with two backs. 115
BRABANTIO. Thou art a villain.
IAGO. You are—a Senator.
BRABANTIO. This thou shalt answer. I know thee, Roderigo.
RODERIGO. Sir, I will answer anything. But I beseech you
If 't be your pleasure and most wise consent,
As partly I find it is, that your fair daughter, 120
At this odd-even° and dull watch o' the night,
Transported with no worse nor better guard
But with a knave of common hire, a gondolier,
To the gross clasps of a lascivious Moor—
If this be known to you, and your allowance,° 125
We then have done you bold and saucy wrongs.
But if you know not this, my manners tell me
We have your wrong rebuke. Do not believe
That, from the sense of all civility,°
I thus would play and trifle with your reverence. 130
Your daughter, if you have not given her leave,
I say again, hath made a gross revolt,
Tying her duty, beauty, wit, and fortunes
In an extravagant° and wheeling° stranger
Of here and everywhere. Straight satisfy yourself. 135

---

106. **grange:** lonely farm 110. **Barbary:** Moorish 111. **nephews:** grandsons 112. **cousins:**
near relations **jennets:** Moorish ponies **germans:** kinsmen 121. **odd-even:** about midnight
125. **your allowance:** by your permission 129. **from . . . civility:** contrary to all decency
[Eds.] 134. **extravagant:** vagabond **wheeling:** wandering

If she be in her chamber or your house,
Let loose on me the justice of the state
For thus deluding you.
BRABANTIO.   Strike on the tinder,° ho!
Give me a taper!° Call up all my people!
This accident is not unlike my dream.   140
Belief of it oppresses me already.
Light, I say! Light! (*Exit above.*)
IAGO.   Farewell, for I must leave you.
It seems not meet, nor wholesome to my place,°
To be produced—as if I stay I shall—
Against the Moor. For I do know the state,   145
However this may gall him with some check,
Cannot with safety cast° him. For he's embarked
With such loud reason to the Cyprus wars,
Which even now stand in act,° that, for their souls,
Another of his fathom they have none   150
To lead their business. In which regard,
Though I do hate him as I do Hell pains,
Yet for necessity of present life
I must show out a flag and sign of love,
Which is indeed but sign. That you shall surely find him,   155
Lead to the Sagittary° the raisèd search,
And there will I be with him. So farewell.
(*Exit* IAGO. *Enter, below,* BRABANTIO, *in his nightgown,*°
and SERVANTS *with torches.*)
BRABANTIO. It is too true an evil. Gone she is,
And what's to come of my despisèd time
Is naught but bitterness. Now, Roderigo,   160
Where didst thou see her? Oh, unhappy girl!
With the Moor, say'st thou? Who would be a father!
How didst thou know 'twas she? Oh, she deceives me
Past thought! What said she to you? Get more tapers.
Raise all my kindred. Are they married, think you?   165
RODERIGO. Truly, I think they are.
BRABANTIO. Oh Heaven! How got she out? Oh, treason of the blood!
Fathers, from hence trust not your daughters' minds
By what you see them act. Are there not charms°

---

138. **tinder:** the primitive method of making fire, used before the invention of matches   139.
taper: candle   143. **place:** i.e., as Othello's officer   147. **cast:** dismiss from service   149. **stand
in act:** are under way [Eds.]   156. **Sagittary:** presumably some inn in Venice [Eds.]   157. s.d.
nightgown: dressing-gown [Eds.]

By which the property° of youth and maidhood   170
May be abused?° Have you not read, Roderigo,
Of some such thing?
RODERIGO.   Yes, sir, I have indeed.
BRABANTIO. Call up my brother.—Oh, would you had had her!—
Some one way, some another.—Do you know
Where we may apprehend her and the Moor?   175
RODERIGO. I think I can discover him, if you please
To get good guard and go along with me.
BRABANTIO. Pray you, lead on. At every house I'll call,
I may command° at most. Get weapons, ho!
And raise some special officers of night.   180
On, good Roderigo, I'll deserve your pains.° (*Exeunt.*)

SCENE 2. Another street.

Enter OTHELLO, IAGO, *and* ATTENDANTS *with torches.*
IAGO. Though in the trade of war I have slain men,
Yet do I hold it very stuff o' the conscience
To do no contrivèd murder. I lack iniquity
Sometimes to do me service. Nine or ten times
I had thought to have yerked him° here under the ribs,   5
OTHELLO. 'Tis better as it is.
IAGO.   Nay, but he prated
And spoke such scurvy and provoking terms
Against your honor
That, with the little godliness I have,
I did full hard forbear him. But I pray you, sir,   10
Are you fast married? Be assured of this,
That the Magnifico is much beloved,
And hath in his effect a voice potential
As double as° the Duke's. He will divorce you,
Or put upon you what restraint and grievance   15
The law, with all his might to enforce it on,
Will give him cable.
OTHELLO.   Let him do his spite.
My services which I have done the signiory°
Shall out-tongue his complaints. 'Tis yet to know°—

---

169. charms: magic spells 170. property: nature 171. abused: deceived 179. command: find
supporters 181. deserve your pains: reward your labor 5. yerked him: stabbed Brabantio [Eds.]
13–14. potential . . . as: twice as powerful as 18. signiory: state of Venice 19. yet to know:
not widely known [Eds.]

Which, when I know that boasting is an honor,   20
I shall promulgate—I fetch my life and being
From men of royal siege,° and my demerits°
May speak unbonneted to as proud a fortune
As this that I have reached. For know, Iago,
But that I love the gentle Desdemona,   25
I would not my unhousèd° free condition
Put into circumscription and confine
For the sea's worth. But look! What lights come yond?

IAGO. Those are the raisèd father and his friends.
You were best go in.

OTHELLO.   Not I, I must be found.   30
My parts, my title, and my perfect soul°
Shall manifest me rightly. Is it they?

IAGO. By Janus, I think no.

(*Enter* CASSIO, *and certain* OFFICERS *with torches.*)

OTHELLO. The servants of the Duke, and my Lieutenant.
The goodness of the night upon you, friends!   35
What is the news?

CASSIO.   The Duke does greet you, General,
And he requires your haste-posthaste appearance,
Even on the instant.

OTHELLO.   What is the matter, think you?

CASSIO. Something from Cyprus, as I may divine.
It is a business of some heat. The galleys   40
Have sent a dozen sequent messengers
This very night at one another's heels,
And many of the consuls, raised and met,
Are at the Duke's already. You have been hotly called for
When, being not at your lodging to be found,   45
The Senate hath sent about three several° quests
To search you out.

OTHELLO.   'Tis well I am found by you.
I will but spend a word here in the house
And go with you. (*Exit.*)

CASSIO.   Ancient, what makes he here?

IAGO. Faith, he tonight hath boarded a land carrack.°   50
If it prove lawful prize, he's made forever.

CASSIO. I do not understand.

---

22. **siege:** rank [Eds.]   **demerits:** deserts   26. **unhousèd:** unmarried   31. **perfect soul:** clear
conscience [Eds.]   46. **several:** separate   50. **carrack:** large merchant ship

IAGO.   He's married.

CASSIO.   To who? (*Re-enter* OTHELLO.)

IAGO. Marry,° to—Come, Captain, will you go?

OTHELLO.   Have with you.

CASSIO. Here comes another troop to seek for you.

IAGO. It is Brabantio. General, be advised,   55
 He comes to bad intent.
 (*Enter* BRABANTIO, RODERIGO, *and* OFFICERS *with torches*
  and weapons.)

OTHELLO.   Holloa! Stand there!

RODERIGO. Signior, it is the Moor.

BRABANTIO.   Down with him, thief!
 (*They draw on both sides.*)

IAGO. You, Roderigo! Come, sir, I am for you.

OTHELLO. Keep up° your bright swords, for the dew will rust them.
 Good signior, you shall more command with years   60
 Than with your weapons.

BRABANTIO. O thou foul thief, where hast thou stowed my
 daughter?
 Damned as thou art, thou hast enchanted her.
 For I'll refer me to all things of sense
 If she in chains of magic were not bound,   65
 Whether a maid so tender, fair, and happy,
 So opposite to marriage that she shunned
 The wealthy curlèd darlings of our nation,
 Would ever have, to incur a general mock,
 Run from her guardage° to the sooty bosom   70
 Of such a thing as thou, to fear, not to delight.
 Judge me the world if 'Tis not gross in sense°
 That thou hast practiced on her with foul charms,
 Abused her delicate youth with drugs or minerals
 That weaken motion.° I'll have 't disputed on,°   75
 'Tis probable, and palpable to thinking.
 I therefore apprehend and do attach° thee
 For an abuser of the world, a practicer
 Of arts inhibited and out of warrant.°
 Lay hold upon him. If he do resist,   80
 Subdue him at his peril.

OTHELLO.   Hold your hands,
 Both you of my inclining and the rest.

53. Marry: a mild oath [Eds.] **59. Keep up:** Sheathe **70. guardage:** guardianship **72. gross in sense:** obvious [Eds.] **75. motion:** sense **disputed on:** argued in the law courts [Eds.] **77. attach:** arrest **79. inhibited . . . warrant:** forbidden and illegal [Eds.]

Were it my cue to fight, I should have known it
Without a prompter. Where will you that I go
To answer this your charge?
BRABANTIO.   To prison, till fit time   85
Of law and course of direct session
Call thee to answer.
OTHELLO.   What if I do obey?
How may the Duke be therewith satisfied,
Whose messengers are here about my side
Upon some present business of the state   90
To bring me to him?
FIRST OFFICER.   'Tis true, most worthy signior.
The Duke's in council, and your noble self
I am sure is sent for.
BRABANTIO.   How? The Duke in council?
In this time of the night? Bring him away.
Mine's not an idle cause. The Duke himself,   95
Or any of my brothers of the state,
Cannot but feel this wrong as 'twere their own.
For if such actions may have passage free,
Bondslaves and pagans shall our statesmen be. (*Exeunt.*)

SCENE 3. A council chamber.

The DUKE *and* SENATORS *sitting at a table,* OFFICERS *attending.*
DUKE. There is no composition° in these news°
That gives them credit.
FIRST SENATOR. Indeed they are disproportioned.
My letters say a hundred and seven galleys.
DUKE. And mine, a hundred and forty.
SECOND SENATOR.   And mine, two hundred.
But though they jump not on a just account°—   5
As in these cases, where the aim reports,°
'Tis oft with difference—yet do they all confirm
A Turkish fleet, and bearing up to Cyprus.
DUKE. Nay, it is possible enough to judgment.
I do not so secure me in the error,°   10
But the main article° I do approve
In fearful° sense.

1. composition: agreement   news: reports   5. jump . . . account: do not agree with an exact
estimate   6. aim reports: i.e., intelligence reports of an enemy's intention often differ in the details
10. I . . . error: I do not consider myself free from danger, because the reports may not all be
accurate.   11. main article: general report   12. fearful: to be feared

SAILOR (*within*).   What ho! What ho! What ho!
FIRST OFFICER. A messenger from the galleys. (*Enter* SAILOR.)
DUKE.   Now, what's the business?
SAILOR. The Turkish preparation makes for Rhodes.
  So was I bid report here to the state   15
  By Signior Angelo.
DUKE. How say you by this charge?
FIRST SENATOR.   This cannot be,
  By no assay of reason. 'Tis a pageant
  To keep us in false gaze. When we consider
  The importancy of Cyprus to the Turk,   20
  And let ourselves again but understand
  That as it more concerns the Turk than Rhodes,
  So may he with more facile question bear it,°
  For that it stands not in such warlike brace
  But altogether lacks the abilities   25
  That Rhodes is dressed in—if we make thought of this,
  We must not think the Turk is so unskillful
  To leave that latest which concerns him first,
  Neglecting an attempt of ease and gain
  To wake and wage a danger profitless.   30
DUKE. Nay, in all confidence, he's not for Rhodes.
FIRST OFFICER. Here is more news. (*Enter a* MESSENGER.)
MESSENGER. The Ottomites,° Reverend and Gracious,
  Steering with due course toward the isle of Rhodes,
  Have there injointed° them with an after-fleet.°   35
FIRST SENATOR. Aye, so I thought. How many, as you guess?
MESSENGER. Of thirty sail. And now they do restem°
  Their backward course, bearing with frank appearance
  Their purposes toward Cyprus. Signior Montano,
  Your trusty and most valiant servitor,   40
  With his free duty recommends° you thus,
  And prays you to believe him.
DUKE. 'Tis certain then for Cyprus.
  Marcus Luccicos, is not he in town?
FIRST SENATOR. He's now in Florence.   45
DUKE. Write from us to him, post-posthaste dispatch.
FIRST SENATOR. Here comes Brabantio and the valiant Moor.

---

23. with . . . it: take it more easily   33. Ottomites: Turks   35. injointed: joined   after-fleet:
second fleet   37. restem: steer again   41. recommends: advises [Eds.]

(*Enter* BRABANTIO, OTHELLO, IAGO, RODERIGO, *and* OFFICERS.)

DUKE. Valiant Othello, we must straight employ you
    Against the general enemy Ottoman.
    (*To* BRABANTIO) I did not see you. Welcome, gentle signior,   50
    We lacked your counsel and your help tonight.

BRABANTIO. So did I yours. Good your Grace, pardon me,
    Neither my place nor aught I heard of business
    Hath raised me from my bed, nor doth the general care
    Take hold on me. For my particular° grief   55
    Is of so floodgate and o'erbearing nature
    That it engluts and swallows other sorrows,
    And it is still itself.

DUKE.   Why, what's the matter?

BRABANTIO. My daughter! Oh, my daughter!

ALL.   Dead?

BRABANTIO.   Aye, to me.
    She is abused, stol'n from me and corrupted   60
    By spells and medicines bought of mountebanks.
    For nature so preposterously to err,
    Being not deficient, blind, or lame of sense,
    Sans° witchcraft could not.

DUKE. Whoe'er he be that in this foul proceeding   65
    Hath thus beguiled your daughter of herself
    And you of her, the bloody book of law
    You shall yourself read in the bitter letter
    After your own sense—yea, though our proper° son
    Stood in your action.

BRABANTIO.   Humbly I thank your Grace.   70
    Here is the man, this Moor, whom now, it seems,
    Your special mandate for the state affairs
    Hath hither brought.

ALL.   We are very sorry for 't.

DUKE (*to* OTHELLO).   What in your own part can you say to this?

BRABANTIO. Nothing but this is so.   75

OTHELLO. Most potent, grave, and reverend signiors,
    My very noble and approved good masters,
    That I have ta'en away this old man's daughter,
    It is most true—true, I have married her.

---

55. particular: personal   64. Sans: Without   69. proper: own

The very head and front of my offending   80
Hath this extent, no more. Rude am I in my speech,
And little blest with the soft phrase of peace,
For since these arms of mine had seven years' pith
Till now some nine moons wasted, they have used
Their dearest action in the tented field;   85
And little of this great world can I speak,
More than pertains to feats of broil and battle,
And therefore little shall I grace my cause
In speaking for myself. Yet, by your gracious patience,
I will a round unvarnished tale° deliver   90
Of my whole course of love—what drugs, what charms,
What conjuration and what mighty magic—
For such proceeding I am charged withal—
I won his daughter.

BRABANTIO.   A maiden never bold,
Of spirit so still and quiet that her motion   95
Blushed at herself, and she—in spite of nature,
Of years, of country, credit,° everything—
To fall in love with what she feared to look on!
It is a judgment maimed and most imperfect
That will confess perfection so could err   100
Against all rules of nature, and must be driven
To find out practices of cunning Hell
Why this should be. I therefore vouch again
That with some mixtures powerful o'er the blood,
Or with some dram conjured to this effect,   105
He wrought upon her.

DUKE.   To vouch this is no proof
Without more certain and more overt test
Than these thin habits and poor likelihoods
Of modern seeming° do prefer against him.

FIRST SENATOR. But, Othello, speak.   110
Did you by indirect and forcèd courses
Subdue and poison this young maid's affections?
Or came it by request, and such fair question
As soul to soul affordeth?

---

90. **round . . . tale:** direct, unadorned account   97. **credit:** reputation   108–9. **thin . . . seeming:** superficial, unlikely, and trivial suppositions [Eds.]

OTHELLO.   I do beseech you
  Send for the lady to the Sagittary,   115
  And let her speak of me before her father.
  If you do find me foul in her report,
  The trust, the office I do hold of you,
  Not only take away, but let your sentence
  Even fall upon my life.
DUKE.   Fetch Desdemona hither.   120
OTHELLO. Ancient, conduct them, you best know the place.
  (*Exeunt* IAGO *and* ATTENDANTS.)
  And till she come, as truly as to Heaven
  I do confess the vices of my blood,
  So justly to your grave ears I'll present
  How I did thrive in this fair lady's love   125
  And she in mine.
DUKE.   Say it, Othello.
OTHELLO. Her father loved me, oft invited me,
  Still° questioned me the story of my life
  From year to year, the battles, sieges, fortunes,
  That I have passed.   130
  I ran it through, even from my boyish days
  To the very moment that he bade me tell it.
  Wherein I spake of most disastrous chances,
  Of moving accidents by flood and field,
  Of hairbreadth 'scapes i' the imminent deadly breach,   135
  Of being taken by the insolent foe
  And sold to slavery, of my redemption thence,
  And portance in my travels' history.
  Wherein of antres° vast and deserts idle,
  Rough quarries, rocks, and hills whose heads touch heaven,   140
  It was my hint to speak—such was the process.
  And of the cannibals that each other eat,
  The anthropophagi,° and men whose heads
  Do grow beneath their shoulders. This to hear
  Would Desdemona seriously incline.   145
  But still the house affairs would draw her thence,
  Which ever as she could with haste dispatch,
  She'd come again, and with a greedy ear
  Devour up my discourse. Which I observing,
  Took once a pliant hour and found good means   150

128. Still: Always   139. antres: caves   143. anthropophagi: cannibals

To draw from her a prayer of earnest heart
That I would all my pilgrimage dilate,
Whereof by parcels she had something heard,
But not intentively. I did consent,
And often did beguile her of her tears   155
When I did speak of some distressful stroke
That my youth suffered. My story being done,
She gave me for my pains a world of sighs.
She swore, in faith, 'twas strange, 'twas passing strange,
'Twas pitiful, 'twas wondrous pitiful.   160
She wished she had not heard it, yet she wished
That Heaven had made her such a man. She thanked me,
And bade me, if I had a friend that loved her,
I should but teach him how to tell my story
And that would woo her. Upon this hint° I spake.   165
She loved me for the dangers I had passed,
And I loved her that she did pity them.
This only is the witchcraft I have used.
Here comes the lady, let her witness it.
(*Enter* DESDEMONA, IAGO, *and* ATTENDANTS.)

DUKE. I think this tale would win my daughter too.   170
Good Brabantio,
Take up this mangled matter at the best.°
Men do their broken weapons rather use
Than their bare hands.

BRABANTIO.   I pray you hear her speak.
If she confess that she was half the wooer,   175
Destruction on my head if my bad blame
Light on the man! Come hither, gentle mistress.
Do you perceive in all this noble company
Where most you owe obedience?

DESDEMONA.   My noble father,
I do perceive here a divided duty.   180
To you I am bound for life and education,
My life and education both do learn me
How to respect you; you are the lord of duty,
I am hitherto your daughter. But here's my husband,
And so much duty as my mother showed   185

---

165. hint: opportunity [Eds.]   172. Take . . . best: Make the best settlement you can of this
confused business.

To you, preferring you before her father,
So much I challenge that I may profess
Due to the Moor my lord.

BRABANTIO.   God be with you! I have done.
Please it your Grace, on to the state affairs.
I had rather to adopt a child than get° it.   190
Come hither, Moor.
I here do give thee that with all my heart
Which, but thou hast already, with all my heart
I would keep from thee. For your sake, jewel,
I am glad at soul I have no other child,   195
For thy escape would teach me tyranny,
To hang clogs on them. I have done, my lord.

DUKE. Let me speak like yourself, and lay a sentence°
Which, as a grise° or step, may help these lovers
Into your favor.   200
When remedies are past, the griefs are ended
By seeing the worst, which late on hopes depended.
To mourn a mischief that is past and gone
Is the next way to draw new mischief on.
What cannot be preserved when fortune takes,   205
Patience her injury a mockery makes.
The robbed that smiles steals something from the thief.
He robs himself that spends a bootless grief.

BRABANTIO. So let the Turk of Cyprus us beguile,
We lose it not so long as we can smile.   210
He bears the sentence well that nothing bears
But the free comfort which from thence he hears.
But he bears both the sentence and the sorrow
That, to pay grief, must of poor patience borrow.
These sentences, to sugar or to gall,   215
Being strong on both sides, are equivocal.
But words are words. I never yet did hear
That the bruised heart was piercèd through the ear.
I humbly beseech you, proceed to the affairs of state.

DUKE. The Turk with a most mighty preparation makes for Cyprus.
Othello, the fortitude of the place is best known to you, and though

---

190 **get:** beget   198. **sentence:** proverbial saying   199. **grise:** degree

we have there a substitute° of most allowed sufficiency, yet opinion,
a sovereign mistress of effects, throws a more safer voice on you. You
must therefore be content to slubber° the gloss of your new fortunes 225
with this more stubborn and boisterous expedition.

OTHELLO. The tyrant custom, most grave Senators,
Hath made the flinty and steel couch of war
My thrice-driven bed of down. I do agnize° 230
A natural and prompt alacrity
I find in hardness,° and do undertake
These present wars against the Ottomites.
Most humbly therefore bending to your state,
I crave fit disposition for my wife,
Due reference of place and exhibition,° 235
With such accommodation and besort°
As levels with her breeding.

DUKE.   If you please,
Be 't at her father's.

BRABANTIO.   I'll not have it so.

OTHELLO. Nor I.

DESDEMONA.   Nor I. I would not there reside, 240
To put my father in impatient thoughts
By being in his eye. Most gracious Duke,
To my unfolding lend your prosperous° ear,
And let me find a charter in your voice
To assist my simpleness. 245

DUKE. What would you, Desdemona?

DESDEMONA. That I did love the Moor to live with him,
My downright violence and storm of fortunes
May trumpet to the world. My heart's subdued
Even to the very quality° of my lord. 250
I saw Othello's visage in his mind,
And to his honors and his valiant parts°
Did I my soul and fortunes consecrate.
So that, dear lords, if I be left behind,
A moth of peace, and he go to the war, 255
The rites for which I love him are bere[f]
And I a heavy interim shall support
By his dear absence. Let me go wit[h]

222. **substitute**: deputy commander [ver]: tarnish 228. **agnize**: confess 230. [hardness**: hardship 234. **exhibition**: [qualities] 235. **besort**: attendants 241. **prosperous**: [favorable] 248. **quality**: profession

OTHELLO. Let her have your voices.
   Vouch with me, Heaven, I therefore beg it not
   To please the palate of my appetite,
   Nor to comply with heat—the young affects   260
   In me defunct°—and proper satisfaction,
   But to be free and bounteous to her mind.°
   And Heaven defend your good souls, that you think
   I will your serious and great business scant
   For she is with me. No, when light-winged toys   265
   Of feathered Cupid seel° with wanton dullness
   My speculative and officed instruments,°
   That my disports° corrupt and taint my business,
   Let housewives make a skillet of my helm,
   And all indign° and base adversities   270
   Make head against my estimation!°
DUKE. Be it as you shall privately determine,
   Either for her stay or going. The affair cries haste,
   And speed must answer 't. You must hence tonight.
DESDEMONA. Tonight, my lord?
DUKE.   This night.
OTHELLO.   With all my heart.   275
DUKE. At nine i' the morning here we'll meet again.
   Othello, leave some officer behind,
   And he shall our commission bring to you,
   With such things else of quality and respect
   As doth import you.
OTHELLO.   So please your Grace, my Ancient,   280
   A man he is of honesty and trust.
   To his conveyance I assign my wife,
   With what else needful your good Grace shall think
   To be sent after me.
DUKE.   Let it be so.
   Good night to everyone. (To BRABANTIO) And, noble signior,   285
   If virtue no delighted beauty lack,
   Your son-in-law is more fair than black.°
FIRST SENATOR. Adieu, brave Moor. Use Desdemona well.

260–61. young . . . defunct: in me
Desdemona's claim that this is a man of youth is dead   262. to . . . mind: Othello repeats
instruments: powers of sight and action minds. 266. seel: close up 267. speculative . . .
ments 270. indign: unworthy 271. e efficiency as your general 268. disports: amuse-
is a beautiful thing in itself, your son-in-law reputation 286–87. If . . . black: If worthiness
lack, has beauty.

BRABANTIO. Look to her, Moor, if thou hast eyes to see.
She has deceived her father, and may thee.   290
(*Exeunt* DUKE, SENATORS, OFFICERS, *etc.*)
OTHELLO. My life upon her faith! Honest Iago,
My Desdemona must I leave to thee.
I prithee, let thy wife attend on her,
And bring them after in the best advantage.
Come, Desdemona, I have but an hour   295
Of love, of worldly matters and direction,
To spend with thee. We must obey the time.
(*Exeunt* OTHELLO *and* DESDEMONA.)
RODERIGO. Iago!
IAGO. What sayest thou, noble heart?
RODERIGO. What will I do, thinkest thou?   300
IAGO. Why, go to bed and sleep.
RODERIGO. I will incontinently° drown myself.
IAGO. If thou dost, I shall never love thee after. Why, thou silly
gentleman!
RODERIGO. It is silliness to live when to live is torment, and then   305
have we a prescription to die when death is our physician.
IAGO. Oh, villainous! I have looked upon the world for four times seven
years, and since I could distinguish betwixt a benefit and an injury
I never found man that knew how to love himself. Ere I would say I
would drown myself for the love of a guinea hen, I would change my
humanity with a baboon.   311
RODERIGO. What should I do? I confess it is my shame to be so fond, but
it is not in my virtue° to amend it.
IAGO. Virtue! A fig! 'Tis in ourselves that we are thus or thus. Our bodies
are gardens, to the which our wills are gardeners. So that if we will plant
nettles or sow lettuce, set hyssop and weed up thyme, supply it with
one gender of herbs or distract it with many, either to have it sterile
with idleness or manured with industry—why, the power and corrigible°
authority of this lies in our wills. If the balance of our lives had not one
scale of reason to poise another of sensuality, the blood and baseness of
our natures would conduct us to most preposterous conclusions. But we
have reason to cool our raging motions, our carnal stings, our unbitted
lusts, whereof I take this that you call love to be a sect or scion.°
RODERIGO. It cannot be.   325

---

302. **incontinently:** immediately   313. **virtue:** strength [Eds.]   319. **corrigible:** correcting,
directing   324. **sect or scion:** Both words mean a slip taken from a tree and planted to produce
a new growth.

IAGO. It is merely a lust of the blood and a permission of the will.
Come, be a man! Drown thyself? Drown cats and blind puppies! I
have professed me thy friend, and I confess me knit to thy deserving
with cables of perdurable toughness. I could never better stead thee
than now. Put money in thy purse, follow thou the wars, defeat
thy favor with an usurped beard°—I say put money in thy purse.
It cannot be that Desdemona should long continue her love to the
Moor—put money in thy purse—nor he his to her. It was a violent
commencement, and thou shalt see an answerable sequestration°—
put but money in thy purse. These Moors are changeable in their
wills.°—Fill thy purse with money. The food that to him now is as
luscious as locusts shall be to him shortly as bitter as coloquintida.°
She must change for youth. When she is sated with his body, she
will find the error of her choice. She must have change, she must—
therefore put money in thy purse. If thou wilt needs damn thyself,
do it a more delicate way than drowning. Make all the money thou
canst.° If sanctimony and a frail vow betwixt an erring° barbarian and
a supersubtle Venetian be not too hard for my wits and all the tribe of
Hell, thou shalt enjoy her—therefore make money. A pox of drowning
thyself! It is clean out of the way. Seek thou rather to be hanged in
compassing thy joy than to be drowned and go without her.   347
RODERIGO. Wilt thou be fast to my hopes if I depend on the issue?
IAGO. Thou art sure of me. Go, make money. I have told thee often, and
I retell thee again and again, I hate the Moor. My cause is hearted,°
thine hath no less reason. Let us be conjunctive in our revenge against
him. If thou canst cuckold him thou dost thyself a pleasure, me a
sport. There are many events in the womb of time which will be
delivered. Traverse, go, provide thy money. We will have more of this
tomorrow. Adieu.   355
RODERIGO. Where shall we meet i' the morning?
IAGO. At my lodging.
RODERIGO. I'll be with thee betimes.
IAGO. Go to, farewell. Do you hear, Roderigo?
RODERIGO. What say you?   360
IAGO. No more of drowning, do you hear?
RODERIGO. I am changed. I'll go sell all my land. (*Exit.*)

330–31. **defeat . . . beard:** disguise your face by growing a beard   334–35. **answerable seques-
tration:** corresponding separation; i.e., reaction   336. **wills:** desires [Eds.]   338. **coloquintida:**
a bitter purgative [Eds.]   342. **Make . . . canst:** Turn all you can into ready cash.   343. **erring:**
vagabond   351. **hearted:** heartfelt

IAGO. Thus do I ever make my fool my purse,
  For I mine own gained knowledge should profane
  If I would time expend with such a snipe   365
  But for my sport and profit. I hate the Moor,
  And it is thought abroad that 'twixt my sheets
  He's done my office. I know not if 't be true,
  But I for mere suspicion in that kind
  Will do as if for surety. He holds me well,   370
  The better shall my purpose work on him.
  Cassio's a proper° man. Let me see now,
  To get his place, and to plume up° my will
  In double knavery—How, how?—Let's see.—
  After some time, to abuse Othello's ear   375
  That he is too familiar with his wife.
  He hath a person and a smooth dispose
  To be suspected,° framed to make women false.
  The Moor is of a free and open nature
  That thinks men honest that but seem to be so,   380
  And will as tenderly be led by the nose
  As asses are.
  I have't. It is engendered. Hell and night
  Must bring this monstrous birth to the world's light. (*Exit.*)

ACT 2

SCENE 1. A seaport in Cyprus. An open place near the wharf.

Enter MONTANO *and two* GENTLEMEN.
MONTANO. What from the cape can you discern at sea?
FIRST GENTLEMAN. Nothing at all. It is a high-wrought flood.
  I cannot 'twixt the heaven and the main
  Descry a sail.
MONTANO. Methinks the wind hath spoke aloud at land,   5
  A fuller blast ne'er shook our battlements.
  If it hath ruffianed so upon the sea,
  What ribs of oak, when mountains melt on them,
  Can hold the mortise? What shall we hear of this?
SECOND GENTLEMAN. A segregation° of the Turkish fleet.   10
  For do but stand upon the foaming shore,
  The chidden billow seems to pelt the clouds,

---

372. **proper:** handsome   373. **plume up:** glorify   377–78. **He . . . suspected:** He has an easy way about him that is naturally suspected.   10. **segregation:** separation

The wind-shakèd surge, with high and monstrous mane,
Seems to cast water on the burning Bear,
And quench the guards of the ever-fixèd Pole.° 15
I never did like molestation view
On the enchafèd flood.

MONTANO.   If that the Turkish fleet
Be not ensheltered and embayed, they are drowned.
It is impossible to bear it out. (*Enter a* THIRD GENTLEMAN.)

THIRD GENTLEMAN. News, lads! Our wars are done. 20
The desperate tempest hath so banged the Turks
That their designment halts. A noble ship of Venice
Hath seen a grievous wreck and sufferance°
On most part of their fleet.

MONTANO. How! Is this true?

THIRD GENTLEMAN.   The ship is here put in, 25
A Veronesa. Michael Cassio,
Lieutenant to the warlike Moor Othello,
Is come on shore, the Moor himself at sea,
And is in full commission here for Cyprus.

MONTANO. I am glad on 't. 'Tis a worthy governor. 30

THIRD GENTLEMAN. But this same Cassio, though he speak of comfort
Touching the Turkish loss, yet he looks sadly
And prays the Moor be safe, for they were parted
With foul and violent tempest.

MONTANO.   Pray Heavens he be,
For I have served him, and the man commands 35
Like a full soldier. Let's to the seaside, ho!
As well to see the vessel that's come in
As to throw out our eyes for brave Othello,
Even till we make the main and the aerial blue
An indistinct regard.

THIRD GENTLEMAN. Come, let's do so. 40
For every minute is expectancy
Of more arrivance. (*Enter* CASSIO.)

CASSIO. Thanks, you the valiant of this warlike isle
That so approve the Moor! Oh, let the heavens
Give him defense against the elements, 45
For I have lost him on a dangerous sea.

MONTANO. Is he well shipped?

14–15. **cast . . . Pole:** drown the constellations [Eds.]   23. **sufferance:** damage

CASSIO. His bark is stoutly timbered, and his pilot
  Of very expert and approved allowance.
  Therefore my hopes, not surfeited to death, 50
  Stand in bold cure.
  (*A cry within:* "A sail, a sail, a sail!" *Enter a* FOURTH GENTLEMAN.)
  What noise?
FOURTH GENTLEMAN. The town is empty. On the brow o' the sea
  Stand ranks of people and they cry "A sail!"
CASSIO. My hopes do shape him for the governor. (*Guns heard.*) 55
SECOND GENTLEMAN. They do discharge their shot of courtesy.
  Our friends, at least.
CASSIO.   I pray you, sir, go forth,
  And give us truth who 'tis that is arrived.
SECOND GENTLEMAN. I shall. (*Exit.*)
MONTANO. But, good Lieutenant, is your General wived? 60
CASSIO. Most fortunately. He hath achieved a maid
  That paragons description and wild fame,
  One that excels the quirks of blazoning pens
  And in the essential vesture of creation
  Does tire the ingener.° (*Re-enter* SECOND GENTLEMAN.)
                How now! Who has put in? 65
SECOND GENTLEMAN.   'Tis one Iago, Ancient to the General.
CASSIO. He has had most favorable and happy speed.
  Tempests themselves, high seas, and howling winds,
  The guttered rocks, and congregated sands,
  Traitors ensteeped to clog the guiltless keel, 70
  As having sense of beauty, do omit
  Their mortal° natures, letting go safely by
  The divine Desdemona.
MONTANO.   What is she?
CASSIO. She that I spake of, our great Captain's captain,
  Left in the conduct of the bold Iago, 75
  Whose footing here anticipates our thoughts
  A sennight's° speed. Great Jove, Othello guard,
  And swell his sail with thine own powerful breath,
  That he may bless this bay with his tall ship,
  Make love's quick pants in Desdemona's arms, 80

63–65. One . . . ingener: One that is too good for the fancy phrases (*quirks*) of painting pens (i.e., poets) and in her absolute perfection wearies the artist (i.e., the painter) ingener: inventor
72. mortal: deadly 77. sennight's: week's

Give renewed fire to our extincted spirits,
And bring all Cyprus comfort.
(*Enter* DESDEMONA, EMILIA, IAGO, RODERIGO, *and* ATTENDANTS.)
                    Oh, behold,
The riches of the ship is come on shore!
Ye men of Cyprus, let her have your knees.
Hail to thee, lady! And the grace of Heaven,   85
Before, behind thee, and on every hand,
Enwheel thee round!

DESDEMONA.   I thank you, valiant Cassio.
What tidings can you tell me of my lord?

CASSIO. He is not yet arrived, nor know I aught
But that he's well and will be shortly here.   90

DESDEMONA. Oh, but I fear—How lost you company?

CASSIO. The great contention of the sea and skies
Parted our fellowship.—But hark! A sail.
(*A cry within:* "A sail, a sail!" *Guns heard.*)

SECOND GENTLEMAN. They give their greeting to the citadel.
This likewise is a friend.

CASSIO.   See for the news. (*Exit* GENTLEMAN.)   95
Good Ancient, you are welcome. (*To* EMILIA) Welcome, mistress.
Let it not gall your patience, good Iago,
That I extend my manners. 'Tis my breeding
That gives me this bold show of courtesy. (*Kissing her.*)

IAGO. Sir, would she give you so much of her lips   100
As of her tongue she oft bestows on me,
You'd have enough.

DESDEMONA.   Alas, she has no speech.

IAGO. In faith, too much,
I find it still when I have list° to sleep.
Marry, before your ladyship, I grant,   105
She puts her tongue a little in her heart
And chides with thinking.

EMILIA. You have little cause to say so.

IAGO. Come on, come on. You are pictures° out of doors,
Bells° in your parlors, wildcats in your kitchens,   110
Saints in your injuries,° devils being offended,
Players in your housewifery, and housewives in your beds.

DESDEMONA. Oh, fie upon thee, slanderer!

---

104. list: desire   109. pictures: i.e., painted and dumb   110. Bells: i.e., ever clacking   111. Saints
. . . injuries: Saints when you hurt anyone else

IAGO. Nay, it is true, or else I am a Turk.
   You rise to play, and go to bed to work.   115
EMILIA. You shall not write my praise.
IAGO.   No, let me not.
DESDEMONA. What wouldst thou write of me if thou shouldst
   praise me?
IAGO. O gentle lady, do not put me to 't,
   For I am nothing if not critical.
DESDEMONA. Come on, assay.°—There's one gone to the harbor?   120
IAGO. Aye, madam.
DESDEMONA (*aside*). I am not merry, but I do beguile
   The thing I am by seeming otherwise.—
   Come, how wouldst thou praise me?
IAGO. I am about it, but indeed my invention   125
   Comes from my pate as birdlime does from frieze°—
   It plucks out brains and all. But my Muse labors,
   And thus she is delivered:
   If she be fair and wise, fairness and wit,
   The one's for use, the other useth it.   130
DESDEMONA. Well praised! How if she be black° and witty?
IAGO. If she be black, and thereto have a wit,
   She'll find a white° that shall her blackness fit.
DESDEMONA. Worse and worse.
EMILIA. How if fair and foolish?   135
IAGO. She never yet was foolish that was fair,
   For even her folly helped her to an heir.
DESDEMONA. These are old fond paradoxes to make fools laugh i' the
   alehouse. What miserable praise hast thou for her that's foul and
   foolish?   140
IAGO. There's none so foul, and foolish thereunto,
   But does foul pranks which fair and wise ones do.
DESDEMONA. Oh, heavy ignorance! Thou praisest the worst best. But what
   praise couldst thou bestow on a deserving woman indeed, one that in
   the authority of her merit did justly put on the vouch of very malice
   itself?°   146
IAGO. She that was ever fair and never proud,
   Had tongue at will° and yet was never loud,
   Never lacked gold and yet went never gay,
   Fled from her wish and yet said "Now I may";   150

---

120. **assay:**   125–26. **my . . . frieze:** my literary effort (*invention*) is as hard to pull out of my head
as frieze (cloth with a nap)   131. **black:** brunette, dark-complexioned [Eds.]   133. **white:** with a
pun on *wight* (line 157), man, person   144–46. **one . . . itself:** one so deserving that even malice
would declare her good   148. **tongue . . . will:** a ready flow of words

She that, being angered, her revenge being nigh,
Bade her wrong stay and her displeasure fly;
She that in wisdom never was so frail
To change the cod's head for the salmon's tail;°
She that could think and ne'er disclose her mind,   155
See suitors following and not look behind;
She was a wight, if ever such wight were—

DESDEMONA. To do what?

IAGO. To suckle fools and chronicle small beer.°

DESDEMONA. Oh, most lame and impotent conclusion! Do not learn
of him, Emilia, though he be thy husband. How say you, Cassio? Is
he not a most profane and liberal° counselor?   162

CASSIO. He speaks home,° madam. You may relish him more in the
soldier than in the scholar.

IAGO (*aside*). He takes her by the palm. Aye, well said, whisper.
With as little a web as this will I ensnare as great a fly as Cassio.
Aye, smile upon her, do, I will gyve thee in thine own courtship.°
You say true, 'tis so indeed. If such tricks as these strip you out of
your Lieutenantry, it had been better you had not kissed your three
fingers° so oft, which now again you are most apt to play the sir° in.
Very good, well kissed! An excellent courtesy! 'Tis so indeed.
Yet again your fingers to your lips? Would they were clyster pipes°
for your sake! (*Trumpet within.*) The Moor! I know his trumpet.   173

CASSIO. 'Tis truly so.

DESDEMONA. Let's meet him and receive him.   175

CASSIO. Lo where he comes! (*Enter* OTHELLO *and* ATTENDANTS.)

OTHELLO. O my fair warrior!°

DESDEMONA.   My dear Othello!

OTHELLO. It gives me wonder great as my content
To see you here before me. O my soul's joy!
If after every tempest come such calms,   180
May the winds blow till they have wakened death!
And let the laboring bark climb hills of seas
Olympus-high, and duck again as low
As Hell's from Heaven! If it were now to die,
'Twere now to be most happy, for I fear   185
My soul hath her content so absolute

---

154. To . . . tail: To prefer the tail end of a good thing to the head of a poor thing   159. suckle
. . . beer: nurse babies and keep petty household accounts (i.e., even the best woman belongs in
the nursery and kitchen) [Eds.]   162. liberal: gross   163. home: bluntly [Eds.]   167. gyve . . .
courtship: trap you with your own show of courtesy [Eds.]   169. kissed . . . fingers: a gesture
of gallantry   170. play the sir: act the fine gentleman   172. clyster pipes: an enema syringe
177. warrior: because she is a soldier's wife

That not another comfort like to this
Succeeds in unknown fate.

DESDEMONA.   The Heavens forbid
But that our loves and comforts should increase,
Even as our days do grow!

OTHELLO.   Amen to that, sweet powers!   190
I cannot speak enough of this content.
It stops me here,° it is too much of joy.
And this, and this, the greatest discords be (*kissing her*)
That e'er our hearts shall make!

IAGO (*aside*).   Oh, you are well tuned now,
But I'll set down the pegs° that make this music,   195
As honest as I am.

OTHELLO.   Come, let us to the castle.
News, friends! Our wars are done, the Turks are drowned.
How does my old acquaintance of this isle?
Honey, you shall be well desired in Cyprus,
I have found great love amongst them. O my sweet,   200
I prattle out of fashion, and I dote
In mine own comforts. I prithee, good Iago,
Go to the bay and disembark my coffers.°
Bring thou the master° to the citadel.
He is a good one, and his worthiness   205
Does challenge much respect. Come, Desdemona,
Once more well met at Cyprus. (*Exeunt all but* IAGO *and* RODERIGO.)

IAGO. Do thou meet me presently at the harbor. Come hither. If thou beest
valiant—as they say base men being in love have then a nobility in their
natures more than is native to them—list me. The Lieutenant tonight
watches on the court of guard. First, I must tell thee this. Desdemona
is directly in love with him.   212

RODERIGO. With him! Why, 'tis not possible.

IAGO. Lay thy finger thus,° and let thy soul be instructed. Mark me
with what violence she first loved the Moor, but for bragging and
telling her fantastical lies. And will she love him still for prating?
Let not thy discreet heart think it. Her eye must be fed, and what
delight shall she have to look on the Devil? When the blood is made

---

192. **here:** i.e., in the heart   195. **set . . . pegs:** i.e., make you sing out of tune. A stringed
instrument was tuned by the pegs.   203. **coffers:** trunks   204. **master:** captain of the ship
214. **thus:** i.e., on the lips

dull with the act of sport, there should be, again to inflame it and to give satiety a fresh appetite, loveliness in favor,° sympathy in years, manners, and beauties, all which the Moor is defective in. Now, for want of these required conveniences, her delicate tenderness will find itself abused, begin to heave the gorge, disrelish and abhor the Moor. Very nature will instruct her in it and compel her to some second choice. Now, sir, this granted—as it is a most pregnant and unforced position°— who stands so eminently in the degree of this fortune as Cassio does? A knave very voluble, no further conscionable° than in putting on the mere form of civil and humane seeming° for the better compassing of his salt° and most hidden loose affection? Why, none, why, none. A slipper° and subtle knave, a finder-out of occasions, that has an eye can stamp and counterfeit advantages,° though true advantage never present itself. A devilish knave! Besides, the knave is handsome, young, and hath all those requisites in him that folly and green minds look after. A pestilent complete knave, and the woman hath found him already.   235

RODERIGO. I cannot believe that in her. She's full of most blest condition.°

IAGO. Blest fig's-end!° The wine she drinks is made of grapes. If she had been blest, she would never have loved the Moor. Blest pudding! Didst thou not see her paddle with the palm of his hand? Didst not mark that?   241

RODERIGO. Yes, that I did, but that was but courtesy.

IAGO. Lechery, by his hand, an index and obscure prologue to the history of lust and foul thoughts. They met so near with their lips that their breaths embraced together. Villainous thoughts, Roderigo! When these mutualities so marshal the way, hard at hand comes the master and main exercise, the incorporate° conclusion. Pish! But, sir, be you ruled by me. I have brought you from Venice. Watch you tonight. For the command, I'll lay 't upon you. Cassio knows you not. I'll not be far from you. Do you find some occasion to anger Cassio, either by speaking too loud, or tainting° his discipline, or from what other course you please which the time shall more favorably minister.

RODERIGO. Well.   253

---

220. **favor:** face 225–26. **pregnant . . . position:** very significant and probable argument 227. **no . . . conscionable:** who has no more conscience 228. **humane seeming:** courteous appearance 229. **salt:** lecherous 230. **slipper:** slippery 231. **stamp . . . advantages:** forge false opportunities 237. **condition:** disposition 238. **fig's-end:** nonsense [Eds.] 247. **incorporate:** bodily 251. **tainting:** disparaging

IAGO. Sir, he is rash and very sudden in choler,° and haply may strike at you. Provoke him, that he may, for even out of that will I cause these of Cyprus to mutiny, whose qualification shall come into no true taste again but by the displanting of Cassio. So shall you have a shorter journey to your desires by the means I shall then have to prefer° them, and the impediment most profitably removed without the which there were no expectation of our prosperity.   260

RODERIGO. I will do this, if I can bring it to any opportunity.

IAGO. I warrant thee. Meet me by and by at the citadel. I must fetch his necessaries ashore. Farewell.

RODERIGO.   Adieu. (*Exit.*)

IAGO. That Cassio loves her, I do well believe it.   265
    That she loves him, 'tis apt and of great credit.°
    The Moor, howbeit that I endure him not,
    Is of a constant, loving, noble nature,
    And I dare think he'll prove to Desdemona
    A most dear husband. Now, I do love her too,   270
    Not out of absolute lust, though peradventure
    I stand accountant for as great a sin,
    But partly led to diet° my revenge
    For that I do suspect the lusty Moor
    Hath leaped into my seat. The thought whereof   275
    Doth like a poisonous mineral gnaw my inwards,
    And nothing can or shall content my soul
    Till I am evened with him, wife for wife.
    Or failing so, yet that I put the Moor
    At least into a jealousy so strong   280
    That judgment cannot cure. Which thing to do,
    If this poor trash of Venice, whom I trash
    For his quick hunting,° stand the putting-on,
    I'll have our Michael Cassio on the hip,
    Abuse him to the Moor in the rank garb°—   285
    For I fear Cassio with my nightcap too—
    Make the Moor thank me, love me, and reward me
    For making him egregiously an ass
    And practicing upon his peace and quiet
    Even to madness. 'Tis here, but yet confused.   290
    Knavery's plain face is never seen till used. (*Exit.*)

---

254. choler: anger   259. prefer: promote   266. apt . . . credit: likely and very creditable
273. diet: feed   282–83. trash . . . hunting: hold back from outrunning the pack [Eds.]
285. rank garb: gross manner; i.e., by accusing him of being Desdemona's lover

SCENE 2. A street.

Enter a HERALD *with a proclamation,* PEOPLE *following.*

HERALD. It is Othello's pleasure, our noble and valiant General, that upon certain tidings now arrived, importing the mere perdition° of the Turkish fleet, every man put himself into triumph°—some to dance, some to make bonfires, each man to what sport and revels his addiction leads him. For, besides these beneficial news, it is the celebration of his nuptial. So much was his pleasure should be proclaimed. All offices° are open, and there is full liberty of feasting from this present hour of five till the bell have told eleven. Heaven bless the isle of Cyprus and our noble General Othello! (*Exeunt.*)

SCENE 3. A hall in the castle.

Enter OTHELLO, DESDEMONA, CASSIO, *and* ATTENDANTS.

OTHELLO. Good Michael, look you to the guard tonight.
  Let's teach ourselves that honorable stop,
  Not to outsport discretion.°
CASSIO. Iago hath directions what to do,
  But notwithstanding with my personal eye   5
  Will I look to 't.
OTHELLO.   Iago is most honest.
  Michael, good night. Tomorrow with your earliest
  Let me have speech with you. (*To* DESDEMONA) Come, my dear love,
  The purchase made, the fruits are to ensue—
  That profit's yet to come 'tween me and you.   10
  Good night. (*Exeunt all but* CASSIO. *Enter* IAGO.)
CASSIO. Welcome, Iago. We must to the watch.
IAGO. Not this hour, Lieutenant, 'tis not yet ten o'clock. Our General cast° us thus early for the love of his Desdemona, who let us not therefore blame. He hath not yet made wanton the night with her, and she is sport for Jove.   16
CASSIO. She's a most exquisite lady.
IAGO. And, I'll warrant her, full of game.
CASSIO. Indeed she's a most fresh and delicate creature.
IAGO. What an eye she has! Methinks it sounds a parley to provocation.   20
CASSIO. An inviting eye, and yet methinks right modest.
IAGO. And when she speaks, is it not an alarum to love?

---

2. **mere perdition:** absolute destruction   3. **put . . . triumph:** celebrate   7. **offices:** the kitchen and buttery—i.e., free food and drink for all   3. **outsport discretion:** let the fun go too far. 14. **cast:** dismissed

CASSIO. She is indeed perfection.

IAGO. Well, happiness to their sheets! Come, Lieutenant, I have a stoup of
    wine, and there without are a brace of Cyprus gallants that would fain
    have a measure to the health of black Othello.   27

CASSIO. Not tonight, good Iago. I have very poor and unhappy brains for
    drinking. I could well wish courtesy would invent some other custom
    of entertainment.   30

IAGO. Oh, they are our friends. But one cup—I'll drink for you.

CASSIO. I have drunk but one cup tonight, and that was craftily qualified°
    too, and behold what innovation it makes here. I am unfortunate in the
    infirmity, and dare not task my weakness with any more.

IAGO. What, man! 'Tis a night of revels. The gallants desire it.   35

CASSIO. Where are they?

IAGO. Here at the door. I pray you call them in.

CASSIO. I'll do 't, but it dislikes me. (*Exit.*)

IAGO. If I can fasten but one cup upon him,
    With that which he hath drunk tonight already,   40
    He'll be as full of quarrel and offense
    As my young mistress' dog. Now my sick fool Roderigo,
    Whom love hath turned almost the wrong side out,
    To Desdemona hath tonight caroused
    Potations pottle-deep, and he's to watch.   45
    Three lads of Cyprus, noble swelling spirits
    That hold their honors in a wary distance,°
    The very elements° of this warlike isle,
    Have I tonight flustered with flowing cups,
    And they watch too. Now, 'mongst this flock of drunkards,   50
    Am I to put our Cassio in some action
    That may offend the isle. But here they come.
    If consequence do but approve my dream,
    My boat sails freely, both with wind and stream.
    (*Re-enter* CASSIO, *with him* MONTANO *and* GENTLEMEN, SERVANTS
        following with wine.)

CASSIO. 'Fore God, they have given me a rouse already.   55

MONTANO. Good faith, a little one—not past a pint, as I am a soldier.

IAGO. Some wine, ho! (*Sings*)
      "And let me the cannikin clink, clink
      And let me the cannikin clink.
      A soldier's a man,   60

32–33. **qualified:** diluted [Eds.]   47. **hold . . . distance:** are very sensitive about their honor
[Eds.]   48. **very elements:** typical specimens

> A life's but a span.°
> Why, then let a soldier drink."
> Some wine, boys!

CASSIO. 'Fore God, an excellent song.

IAGO. I learned it in England, where indeed they are most potent
in potting.° Your Dane, your German, and your swag-bellied
Hollander—Drink, ho!—are nothing to your English.   67

CASSIO. Is your Englishman so expert in his drinking?

IAGO. Why, he drinks you with facility your Dane dead drunk, he sweats
not to overthrow your Almain,° he gives your Hollander a vomit° ere
the next pottle can be filled.   71

CASSIO. To the health of our General!

MONTANO. I am for it, Lieutenant, and I'll do you justice.

IAGO. O sweet England! (*Sings*)

> "King Stephen was a worthy peer,   75
>   His breeches cost him but a crown.
> He held them sixpence all too dear,
>   With that he called the tailor lown.°
>
> "He was a wight of high renown,
>   And thou art but of low degree.   80
> 'Tis pride that pulls the country down.
>   Then take thine auld cloak about thee."

> Some wine, ho!

CASSIO. Why, this is a more exquisite song than the other.

IAGO. Will you hear 't again?   85

CASSIO. No, for I hold him to be unworthy of his place that does those
things. Well, God's above all, and there be souls must be saved and
there be souls must not be saved.

IAGO. It's true, good Lieutenant.

CASSIO. For mine own part—no offense to the General, nor any man of
quality—I hope to be saved.   91

IAGO. And so do I too, Lieutenant.

CASSIO. Aye, but, by your leave, not before me. The Lieutenant is to be
saved before the Ancient. Let's have no more of this, let's to our affairs.
God forgive us our sins! Gentlemen, let's look to our business. Do not
think, gentlemen, I am drunk. This is my Ancient, this is my right
hand and this is my left. I am not drunk now, I can stand well enough
and speak well enough.   98

ALL. Excellent well.

---

61. **span:**   lit., the measure between the thumb and little finger of the outstretched hand; about
9 inches   65–66. **potting:** drinking   70. **Almain:** German   **gives . . . vomit:** drinks as much
as will make a Dutchman throw up   78. **lown:** lout

CASSIO. Why, very well, then, you must not think then that I am drunk.
(*Exit.*)

MONTANO. To the platform, masters. Come, let's set the watch.　101

IAGO. You see this fellow that is gone before.
He is a soldier fit to stand by Caesar
And give direction. And do but see his vice.
'Tis to his virtue a just equinox,　105
The one as long as the other. 'Tis pity of him.
I fear the trust Othello puts him in
On some odd time of his infirmity
Will shake this island.

MONTANO.　　　　　　But is he often thus?

IAGO. 'Tis evermore the prologue to his sleep.　110
He'll watch the horologe a double set,°
If drink rock not his cradle.

MONTANO.　　　　　It were well
The General were put in mind of it.
Perhaps he sees it not, or his good nature
Prizes the virtue that appears in Cassio　115
And looks not on his evils. Is not this true? (*Enter* RODERIGO.)

IAGO (*aside to him*). How now, Roderigo! I pray you, after the Lieutenant.
Go. (*Exit* RODERIGO.)

MONTANO. And 'tis great pity that the noble Moor
Should hazard such a place as his own second　120
With one of an ingraft infirmity.
It were an honest action to say
So to the Moor.

IAGO.　　　　　Not I, for this fair island.
I do love Cassio well, and would do much
To cure him of this evil—But hark! What noise?　125
(*A cry within:* "Help! Help!" *Re-enter* CASSIO, *driving in* RODERIGO.)

CASSIO. 'Zounds! You rogue! You rascal!

MONTANO. What's the matter, Lieutenant?

CASSIO. A knave teach me my duty! But I'll beat the knave into a wicker
bottle.

RODERIGO. Beat me!　130

CASSIO. Dost thou prate, rogue? (*Striking* RODERIGO.)

MONTANO. Nay, good Lieutenant (*staying him*),
　　　　　　　　　　　　　　　I pray you sir, hold
your hand.

CASSIO. Let me go, sir, or I'll knock you o'er the mazzard.°

111. watch . . . set: stay awake the clock twice round　133. mazzard: head

MONTANO. Come, come, you're drunk.

CASSIO. Drunk! (*They fight.*)   135

IAGO (*aside to* RODERIGO). Away, I say. Go out and cry a mutiny.
    (*Exit* RODERIGO.)
    Nay, good Lieutenant! God's will, gentlemen!
    Help, ho!—Lieutenant—sir—Montano—sir—
    Help, masters!—Here's a goodly watch indeed! (*A bell rings.*)
    Who's that that rings the bell?—Diablo, ho!   140
    The town will rise. God's will, Lieutenant, hold—
    You will be ashamed forever. (*Re-enter* OTHELLO *and* ATTENDANTS.)

OTHELLO.   What is the matter here?

MONTANO. 'Zounds, I bleed still, I am hurt to death. (*Faints.*)

OTHELLO. Hold, for your lives!

IAGO. Hold, ho! Lieutenant—sir—Montano—gentlemen—   145
    Have you forgot all sense of place and duty?
    Hold! The General speaks to you. Hold, hold, for shame!

OTHELLO. Why, how now, ho! From whence ariseth this?
    Are we turned Turks, and to ourselves do that
    Which Heaven hath forbid the Ottomites?   150
    For Christian shame, put by this barbarous brawl.
    He that stirs next to carve for his own rage
    Holds his soul light, he dies upon his motion.
    Silence that dreadful bell. It frights the isle
    From her propriety. What is the matter, masters?   155
    Honest Iago, that look'st dead with grieving,
    Speak, who began this? On thy love, I charge thee.

IAGO. I do not know. Friends all but now, even now,
    In quarter and in terms like bride and groom
    Devesting them for bed. And then, but now,   160
    As if some planet had unwitted men,
    Swords out, and tilting one at other's breast
    In opposition bloody. I cannot speak
    Any beginning to this peevish odds,
    And would in action glorious I had lost   165
    Those legs that brought me to a part of it!

OTHELLO. How comes it, Michael, you are thus forgot?°

CASSIO. I pray you, pardon me, I cannot speak.

OTHELLO. Worthy Montano, you were wont be civil.
    The gravity and stillness of your youth   170

---

167. **are thus forgot:** have so forgotten yourself

The world hath noted, and your name is great
In mouths of wisest censure.° What's the matter
That you unlace your reputation thus
And spend your rich opinion° for the name
Of a night brawler? Give me answer to it.   175
MONTANO. Worthy Othello, I am hurt to danger.
Your officer, Iago, can inform you—
While I spare speech, which something now offends me—
Of all that I do know. Nor know I aught
By me that's said or done amiss this night,   180
Unless self-charity° be sometimes a vice,
And to defend ourselves it be a sin
When violence assails us.
OTHELLO.   Now, by Heaven,
My blood begins my safer guides to rule,
And passion, having my best judgment collied,°   185
Assays to lead the way. If I once stir,
Or do but lift this arm, the best of you
Shall sink in my rebuke. Give me to know
How this foul rout began, who set it on,
And he that is approved° in this offense,   190
Though he had twinned with me, both at a birth,
Shall lose me. What! In a town of war,
Yet wild, the people's hearts brimful of fear,
To manage private and domestic quarrel,
In night, and on the court and guard of safety!   195
'Tis monstrous. Iago, who began 't?
MONTANO. If partially affined or leagued in office,
Thou dost deliver more or less than truth,
Thou art no soldier.
IAGO.   Touch me not so near.
I had rather have this tongue cut from my mouth   200
Than it should do offense to Michael Cassio.
Yet I persuade myself to speak the truth
Shall nothing wrong him. Thus it is, General.
Montano and myself being in speech,
There comes a fellow crying out for help,   205
And Cassio following him with determined sword
To execute upon him. Sir, this gentleman

---

172. **censure:** judgment   174. **opinion:** reputation [Eds.]   181. **self-charity:** love for oneself
185. **collied:** darkened   190. **approved:** proved guilty

Steps in to Cassio and entreats his pause.
Myself the crying fellow did pursue
Lest by his clamor—as it so fell out—   210
The town might fall in fright. He, swift of foot,
Outran my purpose, and I returned the rather
For that I heard the clink and fall of swords,
And Cassio high in oath, which till tonight
I ne'er might say before. When I came back—   215
For this was brief—I found them close together,
At blow and thrust, even as again they were
When you yourself did part them.
More of this matter cannot I report.
But men are men, the best sometimes forget.   220
Though Cassio did some little wrong to him,
As men in rage strike those that wish them best,
Yet surely Cassio, I believe, received
From him that fled some strange indignity,
Which patience could not pass.

OTHELLO.   I know, Iago,   225
Thy honesty and love doth mince this matter,
Making it light to Cassio. Cassio, I love thee,
But never more be officer of mine. (*Re-enter* DESDEMONA, *attended.*)
Look, if my gentle love be not raised up!
I'll make thee an example.

DESDEMONA.   What's the matter?   230

OTHELLO. All's well now, sweeting. Come away to bed.
(*To* MONTANO, *who is led off.*)
Sir, for your hurts, myself will be your surgeon.
Lead him off.
Iago, look with care about the town,
And silence those whom this vile brawl distracted.   235
Come, Desdemona. 'Tis the soldier's life
To have their balmy slumbers waked with strife.
(*Exeunt all but* IAGO *and* CASSIO.)

IAGO. What, are you hurt, Lieutenant?

CASSIO. Aye, past all surgery.

IAGO. Marry, Heaven forbid!   240

CASSIO. Reputation, reputation, reputation! Oh, I have lost my reputation!
I have lost the immortal part of myself, and what remains is bestial.
My reputation, Iago, my reputation!

IAGO. As I am an honest man, I thought you had received some bodily wound. There is more sense in that than in reputation. Reputation is an idle and most false imposition, oft got without merit and lost without deserving. You have lost no reputation at all unless you repute yourself such a loser. What, man! There are ways to recover the General again. You are but now cast in his mood,° a punishment more in policy° than in malice—even so as one would beat his offenseless dog to affright an imperious lion.° Sue to him again and he's yours. 252

CASSIO. I will rather sue to be despised than to deceive so good a commander with so slight, so drunken, and so indiscreet an officer. Drunk? And speak parrot°? And squabble? Swagger? Swear? And discourse fustian° with one's own shadow? O thou invisible spirit of wine, if thou hast no name to be known by, let us call thee devil! 258

IAGO. What was he that you followed with your sword? What had he done to you? 260

CASSIO. I know not.

IAGO. Is 't possible?

CASSIO. I remember a mass of things, but nothing distinctly—a quarrel, but nothing wherefore. Oh God, that men should put an enemy in their mouths to steal away their brains! That we should, with joy, pleasance, revel, and applause, transform ourselves into beasts! 266

IAGO. Why, but you are now well enough. How came you thus recovered?

CASSIO. It hath pleased the devil drunkenness to give place to the devil wrath. One unperfectness shows me another, to make me frankly despise myself. 271

IAGO. Come, you are too severe a moraler. As the time, the place, and the condition of this country stands, I could heartily wish this had not befallen. But since it is as it is, mend it for your own good.

CASSIO. I will ask him for my place again, he shall tell me I am a drunkard! Had I as many mouths as Hydra, such an answer would stop them all. To be now a sensible man, by and by a fool, and presently a beast! Oh, strange! Every inordinate cup is unblest, and the ingredient is a devil.

IAGO. Come, come, good wine is a good familiar creature, if it be well used. Exclaim no more against it. And, good Lieutenant, I think you think I love you. 282

---

249. cast . . . mood: dismissed because he is in a bad mood   250. in policy: i.e., because he must appear to be angry before the Cypriots   250–51. even . . . lion: a proverb meaning that when the lion sees the dog beaten, he will know what is coming to him   255. speak parrot: babble   256. fustian: nonsense

CASSIO. I have well approved it, sir. I drunk!

IAGO. You or any man living may be drunk at some time, man. I'll tell you what you shall do. Our General's wife is now the General. I may say so in this respect, for that he hath devoted and given up himself to the contemplation, mark, and denotement of her parts and graces. Confess yourself freely to her, importune her help to put you in your place again. She is of so free, so kind, so apt, so blessed a disposition, she holds it a vice in her goodness not to do more than she is requested. This broken joint between you and her husband entreat her to splinter° and, my fortunes against any lay° worth naming, this crack of your love shall grow stronger than it was before.   293

CASSIO. You advise me well.

IAGO. I protest, in the sincerity of love and honest kindness.

CASSIO. I think it freely, and betimes in the morning I will beseech the virtuous Desdemona to undertake for me. I am desperate of my fortunes if they check me here.

IAGO. You are in the right. Good night, Lieutenant, I must to the watch.

CASSIO. Good night, honest Iago. (*Exit.*)   300

IAGO. And what's he then that says I play the villain?
When this advice is free I give and honest,
Probal° to thinking, and indeed the course
To win the Moor again? For 'tis most easy
The inclining Desdemona to subdue   305
In any honest suit. She's framed as fruitful
As the free elements. And then for her
To win the Moor, were 't to renounce his baptism,
All seals and symbols of redeemèd sin,
His soul is so enfettered to her love   310
That she may make, unmake, do what she list,
Even as her appetite shall play the god
With his weak function.° How am I then a villain
To counsel Cassio to this parallel course,
Directly to his good? Divinity of Hell!   315
When devils will the blackest sins put on,
They do suggest at first with heavenly shows,
As I do now. For whiles this honest fool
Plies Desdemona to repair his fortunes,
And she for him pleads strongly to the Moor,   320
I'll pour this pestilence into his ear,

---

292. **splinter:** put in splints   **lay:** bet   303. **Probal:** Probable   313. **function:** mental faculties [Eds.]

That she repeals° him for her body's lust,
And by how much she strives to do him good,
She shall undo her credit with the Moor.
So will I turn her virtue into pitch,   325
And out of her own goodness make the net
That shall enmesh them all. (*Enter* RODERIGO.)
                                   How now, Roderigo!

RODERIGO. I do follow here in the chase, not like a hound that hunts but
  one that fills up the cry. My money is almost spent, I have been tonight
  exceedingly well cudgeled, and I think the issue will be I shall have so
  much experience from my pains and so, with no money at all and a little
  more wit, return again to Venice.   332

IAGO. How poor are they that have not patience!
  What wound did ever heal but by degrees?
  Thou know'st we work by wit and not by witchcraft,   335
  And wit depends on dilatory Time.
  Does 't not go well? Cassio hath beaten thee,
  And thou by that small hurt hast cashiered Cassio.
  Though other things grow fair against the sun,
  Yet fruits that blossom first will first be ripe.   340
  Content thyself awhile. By the mass, 'tis morning.
  Pleasure and action make the hours seem short.
  Retire thee, go where thou art billeted.
  Away, I say. Thou shalt know more hereafter.
  Nay, get thee gone. (*Exit* RODERIGO.)
                                   Two things are to be done: 345
  My wife must move for Cassio to her mistress,
  I'll set her on,
  Myself the while to draw the Moor apart
  And bring him jump° when he may Cassio find
  Soliciting his wife. Aye, that's the way.   350
  Dull not device by coldness and delay. (*Exit.*)

ACT 3

SCENE 1. Before the castle.

Enter CASSIO *and some* MUSICIANS.

CASSIO. Masters, play here, I will content your pains°—
  Something that's brief, and bid "Good morrow, General."°

322. repeals: calls back   349. jump: at the moment   1. content your pains: reward your labor
2. bid . . . General.": It was a common custom to play or sing a song beneath the bedroom window
of a distinguished guest or of a newly wedded couple on the morning after their wedding night.

(*Music. Enter* CLOWN.)

CLOWN. Why, masters, have your instruments been in Naples, that they
   speak i' the nose thus?

FIRST MUSICIAN. How, sir, how? 5

CLOWN. Are these, I pray you, wind instruments?

FIRST MUSICIAN. Aye, marry are they, sir.

CLOWN. Oh, thereby hangs a tail.

FIRST MUSICIAN. Whereby hangs a tale, sir?

CLOWN. Marry, sir, by many a wind instrument that I know. But, masters,
   here's money for you. And the General so likes your music that he
   desires you, for love's sake, to make no more noise with it. 12

FIRST MUSICIAN. Well, sir, we will not.

CLOWN. If you have any music that may not be heard, to 't again. But, as
   they say, to hear music the General does not greatly care. 15

FIRST MUSICIAN. We have none such, sir.

CLOWN. Then put up your pipes in your bag, for I'll away. Go, vanish into
   air, away! (*Exeunt* MUSICIANS.)

CASSIO. Dost thou hear, my honest friend?

CLOWN. No, I hear not your honest friend, I hear you. 20

CASSIO. Prithee keep up thy quillets.° There's a poor piece of gold for thee.
   If the gentlewoman that attends the General's wife be stirring, tell
   her there's one Cassio entreats her a little favor of speech. Wilt thou
   do this?

CLOWN. She is stirring, sir. If she will stir hither, I shall seem to notify
   unto her. 26

CASSIO. Do, good my friend. (*Exit* CLOWN. *Enter* IAGO.)
                      In happy time, Iago.

IAGO. You have not been abed, then?

CASSIO. Why, no, the day had broke
   Before we parted. I have made bold, Iago, 30
   To send in to your wife. My suit to her
   Is that she will to virtuous Desdemona
   Procure me some access.

IAGO.   I'll send her to you presently,
   And I'll devise a mean to draw the Moor
   Out of the way, that your convérse and business 35
   May be more free.

CASSIO. I humbly thank you for 't. (*Exit* IAGO.)
                      I never knew
   A Florentine more kind and honest. (*Enter* EMILIA.)

EMILIA. Good morrow, good Lieutenant. I am sorry

---

21. **keep . . . quillets:** put away your wisecracks

For your displeasure, but all will sure be well.   40
The General and his wife are talking of it,
And she speaks for you stoutly. The Moor replies
That he you hurt is of great fame in Cyprus
And great affinity,° and that in wholesome wisdom
He might not but refuse you. But he protests he loves you,   45
And needs no other suitor but his likings
To take the safest occasion by the front
To bring you in again.

CASSIO.   Yet I beseech you
If you think fit, or that it may be done,
Give me advantage of some brief discourse   50
With Desdemona alone.

EMILIA.   Pray you, come in.
I will bestow you where you shall have time
To speak your bosom freely.

CASSIO.   I am much bound to you. (*Exeunt.*)

SCENE 2. A room in the castle.

Enter OTHELLO, IAGO, *and* GENTLEMEN.

OTHELLO. These letters give, Iago, to the pilot,
And by him do my duties to the Senate.
That done, I will be walking on the works.°
Repair there to me.

IAGO.   Well, my good lord, I'll do 't.

OTHELLO. This fortification, gentlemen, shall we see 't?   5

GENTLEMEN. We'll wait upon your lordship. (*Exeunt.*)

SCENE 3. The garden of the castle.

Enter DESDEMONA, CASSIO, *and* EMILIA.

DESDEMONA. Be thou assured, good Cassio, I will do
All my abilities in thy behalf.

EMILIA. Good madam, do. I warrant it grieves my husband
As if the case were his.

DESDEMONA. Oh, that's an honest fellow. Do not doubt, Cassio,   5
But I will have my lord and you again
As friendly as you were.

CASSIO.   Bounteous madam,
Whatever shall become of Michael Cassio,
He's never anything but your true servant.

DESDEMONA. I know 't. I thank you. You do love my lord.   10

44. **affinity:** kindred   3. **works:** fortifications

You have known him long, and be you well assured
He shall in strangeness stand no farther off
Than in a politic distance.°

CASSIO.   Aye, but lady,
That policy may either last so long,
Or feed upon such nice and waterish diet,   15
Or breed itself so out of circumstance,
That, I being absent and my place supplied,
My General will forget my love and service.

DESDEMONA. Do not doubt° that. Before Emilia here
I give thee warrant of thy place. Assure thee,   20
If I do vow a friendship, I'll perform it
To the last article. My lord shall never rest.
I'll watch him tame and talk him out of patience,
His bed shall seem a school, his board a shrift.°
I'll intermingle every thing he does   25
With Cassio's suit. Therefore be merry, Cassio,
For thy solicitor shall rather die
Than give thy cause away. (*Enter* OTHELLO *and* IAGO, *at a distance.*)

EMILIA. Madam, here comes my lord.

CASSIO. Madam, I'll take my leave.   30

DESDEMONA. Nay, stay and hear me speak.

CASSIO. Madam, not now. I am very ill at ease,
Unfit for mine own purposes.

DESDEMONA. Well, do your discretion. (*Exit* CASSIO.)

IAGO. Ha! I like not that.   35

OTHELLO. What dost thou say?

IAGO. Nothing, my lord. Or if—I know not what.

OTHELLO. Was not that Cassio parted from my wife?

IAGO. Cassio, my lord! No, sure, I cannot think it,
That he would steal away so guilty-like,
Seeing you coming.   40

OTHELLO.   I do believe 'twas he.

DESDEMONA. How now, my lord!
I have been talking with a suitor here,
A man that languishes in your displeasure.

OTHELLO. Who is 't you mean?   45

DESDEMONA. Why, your Lieutenant, Cassio. Good my lord,
If I have any grace or power to move you,

12–13. He . . . distance: i.e., his apparent coldness to you shall only be so much as his official
position demands for reasons of policy   19. doubt: fear   24. shrift: place of confession [Eds.]

His present reconciliation take.°
For if he be not one that truly loves you,
That errs in ignorance and not in cunning,   50
I have no judgment in an honest face.
I prithee call him back.

OTHELLO.   Went he hence now?

DESDEMONA. Aye, sooth, so humbled
That he hath left part of his grief with me,
To suffer with him. Good love, call him back.   55

OTHELLO. Not now, sweet Desdemona, some other time.

DESDEMONA. But shall 't be shortly?

OTHELLO.   The sooner, sweet, for you.

DESDEMONA. Shall 't be tonight at supper?

OTHELLO.   No, not tonight.

DESDEMONA. Tomorrow dinner then?

OTHELLO.   I shall not dine at home.
I meet the captains at the citadel.   60

DESDEMONA. Why, then tomorrow night or Tuesday morn,
On Tuesday noon, or night, on Wednesday morn.
I prithee name the time, but let it not
Exceed three days. In faith, he's penitent,
And yet his trespass, in our common reason—   65
Save that, they say, the wars must make examples
Out of their best—is not almost° a fault
To incur a private check.° When shall he come?
Tell me, Othello. I wonder in my soul
What you would ask me that I should deny,   70
Or stand so mammering° on. What! Michael Cassio,
That came a-wooing with you, and so many a time
When I have spoke of you dispraisingly
Hath ta'en your part—to have so much to do
To bring him in! Trust me, I could do much—   75

OTHELLO. Prithee, no more. Let him come when he will.
I will deny thee nothing.

DESDEMONA.   Why, this is not a boon.
'Tis as I should entreat you wear your gloves,
Or feed on nourishing dishes, or keep you warm,
Or sue to you to do a peculiar profit   80
To your own person. Nay, when I have a suit

---

48. His . . . take: Accept his immediate apology and forgive him.   67. not almost: hardly
68. check: rebuke   71. mammering: hesitating

Wherein I mean to touch your love indeed,
It shall be full of poise and difficult weight,
And fearful to be granted.
OTHELLO.   I will deny thee nothing.
Whereon I do beseech thee grant me this,   85
To leave me but a little to myself.
DESDEMONA. Shall I deny you? No. Farewell, my lord.
OTHELLO. Farewell, my Desdemona. I'll come to thee straight.
DESDEMONA. Emilia, come. Be as your fancies teach you.
Whate'er you be, I am obedient.   90
(*Exeunt* DESDEMONA *and* EMILIA.)
OTHELLO. Excellent wretch! Perdition catch my soul
But I do love thee! And when I love thee not,
Chaos is come again.
IAGO. My noble lord—
OTHELLO.   What dost thou say, Iago?
IAGO. Did Michael Cassio, when you wooed my lady,   95
Know of your love?
OTHELLO. He did, from first to last. Why dost thou ask?
IAGO. But for a satisfaction of my thought,
No further harm.
OTHELLO.   Why of thy thought, Iago?
IAGO. I did not think he had been acquainted with her.   100
OTHELLO. Oh yes, and went between us very oft.
IAGO. Indeed!
OTHELLO. Indeed! Aye, indeed. Discern'st thou aught in that?
Is he not honest?
IAGO.   Honest, my lord!
OTHELLO.   Honest! Aye, honest.
IAGO. My lord, for aught I know.
OTHELLO.   What dost thou think?   105
IAGO. Think, my lord!
OTHELLO. Think, my lord! By Heaven, he echoes me
As if there were some monster in his thought
Too hideous to be shown. Thou dost mean something.
I heard thee say even now that thou likedst not that   110
When Cassio left my wife. What didst not like?
And when I told thee he was of my counsel
In my whole course of wooing, thou criedst "Indeed!"
And didst contract and purse thy brow together
As if thou then hadst shut up in thy brain   115
Some horrible conceit. If thou dost love me,

Show me thy thought.

IAGO. My lord, you know I love you.

OTHELLO.   I think thou dost,
And for I know thou'rt full of love and honesty
And weigh'st thy words before thou givest them breath,   120
Therefore these stops of thine fright me the more.
For such things in a false disloyal knave
Are tricks of custom, but in a man that's just
They're close delations,° working from the heart,
That passion cannot rule.

IAGO.   For Michael Cassio,   125
I dare be sworn I think that he is honest.

OTHELLO. I think so too.

IAGO.   Men should be what they seem,
Or those that be not, would they might seem none!°

OTHELLO. Certain, men should be what they seem.

IAGO. Why, then I think Cassio's an honest man.   130

OTHELLO. Nay, yet there's more in this.
I prithee speak to me as to thy thinkings,
As thou dost ruminate, and give thy worst of thoughts
The worst of words.

IAGO.   Good my lord, pardon me.
Though I am bound to every act of duty,   135
I am not bound to that all slaves are free to.
Utter my thoughts? Why, say they are vile and false,
As where's that palace whereinto foul things
Sometimes intrude not? Who has a breast so pure
But some uncleanly apprehensions   140
Keep leets° and law days, and in session sit
With meditations lawful?

OTHELLO. Thou dost conspire against thy friend, Iago,
If thou but think'st him wronged and makest his ear
A stranger to thy thoughts.

IAGO.   I do beseech you—   145
Though I perchance am vicious in my guess,
As, I confess, it is my nature's plague
To spy into abuses, and oft my jealousy°
Shapes faults that are not—that your wisdom yet,
From one that so imperfectly conceits,°   150
Would take no notice, nor build yourself a trouble

---

124. **close delations:** concealed accusations   128. **seem none:** i.e., not seem to be honest men
141. **leets:** courts   148. **jealousy:** suspicion   150. **conceits:** conceives

Out of his scattering and unsure observance.°
It were not for your quiet nor your good,
Nor for my manhood, honesty, or wisdom,
To let you know my thoughts.
OTHELLO.   What dost thou mean?   155
IAGO. Good name in man and woman, dear my lord,
   Is the immediate jewel of their souls.
   Who steals my purse steals trash—'tis something, nothing,
   'Twas mine, 'tis his, and has been slave to thousands—
   But he that filches from me my good name   160
   Robs me of that which not enriches him
   And makes me poor indeed.
OTHELLO. By Heaven, I'll know thy thoughts.
IAGO. You cannot, if my heart were in your hand,
   Nor shall not, whilst 'tis in my custody.   165
OTHELLO. Ha!
IAGO.   Oh, beware, my lord, of jealousy.
   It is the green-eyed monster which doth mock
   The meat it feeds on. That cuckold lives in bliss
   Who, certain of his fate, loves not his wronger.°
   But, oh, what damnèd minutes tells he o'er   170
   Who dotes, yet doubts, suspects, yet strongly loves!
OTHELLO. Oh misery!
IAGO. Poor and content is rich, and rich enough,
   But riches fineless° is as poor as winter
   To him that ever fears he shall be poor.   175
   Good God, the souls of all my tribe defend
   From jealousy!
OTHELLO.   Why, why is this?
   Think'st thou I'd make a life of jealousy,
   To follow still the changes of the moon
   With fresh suspicions? No, to be once in doubt   180
   Is once to be resolved.° Exchange me for a goat
   When I shall turn the business of my soul
   To such exsufflicate° and blown surmises,
   Matching thy inference.° 'Tis not to make me jealous
   To say my wife is fair, feeds well, loves company,   185

---

152. **observance:** observation   168–69. **That . . . wronger:** i.e., the cuckold who hates his
wife and knows her falseness is not tormented by suspicious jealousy.   174. **fineless:** limitless
180–81. **to . . . resolved:** whenever I find myself in doubt I at once seek out the truth.   182–84.
When . . . inference: When I shall allow that which concerns me most dearly to be influenced by
such trifling suggestions as yours   **exsufflicate:** blown up like a bubble

Is free of speech, sings, plays, and dances well.
Where virtue is, these are more virtuous.
Nor from mine own weak merits will I draw
The smallest fear or doubt of her revolt,
For she had eyes, and chose me. No, Iago,   190
I'll see before I doubt, when I doubt, prove,
And on the proof, there is no more but this—
Away at once with love or jealousy!

IAGO. I am glad of it, for now I shall have reason
To show the love and duty that I bear you   195
With franker spirit. Therefore, as I am bound,
Receive it from me. I speak not yet of proof.
Look to your wife. Observe her well with Cassio.
Wear your eye thus, not jealous nor secure.°
I would not have your free and noble nature   200
Out of self-bounty° be abused. Look to 't.
I know our country disposition well.
In Venice° they do let Heaven see the pranks
They dare not show their husbands. Their best conscience
Is not to leave 't undone, but keep 't unknown.   205

OTHELLO. Dost thou say so?

IAGO. She did deceive her father, marrying you,
And when she seemed to shake and fear your looks,
She loved them most.

OTHELLO.   And so she did.

IAGO.   Why, go to, then.
She that so young could give out such a seeming   210
To seel° her father's eyes up close as oak—
He thought 'twas witchcraft—but I am much to blame.
I humbly do beseech you of your pardon
For too much loving you.

OTHELLO.   I am bound to thee forever.

IAGO. I see this hath a little dashed your spirits.   215

OTHELLO. Not a jot, not a jot.

IAGO.   I' faith, I fear it has.
I hope you will consider what is spoke
Comes from my love. But I do see you're moved.
I am to pray you not to strain my speech
To grosser issues nor to larger reach   220

---

199. **secure:** overconfident   201. **self-bounty:** natural goodness   203. **In Venice:** Venice was
notorious for its loose women; the Venetian courtesans were among the sights of Europe and were
much commented upon by travelers.   211. **seel:** blind

Than to suspicion.

OTHELLO. I will not.

IAGO.   Should you do so, my lord,
My speech should fall into such vile success
As my thoughts aim not at. Cassio's my worthy friend.—
My lord, I see you're moved.

OTHELLO.   No, not so much moved.   225
I do not think but Desdemona's honest.°

IAGO. Long live she so! And long live you to think so!

OTHELLO. And yet, how nature erring from itself—

IAGO. Aye, there's the point. As—to be bold with you—
Not to affect° many proposèd matches   230
Of her own clime, complexion, and degree,
Whereto we see in all things nature tends°—
Foh! One may smell in such a will most rank,°
Foul disproportion, thoughts unnatural.
But pardon me. I do not in position   235
Distinctly speak of her, though I may fear
Her will, recoiling to her better judgment,
May fall to match° you with her country forms,°
And happily° repent.

OTHELLO.   Farewell, farewell.
If more thou dost perceive, let me know more.   240
Set on thy wife to observe. Leave me, Iago.

IAGO (*going*). My lord, I take my leave.

OTHELLO. Why did I marry? This honest creature doubtless
Sees and knows more, much more, than he unfolds.

IAGO (*returning*). My lord, I would I might entreat your honor   245
To scan this thing no further. Leave it to time.
Though it be fit that Cassio have his place,
For sure he fills it up with great ability,
Yet if you please to hold him off awhile,
You shall by that perceive him and his means.   250
Note if your lady strain his entertainment°
With any strong or vehement importunity—
Much will be seen in that. In the meantime,
Let me be thought too busy in my fears—

---

226. **honest:** When applied to Desdemona, "honest" means "chaste," but applied to Iago it has the modern meaning of "open and sincere."   230. **affect:** be inclined to   232. **in . . . tends:** i.e., a woman naturally marries a man of her own country, color, and rank.   233. **will . . . rank:** desire most lustful   238. **match:** compare   **country forms:** the appearance of her countrymen, i.e., white men   239. **happily:** haply, by chance   251. **strain his entertainment:** urge you to receive him

As worthy cause I have to fear I am—   255
And hold her free, I do beseech your Honor.
OTHELLO. Fear not my government.°
IAGO. I once more take my leave. (*Exit.*)
OTHELLO. This fellow's of exceeding honesty,
And knows all qualities, with a learned spirit,   260
Of human dealings. If I do prove her haggard,°
Though that her jesses° were my dear heartstrings,
I'd whistle her off and let her down the wind
To prey at fortune.° Haply, for° I am black
And have not those soft parts of conversation   265
That chamberers° have, or for I am declined
Into the vale of years—yet that's not much—
She's gone, I am abused, and my relief
Must be to loathe her. Oh, curse of marriage,
That we can call these delicate creatures ours,   270
And not their appetites! I had rather be a toad
And live upon the vapor of a dungeon
Than keep a corner in the thing I love
For others' uses. Yet, 'tis the plague of great ones,
Prerogatived are they less than the base.   275
'Tis destiny unshunnable, like death.
Even then this forkèd plague° is fated to us
When we do quicken.° Desdemona comes.
(*Re-enter* DESDEMONA *and* EMILIA.)
If she be false, oh, then Heaven mocks itself!
I'll not believe 't.
DESDEMONA.   How now, my dear Othello!   280
Your dinner, and the generous° islanders
By you invited, do attend your presence.
OTHELLO. I am to blame.
DESDEMONA.   Why do you speak so faintly?
Are you not well?
OTHELLO. I have a pain upon my forehead here.   285
DESDEMONA. Faith, that's with watching,° 'twill away again.
Let me but bind it hard, within this hour

---

257. **government:** self-control   261. **haggard:** a wild hawk   262. **jesses:** the straps attached
to a hawk's legs   261–64. **If . . . fortune:** Othello keeps up the imagery of falconry throughout.
He means: If I find that she is wild, I'll whistle her off the game and let her go where she will, for
she's not worth keeping.   264. **Haply, for:** Perhaps, because [Eds.]   266. **chamberers:** playboys
277. **forkèd plague:** i.e., to be a cuckold   278. **quicken:** stir in our mother's womb
281. **generous:** noble   286. **watching:** lack of sleep

It will be well.

OTHELLO.   Your napkin° is too little,

(*He puts the handkerchief from him, and it drops.*)

Let it alone. Come, I'll go in with you.

DESDEMONA. I am very sorry that you are not well.   290

(*Exeunt* OTHELLO *and* DESDEMONA.)

EMILIA. I am glad I have found this napkin.

This was her first remembrance from the Moor.

My wayward° husband hath a hundred times

Wooed me to steal it, but she so loves the token,

For he conjured° her she should ever keep it,   295

That she reserves it evermore about her

To kiss and talk to. I'll have the work ta'en out,°

And give 't to Iago. What he will do with it

Heaven knows, not I.

I nothing know, but for his fantasy.° (*Re-enter* IAGO.)   300

IAGO. How now! What do you here alone?

EMILIA. Do not you chide, I have a thing for you.

IAGO. A thing for me? It is a common thing—

EMILIA. Ha!

IAGO. To have a foolish wife.   305

EMILIA. Oh, is that all? What will you give me now

For that same handkerchief?

IAGO.   What handkerchief?

EMILIA. What handkerchief!

Why, that the Moor first gave to Desdemona,

That which so often you did bid me steal.   310

IAGO. Hast stol'n it from her?

EMILIA. No, faith, she let it drop by negligence,

And, to the advantage, I being here took 't up.

Look, here it is.

IAGO.   A good wench. Give it me.

EMILIA. What will you do with 't, that you have been so earnest   315

To have me filch it?

IAGO (*snatching it*). Why, what's that to you?

EMILIA. If 't be not for some purpose of import,

Give 't me again. Poor lady, she'll run mad

When she shall lack it.

IAGO. Be not acknown on 't,° I have use for it.   320

Go, leave me. (*Exit* EMILIA.)

288. napkin: handkerchief   293. wayward: unaccountable   295. conjured: begged with an oath
297. work . . . out: pattern copied   300. fantasy: whim   320. Be . . . 't: Know nothing about it

I will in Cassio's lodging lose this napkin,
And let him find it. Trifles light as air
Are to the jealous confirmations strong
As proofs of Holy Writ. This may do something.   325
The Moor already changes with my poison.
Dangerous conceits° are in their natures poisons,
Which at the first are scarce found to distaste,
But, with a little, act upon the blood,
Burn like the mines of sulphur. I did say so.°   330
Look where he comes! (*Re-enter* OTHELLO.)
            Not poppy,° nor mandragora,°
Nor all the drowsy syrups of the world,
Shall ever medicine thee to that sweet sleep
Which thou owedst° yesterday.

OTHELLO.   Ha! Ha! False to me?
IAGO. Why, how now, General! No more of that.   335
OTHELLO. Avaunt! Be gone! Thou hast set me on the rack.
I swear 'tis better to be much abused
Than but to know 't a little.

IAGO.   How now, my lord!
OTHELLO. What sense had I of her stol'n hours of lust?
I saw 't not, thought it not, it harmed not me.   340
I slept the next night well, was free and merry.
I found not Cassio's kisses on her lips.
He that is robbed, not wanting° what is stol'n,
Let him not know 't and he's not robbed at all.

IAGO. I am sorry to hear this.   345
OTHELLO. I had been happy if the general camp,
Pioners° and all, had tasted her sweet body,
So I had nothing known. Oh, now forever
Farewell the tranquil mind! Farewell content!
Farewell the plumèd troop and the big wars   350
That make ambition virtue! Oh farewell,
Farewell the neighing steed and the shrill trump,
The spirit-stirring drum, the ear-piercing fife,
The royal banner, and all quality,
Pride, pomp, and circumstance of glorious war!   355
And, O you mortal engines,° whose rude throats
The immortal Jove's dread clamors counterfeit,

---

327. **conceits:** ideas [Eds.]   330. **I . . . so:** As Iago says this, Othello is seen approaching, with all the signs of his agitation outwardly visible.   331. **poppy:** opium **mandragora:** called also mandrake—a root used as a drug to bring sleep   334. **owedst:** owned   343. **wanting:** missing
347. **Pioners:** Pioneers, the lowest type of soldier   356. **mortal engines:** deadly cannon

Farewell! Othello's occupation's gone!

IAGO. Is 't possible, my lord?

OTHELLO. Villain, be sure thou prove my love a whore,   360
Be sure of it, give me the ocular proof.
Or by the worth of man's eternal soul,
Thou hadst been better have been born a dog
Than answer my waked wrath!

IAGO.   Is 't come to this?

OTHELLO. Make me to see 't, or at the least so prove it   365
That the probation° bear no hinge nor loop
To hang a doubt on, or woe upon thy life!

IAGO. My noble lord—

OTHELLO. If thou dost slander her and torture me,
Never pray more, abandon all remorse.°   370
On horror's head horrors accumulate,
Do deeds to make Heaven weep, all earth amazed,
For nothing canst thou to damnation add
Greater than that.

IAGO.   Oh, grace! Oh, Heaven defend me!
Are you a man? Have you a soul or sense?   375
God be wi' you, take mine office. O wretched fool,
That livest to make thine honesty a vice!
O monstrous world! Take note, take note, O world,
To be direct and honest is not safe.
I thank you for this profit, and from hence   380
I'll love no friend, sith° love breeds such offense.

OTHELLO. Nay, stay. Thou shouldst be honest.

IAGO. I should be wise, for honesty's a fool,
And loses that it works for.

OTHELLO.   By the world,
I think my wife be honest, and think she is not.   385
I think that thou are just, and think thou art not.
I'll have some proof. Her name, that was as fresh
As Dian's° visage, is now begrimed and black
As mine own face. If there be cords, or knives,
Poison, or fire, or suffocating streams,   390
I'll not endure it. Would I were satisfied!

IAGO. I see, sir, you are eaten up with passion.
I do repent me that I put it to you.
You would be satisfied?

OTHELLO.   Would! Nay, I will.

366. probation: proof   370. remorse: pity   381. sith: since   388. Dian: Diana, goddess of chastity

IAGO. And may, but how? How satisfied, my lord?   395
    Would you, the supervisor,° grossly gape on?
    Behold her topped?
OTHELLO.   Death and damnation! Oh!
IAGO. It were a tedious difficulty, I think,
    To bring them to that prospect. Damn them then,
    If ever mortal eyes do see them bolster°   400
    More than their own! What then? How then?
    What shall I say? Where's satisfaction?
    It is impossible you should see this,
    Were they as prime° as goats, as hot as monkeys,
    As salt° as wolves in pride,° and fools as gross   405
    As ignorance made drunk. But yet I say
    If imputation° and strong circumstances,
    Which lead directly to the door of truth,
    Will give you satisfaction, you may have 't.
OTHELLO. Give me a living reason she's disloyal.   410
IAGO. I do not like the office.
    But sith I am entered in this cause so far,
    Pricked to 't by foolish honesty and love,
    I will go on. I lay with Cassio lately,
    And being troubled with a raging tooth,   415
    I could not sleep.
    There are a kind of men so loose of soul
    That in their sleeps will mutter their affairs.
    One of this kind is Cassio.
    In sleep I heard him say "Sweet Desdemona,   420
    Let us be wary, let us hide our loves."
    And then, sir, would he gripe° and wring my hand,
    Cry "O sweet creature!" and then kiss me hard,
    As if he plucked up kisses by the roots
    That grew upon my lips. Then laid his leg   425
    Over my thigh, and sighed and kissed, and then
    Cried "Cursed fate that gave thee to the Moor!"
OTHELLO. Oh, monstrous! Monstrous!
IAGO.   Nay, this was but his dream.
OTHELLO. But this denoted a foregone conclusion.
    'Tis a shrewd doubt,° though it be but a dream.   430
IAGO. And this may help to thicken other proofs

---

396. **supervisor:** looker-on 400. **bolster:** sleep together 404. **prime:** lustful 405. **salt:**
eager **pride:** in heat 407. **imputation:** probability 422. **gripe:** grip 430. **shrewd**
doubt: bitter suspicion

That do demonstrate thinly.

OTHELLO.   I'll tear her all to pieces.

IAGO. Nay, but be wise. Yet we see nothing done.
　　She may be honest yet. Tell me this:
　　Have you not sometimes seen a handkerchief   435
　　Spotted with strawberries in your wife's hand?

OTHELLO. I gave her such a one, 'twas my first gift.

IAGO. I know not that. But such a handkerchief—
　　I am sure it was your wife's—did I today
　　See Cassio wipe his beard with.

OTHELLO.   If it be that—   440

IAGO. If it be that, or any that was hers,
　　It speaks against her with the other proofs.

OTHELLO. Oh, that the slave had forty thousand lives!
　　One is too poor, too weak, for my revenge.
　　Now do I see 'tis true. Look here, Iago,   445
　　All my fond love thus do I blow to Heaven—
　　'Tis gone.
　　Arise, black Vengeance, from thy hollow cell!
　　Yield up, O Love, thy crown and hearted throne
　　To tyrannous hate! Swell, bosom, with thy fraught,°   450
　　For 'tis of aspics'° tongues!

IAGO.   Yet be content.

OTHELLO. Oh, blood, blood, blood!

IAGO. Patience, I say. Your mind perhaps may change.

OTHELLO. Never, Iago. Like to the Pontic Sea,
　　Whose icy current and compulsive course   455
　　Ne'er feels retiring ebb but keeps due on
　　To the Propontic and the Hellespont;
　　Even so my bloody thoughts, with violent pace,
　　Shall ne'er look back, ne'er ebb to humble love,
　　Till that a capable° and wide revenge   460
　　Swallow them up. Now, by yond marble Heaven,
　　In the due reverence of a sacred vow (*kneels*)
　　I here engage my words.

IAGO.   Do not rise yet. (*Kneels.*)
　　Witness, you ever burning lights above,
　　You elements that clip° us round about,   465
　　Witness that here Iago doth give up
　　The execution of his wit,° hands, heart,

450. **fraught:** freight   451. **aspics':** asps'   460. **capable:** comprehensive   465. **clip:** embrace
467. **wit:**   mind [Eds.]

To wronged Othello's service! Let him command,
And to obey shall be in me remorse,°
What bloody business ever. (*They rise.*)
OTHELLO.   I greet thy love,   470
Not with vain thanks, but with acceptance bounteous,
And will upon the instant put thee to 't.
Within these three days let me hear thee say
That Cassio's not alive.
IAGO. My friend is dead. 'Tis done at your request.   475
But let her live.
OTHELLO. Damn her, lewd minx! Oh, damn her!
Come, go with me apart. I will withdraw,
To furnish me with some swift means of death
For the fair devil. Now art thou my Lieutenant.   480
IAGO. I am your own forever. (*Exeunt.*)

SCENE 4. Before the castle.

Enter DESDEMONA, EMILIA, *and* CLOWN.

DESDEMONA. Do you know, sirrah, where Lieutenant Cassio lies?
CLOWN. I dare not say he lies anywhere.
DESDEMONA. Why, man?
CLOWN. He's a soldier, and for one to say a soldier lies is stabbing.
DESDEMONA. Go to. Where lodges he?   5
CLOWN. To tell you where he lodges is to tell you where I lie.
DESDEMONA. Can anything be made of this?
CLOWN. I know not where he lodges, and for me to devise a lodging, and
say he lies here or he lies there, were to lie in mine own throat.
DESDEMONA. Can you inquire him out and be edified by report?°   10
CLOWN. I will catechize the world for him; that is, make questions and by
them answer.
DESDEMONA. Seek him, bid him come hither. Tell him I have moved my
lord on his behalf and hope all will be well.
CLOWN. To do this within the compass of man's wit, and therefore I
will attempt the doing it. (*Exit.*)   16
DESDEMONA. Where should I lose that handkerchief, Emilia?
EMILIA. I know not, madam.
DESDEMONA. Believe me, I had rather have lost my purse
Full of crusados. And, but my noble Moor   20
Is true of mind and made of no such baseness

---

469. **remorse:** solemn obligation   10. **edified by report:** enlightened by the information.
Desdemona speaks with mock pomposity.

As jealous creatures are, it were enough
To put him to ill thinking.
EMILIA.   Is he not jealous?
DESDEMONA. Who, he? I think the sun where he was born
Drew all such humors from him.
EMILIA.   Look where he comes.   25
DESDEMONA. I will not leave him now till Cassio
Be called to him. (*Enter* OTHELLO.)
                              How is 't with you, my lord?
OTHELLO. Well, my good lady. (*Aside*) Oh, hardness to dissemble!
How do you, Desdemona?
DESDEMONA.   Well, my good lord.
OTHELLO. Give me your hand. This hand is moist,° my lady.   30
DESDEMONA. It yet has felt no age nor known no sorrow.
OTHELLO. This argues fruitfulness and liberal heart.
Hot, hot, and moist—this hand of yours requires
A sequester from liberty, fasting and prayer,
Much castigation, exercise devout.   35
For here's a young and sweating devil here,
That commonly rebels. 'Tis a good hand,
A frank one.
DESDEMONA. You may indeed say so,
For 'twas that hand that gave away my heart.
OTHELLO. A liberal° hand. The hearts of old gave hands,   40
But our new heraldry is hands, not hearts.°
DESDEMONA. I cannot speak of this. Come now, your promise.
OTHELLO. What promise, chuck?°
DESDEMONA. I have sent to bid Cassio come speak with you.
OTHELLO. I have a salt and sorry rheum offends me.   45
Lend me thy handkerchief.
DESDEMONA.   Here, my lord.
OTHELLO. That which I gave you.
DESDEMONA.   I have it not about me.
OTHELLO. Not?
DESDEMONA. No indeed, my lord.
OTHELLO. That's a fault. That handkerchief
Did an Egyptian to my mother give.   50

---

30. **moist:** A hot moist palm was believed to show desire. 40. **liberal:** overgenerous 40–41. **The . . . hearts:** Once love and deeds went together, but now it is all deeds (i.e., faithlessness) and no love. 43. **chuck:** A term of affection, but not the kind of word with which a person of Othello's dignity would normally address his wife. He is beginning to treat her with contemptuous familiarity.

She was a charmer, and could almost read
The thoughts of people. She told her while she kept it
'Twould make her amiable and subdue my father
Entirely to her love, but if she lost it
Or made a gift of it, my father's eye   55
Should hold her loathèd and his spirits should hunt
After new fancies. She dying gave it me,
And bid me, when my fate would have me wive,
To give it her. I did so. And take heed on 't,
Make it a darling like your precious eye.   60
To lose 't or give 't away were such perdition
As nothing else could match.
DESDEMONA.   Is 't possible?
OTHELLO. 'Tis true. There's magic in the web of it.
A sibyl that had numbered in the world
The sun to course two hundred compasses   65
In her prophetic fury sewed the work.
The worms were hallowed that did breed the silk,
And it was dyed in mummy which the skillful
Conserved° of maiden's hearts.
DESDEMONA.   Indeed! Is 't true?
OTHELLO. Most veritable, therefore look to 't well.   70
DESDEMONA. Then would God that I had never seen 't.
OTHELLO. Ha! Wherefore?
DESDEMONA. Why do you speak so startingly and rash?
OTHELLO. Is 't lost? Is 't gone? Speak, is it out o' the way?
DESDEMONA. Heaven bless us!   75
OTHELLO. Say you?
DESDEMONA. It is not lost, but what an if it were?
OTHELLO. How!
DESDEMONA. I say it is not lost.
OTHELLO.   Fetch 't, let me see it.
DESDEMONA. Why, so I can, sir, but I will not now.   80
This is a trick to put me from my suit.
Pray you let Cassio be received again.
OTHELLO. Fetch me the handkerchief. My mind misgives.
DESDEMONA. Come, come,
You'll never meet a more sufficient man.   85
OTHELLO. The handkerchief!
DESDEMONA.   I pray talk me of Cassio.

69. **Conserved:** Prepared

OTHELLO. The handkerchief!

DESDEMONA.   A man that all this time

Hath founded his good fortunes on your love,

Shared dangers with you—

OTHELLO. The handkerchief!   90

DESDEMONA. In sooth, you are to blame.

OTHELLO. Away! (*Exit.*)

EMILIA. Is not this man jealous?

DESDEMONA. I ne'er saw this before.

Sure there's some wonder in this handkerchief.   95

I am most unhappy in the loss of it.

EMILIA. 'Tis not a year or two shows us a man.°

They are all but stomachs and we all but food.

They eat us hungerly, and when they are full

They belch us. Look you, Cassio and my husband.   100

(*Enter* CASSIO *and* IAGO.)

IAGO. There is no other way, 'Tis she must do 't.

And, lo, the happiness!° Go and impórtune her.

DESDEMONA. How now, good Cassio! What's the news with you?

CASSIO. Madam, my former suit. I do beseech you

That by your virtuous means I may again   105

Exist, and be a member of his love

Whom I with all the office of my heart

Entirely honor. I would not be delayed.

If my offense be of such mortal kind

That nor my service past nor present sorrows   110

Nor purposed merit in futurity

Can ransom me into his love again,

But to know so must be my benefit.

So shall I clothe me in a forced content

And shut myself up in some other course   115

To Fortune's alms.

DESDEMONA.   Alas, thrice-gentle Cassio!

My advocation° is not now in tune.

My lord is not my lord, nor should I know him

Were he in favor° as in humor altered.

So help me every spirit sanctified,   120

As I have spoken for you all my best

And stood within the blank° of his displeasure

---

97. 'Tis . . . man: It does not take a couple of years to discover the nature of a man; i.e., he soon shows his real nature.   102. And . . . happiness!: What good luck, here she is!   117. advocation: advocacy   119. favor: face [Eds.]   122. blank: aim

For my free speech! You must awhile be patient.
What I can do I will, and more I will
Than for myself I dare. Let that suffice you.   125
IAGO. Is my lord angry?
EMILIA.   He went hence but now,
And certainly in strange unquietness.
IAGO. Can he be angry? I have seen the cannon
When it hath blown his ranks into the air,
And, like the Devil, from his very arm   130
Puffed his own brother, and can he be angry?
Something of moment then. I will go meet him.
There's matter in 't indeed if he be angry.
DESDEMONA. I prithee do so. (*Exit* IAGO.)
                                     Something sure of state,
Either from Venice, or some unhatched practice   135
Made demonstrable° here in Cyprus to him,
Hath puddled his clear spirit. And in such cases
Men's natures wrangle with inferior things,
Though great ones are their object. 'Tis even so,
For let our finger ache and it induces   140
Our other healthful members even to that sense
Of pain. Nay, we must think men are not gods,
Nor of them look for such observancy
As fits the bridal.° Beshrew me much, Emilia,
I was, unhandsome warrior° as I am,   145
Arraigning his unkindness with my soul,
But now I find I had suborned the witness,°
And he's indicted falsely.
EMILIA. Pray Heaven it be state matters, as you think,
And no conception nor no jealous toy°   150
Concerning you.
DESDEMONA. Alas the day, I never gave him cause!
EMILIA. But jealous souls will not be answered so.
They are not ever jealous for the cause,
But jealous for they are jealous. 'Tis a monster   155
Begot upon itself, born on itself.
DESDEMONA. Heaven keep that monster from Othello's mind!

135–36. unhatched . . . demonstrable: some plot, not yet matured, which has been revealed
144. bridal: honeymoon   145. unhandsome warrior: clumsy soldier. Desdemona continually
thinks of herself as Othello's companion in arms. Cf. 1.3.248 ff.   147. suborned the witness:
corrupted the evidence; i.e., misunderstood his behavior [Eds.]   150. jealous toy: silly suspicion

EMILIA. Lady, amen.

DESDEMONA. I will go seek him. Cassio, walk hereabout.
If I do find him fit, I'll move your suit,   160
And seek to effect it to my uttermost.

CASSIO. I humbly thank your ladyship.

(*Exeunt* DESDEMONA *and* EMILIA. *Enter* BIANCA.)

BIANCA. Save you, friend Cassio!

CASSIO.   What make you from home?
How is it with you, my most fair Bianca?
I' faith, sweet love, I was coming to your house.   165

BIANCA. And I was going to your lodging, Cassio.
What, keep a week away? Seven days and nights?
Eightscore eight hours? And lovers' absent hours,
More tedious than the dial eightscore times?
Oh, weary reckoning!

CASSIO.   Pardon me, Bianca.   170
I have this while with leaden thoughts been pressed,
But I shall in a more continuate time
Strike off this score of absence. Sweet Bianca,

(*Giving her* DESDEMONA'S *handkerchief.*)

Take me this work out.

BIANCA.   O Cassio, whence came this?
This is some token from a newer friend.   175
To the felt absence now I feel a cause.
Is 't come to this? Well, well.

CASSIO.   Go to, woman!
Throw your vile guesses in the Devil's teeth,
From whence you have them. You are jealous now
That this is from some mistress, some remembrance.   180
No, by my faith, Bianca.

BIANCA.   Why, whose is it?

CASSIO. I know not, sweet. I found it in my chamber.
I like the work well. Ere it be demanded—
As like enough it will—I'd have it copied.
Take it, and do 't, and leave me for this time.   185

BIANCA. Leave you! Wherefore?

CASSIO. I do attend here on the General,
And think it no addition,° nor my wish
To have him see me womaned.°

BIANCA.   Why, I pray you?

188. addition: honor   189. womaned: with a woman

CASSIO. Not that I love you not.

BIANCA.   But that you do not love me. 190
 I pray you bring me on the way a little,
 And say if I shall see you soon at night.

CASSIO. 'Tis but a little way that I can bring you,
 For I attend here. But I'll see you soon.

BIANCA. 'Tis very good, I must be circumstanced.° (*Exeunt.*) 195

ACT 4

SCENE 1. Cyprus. Before the castle.

    Enter OTHELLO *and* IAGO.

IAGO. Will you think so?

OTHELLO.   Think so, Iago!

IAGO.   What,
 To kiss in private?

OTHELLO.   An unauthorized kiss.

IAGO. Or to be naked with her friend in bed
 An hour or more, not meaning any harm?   5

OTHELLO. Naked in bed, Iago, and not mean harm!
 It is hypocrisy against the Devil.
 They that mean virtuously and yet do so,
 The Devil their virtue tempts and they tempt Heaven.

IAGO. So they do nothing, 'tis a venial° slip.
 But if I give my wife a handkerchief—   10

OTHELLO. What then?

IAGO. Why, then, 'tis hers, my lord, and being hers,
 She may, I think, bestow 't on any man.

OTHELLO. She is protectress of her honor too.
 May she give that?   15

IAGO. Her honor is an essence that's not seen.
 They have it very oft that have it not.
 But for the handkerchief—

OTHELLO. By Heaven, I would most gladly have forgot it.
 Thou said'st—oh, it comes o'er my memory,   20
 As doth the raven o'er the infected house
 Boding to all°—he had my handkerchief.

IAGO. Aye, what of that?

OTHELLO.   That's not so good now.

---

195. circumstanced: put off   9. venial: pardonable   21–22. As doth the raven ... all: As an evil
omen (such as a raven overhead) brings evil tidings to all who live in a plague-infested house [Eds.]

IAGO.   What
If I had said I had seen him do you wrong?
Or heard him say—as knaves be such abroad,
Who having, by their own importunate suit,   25
Or voluntary dotage of some mistress,
Convincèd or supplied° them, cannot choose
But they must blab—
OTHELLO.   Hath he said anything?
IAGO. He hath, my lord, but be you well assured,   30
No more than he'll unswear.
OTHELLO.   What hath he said?
IAGO. Faith, that he did—I know not what he did.
OTHELLO. What? What?
IAGO. Lie—
OTHELLO. With her?
IAGO.   With her, on her, what you will.   34
OTHELLO. Lie° with her! Lie on her!—We say lie on her when they
belie her. —Lie with her. 'Zounds, that's fulsome!° Handkerchief—
confessions—handkerchief!—To confess, and be hanged for his labor.
First to be hanged, and then to confess. I tremble at it. Nature would
not invest herself in such shadowing passion without some instruction.°
It is not words that shake me thus. Pish! Noses, ears, and lips. Is 't
possible?—Confess?—Handkerchief?—Oh, devil! (*Falls in a trance.*)   41
IAGO. Work on,
My medicine, work! Thus credulous fools are caught,
And many worthy and chaste dames even thus,
All guiltless, meet reproach. What ho! My lord!   45
My lord, I say! Othello! (*Enter* CASSIO.)
                              How now, Cassio!
CASSIO. What's the matter?
IAGO. My lord is fall'n into an epilepsy.
This is his second fit, he had one yesterday.
CASSIO. Rub him about the temples.
IAGO.   No, forbear,   50
The lethargy° must have his quiet course.
If not, he foams at mouth and by and by
Breaks out to savage madness. Look, he stirs.
Do you withdraw yourself a little while,

---

28. **Convincèd or supplied:** Overcome or satisfied their desires   35–41. **Lie . . . devil:** Othello
breaks into incoherent muttering before he falls down in a fit.   36. **fulsome:** disgusting
38–40. **Nature . . . instruction:** Nature would not fill me with such overwhelming emotion
unless there was some cause.   51. **lethargy:** epileptic fit

He will recover straight. When he is gone,   55
I would on great occasion speak with you. (*Exit* CASSIO.)
How is it, General? Have you not hurt your head?°
OTHELLO. Dost thou mock me?
IAGO.   I mock you! No, by Heaven.
Would you would bear your fortune like a man!
OTHELLO. A hornèd man's a monster and a beast.   60
IAGO. There's many a beast, then, in a populous city,
And many a civil monster.
OTHELLO. Did he confess it?
IAGO.   Good sir, be a man.
Think every bearded fellow that's but yoked°
May draw with you.° There's millions now alive   65
That nightly lie in those unproper beds
Which they dare swear peculiar.° Your case is better.
Oh, 'tis the spite of Hell, the Fiend's arch-mock,
To lip° a wanton in a secure couch°
And to suppose her chaste! No, let me know,   70
And knowing what I am, I know what she shall be.
OTHELLO. Oh, thou art wise, 'tis certain.
IAGO.   Stand you awhile apart,
Confine yourself but in a patient list.°
Whilst you were here o'erwhelmèd with your grief—
A passion most unsuiting such a man—   75
Cassio came hither. I shifted him away,
And laid good 'scuse upon your ecstasy,°
Bade him anon return and here speak with me,
The which he promised. Do but encave yourself,
And mark the fleers, the gibes, and notable scorns,   80
That dwell in every region of his face.
For I will make him tell the tale anew,
Where, how, how oft, how long ago, and when
He hath and is again to cope° your wife.
I say but mark his gesture. Marry, patience,   85
Or I shall say you are all in all in spleen,
And nothing of a man.

---

57. **Have . . . head?:** With brutal cynicism Iago asks whether Othello is suffering from cuckold's
headache. 64. **yoked:** married 65. **draw with you:** be your yoke fellow 66–67. **That . . .**
peculiar: That lie nightly in beds which they believe are their own but which others have shared
69. **lip:** kiss **secure couch:** literally., a carefree bed; i.e., a bed which has been used by the wife's
lover, but secretly 73. **patient list:** confines of patience 77. **ecstasy:** fit 84. **cope:** encounter

OTHELLO.   Dost thou hear, Iago?
  I will be found most cunning in my patience,
  But—dost thou hear?—most bloody.

IAGO.   That's not amiss.
  But yet keep time in all. Will you withdraw? (OTHELLO *retires.*)   90
  Now will I question Cassio of Bianca,
  A housewife° that by selling her desires
  Buys herself bread and clothes. It is a creature
  That dotes on Cassio, as 'tis the strumpet's plague
  To beguile many and be beguiled by one.   95
  He, when he hears of her, cannot refrain
  From the excess of laughter. Here he comes. (*Re-enter* CASSIO.)
  As he shall smile, Othello shall go mad,
  And his unbookish° jealousy must construe
  Poor Cassio's smiles, gestures, and light behavior   100
  Quite in the wrong. How do you now, Lieutenant?

CASSIO. The worser that you give me the addition°
  Whose want even kills me.

IAGO. Ply Desdemona well, and you are sure on 't.
  Now, if this suit lay in Bianca's power,   105
  How quickly should you speed!

CASSIO.   Alas, poor caitiff!°

OTHELLO. Look how he laughs already!

IAGO. I never knew a woman love man so.

CASSIO. Alas, poor rogue! I think i' faith, she loves me.

OTHELLO. Now he denies it faintly and laughs it out.   110

IAGO. Do you hear, Cassio?

OTHELLO.   Now he impórtunes him
  To tell it o'er. Go to. Well said, well said.

IAGO. She gives it out that you shall marry her.
  Do you intend to?

CASSIO. Ha, ha, ha!   115

OTHELLO. Do you triumph, Roman?° Do you triumph?

CASSIO. I marry her! What, a customer!° I prithee bear some charity to my
  wit. Do not think it so unwholesome. Ha, ha, ha!

OTHELLO. So, so, so, so. They laugh that win.

IAGO. Faith, the cry goes that you shall marry her.   120

CASSIO. Prithee say true.

---

92. **housewife:** hussy   99. **unbookish:** unlearned   102. **addition:** title (Lieutenant) which he
has lost   106. **caitiff:** wretch   116. **triumph, Roman:** The word "triumph" suggests "Roman"
because the Romans celebrated their victories with triumphs, elaborate shows, and processions.
117. **customer:** harlot

IAGO. I am a very villain else.

OTHELLO. Have you scored° me? Well.

CASSIO. This is the monkey's own giving out. She is persuaded I
will marry her out of her own love and flattery, not out of my
promise.   126

OTHELLO. Iago beckons me, now he begins the story.

CASSIO. She was here even now. She haunts me in every place. I was the
other day talking on the sea bank with certain Venetians, and thither
comes the bauble, and, by this hand, she falls me thus about my
neck—   131

OTHELLO. Crying "O dear Cassio!" as it were. His gesture imports it.

CASSIO. So hangs and lolls and weeps upon me, so hales and pulls me. Ha,
ha, ha!

OTHELLO. Now he tells how she plucked him to my chamber. Oh,
I see that nose of yours, but not that dog I shall throw it to.   136

CASSIO. Well, I must leave her company.

IAGO. Before me!° Look where she comes.

CASSIO. 'Tis such another fitchew!° Marry, a perfumed one.

(Enter BIANCA.*)*

What do you mean by this haunting of me?   140

BIANCA. Let the Devil and his dam haunt you! What did you mean by that
same handkerchief you gave me even now? I was a fine fool to take it.
I must take out the work? A likely piece of work, that you should find
it in your chamber and not know who left it there! This is some minx's
token, and I must take out the work? There, give it your hobby-horse.
Wheresoever you had it, I'll take out no work on 't.   146

CASSIO. How now, my sweet Bianca! How now! How now!

OTHELLO. By Heaven, that should be my handkerchief!

BIANCA. An° you'll come to supper tonight, you may. An you will not,
come when you are next prepared for. *(Exit.)*   150

IAGO. After her, after her.

CASSIO. Faith, I must, she'll rail i' the street else.

IAGO. Will you sup there?

CASSIO. Faith, I intend so.

IAGO. Well, I may chance to see you, for I would very fain
speak with you.   156

CASSIO. Prithee, come, will you?

IAGO. Go to. Say no more. *(Exit* CASSIO.*)*

OTHELLO *(advancing).* How shall I murder him, Iago?

123. **scored:** marked, as with a blow from a whip   138. **Before me!:** By my soul!
139. **fitchew:** polecat   149. **An:** If

IAGO. Did you perceive how he laughed at his vice? 160

OTHELLO. Oh, Iago!

IAGO. And did you see the handkerchief?

OTHELLO. Was that mine?

IAGO. Yours, by this hand. And to see how he prizes the foolish woman your wife? She gave it him, and he hath given it his whore. 165

OTHELLO. I would have him nine years a-killing. A fine woman! A fair woman! A sweet woman!

IAGO. Nay, you must forget that.

OTHELLO. Aye, let her rot, and perish, and be damned tonight, for she shall not live. No, my heart is turned to stone, I strike it and it hurts my hand. Oh, the world hath not a sweeter creature. She might lie by an emperor's side, and command him tasks. 172

IAGO. Nay, that's not your way.°

OTHELLO. Hang her! I do but say what she is, so delicate with her needle, an admirable musician—oh, she will sing the savageness out of a bear—of so high and plenteous wit and invention— 176

IAGO. She's the worse for all this.

OTHELLO. Oh, a thousand times. And then, of so gentle a condition!

IAGO. Aye, too gentle.

OTHELLO. Nay, that's certain. But yet the pity of it, Iago! O Iago, the pity of it, Iago! 181

IAGO. If you are so fond over her iniquity, give her patent to offend, for if it touch not you, it comes near nobody.

OTHELLO. I will chop her into messes.° Cuckold me!

IAGO. Oh, 'tis foul in her.

OTHELLO. With mine officer! 185

IAGO. That's fouler.

OTHELLO. Get me some poison, Iago, this night. I'll not expostulate with her, lest her body and beauty unprovide my mind again. This night, Iago. 190

IAGO. Do it not with poison, strangle her in her bed, even the bed she hath contaminated.

OTHELLO. Good, good. The justice of it pleases. Very good.

IAGO. And for Cassio, let me be his undertaker.° You shall hear more by midnight. 195

OTHELLO. Excellent good. (*A trumpet within.*) What trumpet is that same?

IAGO. Something from Venice, sure. 'Tis Lodovico Come from the Duke. And see, your wife is with him. (*Enter* LODOVICO, DESDEMONA, *and* ATTENDANTS.)

---

173. Nay . . . way: i.e., don't get soft thoughts about her   184. messes: mincemeat [Eds.]
194. be his undertaker: undertake to manage his business. In Shakespeare's plays the word does *not* mean "mortician."

LODOVICO. God save the worthy General!   200
OTHELLO. With all my heart, sir.
LODOVICO. The Duke and Senators of Venice greet you. (*Gives him a letter.*)
OTHELLO. I kiss the instrument of their pleasures.
   (*Opens the letter, and reads.*)
DESDEMONA. And what's the news, good Cousin Lodovico?
IAGO. I am very glad to see you, signior.   205
   Welcome to Cyprus.
LODOVICO. I thank you. How does Lieutenant Cassio?
IAGO. Lives, sir.
DESDEMONA. Cousin, there's fall'n between him and my lord
   An unkind breach, but you shall make all well.   210
OTHELLO. Are you sure of that?
DESDEMONA. My lord?
OTHELLO (*reads*). "This fail you not to do, as you will—".
LODOVICO. He did not call, he's busy in the paper.
   Is there division 'twixt my lord and Cassio?   215
DESDEMONA. A most unhappy one. I would do much
   To atone° them, for the love I bear to Cassio.
OTHELLO. Fire and brimstone!
DESDEMONA.   My lord?
OTHELLO.   Are you wise?°
DESDEMONA. What, is he angry?
LODOVICO.   Maybe the letter moved him,
   For, as I think, they do command him home,   220
   Deputing Cassio in his government.
DESDEMONA. By my troth, I am glad on 't.
OTHELLO.   Indeed!
DESDEMONA.   My lord?
OTHELLO. I am glad to see you mad.
DESDEMONA.   Why, sweet Othello?
OTHELLO. Devil! (*Striking her.*)
DESDEMONA. I have not deserved this.   225
LODOVICO. My lord, this would not be believed in Venice
   Though I should swear I saw 't. 'Tis very much.
   Make her amends, she weeps.
OTHELLO.   O devil, devil!
   If that the earth could teem with a woman's tears,
   Each drop she falls would prove a crocodile.°   230
   Out of my sight!

217. **atone:** reconcile   218. **Are you wise?:** i.e., in saying you bear love to Cassio   229–30. **If . . . crocodile:** If the earth could breed from woman's tears, each tear that she lets fall would become a crocodile. It was believed that the crocodile would cry and sob to attract the sympathetic passer-by, who was then snapped up.

DESDEMONA.　　I will not stay to offend you. (*Going.*)

LODOVICO. Truly, an obedient lady.

　　I do beseech your lordship, call her back.

OTHELLO. Mistress!

DESDEMONA. My lord?　　　　　　　　　　　　　　　　235

OTHELLO. What would you with her, sir?

LODOVICO.　　　　　　　　　　Who, I, my lord?

OTHELLO. Aye, you did wish that I would make her turn.

　　Sir, she can turn and turn, and yet go on

　　And turn again. And she can weep, sir, weep.

　　And she's obedient, as you say, obedient,　　　　　240

　　Very obedient.—Proceed you in your tears—

　　Concerning this, sir—oh, well-painted passion!°—

　　I am commanded home.—Get you away.

　　I'll send for you anon.—Sir, I obey the mandate,

　　And will return to Venice.—Hence, avaunt! (*Exit* DESDEMONA.)

　　Cassio shall have my place. And, sir, tonight,　　246

　　I do entreat that we may sup together.

　　You are welcome, sir, to Cyprus.—Goats and monkeys! (*Exit.*)

LODOVICO. Is this the noble Moor whom our full Senate

　　Call all-in-all sufficient? This the nature　　　　250

　　Whom passion could not shake? Whose solid virtue

　　The shot of accident nor dart of chance

　　Could neither graze nor pierce?

IAGO.　　　　　　　　　　He is much changed.

LODOVICO. Are his wits safe? Is he not light of brain?

IAGO. He's that he is. I may not breathe my censure°　　255

　　What he might be. If what he might he is not,

　　I would to Heaven he were!

LODOVICO.　　　　　　　　What, strike his wife!

IAGO. Faith, that was not so well, yet would I knew

　　That stroke would prove the worst!

LODOVICO.　　　　　　　　　Is it his use?

　　Or did the letters work upon his blood,　　　　260

　　And new-create this fault?

IAGO.　　　　　　　　Alas, alas!

　　It is not honesty in me to speak

　　What I have seen and known. You shall observe him,

　　And his own courses will denote him so

---

242. passion: emotion [Eds.]　　255. censure: opinion [Eds.]

That I may save my speech. Do but go after,   265
And mark how he continues.

LODOVICO. I am sorry that I am deceived in him. (*Exeunt.*)

SCENE 2. A room in the castle.

Enter OTHELLO *and* EMILIA.

OTHELLO. You have seen nothing, then?

EMILIA. Nor ever heard, nor ever did suspect.

OTHELLO. Yes, you have seen Cassio and she together.

EMILIA. But then I saw no harm, and then I heard
Each syllable that breath made up between them.   5

OTHELLO. What, did they never whisper?

EMILIA.   Never, my lord.

OTHELLO. Nor send you out o' the way?

EMILIA. Never.

OTHELLO. To fetch her fan, her gloves, her mask, nor nothing?

EMILIA. Never, my lord.   10

OTHELLO. That's strange.

EMILIA. I durst, my lord, to wager she is honest,
Lay down my soul at stake. If you think other,
Remove your thought, it doth abuse your bosom.
If any wretch have put this in your head,   15
Let Heaven requite it with the serpent's curse!
For if she be not honest, chaste, and true,
There's no man happy, the purest of their wives
Is foul as slander.

OTHELLO.   Bid her come hither. Go. (*Exit* EMILIA.)
She says enough. Yet she's a simple bawd   20
That cannot say as much. This is a subtle whore,
A closet lock and key of villainous secrets.
And yet she'll kneel and pray, I have seen her do 't.

(*Enter* DESDEMONA *with* EMILIA.)

DESDEMONA. My lord, what is your will?

OTHELLO.   Pray, chuck, come hither.

DESDEMONA. What is your pleasure?

OTHELLO.   Let me see your eyes.   25
Look in my face.

DESDEMONA.   What horrible fancy's this?

OTHELLO (*to* EMILIA). Some of your function,° mistress.

---

27. Some . . . function: Get about your business, i.e., prostitution. Othello pretends that Emilia is keeper of a brothel and Desdemona one of the women.

Leave procreants alone and shut the door,
Cough, or cry hem, if anybody come.
Your mystery,° your mystery. Nay, dispatch. (*Exit* EMILIA.)   30
DESDEMONA. Upon my knees, what doth your speech import?
   I understand a fury in your words,
   But not the words.
OTHELLO.   Why, what art thou?
DESDEMONA. Your wife, my lord, your true and loyal wife.
OTHELLO. Come, swear it, damn thyself,   35
   Lest, being like one of Heaven,° the devils themselves
   Should fear to seize thee. Therefore be double-damned.
   Swear thou art honest.
DESDEMONA.   Heaven doth truly know it.
OTHELLO. Heaven truly knows that thou art false as Hell.
DESDEMONA. To whom, my lord? With whom? How am I false?   40
OTHELLO. O Desdemona! Away! Away! Away!
DESDEMONA. Alas the heavy day! Why do you weep!
   Am I the motive of these tears, my lord?
   If haply you my father do suspect
   An instrument of this your calling-back,   45
   Lay not your blame on me. If you have lost him,
   Why, I have lost him too.
OTHELLO.   Had it pleased Heaven
   To try me with affliction, had they rained
   All kinds of sores and shames on my bare head,
   Steeped me in poverty to the very lips,   50
   Given to captivity me and my utmost hopes,
   I should have found in some place of my soul
   A drop of patience. But, alas, to make me
   A fixèd figure for the time of scorn
   To point his slow unmoving finger at!   55
   Yet could I bear that too, well, very well.
   But there where I have garnered up my heart,
   Where either I must live or bear no life,
   The fountain from the which my current runs
   Or else dries up—to be discarded thence!   60
   Or keep it as a cistern for foul toads
   To knot and gender in! Turn thy complexion there,
   Patience, thou young and rose-lipped cherubin—
   Aye, there, look grim as Hell!

---

30. **mystery:** profession   36. **being . . . Heaven:** because you look like an angel

DESDEMONA. I hope my noble lord esteems me honest. 65

OTHELLO. Oh, aye, as summer flies are in the shambles,°
That quicken even with blowing.° O thou weed,
Who art so lovely fair and smell'st so sweet
That the sense aches at thee, would thou hadst ne'er been born!

DESDEMONA. Alas, what ignorant sin have I committed? 70

OTHELLO. Was this fair paper,° this most goodly book,
Made to write "whore" upon? What committed!
Committed! O thou public commoner!°
I should make very forges of my cheeks
That would to cinders burn up modesty 75
Did I but speak thy deeds. What committed!
Heaven stops the nose at it, and the moon winks.
The bawdy wind, that kisses all it meets,
Is hushed within the hollow mine of earth
And will not hear it. What committed! 80
Impudent strumpet!

DESDEMONA.   By Heaven, you do me wrong.

OTHELLO. Are not you a strumpet?

DESDEMONA.   No, as I am a Christian.
If to preserve this vessel for my lord
From any other foul unlawful touch
Be not to be a strumpet, I am none. 85

OTHELLO. What, not a whore?

DESDEMONA.   No, as I shall be saved.

OTHELLO. Is 't possible?

DESDEMONA. Oh, Heaven forgive us!

OTHELLO.   I cry you mercy, then.
I took you for that cunning whore of Venice
That married with Othello. (*Raising his voice*) You mistress, 90
That have the office opposite to Saint Peter,
And keep the gate of Hell! (*Re-enter* EMILIA.)
                         You, you, aye, you!
We have done our course, there's moncy for your pains.
I pray you turn the key, and keep our counsel. (*Exit.*)

EMILIA. Alas, what does this gentleman conceive? 95
How do you, madam? How do you, my good lady?

DESDEMONA. Faith, half-asleep.

EMILIA. Good madam, what's the matter with my lord?

---

66. **shambles:** slaughterhouse   67. **quicken . . . blowing:** come to life as soon as the eggs are laid
71. **fair paper:** i.e., her white body   73. **public commoner:** one who offers herself to all comers

DESDEMONA. With who?

EMILIA. Why, with my lord, madam.   100

DESDEMONA. Who is thy lord?

EMILIA.   He that is yours, sweet lady.

DESDEMONA. I have none. Do not talk to me, Emilia.
   I cannot weep, nor answer have I none
   But what should go by water.° Prithee tonight
   Lay on my bed my wedding sheets. Remember,   105
   And call thy husband hither.

EMILIA.   Here's a change indeed! (*Exit.*)

DESDEMONA. 'Tis meet I should be used so, very meet.
   How have I been behaved that he might stick
   The small'st opinion on my least misuse?°
   (*Re-enter* EMILIA *with* IAGO.)

IAGO. What is your pleasure, madam? How is 't with you?   110

DESDEMONA. I cannot tell. Those that do teach young babes
   Do it with gentle means and easy tasks.
   He might have chid me so, for, in good faith,
   I am a child to chiding.

IAGO.   What's the matter, lady?

EMILIA. Alas, Iago, my lord hath so bewhored her,   115
   Thrown such despite and heavy terms upon her,
   As true hearts cannot bear.

DESDEMONA. Am I that name, Iago?

IAGO.   What name, fair lady?

DESDEMONA. Such as she says my lord did say I was.

EMILIA. He called her whore. A beggar in his drink   120
   Could not have laid such terms upon his callet.°

IAGO. Why did he so?

DESDEMONA. I do not know. I am sure I am none such.

IAGO. Do not weep, do not weep. Alas the day!

EMILIA. Hath she forsook so many noble matches,   125
   Her father and her country and her friends,
   To be called whore? Would it not make one weep?

DESDEMONA. It is my wretched fortune.

IAGO.   Beshrew him for 't!
   How comes this trick upon him?

DESDEMONA.   Nay, Heaven doth know.

EMILIA. I will be hanged if some eternal villain,   130
   Some busy and insinuating rogue,

---

104. **go by water:** be expressed in tears   109. **misuse:** mistake   121. **callet:** slut [Eds.]

Some cogging, cozening slave, to get some office,
Have not devised this slander. I'll be hanged else.
IAGO. Fie, there is no such man, it is impossible.
DESDEMONA. If any such there be, heaven pardon him!   135
EMILIA. A halter pardon him! And Hell gnaw his bones!
Why should he call her whore? Who keeps her company?
What place? What time? What form? What likelihood?
The Moor's abused by some most villainous knave,
Some base notorious knave, some scurvy fellow.   140
O Heaven, that such companions° Thou'dst unfold,°
And put in every honest hand a whip
To lash the rascals naked through the world
Even from the east to the west!
IAGO.   Speak withindoor.°
EMILIA. Oh, fie upon them! Some such squire he was   145
That turned your wit the seamy side without,
And made you to suspect me with the Moor.
IAGO. You are a fool. Go to.°
DESDEMONA.   O good Iago,
What shall I do to win my lord again?
Good friend, go to him, for, by this light of Heaven,   150
I know not how I lost him. Here I kneel.
If e'er my will did trespass 'gainst his love
Either in discourse of thought or actual deed,
Or that mine eyes, mine ears, or any sense
Delighted them in any other form,   155
Or that I do not yet,° and ever did,
And ever will, though he do shake me off
To beggarly divorcement, love him dearly,
Comfort forswear me! Unkindness may do much,
And his unkindness may defeat my life,   160
But never taint my love. I cannot say "whore,"
It doth abhor me now I speak the word.
To do the act that might the addition° earn
Not the world's mass of vanity° could make me.
IAGO. I pray you be content, 'tis but his humor.   165
The business of the state does him offense,
And he does chide with you.

---

141. **companions:** low creatures   **unfold:** bring to light   144. **Speak withindoor:** Don't shout
so loud that all the street will hear you.   148. **Go to:** an expression of derision   156. **yet:** still
[Eds.]   163. **addition:** title   164. **vanity:** i.e., riches

DESDEMONA.   If 'twere no other—

IAGO. 'Tis but so, I warrant. (*Trumpets within.*)
Hark how these instruments summon to supper!
The messengers of Venice stay the meat.°   170
Go in, and weep not, all things shall be well.
(*Exeunt* DESDEMONA *and* EMILIA. *Enter* RODERIGO.)
How now, Roderigo!

RODERIGO. I do not find that thou dealest justly with me.

IAGO. What in the contrary?

RODERIGO. Every day thou daffest me with some device, Iago, and rather,
as it seems to me now, keepest from me all conveniency than suppliest
me with the least advantage of hope. I will indeed no longer endure
it, nor am I yet persuaded to put up in peace what already I have
foolishly suffered.   179

IAGO. Will you hear me, Roderigo?

RODERIGO. Faith, I have heard too much, for your words and performances
are no kin together.

IAGO. You charge me most unjustly.

RODERIGO. With naught but truth. I have wasted myself out of my means.
The jewels you have had from me to deliver to Desdemona would half
have corrupted a votarist.° You have told me she hath received them,
and returned me expectations and comforts of sudden respect and
acquaintance, but I find none.   188

IAGO. Well, go to, very well.

RODERIGO. Very well! Go to! I cannot go to, man, nor 'tis not very well. By this
hand, I say 'tis very scurvy, and begin to find myself fopped in it.   192

IAGO. Very well.

RODERIGO. I tell you 'tis not very well. I will make myself known to
Desdemona. If she will return me my jewels, I will give over my suit
and repent my unlawful solicitation. If not, assure yourself I will seek
satisfaction of you.   197

IAGO. You have said now.°

RODERIGO. Aye, and said nothing but what I protest intendment of doing.

IAGO. Why, now I see there's mettle in thee, and even from this instant
do build on thee a better opinion than ever before. Give me thy hand,
Roderigo. Thou hast taken against me a most just exception, but yet I
protest I have dealt most directly in thy affair.   204

RODERIGO. It hath not appeared.

---

170. **meat:** serving of supper   186. **votarist:** nun   198. **You . . . now:** or in modern slang,
"Oh yeah."

IAGO. I grant indeed it hath not appeared, and your suspicion is not without wit and judgment. But, Roderigo, if thou hast that in thee indeed which I have greater reason to believe now than ever—I mean purpose, courage, and valor—this night show it. If thou the next night following enjoy not Desdemona, take me from this world with treachery and devise engines° for my life.   211

RODERIGO. Well, what is it? Is it within reason and compass?

IAGO. Sir, there is especial commission come from Venice to depute Cassio in Othello's place.

RODERIGO. Is that true? Why, then Othello and Desdemona return again to Venice.   216

IAGO. Oh, no. He goes into Mauritania, and takes away with him the fair Desdemona, unless his abode be lingered here by some accident, wherein none can be so determinate as the removing of Cassio.

RODERIGO. How do you mean, "removing of" him?   220

IAGO. Why, by making him uncapable of Othello's place, knocking out his brains.

RODERIGO. And that you would have me to do?

IAGO. Aye, if you dare do yourself a profit and a right. He sups tonight with a harlotry,° and thither will I go to him. He knows not yet of his honorable fortune. If you will watch his going thence, which I will fashion to fall out between twelve and one, you may take him at your pleasure. I will be near to second your attempt, and he shall fall between us. Come, stand not amazed at it, but go along with me. I will show you such a necessity in his death that you shall think yourself bound to put it on him. It is now high suppertime and the night grows to waste. About it.   232

RODERIGO. I will hear further reason for this.

IAGO. And you shall be satisfied. (*Exeunt.*)

SCENE 3. Another room in the castle.

Enter OTHELLO, LODOVICO, DESDEMONA, EMILIA, *and* ATTENDANTS.

LODOVICO. I do beseech you, sir, trouble yourself no further.

OTHELLO. Oh, pardon me, 'twill do me good to walk.

LODOVICO. Madam, good night. I humbly thank your ladyship.

DESDEMONA. Your Honor is most welcome.

OTHELLO.   Will you walk, sir?

    Oh—Desdemona—   5

DESDEMONA. My lord?

---

211. **engines:** instruments of torture   225. **harlotry:** harlot

OTHELLO. Get you to bed on the instant, I will be returned forthwith.
  Dismiss your attendant there. Look it be done.
DESDEMONA. I will, my lord.
  (*Exeunt* OTHELLO, LODOVICO, *and* ATTENDANTS.)
EMILIA. How goes it now? He looks gentler than he did.   10
DESDEMONA. He says he will return incontinent.°
  He hath commanded me to go to bed,
  And bade me to dismiss you.
EMILIA.   Dismiss me!
DESDEMONA. It was his bidding, therefore, good Emilia,
  Give me my nightly wearing, and adieu.   15
  We must not now displease him.
EMILIA. I would you had never seen him!
DESDEMONA. So would not I. My love doth so approve him
  That even his stubbornness, his checks, his frowns—
  Prithee, unpin me—have grace and favor in them.   20
EMILIA. I have laid those sheets you bade me on the bed.
DESDEMONA. All's one. Good faith, how foolish are our minds!
  If I do die before thee, prithee shroud me
  In one of those same sheets.
EMILIA.   Come, come, you talk.
DESDEMONA. My mother had a maid called Barbary.   25
  She was in love, and he she loved proved mad
  And did forsake her. She had a song of "willow"°—
  An old thing 'twas, but it expressed her fortune,
  And she died singing it. That song tonight
  Will not go from my mind. I have much to do   30
  But to go hang my head all at one side
  And sing it like poor Barbary. Prithee, dispatch.
EMILIA. Shall I go fetch your nightgown?
DESDEMONA.   No, unpin me here.
  This Lodovico is a proper man.
EMILIA. A very handsome man.   35
DESDEMONA. He speaks well.
EMILIA. I know a lady in Venice would have walked barefoot to Palestine
  for a touch of his nether lip.
DESDEMONA (*singing*).
  "The poor soul sat sighing by a sycamore tree,
    Sing all a green willow.
  Her hand on her bosom, her head on her knee,   40
    Sing willow, willow, willow.

---

11. **incontinent:** immediately   27. **willow:** the emblem of the forlorn lover

The fresh streams ran by her, and murmured her moans,
   Sing willow, willow, willow.
Her salt tears fell from her, and softened the stones—"   45
Lay by these—(*singing*)
      "Sing willow, willow, willow,"
Prithee, hie thee, he'll come anon.—(*singing*)
      "Sing all a green willow must be my garland.
   Let nobody blame him, his scorn I approve—"   50
Nay, that's not next. Hark! Who is 't that knocks?
EMILIA. It's the wind.
DESDEMONA (*singing*).
      "I called my love false love, but what said he then?
         Sing willow, willow, willow.
      If I court moe° women, you'll couch with moe men."   55
So get thee gone, good night. Mine eyes do itch.
Doth that bode weeping?
EMILIA.   'Tis neither here nor there.
DESDEMONA. I have heard it said so. Oh, these men, these men!
Dost thou in conscience think—tell me, Emilia—
That there be women do abuse their husbands   60
In such gross kind?
EMILIA.   There be some such, no question.
DESDEMONA. Wouldst thou do such a deed for all the world?
EMILIA. Why, would not you?
DESDEMONA.   No, by this heavenly light!
EMILIA. Nor I neither by this heavenly light.
I might do 't as well i' the dark.   65
DESDEMONA. Would thou do such a deed for all the world?
EMILIA. The world's a huge thing. It is a great price
For a small vice.
DESDEMONA.   In troth, I think thou wouldst not.
EMILIA. In troth, I think I should, and undo 't when I had done. Marry, I
   would not do such a thing for a joint ring,° nor for measures of lawn,°
   nor for gowns, petticoats, nor caps, nor any petty exhibition,° but for the
   whole world—why, who would not make her husband a cuckold to
   make him a monarch? I should venture Purgatory for 't.   73
DESDEMONA. Beshrew me if I would do such a wrong for the whole world.
EMILIA. Why, the wrong is but a wrong i' the world, and having the world
for your labor, 'tis a wrong in your own world and you might quickly
make it right.   77

55. moe: more   70. joint ring: ring made in two pieces, a lover's gift   measures of lawn:
lengths of finest linen [Eds.]   71. petty exhibition: small allowance of money

DESDEMONA. I do not think there is any such woman.

EMILIA. Yes, a dozen, and as many to the vantage as would store the world
they played for.
But I do think it is their husbands' faults
If wives do fall. Say that they slack their duties
And pour our treasures into foreign laps,
Or else break out in peevish jealousies, 85
Throwing restraint upon us, or say they strike us,
Or scant our former having in despite,°
Why, we have galls,° and though we have some grace,
Yet have we some revenge. Let husbands know
Their wives have sense like them. They see and smell 90
And have their palates both for sweet and sour,
As husbands have. What is it that they do
When they change us for others? Is it sport?
I think it is. And doth affection breed it?
I think it doth. Is 't frailty that thus errs? 95
It is so too. And have not we affections,
Desires for sport, and frailty, as men have?
Then let them use us well. Else let them know
The ills we do, their ills instruct us so.

DESDEMONA. Good night, good night. Heaven me such uses send, 100
Not to pick bad from bad, but by bad mend! (*Exeunt.*)

ACT 5

SCENE 1. Cyprus. A street.

Enter IAGO *and* RODERIGO.

IAGO. Here, stand behind this bulk, straight will he come.
Wear thy good rapier bare, and put it home.
Quick, quick, fear nothing. I'll be at thy elbow.
It makes us, or it mars us. Think on that,
And fix most firm thy resolution. 5

RODERIGO. Be near at hand. I may miscarry in 't.

IAGO. Here, at thy hand. Be bold, and take thy stand. (*Retires.*)

RODERIGO. I have no great devotion to the deed,
And yet he hath given me satisfying reasons.
'Tis but a man gone. Forth, my sword. He dies. 10

IAGO. I have rubbed this young quat° almost to the sense,°

87. scant . . . despite: for spite cut down our allowance   88. galls: bile, the cause of bitterness
11. quat: pimple sense: quick

And he grows angry. Now, whether he kill Cassio,
Or Cassio him, or each do kill the other,
Every way makes my gain. Live Roderigo,°
He calls me to a restitution large   15
Of gold and jewels that I bobbed from him
As gifts to Desdemona.
It must not be. If Cassio do remain,
He hath a daily beauty in his life
That makes me ugly,° and besides, the Moor   20
May unfold me to him. There stand I in much peril.
No, he must die. Be 't so. I hear him coming. (*Enter* CASSIO.)

RODERIGO. I know his gait, 'tis he. Villain, thou diest!
(*Makes a pass at* CASSIO.)

CASSIO. That thrust had been mine enemy indeed
But that my coat is better than thou know'st.   25
I will make proof of thine. (*Draws, and wounds* RODERIGO.)

RODERIGO.   Oh, I am slain!
(IAGO *from behind wounds* CASSIO *in the leg, and exits.*)

CASSIO. I am maimed for ever. Help, ho! Murder! Murder!
(*Falls. Enter* OTHELLO.)

OTHELLO. The voice of Cassio. Iago keeps his word.

RODERIGO. Oh, villain that I am!

OTHELLO.   It is even so.

CASSIO. Oh, help, ho! Light! A surgeon!   30

OTHELLO. 'Tis he. O brave Iago, honest and just,
That hast such noble sense of thy friend's wrong!
Thou teachest me. Minion,° your dear friend lies dead,
And your unblest fate hies. Strumpet, I come!
Forth of my heart those charms, thine eyes, are blotted.   35
Thy bed lust-stained shall with lust's blood be spotted.
(*Exit. Enter* LODOVICO *and* GRATIANO.)

CASSIO. What ho! No watch?° No passage?° Murder! Murder!

GRATIANO. 'Tis some mischance, the cry is very direful.

CASSIO. Oh, help!

LODOVICO. Hark!   40

RODERIGO. Oh, wretched villain!

LODOVICO. Two or three groan. It is a heavy° night.

---

14. **Live Roderigo:** If Roderigo lives [Eds.]   19–20. **He . . . ugly:** By comparison with him I am
a poor thing. Iago is conscious of his lack of social graces.   33. **Minion:**   Darling, in a bad sense
37. **watch:** police   **No passage?:** Nobody passing?   42. **heavy:** thick

These may be counterfeits. Let's think 't unsafe
To come in to the cry without more help.

RODERIGO. Nobody come? Then I shall bleed to death. 45

LODOVICO. Hark! (*Re-enter* IAGO, *with a light.*)

GRATIANO. Here's one comes in his shirt, with light and weapons.

IAGO. Who's there? Whose noise is this that cries on murder?

LODOVICO. We do not know.

IAGO. Did not you hear a cry?

CASSIO. Here, here! For Heaven's sake, help me!

IAGO. What's the matter? 50

GRATIANO. This is Othello's Ancient, as I take it.

LODOVICO. The same indeed, a very valiant fellow.

IAGO. What are you here that cry so grievously?

CASSIO. Iago? Oh, I am spoiled, undone by villains! Give me
some help. 55

IAGO. Oh me, Lieutenant! What villains have done this?

CASSIO. I think that one of them is hereabout,
And cannot make away.

IAGO. Oh, treacherous villains!
(*To* LODOVICO *and* GRATIANO) What are you there?
Come in and give some help.

RODERIGO. Oh, help me here! 60

CASSIO. That's one of them.

IAGO. Oh, murderous slave! Oh, villain!
(*Stabs* RODERIGO.)

RODERIGO. Oh, damned Iago! Oh, inhuman dog!

IAGO. Kill men i' the dark! Where be these bloody thieves?
How silent is this town! Ho! Murder! Murder!
What may you be? Are you of good or evil? 65

LODOVICO. As you shall prove us, praise us.

IAGO. Signior Lodovico?

LODOVICO. He, sir.

IAGO. I cry your mercy. Here's Cassio hurt by villains.

GRATIANO. Cassio! 70

IAGO. How is 't, brother?

CASSIO. My leg is cut in two.

IAGO. Marry, Heaven forbid!
Light, gentlemen. I'll bind it with my shirt. (*Enter* BIANCA.)

BIANCA. What is the matter, ho? Who is 't that cried?

IAGO. Who is 't that cried! 75

BIANCA. Oh, my dear Cassio! My sweet Cassio!
  Oh, Cassio, Cassio, Cassio!
IAGO. Oh, notable strumpet! Cassio, may you suspect
  Who they should be that have thus mangled you?
CASSIO. No.   80
GRATIANO. I am sorry to find you thus. I have been to seek you.
IAGO. Lend me a garter. Oh, for a chair,
  To bear him easily hence!
BIANCA. Alas, he faints! Oh, Cassio, Cassio, Cassio!
IAGO. Gentlemen all, I do suspect this trash   85
  To be a party in this injury.
  Patience awhile, good Cassio. Come, come
  Lend me a light. Know we this face or no?
  Alas, my friend and my dear countryman
  Roderigo? No—yes, sure. Oh Heaven! Roderigo.   90
GRATIANO. What, of Venice?
IAGO. Even he, sir. Did you know him?
GRATIANO.   Know him! Aye.
IAGO. Signior Gratiano? I cry you gentle pardon.
  These bloody accidents must excuse my manners,
  That so neglected you.
GRATIANO.   I am glad to see you.   95
IAGO. How do you, Cassio? Oh, a chair, a chair!
GRATIANO. Roderigo!
IAGO. He, he, 'tis he. (*A chair brought in.*) Oh, that's well said, the chair.
  Some good man bear him carefully from hence.
  I'll fetch the General's surgeon. (*To* BIANCA) For you, mistress,   100
  Save you your labor. He that lies slain here, Cassio,
  Was my dear friend. What malice between you?
CASSIO. None in the world, nor do I know the man.
IAGO (*to* BIANCA). What, look you pale? Oh, bear him out o' the air.
(CASSIO *and* RODERIGO *are borne off.*)
  Stay you, good gentlemen. Look you pale, mistress?   105
  Do you perceive the gastness of her eye?
  Nay, if you stare, we shall hear more anon.
  Behold her well, I pray you look upon her.
  Do you see, gentlemen? Nay, guiltiness will speak,
  Though tongues were out of use. (*Enter* EMILIA.)   110
EMILIA. 'Las, what's the matter? What's the matter, husband?
IAGO. Cassio hath here been set on in the dark
  By Roderigo and fellows that are 'scaped.
  He's almost slain, and Roderigo dead.

EMILIA. Alas, good gentleman! Alas, good Cassio! 115

IAGO. This is the fruit of whoring. Prithee, Emilia,
Go know of Cassio where he supped tonight.
What, do you shake at that?

BIANCA. He supped at my house, but I therefore shake not.

IAGO. Oh, did he so? I charge you, go with me. 120

EMILIA. Fie, fie upon thee, strumpet!

BIANCA. I am no strumpet, but of life as honest
As you that thus abuse me.

EMILIA.   As I! Foh! Fie upon thee!

IAGO. Kind gentlemen, let's go see poor Cassio dressed.°
Come, mistress, you must tell's another tale. 125
Emilia, run you to the citadel,
And tell my lord and lady what hath happened!
Will you go on afore? I pray. (*Aside*) This is the night
That either makes me or fordoes me quite. (*Exeunt.*)

SCENE 2. A bedchamber in the castle.
DESDEMONA in bed asleep, a light burning.

Enter OTHELLO.

OTHELLO. It is the cause,° it is the cause, my soul.
Let me not name it to you, you chaste stars!
It is the cause. Yet I'll not shed her blood,
Nor scar that whiter skin of hers than snow
And smooth as monumental alabaster. 5
Yet she must die, else she'll betray more men.
Put out the light, and then put out the light.
If I quench thee, thou flaming minister,°
I can again thy former light restore,
Should I repent me. But once put out thy light, 10
Thou cunning'st° pattern of excelling nature,
I know not where is that Promethean heat
That can thy light relume. When I have plucked the rose,
I cannot give it vital growth again,
It needs must wither. I'll smell it on the tree. (*Kissing her*) 15
Ah, balmy breath, that dost almost persuade
Justice to break her sword! One more, one more.

---

124. **dressed:** i.e., his wound dressed   1. **It . . . cause:** The meaning of the opening lines of this speech has been much discussed. The *cause* is Desdemona's supposed faithlessness; Othello, at this moment, sees himself as embodied justice, the avenger of man betrayed by woman. **8. minister:** servant   11. **cunning'st:** most skillfully made

Be thus when thou art dead, and I will kill thee,
And love thee after. One more, and this the last.
So sweet was ne'er so fatal. I must weep, 20
But they are cruel tears. This sorrow's heavenly,
It strikes where it doth love. She wakes.

DESDEMONA. Who's there? Othello?

OTHELLO. Aye, Desdemona.

DESDEMONA. Will you come to bed, my lord?

OTHELLO. Have you prayed tonight, Desdemona?

DESDEMONA. Aye, my lord. 25

OTHELLO. If you bethink yourself of any crime
Unreconciled as yet to Heaven and grace,
Solicit for it straight.

DESDEMONA. Alas, my lord, what may you mean by that?

OTHELLO. Well, do it, and be brief. I will walk by. 30
I would not kill thy unprepared spirit.
No, Heaven forfend! I would not kill thy soul.

DESDEMONA. Talk you of killing?

OTHELLO. Aye, I do.

DESDEMONA. Then Heaven
Have mercy on me!

OTHELLO. Amen, with all my heart!

DESDEMONA. If you say so, I hope you will not kill me. 35

OTHELLO. Hum!

DESDEMONA. And yet I fear you, for you are fatal then
When your eyes roll so. Why I should fear I know not,
Since guiltiness I know not, but yet I feel I fear.

OTHELLO. Think on thy sins.

DESDEMONA. They are loves I bear to you. 40

OTHELLO. Aye, and for that thou diest.

DESDEMONA. That death's unnatural that kills for loving.
Alas, why gnaw you so your nether lip?
Some bloody passion shakes your very frame.
These are portents, but yet I hope, I hope, 45
They do not point on me.

OTHELLO. Peace, and be still!

DESDEMONA. I will so. What's the matter?

OTHELLO. That handkerchief which I so loved and gave thee
Thou gavest to Cassio.

DESDEMONA. No, by my life and soul!
Send for the man, and ask him.

OTHELLO.   Sweet soul, take heed,   50
  Take heed of perjury, thou art on thy deathbed.
DESDEMONA. Aye, but not yet to die.
OTHELLO.   Yes, presently.°
  Therefore confess thee freely of thy sin,
  For to deny each article with oath
  Cannot remove nor choke the strong conception   55
  That I do groan withal. Thou art to die.
DESDEMONA. Then Lord have mercy on me!
OTHELLO.   I say amen.
DESDEMONA. And have you mercy too! I never did
  Offend you in my life, never loved Cassio
  But with such general warranty of Heaven   60
  As I might love. I never gave him token.
OTHELLO. By Heaven, I saw my handkerchief in 's hand.
  O perjured woman! Thou dost stone° my heart,
  And makest me call what I intend to do
  A murder, which I thought a sacrifice.   65
  I saw the handkerchief.
DESDEMONA.   He found it, then,
  I never gave it him. Send for him hither.
  Let him confess a truth.
OTHELLO.   He hath confessed.
DESDEMONA. What, my lord?
OTHELLO. That he hath used thee.
DESDEMONA.   How? Unlawfully?
OTHELLO.   Aye.   70
DESDEMONA. He will not say so.
OTHELLO.   No, his mouth is stopped.
  Honest Iago hath ta'en order for 't.
DESDEMONA. Oh, my fear interprets! What, is he dead?
OTHELLO. Had all his hairs been lives, my great revenge
  Had stomach for them all.   75
DESDEMONA. Alas, he is betrayed, and I undone!
OTHELLO. Out, strumpet! Weep'st thou for him to my face?
DESDEMONA. Oh, banish me, my lord, but kill me not!
OTHELLO. Down, strumpet!
DESDEMONA. Kill me tomorrow, let me live tonight!   80
OTHELLO. Nay, if you strive—
DESDEMONA. But half an hour!

---

52. **presently:** at once   63. **stone:** turn to stone

OTHELLO. Being done, there is no pause.

DESDEMONA. But while I say one prayer!

OTHELLO. It is too late. (*He stifles her.*)

EMILIA (*within*). My lord, my lord! What ho! My lord, my lord!

OTHELLO. What noise is this? Not dead? Not yet quite dead?   85
 I that am cruel am yet merciful,
 I would not have thee linger in thy pain.
 So, so.

EMILIA (*within*). What ho! My lord, my lord!

OTHELLO. Who's there?

EMILIA (*within*). Oh, good my lord, I would speak a word with you!

OTHELLO. Yes, 'tis Emilia. By and by. She's dead.   90
 'Tis like she comes to speak of Cassio's death.
 The noise was here. Ha! No more moving?
 Still as the grave. Shall she come in? Were 't good?
 I think she stirs again. No. What's best to do?
 If she come in, she'll sure speak to my wife.   95
 My wife! My wife! What wife? I have no wife.
 Oh, insupportable! Oh, heavy hour!
 Methinks it should be now a huge eclipse
 Of sun and moon, and that the affrighted globe
 Should yawn° at alteration.

EMILIA (*within*). I do beseech you   100
 That I may speak with you, O good my lord!

OTHELLO. I had forgot thee. Oh, come in, Emilia.
 Soft, by and by. Let me the curtains° draw.
 What art thou? (*Unlocks the door. Enter* EMILIA.)
 What's the matter with thee now?

EMILIA. Oh, my good lord, yonder's foul murders done!   105

OTHELLO. What, now?

EMILIA. But now, my lord.

OTHELLO. It is the very error of the moon.
 She comes more nearer earth than she was wont
 And makes men mad.   110

EMILIA. Cassio, my lord, hath killed a young Venetian
 Called Roderigo.

OTHELLO. Roderigo killed!
 And Cassio killed!

EMILIA. No, Cassio is not killed.

---

100. **yawn:** split open in an earthquake [Eds.]   103. **curtains:** i.e., of the bed

OTHELLO. Not Cassio killed! Then murder's out of tune,
And sweet revenge grows harsh.   115
DESDEMONA. Oh, falsely, falsely murdered!
EMILIA.   Alas, what cry is that?
OTHELLO. That! What?
EMILIA. Out and alas! That was my lady's voice.
Help! Help, ho! Help! O lady, speak again!
Sweet Desdemona! O sweet mistress, speak!   120
DESDEMONA. A guiltless death I die.
EMILIA. Oh, who hath done this deed?
DESDEMONA. Nobody, I myself. Farewell.
Commend me to my kind lord. Oh, farewell! (*Dies.*)
OTHELLO. Why, how should she be murdered?
EMILIA.   Alas, who knows?   125
OTHELLO. You heard her say herself it was not I.
EMILIA. She said so. I must needs report the truth.
OTHELLO. She's like a liar gone to burning Hell.
'Twas I that killed her.
EMILIA.   Oh, the more angel she,
And you the blacker devil!   130
OTHELLO. She turned to folly, and she was a whore.
EMILIA. Thou dost belie her, and thou art a devil.
OTHELLO. She was false as water.
EMILIA.   Thou art rash as fire to say
That she was false. Oh, she was heavenly true!
OTHELLO. Cassio did top her, ask thy husband else.   135
Oh, I were damned beneath all depth in Hell
But that I did proceed upon just grounds
To this extremity. Thy husband knew it all.
EMILIA. My husband!
OTHELLO. Thy husband.   140
EMILIA. That she was false to wedlock?
OTHELLO. Aye, with Cassio. Nay, had she been true,
If Heaven would make me such another world
Of one entire and perfect chrysolite,
I'd not have sold her for it.
EMILIA.   My husband!   145
OTHELLO. Aye, 'twas he that told me first.
An honest man he is, and hates the slime
That sticks on filthy deeds.
EMILIA.   My husband!
OTHELLO. What needs this iteration, woman? I say thy husband.

EMILIA. Oh, mistress, villainy hath made mocks with love!   150
  My husband say that she was false!

OTHELLO.   He, woman.
  I say thy husband. Dost understand the word?
  My friend, thy husband, honest, honest Iago.

EMILIA. If he say so, may his pernicious soul
  Rot half a grain a day! He lies to the heart.   155
  She was too fond of her most filthy bargain.

OTHELLO. Ha!

EMILIA. Do thy worst.
  This deed of thine is no more worthy Heaven
  Than thou wast worthy her.

OTHELLO.   Peace, you were best.   160

EMILIA. Thou hast not half that power to do me harm
  As I have to be hurt. O gull! O dolt!
  As ignorant as dirt! Thou hast done a deed—
  I care not for thy sword, I'll make thee known,
  Though I lost twenty lives. Help! Help! ho! Help!   165
  The Moor hath killed my mistress! Murder! Murder!

  (*Enter* MONTANO, GRATIANO, IAGO, *and others.*)

MONTANO. What is the matter? How now, General!

EMILIA. Oh, are you come, Iago? You have done well,
  That men must lay their murders on your neck.

GRATIANO. What is the matter?   170

EMILIA. Disprove this villain, if thou be'st a man.
  He says thou told'st him that his wife was false.
  I know thou didst not, thou'rt not such a villain.
  Speak, for my heart is full.

IAGO. I told him what I thought, and told no more   175
  Than what he found himself was apt and true.

EMILIA. But did you ever tell him she was false?

IAGO. I did.

EMILIA. You told a lie, an odious, damnèd lie,
  Upon my soul, a lie, a wicked lie!   180
  She false with Cassio! Did you say with Cassio?

IAGO. With Cassio, mistress. Go to, charm your tongue.°

EMILIA. I will not charm my tongue, I am bound to speak.
  My mistress here lies murdered in her bed.

ALL. Oh, Heavens forfend!   185

EMILIA. And your reports have set the murder on.

---

182. charm your tongue: be silent

OTHELLO. Nay, stare not, masters. It is true indeed.

GRATIANO. 'Tis a strange truth.

MONTANO. Oh, monstrous act!

EMILIA.   Villainy, villainy, villainy!
I think upon 't. I think I smell 't. Oh, villainy!   190
I thought so then. I'll kill myself for grief.
Oh, villainy, villainy!

IAGO. What, are you mad? I charge you, get you home.

EMILIA. Good gentlemen, let me have leave to speak.
'Tis proper I obey him, but not now.   195
Perchance, Iago, I will ne'er go home.

OTHELLO. Oh! Oh! Oh! (*Falling on the bed.*)

EMILIA.   Nay, lay thee down and roar,
For thou has killed the sweetest innocent
That e'er did lift up eye.

OTHELLO (*rising*).   Oh, she was foul!
I scarce did know you, Uncle. There lies your niece,   200
Whose breath indeed these hands have newly stopped.
I know this act shows horrible and grim.

GRATIANO. Poor Desdemona! I am glad thy father's dead.
Thy match was mortal to him, and pure grief
Shore his old thread in twain. Did he live now,   205
This sight would make him do a desperate turn—
Yea, curse his better angel from his side,
And fall to reprobation.°

OTHELLO. 'Tis pitiful, but yet Iago knows
That she with Cassio hath the act of shame   210
A thousand times committed. Cassio confessed it.
And she did gratify his amorous works
With that recognizance and pledge of love
Which I first gave her, I saw it in his hand.
It was a handkerchief, an antique token   215
My father gave my mother.

EMILIA. Oh, Heaven! Oh, heavenly powers!

IAGO. 'Zounds! Hold your peace.

EMILIA.   'Twill out, 'twill out. I peace!
No, I will speak as liberal as the north.°
Let Heaven and men and devils, let them all,   220
All, all, cry shame against me, yet I'll speak.

---

208. reprobation: damnation; i.e., by self-murder   **219. liberal . . . north:** as freely as the north
wind, which is loud and bitter

IAGO. Be wise, and get you home.

EMILIA.   I will not.

   (IAGO *offers to stab* EMILIA.)

GRATIANO.   Fie!

   Your sword upon a woman!

EMILIA. O thou dull Moor! That handkerchief thou speak'st of

   I found by fortune and did give my husband,   225

   For often with a solemn earnestness,

   More than indeed belonged to such a trifle,

   He begged of me to steal it.

IAGO.   Villainous whore!

EMILIA. She give it Cassio! No, alas, I found it,

   And I did give 't my husband.

IAGO.   Filth, thou liest!   230

EMILIA. By Heaven, I do not, I do not, gentlemen.

   Oh, murderous coxcomb! What should such a fool

   Do with so good a wife!

OTHELLO.   Are there no stones° in Heaven

   But what serve for the thunder? Precious villain!

   (*He runs at* IAGO. IAGO, *from behind, stabs* EMILIA, *and exits.*)

GRATIANO. The woman falls. Sure, he hath killed his wife.   235

EMILIA. Aye. Aye. Oh, lay me by my mistress' side.

GRATIANO. He's gone, but his wife's killed.

MONTANO. 'Tis a notorious villain. Take you this weapon,

   Which I have here recovered from the Moor.

   Come, guard the door without, let him not pass,   240

   But kill him rather. I'll after that same villain,

   For 'tis a damnèd slave. (*Exeunt all but* OTHELLO *and* EMILIA.)

OTHELLO.   I am not valiant neither,

   But every puny whipster gets my sword.

   But why should honor outlive honesty?

   Let it go all.

EMILIA.   What did thy song bode, lady?   245

   Hark, canst thou hear me? I will play the swan,

   And die in music. (*Singing*)

                    "Willow, willow, willow."

   Moor, she was chaste. She loved thee, cruel Moor,

   So come my soul to bliss as I speak true.

   So speaking as I think, I die, I die. (*Dies.*)   250

OTHELLO. I have another weapon in this chamber.

---

233. stones: thunderbolts

It is a sword of Spain, the ice brook's temper.—
Oh, here it is. Uncle, I must come forth.
GRATIANO (*within*). If thou attempt it, it will cost thee dear.
Thou hast no weapon, and perforce must suffer.   255
OTHELLO. Look in upon me then, and speak with me,
Or, naked° as I am, I will assault thee. (*Re-enter* GRATIANO.)
GRATIANO. What is the matter?
OTHELLO.   Behold, I have a weapon,
A better never did itself sustain
Upon a soldier's thigh. I have seen the day   260
That with this little arm and this good sword
I have made my way through more impediments
Than twenty times your stop. But, oh, vain boast!
Who can control his fate? 'Tis not so now.
Be not afraid, though you do see me weaponed.   265
Here is my journey's end, here is my butt°
And very sea mark of my utmost sail.
Do you go back dismayed? 'Tis a lost fear.
Man but a rush° against Othello's breast,
And he retires. Where should Othello go?   270
Now, how dost thou look now? O ill-starred wench!
Pale as thy smock! When we shall meet at compt,°
This look of thine will hurl my soul from Heaven
And fiends will snatch at it. Cold, cold, my girl!
Even like thy chastity. Oh, cursèd slave!   275
Whip me, ye devils,
From the possession of this heavenly sight!
Blow me about in winds! Roast me in sulphur!
Wash me in steep-down gulfs of liquid fire!
O Desdemona! Desdemona! Dead!   280
Oh! Oh! Oh!
(*Enter* LODOVICO, MONTANO, CASSIO *carried in a chair, and* OFFICERS
with IAGO, *prisoner.*)
LODOVICO. Where is this rash and most unfortunate man?
OTHELLO. That's he that was Othello. Here I am.
LODOVICO. Where is the viper? Bring the villain forth.
OTHELLO. I look down toward his feet,° but that's a fable.   285
If that thou be'st a devil, I cannot kill thee. (*Wounds* IAGO.)

---

257. **naked:** unarmed   266. **butt:** aim   269. **Man . . . rush:** Attack with only a reed
272. **compt:** account; i.e., the Day of Judgment   285. **toward his feet:** i.e., to see if he has the
cloven hoof of a devil

LODOVICO. Wrench his sword from him.

IAGO.   I bleed, sir, but not killed.

OTHELLO. I am not sorry neither. I'd have thee live,
    For, in my sense, 'tis happiness to die.

LODOVICO. O thou Othello, that wert once so good,   290
    Fall'n in the practice° of a damnèd slave,
    What shall be said to thee?

OTHELLO.   Why, anything.
    An honorable murderer, if you will,
    For naught did I in hate, but all in honor.

LODOVICO. This wretch hath part confessed his villainy.   295
    Did you and he consent in Cassio's death?

OTHELLO. Aye.

CASSIO. Dear General, I never gave you cause.

OTHELLO. I do believe it, and I ask your pardon.
    Will you, I pray, demand that demi-devil   300
    Why he hath thus ensnared my soul and body?

IAGO. Demand me nothing. What you know, you know.
    From this time forth I never will speak word.

LODOVICO. What, not to pray?

GRATIANO.   Torments will ope your lips.

OTHELLO. Well, thou dost best.   305

LODOVICO. Sir, you shall understand what hath befall'n,
    Which, as I think, you know not. Here is a letter
    Found in the pocket of the slain Roderigo,
    And here another. The one of them imports
    The death of Cassio to be undertook   310
    By Roderigo.

OTHELLO. Oh, villain!

CASSIO.   Most heathenish and most gross!

LODOVICO. Now here's another discontented paper,
    Found in his pocket too. And this, it seems,
    Roderigo meant to have sent this damnèd villain   315
    But that, belike, Iago in the interim
    Came in and satisfied him.

OTHELLO.   Oh, the pernicious caitiff!
    How come you, Cassio, by that handkerchief
    That was my wife's?

CASSIO.   I found it in my chamber.

---

291. Fall'n . . . practice: Destroyed by the plotting

And he himself confessed but even now   320
That there he dropped it for a special purpose
Which wrought to his desire.

OTHELLO.   O fool! Fool! Fool!

CASSIO. There is besides in Roderigo's letter
How he upbraids Iago, that he made him
Brave° me upon the watch, whereon it came   325
That I was cast.° And even but now he spake
After long seeming dead, Iago hurt him,
Iago set him on.

LODOVICO. You must forsake this room, and go with us.
Your power and your command is taken off,   330
And Cassio rules in Cyprus. For this slave,
If there be any cunning cruelty
That can torment him much and hold him long,°
It shall be his. You shall close prisoner rest
Till that the nature of your fault be known   335
To the Venetian state. Come, bring away.

OTHELLO. Soft you, a word or two before you go.
I have done the state some service, and they know 't.
No more of that. I pray you, in your letters,
When you shall these unlucky deeds relate,   340
Speak of me as I am, nothing extenuate,
Nor set down aught in malice. Then must you speak
Of one that loved not wisely but too well;
Of one not easily jealous, but, being wrought,
Perplexed in the extreme; of one whose hand,   345
Like the base Indian, threw a pearl away
Richer than all his tribe; of one whose subdued eyes,
Albeit unusèd to the melting mood,
Drop tears as fast as the Arabian trees
Their medicinable gum. Set you down this,   350
And say besides that in Aleppo once,
Where a malignant and a turbaned Turk
Beat a Venetian and traduced the state,
I took by the throat the circumcisèd dog
And smote him, thus. (*Stabs himself.*)   355

LODOVICO. Oh, bloody period!

GRATIANO.   All that's spoke is marred.

---

325. **Brave:** Insult   326. **cast:** dismissed   333. **long:** i.e., in dying

OTHELLO. I kissed thee ere I killed thee. No way but this,
 Killing myself, to die upon a kiss. (*Falls on the bed, and dies.*)
CASSIO. This did I fear, but thought he had no weapon,
 For he was great of heart.
LODOVICO (*to* IAGO).   O Spartan° dog,   360
 More fell° than anguish, hunger, or the sea!
 Look on the tragic loading of this bed:
 This is thy work. The object poisons sight,
 Let it be hid.° Gratiano, keep the house,
 And seize upon the fortunes of the Moor,   365
 For they succeed on you. To you, Lord Governor,
 Remains the censure of this hellish villain,
 The time, the place, the torture.
 Oh, enforce it!
 Myself will straight aboard, and to the state   370
 This heavy act with heavy heart relate. (*Exeunt.*)

QUESTIONS

1. In what ways is Othello, in the first two acts, shown to be a person of extraordinary quality?
2. Is Othello a person jealous "by nature"? Does he show any disposition to jealousy in the first two acts? What does he say about himself in his final soliloquy? (There has been much critical controversy over the psychological probability of Othello's being roused so quickly to such a high pitch of jealousy in Act 3. Some have explained it by attributing a predisposition to jealousy in Othello; others have attributed it to the almost superhuman Machiavellian cleverness of Iago, which would have taken in any husband. In general, however, Shakespeare was less interested in psychological consistency and the subtle tracing of motivation—which are modern interests—than he was in theatrical effectiveness and the orchestration of emotions. Perhaps the question we should properly ask is not "How probable is Othello's jealousy?" but "How vital and effective has Shakespeare rendered it?")
3. Who is more naturally suspicious of human nature—Othello or Iago?
4. Is something of Othello's nobility manifested even in the scale of his jealousy? How does he respond to his conviction that Desdemona has been unfaithful to him? Would a lesser man have responded in the same way? Why or why not?
5. How does Othello's final speech reestablish his greatness?
6. What are Iago's motivations in his actions toward Othello, Cassio, and Roderigo? What is his philosophy? How does his technique in handling Roderigo differ from his technique in handling Othello and Cassio? Why?

360. Spartan: i.e., hardhearted   361. fell: cruel   364. Let . . . hid: At these words the curtains are closed across the inner stage (or chamber, if this scene was acted aloft), concealing all three bodies.

7. In rousing Othello's suspicions against Desdemona (3.3), Iago uses the same technique, in part, that he had used with Othello in inculpating Cassio (2.3) and that he later uses with Lodovico in inculpating Othello (4.2). What is this technique? Why is it effective? How does he change his tactics in the opening of 4.1?

8. What opinions of Iago, before his exposure, are expressed by Othello, Desdemona, Cassio, and Lodovico? Is Othello the only one taken in by him? Does his own wife think him capable of villainy?

9. Though Othello is the protagonist, the majority of soliloquies and asides are given to Iago. Why?

10. The difference between Othello and Desdemona that Iago plays on most is that of color, and, reading the play today, we may be tempted to see the play as being centrally about race relations. However, only one other character, besides Othello, makes much of this difference in color. Which one? Is this character sympathetically portrayed? What attitude toward Othello himself, and his marriage, is taken by the Duke, Cassio, Lodovico, Emilia, Desdemona herself? What differences between Othello and Desdemona, besides color, are used by Iago to undermine Othello's confidence in Desdemona's fidelity? What differences between them does Othello himself take into account?

11. What are Desdemona's principal character traits? In what ways are she and Emilia character foils? Is she entirely discreet in pleading Cassio's case to Othello? Why or why not? Why does she lie about the handkerchief (3.4)?

12. Like Sophocles in *Oedipus Rex,* Shakespeare makes extensive use of dramatic irony in this play. Point out effective examples.

13. Unlike *Oedipus Rex, Othello* contains comedy. For what purposes is it used? What larger difference in effect between *Othello* and *Oedipus Rex* does this use of comedy contribute to?

14. Find several occasions when chance and coincidence are involved in the plot (for example, Bianca's entry in 4.1). How important are these to the development of the plot? To what extent do they *cause* subsequent events to happen?

15. As much responsible as any other quality for the original popularity and continued vitality of *Othello* is its poetry. What are some of the prominent characteristics of that poetry (language, imagery, rhythm)? What speeches are particularly memorable or effective? Though most of the play is written in blank verse, some passages are written in rhymed iambic pentameter couplets and others in prose. Can you suggest any reasons for Shakespeare's use of these other mediums?

16. How would the effect of the play have been different if Othello had died *before* discovering Desdemona's innocence?

MOLIÈRE
The Misanthrope

Characters

ALCESTE, *in love with Célimène*
PHILINTE, *Alceste's friend*
ORONTE, *in love with Célimène*
CÉLIMÈNE, *Alceste's beloved*
ELIANTE, *Célimène's cousin*
ARSINOÉ, *a friend of Célimène's*

ACASTE ⎱ *marquesses*
CLITANDRE ⎰
BASQUE, *Célimène's servant*
A GUARD *of the Marshalsea*
DUBOIS, *Alceste's valet*

The scene throughout is in Célimène's house at Paris

ACT I

SCENE I

Enter ALCESTE *and* PHILINTE.

PHILINTE. Now, what's got into you?

ALCESTE (*seated*).   Kindly leave me alone.

PHILINTE. Come, come, what is it? This lugubrious tone . . .

ALCESTE. Leave me, I said; you spoil my solitude.

PHILINTE. Oh, listen to me, now, and don't be rude.

ALCESTE. I choose to be rude, Sir, and to be hard of hearing.   5

PHILINTE. These ugly moods of yours are not endearing;
    Friends though we are, I really must insist . . .

ALCESTE (*abruptly rising*). Friends? Friends, you say? Well, cross me off
    your list.
    I've been your friend till now, as you well know;
    But after what I saw a moment ago   10
    I tell you flatly that our ways must part.
    I wish no place in a dishonest heart.

THE MISANTHROPE   First performed in 1666 in Paris during the reign of the "Sun King" (Louis XIV), a time in social and aristocratic circles when great emphasis was placed on elegance in dress, manners, and taste. Translated by Richard Wilbur. Molière (1622–1673) was born Jean-Baptiste Poquelin in Paris and was given excellent schooling by his father, a successful upholsterer employed by the court. He took "Molière" as his stage name when, at the age of twenty-one, he joined a traveling group of players. The rest of his life was spent in the theater as actor, manager, and author. Though twice sent to prison for debts, and often in trouble with the civil authorities for his writing, he enjoyed a certain amount of royal favor after his establishment in Paris in 1658.

PHILINTE. Why, what have I done, Alceste? Is this quite just?

ALCESTE. My God, you ought to die of self-disgust.
I call your conduct inexcusable, Sir,   15
And every man of honor will concur.
I see you almost hug a man to death,
Exclaim for joy until you're out of breath,
And supplement these loving demonstrations
With endless offers, vows, and protestations;   20
Then when I ask you "Who was that?" I find
That you can barely bring his name to mind!
Once the man's back is turned, you cease to love him,
And speak with absolute indifference of him!
By God, I say it's base and scandalous   25
To falsify the heart's affections thus;
If I caught myself behaving in such a way,
I'd hang myself for shame, without delay.

PHILINTE. It hardly seems a hanging matter to me;
I hope that you will take it graciously   30
If I extend myself a slight reprieve,
And live a little longer, by your leave.

ALCESTE. How dare you joke about a crime so grave?

PHILINTE. What crime? How else are people to behave?

ALCESTE. I'd have them be sincere, and never part   35
With any word that isn't from the heart.

PHILINTE. When someone greets us with a show of pleasure,
It's but polite to give him equal measure,
Return his love the best that we know how,
And trade him offer for offer, vow for vow.   40

ALCESTE. No, no, this formula you'd have me follow,
However fashionable, is false and hollow,
And I despise the frenzied operations
Of all these barterers of protestations,
These lavishers of meaningless embraces,   45
These utterers of obliging commonplaces,
Who court and flatter everyone on earth
And praise the fool no less than the man of worth.
Should you rejoice that someone fondles you,
Offers his love and service, swears to be true,   50
And fills your ears with praises of your name,
When to the first damned fop he'll say the same?
No, no: no self-respecting heart would dream
Of prizing so promiscuous an esteem;
However high the praise, there's nothing worse   55

Than sharing honors with the universe.
Esteem is founded on comparison:
To honor all men is to honor none.
Since you embrace this indiscriminate vice,
Your friendship comes at far too cheap a price; 60
I spurn the easy tribute of a heart
Which will not set the worthy man apart:
I choose, Sir, to be chosen; and in fine,
The friend of mankind is no friend of mine.

PHILINTE. But in polite society, custom decrees 65
That we show certain outward courtesies . . .

ALCESTE. Ah, no! we should condemn with all our force
Such false and artificial intercourse.
Let men behave like men; let them display
Their inmost hearts in everything they say; 70
Let the heart speak, and let our sentiments
Not mask themselves in silly compliments.

PHILINTE. In certain cases it would be uncouth
And most absurd to speak the naked truth;
With all respect for your exalted notions, 75
It's often best to veil one's true emotions.
Wouldn't the social fabric come undone
If we were wholly frank with everyone?
Suppose you met with someone you couldn't bear;
Would you inform him of it then and there? 80

ALCESTE. Yes.

PHILINTE.   Then you'd tell old Emilie it's pathetic
The way she daubs her features with cosmetic
And plays the gay coquette at sixty-four?

ALCESTE. I would.

PHILINTE.   And you'd call Dorilas a bore,
And tell him every ear at court is lame 85
From hearing him brag about his noble name?

ALCESTE. Precisely.

PHILINTE.   Ah, you're joking.

ALCESTE.   Au contraire:°
In this regard there's none I'd choose to spare.
All are corrupt; there's nothing to be seen
In court or town but aggravates my spleen. 90
I fall into deep gloom and melancholy

87. *Au contraire:* On the contrary

When I survey the scene of human folly,
Finding on every hand base flattery,
Injustice, fraud, self-interest, treachery . . .
Ah, it's too much; mankind has grown so base,   95
I mean to break with the whole human race.
PHILINTE. This philosophic rage is a bit extreme;
    You've no idea how comical you seem;
    Indeed, we're like those brothers in the play
    Called *School for Husbands,* one of whom was prey . . .°   100
ALCESTE. Enough, now! None of your stupid similes.
PHILINTE. Then let's have no more tirades, if you please.
    The world won't change, whatever you say or do;
    And since plain speaking means so much to you,
    I'll tell you plainly that by being frank   105
    You've earned the reputation of a crank,
    And that you're thought ridiculous when you rage
    And rant against the manners of the age.
ALCESTE. So much the better; just what I wish to hear.
    No news could be more grateful to my ear.   110
    All men are so detestable in my eyes,
    I should be sorry if they thought me wise.
PHILINTE. Your hatred's very sweeping, is it not?
ALCESTE. Quite right: I hate the whole degraded lot.
PHILINTE. Must all poor human creatures be embraced,   115
    Without distinction, by your vast distaste?
    Even in these bad times, there are surely a few . . .
ALCESTE. No, I include all men in one dim view:
    Some men I hate for being rogues; the others
    I hate because they treat the rogues like brothers,   120
    And, lacking a virtuous scorn for what is vile,
    Receive the villain with a complaisant smile.
    Notice how tolerant people choose to be
    Toward that bold rascal who's at law with me.
    His social polish can't conceal his nature;   125
    One sees at once that he's a treacherous creature;
    No one could possibly be taken in
    By those soft speeches and that sugary grin.

---

100. *School . . . prey: School for Husbands* is an earlier play by Molière. The chief characters are
two brothers, one of whom, puritanical and suspicious, mistrusts the fashions and customs of the
world, shuts up his ward and fiancée to keep her from infection by them, and is outwitted and
betrayed by her. The other, more amiable and easygoing, allows his ward a free rein and is rewarded
with her love.

The whole world knows the shady means by which
The low-brow's grown so powerful and rich, 130
And risen to a rank so bright and high
That virtue can but blush, and merit sigh.
Whenever his name comes up in conversation,
None will defend his wretched reputation;
Call him knave, liar, scoundrel, and all the rest, 135
Each head will nod, and no one will protest.
And yet his smirk is seen in every house,
He's greeted everywhere with smiles and bows,
And when there's any honor that can be got
By pulling strings, he'll get it, like as not. 140
My God! It chills my heart to see the ways
Men come to terms with evil nowadays;
Sometimes, I swear, I'm moved to flee and find
Some desert land unfouled by humankind.

PHILINTE. Come, let's forget the follies of the times 145
And pardon mankind for its petty crimes;
Let's have an end of rantings and of railings,
And show some leniency toward human failings.
This world requires a pliant rectitude;
Too stern a virtue makes one stiff and rude; 150
Good sense views all extremes with detestation,
And bids us to be noble in moderation.
The rigid virtues of the ancient days
Are not for us; they jar with all our ways
And ask of us too lofty a perfection. 155
Wise men accept their times without objection,
And there's no greater folly, if you ask me,
Than trying to reform society.
Like you, I see each day a hundred and one
Unhandsome deeds that might be better done, 160
But still, for all the faults that meet my view,
I'm never known to storm and rave like you.
I take men as they are, or let them be,
And teach my soul to bear their frailty;
And whether in court or town, whatever the scene, 165
My phlegm's as philosophic as your spleen.

ALCESTE. This phlegm which you so eloquently commend,
Does nothing ever rile it up, my friend?
Suppose some man you trust should treacherously
Conspire to rob you of your property, 170

And do his best to wreck your reputation?
Wouldn't you feel a certain indignation?

PHILINTE. Why, no. These faults of which you complain
Are part of human nature, I maintain,
And it's no more a matter of disgust   175
That men are knavish, selfish and unjust,
Than that the vulture dines upon the dead,
And wolves are furious, and apes ill-bred.

ALCESTE. Shall I see myself betrayed, robbed, torn to bits,
And not . . . Oh, let's be still and rest our wits.   180
Enough of reasoning, now. I've had my fill.

PHILINTE. Indeed, you would do well, Sir, to be still.
Rage less at your opponent, and give some thought
To how you'll win this lawsuit that he's brought.

ALCESTE. I assure you I'll do nothing of the sort.   185

PHILINTE. Then who will plead your case before the court?

ALCESTE. Reason and right and justice will plead for me.

PHILINTE. Oh, Lord. What judges do you plan to see?

ALCESTE. Why, none. The justice of my cause is clear.

PHILINTE. Of course, man; but there's politics to fear . . .   190

ALCESTE. No, I refuse to lift a hand. That's flat.
I'm either right, or wrong.

PHILINTE.   Don't count on that.

ALCESTE. No, I'll do nothing.

PHILINTE.   Your enemy's influence
Is great, you know . . .

ALCESTE.   That makes no difference.

PHILINTE. It will; you'll see.

ALCESTE.   Must honor bow to guile?   195
If so, I shall be proud to lose the trial.

PHILINTE. Oh, really . . .

ALCESTE.   I'll discover by this case
Whether or not men are sufficiently base
And impudent and villainous and perverse
To do me wrong before the universe.   200

PHILINTE. What a man!

ALCESTE.   Oh, I could wish, whatever the cost,
Just for the beauty of it, that my trial were lost.

PHILINTE. If people heard you talking so, Alceste,
They'd split their sides. Your name would be a jest.

ALCESTE. So much the worse for jesters.

PHILINTE.   May I enquire   205

Whether this rectitude you so admire,
And these hard virtues you're enamored of
Are qualities of the lady whom you love?
It much surprises me that you, who seem
To view mankind with furious disesteem,   210
Have yet found something to enchant your eyes
Amidst a species which you do despise.
And what is more amazing, I'm afraid,
Is the most curious choice your heart has made.
The honest Eliante is fond of you,   215
Arsinoé, the prude, admires you too;
And yet your spirit's been perversely led
To choose the flighty Célimène instead,
Whose brittle malice and coquettish ways
So typify the manners of our days.   220
How is it that the traits you most abhor
Are bearable in this lady you adore?
Are you so blind with love that you can't find them?
Or do you contrive, in her case, not to mind them?

ALCESTE. My love for that young widow's not the kind   225
    That can't perceive defects; no, I'm not blind.
    I see her faults, despite my ardent love,
    And all I see I fervently reprove.
    And yet I'm weak; for all her falsity,
    That woman knows the art of pleasing me,   230
    And though I never cease complaining of her,
    I swear I cannot manage not to love her.
    Her charm outweighs her faults; I can but aim
    To cleanse her spirit in my love's pure flame.

PHILINTE. That's no small task; I wish you all success.   235
    You think then that she loves you?

ALCESTE.   Heavens, yes!
    I wouldn't love her did she not love me.

PHILINTE. Well, if her taste for you is plain to see,
    Why do these rivals cause you such despair?

ALCESTE. True love, Sir, is possessive, and cannot bear   240
    To share with all the world. I'm here today
    To tell her she must send that mob away.

PHILINTE. If I were you, and had your choice to make,
    Eliante, her cousin, would be the one I'd take;
    That honest heart, which cares for you alone,   245
    Would harmonize far better with your own.

ALCESTE. True, true: each day my reason tells me so;
But reason doesn't rule in love, you know.
PHILINTE. I fear some bitter sorrow is in store;
This love . . .

SCENE 2*

Enter ORONTE.

ORONTE (*to* ALCESTE). The servants told me at the door   250
That Eliante and Célimène were out,
But when I heard, dear Sir, that you were about,
I came to say, without exaggeration,
That I hold you in the vastest admiration,
And that it's always been my dearest desire   255
To be the friend of one I so admire.
I hope to see my love of merit requited,
And you and I in friendship's bond united.
I'm sure you won't refuse—if I may be frank—
A friend of my devotedness—and rank. (*During this speech of* ORONTE'S,
ALCESTE *is abstracted, and seems unaware that he is being spoken to. He only*
breaks off his reverie when ORONTE *says*)
It was for you, if you please, that my words were intended.   261
ALCESTE. For me, Sir?
ORONTE.   Yes, for you. You're not offended?
ALCESTE. By no means. But this much surprises me . . .
The honor comes most unexpectedly . . .
ORONTE. My high regard should not astonish you;   265
The whole world feels the same. It is your due.
ALCESTE. Sir . . .
ORONTE   Why, in all the State there isn't one
Can match your merits; they shine, Sir, like the sun.
ALCESTE. Sir . . .
ORONTE.   You are higher in my estimation
Than all that's most illustrious in the nation.   270
ALCESTE. Sir . . .
ORONTE.   If I lie, may heaven strike me dead!
To show you that I mean what I have said,

---

*In English and in most modern plays, a scene is a continuous section of the action in one setting,
and acts are not usually divided into scenes unless there is a shift in setting or a shift in time. In
older French drama, however, a scene is any portion of the play involving one group of characters,
and a new scene begins, without interruption of the action, whenever any important character
enters or exits.

Permit me, Sir, to embrace you most sincerely,
And swear that I will prize our friendship dearly.
Give me your hand. And now, Sir, if you choose,   275
We'll make our vows.
ALCESTE.   Sir . . .
ORONTE.   What! You refuse?
ALCESTE. Sir, it's a very great honor you extend:
But friendship is a sacred thing, my friend;
It would be profanation to bestow
The name of friend on one you hardly know.   280
All parts are better played when well-rehearsed;
Let's put off friendship, and get acquainted first.
We may discover it would be unwise
To try to make our natures harmonize.
ORONTE. By heaven! You're sagacious to the core;   285
This speech has made me admire you even more.
Let time, then, bring us closer day by day;
Meanwhile, I shall be yours in every way.
If, for example, there should be anything
You wish at court, I'll mention it to the King.   290
I have his ear, of course; it's quite well known
That I am much in favor with the throne.
In short, I am your servant. And now, dear friend,
Since you have such fine judgment, I intend
To please you, if I can, with a small sonnet   295
I wrote not long ago. Please comment on it,
And tell me whether I ought to publish it.
ALCESTE. You must excuse me, Sir; I'm hardly fit
To judge such matters.
ORONTE.   Why not?
ALCESTE.   I am, I fear,
Inclined to be unfashionably sincere.
ORONTE. Just what I ask; I'd take no satisfaction   300
In anything but your sincere reaction.
I beg you not to dream of being kind.
ALCESTE. Since you desire it, Sir, I'll speak my mind.
ORONTE. *Sonnet.* It's a sonnet . . . *Hope* . . . The poem's addressed   305
To a lady who wakened hopes within my breast.
Hope . . . this is not the pompous sort of thing,
Just modest little verses, with a tender ring.
ALCESTE. Well, we shall see.
ORONTE.   *Hope* . . . I'm anxious to hear
Whether the style seems properly smooth and clear,   310

And whether the choice of words is good or bad.

ALCESTE. We'll see, we'll see.

ORONTE.   Perhaps I ought to add
That it took me only a quarter-hour to write it.

ALCESTE. The time's irrelevant, Sir: kindly recite it.

ORONTE (*reading*). Hope comforts us awhile, 'tis true,   315
          Lulling our cares with careless laughter,
          And yet such joy is full of rue,
          My Phyllis, if nothing follows after.

PHILINTE. I'm charmed by this already; the style's delightful.

ALCESTE (*sotto voce, to* PHILINTE). How can you say that? Why, the
     thing is frightful.   320

ORONTE.   Your fair face smiled on me awhile,
          But was it kindness so to enchant me?
          'Twould have been fairer not to smile,
          If hope was all you meant to grant me.

PHILINTE. What a clever thought! How handsomely you phrase it!   325

ALCESTE (*sotto voce, to* PHILINTE). You know the thing is trash. How
     dare you praise it?

ORONTE.   If it's to be my passion's fate
          Thus everlastingly to wait,
          Then death will come to set me free:
          For death is fairer than the fair;   330
          Phyllis, to hope is to despair
          When one must hope eternally.

PHILINTE. The close is exquisite—full of feeling and grace.

ALCESTE (*sotto voce, aside*). Oh, blast the close; you'd better close
     your face
Before you send your lying soul to hell.   335

PHILINTE. I can't remember a poem I've liked so well.

ALCESTE (*sotto voce, aside*). Good Lord!

ORONTE (*to* PHILINTE).   I fear you're flattering me a bit.

PHILINTE. Oh, no!

ALCESTE (*sotto voce, aside*). What else d'you call it, you hypocrite?

ORONTE (*to* ALCESTE). But you, Sir, keep your promise now: don't shrink
From telling me sincerely what you think.   340

ALCESTE. Sir, these are delicate matters; we all desire
To be told that we've the true poetic fire.
But once, to one whose name I shall not mention,
I said, regarding some verse of his invention,
That gentlemen should rigorously control   345

That itch to write which often afflicts the soul;
That one should curb the heady inclination
To publicize one's little avocation;
And that in showing off one's works of art
One often plays a very clownish part.   350
ORONTE. Are you suggesting in a devious way
That I ought not . . .
ALCESTE.   Oh, that I do not say.
Further, I told him that no fault is worse
Than that of writing frigid, lifeless verse,
And that the merest whisper of such a shame   355
Suffices to destroy a man's good name.
ORONTE. D'you mean to say my sonnet's dull and trite?
ALCESTE. I don't say that. But I went on to cite
Numerous cases of once-respected men
Who came to grief by taking up the pen.   360
ORONTE. And am I like them? Do I write so poorly?
ALCESTE. I don't say that. But I told this person, "Surely
You're under no necessity to compose;
Why you should wish to publish, heaven knows.
There's no excuse for printing tedious rot   365
Unless one writes for bread, as you do not.
Resist temptation, then, I beg of you;
Conceal your pastimes from the public view;
And don't give up, on any provocation,
Your present high and courtly reputation,   370
To purchase at a greedy printer's shop
The name of silly author and scribbling fop."
These were the points I tried to make him see.
ORONTE. I sense that they are also aimed at me;
But now—about my sonnet—I'd like to be told . . .   375
ALCESTE. Frankly, that sonnet should be pigeonholed.
You've chosen the worst models to imitate.
The style's unnatural. Let me illustrate:

For example, Your fair face smiled on me awhile,
Followed by, 'Twould have been fairer not to smile!   380
Or this: such joy is full of rue;
Or this: For death is fairer than the fair;
Or, Phyllis, to hope is to despair
When one must hope eternally!

This artificial style, that's all the fashion,   385
Has neither taste, nor honesty, nor passion;
It's nothing but a sort of wordy play,
And nature never spoke in such a way.
What, in this shallow age, is not debased?
Our fathers, though less refined, had better taste;   390
I'd barter all that men admire today
For one old love-song I shall try to say:

> If the King had given me for my own
> Paris, his citadel,
> And I for that must leave alone   395
> Her whom I love so well,
> I'd say then to the Crown,
> Take back your glittering town;
> My darling is more fair, I swear,
> My darling is more fair.   400

The rhyme's not rich, the style is rough and old,
But don't you see that it's the purest gold
Beside the tinsel nonsense now preferred,
And that there's passion in its every word?

> If the King had given me for my own   405
> Paris, his citadel,
> And I for that must leave alone
> Her whom I love so well,
> I'd say then to the Crown,
> Take back your glittering town;   410
> My darling is more fair, I swear,
> My darling is more fair.

There speaks a loving heart. (*To* PHILINTE) You're laughing, eh?
Laugh on, my precious wit. Whatever you say,
I hold that song's worth all the bibelots   415
That people hail today with ah's and oh's.
ORONTE. And I maintain my sonnet's very good.
ALCESTE. It's not at all surprising that you should.
    You have your reasons; permit me to have mine
    For thinking that you cannot write a line.   420
ORONTE. Others have praised my sonnet to the skies.
ALCESTE. I lack their art of telling pleasant lies.
ORONTE. You seem to think you've got no end of wit.
ALCESTE. To praise your verse, I'd need still more of it.
ORONTE. I'm not in need of your approval, Sir.   425

ALCESTE. That's good; you couldn't have it if you were.
ORONTE. Come now, I'll lend you the subject of my sonnet;
  I'd like to see you try to improve upon it.
ALCESTE. I might, by chance, write something just as shoddy;
  But then I wouldn't show it to everybody. 430
ORONTE. You're most opinionated and conceited.
ALCESTE. Go find your flatterers, and be better treated.
ORONTE. Look here, my little fellow, pray watch your tone.
ALCESTE. My great big fellow, you'd better watch your own.
PHILINTE (*stepping between them*). Oh, please, please, gentlemen!
  This will never do. 435
ORONTE. The fault is mine, and I leave the field to you.
  I am your servant. Sir, in every way.
ALCESTE. And I, Sir, am your most abject valet. (*Exit* ORONTE.)

SCENE 3

PHILINTE. Well, as you see, sincerity in excess
  Can get you into a very pretty mess; 440
  Oronte was hungry for appreciation . . .
ALCESTE. Don't speak to me.
PHILINTE.   What?
ALCESTE.   No more conversation.
PHILINTE. Really, now . . .
ALCESTE.   Leave me alone.
PHILINTE.   If I . . .
ALCESTE.   Out of my sight!
PHILINTE. But what . . .
ALCESTE.   I won't listen.
PHILINTE.   But . . .
ALCESTE.   Silence!
PHILINTE.   Now, is it polite . . .
ALCESTE. By heaven, I've had enough. Don't follow me. 445
PHILINTE. Ah, you're just joking. I'll keep you company. (*Exeunt.*)

ACT 2

SCENE 1

  Enter ALCESTE *and* CÉLIMÈNE
ALCESTE. Shall I speak plainly, Madam? I confess
  Your conduct gives me infinite distress,
  And my resentment's grown too hot to smother.
  Soon, I foresee, we'll break with one another.

If I said otherwise, I should deceive you; 5
Sooner or later, I shall be forced to leave you,
And if I swore that we shall never part,
I should misread the omens of my heart.
CÉLIMÈNE. You kindly saw me home, it would appear,
So as to pour invectives in my ear. 10
ALCESTE. I've no desire to quarrel. But I deplore
Your inability to shut the door
On all these suitors who beset you so.
There's what annoys me, if you care to know.
CÉLIMÈNE. Is it my fault that all these men pursue me? 15
Am I to blame if they're attracted to me?
And when they gently beg an audience,
Ought I to take a stick and drive them hence?
ALCESTE. Madam, there's no necessity for a stick;
A less responsive heart would do the trick. 20
Of your attractiveness I don't complain;
But those your charms attract, you then detain
By a most melting and receptive manner,
And so enlist their hearts beneath your banner.
It's the agreeable hopes which you excite 25
That keep these lovers round you day and night;
Were they less liberally smiled upon,
That sighing troop would very soon be gone.
But tell me, Madam, why it is that lately
This man Clitandre interests you so greatly? 30
Because of what high merits do you deem
Him worthy of the honor of your esteem?
Is it that your admiring glances linger
On the splendidly long nail of his little finger?
Or do you share the general deep respect 35
For the blond wig he chooses to affect?
Are you in love with his embroidered hose?
Do you adore his ribbons and his bows?
Or is it that this paragon bewitches
Your tasteful eye with his vast German breeches? 40
Perhaps his giggle, or his falsetto voice,
Makes him the latest gallant of your choice?
CÉLIMÈNE. You're much mistaken to resent him so.
Why I put up with him you surely know:
My lawsuit's very shortly to be tried, 45
And I must have his influence on my side.

ALCESTE. Then lose your lawsuit, Madam, or let it drop;
    Don't torture me by humoring such a fop.
CÉLIMÈNE. You're jealous of the whole world, Sir.
ALCESTE.   That's true,
    Since the whole world is well-received by you.   50
CÉLIMÈNE. That my good nature is so unconfined
    Should serve to pacify your jealous mind;
    Were I to smile on one, and scorn the rest,
    Then you might have some cause to be distressed.
ALCESTE. Well, if I mustn't be jealous, tell me, then,   55
    Just how I'm better treated than other men.
CÉLIMÈNE. You know you have my love. Will that not do?
ALCESTE. What proof have I that what you say is true?
CÉLIMÈNE. I would expect, Sir, that my having said it
    Might give the statement a sufficient credit.   60
ALCESTE. But how can I be sure that you don't tell
    The selfsame thing to other men as well?
CÉLIMÈNE. What a gallant speech! How flattering to me!
    What a sweet creature you make me out to be!
    Well then, to save you from the pangs of doubt,   65
    All that I've said I hereby cancel out;
    Now, none but yourself shall make a monkey of you:
    Are you content?
ALCESTE.   Why, why am I doomed to love you?
    I swear that I shall bless the blissful hour
    When this poor heart's no longer in your power!   70
    I make no secret of it: I've done my best
    To exorcise this passion from my breast;
    But thus far all in vain; it will not go;
    It's for my sins that I must love you so.
CÉLIMÈNE. Your love for me is matchless, Sir; that's clear.   75
ALCESTE. Indeed, in all the world it has no peer;
    Words can't describe the nature of my passion,
    And no man ever loved in such a fashion.
CÉLIMÈNE. Yes, it's a brand-new fashion, I agree:
    You show your love by castigating me,   80
    And all your speeches are enraged and rude.
    I've never been so furiously wooed.
ALCESTE. Yet you could calm that fury, if you chose.
    Come, shall we bring our quarrels to a close?
    Let's speak with open hearts, then, and begin . . .   85

SCENE 2

Enter BASQUE.

CÉLIMÈNE. What is it?

BASQUE.   Acaste is here.

CÉLIMÈNE.   Well, send him in. (*Exit* BASQUE.)

SCENE 3

ALCESTE. What! Shall we never be alone at all?
  You're always ready to receive a call,
  And you can't bear, for ten ticks of the clock,
  Not to keep open house for all who knock.   90

CÉLIMÈNE. I couldn't refuse him: he'd be most put out.

ALCESTE. Surely that's not worth worrying about.

CÉLIMÈNE. Acaste would never forgive me if he guessed
  That I consider him a dreadful pest.

ALCESTE. If he's a pest, why bother with him then?   95

CÉLIMÈNE. Heavens! One can't antagonize such men;
  Why, they're the chartered gossips of the court,
  And have a say in things of every sort.
  One must receive them, and be full of charm;
  They're no great help, but they can do you harm,   100
  And though your influence be ever so great,
  They're hardly the best people to alienate.

ALCESTE. I see, dear lady, that you could make a case
  For putting up with the whole human race;
  These friendships that you calculate so nicely . . .   105

SCENE 4

Enter BASQUE.

BASQUE. Madam, Clitandre is here as well.

ALCESTE.   Precisely.

CÉLIMÈNE. Where are you going?

ALCESTE.   Elsewhere.

CÉLIMÈNE.   Stay.

ALCESTE.   No, no.

CÉLIMÈNE. Stay, Sir.

ALCESTE.   I can't.

CÉLIMÈNE.   I wish it.

ALCESTE.   No, I must go.
  I beg you, Madam, not to press the matter;
  You know I have no taste for idle chatter.   110

CÉLIMÈNE. Stay: I command you.

ALCESTE.   No, I cannot stay.

CÉLIMÈNE. Very well; you have my leave to go away.

SCENE 5

    Enter ELIANTE *and* PHILINTE.

ELIANTE (*to* CÉLIMÈNE). The Marquesses have kindly come to call.

    Were they announced?

CÉLIMÈNE.   Yes. Basque, bring chairs for all.

    (BASQUE *provides the chairs, and exits. To* ALCESTE)

    You haven't gone?

ALCESTE.   No; and I shan't depart   115

    Till you decide who's foremost in your heart.

CÉLIMÈNE. Oh, hush.

ALCESTE.   It's time to choose; take them or me.

CÉLIMÈNE. You're mad.

ALCESTE.   I'm not, as you shall shortly see.

CÉLIMÈNE. Oh?

ALCESTE.   You'll decide.

CÉLIMÈNE.   You're joking now, dear friend.

ALCESTE. No, no; you'll choose; my patience is at an end.   120

    (*Enter* CLITANDRE *and* ACASTE.)

CLITANDRE. Madam, I come, from court, where poor Cléonte

    Behaved like a perfect fool, as is his wont.

    Has he no friend to counsel him, I wonder,

    And teach him less unerringly to blunder?

CÉLIMÈNE. It's true, the man's a most accomplished dunce;   125

    His gauche behavior charms the eye at once;

    And every time one sees him, on my word,

    His manner's grown a trifle more absurd.

ACASTE. Speaking of dunces, I've just now conversed

    With old Damon, who's one of the very worst;   130

    I stood a lifetime in the broiling sun

    Before his dreary monologue was done.

CÉLIMÈNE. Oh, he's a wondrous talker, and has the power

    To tell you nothing hour after hour:

    If, by mistake, he ever came to the point,   135

    The shock would put his jawbone out of joint.

ELIANTE (*to* PHILINTE). The conversation takes its usual turn,

    And all our dear friends' ears will shortly burn.

CLITANDRE. Timante's a character. Madam.

CÉLIMÈNE.   Isn't he, though?

    A man of mystery from top to toe,   140

    Who moves about in a romantic mist

On secret missions which do not exist.
His talk is full of eyebrows and grimaces;
How tired one gets of his momentous faces;
He's always whispering something confidential   145
Which turns out to be quite inconsequential;
Nothing's too slight for him to mystify;
He even whispers when he says "good-by."

ACASTE. Tell us about Géralde.

CÉLIMÈNE.   That tiresome ass.
He mixes only with the titled class,   150
And fawns on dukes and princes, and is bored
With anyone who's not at least a lord.
The man's obsessed with rank, and his discourses
Are all of hounds and carriages and horses;
He uses Christian names with all the great,   155
And the word Milord, with him, is out of date.

CLITANDRE. He's very taken with Bélise, I hear.

CÉLIMÈNE. She is the dreariest company, poor dear.
Whenever she comes to call, I grope about
To find some topic which will draw her out,   160
But, owing to her dry and faint replies,
The conversation wilts, and droops, and dies.
In vain one hopes to animate her face
By mentioning the ultimate commonplace;
But sun or shower, even hail or frost   165
Are matters she can instantly exhaust.
Meanwhile her visit, painful though it is,
Drags on and on through mute eternities,
And though you ask the time, and yawn, and yawn,
She sits there like a stone and won't be gone   170

ACASTE. Now for Adraste.

CÉLIMÈNE.   Oh, that conceited elf
Has a gigantic passion for himself;
He rails against the court, and cannot bear it
That none will recognize his hidden merit;
All honors given to others give offense   175
To his imaginary excellence.

CLITANDRE. What about young Cléon? His house, they say,
Is full of the best society, night and day.

CÉLIMÈNE. His cook has made him popular, not he:
It's Cléon's table that people come to see.   180

ELIANTE. He gives a splendid dinner, you must admit.

CÉLIMÈNE. But must he serve himself along with it?
    For my taste, he's a most insipid dish
    Whose presence sours the wine and spoils the fish.
PHILINTE. Damis, his uncle, is admired no end.   185
    What's your opinion, Madam?
CÉLIMÈNE.   Why, he's my friend.
PHILINTE. He seems a decent fellow, and rather clever.
CÉLIMÈNE. He works too hard at cleverness, however.
    I hate to see him sweat and struggle so
    To fill his conversation with bons mots.   190
    Since he's decided to become a wit
    His taste's so pure that nothing pleases it;
    He scolds at all the latest books and plays,
    Thinking that wit must never stoop to praise,
    That finding fault's a sign of intellect,   195
    That all appreciation is abject,
    And that by damning everything in sight
    One shows oneself in a distinguished light.
    He's scornful even of our conversations:
    Their trivial nature sorely tries his patience;   200
    He folds his arms, and stands above the battle,
    And listens sadly to our childish prattle.
ACASTE. Wonderful, Madam! You've hit him off precisely.
CLITANDRE. No one can sketch a character so nicely.
ALCESTE. How bravely, Sirs, you cut and thrust at all   205
    These absent fools, till one by one they fall:
    But let one come in sight, and you'll at once
    Embrace the man you lately called a dunce,
    Telling him in a tone sincere and fervent
    How proud you are to be his humble servant.   210
CLITANDRE. Why pick on us? Madame's been speaking, Sir,
    And you should quarrel, if you must, with her.
ALCESTE. No, no, by God, the fault is yours, because
    You lead her on with laughter and applause,
    And make her think that she's the more delightful   215
    The more her talk is scandalous and spiteful.
    Oh, she would stoop to malice far, far less
    If no such claque approved her cleverness.
    It's flatterers like you whose foolish praise
    Nourishes all the vices of these days.   220
PHILINTE. But why protest when someone ridicules
    Those you'd condemn, yourself, as knaves or fools?

CÉLIMÈNE. Why, Sir? Because he loves to make a fuss.
  You don't expect him to agree with us,
  When there's an opportunity to express   225
  His heaven-sent spirit of contrariness?
  What other people think, he can't abide;
  Whatever they say, he's on the other side;
  He lives in deadly terror of agreeing;
  'Twould make him seem an ordinary being.   230
  Indeed, he's so in love with contradiction,
  He'll turn against his most profound conviction
  And with a furious eloquence deplore it,
  If only someone else is speaking for it.
ALCESTE. Go on, dear lady, mock me as you please;   235
  You have your audience in ecstasies.
PHILINTE. But what she says is true: you have a way
  Of bridling at whatever people say;
  Whether they praise or blame, your angry spirit
  Is equally unsatisfied to hear it.   240
ALCESTE. Men, Sir, are always wrong, and that's the reason
  That righteous anger's never out of season;
  All that I hear in all their conversation
  Is flattering praise or reckless condemnation.
CÉLIMÈNE. But . . .
ALCESTE.   No, no, Madam, I am forced to state   245
  That you have pleasures which I deprecate,
  And that these others, here, are much to blame
  For nourishing the faults which are your shame.
CLITANDRE. I shan't defend myself, Sir; but I vow
  I'd thought this lady faultless until now.   250
ACASTE. I see her charms and graces, which are many;
  But as for faults, I've never noticed any.
ALCESTE. I see them, Sir; and rather than ignore them,
  I strenuously criticize her for them.
  The more one loves, the more one should object   255
  To every blemish, every least defect.
  Were I this lady, I would soon get rid
  Of lovers who approved of all I did,
  And by their slack indulgence and applause
  Endorsed my follies and excused my flaws.   260
CÉLIMÈNE. If all hearts beat according to your measure,

The dawn of love would be the end of pleasure;
And love would find its perfect consummation
In ecstasies of rage and reprobation.
ELIANTE. Love, as a rule, affects men otherwise,   265
And lovers rarely love to criticize.
They see their lady as a charming blur,
And find all things commendable in her.
If she has any blemish, fault, or shame,
They will redeem it by a pleasing name.   270
The pale-faced lady's lily-white, perforce;
The swarthy one's a sweet brunette, of course;
The spindly lady has a slender grace;
The fat one has a most majestic pace;
The plain one, with her dress in disarray,   275
They classify as *beauté négligée;*°
The hulking one's a goddess in their eyes,
The dwarf, a concentrate of Paradise;
The haughty lady has a noble mind;
The mean one's witty, and the dull one's kind;   280
The chatterbox has liveliness and verve,
The mute one has a virtuous reserve.
So lovers manage, in their passion's cause,
To love their ladies even for their flaws.
ALCESTE. But I still say . . .
CÉLIMÈNE.   I think it would be nice   285
To stroll around the gallery once or twice.
What! You're not going, Sirs?
CLITANDRE and ACASTE.   No, Madam, no.
ALCESTE. You seem to be in terror lest they go.
Do what you will, Sirs; leave, or linger on,
But I shan't go till after you are gone.   290
ACASTE. I'm free to linger, unless I should perceive
Madame is tired, and wishes me to leave.
CLITANDRE. And as for me, I needn't go today
Until the hour of the King's *coucher.*°
CÉLIMÈNE (*to* ALCESTE). You're joking, surely?
ALCESTE.   Not in the least; we'll see
Whether you'd rather part with them, or me.   296

---

276. *beauté négligée*: careless beauty   294. *coucher:* bedtime (the King's going-to-bed was a
ceremonial occasion)

SCENE 6

Enter BASQUE.

BASQUE (*to* ALCESTE). Sir, there's a fellow here who bids me state
That he must see you, and that it can't wait.
ALCESTE. Tell him that I have no such pressing affairs.
BASQUE. It's a long tailcoat that this fellow wears,   300
With gold all over.
CÉLIMÈNE (*to* ALCESTE) You'd best go down and see.
Or—have him enter. (*Exit* BASQUE.)

SCENE 7

Enter GUARD.

ALCESTE (*confronting the guard*). Well, what do you want with me?
Come in, Sir.
GUARD.   I've a word, Sir, for your ear.
ALCESTE. Speak it aloud, Sir; I shall strive to hear.
GUARD. The Marshals have instructed me to say   305
You must report to them without delay.
ALCESTE. Who? Me, Sir?
GUARD.   Yes, Sir; you.
ALCESTE.   But what do they want?
PHILINTE (*to* ALCESTE). To scotch your silly quarrel with Oronte.
CÉLIMÈNE (*to* PHILINTE). What quarrel?
PHILINTE.   Oronte and he have fallen out
Over some verse he spoke his mind about;   310
The Marshals wish to arbitrate the matter.
ALCESTE. Never shall I equivocate or flatter!
PHILINTE. You'd best obey their summons; come, let's go.
ALCESTE. How can they mend our quarrel, I'd like to know?
Am I to make a cowardly retraction,   315
And praise those jingles to his satisfaction?
I'll not recant; I've judged that sonnet rightly.
It's bad.
PHILINTE. But you might say so more politely. . . .
ALCESTE. I'll not back down; his verses make me sick.
PHILINTE. If only you could be more politic!   320
But come, let's go.
ALCESTE.   I'll go, but I won't unsay
A single word.
PHILINTE.   Well, let's be on our way.
ALCESTE. Till I am ordered by my lord the King

To praise that poem, I shall say the thing
Is scandalous, by God, and that the poet   325
Ought to be hanged for having the nerve to show it.
(*To* CLITANDRE *and* ACASTE, *who are laughing*)
By heaven, Sirs, I really didn't know
That I was being humorous.

CÉLIMÈNE.   Go, Sir, go;
Settle your business.

ALCESTE.   I shall, and when I'm through,
I shall return to settle things with you. (*Exeunt.*)   330

ACT 3

SCENE 1

   Enter CLITANDRE *and* ACASTE.

CLITANDRE. Dear Marquess, how contented you appear;
All things delight you, nothing mars your cheer.
Can you, in perfect honesty, declare
That you've a right to be so debonair?

ACASTE. By Jove, when I survey myself, I find   5
No cause whatever for distress of mind.
I'm young and rich; I can in modesty
Lay claim to an exalted pedigree;
And owing to my name and my condition
I shall not want for honors and position.   10
Then as to courage, that most precious trait,
I seem to have it, as was proved of late
Upon the field of honor, where my bearing,
They say, was very cool and rather daring.
I've wit, of course; and taste in such perfection   15
That I can judge without the least reflection,
And at the theater, which is my delight,
Can make or break a play on opening night,
And lead the crowd in hisses or bravos,
And generally be known as one who knows.   20
I'm clever, handsome, gracefully polite;
My waist is small, my teeth are strong and white;
As for my dress, the world's astonished eyes
Assure me that I bear away the prize.
I find myself in favor everywhere,   25
Honored by men, and worshiped by the fair;
And since these things are so, it seems to me

I'm justified in my complacency.
CLITANDRE. Well, if so many ladies hold you dear,
Why do you press a hopeless courtship here?   30
ACASTE. Hopeless, you say? I'm not the sort of fool
That likes his ladies difficult and cool.
Men who are awkward, shy, and peasantish
May pine for heartless beauties, if they wish,
Grovel before them, bear their cruelties,   35
Woo them with tears and sighs and bended knees,
And hope by dogged faithfulness to gain
What their poor merits never could obtain.
For men like me however, it makes no sense
To love on trust, and foot the whole expense.   40
Whatever any lady's merits be,
I think, thank God, that I'm as choice as she;
That if my heart is kind enough to burn
For her, she owes me something in return;
And that in any proper love affair   45
The partners must invest an equal share.
CLITANDRE. You think, then, that our hostess favors you?
ACASTE. I've reason to believe that that is true.
CLITANDRE. How did you come to such a mad conclusion?
You're blind, dear fellow. This is sheer delusion.   50
ACASTE. All right, then: I'm deluded and I'm blind.
CLITANDRE. Whatever put the notion in your mind?
ACASTE. Delusion.
CLITANDRE.   What persuades you that you're right?
ACASTE. I'm blind.
CLITANDRE.   But have, you any proofs to cite?
ACASTE. I tell you I'm deluded.
CLITANDRE.   Have you, then,   55
Received some secret pledge from Célimène?
ACASTE. Oh, no: she scorns me.
CLITANDRE.   Tell me the truth, I beg.
ACASTE. She just can't bear me.
CLITANDRE.   Ah, don't pull my leg.
Tell me what hope she's given you, I pray.
ACASTE. I'm hopeless, and it's you who win the day.   60
She hates me thoroughly, and I'm so vexed
I mean to hang myself on Tuesday next.
CLITANDRE. Dear Marquess, let us have an armistice

And make a treaty. What do you say to this?
If ever one of us can plainly prove 65
That Célimène encourages his love,
The other must abandon hope, and yield,
And leave him in possession of the field.
ACASTE. Now, there's a bargain that appeals to me;
With all my heart, dear Marquess, I agree. 70
But hush.

SCENE 2

Enter CÉLIMÈNE.

CÉLIMÈNE.   Still here?
CLITANDRE.   'Twas love that stayed our feet.
CÉLIMÈNE. I think I heard a carriage in the street.
Whose is it? D'you know?

SCENE 3

Enter BASQUE.

BASQUE.   Arsinoé is here,
Madame.
CÉLIMÈNE. Arsinoé, you say? Oh, dear.
BASQUE. Eliante is entertaining her below. 75
CÉLIMÈNE. What brings the creature here, I'd like to know?
ACASTE. They say she's dreadfully prudish, but in fact
I think her piety . . .
CÉLIMÈNE.   It's all an act.
At heart she's worldly, and her poor success
In snaring men explains her prudishness. 80
It breaks her heart to see the beaux and gallants
Engrossed by other women's charms and talents,
And so she's always in a jealous rage
Against the faulty standards of the age.
She lets the world believe that she's a prude 85
To justify her loveless solitude,
And strives to put a brand of moral shame
On all the graces that she cannot claim.
But still she'd love a lover; and Alceste
Appears to be the one she'd love the best. 90
His visits here are poison to her pride;
She seems to think I've lured him from her side;
And everywhere, at court or in the town,
The spiteful, envious woman runs me down.

In short, she's just as stupid as can be,   95
Vicious and arrogant in the last degree,
And . . .

SCENE 4

Enter ARSINOÉ.

CÉLIMÈNE. Ah! What happy chance has brought you here?
   I've thought about you ever so much, my dear.
ARSINOÉ. I've come to tell you something you should know.
CÉLIMÈNE. How good of you to think of doing so!   100
   (CLITANDRE *and* ACASTE *go out, laughing.*)

SCENE 5

ARSINOÉ. It's just as well those gentlemen didn't tarry.
CÉLIMÈNE. Shall we sit down?
ARSINOÉ.   That won't be necessary.
   Madam, the flame of friendship ought to burn
   Brightest in matters of the most concern,
   And as there's nothing which concerns us more   105
   Than honor, I have hastened to your door
   To bring you, as your friend, some information
   About the status of your reputation.
   I visited, last night, some virtuous folk,
   And, quite by chance, it was of you they spoke;   110
   There was, I fear, no tendency to praise
   Your light behavior and your dashing ways.
   The quantity of gentlemen you see
   And your by now notorious coquetry
   Were both so vehemently criticized   115
   By everyone, that I was much surprised.
   Of course, I needn't tell you where I stood;
   I came to your defense as best I could,
   Assured them you were harmless, and declared
   Your soul was absolutely unimpaired.   120
   But there are some things, you must realize,
   One can't excuse, however hard one tries,
   And I was forced at last into conceding
   That your behavior, Madam, is misleading,
   That it makes a bad impression, giving rise   125
   To ugly gossip and obscene surmise,
   And that if you were more *overtly* good,

You wouldn't be so much misunderstood.
Not that I think you've been unchaste—no! no!
The saints preserve me from a thought so low!   130
But mere good conscience never did suffice:
One must avoid the outward show of vice.
Madam, you're too intelligent, I'm sure,
To think my motives anything but pure
In offering you this counsel—which I do   135
Out of a zealous interest in you.

CÉLIMÈNE. Madam, I haven't taken you amiss;
I'm very much obliged to you for this;
And I'll at once discharge the obligation
By telling you about *your* reputation.   140
You've been so friendly as to let me know
What certain people say of me, and so
I mean to follow your benign example
By offering you a somewhat similar sample.
The other day, I went to an affair   145
And I found some most distinguished people there
Discussing piety, both false and true.
The conversation soon came round to you.
Alas! Your prudery and bustling zeal
Appeared to have a very slight appeal.   150
Your affectation of a grave demeanor,
Your endless talk of virtue and of honor,
The aptitude of your suspicious mind
For finding sin where there is none to find,
Your towering self-esteem, that pitying face   155
With which you contemplate the human race,
Your sermonizings and your sharp aspersions
On people's pure and innocent diversions—
All these were mentioned, Madam, and, in fact,
Were roundly and concertedly attacked.   160
"What good," they said, "are all these outward shows,
When everything belies her pious pose?
She prays incessantly; but then, they say,
She beats her maids and cheats them of their pay;
She shows her zeal in every holy place,   165
But still she's vain enough to paint her face;
She holds that naked statues are immoral,
But with a naked *man* she'd have no quarrel."
Of course, I said to everybody there

That they were being viciously unfair;   170
But still they were disposed to criticize you,
And all agreed that someone should advise you
To leave the morals of the world alone,
And worry rather more about your own.
They felt that one's self-knowledge should be great   175
Before one thinks of setting others straight;
That one should learn the art of living well
Before one threatens other men with hell,
And that the Church is best equipped, no doubt,
To guide our souls and root our vices out.   180
Madam, you're too intelligent, I'm sure,
To think my motives anything but pure
In offering you this counsel—which I do
Out of a zealous interest in you.

ARSINOÉ. I dared not hope for gratitude, but I   185
Did not expect so acid a reply;
I judge, since you've been so extremely tart,
That my good counsel pierced you to the heart.

CÉLIMÈNE. Far from it, Madam. Indeed, it seems to me
We ought to trade advice more frequently.   190
One's vision of oneself is so defective
That it would be an excellent corrective.
If you are willing, Madam, let's arrange
Shortly to have another frank exchange
In which we'll tell each other, *entre nous,*°   195
What you've heard tell of me, and I of you.

ARSINOÉ. Oh, people never censure you, my dear;
It's me they criticize. Or so I hear.

CÉLIMÈNE. Madam, I think we either blame or praise
According to our taste and length of days.   200
There is a time of life for coquetry,
And there's a season, too, for prudery.
When all one's charms are gone, it is, I'm sure,
Good strategy to be devout and pure:
It makes one seem a little less forsaken.   205
Some day, perhaps, I'll take the road you've taken:
Time brings all things. But I have time aplenty,
And see no cause to be a prude at twenty.

ARSINOÉ. You give your age in such a gloating tone
That one would think I was an ancient crone;   210

195. *entre nous*: between ourselves

We're not so far apart, in sober truth,
That you can mock me with a boast of youth!
Madam, you baffle me. I wish I knew
What moves you to provoke me as you do.

CÉLIMÈNE. For my part, Madam, I should like to know   215
Why you abuse me everywhere you go.
Is it my fault, dear lady, that your hand
Is not, alas, in very great demand?
If men admire me, if they pay me court
And daily make me offers of the sort   220
You'd dearly love to have them make to you,
How can I help it? What would you have me do?
If what you want is lovers, please feel free
To take as many as you can from me.

ARSINOÉ. Oh, come. D'you think the world is losing sleep   225
Over that flock of lovers which you keep,
Or that we find it difficult to guess
What price you pay for their devotedness?
Surely you don't expect us to suppose
Mere merit could attract so many beaux?   230
It's not your virtue that they're dazzled by;
Nor is it virtuous love for which they sigh.
You're fooling no one, Madam; the world's not blind;
There's many a lady heaven has designed
To call men's noblest, tenderest feelings out,   235
Who has no lovers dogging her about;
From which it's plain that lovers nowadays
Must be acquired in bold and shameless ways,
And only pay one court for such reward
As modesty and virtue can't afford.   240
Then don't be quite so puffed up, if you please,
About your tawdry little victories;
Try, if you can, to be a shade less vain,
And treat the world with somewhat less disdain.
If one were envious of your amours,   245
One soon could have a following like yours;
Lovers are no great trouble to collect
If one prefers them to one's self-respect.

CÉLIMÈNE. Collect them then, my dear; I'd love to see
You demonstrate that charming theory;   250
Who knows, you might . . .

ARSINOÉ.   Now, Madam, that will do;
  It's time to end this trying interview.
  My coach is late in coming to your door,
  Or I'd have taken leave of you before.
CÉLIMÈNE. Oh, please don't feel that you must rush away;   255
  I'd be delighted, Madam, if you'd stay.
  However, lest my conversation bore you,
  Let me provide some better company for you;
  This gentleman, who comes most apropos,
  Will please you more than I could do, I know.   260

SCENE 6

  Enter ALCESTE.

CÉLIMÈNE. Alceste, I have a little note to write
  Which simply must go out before tonight;
  Please entertain *Madame;* I'm sure that she
  Will overlook my incivility. (*Exit.*)

SCENE 7

ARSINOÉ. Well, Sir, our hostess graciously contrives   265
  For us to chat until my coach arrives;
  And I shall be forever in her debt
  For granting me this little tête-á-tête.
  We women very rightly give our hearts
  To men of noble character and parts,   270
  And your especial merits, dear Alceste,
  Have roused the deepest sympathy in my breast.
  Oh, how I wish they had sufficient sense
  At court, to recognize your excellence!
  They wrong you greatly, Sir. How it must hurt you   275
  Never to be rewarded for your virtue!
ALCESTE. Why, Madam, what cause have I to feel aggrieved?
  What great and brilliant thing have I achieved?
  What service have I rendered to the King
  That I should look to him for anything?   280
ARSINOÉ. Not everyone who's honored by the State
  Has done great services. A man must wait
  Till time and fortune offer him the chance.
  Your merit, Sir, is obvious at a glance,
  And . . .
ALCESTE. Ah, forget my merit; I'm not neglected.   285

The court, I think, can hardly be expected
To mine men's souls for merit, and unearth
Our hidden virtues and our secret worth.

ARSINOÉ. *Some* virtues, though, are far too bright to hide;
Yours are acknowledged, Sir, on every side.   290
Indeed, I've heard you warmly praised of late
By persons of considerable weight.

ALCESTE. This fawning age has praise for everyone,
And all distinctions, Madam, are undone.
All things have equal honor nowadays,   295
And no one should be gratified by praise.
To be admired, one only need exist,
And every lackey's on the honors list.

ARSINOÉ. I only wish, Sir, that you had your eye
On some position at court, however high;   300
You'd only have to hint at such a notion
For me to set the proper wheels in motion;
I've certain friendships I'd be glad to use
To get you any office you might choose.

ALCESTE. Madam, I fear that any such ambition   305
Is wholly foreign to my disposition.
The soul God gave me isn't of the sort
That prospers in the weather of a court.
It's all too obvious that I don't possess
The virtues necessary for success.   310
My one great talent is for speaking plain;
I've never learned to flatter or to feign;
And anyone so stupidly sincere
Had best not seek a courtier's career.
Outside the court, I know, one must dispense   315
With honors, privilege, and influence;
But still one gains the right, forgoing these,
Not to be tortured by the wish to please.
One needn't live in dread of snubs and slights,
Nor praise the verse that every idiot writes,   320
Nor humor silly Marquesses, nor bestow
Politic sighs on Madam So-and-so.

ARSINOÉ. Forget the court, then; let the matter rest.
But I've another cause to be distressed
About your present situation, Sir.   325
It's to your love affair that I refer.
She whom you love, and who pretends to love you,

Is, I regret to say, unworthy of you.

ALCESTE. Why, Madam! Can you seriously intend
To make so grave a charge against your friend? 330

ARSINOÉ. Alas, I must. I've stood aside too long
And let that lady do you grievous wrong;
But now my debt to conscience shall be paid:
I tell you that your love has been betrayed.

ALCESTE. I thank you, Madam; you're extremely kind. 335
Such words are soothing to a lover's mind.

ARSINOÉ. Yes, though she *is* my friend, I say again
You're very much too good for Célimène.
She's wantonly misled you from the start.

ALCESTE. You may be right; who knows another's heart? 340
But ask yourself if it's the part of charity
To shake my soul with doubts of her sincerity.

ARSINOÉ. Well, if you'd rather be a dupe than doubt her,
That's your affair. I'll say no more about her.

ALCESTE. Madam, you know that doubt and vague suspicion 345
Are painful to a man in my position;
It's most unkind to worry me this way
Unless you've some real proof of what you say.

ARSINOÉ. Sir, say no more: all doubt shall be removed,
And all that I've been saying shall be proved. 350
You've only to escort me home, and there
We'll look into the heart of this affair.
I've ocular evidence which will persuade you
Beyond a doubt, that Célimène's betrayed you.
Then, if you're saddened by that revelation, 355
Perhaps I can provide some consolation. (*Exeunt.*)

ACT 4

SCENE 1

 Enter PHILINTE *and* ELIANTE.

PHILINTE. Madam, he acted like a stubborn child;
I thought they never would be reconciled;
In vain we reasoned, threatened, and appealed;
He stood his ground and simply would not yield.
The Marshals, I feel sure, have never heard 5
An argument so splendidly absurd.
"No, gentlemen," said he, "I'll not retract.
His verse is bad: extremely bad, in fact.
Surely it does the man no harm to know it.

Does it disgrace him, not to be a poet? 10
A gentleman may be respected still,
Whether he writes a sonnet well or ill.
That I dislike his verse should not offend him;
In all that touches honor, I commend him;
He's noble, brave, and virtuous—but I fear 15
He can't in truth be called a sonneteer.
I'll gladly praise his wardrobe; I'll endorse
His dancing, or the way he sits a horse;
But, gentlemen, I cannot praise his rhyme.
In fact, it ought to be a capital crime 20
For anyone so sadly unendowed
To write a sonnet, and read the thing aloud."
At length he fell into a gentler mood
And, striking a concessive attitude,
He paid Oronte the following courtesies: 25
"Sir, I regret that I'm so hard to please,
And I'm profoundly sorry that your lyric
Failed to provoke me to a panegyric."
After these curious words, the two embraced,
And then the hearing was adjourned—in haste. 30
ELIANTE. His conduct has been very singular lately;
Still, I confess that I respect him greatly.
The honesty in which he takes such pride
Has—to my mind—its noble, heroic side.
In this false age, such candor seems outrageous; 35
But I could wish that it were more contagious.
PHILINTE. What most intrigues me in our friend Alceste
Is the grand passion that rages in his breast.
The sullen humors he's compounded of
Should not, I think, dispose his heart to love; 40
But since they do, it puzzles me still more
That he should choose your cousin to adore.
ELIANTE. It does, indeed, belie the theory
That love is born of gentle sympathy,
And that the tender passion must be based 45
On sweet accords of temper and of taste.
PHILINTE. Does she return his love, do you suppose?
ELIANTE. Ah, that's a difficult question, Sir. Who knows?
How can we judge the truth of her devotion?
Her heart's a stranger to its own emotion. 50
Sometimes it thinks it loves, when no love's there;

At other times it loves quite unaware.
PHILINTE. I rather think Alceste is in for more
Distress and sorrow than he's bargained for;
Were he of my mind, Madam, his affection   55
Would turn in quite a different direction,
And we would see him more responsive to
The kind regard which he receives from you.
ELIANTE. Sir, I believe in frankness, and I'm inclined,
In matters of the heart, to speak my mind.   60
I don't oppose his love for her; indeed,
I hope with all my heart that he'll succeed,
And were it in my power, I'd rejoice
In giving him the lady of his choice.
But if, as happens frequently enough   65
In love affairs, he meets with a rebuff—
If Célimène should grant some rival's suit—
I'd gladly play the role of substitute;
Nor would his tender speeches please me less
Because they'd once been made without success.   70
PHILINTE. Well, Madam, as for me, I don't oppose
Your hopes in this affair; and heaven knows
That in my conversations with the man
I plead your cause as often as I can.
But if those two should marry, and so remove   75
All chance that he will offer you his love,
Then I'll declare my own, and hope to see
Your gracious favor pass from him to me.
In short, should you be cheated of Alceste,
I'd be most happy to be second best.   80
ELIANTE. Philinte, you're teasing.
PHILINTE.   Ah, Madam, never fear;
No words of mine were ever so sincere,
And I shall live in fretful expectation
Till I can make a fuller declaration.

SCENE 2

Enter ALCESTE.

ALCESTE. Avenge me, Madam! I must have satisfaction,   85
Or this great wrong will drive me to distraction!
ELIANTE. Why, what's the matter? What's upset you so?
ALCESTE. Madam, I've had a mortal, mortal blow.
If Chaos repossessed the universe,

I swear I'd not be shaken any worse.   90
I'm ruined . . . I can say no more . . . My soul . . .
ELIANTE. Do try, Sir, to regain your self-control.
ALCESTE. Just heaven! Why were so much beauty and grace
Bestowed on one so vicious and so base?
ELIANTE. Once more, Sir, tell us . . .
ALCESTE.   My world has gone to wrack;   95
I'm—I'm betrayed; she's stabbed me in the back:
Yes, Célimène (who would have thought it of her?)
Is false to me, and has another lover.
ELIANTE. Are you quite certain? Can you prove these things?
PHILINTE. Lovers are prey to wild imaginings   100
And jealous fancies. No doubt there's some mistake . . .
ALCESTE. Mind your own business, Sir, for heaven's sake.
(*To* ELIANTE) Madam, I have the proof that you demand
Here in my pocket, penned by her own hand.
Yes, all the shameful evidence one could want   105
Lies in this letter written to Oronte—
Oronte! whom I felt sure she couldn't love,
And hardly bothered to be jealous of.
PHILINTE. Still, in a letter, appearances may deceive;
This may not be so bad as you believe.   110
ALCESTE. Once more I beg you, Sir, to let me be;
Tend to your own affairs; leave mine to me.
ELIANTE. Compose yourself; this anguish that you feel . . .
ALCESTE. Is something, Madam, you alone can heal.
My outraged heart, beside itself with grief,   115
Appeals to you for comfort and relief.
Avenge me on your cousin, whose unjust
And faithless nature has deceived my trust;
Avenge a crime your pure soul must detest.
ELIANTE. But how, Sir?
ALCESTE.   Madam, this heart within my breast 120
Is yours; pray take it; redeem my heart from her,
And so avenge me on my torturer.
Let her be punished by the fond emotion,
The ardent love, the bottomless devotion,
The faithful worship which this heart of mine   125
Will offer up to yours as to a shrine.
ELIANTE. You have my sympathy, Sir, in all you suffer;
Nor do I scorn the noble heart you offer;
But I suspect you'll soon be mollified,

And this desire for vengeance will subside.   130
When some beloved hand has done us wrong
We thirst for retribution—but not for long;
However dark the deed that she's committed,
A lovely culprit's very soon acquitted.
Nothing's so stormy as an injured lover,   135
And yet no storm so quickly passes over.
ALCESTE. No, Madam, no—this is no lovers' spat;
I'll not forgive her; it's gone too far for that;
My mind's made up; I'll kill myself before
I waste my hopes upon her any more.   140
Ah, here she is. My wrath intensifies.
I shall confront her with her tricks and lies,
And crush her utterly, and bring you then
A heart no longer slave to Célimène.

SCENE 3

Enter CÉLIMÈNE.

ALCESTE (*aside*). Sweet heaven, help me to control my passion.   145
CÉLIMÈNE (*aside, to* ALCESTE). Oh, Lord. Why stand there staring in
        that fashion?
And what d'you mean by those dramatic sighs,
And that malignant glitter in your eyes?
ALCESTE. I mean that sins which cause the blood to freeze
Look innocent beside your treacheries;   150
That nothing Hell's or Heaven's wrath could do
Ever produced so bad a thing as you.
CÉLIMÈNE. Your compliments were always sweet and pretty.
ALCESTE. Madam, it's not the moment to be witty.
No, blush and hang your head; you've ample reason,   155
Since I've the fullest evidence of your treason.
Ah, this is what my sad heart prophesied;
Now all my anxious fears are verified;
My dark suspicion and my gloomy doubt
Divined the truth, and now the truth is out.   160
For all your trickery, I was not deceived;
It was my bitter stars that I believed.
But don't imagine that you'll go scot-free;
You shan't misuse me with impunity.
I know that love's irrational and blind;   165
I know the heart's not subject to the mind,
And can't be reasoned into beating faster;

I know each soul is free to choose its master;
Therefore had you but spoken from the heart,
Rejecting my attentions from the start,   170
I'd have no grievance, or at any rate
I could complain of nothing but my fate.
Ah, but so falsely to encourage me—
That was a treason and a treachery
For which you cannot suffer too severely,   175
And you shall pay for that behavior dearly.
Yes, now I have no pity, not a shred;
My temper's out of hand; I've lost my head;
Shocked by the knowledge of your double-dealings,
My reason can't restrain my savage feelings;   180
A righteous wrath deprives me of my senses,
And I won't answer for the consequences.

CÉLIMÈNE. What does this outburst mean? Will you please explain?
Have you, by any chance, gone quite insane?

ALCESTE. Yes, yes, I went insane the day I fell   185
A victim to your black and fatal spell,
Thinking to meet with some sincerity
Among the treacherous charms that beckoned me.

CÉLIMÈNE. Pooh. Of what treachery can you complain?

ALCESTE. How sly you are, how cleverly you feign!   190
But you'll not victimize me any more.
Look: here's a document you've seen before.
This evidence, which I acquired today,
Leaves you, I think, without a thing to say.

CÉLIMÈNE. Is this what sent you into such a fit?   195

ALCESTE. You should be blushing at the sight of it.

CÉLIMÈNE. Ought I to blush? I truly don't see why.

ALCESTE. Ah, now you're being bold as well as sly;
Since there's no signature, perhaps you'll claim . . .

CÉLIMÈNE. I wrote it, whether or not it bears my name.   200

ALCESTE. And you can view with equanimity
This proof of your disloyalty to me!

CÉLIMÈNE. Oh, don't be so outrageous and extreme.

ALCESTE. You take this matter lightly, it would seem.
Was it no wrong to me, no shame to you,   205
That you should send Oronte this billet-doux?

CÉLIMÈNE. Oronte! Who said it was for him?

ALCESTE.   Why, those
Who brought me this example of your prose.

But what's the difference? If you wrote the letter 210
To someone else, it pleases me no better.
My grievance and your guilt remain the same.
CÉLIMÈNE. But need you rage, and need I blush for shame,
If this was written to a *woman* friend?
ALCESTE. Ah! Most ingenious. I'm impressed no end;
And after that incredible evasion 215
Your guilt is clear. I need no more persuasion.
How dare you try so clumsy a deception?
D'you think I'm wholly wanting in perception?
Come, come, let's see how brazenly you'll try
To bolster up so palpable a lie: 220
Kindly construe this ardent closing section
As nothing more than sisterly affection!
Here, let me read it. Tell me, if you dare to,
That this is for a woman . . .
CÉLIMÈNE.   I don't care to.
What right have you to badger and berate me, 225
And so highhandedly interrogate me?
ALCESTE. Now, don't be angry; all I ask of you
Is that you justify a phrase or two . . .
CÉLIMÈNE. No, I shall not. I utterly refuse,
And you may take those phrases as you choose. 230
ALCESTE. Just show me how this letter could be meant
For a woman's eyes, and I shall be content.
CÉLIMÈNE. No, no, it's for Oronte; you're perfectly right.
I welcome his attentions with delight,
I prize his character and his intellect, 235
And everything is just as you suspect.
Come, do your worst now; give your rage free rein;
But kindly cease to bicker and complain.
ALCESTE (*aside*). Good God! Could anything be more inhuman?
Was ever a heart so mangled by a woman? 240
When I complain of how she has betrayed me,
She bridles, and commences to upbraid me!
She tries my tortured patience to the limit;
She won't deny her guilt; she glories in it!
And yet my heart's too faint and cowardly 245
To break these chains of passion, and be free,
To scorn her as it should, and rise above
This unrewarded, mad, and bitter love.
(*To* CÉLIMÈNE) Ah, traitress, in how confident a fashion

You take advantage of my helpless passion,   250
And use my weakness for your faithless charms
To make me once again throw down my arms!
But do at least deny this black transgression;
Take back that mocking and perverse confessíon;   255
Defend this letter and your innocence,
And I, poor fool, will aid in your defense.
Pretend, pretend, that you are just and true,
And I shall make myself believe in you.

CÉLIMÈNE. Oh, stop it. Don't be such a jealous dunce,
Or I shall leave off loving you at once.   260
Just why should I *pretend?* What could impel me
To stoop so low as that? And kindly tell me
Why, if I loved another, I shouldn't merely
Inform you of it, simply and sincerely!
I've told you where you stand, and that admission   265
Should altogether clear me of suspicion;
After so generous a guarantee,
What right have you to harbor doubts of me?
Since women are (from natural reticence)
Reluctant to declare their sentiments,   270
And since the honor of our sex requires
That we conceal our amorous desires,
Ought any man for whom such laws are broken
To question what the oracle has spoken?
Should he not rather feel an obligation   275
To trust that most obliging declaration?
Enough, now. Your suspicions quite disgust me;
Why should I love a man who doesn't trust me?
I cannot understand why I continue,
Fool that I am, to take an interest in you.   280
I ought to choose a man less prone to doubt,
And give you something to be vexed about.

ALCESTE. Ah, what a poor enchanted fool I am;
These gentle words, no doubt, were all a sham;
But destiny requires me to entrust   285
My happiness to you, and so I must.
I'll love you to the bitter end, and see
How false and treacherous you dare to be.

CÉLIMÈNE. No, you don't really love me as you ought.

ALCESTE. I love you more than can be said or thought;   290
Indeed, I wish you were in such distress

That I might show my deep devotedness.
Yes, I could wish that you were wretchedly poor,
Unloved, uncherished, utterly obscure;
That fate had set you down upon the earth   295
Without possessions, rank, or gentle birth;
Then, by the offer of my heart, I might
Repair the great injustice of your plight;
I'd raise you from the dust, and proudly prove
The purity and vastness of my love.   300
CÉLIMÈNE. This is a strange benevolence indeed!
God grant that I may never be in need . . .
Ah, here's Monsieur Dubois, in quaint disguise.

SCENE 4

Enter DUBOIS.
ALCESTE. Well, why this costume? Why those frightened eyes?
What ails you?
DUBOIS.   Well, Sir, things are most mysterious.   305
ALCESTE. What do you mean?
DUBOIS.   I fear they're very serious.
ALCESTE. What?
DUBOIS.   Shall I speak more loudly?
ALCESTE.   Yes; speak out.
DUBOIS. Isn't there someone here, Sir?
ALCESTE.   Speak, you lout!
Stop wasting time.
DUBOIS.   Sir, we must slip away.
ALCESTE. How's that?
DUBOIS.   We must decamp without delay.   310
ALCESTE. Explain yourself.
DUBOIS.   I tell you we must fly.
ALCESTE. What for?
DUBOIS.   We mustn't pause to say good-by.
ALCESTE. Now what d'you mean by all of this, you clown?
DUBOIS. I mean, Sir, that we've got to leave this town.
ALCESTE. I'll tear you limb from limb and joint from joint   315
If you don't come more quickly to the point.
DUBOIS. Well, Sir, today a man in a black suit,
Who wore a black and ugly scowl to boot,
Left us a document scrawled in such a hand
As even Satan couldn't understand.   320
It bears upon your lawsuit, I don't doubt;

But all hell's devils couldn't make it out.
ALCESTE. Well, well, go on. What then? I fail to see
    How this event obliges us to flee.
DUBOIS. Well, Sir: an hour later, hardly more,   325
    A gentleman who's often called before
    Came looking for you in an anxious way.
    Not finding you, he asked me to convey
    (Knowing I could be trusted with the same)
    The following message . . . Now, what *was* his name?   330
ALCESTE. Forget his name, you idiot. What did he say?
DUBOIS. Well, it was one of your friends, Sir, anyway.
    He warned you to begone, and he suggested
    That if you stay, you may well be arrested.
ALCESTE. What? Nothing more specific? Think, man, think!   335
DUBOIS. No, Sir. He had me bring him pen and ink,
    And dashed you off a letter which, I'm sure,
    Will render things distinctly less obscure.
ALCESTE. Well—let me have it!
CÉLIMÈNE.   What *is* this all about?
ALCESTE. God knows; but I have hopes of finding out.   340
    How long am I to wait, you blitherer?
DUBOIS (*after a protracted search for the letter*). I must have left it on
    your table, Sir.
ALCESTE. I ought to . . .
CÉLIMÈNE.   No, no, keep your self-control;
    Go find out what's behind his rigmarole.
ALCESTE. It seems that fate, no matter what I do,   345
    Has sworn that I may not converse with you;
    But, Madam, pray permit your faithful lover
    To try once more before the day is over. (*Exeunt.*)

ACT 5

SCENE I

    Enter ALCESTE *and* PHILINTE.
ALCESTE. No, it's too much. My mind's made up, I tell you.
PHILINTE. Why should this blow, however hard, compel you . . .
ALCESTE. No, no, don't waste your breath in argument;
    Nothing you say will alter my intent;
    This age is vile, and I've made up my mind   5
    To have no further commerce with mankind.
    Did not truth, honor, decency, and the laws

Oppose my enemy and approve my cause?
My claims were justified in all men's sight;
I put my trust in equity and right;   10
Yet, to my horror and the world's disgrace,
Justice is mocked, and I have lost my case!
A scoundrel whose dishonesty is notorious
Emerges from another lie victorious!
Honor and right condone his brazen fraud,
While rectitude and decency applaud!   15
Before his smirking face, the truth stands charmed,
And virtue conquered, and the law disarmed!
His crime is sanctioned by a court decree!
And not content with what he's done to me,   20
The dog now seeks to ruin me by stating
That I composed a book now circulating,
A book so wholly criminal and vicious
That even to speak its title is seditious!
Meanwhile Oronte, my rival, lends his credit   25
To the same libelous tale, and helps to spread it!
Oronte! a man of honor and of rank,
With whom I've been entirely fair and frank;
Who sought me out and forced me, willy-nilly,
To judge some verse I found extremely silly;   30
And who, because I properly refused
To flatter him, or see the truth abused,
Abets my enemy in a rotten slander!
There's the reward of honesty and candor!
The man will hate me to the end of time   35
For failing to commend his wretched rhyme!
And not this man alone, but all humanity
Do what they do from interest and vanity;
They prate of honor, truth, and righteousness,
But lie, betray, and swindle nonetheless.   40
Come then: man's villainy is too much to bear;
Let's leave this jungle and this jackal's lair.
Yes! treacherous and savage race of men,
You shall not look upon my face again.

PHILINTE. Oh, don't rush into exile prematurely;   45
    Things aren't as dreadful as you make them, surely.
    It's rather obvious, since you're still at large,
    That people don't believe your enemy's charge.
    Indeed, his tale's so patently untrue

That it may do more harm to him than you.   50

ALCESTE. Nothing could do that scoundrel any harm:
His frank corruption is his greatest charm,
And, far from hurting him, a further shame
Would only serve to magnify his name.

PHILINTE. In any case, his bald prevarication   55
Has done no injury to your reputation,
And you may feel secure in that regard.
As for your lawsuit, it should not be hard
To have the case reopened, and contest
This judgment . . .

ALCESTE.   No, no, let the verdict rest.   60
Whatever cruel penalty it may bring,
I wouldn't have it changed for anything.
It shows the times' injustice with such clarity
That I shall pass it down to our posterity
As a great proof and signal demonstration   65
Of the black wickedness of this generation.
It may cost twenty thousand francs; but I
Shall pay their twenty thousand, and gain thereby
The right to storm and rage at human evil,
And send the race of mankind to the devil.   70

PHILINTE. Listen to me . . .

ALCESTE.   Why? What can you possibly say?
Don't argue. Sir; your labor's thrown away.
Do you propose to offer lame excuses
For men's behavior and the times' abuses?

PHILINTE. No, all you say I'll readily concede: 75
This is a low, dishonest age indeed;
Nothing but trickery prospers nowadays,
And people ought to mend their shabby ways.
Yes, man's a beastly creature; but must we then
Abandon the society of men?   80
Here in the world, each human frailty
Provides occasion for philosophy,
And that is virtue's noblest exercise;
If honesty shone forth from all men's eyes,
If every heart were frank and kind and just,   85
What could our virtues do but gather dust
(Since their employment is to help us bear
The villainies of men without despair)?
A heart well-armed with virtue can endure . . .

ALCESTE. Sir, you're a matchless reasoner, to be sure;   90
  Your words are fine and full of cogency;
  But don't waste time and eloquence on me,
  My reason bids me go, for my own good.
  My tongue won't lie and flatter as it should;
  God knows what frankness it might next commit,   95
  And what I'd suffer on account of it.
  Pray let me wait for Célimène's return
  In peace and quiet. I shall shortly learn,
  By her response to what I have in view,
  Whether her love for me is feigned or true.   100

PHILINTE. Till then, let's visit Eliante upstairs.

ALCESTE. No, I am too weighed down with somber cares.
  Go to her, do; and leave me with my gloom
  Here in the darkened corner of this room.

PHILINTE. Why, that's no sort of company, my friend;   105
  I'll see if Eliante will not descend. (*Exit.* ALCESTE *withdraws.*)

SCENE 2

Enter ORONTE *and* CÉLIMÈNE.

ORONTE. Yes, Madam, if you wish me to remain
  Your true and ardent lover, you must deign
  To give me some more positive assurance.
  All this suspense is quite beyond endurance.   110
  If your heart shares the sweet desires of mine,
  Show me as much by some convincing sign;
  And here's the sign I urgently suggest:
  That you no longer tolerate Alceste,
  But sacrifice him to my love, and sever   115
  All your relations with the man forever.

CÉLIMÈNE. Why do you suddenly dislike him so?
  You praised him to the skies not long ago.

ORONTE. Madam, that's not the point. I'm here to find
  Which way your tender feelings are inclined.   120
  Choose, if you please, between Alceste and me,
  And I shall stay or go accordingly.

ALCESTE (*emerging from the corner*). Yes, Madam, choose; this
      gentleman's demand
  Is wholly just, and I support his stand.
  I too am true and ardent; I too am here   125
  To ask you that you make your feelings clear.
  No more delays, now; no equivocation;

The time has come to make your declaration.

ORONTE. Sir, I've no wish in any way to be
    An obstacle to your felicity. 130

ALCESTE. Sir, I've no wish to share her heart with you;
    That may sound jealous, but at least it's true.

ORONTE. If, weighing us, she leans in your direction . . .

ALCESTE. If she regards you with the least affection . . .

ORONTE. I swear I'll yield her to you there and then. 135

ALCESTE. I swear I'll never see her face again.

ORONTE. Now, Madam, tell us what we've come to hear.

ALCESTE. Madam, speak openly and have no fear.

ORONTE. Just say which one is to remain your lover.

ALCESTE. Just name one name, and it will all be over. 140

ORONTE. What! Is it possible that you're undecided?

ALCESTE. What! Can your feelings possibly be divided?

CÉLIMÈNE. Enough: this inquisition's gone too far:
    How utterly unreasonable you are!
    Not that I couldn't make the choice with ease; 145
    My heart has no conflicting sympathies;
    I know full well which one of you I favor,
    And you'd not see me hesitate or waver.
    But how can you expect me to reveal
    So cruelly and bluntly what I feel? 150
    I think it altogether too unpleasant
    To choose between two men when both are present;
    One's heart has means more subtle and more kind
    Of letting its affections be divined,
    Nor need one be uncharitably plain 155
    To let a lover know he loves in vain.

ORONTE. No, no, speak plainly; I for one can stand it.
    I beg you to be frank.

ALCESTE.   And I demand it.
    The simple truth is what I wish to know,
    And there's no need for softening the blow. 160
    You've made an art of pleasing everyone,
    But now your days of coquetry are done:
    You have no choice now, Madam, but to choose,
    For I'll know what to think if you refuse;
    I'll take your silence for a clear admission 165
    That I'm entitled to my worst suspicion.

ORONTE. I thank you for this ultimatum, Sir,
    And I may say I heartily concur.

CÉLIMÈNE. Really, this foolishness is very wearing:
  Must you be so unjust and overbearing?   170
  Haven't I told you why I must demur?
  Ah, here's Eliante; I'll put the case to her.

SCENE 3

Enter ELIANTE.

CÉLIMÈNE. Cousin, I'm being persecuted here
  By these two persons, who, it would appear,
  Will not be satisfied till I confess   175
  Which one I love the more, and which the less,
  And tell the latter to his face that he
  Is henceforth banished from my company.
  Tell me, has ever such a thing been done?
ELIANTE. You'd best not turn to me; I'm not the one   180
  To back you in a matter of this kind:
  I'm all for those who frankly speak their mind.
ORONTE. Madam, you'll search in vain for a defender.
ALCESTE. You're beaten, Madam, and may as well surrender.
ORONTE. Speak, speak, you must; and end this awful strain.   185
ALCESTE. Or don't, and your position will be plain.
ORONTE. A single word will close this painful scene.
ALCESTE. But if you're silent, I'll know what you mean.

SCENE 4

Enter ACASTE, CLITANDRE, *and* ARSINOÉ

ACASTE (*to* CÉLIMÈNE). Madam, with all due deference, we two
  Have come to pick a little bone with you.   190
CLITANDRE (*to* ORONTE *and* ALCESTE). I'm glad you're present, Sirs; as
      you'll soon learn,
  Our business here is also your concern.
ARSINOÉ (*to* CÉLIMÈNE). Madam, I visit you so soon again
  Only because of these two gentlemen,
  Who came to me indignant and aggrieved   195
  About a crime too base to be believed.
  Knowing your virtue, having such confidence in it,
  I couldn't think you guilty for a minute,
  In spite of all their telling evidence;
  And, rising above our little difference,   200
  I've hastened here in friendship's name to see
  You clear yourself of this great calumny.

ACASTE. Yes, Madam, let us see with what composure
   You'll manage to respond to this disclosure.
   You lately sent Clitandre this tender note.   205
CLITANDRE. And this one, for Acaste, you also wrote.
ACASTE (*to* ORONTE *and* ALCESTE). You'll recognize this writing. Sirs, I
      think;
   The lady is so free with pen and ink
   That you must know it all too well, I fear.
   But listen: this is something you should hear.   210

   "How absurd you are to condemn my lightheartedness in society,
and to accuse me of being happiest in the company of others. Nothing
could be more unjust; and if you do not come to me instantly and beg
pardon for saying such a thing, I shall never forgive you as long as I live.
Our big bumbling friend the Viscount . . ."   215

   What a shame that he's not here.

   "Our big bumbling friend the Viscount, whose name stands first
in your complaint, is hardly a man to my taste; and ever since the day I
watched him spend three-quarters of an hour spitting into a well, so as
to make circles in the water, I have been unable to think highly of him.
As for the little Marquess . . ."   221

   In all modesty, gentlemen, that is I.

   "As for the little Marquess, who sat squeezing my hand for such a
long while yesterday, I find him in all respects the most trifling creature
alive; and the only things of value about him are his cape and his sword.
As for the man with the green ribbons . . ."   226

   (*To* ALCESTE) It's your turn now, Sir.

   "As for the man with the green ribbons, he amuses me now and
then with his bluntness and his bearish ill-humor; but there are many
times indeed when I think him the greatest bore in the world. And as
for the sonneteer . . ."   231

   (*To* ORONTE) Here's your helping.

   "And as for the sonneteer, who has taken it into his head to be witty,
and insists on being an author in the teeth of opinion, I simply cannot
be bothered to listen to him, and his prose wearies me quite as much as
his poetry. Be assured that I am not always so well-entertained as you
suppose; that I long for your company, more than I dare to say, at all
these entertainments to which people drag me; and that the presence of
those one loves is true and perfect seasoning to all one's pleasures."   239

CLITANDRE. And now for me.

   "Clitandre, whom you mention, and who so pesters me with his
saccharine speeches, is the last man on earth for whom I could feel any

affection. He is quite mad to suppose that I love him, and so are you,
to doubt that you are loved. Do come to your senses; exchange your
suppositions for his; and visit me as often as possible, to help me bear
the annoyance of his unwelcome attentions." 246

It's a sweet character that these letters show,
And what to call it, Madam, you well know.
Enough. We're off to make the world acquainted
With this sublime self-portrait that you've painted. 250
ACASTE. Madam, I'll make you no farewell oration;
No, you're not worthy of my indignation.
Far choicer hearts than yours, as you'll discover,
Would like this little Marquess for a lover. (*Exeunt* ACASTE *and*
CLITANDRE.)

SCENE 5

ORONTE. So! After all those loving letters you wrote, 225
You turn on me like this, and cut my throat!
And your dissembling, faithless heart, I find,
Has pledged itself by turns to all mankind!
How blind I've been! But now I clearly see;
I thank you, Madam, for enlightening me. 260
My heart is mine once more, and I'm content;
The loss of it shall be your punishment.
(*To* ALCESTE) Sir, she is yours; I'll seek no more to stand
Between your wishes and this lady's hand. (*Exit.*)

SCENE 6

ARSINOÉ (*to* CÉLIMÈNE). Madam, I'm forced to speak. I'm far too
stirred 265
To keep my counsel, after what I've heard.
I'm shocked and staggered by your want of morals.
It's not my way to mix in others' quarrels;
But really, when this fine and noble spirit,
This man of honor and surpassing merit, 270
Laid down the offering of his heart before you,
How *could* you . . .
ALCESTE.   Madam, permit me, I implore you,
To represent myself in this debate.
Don't bother, please, to be my advocate.
My heart, in any case, could not afford 275
To give your services their due reward;
And if I chose, for consolation's sake,
Some other lady, t'would not be you I'd take.

ARSINOÉ. What makes you think you could, Sir? And how dare you
Imply that I've been trying to ensnare you?   280
If you can for a moment entertain
Such flattering fancies, you're extremely vain.
I'm not so interested as you suppose
In Célimène's discarded gigolos.
Get rid of that absurd illusion, do.   285
Women like me are not for such as you.
Stay with this creature, to whom you're so attached;
I've never seen two people better matched. (*Exit.*)

SCENE 7

ALCESTE (*to* CÉLIMÈNE). Well, I've been still throughout this exposé,
Till everyone but me has said his say.   290
Come, have I shown sufficient self-restraint?
And may I now . . .
CÉLIMÈNE.   Yes, make your just complaint.
Reproach me freely, call me what you will;
You've every right to say I've used you ill.
I've wronged you, I confess it; and in my shame   295
I'll make no effort to escape the blame.
The anger of those others I could despise;
My guilt toward you I sadly recognize.
Your wrath is wholly justified, I fear,
I know how culpable I must appear,   300
I know all things bespeak my treachery,
And that, in short, you've grounds for hating me.
Do so; I give you leave.
ALCESTE.   Ah, traitress—how,
How should I cease to love you, even now?
Though mind and will were passionately bent   305
On hating you, my heart would not consent.
(*To* ELIANTE *and* PHILINTE) Be witness to my madness, both of you;
See what infatuation drives one to;
But wait; my folly's only just begun,
And I shall prove to you before I'm done   310
How strange the human heart is, and how far
From rational we sorry creatures are.
(*To* CÉLIMÈNE) Woman, I'm willing to forget your shame,
And clothe your treacheries in a sweeter name;
I'll call them youthful errors, instead of crimes,   315
And lay the blame on these corrupting times.

My one condition is that you agree
To share my chosen fate, and fly with me
To that wild, trackless solitary place
In which I shall forget the human race.   320
Only by such a course can you atone
For those atrocious letters; by that alone
Can you remove my present horror of you,
And make it possible for me to love you.

CÉLIMÈNE. What! *I* renounce the world at my young age,   325
And die of boredom in some hermitage?

ALCESTE. Ah, if you really loved me as you ought,
You wouldn't give the world a moment's thought;
Must you have me, and all the world beside?

CÉLIMÈNE. Alas, at twenty one is terrified   330
Of solitude. I fear I lack the force
And depth of soul to take so stern a course.
But if my hand in marriage will content you,
Why, there's a plan which I might well consent to,
And . . .

ALCESTE. No, I detest you now. I could excuse   335
Everything else, but since you thus refuse
To love me wholly, as a wife should do,
And see the world in me, as I in you,
Go! I reject your hand, and disenthrall
My heart from your enchantments, once for all.   340
   (*Exit* CÉLIMÈNE.)

SCENE 8

ALCESTE (*to* ELIANTE). Madam, your virtuous beauty has no peer,
Of all this world, you only are sincere;
I've long esteemed you highly, as you know;
Permit me ever to esteem you so,
And if I do not now request your hand,   345
Forgive me. Madam, and try to understand.
I feel unworthy of it; I sense that fate
Does not intend me for the married state,
That I should do you wrong by offering you
My shattered heart's unhappy residue,   350
And that in short . . . .

ELIANTE.   Your argument's well taken:
Nor need you fear that I shall feel forsaken.
Were I to offer him this hand of mine,
Your friend Philinte, I think, would not decline.

PHILINTE. Ah, Madam, that's my heart's most cherished goal,   355
    For which I'd gladly give my life and soul.
ALCESTE (*to* ELIANTE *and* PHILINTE). May you be true to all you now
    profess,
    And so deserve unending happiness.
    Meanwhile, betrayed and wronged in everything,
    I'll flee this bitter world where vice is king,   360
    And seek some spot unpeopled and apart
    Where I'll be free to have an honest heart. (*Exit.*)
PHILINTE. Come, Madam, let's do everything we can
    To change the mind of this unhappy man. (*Exeunt.*)

QUESTIONS

1. How does the argument between Alceste and Philinte in the opening scene state the play's major thematic conflict? Which of the two philosophies expressed is the more idealistic? Which more realistic? Is either or are both of them extreme?

2. What are the attitudes of Célimène, Eliante, and Arsinoé toward Alceste? Do they respect him? Why or why not?

3. *The Misanthrope* is generally acknowledged to be one of the world's greatest comedies, but, at the same time, it is an atypical one, both in its hero and in its ending. In what ways does Alceste approach the stature of a tragic hero? In what way is the ending unlike a comic ending?

4. Alceste is in conflict with social convention, with social injustice, and with Célimène. Does he discriminate between them as to their relative importance? Discuss.

5. Are there any indications in the opening scene that the motivations behind Alceste's hatred of social convention are not as unmixed as he thinks them?

6. Alceste declares himself not blind to Célimène's faults. Is he blind in any way about his relationship with Célimène? If so, what does his blindness spring from?

7. What do Alceste's reasons for refusing to appeal his lawsuit (5.1) and his wish that Célimène were "Unloved, uncherished, utterly obscure" so that he might raise her "from the dust" (4.3) tell us about his character?

8. What are Célimène's good qualities? What are her bad ones? In what ways are she and Alceste foils? Might Célimène have been redeemed had Alceste been able to accept her without taking her from society?

9. How is the gossip session between Acaste, Clitandre, and Célimène (2.5) a double-edged satire? Which of Célimène's satirical portraits is the finest? How accurate is Célimène's portrait of Alceste?

10. Which is the more scathingly satirized—Alceste, or the society in which he lives? Why?

11. What character in the play most nearly represents a desirable norm of social behavior? Why?

12. What characteristics keep Alceste from being a tragic hero? What keeps the ending from being a tragic ending?

13. The verse form used by Richard Wilbur in translating Molière's play is quite different from that used by Shakespeare in *Othello*. Describe the differences. What relation is there between the poetic style of each play and its subject matter?

14. Compare *The Misanthrope* and *A Doll House* as plays dealing with a character in conflict with the norms of a society. How are the characters of Alceste and Nora similar? How are they different? Which is portrayed by the playwright with greater sympathy? Why?

15. Are politeness and hypocrisy the same thing? If not, distinguish between them.

ANTON CHEKHOV

A Marriage Proposal

Characters

LOMOV

CHUBUKOV

NATALIA

Chubukov's mansion—the living room. LOMOV *enters, formally dressed in evening jacket, white gloves, top hat. He is nervous from the start.*

CHUBUKOV (*rising*). Well, look who's here! Ivan Vassilevitch! (*Shakes his hand warmly.*) What a surprise, old man! How are you?

LOMOV. Oh, not too bad. And you?

CHUBUKOV. Oh, we manage, we manage. Do sit down, please. You know, you've been neglecting your neighbors, my dear fellow. It's been ages. Say, why the formal dress? Tails, gloves, and so forth. Where's the funeral, my boy? Where are you headed?

LOMOV. Oh, nowhere. I mean, here; just to see you, my dear Stepan Stepanovitch.

CHUBUKOV. Then why the full dress, old boy? It's not New Year's, and so forth.

LOMOV. Well, you see, it's like this. I have come here, my dear Stepan Stepanovitch, to bother you with a request. More than once, or twice, or more than that, it has been my privilege to apply to you for assistance in things, and you've always, well, responded. I mean, well, you have. Yes. Excuse me, I'm getting all mixed up. May I have a glass of water, my dear Stepan Stepanovitch? (*Drinks.*)

A MARRIAGE PROPOSAL First produced in 1890. Translated from the Russian by Eric Bentley. For biographical information about Anton Chekhov (1860–1904), see the note to the short story "Misery" (page 217). In addition to being a prolific and innovative short-story writer, Chekhov was a highly productive playwright, producing in his short life such masterpieces as *The Cherry Orchard, Three Sisters, Uncle Vanya,* and *The Seagull,* as well as many one-act plays such as "A Marriage Proposal," which can best be described as a comic farce.

CHUBUKOV (*aside*). Wants to borrow some money. Not a chance! (*Aloud.*) What can I do for you my dear friend?

LOMOV. Well, you see, my dear Stepanitch . . . Excuse me, I mean Stepan my Dearovitch . . . No, I mean, I get all confused, as you can see. To make a long story short, you're the only one who can help me. Of course, I don't deserve it, and there's no reason why I should expect you to, and all that.

CHUBUKOV. Stop beating around the bush! Out with it!

LOMOV. In just a minute. I mean, now, right now. The truth is, I have come to ask the hand . . . I mean, your daughter, Natalia Stepanovna, I, I want to marry her!

CHUBUKOV (*overjoyed*). Great heavens! Ivan Vassilevitch! Say it again!

LOMOV. I have come humbly to ask for the hand . . .

CHUBUKOV (*interrupting*). You're a prince! I'm overwhelmed, delighted, and so forth. Yes, indeed, and all that! (*Hugs and kisses* LOMOV.) This is just what I've been hoping for. It's my fondest dream come true. (*Sheds a tear.*) And, you know, I've always looked upon you, my boy, as if you were my own son. May God grant to both of you His Mercy and His Love, and so forth. Oh, I have been wishing for this . . . But why am I being so idiotic? It's just that I'm off my rocker with joy, my boy! Completely off my rocker! Oh, with all my soul I'm . . . I'll go get Natalia, and so forth.

LOMOV (*deeply moved*). Dear Stepan Stepanovitch, do you think she'll agree?

CHUBUKOV. Why, of course, old friend. Great heavens! As if she wouldn't! Why she's crazy for you! Good God! Like a love-sick cat, and so forth. Be right back. (*Leaves.*)

LOMOV. God, it's cold. I'm gooseflesh all over, as if I had to take a test. But the main thing is, to make up my mind, and keep it that way. I mean, if I take time out to think, or if I hesitate, or talk about it, or have ideals, or wait for real love, well, I'll just never get married! Brrrr, it's cold! Natalia Stepanovna is an excellent housekeeper. She's not too bad looking. She's had a good education. What more could I ask? Nothing. I'm so nervous, my ears are buzzing. (*Drinks.*) Besides, I've just got to get married. I'm thirty-five already. It's sort of a critical age. I've got to settle down and lead a regular life. I mean, I'm always getting palpitations, and I'm nervous, and I get upset so easy. Look, my lips are quivering, and my eyebrow's twitching. The worst thing is the night. Sleeping. I get into bed, doze off, and, suddenly, something inside me jumps. First my head snaps, and then my shoulder blade, and I roll out of bed like a lunatic and try to walk it off. Then I try to go back to sleep, but, as soon as I do, something jumps again! Twenty times a night, sometimes . . . (NATALIA STEPANOVNA *enters.*)

NATALIA. Oh, it's only you. All Papa said was: "Go inside, there's a merchant come to collect his goods." How do you do, Ivan Vassilevitch?

LOMOV. How do you do, dear Natalia Stepanovna?

NATALIA. Excuse my apron, and not being dressed. We're shelling peas. You haven't been around lately. Oh, do sit down. *(They do.)* Would you like some lunch?

LOMOV. No thanks, I had some.

NATALIA. Well, then smoke if you want. *(He doesn't.)* The weather's nice today . . . but yesterday, it was so wet the workmen couldn't get a thing done. Have you got much hay in? I felt so greedy I had a whole field done, but now I'm not sure I was right. With the rain it could rot, couldn't it? I should have waited. But why are you so dressed up? Is there a dance or something? Of course, I must say you look splendid, but . . . Well, tell me, why are you so dressed up?

LOMOV *(excited).* Well, you see, my dear Natalia Stepanovna, the truth is, I made up my mind to ask you to . . . well, to, listen to me. Of course, it'll probably surprise you and even maybe make you angry, but . . . *(Aside.)* God it's cold in here!

NATALIA. Why, what do you mean? *(A pause.)* Well?

LOMOV. I'll try to get it over with. I mean, you know, my dear Natalia Stepanovna that I've known, since childhood, even, known, and had the privilege of knowing, your family. My late aunt, and her husband, who, as you know, left me my estate, they always had the greatest respect for your father, and your late mother. The Lomovs and the Chubukovs have always been very friendly, you might even say affectionate. And, of course, you know, our land borders on each other's. My Oxen Meadows touch your birch grove . . .

NATALIA. I hate to interrupt you, my dear Ivan Vassilevitch, but you said: "my Oxen Meadows." Do you really think they're yours?

LOMOV. Why of course they're mine.

NATALIA. What do you mean? The Oxen Meadows are ours, not yours!

LOMOV. Oh, no, my dear Natalia Stepanovna, they're mine.

NATALIA. Well, this is the first I've heard about it! Where did you get that idea?

LOMOV. Where? Why, I mean the Oxen Meadows that are wedged between your birches and the marsh.

NATALIA. Yes, of course, they're ours.

LOMOV. Oh, no, you're wrong, my dear Natalia Stepanovna, they're mine.

NATALIA. Now, come, Ivan Vassilevitch! How long have they been yours?

LOMOV. How long? Why, as long as I can remember!

NATALIA. Well, really, you can't expect me to believe that!

LOMOV. But, you can see for yourself in the deed, my dear Natalia
Stepanovna. Of course, there was once a dispute about them, but
everyone knows they're mine now. There's nothing to argue about.
There was a time when my aunt's grandmother let your father's
grandfather's peasants use the land, but they were supposed to bake
bricks for her in return. Naturally, after a few years they began to act
as if they owned it, but the real truth is . . .

NATALIA. That has nothing to do with the case! Both my grandfather and
my great-grandfather said that their land went as far as the marsh,
which means that the Meadows are ours! There's nothing whatever to
argue about. It's foolish.

LOMOV. But I can show you the deed, Natalia Stepanovna.

NATALIA. You're just making fun of me . . . Great heavens! Here we
have the land for hundreds of years, and suddenly you try to tell
us it isn't ours. What's wrong with you, Ivan Vassilevitch? Those
meadows aren't even fifteen acres, and they're not worth three
hundred rubles, but I just can't stand unfairness! I just can't stand
unfairness!

LOMOV. But, you must listen to me. Your father's grandfather's peasants,
as I've already tried to tell you, then were supposed to bake bricks for
my aunt's grandmother. And my aunt's grandmother, why, she wanted
to be nice to them . . .

NATALIA. It's just nonsense, this whole business about aunts and
grandfathers and grandmothers. The Meadows are ours! That's all
there is to it!

LOMOV. They're mine!

NATALIA. Ours! You can go on talking for two days, and you can put on
fifteen evening coats and twenty pairs of gloves, but I tell you they're
ours, ours, ours!

LOMOV. Natalia Stepanovna, I don't want the Meadows! I'm just acting on
principle. If you want, I'll give them to you.

NATALIA. I'll give them to *you!* Because they're ours! And that's all
there is to it! And if I may say so, your behavior, my dear Ivan
Vassilevitch, is very strange. Until now, we've always considered
you a good neighbor, even a friend. After all, last year we lent
you our threshing machine, even though it meant putting off our
own threshing until November. And here you are treating us
like a pack of gypsies. Giving me my own land, indeed! Really!
Why that's not being a good neighbor. It's sheer impudence, that's
what it is . . .

LOMOV. Oh, so you think I'm just a land-grabber? My dear lady, I've never grabbed anybody's land in my whole life, and no one's going to accuse me of doing it now! (*Quickly walks over to the pitcher and drinks some more water.*) The Oxen Meadows are mine!

NATALIA. That's a lie. They're ours!

LOMOV. Mine!

NATALIA. A lie! I'll prove it. I'll send my mowers out there today!

LOMOV. What?

NATALIA. My mowers will mow it today!

LOMOV. I'll kick them out!

NATALIA. You just dare!

LOMOV (*clutching his heart*). The Oxen Meadows are mine! Do you understand? Mine!

NATALIA. Please don't shout! You can shout all you want in your own house, but here I must ask you to control yourself.

LOMOV. If my heart wasn't palpitating the way it is, if my insides weren't jumping like mad, I wouldn't talk to you so calmly. (*Yelling.*) The Oxen Meadows are mine!

NATALIA. Ours!

LOMOV. Mine!

NATALIA. Ours!

LOMOV. Mine! (*Enter* CHUBUKOV.)

CHUBUKOV. What's going on? Why all the shouting?

NATALIA. Papa, will you please inform this gentleman who owns the Oxen Meadows, he or we?

CHUBUKOV (*to* LOMOV). Why, they're ours, old fellow.

LOMOV. But how can they be yours, my dear Stepan Stepanovitch? Be fair. Perhaps my aunt's grandmother did let your grandfather's peasants work the land, and maybe they did get so used to it that they acted as if it was their own, but . . .

CHUBUKOV. Oh, no, no . . . my dear boy. You forget something. The reason the peasants didn't pay your aunt's grandmother, and so forth, was that the land was disputed, even then. Since then it's been settled. Why, everyone knows it's ours.

LOMOV. I can prove it's mine.

CHUBUKOV. You can't prove a thing, old boy.

LOMOV. Yes I can!

CHUBUKOV. My dear lad, why yell like that? Yelling doesn't prove a thing. Look, I'm not after anything of yours, just as I don't intend to give up anything of mine. Why should I? Besides, if you're going to keep arguing about it, I'd just as soon give the land to the peasants, so there!

LOMOV. There nothing! Where do you get the right to give away someone else's property?

CHUBUKOV. I certainly ought to know if I have the right or not.
And you had better realize it, because, my dear young man, I am not used to being spoken to in that tone of voice, and so forth. Besides which, my dear young man, I am twice as old as you are, and I ask you to speak to me without getting yourself into such a tizzy, and so forth!

LOMOV. Do you think I'm a fool? First you call my property yours, and then you expect me to keep calm and polite! Good neighbors don't act like that, my dear Stepan Stepanovitch. You're no neighbor, you're a land grabber!

CHUBUKOV. What was that? What did you say?

NATALIA. Papa, send the mowers out to the meadows at once!

CHUBUKOV. What did you say, sir?

NATALIA. The Oxen Meadows are ours, and we'll never give them up, never, never, never, never!

LOMOV. We'll see about that. I'll go to court. I'll show you!

CHUBUKOV. Go to court? Well, go to court, and so forth! I know you, just waiting for a chance to go to court, and so forth. You pettifogging shyster, you! All of your family is like that. The whole bunch of them!

LOMOV. You leave my family out of this! The Lomovs have always been honorable, upstanding people, and not a one of them was ever tried for embezzlement, like your grandfather was.

CHUBUKOV. The Lomovs are a pack of lunatics, the whole bunch of them!

NATALIA. The whole bunch!

CHUBUKOV. Your grandfather was a drunkard, and what about your other aunt, the one who ran away with the architect? And so forth.

NATALIA. And so forth!

LOMOV. Your mother was a hunch back! *(Clutches at his heart.)* Oh, I've got a stitch in my side . . . My head's whirling . . . Help! Water!

CHUBUKOV. Your father was a rum-soaked gambler.

NATALIA. And your aunt was queen of the scandalmongers!

LOMOV. My left foot's paralyzed. You're a plotter . . . Oh, my heart. It's an open secret that in the last elections you brib . . . I'm seeing stars! Where's my hat?

NATALIA. It's a low-mean, spiteful . . .

CHUBUKOV. And you're a two-face, malicious schemer!

LOMOV. Here's my hat . . . Oh, my heart . . . Where's the door? How do I get out of here? . . . Oh, I think I'm going to die . . . My foot's numb. *(Goes.)*

CHUBUKOV (*following him*). And don't you ever set foot in my house again!

NATALIA. Go to court, indeed! We'll see about that! (LOMOV *staggers out.*)

CHUBUKOV. The devil with him! (*Gets a drink, walks back and forth, excited.*)

NATALIA. What a rascal! How can you trust your neighbors after an incident like that?

CHUBUKOV. The villain! The scarecrow!

NATALIA. He's a monster! First he tries to steal our land, and then he has the nerve to yell at you.

CHUBUKOV. Yes, and that turnip, that stupid rooster, has the gall to make a proposal. Some proposal!

NATALIA. What proposal?

CHUBUKOV. Why, he came to propose to you.

NATALIA. To propose? To me? Why didn't you tell me before?

CHUBUKOV. So he gets all dressed up in his formal clothes. That stuffed sausage, that dried up cabbage!

NATALIA. To propose to me? Ohhhh! (*Falls into a chair and starts wailing.*) Bring him back! Back! Go get him! Bring him back! Ohhhh!

CHUBUKOV. Bring who back?

NATAILA. Hurry up, hurry up! I'm sick. Get him! (*Complete hysterics.*)

CHUBUKOV. What for? (*To her*) What's the matter with you? (*Clutches his head.*) Oh, what a fool I am! I'll shoot myself! I'll hang myself! I ruined her chances!

NATALIA. I'm dying. Get him!

CHUBUKOV. All right, all right, right away! Only don't yell! (*He runs out.*)

NATALIA. What are they doing to me? Get him! Bring him back! Bring him back! (*A pause.* CHUBUKOV *runs in.*)

CHUBUKOV. He's coming, and so forth, the snake. Oof! You talk to him. I'm not in the mood.

NATALIA (*wailing*). Bring him back! Bring him back!

CHUBUKOV (*yelling*). I told you, he's coming! Oh Lord, what agony to be the father of a grown-up daughter. I'll cut my throat some day, I swear I will. (*To her.*) We cursed him, we insulted him, abused him, kicked him out, and now . . . because you, you . . .

NATALIA. Me? It was all your fault!

CHUBUKOV. My fault? What do you mean my fau . . . ? (LOMOV *appears in the doorway.*) Talk to him yourself! (*Goes out.* LOMOV *enters, exhausted.*)

LOMOV. What palpitations! My heart! And my foot's absolutely asleep. Something keeps giving me a stitch in the side . . .

NATALIA. You must forgive us, Ivan Vassilevitch. We all got too excited. I remember now. The Oxen Meadows are yours.

LOMOV. My heart's beating something awful. My Meadows. My eyebrows, they're both twitching!

NATALIA. Yes, the Meadows are all yours, yes, yours. Do sit down. *(They sit.)* We were wrong, of course.

LOMOV. I argued on principle. My land isn't worth so much to me, but the principle . . .

NATALIA. Oh, yes, of course, the principle, that's what counts. But let's change the subject.

LOMOV. Besides, I have evidence. You see, my aunt's grandmother let your father's grandfather's peasants use the land . . .

NATALIA. Yes, yes, yes, but forget all that. *(Aside.)* I wish I knew how to get him going. *(Aloud)* Are you going to start hunting soon?

LOMOV. After the harvest I'll try for grouse. But oh, my dear Natalia Stepanovna, have you heard about the bad luck I've had? You know my dog, Guess? He's gone lame.

NATALIA. What a pity. Why?

LOMOV. I don't know. He must have twisted his leg, or got in a fight, or something. *(Sighs.)* My best dog, to say nothing of the cost. I paid Mironov 125 rubles for him.

NATALIA. That was too high, Ivan Vassilevitch.

LOMOV. I think it was quite cheap. He's a first class dog.

NATALIA. Why Papa only paid 85 rubles for Squeezer, and he's much better than Guess.

LOMOV. Squeezer better than Guess! What an idea! *(Laughs.)* Squeezer better than Guess!

NATALIA. Of course he's better. He may still be too young but on points and pedigree, he's a better dog even than any Volchanetsky owns.

LOMOV. Excuse me, Natalia Stepanovna, but you're forgetting he's overshot, and overshot dogs are bad hunters.

NATALIA. Oh, so he's overshot, is he? Well, this is the first time I've heard about it.

LOMOV. Believe me, his lower jaw is shorter than his upper.

NATALIA. You've measured them?

LOMOV. Yes, he's all right for pointing, but if you want him to retrieve . . .

NATALIA. In the first place, our Squeezer is a thoroughbred, the son of Harness and Chisel, while your mutt doesn't even have a pedigree. He's as old and worn out as a pedlar's horse.

LOMOV. He may be old, but I wouldn't take five Squeezers for him. How can you argue? Guess is a dog, Squeezer's a laugh. Anyone you can name has a dog like Squeezer hanging around somewhere. They're under every bush. If he only cost twenty-five rubles you got cheated.

NATALIA. The devil is in you today, Ivan Vassilevitch! You want to contradict everything. First you pretend the Oxen Meadows are yours, and now you say Guess is better than Squeezer. People should say what they really mean, and you know Squeezer is a hundred times better than Guess. Why say he isn't?

LOMOV. So, you think I'm a fool or a blind man,—Natalia Stepanovna! Once and for all, Squeezer is overshot!

NATALIA. He is not!

LOMOV. He is so!

NATALIA. He is not!

LOMOV. Why shout, my dear lady?

NATALIA. Why talk such nonsense? It's terrible. Your Guess is old enough to be buried, and you compare him with Squeezer!

LOMOV. I'm sorry, I can't go on. My heart . . . it's palpitating!

NATALIA. I've always noticed that the hunters who argue most don't know a thing.

LOMOV. Please! Be quiet a moment. My heart's falling apart . . . *(Shouts.)* Shut up!

NATALIA: I'm not going to shut up until you admit that Squeezer's a hundred times better than Guess.

LOMOV. A hundred times worse! His head . . . My eyes . . . shoulder . . .

NATALIA. Guess is half-dead already!

LOMOV *(weeping)*. Shut up! My heart's exploding!

NATALIA. I won't shut up! (CHUBUKOV *comes in.*)

CHUBUKOV. What's the trouble now?

NATALIA. Papa, will you please tell us which is the better dog, his Guess or our Squeezer?

LOMOV. Stepan Stepanovitch, I implore you to tell me just one thing; is your Squeezer overshot or not? Yes or no?

CHUBUKOV. Well what if he is? He's still the best dog in the neighborhood, and so forth.

LOMOV. Oh, but isn't my dog, Guess, better? Really?

CHUBUKOV. Don't get yourself so fraught up, old man. Of course, your dog has his good points—thoroughbred, firm on his feet, well sprung ribs, and so forth. But, my dear fellow, you've got to admit he has two defects; he's old and he's short in the muzzle.

LOMOV. Short in the muzzle? Oh, my heart! Let's look at the facts! On the Marusin-sky hunt my dog ran neck and neck with the Count's, while Squeezer was a mile behind them . . .

CHUBUKOV. That's because the Count's groom hit him with a whip.

LOMOV. And he was right, too! We were fox hunting; what was your dog chasing sheep for?

CHUBUKOV. That's a lie! Look, I'm going to lose my temper . . .
(*Controlling himself.*) my dear friend, so let's stop arguing, for that
reason alone. You're only arguing because we're all jealous of
somebody else's dog. Who can help it? As soon as you realize some
dog is better than yours, in this case our dog, you start in with this
and that, and the next thing you know—pure jealousy! I remember
the whole business.

LOMOV. I remember too!

CHUBUKOV (*mimicking*). "I remember too!" What do you remember?

LOMOV. My heart . . . my foot's asleep . . . I can't . . .

NATALIA (*mimicking*). "My heart . . . my foot's asleep." What kind of a
hunter are you? You should be hunting cockroaches in the kitchen,
not foxes. "My heart!"

CHUBUKOV. Yes, what kind of a hunter are you anyway? You should be
sitting at home with your palpitations, not tracking down animals.
You don't hunt anyhow. You just go out to argue with people and
interfere with their dogs, and so forth. For God's sake, let's change
the subject before I lose my temper. Anyway, you're just not a hunter.

LOMOV. But you, you're a hunter? Ha! You only go hunting to get in good
with the count, and to plot, and intrigue, and scheme . . . Oh, my
heart! You're a schemer, that's what!

CHUBUKOV. What's that? Me a schemer? (*Shouting.*) Shut up!

LOMOV. A schemer!

CHUBUKOV. You infant! You puppy!

LOMOV. You old rat! You Jesuit!

CHUBUKOV. You shut up, or I'll shoot you down like a partridge!
You idiot!

LOMOV. Everyone knows that—oh, my heart—that your wife used to beat
you . . . Oh, my feet . . . my head . . . I'm seeing stars . . . I'm going
to faint! (*He drops into an armchair.*) Quick, a doctor! (*Faints.*)

CHUBUKOV (*going on, oblivious*). Baby! Weakling! Idiot! I'm getting sick.
(*Drinks water.*) Me! I'm sick!

NATALIA. What kind of a hunter are you? You can't even sit on a horse! (*To
her father.*) Papa, what's the matter with him? Look, papa! (*Screaming.*)
Ivan Vassilevitch! He's dead.

CHUBUKOV. I'm choking, I can't breathe . . . Give me air.

NATALIA. He's dead! (*Pulling* LOMOV's *sleeve.*) Ivan Vassilevitch!
Ivan Vassilevitch! What have you done to me? He's dead! (*She falls into
an armchair. Screaming hysterically.*) A doctor! A doctor! A doctor!

CHUBUKOV. Ohhhh . . . What's the matter? What happened?

NATALIA (*wailing*). He's dead! He's dead!

CHUBUKOV. Who's dead *(Looks at* LOMOV.) My God, he is! Quick! Water! A doctor! *(Puts glass to* LOMOV's *lips.)* Here, drink this! Can't drink it—he must be dead, and so forth . . . Oh what a miserable life! Why don't I shoot myself! I should have cut my throat long ago! What am I waiting for? Give me a knife! Give me a pistol! (LOMOV *stirs.)* Look, he's coming to. Here, drink some water. That's it.

LOMOV. I'm seeing stars . . . misty . . . Where am I?

CHUBUKOV. Just you hurry up and get married, and then the devil with you! She accepts. *(Puts* LOMOV's *hand in* NATALIA's.) She accepts and so forth! I give you my blessing, and so forth! Only leave me in peace!

LOMOV *(getting up).* Huh? What? Who?

CHUBUKOV. She accepts! Well? Kiss her, damn you!

NATALIA. He's alive! Yes, yes, I accept.

CHUBUKOV. Kiss each other!

LOMOV. Huh? Kiss? Kiss who? *(They kiss.)* That's nice. I mean, excuse me, what happened? Oh, now I get it . . . my heart . . . those stars . . . I'm very happy, Natalia Stepanovna. *(Kisses her hand.)* My foot's asleep.

NATALIA. I . . . I'm happy too.

CHUBUKOV. What a load off my shoulders! Whew!

NATALIA. Well, now maybe you'll admit that Squeezer is better than Guess?

LOMOV. Worse!

NATALIA. Better!

CHUBUKOV. What a way to enter matrimonial bliss! Let's have some champagne!

LOMOV. He's worse!

NATALIA. Better! Better, better, better, better!

CHUBUKOV *(trying to shout her down).* Champagne! Bring some champagne! Champagne! Champagne!

QUESTIONS

1. What are the sources of humor in this play? Identify them, and discuss their effectiveness.
2. Why is Lomov proposing to Natalia? Why is she interested in accepting him?
3. Discuss the comic interplay among the characters. Is any one of them more likable than the other two? If so, which one? Why?
4. Why do the three characters argue about the land ownership and about the relative merits of their dogs? How does the triviality of their arguments contribute to the comic effect of the dialogue?
5. Locate passages that illustrate the status of women in the nineteenth century. Discuss this theme, and discuss other "serious" themes in the play.
6. Are there "absurd" elements in the play's comedy? If so, what are they?

OSCAR WILDE

The Importance of Being Earnest

A Trivial Comedy for Serious People

THE PERSONS OF THE PLAY

JOHN WORTHING, J.P.
ALGERNON MONCRIEFF
REV. CANON CHASUBLE, D.D.
MERRIMAN, *Butler*
LANE, *Manservant*
LADY BRACKNELL
HON. GWENDOLEN FAIRFAX
CECILY CARDEW
MISS PRISM, *Governess*

THE SCENES OF THE PLAY

ACT I: *Algernon Moncrieff's flat in Half-Moon Street, W.*
ACT II: *The garden at the Manor House, Woolton*
ACT III: *Drawing-room at the Manor House, Woolton*
TIME. *The Present*

FIRST ACT

SCENE. *Morning-room in* ALGERNON's *flat in Half-Moon Street. The room is luxuriously and artistically furnished. The sound of a piano is heard in the adjoining room.*

(LANE *is arranging afternoon tea on the table and, after the music has ceased,* ALGERNON *enters.*)
ALGERNON. Did you hear what I was playing, Lane?
LANE. I didn't think it polite to listen, sir.

THE IMPORTANCE OF BEING EARNEST First produced in 1895. Oscar Wilde (1854–1900) was born in Ireland but spent most of his adult life traveling throughout Europe. He wrote excellent fiction and poetry but is best known as a dramatist; in addition to the play printed here, prominent titles are *Lady Windemere's Fan* (1892) and *A Woman of No Importance* (1893). In his plays, notable for their witty, sparkling dialogue, Wilde satirized the pretensions of Britain's upper classes. Though he married and fathered two children, Wilde was a gay man and, subject to the repressive laws of the time, was imprisoned for "gross indecency"; his two years in prison resulted in one of his finest works, "The Ballad of Reading Gaol." Suffering from meningitis, Wilde died at age forty-six.

ALGERNON. I'm sorry for that, for your sake. I don't play accurately—anyone can play accurately—but I play with wonderful expression. As far as the piano is concerned, sentiment is my forte. I keep science for Life.

LANE. Yes, sir.

ALGERNON. And, speaking of the science of Life, have you got the cucumber sandwiches cut for Lady Bracknell?

LANE. Yes, sir. (*Hands them on a salver.*)

ALGERNON (*Inspects them, takes two, and sits down on the sofa*). Oh! . . . by the way, Lane, I see from your book that on Thursday night, when Lord Shoreman and Mr. Worthing were dining with me, eight bottles of champagne are entered as having been consumed.

LANE. Yes, sir; eight bottles and a pint.

ALGERNON. Why is it that at a bachelor's establishment the servants invariably drink the champagne? I ask merely for information.

LANE. I attribute it to the superior quality of the wine, sir. I have often observed that in married households the champagne is rarely of a first-rate brand.

ALGERNON. Good heavens! Is marriage so demoralizing as that?

LANE. I believe it is a very pleasant state, sir. I have had very little experience of it myself up to the present. I have only been married once. That was in consequence of a misunderstanding between myself and a young person.

ALGERNON (*Languidly*). I don't know that I am much interested in your family life, Lane.

LANE. No, sir; it is not a very interesting subject. I never think of it myself.

ALGERNON. Very natural, I am sure. That will do, Lane, thank you.

LANE. Thank you, sir. (LANE *goes out.*)

ALGERNON. Lane's views on marriage seem somewhat lax. Really, if the lower orders don't set us a good example, what on earth is the use of them? They seem, as a class, to have absolutely no sense of moral responsibility. (*Enter* LANE.)

LANE. Mr. Ernest Worthing. (*Enter* JACK. LANE *goes out.*)

ALGERNON. How are you, my dear Ernest? What brings you up to town?

JACK. Oh, pleasure, pleasure! What else should bring one anywhere? Eating as usual, I see, Algy!

ALGERNON (*stiffly*). I believe it is customary in good society to take some slight refreshment at five o'clock. Where have you been since last Thursday?

JACK (*sitting down on the sofa*). In the country.

ALGERNON. What on earth do you do there?

JACK (*pulling off his gloves*). When one is in town one amuses oneself. When one is in the country one amuses other people. It is excessively boring.

ALGERNON. And who are the people you amuse?

JACK (*airily*). Oh, neighbors, neighbors.

ALGERNON. Got nice neighbors in your part of Shropshire?

JACK. Perfectly horrid! Never speak to one of them.

ALGERNON. How immensely you must amuse them! (*Goes over and takes sandwich.*) By the way, Shropshire is your county, is it not?

JACK. Eh? Shropshire? Yes, of course. Hallo! Why all these cups? Why cucumber sandwiches? Why such reckless extravagance in one so young? Who is coming to tea?

ALGERNON. Oh! merely Aunt Augusta and Gwendolen.

JACK. How perfectly delightful!

ALGERNON. Yes, that is all very well; but I am afraid Aunt Augusta won't quite approve of your being here.

JACK. May I ask why?

ALGERNON. My dear fellow, the way you flirt with Gwendolen is perfectly disgraceful. It is almost as bad as the way Gwendolen flirts with you.

JACK. I am in love with Gwendolen. I have come up to town expressly to propose to her.

ALGERNON. I thought you had come up for pleasure? . . . I call that business.

JACK. How utterly unromantic you are!

ALGERNON. I really don't see anything romantic in proposing. It is very romantic to be in love. But there is nothing romantic about a definite proposal. Why, one may be accepted. One usually is, I believe. Then the excitement is all over. The very essence of romance is uncertainty. If ever I get married, I'll certainly try to forget the fact.

JACK. I have no doubt about that, dear Algy. The Divorce Court was specially invented for people whose memories are so curiously constituted.

ALGERNON. Oh, there is no use speculating on that subject. Divorces are made in Heaven—(JACK *puts out his hand to take a sandwich.* ALGERNON *at once interferes.*) Please don't touch the cucumber sandwiches. They are ordered specially for Aunt Augusta. (*Takes one and eats it.*)

JACK. Well, you have been eating them all the time.

ALGERNON. That is quite a different matter. She is my aunt. (*Takes plate from below.*) Have some bread and butter. The bread and butter is for Gwendolen. Gwendolen is devoted to bread and butter.

JACK (*advancing to table and helping himself*). And very good bread and butter it is too.

ALGERNON. Well, my dear fellow, you need not eat as if you were going to eat it all. You behave as if you were married to her already. You are not married to her already, and I don't think you ever will be.

JACK. Why on earth do you say that?

ALGERNON. Well, in the first place, girls never marry the men they flirt with. Girls don't think it right.

JACK. Oh, that is nonsense!

ALGERNON. It isn't. It is a great truth. It accounts for the extraordinary number of bachelors that one sees all over the place. In the second place, I don't give my consent.

JACK. Your consent!

ALGERNON. My dear fellow, Gwendolen is my first cousin. And before I allow you to marry her, you will have to clear up the whole question of Cecily. (*Rings bell.*)

JACK. Cecily! What on earth do you mean? What do you mean, Algy, by Cecily! I don't know any one of the name of Cecily. (*Enter* LANE.)

ALGERNON. Bring me that cigarette case Mr. Worthing left in the smoking-room the last time he dined here.

LANE. Yes, sir. (LANE *goes out.*)

JACK. Do you mean to say you have had my cigarette case all this time? I wish to goodness you had let me know. I have been writing frantic letters to Scotland Yard about it. I was very nearly offering a large reward.

ALGERNON. Well, I wish you would offer one. I happen to be more than usually hard up.

JACK. There is no good offering a large reward now that the thing is found (*Enter* LANE *with the cigarette case on a salver.* ALGERNON *takes it at once,* LANE *goes out.*)

ALGERNON. I think that is rather mean of you, Ernest, I must say. (*Opens case and examines it.*) However, it makes no matter, for, now that I look at the inscription inside, I find that the thing isn't yours after all.

JACK. Of course it's mine. (*Moving to him.*) You have seen me with it a hundred times, and you have no right whatsoever to read what is written inside. It is a very un-gentlemanly thing to read a private cigarette case.

ALGERNON. Oh! it is absurd to have a hard and fast rule about what one should read and what one shouldn't. More than half of modern culture depends on what one shouldn't read.

JACK. I am quite aware of the fact, and I don't propose to discuss modern culture. It isn't the sort of thing one should talk of in private. I simply want my cigarette case back.

ALGERNON. Yes; but this isn't your cigarette case. This cigarette case is a present from someone of the name of Cecily, and you said you didn't know anyone of that name.

JACK. Well, if you want to know, Cecily happens to be my aunt.

ALGERNON. Your aunt!

JACK. Yes. Charming old lady she is, too. Lives at Tunbridge Wells. Just give it back to me, Algy.

ALGERNON (*retreating to back of sofa*). But why does she call herself little Cecily if she is your aunt and lives at Tunbridge Wells? (*Reading.*) "From little Cecily with her fondest love."

JACK (*moving to sofa and kneeling upon it*). My dear fellow, what on earth is there in that? Some aunts are tall, some aunts are not tall. That is a matter that surely an aunt may be allowed to decide for herself. You seem to think that every aunt should be exactly like your aunt! That is absurd. For Heaven's sake give me back my cigarette case. (*Follows* ALGERNON *round the room.*)

ALGERNON. Yes. But why does your aunt call you her uncle? "From little Cecily with her fondest love to her dear Uncle Jack." There is no objection, I admit, to an aunt being a small aunt, but why an aunt, no matter what her size may be, should call her own nephew her uncle, I can't quite make out. Besides, your name isn't Jack at all; it is Ernest.

JACK. It isn't Ernest; it's Jack.

ALGERNON. You have always told me it was Ernest. I have introduced you to every one as Ernest. You answer to the name of Ernest. You look as if your name was Ernest. You are the most earnest-looking person I ever saw in my life. It is perfectly absurd your saying that your name isn't Ernest. It's on your cards. Here is one of them. (*Taking it from case.*) 'Mr. Ernest Worthing, B.4, The Albany.' I'll keep this as a proof that your name is Ernest if ever you attempt to deny it to me, or to Gwendolen, or to anyone else. (*Puts the card in his pocket.*)

JACK. Well, my name is Ernest in town and Jack in the country, and the cigarette case was given to me in the country.

ALGERNON. Yes, but that does not account for the fact that your small Aunt Cecily, who lives at Tunbridge Wells, calls you her dear uncle. Come, old boy, you had much better have the thing out at once.

JACK. My dear Algy, you talk exactly as if you were a dentist. It is very vulgar to talk like a dentist when one isn't a dentist. It produces a false impression.

ALGERNON. Well, that is exactly what dentists always do. Now, go on! Tell me the whole thing. I may mention that I have always suspected you of being a confirmed and secret Bunburyist; and I am quite sure of it now.

JACK. Bunburyist? What on earth do you mean by a Bunburyist?

ALGERNON. I'll reveal to you the meaning of that incomparable expression as soon as you are kind enough to inform me why you are Ernest in town and Jack in the country.

JACK. Well, produce my cigarette case first.

ALGERNON. Here it is. *(Hands cigarette case.)* Now produce your explanation, and pray make it improbable. *(Sits on sofa.)*

JACK. My dear fellow, there is nothing improbable about my explanation at all. In fact it's perfectly ordinary. Old Mr. Thomas Cardew, who adopted me when I was a little boy, made me in his will guardian to his granddaughter, Miss Cecily Cardew. Cecily, who addresses me as her uncle from motives of respect that you could not possibly appreciate, lives at my place in the country under the charge of her admirable governess, Miss Prism.

ALGERNON. Where is that place in the country, by the way?

JACK. That is nothing to you, dear boy. You are not going to be invited. . . . I may tell you candidly that the place is not in Shropshire.

ALGERNON. I suspected that, my dear fellow! I have Bunburyed all over Shropshire on two separate occasions. Now, go on. Why are you Ernest in town and Jack in the country?

JACK. My dear Algy, I don't know whether you will be able to understand my real motives. You are hardly serious enough. When one is placed in the position of guardian, one has to adopt a very high moral tone on all subjects. It's one's duty to do so. And as a high moral tone can hardly be said to conduce very much to either one's health or one's happiness, in order to get up to town I have always pretended to have a younger brother of the name of Ernest, who lives in the Albany, and gets into the most dreadful scrapes. That, my dear Algy, is the whole truth pure and simple.

ALGERNON. The truth is rarely pure and never simple. Modern life would be very tedious if it were either, and modern literature a complete impossibility!

JACK. That wouldn't be at all a bad thing.

ALGERNON. Literary criticism is not your forte, my dear fellow. Don't try it. You should leave that to people who haven't been at a University. They do it so well in the daily papers. What you really are is a Bunburyist. I was quite right in saying you were a Bunburyist. You are one of the most advanced Bunburyists I know.

JACK. What on earth do you mean?

ALGERNON. You have invented a very useful younger brother called Ernest, in order that you may be able to come up to town as often as you like. I have invented an invaluable permanent invalid called Bunbury, in order that I may be able to go down into the country whenever I choose. Bunbury is perfectly invaluable. If it wasn't for Bunbury's extraordinary bad health, for instance, I wouldn't be able to dine with you at Willis's tonight, for I have been really engaged to Aunt Augusta for more than a week.

JACK. I haven't asked you to dine with me anywhere tonight.

ALGERNON. I know. You are absurdly careless about sending out invitations. It is very foolish of you. Nothing annoys people so much as not receiving invitations.

JACK. You had much better dine with your Aunt Augusta.

ALGERNON. I haven't the smallest intention of doing anything of the kind. To begin with, I dined there on Monday, and once a week is quite enough to dine with one's own relations. In the second place, whenever I do dine there I am always treated as a member of the family, and sent down with either no woman at all, or two. In the third place, I know perfectly well whom she will place me next to, tonight. She will place me next Mary Farquhar, who always flirts with her own husband across the dinner-table. That is not very pleasant. Indeed, it is not even decent . . . and that sort of thing is enormously on the increase. The amount of women in London who flirt with their own husbands is perfectly scandalous. It looks so bad. It is simply washing one's clean linen in public. Besides, now that I know you to be a confirmed Bunburyist I naturally want to talk to you about Bunburying. I want to tell you the rules.

JACK. I'm not a Bunburyist at all. If Gwendolen accepts me, I am going to kill my brother, indeed I think I'll kill him in any case. Cecily is a little too much interested in him. It is rather a bore. So I am going to get rid of Ernest. And I strongly advise you to do the same with Mr. . . . with your invalid friend who has the absurd name.

ALGERNON. Nothing will induce me to part with Bunbury, and if you ever get married, which seems to me extremely problematic, you will be very glad to know Bunbury. A man who marries without knowing Bunbury has a very tedious time of it.

JACK. That is nonsense. If I marry a charming girl like Gwendolen, and she is the only girl I ever saw in my life that I would marry, I certainly won't want to know Bunbury.

ALGERNON. Then your wife will. You don't seem to realize, that in married life three is company and two is none.

JACK (*sententiously*). That, my dear young friend, is the theory that the corrupt French Drama has been propounding for the last fifty years.

ALGERNON. Yes; and that the happy English home has proved in half the time.

JACK. For heaven's sake, don't try to be cynical. It's perfectly easy to be cynical.

ALGERNON. My dear fellow, it isn't easy to be anything nowadays. There's such a lot of beastly competition about. (*The sound of an electric bell is heard.*) Ah! that must be Aunt Augusta. Only relatives, or creditors, ever ring in that Wagnerian manner. Now, if I get her out of the way for ten minutes, so that you can have an opportunity for proposing to Gwendolen, may I dine with you tonight at Willis's?

JACK. I suppose so, if you want to.

ALGERNON. Yes, but you must be serious about it. I hate people who are not serious about meals. It is shallow of them. (*Enter* LANE.)

LANE. **Lady** Bracknell and Miss Fairfax. (ALGERNON *goes forward to meet them. Enter* LADY BRACKNELL *and* GWENDOLEN.)

LADY BRACKNELL. Good afternoon, dear Algernon, I hope you are behaving very well.

ALGERNON. I'm feeling very well, Aunt Augusta.

LADY BRACKNELL. That's not quite the same thing. In fact the two things rarely go together. (*Sees* JACK *and bows to him with icy coldness.*)

ALGERNON (to GWENDOLEN). Dear me, you are smart!

GWENDOLEN. I am always smart! Am I not, Mr. Worthing?

JACK. You're quite perfect, Miss Fairfax.

GWENDOLEN. Oh! I hope I am not that. It would leave no room for developments, and I intend to develop in many directions. (GWENDOLEN *and* JACK *sit down together in the corner.*)

LADY BRACKNELL. I'm sorry if we are a little late, Algernon, but I was obliged to call on dear Lady Harbury. I hadn't been there since her poor husband's death. I never saw a woman so altered; she looks quite twenty years younger. And now I'll have a cup of tea, and one of those nice cucumber sandwiches you promised me.

ALGERNON. Certainly, Aunt Augusta. (*Goes over to tea-table.*)

LADY BRACKNELL. Won't you come and sit here, Gwendolen?

GWENDOLEN. Thanks, mamma, I'm quite comfortable where I am.

ALGERNON (*picking up empty plate in horror*). Good heavens! Lane! Why are there no cucumber sandwiches? I ordered them specially.

LANE (*Gravely*). There were no cucumbers in the market this morning, sir. I went down twice.

ALGERNON. No cucumbers!

LANE. No, sir. Not even for ready money.

ALGERNON. That will do, Lane, thank you.

LANE. Thank you, sir. *(Goes out.)*

ALGERNON. I am greatly distressed, Aunt Augusta, about there being no cucumbers, not even for ready money.

LADY BRACKNELL. It really makes no matter, Algernon. I had some crumpets with Lady Harbury, who seems to me to be living entirely for pleasure now.

ALGERNON. I hear her hair has turned quite gold from grief.

LADY BRACKNELL. It certainly has changed its colour. From what cause I, of course, cannot say. (ALGERNON *crosses and hands tea.)* Thank you, I've quite a treat for you tonight, Algernon. I am going to send you down with Mary Farquhar. She is such a nice woman, and so attentive to her husband. It's delightful to watch them.

ALGERNON. I am afraid, Aunt Augusta, I shall have to give up the pleasure of dining with you tonight after all.

LADY BRACKNELL *(frowning)*. I hope not, Algernon. It would put my table completely out. Your uncle would have to dine upstairs. Fortunately he is accustomed to that.

ALGERNON. It is a great bore, and, I need hardly say, a terrible disappointment to me, but the fact is I have just had a telegram to say that my poor friend Bunbury is very ill again. (*Exchanges glances with* JACK.) They seem to think I should be with him.

LADY BRACKNELL. It is very strange. This Mr. Bunbury seems to suffer from curiously bad health.

ALGERNON. Yes; poor Bunbury is a dreadful invalid.

LADY BRACKNELL. Well, I must say, Algernon, that I think it is high time that Mr. Bunbury made up his mind whether he was going to live or to die. This shillyshallying with the question is absurd. Nor do I in any way approve of the modern sympathy with invalids. I consider it morbid. Illness of any kind is hardly a thing to be encouraged in others. Health is the primary duty of life. I am always telling that to your poor uncle, but he never seems to take much notice . . . as far as any improvement in his ailment goes. I should be much obliged if you would ask Mr. Bunbury, from me, to be and kind enough not to have a relapse on Saturday, for I rely on you to arrange my music for me. It is my last reception, and one wants something that will encourage conversation, particularly at the end of the season when everyone has practically said whatever they had to say, which, in most cases, was probably not much.

ALGERNON. I'll speak to Bunbury, Aunt Augusta, if he is still conscious, and I think I can promise you he'll be all right by Saturday. Of course the music is a great difficulty. You see, if one plays good music, people don't listen, and if one plays bad music people don't talk. But I'll run over the program I've drawn out, if you will kindly come into the next room for a moment.

LADY BRACKNELL. Thank you, Algernon. It is very thoughtful of you. (*Rising, and following* ALGERNON.) I'm sure the program will be delightful, after a few expurgations. French songs I cannot possibly allow. People always seem to think that they are improper, and either look shocked, which is vulgar, or laugh, which is worse. But German sounds a thoroughly respectable language, and, indeed I believe is so. Gwendolen, you will accompany me.

GWENDOLEN. Certainly, mamma. (LADY BRACKNELL *and* ALGERNON *go into the music-room,* GWENDOLEN *remains behind.*)

JACK. Charming day it has been, Miss Fairfax.

GWENDOLEN. Pray don't talk to me about the weather, Mr. Worthing. Whenever people talk to me about the weather, I always feel quite certain that they mean something else. And that makes me so nervous.

JACK. I do mean something else.

GWENDOLEN. I thought so. In fact, I am never wrong.

JACK. And I would like to be allowed to take advantage of Lady Bracknell's temporary absence. . . .

GWENDOLEN. I would certainly advise you to do so. Mamma has a way of coming back suddenly into a room that I have often had to speak to her about.

JACK (*nervously*). Miss Fairfax, ever since I met you I have admired you more than any girl . . . I have ever met since . . . I met you.

GWENDOLEN. Yes, I am quite well aware of the fact. And I often wish that in public, at any rate, you had been more demonstrative. For me you have always had an irresistible fascination. Even before I met you I was far from indifferent to you. (JACK *looks at her in amazement.*) We live, as I hope you know, Mr. Worthing, in an age of ideals. The fact is constantly mentioned in the more expensive monthly magazines, and has reached the provincial pulpits, I am told; and my ideal has always been to love someone of the name of Ernest. There is something in that name that inspires absolute confidence. The moment Algernon first mentioned to me that he had a friend called Ernest, I knew I was destined to love you.

JACK. You really love me, Gwendolen?

GWENDOLEN. Passionately!

JACK. Darling! You don't know how happy you've made me.

GWENDOLEN. My own Ernest!

JACK. But you don't really mean to say that you couldn't love me if my name wasn't Ernest?

GWENDOLEN. But your name is Ernest.

JACK. Yes, I know it is. But supposing it was something else? Do you mean to say you couldn't love me then?

GWENDOLEN (*glibly*). Ah! that is clearly a metaphysical speculation, and like most metaphysical speculations has very little reference at all to the actual facts of real life, as we know them.

JACK. Personally, darling, to speak quite candidly, I don't much care about the name of Ernest. . . . I don't think the name suits me at all.

GWENDOLEN. It suits you perfectly. It is a divine name. It has music of its own. It produces vibrations.

JACK. Well, really, Gwendolen, I must say that I think there are lots of other much nicer names. I think Jack, for instance, a charming name.

GWENDOLEN. Jack? . . . No, there is very little music in the name Jack, if any at all, indeed. It does not thrill. It produces absolutely no vibrations. . . . I have known several Jacks, and they all, without exception, were more than usually plain. Besides, Jack is a notorious domesticity for John! And I pity any woman who is married to a man called John. She would probably never be allowed to know the entrancing pleasure of a single moment's solitude. The only really safe name is Ernest.

JACK. Gwendolen, I must get christened at once—I mean we must get married at once. There is no time to be lost.

GWENDOLEN. Married, Mr. Worthing?

JACK (*astounded*). Well . . . surely. You know that I love you, and you led me to believe, Miss Fairfax, that you were not absolutely indifferent to me.

GWENDOLEN. I adore you. But you haven't proposed to me yet. Nothing has been said at all about marriage. The subject has not even been touched on.

JACK. Well . . . may I propose to you now?

GWENDOLEN. I think it would be an admirable opportunity. And to spare you any possible disappointment, Mr. Worthing, I think it only fair to tell you quite frankly beforehand that I am fully determined to accept you.

JACK. Gwendolen!

GWENDOLEN. Yes, Mr. Worthing, what have you got to say to me?

JACK. You know what I have got to say to you.

GWENDOLEN. Yes, but you don't say it.

JACK. Gwendolen, will you marry me? (*Goes on his knees.*)

GWENDOLEN. Of course I will, darling. How long you have been about it! I am afraid you have had very little experience in how to propose.

JACK. My own one, I have never loved any one in the world but you.

GWENDOLEN. Yes, but men often propose for practice. I know my brother Gerald does. All my girl-friends tell me so. What wonderfully blue eyes you have, Ernest! They are quite, quite blue. I hope you will always look at me just like that, especially when there are other people present. (*Enter* LADY BRACKNELL.)

LADY BRACKNELL. Mr. Worthing! Rise, sir, from this semirecumbent posture. It is most indecorous.

GWENDOLEN. Mamma! (*He tries to rise; she restrains him.*) I must beg you to retire. This is no place for you. Besides, Mr. Worthing has not quite finished yet.

LADY BRACKNELL. Finished what, may I ask?

GWENDOLEN. I am engaged to Mr. Worthing, mamma. (*They rise together.*)

LADY BRACKNELL. Pardon me, you are not engaged to any one. When you do become engaged to some one, I, or your father, should his health permit him, will inform you of the fact. An engagement should come on a young girl as a surprise, pleasant or unpleasant, as the case may be. It is hardly a matter that she could be allowed to arrange for herself. . . . And now I have a few questions to put to you, Mr. Worthing. While I am making these inquiries, you, Gwendolen, will wait for me below in the carriage.

GWENDOLEN (*reproachfully*). Mamma!

LADY BRACKNELL. In the carriage, Gwendolen! (GWENDOLEN *goes to the door. She and* JACK *blow kisses to each other behind* LADY BRACKNELL's *back.* LADY BRACKNELL *looks vaguely about as if she could not understand what the noise was. Finally turns round.*) Gwendolen, the carriage!

GWENDOLEN. Yes, mamma. (*Goes out, looking back at* JACK.)

LADY BRACKNELL (*sitting down*). You can take a seat, Mr. Worthing. (*Looks in her pocket for note-book and pencil.*)

JACK. Thank you, Lady Bracknell. I prefer standing.

LADY BRACKNELL (*pencil and note-book in hand*). I feel bound to tell you that you are not down on my list of eligible young men, although I have the same list as the dear Duchess of Bolton has. We work together, in fact. However, I am quite ready to enter your name, should your answers be what a really affectionate mother requires. Do you smoke?

JACK. Well, yes, I must admit I smoke.

LADY BRACKNELL. I am glad to hear it. A man should always have an occupation of some kind. There are far too many idle men in London as it is. How old are you?

JACK. Twenty-nine.

LADY BRACKNELL. A very good age to be married at. I have always been of opinion that a man who desires to get married should know either everything or nothing. Which do you know?

JACK (*after some hesitation*). I know nothing, Lady Bracknell.

LADY BRACKNELL. I am pleased to hear it. I do not approve of anything that tampers with natural ignorance. Ignorance is like a delicate exotic fruit; touch it and the bloom is gone. The whole theory of modern education is radically unsound. Fortunately in England, at any rate, education produces no effect whatsoever. If it did, it would prove a serious danger to the upper classes, and probably lead to acts of violence in Grosvenor Square. What is your income?

JACK. Between seven and eight thousand a year.

LADY BRACKNELL (*makes a note in her book*). In land, or in investments?

JACK. In investments, chiefly.

LADY BRACKNELL. That is satisfactory. What between the duties expected of one during one's lifetime, and the duties exacted from one after one's death, land has ceased to be either a profit or a pleasure. It gives one position, and prevents one from keeping it up. That's all that can be said about land.

JACK. I have a country house with some land, of course, attached to it, about fifteen hundred acres, I believe; but I don't depend on that for my real income. In fact, as far as I can make out, the poachers are the only people who make anything out of it.

LADY BRACKNELL. A country house! How many bedrooms? Well, that point can be cleared up afterwards. You have a town house, I hope? A girl with a simple, unspoiled nature, like Gwendolen, could hardly be expected to reside in the country.

JACK. Well, I own a house in Belgrave Square, but it is let by the year to Lady Bloxham. Of course, I can get it back whenever I like, at six months' notice.

LADY BRACKNELL. Lady Bloxham? I don't know her.

JACK. Oh, she goes about very little. She is a lady considerably advanced in years.

LADY BRACKNELL. Ah, nowadays that is no guarantee of respectability of character. What number in Belgrave Square?

JACK. 149.

LADY BRACKNELL (*shaking her head*). The unfashionable side. I thought there was something. However, that could easily be altered.

JACK. Do you mean the fashion, or the side?

LADY BRACKNELL (*sternly*). Both, if necessary, I presume. What are your politics?

JACK. Well, I am afraid 1 really have none. I am a Liberal Unionist.

LADY BRACKNELL. Oh, they count as Tories. They dine with us. Or come in the evening, at any rate. Now to minor matters. Are your parents living?

JACK. I have lost both my parents.

LADY BRACKNELL. To lose one parent, Mr. Worthing, may be regarded as a misfortune; to lose both looks like carelessness. Who was your father? He was evidently a man of some wealth. Was he born in what the Radical papers call the purple of commerce, or did he rise from the ranks of the aristocracy?

JACK. I am afraid I really don't know. The fact is, Lady Bracknell, I said I had lost my parents. It would be nearer the truth to say that my parents seem to have lost me. . . . I don't actually know who I am by birth. I was . . . well, I was found.

LADY BRACKNELL. Found!

JACK. The late Mr. Thomas Cardew, an old gentleman of a very charitable and kindly disposition, found me, and gave me the name of Worthing, because he happened to have a first-class ticket for Worthing in his pocket at the time. Worthing is a place in Sussex. It is a seaside resort.

LADY BRACKNELL. Where did the charitable gentleman who had a first-class ticket for this seaside resort find you?

JACK (*gravely*). In a hand-bag.

LADY BRACKNELL. A hand-bag?

JACK (*very seriously*). Yes, Lady Bracknell. I was in a hand-bag—a somewhat large, black leather hand-bag, with handles to it—an ordinary hand-bag in fact.

LADY BRACKNELL. In what locality did this Mr. James, or Thomas, Cardew come across this ordinary hand-bag?

JACK. In the cloak-room at Victoria Station. It was given to him in mistake for his own.

LADY BRACKNELL. The cloak-room at Victoria Station?

JACK. Yes. The Brighton line.

LADY BRACKNELL. The line is immaterial. Mr. Worthing, I confess I feel somewhat bewildered by what you have just told me. To be born, or at any rate bred, in a hand-bag, whether it had handles or not, seems to me to display a contempt for the ordinary decencies of family life that reminds one of the worst excesses of the French Revolution. And I presume you know what that unfortunate movement led to? As for the particular locality in which the hand-bag was found, a cloak-room at a railway station might serve to conceal a social indiscretion—has probably, indeed, been used for that purpose before now—but it could hardly be regarded as an assured basis for a recognized position in good society.

JACK. May I ask you then what you would advise me to do? I need hardly say I would do anything in the world to ensure Gwendolen's happiness.

LADY BRACKNELL. I would strongly advise you, Mr. Worthing, to try and acquire some relations as soon as possible, and to make a definite effort to produce at any rate one parent, of either sex, before the season is quite over.

JACK. Well, I don't see how I could possibly manage to do that. I can produce the hand-bag at any moment. It is in my dressing-room at home. I really think that should satisfy you, Lady Bracknell.

LADY BRACKNELL. Me, sir! What has it to do with me? You can hardly imagine that I and Lord Bracknell would dream of allowing our only daughter—a girl brought up with the utmost care—to marry into a cloak-room, and form an alliance with a parcel. Good morning, Mr. Worthing! (LADY BRACKNELL *sweeps out in majestic indignation.*)

JACK. Good morning! (ALGERNON, *from the other room, strikes up the Wedding March.* JACK *looks perfectly furious and goes to the door.*) For goodness' sake don't play that ghastly tune, Algy! How idiotic you are! (*The music stops and* ALGERNON *enters cheerily.*)

ALGERNON. Didn't it go off all right, old boy? You don't mean to say Gwendolen refused you? I know it is a way she has. She is always refusing people. I think it is most ill-natured of her.

JACK. Oh, Gwendolen is as right as a trivet. As far as she is concerned, we are engaged. Her mother is perfectly unbearable. Never met such a Gorgon. . . . I don't really know what a Gorgon is like, but I am quite sure that Lady Bracknell is one. In any case, she is a monster, without being a myth, which is rather unfair. . . . I beg your pardon, Algy, I suppose I shouldn't talk about your own aunt in that way before you.

ALGERNON. My dear boy, I love hearing my relations abused. It is the only thing that makes me put up with them at all. Relations are simply a tedious pack of people, who haven't got the remotest knowledge of how to live, nor the smallest instinct about when to die.

JACK. Oh, that is nonsense!

ALGERNON. It isn't!

JACK. Well, I won't argue about the matter. You always want to argue about things.

ALGERNON. That is exactly what things were originally made for.

JACK. Upon my word, if I thought that, I'd shoot myself. . . . (*A pause.*) You don't think there is any chance of Gwendolen becoming like her mother in about a hundred and fifty years, do you, Algy?

ALGERNON. All women become like their mothers. That is their tragedy. No man does. That's his.

JACK. Is that clever?

ALGERNON. It is perfectly phrased! and quite as true as any observation in civilized life should be.

JACK. I am sick to death of cleverness. Everybody is clever nowadays. You can't go anywhere without meeting clever people. The thing has become an absolute public nuisance. I wish to goodness we had a few fools left.

ALGERNON. We have.

JACK. I should extremely like to meet them. What do they talk about?

ALGERNON. The fools? Oh! about the clever people, of course.

JACK. What fools.

ALGERNON. By the way, did you tell Gwendolen the truth about your being Ernest in town, and Jack in the country?

JACK (*in a very patronizing manner*). My dear fellow, the truth isn't quite the sort of thing one tells to a nice, sweet, refined girl. What extraordinary ideas you have about the way to behave to a woman!

ALGERNON. The only way to behave to a woman is to make love to her, if she is pretty, and to someone else, if she is plain.

JACK. Oh, that is nonsense.

ALGERNON. What about your brother? What about the profligate Ernest?

JACK. Oh, before the end of the week I shall have got rid of him. I'll say he died in Paris of apoplexy. Lots of people die of apoplexy, quite suddenly, don't they?

ALGERNON. Yes, but it's hereditary, my dear fellow. It's a sort of thing that runs in families. You had much better say a severe chill.

JACK. You are sure a severe chill isn't hereditary, or anything of that kind?

ALGERNON. Of course it isn't!

JACK. Very well, then. My poor brother Ernest is carried off suddenly, in Paris, by a severe chill. That gets rid of him.

ALGERNON. But I thought you said that . . . Miss Cardew was a little too much interested in your poor brother Ernest? Won't she feel his loss a good deal?

JACK. Oh, that is all right. Cecily is not a silly romantic girl, I am glad to say. She has got a capital appetite, goes long walks, and pays no attention at all to her lessons.

ALGERNON. I would rather like to see Cecily.

JACK. I will take very good care you never do. She is excessively pretty, and she is only just eighteen.

ALGERNON. Have you told Gwendolen yet that you have an excessively pretty ward who is only just eighteen?

JACK. Oh! one doesn't blurt these things out to people. Cecily and Gwendolen are perfectly certain to be extremely great friends. I'll bet you anything you like that half an hour after they have met, they will be calling each other sister.

ALGERNON. Women only do that when they have called each other a lot of other things first. Now, my dear boy, if we want to get a good table at Willis's, we really must go and dress. Do you know it is nearly seven?

JACK (*irritably*). Oh! it always is nearly seven.

ALGERNON. I'm hungry.

JACK. I never knew you when you weren't. . . .

ALGERNON. What shall we do after dinner? Go to a theatre?

JACK. Oh, no! I loathe listening.

ALGERNON. Well, let us go to the Club?

JACK. Oh, no! I hate talking.

ALGERNON. Well, we might trot round to the Empire at ten?

JACK: Oh, no! I can't bear looking at things. It is so silly.

ALGERNON. Well, what shall we do?

JACK. Nothing!

ALGERNON. It is awfully hard work doing nothing. However, I don't mind hard work where there is no definite object of any kind. (*Enter* LANE.)

LANE. Miss Fairfax. (*Enter* GWENDOLEN. LANE *goes out.*)

ALGERNON. Gwendolen, upon my word!

GWENDOLEN. Algy, kindly turn your back. I have something very particular to say to Mr. Worthing.

ALGERNON. Really, Gwendolen, I don't think I can allow this at all.

GWENDOLEN. Algy, you always adopt a strictly immoral attitude towards life. You are not quite old enough to do that. (ALGERNON *retires to the fireplace.*)

JACK. My own darling!

GWENDOLEN. Ernest, we may never be married. From the expression on mamma's face I fear we never shall. Few parents nowadays pay any regard to what their children say to them. The old-fashioned respect for the young is fast dying out. Whatever influence I ever had over mamma, I lost at the age of three. But although she may prevent us from becoming man and wife, and I may marry someone else, and marry often, nothing that she can possibly do can alter my eternal devotion to you.

JACK. Dear Gwendolen!

GWENDOLEN. The story of your romantic origin, as related to me by mamma, with unpleasing comments, has naturally stirred the deeper fibers of my nature. Your Christian name has an irresistible fascination. The simplicity of your character makes you exquisitely incomprehensible to me. Your town address at the Albany I have. What is your address in the country?

JACK. The Manor House, Woolton, Hertfordshire. (ALGERNON, *who has been carefully listening, smiles to himself, and writes the address on his shirt-cuff. Then picks up the* Railway Guide.)

GWENDOLEN. There is a good postal service, I suppose? It may be necessary to do something desperate. That of course will require serious consideration. I will communicate with you daily.

JACK. My own one!

GWENDOLEN. How long do you remain in town?

JACK. Till Monday.

GWENDOLEN. Good! Algy, you may turn round now.

ALGERNON. Thanks, I've turned round already.

GWENDOLEN. You may also ring the bell.

JACK. You will let me see you to your carriage, my own darling?

GWENDOLEN. Certainly.

JACK (*to* LANE, *who now enters*). I will see Miss Fairfax out.

LANE. Yes, sir. (JACK and GWENDOLEN *go off*). LANE *presents several letters on a salver, to* ALGERNON. *It is to be surmised that they are bills, as* ALGERNON, *after looking at the envelopes, tears them up.*)

ALGERNON. A glass of sherry, Lane.

LANE. Yes, sir.

ALGERNON. Tomorrow, Lane, I'm going Bunburying.

LANE. Yes, sir.

ALGERNON. I shall probably not be back till Monday. You can put up my dress clothes, my smoking jacket, and all the Bunbury suits . . .

LANE. Yes, sir. (*Handing sherry.*)

ALGERNON. I hope tomorrow will be a fine day, Lane.

LANE. It never is, sir.

ALGERNON. Lane, you're a perfect pessimist.

LANE. I do best to give satisfaction, sir. (*Enter* JACK. LANE *goes off.*)

JACK. There's a sensible, intellectual girl! the only girl I ever cared for in my life. (ALGERNON *is laughing immoderately.*) What on earth are you so amused at?

ALGERNON. Oh, I'm a little anxious about poor Bunbury, that is all.

JACK. If you don't take care, your friend Bunbury will get you into a serious scrape some day.

ALGERNON. I love scrapes. They are the only things that are never serious.

JACK. Oh, that's nonsense, Algy. You never talk anything but nonsense.

ALGERNON. Nobody ever does. (JACK *looks indignantly at him, and leaves the room.* ALGERNON *lights a cigarette, reads his shirt-cuff, and smiles.*)

ACT DROP

SECOND ACT

SCENE: *Garden at the Manor House. A flight of grey stone steps leads up to the house. The garden, an old-fashioned one, full of roses. Time of year, July. Basket chairs, and a table covered with books, are set under a large yew-tree.*

(MISS PRISM *discovered seated at the table.* CECILY *is at the back, watering flowers.*)

MISS PRISM (*calling*). Cecily, Cecily! Surely such a utilitarian occupation as the watering of flowers is rather Moulton's duty than yours? Especially at a moment when intellectual pleasures await you. Your German grammar is on the table. Pray open it at page fifteen. We will repeat yesterday's lesson.

CECILY (*coming over very slowly*). But I don't like German. It isn't at all a becoming language. I know perfectly well that I look quite plain after my German lesson.

MISS PRISM. Child, you know how anxious your guardian is that you should improve yourself in every way. He laid particular stress on your German, as he was leaving for town yesterday. Indeed, he always lays stress on your German when he is leaving for town.

CECILY. Dear Uncle Jack is so very serious! Sometimes he is so serious that I think he cannot be quite well.

MISS PRISM (*drawing herself up*). Your guardian enjoys the best of health, and his gravity of demeanour is especially to be commended in one so comparatively young as he is. I know no one who has a higher sense of duty and responsibility.

CECILY. I suppose that is why he often looks a little bored when we three are together.

MISS PRISM. Cecily! I am surprised at you. Mr. Worthing has many troubles in his life. Idle merriment and triviality would be out of place in his conversation. You must remember his constant anxiety about that unfortunate young man his brother.

CECILY. I wish Uncle Jack would allow that unfortunate young man, his brother, to come down here sometimes. We might have a good influence over him, Miss Prism. I am sure you certainly would. You know German, and geology, and things of that kind influence a man very much. (CECILY *begins to write in her diary*.)

MISS PRISM (*shaking her head*). I do not think that even I could produce any effect on a character that according to his own brother's admission is irretrievably weak and vacillating. Indeed I am not sure that I would desire to reclaim him. I am not in favour of this modern mania for turning bad people into good people at a moment's notice. As a man sows so let him reap. You must put away your diary, Cecily. I really don't see why you should keep a diary at all.

CECILY. I keep a diary in order to enter the wonderful secrets of my life. If I didn't write them down, I should probably forget all about them.

MISS PRISM. Memory, my dear Cecily, is the diary that we all carry about with us.

CECILY. Yes, but it usually chronicles the things that have never happened, and couldn't possibly have happened. I believe that Memory is responsible for nearly all the three-volume novels that Mudie sends us.

MISS PRISM. Do not speak slightingly of the three-volume novel, Cecily. I wrote one myself in earlier days.

CECILY. Did you really, Miss Prism? How wonderfully clever you are! I hope it did not end happily? I don't like novels that end happily. They depress me so much.

MISS PRISM. The good ended happily, and the bad unhappily. That is what Fiction means.

CECILY. I suppose so. But it seems very unfair. And was your novel ever published?

MISS PRISM. Alas! no. The manuscript unfortunately was abandoned. (CECILY *starts.*) I used the word in the sense of lost or mislaid. To your work, child, these speculations are profitless.

CECILY (*smiling*). But I see dear Dr. Chasuble coming up through the garden.

MISS PRISM (*rising and advancing*). Dr. Chasuble! This is indeed a pleasure. (*Enter* CANON CHASUBLE.)

CHASUBLE. And how are we this morning? Miss Prism, you are, I trust, well?

CECILY. Miss Prism has just been complaining of a slight headache. I think it would do her so much good to have a short stroll with you in the Park, Dr. Chasuble.

MISS PRISM. Cecily, I have not mentioned anything about a headache.

CECILY. No, dear Miss Prism, I know that, but I felt instinctively that you had a headache. Indeed I was thinking about that, and not about my German lesson, when the Rector came in.

CHASUBLE. I hope, Cecily, you are not inattentive.

CECILY. Oh, I am afraid I am.

CHASUBLE. That is strange. Were I fortunate enough to be Miss Prism's pupil, I would hang upon her lips. (MISS PRISM *glares.*) I spoke metaphorically.—My metaphor was drawn from bees. Ahem! Mr. Worthing, I suppose, has not returned from town yet?

MISS PRISM. We do not expect him till Monday afternoon.

CHASUBLE. Ah yes, he usually likes to spend his Sunday in London. He is not one of those whose sole aim is enjoyment, as, by all accounts, that unfortunate young man his brother seems to be. But I must not disturb Egeria and her pupil any longer.

MISS PRISM. Egeria? My name is Laetitia, Doctor.

CHASUBLE (*bowing*). A classical allusion merely, drawn from the Pagan authors. I shall see you both no doubt at Evensong?

MISS PRISM. I think, dear Doctor, I will have a stroll with you. I find I have a headache after all, and a walk might do it good.

CHASUBLE. With pleasure, Miss Prism, with pleasure. We might go as far as the schools and back.

MISS PRISM. That would be delightful. Cecily, you will read your Political Economy in my absence. The chapter on the Fall of the Rupee you may omit. It is somewhat too sensational. Even these metallic problems have their melodramatic side. (*Goes down the garden with* DR. CHASUBLE.)

CECILY (*picks up books and throws them back on table*). Horrid Political Economy! Horrid Geography! Horrid, horrid German! (*Enter* MERRIMAN *with a card on a salver.*)

MERRIMAN. Mr. Ernest Worthing has just driven over from the station. He has brought his luggage with him.

CECILY (*takes the card and reads it*). 'Mr. Ernest Worthing, B.4, The Albany, W.' Uncle Jack's brother! Did you tell him Mr. Worthing was in town?

MERRIMAN. Yes, Miss. He seemed very much disappointed. I mentioned that you and Miss Prism were in the garden. He said he was anxious to speak to you privately for a moment.

CECILY. Ask Mr. Ernest Worthing to come here. I suppose you had better talk to the housekeeper about a room for him.

MERRIMAN. Yes, Miss. (MERRIMAN *goes off.*)

CECILY. I have never met any really wicked person before. I feel rather frightened. I am so afraid he will look just like every one else. (*Enter* ALGERNON, *very gay and debonair.*) He does!

ALGERNON (*raising his hat*). You are my little cousin Cecily, I'm sure.

CECILY. You are under some strange mistake. I am not little. In fact, I believe I am more than usually tall for my age. (ALGERNON *is rather taken aback.*) But I am your cousin Cecily. You, I see from your card, are Uncle Jack's brother, my cousin Ernest, my wicked cousin Ernest.

ALGERNON. Oh! I am not really wicked at all, Cousin Cecily. You mustn't think that I am wicked.

CECILY. If you are not, then you have certainly been deceiving us all in a very inexcusable manner. I hope you have not been leading a double life, pretending to be wicked and being really good all the time. That would be hypocrisy.

ALGERNON (*looks at her in amazement*). Oh! Of course I have been rather reckless.

CECILY. I am glad to hear it.

ALGERNON. In fact, now you mention the subject, I have been very bad in my own small way.

CECILY. I don't think you should be so proud of that, though I am sure it must have been very pleasant.

ALGERNON. It is much pleasanter being here with you.

CECILY. I can't understand how you are here at all. Uncle Jack won't be back till Monday afternoon.

ALGERNON. That is a great disappointment. I am obliged to go up by the first train on Monday morning. I have a business appointment that I am anxious . . . to miss!

CECILY. Couldn't you miss it anywhere but in London?

ALGERNON. No, the appointment is in London.

CECILY. Well, I know, of course, how important it is not to keep a business engagement, if one wants to retain any sense of the beauty of life, but still I think you had better wait till Uncle Jack arrives. I know he wants to speak to you about your emigrating.

ALGERNON. About my what?

CECILY. Your emigrating. He has gone up to buy your outfit.

ALGERNON. I certainly wouldn't let Jack buy my outfit. He has no taste in neckties at all.

CECILY. I don't think you will require neckties. Uncle Jack is sending you to Australia.

ALGERNON. Australia! I'd sooner die.

CECILY. Well, he said at dinner on Wednesday night, that you would have to choose between this world, the next world, and Australia.

ALGERNON. Oh, well! The accounts I have received of Australia and the next world are not particularly encouraging. This world is good enough for me, Cousin Cecily.

CECILY. Yes, but are you good enough for it?

ALGERNON. I'm afraid I'm not that. That is why I want you to reform me. You might make that your mission, if you don't mind, Cousin Cecily.

CECILY. I'm afraid I've no time, this afternoon.

ALGERNON. Well, would you mind my reforming myself this afternoon?

CECILY. It is rather Quixotic of you. But I think you should try.

ALGERNON. I will. I feel better already.

CECILY. You are looking a little worse.

ALGERNON. That is because I am hungry.

CECILY. How thoughtless of me. I should have remembered that when one is going to lead an entirely new life, one requires regular and wholesome meals. Won't you come in?

ALGERNON. Thank you. Might I have a buttonhole first? I have never any appetite unless I have a buttonhole first.

CECILY. A Maréchal Niel? (*Picks up scissors.*)

ALGERNON. No, I'd sooner have a pink rose.

CECILY. Why? (*Cuts a flower.*)

ALGERNON. Because you are like a pink rose, Cousin Cecily.

CECILY. I don't think it can be right for you to talk to me like that. Miss Prism never says such things to me.

ALGERNON. Then Miss Prism is a short-sighted old lady. (CECILY *puts the rose in his buttonhole.*) You are the prettiest girl I ever saw.

CECILY. Miss Prism says that all good looks are a snare.

ALGERNON. They are a snare that every sensible man would like to be caught in.

CECILY. Oh, I don't think I would care to catch a sensible man. I shouldn't know what to talk to him about. (*They pass into the house.* MISS PRISM *and* DR. CHASUBLE *return.*)

MISS PRISM. You are too much alone, dear Dr. Chasuble. You should get married. A misanthrope I can understand—a womanthrope, never!

CHASUBLE (*with a scholar's shudder*). Believe me, I do not deserve so neologistic a phrase. The precept as well as the practice of the Primitive Church was distinctly against matrimony.

MISS PRISM (*sententiously*). That is obviously the reason why the Primitive Church has not lasted up to the present day. And you do not seem to realize, dear Doctor, that by persistently remaining single, a man converts himself into a permanent public temptation. Men should be more careful; this very celibacy leads weaker vessels astray.

CHASUBLE. But is a man not equally attractive when married?

MISS PRISM. No married man is ever attractive except to his wife.

CHASUBLE. And often, I've been told, not even to her.

MISS PRISM. That depends on the intellectual sympathies of the woman. Maturity can always be depended on. Ripeness can be trusted. Young women are green. (DR. CHASUBLE *starts.*) I spoke horticulturally. My metaphor was drawn from fruits. But where is Cecily?

CHASUBLE. Perhaps she followed us to the schools. (*Enter* JACK *slowly from the back of the garden. He is dressed in the deepest mourning, with crepe hatband and black gloves.*)

MISS PRISM. Mr. Worthing!

CHASUBLE. Mr. Worthing? This is indeed a surprise. We did not look for you till Monday afternoon.

JACK (*shakes* MISS PRISM'S *hand in a tragic manner*). I have returned sooner than I expected. Dr. Chasuble, I hope you are well?

CHASUBLE. Dear Mr. Worthing, I trust this garb of woe does not betoken some terrible calamity?

JACK. My brother.

MISS PRISM. More shameful debts and extravagance?

CHASUBLE. Still leading his life of pleasure?

JACK (*shaking his head*). Dead!

CHASUBLE. Your brother Ernest dead?

JACK. Quite dead.

MISS PRISM. What a lesson for him! I trust he will profit by it.

CHASUBLE. Mr. Worthing, I offer you my sincere condolence. You have at least the consolation of knowing that you were always the most generous and forgiving of brothers.

JACK. Poor Ernest! He had many faults, but it is a sad, sad blow.

CHASUBLE. Very sad indeed. Were you with him at the end?

JACK. No. He died abroad; in Paris, in fact. I had a telegram last night from the manager of the Grand Hotel.

CHASUBLE. Was the cause of death mentioned?

JACK. A severe chill, it seems.

MISS PRISM. As a man sows, so shall he reap.

CHASUBLE (*raising his hand*). Charity, dear Miss Prism, charity! None of us are perfect. I myself am peculiarly susceptible to draughts. Will the interment take place here?

JACK. No. He seems to have expressed a desire to be buried in Paris.

CHASUBLE. In Paris! (*Shakes his head.*) I fear that hardly points to any very serious state of mind at the last. You would no doubt wish me to make some slight allusion to this tragic domestic affliction next Sunday. (JACK *presses his hand convulsively.*) My sermon on the meaning of the manna in the wilderness can be adapted to almost any occasion, joyful, or, as in the present case, distressing. (*All sigh.*) I have preached it at harvest celebrations, christenings, confirmations, on days of humiliation and festal days. The last time I delivered it was in the Cathedral, as a charity sermon on behalf of the Society for the Prevention of Discontent among the Upper Orders. The Bishop, who was present, was much struck by some of the analogies I drew.

JACK. Ah! that reminds me, you mentioned christenings I think,
Dr. Chasuble? I suppose you know how to christen all right?
(DR. CHASUBLE *looks astounded.*) I mean, of course, you are continually
christening, aren't you?

MISS PRISM. It is, I regret to say, one of the Rector's most constant duties
in this parish. I have often spoken to the poorer classes on the subject.
But they don't seem to know what thrift is.

CHASUBLE. But is there any particular infant in whom you are
interested, Mr. Worthing? Your brother was, I believe, unmarried,
was he not?

JACK. Oh yes.

MISS PRISM (*bitterly*). People who live entirely for pleasure usually are.

JACK. But it is not for any child, dear Doctor. I am very fond of children.
No! the fact is, I would like to be christened myself, this afternoon, if
you have nothing better to do.

CHASUBLE. But surely, Mr. Worthing, you have been christened already?

JACK. I don't remember anything about it.

CHASUBLE. But have you any grave doubts on the subject?

JACK. I certainly intend to have. Of course I don't know if the thing
would bother you in any way, or if you think I am a little too old now.

CHASUBLE. Not at all. The sprinkling, and, indeed, the immersion of
adults is a perfectly canonical practice.

JACK. Immersion!

CHASUBLE. You need have no apprehensions. Sprinkling is all that is
necessary, or indeed I think advisable. Our weather is so changeable.
At what hour would you wish the ceremony performed?

JACK. Oh, I might trot round about five if that would suit you.

CHASUBLE. Perfectly, perfectly! In fact I have two similar ceremonies to
perform at that time. A case of twins that occurred recently in one of
the outlying cottages on your own estate. Poor Jenkins the carter, a
most hard-working man.

JACK. Oh! I don't see much fun in being christened along with other
babies. It would be childish. Would half-past five do?

CHASUBLE. Admirably! Admirably! (*Takes out watch.*) And now,
dear Mr. Worthing, I will not intrude any longer into a house
of sorrow. I would merely beg you not to be too much bowed
down by grief. What seem to us bitter trials are often blessings in
disguise.

MISS PRISM. This seems to me a blessing of an extremely obvious kind.
(*Enter* CECILY *from the house.*)

CECILY. Uncle Jack! Oh, I am pleased to see you back. But what horrid
clothes you have got on. Do go and change them.

MISS PRISM. Cecily!

CHASUBLE. My child! my child. (CECILY *goes toward* JACK; *he kisses her brow in a melancholy manner.*)

CECILY. What is the matter, Uncle Jack? Do look happy! You look as if you had toothache, and I have got such a surprise for you. Who do you think is in the dining-room? Your brother!

JACK. Who?

CECILY. Your brother Ernest. He arrived about half an hour ago.

JACK. What nonsense! I haven't got a brother.

CECILY. Oh, don't say that. However badly he may have behaved to you in the past he is still your brother. You couldn't be so heartless as to disown him. I'll tell him to come out. And you will shake hands with him, won't you, Uncle Jack? (*Runs back into the house.*)

CHASUBLE. These are very joyful tidings.

MISS PRISM. After we had all been resigned to his loss, his sudden return seems to me peculiarly distressing.

JACK. My brother is in the dining-room? I don't know what it all means. I think it is perfectly absurd. (*Enter* ALGERNON *and* CECILY *hand in hand. They come slowly up to* JACK.)

JACK. Good heavens! (*Motions* ALGERNON *away.*)

ALGERNON. Brother John, I have come down from town to tell you that I am very sorry for all the trouble I have given you, and that I intend to lead a better life in the future. (JACK *glares at him and does not take his hand.*)

CECILY. Uncle Jack, you are not going to refuse your own brother's hand?

JACK. Nothing will induce me to take his hand. I think his coming down here disgraceful. He knows perfectly well why.

CECILY. Uncle Jack, do be nice. There is some good in everyone. Ernest has just been telling me about his poor invalid friend Mr. Bunbury whom he goes to visit so often. And surely there must be much good in one who is kind to an invalid, and leaves the pleasures of London to sit by a bed of pain.

JACK. Oh! he has been talking about Bunbury, has he?

CECILY. Yes, he has told me all about poor Mr. Bunbury, and his terrible state of health.

JACK. Bunbury! Well, I won't have him talk to you about Bunbury or about anything else. It is enough to drive one perfectly frantic.

ALGERNON. Of course I admit that the faults were all on my side. But I must say that I think that Brother John's coldness to me is peculiarly painful. I expected a more enthusiastic welcome especially considering it is the first time I have come here.

CECILY. Uncle Jack, if you don't shake hands with Ernest, I will never forgive you.

JACK. Never forgive me?

CECILY. Never, never, never!

JACK. Well, this is the last time I shall ever do it. (*Shakes hands with* ALGERNON *and glares.*)

CHASUBLE. It's pleasant, is it not, to see so perfect a reconciliation? I think we might leave the two brothers together.

MISS PRISM. Cecily, you will come with us.

CECILY. Certainly, Miss Prism. My little task of reconciliation is over.

CHASUBLE. You have done a beautiful action today, dear child.

MISS PRISM. We must not be premature in our judgments.

CECILY. I feel very happy. (*They all go off except* JACK *and* ALGERNON.)

JACK. You young scoundrel, Algy, you must get out of this place as soon as possible. I don't allow any Bunburying here. (*Enter* MERRIMAN.)

MERRIMAN. I have put Mr. Ernest's things in the room next to yours, sir. I suppose that is all right?

JACK. What?

MERRIMAN. Mr. Ernest's luggage, sir. I have unpacked it and put it in the room next to your own.

JACK. His luggage?

MERRIMAN. Yes, sir. Three portmanteaus, a dressing-case, two hatboxes, and a large luncheon-basket.

ALGERNON. I am afraid I can't stay more than a week this time.

JACK. Merriman, order the dog-cart at once. Mr. Ernest has been suddenly called back to town.

MERRIMAN. Yes, sir. (*Goes back into the house.*)

ALGERNON. What a fearful liar you are, Jack. I have not been called back to town at all.

JACK. Yes, you have.

ALGERNON. I haven't heard any one call me.

JACK. Your duty as a gentleman calls you back.

ALGERNON. My duty as a gentleman has never interfered with my pleasures in the smallest degree.

JACK. I can quite understand that.

ALGERNON. Well, Cecily is a darling.

JACK. You are not to talk of Miss Cardew like that. I don't like it.

ALGERNON. Well, I don't like your clothes. You look perfectly ridiculous in them. Why on earth don't you go up and change? It is perfectly childish to be in deep mourning for a man who is actually staying for a whole week with you in your house as a guest. I call it grotesque.

JACK. You are certainly not staying with me for a whole week as a guest or anything else. You have got to leave . . . by the four-five train.

ALGERNON. I certainly won't leave you so long as you are in mourning. It would be most unfriendly. If I were in mourning you would stay with me, I suppose. I should think it very unkind if you didn't.

JACK. Well, will you go if I change my clothes?

ALGERNON. Yes, if you are not too long. I never saw anybody take so long to dress, and with such little result.

JACK. Well, at any rate, that is better than being always over-dressed as you are.

ALGERNON. If I am occasionally a little over-dressed, I make up for it by being always immensely over-educated.

JACK. Your vanity is ridiculous, your conduct an outrage, and your presence in my garden utterly absurd. However, you have got to catch the four-five, and I hope you will have a pleasant journey back to town. This Bunburying, as you call it, has not been a great success for you. (*Goes into the house.*)

ALGERNON. I think it has been a great success. I'm in love with Cecily, and that is everything. (*Enter* CECILY *at the back of the garden. She picks up the can and begins to water the flowers.*) But I must see her before I go, and make arrangements for another Bunbury. Ah, there she is.

CECILY. Oh, I merely came back to water the roses. I thought you were with Uncle Jack.

ALGERNON. He's gone to order the dog-cart for me.

CECILY. Oh, is he going to take you for a nice drive?

ALGERNON. He's going to send me away.

CECILY. Then have we got to part?

ALGERNON. I am afraid so. It's a very painful parting.

CECILY. It is always painful to part from people whom one has known for a very brief space of time. The absence of old friends one can endure with equanimity. But even a momentary separation from any one to whom one has just been introduced is almost unbearable.

ALGERNON. Thank you. (*Enter* MERRIMAN.)

MERRIMAN. The dog-cart is at the door, sir. (ALGERNON *looks appealingly at* CECILY.)

CECILY. It can wait, Merriman . . . for . . . five minutes.

MERRIMAN. Yes, Miss. (*Exit* MERRIMAN.)

ALGERNON. I hope, Cecily, I shall not offend you if I state quite frankly and openly that you seem to me to be in every way the visible personification of absolute perfection.

CECILY. I think your frankness does you great credit, Ernest. If you will allow me, I will copy your remarks into my diary. (*Goes over to table and begins writing in diary.*)

ALGERNON. Do you really keep a diary? I'd give anything to look at it. May I?

CECILY. Oh no. (*Puts her hand over it.*) You see, it is simply a very young girl's record of her own thoughts and impressions, and consequently meant for publication. When it appears in volume form I hope you will order a copy. But pray, Ernest, don't stop. I delight in taking down from dictation. I have reached "absolute perfection." You can go on. I am quite ready for more.

ALGERNON (*somewhat taken aback*). Ahem! Ahem!

CECILY. Oh, don't cough, Ernest. When one is dictating one should speak fluently and not cough. Besides, I don't know how to spell a cough. (*Writes as* ALGERNON *speaks.*)

ALGERNON (*speaking very rapidly*). Cecily, ever since I first looked upon your wonderful and incomparable beauty, I have dared to love you wildly, passionately, devotedly, hopelessly.

CECILY. I don't think that you should tell me that you love me wildly, passionately, devotedly, hopelessly. Hopelessly doesn't seem to make much sense, does it?

ALGERNON. Cecily. (*Enter* MERRIMAN.)

MERRIMAN. The dog-cart is waiting, sir.

ALGERNON. Tell it to come round next week, at the same hour.

MERRIMAN (*looks at* CECILY, *who makes no sign*). Yes, sir. (MERRIMAN *retires.*)

CECILY. Uncle Jack would be very much annoyed if he knew you were staying on till next week, at the same hour.

ALGERNON. Oh, I don't care about Jack. I don't care for anybody in the whole world but you. I love you, Cecily. You will marry me, won't you?

CECILY. You silly boy! Of course. Why, we have been engaged for the last three months.

ALGERNON. For the last three months?

CECILY. Yes, it will be exactly three months on Thursday.

ALGERNON. But how did we become engaged?

CECILY. Well, ever since dear Uncle Jack first confessed to us that he had a younger brother who was very wicked and bad, you of course have formed the chief topic of conversation between myself and Miss Prism. And of course a man who is much talked about is always very attractive. One feels there must be something in him, after all. I daresay it was foolish of me, but I fell in love with you, Ernest.

ALGERNON. Darling. And when was the engagement actually settled?

CECILY. On the 14th of February last. Worn out by your entire ignorance of my existence, I determined to end the matter one way or the other, and after a long struggle with myself I accepted you under this dear old tree here. The next day I bought this little ring in your name, and this is the little bangle with the true lover's knot I promised you always to wear.

ALGERNON. Did I give you this? It's very pretty, isn't it?

CECILY. Yes, you've wonderfully good taste, Ernest. It's the excuse I've always given for your leading such a bad life. And this is the box in which I keep all your dear letters. (*Kneels at table, opens box, and produces letters tied up with blue ribbon.*)

ALGERNON. My letters! But, my own sweet Cecily, I have never written you any letters.

CECILY. You need hardly remind me of that, Ernest. I remember only too well that I was forced to write your letters for you. I wrote always three times a week, and sometimes oftener.

ALGERNON. Oh, do let me read them, Cecily?

CECILY. Oh, I couldn't possibly. They would make you far too conceited. (*Replaces box.*) The three you wrote me after I had broken off the engagement are so beautiful, and so badly spelled, that even now I can hardly read them without crying a little.

ALGERNON. But was our engagement ever broken off?

CECILY. Of course it was. On the 22nd of last March. You can see the entry if you like. (*Shows diary.*) 'Today I broke off my engagement with Ernest. I feel it is better to do so. The weather still continues charming.'

ALGERNON. But why on earth did you break it off? What had I done? I had done nothing at all. Cecily, I am very much hurt indeed to hear you broke it off. Particularly when the weather was so charming.

CECILY. It would hardly have been a really serious engagement if it hadn't been broken off at least once. But I forgave you before the week was out.

ALGERNON (*crossing to her, and kneeling*). What a perfect angel you are, Cecily.

CECILY. You dear romantic boy. (*He kisses her, she puts her fingers through his hair.*) I hope your hair curls naturally, does it?

ALGERNON. Yes, darling, with a little help from others.

CECILY. I am so glad.

ALGERNON. You'll never break off our engagement again, Cecily?

CECILY. I don't think I could break it off now that I have actually met you. Besides, of course, there is the question of your name.

ALGERNON. Yes, of course. (*Nervously.*)

CECILY. You must not laugh at me, darling, but it had always been a girlish dream of mine to love some one whose name was Ernest. (ALGERNON *rises,* CECILY *also.*) There is something in that name that seems to inspire absolute confidence. I pity any poor married woman whose husband is not called Ernest.

ALGERNON. But, my dear child, do you mean to say you could not love me if I had some other name?

CECILY. But what name?

ALGERNON. Oh, any name you like—Algernon—for instance . . .

CECILY. But I don't like the name of Algernon.

ALGERNON. Well, my own dear, sweet, loving little darling, I really can't see why you should object to the name of Algernon. It is not at all a bad name. In fact, it is rather an aristocratic name. Half of the chaps who get into the Bankruptcy Court are called Algernon. But seriously, Cecily . . . (*Moving to her.*) if my name was Algy, couldn't you love me?

CECILY (*rising*). I might respect you, Ernest, I might admire your character, but I fear that I should not be able to give you my undivided attention.

ALGERNON. Ahem! Cecily! (*Picking up hat.*) Your Rector here is, I suppose, thoroughly experienced in the practice of all the rites and ceremonials of the Church?

CECILY. Oh, yes. Dr. Chasuble is a most learned man. He has never written a single book, so you can imagine how much he knows.

ALGERNON. I must see him at once on a most important christening—I mean on most important business.

CECILY. Oh!

ALGERNON. I shan't be away more than half an hour.

CECILY. Considering that we have been engaged since February the 14th, and that I only met you to-day for the first time, I think it is rather hard that you should leave me for so long a period as half an hour. Couldn't you make it twenty minutes?

ALGERNON. I'll be back in no time. (*Kisses her and rushes down the garden.*)

CECILY. What an impetuous boy he is! I like his hair so much. I must enter his proposal in my diary. (*Enter* MERRIMAN.)

MERRIMAN. A Miss Fairfax has just called to see Mr. Worthing. On very important business, Miss Fairfax states.

CECILY. Isn't Mr. Worthing in his library?

MERRIMAN. Mr. Worthing went over in the direction of the Rectory some time ago.

CECILY. Pray ask the lady to come out here; Mr. Worthing is sure to be back soon. And you can bring tea.

MERRIMAN. Yes, Miss. (*Goes out.*)

CECILY. Miss Fairfax! I suppose one of the many good elderly women who are associated with Uncle Jack in some of his philanthropic work in London. I don't quite like women who are interested in philanthropic work. I think it is so forward of them. (*Enter* MERRIMAN.)

MERRIMAN. Miss Fairfax. (*Enter* GWENDOLEN. *Exit* MERRIMAN.)

CECILY (*advancing to meet her*). Pray let me introduce myself to you. My name is Cecily Cardew.

GWENDOLEN. Cecily Cardew? (*Moving to her and shaking hands.*) What a very sweet name! Something tells me that we are going to be great friends. I like you already more than I can say. My first impressions of people are never wrong.

CECILY. How nice of you to like me so much after we have known each other such a comparatively short time. Pray sit down.

GWENDOLEN (*still standing up*). I may call you Cecily, may I not?

CECILY. With pleasure!

GWENDOLEN. And you will always call me Gwendolen, won't you?

CECILY. If you wish.

GWENDOLEN. Then that is all quite settled, is it not?

CECILY. I hope so. (*A pause. They both sit down together.*)

GWENDOLEN. Perhaps this might be a favourable opportunity for my mentioning who I am. My father is Lord Bracknell. You have never heard of papa, I suppose?

CECILY. I don't think so.

GWENDOLEN. Outside the family circle, papa, I am glad to say, is entirely unknown. I think that is quite as it should be. The home seems to me to be the proper sphere for the man. And certainly once a man begins to neglect his domestic duties he becomes painfully effeminate, does he not? And I don't like that. It makes men so very attractive. Cecily, mamma, whose views on education are remarkably strict, has brought me up to be extremely short-sighted; it is part of her system; so do you mind my looking at you through my glasses?

CECILY. Oh! not at all, Gwendolen. I am very fond of being looked at.

GWENDOLEN (*after examining* CECILY *carefully through a lorgnette*). You are here on a short visit, I suppose.

CECILY. Oh no! I live here.

GWENDOLEN (*severely*). Really? Your mother, no doubt, or some female relative of advanced years, resides here also?

CECILY. Oh no! I have no mother, nor, in fact, any relations.

GWENDOLEN. Indeed?

CECILY. My dear guardian, with the assistance of Miss Prism, has the arduous task of looking after me.

GWENDOLEN. Your guardian?

CECILY. Yes, I am Mr. Worthing's ward.

GWENDOLEN. Oh! It is strange he never mentioned to me that he had a ward. How secretive of him! He grows more interesting hourly. I am not sure, however, that the news inspires me with feelings of unmixed delight. *(Rising and going to her.)* I am very fond of you, Cecily; I have liked you ever since I met you! But I am bound to state that now that I know that you are Mr. Worthing's ward, I cannot help expressing a wish you were—well, just a little older than you seem to be—and not quite so very alluring in appearance. In fact, if I may speak candidly—

CECILY. Pray do! I think that whenever one has anything unpleasant to say, one should always be quite candid.

GWENDOLEN. Well, to speak with perfect candour, Cecily, I wish that you were fully forty-two, and more than usually plain for your age. Ernest has a strong upright nature. He is the very soul of truth and honor. Disloyalty would be as impossible to him as deception. But even men of the noblest possible moral character are extremely susceptible to the influence of the physical charms of others. Modern, no less than Ancient History, supplies us with many most painful examples of what I refer to. If it were not so, indeed, History would be quite unreadable.

CECILY. I beg your pardon, Gwendolen, did you say Ernest?

GWENDOLEN. Yes.

CECILY. Oh, but it is not Mr. Ernest Worthing who is my guardian. It is his brother—his elder brother.

GWENDOLEN *(sitting down again)*. Ernest never mentioned to me that he had a brother.

CECILY. Sorry to say they have not been on good terms for a long time.

GWENDOLEN. Ah! that accounts for it. And now that I think of it I have never heard any man mention his brother. The subject seems distasteful to most men. Cecily, you have lifted a load from my mind. I was growing almost anxious. It would have been terrible if any cloud had come across a friendship like ours, would it not? Of course you are quite, quite sure that it is not Mr. Ernest Worthing who is your guardian?

CECILY. Quite sure. *(A pause.)* In fact, I am going to be his.

GWENDOLEN *(inquiringly)*. I beg your pardon?

CECILY *(rather shy and confidingly)*. Dearest Gwendolen, there is no reason why I should make a secret of it to you. Our little county newspaper is sure to chronicle the fact next week. Mr. Ernest Worthing and I are engaged to be married.

GWENDOLEN (*quite politely, rising*). My darling Cecily, I think there must be some slight error. Mr. Ernest Worthing is engaged to me. The announcement will appear in the *Morning Post* on Saturday at the latest.

CECILY (*very politely, rising*). I am afraid you must be under some misconception. Ernest proposed to me exactly ten minutes ago. (*Shows diary.*)

GWENDOLEN (*examines through her lorgnette carefully*). It is very curious, for he asked me to be his wife yesterday afternoon at 5:30. If you would care to verify the incident, pray do so. (*Produces diary of her own.*) I never travel without my diary. One should always have something sensational to read in the train. I am so sorry, dear Cecily, if it is any disappointment to you, but I am afraid I have the prior claim.

CECILY. It would distress me more than I can tell you, dear Gwendolen, if it caused you any mental or physical anguish, but I feel bound to point out that since Ernest proposed to you he clearly has changed his mind.

GWENDOLEN (*meditatively*). If the poor fellow has been entrapped into any foolish promise, I shall consider it my duty to rescue him at once, and with a firm hand.

CECILY (*thoughtfully and sadly*). Whatever unfortunate entanglement my dear boy may have got into, I will never reproach him with it after we are married.

GWENDOLEN. Do you allude to me, Miss Cardew, as an entanglement? You are presumptuous. On an occasion of this kind it becomes more than a moral duty to speak one's mind. It becomes a pleasure.

CECILY. Do you suggest, Miss Fairfax, that I entrapped Ernest into an engagement? How dare you? This is no time for wearing the shallow mask of manners. When I see a spade I call it a spade.

GWENDOLEN (*satirically*). I am glad to say that I have never seen a spade. It is obvious that our social spheres have been widely different. (*Enter* MERRIMAN, *followed by the footman. He carries a salver, table cloth, and plate stand.* CECILY *is about to retort. The presence of the servants exercises a restraining influence under which both girls chafe.*)

MERRIMAN. Shall I lay tea here as usual, Miss?

CECILY (*sternly, in a calm voice*). Yes, as usual. (MERRIMAN *begins to clear table and lay cloth. A long pause.* CECILY *and* GWENDOLEN *glare at each other.*)

GWENDOLEN. Are there many interesting walks in the vicinity, Miss Cardew?

CECILY. Oh! yes! a great many. From the top of one of the hills quite close one can see five counties.

GWENDOLEN. Five counties! I don't think I should like that; I hate crowds.

CECILY (*sweetly*). I suppose that is why you live in town? (GWENDOLEN *bites her lip and beats her foot nervously with her parasol.*)

GWENDOLEN (*looking around*). Quite a well-kept garden this is, Miss Cardew.

CECILY. So glad you like it, Miss Fairfax.

GWENDOLEN. I had no idea there were any flowers in the country.

CECILY. Oh, flowers are as common here, Miss Fairfax, as people are in London.

GWENDOLEN. Personally I cannot understand how anybody manages to exist in the country, if anybody who is anybody does. The country always bores me to death.

CECILY. Ah! This is what the newspapers call agricultural depression, is it not? I believe the aristocracy are suffering very much from it just at present. It is almost an epidemic amongst them, I have been told. May I offer you some tea, Miss Fairfax?

GWENDOLEN (*with elaborate politeness*). Thank you. (*Aside.*) Detestable girl! But I require tea!

CECILY (*sweetly*). Sugar?

GWENDOLEN (*superciliously*). No, thank you. Sugar is not fashionable any more. (CECILY *looks angrily at her, takes up the tongs and puts four lumps of sugar into the cup.*)

CECILY (*severely*). Cake or bread and butter?

GWENDOLEN (*In a bored manner*). Bread and butter, please. Cake is rarely seen at the best houses nowadays.

CECILY (*cuts a very large slice of cake and puts it on the tray*). Hand that to Miss Fairfax. (MERRIMAN *does so, and goes out with footman.*
GWENDOLEN *drinks the tea and makes a grimace. Puts down cup at once, reaches out her hand to the bread and butter, looks at it, and finds it is cake. Rises in indignation.*)

GWENDOLEN. You have filled my tea with lumps of sugar, and though I asked most distinctly for bread and butter, you have given me cake. I am known for the gentleness of my disposition, and the extraordinary sweetness of my nature, but I warn you, Miss Cardew, you may go too far.

CECILY (*rising*). To save my poor, innocent, trusting boy from the machinations of any other girl there are no lengths to which I would not go.

GWENDOLEN. From the moment I saw you I distrusted you. I felt that you were false and deceitful. I am never deceived in such matters. My first impressions of people are invariably right.

CECILY. It seems to me, Miss Fairfax, that I am trespassing on your valuable time. No doubt you have many other calls of a similar character to make in the neighborhood. (*Enter* JACK.)

GWENDOLEN (*catching sight of him*). Ernest! My own Ernest!

JACK. Gwendolen! Darling! (*Offers to kiss her.*)

GWENDOLEN (*drawing back*). A moment! May I ask if you are engaged to be married to this young lady? (*Points to* CECILY.)

JACK (*laughing*). To dear little Cecily! Of course not! What could have put such an idea into your pretty little head?

GWENDOLEN. Thank you. You may! (*Offers her cheek.*)

CECILY (*very sweetly*). I knew there must be some misunderstanding, Miss Fairfax. The gentleman whose arm is at present round your waist is my guardian, Mr. John Worthing.

GWENDOLEN. I beg your pardon?

CECILY. This is Uncle Jack.

GWENDOLEN (*receding*). Jack! Oh! (*Enter* ALGERNON.)

CECILY. Here is Ernest.

ALGERNON (*goes straight over to* CECILY *without noticing anyone else*). My own love! (*Offers to kiss her.*)

CECILY (*drawing back*). A moment, Ernest! May I ask you—are you engaged to be married to this young lady?

ALGERNON (*looking round*). To what young lady? Good heavens! Gwendolen!

CECILY. Yes: to good heavens, Gwendolen, I mean to Gwendolen.

ALGERNON (*laughing*). Of course not! What could have put such an idea into your pretty little head?

CECILY. Thank you. (*Presenting her cheek to be kissed.*) You may.
(ALGERNON *kisses her.*)

GWENDOLEN. I felt there was some slight error, Miss Cardew. The gentleman who is now embracing you is my cousin, Mr. Algernon Moncrieff.

CECILY (*breaking away from* ALGERNON). Algernon Moncrieff! Oh! (*The two girls move toward each other and put their arms round each other's waists as if for protection.*)

CECILY. Are you called Algernon?

ALGERNON. I cannot deny it.

CECILY. Oh!

GWENDOLEN. Is your name really John?

JACK (*standing rather proudly*). I could deny it if I liked. I could deny anything if I liked. But my name certainly is John. It has been John for years.

CECILY (*to* GWENDOLEN). A gross deception has been practiced on both
of us.

GWENDOLEN. My poor wounded Cecily!

CECILY. My sweet wronged Gwendolen!

GWENDOLEN (*slowly and seriously*). You will call me sister, will you not?
(*They embrace.* JACK *and* ALGERNON *groan and walk up and down.*)

CECILY (*rather brightly*). Here is just one question I would like to be
allowed to ask my guardian.

GWENDOLEN. An admirable idea! Mr. Worthing, there is just one question
I would like to be permitted to put to you. Where is your brother
Ernest? We are both engaged to be married to your brother Ernest, so
it is a matter of some importance to us to know where your brother
Ernest is at present.

JACK (*slowly and hesitatingly*). Gwendolen—Cecily—it is very painful for
me to be forced to speak the truth. It is the first time in my life that
I have ever been reduced to such a painful position, and I am really
quite inexperienced in doing anything of the kind. However, I will
tell you quite frankly that I have no brother Ernest. I have no brother
at all. I never had a brother in my life, and I certainly have not the
smallest intention of ever having one in the future.

CECILY (*surprised*). No brother at all?

JACK (*cheerily*). None!

GWENDOLEN (*severely*). Had you never a brother of any kind?

JACK (*pleasantly*). Never. Not even of any kind.

GWENDOLEN. I am afraid it is quite clear, Cecily, that neither of us is
engaged to be married to anyone.

CECILY. It is not a very pleasant position for a young girl suddenly to find
herself in. Is it?

GWENDOLEN. Let us go into the house. They will hardly venture to come
after us there.

CECILY. No, men are so cowardly, aren't they? (*They retire into the house with
scornful looks.*)

JACK. This ghastly state of things is what you call Bunburying I suppose?

ALGERNON. Yes, and a perfectly wonderful Bunbury it is. The most
wonderful Bunbury I have ever had in my life.

JACK. Well, you've no right whatsoever to Bunbury here.

ALGERNON. That is absurd. One has a right to Bunbury anywhere one
chooses. Every serious Bunburyist knows that.

JACK. Serious Bunburyist? Good heavens!

ALGERNON. Well, one must be serious about something, if one wants to
have any amusement in life. I happen to be serious about Bunburying.
What on earth you are serious about I haven't got the remotest idea.

About everything, I should fancy. You have such an absolutely
trivial nature.

JACK. Well, the only small satisfaction I have in the whole of this
wretched business is that your friend Bunbury is quite exploded. You
won't be able to run down to the country quite so often as you used to
do, dear Algy. And a very good thing too.

ALGERNON. Your brother is a little off color, isn't he, dear Jack? You won't
be able to disappear to London quite so frequently as your wicked
custom was. And not a bad thing either.

JACK. As for your conduct toward Miss Cardew. I must say that your
taking in a sweet, simple, innocent girl like that is quite inexcusable.
To say nothing of the fact that she is my ward.

ALGERNON. I can see no possible defence at all for your deceiving a
brilliant, clever, thoroughly experienced young lady like Miss Fairfax.
To say nothing of the fact that she is my cousin.

JACK. I wanted to be engaged to Gwendolen, that is all. I love her.

ALGERNON. Well, I simply wanted to be engaged to Cecily. I adore her.

JACK. There is certainly no chance of your marrying Miss Cardew.

ALGERNON. I don't think there is much likelihood, Jack, of you and Miss
Fairfax being united.

JACK. Well, that is no business of yours.

ALGERNON. If it was my business, I wouldn't talk about it. (*Begins to eat
muffins.*) It is very vulgar to talk about one's business. Only people like
stockbrokers do that, and then merely at dinner parties.

JACK. How you can sit there, calmly eating muffins when we are in this
horrible trouble, I can't make out. You seem to me to be perfectly
heartless.

ALGERNON. Well, I can't eat muffins in an agitated manner. The butter
would probably get on my cuffs. One should always eat muffins quite
calmly. It is the only way to eat them.

JACK. I say it's perfectly heartless your eating muffins at all, under the
circumstances.

ALGERNON. When I am in trouble, eating is the only thing that consoles
me. Indeed, when I am in really great trouble, as any one who knows
me intimately will tell you, I refuse everything except food and drink.
At the present moment I am eating muffins because I am unhappy.
Besides, I am particularly fond of muffins. (*Rising.*)

JACK (*rising*). Well, there is no reason why you should eat them all in that
greedy way. (*Takes muffins from* ALGERNON.)

ALGERNON (*offering tea-cake*). I wish you would have tea-cake instead.
I don't like tea-cake.

JACK. Good heavens! I suppose a man may eat his own muffins in his own garden.

ALGERNON. But you have just said it was perfectly heartless to eat muffins.

JACK. I said it was perfectly heartless of you, under the circumstances. That is a very different thing.

ALGERNON. That may be. But the muffins are the same. *(He seizes the muffin-dish from* JACK.*)*

JACK. Algy, I wish to goodness you would go.

ALGERNON. You can't possibly ask me to go without having some dinner. It's absurd. I never go without my dinner. No one ever does, except vegetarians and people like that. Besides I have just made arrangements with Dr. Chasuble to be christened at a quarter to six under the name of Ernest.

JACK. My dear fellow, the sooner you give up that nonsense the better. I made arrangements this morning with Dr Chasuble to be christened myself at 5:30, and I naturally will take the name of Ernest. Gwendolen would wish it. We can't both be christened Ernest. It's absurd. Besides, I have a perfect right to be christened if I like. There is no evidence at all that I have ever been christened by anybody. I should think it extremely probable I never was, and so does Dr. Chasuble. It is entirely different in your case. You have been christened already.

ALGERNON. Yes, but I have not been christened for years.

JACK. Yes, but you have been christened. That is the important thing.

ALGERNON. Quite so. So I know my constitution can stand it. If you are not quite sure about your ever having been christened, I must say I think it rather dangerous your venturing on it now. It might make you very unwell. You can hardly have forgotten that someone very closely connected with you was very nearly carried off this week in Paris by a severe chill.

JACK. Yes, but you said yourself that a severe chill was not hereditary.

ALGERNON. It usen't to be, I know—but I daresay it is now. Science is always making wonderful improvements in things.

JACK *(picking up the muffin-dish)*. Oh, that is nonsense; you are always talking nonsense.

ALGERNON. Jack, you are at the muffins again! I wish you wouldn't. There are only two left. *(Takes them.)* I told you I was particularly fond of muffins.

JACK. But I hate tea-cake.

ALGERNON. Why on earth then do you allow tea-cake to be served up for your guests? What ideas you have of hospitality!

JACK. Algernon! I have already told you to go. I don't want you here. Why don't you go!

ALGERNON. I haven't quite finished my tea yet! and there is still one muffin left. (JACK *groans, and sinks into a chair.* ALGERNON *continues eating.*)

ACT DROP

THIRD ACT

SCENE: Drawing-room at the Manor House

(GWENDOLEN *and* CECILY *are at the window, looking out into the garden.*)

GWENDOLEN. The fact that they did not follow us at once into the house, as anyone else would have done, seems to me to show that they have some sense of shame left.

CECILY. They have been eating muffins. That looks like repentance.

GWENDOLEN (*after a pause*). They don't seem to notice us at all. Couldn't you cough?

CECILY. But I haven't got a cough.

GWENDOLEN. They're looking at us. What effrontery!

CECILY. They're approaching. That's very forward of them.

GWENDOLEN. Let us preserve a dignified silence.

CECILY. Certainly. It's the only thing to do now. (*Enter* JACK *followed by* ALGERNON. *They whistle some dreadful popular air from a British Opera.*)

GWENDOLEN. This dignified silence seems to produce an unpleasant effect.

CECILY. A most distasteful one.

GWENDOLEN. But we will not be the first to speak.

CECILY. Certainly not.

GWENDOLEN. Mr. Worthing, I have something very particular to ask you. Much depends on your reply.

CECILY. Gwendolen, your common sense is invaluable. Mr. Moncrieff, kindly answer me the following question. Why did you pretend to be my guardian's brother?

ALGERNON. In order that I might have an opportunity of meeting you.

CECILY (*to* GWENDOLEN). That certainly seems a satisfactory explanation, does it not?

GWENDOLEN. Yes, dear, if you can believe him.

CECILY. I don't. But that does not affect the wonderful beauty of his answer.

GWENDOLEN. True. In matters of grave importance, style, not sincerity, is the vital thing. Mr. Worthing, what explanation can you offer to me for pretending to have a brother? Was it in order that you might have an opportunity of coming up to town to see me as often as possible?

JACK. Can you doubt it, Miss Fairfax?

GWENDOLEN. I have the gravest doubts upon the subject. But I intend to crush them. This is not the moment for German scepticism. *(Moving to* CECILY.*)* Their explanations appear to be quite satisfactory, especially Mr. Worthing's. That seems to me to have the stamp of truth upon it.

CECILY. I am more than content with what Mr. Moncrieff said. His voice alone inspires one with absolute credulity.

GWENDOLEN. Then you think we should forgive them?

CECILY. Yes. I mean no.

GWENDOLEN. True! I had forgotten. There are principles at stake that one cannot surrender. Which of us should tell them? The task is not a pleasant one.

CECILY. Could we not both speak at the same time?

GWENDOLEN. An excellent idea! I nearly always speak at the same time as other people. Will you take the time from me?

CECILY. Certainly. (GWENDOLEN *beats time with uplifted finger.*)

GWENDOLEN and CECILY *(speaking together).* Your Christian names are still an insuperable barrier. That is all!

JACK and ALGERNON *(speaking together).* Our Christian names! Is that all? But we are going to be christened this afternoon.

GWENDOLEN *(to* JACK*).* For my sake you are prepared to do this terrible thing?

JACK. I am.

CECILY *(to* ALGERNON*).* To please me you are ready to face this fearful ordeal?

ALGERNON. I am!

GWENDOLEN. How absurd to talk of the equality of the sexes! Where questions of self-sacrifice are concerned, men are infinitely beyond us.

JACK. We are. (*Clasps hands with* ALGERNON.)

CECILY. They have moments of physical courage of which we women know absolutely nothing.

GWENDOLEN *(to* JACK*).* Darling!

ALGERNON *(to* CECILY*).* Darling! *(They fall into each other's arms.) (Enter* MERRIMAN. *When he enters he coughs loudly, seeing the situation.)*

MERRIMAN. Ahem! Ahem! Lady Bracknell.

JACK. Good heavens! (*Enter* LADY BRACKNELL. *The couples separate in alarm. Exit* MERRIMAN.)

LADY BRACKNELL. Gwendolen! What does this mean?

GWENDOLEN. Merely that I am engaged to be married to Mr. Worthing, mamma.

LADY BRACKNELL. Come here. Sit down. Sit down immediately. Hesitation of any kind is a sign of mental decay in the young, of physical weakness in the old. (*Turns to* JACK.) Apprised, sir, of my daughter's sudden flight by her trusty maid, whose confidence I purchased by means of a small coin, I followed her at once by a luggage train. Her unhappy father is, I am glad to say, under the impression that she is attending a more than usually lengthy lecture by the University Extension Scheme on the Influence of a Permanent Income on Thought. I do not propose to undeceive him. Indeed I have never undeceived him on any question. I would consider it wrong. But of course, you will clearly understand that all communication between yourself and my daughter must cease immediately from this moment. On this point, as indeed on all points, I am firm.

JACK. I am engaged to be married to Gwendolen, Lady Bracknell!

LADY BRACKNELL. You are nothing of the kind, sir. And now as regards Algernon! . . . Algernon!

ALGERNON. Yes, Aunt Augusta.

LADY BRACKNELL. May I ask if it is in this house that your invalid friend Mr. Bunbury resides?

ALGERNON (*stammering*). Oh! No! Bunbury doesn't live here. Bunbury is somewhere else at present. In fact, Bunbury is dead.

LADY BRACKNELL. Dead! When did Mr. Bunbury die? His death must have been extremely sudden.

ALGERNON (*airily*). Oh! I killed Bunbury this afternoon. I mean poor Bunbury died this afternoon.

LADY BRACKNELL. What did he die of?

ALGERNON. Bunbury? Oh, he was quite exploded.

LADY BRACKNELL. Exploded! Was he the victim of a revolutionary outrage? I was not aware that Mr. Bunbury was interested in social legislation. If so, he is well punished for his morbidity.

ALGERNON. My dear Aunt Augusta, I mean he was found out! The doctors found out that Bunbury could not live, that is what I mean—so Bunbury died.

LADY BRACKNELL. He seems to have had great confidence in the opinion of his physicians. I am glad, however, that he made up his mind at the last to some definite course of action, and acted under proper medical advice. And now that we have finally got rid of this Mr. Bunbury, may I ask, Mr. Worthing, who is that young person whose hand my nephew Algernon is now holding in what seems to me a peculiarly unnecessary manner?

JACK. That lady is Miss Cecily Cardew, my ward, (LADY BRACKNELL *bows coldly to* CECILY.)

ALGERNON. I am engaged to be married to Cecily, Aunt Augusta.

LADY BRACKNELL. I beg your pardon?

CECILY. Mr. Moncrieff and I are engaged to be married, Lady Bracknell.

LADY BRACKNELL (*with a shiver, crossing to the sofa and sitting down*). I do not know whether there is anything peculiarly exciting in the air of this particular part of Hertfordshire, but the number of engagements that go on seems to me considerably above the proper average that statistics have laid down for our guidance. I think some preliminary inquiry on my part would not be out of place. Mr. Worthing, is Miss Cardew at all connected with any of the larger railway stations in London? I merely desire information. Until yesterday I had no idea that there were any families or persons whose origin was a Terminus. (JACK *looks perfectly furious, but restrains himself.*)

JACK (*In a cold, clear voice*). Miss Cardew is the granddaughter of the late Mr. Thomas Cardew of 149 Belgrave Square, S.W.; Gervase Park, Dorking, Surrey; and the Sporran, Fifeshire, N.B.

LADY BRACKNELL. That sounds not unsatisfactory. Three addresses always inspire confidence, even in tradesmen. But what proof have I of their authenticity?

JACK. I have carefully preserved the Court Guides of the period. They are open to your inspection, Lady Bracknell.

LADY BRACKNELL. (*grimly*). I have known strange errors in that publication.

JACK. Miss Cardew's family solicitors are Messrs. Markby, Markby, and Markby.

LADY BRACKNELL. Markby, Markby, and Markby? A firm of the very highest position in their profession. Indeed I am told that one of the Mr. Markby's is occasionally to be seen at dinner parties. So far I am satisfied.

JACK (*very irritably*). How extremely kind of you, Lady Bracknell! I have also in my possession, you will be pleased to hear, certificates of Miss Cardew's birth, baptism, whooping cough, registration, vaccination, confirmation, and the measles; both the German and the English variety.

LADY BRACKNELL. Ah! A life crowded with incident, I see; though perhaps somewhat too exciting for a young girl. I am not myself in favor of premature experiences. (*Rises. Looks at her watch.*) Gwendolen! the time approaches for our departure. We have not a moment to lose. As a matter of form, Mr. Worthing, I had better ask you if Miss Cardew has any little fortune?

JACK. Oh! about a hundred and thirty thousand pounds in the Funds. That is all. Good-bye, Lady Bracknell. So pleased to have seen you.

LADY BRACKNELL. (*sitting down again*). A moment, Mr. Worthing. A hundred and thirty thousand pounds! And in the Funds! Miss Cardew seems to me a most attractive young lady, now that I look at her. Few girls of the present day have any really solid qualities, any of the qualities that last, and improve with time. We live, I regret to say, in an age of surfaces. (*To* CECILY.) Come over here, dear. (CECILY *goes across.*) Pretty child! your dress is sadly simple, and your hair seems almost as Nature might have left it. But we can soon alter all that. A thoroughly experienced French maid produces a really marvellous result in a very brief space of time. I remember recommending one to young Lady Lancing, and after three months her own husband did not know her.

JACK. And after six months nobody knew her.

LADY BRACKNELL. (*glares at* JACK *for a few moments. Then bends, with a practised smile to* CECILY). Kindly turn round, sweet child, (CECILY *turns completely round.*) No, the side view is what I want. (CECILY *presents her profile.*) Yes, quite as I expected. There are distinct social possibilities in your profile. The two weak points in our age are its want of principle and its want of profile. The chin a little higher, dear. Style largely depends on the way the chin is worn. They are worn very high, just at present, Algernon!

ALGERNON. Yes, Aunt Augusta!

LADY BRACKNELL. There are distinct social possibilities in Miss Cardew's profile.

ALGERNON. Cecily is the sweetest, dearest, prettiest girl in the whole world. And I don't care twopence about social possibilities.

LADY BRACKNELL. Never speak disrespectfully of Society, Algernon. Only people who can't get into it do that. (*To* CECILY.) Dear child, of course you know that Algernon has nothing but his debts to depend upon. But I do not approve of mercenary marriages. When I married Lord Bracknell I had no fortune of any kind. But I never dreamed for a moment of allowing that to stand in my way. Well, I suppose I must give my consent.

ALGERNON. Thank you, Aunt Augusta.

LADY BRACKNELL. Cecily, you may kiss me!

CECILY (*kisses her*). Thank you, Lady Bracknell.

LADY BRACKNELL. You may also address me as Aunt Augusta for the future.

CECILY. Thank you, Aunt Augusta.

LADY BRACKNELL. The marriage, I think, had better take place quite soon.

ALGERNON. Thank you, Aunt Augusta.

CECILY. Thank you, Aunt Augusta.

LADY BRACKNELL. To speak frankly, I am not in favor of long engagements. They give people the opportunity of finding out each other's character before marriage, which I think is never advisable.

JACK. I beg your pardon for interrupting you, Lady Bracknell, but this engagement is quite out of the question. I am Miss Cardew's guardian, and she cannot marry without my consent until she comes of age. That consent I absolutely decline to give.

LADY BRACKNELL. Upon what grounds, may I ask? Algernon is an extremely, I may almost say an ostentatiously, eligible young man. He has nothing, but he looks everything. What more can one desire?

JACK. It pains me very much to have to speak frankly to you, Lady Bracknell, about your nephew, but the fact is that I do not approve at all of his moral character. I suspect him of being untruthful. (ALGERNON *and* CECILY *look at him in indignant amazement.*)

LADY BRACKNELL. Untruthful! My nephew Algernon? Impossible! He is an Oxonian.

JACK. I fear there can be no possible doubt about the matter. This afternoon during my temporary absence in London on an important question of romance, he obtained admission to my house by means of the false pretence of being my brother. Under an assumed name he drank, I've just been informed by my butler, an entire pint bottle of my Perrier-Jouet, Brut, '89; wine I was specially reserving for myself. Continuing his disgraceful deception, he succeeded in the course of the afternoon in alienating the affections of my only ward. He subsequently stayed to tea, and devoured every single muffin. And what makes his conduct all the more heartless is, that he was perfectly well aware from the first that I have no brother, that I never had a brother, and that I don't intend to have a brother, not even of any kind. I distinctly told him so myself yesterday afternoon.

LADY BRACKNELL. Ahem! Mr. Worthing, after careful consideration I have decided entirely to overlook my nephew's conduct to you.

JACK. That is very generous of you, Lady Bracknell. My own decision, however, is unalterable. I decline to give my consent.

LADY BRACKNELL. (*to* CECILY). Come here, sweet child. (CECILY *goes over.*) How old are you, dear?

CECILY. Well, I am really only eighteen, but I always admit to twenty when I go to evening parties.

LADY BRACKNELL. You are perfectly right in making some slight alteration. Indeed, no woman should ever be quite accurate about her age. It looks so calculating. . . . . (*In a meditative manner.*) Eighteen, but admitting to twenty at evening parties. Well, it will not be very long before you are of age and free from the restraints of tutelage.

So I don't think your guardian's consent is, after all, a matter of any importance.

JACK. Pray excuse me, Lady Bracknell, for interrupting you again, but it is only fair to tell you that according to the terms of her grandfather's will Miss Cardew does not come legally of age till she is thirty-five.

LADY BRACKNELL. That does not seem to me to be a grave objection. Thirty-five is a very attractive age. London society is full of women of the very highest birth who have, of their own free choice, remained thirty-five for years. Lady Dumbleton is an instance in point. To my own knowledge she has been thirty-five ever since she arrived at the age of forty, which was many years ago now. I see no reason why our dear Cecily should not be even still more attractive at the age you mention than she is at present. There will be a large accumulation of property.

CECILY. Algy, could you wait for me till I was thirty-five?

ALGERNON. Of course I could, Cecily. You know I could.

CECILY. Yes, I felt it instinctively, but I couldn't wait all that time. I hate waiting even five minutes for anybody. It always makes me rather cross. I am not punctual myself, I know, but I do like punctuality in others, and waiting, even to be married, is quite out of the question.

ALGERNON. Then what is to be done, Cecily?

CECILY. I don't know, Mr. Moncrieff.

LADY BRACKNELL. My dear Mr. Worthing, as Miss Cardew states positively that she cannot wait till she is thirty-five—a remark which I am bound to say seems to me to show a somewhat impatient nature—I would beg of you to reconsider your decision.

JACK. But my dear Lady Bracknell, the matter is entirely in your own hands. The moment you consent to my marriage with Gwendolen, I will most gladly allow your nephew to form an alliance with my ward.

LADY BRACKNELL (*rising and drawing herself up*). You must be quite aware that what you propose is out of the question.

JACK. Then a passionate celibacy is all that any of us can look forward to.

LADY BRACKNELL. That is not the destiny I propose for Gwendolen. Algernon, of course, can choose for himself. (*Pulls out her watch.*) Come, dear (GWENDOLEN *rises.*), we have already missed five, if not six, trains. To miss any more might expose us to comment on the platform. (*Enter DR. CHASUBLE.*)

CHASUBLE. Everything is quite ready for the christenings.

LADY BRACKNELL. The christenings, sir! Is not that somewhat premature?

CHASUBLE (*looking rather puzzled, and pointing to* JACK *and* ALGERNON). Both these gentlemen have expressed a desire for immediate baptism.

LADY BRACKNELL. At their age? The idea is grotesque and irreligious! Algernon, I forbid you to be baptized. I will not hear of such excesses. Lord Bracknell would be highly displeased if he learned that that was the way in which you wasted your time and money.

CHASUBLE. Am I to understand then that there are to be no christenings at all this afternoon?

JACK. I don't think that, as things are now, it would be of much practical value to either of us, Dr. Chasuble.

CHASUBLE. I am grieved to hear such sentiments from you, Mr. Worthing. They savor of the heretical views of the Anabaptists, views that I have completely refuted in four of my unpublished sermons. However, as your present mood seems to be one peculiarly secular, I will return to the church at once. Indeed, I have just been informed by the pew-opener that for the last hour and a half Miss Prism has been waiting for me in the vestry.

LADY BRACKNELL (*starting*). Miss Prism! Did I hear you mention a Miss Prism?

CHASUBLE. Yes, Lady Bracknell. I am on my way to join her.

LADY BRACKNELL. Pray allow me to detain you for a moment. This matter may prove to be one of vital importance to Lord Bracknell and myself. Is this Miss Prism a female of repellent aspect, remotely connected with education?

CHASUBLE (*somewhat indignantly*). She is the most cultivated of ladies, and the very picture of respectability.

LADY BRACKNELL. It is obviously the same person. May I ask what position she holds in your household?

CHASUBLE (*severely*). I am a celibate, madam.

JACK (*interposing*). Miss Prism, Lady Bracknell, has been for the last three years Miss Cardew's esteemed governess and valued companion.

LADY BRACKNELL. In spite of what I hear of her, I must see her at once. Let her be sent for.

CHASUBLE (*looking off*). She approaches; she is nigh. (*Enter* MISS PRISM *hurriedly.*)

MISS PRISM. I was told you expected me in the vestry, dear Canon. I have been waiting for you there for an hour and three-quarters. (*Catches sight of* LADY BRACKNELL, *who has fixed her with a stony glare.* MISS PRISM *grows pale and quails. She looks anxiously round as if desirous to escape.*)

LADY BRACKNELL (*in a severe, judicial voice*). Prism! (MISS PRISM *bows her head in shame.*) Come here, Prism! (MISS PRISM *approaches in a humble manner.*) Prism! Where is that baby? (*General consternation. The Canon starts back in horror.* ALGERNON *and* JACK *pretend to be anxious to shield* CECILY *and* GWENDOLEN *from hearing the details of a terrible public scandal.*) Twenty-eight years ago, Prism, you left Lord Bracknell's house, Number 104, Upper Grosvenor Street, in charge of a perambulator that contained a baby of the male sex. You never returned. A few weeks later, through the elaborate investigations of the Metropolitan police, the perambulator was discovered at midnight standing by itself in a remote corner of Bayswater. It contained the manuscript of a three-volume novel of more than usually revolting sentimentality. (MISS PRISM *starts in involuntary indignation.*) But the baby was not there. (*Everyone looks at* MISS PRISM.) Prism! Where is that baby? (*A pause.*)

MISS PRISM. Lady Bracknell, I admit with shame that I do not know. I only wish I did. The plain facts of the case are these. On the morning of the day you mention, a day that is for ever branded on my memory, I prepared as usual to take the baby out in its perambulator. I had also with me a somewhat old, but capacious hand-bag in which I had intended to place the manuscript of a work of fiction that I had written during my few unoccupied hours. In a moment of mental abstraction, for which I can never forgive myself, I deposited the manuscript in the bassinette and placed the baby in the hand-bag.

JACK (*who has been listening attentively*). But where did you deposit the hand-bag?

MISS PRISM. Do not ask me, Mr. Worthing.

JACK. Miss Prism, this is a matter of no small importance to me. I insist on knowing where you deposited the hand-bag that contained that infant.

MISS PRISM. I left it in the cloak-room of one of the larger railway stations in London.

JACK. What railway station?

MISS PRISM (*quite crushed*). Victoria. The Brighton line. (*Sinks into a chair.*)

JACK. I must retire to my room for a moment. Gwendolen, wait here for me.

GWENDOLEN. If you are not too long, I will wait here for you all my life. (*Exit* JACK *in great excitement.*)

CHASUBLE. What do you think this means, Lady Bracknell?

LADY BRACKNELL. I dare not even suspect, Dr. Chasuble. I need hardly tell you that in families of high position strange coincidences are not supposed to occur. They are hardly considered the thing. (*Noises heard overhead as if some one was throwing trunks about. Every one looks up.*)

CECILY. Uncle Jack seems strangely agitated.

CHASUBLE. Your guardian has a very emotional nature.

LADY BRACKNELL. This noise is extremely unpleasant. It sounds as if he was having an argument. I dislike arguments of any kind. They are always vulgar, and often convincing.

CHASUBLE (*looking up*). It has stopped now. (*The noise is redoubled.*)

LADY BRACKNELL. I wish he would arrive at some conclusion.

GWENDOLEN. This suspense is terrible. I hope it will last. (*Enter* JACK *with a hand-bag of black leather in his hand.*)

JACK (*rushing over to* MISS PRISM). Is this the hand-bag, Miss Prism? Examine it carefully before you speak. The happiness of more than one life depends on your answer.

MISS PRISM (*calmly*). It seems to be mine. Yes, here is the injury it received through the upsetting of a Gower Street omnibus in younger and happier days. Here is the stain on the lining caused by the explosion of a temperance beverage, an incident that occurred at Leamington. And here, on the lock, are my initials. I had forgotten that in an extravagant mood I had had them placed there. The bag is undoubtedly mine. I am delighted to have it so unexpectedly restored to me. It has been a great inconvenience being without it all these years.

JACK (*in a pathetic voice*). Miss Prism, more is restored to you than this hand-bag. I was the baby you placed in it.

MISS PRISM (*amazed*). You?

JACK (*embracing her*). Yes . . . mother!

MISS PRISM (*recoiling in indignant astonishment*). Mr. Worthing. I am unmarried!

JACK. Unmarried! I do not deny that is a serious blow. But after all, who has the right to cast a stone against one who has suffered? Cannot repentance wipe out an act of folly? Why should there be one law for men, and another for women? Mother, I forgive you. (*Tries to embrace her again.*)

MISS PRISM (*still more indignant*). Mr. Worthing, there is some error. (*Pointing to* LADY BRACKNELL.) There is the lady who can tell you who you really are.

JACK (*after a pause*). Lady Bracknell, I hate to seem inquisitive, but would you kindly inform me who I am?

LADY BRACKNELL. I am afraid that the news I have to give you will not altogether please you. You are the son of my poor sister, Mrs. Moncrieff, and consequently Algernon's elder brother.

JACK. Algy's elder brother! Then I have a brother after all. I knew I had a brother! I always said I had a brother! Cecily—how could you have ever doubted that I had a brother? (*Seizes hold of* ALGERNON.) Dr. Chasuble, my unfortunate brother. Miss Prism, my unfortunate brother. Gwendolen, my unfortunate brother. Algy, you young scoundrel, you will have to treat me with more respect in the future. You have never behaved to me like a brother in all your life.

ALGERNON. Well, not till to-day, old boy, I admit. I did my best, however, though I was out of practice. (*Shakes hands.*)

GWENDOLEN (*to* JACK). My own! But what own are you? What is your Christian name, now that you have become some one else?

JACK. Good heavens! . . . . I had quite forgotten that point. Your decision on the subject of my name is irrevocable, I suppose?

GWENDOLEN. I never change, except in my affections.

CECILY. What a noble nature you have, Gwendolen!

JACK. Then the question had better be cleared up at once. Aunt Augusta, a moment. At the time when Miss Prism left me in the hand-bag, had I been christened already?

LADY BRACKNELL. Every luxury that money could buy, including christening, had been lavished on you by your fond and doting parents.

JACK. Then I was christened! That is settled. Now, what name was I given? Let me know the worst.

LADY BRACKNELL. Being the eldest son you were naturally christened after your father.

JACK (*irritably*). Yes, but what was my father's Christian name?

LADY BRACKNELL (*meditatively*). I cannot at the present moment recall what the General's Christian name was. But I have no doubt he had one. He was eccentric, I admit. But only in later years. And that was the result of the Indian climate, and marriage, and indigestion, and other things of that kind.

JACK. Algy! Can't you recollect what our father's Christian name was?

ALGERNON. My dear boy, we were never even on speaking terms. He died before I was a year old.

JACK. His name would appear in the Army Lists of the period, I suppose, Aunt Augusta?

LADY BRACKNELL. The General was essentially a man of peace, except in his domestic life. But I have no doubt his name would appear in any military directory.

JACK. The Army Lists of the last forty years are here. These delightful records should have been my constant study. (*Rushes to bookcase and tears the books out.*) M. Generals . . . Mallam, Maxbohm, Magley— what ghastly names they have—Markby, Migsby, Mobbs, Moncrieff! Lieutenant 1840, Captain, Lieutenant-Colonel, Colonel, General 1869, Christian names, Ernest John. (*Puts book very quietly down and speaks quite calmly.*) I always told you, Gwendolen, my name was Ernest, didn't I? Well, it is Ernest after all. I mean it naturally is Ernest.

LADY BRACKNELL. Yes, I remember now that the General was called Ernest. I knew I had some particular reason for disliking the name.

GWENDOLEN. Ernest! My own Ernest! I felt from the first that you could have no other name!

JACK. Gwendolen, it is a terrible thing for a man to find out suddenly that all his life he has been speaking nothing but the truth. Can you forgive me?

GWENDOLEN. I can. For I feel that you are sure to change.

JACK. My own one!

CHASUBLE (*to* MISS PRISM). Laetitia! (*Embraces her.*)

MISS PRISM (*enthusiastically*). Frederick! At last!

ALGERNON. Cecily! (*Embraces her.*) At last!

JACK. Gwendolen! (*Embraces her.*) At last!

LADY BRACKNELL. My nephew, you seem to be displaying signs of triviality.

JACK. On the contrary, Aunt Augusta, I've now realized for the first time in my life the vital Importance of Being Earnest.

TABLEAU

Curtain

QUESTIONS

1. Describe the society depicted in this play. What are its codes of behavior? Do the characters follow its codes or breach them? Which characters represent the enforcement of the codes, and which characters are more subversive?
2. Discuss the comic effects of the play. Many commentators agree that Lady Bracknell has some of the funniest lines: what is the source of their humor? Does she intend to be funny?
3. Discuss the relationship between Algernon and Jack. Which of them is the more admirable? Is either of them "earnest"?
4. What view of marriage does the play provide? Is marriage a positive or a destructive institutuion, as depicted here?
5. Contrast the characterizations of Cecily and Gwendolen. Is either of them hypocritical in her behavior? Does either undergo a significant change in the course of the play?
6. Map the play's structure, its twists and turns. How does the plot arrangement help to illustrate the play's characters and its theme?
7. Focus on the ending. Is the resolution satisfying? Why or why not?

SUGGESTIONS FOR WRITING

1. One of the structural devices regularly used by Shakespeare is contrast in tone, content, or effect. In tragedies, he follows a scene of high seriousness with a comic scene (commonly called **comic relief,** because like a "relief

map," it delineates for us by contrast the heights of emotion that we have just experienced). Conversely, in comedies, we often encounter actions that threaten dire consequences or remind the audience of the less pleasant side of life (no one has labeled this "tragic relief," though that might be an appropriate term). Using "Time Flies," "Los Vendidos," *The Misanthrope*, or "A Marriage Proposal," write an essay that explores the emotional effects of these contrasts.

2. Using one of the plays in this chapter, write an essay demonstrating the idea that the conclusion of a tragedy or of a comedy has a mixed effect on the audience—that tragedy does not produce unmitigated woe and depression, that comedy leaves its audience not only laughing but with a renewed sense of its own limitations.

3. Explore the emotional effects of the conclusions of one or more of the following: Glaspell's "Trifles," Albee's "The Sandbox," Ibsen's *A Doll House*, Williams's *The Glass Menagerie*.

4. Write an essay about one of the eight plays in chapters 1 and 2 showing it to be an example of one of the four dramatic categories defined in this chapter— tragedy, comedy, melodrama, or farce. If your choice does not wholly fit into one of the categories, explore the ways in which it has characteristics of more than one of them.

PRACTICE AP WRITING PROMPTS ▰▰▰▰

Sophocles, *Oedipus Rex* (pp. 1247–1292)

The following prompt is similar to one that might appear on the AP Literature and Composition Exam, Question 3. Apply this prompt to *Oedipus Rex* or to another work in which a character is engaged in a search for truth.

Choose a novel or play in which a character is engaged in a relentless search for truth. In a well-written essay, analyze the character's motivation in seeking truth, the outcome and consequences of the search, and the significance of this search on the meaning of the work as a whole. Avoid merely providing a plot summary.

William Shakespeare, *Othello, the Moor of Venice* (pp. 1293–1386)

The following prompt is similar to one that might appear on the AP Literature and Composition Exam in the free response section. Though it may be obvious to you that *Othello* is a suitable choice for this prompt, you may wish to consider other works of literary merit that you could select if you came upon this prompt on your exam:

The great Spanish playwright Lope de Vega said, "There is no greater glory than love, nor any greater punishment than jealousy." Choose a novel, play, or epic poem of literary merit in which a character is affected by the conflicting emotions of love and jealousy. Analyze the development of the character's conflict, and show how it contributes to the meaning of the work as a whole. Do not merely summarize the plot.

(Note: See the chapter on "Preparing to Succeed on the Advanced Placement Literature Examination" for a discussion about how to avoid providing a mere plot summary.)

Molière, *The Misanthrope* (pp. 1387–1438)

The excerpt from *The Misanthrope* in the first prompt below is the length of most passages that are the focus of AP Literature Exam Question 2 prompts. Answer the second prompt, which emulates a typical Question 3, with *The Misanthrope* or another play or novel in which a similar character appears.

1. Read carefully lines 1–96 of Molière's *The Misanthrope*. Then, in a well-organized essay, analyze the conflicting viewpoints of Philinte and Alceste toward the manners of society, showing how their dispute creates the author's intended effect.

2. In some works of literature, characters may be astute critics of others while failing to see themselves with the same sharp focus. Choose such a character from a novel or play. Then write an essay in which you analyze the contradiction between the character's personal misperceptions and his or her criticisms of the surrounding society. Show how this contradiction reveals the meaning of the work as a whole.

Plays for
Further Reading

EUGENE O'NEILL

Before Breakfast

Character

MRS. ROWLAND

SCENE. *A small room serving both as kitchen and dining room in a flat on Christopher Street, New York City. In the rear, to the right, a door leading to the outer hallway. On the left of the doorway, a sink, and a two-burner gas stove. Over the stove, and extending to the left wall, a wooden closet for dishes, etc. On the left, two windows looking out on a fire escape where several potted plants are dying of neglect. Before the windows, a table covered with oilcloth. Two canebottomed chairs are placed by the table. Another stands against the wall to the right of door in rear. In the right wall, rear, a doorway leading into a bedroom. Farther forward, different articles of a man's and a woman's clothing are hung on pegs. A clothes line is strung from the left corner, rear, to the right wall, forward.*

It is about eight-thirty in the morning of a fine, sunshiny day in the early fall.

MRS. ROWLAND *enters from the bedroom, yawning, her hands still busy putting the finishing touches on a slovenly toilet by sticking hairpins into her hair which is bunched up in a drab-colored mass on top of her round head. She is of medium height and inclined to a shapeless stoutness, accentuated by her formless blue dress, shabby and worn. Her face is characterless, with small, regular features and eyes of a nondescript blue. There is a pinched expression about her eyes and nose and her weak, spiteful mouth. She is in her early twenties but looks much older.*

She comes to the middle of the room and yawns, stretching her arms to their full length. Her drowsy eyes stare about the room with the irritated look of one to whom a long sleep has not been a long rest. She goes wearily to the clothes hanging on the right and takes an apron from a hook. She ties it about her waist, giving vent to an exasperated "damn" when the knot fails to obey her clumsy fingers. Finally gets it tied and goes slowly to the gas stove and lights one burner. She fills the coffee pot at the sink and sets it over the flame. Then slumps down into a chair by the table and puts a hand over her forehead as if she were suffering from headache. Suddenly her face brightens as though she had remembered something, and she casts a quick glance at the dish closet; then looks sharply at the bedroom door and listens intently for a moment or so.

BEFORE BREAKFAST First produced in 1916. Eugene O'Neill (1888–1953) is widely considered one of America's most important playwrights. In addition to such celebrated full-length plays as *Mourning Becomes Electra* (1931), *The Iceman Cometh* (1939), and *Long Day's Journey into Night* (1941), he wrote many excellent one-acts, including "Before Breakfast" and "Bound East for Cardiff" (1914). Despite his struggles with depression and alcoholism, he was a prolific writer, winning the Pulitzer Prize for Drama four times. He won the Nobel Prize for Literature in 1936.

MRS. ROWLAND (*In a low voice*). Alfred! Alfred! (*There is no answer from the next room and she continues suspiciously in a louder tone*) You needn't pretend you're asleep. (*There is no reply to this from the bedroom, and, reassured, she gets up from her chair and tiptoes cautiously to the dish closet. She slowly opens one door, taking great care to make no noise, and slides out, from their hiding place behind the dishes, a bottle of Gordon gin and a glass. In doing so she disturbs the top dish, which rattles a little. At this sound she starts guiltily and looks with sulky defiance at the doorway to the next room.*)

(*Her voice trembling*) Alfred!

(*After a pause, during which she listens for any sound, she takes the glass and pours out a large drink and gulps it down; then hastily returns the bottle and glass to their hiding place. She closes the closet door with the same care as she had opened it, and, heaving a great sigh of relief sinks down into her chair again. The large dose of alcohol she has taken has an almost immediate effect. Her features become more animated, she seems to gather energy, and she looks at the bedroom door with a hard, vindictive smile on her lips. Her eyes glance quickly about the room and are fixed on a man's coat and vest which hang from a hook at right. She moves stealthily over to the open doorway and stands there, out of sight of anyone inside, listening for any movement.*)

(*Calling in a half-whisper*) Alfred!

(*Again there is no reply. With a swift movement she takes the coat and vest from the hook and returns with them to her chair. She sits down and takes the various articles out of each pocket but quickly puts them back again. At last, in the inside pocket of the vest, she finds a letter.*)

(*Looking at the handwriting—slowly to herself*) Hmm! I knew it.

(*She opens the letter and reads it. At first her expression is one of hatred and rage, but as she goes on to the end it changes to one of triumphant malignity. She remains in deep thought for a moment, staring before her, the letter in her hands, a cruel smile on her lips. Then she puts the letter back in the pocket of the vest, and still careful not to awaken the sleeper, hangs the clothes up again on the same hook, and goes to the bedroom door and looks in.*)

(*In a loud, shrill voice*) Alfred! (*Still louder*) Alfred! (*There is a muffled, yawning groan from the next room*) Don't you think it's about time you got up? Do you want to stay in bed all day? (*Turning around and coming back to her chair*) Not that I've got any doubts about your being lazy enough to stay in bed forever. (*She sits down and looks out of the window, irritably*) Goodness knows what time it is. We haven't even got any way of telling the time since you pawned your watch like a fool. The last valuable thing we had, and you knew it. It's been nothing but pawn, pawn, pawn, with you—anything to put off getting a job, anything to get out of going to work like a man. (*She taps the floor with her foot nervously, biting her lips.*)

(*After a short pause*) Alfred! Get up, do you hear me? I want to make that bed before I go out. I'm sick of having this place in a continual mess on your account. (*With a certain vindictive satisfaction*) Not that we'll be here long unless you manage to get some money some place. Heaven knows I do my part—and more—going out to sew every day while you play the gentleman and loaf around barrooms with that good-for-nothing lot of artists from the Square.

(*A short pause during which she plays nervously with a cup and saucer on the table.*)

And where are you going to get money, I'd like to know? The rent's due this week and you know what the landlord is. He won't let us stay a minute over our time. You say you *can't* get a job. That's a lie and you know it. You never even look for one. All you do is moon around all day writing silly poetry and stories that no one will buy—and no wonder they won't. I notice I can always get a position, such as it is; and it's only that which keeps us from starving to death.

(*Gets up and goes over to the stove—looks into the coffee pot to see if the water is boiling; then comes back and sits down again.*)

You'll have to get money today some place. I can't do it all, and I won't do it all. You've got to come to your senses. You've got to beg, borrow, or steal it somewheres. (*With a contemptuous laugh*) But where, I'd like to know? You're too proud to beg, and you've borrowed the limit, and you haven't the nerve to steal.

(*After a pause—getting up angrily*) Aren't you up yet, for heaven's sake? It's just like you to go to sleep again, or pretend to. (*She goes to the bedroom door and looks in*) Oh, you are up. Well, it's about time. You needn't look at me like that. Your airs don't fool me a bit any more. I know you too well—better than you think I do—you and your goings-on. (*Turning away from the door—meaningly*) I know a lot of things, my dear. Never mind what I know, now. I'll tell you before I go, you needn't worry. (*She comes to the middle of the room and stands there, frowning.*)

(*Irritably*) Hmm! I suppose I might as well get breakfast ready— not that there's anything much to get. (*Questioningly*) Unless you have some money? (*She pauses for an answer from the next room which does not come*) Foolish question! (*She gives a short, hard laugh*) I ought to know you better than that by this time. When you left here in such a huff last night I knew what would happen. You can't be trusted for a second. A nice condition you came home in! The fight we had was only an excuse for you to make a beast of yourself. What was the use pawning your watch if all you wanted with the money was to waste it in buying drink?

(*Goes over to the dish closet and takes out plates, cups, etc., while she is talking.*)

Hurry up! It don't take long to get breakfast these days, thanks to you. All we got this morning is bread and butter and coffee; and you wouldn't even have that if it wasn't for me sewing my fingers off. (*She slams the loaf of bread on the table with a bang.*)

The bread's stale. I hope you'll like it. *You* don't deserve any better, but I don't see why *I* should suffer.

(*Going over to the stove*) The coffee'll be ready in a minute, and you needn't expect me to wait for you.

(*Suddenly with great anger*) What on earth are you doing all this time? (*She goes over to the door and looks in*) Well, you're *almost* dressed at any rate. I expected to find you back in bed. That'd be just like you. How awful you look this morning! For heaven's sake, shave! You're disgusting! You look like a tramp. No wonder no one will give you a job. I don't blame them—when you don't even look half-way decent. (*She goes to the stove*) There's plenty of hot water right here. You've got no excuse. (*Gets a bowl and pours some of the water from the coffee pot into it*) Here.

(*He reaches his hand into the room for it. It is a sensitive hand with slender fingers. It trembles and some of the water spills on the floor.*)

(*Tauntingly*) Look at your hand tremble. You'd better give up drinking. You can't stand it. It's just your kind that get the D.T.'s. *That would be* the last straw! (*Looking down at the floor*) Look at the mess you've made of this floor—cigarette butts and ashes all over the place. Why can't you put them on a plate? No, you wouldn't be considerate enough to do that. You never think of me. You don't have to sweep the room and that's all you care about.

(*Takes the broom and commences to sweep viciously, raising a cloud of dust. From the inner room comes the sound of a razor being stropped.*)

(*Sweeping*) Hurry up! It must be nearly time for me to go. If I'm late I'm liable to lose my position, and then I couldn't support you any longer. (*As an afterthought she adds sarcastically*) And then you'd have to go to work or something dreadful like that. (*Sweeping under the table*) What I want to know is whether you're going to look for a job today or not. You know your family won't help us any more. They've had enough of you, too. (*After a moment's silent sweeping*) I'm about sick of all this life. I've a good notion to go home, if I wasn't too proud to let them know what a failure you've been—you, the millionaire Rowland's only son, the Harvard graduate, the poet, the catch of the town—Huh! (*With bitterness*) There wouldn't be many of them now envy my catch if they knew the truth. What has our marriage been, I'd like to know? Even before your *millionaire* father died owing everyone in the world money, you certainly never wasted any of your time on your wife. I suppose you thought I'd ought to be glad you were *honorable* enough to marry after getting me into trouble. You were ashamed of me with your fine friends because my father's only a grocer, that's what you were. At least he's honest, which is more than anyone could say about yours. (*She is sweeping steadily toward the door. Leans on her broom for a moment.*)

You hoped everyone'd think you'd been forced to marry me, and pity you, didn't you? You didn't hesitate much about telling me you loved me, and making me believe your lies, before it happened, did you? You made me think you didn't want your father to buy me off as he tried to do. I know better now. I haven't lived with you all this time for nothing. (*Somberly*) It's lucky the poor thing was bom dead, after all. What a father you'd have been!

(*Is silent, brooding moodily for a moment—then she continues with a sort of savage joy.*)

But I'm not the only one who's got you to thank for being unhappy. There's one other, at least, and *she* can't hope to marry you now. (*She puts her head into the next room*) How about Helen? (*She starts back from the doorway, half frightened.*)

Don't look at me that way! Yes, I read her letter. What about it? I got a right to. I'm your wife. And I know all there is to know, so don't lie. You needn't stare at me so. You can't bully me with your superior airs any longer. Only for me you'd be going without breakfast this very morning. (*She sets the broom back in the corner—whiningly*) You never did have any gratitude for what I've done. (*She comes to the stove and puts the coffee into the pot*) The coffee's ready. I'm not going to wait for you. (*She sits down in her chair again.*)

(*After a pause—puts her hand to her head—fretfully*) My head aches so this morning. It's a shame I've got to go to work in a stuffy room all day in my condition. And I wouldn't if you were half a man. By rights I ought to be lying on my back instead of you. You know how sick I've been this last year, and yet you object when I take a little something to keep up my spirits. You even didn't want me to take that tonic I got at the drug store. (*With a hard laugh*) I know you'd be glad to have me dead and out of your way; then you'd be free to run after all these silly girls that think you're such a wonderful, misunderstood person—this Helen and the others. (*There is a sharp exclamation of pain from the next room.*)

(*With satisfaction*) There! I knew you'd cut yourself. It'll be a lesson to you. You know you oughtn't to be running around nights drinking with your nerves in such an awful shape. (*She goes to the door and looks in.*)

What makes you so pale? What are you staring at yourself in the mirror that way for? For goodness sake, wipe that blood off your face! (*With a shudder*) It's horrible. (*In relieved tones*) There, that's better. I never could stand the sight of blood. (*She shrinks back from the door a little*) You better give up trying and go to a barber shop. Your hand shakes dreadfully. Why do you stare at me like that? (*She turns away from the door*) Are you still mad at me about that letter? (*Defiantly*) Well, I had a right to read it. I'm your wife. (*She comes to the chair and sits down again. After a pause.*)

I knew all the time you were running around with someone. Your lame excuses about spending the time at the library didn't fool me. Who is this Helen, anyway? One of those artists? Or does she write poetry, too? Her letter sounds that way. I'll bet she told you your things were the best ever, and you believed her, like a fool.

Is she young and pretty? I was young and pretty, too, when you fooled me with your fine, poetic talk; but life with you would soon wear anyone down. What I've been through!

(*Goes over and takes the coffee off the stove*) Breakfast is ready. (*With a contemptuous glance*) Breakfast! (*Pours out a cup of coffee for herself and puts the pot on the table.*) Your coffee'll be cold. What are you doing—still shaving, for heaven's sake? You'd better give it up. One of these mornings you'll give yourself a serious cut. (*She cuts off bread and butters it. During the following speeches she eats and sips her coffee.*)

I'll have to run as soon as I've finished eating. One of us has got to work. (*Angrily*) Are you going to look for a job today or aren't you? I should think some of your fine friends would help you, if they really think you're so much. But I guess they just like to hear you talk. (*Sits in silence for a moment.*)

I'm sorry for this Helen, whoever she is. Haven't you got any feelings for other people? What will her family say? I see she mentions them in her letter. What is she going to do—have the child—or go to one of those doctors? That's a nice thing, I must say. Where can she get the money? Is she rich? (*She waits for some answer to this volley of questions.*)

Hmm! You won't tell me anything about her, will you? Much I care. Come to think of it, I'm not so sorry for her after all. She knew what she was doing. She isn't any schoolgirl, like I was, from the looks of her letter. Does she know you're married? Of course, she must. All your friends know about your unhappy marriage. I know they pity you, but they don't know my side of it. They'd talk different if they did.

(*Too busy eating to go on for a second or so.*)

This Helen must be a fine one, if she knew you were married. What does she expect, then? That I'll divorce you and let her marry you?

Does she think I'm crazy enough for that—after all you've made me go through? I guess not! And you can't get a divorce from me and you know it. No one can say *I've* ever done anything wrong. (*Drinks the last of her cup of coffee.*)

She deserves to suffer, that's all I can say. I'll tell you what I think; I think your Helen is no better than a common streetwalker, that's what I think. (*There is a stifled groan of pain from the next room.*)

Did you cut yourself again? Serves you right. (*Gets up and takes off her apron*) Well, I've got to run along. (*Peevishly*) This is a fine life for me to be leading! I won't stand for your loafing any longer. (*Something catches her ear and she pauses and listens intently*) There! You've overturned the water all over everything. Don't say you haven't. I can hear it dripping on the floor. (*A vague expression of fear comes over her face*) Alfred! Why don't you answer me?

(*She moves slowly toward the room. There is the noise of a chair being overturned and something crashes heavily to the floor. She stands, trembling with fright.*)

Alfred! Alfred! Answer me! What is it you knocked over? Are you still drunk? (*Unable to stand the tension a second longer she rushes to the door of the bedroom.*)

Alfred!

(*She stands in the doorway looking down at the floor of the inner room, transfixed with horror. Then she shrieks wildly and runs to the other door, unlocks it and frenziedly pulls it open, and runs shrieking madly into the outer hallway.*)

(THE CURTAIN FALLS)

QUESTIONS

1. Discuss the subject matter of "Before Breakfast." What kind of marriage does the couple have? What is the source of conflict?
2. The play is set in the Greenwich Village section of New York City. Why do the Rowlands live there? How is the setting related to Mr. Rowland's profession?
3. Why does Mr. Rowland not appear onstage? What effects does the play achieve by his absence?
4. Analyze Mrs. Rowland's characterization. Is she sympathetic in any way? Why or why not?
5. Could this play be considered a tragedy? Why or why not?
6. What happens to Mr. Rowland near the end of the play? What is the final effect of the play's ending?
7. Do some Internet research into Eugene O'Neill's life story. In what ways might this play be dealing with autobiographical themes?

MEREDITH OAKES
Mind the Gap

Characters

GINNY, *a mother*   *A London Underground* GUARD
LAWRENCE, *her son, fourteen*   *Passengers*
EMMA, *another mother*

SCENE. A station platform and the interior of a train of the Underground. The noise of the train when it is moving, and the silence when it is stopped, are central to the action. The dialogue can pause at the performers' discretion.

LAWRENCE *and* GINNY *are waiting for a train.* GINNY *sits.* LAWRENCE *stands nearby.* EMMA *approaches them.*

EMMA (*brusque*). Orthodontist is it?
GINNY. Emma. I was in a different movie.°
EMMA. What's he doing off school?
GINNY (*calls*). Lawrence. Say hullo to Emma, darling.
LAWRENCE. Hullo Emma darling. (*Turns away.*)
GINNY (*wearily*). They're amusing, aren't they.
EMMA. Mine aren't amusing.
GINNY. But isn't Nicholas so sweet with his trombone.
EMMA. Lawrence doesn't play?
GINNY. No, it seems to be weight training with us. They will pick the most expensive thing, won't they, and it's such a worry, isn't it, the brain damage, the house full of dumbbells . . .
EMMA. Where are you taking him?
GINNY. Lawrence, tell Emma about Mönchengladbach. He went to Mönchengladbach at Easter, didn't you Spoffy. On exchange.°

MIND THE GAP.   First performed in 1995. Meredith Oakes was born in 1946 in Sydney, Australia, and educated at the University of Sydney. She moved to London in 1971 and worked in music journalism. Her first play production was in 1993 at the Royal National Theatre studio, and since then she has had plays mounted by two of the most prestigious companies featuring new playwrights, the Royal Court Theatre and the Hampstead Theatre (where *Mind the Gap* was performed). She is married and the mother of two children. The title "mind the gap" quotes a recorded loudspeaker announcement in stations of the London Underground (i.e., subway) warning passengers of a dangerous space between the station platform and the cars of the train.

I was in a different movie: My mind was somewhere else. **Mönchengladbach . . . exchange:** He has been in a student exchange program in a small industrial city in northwest Germany.

LAWRENCE. I went to Mönchengladbach on exchange.

EMMA. I thought Mönchengladbach was nothing but factories.

LAWRENCE. It is.

GINNY. Lawrence stayed with a lovely family in the hills.

EMMA. Mönchengladbach hasn't got any hills. Why aren't you at school, Lawrence?

GINNY. I seem to be taking him to a careers adviser. He doesn't have a clue what to do with himself and yet I'm sure there must be something . . .

EMMA (*to* LAWRENCE). Haven't you had your appointment then?

GINNY. Oh we went and saw the woman at the school. It's just the basic, though, isn't it.

EMMA. Nothing wrong with the basic, is there?

GINNY. Well you get what you pay for, don't you. Did you enjoy the Easter Concert? It was exhausting to organize but such fun, honestly.

EMMA. Yes, they played well, didn't they.

GINNY. Do you know, I didn't listen to them, I used the time to write them their thank you letters, I find I have to prioritize, don't you, I envy these women that go out to work, I'm sure they don't have nearly as much to do as us. Here's the train, goodness knows where it's been.

EMMA. It's been to Wimbledon.

GINNY. Are you going far?

EMMA. Not far. Just to work.

GINNY (*drops her voice*). Emma, I didn't know. (*They get into the train and sit down together. Other passengers are in evidence, close enough to hear what's being said when it's stationary but not when it's moving.* GINNY *makes the following remark in a hushed voice.*) I honestly didn't know you were working. (*Pause.*) Patrick's all right, is he? Things are so difficult at the moment. (EMMA *nods.*) Half the people we used to know are out of work. (EMMA *nods.*) We shan't know anyone soon. (*The train starts.*)

EMMA. Patrick won't push.

GINNY. I expect working at a job that interests you is nice, isn't it?

EMMA. I wouldn't know.

GINNY. Weren't you something before you were married?

EMMA. Physiotherapist.

GINNY. You'd have to be so strong.

EMMA. I am strong.

GINNY. And caring. (EMMA *shrugs.*) So you're pummelling people into shape, are you?

EMMA. Companies get me in to massage them. My biggest client is a debt collector. Repeated strain injury.

GINNY. Really.

EMMA. I can't understand how so many people in our position fail to see the writing on the wall.

GINNY. Oh the graffitti, they never catch them do they.

EMMA. People like us can't afford silly ideas.

GINNY. Michael and I can still afford most things.

EMMA. I've told the boys there's always the comprehensive.°

GINNY. I'm sure you're exaggerating, Emma. Where would we be without your boys?

EMMA. They'd still be here you know. They'd be changing schools, not turning into werewolves.

GINNY. I don't know, I mean surely you could sell your lovely house.

EMMA. Patrick needs something to cling to. He's being swallowed by the overdraft. Keep this to yourself, but we're really in deep—(*The train stops.*)

GINNY. Southfields.

EMMA (*getting up to go*). Have fun with the careers adviser, Lawrence.

LAWRENCE. Yeah, thanks.

GINNY. Let me know about your lovely house! (EMMA *is gone. Silence.*) Do you want your ticket darling?

LAWRENCE. No thanks.

GINNY. Silly of me, I should have given it you at the barrier.° Mothers, aren't we a pain. (*The train starts. While the train is moving,* GINNY *talks to* LAWRENCE *in a different tone.*) Of all the people who could possibly have seen us.

LAWRENCE. What's your problem?

GINNY. That woman is so sadistically unpretentious. I suppose those who can't pretend, don't. What am I going to do?

LAWRENCE. She thinks it's the careers adviser.

GINNY. She won't rest until she's found the name, she'll have her eye on us from this moment on. People are always wanting to catch one out. That's all some of these people ever think of, they imagine we have such a wonderful life you know, heaven knows I play my part.

LAWRENCE. I told you to take the car.

GINNY. I said I'm not taking the car. (*Silence.*) You never stop, do you. You never stop getting at me until I give way to you. (*Silence.*) No car, Lawrence. We're taking the train.

LAWRENCE. If she sees you, you've only got yourself to blame, right?

GINNY. Oh no, Lawrence. Wrong. It's no use trying to twist things around to suit yourself. If it weren't for you, we wouldn't be here. Would we? (*Silence.*) There's no need to answer that.

Comprehensive: state-supported secondary school   **barrier:** entry to the station platform where tickets are inspected

LAWRENCE. If you don't want to be here, why are we going?

GINNY. We're going because you've made it necessary. You've left me no alternative.

LAWRENCE. So why couldn't we go in the car?

GINNY. Because I'm not taking the car to Brixton.°

LAWRENCE. Why not?

GINNY. Are you mad? Because it's not a place I want to take the car to.

LAWRENCE. Why the fuck isn't it a place you want to take the car to?

GINNY. Have you ever been to Brixton?

LAWRENCE. Yes.

GINNY. You've been to Brixton. For God's sake, Lawrence. You're fourteen.

LAWRENCE. What's wrong with Brixton?

GINNY. You're doing this deliberately.

LAWRENCE. What's wrong with Brixton?

GINNY. There's nowhere to park in Brixton.

LAWRENCE. Yes there is.

GINNY. I wouldn't know.

LAWRENCE. People park all over Brixton.

GINNY. So that's what you want me to do. The hell with everything, the hell with the car, park it all over Brixton like everyone else. I wonder why you're so determined to expose me to that.

LAWRENCE. You're so stupid. You're so fucking stupid.

GINNY. You simply can't discuss a thing sensibly, can you. Not with me. Not with your mother. You work yourself into a frenzy.

LAWRENCE. Fuck you!

GINNY. That's enough Lawrence, if you continue like this I'm going to pull the lever° and stop the train. Don't think I won't do it. I'm quite impulsive, you know.

LAWRENCE. All I'm saying is we ought to have taken the car.

GINNY. Oh for God's sake, do you think I like going to this place?

LAWRENCE. So why didn't you pick a guy near us?

GINNY. It isn't up to me to choose where the wretched man lives. (*Train is stopping. Silence.*)

LAWRENCE. Stephen's dad's a psychiatrist. He lives in Richmond.°

GINNY. Which one is Stephen, darling? Do I know him? I get so confused with all your friends trooping in and out. Is he the one with the ring through his nose?

LAWRENCE. I don't know the guy, he's just a guy in my class. I only mention him because his dad's a—

Brixton: known as a rough, racially mixed working-class district   **Lever:** switch to stop the train in an emergency (false alarms are heavily fined)   **Richmond:** an upper-class suburb

GINNY. They live in Richmond, do they? Where in Richmond?

LAWRENCE. Fucked if I know.

GINNY. Pardon, I didn't hear what you said.

LAWRENCE. Look, the point I was making is that you don't have to take me all the way to Brixton just to see a—

GINNY. What's become of your class list of addresses? Did they give you one this year? They usually type them out, don't they, and distribute them, I think it's so sensible, quite interesting to see the names, isn't it, quite multicultural your school, and of course then you can see where everyone lives. Did you give it me? I can't remember. We usually have it pinned up on the notice board in the kitchen. (*The train has started again.* GINNY *resumes her private voice.*) Do you want the whole carriage to know where you're going? You seem to be regarding this as some kind of joke. It's very far from a joke. A history of instability. That's what you're about to have.

LAWRENCE. Do you have to keep raking over the future?

GINNY. It's all very well for us to be enlightened about that sort of thing, which I am, because your father's poor cousin Elizabeth has been in analysis for years and you'd never know really, if she didn't insist on telling one which I always think is peculiar, she lacks the normal inhibitions . . . but I think it's terribly important for you to go into this experience in a positive frame of mind, purely for your own sake, because you want to get the most out of it, Lawrence, that's what we're paying for. I'd like to think that this young man could become a friend to you, someone to discuss things with that you might not want to say to me directly. Are there things like that Lawrence? (*Silence.*) I've done everything I could to avoid it coming to this, but all my initiatives have failed, haven't they. I shall have to admit when he questions me that all my initiatives have failed. I expect he will question me, won't he, don't you think? They like to involve the family don't they. I hope he won't ask me all sorts of embarrassing questions, the truth can be nasty, but let's leave your father out of this shall we. Anyway I defy some psychiatrist to make me talk, Lawrence.

LAWRENCE. I defy him to make you stop.

GINNY. Of course if there are things he wants to check with me, I shall cooperate. Because we don't want to be at cross purposes, do we. We want to know that everyone's being fair in what they say, we don't want this poor young man being used as an excuse to slag one another off,° Lawrence. As for my credentials as a mother, well frankly I

Slag one another off: criticize or insult one another.

think they'll stand up to examination. I don't feel I have anything to apologize for in that department. I wonder, should I have worn the cashmere dress, what do you think, the grey one, only I didn't want to walk in there looking like some bimbo who only ever thinks of her appearance.

LAWRENCE. What's it matter?

GINNY. Lawrence, I'm trying hard to be agreeable! It isn't easy! I don't know what it is that makes it so impossible for you to participate in the slightest thing that might give me pleasure.

LAWRENCE. Like being dragged off to have my head shrunk.

GINNY. Well you certainly haven't been worried about expanding it. (*Train is stopping. They sit in silence until it starts again.*) There's not really any reason for all this self-destructive behavior. Not if it's aimed at me, Lawrence.

LAWRENCE. If it's aimed at you, it isn't self-destructive, is it.

GINNY. Because if you do finally succeed in killing yourself with the life you lead I might just heave an enormous sigh of relief. What a terrible thing to say. How could I say such a terrible thing? This is what you've brought me to, Lawrence, I simply don't recognize myself any more. I was never meant to be horrid and cross and ugly, I was innocent, I was meant to be cared for. I pity any woman as stupid as I've been, all those years imagining my child would care for me. What an old-fashioned idea that's turned out to be. When I first took you to nursery school you couldn't bear me to leave you, tears flying everywhere. I'd have to change my skirt when I got home, there'd be sopping wet patches where you'd put your little face. Then one day that big teacher with the mustache said, "Don't worry Mrs. Amherst, five minutes after you're gone he's playing with the others as good as gold." Well, I didn't believe her of course. So do you know what I did? I squeezed around the side of the building and climbed on to the dustbins so I could see you all through the window. I couldn't believe my eyes, there you were running around with two other little boys, as happy as if I didn't exist. Those little drawings and messages I used to get, "Mummy I love you forever," you always knew how to make the grand gesture, didn't you. Love. You don't understand the meaning of the word. I've become bitter, Lawrence. I never expected to become a bitter person. You think you're bitter, I expect. I promise you, your bitterness is childsplay next to mine. I wanted a companion in this life to confide in, to laugh with, Lawrence, for heaven's sake, how long is it since you've laughed with me, why can't we laugh together for heaven's sake? All I wanted was someone to feel sorry for me when I cried and tell me when my clothes didn't suit me, to understand my side of things even when I might be hiding my feelings, because I don't complain even when there's a great deal to complain of. But let's not talk about your father. I wanted my child to see me as I really am, that's all. But you have your own view. I used to think of you as my little guardian angel. I used to think there was nothing you didn't understand. We communicated perfectly until you learned to talk. (*Silence.*) Your father and I confused you with clothes and money and electronic toys, we weakened your hold on reality. All of that is going to have to change. All of that is going to have to be earned. I'm sure the shrink in Brixton will agree. Judgment Day, Lawrence. As for the time you took money from my purse. Well of course it's symbolic.

LAWRENCE. Symbolic, yeah.

GINNY. The child stealing money from the mother's purse is actually trying to steal from her the love and attention which it feels for some reason it isn't able to get in the usual way. Don't ask me why you feel like that.

LAWRENCE. I was skint.°

GINNY. You know who Freud was, do you? Freud knew all about people like you. Freud discovered the subconscious of people like you, because what we see is only the tip of the iceberg, there's a great deal more unfortunately. Have you heard of the Oedipus Complex, in which sons want to marry their mothers it seems? Nothing to be ashamed of Lawrence, Freud says it's quite normal. But their mothers are already married, aren't they. Their mothers couldn't marry someone young enough to be their son, could they. They would have to say no, Lawrence. I'm sorry.

LAWRENCE. Don't worry about it.

GINNY. The point is, we understand that all this difficult behavior of yours relates to the fact that you're terribly dependent on me, if you could only admit it. If a person is the center of our lives, surely we should be able to tell them, give them some flowers, I don't know, I don't see why we have to be so repressed and English about these things, do you? If you could still say to me, as you did when you were so little and sweet, "Mummy I love you forever," it would solve so many problems. I truly believe that if you could come to terms with this thing, we shouldn't even be going on this wild goose chase to Brixton. We could get off this horrible train and take a taxi home. We'd be there in a quarter of an hour and you could still have the day off school, we could get you a video on the way and some cigarettes if you must, we could have fun

Skint: out of money

together Lawrence, it feels like centuries since I've had fun. For God's sake why don't you just say the word and we'll go home.

LAWRENCE. What word.

GINNY. Mummy I love you forever! (*Train stops.* GINNY *reverts to her "public" voice.*) We must get you some socks.

LAWRENCE. My feet are growing.

GINNY. They can't be, Spoff, not again.

LAWRENCE. I need some boots.

GINNY. Couldn't it be shoes this time darling. You all insist on these enormous boots. Don't you get tired lifting your feet up and down? You all look so exhausted all the time, those boots are draining you.

LAWRENCE. Only they're getting tight.

GINNY. Then we'd better do something about it, hadn't we. That's another blow to the poor old exchequer. Where's the best place darling, is it Kensington?

LAWRENCE. Catford.°

GINNY. I wish I'd been free to choose my own clothes when I was young. I think it's so important to choose one's own clothes at your age, after all you've got the rest of your life to be nicely dressed, haven't you? (*The train starts. Silence.*) Well?

LAWRENCE. What.

GINNY. Isn't there anything you can say?

LAWRENCE. I don't know.

GINNY. You don't know.

LAWRENCE. Look. You don't make it easy. All right?

GINNY. Oh Lawrence, let's not fight any more.

LAWRENCE. I'm not fighting.

GINNY. Look me in the eyes and say that.

LAWRENCE (*intensely embarrassed, looking her in the eyes*). I'm not fighting.

GINNY. Oh Lawrence I do love you.

LAWRENCE. When can we get the boots then?

GINNY. We paid sixty pounds for a new pair of boots only a month ago. I don't believe your feet have grown. You simply have no sense of proportion. I'm having to pay this man seventy you realize, this psychiatrist of yours, seventy pounds the first session is what he charges, they let you pay them for the sake of your self-respect, and I suppose one's self-respect is bound to cost, anyway there it is, I'm afraid that's your boots for this month.

LAWRENCE. Bollocks,° you can afford it.

Catford: upper- and lower-class districts **Bollocks:** (slang) testicles

GINNY. It's starting again, isn't it Lawrence.

LAWRENCE. What is?

GINNY. You deny it, do you? You deny that it's starting again.

LAWRENCE. Deny what?

GINNY. As soon as I give way to you an inch it starts. You're materialistic, Lawrence. You're absolutely hung up on possessions. Why? It's not as if you were poor or anything embarrassing like that.

LAWRENCE. Oh for Christ's sake.

GINNY. You're not very sincere, are you. You don't inspire me with much confidence honestly. I think you're cold, Lawrence. Calculating and cold. I think you'd walk over my dead body to get what you want. There isn't much you hold sacred, is there. I expect you're right Lawrence. Why should we hold a little thing like our mother and father sacred? It's every man for himself, isn't it. I ought to take a leaf out of your book. I've sacrificed myself for fifteen years and nothing to show for it, perhaps it's time I forgot about you and started looking for others to appreciate me. Don't imagine it doesn't happen. I could name you two women who are certainly no younger than I am, both with sons at the school, one of them in particular I'm thinking of, Angela met her out walking the dog and said, "How have you been keeping Helen"—never mind the name, and she replied, "I'm afraid I've been in bed all week." So naturally Angela said, oh you poor thing, this flu is really terrible, and do you know what she said, "Not with the flu, with Wayne." Wayne. A toy boy,° Lawrence. What do you think? Don't you think it would do me good? I ought to try it with your young psychiatrist perhaps, I'm sure with the benefit of all that training he'd know what I need. You haven't seen him, have you, he's blond with mobile features, well I'm still bloody mobile actually, tennis four times a week—besides men aren't choosy, are they—(*While she's saying this,* LAWRENCE *is pulling the lever to call the guard.*) Lawrence! What are you doing? Leave it alone. (*She jumps up and struggles with him. He pulls the lever and the train pulls into a station with the doors shut. Silence. When* GINNY *speaks again, she's trying to regain her "public" voice.*) What a stupid accident darling, why do you have to fidget with everything. (*She sits down.*) You've given everyone a dreadful fright.

LAWRENCE. (*vaguely, to passengers staring at him*). Sorry. Sorry.

GINNY. Sit down Lawrence, sit down or I'll scream. There's nothing to be upset about. (*He sits.*) At least we know those peculiar things work now, I've always wondered, haven't you? (GUARD *arrives.*)

Toy boy: young male lover

GUARD. What's the problem here?

GINNY. I'm terribly sorry, my son made the stupidest mistake, he honestly didn't mean it, did you Spoff, he just fell on it as the train moved.

LAWRENCE. I did it on purpose.

GINNY. This isn't the time for jokes, darling.

LAWRENCE. I did it because I'm mad.

GINNY. Stop it, Lawrence.

LAWRENCE. She's taking me to see the shrink.

GINNY. We're going to consult a careers adviser, his father wants him to be a lawyer, he certainly knows how to dominate a room.

LAWRENCE. We're going to see a psychiatrist.

GUARD. I don't give a monkeys if you're going to see Santa Claus.

LAWRENCE. I'm in a different movie.

GINNY. This is absurd, Lawrence. (*To* GUARD) You need a sense of humor, don't you.

GUARD. You must do.

LAWRENCE. Yes, I'm funny, aren't I, ha ha ha.

GUARD. Do you have some form of identification, madam?

GINNY. I'll give you my driving license, his name is Lawrence, his father's an absolute workaholic and we live in Wimbledon as you see, it isn't a flat it's a house.

GUARD. Are you able to assume responsibility for your son, madam?

GINNY. Do you take American Express?

LAWRENCE. She's not my mother. She's nothing like my mother. My mother's dead. This woman is mad.

GUARD. I have to take your particulars, madam, and you will receive a summons. (*He's writing down the name and address, using* GINNY's *driving license as a guide.*)

LAWRENCE (*to* GUARD). Don't leave me alone with her. Take me with you.

GUARD. I can't do that, you ain't housetrained.

LAWRENCE. Scream if you're mad. (*He screams.*)

GINNY (*in an undertone*). Stop it. I'll get you the boots. (LAWRENCE *is about to scream again.*) And a leather jacket, all right?

LAWRENCE. Green one.

GINNY (*in an undertone*). Yes.

LAWRENCE (*to* GUARD). Thank you for your prompt action, officer. People might have been killed.

GUARD. We can still hope. (*He leaves.*)

LAWRENCE (*calling after him*). Thank you. (*As the* GUARD *regains his post, the doors open.*)

GINNY. We do make things complicated for ourselves, don't we Lawrence. There isn't any need for things to be so complicated is there? Is there?

LAWRENCE. No.

GINNY. So let's keep it simple, shall we. Simple things are always so expensive. Where shall we go?

LAWRENCE. I thought we were going to Brixton.

GINNY. They won't have those boots in Brixton, darling, and this jacket, where can we get a green one, the Kings Road I expect, we could have a pancake.

LAWRENCE. Hackney.°

GINNY. Is there a train to Hackney?

LAWRENCE. Better take the car. (*The train starts.*)

GINNY. Yes, perhaps we'd better take the car.

QUESTIONS

1. What does the encounter with Emma reveal about Ginny's values? Why does Ginny speak in two voices, "public" when the train is quiet and not moving, and "private" at other times?

2. What is the significance of Ginny's concern about parking in Brixton, her description to the guard of her house in Wimbledon, the shopping areas that she offers to take Lawrence to? How are Lawrence's references to other areas relevant to the situation between him and his mother?

3. Ginny speaks of Lawrence's materialistic values and of his dependence on her. How are these remarks ironic?

4. What can you infer about the relationship between Ginny and her husband? How is it implied by Ginny's hope that Lawrence would become her "guardian angel"?

5. There is no specific information about why Lawrence is being taken to a psychiatrist. What can you infer from his mother's remarks about his behavior? What can you infer from Lawrence's speeches and actions?

6. Who seems to you to be more in need of counseling, Lawrence or Ginny? Explain.

7. The title of the play refers to the dangerous space between a station platform and the train, warning the passengers to be aware ("mind") of the physical danger of falling between them. What other kinds of "gap" is the play concerned with?

King's Road . . . Hackney: a shopping street for youthful modern clothes; a working-class district northeast of London

LORRAINE HANSBERRY

A Raisin in the Sun

To Mama: in gratitude for the dream

Characters

RUTH YOUNGER	JOSEPH ASAGAI
TRAVIS YOUNGER	GEORGE MURCHISON
WALTER LEE YOUNGER (*Brother*)	KARL LINDNER
BENEATHA YOUNGER	BOBO
LENA YOUNGER (*Mama*)	MOVING MEN

The action of the play is set in Chicago's Southside, sometime between World War II and the present.

ACT I

SCENE I. *Friday morning*

SCENE II. *The following morning*

ACT II

SCENE I. *Later, the same day*

SCENE II. *Friday night, a few weeks later*

SCENE III. *Saturday, moving day, one week later*

ACT III

An hour later

What happens to a dream deferred?
Does it dry up
Like a raisin in the sun?
Or fester like a sore—

A RAISIN IN THE SUN: First produced in 1959. Lorraine Hansberry (1930–1965) was a major voice in African American literature in the twentieth century who, before fulfilling her promise as a playwright, died of cancer at the age of thirty-four. Hansberry's best-known work, *A Raisin in the Sun* was the first play by a black woman to be produced on Broadway, where it ran for almost two years. In 1961, the play was made into a film starring Sidney Poitier.

And then run?
Does it stink like rotten meat?
Or crust and sugar over—
Like a syrupy sweet?

Maybe it just sags
Like a heavy load.

Or does it explode?

Langston Hughes[1]

ACT I

SCENE I. *The* YOUNGER *living room would be a comfortable and well-ordered room if it were not for a number of indestructible contradictions to this state of being. Its furnishings are typical and undistinguished and their primary feature now is that they have clearly had to accommodate the living of too many people for too many years—and they are tired. Still, we can see that at some time, a time probably no longer remembered by the family (except perhaps for* MAMA), *the furnishings of this room were actually selected with care and love and even hope—and brought to this apartment and arranged with taste and pride.*

That was a long time ago. Now the once loved pattern of the couch upholstery has to fight to show itself from under acres of crocheted doilies and couch covers which have themselves finally come to be more important than the upholstery. And here a table or a chair has been moved to disguise the worn places in the carpet; but the carpet has fought back by showing its weariness, with depressing uniformity, elsewhere on its surface.

Weariness has, in fact, won in this room. Everything has been polished, washed, sat on, used, scrubbed too often. All pretenses but living itself have long since vanished from the very atmosphere of this room.

Moreover, a section of this room, for it is not really a room unto itself, though the landlord's lease would make it seem so, slopes backward to provide a small kitchen area, where the family prepares the meals that are eaten in the living room proper, which must also serve as dining room. The single window that has been provided for these "two" rooms is located in this kitchen area. The sole natural light the family may enjoy in the course of a day is only that which fights its way through this little window.

At left, a door leads to a bedroom which is shared by MAMA *and her daughter,* BENEATHA. *At right, opposite, is a second room (which in the beginning of the life of this apartment was probably a breakfast room), which serves as a bedroom for* WALTER *and his wife,* RUTH.

Time: Sometime between World War II and the present.
Place: Chicago's Southside.
At rise: It is morning dark in the living room. TRAVIS *is asleep on the make-down bed at center. An alarm clock sounds from within the bedroom at right, and presently* RUTH *enters from that room and closes the door behind her. She crosses sleepily toward the window. As she passes her sleeping son she reaches down and shakes him a little. At the window she raises the shade and a dusky Southside morning light comes in feebly. She fills a pot with water and puts it on to boil. She calls to the boy, between yawns, in a slightly muffled voice.*

RUTH *is about thirty. We can see that she was a pretty girl, even exceptionally so, but now it is apparent that life has been little that she expected, and disappointment has already begun to hang in her face. In a few years, before thirty-five even, she will be known among her people as a "settled woman."*

She crosses to her son and gives him a good, final, rousing shake.

RUTH. Come on now, boy, it's seven thirty! (*Her son sits up at last, in a stupor of sleepiness.*) I say hurry up, Travis! You ain't the only person in the world got to use a bathroom! (*The child, a sturdy, handsome little boy of ten or eleven, drags himself out of the bed and almost blindly takes his towels and "today's clothes" from drawers and a closet and goes out to the bathroom, which is in an outside hall and which is shared by another family or families on the same floor.* RUTH *crosses to the bedroom door at right and opens it and calls in to her husband.*) Walter Lee! . . . It's after seven thirty! Lemme see you do some waking up in there now! (*She waits.*) You better get up from there, man! It's after seven thirty I tell you. (*She waits again.*) All right, you just go ahead and lay there and next thing you know Travis be finished and Mr. Johnson'll be in there and you'll be fussing and cussing round here like a mad man! And be late too! (*She waits, at the end of patience.*) Walter Lee—it's time for you to get up!

(*She waits another second and then starts to go into the bedroom, but is apparently satisfied that her husband has begun to get up. She stops, pulls the door to, and returns to the kitchen area. She wipes her face with a moist cloth and runs her fingers through her sleep-disheveled hair in a vain effort and ties an apron around her housecoat. The bedroom door at right opens and her husband stands in the doorway in his pajamas, which are rumpled and mismated. He is a lean, intense young man in his middle thirties, inclined to quick nervous movements and erratic speech habits—and always in his voice there is a quality of indictment.*)

WALTER. Is he out yet?

RUTH. What you mean *out*? He ain't hardly got in there good yet.

WALTER (*wandering in, still more oriented to sleep than to a new day*). Well, what was you doing all that yelling for if I can't even get in there yet? (*Stopping and thinking*) Check coming today?

RUTH. They *said* Saturday and this is just Friday and I hopes to God you ain't going to get up here first thing this morning and start talking to me 'bout no money—'cause I 'bout don't want to hear it.

WALTER. Something the matter with you this morning?

RUTH. No—I'm just sleepy as the devil. What kind of eggs you want?

WALTER. Not scrambled. (RUTH *starts to scramble eggs.*) Paper come? (RUTH *points impatiently to the rolled up* Tribune *on the table, and he gets it and spreads it out and vaguely reads the front page.*) Set off another bomb yesterday.

RUTH (*maximum indifference*). Did they?

WALTER (*looking up*). What's the matter with you?

RUTH. Ain't nothing the matter with me. And don't keep asking me that this morning.

WALTER. Ain't nobody bothering you. (*Reading the news of the day absently again*) Say Colonel McCormick is sick.

RUTH. (*affecting tea-party interest*). Is he now? Poor thing.

WALTER (*sighing and looking at his watch*). Oh, me. (*He waits.*) Now what is that boy doing in that bathroom all this time? He just going to have to start getting up earlier. I can't be being late to work on account of him fooling around in there.

RUTH (*turning on him*). Oh, no he ain't going to be getting up no earlier no such thing! It ain't his fault that he can't get to bed no earlier nights 'cause he got a bunch of crazy good-for-nothing clowns sitting up running their mouths in what is supposed to be his bedroom after ten o'clock at night. . . .

WALTER. That's what you mad about, ain't it? The things I want to talk about with my friends just couldn't be important in your mind, could they?

(*He rises and finds a cigarette in her handbag on the table and crosses to the little window and looks out, smoking and deeply enjoying this first one.*)

RUTH (*almost matter of factly, a complaint too automatic to deserve emphasis*). Why you always got to smoke before you eat in the morning?

WALTER (*at the window*). Just look at 'em down there. . . . Running and racing to work . . . (*he turns and faces his wife and watches her a moment at the stove, and then, suddenly*) You look young this morning, baby.

RUTH (*indifferently*). Yeah?

WALTER. Just for a second—stirring them eggs. It's gone now—just for a second it was—you looked real young again. (*Then, drily*) It's gone now—you look like yourself again.

RUTH. Man, if you don't shut up and leave me alone.

WALTER (*looking out to the street again*). First thing a man ought to learn in life is not to make love to no colored woman first thing in the morning. You all some evil people at eight o'clock in the morning.

(TRAVIS *appears in the hall doorway, almost fully dressed and quite wide awake now, his towels and pajamas across his shoulders. He opens the door and signals for his father to make the bathroom in a hurry.*)

TRAVIS (*watching the bathroom*). Daddy, come on!

(WALTER *gets his bathroom utensils and flies out to the bathroom.*)

RUTH. Sit down and have your breakfast, Travis.

TRAVIS. Mama, this is Friday. (*Gleefully*) Check coming tomorrow, huh?

RUTH. You get your mind off money and eat your breakfast.

TRAVIS (*eating*). This is the morning we supposed to bring the fifty cents to school.

RUTH. Well, I ain't got no fifty cents this morning.

TRAVIS. Teacher say we have to.

RUTH. I don't care what teacher say. I ain't got it. Eat your breakfast, Travis.

TRAVIS. I *am* eating.

RUTH. Hush up now and just eat!

(*The boy gives her an exasperated look for her lack of understanding, and eats grudgingly.*)

TRAVIS. You think Grandmama would have it?

RUTH. No! And I want you to stop asking your grandmother for money, you hear me?

TRAVIS (*outraged*). Gaaaleee! I don't ask her, she just gimme it sometimes!

RUTH. Travis Willard Younger—I got too much on me this morning to be—

TRAVIS. Maybe Daddy—

RUTH. *Travis!*

(*The boy hushes abruptly. They are both quiet and tense for several seconds.*)

TRAVIS (*presently*). Could I maybe go carry some groceries in front of the supermarket for a little while after school then?

RUTH. Just hush, I said. (TRAVIS *jabs his spoon into his cereal bowl viciously, and rests his head in anger upon his fists.*) If you through eating, you can get over there and make up your bed.

(*The boy obeys stiffly and crosses the room, almost mechanically, to the bed and more or less carefully folds the covering. He carries the bedding into his mother's room and returns with his books and cap.*)

TRAVIS (*sulking and standing apart from her unnaturally*). I'm gone.

RUTH (*looking up from the stove to inspect him automatically*). Come here. (*He crosses to her and she studies his head.*) If you don't take this comb and fix this here head, you better! (TRAVIS *puts down his books with a great sigh of oppression, and crosses to the mirror. His mother mutters under her breath about his "stubbornness."*) 'Bout to march out of here with that head looking just like chickens slept in it! I just don't know where you get your slubborn ways. . . . And get your jacket, too. Looks chilly out this morning.

TRAVIS (*with conspicuously brushed hair and jacket*). I'm gone.

RUTH. Get carfare and milk money—(*waving one finger*)—and not a single penny for no caps, you hear me?

TRAVIS (*with sullen politeness*). Yes'm.

(*He turns in outrage to leave. His mother watches after him as in his frustration he approaches the door almost comically. When she speaks to him, her voice has become a very gentle tease.*)

RUTH (*mocking; as she thinks he would say it*). Oh, Mama makes me so mad sometimes, I don't know what to do! (*She waits and continues to his back as he stands stock-still in front of the door.*) I wouldn't kiss that woman good-bye for nothing in this world this morning! (*The boy finally turns around and rolls his eyes at her, knowing the mood has changed and he is vindicated; he does not, however, move toward her yet.*) Not for nothing in this world! (*She finally laughs aloud at him and holds out her arms to him and we see that it is a way between them, very old and practiced. He crosses to her and allows her to embrace him warmly but keeps his face fixed with masculine rigidity. She holds him back from her presently and looks at him and runs her fingers over the features of his face. With utter gentleness—*) Now—whose little old angry man are you?

TRAVIS (*the masculinity and gruffness start to fade at last*). Aw gaalee—Mama . . .

RUTH (*mimicking*). Aw—gaaaaalleeeee, Mama! (*She pushes him, with rough playfulness and finality, toward the door.*) Get on out of here or you going to be late.

TRAVIS (*in the face of love, new aggressiveness*). Mama, could I *please* go carry groceries?

RUTH. Honey, it's starting to get so cold evenings.

WALTER (*coming in from the bathroom and drawing a make-believe gun from a make-believe holster and shooting at his son*). What is it he wants to do?

RUTH. Go carry groceries after school at the supermarket.

WALTER Well, let him go . . .

TRAVIS (*quickly, to the ally*). I *have* to—she won't gimme the fifty cents. . . .

WALTER (*to his wife only*). Why not?

RUTH (*simply, and with flavor*). 'Cause we don't have it.

WALTER (*to* RUTH *only*). What you tell the boy things like that for? (*Reaching down into his pants with a rather important gesture*) Here, son—

(*He hands the boy the coin, but his eyes are directed to his wife's.* TRAVIS *takes the money happily.*)

TRAVIS. Thanks, Daddy.

(*He starts out.* RUTH *watches both of them with murder in her eyes.* WALTER *stands and stares back at her with defiance, and suddenly reaches into his pocket again on an afterthought.*)

WALTER (*without even looking at his son, still staring hard at his wife*). In fact, here's another fifty cents. . . . Buy yourself some fruit today—or take a taxicab to school or something!

TRAVIS. Whoopee—

(*He leaps up and clasps his father around the middle with his legs, and they face each other in mutual appreciation; slowly* WALTER LEE *peeks around the boy to catch the violent rays from his wife's eyes and draws his head back as if shot.*)

WALTER. You better get down now—and get to school, man.

TRAVIS (*at the door*). O.K. Good-bye. (*He exits.*)

WALTER (*after him, pointing with pride*). That's *my* boy. (*She looks at him in disgust and turns back to her work.*) You know what I was thinking 'bout in the bathroom this morning?

RUTH. No.

WALTER. How come you always try to be so pleasant!

RUTH. What is there to be pleasant 'bout!

WALTER. You want to know what I was thinking 'bout in the bathroom or not!

RUTH. I know what you thinking 'bout.

WALTER (*ignoring her*). 'Bout what me and Willy Harris was talking about last night.

RUTH (*immediately—a refrain*). Willy Harris is a good-for-nothing loud mouth.

WALTER. Anybody who talks to me has got to be a good-for-nothing loud mouth, ain't he? And what you know about who is just a good-for-nothing loud mouth? Charlie Atkins was just a "good-for-nothing loud mouth" too, wasn't he! When he wanted me to go in the dry-cleaning business with him. And now—he's grossing a hundred thousand a year. A hundred thousand dollars a year! You still call *him* a loud mouth!

RUTH (*bitterly*). Oh, Walter Lee. . . . (*She folds her head on her arms over the table.*)

WALTER (*rising and coming to her and standing over her*). You tired, ain't you? Tired of everything. Me, the boy, the way we live—this beat-up hole—everything. Ain't you? (*She doesn't look up, doesn't answer.*) So tired—moaning and groaning all the time, but you wouldn't do nothing to help, would you? You couldn't be on my side that long for nothing, could you?

RUTH. Walter, please leave me alone.

WALTER. A man needs for a woman to back him up. . . .

RUTH. Walter—

WALTER. Mama would listen to you. You know she listen to you more than she do me and Bennie. She think more of you. All you have to do is just sit down with her when you drinking your coffee one morning and talking 'bout things like you do and—(*he sits down beside her and demonstrates graphically what he thinks her methods and tone should be*)—you just sip your coffee, see, and say easy like that you been thinking 'bout that deal Walter Lee is so interested in, 'bout the store and all, and sip some more coffee, like what you saying ain't really that important to you—And the next thing you know, she be listening good and asking you questions and when I come home—I can tell her the details. This ain't no fly-by-night proposition, baby. I mean we figured it out, me and Willy and Bobo.

RUTH (*with a frown*). Bobo?

WALTER. Yeah. You see, this little liquor store we got in mind cost seventy-five thousand and we figured the initial investment on the place be 'bout thirty thousand, see. That be ten thousand each. Course, there's a couple of hundred you got to pay so's you don't spend your life just waiting for them clowns to let your license get approved—

RUTH. You mean graft?

WALTER (*frowning impatiently*). Don't call it that. See there, that just goes to show you what women understand about the world. Baby, don't *nothing* happen for you in this world 'less you pay *somebody* off!

RUTH. Walter, leave me alone! (*She raises her head and stares at him vigorously—then says, more quietly*) Eat your eggs, they gonna be cold.

WALTER (*straightening up from her and looking off*). That's it. There you are. Man say to his woman: I got me a dream. His woman say: Eat your eggs. (*Sadly, but gaining in power*) Man say: I got to take hold of this here world, baby! And a woman will say: Eat your eggs and go to work. (*Passionately now*) Man say: I got to change my life, I'm choking to death, baby! And his woman say—(*in utter anguish as he brings his fists down on his thighs*)—Your eggs is getting cold!

RUTH (*softly*). Walter, that ain't none of our money.

WALTER (*not listening at all or even looking at her*). This morning, I was lookin' in the mirror and thinking about it. . . . I'm thirty-five years old; I been married eleven years and I got a boy who sleeps, in the living room—(*very, very quietly*)—and all I got to give him is stories about how rich white people live. . . .

RUTH. Eat your eggs, Walter.

WALTER. *Damn my eggs . . . damn all the eggs that ever was!*

RUTH. Then go to work.

WALTER (*looking up at her*). See—I'm trying to talk to you 'bout myself—(*shaking his head with the repetition*)—and all you can say is eat them eggs and go to work.

RUTH (*wearily*). Honey, you never say nothing new. I listen to you every day, every night and every morning, and you never say nothing new. (*Shrugging*) So you would rather *be* Mr. Arnold than be his chauffeur. So—I would *rather* be living in Buckingham Palace.

WALTER. That is just what is wrong with the colored woman in this world. . . . Don't understand about building their men up and making 'em feel like they somebody. Like they can do something.

RUTH (*drily, but to hurt*). There *are* colored men who do things.

WALTER. No thanks to the colored woman.

RUTH. Well, being a colored woman, I guess I can't help myself none.

(*She rises and gets the ironing board and sets it up and attacks a huge pile of rough-dried clothes, sprinkling them in preparation for the ironing and then rolling them into tight fat balls.*)

WALTER (*mumbling*). We one group of men tied to a race of women with small minds.

(*His sister* BENEATHA *enters. She is about twenty, as slim and intense as her brother. She is not as pretty as her sister-in-law, but her lean, almost intellectual face has a handsomeness of its own. She wears a bright-red flannel nightie, and her thick hair stands wildly about her head. Her speech is a mixture of many things; it is different from the rest of the family's insofar as education has per-meated her sense of English—and perhaps the Midwest rather than the South has finally—at last—won out in her inflection; but not altogether, because over all of it is a soft slurring and transformed use of vowels which is the decided influence of the Southside. She passes through the room without looking at either* RUTH *or* WALTER *and goes to the outside door and looks, a little blindly, out to the bathroom. She sees that it has been lost to the Johnsons. She closes the door with a sleepy vengeance and crosses to the table and sits down a little defeated.*)

BENEATHA. I am going to start timing those people.

WALTER. You should get up earlier.

BENEATHA (*her face in her hands. She is still fighting the urge to go back to bed*). Really—would you suggest dawn? Where's the paper?

WALTER (*pushing the paper across the table to her as he studies her almost clini-cally, as though he has never seen her before*). You a horrible-looking chick at this hour.

BENEATHA (*drily*). Good morning, everybody.

WALTER (*senselessly*). How is school coming'?

BENEATHA (*in the same spirit*). Lovely. Lovely. And you know, biology is the greatest. (*Looking up at him*) I dissected something that looked just like you yesterday.

WALTER. I just wondered if you've made up your mind and everything.

BENEATHA (*gaining in sharpness and impatience*). And what did I answer yesterday morning—and the day before that?

RUTH (*from the ironing board, like someone disinterested and old*). Don't be so nasty, Bennie.

BENEATHA (*still to her brother*). And the day before that and the day before that!

WALTER (*defensively*). I'm interested in you. Something wrong with that? Ain't many girls who decide—

WALTER *and* BENEATHA (*in unison*). —"to be a doctor."

(*Silence.*)

WALTER. Have we figured out yet just exactly how much medical school is going to cost?

RUTH. Walter Lee, why don't you leave that girl alone and get out of here to work?

BENEATHA (*exits to the bathroom and bangs on the door*). Come on out of there, please! (*She comes back into the room.*)

WALTER (*looking at his sister intently*). You know the check is coming tomorrow.

BENEATHA (*turning on him with a sharpness all her own*). That money belongs to Mama, Walter, and it's for her to decide how she wants to use it. I don't care if she wants to buy a house or a rocket ship or just nail it up somewhere and look at it. It's hers. Not ours—*hers*.

WALTER (*bitterly*). Now ain't that fine! You just got your mother's interest at heart, ain't you, girl? You such a nice girl—but if Mama got that money she can always take a few thousand and help you through school too—can't she?

BENEATHA. I have never asked anyone around here to do anything for me!

WALTER. No! And the line between asking and just accepting when the time comes is big and wide—ain't it!

BENEATHA (*with fury*). What do you want from me, Brother—that I quit school or just drop dead, which!

WALTER. I don't want nothing but for you to stop acting holy 'round here. Me and Ruth done made some sacrifices for you—why can't you do something for the family?

RUTH. Walter, don't be dragging me in it.

WALTER. You are in it—Don't you get up and go work in somebody's kitchen for the last three years to help put clothes on her back?

RUTH. Oh, Walter—that's not fair. . . .

WALTER. It ain't that nobody expects you to get on your knees and say thank you, Brother; thank you, Ruth; thank you, Mama—and thank you, Travis, for wearing the same pair of shoes for two semesters—

BENEATHA (*dropping to her knees*). Well—I *do*—all right?—thank everybody . . . and forgive me for ever wanting to be anything at all . . . forgive me, forgive me!

RUTH. Please stop it! Your mama'll hear you.

WALTER. Who the hell told you you had to be a doctor? If you so crazy 'bout messing 'round with sick people—then go be a nurse like other women—or just get married and be quiet. . . .

BENEATHA. Well—you finally got it said. . . . It took you three years but you finally got it said. Walter, give up; leave me alone—it's Mama's money.

WALTER. *He was my father, too!*

BENEATHA. So what? He was mine, too—and Travis' grandfather—but the insurance money belongs to Mama. Picking on me is not going to make her give it to you to invest in any liquor stores—(*underbreath, dropping into a chair*)—and I for one say, God bless Mama for that!

WALTER (*to* RUTH). See—did you hear? Did you hear!

RUTH. Honey, please go to work.

WALTER. Nobody in this house is ever going to understand me.

BENEATHA. Because you're a nut.

WALTER. Who's a nut?

BENEATHA. You—you are a nut. Thee is mad, boy.

WALTER (*looking at his wife and his sister from the door, very sadly*). The world's most backward race of people, and that's a fact.

BENEATHA (*turning slowly in her chair*). And then there are all those prophets who would lead us out of the wilderness—(WALTER *slams out of the house.*)—into the swamps!

RUTH. Bennie, why you always gotta be pickin' on your brother? Can't you be a little sweeter sometimes? (*Door opens.* WALTER *walks in.*)

WALTER (*to* RUTH). I need some money for carfare.

RUTH (*looks at him, then warms; teasing, but tenderly*). Fifty cents? (*She goes to her bag and gets money.*) Here, take a taxi.

 (WALTER *exits.* MAMA *enters. She is a woman in her early sixties, full-bodied and strong. She is one of those women of a certain grace and beauty who wear it so unobtrusively that it takes a while to notice. Her dark-brown face is surrounded by the total whiteness of her hair, and, being a woman who has adjusted to many things in life and overcome many more, her face is full of strength. She has, we can see, wit and faith of a kind that keep her eyes lit and full of interest and expectancy. She is, in a word, a beautiful woman. Her bearing is perhaps most like the noble bearing of the women of the Hereros of Southwest Africa—rather as if she imagines that as she walks she still bears a basket or a vessel upon her head. Her speech, on the other hand, is as careless as her carriage is precise—she is inclined to slur everything—but her voice is perhaps not so much quiet as simply soft.*)

MAMA. Who that 'round here slamming doors at this hour?

 (*She crosses through the room, goes to the window, opens it, and brings in a feeble little plant growing doggedly in a small pot on the window sill. She feels the dirt and puts it back out.*)

RUTH. That was Walter Lee. He and Bennie was at it again.

MAMA. My children and they tempers. Lord, if this little old plant don't get more sun than it's been getting it ain't never going to see spring again. (*She turns from the window.*) What's the matter with you this morning, Ruth? You looks right peaked. You aiming to iron all them things? Leave some for me. I'll get to 'em this afternoon. Bennie honey, it's too drafty for you to be sitting 'round half dressed. Where's your robe?

BENEATHA. In the cleaners.

MAMA. Well, go get mine and put it on.

BENEATHA. I'm not cold, Mama, honest.

MAMA. I know—but you so thin. . . .

BENEATHA (*irritably*). Mama, I'm not cold.

MAMA (*seeing the make-down bed as* TRAVIS *has left it*). Lord have mercy, look at that poor bed. Bless his heart—he tries, don't he? (*She moves to the bed* TRAVIS *has sloppily made up.*)

RUTH. No—he don't half try at all 'cause he knows you going to come along behind him and fix everything. That's just how come he don't know how to do nothing right now—you done spoiled that boy so.

MAMA. Well—he's a little boy. Ain't supposed to know 'bout housekeeping. My baby, that's what he is. What you fix for his breakfast this morning?

RUTH (*angrily*). I feed my son, Lena!

MAMA. I ain't meddling—(*underbreath; busy-bodyish*) I just noticed all last week he had cold cereal, and when it starts getting this chilly in the fall a child ought to have some hot grits or something when he goes out in the cold—

RUTH (*furious*). I gave him hot oats—is that all right!

MAMA. I ain't meddling. (*Pause.*) Put a lot of nice butter on it? (RUTH *shoots her an angry look and does not reply.*) He likes lots of butter.

RUTH (*exasperated*). Lena—

MAMA (*to* BENEATHA. MAMA *is inclined to wander conversationally sometimes*). What was you and your brother fussing 'bout this morning?

BENEATHA. It's not important, Mama.

  (*She gets up and goes to look out at the bathroom, which is apparently free, and she picks up her towels and rushes out.*)

MAMA. What was they fighting about?

RUTH. Now you know as well as I do.

MAMA (*shaking her head*). Brother still worrying his self sick about that money?

RUTH. You know he is.

MAMA. You had breakfast?

RUTH. Some coffee.

MAMA. Girl, you better start eating and looking after yourself better. You almost thin as Travis.

RUTH. Lena—

MAMA. Un-hunh?

RUTH. What are you going to do with it?

MAMA. Now don't you start, child. It's too early in the morning to be talking about money. It ain't Christian.

RUTH. It's just that he got his heart set on that store—

MAMA. You mean that liquor store that Willy Harris want him to invest in?

RUTH. Yes—

MAMA. We ain't no business people, Ruth. We just plain working folks.

RUTH. Ain't nobody business people till they go into business. Walter Lee say colored people ain't never going to start getting ahead till they start gambling on some different kinds of things in the world—investments and things.

MAMA. What done got into you, girl? Walter Lee done finally sold you on investing.

RUTH. No. Mama, something is happening between Walter and me. I don't know what it is—but he needs something—something I can't give him any more. He needs this chance, Lena.

MAMA (*frowning deeply*). But liquor, honey—

RUTH. Well—like Walter say—I spec people going to always be drinking themselves some liquor.

MAMA. Well—whether they drinks it or not ain't none of my business. But whether I go into business selling it to 'em *is*, and I don't want that on my ledger this late in life. (*Stopping suddenly and studying her daughter-in-law*) Ruth Younger, what's the matter with you today? You look like you could fall over right there.

RUTH. I'm tired.

MAMA. Then you better stay home from work today.

RUTH. I can't stay home. She'd be calling up the agency and screaming at them, "My girl didn't come in today—send me somebody! My girl didn't come in!" Oh, she just have a fit. . . .

MAMA. Well, let her have it. I'll just call her up and say you got the flu—

RUTH (*laughing*). Why the flu?

MAMA. 'Cause it sounds respectable to 'em. Something white people get, too. They know 'bout the flu. Otherwise they think you been cut up or something when you tell 'em you sick.

RUTH. I got to go in. We need the money.

MAMA. Somebody would of thought my children done all but starved to death the way they talk about money here late. Child, we got a great big old check coming tomorrow.

RUTH (*sincerely, but also self-righteously*). Now that's your money. It ain't got nothing to do with me. We all feel like that—Walter and Bennie and me—even Travis.

MAMA (*thoughtfully, and suddenly, very far away*). Ten thousand dollars—

RUTH. Sure is wonderful.

MAMA. Ten thousand dollars.

RUTH. You know what you should do, Miss Lena? You should take yourself a trip somewhere. To Europe or South America or someplace—

MAMA (*throwing up her hands at the thought*). Oh, child!

RUTH. I'm serious. Just pack up and leave! Go on away and enjoy yourself some. Forget about the family and have yourself a ball for once in your life—

MAMA (*drily*). You sound like I'm just about ready to die. Who'd go with me? What I look like wandering 'round Europe by myself?

RUTH. Shoot—these here rich white women do it all the time. They don't think nothing of packing up they suitcases and piling on one of them big steamships and—swoosh!—they gone, child.

MAMA. Something always told me I wasn't no rich white woman.

RUTH. Well—what are you going to do with it then?

MAMA. I ain't rightly decided. (*Thinking. She speaks now with emphasis.*) Some of it got to be put away for Beneatha and her schoolin'—and ain't nothing going to touch that part of it. Nothing. (*She waits several seconds, trying to make up her mind about something, and looks at* RUTH *a little tentatively before going on.*) Been thinking that we maybe could meet the notes on a little old two-story somewhere, with a yard where Travis could play in the summertime, if we use part of the insurance for a down payment and everybody kind of pitch in. I could maybe take on a little day work again, few days a week—

RUTH (*studying her mother-in-law furtively and concentrating on her ironing, anxious to encourage without seeming to*). Well, Lord knows, we've put enough rent into this here rat trap to pay for four houses by now . . .

MAMA (*looking up at the words "rat trap" and then looking around and leaning back and sighing—in a suddenly reflective mood—*). "Rat trap"—yes, that's all it is. (*Smiling*) I remember just as well the day me and Big Walter moved in here. Hadn't been married but two weeks and wasn't planning on living here no more than a year. (*She shakes her head at the dissolved dream.*) We was going to set away, little by little, don't you know, and buy a little place out in Morgan Park. We had even picked out the house. (*Chuckling a little*) Looks right dumpy today. But Lord, child, you should know all the dreams I had 'bout buying that house and fixing it up and making me a little garden in the back—(*She waits and stops smiling.*) And didn't none of it happen. (*Dropping her hands in a futile gesture.*)

RUTH (*keeps her head down, ironing*). Yes, life can be a barrel of disappointments, sometimes.

MAMA. Honey, Big Walter would come in here some nights back then and slump down on that couch there and just look at the rug, and look at me and look at the rug and then back at me—and I'd know he was down then . . . really down. (*After a second, very long and thoughtful pause; she is seeing back to times that only she can see.*) And then, Lord, when I lost that baby—little Claude—I almost thought I was going to lose Big Walter too. Oh, that man grieved hisself! He was one man to love his children.

RUTH. Ain't nothin' can tear at you like losin' your baby.

MAMA. I guess that's how come that man finally worked hisself to death like he done. Like he was fighting his own war with this here world that took his baby from him.

RUTH. He sure was a fine man, all right. I always liked Mr. Younger.

MAMA. Crazy 'bout his children! God knows there was plenty wrong with Walter Younger—hard-headed, mean, kind of wild with women— plenty wrong with him. But he sure loved his children. Always wanted them to have something—be something. That's where Brother gets all these notions, I reckon. Big Walter used to say, he'd get right wet in the eyes sometimes, lean his head back with the water standing in his eyes and say, "Seem like God didn't see fit to give the black man nothing but dreams—but He did give us children to make them dreams seem worth while." (*She smiles.*) He could talk like that, don't you know.

RUTH. Yes, he sure could. He was a good man, Mr. Younger.

MAMA. Yes, a fine man—just couldn't never catch up with his dreams, that's all.

(BENEATHA *comes in, brushing her hair and looking up to the ceiling, where the sound of a vacuum cleaner has started up.*)

BENEATHA. What could be so dirty on that woman's rugs that she has to vacuum them every single day?

RUTH. I wish certain young women 'round here who I could name would take inspiration about certain rugs in a certain apartment I could also mention.

BENEATHA (*shrugging*). How much cleaning can a house need, for Christ's sakes.

MAMA (*not liking the Lord's name used thus*). Bennie!

RUTH. Just listen to her—just listen!

BENEATHA. Oh, God!

MAMA. If you use the Lord's name just one more time—

BENEATHA (*a bit of a whine*). Oh, Mama—

RUTH. Fresh—just fresh as salt, this girl!

BENEATHA (*drily*). Well—if the salt loses its savor—

MAMA. Now that will do. I just ain't going to have you 'round here reciting the scriptures in vain—you hear me?

BENEATHA. How did I manage to get on everybody's wrong side by just walking into a room?

RUTH. If you weren't so fresh—

BENEATHA. Ruth, I'm twenty years old.

MAMA. What time you be home from school today?

BENEATHA. Kind of late. (*With enthusiasm*) Madeline is going to start my guitar lessons today.

(MAMA *and* RUTH *look up with the same expression.*)

MAMA. Your *what* kind of lessons?

BENEATHA. Guitar.

RUTH. Oh, Father!

MAMA. How come you done taken it in your mind to learn to play the guitar?

BENEATHA. I just want to, that's all.

MAMA (*smiling*). Lord, child, don't you know what to do with yourself? How long it going to be before you get tired of this now—like you got tired of that little play-acting group you joined last year? (*Looking at* RUTH) And what was it the year before that?

RUTH. The horseback-riding club for which she bought that fifty-five-dollar riding habit that's been hanging in the closet ever since!

MAMA (*to* BENEATHA). Why you got to flit so from one thing to another, baby?

BENEATHA (*sharply*). I just want to learn to play the guitar. Is there anything wrong with that?

MAMA. Ain't nobody trying to stop you. I just wonders sometimes why you has to flit so from one thing to another all the time. You ain't never done nothing with all that camera equipment you brought home—

BENEATHA. I don't flit! I—I experiment with different forms of expression—

RUTH. Like riding a horse?

BENEATHA. —People have to express themselves one way or another.

MAMA. What is it you want to express?

BENEATHA (*angrily*). Me! (MAMA *and* RUTH *look at each other and burst into raucous laughter.*) Don't worry—I don't expect you to understand.

MAMA (*to change the subject*). Who you going out with tomorrow night?

BENEATHA (*with displeasure*). George Murchison again.

MAMA (*pleased*). Oh—you getting a little sweet on him?

RUTH. You ask me, this child ain't sweet on nobody but herself— (*Underbreath*) Express herself!

(*They laugh.*)

BENEATHA. Oh—I like George all right, Mama. I mean I like him enough to go out with him and stuff, but—

RUTH (*for devilment*). What does *and stuff* mean?

BENEATHA. Mind your own business.

MAMA. Stop picking at her now, Ruth. (*A thoughtful pause, and then a suspicious sudden look at her daughter as she turns in her chair for emphasis*) What *does* it mean?

BENEATHA (*wearily*). Oh, I just mean I couldn't ever really be serious about George. He's—he's so shallow.

RUTH. Shallow—what do you mean he's shallow? He's *rich!*

MAMA. Hush, Ruth.

BENEATHA. I know he's rich. He knows he's rich, too.

RUTH. Well—what other qualities a man got to have to satisfy you, little girl?

BENEATHA. You wouldn't even begin to understand. Anybody who married Walter could not possibly understand.

MAMA (*outraged*). What kind of way is that to talk about your brother?

BENEATHA. Brother is a flip—let's face it.

MAMA (*to* RUTH, *helplessly*). What's a flip?

RUTH (*glad to add kindling*). She's saying he's crazy.

BENEATHA. Not crazy. Brother isn't really crazy yet—he—he's an elaborate neurotic.

MAMA. Hush your mouth!

BENEATHA. As for George. Well. George looks good—he's got a beautiful car and he takes me to nice places and, as my sister-in-law says, he is probably the richest boy I will ever get to know and I even like him sometimes—but if the Youngers are sitting around waiting to see if their little Bennie is going to tie up the family with the Murchisons, they are wasting their time.

RUTH. You mean you wouldn't marry George Murchison if he asked you someday? That pretty, rich thing? Honey, I knew you was odd—

BENEATHA. No I would not marry him if all I felt for him was what I feel now. Besides, George's family wouldn't really like it.

MAMA. Why not?

BENEATHA. Oh, Mama—The Murchisons are honest-to-God-real-*live*-rich colored people, and the only people in the world who are more snobbish than rich white people are rich colored people. I thought everybody knew that. I've met Mrs. Murchison. She's a scene!

MAMA. You must not dislike people 'cause they well off, honey.

BENEATHA. Why not? It makes just as much sense as disliking people 'cause they are poor, and lots of people do that.

RUTH (*a wisdom-of-the-ages manner. To* MAMA). Well, she'll get over some of this—

BENEATHA. Get over it? What are you talking about, Ruth? Listen, I'm going to be a doctor. I'm not worried about who I'm going to marry yet—if I ever get married.

MAMA *and* RUTH. *If!*

MAMA. Now, Bennie—

BENEATHA. Oh, I probably will . . . but first I'm going to be a doctor, and George, for one, still thinks that's pretty funny. I couldn't be bothered with that, I am going to be a doctor and everybody around here better understand that!

MAMA (*kindly*). 'Course you going to be a doctor, honey, God willing.

BENEATHA (*drily*). God hasn't got a thing to do with it.

MAMA. Beneatha—that just wasn't necessary.

BENEATHA. Well—neither is God. I get sick of hearing about God.

MAMA. Beneatha!

BENEATHA. I mean it! I'm just tired of hearing about God all the time. What has He got to do with anything? Does He pay tuition?

MAMA. YOU 'bout to get your fresh little jaw slapped!

RUTH. That's just what she needs, all right!

BENEATHA. Why? Why can't I say what I want to around here, like everybody else?

MAMA. It don't sound nice for a young girl to say things like that—you wasn't brought up that way. Me and your father went to trouble to get you and Brother to church every Sunday.

BENEATHA. Mama, you don't understand. It's all a matter of ideas, and God is just one idea I don't accept. It's not important, I am not going out and be immoral or commit crimes because I don't believe in God. I don't even think about it. It's just that I get tired of Him getting credit for all the things the human race achieves through its own stubborn effort. There simply is no blasted God—there is only man and it is he who makes miracles!

(MAMA *absorbs this speech, studies her daughter and rises slowly and crosses to* BENEATHA *and slaps her powerfully across the face. After, there is only silence and the daughter drops her eyes from her mother's face, and* MAMA *is very tall before her.*)

MAMA. Now—you say after me, in my mother's house there is still God. (*There is a long pause and* BENEATHA *stares at the floor wordlessly.* MAMA *repeats the phrase with precision and cool emotion.*) In my mother's house there is still God.

BENEATHA. In my mother's house there is still God.

(*A long pause*)

MAMA (*walking away from* BENEATHA, *too disturbed for triumphant posture. Stopping and turning back to her daughter*). There are some ideas we ain't going to have in this house. Not long as I am at the head of this family.

BENEATHA. Yes, ma'am.

(MAMA *walks out of the room.*)

RUTH (*almost gently, with profound understanding*). You think you a woman, Bennie—but you still a little girl. What you did was childish—so you got treated like a child.

BENEATHA. I see. (*Quietly*) I also see that everybody thinks it's all right for Mama to be a tyrant. But all the tyranny in the world will never put a God in the heavens! (*She picks up her books and goes out.*)

RUTH (*goes to* MAMA's *door*). She said she was sorry.

MAMA (*coming out, going to her plant*). They frightens me, Ruth. My children.

RUTH. You got good children, Lena. They just a little off sometimes—but they're good.

MAMA. No—there's something come down between me and them that don't let us understand each other and I don't know what it is. One done

almost lost his mind thinking 'bout money all the time and the other
done commence to talk about things I can't seem to understand in no
form or fashion. What is it that's changing, Ruth?

RUTH (*soothingly, older than her years*). Now . . . you taking it all too seriously.
You just got strong-willed children and it takes a strong woman like
you to keep 'em in hand.

MAMA (*looking at her plant and sprinkling a little water on it*). They spirited
all right, my children. Got to admit they got spirit—Bennie and
Walter. Like this little old plant that ain't never had enough sunshine or
nothing—and look at it. . . .

(*She has her back to* RUTH, *who has had to stop ironing and lean against
something and put the back of her hand to her forehead.*)

RUTH (*trying to keep* MAMA *from noticing*). You . . . sure . . . loves that little
old thing, don't you? . . .

MAMA. Well, I always wanted me a garden like I used to see sometimes
at the back of the houses down home. This plant is close as I ever got
to having one. (*She looks out of the window as she replaces the plant.*) Lord,
ain't nothing as dreary as the view from this window on a dreary day, is
there? Why ain't you singing this morning, Ruth? Sing that "No Ways
Tired." That song always lifts me up so—(*She turns at last to see that*
RUTH *has slipped quietly into a chair, in a state of semiconsciousness.*) Ruth!
Ruth honey—what's the matter with you . . . Ruth!

CURTAIN

SCENE II. *It is the following morning; a Saturday morning, and house
cleaning is in progress at the* YOUNGERS. *Furniture has been shoved hither and
yon and* MAMA *is giving the kitchen-area walls a washing down.* BENEATHA,
*in dungarees, with a handkerchief tied around her face, is spraying insecticide
into the cracks in the walls. As they work, the radio is on and a Southside
disc-jockey program is inappropriately filling the house with a rather exotic
saxophone blues.* TRAVIS, *the sole idle one, is leaning on his arms, looking out
of the window.*

TRAVIS. Grandmama, that stuff Bennie is using smells awful. Can I go
downstairs, please?

MAMA. Did you get all them chores done already? I ain't see you doing much.

TRAVIS. Yes'm—finished early. Where did Mama go this morning?

MAMA (*looking at* BENEATHA). She had to go on a little errand.

TRAVIS. Where?

MAMA. To tend to her business.

TRAVIS. Can I go outside then?

MAMA. Oh, I guess so. You better stay right in front of the house,
though . . . and keep a good lookout for the postman.

TRAVIS. Yes'm. (*He starts out and decides to give his* AUNT BENEATHA *a good swat on the legs as he passes her.*) Leave them poor little old cockroaches alone, they ain't bothering you none.

(*He runs as she swings the spray gun at him both viciously and playfully.* WALTER *enters from the bedroom and goes to the phone.*)

MAMA. Look out there, girl, before you be spilling some of that stuff on that child!

TRAVIS (*teasing*). That's right—look out now! (*He exits.*)

BENEATHA (*drily*). I can't imagine that it would hurt him—it has never hurt the roaches.

MAMA. Well, little boys' hides ain't as tough as Southside roaches.

Walter (*into phone*). Hello—Let me talk to Willy Harris.

MAMA. You better get over there behind the bureau. I seen one marching out of there like Napoleon yesterday.

WALTER. Hello. Willy? It ain't come yet. It'll be here in a few minutes. Did the lawyer give you the papers?

BENEATHA. There's really only one way to get rid of them, Mama—

MAMA. How?

BENEATHA. Set fire to this building.

WALTER. Good. Good. I'll be right over.

BENEATHA. Where did Ruth go, Walter?

WALTER. I don't know. (*He exits abruptly.*)

BENEATHA. Mama, where did Ruth go?

MAMA (*looking at her with meaning*). To the doctor, I think.

BENEATHA. The doctor? What's the matter? (*They exchange glances.*) You don't think—

MAMA (*with her sense of drama*). Now I ain't saying what I think. But I ain't never been wrong 'bout a woman neither.

(*The phone rings.*)

BENEATHA (*at the phone*). Hay-lo . . . (*Pause, and a moment of recognition*) Well—when did you get back! . . . And how was it? . . . Of course I've missed you—in my way. . . . This morning? No . . . house cleaning and all that and Mama hates it if I let people come over when the house is like this. . . . You *have*? Well, that's different. . . . What is it—Oh, what the hell, come on over. . . . Right, see you then. (*She hangs up.*)

MAMA (*who has listened vigorously, as is her habit*). Who is that you inviting over here with this house looking like this? You ain't got the pride you was born with!

BENEATHA. Asagai doesn't care how houses look, Mama—he's an intellectual.

MAMA. *Who?*

BENEATHA. Asagai—Joseph Asagai. He's an African boy I met on campus. He's been studying in Canada all summer.

MAMA. What's his name?

BENEATHA. Asagai, Joseph. Ah-sah-guy . . . He's from Nigeria.

MAMA. Oh, that's the little country that was founded by slaves way back....

BENEATHA. No, Mama—that's Liberia.

MAMA. I don't think I never met no African before.

BENEATHA. Well, do me a favor and don't ask him a whole lot of ignorant questions about Africans. I mean, do they wear clothes and all that—

MAMA. Well, now, I guess if you think we so ignorant 'round here maybe you shouldn't bring your friends here—

BENEATHA. It's just that people ask such crazy things. All anyone seems to know about when it comes to Africa is Tarzan—

MAMA (*indignantly*). Why should I know anything about Africa?

BENEATHA. Why do you give money at church for the missionary work?

MAMA. Well, that's to help save people.

BENEATHA. You mean to save them from *heathenism*—

MAMA (*innocently*). Yes.

BENEATHA. I'm afraid they need more salvation from the British and the French.

(RUTH *comes in forlornly and pulls off her coat with dejection. They both turn to look at her.*)

RUTH (*dispiritedly*). Well, I guess from all the happy faces—everybody knows.

BENEATHA. You pregnant?

MAMA. Lord have mercy, I sure hope it's a little old girl. Travis ought to have a sister.

(BENEATHA *and* RUTH *give her a hopeless look for this grandmotherly enthusiasm.*)

BENEATHA. How far along are you?

RUTH. Two months.

BENEATHA. Did you mean to? I mean did you plan it or was it an accident?

MAMA. What do you know about planning or not planning?

BENEATHA. Oh, Mama.

RUTH (*wearily*). She's twenty years old, Lena.

BENEATHA. Did you plan it, Ruth?

RUTH. Mind your own business.

BENEATHA. It is my business—where is he going to live, on the *roof*? (*There is silence following the remark as the three women react to the sense of it.*) Gee—I didn't mean that, Ruth, honest. Gee, I don't feel like that at all. I—I think it is wonderful.

RUTH (*dully*). Wonderful.

BENEATHA. Yes—really.

MAMA (*looking at* RUTH, *worried*). Doctor say everything going to be all right?

RUTH (*far away*). Yes—she says everything is going to be fine. . . .

MAMA (*immediately suspicious*). "She"—What doctor you went to?

(RUTH *folds over, near hysteria.*)

MAMA (*worriedly hovering over* RUTH). Ruth honey—what's the matter with you—you sick?

(RUTH *has her fists clenched on her thighs and is fighting hard to suppress a scream, that seems to be rising in her.*)

BENEATHA. What's the matter with her, Mama?

MAMA (*working her fingers in* RUTH'S *shoulder to relax her*). She be all right. Women gets right depressed sometimes when they get her way. (*Speaking softly, expertly, rapidly*) Now you just relax. That's right . . . just lean back, don't think 'bout nothing at all . . . nothing at all—

RUTH. I'm all right. . . .

(*The glassy-eyed look melts and then she collapses into a fit of heavy sobbing. The bell rings.*)

BENEATHA. Oh, my God—that must be Asagai.

MAMA (*to* RUTH). Come on now, honey. You need to lie down and rest awhile . . . then have some nice hot food.

(*They exit,* RUTH'S *weight on her mother-in-law.* BENEATHA, *herself profoundly disturbed, opens the door to admit a rather dramatic-looking young man with a large package.*)

ASAGAI. Hello, Alaiyo—

BENEATHA (*holding the door open and regarding him with pleasure*). Hello . . . (*Long pause*) Well—come in. And please excuse everything. My mother was very upset about my letting anyone come here with the place like this.

ASAGAI (*coming into the room*). You look disturbed too. . . . Is something wrong?

BENEATHA (*still at the door, absently*). Yes . . . we've all got acute ghetto-itus. (*She smiles and comes toward him, finding a cigarette and sitting.*) So—sit down! How was Canada?

ASAGAI (*a sophisticate*). Canadian.

BENEATHA (*looking at him*). I'm very glad you are back.

ASAGAI (*looking back at her in turn*). Are you really?

BENEATHA. Yes—very.

ASAGAI. Why—you were quite glad when I went away. What happened?

BENEATHA. You went away.

ASAGAI. Ahhhhhhhh.

BENEATHA. Before—you wanted to be so serious before there was time.

ASAGAI. How much time must there be before one knows what one feels?

BENEATHA (*stalling this particular conversation. Her hands pressed together, in a deliberately childish gesture*). What did you bring me?

ASAGAI (*handing her the package*). Open it and see.

BENEATHA (*eagerly opening the package and drawing out some records and the colorful robes of a Nigerian woman*). Oh, Asagai! . . . You got them for me! . . . How beautiful . . . and the records too! (*She lifts out the robes and runs to the mirror with them and holds the drapery up in front of herself.*)

ASAGAI (*coming to her at the mirror*). I shall have to teach you how to drape it properly. (*He flings the material about her for the moment and stands back to look at her.*) Ah—Oh-pay-gay-day, oh-gbah-mu-shay. (*A Yo-ruba exclamation for admiration*) You wear it well . . . very well . . . mutilated hair and all.

BENEATHA (*turning suddenly*). My hair—what's wrong with my hair?

ASAGAI (*shrugging*). Were you born with it like that?

BENEATHA (*reaching up to touch it*). No . . . of course not. (*She looks back to the mirror, disturbed.*)

ASAGAI (*smiling*). How then?

BENEATHA. You know perfectly well how . . . as crinkly as yours . . . that's how.

ASAGAI. And it is ugly to you that way?

BENEATHA (*quickly*). Oh, no—not ugly . . . (*More slowly, apologetically*) But it's so hard to manage when it's, well—raw.

ASAGAI. And so to accommodate that—you mutilate it every week?

BENEATHA. It's not mutilation!

ASAGAI (*laughing aloud at her seriousness*). Oh . . . please! I am only teasing you because you are so very serious about these things. (*He stands back from her and folds his arms across his chest as he watches her pulling at her hair and frowning in the mirror.*) Do you remember the first time you met me at school? . . . (*He laughs.*) You came up to me and you said—and I thought you were the most serious little thing I had ever seen—you said: (*He imitates her.*) "Mr. Asagai—I want very much to talk with you. About Africa. You see, Mr. Asagai, I am looking for my *identity!*" (*He laughs.*)

BENEATHA (*turning to him, not laughing*). Yes—(*Her face is quizzical, profoundly disturbed.*)

ASAGAI (*still teasing and reaching out and taking her face in his hands and turning her profile to him*). Well . . . it is true that this is not so much a profile of a Hollywood queen as perhaps a queen of the Nile—(*A mock dismissal of the importance of the question*) But what does it matter? Assimilationism is so popular in your country.

BENEATHA (*wheeling, passionately, sharply*). I am not an assimilationist!

ASAGAI (*the protest hangs in the room for a moment and* ASAGAI *studies her, his laughter fading*). Such a serious one. (*There is a pause.*) So—you like the robes? You must take excellent care of them—they are from my sister's personal wardrobe.

BENEATHA (*with incredulity*). You—you sent all the way home—for me?

ASAGAI (*with charm*). For you—I would do much more. . . . Well, that is what I came for. I must go.

BENEATHA. Will you call me Monday?

ASAGAI. Yes . . . We have a great deal to talk about. I mean about identity and time and all that.

BENEATHA. Time?

ASAGAI. Yes. About how much time one needs to know what one feels.

BENEATHA. You never understood that there is more than one kind of feeling which can exist between a man and a woman—or, at least, there should be.

ASAGAI (*shaking his head negatively but gently*). No. Between a man and a woman there need be only one kind of feeling. I have that for you. . . . Now even . . . right this moment. . . .

BENEATHA. I know—and by itself—it won't do. I can find that anywhere.

ASAGAI. For a woman it should be enough.

BENEATHA. I know—because that's what it says in all the novels that men write. But it isn't. Go ahead and laugh—but I'm not interested in being someone's little episode in America or—(*with feminine vengeance*)—one of them! (ASAGAI *has burst into laughter again.*) That's funny as hell, huh!

ASAGAI. It's just that every American girl I have known has said that to me. White—black—in this you are all the same. And the same speech, too!

BENEATHA (*angrily*). Yuk, yuk, yuk!

ASAGAI. It's how you can be sure that the world's most liberated women are not liberated at all. You all talk about it too much!

(MAMA *enters and is immediately all social charm because of the presence of a guest.*)

BENEATHA. Oh—Mama—this is Mr. Asagai.

MAMA. How do you do?

ASAGAI (*total politeness to an elder*). How do you do, Mrs. Younger. Please forgive me for coming at such an outrageous hour on a Saturday.

MAMA. Well, you are quite welcome. I just hope you understand that our house don't always look like this. (*Chatterish*) You must come again. I would love to hear all about—(*not sure of the name*)—your country. I think it's so sad the way our American Negroes don't know nothing about Africa 'cept Tarzan and all that. And all that money they pour into these churches when they ought to be helping you people over there drive out them French and Englishmen done taken away your land.

(*The mother flashes a slightly superior look at her daughter upon completion of the recitation.*)

ASAGAI (*taken aback by this sudden and acutely unrelated expression of sympathy*). Yes . . . yes.

MAMA (*smiling at him suddenly and relaxing and looking him over*). How many miles is it from here to where you come from?

ASAGAI. Many thousands.

MAMA (*looking at him as she would* WALTER). I bet you don't half look after yourself, being away from your mama either. I spec you better come 'round here from time to time and get yourself some decent home-cooked meals. . . .

ASAGAI (*moved*). Thank you. Thank you very much. (*They are all quiet, then*—) Well . . . I must go. I will call you Monday, Alaiyo.

MAMA. What's that he call you?

ASAGAI. Oh—"Alaiyo." I hope you don't mind. It is what you would call a nickname, I think. It is a Yoruba word. I am a Yoruba.

MAMA (*looking at* BENEATHA). I—I thought he was from—

ASAGAI (*understanding*). Nigeria is my country. Yoruba is my tribal origin—

BENEATHA. You didn't tell us what Alaiyo means . . . for all I know, you might be calling me Little Idiot or something. . . .

ASAGAI. Well . . . let me see . . . I do not know how just to explain it. . . . The sense of a thing can be so different when it changes languages.

BENEATHA. You're evading.

ASAGAI. No—really it is difficult. . . . (*Thinking*) It means . . . it means One for Whom Bread—Food—Is Not Enough. (*He looks at her.*) Is that all right?

BENEATHA (*understanding, softly*). Thank you.

MAMA (*looking from one to the other and not understanding any of it*). Well . . . that's nice. . . . You must come see us again—Mr.—

ASAGAI. Ah-sah-guy . . .

MAMA. Yes . . . Do come again.

ASAGAI. Good-bye. (*He exits.*)

MAMA (*after him*). Lord, that's a pretty thing just went out here! (*Insinuatingly, to her daughter*) Yes, I guess I see why we done commence to get so interested in Africa 'round here. Missionaries my aunt Jenny! (*She exits.*)

BENEATHA. Oh, Mama! . . .

(*She picks up the Nigerian dress and holds it up to her in front of the mirror again. She sets the headdress on haphazardly and then notices her hair again and clutches at it and then replaces the headdress and frowns at herself. Then she starts to wriggle in front of the mirror as she thinks a Nigerian woman might.* TRAVIS *enters and regards her.*)

TRAVIS. You cracking up?

BENEATHA. Shut up.

(*She pulls the headdress off and looks at herself in the mirror and clutches at her hair again and squinches her eyes as if trying to imagine something. Then, suddenly, she gets her raincoat and kerchief and hurriedly prepares for going out.*)

MAMA (*coming back into the room*). She's resting now. Travis, baby, run next door and ask Miss Johnson to please let me have a little kitchen cleanser. This here can is empty as Jacob's kettle.

TRAVIS. I just come in.

MAMA. Do as you told. (*He exits and she looks at her daughter.*) Where you going?

BENEATHA (*halting at the door*). To become a queen of the Nile!

(*She exits in a breathless blaze of glory.* RUTH *appears in the bedroom doorway.*)

MAMA. Who told you to get up?

RUTH. Ain't nothing wrong with me to be lying in no bed for. Where did Bennie go?

MAMA (*drumming her fingers*). Far as I could make out—to Egypt. (RUTH *just looks at her.*) What time is it getting to?

RUTH. Ten twenty. And the mailman going to ring that bell this morning just like he done every morning for the last umpteen years.

(TRAVIS *comes in with the cleanser can.*)

TRAVIS. She say to tell you that she don't have much.

MAMA (*angrily*). Lord, some people I could name sure is tight-fisted! (*Directing her grandson*) Mark two cans of cleanser down on the list there. If she that hard up for kitchen cleanser, I sure don't want to forget to get her none!

RUTH. Lena—maybe the woman is just short on cleanser—

MAMA (*not listening*). —Much baking powder as she done borrowed from me all these years, she could of done gone into the baking business!

(*The bell sounds suddenly and sharply and all three are stunned—serious and silent—mid-speech. In spite of all the other conversations and distractions of the morning, this is what they have been waiting for, even* TRAVIS, *who looks helplessly from his mother to his grandmother.* RUTH *is the first to come to life again.*)

RUTH (*to* TRAVIS). Get down them steps, boy!

(TRAVIS *snaps to life and flies out to get the mail.*)

MAMA (*her eyes wide, her hand to her breast*). You mean it done really come?

RUTH (*excitedly*). Oh, Miss Lena!

MAMA (*collecting herself*). Well . . . I don't know what we all so excited about 'round here for. We known it was coming for months.

RUTH. That's a whole lot different from having it come and being able to hold it in your hands . . . a piece of paper worth ten thousand dollars. . . . (TRAVIS *bursts back into the room. He holds the envelope high above his head, like a little dancer, his face is radiant and he is breathless. He moves to his grandmother with sudden slow ceremony and puts the envelope into her hands. She accepts it, and then merely holds it and looks at it.*) Come on! Open it . . . Lord have mercy, I wish Walter Lee was here!

TRAVIS. Open it, Grandmama!

MAMA (*staring at it*). Now you all be quiet. It's just a check.

RUTH. *Open it.* . . .

MAMA (*still staring at it*). Now don't act silly. . . . We ain't never been no people to act silly 'bout no money—

RUTH (*swiftly*). We ain't never had none before—*open it!*

(MAMA *finally makes a good strong tear and pulls out the thin blue slice of paper and inspects it closely. The boy and his mother study it raptly over* MAMA's *shoulders.*)

MAMA. Travis! (*She is counting off with doubt.*) Is that the right number of zeros.

TRAVIS. Yes'm . . . ten thousand dollars. Gaalee, Grandmama, you rich.

MAMA (*She holds the check away from her, still looking at it. Slowly her face sobers into a mask of unhappiness*). Ten thousand dollars. (*She hands it to* RUTH.)

Put it away somewhere, Ruth. (*She does not look at* RUTH; *her eyes seem to be seeing something somewhere very far off.*) Ten thousand dollars they give you. Ten thousand dollars.

TRAVIS (*to his mother, sincerely*). What's the matter with Grandmama—don't she want to be rich?

RUTH (*distractedly*). You go on out and play now, baby. (TRAVIS *exits.* MAMA *starts wiping dishes absently, humming intently to herself.* RUTH *turns to her, with kind exasperation.*) You're gone and got yourself upset.

MAMA (*not looking at her*). I spec if it wasn't for you all . . . I would just put that money away or give it to the church or something.

RUTH. Now what kind of talk is that. Mr. Younger would just be plain mad if he could hear you talking foolish like that.

MAMA (*stopping and staring off*). Yes . . . he sure would. (*Sighing*) We got enough to do with that money, all right. (*She halts then, and turns and looks at her daughter-in-law hard;* RUTH *avoids her eyes and* MAMA *wipes her hands with finality and starts to speak firmly to* RUTH.) Where did you go today, girl?

RUTH. To the doctor.

MAMA (*impatiently*). Now, Ruth . . . you know better than that. Old Doctor Jones is strange enough in his way but there ain't nothing 'bout him make somebody slip and call him "she"—like you done this morning.

RUTH. Well, that's what happened—my tongue slipped.

MAMA. You went to see that woman, didn't you?

RUTH (*defensively, giving herself away*). What woman you talking about?

MAMA (*angrily*). That woman who—

(WALTER *enters in great excitement.*)

WALTER. Did it come?

MAMA (*quietly*). Can't you give people a Christian greeting before you start asking about money?

WALTER (*to* RUTH). Did it come? (RUTH *unfolds the check and lays it quietly before him, watching him intently with thoughts of her own.* WALTER *sits down and grasps it close and counts off the zeros.*) Ten thousand dollars— (*He turns suddenly, frantically to his mother and draws some papers out of his breast pocket.*) Mama—look. Old Willy Harris put everything on paper—

MAMA. Son—I think you ought to talk to your wife. . . . I'll go on out and leave you alone if you want—

WALTER. I can talk to her later— Mama, look—

MAMA. Son—

WALTER. WILL SOMEBODY PLEASE LISTEN TO ME TODAY!

MAMA (*quietly*). I don't 'low no yellin' in this house, Walter Lee, and you know it—(WALTER *stares at them in frustration and starts to speak several times.*) And there ain't going to be no investing in no liquor stores. I don't aim to have to speak on that again.

(*A long pause*)

WALTER. Oh—so you don't aim to have to speak on that again? So *you* have decided. . . . (*Crumpling his papers*) Well, *you* tell that to my boy tonight when you put him to sleep on the living-room couch. . . . (*Turning to* MAMA *and speaking directly to her*) Yeah—and tell it to my wife, Mama, tomorrow when she has to go out of here to look after somebody else's kids. And tell it to *me*, Mama, every time we need a new pair of curtains and I have to watch *you* go out and work in somebody's kitchen. Yeah, you tell me then!

(WALTER *starts out.*)

RUTH. Where you going?

WALTER. I'm going out!

RUTH. Where?

WALTER. Just out of this house somewhere—

RUTH (*getting her coat*). I'll come too.

WALTER. I don't want you to come!

RUTH. I got something to talk to you about, Walter.

WALTER. That's too bad.

MAMA (*still quietly*). Walter Lee—(*She waits and he finally turns and looks at her.*) Sit down.

WALTER. I'm a grown man, Mama.

MAMA. Ain't nobody said you wasn't grown. But you still in my house and my presence. And as long as you are—you'll talk to your wife civil. Now sit down.

RUTH (*suddenly*). Oh, let him go on out and drink himself to death! He makes me sick to my stomach! (*She flings her coat against him.*)

WALTER (*violently*). And you turn mine too, baby! (RUTH *goes into their bedroom and slams the door behind her.*) That was my greatest mistake—

MAMA (*still quietly*). Walter, what is the matter with you?

WALTER. Matter with me? Ain't nothing the matter with *me!*

MAMA. Yes there is. Something eating you up like a crazy man. Something more than me not giving you this money. The past few years I been watching it happen to you. You get all nervous acting and kind of wild in the eyes—(WALTER *jumps up impatiently at her words.*) I said sit there now, I'm talking to you!

WALTER. Mama—I don't need no nagging at me today.

MAMA. Seem like you getting to a place where you always tied up in some kind of knot about something. But if anybody ask you 'bout it you just yell at 'em and bust out the house and go out and drink somewheres. Walter Lee, people can't live with that. Ruth's a good, patient girl in her way—but you getting to be too much. Boy, don't make the mistake of driving that girl away from you.

WALTER. Why—what she do for me?

MAMA. She loves you.

WALTER. Mama—I'm going out. I want to go off somewhere and be by myself for a while.

MAMA. I'm sorry 'bout your liquor store, son. It just wasn't the thing for us to do. That's what I want to tell you about—

WALTER. I got to go out, Mama—(*He rises.*)

MAMA. It's dangerous, son.

WALTER. What's dangerous?

MAMA. When a man goes outside his home to look for peace.

WALTER (*beseechingly*). Then why can't there never be no peace in this house then?

MAMA. You done found it in some other house?

WALTER. No—there ain't no woman! Why do women always think there's a woman somewhere when a man gets restless. (*Coming to her*) Mama— Mama—I want so many things. . . .

MAMA. Yes, son—

WALTER. I want so many things that they are driving me kind of crazy. . . . Mama—look at me.

MAMA. I'm looking at you. You a good-looking boy. You got a job, a nice wife, a fine boy and—

WALTER. A job. (*Looks at her*) Mama, a job? I open and close car doors all day long. I drive a man around in his limousine and I say, "Yes, sir; no, sir; very good, sir; shall I take the Drive, sir?" Mama, that ain't no kind of job . . . that ain't nothing at all. (*Very quietly*) Mama, I don't know if I can make you understand.

MAMA. Understand what, baby?

WALTER (*quietly*). Sometimes it's like I can see the future stretched out in front of me—just plain as day. The future, Mama. Hanging over there at the edge of my days. Just waiting for me—a big, looming blank space— full of *nothing*. Just waiting for *me*. (*Pause*) Mama—sometimes when I'm downtown and I pass them cool, quiet-looking restaurants where them white boys are sitting back and talking 'bout things . . . sitting there turning deals worth millions of dollars . . . sometimes I see guys don't look much older than me—

MAMA. Son—how come you talk so much 'bout money?

WALTER (*with immense passion*). Because it is life, Mama!

MAMA (*quietly*). Oh— (*Very quietly*) So now it's life. Money is life. Once upon a time freedom used to be life—now it's money. I guess the world really do change. . . .

WALTER. No—it was always money, Mama. We just didn't know about it.

MAMA. No . . . something has changed. (*She looks at him.*) You something new, boy. In my time we was worried about not being lynched and get- ting to the North if we could and how to stay alive and still have a pinch of dignity too. . . . Now here come you and Beneatha—talking 'bout things we ain't never even thought about hardly, me and your daddy. You ain't satisfied or proud of nothing we done. I mean that you had a home; that we kept you out of trouble till you was grown; that you don't have to ride to work on the back of nobody's streetcar—You my children—but how different we done become.

WALTER. You just don't understand, Mama, you just don't understand.

MAMA. Son—do you know your wife is expecting another baby? (WALTER *stands, stunned, and absorbs what his mother has said.*) That's what she wanted to talk to you about. (WALTER *sinks down into a chair.*) This ain't for me to be telling—but you ought to know. (*She waits.*) I think Ruth is thinking 'bout getting rid of that child.

WALTER (*slowly understanding*). No—no—Ruth wouldn't do that.

MAMA. When the world gets ugly enough—a woman will do anything for her family. *The part that's already living.*

WALTER. You don't know Ruth, Mama, if you think she would do that.
    (RUTH *opens the bedroom door and stands there a little limp.*)

RUTH (*beaten*). Yes I would too, Walter. (*Pause*) I gave her a five-dollar down payment.

    (*There is total silence as the man stares at his wife and the mother stares at her son.*)

MAMA (*presently*). Well— (*Tightly*) Well—son, I'm waiting to hear you say something. . . . I'm waiting to hear how you be your father's son. Be the man he was. . . . (*Pause*) Your wife say she going to destroy your child. And I'm waiting to hear you talk like him and say we a people who give children life, not who destroys them— (*She rises.*) I'm waiting to see you stand up and look like your daddy and say we done give up one baby to poverty and that we ain't going to give up nary another one. . . . I'm waiting.

WALTER. Ruth—

MAMA. If you a son of mine, tell her! (WALTER *turns, looks at her and can say nothing. She continues, bitterly.*) You . . . you are a disgrace to your father's memory. Somebody get me my hat.

                                                                CURTAIN

ACT II

SCENE I.

Time: Later the same day.

At rise: RUTH *is ironing again. She has the radio going. Presently* BENEATHA's *bedroom door opens and* RUTH's *mouth falls and she puts down the iron in fascination.*

RUTH. What have we got on tonight!

BENEATHA (*emerging grandly from the doorway so that we can see her thoroughly robed in the costume* ASAGAI *brought*). You are looking at what a well-dressed Nigerian woman wears— (*She parades for* RUTH, *her hair completely hidden by the headdress; she is coquettishly fanning herself with an ornate*

oriental fan, mistakenly more like Butterfly than any Nigerian that ever was.)
Isn't it beautiful? (*She promenades to the radio and, with an arrogant flourish,
turns off the good loud blues that is playing.*) Enough of this assimilationist
junk! (RUTH *follows her with her eyes as she goes to the phonograph and puts
on a record and turns and waits ceremoniously for the music to come up. Then,
with a shout*—) OCOMOGOSIAY!

(Ruth *jumps. The music comes up, a lovely Nigerian melody.* BENEATHA
listens, enraptured, her eyes far away—"back to the past." She begins to dance.
RUTH *is dumfounded.*)

RUTH. What kind of dance is that?

BENEATHA. A folk dance.

RUTH (*Pearl Bailey*). What kind of folks do that, honey?

BENEATHA. It's from Nigeria. It's a dance of welcome.

RUTH. Who you welcoming?

BENEATHA. The men back to the village.

RUTH. Where they been?

BENEATHA. How should I know—out hunting or something. Anyway, they
are coming back now. . . .

RUTH. Well, that's good.

BENEATHA (*with the record*).

*Alundi, alundi
Alundi alunya
Jop pu a jeepua
Ang gu soooooooooo*

*Ai yai yae . . .
Ay eh aye—alundi . . .*

(WALTER *comes in during this performance; he has obviously been drinking. He
leans against the door heavily and watches his sister, at first with distaste. Then his
eyes look off—"back to the past"—as he lifts both his fists to the roof, screaming.*)

WALTER. YEAH . . . AND ETHIOPIA STRETCH FORTH HER HANDS
AGAIN! . . .

RUTH (*drily, looking at him*). Yes—and Africa sure is claiming her own
tonight. (*She gives them both up and starts ironing again.*)

WALTER (*all in a drunken, dramatic shout*). Shut up! . . . I'm digging them
drums . . . them drums move me! . . . (*He makes his weaving way to his
wife's face and leans in close to her.*) In my *heart of hearts*—(*he thumps his
chest*)—I am much warrior!

RUTH (*without even looking up*). In your heart of hearts you are much drunkard.

WALTER (*coming away from her and starting to wander around the room, shouting*).
Me and Jomo . . . (*Intently, in his sister's face. She has stopped dancing to*

watch him in this unknown mood.) That's my man, Kenyatta. (*Shouting and thumping his chest*) FLAMING SPEAR! HOT DAMN! (*He is suddenly in possession of an imaginary spear and actively spearing enemies all over the room.*) OCOMOGOSIAY . . . THE LION IS WAKING . . . OWIMOWEH! (*He pulls his shirt open and leaps up on a table and gestures with his spear. The bell rings.* RUTH *goes to answer.*)

BENEATHA (*to encourage* WALTER, *thoroughly caught up with this side of him*). OCOMOGOSIAY, FLAMING SPEAR!

WALTER (*on the table, very far gone, his eyes pure glass sheets. He sees what we cannot, that he is a leader of his people, a great chief, a descendant of Chaka, and that the hour to march has come.*) Listen, my black broth—ers—

BENEATHA. OCOMOGOSIAY!

WALTER. —Do you hear the waters rushing against the shores of the coastlands—

BENEATHA. OCOMOGOSIAY!

WALTER. —Do you hear the screeching of the cocks in yonder hills beyond where the chiefs meet in council for the coming of the mighty war—

BENEATHA. OCOMOGOSIAY!

WALTER. —Do you hear the beating of the wings of the birds flying low over the mountains and the low places of our land—

(RUTH *opens the door.* GEORGE MURCHISON *enters.*)

BENEATHA. OCOMOGOSIAY!

WALTER. —Do you hear the singing of the women, singing the war songs of our fathers to the babies in the great houses . . . singing the sweet war songs? OH, DO YOU HEAR, MY BLACK BROTHERS!

BENEATHA (*completely gone*). We hear you, Flaming Spear—

WALTER. Telling us to prepare for the greatness of the time— (*To* GEORGE) Black Brother! (*He extends his hand for the fraternal clasp.*)

GEORGE. Black Brother, hell!

RUTH (*having had enough, and embarrassed for the family*). Beneatha, you got company—what's the matter with you? Walter Lee Younger, get down off that table and stop acting like a fool. . . .

(WALTER *comes down off the table suddenly and makes a quick exit to the bathroom.*)

RUTH. He's had a little to drink. . . . I don't know what her excuse is.

GEORGE (*to* BENEATHA). Look honey, we're going *to* the theater—we're not going to be *in* it . . . so go change, huh?

RUTH. You expect this boy to go out with you looking like that?

BENEATHA (*looking at* GEORGE). That's up to George. If he's ashamed of his heritage—

GEORGE. Oh, don't be so proud of yourself, Bennie—just because you look eccentric.

BENEATHA. How can something that's natural be eccentric?

GEORGE. That's what being eccentric means—being natural. Get dressed.

BENEATHA. I don't like that, George.

RUTH. Why must you and your brother make an argument out of everything people say?

BENEATHA. Because I hate assimilationist Negroes!

RUTH. Will somebody please tell me what assimila-whoever means!

GEORGE. Oh, it's just a college girl's way of calling people Uncle Toms—but that isn't what it means at all.

RUTH. Well, what does it mean?

BENEATHA (*cutting* GEORGE *off and staring at him as she replies to* RUTH). It means someone who is willing to give up his own culture and submerge himself completely in the dominant, and in this case, *oppressive* culture!

GEORGE. Oh, dear, dear, dear! Here we go! A lecture on the African past! On our Great West African Heritage! In one second we will hear all about the great Ashanti empires; the great Songhay civilizations; and the great sculpture of Bénin—and then some poetry in the Bantu—and the whole monologue will end with the word *heritage!* (*Nastily*) Let's face it, baby, your heritage is nothing but a bunch of raggedy-assed spirituals and some grass huts!

BENEATHA. *Grass huts!* (RUTH *crosses to her and forcibly pushes her toward the bedroom.*) See there . . . you are standing there in your splendid ignorance talking about people who were the first to smelt iron on the face of the earth! (RUTH *is pushing her through the door.*) The Ashanti were performing surgical operations when the English—(RUTH *pulls the door to, with* BENEATHA *on the other side, and smiles graciously at* GEORGE. BENEATHA *opens the door and shouts the end of the sentence defiantly at* GEORGE)—were still tattooing themselves with blue dragons. . . . (*She goes back inside.*)

RUTH. Have a seat, George. (*They both sit.* RUTH *folds her hands rather primly on her lap, determined to demonstrate the civilization of the family.*) Warm, ain't it? I mean for September. (*Pause*) Just like they always say about Chicago weather: If it's too hot or cold for you, just wait a minute and it'll change. (*She smiles happily at this cliché of clichés.*) Everybody say it's got to do with them bombs and things they keep setting off. (*Pause*) Would you like a nice cold beer?

GEORGE. No, thank you. I don't care for beer. (*He looks at his watch.*) I hope she hurries up.

RUTH. What time is the show?

GEORGE. It's an eight-thirty curtain. That's just Chicago, though. In New York standard curtain time is eight forty. (*He is rather proud of this knowledge.*)

RUTH (*properly appreciating it*). You get to New York a lot?

GEORGE (*offhand*). Few times a year.

RUTH. Oh—that's nice. I've never been to New York.

(WALTER *enters. We feel he has relieved himself, but the edge of unreality is still with him.*)

WALTER. New York ain't got nothing Chicago ain't. Just a bunch of hustling people all squeezed up together—being "Eastern." (*He turns his face into a screw of displeasure.*)

GEORGE. Oh—you've been?

WALTER. *Plenty* of times.

RUTH (*shocked at the lie*). Walter Lee Younger!

WALTER (*staring her down*). Plenty! (*Pause*) What we got to drink in this house? Why don't you offer this man some refreshment? (*To* GEORGE) They don't know how to entertain people in this house, man.

GEORGE. Thank you—I don't really care for anything.

WALTER (*feeling his head; sobriety coming*). Where's Mama?

RUTH. She ain't come back yet.

Walter (*looking* MURCHISON *over from head to toe, scrutinizing his carefully casual tweed sports jacket over cashmere V-neck sweater over soft eyelet shirt and tie, and soft slacks, finished off with white buckskin shoes*). Why all you college boys wear them fairyish-looking white shoes?

RUTH. Walter Lee!

(GEORGE MURCHISON *ignores the remark.*)

WALTER (*to* RUTH). Well, they look crazy as hell—white shoes, cold as it is.

RUTH. (*crushed*). You have to excuse him—

WALTER. No he don't! Excuse me for what? What you always excusing me for! I'll excuse myself when I needs to be excused! (*A pause*) They look as funny as them black knee socks Beneatha wears out of here all the time.

RUTH. It's the college *style*, Walter.

WALTER. Style, hell. She looks like she got burnt legs or something!

RUTH. Oh, Walter—

WALTER (*an irritable mimic*). Oh, Walter! Oh, Walter! (*To* MURCHISON) How's your old man making out? I understand you all going to buy that big hotel on the Drive? (*He finds a beer in the refrigerator, wanders over to* MURCHISON, *sipping and wiping his lips with the back of his hand, and straddling a chair backwards to talk to the other man.*) Shrewd move. Your old man is all right, man. (*Tapping his head and half winking for emphasis*) I mean he knows how to operate. I mean he thinks *big*, you know what I mean, I mean for a *home*, you know? But I think he's kind of running out of ideas now. I'd like to talk to him. Listen, man, I got some plans that could turn this city upside down. I mean I think like he does. *Big*. Invest big, gamble big, hell, lose *big* if you have to, you know what I mean. It's hard to find a man on this whole Southside who understands my kind of thinking—you dig? (*He scrutinizes* MURCHISON *again, drinks his beer, squints his eyes and leans in close, confidential, man to man.*) Me and you ought to sit down and talk sometimes, man. Man, I got me some ideas. . . .

MURCHISON (*with boredom*). Yeah—sometimes we'll have to do that, Walter.

WALTER (*understanding the indifference, and offended*). Yeah—well, when you get the time, man. I know you a busy little boy.

RUTH. Walter, please—

WALTER (*bitterly, hurt*). I know ain't nothing in this world as busy as you colored college boys with your fraternity pins and white shoes. . . .

RUTH (*covering her face with humiliation*). Oh, Walter Lee—

WALTER. I see you all all the time—with the books tucked under your arms—going to your (*British A—a mimic*) "clahsses." And for what! What the hell you learning over there? Filling up your heads—(*counting off on his fingers*)—with the sociology and the psychology—but they teaching you how to be a man? How to take over and run the world? They teaching you how to run a rubber plantation or a steel mill? Naw—just to talk proper and read books and wear white shoes. . . .

GEORGE (*looking at him with distaste, a little above it all*). You're all wacked up with bitterness, man.

WALTER (*intently, almost quietly, between the teeth, glaring at the boy*). And you—ain't you bitter, man? Ain't you just about had it yet? Don't you see no stars gleaming that you can't reach out and grab? You happy?—You contented son-of-a-bitch—you happy? You got it made? Bitter? Man, I'm a volcano. Bitter? Here I am a giant—surrounded by ants! Ants who can't even understand what it is the giant is talking about.

RUTH (*passionately and suddenly*). Oh, Walter—ain't you with nobody!

WALTER (*violently*). No! 'Cause ain't nobody with me! Not even my own mother!

RUTH. Walter, that's a terrible thing to say!

    (BENEATHA *enters, dressed for the evening in a cocktail dress and earrings.*)

GEORGE. Well—hey, you look great.

BENEATHA. Let's go, George. See you all later.

RUTH. Have a nice time.

GEORGE. Thanks. Good night. (*To* WALTER, *sarcastically*) Good night, *Prometheus.* (BENEATHA *and* GEORGE *exit.*)

WALTER (*to* RUTH). Who is Prometheus?

RUTH. I don't know. Don't worry about it.

WALTER (*in fury, pointing after* GEORGE). See there—they get to a point where they can't insult you man to man—they got to go talk about something ain't nobody never heard of!

RUTH. How do you know it was an insult? (*To humor him*) Maybe Prometheus is a nice fellow.

WALTER. Prometheus! I bet there ain't even no such thing! I bet that simple-minded clown—

RUTH. Walter— (*She stops what she is doing and looks at him.*)

WALTER (*yelling*). Don't start!

RUTH. Start what?

WALTER. Your nagging! Where was I? Who was I with? How much money did I spend?

RUTH (*plaintively*). Walter Lee—why don't we just try to talk about it. . . .

WALTER (*not listening*). I been out talking with people who understand me. People who care about the things I got on my mind.

RUTH (*wearily*). I guess that means people like Willy Harris.

WALTER. Yes, people like Willy Harris.

RUTH (*with a sudden flash of impatience*). Why don't you all just hurry up and go into the banking business and stop talking about it!

WALTER. Why? You want to know why? 'Cause we all tied up in a race of people that don't know how to do nothing but moan, pray and have babies!

(*The line is too bitter even for him and he looks at her and sits down.*)

RUTH. Oh, Walter . . . (*Softly*) Honey, why can't you stop fighting me?

WALTER (*without thinking*). Who's fighting you? Who even cares about you?

(*This line begins the retardation of his mood.*)

RUTH. Well— (*She waits a long time, and then with resignation starts to put away her things.*) I guess I might as well go on to bed. . . . (*More or less to herself*) I don't know where we lost it . . . but we have. . . . (*Then, to him*) I—I'm sorry about this new baby, Walter. I guess maybe I better go on and do what I started . . . I guess I just didn't realize how bad things was with us . . . I guess I just didn't really realize—(*She starts out to the bedroom and stops.*) You want some hot milk?

WALTER. Hot milk?

RUTH. Yes—hot milk.

WALTER. Why hot milk?

RUTH. 'Cause after all that liquor you come home with you ought to have something hot in your stomach.

WALTER. I don't want no milk.

RUTH. You want some coffee then?

WALTER. No, I don't want no coffee. I don't want nothing hot to drink. (*Almost plaintively*) Why you always trying to give me something to eat?

RUTH (*standing and looking at him helplessly*). What else can I give you, Walter Lee Younger?

(*She stands and looks at him and presently turns to go out again. He lifts his head and watches her going away from him in a new mood which began to emerge when he asked her "Who cares about you?"*)

WALTER. It's been rough, ain't it, baby? (*She hears and stops but does not turn around and he continues to her back.*) I guess between two people there ain't never as much understood as folks generally thinks there is. I mean like between me and you— (*She turns to face him.*) How we gets to the place where we scared to talk softness to each other. (*He waits, thinking hard himself.*) Why you think it got to be like that? (*He is thoughtful, almost as a child would be.*) Ruth, what is it gets into people ought to be close?

RUTH. I don't know, honey. I think about it a lot.

WALTER. On account of you and me, you mean? The way things are with us. The way something done come down between us.

RUTH. There ain't so much between us, Walter. . . . Not when you come to me and try to talk to me. Try to be with me . . . a little even.

WALTER (*total honesty*). Sometimes . . . sometimes . . . I don't even know how to try.

RUTH. Walter—

WALTER. Yes?

RUTH (*coming to him, gently and with misgiving, but coming to him*). Honey . . . life don't have to be like this. I mean sometimes people can do things so that things are better. . . . You remember how we used to talk when Travis was born . . . about the way we were going to live . . . the kind of house . . . (*She is stroking his head.*) Well, it's all starting to slip away from us. . . .

(MAMA *enters, and* WALTER *jumps up and shouts at her.*)

WALTER. Mama, where have you been?

MAMA. My—them steps is longer than they used to be. Whew! (*She sits down and ignores him.*) How you feeling this evening, Ruth?

(RUTH *shrugs, disturbed some at having been prematurely interrupted and watching her husband knowingly.*)

WALTER. Mama, where have you been all day?

MAMA (*still ignoring him and leaning on the table and changing to more comfortable shoes*). Where's Travis?

RUTH. I let him go out earlier and he ain't come back yet. Boy, is he going to get it!

WALTER. Mama!

MAMA (*as if she has heard him for the first time*). Yes, son?

WALTER. Where did you go this afternoon?

MAMA. I went downtown to tend to some business that I had to tend to.

WALTER. What kind of business?

MAMA. You know better than to question me like a child, Brother.

WALTER (*rising and bending over the table*). Where were you, Mama? (*Bringing his fists down and shouting*) Mama, you didn't go do something with that insurance money, something crazy?

(*The front door opens slowly, interrupting him, and* TRAVIS *peeks his head in, less than hopefully.*)

TRAVIS (*to his mother*). Mama, I—

RUTH. "Mama I" nothing! You're going to get it, boy! Get on in that bedroom and get yourself ready!

TRAVIS. But I—

MAMA. Why don't you all never let the child explain hisself.

RUTH. Keep out of it now, Lena.

(Mama *clamps her lips together, and* RUTH *advances toward her son menacingly.*)

RUTH. A thousand times I have told you not to go off like that—

MAMA (*holding out her arms to her grandson*). Well—at least let me tell him something. I want him to be the first one to hear. . . . Come here, Travis. (*The boy obeys, gladly.*) Travis—(*she takes him by the shoulder and looks into his face*)—you know that money we got in the mail this morning?

TRAVIS. Yes'm—

MAMA. Well—what you think your grandmama gone and done with that money?

TRAVIS. I don't know, Grandmama.

Mama (*putting her finger on his nose for emphasis*). She went out and she bought you a house! (*The explosion comes from* WALTER *at the end of the revelation and he jumps up and turns away from all of them in a fury.* MAMA *continues, to* TRAVIS) You glad about the house? It's going to be yours when you get to be a man.

TRAVIS. Yeah—I always wanted to live in a house.

MAMA. All right, gimme some sugar then—(TRAVIS *puts his arms around her neck as she watches her son over the boy's shoulder. Then, to* TRAVIS, *after the embrace*) Now when you say your prayers tonight, you thank God and your grandfather—'cause it was him who give you the house—in his way.

RUTH (*taking the boy from* MAMA *and pushing him toward the bedroom*). Now you get out of here and get ready for your beating.

TRAVIS. Aw, Mama—

RUTH. Get on in there—(*Closing the door behind him and turning radiantly to her mother-in-law*) So you went and did it!

MAMA (*quietly, looking at her son with pain*). Yes, I did.

RUTH (*raising both arms classically*). Praise God! (*Looks at* WALTER *a moment, who says nothing. She crosses rapidly to her husband.*) Please, honey—let me be glad . . . you be glad too. (*She has laid her hands on his shoulders, but he shakes himself free of her roughly, without turning to face her.*) Oh, Walter . . . a home . . . a home. (*She comes back to* MAMA.) Well—where is it? How big is it? How much it going to cost?

MAMA. Well—

RUTH. When we moving?

MAMA (*smiling at her*). First of the month.

RUTH (*throwing back her head with jubilance*). Praise God!

MAMA (*tentatively, still looking at her son's back turned against her and* RUTH). It's—it's a nice house too. . . . (*She cannot help speaking directly to him. An imploring quality in her voice, her manner, makes her almost like a girl now.*) Three bedrooms—nice big one for you and Ruth. . . . Me and Beneatha still have to share our room, but Travis have one of his own—and (*with difficulty*) I figure if the—new baby—is a boy, we could get one of them double-decker outfits. . . . And there's a yard with a little patch of dirt where I could maybe get to grow me a few flowers. . . . And a nice big basement. . . .

RUTH. Walter honey, be glad—

MAMA (*still to his back, fingering things on the table*). 'Course I don't want to make it sound fancier than it is. . . . It's just a plain little old house—but it's made good and solid—and it will be *ours*. Walter Lee—it makes a difference in a man when he can walk on floors that belong to *him*. . . .

RUTH. Where is it?

MAMA (*frightened at this telling*). Well—well—it's out there in Clybourne Park—

(RUTH's *radiance fades abruptly, and* WALTER *finally turns slowly to face his mother with incredulity and hostility.*)

RUTH. Where?

MAMA (*matter-of-factly*). Four o six Clybourne Street, Clybourne Park.

RUTH. Clybourne Park? Mama, there ain't no colored people living in Clybourne Park.

MAMA (*almost idiotically*). Well, I guess there's going to be some now.

WALTER (*bitterly*). So that's the peace and comfort you went out and bought for us today!

MAMA (*raising her eyes to meet his finally*). Son—I just tried to find the nicest place for the least amount of money for my family.

RUTH (*trying to recover from the shock*). Well—well—'course I ain't one never been 'fraid of no crackers, mind you—but—well, wasn't there no other houses nowhere?

MAMA. Them houses they put up for colored in them areas way out all seem to cost twice as much as other houses. I did the best I could.

RUTH (*struck senseless with the news, in its various degrees of goodness and trouble, she sits a moment, her fists propping her chin in thought, and then she starts to rise, bringing her fists down with vigor, the radiance spreading from cheek to cheek again*). Well—well!—All I can say is—if this is my time in life— *my time*—to say good-bye—(*and she builds with momentum as she starts to circle the room with an exuberant, almost tearfully happy release*)—to these Goddamned cracking walls!—(*she pounds the walls*)—and these marching roaches!—(*she wipes at an imaginary army of marching roaches*)—and this cramped little closet which ain't now or never was no kitchen! . . . then I say it loud and good, Hallelujah! and good-bye misery. . . . I don't never want to see your ugly face again! (*She laughs joyously, having practically destroyed the apartment, and flings her arms up and lets them come down happily, slowly, reflectively, over her abdomen, aware for the first time perhaps that the life therein pulses with happiness and not despair.*) Lena?

MAMA (*moved, watching her happiness*). Yes, honey?

RUTH (*looking off*). Is there—is there a whole lot of sunlight?

MAMA (*understanding*). Yes, child, there's a whole lot of sunlight.

> (*Long pause.*)

RUTH (*collecting herself and going to the door of the room* TRAVIS *is in*). Well—I guess I better see 'bout Travis. (*To* MAMA) Lord, I sure don't feel like whipping nobody today! (*She exits.*)

MAMA (*the mother and son are left alone now and the mother waits a long time, considering deeply, before she speaks*). Son—you—you understand what I done, don't you? (WALTER *is silent and sullen.*) I—I just seen my family falling apart today . . . just falling to pieces in front of my eyes. . . . We couldn't of gone on like we was today. We was going backwards 'stead of forwards—talking 'bout killing babies and wishing each other was dead. . . . When it gets like that in life—you just got to do something different, push on out and do something bigger. . . . (*She waits.*) I wish you say something, son . . . I wish you'd say how deep inside you you think I done the right thing—

WALTER (*crossing slowly to his bedroom door and finally turning there and speaking measuredly*). What you need me to say you done right for? *You* the head of this family. You run our lives like you want to. It was your money and you did what you wanted with it. So what you need for me to say it was all right for? (*Bitterly, to hurt her as deeply as he knows is possible*) So you butchered up a dream of mine—you—who always talking 'bout your children's dreams. . . .

MAMA. Walter Lee—

> (*He just closes the door behind him.* MAMA *sits alone, thinking heavily.*)

CURTAIN

SCENE II.

> *Time: Friday night, a few weeks later.*
>
> *At rise: Packing crates mark the intention of the family to move.* BENEATHA *and* GEORGE *come in, presumably from an evening out again.*

GEORGE. O.K . . . . O.K., whatever you say. . . . (*They both sit on the couch. He tries to kiss her. She moves away.*) Look, we've had a nice evening; let's not spoil it, huh? . . .

> (*He again turns her head and tries to nuzzle in and she turns away from him, not with distaste but with momentary lack of interest; in a mood to pursue what they were talking about.*)

BENEATHA. I'm *trying* to talk to you.

GEORGE. We always talk.

BENEATHA. Yes—and I love to talk.

GEORGE (*exasperated; rising*). I know it and I don't mind it sometimes . . . I want you to cut it out, see—The moody stuff, I mean. I don't like it. You're a nice-looking girl . . . all over. That's all you need, honey, forget the atmosphere. Guys aren't going to go for the atmosphere—they're going to go for what they see. Be glad for that. Drop the Garbo routine. It doesn't go with you. As for myself, I want a nice—(*groping*)—simple (*thoughtfully*)—sophisticated girl . . . not a poet—O.K.?

(*She rebuffs him again and he starts to leave.*)

BENEATHA. Why are you angry?

GEORGE. Because this is stupid! I don't go out with you to discuss the nature of "quiet desperation" or to hear all about your thoughts—because the world will go on thinking what it thinks regardless—

BENEATHA. Then why read books? Why go to school?

GEORGE (*with artificial patience, counting on his fingers*). It's simple. You read books—to learn facts—to get grades—to pass the course—to get a degree. That's all—it has nothing to do with thoughts.

(*A long pause.*)

BENEATHA. I see. (*A longer pause as she looks at him*) Good night, George.

(GEORGE *looks at her a little oddly, and starts to exit. He meets* MAMA *coming in.*)

GEORGE. Oh—hello, Mrs. Younger.

MAMA Hello, George, how you feeling?

GEORGE. Fine—fine, how are you?

MAMA. Oh, a little tired. You know them steps can get you after a day's work. You all have a nice time tonight?

GEORGE. Yes—a fine time. Well, good night.

MAMA. Good night. (*He exits.* MAMA *closes the door behind her.*) Hello, honey. What you sitting like that for?

BENEATHA. I'm just sitting.

MAMA. Didn't you have a nice time?

BENEATHA. No.

MAMA. No? What's the matter?

BENEATHA. Mama, George is a fool—honest. (*She rises.*)

MAMA (*hustling around unloading the packages she has entered with. She stops*). Is he, baby?

BENEATHA. Yes. (BENEATHA *makes up* TRAVIS' *bed as she talks.*)

MAMA. You sure?

BENEATHA. Yes.

MAMA. Well—I guess you better not waste your time with no fools.

(BENEATHA *looks up at her mother, watching her put groceries in the refrigerator. Finally she gathers up her things and starts into the bedroom. At the door she stops and looks back at her mother.*)

BENEATHA. Mama—

MAMA. Yes, baby—

BENEATHA. Thank you.

MAMA. For what?

BENEATHA. For understanding me this time.

(She exits quickly and the mother stands, smiling a little, looking at the place where BENEATHA *just stood.* RUTH *enters.)*

RUTH. Now don't you fool with any of this stuff, Lena—

MAMA. Oh, I just thought I'd sort a few things out.

(The phone rings. RUTH *answers.)*

RUTH *(at the phone).* Hello—Just a minute. *(Goes to the door)* Walter, it's Mrs. Arnold. *(Waits. Goes back to the phone. Tense)* Hello. Yes, this is his wife speaking . . . He's lying down now. Yes . . . well, he'll be in tomorrow. He's been very sick. Yes—I know we should have called, but we were so sure he'd be able to come in today. Yes—yes, I'm very sorry. Yes. Thank you very much. *(She hangs up.* WALTER *is standing in the doorway of the bedroom behind her.)* That was Mrs. Arnold.

WALTER *(indifferently).* Was it?

RUTH. She said if you don't come in tomorrow that they are getting a new man. . . .

WALTER. Ain't that sad—ain't that crying sad.

RUTH. She said Mr. Arnold has had to take a cab for three days. . . . Walter, you ain't been to work for three days! *(This is a revelation to her.)* Where you been, Walter Lee Younger? *(WALTER *looks at her and starts to laugh.)* You're going to lose your job.

WALTER. That's right . . .

RUTH. Oh, Walter, and with your mother working like a dog every day—

WALTER. That's sad too—Everything is sad.

MAMA. What you been doing for these three days, son?

WALTER. Mama—you don't know all the things a man what got leisure can find to do in this city. . . . What's this—Friday night? Well— Wednesday I borrowed Willy Harris' car and I went for a drive . . . just me and myself and I drove and drove . . . Way out . . . way past South Chicago, and I parked the car and I sat and looked at the steel mills all day long. I just sat in the car and looked at them big black chimneys for hours. Then I drove back and I went to the Green Hat. *(Pause)* And Thursday—Thursday I borrowed the car again and I got in it and I pointed it the other way and I drove the other way—for hours—way, way up to Wisconsin, and I looked at the farms. I just drove and looked at the farms. Then I drove back and I went to the Green Hat. *(Pause)* And today—today I didn't get the car. Today I just walked. All over the South side. And I looked at the Negroes and they looked at me and finally I just sat down on the curb at Thirty-ninth and South Parkway and I just sat there and watched the Negroes go by. And then I went to

the Green Hat. You all sad? You all depressed? And you know where I
am going right now—

   (RUTH *goes out quietly.*)

MAMA. Oh, Big Walter, is this the harvest of our days?

WALTER. You know what I like about the Green Hat? (*He turns the radio on
and a steamy, deep blues pours into the room.*) I like this little cat they got
there who blows a sax. . . . He blows. He talks to me. He ain't but 'bout
five feet tall and he's got a conked head and his eyes is always closed and
he's all music—

MAMA (*rising and getting some papers out of her handbag*). Walter—

WALTER. And there's this other guy who plays the piano . . . and they got
a sound. I mean they can work on some music. . . . They got the best
little combo in the world in the Green Hat. . . . You can just sit there
and drink and listen to them three men play and you realize that don't
nothing matter worth a damn, but just being there—

MAMA. I've helped do it to you, haven't I, son? Walter, I been wrong.

WALTER. Naw—you ain't never been wrong about nothing, Mama.

MAMA. Listen to me, now. I say I been wrong, son. That I been doing to
you what the rest of the world been doing to you. (*She stops and he
looks up slowly at her and she meets his eyes pleadingly.*) Walter—what you
ain't never understood is that I ain't got nothing, don't own nothing, ain't never really wanted nothing that wasn't for you. There ain't
nothing as precious to me. . . . There ain't nothing worth holding on
to, money, dreams, nothing else—if it means—if it means it's going
to destroy my boy. (*She puts her papers in front of him and he watches her
without speaking or moving.*) I paid the man thirty-five hundred dollars
down on the house. That leaves sixty-five hundred dollars. Monday
morning I want you to take this money and take three thousand dollars and put it in a savings account for Beneatha's medical schooling.
The rest you put in a checking account—with your name on it. And
from now on any penny that come out of it or that go in it is for you
to look after. For you to decide. (*She drops her hands a little helplessly.*)
It ain't much, but it's all I got in the world and I'm putting it in your
hands. I'm telling you to be the head of this family from now on like
you supposed to be.

WALTER (*stares at the money*). You trust me like that, Mama?

MAMA. I ain't never stop trusting you. Like I ain't never stop loving you.

   (*She goes out, and* WALTER *sits looking at the money on the table as the
music continues in its idiom, pulsing in the room. Finally, in a decisive gesture,
he gets up, and, in mingled joy and desperation, picks up the money. At the same
moment,* TRAVIS *enters for bed.*)

TRAVIS. What's the matter, Daddy? You drunk?

WALTER (*sweetly, more sweetly than we have ever known him*). No, Daddy ain't
drunk. Daddy ain't going to never be drunk again. . . .

TRAVIS. Well, good night, Daddy.

(The FATHER *has come from behind the couch and leans over, embracing
his son.*)

WALTER. Son, I feel like talking to you tonight.

TRAVIS. About what?

WALTER. Oh, about a lot of things. About you and what kind of man you
going to be when you grow up. . . . Son—son, what do you want to be
when you grow up?

TRAVIS. A bus driver.

WALTER (*laughing a little*). A what? Man, that ain't nothing to want to be!

TRAVIS. Why not?

WALTER. 'Cause, man—it ain't big enough—you know what I mean.

TRAVIS. I don't know then. I can't make up my mind. Sometimes Mama asks
me that too. And sometimes when I tell her I just want to be like you—she
says she don't want me to be like that and sometimes she says she does. . . .

WALTER (*gathering him up in his arms*). You know what, Travis? In seven years
you going to be seventeen years old. And things is going to be very different with us in seven years, Travis. . . . One day when you are seventeen
I'll come home—home from my office downtown somewhere—

TRAVIS. You don't work in no office, Daddy.

WALTER. No—but after tonight. After what your daddy gonna do tonight,
there's going to be offices—a whole lot of offices. . . .

TRAVIS. What you gonna do tonight, Daddy?

WALTER. You wouldn't understand yet, son, but your daddy's gonna make
a transaction . . . a business transaction that's going to change our
lives. . . . That's how come one day when you 'bout seventeen years old
I'll come home and I'll be pretty tired, you know what I mean, after a
day of conferences and secretaries getting things wrong the way they
do . . . 'cause an executive's life is hell, man—(*The more he talks, the farther
away he gets.*) And I'll pull the car up on the driveway . . . just a plain black
Chrysler, I think, with white walls—no—black tires. More elegant. Rich
people don't have to be flashy . . . though I'll have to get something a
little sportier for Ruth—maybe a Cadillac convertible to do her shopping
in. . . . And I'll come up the steps to the house and the gardener will be
clipping away at the hedges and he'll say, "Good evening, Mr. Younger."
And I'll say, "Hello, Jefferson, how are you this evening?" And I'll go
inside and Ruth will come downstairs and meet me at the door and we'll
kiss each other and she'll take my arm and we'll go up to your room to
see you sitting on the floor with the catalogues of all the great schools in
America around you. . . . All the great schools in the world! And—and
I'll say, all right son—it's your seventeenth birthday, what is it you've

decided? . . . Just tell me where you want to go to school and you'll *go.* Just tell me, what it is you want to be—and you'll be it. . . . Whatever you want to be—Yessir! (*He holds his arms open for* TRAVIS.) You just name it, son . . . (TRAVIS *leaps into them.*) and I hand you the world!

(WALTER's *voice has risen in pitch and hysterical promise and on the last line he lifts* TRAVIS *high.*)

BLACKOUT

SCENE III.

Time: Saturday, moving day, one week later.

Before the curtain rises, RUTH's *voice, a strident, dramatic church alto cuts through the silence.*

It is, in the darkness a triumphant surge, a penetrating statement of expectation: "Oh, Lord, I don't feel no ways tired! Children, oh, glory hallelujah!"

As the curtain rises we see that RUTH *is alone in the living room, finishing up the family's packing. It is moving day. She is nailing crates and tying cartons.* BENEATHA *enters, carrying a guitar case, and watches her exuberant sister-in-law.*

RUTH. Hey!

BENEATHA (*putting away the case*). Hi.

RUTH (*pointing at a package*). Honey—look in that package there and see what I found on sale this morning at the South Center. (RUTH *gets up and moves to the package and draws out some curtains.*) Lookahere— hand-turned hems!

BENEATHA. How do you know the window size out there?

RUTH (*who hadn't thought of that*). Oh—Well, they bound to fit something in the whole house. Anyhow, they was too good a bargain to pass up. (RUTH *slaps her head, suddenly remembering something.*) Oh, Bennie—I meant to put a special note on that carton over there. That's your mamma's good china and she wants 'em to be very careful with it.

BENEATHA. I'll do it.

(BENEATHA *finds a piece of paper and starts to draw large letters on it.*)

RUTH. You know what I'm going to do soon as I get in that new house?

BENEATHA. What?

RUTH. Honey—I'm going to run me a tub of water up to here. . . .

(*With her fingers practically up to her nostrils*) And I'm going to get in it—and I am going to sit . . . and sit . . . and sit in that hot water and the first person who knocks to tell *me* to hurry up and come out—

BENEATIIA. Gets shot at sunrise.

RUTH (*laughing happily*). You said it, sister! (*Noticing how large* BENEATHA *is absent-mindedly making the note*) Honey, they ain't going to read that from no airplane.

BENEATHA (*laughing herself*). I guess I always think things have more emphasis if they are big, somehow.

RUTH (*looking up at her and smiling*). You and your brother seem to have that as a philosophy of life. Lord, that man—done changed so 'round here. You know—you know what we did last night? Me and Walter Lee?

BENEATHA. What?

RUTH (*smiling to herself*). We went to the movies. (*Looking at* BENEATHA *to see if she understands*) We went to the movies. You know the last time me and Walter went to the movies together?

BENEATHA. No.

RUTH. Me neither. That's how long it been. (*Smiling again*) But we went last night. The picture wasn't much good, but that didn't seem to matter. We went—and we held hands.

BENEATHA. Oh, Lord!

RUTH. We held hands—and you know what?

BENEATHA. What?

RUTH. When we come out of the show it was late and dark and all the stores and things was closed up . . . and it was kind of chilly and there wasn't many people on the streets . . . and we was still holding hands, me and Walter.

BENEATHA. You're killing me.

(WALTER *enters with a large package. His happiness is deep in him; he cannot keep still with his new-found exuberance. He is singing and wiggling and snapping his fingers. He puts his package in a corner and puts a phonograph record, which he has brought in with him, on the record player. As the music comes up he dances over to* RUTH *and tries to get her to dance with him. She gives in at last to his raunchiness and in a fit of giggling allows herself to be drawn into his mood and together they deliberately burlesque an old social dance of their youth.*)

BENEATHA (*regarding them a long time as they dance, then drawing in her breath for a deeply exaggerated comment which she does not particularly mean*). Talk about—olddddddddddd-fashionedddddddd—Negroes!

WALTER (*stopping momentarily*). What kind of Negroes?

(*He says this in fun. He is not angry with her today, nor with anyone. He starts to dance with his wife again.*)

BENEATHA. Old-fashioned.

WALTER (*as he dances with* RUTH). You know, when these *New Negroes* have their convention—(*pointing at his sister*)—that is going to be the chairman of the Committee on Unending Agitation. (*He goes on dancing, then stops.*) Race, race, race! . . . Girl, I do believe you are the first person in the history of the entire human race to successfully brainwash yourself. (BENEATHA *breaks up and he goes on dancing. He stops again, enjoying his tease.*) Damn, even the N double ACP takes a holiday sometimes! (BENEATHA *and* RUTH *laugh. He dances with* RUTH *some more and starts to laugh and stops and pantomimes someone over an operating table.*) I can just see that chick someday looking down at some poor cat on an operating table before she starts to slice him, saying . . . (*pulling his sleeves back maliciously*) "By the way, what are your views on civil rights down there? . . . " (*He laughs at her again and starts to dance happily. The bell sounds.*)

BENEATHA. Sticks and stones may break my bones but . . . words will never hurt me!

    (BENEATHA *goes to the door and opens it as* WALTER *and* RUTH *go on with the clowning.* BENEATHA *is somewhat surprised to see a quiet-looking middle-aged white man in a business suit holding his hat and a briefcase in his hand and consulting a small piece of paper.*)

MAN. Uh—how do you do, miss. I am looking for a Mrs.—(*he looks at the slip of paper*) Mrs. Lena Younger?

BENEATHA (*smoothing her hair with slight embarrassment*). Oh—yes, that's my mother. Excuse me. (*She closes the door and turns to quiet the other two.*) Ruth! Brother! Somebody's here. (*Then she opens the door. The man casts a curious quick glance at all of them.*) Uh—come in please.

MAN (*coming in*). Thank you.

BENEATHA. My mother isn't here just now. Is it business?

MAN. Yes . . . well, of a sort.

WALTER (*freely, the Man of the House*). Have a seat. I'm Mrs. Younger's son. I look after most of her business matters.

    (RUTH *and* BENEATHA *exchange amused glances.*)

MAN (*regarding* WALTER, *and sitting*). Well—My name is Karl Lindner . . .

WALTER (*stretching out his hand*). Walter Younger. This is my wife— (RUTH *nods politely*)—and my sister.

LINDNER. How do you do.

WALTER (*amiably, as he sits himself easily on a chair, leaning with interest forward on his knees and looking expectantly into the newcomer's face*). What can we do for you, Mr. Lindner!

LINDNER (*some minor shuffling of the hat and briefcase on his knees*). Well—I am a representative of the Clybourne Park Improvement Association—

WALTER (*pointing*). Why don't you sit your things on the floor?

LINDNER. Oh—yes. Thank you. (*He slides the briefcase and hat under the chair.*) And as I was saying—I am from the Clybourne Park Improvement Association and we have had it brought to our attention at the last meeting that you people—or at least your mother—has bought a piece of residential property at—(*he digs for the slip of paper again*)—four o six Clybourne Street. . . .

WALTER. That's right. Care for something to drink? Ruth, get Mr. Lindner a beer.

LINDNER (*upset for some reason*). Oh—no, really. I mean thank you very much, but no thank you.

RUTH (*innocently*). Some coffee?

LINDNER. Thank you, nothing at all.

(BENEATHA *is watching the man carefully.*)

LINDNER. Well, I don't know how much you folks know about our organization. (*He is a gentle man; thoughtful and somewhat labored in his manner.*) It is one of those community organizations set up to look after—oh, you know, things like block upkeep and special projects and we also have what we call our New Neighbors Orientation Committee. . . .

BENEATHA (*drily*). Yes—and what do they do?

LINDNER (*turning a little to her and then returning the main force to* WALTER). Well—it's what you might call a sort of welcoming committee, I guess. I mean they, we, I'm the chairman of the committee—go around and see the new people who move into the neighborhood and sort of give them the lowdown on the way we do things out in Clybourne Park.

BENEATHA (*with appreciation of the two meanings, which escape* RUTH *and* WALTER). Un-huh.

LINDNER. And we also have the category of what the association calls— (*he looks elsewhere*)—uh—special community problems. . . .

BENEATHA. Yes—and what are some of those?

WALTER. Girl, let the man talk.

LINDNER (*with understated relief*). Thank you. I would sort of like to explain this thing in my own way. I mean I want to explain to you in a certain way.

WALTER. Go ahead.

LINDNER. Yes. Well. I'm going to try to get right to the point. I'm sure we'll all appreciate that in the long run.

BENEATHA. Yes.

LINDNER. Well—

WALTER. Be still now!

LINDNER. Well—

RUTH (*still innocently*). Would you like another chair—you don't look comfortable.

LINDNER (*more frustrated than annoyed*). No, thank you very much. Please. Well—to get right to the point I—(*a great breath, and he is off at last*) I am sure you people must be aware of some of the incidents which have happened in various parts of the city when colored people have moved into certain areas—(BENEATHA *exhales heavily and starts tossing a piece of fruit up and down in the air.*) Well—because we have what I think is going to be a unique type of organization in American community life—not only do we deplore that kind of thing—but we are trying to do something about it. (BENEATHA *stops tossing and turns with a new and quizzical interest to the man.*) We feel—(*gaining confidence in his mission because of the interest in the faces of the people he is talking to*)—we feel that most of the trouble in this world, when you come right down to it—(*he hits his knee for emphasis*)—most of the trouble exists because people just don't sit down and talk to each other.

RUTH (*nodding as she might in church, pleased with the remark*). You can say that again, mister.

LINDNER (*more encouraged by such affirmation*). That we don't try hard enough in this world to understand the other fellow's problem. The other guy's point of view.

RUTH. Now that's right.

(BENEATHA *and* WALTER *merely watch and listen with genuine interest.*)

LINDNER. Yes—that's the way we feel out in Clybourne Park. And that's why I was elected to come here this afternoon and talk to you people. Friendly like, you know, the way people should talk to each other and see if we couldn't find some way to work this thing out. As I say, the whole business is a matter of *caring* about the other fellow. Anybody can see that you are a nice family of folks, hard-working and honest I'm sure. (BENEATHA *frowns slightly, quizzically, her head tilted regarding him.*) Today everybody knows what it means to be on the outside of *something*. And of course, there is always somebody who is out to take the advantage of people who don't always understand.

WALTER. What do you mean?

LINDNER. Well—you see our community is made up of people who've worked hard as the dickens for years to build up that little community. They're not rich and fancy people; just hard-working, honest people who don't really have much but those little homes and a dream of the kind of community they want to raise their children in. Now, I don't say we are perfect and there is a lot wrong in some of the things they want. But you've got to admit that a man, right or wrong, has the right to want to have the neighborhood he lives in a certain kind of way. And at the moment the overwhelming majority of our people out there feel that people get along better, take more of a common interest in the life of the community, when they share a common background. I want you to believe me when I tell you that race prejudice simply doesn't enter into it. It is a matter of the people of Clybourne Park believing, rightly or wrongly, as I say, that for the happiness of all concerned that our Negro families are happier when they live in their *own* communities.

BENEATHA (*with a grand and bitter gesture*). This, friends, is the Welcoming Committee!

WALTER (*dumbfounded, looking at* LINDNER). Is this what you came marching all the way over here to tell us?

LINDNER. Well, now we've been having a fine conversation. I hope you'll hear me all the way through.

WALTER (*tightly*). Go ahead, man.

LINDNER. You see—in the face of all things I have said, we are prepared to make your family a very generous offer. . . .

BENEATHA. Thirty pieces and not a coin less!

WALTER. Yeah?

LINDNER (*putting on his glasses and drawing a form out of the briefcase*). Our association is prepared, through the collective effort of our people, to buy the house from you at a financial gain to your family.

RUTH. Lord have mercy, ain't this the living gall!

WALTER. All right, you through?

LINDNER. Well, I want to give you the exact terms of the financial arrangement—

WALTER. We don't want to hear no exact terms of no arrangements. I want to know if you got any more to tell us 'bout getting together?

LINDNER (*taking off his glasses*). Well—I don't suppose that you feel. . . .

WALTER. Never mind how I feel—you got any more to say 'bout how people ought to sit down and talk to each other? . . . Get out of my house, man. (*He turns his back and walks to the door.*)

LINDNER (*looking around at the hostile faces and reaching and assembling his hat and briefcase*). Well—I don't understand why you people are reacting this way. What do you think you are going to gain by moving into a neighborhood where you just aren't wanted and where some elements—well—people can get awful worked up when they feel that their whole way of life and everything they've ever worked for is threatened.

WALTER. Get out.

LINDNER (*at the door, holding a small card*). Well—I'm sorry it went like this.

WALTER. Get out.

LINDNER (*almost sadly, regarding* WALTER). You just can't force people to change their hearts, son.

   (*He turns and puts his card on a table and exits.* WALTER *pushes the door to with stinging hatred, and stands looking at it.* RUTH *just sits and* BENEATHA *just stands. They say nothing.* MAMA *and* TRAVIS *enter.*)

MAMA. Well—this all the packing got done since I left out of here this morning. I testify before God that my children got all the energy of the dead. What time the moving men due?

BENEATHA. Four o'clock. You had a caller, Mama. (*She is smiling, teasingly.*)

MAMA. Sure enough—who?

BENEATHA (*her arms folded saucily*) The Welcoming Committee.

   (WALTER *and* RUTH *giggle.*)

MAMA (*innocently*). Who?

BENEATHA. The Welcoming Committee. They said they're sure going to be glad to see you when you get there.

WALTER (*devilishly*). Yeah, they said they can't hardly wait to see your face. (*Laughter.*)

MAMA (*sensing their facetiousness*). What's the matter with you all?

WALTER. Ain't nothing the matter with us. We just telling you 'bout the gentleman who came to see you this afternoon. From the Clybourne Park Improvement Association.

MAMA. What he want?

RUTH (*in the same mood as* BENEATHA *and* WALTER). To welcome you, honey.

WALTER. He said they can't hardly wait. He said the one thing they don't have, that they just *dying* to have out there is a fine family of colored people! (*To* RUTH *and* BENEATHA) Ain't that right!

RUTH *and* BENEATHA (*mockingly*). Yeah! He left his card in case—
    (*They indicate the card, and* MAMA *picks it up and throws it on the floor— understanding and looking off as she draws her chair up to the table on which she has put her plant and some sticks and some cord.*)

MAMA. Father, give us strength. (*Knowingly—and without fun*) Did he threaten us?

BENEATHA. Oh—Mama—they don't do it like that any more. He talked Brotherhood. He said everybody ought to learn how to sit down and hate each other with good Christian fellowship.
    (*She and* WALTER *shake hands to ridicule the remark.*)

MAMA (*sadly*). Lord, protect us. . . .

RUTH. You should hear the money those folks raised to buy the house from us. All we paid and then some.

BENEATHA. What they think we going to do—eat 'em?

RUTH. No, honey, marry 'em.

MAMA (*shaking her head*). Lord, Lord, Lord. . . .

RUTH. Well—that's the way the crackers crumble. Joke.

BENEATHA (*laughingly noticing what her mother is doing*). Mama, what are you doing?

MAMA. Fixing my plant so it won't get hurt none on the way. . . .

BENEATHA. Mama, you going to take *that* to the new house?

MAMA. Un-huh—

BENEATHA. That raggedy-looking old thing?

MAMA (*stopping and looking at her*). It expresses *me.*

RUTH (*with delight, to* BENEATHA). So there, Miss Thing!
    (*WALTER comes to* MAMA *suddenly and bends down behind her and squeezes her in his arms with all his strength. She is overwhelmed by the suddenness of it and, though delighted, her manner is like that of* RUTH *with* TRAVIS.)

MAMA. Look out now, boy! You make me mess up my thing here!

WALTER (*his face lit, he slips down on his knees beside her, his arms still about her*). Mama . . . you know what it means to climb up in the chariot?

MAMA (*gruffly, very happy*). Get on away from me now. . . .

RUTH (*near the gift-wrapped package, trying to catch* WALTER's *eye*). Psst—

WALTER. What the old song say, Mama. . . .

RUTH. Walter—Now? (*She is pointing at the package.*)

WALTER (*speaking the lines, sweetly, playfully, in his mother's face*).

I got wings . . . you got wings . . .
All God's children got wings . . .

MAMA. Boy—get out of my face and do some work. . . .

WALTER.

When I get to heaven gonna put on my wings.
Gonna fly all over God's heaven . . .

BENEATHA (*teasingly, from across the room*). Everybody talking 'bout heaven ain't going there!

WALTER (*to* RUTH, *who is carrying the box across to them*). I don't know, you think we ought to give her that. . . . Seems to me she ain't been very appreciative around here.

MAMA (*eying the box, which is obviously a gift*). What is that?

WALTER (*taking it from* RUTH *and putting it on the table in front of* MAMA). Well—what you all think? Should we give it to her?

RUTH. Oh—she was pretty good today.

MAMA. I'll good you— (*She turns her eyes to the box again.*)

BENEATHA. Open it, Mama.

(*She stands up, looks at it, turns and looks at all of them, and then presses her hands together and does not open the package.*)

WALTER (*sweetly*). Open it, Mama. It's for you. (MAMA *looks in his eyes. It is the first present in her life without its being Christmas. Slowly she opens her package and lifts out, one by one, a brand-new sparkling set of gardening tools.* WALTER *continues, prodding*) Ruth made up the note—read it . . .

MAMA (*picking up the card and adjusting her glasses*). "To our own Mrs. Miniver—Love from Brother, Ruth and Beneatha." Ain't that lovely. . . .

TRAVIS (*tugging at his father's sleeve*). Daddy, can I give her mine now?

WALTER. All right, son. (TRAVIS *flies to get his gift.*) Travis didn't want to go in with the rest of us, Mama. He got his own. (*Somewhat amused*) We don't know what it is. . . .

TRAVIS (*racing back in the room with a large hatbox and putting it in front of his grandmother*). Here!

MAMA. Lord have mercy, baby. You done gone and bought your grandmother a hat?

TRAVIS (*very proud*). Open it!

(*She does and lifts out an elaborate, but very elaborate, wide gardening hat, and all the adults break up at the sight of it.*)

RUTH. Travis, honey, what is that?

TRAVIS (*who thinks it is beautiful and appropriate*). It's a gardening hat! Like the ladies always have on in the magazines when they work in their gardens.

BENEATHA (*giggling fiercely*). Travis—we were trying to make Mama Mrs. Miniver—not Scarlett O'Hara!

MAMA (indignantly). What's the matter with you all! This here is a beautiful hat! (*Absurdly*) I always wanted me one just like it!

(*She pops it on her head to prove it to her grandson, and the hat is ludicrous and considerably oversized.*)

RUTH. Hot dog! Go, Mama!

WALTER (*doubled over with laughter*). I'm sorry, Mama—but you look like you ready to go out and chop you some cotton sure enough!

(*They all laugh except* MAMA, *out of deference to* TRAVIS' *feelings.*)

MAMA (*gathering the boy up to her*). Bless your heart—this is the prettiest hat I ever owned—(WALTER, RUTH, *and* BENEATHA *chime in noisily, festively and insincerely congratulating* TRAVIS *on his gift.*) What are we all standing around here for? We ain't finished packin' yet. Bennie, you ain't packed one book.

(*The bell rings.*)

BENEATHA. That couldn't be the movers . . . it's not hardly two good yet—

(BENEATHA *goes into her room.* MAMA *starts for door.*)

WALTER (*turning, stiffening*). Wait—wait—I'll get it. (*He stands and looks at the door.*)

MAMA. You expecting company, son?

WALTER (*just looking at the door*). Yeah—yeah. . . .

(MAMA *looks at* RUTH, *and they exchange innocent and unfrightened glances.*)

MAMA (*not understanding*). Well, let them in, son.

BENEATHA (*from her room*). We need some more string.

MAMA. Travis—you run to the hardware and get me some string cord.

(MAMA *goes out and* WALTER *turns and looks at* RUTH. TRAVIS *goes to a dish for money.*)

RUTH. Why don't you answer the door, man?

WALTER (*suddenly bounding across the floor to her*). 'Cause sometimes it hard to let the future begin! (*Stooping down in her face*)

I got wings! You got wings!
All God's children got wings!

(*He crosses to the door and throws it open. Standing there is a very slight little man in a not too prosperous business suit and with haunted frightened eyes and a hat pulled down tightly, brim up, around his forehead.* TRAVIS *passes between the men and exits.* WALTER *leans deep in the man's face, still in his jubilance.*)

> When I get to heaven gonna put on my wings.
> Gonna fly all over God's heaven . . .

(The little man just stares at him.)

> Heaven—

(Suddenly he stops and looks past the little man into the empty hallway.) Where's Willy, man?

BOBO. He ain't with me.

WALTER *(not disturbed).* Oh—come on in. You know my wife.

BOBO *(dumbly, taking off his hat).* Yes—h'you, Miss Ruth.

RUTH *(quietly, a mood apart from her husband already, seeing* BOBO*).* Hello, Bobo.

WALTER. You right on time today. . . . Right on time. That's the way! *(He slaps* BOBO *on his back.)* Sit down . . . lemme hear.

*(*RUTH *stands stiffly and quietly in back of them, as though somehow she senses death, her eyes fixed on her husband.)*

BOBO *(his frightened eyes on the floor, his hat in his hands).* Could I please get a drink of water, before I tell you about it, Walter Lee?

*(*WALTER *does not take his eyes off the man.* RUTH *goes blindly to the tap and gets a glass of water and brings it to* BOBO*).*

WALTER. There ain't nothing wrong, is there?

BOBO. Lemme tell you—

WALTER. Man—didn't nothing go wrong?

BOBO. Lemme tell you—Walter Lee. *(Looking at* RUTH *and talking to her more than to* WALTER*)* You know how it was. I got to tell you how it was. I mean first I got tell you how it was all the way . . . I mean about the money I put in, Walter Lee. . . .

WALTER *(with taut agitation now).* What about the money you put in?

BOBO. Well—it wasn't much as we told you—me and Willy—*(He stops.)* I'm sorry, Walter. I got a bad feeling about it. I got a real bad feeling about it. . . .

WALTER. Man, what you telling me about all this for? . . . Tell me what happened in Springfield. . . .

BOBO. Springfield.

RUTH *(like a dead woman).* What was supposed to happen in Springfield?

BOBO *(to her).* This deal that me and Walter went into with Willy—Me and Willy was going to go down to Springfield and spread some money 'round so's we wouldn't have to wait so long for the liquor license. . . . That's what we were going to do. Everybody said that was the way you had to do, you understand, Miss Ruth?

WALTER. Man—what happened down there?

BOBO (*a pitiful man, near tears*). I'm trying to tell you, Walter.

WALTER (*screaming at him suddenly*). THEN TELL ME, GODDAMMIT . . . WHAT'S THE MATTER WITH YOU?

BOBO. Man . . . I didn't go to no Springfield, yesterday.

WALTER (*halted, life hanging in the moment*). Why not?

BOBO (*the long way, the hard way to tell*). 'Cause I didn't have no reasons to. . . .

WALTER. Man, what are you talking about!

BOBO. I'm talking about the fact that when I got to the train station yesterday morning—eight o'clock like we planned . . . Man—*Willy didn't never show up.*

WALTER. Why . . . where was he . . . where is he?

BOBO. That's what I'm trying to tell you . . . I don't know . . . I waited six hours . . . I called his house . . . and I waited . . . six hours . . . I waited in that train station six hours . . . (*Breaking into tears*) That was all the extra money I had in the world. . . . (*Looking up at* WALTER *with the tears running down his face*) Man, *Willy is gone.*

WALTER. Gone, what you mean Willy is gone? Gone where? You mean he went by himself. You mean he went off to Springfield by himself—to take care of getting the license—(*Turns and looks anxiously at* RUTH) You mean maybe he didn't want too many people in on the business down there? (*Looks to* Ruth *again, as before*) You know Willy got his own ways. (*Looks back to* BOBO) Maybe you was late yesterday and he just went on down there without you. Maybe—maybe—he's been callin' you at home tryin' to tell you what happened or something. Maybe—maybe—he just got sick. He's somewhere—he's got to be somewhere. We just got to find him—me and you got to find him. (*Grabs* BOBO *senselessly by the collar and starts to shake him*) We got to!

BOBO (*in sudden angry, frightened agony*). What's the matter with you, Walter! *When a cat take off with your money he don't leave you no maps!*

WALTER (*turning madly, as though he is looking for* WILLY *in the very room*). Willy! . . . Willy . . . don't do it. . . . Please don't do it. . . . Man, not with that money . . . Man, please, not with that money . . . Oh, God . . . Don't let it be true. . . . (*He is wandering around, crying out for* WILLY *and looking for him or perhaps for help from God.*) Man . . . I trusted you . . . Man, I put my life in your hands. . . . (*He starts to crumple down on the floor as* RUTH *just covers her face in horror.* MAMA *opens the door and comes into the room, with* BENEATHA *behind her.*) Man . . . (*He starts to pound the floor with his fists, sobbing wildly.*) That money is made out of my father's flesh. . . .

BOBO (*standing over him helplessly*). I'm sorry, Walter. . . . (*Only* WALTER'S *sobs reply.* BOBO *puts on his hat.*) I had my life staked on this deal, too. . . . (*He exits.*)

MAMA (*to* WALTER). Son—(*She goes to him, bends down to him, talks to his bent head.*) Son . . . Is it gone? Son, I gave you sixty-five hundred dollars. Is it gone? All of it? Beneatha's money too?

WALTER (*lifting his head slowly*). Mama . . . I never . . . went to the bank at all. . . .

MAMA (*not wanting to believe him*). You mean . . . your sister's school money . . . you used that too . . . Walter? . . .

WALTER. Yessss! . . . All of it. . . . It's all gone. . . .

(*There is total silence.* RUTH *stands with her face covered with her hands;* BENEATHA *leans forlornly against a wall, fingering a piece of red ribbon from the mother's gift.* MAMA *stops and looks at her son without recognition and then, quite without thinking about it, starts to beat him senselessly in the face.* BENEATHA *goes to them and stops it.*)

BENEATHA. MAMA!

(MAMA *stops and looks at both of her children and rises slowly and wanders vaguely, aimlessly away from them.*)

MAMA. I seen . . . him . . . night after night . . . come in . . . and look at that rug . . . and then look at me . . . the red showing in his eyes . . . the veins moving in his head. . . . I seen him grow thin and old before he was forty . . . working and working and working like somebody's old horse . . . killing himself . . . and you—you give it all away in a day. . . .

BENEATHA. Mama—

MAMA. Oh, God . . . (*She looks up to Him.*) Look down here—and show me the strength.

BENEATHA. Mama—

MAMA (*folding over*). Strength . . .

BENEATHA (*plaintively*). Mama . . .

MAMA. Strength!

CURTAIN

ACT III

An hour later.

At curtain, there is a sullen light of gloom in the living room, gray light not unlike that which began the first scene of Act I. At left we can see WALTER *within his room, alone with himself. He is stretched out on the bed, his shirt out and open, his arms under his head. He does not smoke, he does not cry out, he merely lies there, looking up at the ceiling, much as if he were alone in the world.*

In the living room BENEATHA *sits at the table, still surrounded by the now almost ominous packing crates. She sits looking off. We feel that this is a mood struck perhaps an hour before, and it lingers now, full of the empty sound of profound*

(*He exits.* BENEATHA *sits on alone. Presently* WALTER *enters from his room and starts to rummage through things, feverishly looking for something. She looks up and turns in her seat.*)

BENEATHA (*hissingly*). Yes—just look at what the New World hath wrought! . . . Just look! (*She gestures with bitter disgust.*) There he is! *Monsieur le petit bourgeois noir*—himself! There he is—Symbol of a Rising Class! Entrepreneur! Titan of the system! (WALTER *ignores her completely and continues frantically and destructively looking for something and hurling things to floor and tearing things out of their place in his search.* BENEATHA *ignores the eccentricity of his actions and goes on with the monologue of insult.*) Did you dream of yachts on Lake Michigan, Brother? Did you see yourself on that Great Day sitting down at the Conference Table, surrounded by all the mighty bald-headed men in America? All halted, waiting, breathless, waiting for your pronouncements on industry? Waiting for you—Chairman of the Board? (WALTER *finds what he is looking for—a small piece of white paper—and pushes it in his pocket and puts on his coat and rushes out without ever having looked at her. She shouts after him.*) I look at you and I see the final triumph of stupidity in the world!

(*The door slams and she returns to just sitting again.* RUTH *comes quickly out of* MAMA's *room.*)

RUTH. Who was that?

BENEATHA. Your husband.

RUTH. Where did he go?

BENEATHA. Who knows—maybe he has an appointment at U.S. Steel.

RUTH (*anxiously, with frightened eyes*). You didn't say nothing bad to him, did you?

BENEATHA. Bad? Say anything bad to him? No—I told him he was a sweet boy and full of dreams and everything is strictly peachy keen, as the ofay kids say!

(MAMA *enters from her bedroom. She is lost, vague, trying to catch hold, to make some sense of her former command of the world, but it still eludes her. A sense of waste overwhelms her gait; a measure of apology rides on her shoulders. She goes to her plant, which has remained on the table, looks at it, picks it up and takes it to the window sill and sits it outside, and she stands and looks at it a long moment. Then she closes the window, straightens her body with effort and turns around to her children.*)

MAMA. Well—ain't it a mess in here, though? (*A false cheerfulness, a beginning of something*) I guess we all better stop moping around and get some work done. All this unpacking and everything we got to do. (RUTH *raises her head slowly in response to the sense of the line; and* BENEATHA *in similar manner turns very slowly to look at her mother.*) One of you all better call the moving people and tell 'em not to come.

RUTH. Tell 'em not to come?

MAMA. Of course, baby. Ain't no need in 'em coming all the way here and having to go back. They charges for that too. (*She sits down, fingers to her brow, thinking.*) Lord, ever since I was a little girl, I always remembers people saying, "Lena—Lena Eggleston, you aims too high all the time. You needs to slow down and see life a little more like it is. Just slow down some." That's what they always used to say down home—"Lord, that Lena Eggleston is a high-minded thing. She'll get her due one day!"

RUTH. No, Lena. . . .

MAMA. Me and Big Walter just didn't never learn right.

RUTH. Lena, no! We gotta go. Bennie—tell her. . . . (*She rises and crosses to* BENEATHA *with her arms outstretched.* BENEATHA *doesn't respond.*) Tell her we can still move . . . the notes ain't but a hundred and twenty-five a month. We got four grown people in this house—we can work. . . .

MAMA (*to herself*). Just aimed too high all the time—

RUTH (*turning and going to* MAMA *fast—the words pouring out with urgency and desperation*). Lena—I'll work. . . . I'll work twenty hours a day in all the kitchens in Chicago. . . . I'll strap my baby on my back if I have to and scrub all the floors in America and wash all the sheets in America if I have to—but we got to move. . . . We got to get out of here. . . .

(MAMA *reaches out absently and pats* RUTH's *hand.*)

MAMA. No—I see things differently now. Been thinking 'bout some of the things we could do to fix this place up some. I seen a second-hand bureau over on Maxwell Street just the other day that could fit right there. (*She points to where the new furniture might go.* RUTH *wanders away from her.*) Would need some new handles on it and then a little varnish and then it look like something brand-new. And—we can put up them new curtains in the kitchen. . . . Why this place be looking fine. Cheer us all up so that we forget trouble ever came. . . . (*To* RUTH) And you could get some nice screens to put up in your room round the baby's bassinet. . . . (*She looks at both of them, pleadingly.*) Sometimes you just got to know when to give up some things . . . and hold on to what you got. (WALTER *enters from the outside, looking spent and leaning against the door, his coat hanging from him.*)

MAMA. Where you been, son?

WALTER (*breathing hard*). Made a call.

MAMA. To who, son?

WALTER. To The Man.

MAMA. What man, baby?

WALTER. The Man, Mama. Don't you know who The Man is?

RUTH. Walter Lee?

WALTER. *The Man.* Like the guys in the streets say—The Man. Captain Boss—Mistuh Charley . . . Old Captain Please Mr. Bossman . . .

BENEATHA (*suddenly*). Lindner!

WALTER. That's right! That's good. I told him to come right over.

BENEATHA (*fiercely, understanding*). For what? What do you want to see him for!

WALTER (*looking at his sister*). We going to do business with him.

MAMA. What you talking 'bout, son?

WALTER. Talking 'bout life, Mama. You all always telling me to see life like it is. Well—I laid in there on my back today . . . and I figured it out. Life just like it is. Who gets and who don't get. (*He sits down with his coat on and laughs.*) Mama, you know it's all divided up. Life is. Sure enough. Between the takers and the "tooken." (*He laughs.*) I've figured it out finally. (*He looks around at them.*) Yeah. Some of us always getting "tooken." (*He laughs.*) People like Willy Harris, they don't never get "tooken." And you know why the rest of us do? 'Cause we all mixed up. Mixed up bad. We get to looking 'round for the right and the wrong; and we worry about it and cry about it and stay up nights trying to figure out 'bout the wrong and the right of things all the time. . . . And all the time, man, them takers is out there operating, just taking and taking. Willy Harris? Shoot—Willy Harris don't even count. He don't even count in the big scheme of things. But I'll say one thing for old Willy Harris . . . he's taught me something. He's taught me to keep my eye on what counts in this world. Yeah—(*shouting out a little*) Thanks, Willy!

RUTH. What did you call that man for, Walter Lee?

WALTER. Called him to tell him to come on over to the show. Gonna put on a show for the man. Just what he wants to see. You see, Mama, the man came here today and he told us that them people out there where you want us to move—well they so upset they willing to pay us not to move out there. (*He laughs again.*) And—and oh, Mama—you would of been proud of the way me and Ruth and Bennie acted. We told him to get out . . . Lord have mercy! We told the man to get out. Oh, we was some proud folks this afternoon, yeah. (*He lights a cigarette.*) We were still full of that old-time stuff. . . .

RUTH (*coming toward him slowly*). You talking 'bout taking them people's money to keep us from moving in that house?

WALTER. I ain't just talking 'bout it, baby—I'm telling you that's what's going to happen.

BENEATHA. Oh, God! Where is the bottom! Where is the real honest-to-God bottom so he can't go any farther!

WALTER. See—that's old stuff. You and that boy that was here today. You all want everybody to carry a flag and a spear and sing some marching songs, huh? You wanna spend your life looking into things and trying to find the right and the wrong part, huh? Yeah. You know what's going to happen to that boy someday—he'll find himself sitting in a dungeon, locked in forever—and the takers will have the key! Forget it, baby! There ain't no causes—there ain't nothing but taking in this world, and he who takes most is smartest—and it don't make a damn bit of difference *how.*

MAMA. You making something inside me cry, son. Some awful pain inside me.

WALTER. Don't cry, Mama. Understand. That white man is going to walk in that door able to write checks for more money than we ever had. It's important to him and I'm going to help him . . . I'm going to put on the show, Mama.

MAMA. Son—I come from five generations of people who was slaves and sharecroppers—but ain't nobody in my family never let nobody pay 'em no money that was a way of telling us we wasn't fit to walk the earth. We ain't never been that poor. (*Raising her eyes and looking at him*) We ain't never been that dead inside.

BENEATHA. Well—we are dead now. All the talk about dreams and sunlight that goes on in this house. All dead.

WALTER. What's the matter with you all! I didn't make this world! It was give to me this way! Hell, yes, I want me some yachts someday! Yes, I want to hang some real pearls 'round my wife's neck. Ain't she supposed to wear no pearls? Somebody tell me—tell me, who decides which women is suppose to wear pearls in this world. I tell you I am a *man*— and I think my wife should wear some pearls in this world!

(*This last line hangs a good while and* WALTER *begins to move about the room. The word "Man" has penetrated his consciousness; he mumbles it to himself repeatedly between strange agitated pauses as he moves about.*)

MAMA. Baby, how you going to feel on the inside?

WALTER. Fine! . . . Going to feel fine . . . a man. . . .

MAMA. You won't have nothing left then, Walter Lee.

WALTER (*coming to her*). I'm going to feel fine, Mama. I'm going to look that son-of-a-bitch in the eyes and say—(*he falters*)—and say, "All right, Mr. Lindner—(*he falters even more*)—that's your neighborhood out there. You got the right to keep it like you want. You got the right to have it like you want. Just write the check and—the house is yours." And, and I am going to say— (*His voice almost breaks.*) And you—you people just put the money in my hand and you won't have to live next to this bunch of stinking niggers! . . . (*He straightens up and moves away from his mother, walking around the room.*) Maybe—maybe I'll just get down on my black knees. . . . (*He does so;* RUTH *and* BENNIE *and* MAMA *watch him in frozen horror.*) Captain, Mistuh, Bossman. (*He starts crying.*) A-hee-hee-hee! (*Wringing his hands in profoundly anguished imitation*) Yasssssuh! Great White Father, just gi' ussen de money, fo' God's sake, and we's ain't gwine come out deh and dirty up yo' white folks neighborhood. . . .

(*He breaks down completely, then gets up and goes into the bedroom.*)

BENEATHA. That is not a man. That is nothing but a toothless rat.

MAMA. Yes—death done come in this here house. (*She is nodding, slowly, reflectively.*) Done come walking in my house. On the lips of my children. You what supposed to be my beginning again. You—what supposed to be my harvest. (*To* BENEATHA) You—you mourning your brother?

BENEATHA. He's no brother of mine.

MAMA. What you say?

BENEATHA. I said that that individual in that room is no brother of mine.

MAMA. That's what I thought you said. You feeling like you better than he is today? (BENEATHA *does not answer.*) Yes? What you tell him a minute ago? That he wasn't a man? Yes? You give him up for me? You done wrote his epitaph too—like the rest of the world? Well, who give you the privilege?

BENEATHA. Be on my side for once! You saw what he just did, Mama! You saw him—down on his knees. Wasn't it you who taught me—to despise any man who would do that. Do what he's going to do.

MAMA. Yes—I taught you that. Me and your daddy. But I thought I taught you something else too . . . I thought I taught you to love him.

BENEATHA. Love him? There is nothing left to love.

MAMA. There is always something left to love. And if you ain't learned that, you ain't learned nothing. (*Looking at her*) Have you cried for that boy today? I don't mean for yourself and for the family 'cause we lost the money. I mean for him; what he been through and what it done to him. Child, when do you think is the time to love somebody the most; when they done good and made things easy for everybody? Well then, you ain't through learning—because that ain't the time at all. It's when he's at his lowest and can't believe in hisself 'cause the world done whipped him so. When you starts measuring somebody, measure him right, child, measure him right. Make sure you done taken into account what hills and valleys he come through before he got to wherever he is.

(TRAVIS *bursts into the room at the end of the speech, leaving the door open.*)

TRAVIS. Grandmama—the moving men are downstairs! The truck just pulled up.

MAMA (*turning and looking at him*). Are they, baby? They downstairs?

(*She sighs and sits.* LINDNER *appears in the doorway. He peers in and knocks lightly, to gain attention, and comes in. All turn to look at him.*)

LINDNER (*hat and briefcase in hand*). Uh—hello . . .

(RUTH *crosses mechanically to the bedroom door and opens it and lets it swing open freely and slowly as the lights come up on* WALTER *within, still in his coat, sitting at the far corner of the room. He looks up and out through the room to* LINDNER.)

RUTH. He's here.

(*A long minute passes and* WALTER *slowly gets up.*)

LINDNER (*coming to the table with efficiency, putting his briefcase on the table and starting to unfold papers and unscrew fountain pens*). Well, I certainly was glad to hear from you people. (WALTER *has begun the trek out of the room, slowly and awkwardly, rather like a small boy, passing the back of his sleeve across his mouth from time to time.*) Life can really be so much simpler than people let it be most of the time. Well—with whom do I negotiate? You, Mrs. Younger, or your son here? (MAMA *sits with her hands folded on her lap and her eyes closed as* WALTER *advances.* TRAVIS *goes close to* LINDNER *and looks at the papers curiously.*) Just some official papers, sonny.

RUTH. Travis, you go downstairs.

MAMA (*opening her eyes and looking into* WALTER'S). No. Travis, you stay right here. And you make him understand what you doing, Walter Lee. You teach him good. Like Willy Harris taught you. You show where our five generations done come to. Go ahead, son—

WALTER (*looks down into his boy's eyes.* TRAVIS *grins at him merrily and* WALTER *draws him beside him with his arm lightly around his shoulders*). Well, Mr. Lindner. (BENEATHA *turns away.*) We called you— (*there is a profound, simple groping quality in his speech*)—because, well, me and my family—(*He looks around and shifts from one foot to the other.*) Well—we are very plain people. . . .

LINDNER. Yes—

WALTER. I mean—I have worked as a chauffeur most of my life—and my wife here, she does domestic work in people's kitchens. So does my mother. I mean—we are plain people. . . .

LINDNER. Yes, Mr. Younger—

WALTER (*really like a small boy, looking down at his shoes and then up at the man*). And—uh—well, my father, well, he was a laborer most of his life.

LINDNER (*absolutely confused*). Uh, yes—

WALTER (*looking down at his toes once again*). My father almost beat a man to death once because this man called him a bad name or something, you know what I mean?

LINDNER. No, I'm afraid I don't.

WALTER (*finally straightening up*). Well, what I mean is that we come from people who had a lot of pride. I mean—we are very proud people. And that's my sister over there and she's going to be a doctor—and we are very proud—

LINDNER. Well—I am sure that is very nice, but—

WALTER (*starting to cry and facing the man eye to eye*). What I am telling you is that we called you over here to tell you that we are very proud and that this is—this is my son, who makes the sixth generation of our family in this country, and that we have all thought about your offer and we have decided to move into our house because my father—my father—he earned it. (MAMA *has her eyes closed and is rocking back and forth as though she were in church, with her head nodding the amen yes.*) We don't want to make no trouble for nobody or fight no causes—but we will try to be good neighbors. That's all we got to say. (*He looks the man absolutely in the eyes.*) We don't want your money. (*He turns and walks away from the man.*)

LINDNER (*looking around at all of them*). I take it then that you have decided to occupy.

BENEATHA. That's what the man said.

LINDNER (*to* MAMA *in her reverie*). Then I would like to appeal to you, Mrs. Younger. You are older and wiser and understand things better I am sure. . . .

MAMA (*rising*). I am afraid you don't understand. My son said we was going to move and there ain't nothing left for me to say. (*Shaking her head with double meaning*) You know how these young folks is nowadays, mister. Can't do a thing with 'em. Good-bye.

LINDNER (*folding up his materials*). Well—if you are that final about it. . . . There is nothing left for me to say. (*He finishes. He is almost ignored by the family, who are concentrating on* WALTER LEE. *At the door* LINDNER *halts and looks around.*) I sure hope you people know what you're doing. (*He shakes his head and exits.*)

RUTH (*looking around and coming to life*). Well, for God's sake—if the moving men are here—LET'S GET THE HELL OUT OF HERE!

MAMA (*into action*). Ain't it the truth! Look at all this here mess. Ruth, put Travis' good jacket on him. . . . Walter Lee, fix your tie and tuck your shirt in, you look just like somebody's hoodlum. Lord have mercy, where is my plant? (*She flies to get it amid the general hustling of the family, who are deliberately trying to ignore the nobility of the past moment.*) You all start on down. . . . Travis child, don't go empty-handed. . . . Ruth, where did I put that box with my skillets in it? I want to be in charge of it myself . . . I'm going to make us the biggest dinner we ever ate tonight. . . . Beneatha, what's the matter with them stockings? Pull them things up, girl. . . .

(*The family starts to file out as two moving men appear and begin to carry out the heavier pieces of furniture, bumping into the family as they move about.*)

BENEATHA. Mama, Asagai—asked me to marry him today and go to Africa—

MAMA (*in the middle of her getting-ready activity*). He did? You ain't old enough to marry nobody—(*Seeing the moving men lifting one of her chairs precariously*) Darling, that ain't no bale of cotton, please handle it so we can sit in it again. I had that chair twenty-five years. . . .

(*The movers sigh with exasperation and go on with their work.*)

BENEATHA (*girlishly and unreasonably trying to pursue the conversation*). To go to Africa, Mama—be a doctor in Africa. . . .

MAMA (*distracted*). Yes, baby—

WALTER. Africa! What he want you to go to Africa for?

BENEATHA. To practice there. . . .

WALTER. Girl, if you don't get all them silly ideas out your head! You better marry yourself a man with some loot. . . .

BENEATHA (*angrily, precisely as in the first scene of the play*). What have you got to do with who I marry!

WALTER. Plenty. Now I think George Murchison—

(*He and* BENEATHA *go out yelling at each other vigorously;* BENEATHA *is heard saying that she would not marry* GEORGE MURCHISON *if he were Adam and she were Eve, etc. The anger is loud and real till their voices diminish.* RUTH *stands at the door and turns to* MAMA *and smiles knowingly.*)

MAMA (*fixing her hat at last*). Yeah—they something all right, my children. . . .

RUTH. Yeah—they're something. Let's go, Lena.

MAMA (*stalling, starting to look around at the house*). Yes—I'm coming. Ruth—

RUTH. Yes?

MAMA (*quietly, woman to woman*). He finally come into his manhood today, didn't he? Kind of like a rainbow after the rain. . . .

RUTH (*biting her lip lest her own pride explode in front of* MAMA). Yes, Lena.

(WALTER's *voice calls for them raucously.*)

MAMA (*waving* RUTH *out vaguely*). All right, honey—go on down. I be down directly.

(RUTH *hesitates, then exits.* MAMA *stands, at last alone in the living room, her plant on the table before her as the lights start to come down. She looks around at all the walls and ceilings and suddenly, despite herself, while the children call below, a great heaving thing rises in her and she puts her fist to her mouth, takes a final desperate look, pulls her coat about her, pats her hat and goes out. The lights dim down. The door opens and she comes back in, grabs her plant, and goes out for the last time.*)

CURTAIN

QUESTIONS

1. The play's title derives from a poem by Langston Hughes called "Harlem" (printed on p. 748 of this anthology). Discuss the significance of the play's title and its relationship to the poem.
2. Analyze the characterizations of any of the following, indicating how he or she represents particular facets of twentieth-century African American experience: Walter, Ruth, Beneatha, Mama.
3. Analyze the speeches of the white character, Karl Lindner. How does he differ from the black characters? Is he meant to be admirable? Why or why not?
4. Discuss the play's treatment of gender, focusing on one of the major characters. Are the gender roles as dramatized in the play stereotypical or do they flout familiar stereotypes?
5. How does the playwright handle black dialect in the play? Are the language and dialect appropriate for city-dwelling black characters in the twentieth century?
6. Isolate the play's major themes. Is Hansberry offering us a play with strictly African American themes, or are her themes more universal?

WENDY WASSERSTEIN
Tender Offer

Characters

LISA

PAUL

A girl of around nine is alone in a dance studio. She is dressed in traditional leotards and tights. She begins singing to herself, "Nothing Could Be Finer Than to Be in Carolina." She maps out a dance routine, including parts for the chorus. She builds to a finale. A man, Paul, around thirty-five, walks in. He has a sweet, though distant demeanor. As he walks in, Lisa notices him and stops.

PAUL. You don't have to stop, sweetheart.
LISA. That's okay.
PAUL. Looked very good.
LISA. Thanks.
PAUL. Don't I get a kiss hello?
LISA. Sure.
PAUL (*embraces her*). Hi, Tiger.
LISA. Hi, Dad.
PAUL. I'm sorry I'm late.

TENDER OFFER First produced in 1983. Wendy Wasserstein (1950–2006) was born and raised in Brooklyn and earned degrees from Mount Holyoke, City College of New York, and Yale Drama School. She won a Tony award and Pulitzer Prize for her second play, *The Heidi Chronicles*, in 1989.

LISA. That's okay.

PAUL. How'd it go?

LISA. Good.

PAUL. Just good?

LISA. Pretty good.

PAUL. "Pretty good." You mean you got a lot of applause or "pretty good" you could have done better.

LISA. Well, Courtney Palumbo's mother thought I was pretty good. But you know the part of the middle when everybody's supposed to freeze and the big girl comes out. Well, I think I moved a little bit.

PAUL. I thought what you were doing looked very good.

LISA. Daddy, that's not what I was doing. That was tap-dancing I made that up.

PAUL. Oh. Well it looked good. Kind of sexy.

LISA. Yuch!

PAUL. What do you mean "yuch"?

LISA. Just yuch!

PAUL. You don't want to be sexy?

LISA. I don't care.

PAUL. Let's go Tiger. I promised your mother I'd get you home in time for dinner.

LISA. I can't find my leg warmers.

PAUL. You can't find your what?

LISA. Leg warmers. I can't go home till I find my leg warmers.

PAUL. I don't see you looking for them.

LISA. I was waiting for you.

PAUL. Oh.

LISA. Daddy.

PAUL. What?

LISA. Nothing.

PAUL. Where do you think you left them?

LISA. Somewhere around here. I can't remember.

PAUL. Well, try to remember, Lisa. We don't have all night.

LISA. I told you. I think somewhere around here.

PAUL. I don't see them. Let's go home now. You'll call the dancing school tomorrow.

LISA. Daddy, I can't go home till I find them. Miss Judy says it's not professional to leave things.

PAUL. Who's Miss Judy?

LISA. She's my ballet teacher. She once danced the lead in *Swan Lake,* and she was a June Taylor dancer.

PAUL. Well, then, I'm sure she'll understand about the leg warmers.

LISA. Daddy, Miss Judy wanted to know why you were late today.

PAUL. Hmmmmmmmm?

LISA. Why were you late?

PAUL. I was in a meeting. Business I'm sorry.

LISA. Why did you tell Mommy you'd come instead of her if you knew you had business?

PAUL. Honey, something just came up. I thought I'd be able to be here. I was looking forward to it.

LISA. I wish you wouldn't make appointments to see me.

PAUL. Hmmmmmmmm?

LISA. You shouldn't make appointments to see me unless you know you're going to come.

PAUL. Of course I'm going to come.

LISA. No, you're not. Talia Robbins told me she's much happier living without her father in the house. Her father used to come home late and go to sleep early.

PAUL. Lisa, stop it. Let's go.

LISA. I can't find my leg warmers.

PAUL. Forget your leg warmers.

LISA. Daddy.

PAUL. What is it?

LISA. I saw this show on television, I think it was WPIX Channel 11. Well, the father was crying about his daughter.

PAUL. Why was he crying? Was she sick?

LISA. No. She was at school. And he was at business. And he just missed her, so he started to cry.

PAUL. What was the name of this show?

LISA. I don't know. I came in in the middle.

PAUL. Well, Lisa, I certainly would cry if you were sick or far away, but I know that you're well and you're home. So no reason to get maudlin.

LISA. What's maudlin?

PAUL. Sentimental, soppy. Frequently used by children who make things up to get attention.

LISA. I am sick! I am sick! I have Hodgkin's disease and a bad itch on my leg.

PAUL. What do you mean you have Hodgkin's disease? Don't say things like that.

LISA. Swoosie Kurtz, she had Hodgkin's disease on a TV movie last year, but she got better and now she's on *Love Sidney*.

PAUL. Who is Swoosie Kurtz?

LISA. She's an actress named after an airplane. I saw her on *Live at Five*.

PAUL. You watch too much television; you should do your homework. Now put your coat on.

LISA. Daddy, I really do have a bad itch on my leg. Would you scratch it?

PAUL. Lisa, you're procrastinating.

LISA. Why do you use words I don't understand? I hate it. You're like Daria Feldman's mother. She always talks in Yiddish to her husband so Daria won't understand.

PAUL. Procrastinating is not Yiddish.

LISA. Well, I don't know what it is.

PAUL. Procrastinating means you don't want to go about your business.

LISA. I don't go to business. I go to school.

PAUL. What I mean is you want to hang around here until you and I are late for dinner and your mother's angry and it's too late for you to do your homework.

LISA. I do not.

PAUL. Well, it sure looks that way. Now put your coat on and let's go.

LISA. Daddy.

PAUL. Honey, I'm tired. Really, later.

LISA. Why don't you want to talk to me?

PAUL. I do want to talk to you. I promise when we get home we'll have a nice talk.

LISA. No, we won't. You'll read the paper and fall asleep in front of the news.

PAUL. Honey, we'll talk on the weekend, I promise. Aren't I taking you to the theater this weekend? Let me look. (*He takes out an appointment book.*) Yes. Sunday. *Joseph and the Amazing Technicolor Raincoat* with Lisa. Okay, Tiger?

LISA. Sure. It's *Dreamcoat.*

PAUL. What?

LISA. Nothing. I think I see my leg warmers. (*She goes to pick them up and an odd-looking trophy.*)

PAUL. What's that?

LISA. It's stupid. I was second best at the dance recital, so they gave me this thing. It's stupid.

PAUL. Lisa.

LISA. What?

PAUL. What did you want to talk about?

LISA. Nothing.

PAUL. Was it about my missing your recital? I'm really sorry, Tiger. I would have liked to have been here.

LISA. That's okay.

PAUL. Honest?

LISA. Daddy, you're prostrastinating.

PAUL. I'm procrastinating. Sit down. Let's talk. How's school?

LISA. Fine.

PAUL. You like it?

LISA. Yup.

PAUL. You looking forward to camp this summer?

LISA. Yup.

PAUL. Is Daria Feldman going back?

LISA. Nope.

PAUL. Why not?

LISA. I don't know. We can go home now. Honest, my foot doesn't itch anymore.

PAUL. Lisa, you know what you do in business when it seems like there's nothing left to say? That's when you really start talking. Put a bid on the table.

LISA. What's a bid?

PAUL. You tell me what you want and I'll tell you what I've got to offer. Like Monopoly. You want Boardwalk, but I'm only willing to give you the Railroads. Now, because you are my daughter I'd throw in Water Works and Electricity. Understand, Tiger?

LISA. No. I don't like board games. You know, Daddy, we could get Space Invaders for our home for thirty-five dollars. In fact, we could get an Osborne System for two thousand. Daria Feldman's parents . . .

PAUL. Daria Feldman's parents refuse to talk to Daria, so they bought a computer to keep Daria busy so they won't have to speak in Yiddish. Daria will probably grow up to be a homicidal maniac lesbian prostitute.

LISA. I know what the word prostitute means.

PAUL. Good. (*Pause.*) You still haven't told me about school. Do you still like your teacher?

LISA. She's okay.

PAUL. Lisa, if we're talking try to answer me.

LISA. I am answering you. Can we go home now, please?

PAUL. Damn it, Lisa, if you want to talk to me . . . . Talk to me!

LISA. I can't wait till I'm old enough so I can make my own money and never have to see you again. Maybe I'll become a prostitute.

PAUL. Young lady, that's enough.

LISA. I hate you, Daddy! I hate you! (*She throws her trophy into the trash bin.*)

PAUL. What'd you do that for?

LISA. It's stupid.

PAUL. Maybe I wanted it.

LISA. What for?

PAUL. Maybe I wanted to put it where I keep your dinosaur and the picture you made of Mrs. Kimbel with the chicken pox.

LISA. You got mad at me when I made that picture. You told me I had to respect Mrs. Kimbel because she was my teacher.

PAUL. That's true. But she wasn't my teacher. I liked her better with the chicken pox. (*Pause.*) Lisa, I'm sorry. I was very wrong to miss your recital, and you don't have to become a prostitute. That's not the type of profession Miss Judy has in mind for you.

LISA. (*mumbles*). No.

PAUL. No. (*Pause.*) So Talia Robbins is really happy her father moved out?

LISA. Talia Robbins picks open the eighth-grade lockers during gym period. But she did that before her father moved out.

PAUL. You can't always judge someone by what they do or what they don't do. Sometimes you come home from dancing school and run upstairs and shut the door, and when I finally get to talk to you, everything is "okay" or "fine." Yup or nope?

LISA. Yup.

PAUL. Sometimes, a lot of times, I come home and fall asleep in front of the television. So you and I spend a lot of time being a little scared of each other. Maybe?

LISA. Maybe.

PAUL. Tell you what. I'll make you a tender offer.

LISA. What?

PAUL. I'll make you a tender offer. That's when one company publishes in the newspaper that they want to buy another company. And the company that publishes is called the Black Knight because they want to gobble up the poor little company. So the poor little company needs to be rescued. And then a White Knight comes along and makes a bigger and better offer so the shareholders won't have to tender shares to the Big Black Knight. You with me?

LISA. Sort of.

PAUL. I'll make you a tender offer like the White Knight. But I don't want to own you. I just want to make a much better offer. Okay?

LISA. (*sort of understanding*). Okay. (*Pause. They sit for a moment.*) Sort of, Daddy, what do you think about? I mean, like when you're quiet what do you think about?

PAUL. Oh, business usually. If I think I made a mistake or if I think I'm doing okay. Sometimes I think about what I'll be doing five years from now and if it's what I hoped it would be five years ago. Sometimes I think about what your life will be like, if Mount Saint Helen's will erupt again. What you'll become if you'll study penmanship or word processing. If you speak kindly of me to your psychiatrist when you are in graduate school. And how the hell I'll pay for your graduate school. And sometimes I try and think what it was I thought about when I was your age.

LISA. Do you ever look out your window at the clouds and try to see which kinds of shapes they are? Like one time, honest, I saw the head of Walter

Cronkite in a flower vase. Really! Like look don't those kinda look like if you turn it upside down, two big elbows or two elephant trunks dancing?

PAUL. Actually still looks like Walter Cronkite in a flower vase to me. But look up a little. See the one that's still moving? That sorta looks like a whale on a thimble.

LISA. Where?

PAUL. Look up to your right.

LISA. I don't see it. Where?

PAUL. The other way.

LISA. Oh, yeah! There's the head and there's the stomach. Yeah! (*Lisa picks up her trophy.*) Hey, Daddy.

PAUL. Hey, Lisa.

LISA. You can have this thing if you want it. But you have to put it like this, because if you put it like that it is gross.

PAUL. You know what I'd like? So I can tell people who come into my office why I have this gross stupid thing on my shelf, I'd like it if you could show me your dance recital.

LISA. Now?

PAUL. We've got time. Mother said she won't be home till late.

LISA. Well, Daddy, during a lot of it I freeze and the big girl in front dances.

PAUL. Well, how 'bout the number you were doing when I walked in?

LISA. Well, see, I have parts for a lot of people in that one, too.

PAUL. I'll dance the other parts.

LISA. You can't dance.

PAUL. Young lady, I played Yvette Mimieux in a *Hasty Pudding* Show.

LISA. Who's Yvette Mimieux?

PAUL. Watch more television. You'll find out. (*Paul stands up.*) So I'm ready. (*He begins singing.*) "Nothing could be finer than to be in Carolina."

LISA. Now I go. In the morning. And now you go. Dum-da.

PAUL (*obviously not a tap dancer*). Da-da-dum.

LISA (*whines*). Daddy!

PAUL (*mimics her*). Lisa! Nothing could be finer . . .

LISA. That looks dumb.

PAUL. Oh, yeah? You think they do this better in *The Amazing Minkcoat?* No way! Now you go—da da da dum.

LISA. Da da da dum.

PAUL. If I had Aladdin's lamp for only a day, I'd make a wish . . .

LISA. Daddy, that's maudlin!

PAUL. I know it's maudlin. And here's what I'd say:

LISA AND PAUL. I'd say that "nothing could be finer than to be in Carolina in the moooooooooooornin'."

QUESTIONS

1. The play contains several references to television and movies. If you don't recognize the names or titles, the Internet has all the necessary information. What purpose is served by these references to popular media? How do they help to characterize Lisa and Paul?
2. What are the sources of conflict between the two characters? Which, if any, are resolved by the conclusion of the play?
3. Explain the possible meanings of the title, and how they are relevant to the play.
4. Briefly describe the plot, and explain how it relates to the theme of the play.
5. Would you describe one or the other of the characters as the protagonist? Is the other character the antagonist?
6. What is the function of the wife/mother who never appears on stage? What would be lost if Paul were the single parent of Lisa?

PRACTICE AP WRITING PROMPTS

Lorraine Hansberry, *A Raisin in the Sun* (pp. 1522–1596)

In *A Raisin in the Sun*, each of the two children of Ruth Younger ("Mama") has a "dream." Walter's dream is to own a liquor store; his sister Beneatha's dream is to become a doctor. Write an essay in which you analyze the way each of their dreams comes to be an obstacle to the other's, and show how understanding this conflict helps us interpret the play as a whole. Do not merely summarize the plot.

EXCERPT FROM OEDIPUS REX BY SOPHOCLES

QUESTIONS 1–10. Carefully read the passage, the conclusion of the play, before choosing your answers.

OEDIPUS: ... Children, where are you?
    Come quickly to my hands: they are your brother's—
    Hands that have brought your father's once clear eyes
    To this way of seeing—

5   Ah dearest ones,
    I had neither sight nor knowledge then, your father By the
    woman who was the source of his own life!
    And i weep for you—having no strength to see you—
    I weep for you when I think of the bitterness

10   That men will visit upon you all your lives.
    What homes, what festivals can you attend
    Without being forced to depart again in tears?
    And when you come to marriageable age,
    Where is the man, my daughters, who would dare

15   Risk the bane that lies on all my children?
    Is there any evil wanting? Your father killed
    His father; sowed the womb of her who bore him;
    Engendered you at the fount of his own existence!
    That is what they will say of you.

20   Then, whom
    Can you ever marry? There are no bridegrooms for you,
    And your lives must wither away in sterile dreaming.
    O Kreon, son of Menoikeus!
    You are the only father my daughters have,

25   since we, their parents, are both of us gone for ever.
    They are your own blood: you will not let them
    Fall into beggary and loneliness;
    You will keep them from the miseries that are mine!
    Take pity on them; see, they are only children,

30   Friendless except for you. Promise me this,
    Great prince, and give me your hand in token of it.
    (Kreon clasps his right hand.)
    Children:
    I could say much, if you could understand me,

35   But as it is, I have only this prayer for you:
    Live where you can, be as happy as you can—
    Happier, please God, than God has made your father.

1. In telling his daughters, "I had neither sight nor knowl-
   edge then, your father / By the woman who was the
   source of his own life!" (lines 6–7), Oedipus means that
   I. he did not know he was their brother
   II. he did not know their mother was his mother
   III. he was their father
   (A) I and II only
   (B) II and III only
   (C) I, II, and III
   (D) I only
   (E) II only

2. In "... the bitterness / That men will visit upon you all
   your lives" (lines 9–10), "visit upon you" means
   (A) forgive you
   (B) thrust upon you
   (C) force you to make a journey
   (D) send you on a sacred pilgrimage
   (E) kill you

3. In "Risk the bane that lies on my children?" (line 15),
   the word "bane" means
   (A) trouble
   (B) death
   (C) running
   (D) laughing
   (E) cheering

4. "Your father killed / His father; sowed the womb of her
   who bore him; / Engendered you at the fount of his own
   existence!" (lines 16–17) refers to
   (A) fratricide and marriage
   (B) regicide and matricide
   (C) intended patricide
   (D) unintended patricide
   (E) premeditated murder

5. In "Is there any evil wanting?" (line 16), the word "want-
   ing" means
   (A) hoping
   (B) lacking
   (C) needing
   (D) filling
   (E) describing

6. Line 17, "sowed the womb of her who bore him," is a metaphoric way of describing the fact that Oedipus
   (A) had sexual relations with his mother
   (B) had farmers who worked for him
   (C) had two mothers
   (D) was naive
   (E) was an exceptional gardener

7. In the lines "you will not let them / Fall into beggary and loneliness" (26–27), the "you" refers to
   (A) Oedipus
   (B) Kreon
   (C) Menoikeus
   (D) the father of Oedipus
   (E) the mother of Oedipus

8. In "There are no bridegrooms for you, / And your lives must wither away in sterile dreaming," (lines 21–22) the word "sterile" gives a vision of a(n)
   (A) austere future
   (B) refreshing past
   (C) crafty reconcilement
   (D) legal conundrum
   (E) after-thought of great expectation

9. "Children, where are you? / Come quickly to my hands: they are your brother's— /" (lines 1–2) emphasizes
   (A) the strange father-and-sibling relationship
   (B) the normal mother-and-daughter relationship
   (C) a definite lack of fatalism
   (D) the essence of hope
   (E) the misguided but happy fortune of Oedipus

10. Lines 36–37, "be as happy as you can— / Happier, please God, than God has made your father," suggest
    (A) their fate is sealed and there will be no hope
    (B) there may be hope that a father's prayer will be answered
    (C) their fate shows that Kreon will kill them
    (D) their fate shows that Oedipus will ask his wife for help
    (E) there is no such a thing as fate in a Greek play

See page 1608 for the answers to this set of questions.

EXCERPT FROM *THE SANDBOX*
BY EDWARD ALBEE

Questions 11–25. Carefully read the following passage, from the first scene, before choosing your answers.

MOMMY (out *over the audience*). Be quiet, Grandma . . . just be
quiet, and wait. (GRANDMA *throws a shovelful of sand at*
MOMMY. *Still out over the audience*) She's throwing sand at
me! You stop that, Grandma; you stop throwing sand at
Mommy! *(To* DADDY) She's throwing sand at me. (DADDY   5
looks around at GRANDMA, *who screams at him.*)

GRANDMA. GRAAAAA!

MOMMY. Don't look at her. Just . . . sit here . . . be very still
. . . and wait. (*To the* MUSICIAN) You . . . uh . . . you go
ahead and do whatever it is you do. *(The* MUSICIAN *plays.*   10
MOMMY *and* DADDY *are fixed, staring out beyond the audience.*
GRANDMA *looks at them, looks at the* MUSICIAN, *looks at the
sandbox, throws down the shovel.*)

GRANDMA. Ah-haaaaaa! Graaaaaa! (*Looks for reaction; gets none.
Now . . . directly to the audience*) Honestly! What a way to   15
treat an old woman! Drag her out of the house . . . stick
her in a car . . . bring her out here from the city . . . dump
her in a pile of sand . . . and leave her here to set. i'm
eighty-six years old! i was married when i was seventeen.
To a farmer. He died when I was thirty. (*To the* MUSICIAN)   20
Will you stop that, please? (*The* MUSICIAN *stops playing.*)
I'm a feeble old woman . . . how do you expect anybody
to hear me over that peep! peep! peep! *(To herself)* There's
no respect around here (*To the* YOUNG MAN) There's no
respect around here!   25

YOUNG MAN (*same smile*). Hi!

GRANDMA (*after a pause, a mild double-take, continues, to the
audience*). My husband died when I was thirty (*indicates-
MOMMY), and I had to raise that big cow over there all by
my lonesome. You can imagine what *that was like*. Lordy!   30
(*To the* YOUNG MAN) Where'd they get *you?*

YOUNG MAN. Oh . . . I've been around for a while.

GRANDMA. I'll bet you have! Heh, heh, heh. Will you look at
you!

35   YOUNG MAN *(flexing his muscles)*. Isn't that something? *(Continues his calisthenics.)*

GRANDMA. Boy, oh boy; I'll say. Pretty good.

YOUNG MAN *(sweetly)* I'll say.

GRANDMA. Where ya from?

40   YOUNG MAN. Southern California.

GRANDMA *(nodding)*. Figgers; figgers. What's your name, honey?

YOUNG MAN. I don't know . . .

GRANDMA (to *the audience*). Bright, too!

45   Young Man. I mean . . . I mean, they haven't given me one yet . . . the studio . . .

11. "What a way to treat an old woman! Drag her out of the house . . . stick her in a car . . . bring her out here from the city . . . dump her in a pile of sand . . . and leave her here to set"(lines 1518) seems to show
    (A) an absurdist's view of the way old people are treated
    (B) life at the beach
    (C) a realist's view of the way old people are treated
    (D) hope for the future
    (E) a pragmatist's view of the way old people are treated

12. The entire passage shows that the author encourages the audience to
    (A) laugh harshly at children at play
    (B) cry sweetly for a misspent youth
    (C) laugh bitterly and draw attention to a dysfunctional family
    (D) smile blithely at life
    (E) stop going to the beach

13. "Will you stop that, please?"(line 21) is addressed to the Musician. All of the following apply to this line EXCEPT
    (A) the play deals with a beginning-of-life ritual
    (B) the actors talk to the sound people
    (C) the situation is absurd
    (D) Grandma appears to be a senile dementia extrovert
    (E) absurd drama philosophically addresses even staging limitations

14. "Grandma (nodding). Figgers; figgers. What's your name, honey?
    YOUNG MAN. I don't know . . .
    GRANDMA (*to the audience*). Bright, too!"(lines 41–44)
    This repartee shows all of the following EXCEPT
    (A) 86-year-old Grandma still has a sense of humor
    (B) the Young Man is intellectually gifted
    (C) the Young Man appears to lack knowledge
    (D) Grandma's bantering fakes an entree into romance
    (E) Grandma's term "Honey"aids her obviously feigned seduction

15. The interlinear scene direction in line 13, "(looks at the sandbox, throws down the shovel)," indicates a subtext that includes all of the following EXCEPT
    (A) because of their treatment old people often simply give up
    (B) Mommy and Daddy needed to be shocked back to reality
    (C) Mommy and Daddy have reacted to Grandma appropriately
    (D) aggressive tendencies of senility are often fleeting
    (E) drama, even absurd drama, is often allegorical

16. When Mommy says, "She's throwing sand at me! You stop that, Grandma; you stop throwing sand at Mommy! (To Daddy) She's throwing sand at me"(lines 3–5), the indication is that Albee
    (A) shows in Mommy's words and actions a loving daughter
    (B) shows that Mommy hates Daddy
    (C) holds a comic mirror up to family relationships
    (D) shows that Daddy really hates Mommy
    (E) seriously depicts matricide

17. In line 29, the "big cow"is
    (A) Grandma
    (B) Daddy
    (C) the Young Man
    (D) Mommy
    (E) the sandbox

18. The entire excerpt shows
    (A) nastiness and lack of kindness on the part of Mommy and Daddy
    (B) no empathy at all for Grandma
    (C) empathy for Mommy and Daddy
    (D) empathy for the Young Man
    (E) real love in this strange family

19. The sandbox itself is
    (A) symbolic of the womb
    (B) representative of the grave
    (C) symbolic of youthful days at the beach
    (D) representative of American soil
    (E) symbolic of our nascent salad days

20. *The Sandbox* addresses all of the following EXCEPT
    (A) the poverty of interpersonal communication
    (B) the essence of theater itself in modern America
    (C) the idea that the limitations of symbolic drama in our media-driven society may also be its greatest asset
    (D) the poor treatment of old people once they are deemed to have no value to society
    (E) the idea that no truly great and seminal ideas can ever come from comedy but must originate in tragedy

21. In a most absurd way, the play deals with
    I. an elderly parent, treated as an infant by her family, protesting her fate
    II. the fact that the roles have changed and the child has now become the parent who is confronting an awareness of death
    III. the fact that the elderly are mocked as being closer to death
    (A) I only
    (B) I and II only
    (C) II and III only
    (D) I, II, and III
    (E) II only

22. In lines 16–17, "Drag her out of the house . . . stick her in a car,"the "her"referred to is
    (A) Mommy
    (B) Grandma
    (C) the sandbox
    (D) the Musician
    (E) an unknown victim

23. The word "figgers"(line 41) is
    (A) a made-up word mimicking the sounds of the words
        for "it figures"
    (B) slang for "you have a nice figure"
    (C) a colloquialism for "it does not compute"
    (D) dialect for "fantastically bigger"
    (E) lingo for "a beach bum"

24. "[T]hat peep! peep! peep!"(line 23) is an example of
    (A) oxymoron
    (B) an image of baby chickens
    (C) onomatopoeia
    (D) an image of sight
    (E) a friend on the Internet and the phone

25. The words "that was like"are italicized in line 30 because
    they
    (A) are just another interlinear scene direction
    (B) indicate to the actor to say them silently
    (C) indicate to the actor to sing them
    (D) indicate to the actor to show optimistic merriment
    (E) indicate to the actor to stress sarcasm

See page 1608 for the answers to this set of questions.

ANSWERS FOR THE AP®
MULTIPLE-CHOICE QUESTIONS

FICTION

Excerpt from "The Lottery" by Shirley Jackson

1. A	2. E	3. B	4. E	5. C
6. C	7. C	8. A	9. E	10. C
11. A	12. E	13. E	14. E	

Excerpt from "A Very Old Man with Enormous Wings" by Gabriel García Marquéz

15. A	16. D	17. C	18. B	19. D
20. E	21. E	22. A	23. D	24. A
25. C	26. D	27. C	28. E	

Excerpt from "Bartleby the Scrivener: A Story of Wall Street" by Herman Melville

29. E	30. B	31. B	32. C	33. C
34. B	35. D	36. B	37. A	38. A
39. C	40. B	41. E	42. C	

POETRY

"A Valediction: Forbidding Mourning" by John Donne

1. B	2. C	3. D	4. C	5. A
6. B	7. C	8. B	9. D	10. C
11. D	12. B	13. A	14. B	15. A

"A Supermarket in California" by Allen Ginsberg

16. D	17. A	18. E	19. B	20. C
21. E	22. A	23. E	24. A	25. A
26. D				

"Mid-Term Break" by Seamus Heaney

27. B	28. A	29. C	30. E	31. C
32. A	33. D	34. D	35. C	36. C
37. C	38. E	39. A		

DRAMA

Excerpt from *Oedipus Rex* by Sophocles

1. C	2. B	3. A	4. D	5. B
6. A	7. B	8. A	9. A	10. B

Excerpt from *The Sandbox* by Edward Albee

11. A	12. C	13. A	14. B	15. C
16. C	17. D	18. A	19. B	20. E
21. D	22. B	23. A	24. C	25. E

GLOSSARY OF TERMS

These definitions sometimes repeat and sometimes differ in language from those in the text. Where they differ, the intention is to give a fuller sense of the term's meaning by allowing the reader a double perspective on it. Page numbers refer to the discussions in the text, which in most but not all cases are fuller than those in the glossary. Multiple page references may indicate separate discussions in the various sections of this book—Fiction, Poetry, Drama.

Absurd, Drama of the A type of drama, allied to *comedy*, radically nonrealistic in both content and presentation, that emphasizes the absurdity, emptiness, or meaninglessness of life. (**page 1100**)

Accent In this book, the same as *stress*. A syllable given more prominence in pronunciation than its neighbors is said to be accented. (**pages 874, 1296**)

Allegory A narrative or description that has a second meaning beneath the surface, often relating each literal term to a fixed, corresponding abstract idea or moral principle; usually, the ulterior meanings belong to a pre-existing system of ideas or principles. (**pages 289–290, 774**)

Alliteration The repetition at close intervals of the initial consonant sounds of accented syllables or important words (for example, *m*ap–*m*oon, *k*ill–*c*ode, *pr*each–*appr*ove). Important words and accented syllables beginning with vowels may also be said to alliterate with each other inasmuch as they all have the same lack of an initial consonant sound (for example, "*I*nebri*a*te of *A*ir— am *I*"). (**page 858**)

Allusion A reference, explicit or implicit, to something in previous literature or history. (The term is reserved by some writers for implicit references only, such as those in "in Just—," [**page 815**]; and "On His Blindness," [**page 816**], but the distinction between the two kinds of reference is not always clear-cut.) (**pages 810–813**)

Anapest A metrical foot consisting of two unaccented syllables followed by one accented syllable (for example, ŭn-dĕr-stánd). (**page 878**)

Anapestic meter A *meter* in which a majority of the feet are anapests. (But see *Triple meter*.) (**page 878**)

Anaphora Repetition of an opening word or phrase in a series of lines. (**page 866**)

Antagonist Any force in a story or play that is in conflict with the *protagonist*. An antagonist may be another person, an aspect of the physical or social environment, or a destructive element in the protagonist's own nature. **(page 98)** See *Conflict*.

Apostrophe A figure of speech in which someone absent or dead or something nonhuman is addressed as if it were alive and present and could reply. **(page 752)**

Approximate rhyme (also known as imperfect rhyme, near rhyme, slant rhyme, or oblique rhyme) A term used for words in a rhyming pattern that have some kind of sound correspondence but are not perfect rhymes. See *Rhyme*. Approximate rhymes occur occasionally in patterns where most of the rhymes are perfect (for example, *push–rush* in "Leda and the Swan," [page 859]), and sometimes are used systematically in place of perfect rhyme.

Artistic unity That condition of a successful literary work whereby all its elements work together for the achievement of its central purpose. In an artistically unified work nothing is included that is irrelevant to the central purpose, nothing is omitted that is essential to it, and the parts are arranged in the most effective order for the achievement of that purpose. **(page 103)**

Aside A brief speech in which a character turns from the person being addressed to speak directly to the audience; a dramatic device for letting the audience know what a character is really thinking or feeling as opposed to what the character pretends to think or feel. **(page 1069)**

Assonance The repetition at close intervals of the vowel sounds of accented syllables or important words (for example, h*a*t–r*a*n–*a*mber, v*ei*n–m*a*de). **(page 858)**

Aubade A poem about dawn; a morning love song; or a poem about the parting of lovers at dawn. **(page 1020)**

Ballad A fairly short narrative poem written in a songlike *stanza* form. Example: "La Belle Dame sans Merci," **(page 1014)**.

Blank verse Unrhymed iambic pentameter. **(page 888)**

Cacophony A harsh, discordant, unpleasant-sounding choice and arrangement of sounds. **(page 902)**

Caesura A speech pause occurring within a line. See *Grammatical pause* and *Rhetorical pause*. **(page 875)**

Catharsis A term used by Aristotle to describe some sort of emotional release experienced by the audience at the end of a successful tragedy. **(pages 1241–1243)**

Chance The occurrence of an event that has no apparent cause in antecedent events or in predisposition of character. **(pages 103–104)**

Character   Any of the persons presented in a story or play. (page 144)

> **Developing (or dynamic) character**   A *character* who during the course of a work undergoes a permanent change in some distinguishing moral qualities or personal traits or outlook. (pages 145–146)
>
> **Flat character**   A *character* whose distinguishing moral qualities or personal traits are summed up in one or two traits. (pages 144–145)
>
> **Foil character**   A minor *character* whose situation or actions parallel those of a major character, and thus by contrast sets off or illuminates the major character; most often the contrast is complimentary to the major character.
>
> **Round character**   A *character* whose distinguishing moral qualities or personal traits are complex and many-sided. (pages 144–145)
>
> **Static character**   A *character* who is the same sort of person at the end of a work as at the beginning. (page 145)
>
> **Stock character**   A stereotyped *character*: one whose nature is familiar to us from prototypes in previous literature. (page 145)

Characterization   The various literary means by which characters are presented. (pages 142–143)

Chorus   A group of actors speaking or chanting in unison, often while going through the steps of an elaborate formalized dance; a characteristic device of Greek drama for conveying communal or group emotion. (pages 1115, 1253)

Climax   The turning point or high point in a *plot*. (page 104)

Coincidence   The chance concurrence of two events having a peculiar correspondence between them. (pages 103–104)

Comedy   A type of drama, opposed to *tragedy*, having usually a happy ending, and emphasizing human limitation rather than human greatness. (pages 1240–1247)

> **Scornful comedy**   A type of *comedy* whose main purpose is to expose and ridicule human folly, vanity, or hypocrisy. (page 1244)
>
> **Romantic comedy**   A type of *comedy* whose likable and sensible main characters are placed in difficulties from which they are rescued at the end of the play, either attaining their ends or having their good fortunes restored. (pages 1244–1245)

Comic relief   In a *tragedy*, a comic scene that follows a scene of seriousness and by contrast intensifies the emotions aroused by the serious scene. (page 1499)

Commercial fiction   Fiction written to meet the taste of a wide popular audience and relying usually on tested formulas for satisfying such taste. (pages 57–62)

Conflict A clash of actions, desires, ideas, or goals in the _plot_ of a story or drama. Conflict may exist between the main _character_ and some other person or persons; between the main character and some external force—physical nature, society, or "fate"; or between the main character and some destructive element in his or her own nature. **(pages 98–99)**

Connotation What a word suggests beyond its basic dictionary definition; a word's overtones of meaning. **(pages 720–722)**

Consonance The repetition at close intervals of the final consonant sounds of accented syllables or important words (for example, book–pla_que_–thic_k_er). **(page 858)**

Continuous form That _form_ of a poem in which the lines follow each other without formal grouping, the only breaks being dictated by units of meaning. **(page 917)**

Couplet Two successive lines, usually in the same _meter_, linked by _rhyme_. **(page 921)**

Dactyl A metrical foot consisting of one accented syllable followed by two unaccented syllables (for example, mér-ři-lў). **(page 878)**

Dactylic meter A _meter_ in which a majority of the feet are dactyls. (But see _Triple meter_.) **(page 878)**

Denotation The basic definition or dictionary meaning of a word. **(page 720)**

Denouement That portion of a _plot_ that reveals the final outcome of its conflicts or the solution of its mysteries.

Deus ex machina ("god from the machine") The resolution of a _plot_ by use of a highly improbable chance or coincidence (so named from the practice of some Greek dramatists of having a god descend from heaven at the last possible minute—in the theater by means of a stage machine—to rescue the _protagonist_ from an impossible situation). **(pages 103, 1246)**

Developing character See _Character_.

Didactic writing Poetry, fiction, or drama having as a primary purpose to teach or preach. **(page 937)**

Dilemma A situation in which a _character_ must choose between two courses of action, both undesirable. **(pages 99–100)**

Dimeter A metrical line containing two feet. **(page 879)**

Direct presentation of character That method of _characterization_ in which the author, by exposition or analysis, tells us directly what a _character_ is like, or has someone else in the story do so. **(pages 143–144)**

Dramatic convention Any dramatic device which, though it departs from reality, is implicitly accepted by author and audience as a means of representing reality. **(pages 1114–1115)**

Dramatic exposition The presentation through dialogue of information about events that occurred before the action of a play, or that occur off-stage or between the staged actions; this may also refer to the presentation of information about individual characters' backgrounds or the general situation (political, historical, etc.) in which the action takes place.

Dramatic framework The situation, whether actual or fictional, realistic or fanciful, in which an author places his or her characters in order to express the *theme*. (page 707)

Dramatic irony See *Irony*.

Dramatic point of view See *Point of view*.

Dramatization The presentation of character or of emotion through the speech or action of characters rather than through exposition, analyses, or description by the author. See *Indirect presentation of character*. (page 144)

Duple meter A *meter* in which a majority of the feet contain two syllables. *Iambic* and *trochaic* are both duple meters. (page 878)

Dynamic character See *Character*.

Editorializing Writing that departs from the narrative or dramatic mode and instructs the reader how to think or feel about the events of a story or the behavior of a *character*. (page 334)

End rhyme Rhymes that occur at the ends of lines. (page 859)

End-stopped line A line that ends with a natural speech pause, usually marked by punctuation. (page 875)

English (or Shakespearean) sonnet A *sonnet* rhyming *ababcdcdefefgg*. Its content or structure ideally parallels the rhyme scheme, falling into three coordinate *quatrains* and a concluding *couplet;* but it is sometimes structured, like the *Italian sonnet*, into *octave* and *sestet*, the principal break in thought coming at the end of the eighth line. (page 921)

Epiphany A moment or event in which a *character* achieves a spiritual insight into life or into her or his own circumstances. (page 145)

Euphony A smooth, pleasant-sounding choice and arrangement of sounds. (page 902)

Expected rhythm The rhythmic expectation set up by the basic *meter* of a poem. (page 886)

Extended figure (also known as *sustained figure*) A *figure of speech* (usually *metaphor*, *simile*, *personification*, or *apostrophe*) sustained or developed through a considerable number of lines or through a whole poem. (page 758)

Extended metaphor See *Extended figure*.

Extended simile See *Extended figure*.

Extrametrical syllables In metrical verse, extra unaccented syllables added at the beginnings or endings of lines; these may be either a feature of the metrical *form* of a poem (example, "Is my team plowing," odd-numbered lines [page 705]) or occur as exceptions to the *form* (example, "Virtue," lines 9 and 11 [page 879]). In *iambic* lines, they occur at the end of the line; in *trochaic*, at the beginning. **(page 878)**

Falling action That segment of the *plot* that comes between the *climax* and the conclusion. **(page 104)**

Fantasy A kind of fiction that pictures creatures or events beyond the boundaries of known reality. **(pages 290–292)**

Farce A type of drama related to *comedy* but emphasizing improbable situations, violent conflicts, physical action, and coarse wit over *characterization* or articulated *plot*. **(page 1246)**

Feminine rhyme A rhyme in which the repeated accented vowel is in either the second or third last syllable of the words involved (for example, *ceil*ing–ap*peal*–ing; *hur*rying–*scur*rying). **(page 859)**

Figurative language Language employing *figures of speech*; language that cannot be taken literally or only literally. **(page 748)**

Figure of speech Broadly, any way of saying something other than the ordinary way; more narrowly (and for the purposes of this book) a way of saying one thing and meaning another. **(pages 748–756)**

First-person point of view See *Point of view*.

Fixed form A *form* of poem in which the length and pattern are prescribed by previous usage or tradition, such as *sonnet*, *villanelle*, and so on. **(pages 919–920)**

Flat character See *Character*.

Foil character See *Character*.

Folk ballad A narrative poem designed to be sung, composed by an anonymous author, and transmitted orally for years or generations before being written down. It has usually undergone modification through the process of oral transmission. **(page 691)**

Foot The basic unit used in the *scansion* or measurement of verse. A foot usually contains one accented syllable and one or two unaccented syllables (the *spondaic foot* is a modification of this principle). **(page 877)**

Form The external pattern or shape of a poem, describable without reference to its content, as *continuous form*, *stanzaic form*, *fixed form* (and their varieties), *free verse*, and *syllabic verse*. See *Structure*. **(page 917)**

Free verse Nonmetrical poetry in which the basic rhythmic unit is the line, and in which pauses, line breaks, and formal patterns develop organically from the requirements of the individual poem rather than from established poetic forms. (page 876)

Grammatical pause (also known as *caesura*) A pause introduced into the reading of a line by a mark of punctuation. (page 887)

Hamartia   In Greek tragedy, a criminal act committed in ignorance of some material fact or even for the sake of a greater good. (page 1241)

Happy ending   An ending in which events turn out well for a sympathetic *protagonist*. (pages 101–102)

Heard rhythm   The actual *rhythm* of a metrical poem as we hear it when it is read naturally. The heard rhythm mostly conforms to but sometimes departs from or modifies the *expected rhythm*. (page 886)

Hexameter   A metrical line containing six feet. (page 879)

Iamb   A metrical *foot* consisting of one unaccented syllable followed by one accented syllable (for example, rĕ-heárse). (page 878)

Iambic meter   A *meter* in which the majority of feet are *iambs*. The most common English meter. (page 878)

Imagery   The representation through language of sense experience. (pages 732–734)

Indeterminate ending   An ending in which the central problem or *conflict* is left unresolved. (pages 102–103)

Indirect presentation of character   That method of *characterization* in which the author shows us a *character* in action, compelling us to infer what the character is like from what is said or done by the character. (pages 143–144)

Internal rhyme   A rhyme in which one or both of the rhyme-words occurs *within* the line. (page 859)

Irony   A situation or a use of language involving some kind of incongruity or discrepancy. (pages 331–333, 795–796) Three kinds of irony are distinguished in this book:

Verbal irony   A *figure of speech* in which what is said is the opposite of what is meant. (pages 331, 795–796)

Dramatic irony   An incongruity or discrepancy between what a *character* says or thinks and what the reader knows to be true (or between what a character perceives and what the author intends the reader to perceive). (pages 332, 797–798)

Irony of situation   A situation in which there is an incongruity between appearance and reality, or between expectation and fulfillment, or between the actual situation and what would seem appropriate. (pages 332–333, 799)

an (or Petrarchan) sonnet A *sonnet* consisting of an *octave* rhyming *abbaabba* and of a *sestet* using any arrangement of two or three additional rhymes, such as *cdcdcd* or *cdecde*. **(pages 920)**

Literary fiction Fiction written with serious artistic intentions, providing an imagined experience yielding authentic insights into some significant aspect of life. **(pages 57–61)**

Masculine rhyme (also known as *single rhyme*) A rhyme in which the repeated accented vowel sound is in the final syllable of the words involved (for example, d*ance–pants*, s*cald–recalled*). **(page 858)**

Melodrama A type of drama related to *tragedy* but featuring sensational incidents, emphasizing *plot* at the expense of *characterization*, relying on cruder conflicts (virtuous *protagonist* versus villainous *antagonist*), and having a *happy ending* in which good triumphs over evil. **(page 1246)**

Metaphor A *figure of speech* in which an implicit comparison is made between two things essentially unlike. It may take one of four forms: (1) that in which the literal term and the figurative term are *both named*; (2) that in which the literal term is *named* and the figurative term *implied*; (3) that in which the literal term is *implied* and the figurative term *named*; (4) that in which *both* the literal and the figurative terms are *implied*. **(pages 748–750)**

Meter The regular patterns of accent that underlie metrical verse; the measurable repetition of accented and unaccented syllables in poetry. **(pages 876–877)**

Metonymy A *figure of speech* in which some significant aspect or detail of an experience is used to represent the whole experience. In this book the single term *metonymy* is used for what are sometimes distinguished as two separate figures: *synecdoche* (the use of the part for the whole) and *metonymy* (the use of something closely related for the thing actually meant). **(pages 753–754)**

Metrical variations Departures from the basic metrical pattern (see *substitution, extrametrical syllables*). **(page 879)**

Monometer A metrical line containing one *foot*. **(page 879)**

Moral A rule of conduct or maxim for living expressed or implied as the "point" of a literary work. Compare *Theme*. **(page 683)**

Motivation The incentives or goals that, in combination with the inherent natures of characters, cause them to behave as they do. In *commercial fiction* actions may be unmotivated, insufficiently motivated, or implausibly motivated. **(page 144)**

Mystery An unusual set of circumstances for which the reader craves an explanation; used to create *Suspense*. **(pages 99–100)**

Narrator In drama a *character* found in some plays who, speaking directly to the audience, introduces the action and provides a string of commentary between the dramatic scenes. The narrator may or may not be a major character in the action itself. (page 1115)

Nonrealistic drama Drama that, in content, presentation, or both, departs markedly from fidelity to the outward appearances of life. (pages 1112–1116)

Objective point of view See *Point of view*.

Octave (1) an eight-line *stanza*. (2) the first eight lines of a *sonnet*, especially one structured in the manner of an *Italian sonnet*. (page 920)

Omniscient point of view See *Point of view*.

Onomatopoeia The use of words that supposedly mimic their meaning in their sound (for example, *boom, click, plop*). (page 900)

Overstatement (or hyperbole) A *figure of speech* in which exaggeration is used in the service of truth. (pages 792–793)

Oxymoron A compact verbal paradox in which two successive words seemingly contradict one another. (page 930)

Paradox A statement or situation containing apparently contradictory or incompatible elements. (page 791)

Paradoxical situation A situation containing apparently but not actually incompatible elements. The celebration of a fifth birthday anniversary by a twenty-year-old man is paradoxical but explainable if the man was born on February 29. The Christian doctrines that Christ was born of a virgin and is both God and man are, for a Christian believer, paradoxes (that is, apparently impossible but true). (page 791)

Paradoxical statement (or verbal paradox) A *figure of speech* in which an apparently self-contradictory statement is nevertheless found to be true. (page 791)

Paraphrase A restatement of the content of a poem designed to make its *prose meaning* as clear as possible. (pages 702–704)

Pentameter A metrical line containing five feet. (page 879)

Personification A *figure of speech* in which human attributes are given to an animal, an object, or a concept. (pages 750–751)

Petrarchan sonnet See *Italian sonnet*.

Phonetic intensive A word whose sound, by an obscure process, to some degree suggests its meaning. As differentiated from *onomatopoetic* words, the meanings of phonetic intensives do not refer explicitly to sounds. (pages 900–901)

Playwright A maker of plays. (page 1068)

Plot The sequence of incidents or events of which a story or play is composed. (page 97)

Plot manipulation A situation in which an author gives the *plot* a twist or turn unjustified by preceding action or by the characters involved. (page 103)

Poeticizing Writing that uses immoderately heightened or distended language to sway the reader's feelings. (page 334)

Point of view The angle of vision from which a story is told. (page 236)
The four basic points of view are as follows:

Omniscient point of view The author tells the story using the third person, knowing all and free to tell us anything, including what the characters are thinking or feeling and why they act as they do. (pages 237–238)

Third-person limited point of view The author tells the story using the third person, but is limited to a complete knowledge of one *character* in the story and tells us only what that one character thinks, feels, sees, or hears. (pages 238–239)

First-person point of view The story is told by one of its characters, using the first person. (pages 239–240)

Objective (or Dramatic) point of view The author tells the story using the third person, but is limited to reporting what the characters say or do; the author does not interpret the characters' behavior or tell us their private thoughts or feelings. (pages 240–241)

Prose meaning That part of a poem's *total meaning* that can be separated out and expressed through *paraphrase*. (page 824)

Prose poem Usually a short composition having the intentions of poetry but written in prose rather than *verse*. (page 876)

Protagonist The central *character* in a story or play. (page 98)

Quatrain (1) A four-line *stanza*. (2) A four-line division of a *sonnet* marked off by its rhyme scheme. (page 921)

Realistic drama Drama that attempts, in content and in presentation, to preserve the illusion of actual, everyday life. (pages 1112–1116)

Refrain A repeated word, phrase, line, or group of lines, normally at some fixed position in a poem written in *stanzaic form*. (page 860)

Rhetorical pause (also known as *caesura*) A natural pause, unmarked by punctuation, introduced into the reading of a line by its phrasing or syntax. (page 887)

Rhetorical poetry Poetry using artificially eloquent language, that is, language too high-flown for its occasion and unfaithful to the full complexity of human experience. (pages 936–937)

Rhetorical stress In natural speech, as in prose and poetic writing, the stressing of words or syllables so as to emphasize meaning and sentence structure. (page 875)

Rhyme The repetition of the accented vowel sound and all succeeding sounds in important or importantly positioned words (for example, *old–cold*, *vane–reign*, *court–report*, *order–recorder*). The above definition applies to *perfect rhyme* and assumes that the accented vowel sounds involved are preceded by differing consonant sounds. If the preceding consonant sound is the same (for example, *manse–romance*, *style–stile*), or if there is no preceding consonant sound in either word (for example, *aisle–isle*, *alter–altar*), or if the same word is repeated in the rhyming position (for example, *hill–hill*), the words are called *identical rhymes*. Both perfect rhymes and identical rhymes are to be distinguished from *approximate rhymes*. (pages 858–859)

Rhyme scheme Any fixed pattern of rhymes characterizing a whole poem or its *stanzas*. (page 918)

Rhythm Any wavelike recurrence of motion or sound. (page 874)

Rising action That development of *plot* in a story or play that precedes and leads up to the *climax*. (page 104)

Romantic comedy See *Comedy*.

Round character See *Character*.

Run-on line A line that has no natural speech pause at its end, allowing the sense to flow uninterruptedly into the succeeding line. (page 875)

Sarcasm Bitter or cutting speech; speech intended by its speaker to give pain to the person addressed. (page 795)

Satire A kind of literature that ridicules human folly or vice with the purpose of bringing about reform or of keeping others from falling into similar folly or vice. (page 795)

Scansion The process of measuring metrical verse, that is, of marking accented and unaccented syllables, dividing the lines into feet, identifying the metrical pattern, and noting significant variations from that pattern. (page 879)

Scornful comedy See *Comedy*.

Sentimentality Unmerited or contrived tender feeling; that quality in a work that elicits or seeks to elicit tears through an oversimplification or falsification of reality. (pages 333–334, 936)

Sentimental poetry Poetry that attempts to manipulate the reader's emotions in order to achieve a greater emotional response than the poem itself really warrants. (A sentimental novel or film is sometimes called, pejoratively, a "tearjerker.") (page 936)

Sestet (1) A six-line *stanza*. (2) The last six lines of a *sonnet* structured on the Italian model. **(page 920)**

Setting The context in time and place in which the action of a story occurs.

Shakespearean sonnet See *English sonnet*.

Simile A *figure of speech* in which an explicit comparison is made between two things essentially unlike. The comparison is made explicit by the use of some such word or phrase as *like, as, than, similar to, resembles*, or *seems*. **(page 748)**

Single rhyme See *Masculine rhyme*.

Situational irony See *Irony*.

Soliloquy A speech in which a *character*, alone on the stage, addresses himself or herself; a soliloquy is a "thinking out loud," a dramatic means of letting an audience know a character's thoughts and feelings. **(page 1069)**

Sonnet A *fixed form* of fourteen lines, normally iambic pentameter, with a rhyme scheme conforming to or approximating one of two main types—the *Italian* or the *English*. **(page 920)**

Spondee A metrical *foot* consisting of two syllables equally or almost equally accented (for example, *trúe–blúe*). **(page 878)**

Stanza A group of lines whose metrical pattern (and usually its rhyme scheme as well) is repeated throughout a poem. **(pages 879, 918)**

Stanzaic form The *form* taken by a poem when it is written in a series of units having the same number of lines and usually other characteristics in common, such as metrical pattern or rhyme scheme. **(page 918)**

Static character See *Character*.

Stock character See *Character*.

Stream of consciousness Narrative that presents the private thoughts of a *character* without commentary or interpretation by the author. **(page 239)**

Stress In this book, the same as *Accent*. But see page 874 (footnote).

Structure The sequential arrangement of plot elements in fiction or drama. **(page 97)** In poetry, the internal organization of content (see *Form*). **(page 917)**

Substitution In metrical verse, the replacement of the expected metrical *foot* by a different one (for example, a *trochee* occurring in an *iambic* line). **(page 879)**

Surprise An unexpected turn in the development of a *plot*. **(page 101)**

Surprise ending A completely unexpected revelation or turn of *plot* at the conclusion of a story or play. **(page 101)**

Suspense   That quality in a story or play that makes the reader eager to discover what happens next and how it will end. (**pages 99–101**)

Sustained figure   See *Extended figure.*

Syllabic verse   *Verse* measured by the number of syllables rather than the number of feet per line. (**page 893**)

Symbol   Something that means *more* than what it is; an object, person, situation, or action that in addition to its literal meaning suggests other meanings as well. (**pages 282–292, 766–767**)

Synecdoche   A *figure of speech* in which a part is used for the whole. In this book it is subsumed under the term *Metonymy.* (**pages 753–754**)

Synesthesia   Presentation of one sense experience in terms usually associated with another sensation. (**page 907**)

Tercet   A three line *stanza* exhibited in *terza rima* and *villanelle* as well as in other poetic forms. (**page 922**)

Terza rima   An interlocking rhyme scheme with the pattern *aba bcb cdc*, etc. (**page 932**)

Tetrameter   A metrical line containing four feet. (**page 879**)

Theme   The central idea or unifying generalization implied or stated by a literary work. (**pages 193–199, 702**)

Third-person limited point of view   See *Point of view.*

Tone   The writer's or speaker's attitude toward the subject, the audience, or herself or himself; the emotional coloring, or emotional meaning, of a work. (**pages 838–842**)

Total meaning   The total experience communicated by a poem. It includes all those dimensions of experience by which a poem communicates— sensuous, emotional, imaginative, and intellectual—and it can be communicated in no other words than those of the poem itself. (**page 824**)

Tragedy   A type of drama, opposed to *comedy*, which depicts the causally related events that lead to the downfall and suffering of the *protagonist*, a person of unusual moral or intellectual stature or outstanding abilities. (**pages 1240–1244**)

Trimeter   A metrical line containing three feet. (**page 879**)

Triple meter   A *meter* in which a majority of the feet contain three syllables. (Actually, if more than 25 percent of the feet in a poem are triple, its effect is more triple than duple, and it ought perhaps to be referred to as triple meter.) *Anapestic* and *dactylic* are both triple meters. (**page 878**)

Trochaic meter   A *meter* in which the majority of feet are trochees. (**page 878**)

Trochee A metrical foot consisting of one accented syllable followed by one unaccented syllable (for example, bár-tĕr). **(page 878)**

Truncation In metric verse, the omission of an unaccented syllable at either end of a line (for example, "Introduction to *Songs of Innocence*," [page 889]). **(page 879)**

Understatement A *figure of speech* that consists of saying less than one means, or of saying what one means with less force than the occasion warrants. **(page 793)**

Unhappy ending An ending that turns out unhappily for a sympathetic *protagonist*. **(page 101)**

Verbal irony See *Irony*.

Verse Metrical language; the opposite of *prose*.

Villanelle A nineteen-line *fixed form* consisting of five tercets rhymed *aba* and a concluding quatrain rhymed *abaa*, with lines 1 and 3 of the first *tercet* serving as refrains in an alternating pattern through line 15 and then repeated as lines 18 and 19. **(pages 922–924)**

COPYRIGHTS AND ACKNOWLEDGMENTS

Reprinted by permission of Farrar, Straus & Giroux, LLC. and Faber &
Faber Ltd. "Church Going" and "Toads" from *The Less Deceived*. Copyright ©
1955 by Philip Larkin. Reprinted with the permission of The Marvell
Press, England and Australia. "Aubade" from *Collected Poems*, edited by
Anthony Thwaite. Copyright © 1988 by The Estate of Philip Larkin.
Reprinted with the permission of Farrar, Straus & Giroux, LLC and Faber &
Faber, Ltd.

D. H. LAWRENCE, "Odour of Chrysanthemums," "Piano," "The
Rocking Horse Winner". Copyright 1933 by the Estate of D. H.
Lawrence and renewed © 1961 by Angelo Ravagli and C. Montague
Weekley, Executors of the Estate of Frieda Lawrence Ravagli and renewed ©
1950 by Frieda Lawrence. Used by permission of Viking Penguin, a
division of Penguin Group (USA) LLC. "The Horse-Dealer's Daughter"
from *Complete Short Stories of D. H. Lawrence*. Copyright 1922 by
Thomas Seltzer, Inc. and renewed © 1950 by Frieda Lawrence. Used by
permission of Viking Penguin, a division of Penguin Group (USA) LLC.

URSULA K. LE GUIN, "The Ones Who Walk Away from Omelas"
from *The Wind's Twelve Quarters*. First appeared in New Dimensions 3
(1973). Copyright © 1973, 2001 by Ursula K. Le Guin. Reprinted by
permission of the Author and the Author's Agent, the Virginia Kidd
Agency, Inc.

SYDNEY LEA, "Bald Sentiment," *The Georgia Review*, Winter 2009.
Copyright © 2009. Reprinted with permission.

DENISE LEVERTOV, "To the Snake" from *Collected Earlier Poems
1940–1960*. Copyright ©1960 by Denise Levertov. Reprinted by permission of New Directions Publishing Corp.

GEORGE CABOT LODGE, "Lower New York: At Dawn" by George
Cabot Lodge.

AUDRE LORDE, "Black Mother Woman" from *Collected Poems of Audre
Lorde*. Copyright © 1973 by Audre Lorde. Used by permission of
W. W. Norton & Company, Inc.

ARCHIBALD MACLEISH, "Ars Poetica" from *Collected Poems,
1917–1982*. Copyright © 1985 by the Estate of Archibald MacLeish.
Reprinted by permission of Houghton Mifflin Harcourt Publishing
Company. All rights reserved.

BERNARD MALAMUD, "The Magic Barrel" from *The Magic Barrel*.
Copyright © 1950, 1958, renewed 1977, 1986 by Bernard Malamud.
Reprinted by permission of Farrar, Straus and Giroux, LLC.

KATHERINE MANSFIELD, "Miss Brill," from *The Short Stories of
Katherine Mansfield*. Copyright © 1923 by Alfred A. Knopf, a divi-

INDEX OF AUTHORS, TITLES, AND FIRST LINES

Authors' names appear in CAPITALS, titles of selections in italics, and first lines of poems in roman type. Numbers in bold face indicate the pages of the selection, and numbers in roman type indicate the pages where the selection is discussed.